A New General Biographical Dictionary
by Hugh James Rose

Address:
HardPress
8345 NW 66TH ST #2561
MIAMI FL 33166-2626
USA
Email: info@hardpress.net

SIGILLUM · UNIVERSITATIS · BRUNENSIS ·
IN DEO SPERAMUS

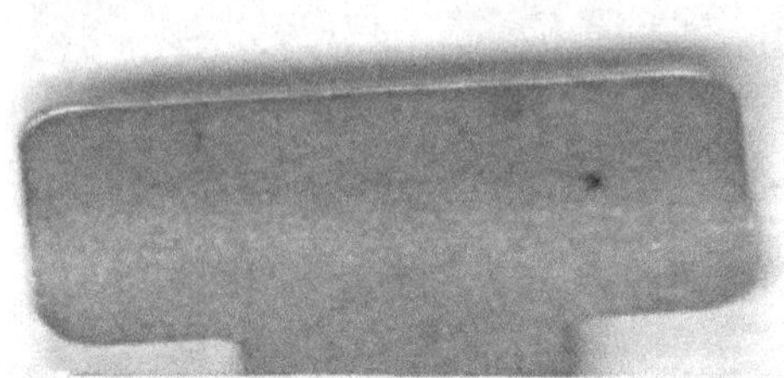

$43.00.

A

NEW GENERAL

BIOGRAPHICAL DICTIONARY.

BEE——BRA.

LONDON:—PRINTED BY RICHARD CLAY,
BREAD STREET HILL.

A

NEW GENERAL

BIOGRAPHICAL DICTIONARY,

PROJECTED AND PARTLY ARRANGED

BY THE LATE

REV. HUGH JAMES ROSE, B.D.

PRINCIPAL OF KING'S COLLEGE, LONDON.

IN TWELVE VOLUMES.

VOL. IV.

LONDON:
B. FELLOWES, LUDGATE STREET;
F. & J. RIVINGTON; E. HODGSON; G. LAWFORD; J. M. RICHARDSON
J. BOHN; J. BAIN; J. DOWDING; G. GREENLAND; A. GREENLAND
F. C. WESTLEY; JAMES BOHN; CAPES & CO.;
T. BOSWORTH; J. & J. J. DEIGHTON, CAMBRIDGE;
AND J. H. PARKER, OXFORD.
1850.

A

BIOGRAPHICAL DICTIONARY.

BEETHOVEN, (Lewis von,) one of the finest musical geniuses that ever existed, but so eccentric in his habits, that the world was long inclined to call him a madman.* He was born on the 17th of December, 1770, at Bonn, on the Rhine, his father occupying the situation of *tenor* at the electoral chapel. It has, however, been said, that his father was Frederic William II. of Prussia, as if none but a royal descent was adequate to his genius. His faculties developed themselves so early, that his father began to instruct him when he was only five years old, but soon found him above his lessons. Hence he gave him over to Van der Enden, one of the best pianists of that time. Subsequently, Neefe, by orders of the elector Maximilian, became Beethoven's master. He initiated the extraordinary child into the works of Sebastian Bach and Händel, which ever excited his reverence and veneration. At the age of eight (so it is said, at least), he excelled as a violin player; and at thirteen, some of his compositions were printed. But it was improvisation and the *fantasia libera*, in which he shone most brightly, and which he first exhibited before the learned composer, Junker, at Cologne, pouring forth a superabundance of rich and brilliant ideas. It was in this sort of boundless ramble, as it were, that his mind found nourishment and scope. In composition, he continually violated the rules of harmony then received. This caused an opposition that often harassed him, and probably injured his temper. The talents which he showed on the organ, induced his patron, the elector, to send him in 1792 to Vienna, to perfect under Haydn his theoretic and practical acquirements. Just in the same way as Corneille had not been able to understand Racine, Haydn was mistaken in Beethoven, whom he thought "not destined to be a musical composer;" and when asked his opinion about him, said drily, "he plays well on the piano." Mozart, however, had shown more penetration. When Beethoven had previously made a visit to Vienna, in 1790, and had executed a *fantasia libera* before him, he cautiously said at first nothing, thinking that it had been previously *practised* and played by heart. But as Beethoven, suspecting this, requested Mozart to give him some theme, and receiving one of a very complicated nature, he followed it extempore, during three-quarters of an hour. Holding his breath, Mozart slipped on tip-toe into the next room, and said to some friends there, "Mark well this young man, you will hear more of him."

When Haydn went to England, he left Beethoven under the care of Albrechtsberger, from whom he received important lessons in counterpoint, as he gratefully acknowledged in his posthumous *Studien*. His reputation as a pianist and composer began now to be established, but it was his *fantasia libera* which carried away every hearer. At that period he also learnt much of ancient and modern languages, history, and the *belles-lettres*, his life being generally spent alone. A musician, however, named Wolff (now forgotten) competed then with him as a player; yet, although rivals, they bore a sincere friendship towards each other. The crowd of amateurs became divided; prince Lichnowsky giving the palm to Beethoven, baron Wetzlar to Wolff. It was in the charming villa of the latter, near Schönbrunn, that contests between the two champions were often prolonged until late at night—nights, which will

* The extraordinary novelty of his works shocked the greatest masters. Haydn considered him but a good pianist, Salleri said he was mad, Neefe prohibited him seriously from composing, and Albrechtsberger talked of putting him in prison. It appears even, that his father died of grief at having a son who did not care about counterpoint. (A. Delrieu, l. c.)

never be forgotten by the few who still remain to remember them. In 1801 his patron, the elector, having died, he determined on remaining at Vienna, then the capital of the musical world. Two of his younger brothers had followed him thither, and on that account, also, he declined a most favourable offer to go to London. Prince Lichnowsky received Beethoven about 1802 as an inmate in his house, but accustomed to compose mostly out of town, amidst mountains and forests, unruly and averse from any system not emanating from himself, he was soon induced to change his quarters. An anecdote is related of Lichnowsky, which shows that he was a prince even in mind. When Beethoven had moved into his palace, he ordered his domestics, that if he and the latter should ring at the same time, the guest should be attended first.

The works which first showed Beethoven's genius as a composer, were his quartets for stringed instruments, which kind of composition also he carried to the very limits of our present conceptions. His intimacy with M. Salieri, and the general desire of the public, led him also to theatrical composition. The result was the opera Leonora, afterwards named Fidelio. It was first performed at Prague (about 1811), with no great success, and was not thoroughly appreciated till much later. The immense power, nay, stress of the orchestra and chorus, laid upon the word *Freyheit* (freedom), was one of the first manifestations of those republican opinions of Beethoven, which showed themselves so strongly in after life. About the same time his oratorio, Christ on the Mount of Olives, the *symfonia heroica*, and *pastorale*, made their appearance.

Beethoven, however, was yet not a man established in the world, having no income but that which his continual exertions procured him from day to day. "At the age of thirty-seven, equivocal trials as a composer, an unhappy amour, a deceived ambition, and a rude behaviour, had made him completely miserable." (Delrieu.) It was Jerome Bonaparte, king of Westphalia, who, in 1809, made Beethoven the first offer of a permanent and honourable situation, as *maître de chapelle* at Cassel. This aroused others, and the archduke Rudolph (his musical pupil), with the princes Lobkowitz and Kinsky, secured to him (in *terms* most flattering) a yearly pension of 4000 florins of paper money (then worth about 70*l.*), on condition of staying in the Austrian dominions. About this time, his bodily afflictions had risen to a height which embittered his life to the utmost degree. He laboured under a defect in hearing, the more tormenting to him, as he felt that he ought to possess that sense more perfectly than any other; in fact, he had possessed it in his younger years, with a nicety very rarely known. His disaster was partially alleviated by marks of respect and sympathy showered upon him — either a medal with his portrait, struck at Paris, or a costly piano sent him by London artists and amateurs, a diploma of the Royal Academy of Sweden, or that of honorary citizenship of Vienna. Beethoven's happiest days were passed between 1817 and 1819. He lived then much at Bruck am Gebürge, a village near Vienna, whence he continually rambled over the adjoining charming country. It was at that time, that his portrait (representing him amidst a bower of foliage) was taken, which is really *himself* — several representations of him being absurd caricatures. An incident, which happened about this time to the writer of this article and some friends, will best picture Beethoven's mode of life. We were once taking a drive to Bruck, when a heavy thunder-storm began to threaten, and, at a mile from the village, burst forth with unusual violence. We made therefore all speed possible, when we perceived a solitary rambler, stalking right across the fields, and making, at times, most eccentric gestures. It was Beethoven. One of our party recognised him first, and waved his hat to him; Beethoven nodded in return, but on he went. Such a man could represent a storm from real and intimate intercourse with nature.

Beethoven had two brothers; the younger, John, was an apothecary, who had become prosperous by his means, but, notwithstanding, continually preyed upon his purse, even when he was ill. Both brothers incessantly meddled with his affairs, and did every thing to alienate him from his friends. But he was so kind as to say of each of them, "He is, after all, my brother." His fame was constantly spreading over half the world, still he lived solitary and retired. In the coffee-room which he frequented at Vienna, he sat alone, self-absorbed, sometimes making strange gestures. But every one treated him most respectfully.

In politics, Beethoven displayed his

usual eccentricity. A symphony of his was to have been dedicated to Bonaparte, when first consul; but before it appeared, its intended patron was an emperor. The composer said immediately, that he would have nothing to do with him, and the title-page was destroyed. The piece, indeed, came forth, but its character was changed from gay to sad, and it bore another title. Thus, too, when he and Goethe were once walking in Carlsbad, during the season, engaged in conversation, the imperial family and other princes came that way. Beethoven would have turned aside, and continued the conversation; but Goethe stopped, and made one of his courtly bows. For this, Beethoven, who had run away, severely reproached him. Hence it is not surprising, that this great composer, although living for thirty years in the Austrian metropolis, never inscribed a line of his music to either the emperor Francis or prince Metternich.

Another of his characteristics was an avarice, that made him ever willing to plead poverty. This gained him 200*l.* from George IV. of Great Britain, when regent. Not long before his death, he applied to the Harmonic Society of London to give a concert for his benefit. He received instantly a present of 100*l.* When he died, however, 10,000 florins were found in an old trunk.

Beethoven was very partial to the son of his elder brother, who, for a time, had been his constant companion. This young man, who greatly abused his kindness, late in the autumn of 1826 came suddenly to Baden, and earnestly besought him to save him from his creditors. On this application, the kind uncle walked a distance of more than twelve miles, and when he reached his house, was drenched with rain. A violent cold ensued, then an inflammation of the lungs, which brought on dropsy. He died on the 26th of March, 1827, at half-past five A.M. Thirty thousand people assisted at his funeral!

Beethoven's countenance was one of those which might be known amongst millions. His frame was strong, but he was only of ordinary size, perhaps even a little under it. His forehead, perhaps one of the finest ever seen, was of extraordinary breadth, and of a form highly symmetrical. His eyes, generally serious and stern, when he was excited became like stars. At moments when occupied by some lofty idea, "his exterior at once underwent a striking alteration, and assumed an aspect visibly inspired and commanding, which, to the bystanders, made his short figure appear as gigantic as his mind."

His principal works are, seventeen quartets, three quintets, five trios, a septuor, for stringed instruments; thirty-three sonatas for the piano alone; nine symphonias, one with choruses; the Battle of Vittoria, symphony; two masses; Christ on the Mount of Olives, oratorio; Adelaide and Armide, cantatas; Egmont, melodrama; Prometheus, ballet; overtures to Coriolanus, the Ruins of Athens, and the Dedication of the Temple; concerts for the piano and for the violin, and a host of other minor compositions. To these we must add his *Studien*, or treatise on harmony and composition—a work full of useful advice for the composer, and showing that Beethoven knew thoroughly those rules of counterpoint, which he seemed to disregard in his compositions. Readers who require a detailed musical review of his works, may consult Schilling's Encyclopedie der Music. Of his vanity as a composer, the following anecdote may give some idea. When Ries spoke of two consecutive fifths, in his violin concert, and expressed some doubt of their correctness, Beethoven said, "Well, and who then has forbidden the use of them?" Ries cited some of the first authorities, when the proud reply was given, "Then *I* allow them. Yo el Rey."

The materials for Beethoven's life are increasing every day. Schindler's Leben is perhaps the most complete, of which M. Moschelles has published an English edition. See also Ferdinand Ries. Biog. Univ. Suppl. Hogarth's Musical History. Polytechnic Journal, 1840. Tait's Magazine, 1841. Le Siècle, 14 Sept. 1840, A. Delrieu.

BEFFA-NEGRINI, (Anthony, 1532—1602,) a poet and miscellaneous writer, born at Asola, in the province of Brescia, and descended from a noble family. He wrote the history of several distinguished houses, a life of the countess Matilda, and some other historical works, of which all have not seen the light. (Biog. Univ.)

BEFFROY DE BEAUVOIR, (Lewis Stephen, 1754—1825,) a native of Laon, of a distinguished but impoverished family. He was an officer of grenadiers when the revolution broke out, and immediately became one of its decided partisans. This was the way to fortune; he filled, in succession, several important offices, and in 1792 was deputed to the National Convention, where he voted for the death of Lewis. From this time, his attention was chiefly turned to finance and agriculture, of which he was made commissioner. On the restoration of the Bourbons he was exiled as a regicide, and he retired to Liège, where he ended his days. He published one or two tracts of no importance. (Biog. Univ. Suppl.)

BEFFROY DE REIGNY, (Lewis Abel, 1757—1811,) brother of the preceding, better known by the name of *Cousin Jacques*, an author who first tried a frivolous style of writing, but afterwards changed it, and his dramatic pieces had considerable success. All his works have a moral tendency, and are replete with honest sentiments, with which he constantly strives to inspire his readers. He rendered himself conspicuous by giving, in 1800, his Dictionnaire Néologique des Hommes et des Choses de la Révolution. Among his numerous works may be remarked, Les Petites Maisons du Parnasse, Poème comique d'un Genre nouveau en Vers et en Prose, Bouillon, 1783, in 8vo. Marlborough, Poème comique en Prose rimée, Londres et Paris, 1783, in 8vo. Histoire de France pendant trois Mois, Paris, 1789, in 8vo. Soirées chantantes, ou le Chansonnier Bourgeois, avec les Airs Notés, Paris, 1802, in 8vo. He composed the music to his operas, and which, if it savour of negligence in style, is very often both easy and agreeable. He died in obscurity at Charenton.

BEGA, (St. Bee,) an Irish virgin, who retired about the middle of the seventh century to a spot in Copeland, near Carlisle, where a religious house was eventually founded to her memory. Her "day" is the 7th of September; or, according to Dempster, who places her amongst the Scottish saints, the 6th of that month. (Butler, Lives of the Saints. Dempster. Strype's Grindal.)

BEGA, (Cornelius, 1620—Aug. 27, 1664,) a painter, born at Haarlem, son of a sculptor named Peter Begyn. He changed his name to Bega in consequence, it is said, of having been disowned by his father for irregularities in conduct. He was a disciple of Ostade, and his pictures, like his master's, represent Dutch peasants regaling and amusing themselves; interiors of Dutch cottages; exteriors with landscape and cattle introduced; all which subjects he treated with great humour of character and excellence of effect. They are not, indeed, equal to the pencilling of Ostade, but his touch was delicate and his colouring lucid. Bega died of the plague which ravaged Holland in 1664, it is said, in consequence of his attendance on a young woman to whom he was tenderly attached, and who, being attacked by the malady, was abandoned by all but her lover. If this story be true, the date of Bega's birth, as stated above, would appear to be correct, rather than that of 1600, as given by M. Durdent in the Biographie Universelle. Bega etched several drolleries, and a set of thirty-four prints, representing alehouse scenes, &c. (Pilkington's and Bryan's Dictionaries. Biog. Univ. Strutt's Dict. of Eng.)

BEGARELLI, (Anthony, about 1498—1565,) a native of Modena, and a most eminent modeller in clay. That city was celebrated for its practitioners in this art, which consisted in modelling all sorts of figures in plaster, stucco, and clay. Guido Mazzoni, otherwise called Paganini, had already made considerable progress in this class of sculpture in 1484; he had had for a rival Giovanni, the father of Nicolo del' Abbate, but Begarelli surpassed as well Mazzoni and Abbate, as all their pupils. He executed figures as large, and sometimes larger than life. In the church and monastery of the Benedictines is preserved a noble collection of them. As he lived long, and worked to the end of his life, he filled the churches of Modena with monuments, groups, and statues, besides others which he modelled for Parma, Mantua, and other places. Vasari praises him for the fine air of his heads, for beautiful drapery, exquisite proportions, and for the colour of marble; relating also, that Michael Angelo said of Begarelli's works, "If this clay were only to become marble, woe betide the ancient statues," a species of eulogy, in the opinion of Lanzi, most desirable to an artist, "in particular when we reflect upon the profound science of Buonarotti, and how tardy he was to praise." Begarelli was also an able designer, and taught that as well as the art of modelling, whence he greatly influenced the art of painting; and to him, in the opinion of Lanzi, we are, in a great measure, to trace that correctness, relief, and foreshortening, and degree of grace, approaching nearly to Raffaelle's, in all of which this part of Lombardy boasted such a conspicuous share. (Lanzi, Stor. Pitt. iv. 29. Biog. Univ.)

BEGAT, (John,) born at Dijon in 1523, who acquired considerable reputation for learning and eloquence as an advocate in that town. He was employed to solicit from Charles IX. the revocation of the edict of the 17th of January, 1562, which tolerated the Calvinists in all parts of the kingdom. His remonstrances were successful, and the edict was recalled. He also opposed, but without the same result, the edict of the 19th of March, in favour of the protestants. He died, president of the parliament of Burgundy, on the 10th of June, 1572. It has been stated that Begat was author of "Remonstrances to Charles IX. on the Edict of 1560," which gave toleration to the protestants, but the edict belongs to 1562, and Begat's Remonstrances, on this occasion, were never printed. His Remonstrances to oppose the edict of March, 1563, were, however, produced at Antwerp the same year, without his consent. Several correct editions were subsequently published, and the work was translated into Latin, Italian, Spanish, and German. A protestant, about this time, published an apology for the king's edict, to which Begat replied, in a work without date or printer's name. He is also the author of a book entitled, Commentarii Rerum Burgundiarum, which has the fault of being replete with anachronisms. (Biog. Univ.)

BEGAULT, (Giles, 1660 — 1725?) canon and archdeacon of Nîmes, a celebrated preacher. His Panegyrics and Sermons have been printed in five volumes. (Biog. Univ. Suppl.)

BEGER, (Laurence,) born at Heidelberg in 1633, the son of a tanner, who, perceiving his talents, gave him a superior education, but required him to study theology. At the death of his father, however, Beger abandoned it, and became librarian to the elector palatine, Charles Lewis. He gained the favour of this prince by his Considerations upon Marriage. The elector desired to marry a young lady, of whom he was enamoured, during the life of his wife, a princess of Hesse-Cassel—a union which he actually accomplished by a left-handed marriage. Beger's work was in favour of polygamy. Prince Charles, son of the elector by his first wife, on the death of his father, compelled him to write a pamphlet on the other side, but it was never printed. Charles Lewis had a passion for collecting coins, and on Beger was laid the task—one very agreeable to his taste and previous pursuits—of describing them. This he did in a work entitled, Thesaurus ex Thesauro Palat. Selectus, Heidelbergæ, 1685. On the death of his patron, in 1685, his collections were dispersed; the coins went to Berlin, and the library to Cassel; but Beger found a better post, as superintendent of the elector of Brandenburg's numismatic collection at Cleves, and from this period date some of his best works. These were, a Description of the Brandenburg Collection; several tracts on particular antiquities, gems, &c.; and an edition of Florus, a work exhibiting more of critical pretence than critical ability. He died in 1705. (Ersch und Gruber.)

BEGER, (Laurence,) an engraver at Berlin, nephew of the preceding. After having worked some time at Berlin, he went to Heidelberg, to Frankfort-on-the-Maine, and lastly, according to Nicolai, to England, in 1711, a circumstance which is disproved by Husgen. Professor Christ says that he engraved, about 1700, at Berlin, a set of twelve anatomical plates, taken from the designs of Vesalius, and adds, that it is likely that the greater part of the plates of antiquities, published by his uncle, under the title of Thesaurus Brandenburgicus, were engraved by Beger. (Heinecken. Strutt's Dict. of Eng.)

BEGEYN. See Begyn.

BEGGI-JAN, the familiar appellation of Shah Mourad Beg, a singular personage, who, in the latter part of the last century, attained sovereign power in the Uzbek kingdom of Bokhara. At the death of his father, the Emir Daniel, who had virtually ruled the country in the name of the pageant monarch Abdul-Ghazi Khan, Beggi-Jan, who made pretensions to the highest degree of ascetic sanctity, declared his determination to take no part in the strife for power which broke out among his numerous brothers; the anarchy, however, into which the country was speedily thrown, and the supplications of the people and the titular king, (who regarded him, in consequence of his *sooffi*, or mystic aspirations, as the especial favourite of heaven,) overcame this feigned reluctance; and he assumed, about 1783, the absolute direction of the state, which he continued to administer till his death in 1800. His accession to power, however, produced no change in his previously adopted habits, which were those of a dervise, or religious mendicant; his support was derived from the sale of whips, which he plaited with his own hands; and, while surrounded by splendid nobles, his only dress was a patched and filthy green robe; but this apparent self-denial and humiliation was the result of deep and crafty policy, and enabled him to retain in willing obedience the fierce tribes, from the Oxus to the Jaxartes, who would have spurned subjection to a less saintly ruler, unendowed with any legitimate claim to their allegiance. His administration of justice, according to the Koran, was rigid and impartial; and the observance of both the precepts and prohibitions of the Moslem law was enforced on the inhabitants of Bokhara with a strictness unknown for many ages in the annals of Islam. His renown, in the double capacity of a saint and a ruler, spread throughout Asia, and he even received more than one embassy from Catharine II. of Russia, with whom he maintained, till her death, a friendly correspondence. Though his foreign policy was generally peaceful, he waged, with spirit and success, a short war against the Affghan monarch, Timour Shah; and the annual predatory excursions which he made during the latter part of his life into Persian Khorassan, are a great blot on his character: thousands of captives being yearly torn from their homes, and sold like cattle in the markets of Bokhara. This extraordinary man, though styled king of Bokhara by many writers, never assumed the royal title. His son Hyder, however, at once set aside the pageant monarch, and proclaimed himself king. He died in 1825, and several of his sons have since reigned in succession. (Malcolm's Persia. Burnes's Bokhara, &c.)

BEGNI, (Julius Cæsar,) a painter of the Roman school, born at Pesara. He was pupil of Antonio Cimatori, and was a bold and animated artist, a good painter of perspective, and in a great degree a follower of the Venetian school, in which he studied and painted. He left many works in Udine, and many more in his native place, executed in a rapid and unfinished style, but possessing good general effect. He died shortly before 1680. (Lanzi, Stor. Pitt. ii. 130.)

BEGON, (Michael,) a magistrate under Lewis XIV., born at Blois in 1638. After having qualified himself for the law in Paris, he returned to his native place, and proving a man of merit, with the advantage of relationship to Colbert, he obtained a succession of honourable posts, in his own country and the French West Indies. He died the 4th of March, 1710. Conceiving the design of publishing the portraits of illustrious Frenchmen of the seventeenth century, he had upwards of two hundred engravings executed at his own cost, which may be seen in Perault's Hommes Illustres, published in 1696—1700. We are told that he left behind him a journal of his residence in America, containing the laws promulgated by him; this, however, was never published. A tribe of American plants was called after him, *Begonia*. (Biog. Univ.)

BEGON, (Stephen,) an advocate in the parliament of Paris. His health compelled him to be carried in a chair to court, where he could not be seen by the judges, without mounting a bench. He was counsel for the duchess of Gevres, when seeking a divorce from her husband. Study was Begon's only occupation, when not in court, and he never slept but when completely exhausted with fatigue. He died in 1726, at what age is not known, after having been thirty-five years an advocate. (Biog. Univ.)

BEGON, (Scipio Jerome, 1681—1753,) second son of Michael Begon, consecrated bishop of Toul in 1723. Besides pastoral letters, charges, and funeral orations, he published, L'Eloge du bien-heureux Père Pierre Fourrier, in 1732; Discours sur l'Avènement du Roi de Pologne, at his solemn reception in the cathedral of Toul, in 1737. This exemplary prelate, distinguished alike for his piety, virtue, learning, and high taste for literature and the fine arts, died lamented and regretted by all ranks of society.

BEGUE, (Nicholas A. le) first an organist of St. Merry at Paris, and after 1678, of the royal chapel, died in 1700. He was a superior performer on his instrument, but became especially notorious for sounding a double or even treble melody. As no one else could do so, he was suspected of having a hidden assistant—a supposition somewhat plausible, as Begue played always at the back part of the organ. This doubt was never cleared up. Some of his piano and organ music, as well as some motettes, were printed at Paris. (Walther. Gerber. Schilling.)

BEGUE DE PRESLE, (Achilles William le,) a French physician, born at Pithiviers, near Orleans. He studied at Paris, where he took the degree of doctor of medicine in 1760, was appointed one of the royal censors, and died May 18, 1807. He wrote a great number of works, and laboured to treat of medicine in a popular manner. He also translated various works: among others, that of Storck on the Medical Nature of Hemlock, and its Use in the Cure of Cancers; also his work on Aconite. He was intimate with J. J. Rousseau, and published an account of the latter days of his friend, which appeared in 1778. He also wrote, but did not publish, a letter on the death of Rousseau, addressed to the Journal de

Paris, which afterwards appeared in the Literary Correspondence of Grimm. He was one of the editors of the Bibliothèque Physico-économique, from 1786 to 1792. His publications deserving notice are:—Le Conservateur de la Santé, La Haye (Paris), 1763, 12mo; Mémoires et Observations sur l'Usage interne du Colchique commun, les Feuilles d'Oranger, et le Vinaigre distillé, Paris, 1764, 12mo; Manuel du Naturaliste pour Paris et ses Environs, Paris, 1766, 8vo; Economie rurale et civile, Paris, 1789, 2 vols, 8vo; Relation ou Notice des derniers Jours de J. J. Rousseau, avec une Addition par J. H. de Magellan, Lond. 1778, 8vo.

BEGUELIN, (Nicholas de, 1714—1789,) a natural philosopher of Switzerland, who sought employment in Prussia, and was entrusted with the education of prince Frederic William, nephew of the great Frederic. In 1764 he lost his post through an act of injustice; twenty years afterwards he was restored, and when his pupil became king of Prussia, he was created a noble, and otherwise honoured; but he did not long enjoy his good fortune. To the royal academy of Berlin he contributed some valuable papers, and he also translated two or three works. (Biog. Univ. Suppl.)

BEGUILLET, (Edme, died 1786,) an advocate and notary of Dijon, wrote several treatises on agricultural subjects, a History of Burgundy, and a History of Paris. (Biog. Univ.)

BEGUIN, (John,) a celebrated French physician and chemist, under Henry IV. He was almoner to Lewis XIII. He visited the mines, and travelled through Italy, Germany, and Hungary. He invented a method of preparing Calomel; and published a Compendium of Chemistry, which went through an immense number of editions. It appeared first at Paris in 1608, in 12mo, under the title of Tyrocinium Chymicum è Naturæ Fonte et manuali Experientia de promptum, Paris, 1608. It was translated into German, with notes, by Jeremiah Barth and Christopher Glücksradt, at Königsberg, in 1618; again, by J. G. Pelshofer, at Wittemberg, in 1634; into Dutch, by Gerard Blaes, or Blasius, at Amsterdam, in 1659; into French, by John Lucas Le Roi, Paris, 1624; and into English, London, 1669, 8vo.

BEGUINOT, (count N. 1747—1808,) a French general, who, when the revolution broke out, was a common soldier. Napoleon, disliking his republicanism, in 1808 ceased to employ him, but conferred some honours upon him. (Biog. Univ. Suppl.)

BEGYN, or BEGEYN, (Abraham,) a Dutch painter, born in 1650. He painted landscapes and cattle in the manner of Nicholas Berchem. His principal residence was at Berlin, where his works were greatly prized, and, according to Houbracken, he was principal painter to the elector of Brandenberg, afterwards king of Prussia. In many collections in Holland, the pictures of Begyn are placed amongst those of the most admired masters. His pencilling is light and free, and his colouring very agreeable. Many of his works are landscapes, with views of rivers, ruins, and pieces of architecture, enriched with figures and a variety of animals. (Pilkington's Dict. Bryan's Dict.)

BEHAGUE, (John Peter Anthony, comte de,) a French general, who entered the service in 1744. In 1791 he was sent to Martinique as governor. To his honour, he adhered to the royal cause, and when he could no longer prevent the colonies from embracing the revolution, he came to England. By the Bourbon princes he was employed to organize insurrections in Brittany, but his advanced age rendered him unfit for service, and he returned to London, where he died early in the present century. (Biog. Univ. Suppl.)

BEHAM, or BOEHEM, the name of two eminent German artists.

1. *Bartel*, or *Bartlemy*, a painter and engraver, born at Nuremberg about 1496, elder brother of the celebrated Hans Sebald Beham. He seems to have resided chiefly in Italy, and to have studied under Marc Antonio Raimondi at Rome and Bologna. As an engraver, he is considered one of the most successful imitators of Marc Antonio. His drawing is masterly, and his heads possess great expression. Many of his plates are without mark, which has sometimes led to mistakes. The prints that bear his signature are marked B B, and are dated from 1520 to 1536. He is supposed to have been in the service of duke William of Bavaria, and to have died in Italy, whither he had been sent by the duke about the year 1540. M. Heinecken gives a copious list of his works. (Heinecken, Dict. des Artistes. Strutt's Dict. of Eng. Bryan's Dict.)

2. *Hans Sebald*, also a painter and engraver, born at Nuremberg in 1500. Heinecken states him to be the nephew of the preceding, but Mr. Strutt observes

that he is generally allowed to have been his brother. He is said to have received instruction in engraving from Bartel, probably before he went to Italy, which he did at an early age. His style resembles that of H. Aldegrever; and, like that artist, he is classed amongst the little masters, from the diminutiveness of his works. He engraved both on copper and wood, and some few etchings have been attributed to him. He possessed considerable genius and a ready invention; drawing correctly, and in a good but gothic style. His draperies are frequently stiff, and loaded with a multiplicity of short, inelegant folds. Many of his engravings are grossly indecent. This forced him to leave his native city and take refuge at Frankfort-on-the-Maine, where he continued to exercise his art. His dissipated habits at length made him quit the brush and burin, and he died a dealer in wine at Frankfort, in 1552. The plates which he executed at Nuremberg are marked with a cipher composed of the letters H. S. P. joined, and are dated from 1519 to 1530. Those engraved at Frankfort are marked with the letters H. S. B. joined, and are dated from 1531 to 1549. His works on copper are very numerous, of which a lengthened catalogue is given by Heinecken. (Strutt's Dict. Biog. Univ. Heinecken.)

BEHAM, (Martin,) a celebrated geographer and navigator of the fifteenth century. His name, by different writers, is altered into Behem, Behaim, Bœhm, Bœhem, Behen, Behemira, &c. All agree that he was born at Nuremberg, in Franconia, of a noble family, originally from Bohemia. Some place his birth in 1430, others in 1436; and a few, without mentioning any particular year, oblige us, from the account they give of his adventures, to fix upon a much earlier date. Again, Cellarius at first, followed afterwards by Riccioli, with a few more, pretended that Beham in 1459 went to pay a visit to Isabella, daughter of John I., king of Portugal, but then regent of Flanders, from whom, having received a vessel, he sailed westward, and discovered the whole group of the Azores, or at least the island of Fayal, where he established a colony; for which discovery he received the government of it, and the dignity of knighthood from John II. Nor is this enough; for the same writers go farther, and following Struvenius' treatise, De vero novi Orbis Inventore, copied by Hartman Schedel in his Latin Chronicle, and the remarks of Mateus on the canon law, &c., pretend that many years before Columbus, Beham had visited America, discovered the Brazils, and the Straits of Magellan, and that what Columbus did was in pursuance of the instructions he received from Beham, whom he met at the island of Madeira. We should not have noticed these extraordinary opinions, which had been confuted since the year 1761 by professor Tozen, and after him by Robertson and others, had they not been revived by M. Otto, a diplomatic agent of the French government, in 1786, who, not aware that such an opinion had been started before, renewed the forgotten dispute in a letter to Dr. Franklin, which was published in the 2d vol. of the Transactions of the American Philosophical Society, held at Philadelphia. In this letter Otto tried to prove his assertion from some records kept in the archives of Nuremberg, and from a globe which Beham had made; and has thus offered the opportunity to writers who knew nothing about the matter to repeat the old story; for, in point of fact, the Azores had been seen by Vanderberg, a navigator of Bruges, in 1431, and visited in 1432 by Velho Cabral, when Beham was scarcely born; and as to the records of Nuremberg, it has been shown that they must have been written after the discovery of Columbus. As to the globe and charts which Beham made, and from which M. Otto and his followers try to prove that Columbus first received the notion of a western continent, it has been proved by Murr, who wrote his life in German, and published a fac-simile of them, (the translation of which, by Jansen, was added to the first voyage round the world by Pigafetta,) that they were made according to the description of Ptolemy, Strabo, Pliny, Marco Polo, and the travels of Sir John Mandeville. Hence Beham's geographical knowledge did not really go beyond Japan in the east, or the Cape Verde islands in the west; and he places between them two islands, which he calls Brandon and Antllia; the first of which does not exist, and the latter, one of the Azores, had long been so called.

Beham studied under the learned John Müller, better known by the Latin name of Regiomontanus. He seems to have paid particular attention to mathematics and navigation, and, like Columbus, with other learned men, to have speculated upon large tracts of land in the western hemisphere. For some time he followed the profession of a merchant, without giving up his favourite studies; and in 1479, being on business at Antwerp, he became acquainted with some Flemings, who were connected with the court of Lisbon, and had formed colonies in the newly discovered islands of the Azores, Fayal, and Pico. At their invitation he accompanied them to Lisbon in 1470, where his great knowledge and skill in making maps insured him a gracious reception. In 1484 he accompanied, as a scientific man, the expedition, under the command of the admiral Don Diego Cam, sent to the western coast of Africa, the knowledge of which previously had scarcely reached Cape St. Catharine, S. lat. 2° 3′. It was then extended to Cape Cross, or De Patrono, in lat. 20°. After nineteen months he returned to Lisbon, where, on account of his services, king John II. conferred on him the honour of knighthood. It seems that about this time Beham went back to Fayal, where he took great pains to improve the state of the colony; and where, in 1486, he married Jane de Macedo, daughter of Job Huerte. The desire of seeing his relations made him, in 1492, the year in which Columbus started on his expedition of discovery, visit Nuremberg, where he passed a whole year, and at the request of his countrymen, made a terrestrial globe. On his return to Portugal he had some brief diplomatic employment; but at the death of king John in 1494, he returned to Fayal, where he lived in peace with his family till the year 1506, when he went once more to Lisbon. He died there on the 29th of July, leaving no other works of record than maps, charts, and the globe above mentioned.

BEHAMB, (John Ferdinand,) born at Presburg, in Hungary, where he first studied. He went then to Strasburg to study law, and became a doctor. He relinquished the protestant faith for the Romish, and settled as an advocate at Lintz, in Austria. He wrote, Notitia Hungariæ Antiquo-moderna Berneggeriana, &c., Argent. 1686, 8vo, and some law books, printed about the same period, at Lintz. (Horányi, Mem. Hung.)

BEHEM, (Bernard,) master of the mint at Halle, in Tyrol, who made for the archduke Sigismond the first dollars with the effigy of that prince, which are fine specimens of the art of those times. He died in 1507, aged 71.

His son, of the same christian name, was appointed by the emperor Maximilian I., in the year 1511, chief master of the mints of Austria and Tyrol. To him is ascribed the sinking of the die for the memorable dollar with the effigy of Lewis I. of Hungary, bearing the date of 1525. (Nagler, Lex. der Künstler.)

BEHM, (John, 1578—1648,) wrote a Chronology from the Creation to the Destruction of Jerusalem by Titus. (Biog. Univ.)

BEHM, (Michael,) born at Königsberg in 1612, studied at Copenhagen, where the great theologian Brochmann became his patron, and at Wittemberg, whence the plague drove him to Leipsic. He was afterwards named a professor of theology at Wittemberg, and the queen dowager of Sweden made him her court preacher; elector Frederic William of Brandenburg sent him to a theological *colloquium charitativum* at Thorn. He wrote, Utrum Christus ob Sanctific. et Missionem in Mundum se Filium Dei appellavit; and some more Latin and German theological works. (Freheri Theatrum Virorum erud. clar.)

BEHM, (Michael,) a common counsellor at Dantzic, about 1630. He took an active part in the disputes then carried on about the Jus Indigenatus in Prussia; and wrote, De Indigenatu sincera Collatio, Gedani, 1669, 4to. (Hoppius, Schediasma.)

BEHMER, (Frederic Ehrenreich,) a lawyer, born at Berlin in 1721, employed by Frederic II. in the preparation of many important diplomatic documents. His Vindiciæ Supremat0̂s in Silesiam Borussici are deposited in the Royal Archives. His greatest work is, Novum Jus Controversum. This work contains fifty-one articles, relative to all portions of jurisprudence, and especially civil law. He died the 16th of April, 1776. (Biog. Univ.)

BEHN, (Aphra,) an English dramatist, poetess, and novel writer, highly popular in the reign of Charles II. when nothing could exceed the licentiousness of the public stage, but the licentiousness of private manners.

She was born in the reign of Charles I., but the year is not known, and, as is stated, of a good family in Canterbury, of the name of Johnson. While she was yet very young, her father was appointed governor of Surinam, but he died on the voyage out, leaving behind him a large family who were with him on the way to the West Indies. They proceeded on their expedition, and resided at Surinam for some years, where Aphra Johnson became intimately acquainted with prince

Oroonoko, whose history she afterwards moulded into the novel that Southern used in writing his tragedy of that name. In Surinam she lost several other relations, and returned to London, where her beauty and abilities procured her a husband in Mr. Behn, an English merchant of a Dutch family. Not long afterwards (her husband, probably, having died in the interval) it is asserted that she was employed by the court of England, at the instance, it would seem, of Charles II. himself, to proceed to the Low Countries, in order to procure and transmit information as to the designs of the Dutch. She went to Antwerp, and there formed, or renewed, an acquaintance with a person of influence and information, named Vander Albert, who let her into the secret of the intention of the Dutch, under de Witt and de Ruyter, to sail up the Thames and burn the English ships at Chatham. This is broadly stated in the Memoirs of Mrs. Behn, but it seems very doubtful, as unquestionably the intelligence that she is reported to have sent over was not credited in London. It looks like an endeavour to give importance to Mrs. Behn's character after the attempt had been made by the Dutch, and to cast an imputation upon the English government for not availing itself of her information.

She continued to reside for some time in Antwerp, and is said to have entered into all the gaieties and gallantries of the city. Why she returned to England does not appear; but sailing from Dunkirk she was wrecked on our coast, and was only saved by boats from the shore. At this period she could not have been much more than twenty-three or twenty-four years old, and it seems probable that during the rest of her life she was mainly indebted to her pen for support. That she was a woman of beauty and gallantry cannot be doubted; and it is asserted, with some appearance of truth, that she devoted herself much to the pleasures of the town. Two of her plays were printed in 1671, the Amorous Prince and the Forced Marriage; and between that year and 1687, she produced no fewer than thirteen other comedies or tragi-comedies, and one tragedy, entitled Abdelazar, which made its appearance in 1677. It is founded upon the old play, long falsely attributed to Marlowe, called Lust's Dominion, (see Dodsley's Old Plays, ii. 311, last edit.); and Dr. Young borrowed considerably from Mrs. Behn in his Revenge. Two of her dramas, The Widow Ranter, and The Younger Brother, were posthumous; the first having been brought out at the Theatre Royal in 1690, and the second at Drury-lane Theatre in 1696. There is no one of her plays totally devoid of merit, although it is evident that she sometimes wrote under the pressure of necessity. Their indecency she seeks to excuse in the preface to her Lucky Chance, 1687, which says that she offended in this respect no more than her neighbours, and that her productions ought not to be examined with greater severity. She had, however, probably better talents than many of these worthless neighbours, and was, besides, a woman.

Of the later portion of her career little has been ascertained, and perhaps the result of an investigation might be anything but satisfactory. In 1684, 1685, and 1688, she published three volumes of miscellanies in verse, including pieces by the earl of Rochester and Sir George Etherage, (a companionship not of the most unexceptionable kind,) together with a translation of Rochefoucault's Maxims. One of her most remarkable pieces is a version of Ovid's Epistle, Œnone to Paris, which, with others, was printed under the sanction of a preface by Dryden, in which he avows that she did not understand Latin. She had not attained her fiftieth year at the time of her death, on the 16th of April, 1689, after a tedious illness; she was buried in the eastern ambulatory of the cloisters of Westminster Abbey. During her life she was very commonly known by the poetical appellation of "the Divine Astræa," a circumstance which misled Langbaine, when, in his account of Dramatic Authors, he called her Mrs. Astræa Behn. Gildon published a collected edition of her separately printed plays, and such was their discreditable popularity, that they reached the eighth edition in 1735.

BEHOURT, (John,) a French grammarian and dramatic poet, born in Normandy about the end of the sixteenth century, professor of the belles-lettres at Rouen for more than forty years; long famed for an abridgement of Despautère's grammar, and author of three plays written for his pupils. They were printed at Rouen in 12mo, and are extremely rare. (Biog. Univ. Suppl.)

BEHR, (Christopher,) professor of eloquence and poetry at Dantzic. He wrote, Exultans Flammula, a poem on the coronation of king John III. Gedani, 1676, folio; and some other festival addresses. (Hoppius, Schediasma.)

BEHR, (George Henry,) a physician and a poet, born at Strasburg, Oct. 16, 1708. He studied medicine, and in 1730 entered as a surgeon to a Swiss regiment in the French service, in which he remained only one year. He then travelled in Germany and Holland, and in the latter country took the degree of a doctor of medicine in 1731. In 1738 he was appointed physician to prince Hohenlohe Waldenbourg. He was made a magistrate of his native place, and he died May 9, 1761. He published many professional works, and also wrote many papers in the Commercium Litterarium Noribergense, and in the Acts of the Academy of the Curious in Nature.

BEHR, (Christian Frederic de, 1739—1831,) general of artillery, marshal of the palace, and president of the council to the king of Wurtemberg. He rose from a very humble station, and during seventy-four years, served five princes of that house. (Biog. Univ. Suppl.)

BEHRENS, (Charles Frederic,) one of the few Germans mentioned in the History of Maritime Discoveries of Older Times. He was a native of Mecklenburg, and embarked with Roggewein upon his expedition "in search of unknown countries." He published an account of his voyage in 1738, and a French translation of this appeared in 1739. A chart is prefixed to the book, on which Behrens has marked the track of the vessels. (Dalrymple, Hist. Coll. Pacif. Ocean. Burney.)

BEHRENS, (Conrad Berthold,) a physician and historian, born at Hildesheim, in Lower Saxony, Aug. 26, 1660. He was physician to the army at Brunswick Lunenburg, and made a campaign into Hungary. Of the house of Brunswick he wrote a history, although he was much engaged in an extensive practice. He died Oct. 4, 1736, having published several medical works, besides many papers in the Ephémérides des Curieux de la Nature, and in the Acts of the Academy of Sciences of Berlin.

BEHRENS, (George Henning,) a German physician, born at Gosslar, in 1662. He practised in his native city, where he died in 1712. He had composed many works; but a fire which consumed Nordhausen in 1710 destroyed all his manuscripts. Only one work of his has been printed, which is a description of the Hartz, entitled Curiöser Harzwold, Nordhausen, 1703, 4to; again in 1708 and 1717. It was translated into English, and published in London, 1730, 8vo.

BEHRENS, (Rodolph Augustine,) a physician, son of C. B. Behrens, born at Brunswick. He practised at Wolfenbuttel, and died of apoplexy at Frankfort-on-the-Maine, Oct. 12, 1747. He furnished many papers to the Commercium Litterarium Noribergense, and published several works.

BEIDHAVI, (Cadhi Nasser-ed-Deen Abu-Said Abdallah Ebn Omar,) a celebrated Moslem divine and commentator on the Koran, born at Beidha, in Farss, but the precise date of his birth is unknown, and at one period cadhi of Shiraz, where he gained high reputation by the equity of his decisions. He afterwards removed to Tabriz, where he died, A.H. 692, (A.D. 1293,) though some accounts place his decease seven years earlier. He was the author of numerous works in Arabic on scholastic and doctrinal subjects, all of which enjoy great reputation; but his fame chiefly rests on his great commentary on the Koran, entitled Anwar al Tensil wa Asraïr al Tawil, The Lights of the Text (of the Koran), and the Mysteries of its Interpretation, a composition which the unanimous consent of Moslem divines has placed at the head of its class, and which has itself been made the basis of many subordinate treatises. He also wrote (by the Arabic title of Nizam-al-Towarikh, or The Rule of Histories,) a chronological work in Persian, extending from the creation of the world to his own time. Other historical works have been also attributed to him, but it is supposed incorrectly. (D'Herbelot. Pocock. Sale's Koran.)

BEIER, (Hartmann, 1516—1577,) a Lutheran minister of Wittemberg, who had the honour of Luther's friendship, and who wrote a Commentary on the Bible, and some other works. (Biog. Univ.)

BEIER, (Adrian,) a lawyer distinguished by his researches into those questions of law which affect industry and the rights of artisans, born at Jena on the 20th of Jan. 1634. He was professor of law in his native place when he died, in 1712. Beier's works are still much regarded in Germany. His principal writings are, 1. Tyro, prudentiæ Juris Opificiarii, &c. 1638. 2. Tractatus de Jure Prohibendi. 3. Boëthus peregrè redux Conspectibus, &c. 4. De Collegiis Opificum. 5. Opus de eo quod circa Carnifices et Excoriatores justum est. (Biog. Univ.)

BEIL, (John David,) a dramatist and

actor, born at Chemnitz in 1754. Though of poor parents, he was sent to Leipsic university, which he soon deserted to join a company of strolling players. While with them he was recommended to the duke of Gotha, for whose theatre he was engaged in 1777. He shone both in tragedy and comedy, and wrote several plays, rich in comic situations, but hasty and superficial compositions. Beil died in August, 1794.

BEINASCHI. See BENASCHI.

BEINGA-DELLA, the last king of Pegu, who conquered Ava, and in 1754, put to death Douipdi, an old man, the last emperor of its ancient dynasty. In the following wars he lost his capital, Pegu, and became the prisoner of Alompra, chief of the Birmans. For some time his captivity was mild, but the inhabitants of Pegu breaking out into rebellion against their conquerors, he was tried, condemned, and put to death by the hand of the public executioner. (Biog. Univ. Suppl.)

BEINL DE BIENENBURG, (Anthony, 1749—1820,) an eminent physician of Vienna, who wrote on the medical administration of an army. (Biog. Univ. Suppl.)

BEINVILLE, (Charles Bartholomew de, died 1641,) a gentleman of Picardy, who wrote in defence of the French against the Spaniards; in other words, a Defence of Cardinal Richelieu against the Cardinal Archbishop of Toledo, governor of the Netherlands under Philip IV. (Biog. Univ.)

BEIREIS, (Godfrey Christopher,) a physician, born at Mülhausen, March 2, 1730, who collected a very fine museum, containing objects of art, curious mechanism, and specimens illustrative of natural history and science in general; which he pretended to have been able to amass by having acquired the power of making gold. He died at a very advanced age, in Sept. 1809, having published some papers on philosophy and natural history in the Miscellaneen Artisischen Inhalts of Meusel, and in the Acts of the Society of Natural History of Berlin, together with some works of no great importance.

BEISCH, (Joachim Francis, 1665—Oct. 16, 1748,) a painter of landscapes and battles, born at Ravensburg, in Swabia, but resided and worked at Munich. He was the son and pupil of William Beisch, a painter of little note, who only painted for amusement. Joachim visited Italy, and painted many of its most striking views. His style of composition resembles that of Gaspar Poussin, though his touch is light, tender, and full of spirit. As an engraver, Beisch has contributed many charming etchings to the portfolios of collectors. There are by him four sets of landscapes, with figures and buildings, amounting together to twenty-six plates, etched with great freedom and spirit. (Bryan's Dict. Biog. Univ.)

BEISSIER, (James,) a celebrated French surgeon, born in 1621. He studied surgery under a renowned military surgeon, Martin d'Alencé. He served in the French army in the Low Countries, and arrived at the rank of surgeon-major. Lewis XIV. would not undertake any campaign without his attendance. When the king assigned the command of the army to the dauphin, and afterwards to the duke of Burgundy, he selected Beissier to accompany the princes in their expeditions, and he recompensed him in the most liberal manner, and even granted to him letters of nobility. Beissier was exceedingly charitable, and contributed largely to the relief of the distressed. In the severe winter of 1709, he even disposed of his carriage and horses to afford assistance to the necessitous. He lived to an advanced age, and passed the latter years of his life in acts of piety and devotion. He died suddenly, June 15, 1712, at the age of ninety-one years, and he was honourably buried in the church of St. Saviour.

BEITAR, an eminent botanist and physician, was born at Malaga. He died at Damascus, A.H. 646, (A.D. 1248-9.) He was the author of several medical and botanical works, some of which still exist in MS. in different European libraries. The most important of them is called Al-jámio 'l-Kabíro fi 'l-adwaiti 'l-mofridati, Collectio magna Simplicium Medicamentorum. It has never been published, either in the original Arabic or in a translation. Casiri remarks that Tournefort makes mention of a translation of Beitár by Galland, but observes that no such work is to be found in the Paris catalogue, in which several of his translations from the Arabic are mentioned. He himself gives the preface of the work, with a Latin translation, from which it will appear what pains were bestowed by the author on his work, and with what injustice it has sometimes been represented as a mere translation of Dioscorides. Russell says (Appendix to his Nat. Hist. of Aleppo) that it is in high estimation in the East, where MSS. of it are common. Bochart in his works has translated many extracts from it. It is divided into four parts, in which the author treats in alphabetical order of all the articles in the animal, vegetable, and mineral kingdoms, that possess any medical properties; and he is so accurate in his descriptions, that he often corrects errors in Galen, Dioscorides, and Ribasius, and mentions facts and details not to be found in their writings. There is a sort of analysis of this work in Dietz's Analecta Medica, Lips. 1833, 8vo. The chapter on the Lemon was translated into Latin, Venet. 1583, 4to, by And. Alpago, and Paris, 1602, 4to. These two works are so rarely to be met with, that Martin Ghizi, a learned physician of Cremona, believing the Latin translation to be still unedited, published it 1758, Cremona, 4to; and in the same year, Valcarenghi published a work entitled, In Ebenbitar Tractatum de malis Limoniis Commentaria, Cremona, 4to. (See Nicoll and Pusey, Catal. MSS. Arab. Bibl. Bodl. p. 585; C. G. Kühn, Additam. ad Ind. Medicor. Arab. à J. A. Fabricio in Bibl. Græc. vol. xiii. Exhibitum, Manip. 4; besides the authors already quoted.)

BEITLER, (William Gottlieb Frederic,) born in 1745 at Reutlingen, in the kingdom of Wirtemberg, appointed professor of mathematics at Milan, and in 1778 astronomer of the Petrina academy there. Many of his observations are given in the scientific journals of Berlin, Petersburg, and Paris; those upon Jupiter's satellites have been of great use to other astronomers. A Nova Analysis Equationum Cubicarum appeared in 4to at Milan, 1778, and a treatise on the planets of our solar system was printed after his death in 1811. (Ersch und Gruber.)

BEITLER. See Beutler.

BEITON, (Athanasius Ivanovitch,) descended from a noble German family, once in the Polish service, but being taken prisoner by the Russians, he entered their army, and greatly distinguished himself against the Chinese. He died at the beginning of the eighteenth century, but the precise time is not known. (Entz. Leks.)

BEJA, (F. Anthony de,) a native of Beja, in Portugal, wrote Tratado de Astrologia Judiciaria, printed about 1530. (Antonio.)

BEJA, (F. Lewis, de Peristrello,) a Portuguese friar, a deputy of the Italian inquisition, and for many years a teacher at Bologna. He was one of the members of a sort of academy, which discussed in the archbishop's palace cases of conscience, in which the decisions of Beja were considered final. He published his decisions under the title, Responsa Casuum Conscientiæ, Bononiæ, 1587. A second vol. was printed at Rome. He wrote other works, some of which passed through several editions. (Antonio, Bibl. Hisp.)

BEJART. The name of a French family, distinguished on the stage.

1. A comrade of Molière's, wounded in the foot, in endeavouring to separate two friends who were fighting. He used crutches afterwards, and such was his success in characters of valets, that other actors of those parts in the provinces affected lameness in imitation of him. He quitted the stage in 1670. (Biog. Univ.)

2. *Elizabeth Armande Cresinde Claire*, sister of the preceding, first married Molière, and secondly Guérin d'Estriche. Molière was not long before he repented of his marriage with her. She quitted the theatre in 1694, and died on the 3d of October, 1700. (*Id.*)

3. *Genevieve*, another sister of the above, married Villeaubrun, afterwards Aubry, who from a master paviour had become a tragic author. She played the parts of waiting maids, and died in 1675. (*Id.*)

BEJOT, (Francis, 1718—1787,) of Montpelier, keeper of the MSS. in the royal library of Paris. He left several works in MS. (Biog. Univ.)

BEK, an engraver, little known in England, by whom we have, among other prints, the portrait of Peter Malmberg, almoner to Charles XII., king of Sweden. (Strutt's Dict. of Eng.) See also Beck.

BEK, (John Philippovitch,) born at Riga in 1735. Having studied at Berlin, he went to St. Petersburg, and was made an army surgeon. In 1773 he was appointed chief surgeon to the grand duke Paul, after whose accession to the throne he was liberally rewarded. He is said to have made public (at the emperor's request) a cure for the tape-worm. He died in 1811. (Entz. Leks.)

BEK, or BEAK, (Anthony,) perhaps the most opulent and magnificent of the ancient English prelacy, except Wolsey. He was consecrated to the see of Durham in 1283, and having, in addition to its ample revenues, a private estate of five thousand marks a-year, he became one of the most conspicuous personages of his day. From the pope he obtained the title of patriarch of Jerusalem, and his own sovereign granted him the Isle of Man. He was, however, long harassed by a dispute with the monastic chapter of his cathedral, arising from his objections to the prior on the ground of incompetency. This involved him in difficulties both at Rome and with the English crown. At length, he recovered the king's favour, and spent his princely resources to the end of life in raising noble piles of building. His episcopal seat of Auckland he converted into a castle, and several other castellated and religious edifices were either built or enlarged by him. He died at Eltham, in 1311. (Collier. Godwin.)

BEK, or BEKH, (Michael Schend von der,) of Greek origin, educated in Holland, and doctor of philosophy and medicine in the university of Padua. He entered into the service of Russia, in the reign of Peter the Great, and in 1725 was appointed chief physician of the military hospital at St. Petersburg. His writings, which are in a style of pure Latinity, show him to have possessed no ordinary degree of knowledge and science. In the first volume of the Acta Physico-Med. Acad. Nat. Cur. (1725), is printed his Præsens Russiæ Litterariæ Status, &c. It appears also, according to Scheben, that he composed a work entitled Lexicon Universale Criticum, which was purloined from him by prince Maurocordato. Like Mead, he was a great antiquary, fond of numismatics and collecting coins. (Evgenii.)

BEKA, (Jerome,) a Carthusian monk of Belgium, prior at Ghent, and afterwards at Dijon. He wrote a great many sermons and epistles, perhaps worthy not to have been forgotten. (Biblioth. Carthus. Swertius.)

BEKESZ, (Gaspar,) a Hungarian nobleman, born in 1540; employed in various missions to the courts of Vienna and Constantinople. At the former his talents so recommended him to Maximilian II., that, on the death of Sigismond, the emperor advised the people of Sedmigradsk to elect him their prince; but his Socinianism and haughtiness caused him to be disliked by the nobles, who made choice of Stephen Batori. Nevertheless, when the latter was elected to the throne of Poland, Bekesz became his staunch and faithful adherent, rendering him important services on many occasions, and particularly at the siege of Dantzic. He died shortly after at Wilna, where he was buried on a hill which has since borne the name of the *Bekeszowa gora*.

BEKETOV, (Nikita Athanascivitch,) born September 8th, 1729. In 1763, he was governor of Astrachan. In this capacity he was a most important benefactor to his country, for, during the whole of his administration, he gave his attention to colonization, agriculture, vines, and silkworms, the mercantile intercourse between Russia and Persia, and the fisheries. On retiring from his government in 1780, Beketov settled at Otrada, a village belonging to him, (at no great distance from the mineral springs of Sarepta, which had been discovered by himself,) where he died July 9th (21), 1794. Beketov had a turn for poetry, and wrote several songs, which were printed in the collection published at Moscow, 1769-70; he also wrote a tragedy entitled, Nicanor, from a subject of Assyrian history; but it was never printed, and was destroyed with other manuscripts and papers by a fire at his residence at Otrada. (Evgenii.)

BEKETOV, (Platon Petrovitch,) born at Simbirsk in 1761, who established, in 1807, a printing office at Moscow, where he published editions of Bogdanovitch and other eminent authors, in what was then considered a very superior style of typography. He became a member of the Russian Historical and Antiquarian Society at Moscow, and when that body was re-organized, and received a new charter, he was elected its president, which office he continued to hold until 1820, when he resigned, in consequence of his declining health. The distinction thus conferred upon him was well merited, for he was a most liberal benefactor to that institution, having enriched its library with a variety of rare manuscripts, books, and coins, both before the collection was destroyed by the conflagration of 1812, and afterwards. He survived his retirement from the presidentship many years, for he did not die until 1836. (Snigerev.)

BEKETOV, (Nikolai Andreevitch,) professor of political economy and diplomacy at Moscow; born May 12 (26), 1790. He died, August 8th (20), 1829. In an autobiographical memoir, inserted in the third volume of the Russian translation of Richter's History of Medicine (which volume and the second were translated by himself), mention is made of several literary productions by him, some of which remain inedited. His treatise on the Commercial Intercourse between the ancient Slavonians and other Nations, and that between Russia and Greece, is printed in the Transactions of the Russian Historical and Antiquarian Society, vol. ii. 1824. Beketov also translated Voltaire's History of Peter the Great, 2 vols, 12mo; and Klopstock's Messiah, 4 vols, 12mo, 1820-1. (Snigerev.)

BEKKER, (Balthazar,) almost the very first to oppose and uproot those absurd superstitions which prevailed, to the disgrace of reason and religion, down to a late period, was the son of a clergyman at Warfhuizen, in Ommelanden, where he was born in 1634. He attacked the prevalent superstitious notions of the times, on the occasion of the great comet of 1680; but it was not until some years afterwards, namely, 1691, that he published his celebrated Betooverde Wereld, in which he boldly attacked the prevalent notions relative to evil spirits, their power and influence; and in consequence of which he was suspended from his duties for two years; but this mark of censure not satisfying the more bigoted of his adversaries, he was afterwards prohibited from preaching by the synod, and deprived of his office. This persecution and disgrace he bore with patient fortitude, and died, in 1698, with sentiments of sincere piety. That some of his speculations in regard to fallen angels and evil spirits were calculated to alarm the scrupulous, is not to be denied; but his book certainly gave a severe shock to those inveterate superstitions which had till then maintained themselves even in the reformed church, and opened a way that was quickly trodden by other writers. (Van Kampen.)

BEKKER, (Elizabeth,) a Dutch authoress, one of the few original writers of novels the language could then boast, born at Vlissengen, 1738. She married Adrian Wolff, a clergyman of the reformed church, in Beemster; but is as frequently spoken of by her maiden as by her marriage name, and we have therefore placed her here under the former. After her husband's death, she and her friend, Agatha Deken, constantly resided together, sharing in each other's literary pursuits, and frequently uniting their talents on the same work. At the time of the disturbances in 1787, they went to reside for awhile in Burgundy, but returned to Holland, where they died at the Hague, in 1804. Both were women of superior abilities, but Elizabeth's forte lay more peculiarly in keenness of observation, lively raillery, partaking occasionally of causticity, and in shrewd remark; while Agatha, who was of a more serious disposition, distinguished herself by the pure morality and sound religious feeling which pervade her compositions. It is difficult, however, to determine what was the exact share of these literary colleagues in those novels which they jointly composed in the epistolary form. Suffice it to say that those productions are still recognised as classical, and as affording admirable pictures of the national character and manners at the time. They consist of Historie van Sara Burgerhart, 2 vols, 8vo, 1782, (translated into French, and published at Lausanne, in 4 vols, 18mo, 1788); Historie von Willem Levend, 8 vols, 8vo, 1784-5; Brievan van Abraham Blankaert, 3 vols, 1787; and Historie van Cornelia Wildschut, 6 vols, 1783. Though now chiefly remembered by the abovementioned works, both possessed also some degree of poetical talent; the former published several elegies and poetical epistles, and a sort of satirical burlesque piece, entitled, De Menuet en de Dominees Pruik, wherein she animadverts with much caustic pleasantry on the over-strained punctilio of some of the members of the high-church; while Agatha wrote Liederen voor den Boerenstand, Leyden, 1804. This very remarkable case of personal and literary friendship loses nothing of its interest by the circumstance of their both departing from life within a very few days of each other, Elizabeth dying on the 5th, and Agatha on the 14th of November, 1804. (Van Kampen. Eichhorn.)

BEKOVITCH, (Prince Alexander,) a Tcherkes, or Circassian by birth, supposed to be descended from some of the *Begs*, *Beks*, or native princes of that country, and who fixed himself in Russia, where he adopted the christian faith, and was taken into great favour by Peter the First. He afterwards suggested to him the policy of subjugating the Caucasian tribes, and rendering them tributary to Russia, urging the expediency of doing so without delay, lest such project should be anticipated by Turkey. For the promotion of this scheme, he recommended that Russia should take possession of and fortify the shores of the Caspian Sea, and enter into alliance with Persia. The war with Sweden prevented the tzar from doing more at the time than sending an ambassador to the Persian court. In 1715, Bekovitch himself was employed in examining the eastern coast of the Caspian, and establishing military stations, preparatory to an expedition against Khiva; upon which last he set out from Astrachan in the spring of 1717, with a force of between seven and eight thousand men. After a laborious march of nearly a month, across the desert, the Russians approached within a few leagues of Khiva, when, contrary to their expectation, they found the enemy prepared to resist them, with a force very much superior to their own, it amounting to 24,000 men. Their valour seemed, however, likely to overcome this formidable obstacle, when Bekovitch suffered himself to be decoyed into the city. Hence he was obliged to send orders to major Von Frankenbeck to withdraw his troops; which command was not obeyed until it had been repeated three times. The reward for his compliance was, that Bekovitch himself was beheaded, and his companion Simonov, who had principally instigated him to enter Khiva, was cut in pieces. Great slaughter was also committed among those without the city; and the expedition terminated in sudden and complete failure. (Entz. Leks.)

BEKTASH, or HADJI-BEKTASH, the name of a celebrated dervise of Amaisian Anatolia, contemporary with Orkhan, the son of Othman, the second prince of the Ottoman line, who, on the formation of the new corps, afterwards so widely famous by the title of *janizaries*, sought to add solemnity to the institution by obtaining the benediction of Bektash, then in the odour of sanctity, on his troops. The ceremony of their consecration by the extended sleeve of the sheikh is universally familiar; but almost every modern writer, including even Gibbon, has followed an error originated by Kantemir, in attributing to the reign of Mourad I. an event which Von Hammer clearly proves, from Turkish authorities, to have taken place under that of his predecessor, Orkhan. An order of dervises founded by Hadji-Bektash, and bearing his name, became in after years widely dispersed through the Ottoman empire, and were especially protected by the janizaries, who regarded them as affiliated members of their own body. But this connexion proved, eventually, fatal to the Bektashis, who were involved in the proscription which overtook their allies in the reign of Mahmood II.

BEL, or BELIUS, (Matthias, 1684—1749,) a native of Orsova in Hungary, Lutheran pastor of Presburg, and rector of the college in that city, wrote some useful works on the history of Hungary. Of these, the most valuable is, Notitia Hungariæ Novæ Historica Geographica, (4 vols, fol. Vienna, 1735,) which obtained him letters of nobility, and the post of historiographer to the emperor Charles VI. His Apparatus ad Historiam Hungariæ, (3 vols, folio,) and his Amplissimæ Historico-criticæ Præfationes, (3 vols, 8vo,) may also be consulted with great advantage. Indeed, to the historian of Hungary, no writer or collector is so valuable. (Biog. Univ.)

BEL, (Charles Andrew, 1717—1782,) son of the preceding, professor and librarian at Leipsic, and counsellor of state to the Saxon elector, was also a man of great learning, though inferior to the father. His edition of Bonfinii Rerum Hungaricarum Decades; and his De Verâ Origine et Epochâ Hunnorum, should be joined with those of the elder Bel. (Biog. Univ.)

BEL, (John James, 1693—1738,) a French writer, born at Bourdeaux, counsellor of the parliament there, wrote some satirical works. His Dictionnaire Néologique contains the vicious words and locations, in alphabetical order, of his most celebrated contemporaries, such as La Motte, Fontenelle, Crebillon, Rollin, and even Voltaire. (Biog. Univ.)

BEL, (John Baptist le,) a Flemish artist, about 1750. He painted mostly heads of old men and women, as well portraits as of his own composition. His portrait is in the Florence gallery, where several of his pictures are to be found. (Fiorillo. Nagler.)

BELA, (the *Cavallero de*,) deserves honourable mention for a great literary undertaking, which, though now in MS., may one day be published in France. In 1748 Bela was made colonel of the Royal Cantabrian regiment. Thirty years of his life were passed in the composition of a History of the Basques, his countrymen. He consulted all that has ever been written on that subject, from the Greeks down to the modern Spaniards; he made no less use of MSS. than of printed books; and, with the most indefatigable industry, he composed, from elements so various, and often so discordant, a complete history of that singular people, who inhabit Alava, Guipuscoa, Biscay, Navarre, Upper and Lower, both on the Spanish and French side of the Pyrenees. It is in 3 vols, folio, and contains 600 pages of MS. in the author's hand-writing. In 1766 it was sent to Paris for publication, but the censors of the press forbade it. No one, indeed, could expect that a Spaniard, still less a Biscayan, should write so as to please the French in matters of history, where the origin, or interests, or prejudices of the two people are at stake. (Biog. Univ. Suppl.)

BELA I. king of Hungary, mounted the throne A.D. 1061, in the place of his brother Andrew, whom he dethroned for attempting to substitute his son Solomon in the succession, which had previously been promised to Bela. His short reign of three years was equitable and prosperous; but the only remarkable event was the assemblage by his orders at Alba-Regalis of the deputies of the towns and districts for the discussion of public affairs, a measure in which may be traced the first germ of the diet of the kingdom. The session was, however, abruptly terminated by the forces of the king, in consequence of the demand of the assembly that paganism should be re-established, the clergy given up to slaughter, and the churches and bells destroyed!—a singular request for a nation which for seventy years past had been nominally christian. Bela was killed A.D. 1064, by the accidental fall of a plank in his palace. He left three sons, two of whom, Geisa and Ladislas, were afterwards kings; but the immediate successor of Bela was his nephew Solomon, son of Andrew.

BELA II. the grandson of Geisa, was placed on the Hungarian throne A.D. 1131, at the death of his cousin Stephen II. notwithstanding his blindness, his eyes having been put out by his uncle Coloman, another son of whom, Borich, (half-brother of Stephen,) vainly contested the crown with him, by the help of Henry the Proud, duke of Bavaria. In 1138, having subdued the districts of Rama, in Servia, he assumed the additional title of king of Rama. An incident scarcely worth commemorating, were it not that it is by a reference to this obscure dominion that Gibbon (ch. lxx. note s,) corrects the error of Giannone, who has supposed that Ladislas of Naples, at the end of the fourteenth century, assumed the title of king of Rome, thus confounding Roma and Rama. Bela died 1141, leaving the character of a wise and just prince; his virtues, however, were sullied by drunkenness, and by acts of cruelty committed under the influence of intoxication. His son Geisa II. succeeded him.

BELA III. grandson of the preceding, and son of Geisa II. succeeded his elder brother, Stephen III. A.D. 1174. He was then resident at the court of the Greek emperor, Manuel Comnenus, whose powerful intervention had been frequently called in during the preceding reign by the civil wars between Stephen and his uncles. The authority of Bela was, however, universally acknowledged, without opposition, and he applied himself diligently to restore order to the distracted monarchy. In 1181 he recovered the important fortress of Zara, with great part of Dalmatia, from Venice; he also annexed part of Croatia and Bulgaria to his dominions, and gained considerable advantages over the Poles and Russians on the opposite frontier of his kingdom. He also made important changes in the internal regulation of the monarchy, the division of which into bannats, or counties, is attributed to him, as is also the institution of the dignity of palatine, or lieutenant-general of the kingdom, the highest station below the throne. Bela III. died A.D. 1196, after an able and prosperous reign, leaving two sons, Emeric and Andrew, who reigned in succession.

BELA IV. grandson of Bela III. succeeded his father Andrew (by whom he had been previously associated in the government) A.D. 1235. The first great event of his reign was the dreadful invasion of Hungary in 1241 and 1242, by a horde of 500,000 Moguls, under Batu, the grandson of Jenghiz-khan. The king and his valiant brother Coloman in vain attempted to withstand in arms the progress of these barbarians. Their troops were overwhelmed in every battle, and only three of all the Hungarian cities and fortresses are said to have escaped merciless slaughter and devastation. The king took refuge in the Adriatic islands, and the country was only released, after two years, from the utmost horrors of fire and sword, by the voluntary retreat of the Moguls. On returning to his desolated kingdom, Bela invited colonies of Germans and Italians to repeople the country; and in 1246 he defeated and killed Frederic the Warlike, duke of Austria, who had availed himself of the distress of Hungary to encroach on its territory: he even attempted to possess himself of Austria, but was routed and taken prisoner (1252) by Ottokar, king of Bohemia; a second attempt in 1260 was defeated by the same means, and Bela was forced, as the price of peace, to cede part of Styria. The last ten years of his reign were peaceful, and by judicious administration he succeeded in restoring to Hungary in some measure the prosperity which had been destroyed by the irruption of the Moguls. He died A.D. 1270, regretted by his subjects as a mild and beneficent ruler, and was succeeded by his son, Stephen IV. Some writers erroneously place his death five years later. (Bonfinius. Miechoritz. Gibbon. De Guignes, &c.)

BELA, or BELLA, (Anthony,) a priest and painter at Cordova, in Spain, also very skilful as a gilder. His works are to be found in that city, where he died in 1676. (Nagler, Lex.)

BELAIR, (A. P. Julian de, 1740—1819,) an officer in the French army, son of a banker at Paris. His father being ruined by extensive speculations, he studied mathematics, entered the army, and obtained the rank of captain, which he held until the dissolution of the legion in 1785. The next two years we find him at Berlin, connected with the periodical press of that capital. Want of encouragement made him return to Paris, where the revolution led him on to fortune. He was in 1792 chief engineer for the defence of Paris. This led him to trace a plan of entrenchments, to commence at St. Denis, and finish at Nogent-sur-Marne, which he proposed to line with six hundred pieces of artillery; materials for these were to be found in the royal statues overthrown by the revolution, and the lead of Versailles was to supply balls. In 1793 he had obtained the rank of general, and served in the North, under Dumourier and Jourdain. On his return to Paris, he engaged in many speculations, which exhausted his resources without benefiting his country, and he died poor. During his long life he wrote many works, on fortification, engineering, and other branches of military tactics. (Biog. Univ. Suppl.)

BELAU, (Nicholas Bruno, 1684—1747,) a painter, born at Magdeburg, who, having been instructed at Berlin by Augustine Zerwesten, finished his studies in Italy. On his return he painted at Berlin, Anspach, Vienna, and other parts of Germany. He died at Barby. We have from him the portrait of Gottlieb van Haesseler, privy counsellor to the king of Prussia, engraved by Bernigeroth, and a dedication to the emperor Charles VI. who is represented on horseback, and to whom a gentleman on his knees presents a book, a folio plate, engraved by G. A. Muller, at Vienna. (Heinecken, Dict. des Artistes.)

BELAY, or BELLAY, a carver of ornaments at Paris, after whom M. Cochin the younger has engraved the Four Seasons, represented by trophies of agricultural implements, and various other plates of ornaments. (Heinecken.)

BELBAI, (Malek-al-Dhaher Abu-Said,) the fifteenth sultan of Egypt, of the race of the Circassian or Borgite Mamlukes, elected to the throne by the beys on the death of sultan Khosh-khadem, A.H. 872 (A.D. 1467), (not 1460, as it is given in D'Herbelot, probably by a typographical error). He was more than seventy years of age at his elevation; but his tyranny and intemperate conduct inspired such general disgust, that after reigning only fifty-six days, he was deposed by common consent; a fate which his successor, Temar-Boga, also shared before the end of the same year. His name, according to D'Herbelot, was sometimes written Ilbai, which is perhaps more accurate, as the Arabs frequently mutilate Turkish names, and the difference between Belbai and Ilbai consists merely in a single point. (Al-Jannabi. Pocock. Prolegomena to Abul-Faraj. D'Herbelot.)

BELBRULE, (T.) a wood engraver, who lived in the time of Henry III. of France, about 1580, of whom Papillon says, that he has seen some ornamental flowers by him engraved very delicately on wood; and a small wood-cut in a book, containing figures of the sibyls, engraved on copper by John Rabel, dedicated to Louisa de Lorraine, wife of king Henry the Third. (Strutt's Dict. of Eng.)

BELCAMP, (John van,) a painter at London, who was employed by Vander Dort to copy the king's pictures. He also painted other works, and died in 1653. His portrait is engraved by Bannerman. (Heinecken, Dict. des Artistes.)

BELCARI, (Maffeo de,) a Florentine noble and poet of the fifteenth century. He filled several offices of the magistracy with considerable credit; his poems are all devotional. (Biog. Univ.)

BELCHER, (Dabridgecourt, commonly pronounced Dapscourt,) a dramatic writer of the Elizabethan era, of whose life very few particulars have been collected. His father, William Belcher, was a gentleman of good descent, residing at Guilsborough, in Northamptonshire. He was a friend of Guillim, the herald, who in his Display of Heraldry has given his achievements, and has spoken of him as "a man very complete in all gentlemanlike qualities, a lover of arts, and a diligent searcher after matters pertaining to honour and antiquity." A few Latin lines are prefixed to the

Display, by William Belcher, from which we extract the following enumeration of early English authors on heraldry:—

"Armorum primus *Wynkyn Meworden*s artem
Protulit, et ternis linguis lustravit eandem:
Accedit *Leghus*: concordat perbene *Boswell*,
Armorioque suo vivi dignatur honoris,
Clarorum clypeis et cristis ornat: eamque
Pulchre nobilitat, generis blazonia, *Ferni*:
Armorum proprium docuit *Wiricius* et usum."

William Belcher married Christiana Dabridgecourt, whose surname he gave as a christian name to his son, who was born about 1580, having been admitted, according to the Biographia Dramatica, at Corpus Christi college, Cambridge, March 2, 1597, and being afterwards, according to Wood, of Christchurch, Oxford, where he took the degree of B.A. in 1600. Very soon after this date he must have married Elizabeth, daughter of Richard Fisher, of Warwick, his eldest son being aged seventeen at the time of his father's death. When he went abroad, or what occasioned him to do so, are circumstances of his life not known; but he appears, from Wood's short notice of him, to have lived much at Utrecht, where, in 1617, he translated from a dramatic piece called Hans Beerpot, his comedy of See Me and See Me Not. This piece was printed in 1618, with a dedication to Sir John Ogle, then in a military command in the Low Countries, and governor of the town and garrison of Utrecht. In the title-page it is said to have been acted "by an honest company of health-drinkers." Perhaps he was an officer of the troops under Sir John Ogle. According to Wood, he wrote several poems, and made other translations, none of which, however, appear to have been printed, and died in the Low Countries in 1621.

BELCHER, (Jonathan, 1681—1757,) governor of Massachusetts and New Jersey, the son of Andrew Belcher, one of the council of the province. His father having paid great attention to his education, he graduated at Harvard college in 1699, and afterwards visited Europe. On his return he lived in Boston as a merchant with great reputation. He was chosen a member of the council, and was sent by the general assembly as an agent of the province to the British court in 1729. On the death of governor Burnet, his majesty nominated him to the government of Massachusetts and New Hampshire in 1730. He quitted the business of merchant of New England on being appointed to the chair of the first magistrate, the dignity of which he supported at the expense of his private fortune. The frankness and sincerity which so much distinguished him caused him to be extremely liberal in his censures both in conversation and letters. This gained him many enemies, and he fell into temporary disgrace; but having vindicated his character, he was restored to the royal favour, and appointed governor of New Jersey, where he arrived in 1747. On taking this situation, he found himself surrounded by numerous difficulties, but all these were conquered by his firmness, prudence, and impartiality. Governor Belcher was remarkable for the gracefulness of his person and the dignity of his deportment, and was distinguished by an integrity which could not be moved, and by justice, the zeal in administering which could be equalled only by his anxiety to have it equally distributed. His piety shed a lustre over all his other qualifications, religion with him not being merely formal, but exhibiting itself in devotion, meekness, humility, justice, truth, and benevolence. When Mr. Whitefield was at Boston in 1740, he treated him with marked respect, and requested him *to spare neither ministers nor rulers*.

BELCHER, (Jonathan,) chief justice of Nova Scotia, second son of the preceding, born about the year 1711, who, having graduated at Harvard college in 1728, came to England, where he was called to the bar. He went after this to Halifax, of which in 1760, being then senior counsellor, he was appointed lieutenant-governor, an office he held until 1763. In 1761, he was appointed chief justice. He died in Halifax, in March 1776.

BELCHIER, (John,) an English surgeon, a native of Kingston, in Surrey, born in 1706. He was educated at Eton, and bound apprentice to the celebrated Cheselden. He distinguished himself by the neatness of his dissections. He was very successful in practice, and chosen surgeon to Guy's Hospital. Being a fellow of the Royal Society, he communicated three papers, published in the Philosophical Transactions, two of which are singular cases, and the other is on the colouring of the bones of animals by giving to them particular kinds of aliment. He was a man of very amiable manners and disposition, and upon his retirement from the office of surgeon to Guy's hospital, he was elected a governor of that institution, and also of the neighbouring hospital of St. Thomas. He died in 1785, and was buried in the chapel attached to Guy's hospital.

BELDENAK, (Jens Andersen,) son of a shoemaker at Börglum, in Aalburg, studied theology, held an appointment as tutor, travelled through Germany and Italy, was appointed bishop in Odensee, and employed by king John of Denmark, amongst other missions, on an embassy to Lubeck, to solicit the interference of the Hanse confederates in obtaining the liberty of queen Christina, a Danish princess, held prisoner by the states of Sweden. He effected the object of his journey, but overstepped his commission so far as to give the Lubeckers a large sum of money for their interference, in the king of Denmark's name, and as his plenipotentiary. The king forgave this boldness, but only in part fulfilled the promise made by his servant. Fourteen years afterwards the successor of this king, Christian II. imprisoned Beldenak on some not very defined ground of complaint, compelled him to the renunciation of his episcopal office, to the payment of a heavy fine, and to a public apology for some free expressions uttered by him against the king and queen. This did not prevent Christian from availing himself of Beldenak's known talents, in a mission to procure the acknowledgment of the right of the king of Denmark to the throne of Sweden. His investiture followed almost immediately upon the embassy. As a reward for this service, he received the bishopric of Strengnäs. He was, however, again imprisoned in 1522 at Hammershuus, on the island of Bornholm, but liberated by the Lubeckers, who had not forgotten his liberality. From another imprisonment under Frederic I. he redeemed himself by the payment of a fine. He closed his active and troubled life in 1532, having before that time laid down his episcopal office. (Ersch und Gruber.)

BELDERBUSCH, (the count Charles Leopold de, 1749—1826,) of Lüneburg, minister for his sovereign, the elector of Cologne, to the French court, down to the period of the revolution. When the reign of terror was past, he returned to Paris, and, by Napoleon, was made prefect of the department of the Oise. On the restoration of the Bourbons, he was naturalized, but no longer employed. He wrote, from time to time, various political tracts. (Biog. Univ. Suppl.)

BELEAGO, or BALEAGO, (Melchior de,) born at Oporto, a professor of the Academy of Lisbon in the reign of John III. He wrote, Oratio de Disciplinarum omnium Studiis ad Universam Academiam Coimbricensem habita, Kal. Oct. 1547, 4to,—probably the prototype of those catalogues of lectures since used in German universities. His Dialectica, *ib.* 1549, was long the text-book in Portuguese academies. (Antonius, Bibl. Hisp. Nova.)

BELEJAMBE, or BELJAMBE, (Peter,) a modern French engraver, born at Rouen in 1752. (Bryan's Dict. Heinecken.)

BELELLI, (Fulgencio, 1682—1742,) of Naples, general of the Augustinians, and vicar-general of the pope, wrote an Exposition of St. Augustine's Opinion on the Mode of Repairing Fallen Human Nature. (Biog. Univ. Suppl.)

BELEM, (Fr. Jerome de,) born near Braga, in Portugal, in 1692, librarian of the convent of Xabregas. The list of his devotional works is singularly long. (Machado.)

BELEM, (Jane de,) a native of Namur, and a common prostitute at Brussels. She finally became the mistress of Henry Vander Nout, when she was greatly instrumental in revolutionizing Brabant in 1789, 1790, 1791. (Biog. Univ. Suppl.)

BELENVEI, (Aimery de,) a troubadour of the thirteenth century, whose songs were celebrated, and whose patrons were the highest in the north of France. He remained some years at the court of Raymund Berenger V., count of Provence. (Biog. Univ.)

BELESTAT, (Peter Langlois de,) physician of the duke d'Anjou, afterwards Henry III. He wrote two works on the Egyptian hieroglyphics. (Biog. Univ.)

BELESTAT, (the marquis de, 1725—1807,) of Haerlem. Voltaire wished to pass him off as the author of a pamphlet against a History of the President Henault—which tract he seems to have written himself, but was ashamed to own.

BELETH, (John,) a native of France, lived in the twelfth century. He taught theology at Paris, and is the author of various works but little known and of no reputation. (Hist. Lit. de France.)

BELFOUR, (Hugo John, 1802 or 3—Sept. 1827,) an English poetical and dramatic writer, admitted to holy orders in May 1826, and appointed to a curacy in Jamaica. His works consist of two dramatic pieces, called the Vampire and Montezuma, which with other poems were published under the assumed name of St. John Dorset. He possessed much facility of composition. (Gent. Mag. xcvii. 570.)

BELFREDOTTI, (Bocchino dei,) sovereign of Volterra in the sixteenth century, who, in the troubles of the time, lost his head upon the scaffold. (Biog. Univ.)

BELGARDE, (N.) a mulatto of Martinique, named governor of that island during the troubles which followed the suspension of general Rochambeau. In those perilous and difficult circumstances, he showed himself an able and courageous man. He was, however, compelled to yield to the English, who stripped him of his temporary power. (Biog. Nouv. des Contemp.)

BELGIUS, or BOLGIUS, a chief of the Gauls, who, about the year 279 before Christ, made an irruption into Macedonia and Illyria, at the head of a considerable army. He defeated and slew Ptolemy Ceraunus, king of the former country. From this period we hear no more of him; but his colleague, Brennus, penetrated into Greece.

BELGRADO, (James, 1704—1789,) a very learned Jesuit of Udino, in Italy, who taught physics, mechanics, and mathematics at Parma. His works might be consulted with advantage by writers on this side of the Alps. They are numerous. (Biog. Univ.)

BELGRAMO, the name of an engraver at Turin. He engraved a large map of the States of Savoy and Piedmont, after the design of John Thomas Borgonio, in 1680. (Heinecken.)

BELGRAVE, (Richard,) a Carmelite friar, in the fourteenth century, who lectured with great applause in the houses of his order.

BELHOMME, (Humbert, 1655—1727,) a native of Bar-le-duc, early professed in the congregation of St. Vannes, who rose to the highest dignities of his order, viz., the reformed Benedictine. His eloquence, his erudition, and the gravity of his manners, made him favourably known to Lorraine, and, we may add, the whole of France. His Historia Mediarni Monasterii in Vosago, or History of the Abbey of Moyen-Moutier, contains some excellent materials for the history of France in general, no less than of Lorraine and the neighbouring provinces. As abbot of that religious house, he collected a large and valuable library, which the republicans of France sold at the price of waste paper. Even his modest tomb did not escape their Vandalism. (Biog. Univ. Suppl.)

BELIDOR, (Bernard Forest de,) a colonel of infantry in the French service. He published various works on civil and military architecture. He died in 1761. His portrait is engraved by J. G. Wille.

BELIGATTI, (Cassio, 1708—1791,) a capucin of Macerata, in the papal states, sent on the mission to India and Thibet, which detained him eighteen years. He returned with a thorough knowledge of the language, and a respectable one of the literature, of that extraordinary people, the Thibetians, who so jealously guard their frontiers against Europeans. He was also well acquainted with the Hindoostani tongue, and partially with the Sanscrit. He had learning enough to be of great use to father Giorgi, in analyzing the Tartar MSS. which had been brought to Europe in 1721, and which no individual of the literary societies founded by Peter the Great had been able to understand. (Biog. Univ. Suppl.)

BELIGH, the name of two modern Turkish poets—the one Mustafa, son of Budshakli Ahmed Efendi, born at Constantinople, went the round of the professorships, and died in 1705. The other, Ismail, born at Brusa, was known under the name of Shahin Emirzádeh. He wrote the amatory history of his own youth, and afterwards put into verse a hundred traditions of the prophet, under the title of Gul Sadberg, (The Rose with a Hundred Leaves.) He also described the beauties of his native city, in a poem of the kind called in Persian, Shahrangéz (Stirrer-up of the City); and collected the history of the sheikhs, poets, and learned men of Brusa, from the time of the conquest to his own, under the title of Wafiat Danishveran (Biographies of the Learned). His last work was a collection of seven hymns, under the Arabic title of Seba' Sayáre (The Seven Planets.) (Von Hammer in Ersch und Gruber.)

BELIN, (Albert, 1610—1677,) of Besançon, a monk of the Benedictine order, bishop of Bellay. Besides some dogmatic and ascetic works, he wrote a book against the Chymists, Aventures du Philosophe Inconnu en la Recherche et Invention de la Pierre Philosophale, and a treatise of Talismans. (Biog. Univ.)

BELIN, or BELLIN, (Francis, 1672—1732,) a French dramatic writer, born at Marseilles. He wrote Mustapha et Zéangir, a tragedy in five acts, represented and printed in 1705, which is also to be found in the Petite Bibliothèque des Théâtres. La Harpe says, that, though this piece is written feebly, there is enough of happy expression to show that he had studied Racine. His other tragedies, Othon, Volonés, and La Mort de Néron, were afterwards played, but have not been printed. (Biog. Univ.)

BELIN, or BELLIN, (Nicholas,) an engraver at Rome, with whom Fuesli, in his dictionary, has confounded Nicoletto da Modena, an engraver, who lived in the sixteenth century. Belin lived in the seventeenth, and engraved some plates for the work, Insignium Romæ Templorum Prospectus, published by James de Rossi, in 1684, in folio; and amongst others, the plan of the church of the Vatican, after the chevalier Bernini, designed by Francis Buffalini. (Heinecken, Dict. des Artistes.)

BELIN DE BALLU, (James Nicholas, 1753—1815,) of Paris, one of the most distinguished Hellenists of France in his day; he held, prior to the revolution, a post in some public office, which enabled him to live while he abandoned himself to his favourite pursuits. He commenced his career by the translation of the Hecuba of Euripides, and he would have proceeded in this path had not his attention been called to the faults in the recent edition of Oppian, by Schneider. To collate MSS. for a new edition of that poet, and to prepare materials for a commentary, were his occupation for some time; but he did not finish the publication, probably through want of encouragement, and the apprehension of an approaching change in the political state of France. However, he had time to publish his translation of Lucian, which he seems to have executed some years before. During the reign of terror, and some time afterwards, he remained in obscurity; and seeing little hope of the restoration of letters in France, he accepted, from Alexander of Russia, the offer of a chair of Greek literature in the university which that emperor had just founded at Charkorf, in the Ukraine. There he remained some years, but he was not happy; and he removed to Moscow, where he happened to be when Bonaparte invaded Russia, and he fled from the ruins of that city to St. Petersburg, where he died. His literary merits are respectable. The poem of Oppian, which, though he did not publish it in the original, he translated into French, proves that he was more than moderately acquainted with Greek antiquities. His translation of Lucian is said to be faithful, but the style is inelegant; and we may add, that one part, at least, of the work has been negligently prepared; the notes, however, display considerable reading. A far more important work, and one on which the fame of M. Belin chiefly rests, is his Histoire Critique de l'Eloquence chez les Grecs, (2 vols, 8vo, Paris, 1813.) It was to be followed by a history of Greek poetry; and this, in its turn, by one of Greek philosophy, until he had formed a complete critical history of Greek literature. Many other publications issued from his pen, but of minor interest, though one of them (Mémoires et Voyage d'un Emigré, written after the manner of the abbé Terasson's Sethos), is said to exhibit an extensive acquaintance with antiquities. (Biog. Univ. Suppl.)

BELING, (Richard,) an Irish Roman catholic, who was the son of Sir Henry Beling, knt. and was born in the year 1613 at Belingstown, in the barony of Balrothe, in the county of Dublin. After receiving the rudiments of education at a grammar school in Dublin, he was placed under the care of some priests, by whom his talents were carefully cultivated, and he was instructed to write Latin fluently and elegantly. He after this became a member of Lincoln's-inn, where he studied some years, and returning home, was engaged in the rebellion of 1641, and attained considerable rank in the insurgent forces. In the February of that year he, at the head of a strong party, besieged the castle of Lismore, but was compelled to retreat before some reinforcements which lord Broghill received. Beling afterwards became a leading member in the supreme council of the confederated Roman catholics at Kilkenny, and also their principal secretary, and was sent ambassador to the pope and other Italian princes to beg assistance for their cause. He brought back with him John Baptist Rinenani, archbishop and prince of Fermo, as papal nuncio, who by reviving the distinction between the old Irish of blood and the old English of Irish birth, divided and weakened the Roman-catholic party. He was, however, opposed by Beling, who thereby became so acceptable to the marquis of Ormond, that he was employed by that nobleman in several transactions, both before and after the restoration. In 1647 he was commissioned to conduct the negotiation for the junction of the Irish army with that of Ormond before the surrender of Dublin to the parliament; and after the restoration he endeavoured three several times, at the instance of Ormond, to induce the Romish synod assembled at Dublin in 1666, to sign a declaration of their loyalty. In this attempt, however, he was not successful. During the time of the protectorate Beling resided in France, but returned to Ireland on the restoration, and through the intercession of Ormond, was repossessed of his estates, and died at Dublin in September 1677. His works are,—1. A sixth book added to Sir Philip Sidney's Arcadia, to which only his initials are appended. This was written by him while at Lincoln's-inn. 2. Vindiciæ Catholicorum Hiberniæ, published under the name of Philopator Irenæus. 3. Annotationes in Johannis Poncii Librum, cui tit. Vindiciæ Eversæ access. Belingi Vindiciæ, Par. 1654. 4. Innocentiæ suæ impetitæ per Rev. Fernensem Vindiciæ, Par. 1652. He is also said to have written a poem, called The Eighth Day.

BELISARIUS, "one of those heroic names," to use the words of Gibbon, "which are familiar to every age and to every nation," is supposed to have been born of humble parents in Thrace, about the end of the fifth or beginning of the sixth century, but nothing certain is known on this point; as his public career, however, opens in the guards of Justinian, then heir to the imperial throne, but who was the son of Gothic peasants of Sardica, it has been conjectured, with probability, that Belisarius drew his origin from the same country. He gradually rose in military rank, and his first important command was on the Mesopotamian and Armenian frontier, where, with the title of general of the East, he withstood for several years, with inferior forces, the arms of the Persians, whom he defeated, A.D. 530, in the sanguinary battle of Dora; but in the ensuing campaign, the rashness of part of his troops, and the misconduct of the auxiliaries, occasioned his sustaining a reverse at Callinicum, in passing the Euphrates, and his courage and conduct alone saved the army from destruction. In 532 he returned to Constantinople, where he married the celebrated Antonina, (see ANTONINA,) a consort who atoned in some measure for her disregard of conjugal fidelity by the zealous care with which she promoted the political interests of her husband; and it is probable that Belisarius owed his appointment, in the following year, to the command of the expedition directed against the Vandals of Africa, as much to the influence of his wife with the empress Theodora, as to his own services in suppressing, at the head of a veteran corps, trained in the Persian war, the famous sedition called *Nika*, in which the factions of the circus, and the mob of Constantinople, anticipated and equalled the enormities of which the hippodrome was similarly made the customary scene, eleven centuries later, by the turbulent janizaries of the Porte. He sailed for the African coast in June 533: his first victory, at Decimum, placed him in possession of the Vandal capital of Carthage; his second triumph completed the overthrow of the kingdom, and the king, Gelimer, who had fled into the interior of Numidia, surrendered to the mercy of the conqueror. The dependencies of the Vandal empire, Sardinia, Corsica, and the Balearic Isles, submitted without resistance; but Belisarius was recalled from the regulation of his new conquests by the jealousy of Justinian, who feared his renewing the kingdom of Africa in his own person. He implicitly obeyed the command, and his return to Constantinople was hailed by a triumph, the first ever seen in that city, and by his investiture with the honour of the sole consulship, A.D. 535. The easy subjugation of Africa inspired the hope of reuniting to the empire its ancient capital of Rome, which, with the kingdom of Italy, was now held by the Ostrogoths; and at the end of the same year, Belisarius again sailed, with very inadequate forces, to effect this enterprise. He easily subdued Sicily, and after crossing to Africa and suppressing a sedition which had broken out there, hastily returned for the invasion of Italy. The domestic dissensions of the Goths made his progress at first almost unopposed; Naples alone sustained a siege of twenty days; and he entered Rome, December 10, 536. But early in the next year, the deposition and death of the effeminate Theodatus, and the substitution of Vitiges on the throne, restored unity and vigour to the Goths, who besieged Rome with an army of 150,000 men. In a skirmish outside the walls, the army was saved from defeat chiefly by the example and personal valour of Belisarius; he sustained, with equal courage and conduct, a blockade of more than a year, and punished, with instant deposition and exile, the treason of pope Sylverius, whom he had detected in an attempt to betray the city to the Gothic king. The long and fruitless siege ruined the army and the spirit of the Goths; and when they at length withdrew, their cities and provinces were rapidly reduced by Belisarius and his lieutenants; but their final reduction was delayed by the mutinous spirit of some of the Roman officers, and by an inroad of the Franks (538-9), who took and destroyed Milan; and it was not till December 539, that Ravenna, the capital and last stronghold of the Gothic kingdom, was compelled by famine to surrender to the Roman general, who had previously refused, on his own risk, to ratify a treaty granted by Justinian to the Gothic ambassadors, and now rejected the homage of the conquered Goths, whose esteem for his valour led them to desire him for their king. But scarcely was Ravenna in the possession of the Romans, when he was again recalled peremptorily to Constantinople, by the timid suspicions of his sovereign. He again obeyed the mandate; and, in 541, was sent to guard the eastern provinces against the arms of the great Nusheerwan, king of Persia, whose progress threatened the total loss of Syria. His consummate generalship enabled him, with immeasurably inferior forces, to frustrate, during two campaigns, the efforts of the great king; but his return to the capital was followed by his disgrace, on pretence of his having spoken with disrespect of the empress. He was heavily fined, and his life was only spared on condition of his reconciliation to his faithless and imperious wife, who still was the confidant and favourite of Theodora. But in the mean time, through the incapacity of their commanders, and the revolt of the Goths under the valiant Totila, the Romans had been nearly dispossessed of Italy; and Belisarius was despatched thither, in 544, as alone able to retrieve his former conquests; but he was left unprovided with troops, stores, or money; and his second Italian campaign was far less glorious than the former. The small number of his forces compelled him to watch and harass, rather than oppose in the field, the progress of Totila; he was repulsed, through the misconduct of his officers, in a gallant attempt to raise the siege of Rome; and the imperial city was retaken, December, 546, by the Gothic king, who spared it from destruction only by the remonstrance of the Roman general. The speedy recapture and successful defence of Rome was the last of the Italian exploits of Belisarius, who succeeded, in 548, in obtaining his recall from a war which he was not furnished with means for bringing to a successful termination; and he returned to Constantinople, where, freed by the death of Theodora from the most powerful of his enemies, and invested with the high dignities of general of the East and count of the domestics, he resided some years in the tranquil enjoyment of his honours, while the destruction of the Goths in Italy was completed by the eunuch Narses. He narrowly escaped from a conspiracy, in which his death had been aimed at as an indispensable preliminary to that of the emperor, by the timely confession of an accomplice; and his last employment in the field, in 559, was signalized by the repulse of a marauding host of Bulgarians, who had even approached and threatened Constantinople. But the last days of the aged general were destined to be clouded by injustice and calamity: a plot was detected in 563 against the emperor, and some of the conspirators, on being subjected to the torture, accused Belisarius of sharing in the design. His long services and unshaken loyalty were instantly forgotten by the emperor. After an examination before the council, his property was sequestered, and he was confined for eight months a close prisoner in his palace; and though his innocence was at length acknowledged, and his freedom and honours restored, he did not long survive the unmerited disgrace to which he had been subjected, dying, March 13, 565. His riches, with the exception of a pittance afforded to his widow, were immediately confiscated by the emperor. The popular tradition that he was deprived of his eyes, and reduced to beg his bread of the passers-by, appears to have no earlier foundation than the Chiliads of Tzetzes, who wrote in the twelfth century. An attempt has been made by lord Mahon, in his late Life of Belisarius, to revive and confirm the story; but it probably originated only in the embellishments of romance, and the historical facts of the ingratitude of Justinian to his great general need no exaggeration to justify the indignation of succeeding ages. Belisarius is described as of lofty stature and dignified appearance; his generosity and frankness of manner attached his followers strongly to his person; and his love of justice has never been impeached, unless when he listened to the suggestions or commands of his wife. His talents, both as a commander and a soldier, were of the highest class; and when we contrast the extent of his conquests and the difficulties which he triumphantly surmounted, with the scanty, ill-disciplined, and heterogeneous armies which he commanded, it must be acknowledged that scarcely any general, in any age, has achieved such important results with means apparently so inadequate; and the charges of rapacity and oppression, which have been brought against his conduct in the last Italian campaigns, are sufficiently explained by the necessity of providing for his troops when left without supplies by the neglect of Justinian. His blind submission to that emperor's caprice and ingratitude was, perhaps, beneath him; as, undoubtedly, was the mean subjection to his own wife in which he lived. "The unconquerable patience and loyalty of Belisarius," says Gibbon, "appear either below or above the character of MAN." The courage which animated him in the field, seems to have deserted him within the precincts of a court. His fidelity, however, to an unworthy sovereign, *then* scarcely considered as a virtue, has been advantageous to his memory under the fixed principles of succession established in later times, which will not bear the name of rebel. The annals of the Lower Empire furnish us with but few great or eminent characters; but far at the head of this scanty list may be safely placed the name of Belisarius. (Procopius. Gibbon. Lord Mahon's Belisarius, &c.)

BELKNAP, (Dr. Jeremy), an American divine, born on the 4th of June, 1744, and died on the 28th of June, 1798. He was one of the founders of the Massachusetts Historical Society; and besides some sermons and other tracts, was the author of a History of New Hampshire, published in 1784-91-92. His patience and accuracy qualified him for historical inquiry; but of natural science he knew little, nor is he recommended by elegance of style. (Americ. Biog. Dict.)

BELL, (Beaupré,) an antiquary of the eighteenth century, descended from Sir Robert Bell, chief baron of the exchequer in the reign of Elizabeth, who married into the Beaupré family, settled at Beaupré hall, in Norfolk, early in the fourteenth century. The antiquary's father, who bore the name of Beaupré also, suffered the family seat to become dilapidated, and hardly allowed necessaries to his son, although he had 500 horses of his own breeding. At his death, the subject of this article succeeded to an estate of 1500*l.* a-year. He was educated at Westminster school; from thence he passed to Trinity college, Cambridge, where he was admitted in 1723; and died, unmarried, of a consumption, on the road to Bath, in August, 1745, at an early age. Much seems to have been expected from the zeal which he evinced, from a very early period of his life, by the antiquaries of the time, Stukeley, Hearne, and others; but he appears not to have left any public and permanent memorial of his own powers in any department of antiquarian research. His strength lay in his knowledge of ancient medals. Stukeley, in his Memoirs of Carausius, says, "My late friend, Mr. Beaupré Bell, a young gentleman of most excellent knowledge in medals, whose immature death is a real loss to this part of learning, was busy in putting out a book like that of Patarol, and left his manuscripts, plates, and coins, to Trinity college, Cambridge." He assisted Blomefield in his History of the County of Norfolk; was a correspondent and literary contributor of Thomas Hearne's; and principal member of the Literary Society which existed in those days at Spalding in Lincolnshire.

BELL, (Dr. Andrew,) a clergyman of the English church, illustrious for naturalizing among its members the Madras system of education. He was born at St. Andrew's, in 1753, and educated in the university there. Some of his early years were spent in America, where, as in every other of his residences, he made himself conspicuous for solid excellence of character. In 1789, he was chaplain to Fort St. George, and minister of St. Mary's at Madras. In that place he undertook, gratuitously, to superintend the male military orphan asylum, and in fulfilling this duty, he adopted arrangements from the native Indian schools, which were subsequently introduced into England, and formed into the national system of education. The system consists in a division of the school into classes; a pairing off of the members of each class into tutors and pupils, so that each pupil has a tutor, and each tutor a pupil; the appointment of a teacher and assistant-teacher to each class, who instruct the tutors; and the general superintendence of a master; the last being the only adult member of the system. Joseph Lancaster, a quaker, has usually passed among dissenters as the introducer of this system into England; but the general current of opinion, supported by documentary evidence, awards the honour of its introduction to Dr. Bell. On that excellent person's arrival in England in 1797, he published An Experiment in Education made at the Male Asylum of

Madras, suggesting a System by which a School or Family may teach itself under the Superintendence of the Master or Parent, 8vo. This piece attracted little notice until Lancaster adopted its principles in arranging a plan of educating the poor without any connexion with the national church. Nothing could be more agreeable to the dissenters, and to all such as lay claim to superior liberality. Hence, Lancaster soon found an abundance of active supporters; and zealous friends of the church began to fear that a system, brought over into Europe by one of their own clergy, would soon become an effective instrument in the hands of persons with very different sentiments from his. This drew Dr. Bell from his retirement, and, in 1807, he undertook the management of some schools for the poor in London and Lambeth; and his admirable system has gone on increasing in popularity, until now (1841) it educates nearly a million children in sound elementary knowledge, and reverential attachment to the church and other institutions of England. Dr. Bell's extraordinary services were acknowledged in his preferments to a prebend of Westminster, and the mastership of Sherborn hospital, Durham. But the opulence which rewarded his life of piety and usefulness, was returned to his grateful country with usurious interest: he bestowed no less than 120,000*l.* in the support of national institutions and public charities. He died at Cheltenham, Jan. 27, 1832, in his 80th year. His remains were brought to town, and interred in Westminster Abbey, with all the distinction due to worth like his. (Annual Obituary. Biog. Univ. Suppl.)

BELL, (John,) the name of a painter, mentioned by Walpole as having worked under Torreggiano. He is mentioned in the Harleian MSS. in an estimate of the expense of the monument to be erected to Henry the Seventh. (Walpole's Anec. of Painting, by Dallaway, i. 176.)

BELL, (William,) a painter born at Newcastle-upon-Tyne. He came to London about the year 1768, and was amongst the first who entered as students of the Royal Academy. In 1771 he obtained the gold medal, for a picture representing Venus soliciting Vulcan to forge the Arms for Æneas. He was patronized by lord Delaval, for whom he painted two views of Seaton Delaval, and the portraits of the family. He died at Newcastle, soon after the year 1800. (Bryan's Dict. App.)

BELL, (Benjamin,) a celebrated surgeon of the eighteenth century, a native of Edinburgh, where he was educated under professor Monro. He travelled on the continent, and visited the principal universities, and after a long stay at Paris, returned to Edinburgh, and devoted himself to practice. He was chosen one of the surgeons to the Royal Infirmary, and elected into the Royal Society. His System of Surgery for a long time held the first place in medical libraries, and may still be referred to with advantage, as it affords a true picture of the state of the art at his time, and does the author credit for his endeavour to divest it of the useless machinery with which it was then encumbered. His first work was on the Theory and Management of Ulcers, Edinb. 1779, 8vo. It was translated into German, Leipsig, 1792, 8vo, and into French by Bosquillon. The seventh edition, published in 1801, was also translated by Adet and Lanigan. He also published a System of Surgery, Edinb. 1782-87, 6 vols, 8vo; the seventh edition, in 1801, in 7 vols, translated into French by Bosquillon, Paris, 1796, 6 vols, 8vo; and into German by E. G. Hebenstreit, Leipsig, 1784-89, 7 vols, 8vo; and again in 1792-99, and 1804-10, 8vo. On Gonorrhœa Virulenta and Lues Venerea, Edinb. 1793, 8vo, 2 vols; second edit. 1797. This was also translated into French by Bosquillon, Paris, 1802, 8vo, and into German, Leipsig, 1794, 8vo; a most able performance. On the Hydrocele, on Sarcocele or Cancer, and other diseases of the Testes, Edinb. 1794, 8vo, translated into German by Hebenstreit, Leipsig, 1795, 8vo.

BELL, (Henry,) an ingenious mechanic, to whom, in a great measure, we owe the introduction of steam navigation into this country, was born at Torpichen, in Linlithgowshire, on the 7th of April, 1767. After having received the ordinary education of a parish school, he began, in 1780, to learn the trade of a stone mason, which in three years he abandoned, and was apprenticed to his uncle, a millwright. When his apprenticeship was terminated, he removed to Borrowstownness, for the purpose of qualifying himself as a ship-modeller, and (1787) took lessons in mechanics. After this he went to London, where he was much employed by the famous Rennie; but returning in 1790 to Scotland, pursued at Glasgow the humble avocations of a carpenter. On the 20th of October,

1797, he was entered a member of the corporation of wrights in that city. It was his intention to have become an undertaker of public works, but from want of capital or unsteadiness of character, he never succeeded in this design. In 1808 he removed to Helensburgh, a village on the Frith of Clyde, where his wife superintended a large inn and the public baths, while he still pursued his mechanical projects, without much regard to his own advantage, or even to their own feasibility. He wished all his plans and the method of their execution to be altogether unlike any hitherto known; and not being very scientific in his calculations, many of his projects were original only because they were impracticable. He was once employed to erect a small pier. This he must needs do on a new principle; but unhappily the first high tide washed away the building. When it was remarked to him that it would have been better had he built the pier in the old fashion, he stoutly denied the assertion, and in spite of experience, sturdily defended his new principle. The scheme of steam navigation had been tried in Scotland on several occasions, and had failed; but in January 1812, Bell constructed a vessel, forty feet in length, which was found capable of ascending the river against a head-tide, at the rate of seven miles an hour. It is hardly possible that Bell should have heard of Fulton's success in America in 1807. The latter end of his life was rendered comfortable by a handsome subscription raised amongst the citizens of Glasgow, and the trustees of the river Clyde allowed him a pension of 100*l*. a year. He died at Helensburgh on the 14th of November, 1830, leaving a widow.

BELL, (John,) a traveller, now nearly forgotten, born at Antermony in the year 1691, who, after having received an excellent education, turned his attention to medicine, and graduated as a physician. In July, 1714, he sailed from England to St. Petersburgh, and soon after his arrival there he attended an ambassador sent from Russia to Persia. He subsequently went with an embassy to China, and reached Pekin, after a journey of sixteen months. After his return, he was employed to accompany an army to Derbent, which the czar sent to the aid of the sovereign of Persia, whose subjects, the Affghans, had seized on Candahar, and made themselves masters of several provinces on the frontiers of India. He returned from this expedition in December 1722, and revisited his native country, from which he proceeded once more to St. Petersburgh, where he arrived in 1734. The Russian chancellor and the English ambassador sent him to Constantinople, where after a time he abandoned the public service, and settled as a merchant. He married, in 1746, a Russian lady, and soon returned to Scotland, where he died at Antermony on the 1st of July, 1780. His Travels from St. Petersburgh, in Russia, to various parts of Asia, were compiled from his notes by professor Barron, of Aberdeen, and published in quarto in 1763.

BELL, (John,) a lieutenant in the Royal Artillery, eldest son of a hatter at Carlisle, where he was born on the 1st of March, 1747. Up to the age of eighteen he assisted in his father's business; but in 1765 he enlisted in the artillery, and in 1766 he embarked for Gibraltar, where he remained for six years. His zeal and ability procured him rapid promotion. He became bombardier in 1775, and was employed for some months recruiting at Carlisle. In 1782 he was paymaster-serjeant and conductor of stores to the artillery encamped on Southsea Common. He was a spectator of the wreck of the *Royal George*, and was anxious to devise some plan for raising or destroying her, an object which has been at length accomplished by the science of colonel Pasley. On the ratification of peace with America, he returned to Woolwich, and was appointed inspector of the proof. In 1793, the duke of Richmond presented him with a commission as second lieutenant in the artillery, and about the same time he was despatched on a secret expedition designed for the destruction of the Dutch fleet in the Texel, but which was abandoned. In January, 1794, he became first lieutenant in the invalid battalion of the same regiment, and died at Queensborough on the 1st of June, 1798. Amongst his inventions may be named that of the "gun proof," by which the soundness of the interior of cannon is ascertained, and which has proved of the greatest utility. A gyn, called "Bell's gyn," is still in use in the Royal Military Repository; an effective petard, a method of destroying ordnance by means of a ponderous weight worked at a high altitude, may also be mentioned. In 1791 he received from the Society of Arts a silver medal, and a premium of five guineas, and in 1793 a further premium of twenty guineas, for useful inventions. Some doubt has been entertained whether he did not anticipate captain Manby in his "apparatus for shipwrecked mariners," (see Trans. Soc. of Arts, vol. xxv.) His invention for destroying sunken ships will be found noticed in the United Service Journal for April 1840, whence this account has been taken.

BELL, (John,) an eminent equity lawyer, born in Cumberland, and educated at Cambridge, where he was fellow of Trinity college, and senior wrangler. He was called to the bar Feb. 1, 1789, and in 1816, nominated king's counsel. He retained through life the Cumberland dialect, as well as a defect in utterance, which caused him to stutter and repeat his words. Even to tell a plain tale in a plain manner, the usual object sought in the chancery courts, was beyond his power; yet he maintained a very high rank at the bar. Lord Eldon is said to have observed to the prince regent, on a question being put who was considered at that time the greatest lawyer, "a gentleman who can neither read, write, walk, nor talk." Walking, from a distortion in his feet, was painful to him, and his writing was all but illegible. Some time before his death, which happened Feb. 6, 1836, he retired from the bar, having realized a princely fortune. (Gent. Mag.)

BELL, (John,) a celebrated surgeon, anatomist, and physiologist, born in Edinburgh, May 12, 1763, and second son of the Rev. William Bell, a clergyman of the Episcopal church of Scotland. He was educated at the High School of his native city, and early manifested a great disposition for medical science. He was therefore placed as a pupil with Mr. Alexander Wood, and attended the regular courses of lectures, and the practice of the celebrated professors Black, Cullen, and Monro Secundus. In August, 1786, he was admitted a fellow of the Royal College of Surgeons of Edinburgh, and in 1790 he built an anatomical theatre in Surgeon's-square, and commenced lectures on anatomy and surgery. He also carried on courses of dissections, and began to form a museum. As this system of private teaching was considered an innovation upon the rights and privileges of the University, he was warmly opposed; but his ardent zeal conquered all opposition, and he became a most successful teacher. He was distinguished by his eloquence and the extent and diversity of his attainments. Endowed with high intellectual powers, he also possessed a fine taste for the beauties of nature and the productions of art. He instructed some of the ablest professional men Scotland has produced, and among others, his brother, the present Sir Charles Bell, now professor of surgery in the University of Edinburgh, who, for some time, assisted him in the duties of teaching.

Mr. Bell's earliest literary production was a System of the Anatomy of the Human Body, the first volume of which appeared in 1793. The work has gone through several editions, the sixth of which appeared in 1826. It has been translated into German by J. C. A. Heinroth and J. C. Rosenmuller, Leipsig, 1806-7, 2 vols, 8vo. A volume of Engravings, to illustrate the structure of the Bones, Muscles, and Joints, was published, London, 1794, 4to, and again, in 1808, the drawings of which were made by Mr. Bell; and a volume, to illustrate the Arteries, in the same manner, by Sir C. Bell, in 1801, 8vo, and again, in 1806 and 1811. Sir Charles Bell also published 2 vols, 4to, of Illustrations of the Brain and Nerves, in 1802 and 1803. All these works are necessary to form a complete set of the anatomy of the human body, a work of high excellence, distinguished by its accuracy and the elegant display of the opinions of the ancients and moderns on the subjects of which it treats. The first surgical work of Mr. Bell was, Discourses on the Nature and Cure of Wounds, Edinburgh, 1793-5, 8vo, again in 1800 and 1812. It was translated into German by J. C. F. Leune, Leipsig, 1798, 2 vols, 8vo.

In 1799, a pamphlet was published under the assumed name of Jonathan Danplucker, affecting to eulogize Mr. Bell, but really representing him as unfit for taking the lead in his profession. It was not allowed to pass unanswered, but henceforth Mr. Bell's System of Surgery, which had been regarded as the text-book of the students, ceased to enjoy either popularity or authority.

In 1803, Mr. Bell made an offer to the government, to embody a corps of young men to be instructed in military surgery, to aid the country in case of invasion, with which it was at that time threatened. The offer was in the first instance accepted, but afterwards declined. Being, by a change in the surgical arrangements at the Infirmary, deprived of his opportunities of operating, Mr. Bell abandoned the duties of teaching, and devoted himself to private practice and to literary composition. He published, The Principles of Surgery, in 3 vols, 4to, London, 1801, 1808; and Letters on Professional Characters, Edinburgh, 1810, 8vo. In 1805 he married the daughter of Dr. Congalton, a retired physician, and remained at Edinburgh until 1817, when the infirm state of his health compelled him to quit his native place and repair to Italy. He died of dropsy at Rome, April 15, 1820. Five years after his decease his widow published, Observations on Italy, from notes made during his tour. It is altogether an elegant production, and contains many excellent remarks upon the various specimens of sculpture, painting, &c., to be met with in that country. Among the notes was found the following, which shows how well he was acquainted with his own danger. "I have seen much of the disappointments of life. I shall not feel them long. Sickness, in an awful and sudden form; loss of blood, in which I lay sinking for many hours, with the feeling of death long protracted, when I felt how painful it was not to come quite to life, yet not to die, (a clamorous dream!) tell that in no long time that must happen, which was lately so near."

BELL, (James,) birth unknown; died at Jamaica, 1801. A celebrated physician, who published a work on a case of "Retroversion of the Uterus, terminating in Abortion and Death."

BELL, (James,) a geographical writer, born at Jedburgh, in 1769, who was bred a weaver, and became a Glasgow manufacturer. Disliking trade, and having a great aptitude for literary labour, he turned his attention to classical tuition. He published A System of Popular and Scientific Geography, 6 vols, and a Gazetteer of England and Wales. He died in 1833. (Biog. Treas.)

BELL, (John,) an intelligent and enterprising London publisher, born 1746, died 1831. To him we owe a neat, but small, edition of the British Poets, in 109 vols, with a Shakspeare, and a British Theatre, of the same size.

BELL, (William,) a learned, exemplary, and liberal divine of the English church, educated at Magdalen college, Cambridge, and some time fellow there. He took his bachelor's degree in 1753, being eighth wrangler. In 1755, he gained one of the senior bachelor's prizes: and for several years he was domestic chaplain to the princess Amelia, aunt to George III. Through that lady's interest, he obtained a prebend of Westminster, in 1765. He also was preferred to the treasurership of St. Paul's cathedral, a dignity endowed with estates leased for lives, and of no great value, unless one or more of them should drop, and compensation be given for a renewal of the term. Dr. Bell was unusually fortunate in such contingencies, and he nobly showed his fitness for the abundance thus unexpectedly conferred upon him. He redeemed the land-tax on each of the three vicarages in his patronage as treasurer, freely making over his purchases as permanent augmentations to those benefices; and he rendered himself conspicuous through life for acts of discerning liberality, so that all who had intercourse with him, still speak of his memory with deep veneration. Such acts, however, would not content him. In 1810, accordingly, he transferred 15,200*l.* three per cent. consols to the university of Cambridge, as a foundation for eight new scholarships, to be bestowed upon sons of clergymen in circumstances insufficient for the expense of an academical education. Dr. Bell, in the course of his life, held several parochial benefices, but long before his death he had resigned all such preferment. He died at his prebendal house in Westminster, in 1816, being then in the 85th year of his age. His whole course was an honour to the church, his patrons, and himself, proving, among innumerable instances of the same kind, that opulence is no where more likely to benefit a country than in the hands of a conscientious clergy.

Dr. Bell's first publication was his bachelor's prize, A Dissertation on the Causes which principally contribute to render a Nation populous, 1756, 4to. He subsequently published, An Inquiry into the Missions of John the Baptist and Jesus Christ, so far as they can be proved from the Circumstances of their Births, and their Connexion with each other, 1761, 8vo. A second edition of this Inquiry appeared in 1797, and to it were then prefixed, Arguments in Proof of the Authenticity of the Narratives of the Births of John and Jesus, contained in the first two Chapters of the Gospels of St. Matthew and St. Luke. In 1774 he published A Sermon, preached at the Consecration of Dr. Thomas, Bishop of Rochester, 4to. In 1780, appeared his Attempt to ascertain and illustrate the Authority, Nature, and Design of the Institution of Christ, commonly called the Lord's Supper, 8vo. In the next year, this piece elicited a letter to him from

Dr. Bagot, eventually bishop of St. Asaph, entitled, An Inquiry whether any Doctrine relating to the Nature and Effects of the Lord's Supper can be justly founded on the Doctrine of our Lord, recorded in the Sixth Chapter of the Gospel of St. John. In 1787, Dr. Bell published a curious piece, left by Peter Francis le Courayer, the courageous, learned, and intelligent champion of English ordinations to a French public, blindly bent upon questioning their validity. This interesting remain was entitled, Déclaration de mes derniers Sentimens sur les différens Dogmes de la Religion. The MS. of this piece was given by Le Courayer to the princess Amelia, with whom Dr. Bell was domesticated at Gunnersbury house, and she left it to him. Such a piece, by such a man, was too interesting to be left in a foreign language, and, accordingly, soon after its appearance, a translation followed, entitled, A Declaration of my Last Sentiments on the different Doctrines of Religion, by the late Pierre François le Courayer, D.D., author of the Dissertation on the Validity of English Ordinations, and translator of the History of the Council of Trent, by Fra. Paolo Sarpi, and of the History of the Reformation, by John Sleidan. The translation was anonymous, but it was ultimately known to have been performed by the Rev. John Calder, who declared it to have been undertaken without any concert with Dr. Bell, to whose claims upon public respect he gave high, but well-merited testimony. (Gent. Mag.)

BELLA, (Giano della,) a Florentine noble of the thirteenth century, who, renouncing the privileges of birth, joined inferior life in resisting the aggressions of superior. Many were the popular complaints of insolence, rapacity, contempt of law, and armed violence, displayed by persons of condition. If a gentleman were guilty of a crime, and was committed to prison by the municipal authorities, the gates were soon broken, and he was borne away in triumph by his party. Giano della Bella organized a force sufficient to protect the administration of justice, and to substitute order for anarchy. But he also attempted to reform the populace. This created enemies; and in 1294, the very tribunal which he had formed for the trial and punishment of delinquents, summoned him to appear before it, and account for his conduct. In disgust he left the place and died in exile. (Biog. Univ.)

BELLA, (Jerome,) a Piedmontese ecclesiastic of the seventeenth century, who, preferring poetry to theology, wrote some pastoral dramas. (Biog. Univ.)

BELLA, (Stephen della, May 18th, 1610—July 22, 1664,) called Della Bella, an eminent engraver, son of a sculptor of Florence, and born in that city. Left an orphan at the age of ten years and a half, he was first placed with a goldsmith, where he employed his leisure time in copying the plates of Callot, which was done with such exactness as to deceive connoisseurs. His amiability procured him many friends, amongst whom was Canta Gallina, a Florentine painter, and Vanni, from whom he received valuable lessons. He attained an extraordinary facility, which he retained all his life, of drawing the human figure, commencing at the feet and finishing at the head. Although he had made great progress in painting, his natural taste prompted him to confine his talents wholly to engraving, more especially to etching, which being the most rapid, was a style equally suited to his activity of mind, and fecundity of genius. Having attracted general notice, especially by his small figures, he was welcomed by all persons of the highest distinction in a visit made to France. Cardinal Richelieu engaged him to engrave the capture of Arras, and the other conquests of Louis XIII. After the death of that minister, Della Bella executed a vast number of subjects for the printsellers of Paris. At the end of ten years, Italians became so unpopular in the war of the Fronde, that he returned to his native city, where the grand duke received him with distinction, granted him a pension, and engaged him to teach drawing to his son, afterwards Cosmo II. A native modesty, coupled with eminent talents and high genius, not only ensured Della Bella the countenance of the house of Medici, but also the patronage of the principal nobles of Florence; and his own goodness of heart prompted him to become in turn the liberal friend of artists less gifted or less fortunate than himself. His last long and painful illness was aggravated by insanity, under a fit of which he died in his native city, at the age of fifty-four years. The grand duke, to honour his memory, placed his portrait in the gallery of the palace, and made an extensive collection of his most celebrated works. Della Bella may be regarded as a model for small subjects; his touch is spirited and picturesque, his execution admirable, and no artist has handled the point with more facility. His earlier works are done in the style of Callot, but he soon adopted one of his own. He designed his subjects, whether historical, battle pieces, sea pieces, landscapes, huntings, animals, or ornaments, for he was equally successful in all, with infinite taste, and his plates produce a clear and brilliant effect. We cease to wonder that some of his works are slightly executed, when we find that they are no less than fourteen hundred in number, a list of which is prefixed to the life of the artist by Ch. Ant. Jombert, 1772, 8vo. Mr. Heinecken also gives a copious catalogue of them. Mr. Strutt, alluding to the useless discussion entered into by some writers respecting the relative merits of this artist and Callot, judiciously says, that he sees no reason to compare them together, especially if the excellence of Della Bella consists in the freedom of his point, and the lightness and elegance of his figures; and that of Callot in the clearness and perspicuity of his designs, the arrangement of his groups, and the firmness of his outline. Mr. Ponce, in the Biographie Universelle, instances, as of pre-eminent excellence, the following works of Della Bella,—a view of the Pont Neuf, very rare, before the cock was placed on the steeple of St. Germain, l'Auxerrois; the prints of S. Prosper and of Parnassus; those of the procession of Corpus Christi, of the Rock, and of the Medici Vase. (Biog. Univ. Heinecken, Dict. des Artistes. Strutt's Dict. Bryan's Dict.)

BELLAGATTA, (Angelo Anthony,) an Italian physician, son of a printer, born at Milan, May 9, 1704. He was originally destined for the church; but his taste led him to medicine. In 1733 he was chosen physician to the city of Arona, which office he filled during nine years. He then entered the church, but an attack of apoplexy prematurely terminated his life, Feb. 2, 1742. He published, Due Littere Filosofiche scritte ad un Amico intorno alla cattarale Influenza seguita in quest' Anno universalmente per tutta Europa, Milan, 1730, 4to. Le Disavventure della Medicina, Trattenimento Fisico, Milan, 1733, 8vo. Ragguaglio dell' Operato del S. Francesco di Paola a 28 di Marzo, 1735, Milan, 1735, 4to. Trattenimento Fisico sopra l'Ignea apparenza osservata nella Notte 16 Dec. 1737, Milan, 1738, 4to.

BELLAIRE, (N.) a French captain of infantry, who served in the Levant, and gave a very correct account of the facts that he had witnessed, entitled Précis des Opérations générales de la Division Française du Levant, Paris, 1805, 8vo. (Biog. des Contemp.)

BELLAMY, (George Anne, April 23, 1733—1788,) an actress, natural daughter of lord Tyrawley, by a daughter of a quaker named Seal, who, before the birth of the subject of this notice, married captain Bellamy. George Anne Bellamy, the first name being given her from her birth taking place on St. George's day, was sent to Boulogne, where she remained for seven years, and then came to England. Being renounced by her father for keeping up a correspondence and intimacy with her mother, she adopted the stage as a profession, and appeared in 1747 at Covent-garden theatre as Monimia, in Otway's Orphan. After playing successfully in London, she went to Dublin, where she was recognised by lord Tyrawley's sister, and introduced to the best society. Garrick for a time refused to play king John to her Constance, on the ground of her youth; but the public compelled him to submit. Her habits being dissolute and extravagant, she suffered occasionally severe distress, and once contemplated suicide by drowning. She was the ostensible writer of an Apology for the Life of George Anné Bellamy, late of Covent-garden Theatre, written by herself, published in London in 1785; but this work is said to have been drawn up by Alexander Bicknell, the editor of Carver's Travels in Africa.

BELLAMY, (Thomas, 1745—1800,) an English miscellaneous writer, born at Kingston-upon-Thames, and bred a hosier. After being engaged in that business for twenty years, he became an author, and produced Sadaski, a novel; Lessons from Life; the Friends, a musical interlude; and other works. He was the original projector of the Monthly Mirror.

BELLAMY, (Joseph,) an American divine, born at New Cheshire in 1719. In 1750 he published a work entitled True Religion delineated. He appears to have devoted himself to the instruction of young men for the pulpit. He died on the 6th of March, 1790. His works, which are not important, appeared in a collected form in 1811.

BELLAMY, (Jacob,) a very celebrated modern Dutch poet, and one of those whose names shine forth with all the greater lustre on account of the humbleness of their origin, was born at Vlissingen, in 1757. His mother being left a widow, in very narrow circumstances, when he was only five years old, was obliged to apprentice him at an early age to a baker. For the duties now expected of him, he soon showed himself totally unfit. Of this the real cause was happily discerned by a preacher named Te Water, who bestowed on him not only notice, but also encouragement, instruction, and advice. At length, when he found him really possessed of talents and application, he exerted himself in his behalf, and with the assistance of Van Ritthem and some other benevolent individuals, liberated Bellamy from his servitude, and sent him, in 1782, to the high school at Utrecht. A new scene, or rather a new world, now opened itself to him, and politics had awakened a tone of excitement and public feeling in that city, which were not without their influence on the youthful poet, who had already given proofs of his patriotic sentiments in some of his earlier attempts. The appearance of his Vaderlandsche Gezangen van Zelandus, in 1785, stamped his reputation at once. This was succeeded by another collection of Gezangen, or lyric compositions and songs, many of which are master-pieces of their kind, and have become not merely popular, but household strains, familiar to every one. Several of them breathe the warmest, but at the same time the purest and most delicate passion, not for a poetical abstraction of a mistress, but for a young lady at Vlissingen, in circumstances much superior to his own. His ardent passion was returned by the object of it, but her parents, naturally enough, discountenanced a suitor who was then almost as obscure as he was poor. They accordingly selected another, a more suitable match for their daughter, in a worldly point of view. The marriage, however, was frustrated by the sudden death of the intended bridegroom, and Bellamy's hopes of ultimate success revived. His position was now altered; and although he had as yet no adequate provision, he was looking forward to distinction in the church. He did not live to enter upon that profession; for notwithstanding a healthy, and even robust constitution, he was attacked by a violent cold, which carried him off, in 1786, at the age of twenty-eight. Bellamy, like Burns, was the poet of nature and feeling; unschooled by formal precepts, but guided more surely by the impulses of his own mind, and the instinct of his taste. The want of an earlier acquaintance with classic models was in some respects rather an advantage to him, as it prevented his use of heathen mythology and heathen ideas, which gives a forced, cold, and pedantic air to so much of modern poetry. He had studied Cats, Vondel, and other native poets, particularly Van Haren's Geuzen, but he did not borrow from or imitate any of them. With the exception of Van Alphen, he was the first who ventured to discard rhyme from Dutch poetry, even in his lyrical productions, trusting to the continuous harmony of rhythm, and to the forcible expression of his language. This innovation was reprobated as a dangerous one by the critics of that day, who considered rhyme a wholesome restraint and distinction, that prevented poetry from sinking into measured prose, divided into lines more perceptible to the eye than the ear. Bellamy's example, indeed, obtained for awhile many imitators, seduced not only by its novelty, but also by its apparent facility. They might have seen that a genuine poetical feeling and expression, peculiarly distinguish the productions of Bellamy, rendering them inimitable by minds inferior to his own. (Von Kampen. De Vries.)

BELLANGE, (James,) a French engraver, born at Chalons about 1610. He studied under Claude Henriot, a painter of Nancy, and afterwards went to Paris, and became a pupil of Simon Vouet. He is little known as a painter, but as an engraver we have many of his works. There is a difference of opinion as to their value, but the prevailing judgment is unfavourable. (Strutt's and Bryan's Dictionaries. Heinecken, Dict. des Artistes.)

BELLANGE, (Thierri,) an eminent French painter of the seventeenth century, born at Nancy about 1596. He was the friend of Callot, and of other young artists who shed a lustre on the peaceful reign of Charles III. duke of Lorraine. He worked under Henriot, a distinguished painter of Champagne, whom the duke engaged in 1596 to embellish his palace and capital, especially to adorn the windows of the principal churches, for Henriot excelled in the art of painting on glass. Bellange, notwithstanding, neither followed the class of painting nor the manner of his master, but adopted a style of his own. Having returned to Paris, he was employed by Simon Vouet to design landscapes and ornaments. He was afterwards employed, with other artists, in decorating various palaces in Paris. Being again invited to Lorraine by Charles III., he painted in fresco a large hall demolished in 1718, and executed other important works. He died at Nancy towards the middle of the seventeenth century. (Biog. Univ. Suppl.)

BELLANGER, (J. A.) an amateur French engraver, who etched several plates after his own designs, with much taste and correctness. He also executed a few plates after Raffaelle, amongst which are the Miracle of the Loaves and Fishes, and the School of Athens. His etchings are dated from 1745 to 1763. (Heinecken. Strutt's Dict. of Eng.)

BELLANTI, (Lucius,) an Italian writer of the fifteenth century, who wrote in defence of astrology, but gives amongst serious errors much good information upon the solar and lunar motions, the elongations of Mercury, and the like.

BELLARDI, (Charles Lewis, 1741—1828,) a physician and botanist of Turin, who published several botanical works, and left several in MS. His position in the University of Turin enabled him to give a new impulse to botany and to natural history in general; and his instructions in medicine led many to imitate him with success.

BELLARMINO, (Robert,) cardinal Bellarmine, the greatest of Romish doctrinal controversialists, whose writings rendered the same service to the papal church in matters of opinion, that those of Baronius did in matters of history. This eminent divine was born at Monte Pulciano, in Tuscany, October 4, 1542. His mother was Cynthia Cervini, sister to pope Marcellus II. In 1560, he enrolled himself among the Jesuits, then straining every nerve to paralyze the Reformation. His talents were immediately seen to be of no ordinary kind; and as he discovered great powers for pulpit oratory, he received a license to preach before age or sacerdotal ordination regularly qualified him for the duty. Immediately did he establish his title to this indulgence at Mondovi, Florence, and Padua. A young man, with powers and disposition so uncommon for benefiting the papal cause, could hardly find in Italy sufficient call or space for his exertions. He proceeded, accordingly, to Flanders, where opinions, branded as heresy by Rome, were boldly and learnedly maintained within the country, and in every neighbouring region. It was at Ghent that he received priest's orders, in 1569, from Jansenius, eventually so famed as the founder of a pious, but ascetic party, in the Romish church. In the following year, Bellarmine became professor of theology at Louvain, being the first Jesuit so employed in that illustrious university. His duties were fulfilled in a manner worthy of the reputation that has ever accompanied his name, and every year added to the expectations entertained of him by the Romish party. Even Protestants were among the crowded congregations that listened while he preached. After a residence of seven years in the Low Countries, he returned to Italy; and in 1577 he delivered controversial lectures at Rome, being the first of his order so employed in that capital. He showed, as usual, most advantageously in this undertaking; and Sixtus V. entertained so high an opinion of him, that he sent him with a legate into France, in 1569, thinking that his assistance would be found invaluable in case of any call for controversial erudition. After about six months he returned to Rome, and his great services were requited by a succession of preferments. In 1599 he was honoured by the dignity of cardinal; a compliment very rarely so well bestowed, but which, it is said, he accepted with extreme reluctance. Three years afterwards he was made archbishop of Capua, but he resigned that see in 1605, being unable to fulfil its duties from attendance required of him as librarian of the Vatican, and constant occupations about the papal court. He continued immersed in these engagements until the early part of 1621, when declining health suggested a pious desire of withdrawing his mind wholly from this world's affairs, before death summoned him to another. He therefore sought religious retirement in a house of his order. He did not live a year there, but died September 17, 1621, having previously charged one of his brethren to testify publicly, that he departed in the full persuasion of those religious opinions which he had so strenuously maintained throughout a laborious and illustrious life.

Bellarmine rapidly became almost the only antagonist noticed by the leading protestants, and he long maintained that honourable position. He is, indeed, even still, the principal authority in the Romish controversy. His own church, however, has never been entirely satisfied with him. He has none of the special pleader's arts. He sought indefatigably for every allegation brought against Romish peculiarities; and he neither concealed nor garbled any thing that seemed in want of an answer. He was evidently too wise, learned, and honest, to value a case merely specious; for none that he did not think a solid one, would he deign to plead. In his magnanimous contempt, however, of all injustice to the adverse party, he naturally displayed many of its more impregnable positions, and laid bare the points best fitted for attacks upon his own. Timid or violent Romish partisans were alarmed or indignant at such controversial integrity. They seem even to have spoken of it as casting a suspicion over the author's own convictions; and injudicious protestants would not fail of representing so much candour as a proof, that it could only have originated in that secret leaning to their own opinions, which must naturally result from an accurate acquaintance with them. Hence, probably, this great man's anxiety, when death was near, to provide for a public announcement of his departure in the belief that owed so much to his exertions. But although Bellarmine gave offence by his integrity to many of the more decided Romanists, in some things he proceeded far enough for all but the most extravagant of their body. He was a zealous advocate for papal pretensions, and attacking James I. under the fictitious name of *Matthew Tortus*, he encouraged English Romanists in refusing, or evading, the oaths imposed by law. His ultramontane doctrines, as these assertions of papal power are termed, brought a formal parliamentary condemnation in France, in 1610, on his treatise against Barclay; and his pernicious interference in English politics drew forth a reply from Bishop Andrewes. Yet, even in his opinions upon the papacy, Bellarmine fell short of the standard set up by some of its partisans. He would not build its authority upon a direct grant from Jesus Christ, although he admitted an indirect one. This admission, however, would not satisfy Sixtus V., and, accordingly, that pontiff condemned his treatise, De Romano Pontifice, as injurious to the see of Rome. This great cardinal's independent spirit was also above any servile adherence to his order. He did not agree with it upon predestination; and he utterly abhorred that relaxed morality which fain would justify means by ends. In spite also of his incessant occupation in controversy, he was, at bottom, a man of amiable temper, and often said, that "an ounce of peace was better than a pound of victory." Admirable, however, as was Bellarmine, it would detract from the usefulness of biography to paint him as faultless. He evidently looked upon his great services to the cause of Romanism with a degree of pride that degenerated into vanity. This weakness appeared in his posthumous life of himself, a work that has been considered as one obstacle to the success of applications made by his own order to have him canonized. Another obstacle has been opposition from France, excited by his disparagement of civil authority. As a saint, however, the Roman populace considered him during life; and at his funeral, it was found necessary to station the pope's Swiss guards around the bier, to keep off the people, who eagerly pressed forward to touch and kiss the body. Every thing that had been used by him was carefully preserved as a sacred relic, serviceable for animating devotion. Nor did popular veneration wait until the termination of his honourable career. When he left Capua, several years before, the inhabitants of that city were deeply moved. Some devoutly kissed his robe as he withdrew; others rubbed their rosaries against it; everybody begged his blessing. As Bellarmine was unquestionably one of the greatest men that ever bore the name of cardinal, and a strong assertor too of papal privileges, though not quite strong enough for a few of their advocates, it may seem surprising that he was not chosen to wear the tiara. His enrolment among the Jesuits is considered as a reason why he was passed over, when an opportunity occurred of thus raising him to the summit of professional dignity; it being thought that foreign powers would have disapproved of a pope from that order, and that if such an individual had actually been elected, his society would have established itself in the Vatican, either permanently, or during a very long period. Bellarmine himself evidently entertained expectations, if not hopes, of the pontifical chair, a solemn vow of his being extant, binding him to disregard the interested claims of kindred, in case of his elevation to it. Notwithstanding, however, his great services to the Romish cause, he really was not very popular among its more artful friends. Hence, when Sir Edwin Sandys was in Italy, in the beginning of the seventeenth century, he could not meet with a copy of his works in any bookseller's shop there, and, accordingly, he considered them prohibited. Spain, too, it was believed, had forbidden their sale; the leading clergy considering their arrangement of Protestant opinions highly favourable for the study of them, and objections to Romanism stated better than confirmations of it. As a linguist, Bellarmine's qualifications have been often thought defective, doubts being thrown upon his knowledge of Greek; and although when young he wrote a Hebrew Grammar, it has been reasonably supposed that he never made any great progress in that language. Some of this great man's early antagonists made other injurious reflections upon him which were still more palpably incapable of proof, and gave thus an advantage to his admirers that was judiciously turned to account. Others, however, who lived with, or near him, did full justice to his unusual industry and stupendous reading, deservedly commending those great abilities which first reduced into a manageable and polished form the mass of controversial matter that before defied any ordinary powers of consideration. Bellarmine's private life was quite worthy of his public reputation; stained by no impurity, dishonoured by no breach of veracity, lowered by no impatience. In person he was not commanding, his stature being below the ordinary standard, and his countenance was far from striking at first sight, although when regarded with attention, it gave sufficient indication of a powerful intellect and a gentle disposition.

Bellarmine's great controversial collection was first published at Ingoldstadt, in three volumes, folio, the first of which appeared in 1587, and the last in 1590. His brother Jesuit, Valentia, took charge of this work through the press, and allowed some alterations in it which the author disapproved. Bellarmine himself, accordingly, revised and corrected the whole, with a view to a new edition, which was printed at Venice. This, having the advantage of such a preparation, ought naturally to possess superior claims to confidence; but it was carelessly printed, and thus really rendered less valuable than its predecessor. The learned author, to remedy the various inaccuracies abroad under his name, published, at Rome, in 1607, a general correction of them, under the title of Recognitio Librorum omnium R. B. ab ipso edita. This tract, with six others, formed an appendix to an edition of the cardinal's Controversies, published at Cologne, in 1615. That edition, accordingly, was extended to four volumes, but is commonly bound in two. Its title is, Roberti Bellarmini e Societate Jesu, S. R. E. Cardinalis Disputationes de Controversiis Christianæ Fidei adversus hujus temporis Hæreticos. Another edition of this great work was published at Paris in 1688, and upon this was formed another, published at Prague, in 1721. Besides this principal production of his pen, other published works of Bellarmine are, a Hebrew Grammar, of which there are several editions; a Commentary on the Psalms; a Short Account of Ecclesiastical Writers; a Treatise upon the Vulgate, explanatory of the Sense in which the Council of Trent pronounced it *Authentic;* a Treatise on the Duty of Bishops; a Catechism; some Ascetic Pieces, and a posthumous Life of himself. Of these productions, the most popular has been the Catechism, but it contains principles so unfavourable to temporal power, than even Maria Theresa, with all her affection for Romish opinions, suppressed it at Vienna in 1775. It has, however, been translated into twelve different languages, and passed through numerous editions. Bellarmine's Ascetic Pieces have also been highly esteemed among members of the Romish communion, and have been translated into most European languages. His Autobiography has tended rather to lower him, by exhibiting a person full of himself, anxious to make the most of all his good qualities, and willing to claim an importance for things on no other intelligible account than his own connexion with them. Of this great man's biographies by others, the earliest appear to be those of Cervini, Sienna, 1622, 8vo; Edward Coffin, an English Jesuit, St. Omer's, 1623; Fuligatti, Rome, 1624, 4to; Didacus Ramirez, a Spanish Jesuit, who died in 1647. (Bayle. Biog. Univ. Launoii Epistolæ.)

BELLART, (Nicholas Francis, 1761—1826.) a celebrated Parisian advocate, whose eminence was first established in 1792, as counsel for individuals brought by revolutionary passions before the sanguinary tribunals of that unhappy time. As a pleader, he was remarkable for the vehemence rather than the force of his reasoning; he appealed to the passions rather than to the understanding;

but he generally captivated his hearers. Napoleon he termed, on his first downfal, "the greatest oppressor that had ever cursed the human race." By Lewis he was rewarded with letters of nobility and with office. On the return of Bonaparte, in March 1815, he fled, and his property was declared forfeited to the crown; but the second restoration proved even more favourable to him than the first. His works, in 6 vols, 8vo, contain little to interest an English reader. (Biog. Univ. Suppl.)

BELLATI, (Anthony Francis,) an Italian Jesuit, famous as a preacher, born at Ferrara in 1665. He took the vows in 1699, and immediately gave his principal attention to the pulpit. He attracted large congregations through most parts of Italy, but a defective constitution obliged him to discontinue these exertions at an early age, and he spent his latter years as rector of the college at Piacenza. Thence he accompanied, in 1714, Elizabeth Farnese, wife to Philip V. of Spain, as far as the frontiers of that country. He died in 1742. Several of his works appeared between the years 1705 and 1731, which were collected after his death in one volume, 4to. Venice, 1742. A second, containing pieces hitherto unpublished, was to follow, but it did not appear. A complete collection of his works, which are all religious and moral, was, however, published at Ferrara, in four volumes, between 1744 and 1748, in the fourth volume of which is a life of the author. He was one of the best writers in his way that Italy produced in the last century. (Biog. Univ.)

BELLATI, (John, 1745—1808,) an Italian painter, who might have been eminent, if he had not turned his attention to mining, which, however, did not enrich him. (Tipaldo, iii. 472.)

BELLATOR, (Presbyter,) whom Trithemius and Lambeccius refer to the ninth century, whilst Cassiodorus, who lived about A.D. 562, calls him "his friend." Of all his works, which were chiefly commentaries upon Scripture, none are known to be extant; but Huet attributes to him the versions of some of Origen's minor pieces. (Cave. Hist. Lit. Fabric. Bibl. Lat.)

BELLAVEINE, (J. N. 1770—1826,) of Verdun, a general in the French army, who rose from the ranks, but was an officer's son. Being obliged to retire from active service by the loss of a leg in battle in 1797, he became eventually an inspector of military schools. For their use he compiled Cours de Mathématiques, Paris, 1813. (Biog. Univ. Suppl.)

BELLAVIA, (Mark Anthony,) a Sicilian artist, who painted in Rome, and is conjectured to have been a scholar of Cortona. (Lanzi, Stor. Pitt. ii. 301.)

BELLAVITA, (Angelo,) a Cremonese painter, who flourished in the year 1420. (Lanzi, Stor. Pitt. iv. 100.)

BELLAY. See BELAY.

BELLAY, (William du,) lord of Langey, under which name he is also known, eldest son of Lewis du Bellay, and Margaret de la Tour Landri, born, at the castle of Glatigny, near Montmirail, about the year 1491, and died on the 9th of January, 1543. He was an excellent general, an able negotiator, and remarkable for obtaining information by means of spies, whom he paid most liberally. By his influence, it is thought, some of the French universities gave judgment in favour of Henry VIII.'s divorce from Catherine of Aragon. Few things undoubtedly were more likely to cement an alliance between Francis and Henry against Charles V. This great political object caused him to be sent upon several embassies into Germany, England, and Italy; for which services he received the knighthood of St. Michael, was made lieutenant-general of the armies of Italy, and viceroy of Piedmont, where he took several towns from the imperialists. At the end of the year 1542, having some important intelligence to communicate to the king, he set out from Turin, though ill at the time, and, becoming worse on the road, he died at St. Saphorin (Symphorien), on the 9th of January following, and was buried in the cathedral of Mans, where a noble monument, with a short and elegant inscription, was erected to his memory.

Du Bellay was not only eminent as a general and a statesman; he was also a scholar, but no courtier, though always at court, his manners being plain to the very edge of rudeness. His principal works are, a Latin history of his own times, in eight books, of which only a few fragments remain, besides three or four books which his brother Martin has inserted into another of his works, entitled his Memoirs; and, lastly, the Epitome of the Antiquities of Gaul, printed with some other small pieces in 1556. Du Verdier also ascribes to him a book on military discipline, but that is an error, however it may have been defended by some of his biographers. The author of that book is Raimond of Pavia, a Gascon gentleman, and a *gend'arme* in the company of the sieur de Negnepellisse in 1528, who, perhaps, might have served under Du Bellay in his Italian wars.

BELLAY, (John du, 1492—1560,) younger brother of the preceding. He soon acquired the favour of Francis I., by whom he was appointed, first, to the see of Bayonne, and subsequently to that of Paris. In 1527, he was sent as ambassador to Henry VIII., king of England, and again in 1533. His diplomatic duties on these occasions were often very far from such as a zealous prelate of the Romish church would willingly have chosen. But John du Bellay even aided his brother William in holding out expectations to the German protestants of some religious movement, like their own, in France. He might, unquestionably, have been sincere in an expectation of this kind. Of his private wishes in its favour, a secret marriage with Madame de Châtillon, of which Brantome gives a curious account, may fairly be taken as an evidence. In 1534 he was sent to Rome, to dissuade Clement VII. from treating Henry of England with indiscreet precipitancy. That monarch had pledged himself to delay, if time were allowed to make his defence by proxy. The pope was won over by Du Bellay to this reasonable indulgence, but Henry's acceptance of the arrangement having accidentally failed of arriving on the day when it was expected, Clement was driven by the emperor's agents into the folly of that rupture which proved final, and relieved England from her long dependence upon Rome.

In 1535 Du Bellay was promoted to the dignity of cardinal, by pope Paul III.; and when, in 1536, Francis went to attack Charles V., who had landed a large army in Provence, he appointed the cardinal lieutenant-general, for the protection of Picardy and Champagne. For his various services Francis appointed him bishop of Limoges in 1541, archbishop of Bourdeaux in 1544, bishop of Mans in 1546. But after the king's death, which took place in the following year, cardinal Du Bellay became the victim of court intrigue, and retired to Rome. There he died, after having built a magnificent palace. He had resigned the sees of Paris and Bourdeaux, but was bishop of Ostia, and dean of the college of cardinals.

Cardinal du Bellay was a man of superior wisdom, eloquence, and knowledge. His love of learning induced him to join Budæus in persuading Francis to found the royal college. Rabelais was a member of his establishment; some say as physician, but others as a dependent of humbler grade. He has left some works in prose and in verse, such as, Harangues, Apologie pour François I., Letters, partly remaining in MS., partly published in Le Grand's Histoire du Divorce de Henri VIII., with some elegies, epigrams, and odes, collected by Robert Etienne, in 1579, 8vo. (Biog. Univ.)

BELLAY, (Martin du,) brother of the two preceding, like them, too, with talents for war, an able negotiator, and a patron of letters, died in 1559, at Glatigny. He was lieutenant-general of Normandy, and prince of Yvetot by his marriage with Elizabeth Chenu, to whom that principality belonged. By him we have the Mémoires Historiques from 1515 to 1547, in ten books, of which the fifth, sixth, and seventh, are derived from the materials left by William du Bellay. These curious memoirs were published by René du Bellay, baron de la Lande, son-in-law of William du Bellay. The best edition of them is by the abbé Lambert, Paris, 1753, 7 vols, 12mo, together with the Memoirs of Marshal Fleuranges, and the Journal of Louisa of Savoy, with notes, and documents, pour servir à l'histoire du règne de François I. (Biog. Univ.)

BELLAY, (René du,) who died bishop of Mans, in 1546, the fourth of these illustrious brothers, distinguished as a scholar by his love of physical science, and as a man, by his active benevolence. (Biog. Univ.)

BELLAY, (Eustace du,) nephew of the preceding, successor to his uncle, John, in the see of Paris. He proved an excellent prelate, and maintained episcopal rights, at Trent, against some who sought authority from the council there to lower them. He thought them to have suffered greatly from the encroachments of the regulars, and viewing the new order of Jesuits with even greater jealousy than any of the older monastic bodies, he opposed its introduction into France. He died in 1565, at Bellay, in Anjou. (Biog. Univ. Le Courayer's Concile de Trente, ii. 354.)

BELLAY, (Joachim du,) of the same noble family, born in 1524 at Liré, in Anjou. The care of his education fell upon an elder brother, who neglected it, and he had scarely reached adult age, when it became his own turn to undertake the guardianship of a nephew. This relative's affairs were deeply embarrassed, and the lawsuits, with other vexations that preyed upon him, brought on an illness of two years' continuance. To beguile time and pain, he read the Greek, Latin, and French poets, and produced some compositions of his own, which procured him access to Francis I., Henry II., and Margaret of Navarre.

Being invited to Rome, in 1549, by his cousin, cardinal John du Bellay, Joachim passed three pleasant years in the society of that prelate, who, like him, was fond of literature and poetry, and who, after that time, entrusted him with the management of his affairs, which obliged him to return to France. There some illnatured people reported to the cardinal that Joachim had spoken ill of him; they even found fault with his conduct and his writings; and some went so far as to accuse him of want of religion. The vexation that he felt at these false accusations brought on his old complaint. Eustace du Bellay, bishop of Paris, affected at his misfortunes, procured him a canonry in his church, which, however, he did not enjoy long, for an apoplectic fit carried him off on the 4th of June, 1559, at the age of thirty-five. In the several epitaphs which were made on him he was styled, "Pater elegantiarum, pater omnium leporum." His French poems were published at Paris in 1561, 4to; and 1597, 12mo; and were much esteemed at the time. His Latin poems were published at Paris in 1569.

BELLE. The name of two French artists.

1. *Alexis Simon*, a portrait painter, who learned the art from Francis de Troy. He practised in Paris, and was a member of the Royal Academy of Painting in that city. He executed, for his amusement, some plates in mezzotinto. Heinecken gives the dates of his birth and death, 1674 and 1734. His wife, Maria Horthemels, was also both a painter and engraver. (Heinecken, Dict. des Artistes. Biog. Univ.)

2. *Clement Lewis Maria Anne*, (Nov. 16, 1722—Sept. 29, 1806,) the son of the preceding, and an historical painter. After the death of his father, which happened whilst he was young, he was placed by his mother under the direction of Le Moyne, and at twenty-three years of age was sent, by her, to Italy to complete his studies. He returned to France in 1759, and two years afterwards was made a member of the Academy; having been nominated successively assistant-professor and professor, and in 1785 associate-rector and rector of that institution. Although his nomination to the office of inspector of the manufactory of the Gobelins in the department of arts, to which he was called in 1755, much interfered with the time that he could devote to painting, he did not fail to produce many pictures of merit; amongst others, the Consecration of the Host, which is in the church of St. Médéric in Paris; Ulysses discovered by his Nurse, the picture he painted on his admission into the Academy; and a Christ, intended to adorn one of the halls of the parliament of Dijon; and, as a proof of his patience, may be cited his tracings of the frescos of Raffaelle in the Vatican, the fidelity and purity of the outline of which are highly esteemed by artists. As a painter, Belle is described as learned in composition, but indifferent in execution. He left a son, who was his pupil, and who succeeded to his place of inspector of the Gobelins. (Biog. Univ.)

BELLEAU, (Remi,) born 1528, died 1577, one of the seven poets honourably known as *la Pléiade Française*. Ronsard called him the painter of nature. Among other works, he published translations in verse of Ecclesiastes, the Canticles, the Odes of Anacreon, and the Phenomena of Aratus. The last edition of his poetical works appeared at Rouen in 1604, 2 vols, 12mo; but that of Paris, 1578, is most esteemed. Belleau's most curious production is a burlesque poem, without date, entitled, Dictamen Metrificum de Bello Huguenotico, which has been often reprinted in collections. (Biog. Univ.)

BELLEBUONI, (Matthew,) an Italian author of the fourteenth century, who translated from the Latin the history of the Trojan war, by Guido delle Colonne. (Biog. Univ.)

BELLECOUR. The name of two French actors.

1. *Gilles Colson*, called Bellicour, originally intended for a painter, but he took to the stage, and made his first appearance December 31, 1750. He excelled in personating dissipated men of fashion. He died on the 19th of Nov. 1778, not 1786. In 1761 he wrote a comedy in prose, in one act, entitled, Les Fausses Apparences, not printed. (Biog. Univ.)

2. *Le Roi Beaumenard*, the wife of the preceding, who filled, during nearly thirty years, the parts of waiting-maids with admirable talent. In 1791 she retired from the stage, but poverty drove

her to return. She died at an advanced age, in August 1799. (Biog. Univ. Biog. des Contemp.)

BELLEE, (Theodore, d. 1600,) a physician of Magusa, who wrote a Latin commentary on the Aphorisms of Hippocrates. (Biog. Univ.)

BELLEFONT, (Bernardine Gigault, Marquis de, 1635—1699,) a French marshal, who headed the expedition into Holland in 1675, and that into Catalonia in 1684. He had previously been ambassador at Madrid and London. (Biog. Univ.)

BELLEFOREST, (Francis de,) born at Sarzan, in Comminges, in 1530, and died at Paris in 1583. Although patronized in early life by the queen of Navarre, sister to Francis I., and brought up to the bar, these advantages were all thrown away. He spent his time for several years in rhyming to get a dinner or a supper. At length he was induced, by the rising taste for historical studies, to write the History of the Nine Kings of France who bore the Name of Charles. This work procured him the office of historiographer of France; and, as such, he attempted the general history of that country, but his failure was so complete as to lose him that office. His works are very numerous.

BELLEGARDE, (Roger de Saint Lary de,) seigneur de Bellegarde, of an ancient family, known since the fifteenth century. He seems to have been destined for the church, but he preferred the army. Forming an intimacy with one of the Italians who accompanied Catharine de' Medici into France, he rose with surprising rapidity. He really rendered, however, very considerable services. For these he was rewarded with the dignity of field-marshal, by royal letters patent, September 6, 1574, received a pension of thirty thousand livres, besides the marquisate of Saluces, with other honours and distinctions, which obtained him the nick-name of *Torrent de la Faveur*. So much favour excited envy, and his credit being undermined with Henry III., he received latterly none but distant and trifling commissions. He died by poison in 1579. He must not be confounded with one of his descendants of the same name, who had the good fortune to obtain the favour of three successive kings; Henry III. made him master of the guard robe, first groom of his chamber, and master of the horse; Henry IV. gave him the government of Burgundy, and made him knight of St. Michael and other orders in 1595; and Lewis XIII., in 1620, raised him to the rank of duke and peer. He died in 1646.

BELLEGARDE, (Octavius,) son of Cesar, governor of Saintonge, and cousin of the above, born in 1587, and educated by the Benedictine monks of Auxerre. Bishop of Conserans in 1614, and archbishop of Sens in 1640. After a useful life, he died in 1646.* He is supposed to have written the book entitled, Augustinus docens Catholicos et vincens Pelagianos, addressed to the clergy of his diocese.

BELLEGARDE, (John Baptist Morvan de,) known as the abbé de Bellegarde, born in 1648, and died in 1734. He was a voluminous translator and compiler, but his works are little known in England.

BELLEGARDE, (Gabriel du Pac de,) and not, as he has been sometimes called, du Parc, born on the 17th October, 1717. From infancy he was remarkably studious and pious. During two years he held a canonry of Lyons; but having identified himself with the Port Royal party, he retired in 1751 to the seminary of Rhynswik, near Utrecht. There he put together the Memoirs on the history of the Bull Unigenitus, in the Netherlands. He subsequently published, 1. A Compendium of the History of the Church of Utrecht. 2. The Life of Van Espen, with a Collection of his Works. 3. An edition of the Works of Arnauld, an immense work, which took four years in printing, and appeared at last at Lausanne in 1782, in 45 vols, 4to, with a Life of the Author, and suitable illustrations. He meditated a similar work on Nicole. Death put an end to his useful and learned labours in 1789.

BELLEGARDE, (Anthony du Bois de, 1740—1825,) an officer in the French army before the revolution, but degraded and exiled for his vices. He then entered the Prussian service, but hastily left it. Being just the man for a revolution, he obtained a seat in the National Assembly, and was active against the unfortunate king. This prominence obtained for him various employments of note while the republic lasted, but Bonaparte would only appoint him to a subordinate office. On the restoration, he was classed among the regicides, and he died in exile. (Biog. Univ. Suppl.)

The Count Henry de, (1758—1831,) a native of Chamberi, and descended from one of the most ancient houses of Savoy, entered the military service, which had been that of his father and uncles. Conceiving that there was little prospect of advantage in his native country, he offered his sword to the Austrians, as his father had offered it to the Saxons, and from 1793 to 1815 he was in constant activity. He was present in most of the great battles of Austria against France. But his military talents were scarcely equal to his civil; though created (in 1806) a field marshal, he was not placed at the head of an army when great interests were at stake; and he was generally entrusted with the government of some province, such as Lombardy, Venice, or Gallicia, for which he was supposed to be better qualified. If the French are to be credited, his character was not unalloyed by dissimulation. (Biog. Univ. Suppl.)

BELLEGINGUE, (Peter, 1759—1826,) a physician of Besançon, who, after being attached to the French armies, retired to his native city, and wrote some odd books. We will waste no words on one who was evidently mad. (Biog. Univ. Suppl.)

BELLEISLE, (Charles Lewis Augustus Fouquet, count of, 1684—1761,) marshal of France, born at the seat of his father, the marquis de Belleisle, Villefranche, in Rouergue. He was properly educated for the military life; and while young, Lewis XIV. gave him a regiment of dragoons. He served with distinction in the Low Countries, in Spain during the war of succession, and after it in the war which the regent, duke of Orleans, declared against Philip V. After a short disgrace, occasioned by a change of ministry, consigning him for a while to the Bastile, he was again employed. In 1732 he was made lieutenant-general; and in the campaigns of the following years down to the peace of 1736, when Lorraine was ceded to France, he played a very distinguished part. The government of Metz, the administration of three bishoprics, and the *baton* of marshal, were his immediate rewards. In the famous war of Frederic the Great and of the Bavarian elector against Maria Theresa, in which the French were their allies, he penetrated into Bohemia, and took Prague. In the following diet of Frankfort, he espoused the cause of the Bavarian elector, who was raised to the throne of the empire as Charles VII. But there was a turn of affairs in Bohemia, which the new emperor had claimed in virtue of his supposed family rights; he returned, was invested in Prague, and forced to retreat. That he showed admirable conduct on this occasion, is allowed by all writers of the period. As governor of Provence and Dauphiny, he defended those provinces against the Sardinians and Austrians. In 1748 he was created a duke; in 1757 he became minister of war, and his administration was a benefit to France. (Biog. Univ.)

BELLEISLE, (Lewis Charles Armand Fouquet, count of, 1693—1746,) brother of the preceding, lieutenant-general in the French armies; served under the marshal in many of the great military operations of the period. He fell at the foot of the Col de l'Assiette, near Exiles and Fénestrelles, while attempting to force a passage through the tremendous defiles of the Alps into the valleys of Piedmont. (Biog. Univ.)

BELLELLI, (Fulgentius, or Francis, 1677—1742,) an Italian ecclesiastic, born at Buccino, librarian of the Bibliotheca Angelica, both under Benedict XIII. and Clement XII. He wrote two works on St. Augustine, against the Jansenists. 1. Mens Augustini de Statu Naturæ rationalis post Peccatum, 1730; and, 2. Mens Augustini de Modo Reparationis Creaturæ post Lapsum, &c. (Tipaldo, iv. 396.)

BELLEND DE ST. JEAN, (Anthony J. 1746—1791,) a French officer of noble family, actively engaged from the early part of 1789 in repressing revolutionary violence in le Quercy. During eighteen months he saved many mansions which had been doomed to the flames; but in May, 1791, his own was beset by about 10,000 people. He had with him only his brother and one servant, but a noble resistance was made, a brisk fire killing many of their savage assailants. When the gates were forced, they took refuge in the cellars, with the view of escaping through a subterraneous passage to a cave near the house. The mob, flocking to the cellars, and finding the entrance closely barricadoed, set fire to the house. In the confusion that ensued, the younger Bellend and the domestic endeavoured to escape; the latter was killed, the former made prisoner and conveyed to Cahors. The elder remained in the cellar, and killed twenty-three of those who ventured to the door; three or four times that number he wounded. At length he ceased to fire; and while conjecture was busy as to the cause, another and a last report was heard,—his last ball had entered his own brain.

His brother, who had served with distinction in the army, was treated with extreme brutality on the way to prison, and when he was put to death, a depraved ingenuity contrived to torture every part of his body with the keenest pain. (Biog. Univ. Suppl.)

BELLENDEN, (Sir, or Dr. John,) a Scottish poet and historian in the sixteenth century, of good family, and eminent abilities. Of his birth and education nothing is known, but his language makes it probable that he studied in France. He was, in fact, a doctor of the Sorbonne, and being highly valued by James V., he obtained a canonry of Ross, and the archdeaconry of Murray. By his royal master's desire, he undertook a translation into the vernacular tongue of the Scottish history, by Hector Boëthius. He fulfilled his task excellently, but used a degree of freedom which renders the translation and the original considerably different from each other. His variations, however, do not impair the value of the work, being, in some cases, corrections of Boëthius, in others, the addition of circumstances probably unknown to him. Hence Bellenden's free version obtained great credit in all parts of Britain. It appeared at Edinburgh, in 1536, with this title, The History and Chronicles of Scotland, compilit and newly correctit and amendit be the Reverend and Noble Clerk, Mr. Hector Boeis, Chanon of Aberdene, translated lately be Mr. John Bellenden, Archdene of Murray, and Chanon of Rosse; at command of James the Fyfte, King of Scottis. The able translator was a zealous Romanist, and active in his opposition to the Reformation. As the stream of public opinion in Scotland was then running another way, he thus must have often found himself uncomfortable among his countrymen, and this may have driven him to Rome, where he seems to have died, in 1560. His poetry also deserves notice, as displaying an enthusiasm which is truly worthy of the art. (Chalmers.)

BELLENDEN, (William,) of whose birth and parentage nothing is known, a native of Scotland; said by Dempster to have been professor of elegant literature at Paris in 1602. He seems to have been a favourite with James VI. and to have been appointed by him Magister Supplicum Libellorum, *i. e.* Reader of petitions, an office apparently bestowed for the purpose of enabling him to lead a life of learned retirement in France. There devoting himself to the study of Cicero more especially, he published, in 1608, his Ciceronis Princeps; in which he detailed the duties of a ruler by bringing from the writings of the Roman orator whatever could bear upon the subject; and to show his thorough acquaintance with the matter in hand, he prefixed a few pages, De Processu et Scriptoribus Rei Politicæ. In this, though no mention is made of any political writer subsequent to the time of Cicero, yet the preface alludes to the Βασιλικὸν Δῶρον, printed at Edinburgh, 1603, containing "His majesties instructions to his dearest sonne Henrie the prince," to whom Bellenden addressed his own volume. In 1612 appeared the Ciceronis Consul Senator Senatusque Romanus, to which was appended the Liber de Statu Prisci Orbis. These three treatises having become very scarce, in consequence, it is said, of the loss of the greater part of the copies at sea, when they were sent from France to England, were reprinted, but in a different order, at London, in 1787, by Dr. Parr. They were accompanied with his celebrated preface, in which he spoke of Burke, Fox, and lord North, as the three English luminaries in oratory and politics. The idea was suggested by Bellenden's work, De Tribus Luminibus Romanorum, a piece originally intended to eulogize Cicero, Seneca, and Pliny. Only the first part of this, that relating to Cicero, appeared at Paris, 1634, folio, (Bellenden having died before he had time to arrange his papers relating to the other two.) From this work Conyers Middleton is thought by Warton in his Essay on Pope, (ii. p. 324,) to have taken the idea of writing Cicero's history in his own words, and also to have taken the whole arrangements, adopted without acknowledgment, by himself.

BELLER, BELLERE, or BELLERUS, (John, d. 1595,) a native of Antwerp, rather celebrated in the annals of typography.

BELLER, (Luke, d. 1564,) believed to be a brother of the preceding, a printer and bookseller; but probably not identical with the Luke Beller who translated into Latin the Voyage du Chevalier Errant, by Cartigny of Valenciennes. (Biog. Univ. Suppl.)

BELLEROSE, (Peter le Messier, so called,) a French comedian, regarded as the first actor who had played with dignity both tragedy and comedy. He died in 1670, twenty-five years after his retirement from the theatre. (Biog. Univ.)

BELLET, (Charles, 1702—1771,) beneficed in the cathedral of Montaubon, author of L'Adoration Chrétienne dans la Dévotion du Rosaire, and Des Droits de la Religion Chrétienne et Catholique sur le Cœur de l'Homme. This work is said to have merit.

Two other persons of this name appear in the literary annals of France:

1. *The Abbé Bellet*, canon of Cadillac, who wrote on natural history and French coins, in the Transactions of the Bourdeaux Academy.

2. *Bellet Verrier*, who early in the last century wrote Mémorial Alphabétique, on subjects of law, police, and finance.

BELLET, (Isaac,) a physician at Bourdeaux. He was a man of very general information, and was made inspector of the mineral waters of France. Haller has erred in printing his name Bellot. He died at Paris, in 1778. He wrote, Lettres sur le Pouvoir de l'Imagination des Femmes enceintes, Paris, 1745, 12mo. This was translated into Italian by J. F. Bianchini, Venez. 1751, folio; and into English, Lond. 1756, 8vo; and again in 1772, 8vo. Histoire de la Conjuration de Catiline, Paris, 1752, 12mo. Exposition des Effets d'un nouveau Remède dénommé Sirop Mercuriel, Paris, 1768, 12mo; 1770, 12mo.

BELLETESTE, (B. 1778—1808,) of Orleans, an orientalist, who in 1798 accompanied the French army into Egypt as interpreter. On his return, he translated from the Turkish the Forty Viziers, and from the Arabic a treatise on precious stones. (Biog. Univ.)

BELLETTI, (John Francis, 1735—1819,) an Italian lawyer and author. He was the son of humble parents, but educated well. He wrote several farces and comedies, (in the dialect of his country,) some orations on sacred subjects, the lives of the popes to Pius VII., beginning the series with St. Peter, and published for many years an annual or almanac, called Solitario Lughese. (Tipaldo, iii. 163.)

BELLEVAL, (Peter Richer de,) a physician and botanist, born at Châlons-sur-Marne, in 1558, director of the botanic garden established by Henry IV. at Montpelier. He was an able teacher of botany, and the first in France who did not confine his views solely to the medicinal properties of plants. A genus of plants, Richeria, has been named after him by Villars, in acknowledgment of his eminence in botanical science. Tournefort and Linnæus have eulogized his labours. He paid unceasing attention to the garden, and at his death it was in a very flourishing condition. It afterwards ran to decay, and was much neglected, until it fell under the superintendence of Magnol. Belleval employed six students to procure plants from various parts of the world at his own expense. The garden suffered during a siege at Montpelier, and this eminent botanist expended not less than 100,000 francs to restore it to its former condition. It contained upwards of 3,000 plants. Belleval died in 1603. He left many manuscripts, which have not been printed; among others to be much regretted, the materials for a Flora of Languedoc, which he proposed to publish and illustrate with 400 plates in 4to. Belleval endeavoured to give to each plant a Greek name, an attempt afterwards pursued by Erhart, but without success. The published works of Belleval are, Onomatologia, seu Nomenclatura Stirpium Horti Regii Monspeliensis, Montp. 1598, 8vo; Paris, 1785, 8vo. This was published by P. M. A. Broussonet, under the title of Opuscules de Richer de Belleval; it contains a list of 2000 plants, arranged in alphabetical order. Recherche des Plantes du Languedoc, Montp. 1603, 4to. Dessein touchant la Recherche des Plantes du Languedoc. Montp. 1605, 4to. Remonstrance et Supplication au Roi Henri IV. touchant la Continuation de la Recherche des Plantes du Languedoc, et peuplement de son Jardin de Montpelier, Montp. 4to.

BELLEVILLE, or TURLUPIN, (Henry Legrand, so called,) a French comedian of great reputation, in the seventeenth century, familiarly known as Turlupin, who died in 1634. There is an engraved portrait of him. (Biog. Univ.)

BELLEVOIS, a painter of sea-pieces, ports, and storms, whose works are in many collections, particularly in Flanders, but of whom no particulars are known. He holds a respectable rank amongst the artists of his class; his touch is light, his colouring clear, but his figures are indifferently drawn. (Pilkington's Dict.)

BELLEVUE, (James de,) a learned lawyer of the fourteenth century, born at Aix in Provence. He wrote, 1. De Usu Feudorum; 2. In Novellas Justin; 3. De Excommunicatione; 4. Disputationes variæ; 5. Practica Juris; 6. De Foro Competenti; 7. Praxis Judiciaria. (Biog. Univ.)

BELLEVUE, (Armand,) a Dominican friar of the same country, related, perhaps, to the preceding, favoured by John

XXII. He wrote a dictionary of the most difficult words in philosophy and theology, which has been several times printed, a course of sermons, and some other religious works.

BELLEY, (Augustine, 1697—1771,) a Norman ecclesiastic, who was first tutor to the sons of the marquis of Balleroy, next secretary to the duke of Orleans. His works consist of antiquarian contributions to the Journal des Savans, and to the publications of his literary friends. (Biog. Univ. Suppl.)

BELLI. See Belly and Billy.

BELLI, (Pascal, 1752—1833,) an Italian architect, originally educated for a painter, placed in 1811 at the head of the commission formed by Napoleon for the preservation of the monuments of antiquity. (Tipaldo, iv. 402.)

BELLI, (Honorius,) a physician and botanist of Vicenza, who practised medicine in his native city, and thence departed for the isle of Candia, then belonging to the Venetians, where he practised, and paid particular attention to botany. Being well acquainted with the ancient Greek, he readily recognised the plants spoken of by the ancients in their works. His labours in this respect have called forth the acknowledgments of M. Petit-Thouars, who considers Belli to have done great service to science. He maintained an active correspondence with the most celebrated botanists of his time, and he is frequently referred to in the writings of John and Caspar Bauhin. He did not publish any work himself, but L'Escluse printed his Letters from Candia from 1594 to 1598, under the title of Epistolæ de Plantis Creticis, Ægyptiisque, novis et rarioribus, as a sequel to his History of Plants, (tom. ii. p. 299.) Pona has also, in the Description of the Plants of Mount Baldo, near Verona, communicated some observations made by Belli. He corrected the errors of Anguillara, Odoni, Belon, and Rauwolf, on the plants of the isle of Crete. The subject received its final completion from the hands of Tournefort, in his Flora of Candia. (Biog. Univ.)

BELLI, (Paul, 1588—1658,) a Jesuit, born at Messina, related to Innocent X. He wrote in Latin a history of the Passion, drawn from the four Evangelists, and a collection of one thousand eulogies of the blessed Virgin. We have besides, in Italian, a sort of tragi-comic representation of the sacrifice of Abraham, published at Roma in 1648, under the name of Lelio Palombo, which has been considered as an anagram. This, however, would turn his name into Ombelli. (Biog. Univ.)

BELLI, (Valerius,) born at Vicenza, after the middle of the sixteenth century, and died in the beginning of the seventeenth, was both an orator and a poet. In 1580 he wrote and spoke at Vicenza the funeral oration at the death of the celebrated architect, Andrew Palladio, and he published several madrigals, Venice, 1599, 12mo, and the Testamento Amoroso, Vicenza, 1612, 12mo. (Biog. Univ.)

BELLI, (Cherubino,) a Sicilian monk, of the seventeenth century, a learned canonist, theologian, and a poet. Before he became a monk, he published at Palermo, under his baptismal name of Girolamo Belli, in 1616—1618 and 1635, in 12mo, Ergasto, an idyll; La Clori, a pastoral drama; and Le Lagrime di Maria Vergine nel Calvario, the first and last in the Sicilian dialect; but on becoming a monk, having changed the name of Girolamo into that of Cherubino, he published, in 1646, under this name, two sacred tragedies, L'Agnese and Il Martirio di Sant' Agata; and in 1652, Il Nascimento del Bambino Gesù, a drama. (Biog. Univ.)

BELLI, (Francis,) an Italian ecclesiastic, born in 1577, who travelled through Holland and France, and died in 1644. By him we have,—1. La Caterina d'Alessandria, a tragedy, in verse, Verona, 1621-22 and 1660, 12mo. 2. L'Esequie del Redentore, a sacred drama in prose, Venice, 1633, 12mo. 3. Osservazioni di F. Belli nei suoi Viaggi d'Olanda e di Francia, Venice, 1632, 4to. 5. Gli accidenti di Cloramindo, a novel, Venice, 1635, 4to; besides other novels, academical discourses, and some lyric poems, which are quoted by Crescimbeni, Istor. della Volgare Poesia, v. 152. (Biog. Univ.)

BELLI, (Charles,) born in Venice in 1742, and died in 1816, a Jesuit, who at the suppression of his order lived a retired and literary life. He translated into Italian the first canto of Klopstok's Messiah, and wrote Il Ventaglia (The Fan,) with some other poems.

There have been many other authors of this name; as *Julius*, who was secretary to cardinal Dietrichstein, in Moravia, and was the author of Hermes Politicus, sive de Peregrinatoria Prudentia, libri iii. Frankfort, 1608, 12mo; and twelve books of commentaries of the war which took place in his time in Germany, entitled, Laurea Austriaca, which, however, has been also ascribed to Nicholas Belli, under whose name appeared the German translation of the original Latin. There were, however, two writers of this same name, who have been often confused, one a political writer, who lived about the beginning of the seventeenth century, but whose native country is unknown. He translated into Latin Garzoni's Piazza Universale, under the title of Emporium Universale. He also wrote Dissertationes Politicæ, tom. iv.

The other, *Nicholas Belli*, a Sicilian ecclesiastic, lived during the latter end of the seventeenth century, and left two volumes of panegyrics, printed at Rome, the first in 1669, 12mo, the second in 1672, 4to. (Biog. Univ.)

BELLI, (Peter,) a celebrated lawyer, born of noble parents at Alba, on the 20th of March, 1502. He was the first, according to Tiraboschi, who made an extensive application of legal science to the usages of war. He was during many years attached to the military establishments of the emperor Charles V. and his son Philip II. Subsequently he was counsellor of state to Emanuel Philibert, of Savoy, and employed by him in many affairs of importance, He died Dec. 31, 1575. He wrote several works, one of which, on military jurisprudence, is yet occasionally consulted. It is entitled, De Re Militari et Bello tractatus, divisus in partes ii. (Biog. Univ. Suppl.)

BELLIARD, (William,) a French writer, born at Blois, in the sixteenth century. During the stay of Margaret de Valois in that city, he presented to her several poems, which procured him the post of her secretary. He printed, in 1578, the first book of his poems, containing Les Délicieuses Amours de Marc-Antoine et de Cléopâtre, les Triomphes d'Amour et de la Mort, and other imitations of Ovid, Petrarch, and Ariosto, 4to, Paris. All his productions are considered worthless. (Biog. Univ.)

BELLIARD, (Augustine Daniel, count de, 1769—1832,) a French general, born in Poitou, who served all the successive governments established in France during his time, from that of the regicides to that of Lewis Philip. In 1831 the zeal which he had shown in the revolution of the preceding year caused him to be sent ambassador to Brussels, where he died. (Biog. Univ. Suppl.)

BELLICARD, (Jerome C. 1726—1786,) a Parisian architect, whom, notwithstanding his ability, the love of gambling brought to ruin. In 1754 he published some Observations on the Antiquities of Herculaneum. (Biog. Univ.)

BELLIER, (Peter,) a French scholar of the sixteenth century, known as a translator of Philo Judæus. He went to Rome, for the purpose of collating MSS. of that author, but finding the Vatican library closed, on account of Pius the Fifth's death, he lost some of his time. After his return, he published his translation of Philo, but it only gives twenty-four parts out of forty. (Biog. Univ. Suppl.)

BELLIEVRE, (Pomponne de, 1529—1607,) chancellor of France, a native of Lyons. He accompanied the duke of Anjou into Poland; and when that prince became king of France as Henry III. he was entrusted with some important negotiations; one to queen Elizabeth in behalf of the unfortunate Mary Stuart. In 1599 he was invested with the chancellorship of the realm; but in four years the seals were taken from him, and given to his rival, Sillery.

Two sons of the chancellor, *Albert* and *Claudius Bellievre*, were successively archbishops of Lyons.

A third son, *Nicolas de Bellievre*, president of the cour à Mortier, deserves honourable mention for his rebuke of cardinal Richelieu, when that minister persuaded Lewis XIII. to sit as one of the judges on the trial of the duke de la Valette. Though the cardinal was present, he expressed to the king the surprise and the sorrow which he felt at seeing on the seat of condemnation one whose prerogative was mercy,—one who should leave condemnation to his judges, and reserve pardon to himself, as the most enviable prerogative.

This noble family became extinct in 1637, in the person of *Papeuse de Bellievre*, first president of the parliament of Paris, who had been ambassador to Italy, Holland, and England. He deserves immortal remembrance as the founder of the general hospital at Paris. He saw the poor deprived of all effectual aid, temporal or spiritual: he called the hospital into existence, and they had both. (Biog. Univ.)

BELLIN, (James Nicholas,) a geographer, born at Paris in 1703. He was a member of the Royal Society of London. He died in 1772. The most important of his works are,—Le Petit Atlas Maritime, 4to, Paris, 1764; Le Neptune Français, fol. 1753; L'Hydrographie Français, fol. Par. 1752—1804. He wrote also a description of the British isles, and another of the Antilles, of the island of Corsica, and the gulf of Venice. His works, taking into consideration the date of their appearance, are not without merit, but exhibit many marks of haste and inaccuracy. (Baur, in Ersch und Gruber.)

BELLIN LA LIBORLIÈRE, (Francis Lewis,) a French writer, born at Poitiers. He produced, in 1799, Celestine, ou les Epoux sans l'être, 4 vols, a romance in Mrs. Radcliffe's manner. It was well received, but severely criticised by the author himself in his next work of fiction, entitled, La Nuit Anglaise. He subsequently wrote some other novels and a play. (Biographie des Contemporains)

BELLIN. See Belin.

BELLINCIONI, (Bernard,) also called Bellinzona, a famous poet of the fifteenth century, born at Florence, but settled at the court of Lewis Sforza, surnamed the Moor, duke of Milan, who loaded him with gifts and benefices. He died at Milan in 1491. His poems, which are in all sorts of metre, were published in 1493, in that city, by Tonzi, in 4to. Their faults are not few, but La Crusca quotes them as an authority for language. Bellincioni was the first to give to some of his poems the title and turn of elegy, and was conspicuous for satire and abuse.

BELLING, (Joseph Erasmus,) an engraver at Augsburg. Besides the portrait of pope Clement XIII. a folio plate, he engraved many devotional subjects. (Heinecken, Dict. des Artistes.)

BELLING, (William Sebastian von,) a celebrated Prussian commander, born about 1719. He commanded in 1758 prince Henry's corps of hussars, distinguished by a black uniform, death's head and cross bones, and the device, "Vincere aut mori." This corps became renowned through the whole army, and eventually was known as Blucher's, but with a less marked uniform. Belling died in 1779. (Ersch und Gruber.)

BELLINGEN, (Fleury de,) a grammarian, supposed to have taught the French language in Holland, and then to have made its origin his especial study. In 1653 he published, Les premiers Essais des Proverbes Français, which he reproduced under this title, Etymologie, ou Explication des Proverbes Français, divisée en trois Livres, par Chapitres en forme de Dialogues, La Haye, 1656, in 8vo. The abbé Goujet esteemed the Illustres Proverbes, as one of the best works that were known on that subject.

BELLINGHAM, (Richard,) governor of Massachusetts, born about the year 1592, in England, and bred to the law. He arrived in America, in 1634, and is remarkable for refusing, with some others, a summons from the crown, in 1664, to go over to England, and answer for themselves. He died on the 7th of December, 1672.

BELLINI. The name of several distinguished Italian artists.

1. *Jacob*, (1405—1470,) an early painter of the Venetian school, better known, according to Lanzi, by the celebrity of his sons than by his own works. These are either destroyed or incapable of identification. He was, according to Ridolfi, a very eminent portrait painter. Oil painting is said to have been taught him by Dominic and Andrew del Castagno. It was then a secret, and he communicated it to his sons. (Pilkington's and Bryan's Dictionaries. Lanzi, Stor. Pitt. ii. 14; iii. 18.)

2. *Gentile*, (1421—1501,) elder son of the preceding, born at Venice, who assumed the name of Gentile in remembrance of his father's instructor. Though an inferior artist to his brother, he was employed on an equal footing with him to adorn the hall of the great council; and when the grand signor sent to Venice for an eminent portrait painter, the senate commissioned Gentile to go to Constantinople, where his works added glory to the Venetian name. Besides many pictures that he painted for Mahomet II. he struck a fine medal for him, bearing his head on one side, and three crowns on the reverse. From this work, which is extremely rare, it appears that Gentile was also a worker of metals, a fact not before adverted to. However inferior to his brother from the harshness of tone in several of his works, there are others of extreme beauty. But he imitated exactly what he saw, even to the peculiarities of expression and the deformities of body presented by his models; and he has introduced, absurdly enough, the dresses of Venice and Turkey amongst the auditors of St. Mark. It is related, but on insufficient authority, that, while at Constantinople, he painted a decollation of St. John the Baptist. The sultan pronounced his work inaccurate, and ordered a slave to be beheaded in his presence, to prove himself a sufficient critic. Alarmed at such a lesson, Gentile took the earliest opportunity of returning home. He was there admitted into the order of St. Mark, and had a pension assigned to him for life. (Lanzi, Stor. Pitt. ii. 15; iii. 33.)

3. *John,* (1426—1516,) brother of the preceding, born also at Venice. He worked upwards of fifty-two years, and his progress of improvement as an artist is easily discernible from his pictures painted in distemper to those executed in oil. Borgini and Ridolfi say that, wishing to learn the latter art, imported into Italy by Antonello da Messina, he introduced himself to that artist as a nobleman of Venice, in order to see him prepare his colours. This anecdote, however, is mentioned by no other authors. Bellini rapidly became an oil painter of celebrity, and executed a great number of admirable works. He was ever improving, even when advanced in life. No example was lost upon him; hence, in the latter years of his honourable career, he conceived his subjects more boldly, gave roundness to his forms, and warmth to his colours. His gradations of tint were more delicate, yet well contrasted, his naked subjects better drawn, and more judicious in their selection, and his style of drapery more elevated; and had he succeeded still further in acquiring a greater degree of softness and delicacy in his contours, he might have been held up as one of the most finished examples of the modern style. Albert Dürer, who visited Venice in 1516, is said to have declared that, although very old, he was still the best painter then living. The class of pictures by him most usually met with are, Madonnas, figures of the Dead Christ, and other devotional subjects, and are to be seen at Bergamo, Vicenza, Venice, and other cities. This artist is generally held to be the founder of the Venetian school. The improvements he introduced into the art of painting were, a greater simplicity in the style of drapery, a generalization or breaking up of the positive colours, and a greater breadth of massing than had been before his time adopted. Nor is he less noted for having been the preceptor of both Giorgione and Titian, who carried to perfection the style of colouring introduced by him. (Lanzi, Stor. Pitt. ii. 15; iii. 32. Biog. Univ.)

4. *Bellin,* a painter of the school of the Bellini, and one of their family, who flourished about 1500, and who imitated their style with great exactness. He painted Madonnas for private individuals, which, as Bellin Bellini is little known, are generally attributed either to Gentile or Giovanni. (Lanzi, Stor. Pitt. iii. 37.)

5. *Philip d'Urbino,* a painter of the Roman school, about 1594, nearly unknown in the history of art, but mentioned by Lanzi as a painter of singular merit. There do not appear to be any of his pictures in his native city of Urbino, but many, both in oil and fresco, are scattered through the March. He is, in general, an imitator of Barocci; but in some of his works he has a vigorous, lively style, powerful colouring, and grandeur of composition. (Lanzi, Stor. Pitt. ii. 129.)

6. *Hyacinth,* a native of Bologna, and a scholar of Francis Albano. He painted in the style of Albano, and his pictures are much in that master's graceful style. (Bryan's Dict.)

BELLINI, (Laurence,) a very celebrated Italian physician and anatomist, born at Florence, September 3, 1643, of parents not in affluent circumstances. Manifesting very early a disposition to study, especially to science, he found a patron in the grand duke, Ferdinand II. By his liberality he was enabled to go to the university of Pisa, where he studied philosophy and mathematics under Alexander Marchetti, medicine and anatomy under Francis Redi, and mechanics under Borelli. The last instructor's lessons were most instrumental in laying the foundations of Bellini's fame, the principles of mechanics being used by him to explain the phenomena of the living body. His progress under education was such as to gain him, when only twenty-two, the professorship of philosophy and theoretical medicine. He so acquitted himself as to pass for a brilliant teacher, and brilliancy, rather than solidity, marked his future career. As an anatomist, however, he made many discoveries, and it is in this department, rather than that of practical medicine, that his reputation is now placed. He was an exceedingly popular teacher, and his discourses were attended by the grand duke himself. During thirty years he filled the chair of anatomy with increasing celebrity, and the number of distinguished pupils spread throughout Italy and other countries have disseminated his fame. At fifty years of age he abandoned his professorship to return to Florence, where he engaged in practice, and enjoyed a pension from the grand duke Ferdinand. He did not confine his studies to the sciences: he also cultivated letters and poetry with success. He died, at the age of sixty years, at Florence, June 8, 1703. His doctrines were readily adopted in his own and foreign countries, and for a length of time prevailed over all other systems of physiological medicine. Pitcairn obtained reputation by their aid at Leyden and in Scotland, and the works of Bellini were translated into many languages. Among his most successful labours must be mentioned his Observations on the Kidneys, published when he was only nineteen years of age. He is the discoverer of the Tubuli Uriniferi; he pointed out the connexion which exists between the nervous and muscular systems, and showed the power of action in the latter to be dependent upon the former. His descriptions of parts are always anatomically correct, but his physiological views are based upon the mechanical philosophy. His medical writings are not deserving of the same degree of praise as his anatomical; they are full of subtleties and speculations, founded upon erroneous principles. His imagination appears to have been too lively for a good practitioner, but well fitted for success in poetry. Some of his poems, indeed, have been published, and with advantage to his reputation. He also furnished many discourses to the Academia della Crusca, which are specimens of an excellent style and a lively wit. He was the author of the following works:—Exercitatio Anatomica de Structurâ et Usu Renum, Florent. 1662, 4to; Strasb. 1664, 8vo; Amst. 1665, 12mo; Patav. 1665, 8vo; Lugd. Bat. 1665, 1711, 1714, 4to. Gustûs Organum novissime deprehensum, Bonon. 1665, 12mo. This is inserted in the Bibliotheca Anatomica of Mangetus, and it also appeared at Leyden in 1711 and 1714 with the preceding work. Gratiarum Actio ad Etruriæ Principem, Pisæ, 1670, 12mo. De Urinis, de Pulsibus, de Missione Sanguinis, de Febribus, de Morbis Capitis et Pectoris, Opus, Bonon. 1683, 4to; Lipsiæ, 1685, 4to; Lugd. Bat. 1718, 4to, which edition was revised by Boerhaave. Consideratio nova de Naturâ et Modo Respirationis. This is to be found in the Ephemerides of the Curious in Nature, vol. ii. Opuscula aliquot ad Archibald. Pitcairnium, Pistoiæ, 1695, 4to; Lugd. Bat. 1714, 1731, 4to. Opera Omnia, Venet. 1708, 1720, 1747, 4to.

BELLINIANO, (Victor,) a Venetian painter, about the year 1526, called Bellini by Vasari, pupil of Giambatista Cima. He painted various historical pieces, in the religious edifices of Venice and its neighbourhood, being particularly happy in architectural display. (Lanzi, Stor. Pitt. iii. 41.)

BELLIS, (Anthony de,) a painter of the Neapolitan school, who died at an early age, in 1656, leaving some of his pictures unfinished. His manner partakes somewhat of that of Guercino, but is in fact founded on the style of Guido. (Lanzi, Stor. Pitt. ii. 275.)

BELLMANN, (Charles Michael,) one of the most original and national of the poets of Sweden, whose delineations of social and domestic life have obtained for him the title of its literary Teniers. He was born at Stockholm in 1741, and his first poetical attempts were serious, and even devotional. Subsequent productions have, however, cast over these an appearance of hypocrisy, Bellmann being eventually known as the bard of mirth and revelry. Though his subjects of this latter class were never elevated, often trivial, or even insignificant, they captivated by the nameless charm which he imparted to them—by their singular felicity of expression, and by a gaiety that was irresistible. Many of his most popular songs, and other poems of that kind, were not written, but were extemporaneous effusions of the moment, when surrounded by his companions in the hours of their festive jollity. Themselves the flashes of the bard's own enthusiasm at such times, it is less to be wondered at that those lyrical *improvisations* should have been enthusiastically welcomed, not only by his own circle, but also by the public, and indeed by all Sweden, for they are still everywhere chaunted by the peasants, and may be heard at every village festival.

Among Bellmann's admirers was Gustavus III., who obtained for him the place of secretary in the royal lottery. Bellmann himself, however, was contented with half the emoluments, and gave the other half to a substitute. He thought of nothing but enjoyment of the passing hour, being really the gay, careless person that his verses paint. He died in 1795, and it is said, that, when he felt his last hour approaching, a few intimate friends were invited to a carousal with him, in the course of which he sang some of his most energetic songs; and, at last addressing to each of his guests in turn a separate stanza, he exclaimed, "Let us die as we have lived, let us die breathing out our soul in song." Yet whether he did, after all, actually expire in the midst of his assembled guests, is left somewhat doubtful by those who tell this tale. He probably, therefore, did not leave the world thus indecently;

though he might really have assembled such a party as that described, at a time when more sober spirits would have been intent upon better things. One of his chief productions is that entitled, Fredmann's Epistolar och Sänger, 2 vols, Stockholm, 1791. After his death, his Skaldestykken were first published in 2 vols, Stockh. 1812; and in the following year another posthumous collection of pieces, entitled Handskrifter, appeared at Upsala. (Marmier, d'Ehrenström.)

BELLMONT, (Philip Francis von,) ordinary professor of national law and history at Erfurt, born at Würzburg, in 1683. He published an inaugural dissertation on the right of punishing a delinquent in his own or a foreign territory; and a programme of the library, with some skeletons of essays for the use of the attendants on his lectures. He died in 1740. (Ersch und Gruber.)

BELLO, (Mark,) a painter of the first epoch of the Venetian school, and a pupil of John Bellini. (Lanzi, Stor. Pitt. iii. 43.)

BELLO, (Philip, 1666—1719,) an advocate and miscellaneous writer of Naples, whose poems, lyrical collections, and life of St. Sabino, attested the respectability of his acquirements, while his great integrity won the esteem of all men. (Biog. Univ. Suppl.)

BELLOC, (John James,) a French surgeon, born at Saint Maurin, near Agen, in 1730, who made improvements in, and suggested some new surgical instruments adapted to cases of polypi of the nasal cavities. He died November 19, 1807, having published several works.

BELLOCQ, (Peter, 1645—1704,) a valet-de-chambre of Louis XIV., the friend of Moliere and Racine, and the author of several satirical pieces. (Biog. Univ.)

BELLONE, (Nicholas,) an Italian civilian, who wrote, among other works, Sopra i quattro Libri delle Institutioni Giustinian. Lione, 1568. (Chiesa Scritt. Piementesi, Torino, 1614, 4to.)

BELLONI, (John,) a citizen of Venice, who died, professor of moral philosophy at Padua, in 1623. He is author of an academical discourse. (Biog. Univ.)

BELLONI, (Joseph,) a sculptor and architect at Venice. There was also a painter of the name of Belloni at Milan. (Heinecken, Dict. des Artistes.)

BELLONI, (Paul,) a learned lawyer, who died at Milan, in April, 1625. He left several works, chiefly on civil law, and not a few Latin discourses, spoken on different occasions.

BELLONI, (Jerome,) a celebrated Roman banker, who by perseverance and integrity acquired an immense fortune, and was made a marquis by Benedict XIV. He published a learned dissertation on commerce, in 1750, which has been often reprinted, with various additions, and translated into the French and German languages. Belloni died in 1761.

BELLORI, (John Peter,) an eminent Italian antiquary, born at Rome, of a respectable family, in 1615, and educated by his maternal uncle, Francis Angeloni, a famous antiquary, and secretary to cardinal Aldobrandini. Becoming famous for acquaintance with antiquities, queen Christina appointed him her librarian, and keeper of her museum. Clement X. also conferred on him the title of antiquary of the city of Rome, where he died in 1696, leaving a fine collection of antiquities, drawings, and prints of all sorts, which was bought by the elector of Brandenburgh, and is now in the museum of the king of Prussia.

BELLOSTE, (Augustine,) a celebrated French surgeon, born at Paris in 1654, who simplified the modes of treatment in vogue in his day. Victor Amadeus, of Savoy, king of Sardinia, tempted him to quit France, and attend upon his mother, the dowager duchess of Savoy, at Turin, to whom he was appointed chief surgeon. He accordingly removed thither, where he died July 15, 1730. An empirical medicine has passed under his name, but he was not the inventor; it has been current in the formularies, and has been described in the Pharmacopœia of Renaudot. He published Chirurgien de l'Hôpital, Paris, 1696, 1698, 1705, 1708, 1716, 8vo, Amst. 1707, 8vo. It was translated into English, Lond. 1732, 12mo; into German by Martin Schurig, Dresden, 1705, 1710, 1724, 8vo; into Italian, Venez. 1710, 1729, 8vo; into Dutch, La Haye, 1701, 8vo; Haarlem, 1725, 1729, 8vo. Suite du Chirurgien de l'Hôpital, du Mercure, des Maladies des Yeux, des Tumeurs encystées, &c. Paris, 1725, 1728, 1734, 12mo.

BELLOT, (Florence Charles,) the son of an eminent physician, born at Abbeville, in May, 1724. He studied medicine, and was at the age of thirty-one appointed to a chair of chemistry in the Royal College of France. He died at fifty, leaving some unfinished works in

MS. He only published a thesis, entitled, Utrum in Cancro Belladonnæ Usus tum internus, tum externus? Paris, 1760, 4to.

BELLOTTI, (Peter, 1625—1700,) a painter of the Venetian school, born at Volgano, on the lake of Garda, and pupil of Girolamo Forabosco, under whom he became an excellent colourist. In historical subjects, he had no great success, but his portraits are excellent, and so are his caricatures. Objections are sometimes made to a minuteness and dryness of style, which led him to distinguish almost every hair; but Boschini seems to consider him almost a prodigy for uniting carefulness and finish with an exquisite delicacy in his tints never before known. In 1668 he was painter to the court at Munich, but he returned to Italy, and died at Garignano. P. A. Pazzi has engraved his portrait, painted by himself. (Lanzi, Stor. Pitt. iii. 178.)

BELLOTTO, (Bernard, 1724—Oct. 17, 1780,) a modern painter and engraver, born at Venice, nephew and pupil of Antonio Canal, called Canaletti. Bernard, in imitation of his uncle, painted views and perspectives, according to Lanzi, approaching so nearly the style of his preceptor, that it is difficult to distinguish their works. After having worked at Vienna, and Dresden, he removed to Warsaw, where he died. M. Heinecken gives a list of his works. (Bryan's Dict. Lanzi, Stor. Pitt. iii. 238.)

BELLOVESUS, a Gaulish Celt, who passed over into Italy in the reign of Tarquinius Priscus. According to Livy, he was nephew of Ambigatus, supreme chieftain of his race. The Celtic territories were then found, as usual among savages, to supply an insufficient range for a growing population. Ambigatus accordingly desired Bellovesus and his brother, Sigovesus, sons of his sister, to seek farther space elsewhere. The latter took a northerly direction; the former led a formidable band towards Italy, which he entered through the defiles of Turin. In the plains of Lombardy, he defeated the Tuscans, triumphed as he proceeded over other tribes, and founded Milan. The news of his success allured other Gallic tribes to his standard, and by degrees their colonies spread over Etruria, Liguria, and to the feet of the Appennines. From this period the whole region was termed Cisalpine Gaul. The establishment of these colonies is referred to A.U.C. 164, which corresponds to A. C. 590. (Liv. v. 34. Biog. Univ.)

BELLOY, BELLOI, and BELOY, (Peter de,) an eminent French lawyer, born at Montauban, about the year 1540, of an ancient family, originally from Brittany. His three elder brothers were killed fighting in the royal army against the Huguenots, and hence his own appearance as an advocate for Henry IV. against the league proved unusually offensive to the more violent Romanists. He did, however, publish, in 1585, a work entitled Apologie Catholique contre les Libelles des Ligueurs, which maintains that Henry's rights to the throne were unaffected by his protestantism, and not amenable to any tribunal of the pope's. This is a profound and luminous production, the more honourable to its author, because he was a zealous Romanist; but it was treated as a defamatory libel by the leaguers, who branded him as a heretic. By their influence he was first imprisoned in the Conciergerie, and afterwards in the Bastille. There he continued for above two years. Henry IV., as a reward for his services and sufferings, made him advocate-general to the parliament of Toulouse. The time of his death is not recorded. Belloi wrote also, De l'Autorité du Roi, et des Crimes qui se committent par les Ligués, 1588, 8vo. Examen du Discours publié contre la Maison royale de France, 1587, 8vo. This work maintains that the king cannot deprive his lawful heir of the succession, and that the zeal of the Lorraine princes for the Romish faith was merely a pretence to gain the throne. It is, however, a fair and moderate production, displaying great erudition, but no bad spirit whatever. Moyens d'Abus et Nullités de la Bulle de Pie V. contre le Roi de Navarre, 1586, 8vo. This treats deeply of the papal authority, and reduces it within just bounds. Recueil de Pièces pour les Universités contre les Jésuites, depuis 1552, jusqu'en 1624, 8vo. Belloi also wrote a curious and interesting work upon the different orders of knighthood, besides treatises upon several legal and contemporary subjects.

BELLOY, (Pius Laurence Buirette de, 1727—1775,) a celebrated French dramatic author, born at St. Flour, in Auvergne, and, losing his father at six years of age, brought up by his uncle, an eminent advocate of the parliament of Paris. He was himself intended for the law, but having a taste for the stage, which his uncle could neither endure nor he control, he fled into the north of

Europe, and under the name of Dormont de Belloy, lived as an actor, passing some years at St. Petersburgh, in the reign of the empress Elizabeth. He returned to Paris in 1758, to bring out his tragedy of Titus; but his uncle having procured an order for his arrest if he attempted to play in France, Belloy fled back to Russia. His uncle dying soon after, he returned to France, and produced his tragedy of Zelmire, which was very successful. His Siege of Calais, in 1765, gained him his highest celebrity. It was acted in all the garrisons of France; represented and printed at St. Domingo; and translated into English, by Denys. The city of Calais sent to the poet letters of citizenship, in a gold box, bearing this inscription,—*Lauream tulit, civicam recipit.* Thenceforth devoted to national subjects, both by taste and by remembrance, Belloy composed Gaston et Bayard, Gabrielle de Vergy, and lastly, Pierre le Cruel. The first of these tragedies had a brilliant success, and opened to him the doors of the French Academy; the second was not played till after his death; the third completely failed; and although subsequently well received, its author had not the satisfaction of knowing it: he had sunk, deeply mortified, into the grave. Gaillard, the friend of Belloy, collected his works, in six vols, Paris, 1779, with a life of the author prefixed. (Biog. Univ.)

BELLOY, (John Baptist,) cardinal, born at Morangles, near Senlis, and educated for the church, but of an ancient family, that had been chiefly remarkable for the military services of its members. In early life, he was made vicar-general, official, and archdeacon of Beauvais, under cardinal de Gèvres. In 1751, he became bishop of Glandèves; and in 1755, being deputed to the famous ecclesiastical assembly of that year, he joined the *Feuillants*, or moderate party, (so called because led by the cardinal de la Rochefoucault, minister *de la feuille des bénéfices*,) and opposed to the *Théatines*, the party professing the principles of an ancient bishop of Mirepoix, who had been of that order. Belloy's aid was requited by the see of Marseilles, that soon became opportunely vacant by the death of Belsunce, famed for his admirable conduct during the plague in that city, but latterly conspicuous for a zealous devotion to the bull *Unigenitus*. The new bishop thus found himself provided with a difficult task, but his discreet and amiable carriage restored peace to the diocese. The revolution drove him from it, and he retired to Chambly, a small town near his native place, without encountering any considerable danger. When the *Concordat* was concluded, he was the first French prelate that answered, by a formal surrender of his see, the pope's recommendation to resign. His example was immediately followed by various other members of the episcopal body, committed more or less to the revolution, and it was so agreeable to the government, then intent upon organizing the hierarchy anew, that he was promoted to the archiepiscopal see of Paris, in 1802. In the following year, his ready obedience to the papal call for resignation was acknowledged by the compliment of a cardinal's hat. He died in 1808, leaving a character for piety and moral worth deeply venerated even by those who thought his policy sometimes dangerously pliant. Buonaparte, then emperor, allowed his remains, by a special privilege, to be interred in the vault of his predecessors, and ordered a monument to be erected as a testimony of his *singular consideration for his episcopal virtues.* (Biog. Univ. Biog. des Contemp.)

BELLUCCI, (Anthony, 1654—1726,) a painter of the modern Venetian school, born at Soligo, in the Trevisano, and a pupil of Domenico Difinico. He combined a delicacy of colouring with much energy and breadth; and though he indulged in deep shades, he disposed of them in grand masses, and enlivened his works by neatness of touch and agreeableness of tone. He appears to great advantage in small figures, which he frequently introduced into the landscapes of Tempesta. He engraved for his amusement the portrait of Correggio. A painter of this name is mentioned by Walpole as having visited England in 1716, from the court of the elector palatine, and who finished, in 1722, a ceiling at Buckingham-house, for which the duchess paid him 500*l*., and also as having been employed by the duke of Chandos at his magnificent seat of Canons. Vertue names a nephew of this Bellucci who went to Ireland, and made a fortune by painting portraits there. Lanzi, in a note, also mentions a son of Antonio Bellucci, named Giovanni Battista, who painted a fine altar-piece at Sorigo, but who abandoned the art of painting to live upon his fortune. (Lanzi, Stor. Pitt. iii. 217. Walpole's Anec. of Painting, by Dallaway, iv. 40. Pilkington's Dict. by Fuseli. Bryan's Dict. Heinecken.)

BELLUCCI, (Thomas,) a botanist of Pistoria, and gardener to the university of Pisa in the seventeenth century, who published a catalogue of all the plants that were cultivated in his time. (Biog. Univ.)

BELLUGA, (Lewis,) descended from the ancient family of Moncada, born at Motril, in Granada, in 1662, and bishop of Carthagena in 1705. On the approach of the Austrian troops in the war of succession, he assisted Philip V. with all his influence, a service for which he was rewarded with the viceroyalty of Granada; but he drew upon himself the anger of the court by his protest against the taxation of the church revenues. His appointment to a cardinal's hat by Clement XI. in 1719, was warmly opposed by the king of Spain; and Belluga, whose feelings of loyalty led him to decline this honour, ran great risk of incurring the displeasure of his spiritual as well as of his civil superior. A reconciliation between the king and the pope, however, gave Belluga the satisfaction of receiving the hat, which he had not used, from the hands of Philip. He died in 1743, after having resided some time in Rome in the character of a Spanish ambassador. (Baur, in Ersch und Gruber.)

BELLUNELLO, (Andrew,) a painter of the Venetian school, called Bellunello da San Vito. His master-piece is a Crucifixion, amongst various Saints, with the date, 1475, in the great council chamber of Udine. It has some merit in regard to size and the distribution of the figures, but displays neither beauty of forms nor colour, and bears greatly the appearance of an ancient piece of tapestry. (Lanzi, Stor. Pitt. iii. 25.)

BELLUNESE, (George, da San Vito,) a very excellent painter of friezes and miniature ornaments, and an able portrait painter, who flourished at San Vito, a place in the Friuli, about the middle of the sixteenth century. (Lanzi, Stor. Pitt. iii. 155.)

BELLUNO, (Victor, Perrin, duke de,) marshal and peer of France, one of the great captains brought forward by the revolution. He was born in 1766 at La Manche, in Lorraine, and entered the artillery service in 1788. He obtained the post of *maréchal de camp* in 1793, at the siege of Toulon, when he commanded the attack on the redoubt l'Aiguilette, the taking of which hastened the evacuation of the place by the English. Having recovered from the effects of two shots received at that siege, he went to the army of the eastern Pyrenees, and served with distinction. Being subsequently employed in Italy, his operations eventually compelled the pope to sign the treaty of Tolentino. During the external peace, which followed the treaty of Campo Formio, he took the command of La Vendée, which he succeeded in finally calming. He returned in 1799 to Italy, and took a most honourable part in the battles of St. Lucie, Alexandria, and Novi. Arrived with his corps on the fields of Montebello, when the attack had already begun, he came still early enough to decide the fate of that day, and five days afterwards he again led the van on the field of Marengo. Stationed to oppose the advance of the Austrian army, he succeeded in so doing for eight hours, till the main body of the French army arrived. Bonaparte presented him with a sword of honour on that occasion. He went next to take the command of the French and Dutch armies, destined, as was said, for an expedition to Louisiana. This did not take place; general Victor remained in Holland, and married at the Hague, where he remained until after the treaty of Amiens, when he was sent as ambassador of the republic to Denmark, and did not return to France till the war broke out with Prussia. He was wounded at Jena, and took part in all the brilliant events of the campaign of 1806. At the battle of Friedland he commanded the first corps of the *grande armée*, and the success of the day was chiefly due to his skilful manœuvres, wherefore Napoleon gave him on the field of battle the baton of a *maréchal de l'empire*. After the battle of Tilsit, he was named governor of Berlin, which situation he retained fifteen months. In 1808 he commanded a corps in Spain, at the head of which he defeated the army of Galicia, and won the battles of Somo Sierra, and Madrid, and in 1809 that of Uclés, where he defeated the duke of Infantado, and made 15,000 prisoners. At Medellin he destroyed the army of Cuesta. His subsequent skilful march through the Sierra-Morena reduced all Andalusia under the French. He afterwards conducted the siege of Cadiz. Called in 1812 to the army in Russia, he commanded the ninth *corps d'armée*, and covered himself with glory at the Beresina. At the battle of Dresden he headed the second *corps d'armée*, and by a most bold manœuvre, made himself master of the positions occupied by the left wing of the allies, and cut off 16,000 Austrians, and made them prisoners. In subsequent battles he showed himself equally brave, though success was now sometimes denied him; yet even during his retreat, he drove the Russians from St. Dizier (January 27, 1814.) Some days afterwards, he drove 15,000 Russians and Prussians out of Brienne. He contributed also to the advantages which Napoleon obtained at Nargis and Villeneuve. Having rested a few hours at Salins, he delayed the occupation of the bridges of Montereau, for which the emperor severely reproached him. He expiated this fault by his bravery at the abbaye de Vaucler (March 7, 1814,) where he passed a *defilée*, defended by sixty pieces of artillery.

At the restoration, Lewis XVIII. bestowed on him several marks of esteem; and when Napoleon returned from Elba, Belluno followed the Bourbons to Belgium, and returned with them to Paris. Such a proof of constancy procured for him new honours, and he was in 1815 chosen to represent the French army at the marriage of the duke of Berry. Being in 1821 minister of war, he was nominated major-general of the army sent against the Spanish constitutionalists. He remained, however, only with it till it passed the Bidassoa, and soon returned to Paris. On the 28th October following, he was placed on what may be called ministerial half-pay, which affected him to that degree, that he first refused the post of ambassador at Vienna, but accepted it afterwards. Since the revolution of 1830, he took no part in public affairs, and died in March, 1841. At the desire of his family, no speech over his grave was pronounced, as is the custom on such occasions. (Biographie des Contemporains, by Arnauld. Journal des Débats, March, 1841.)

BELLUTI, (Bonaventura, 1599—1676,) a friar of Catania, in Sicily, who obtained great reputation in theology and philosophy. His philosophical works, written in Latin, were published in two volumes folio; and after his death were published some pieces written by him on morals. (Biog. Univ.)

BELLY, (James,) a painter and engraver, a native of Chartres, who worked in Italy, where he engraved after the Caraccis. (Heinecken.)

BELMEIS, or BEAUMES, (Richard de,) bishop of London in the reign of Henry I., consecrated 26th of July, 1108, warden of the Welsh Marches, and lieutenant of Shropshire. He expended the whole revenues of his bishopric on the erection of St. Paul's cathedral, in London, purchasing and pulling down the adjoining houses for a churchyard, which he surrounded with a high wall. Bishop Godwin thinks that this wall was entire in his time, though concealed by the houses with which it was covered on all sides. He afterwards built a convent for Regular Canons at St. Osith de Chich, in Essex. (Biog. Brit. Godwin de Præsul.)

BELMISSERO, (Paul,) a physician and Latin poet of the sixteenth century, who translated into Latin verse, Aristotle de Animalibus, and wrote a considerable number of miscellaneous poems. (Biog. Univ.)

BELMONDI, (Peter, 1774—1822,) a periodical writer of Paris, best known as the compiler of a very useful work, Code des Contributions Directes, 3 vols, 8vo, Paris, 1817, &c. (Biog. Univ. Suppl.)

BELMONT, (Aimery de,) a troubadour of Provence, in the time of Raymond Berenger V., some of whose verses remain in the collection of St. Palaye. (Biog. Univ.)

BELMONT. See Beaumont.

BELMONTE, (Lewis de,) a dramatic poet, probably the author of Hazañas de D. G. H. de Mendoza, 1622, 4to. (Antonio.)

BELMONTI, (Peter,) a moral writer and poet, born at Rimini, in 1537, principally known as the author of a posthumous work, Instituzione della Sposa, Rome, 1587, 4to. (Biog. Univ.)

BELOE, (William, 1756—1817,) son of an eminent tradesman at Norwich, where the future author was born. His father failed in early life, but subsequent exertions enabled him to do even more than recover himself; and feeling that nothing can absolve an honourable man from his debts but the payment of them, he took the first opportunity of calling his creditors together, and paid to each the balance due to him, amidst the plaudits of them all. This high-minded man discerned a precocity of talent in his son, which he determined upon improving by a suitable education. He sent him, accordingly, into Yorkshire for instruction by the scholarly father of Dr. Raine, eventually master of Charterhouse school, London, but apparently with no view of training him for any profession more learned than that of surgery. Mr. Raine, however, discerned in him talents fitted for a life of greater erudition, and he recommended his father to place him in a school of *higher* pretensions than his own, and thence to remove him to the university. He was, in compliance with this disinterested advice, transferred to an academy at Stanmore, in Middlesex, then kept by Samuel Parr, certainly one of the most competent classical instructors of his day. From this eminent person's tuition he was rather abruptly removed, in consequence of a persecution raised against him by some of the upper boys, and he spent some time with his family at Norwich, before his admission in the university of Cambridge. He was of Bene't, or Corpus Christi college there; in entering which society he soon found his feelings wounded by something that he considered insolence in two young men of superior condition to his own. He thoughtlessly took revenge in the composition of an epigram, which gave great offence, and excluded him from society that he would have gladly joined. He was thus less tempted into misapplication of his time than he might otherwise have been, and hence, probably, the mortification proved a permanent advantage. In 1779, Beloe took his bachelor's degree, and returned to Norwich. His old instructor, Dr. Parr, was now there as master of the grammar-school, and he invited him to become his assistant, a satisfactory testimonial to Beloe's conduct at Stanmore. He now married, and became curate of Earlham, in his native county, and it is another honourable testimony to his worth that when the living became vacant, he was chosen to fill it. He soon found, however, this little vicarage a most insufficient provision; it being the nature, indeed, of such preferments to place individuals in a position which cannot be supported with any comfort, or hardly at all, without private fortune. Beloe, wanting this advantage, determined upon a removal to London, in the hope of rising there by his talents and industry, to some situation of ease and independence. He sought, immediately, employment from the publishers, and was more in their pay, during several years, than almost any other of his contemporaries. In those days, periodical writing was very much in the hands of dissenters, the clerical part of whom are naturally prejudiced against the church, and possess very little accurate knowledge of it. Beloe did not, of course, in these respects resemble the bulk of professed authors, although youth, and want of introduction, must have denied him any sufficient acquaintance with ecclesiastical questions. For mere politics, however, he was furnished with no corrective; on the contrary, family engagements threw him, during all the heat and violence of the American war, among determined advocates of the colonial party. Dr. Parr, too, had been both his instructor and patron. His condition, besides, was difficult and struggling. These things, added to the warmth inseparable from his years, and his very limited means of obtaining good information, rendered young Beloe a partizan of those opinions which their friends complacently denominated liberal. But as the French revolution advanced, unfolding a character of sanguinary selfishness, many of those who had hastily approved its earlier stages, pressed emulously forward with acknowledgments of error. Beloe was one of these. In conjunction with archdeacon Nares, he undertook the British Critic, a review that advocated constitutional principles in religion and politics. The party with which he had formerly been connected, enraged by his secession, attributed it to a sordid spirit of calculation. But, undoubtedly, there is enough to account for it, without any uncharitable imputation, in greater maturity of judgment, better information, and observation of the revolutionists in France. That Beloe, however, might have reckoned upon some temporal advantage from his change of sentiments is highly probable, and not discreditable; it being reasonable, that he who labours in defence of others, should receive a reasonable reward from his exertions. He did not, however, obtain any considerable preferment, although enough to provide respectably for his declining years. In 1796 he was presented by the lord chancellor, Loughborough, afterwards earl of Rosslyn, to the rectory of Allhallows, London-wall. In the following year, Bishop Pretyman collated him to a stall in Lincoln cathedral; and in 1805, Bishop Porteus to one in St. Paul's. This last, being the prebend of St. Pancras, was the best endowed of all his preferments; but unless the owner should be fortunate with fines, he might receive but little from it during many years. Beloe, in fact, although possessed of preferment which makes a great shew on paper, had really never an income from the church of any considerable amount. He was, therefore, in 1804, glad of an appointment in the British Museum, as assistant-librarian, and probably might have retained it to his death, notwithstanding his preferment in the following year to a prebend of St. Paul's, had he not been shamefully deceived by a person allowed to use the books and drawings under his care. His constitution appears never to have been robust, and incessant labour, aided in its wearing operation upon a temperament highly sensitive by various painful incidents, brought him to the grave when he had only just entered into his sixtieth year. He left behind him the character of a religious, amiable, and accomplished man.

The following are Beloe's publications:—1. Ode to Miss Boscawen, 1783. 2. The Rape of Helen, from the Greek, with Notes, 1786. 3. Poems and Translations, 1788. 4. The History of Herodotus, from the Greek, with Notes, 4 vols, 8vo, 1791. This work had the honour of a favourable notice from Larcher, the learned French translator of the original, from whose labours it is enriched by many valuable notes, and Beloe has availed himself besides of the discoveries recently made in Africa. 5. Translation of Alciphron's Epistles, 1791. 6. Translation of the Attic Nights of Aulus Gellius, 1795. 7. Miscellanies, *viz.* Poems, Classical Extracts, and Oriental Apologues, 3 vols, 12mo, 1795. 8. Translation of the Arabian Nights Entertainments, from the French, 4 vols, 12mo. 9. Joseph, translated from the French of M. Bitaubé, 2 vols, 12mo. 10. Anecdotes of Literature and Scarce Books, 6 vols, 8vo, published between 1806 and 1812. 11. Brief Memoirs of the Leaders of the French Revolution. 12. The Sexagenarian, or Memoirs of a Literary Life. This was a posthumous work, edited by a friend, and published in 1818. Mr. Beloe was also at one time sole editor of the British Critic, and for many years he was joint-conductor with archdeacon Nares. The connexion of these two clergymen with that periodical terminated with the forty-second volume. Another of Beloe's joint labours was upon a Biographical Dictionary, in 15 vols, 8vo, which he undertook in conjunction with the Rev. W. Tooke, late chaplain to the British factory in Russia, Mr. Morrison, and the Rev. R. Nares. (Annual Biog. Gent.'s Mag.)

BELON, (Peter, 1517—1564,) a celebrated French physician and naturalist, born at Soulletière, in Maine. Of his family nothing is known, but he met with patrons, by whose kindness he received a good education and the means of travelling.

Belon departed for Candia in 1546, where he remained some time studying the plants of that island, and afterwards repaired to Constantinople. He visited Lemnos, Mount Athos, and Thessalonica, whence he returned to Constantinople, and then took his departure for Egypt, from which he passed to Mount Sinai and Jerusalem. He again returned to Constantinople and visited Natolia, embarked at Gallipoli, arrived at Venice, where he made a short stay, and then departed for Cività-Vecchia and Rome. He returned to France with a valuable collection, having been absent three years. He then published some works, which were well received, but notwithstanding in 1554 he failed of obtaining a license to practise medicine. This disappointment arose from the interruption of his academic course made by his travels. He was, however, in 1557 received as a bachelor extraordinary, and he ultimately obtained his degree in 1560. At the time of his death, he was meditating an important work upon agriculture, but returning one day from Paris, he was assassinated in the *Bois de Boulogne*. He must be regarded as one of the most distinguished naturalists of the sixteenth century; and, with Gesner, a founder of natural history at the restoration of letters. He is also to be remembered as one of the earliest cultivators of comparative anatomy. He described, with much fidelity, the countries he visited, and minutely detailed their natural productions. His erudition renders his works particularly interesting. Plumier has consecrated a genus of American plants, the *Bellonia*, to his memory, and in acknowledgment of the services he had rendered to botanical science. He published:—Histoire Naturelle des estranges Poissons Marins, avec leurs Portraicts gravés en bois: plus le vraie Peincture et Description du Daulphin et de plusieurs autres Rares de son Espèce, Paris, 1551, 4to. De Aquatilibus libri duo, cum Iconibus ad Vivam ipsorum Effigiem quoad fieri potuit, Paris, 1553, 8vo. La Nature et Diversité des Poissons, avec leurs Pourtraicts représentés au plus près du Naturel, Paris, 1555, 8vo. De la Nature et Diversité des Poissons, avec leurs Descriptions et naifs Pourtraicts, en sept livres, Paris, 1555, fol. Histoire des Poissons, Paris, 1555, 4to, in French and Latin. Les Observations de plusieurs Singularités et Choses mémorables trouvées en Grèce, Asie, Judée, Egypte, Arabie, et autres Pays estranges, redigées en trois livres, Paris, 1553, 1554, 1555, 1558, 4to; Anvers, 1555, 4to; translated into Latin by Charles de l'Ecluse, Anvers, 1589, 4to; and into German, in the Sammlung der Merkwuerdigsten Reisen in der Orient de Paulus. The Latin translation was reprinted in the collection De Exoticis, (Anvers, 1605, fol.) De Arboribus coniferis, resiniferis, aliisque nonnullis sempiternâFronde viventibus, cum earundem Iconibus ad vivum expressis; item de Melle Cedrino, Cedriâ, Agarico, Resinis et iis quæ ex Coniferis proficiscuntur, Paris, 1553, 4to. De admirabili Operum antiquorum et Rerum suspiciendarum Præstantiâ liber, quo de Ægyptiis Pyramidibus, de Obeliscis, de Labyrinthis sepulchralibus et de Antiquorum Sepulturis agitur, Paris, 1553, 4to. L'Histoire de la Nature des Oiseaux, Paris, 1555, fol. Pourtraicts d'Oiseaux, Animaux, Serpents, Herbes, Arbres, Hommes et Femmes d'Arabie et d'Egypte, Paris, 1557, 1618, 4to. Remontrance sur le Défaut de Labour et Culture des Plantes, et de la Connoissance d'Icelles, &c. Paris, 1558, 8vo; translated into Latin by Charles de l'Ecluse, Anvers, 1589, 8vo.

BELORADO, (John de,) a Benedictine friar, and abbot of the convent of St. Peter, at Cardeña, in Spain. He wrote Coronica del famoso Cavallero Cid Ruy Dias de Bivar. Burgos, 1593, fol. (Antonio.)

BELOSELSKY, (Prince,) born at Petersburgh in 1757, died there in 1809; in early youth, sent by the empress Catharine II. to the court of Turin, but the count Panin recalled him, from jealousy of his talents, it has been said, but probably from thinking them rather fit for literature than business. Beloselsky consoled himself under this disgrace by consecrating an ample fortune to the protection of art and the cultivation of letters. He published, 1. Dyanyologie, ou Tableau de l'Entendement, 8vo. 2. De la Musique en Italie, 8vo. 3. Poésies Françaises d'un Prince étranger, 8vo. In these works he displayed the most varied knowledge, and a talent for French poetry so extraordinary, that Voltaire placed him by the side of the count Schouvalow, author of l'Epître à Ninon. When a sanguinary spirit of spoliation stalked abroad in France, under the name of liberty, Beloselsky nobly found another use for the opulence with which Providence had entrusted him. His mansion was ever open to enlightened Frenchmen, driven by revolutionary violence and cupidity from their homes. (Biog. Univ.)

BELOT, (John,) born at Blois, at the end of the sixteenth century, an advocate of the privy council of Lewis XIII., connected with Lachambre and other members of the *Académie Française*, then just established. Belot was of opinion that scientific works should not be written in the vernacular tongue; Lachambre differed from this opinion, and a controversy ensued. Belot announced a work, called La France, ou la Monarchie parfaite, which never appeared. Some authors think him the same with Michael Belot, who published in 1666, Mémoires de Guillaume Ribier, to which is appended a life of cardinal Sadolet. (Biog. Univ.)

BELOT, (John,) pastor of Mil-Monts, born towards the end of the sixteenth century, a pretended adept in the occult sciences. He published l'Œuvre des Œuvres, in 1623, and afterwards a book on Chiromancy and Physiognomy, works occasionally sought by book collectors. (Biog. Univ.)

BELOT, (Madame, d. 1805,) of Chaillot, the widow of an advocate, who translated Hume's England, Johnson's Rasselas, and other English works, into French. She also wrote some original pieces in her own language, one of which especially, entitled Reflexions d'une Provinciale sur le Discours de J. J. Rousseau, touchant l'Inégalité des Conditions, has been highly commended. (Biog. Univ.)

BELOW, (Jacob Frederic,) a Swedish physician and naturalist, born at Stockholm, in 1669, where he practised medicine for many years. Charles XII. called him into Saxony in 1705, and made him physician to the army. He was taken prisoner, and conducted to Moscow, where he was engaged in his profession with success. He died in 1716, having only published some small academical works. (Biog. Univ.)

BELPRATO, (John Vincent,) count of Aversa, in the kingdom of Naples. He lived in the sixteenth century, and was of Spanish extraction. His contemporaries considered him an excellent linguist and poet. His principal works are translations from the Latin into Italian; but some poems of his are dispersed in various collections, and there is also of his a published dialogue on the nature and rules of the sonnet, entitled La Veronica, o del Sonetto. Genoa, 1589, 8vo. (Biog. Univ.)

BELSHAM, (Thomas,) an English theologian, of considerable note among the Socinians of his day, son of a dissenting minister at Bedford, where he was born, April 15, 1750. He was regularly educated for his father's profession, and being chosen pastor of an old presbyterian congregation at Worcester, he settled there in 1778. In 1781, he returnd to the academy at Daventry, where he had been educated for the ministry, as principal tutor and director. From this appointment he retired in 1789, on embracing the opinions then strenuously advocated by Dr. Priestley, and rendered especially conspicuous by Mr. Lindsey's resignation of a Yorkshire vicarage on their account. Mr. Belsham, however, thus rendered himself acceptable to a religious body that had recently established an academy at Hackney, and he became tutor there. At his suggestion, the Unitarian Society for Promoting Christian Knowledge and the Practice of Virtue was founded in 1791. In 1794, on Dr. Priestley's removal to America, Mr. Belsham was elected to succeed him as minister of a congregation at Hackney. This was a fortunate circumstance for him, as in 1796 the Hackney College was dissolved.

Mr. Belsham continued minister of the congregation at Hackney till 1805, when he became minister of the congregation originally collected in Essex-street chapel, London, by Mr. Lindsey, and of which Dr. Disney, another clerical seceder from the church on Socinian grounds, had recently been pastor. In this situation he continued until 1826, when the infirmities of age compelled him to retire. He died at Hampstead, November 11, 1829.

His numerous publications were all in the departments of metaphysics and theology, and not a few of them controversial. Passing over the occasional sermons which he published, there are two volumes of his Discourses, Doctrinal and Practical; Discourses on the Evidence of the Christian Religion; Elements of Logic and Mental Philosophy; A Calm Enquiry into the Scripture Doctrine concerning the Person of Christ; and a New Translation and Exposition of the Epistles of Saint Paul. He had a principal share in the preparation of a New Version of the New Testament, published in 1808, by the Unitarian Society, of which he was the founder, and called an *Improved* Version, but evidently prepared by persons without sufficient scholarship for any real improvement. (Gent.'s Mag.)

BELSHAM, (William,) younger brother of the preceding, an English political writer and historian, born in 1753. He commenced his literary career in 1789 by publishing some political and historical essays, which went through several editions. These were followed by similar essays on almost all the various topics of the day; and in 1793 he published, Memoirs of the Kings of Great Britain of the House of Brunswick Lunenburg, 2 vols, 8vo. In 1795 appeared in four volumes his Memoirs of the Reign of George III. to the Session of Parliament ending 1793. A fifth and a sixth volume followed in 1801. In 1798 he published, in 2 vols, 8vo, History of Great Britain, from the Revolution to the Accession of the House of Hanover. In 1806 these were all brought into one body in his History of Great Britain to the conclusion of the Peace of Amiens in 1802, in 12 vols. Mr. Belsham was a decided Whig partisan, and being resident at one time at Bedford, he became intimate with the late Mr. Whitbread. Others, then in opposition, were also glad of his acquaintance, thinking his works likely to serve their cause. He died at Hammersmith, aged seventy-five. (Gent.'s Mag.)

BELSUNCE, (Henry Francis Xavier de, 1671—1755,) a French prelate, immortalized by his truly christian conduct during the plague of Marseilles. He was born in Perigord, of an ancient family, that came from Navarre. At twenty, he entered among the Jesuits, a step which influenced his future life; in the end disadvantageously. After a residence of some years with this order, he became grand vicar of Agen, and in 1709, he was promoted to the see of Marseilles. In 1720, and the following year, his flock was visited by a frightful pestilence, and he then emulated Charles Boromeo, who nobly disregarded every personal consideration upon a similar occasion, at Milan. Belsunce, like the Italian metropolitan, was in every infected quarter, bearing aid, both spiritual and temporal, to the sick and dying, shaming into action lay authorities, both civil and military, and exhibiting a finished picture of holy zeal. Happily the contagion spared him, and he thus carried his invaluable services to the end of this distressing time. Pope has finely introduced his providential exemption from the scourge that swept away such multitudes on every side,

"Why drew Marseilles' good bishop purer breath,
When Nature sicken'd, and each gale was death?"
ESSAY ON MAN, IV. 108.

Such admirable self-devotion procured for Belsunce an offer, in 1723, of the bishopric of Laon, with its appendant peerage and ducal coronet, but he declined it, as he did also the archiepiscopal see of Bordeaux, in 1729; being unwilling to leave his charge at Marseilles, endeared to him as the source of the purest reputation within human reach. As some compensation for these high-minded refusals, two rich abbeys were conferred upon him; and although he did not choose an archbishopric, Clement II. paid him the archiepiscopal compliment of transmitting to him a pall, in 1731. Unhappily, this admirable prelate's latter years denied him the tranquillity that earlier sacrifices had so richly earned. His Jesuitic prepossessions engaged him in an obstinate conflict with Jansenism. At a former period, Huguenot opinions had been discountenanced by a refusal of the sacraments to such as could not produce certificates of confession signed by unsuspected clergymen. This narrow policy was now revived as an instrument against Jansenism, and Belsunce was the first bishop that approved it. He was thus betrayed into collision with the civil authorities, by which his mistaken zeal was perseveringly opposed, but with a feeling of deep regret at such a necessity with such a man. He was even tempted into accusations against a religious society at Marseilles, opposed to him, that were completely refuted; and when he died, his indiscret zeal against Jansenism had filled the diocese of Marseilles with bitterness and confusion. A college of Jesuits, bearing his name, was founded by him. While grand vicar of Agen, he published an account of his aunt, entitled, Abrégé de la Vie de Susanne Henriette de Foix, Agen, 1707, 12mo. While bishop, he published several pastoral instructions, chiefly levelled against Jansenism, and a work entitled L'Antiquité de l'Eglise de Marseille, et la Succession de ses Evêques, Marseille, 1747-51, 3 vols, 4to. This has been considered as really the work of some Jesuit to whom Belsunce allowed the use of his name. It is a work disfigured by the introduction of some legendary tales as authentic history. (Biog. Univ.)

BELSUNCE, (Count of,) of the same noble family, second major of an infantry regiment, quartered at Caen in 1790. Having acted with decision there to preserve the peace, he was murdered by the mob, and his bleeding heart carried about in triumph. It has been said that Charlotte Corday was his mistress, and then conceived that hatred against the infamous Marat, which induced her to murder him; but this assertion is without foundation.

BELTRAFFIO, (John Anthony, 1467—1516,) a gentleman of Milan, who was a pupil of Vinci, and an amateur artist. Some of his works are at Milan, but his best is at Bologna. It exhibits the exact study of his school in the air of the heads, is judicious in its composition, and softened in its outlines; but his design is rather more dry than that of his fellow pupils, owing, perhaps, to his early education under the Milanese artists. (Lanzi, Stor. Pitt. iv. 163.)

BELTRAM, (D. John de Guevara,) a Spanish ecclesiastic, of distinguished learning, especially in jurisprudence, born at Medina de las Torres, and educated at Salamanca. In 1614 he was promoted to the see of Compostella, and died in 1622, aged eighty. His printed works are, Propugnaculum ecclesiasticæ libertatis, adversus Leges Venetiis latas. Rom. 1607, 4to. This is said to have been written by desire of pope Paul V. Discursos del Principio, y Origen y Uso de la Monarquia de Sicilia, Pinciæ, 1605, fol. This work was written against a disquisition in the Annals of Baronius. He also wrote some other pieces, which have not been printed, except, perhaps, a Defence of Philip the Second's claims to the Crown of Portugal. (Antonio.)

BELTRAMELLI, (Joseph, 1734—1816,) a noble and opulent native of Bergamo, but educated at Bologna, where he also gained a knowledge of painting. To enlarge his mind, he not merely visited but resided in the chief cities of Europe. The expense impaired his fortune, and the revolutionary wars completely ruined him. But he bore his reverses with fortitude, and obtained an honourable subsistence as professor of eloquence in his native city. His publications relate to the literature and arts of Italy. (Biog. Univ. Suppl.)

BELTRAMI, (Fabricius,) a Siennese, whose only published work is, Discorso intorno alle imprese comuni academiche. Perusa, 1612, 4to. (Biog. Univ.)

BELTRAN, (James,) who published, with Vincent Ferrandis, like himself a Valencian, in the dialect of that province, Obres contemplatives e de molta devocio trobades en Loors de la sanctissima Creu. Valentia, 1615, 4to. This poem is very rare. (Antonio.)

BELTRAND, (Herman Dominic,) a Spanish sculptor and architect, born at Vittoria, in Biscay, in the sixteenth century. He went to Italy, and became so able that Palomino Velasco does not hesitate to place him above the most famous artists of his time. His chief model was Michael Angelo, and many statues of Christ, of the natural size, executed by him, are worthy of that illustrious master. Beltrand died in 1590, at a very advanced age. (Biog. Univ.)

BELTRANO, (Octavius,) a bookseller, printer, and author, of Naples, in the seventeenth century, who wrote, with some minor works, Breve Descrizione del Regno di Napoli. Naples, 1640, 4to. It has been often reprinted. (Biog. Univ.)

BELTRANO, (Augustine,) a painter of the Neapolitan school, born at Naples, and a pupil of Massanio Stanzioni. He became a good fresco painter, and a colourist in oil of no common merit. His wife, Aniella di Rosa, niece of Francis di Rosa, called Pacicco, was his fellow pupil under Massanio, and painted in the same style as her husband. They worked in conjunction, and often prepared pictures which their master afterwards finished, so that they were sold as his own. She was murdered by her husband from jealousy, 1649, when about thirty-six years of age. Beltrano died in 1665. (Lanzi, Stor. Pitt. ii. 275.)

BELTRANO, (Francis Paul, 1745—1802,) a celebrated Sicilian jurist. His wealthy parents gave him an excellent education, and brought him up to the law, which he studied without neglecting other branches of knowledge, especially philosophy. When master of his profession, he reduced a mass of confused enactments into a system, in a work entitled, Elementa juris privati Siculi, Palermo, 1774, 2 vols, 12mo. (Biographia degli Uomini illustri della Sicilia, Napoli, 1817, 2 vols, 4to.)

BELUS, king of Babylon, father of Ninus, who reigned over all Assyria. Belus appears to have come from Egypt, at a period long anterior to the historical knowledge of Greece. (Stephani Dictionarum. Larcher *apud* Beloe. Herod. i. 181.)

BELVEDERE, (Ab. Andrew, 1646—1732,) a Neapolitan artist, pupil of Recco, who excelled in painting hunting, fowling, and fishing pieces, and others of a similar nature. (Lanzi, Stor. Pitt. ii. 289.)

BELVEZER, (Aymeric de,) a Provençal poet, who flourished about the year 1233, and sang in his native dialect the praises of a Gascon lady, with whom he was in love, until he was retained at the court of Raymond Berenger, count of Provence. There he fell again in love with a princess of "prodigious beauty, most unexceptionable character, and conversant in all the seven liberal sciences." His poems, however, did not prevent her from entering a nunnery; and our poet, after sending her a poem, entitled Les Amours de son Ingrata, died of grief in 1264.

BELVISO, (Jacopo, or Giacomo,) an eminent Italian scholar, born at Bologna, towards the latter end of the thirteenth century. He was professor of law in his native city, but induced by the factions that distracted it to accept an invitation from Charles II. king of Naples. He remained in that country, with an honourable and liberal provision, until the death of Charles, in 1309. He then accepted the law professorship at Perugia. But the strong measures which the government of Bologna adopted, about the year 1320, to oblige all native professors to come back to that university, obliged Belviso to return to Bologna, where he was received with extraordinary honours, and where he died in 1335. It has been remarked, that, although the Belvisi generally were Ghibellines, he was a Guelph.

BELYARD, (Simon,) a French poet, little known, who lived at the end of the sixteenth century, and wrote a tragedy in five acts, called, Le Guysien, ou Perfidie tyrannique commise par Henry de Valois, ès—persounes des Princes Louis de Lorraine, cardinal, et Henry de Lorraine, duc de Guyse. Troyes, 1592, 8vo. It is a very moderate production, but sought from its extreme rarity. A pastoral is commonly at the end of it, entitled Charlot, Eglogue à onze Personnages sur les Misères de la France, et la Miraculeuse Déliverance du Duc de Guyse, Troyes, 1592, 8vo. Of these the duke de la Vallière says, that the pastoral is well written for the time, and that it is wonderful that the same author has written a very bad tragedy and a charming pastoral. (Biog. Univ.)

BELZONI, (John Baptist,) born at Padua, about the year 1774, of a family originally from Rome. There he passed much of his youth, with an intention of adopting the monastic life, but the French invasion drove him to think of some other course. In 1803 he arrived in England, being then a remarkably fine young man, six feet seven inches high, proportionably stout, and recommended, besides, by a countenance highly prepossessing. He had acquired at Rome a knowledge of hydraulics, and an exhibition, founded on this science, gained him a maintenance in various parts of the United Kingdom. When this resource failed, he exhibited feats of strength. Finding this attraction on the wane, he sailed from Britain, and wandered over various parts of the Spanish peninsula. In 1815 he visited Egypt, with a view to construct an hydraulic machine, more fit for irrigation than the clumsy contrivances in use there. The pacha engaged him to supply one for his garden at Zubra, near Cairo; but it failed from native opposition. Through the recommendation of Mr. Burckhardt, he was then employed by Mr. Salt, the British consul, to remove the colossal bust, commonly, but incorrectly, called the Young Memnon, which he did with great ingenuity, and shipped it for England, where it was deposited in the British Museum. In the mean time he made an excursion in Upper Egypt as far as the second cataract; was the first to open the temple of Ipsambul, cut in the side of a mountain, and almost entirely choked by sand, which he cleared. In 1817 he made a second journey in Upper Egypt; made excavations at Carnac, and found a colossal head of granite, also in the British Museum, with other interesting antiquities. Animated by so much success, he continued his discoveries, and opened in Beban-el-Molouk, the most perfect and magnificent of known Egyptian tombs. It has several chambers, covered with paintings, probably of the ancient mysteries for the most part, although some of them may represent funeral rites upon the grandest scale. Accurate drawings being made of the wonders thus disinterred, Belzoni exhibited an exact resemblance of the two principal chambers, in London, in 1821. It was a most interesting exhibition, and proved highly popular; but when tried at Paris, in the next season, it was not equally fortunate. Before Belzoni left Egypt, he also entered, in 1818, the second of the great pyramids of Ghizeh, known as that of Cephrenes, and believed since the days of Herodotus to be without internal chambers. In this he found a sarcophagus, containing some bones, thought to be those of a king, but found to be those of a cow; a strong presumption that the pyramids are not of sepulchral but of religious origin, the cow being still a sacred object among oriental pagans. Belzoni likewise went to Esné, crossed the Desert to the Red Sea, discovered the ruins of Berenice, visited the Lake Mœris, and the small oasis, which he erroneously supposed to be that of Jupiter Ammon. In the September of 1819 he left Egypt, visited his native town of Padua, where a medal was struck in commemoration of his discoveries; and on his return to England, he published a Narrative of the Operations and recent Discoveries within the Pyramids, Temples, Tombs, and Excavations in Egypt and Nubia; and of a Journey to the coast of the Red Sea, in search of the ancient Berenice, and another to the Oasis of Jupiter Ammon, London, 1820, 4to, with an atlas. In 1823 he set out again for Africa, with the intention of reaching Timbuctoo, landed at Tangiers, proceeded to Fez, where he left his wife, who was an Englishwoman, and reached the Bight of Benin, which he seems to have guessed to be the direct way to the Niger. With every appearance of success he now began his journey, when he was attacked by a dysentery, which carried him off on the 3d of December, 1823, at a place called Gato, in the kingdom of Benin. He was buried under a large tree, and a simple inscription was placed on his tomb.

BEM, (Magnus von,) governor of Kamtchatka, from 1772 to 1779, and a distinguished benefactor to that remote region, although little aided by the Russian government. In the summer of 1775, he made an excursion of upwards of 200 versts on foot, in order to meet the companions of captain Cook, who on their return home represented to the government the friendly services they had received at his hands. Weakened at length by the labours and privations voluntarily undergone to serve his province, he obtained his recall in 1779; after which no further notice of him can be traced. (Entz. Leks.)

BEMBO. The name of two painters of the Cremonese school.

1. Boniface, or *Fazio*, called Da Valdarno, a distinguished artist, employed by the court of Milan as early as 1461. He was spirited in his attitudes, glowing in his colours, and grand in his draperies, though deficient in imagination. (Lanzi, Stor. Pitt. iv. 100.)

2. John Francis, called *Il Vetraro*, younger brother of the preceding, and also his pupil, whose pictures prove him to have added dignity to the Lombard school, and to have improved upon the ancient manner. (Lanzi, Stor. Pitt. iv. 106.)

BEMBO, (Bernard,) a Venetian senator, born in Venice in 1433. Of his elder brothers, Francis and Mark, the former was bishop of Venice, the latter a renowned captain, and he himself, from early youth, was in public employments. In 1481 he was elected chief magistrate of Ravenna. There, finding that Dante had been buried in the church of St. Francis without any monument, he raised a fine marble mausoleum at his own expense, with a bust of the poet, and an inscription in Latin verses. He died in 1519, with the reputation of a learned man. Some of his Latin letters have been published among those of Sabellicus, and the Petrarca Redivivus of Tomasini.

BEMBO, (Peter, cardinal,) son of the preceding, and Helena Marcella, born at Venice in 1470. When scarcely eight years old, he accompanied his father, then sent ambassador to Florence, where he remained two years. On his return to Venice he learned the Latin language. Greek he acquired at Messina, under Constantine Lascaris, and he studied philosophy at Padua. He first gained popularity from a literary essay, written while he resided at Asolo, a little town near Treviso, then the abode of Catharine Cornaro, widow of James Lusignano, the last king of Cyprus. She resigned her kingdom to the Venetian senate, and enjoyed a splendid income, yet retaining the title of queen, and shedding a lustre upon it by refined manners, cultivated talents, and elegant taste. In September 1496, on the marriage of her favourite lady-in-waiting, she gave a splendid entertainment, to which she invited many persons of distinction, and among them young Bembo. Prevailing manners caused upon such occasions, tournaments, pageants, and banquets, intermixed with sprightly conversations, and discussions upon love, eulogizing its properties to bless mankind, or branding it as the bane of human happiness. Bembo, who had taken an active part in these discussions, conceived from them the plan of a work which, from the name of the place, he called Gli Asolani. It is, or pretends to be, a collection of what was said on that occasion, on the nature, quality, and effects of love, distinguishing the pure sentiment from the grossness of passion, and ending in a moral strain on the contemplation of divine love, after the metaphysical reasoning of Plato's philosophy, which was then much in vogue in Italy. This work proved highly attractive to readers of both sexes, and no one could mix in the Italian society of that day without knowing something about it.

In 1498 Bembo went to join his father, who had been, the year before, sent as vicedomino to Ferrara, where, besides contracting friendships with Tebaldeo, Sadoleto, and Hercules Strozzi, he obtained the favour of the young prince, Alfonso d'Este. On his return to Venice, he became a member of the celebrated academy there, founded by Aldo Manuzio; and when, in 1502, prince Alfonso married Lucretia Borgia, daughter of pope Alexander VI., one of the most beautiful and vicious women of her age, Bembo often visited Ferrara and became her favourite. In 1506 he went to Urbino, then famed for the most magnificent of the Italian courts. There he dwelt six years, cherished by the duke Guidobaldo of Montefeltro, and by his virtuous wife, Elisabeth Gonzaga. He now began to write Italian poetry, imitating the style of Petrarch. He became also acquainted with Julian de' Medici, third son of the great Laurence, and brother to cardinal John, who soon after became Leo X. At Urbino, too, after the death of Guidobaldo, which was soon followed by that of the duchess, Bembo left a token of his gratitude to the memory of these amiable sovereigns, by writing a composition, entitled De Guido Ubaldo Fenetrio (and not Feltrio) deque Elisabetha Gonzaga Urbini Ducibus. It is a dialogue between himself, Sadoleto, Beroaldo, and Sigismond da Foligno, really interesting, written with sincerity and true feeling. The sketch of the duchess is a touching specimen of real pathos, for she, like her relative, Lucretia Gonzaga, was a bright specimen of Italian female character in the midst of a corrupt age.

Leaving now Urbino, in 1512, he accompanied Julian to Rome, and there, having had the good fortune to decipher an ancient Latin MS. sent to pope Julius II., he was rewarded by that pontiff with ecclesiastical preferment. At his death, which took place in the following year, Leo X. was elected pope, and he appointed Bembo one of his secretaries, with the salary of 3000 scudi (about 600*l.*) Rome at that time was the seat of licentiousness, as well as learning, and Bembo's natural disposition did not allow him to withstand the general example. He formed a connexion with a beautiful young woman of the name of

Morosina, which he continued till her death in 1535. By her he had two sons, the eldest of whom died in his infancy; the second, Torquato, became a canon at Padua; and one daughter, Helen, who married Peter Grandenigo, a Venetian nobleman, and a descendant of the doge of the same name, that altered the Venetian constitution and established the terrible council of ten.

After Leo's death, in 1521, Bembo fixed his residence at Padua; and, being amply provided with ecclesiastical benefices, he began to gratify his taste for literature, collecting a valuable and extensive library, and a cabinet of rare medals, and establishing a magnificent botanic garden. In 1525, he completed a work on the Italian language, which he dedicated to cardinal de' Medici, afterwards pope Clement VII., and published at Venice, under the title of Prose di M. Pietro Bembo, nelle quali si ragiona della Volgar Lingua, divise in tre libri. It is one of the earliest works on the rules of the Italian language, and has gone through several editions. In 1529 he received from the council of ten a commission to write the History of Venice, beginning from the year 1487, where Sabellico had left it. It was his intention to have continued it to the year 1521, but he could only carry it down to the death of Julius II. in 1513. It was published in 1551, four years after his death, under the title of Historiæ Venetæ libri xii. His Italian translation of the same was also published, after his death, in 1552, and republished in 1790 by Monelli, the librarian of St. Mark, in 2 vols, 4to, with a fine likeness of the author, engraven by Bartolozzi, from a painting by Titian. This work of Bembo, though written in a style elegant and correct, has been severely criticized for a servile and affected imitation of Cicero. This blemish is common to all his Latin compositions, and it has gone so far, as to make him speak of the pope as *earthly vicar of the immortal gods*, and of some bad wood, given for the Virgin Mary's house at Loretto, as a mockery not only to the pontiff, but to *the goddess herself likewise*. Bembo's history has also been censured for the omission of dates; a fault general in his day, but rendering it almost impossible to assign their proper places to events. Lastly, it has been taxed with deficiency of information as to the springs of action. This arose, however, Foscarini says, from the historian's ecclesiastical profession, which the Venetian government considered as a bar to unrestrained admittance among its archives. Bembo was still writing the Venetian history in studious retirement at Padua, and leading an exemplary life, when, in 1539, Paul III. unexpectedly sent him a cardinal's hat, which, after some hesitation, he accepted, and went to Rome, where, taking priest's orders, he resided for the remainder of his life. He died in 1547, celebrated as one of the best writers in verse and prose, in Latin and Italian, that his illustrious age produced. His pen is, however, blemished by some obscenities, which are the more offensive, because he spent his life in connexion with the church, and ultimately became a cardinal. But justice requires us to remember, that such unhappy sallies are so far from being chargeable upon his later years, that he took measures to suppress them, and that his earlier days were not spent in a character strictly clerical. He has been thought inclinable to protestantism, from his acquaintance with some accomplished converts to it. He seems, however, to have been actuated in these associations, merely by a wish to hold commerce with learning and ability. Perhaps he regarded little the religious bias of those in whom he found such recommendations. His different works, after having separately passed through several editions, were collected into 4 vols, fol. at Venice, in 1729, by Hertzhauser, with a life of the author. (Bayle.)

BEMBO, (John,) doge of Venice, born in 1535, succeeded, in 1615, Mark Anthony Memmo at a time when the republic was at war with both Austria and Spain. The peace concluded at Paris in Sept. 1617, did not put an end to its trouble and dangers; for the marquis of Bedmar, Spanish ambassador at Venice, assisted by the duke of Ossuna, viceroy of Naples, and by Don Pedro de Toledo, governor of Milan, entered into a terrible conspiracy, which intended the entire destruction of the Venetian government. Bembo, however, died before it was discovered, in March 1618.

BEMBO, (Dardi,) a Venetian nobleman and scholar, who died prematurely in 1633. He translated into Italian, 1st, all the works of Plato, which were published at Venice, 1601, in 5 vols, 12mo; and again in 1742, 3 vols, 4to. 2dly, The Commentary of Hierocles on the Golden Verses of Pythagoras, Venice, 1603, 4to. 3dly, The Treatise of Timæus of Locri on the Anima Mundi, Venice, 1607, 12mo; and, lastly, the Discourses of Theodoret, Venice, 1617, 4to.

BEMBUS, (Matthew,) a learned Pole, who became a Jesuit in 1587, and died very aged, leaving various works, both in Latin and Polish, little known out of his own country. (Alegambe, Script. Soc. Jesu.)

BEME, so called because of a Bohemian family, though he seems himself to have been born in Wirtemberg. His name was *Charles Dianowitz*, and he was brought up by the duke of Guise. In the massacre of St. Bartholomew's day, he murdered the admiral de Coligni, and threw his corpse out of a window. To this crime he owes his notoriety. It has been said to have procured for him a natural daughter of the cardinal of Lorraine, brother to the duke of Guise, as a wife. During the troubles that succeeded the massacre, this man of blood was taken prisoner by the protestants, and kept for some time in fear of an agonizing death by the hands of an executioner. He succeeded, however, in corrupting his guard, and escaped; but he was quickly overtaken, and killed upon the spot.

BEMETZRIEDER, an eccentric German, who wrote several works on theoretical music, of which one, printed at Paris in 1780, was translated into English by Giffard Bernard. (Schilling's Encyclopedie der Music.)

BEMMEL, (William van, 1630—1708,) a Dutch painter, born at Utrecht, who studied under Herman Zaft Leven, and travelled to Rome for improvement. Eventually he settled at Nuremberg, and met with great encouragement. His works are remarkable for a just distribution of light and shades. They are generally landscapes, with ruins and other incidental things introduced, and are rare in England. The artist died at Nuremberg, according to Mr. Bryan, in 1703. He had a son, John George, born at Nuremberg in 1669, and died in 1723, who acquired reputation as a battle painter. Mention is made of a third of the name, Peter van, either a younger son or grandson of William, born at Nuremberg in 1689, who painted landscape, but whose works are little known out of his native city. He died in 1723. There appears to be a fourth of the name, M. D. Bemmel, whose name is attached to a portrait of Harvey, which Houbraken engraved in 1739. (Biog. Univ. Bryan's Dict. Heinecken, Dict. des Artistes.)

BEMMELEN, (Abraham van, 1763—1822,) a Dutch professor of mathematics and mechanics, who wrote some good elementary treatises. (Biog. Univ. Suppl.)

BEN ALOGIAIM, a physician and astrologer, mentioned by the anonymous anthor of the Arabica Philosophorum Bibliotheca, (quoted by Casiri, Bibl. Arabico-Hisp. Escur. tom. i. p. 417,) as having acquired great celebrity in Persia and Assyria, under the Bouzah dynasty. He died A.H. 430, (A.D. 1038-9.)

BEN SEV, a learned Polish Jew, born in 1763. His early progress in the Talmud and its grammatical construction excited expectations which his after career fulfilled. When twenty-one years old he wrote a commentary on a Hebrew philosophical work (Emunot Vedeul). A few years afterwards he published a valuable Hebrew grammar, under the title of Talmud Leshon Ivri, of which a new edition was printed at Vienna in 1806. Not long after this publication appeared his Sirach, a translation from the Syriac, with a commentary. His last literary labours were, an Elementary Work for Youth, a Lexicon, and a Treatise on Faith. His extraordinary application destroyed his health, and he died at Vienna in 1811. He would answer, when he was entreated to spare himself in his studies, "that it lay in the nature of the best men to offer themselves up for the good of their nation, and for the increase of its prosperity." (Ersch und Gruber.)

BENABEN, (L. G. J. Marie, 1774—1832,) a native of Toulouse, who served in Egypt in the commissariat under Bonaparte, but subsequently became professor in several French universities. Eventually he gained his living as a political writer, and produced numerous pieces of temporary interest. (Biog. Univ. Suppl.)

BENAGLIO, (Alexander,) an ecclesiastic and preacher of Bergamo, born about 1600. He wrote, Lettera consolatoria. . . .per l'occasione della Peste, Bergamo, 1631; Intuito generale agli essercitii spirituali—nella Congregatione dell' Annontiata, *ibid.* 1648. He left many MSS. (Calvi, Scritt. Bergam.)

BENALCAZAR, (Sebastian,) one of the leaders who, in 1532, assisted Pizarro in the conquest of Peru. The following year he was employed in the conquest of Quito, which he annexed to the Spanish crown, and which he governed as viceroy of Charles V. In 1539 he was arbitrarily deprived of his office by Pizarro, whose ambitious views he would not promote. Faithful to the royal party, he assisted

Vaca de Castro to gain the battle of Chupas. In 1544 he was nominated to the government of Popayan, but the following year he was defeated by Gonzalo Pizarro, brother of the Peruvian conqueror, who had rebelled against the sovereign of Spain. Contrary to expectation, his life was spared, and he died in the peaceable enjoyment of his authority. (Biog. Univ.)

BENAMATI, (Guidobaldo,) an Italian poet, who died in 1653. He has left, among numerous poetical productions, 1. L'Alvida, favola Boschereccia, Parma, 1614, in 8vo. 2. La Selva del Sole, Perugia, 1640, 12mo. 3. La Vittoria Navale, poema eroico, Bologna, 1646.

BENANI, (Francis,) a very early Italian painter, by whom there is a whole length picture of St. Jerome holding a crucifix in his hand. It possesses all the characteristics attributed by Lanzi to Italian painting in the thirteenth century. Near the bottom of the picture is a label, inscribed Franciscus Benanus, Filius Petri Ablada. The size of it is two feet eight inches by two feet two inches, on panel covered with gypsum. The colours were probably prepared with eggs, as usual before the invention of painting in oil, and to which an absorbent ground of lime, or gypsum, seems to have been indispensable. Pictures executed in this manner have preserved their colouring to the present day. (Roscoe's Translation of Lanzi, i. 16, note.)

BENARD, (Laurence,) a learned Benedictine, who died in 1620, after having been engaged, under sanction of Lewis XIII., upon plans for monastic reform, then much required. He wrote—1. De l'Esprit des Ordres Religieux, a dissertation, followed by the Traduction des Dialogues de Sainte Grégoire-le-Grand, Paris, 1616, 8vo. 2. La Police regulière tirée de la règle de Saint Benoit. This he dedicated to the cardinal de Retz.

BENARD. The name of two French artists.

1. *J. F.* an engraver at Paris about 1672, who engraved architectural and ornamental subjects. (Bryan's Dict.)

2. *John Baptist*, or *Besnard*, a painter at Paris, after whom there are several plates engraven, one dated 1755. It represents a Dance of Villagers. (Heinecken, Dict. des Artistes.)

BENASCHI, or BEINASCHI, (John Baptist, 1636—1688, or 1690,) a painter, born at Turin, whose principal works are cupolas, ceilings, and the like. In his design he had great variety, never in his many pictures repeating an attitude, and was eminent for his excellence of foreshortening. In his colours he was good so long as he followed the steps of Lanfranco, of whom he is erroneously supposed to have been a pupil; but when he strove to be more vigorous in his style he became dark and heavy. He had a daughter, Angela, who went to Rome with him, and painted portraits in an agreeable style. She was born in 1666, and was living in 1717. The name of this artist is written also Bernaschi, which has given occasion for the belief that there were three artists, but this is not so. (Lanzi, Stor. Pitt. ii. 283.)

BENAVENTE, (Christopher de, y Benavides,) a native of Placentia in Spain, knight of St. Jago, counsellor of war to Philip IV., and tutor in the royal family. He wrote, Advertencias para Reyes, Principes y Embaxadores, Madrid, 1634, 4to. (Antonio.)

BENAVENTE, (John de Quiñones de,) a Spanish lawyer, who died in 1650. His habits were decidedly literary, and he collected a large library; but although he published several tracts, they are of little general interest. (Antonio.)

BENAVENTE, (Lewis de,) a Spanish dramatic writer of the seventeenth century, with admirable talents for *entremeses*. A set of these he published in 1645. (Antonio.)

BENAVENTE, or MOTOLINEA, (Toribius de,) born at Benavente, in Old Castile, one of the twelve Franciscan friars who first went as missionaries into Mexico. He died there, after great success, being the last survivor of his party. He wrote, but did not print, some pieces relating to the native Mexican population, and the mission in which he was engaged. One of his tracts, however, Vida y Muerte de los tres Niños principales de la Ciudad de Tlascala, que murieron por la Confession de la Fee, was translated into Mexican, and printed at Mexico, 1601, 8vo. Benavente wrote also several religious tracts in the language, and for the use of the Mexicans. (F. Gonzaga de Orig. Seraph. Relig. Romæ, 1587, fol. Antonio.)

BENAVIDES, (Didacus de Villalobos,) born at Mexico, but son of a Spanish knight. He was engaged in the Spanish campaigns against Holland and France, which occasioned him to write Commentarios de las Cosas sucedidas en los Paises baxos, Madrid, 1612, 4to. To the MS. of this work a strange accident happened. The author was made prisoner, on his voyage to Spain, by the Dutch, who, although they set him at liberty, could never be prevailed upon to restore the MS. He wrote it, however, again from memory and some stray leaves. (A. L. de Haro, Nobiliarium. Antonio.)

BENAVIDES, (Alphonso de,) a Spanish Observatine friar, head of a mission to New Mexico. He addressed to Philip IV. a Spanish treatise connected with his duties there, printed at Madrid in 1630. Of this a Latin translation appeared at Saltzburg in 1634, with the following title: Relatio de magnis Thesauris spirit. et temporal. D. adjuv. in Novo Mexico detectis. (Antonio.)

BENAVIDES, (Peter Arias de,) a Spanish medical man, who chiefly practised among the Indians of America. He is remarkable for publishing, in his own language, in 1567, one of the first books on Syphilis. It is in a work detailing various Indian modes of cure, and professing to reveal secrets hitherto unwritten. (Antonio.)

BENAVIDES, (Vincent de, 1637—1703,) a Spanish painter, born at Oran, in Africa, excellent in architecture and perspective, but less successful in painting the figure. He worked in distemper and fresco, chiefly at Madrid. (Pilkington.)

BENAVIDES, (Mark, 1489—1582,) an eminent legal professor in the university of Padua. He was born in that city, and no offers, however alluring, could induce him to leave it. Charles V. did homage to his talents by creating him a count, and pope Pius IV. by granting him the honour of knighthood. He wrote several legal treatises, remarkable alike for their acuteness and erudition. But his pen was not confined to his profession, and his purely literary efforts procured him the esteem of the eminent writers of his age. (Biog. Univ. Suppl.)

BENAZECH, (Peter Paul,) a designer and engraver, said to have been born in London about 1744. He was the pupil of Vivares, and, according to Basan, worked some time at Paris, but returned to London. There was another artist, and perhaps also a third, of the same surname. (Bryan's Dict. Heinecken, Dict. des Artistes. Strutt's Dict. of Eng. Edwards's Anecdotes of Painting, 225.)

BENBOW, (John,) a renowned admiral of England. The surname of this brave and intrepid seaman has been confounded with that of *Bembo*, a Venetian admiral of the fifteenth century; and sundry biographers, in ignorance of his real origin, have pronounced it *low*. He was in fact, however, the son of colonel John Benbow, a Shropshire gentleman, who bore a conspicuous part in the memorable battle of Worcester. In this conflict (so fatal to the royal cause,) he was taken prisoner, and by a well-timed and fortunate flight, escaped the fate of his murdered brother. During the usurpation, the father of our subject was compelled to remain in retirement, and at the restoration, was glad to accept a subordinate post in the Tower, but it barely supplied enough to provide himself and family with ordinary comfort. Thus was the former colonel fallen, when, some short time before the first Dutch war, the king paid a visit to the Tower for the purpose of inspecting the arms and military stores. The hoary-headed pensioner soon attracted the notice of Charles, whose quick eye at once recognised the features of his former firm and faithful adherent. "My old Worcester friend, colonel Benbow!" exclaimed the king, advancing to embrace the aged officer; "what do you here?" "I have a place of four-score pounds a year," returned the colonel, "in which I serve your majesty as cheerfully as if it brought me in four thousand." "Alas," said the king, "is that *all* that could be found for an old Worcester friend! Colonel Legge, bring this gentleman to me to-morrow, and I will provide for him and his family as it becomes me." But, according to Campbell's informant, short as the time was, the colonel did not live to receive, or even to claim the effects of his majesty's gracious promise. His sense of his sovereign's condescension and goodness so overcame his spirits, that sitting down on a bench he breathed his last before the king was well out of the Tower.

Touching the fulfilment of Charles's promised provision for the family of his "Worcester friend," contemporary writers are all silent. The subsequent condition of the colonel's children would, however, induce the more than probable belief, that in his insatiable pursuit of pleasure, the king thought no more of the matter.

Thrown upon the wide world, young Benbow, at an early age, embarked in the commercial marine. In this laborious and short-handed service he manfully made his way, eventually becoming both master and owner of some of the best equipped and desirable vessels employed in the Mediterranean trade. When in command of a trading vessel, named the *Benbow-frigate*, as also of the *Malaga merchant*, he had been repeatedly attacked by piratical cruisers; and in each instance, although his ferocious opponents had recourse to boarding, they were either repulsed or left dead upon his deck.

According to Mr. Paul Calton, of Milton in Berkshire, son-in-law of Benbow, the captain was attacked, in 1686, on his passage to Cadiz, in his own vessel, the *Benbow-frigate*, by a Sallee corsair. His complement of men was very inferior, but he defended himself with the utmost bravery. At last, the Moors boarded him, but were quickly beaten out of his ship again, with the loss of thirteen men. The heads of these Benbow cut off, and threw them into a tub of brine. When he landed at Cadiz, a negro servant followed him with the Moors' heads in a sack. "What have you here?" inquired the custom-house officers. "Salt provisions for my own use," the captain answered, declining to allow an examination of the sack. He was told, however, that his bare word could not be taken, unless under sanction of the superior authorities. To these he willingly repaired, and was treated with great politeness, but informed that an inspection of the sack's contents was indispensable. "Cæsar, throw them down upon the table," said Benbow, "and, gentlemen, if you like them, they are at your service." The Spaniards were exceedingly struck at the sight of the Moors' heads, and no less astonished at the account of the captain's adventure, who with so small a force, had been able to defeat such a number of barbarians.

In 1689, he received his commission as *captain* of the *York;* which commission, there is now every reason to believe, was the *first* that he obtained in the royal navy. In the succeeding year, the earl of Torrington, anxious to secure the services of a practical and trustworthy seaman, competent to discharge the several onerous and arduous duties which devolve while at sea on the master of the fleet, prevailed on Benbow to take upon himself this responsible post. In this capacity, though none of his biographers mention it, he served in the ill-advised and disastrous battle of Beachy Head. After this unfortunate affair, he resumed the command of a single ship, and became an active and successful cruiser in the Channel.

Having already attained the rank of commodore, he was now, November 1695, entrusted with the command of a detached squadron, destined to bombard the town of St. Maloes. He appeared off the port on the 15th of the same month; and after anchoring his ships in positions best suited to commence operations, he opened on the town, and particularly on the Quince fort, a furious fire. Although twice compelled to remove his mortar-vessels, and to shift with the falling tide the several positions of his largest and best battering ships; still for three successive days was there little cessation in the discharge of shot and shell. On the fourth evening, taking advantage of the wind veering round dead on the shore, he sent in a fire-ship, or rather an explosion-vessel, of a novel construction; but in consequence of this vessel, or "infernal," (as aptly called by the seamen of the squadron,) grounding at a greater distance from the town than that at which it was intended to place her, the explosion produced not to the enemy the extent of damage which must have inevitably ensued had she reached her assigned station. Still the shock has been represented as terrible beyond description. It shook the town like an earthquake, broke windows for three leagues around, and shattered the roofs of three hundred houses. A considerable portion of the town wall fell to the ground; and had there been embarked sufficient troops in the squadron, the place might readily have been taken. Nevertheless a landing was effected and enough done to make all England feel the irresistible power of her wooden walls, when manned by skill and courage.

In the succeeding operations against Dunkirk and Calais, Benbow, acting in each instance under Sir Cloudesley Shovel, met not with the same success that attended the better supported assault of St. Maloes. At Calais he was wounded in the leg; and to mark the royal approbation of his zeal and ardour in that attack, he was immediately on his return home promoted to the rank of rear-admiral of the blue. On hoisting his flag, he had assigned to him the harassing and unprofitable service of watching the enemy in Dunkirk. Despite of his vigilance, the flying squadron under the celebrated Bart contrived, under cover of a fog, to depart port: a severe vexation to him, for he had long looked for an opportunity to measure strength with this dexterous and successful cruizer.

After the treaty of Ryswick was ratified, considerable doubts still existed as to the policy which Lewis XIV. would pursue upon the death of Charles II. of Spain. It was therefore deemed expedient to despatch a naval force to the West Indies, so as to be in readiness to act in that quarter in the event of a renewal of war with France. The command of this squadron was given to Benbow, who arrived at Barbadoes in January 1699. Having distributed troops for the defence of the Leeward Islands, he proceeded to Carthagena, where by spirited and well-timed remonstrances he procured the restitution of several English vessels that had been seized by the Spaniards by way of reprisal for the settlement made by the Scots on the isthmus of Darien. At the instigation of the Jamaica merchants, he subsequently proceeded on a similar mission to Porto Bello; but here, though full satisfaction had been promised, it does not appear that the promise had been ever fulfilled.

On his return to England, in June 1700, he was advanced to the rank of vice-admiral, and again sent to blockade Dunkirk, a duty particularly arduous, because serious apprehensions were then entertained of invasion from that quarter. But Benbow assuring the government that there was little ground for alarm, it was determined he should resume his command in the Western world, taking with him a more efficient force than that which he commanded in the previous year. The king, however, unwilling to subject the vice-admiral to such incessant exertion, particularly as he had but recently returned from this "sickly station," commanded the minister to nominate another officer. Several names were submitted to the king, none of which meeting with his approval, William is *stated* to have said,—"No, these are all fresh-water *beaus;* the service requires a *beau* of another sort. Honest Ben-*bow* must go, after all." The king accordingly sent for the admiral, asked him whether he was willing to accept the West India command, assuring him that if he expressed a disinclination to serve on that station, he should not be the least displeased. Benbow, who was a plain blunt seaman, merely said, that "he knew no difference of climates, or thought an officer had any right to choose his station, and that at all times he was both ready and willing to proceed to any part of the world to which his majesty thought proper to send him."

Receiving his appointment, Benbow hoisted his flag on board the *Breda* (70), and with a squadron of ten sail of the line, departed Spithead about the end of August 1701. On the 3d of November he arrived at Barbadoes.

As soon as Benbow had been apprised of the war with France, measures were promptly taken to act on the offensive. In the middle of May, rear-admiral Whetstone arrived from England with a reinforcement. Benbow continued at Jamaica, occasionally sending out cruizers to pick up prizes and gain intelligence. On the 11th of July the squadron under his orders departed Port Royal; that under Whetstone was already at sea in pursuit of a detached force commanded by M. Du Casse. Benbow, in search of the same squadron, pursued in another direction, when on the evening of the 19th of August, he descried, close in with the coast of St. Martha, several vessels of war running leisurely along the land. On approaching sufficiently near to ascertain their exact strengths and characters, he found that they were the very ships of which he and Whetstone had been in such anxious search. This force consisted of four two-decked ships, one Dutch-built vessel, carrying between thirty and forty guns, another mounting the same metal, and full of troops, a sloop, and three craft of a smaller size. Benbow's force, and order of battle, was on this day as follows:—

Defiance, capt. Richard Kirkby	64
Windsor, capt. John Constable	60
Pendennis, capt. Thos. Hudson	48
Breda, vice-admiral Benbow, capt. Fogg .	70
Greenwich, capt. Wade	54
Ruby, capt. Geo. Walton	48
Falmouth, capt. S. Vincent	48

In consequence of the British line of battle being tardily formed, the sternmost ships occupying considerable time in reaching their assigned stations, Benbow, though still closing with the enemy, was not desirous to commence the attack until his van ship had reached abreast of the leader of the French line; but before this could be effected, the French rear opened their fire on the British force, and, contrary to his intention, compelled the vice-admiral to engage. The *Defiance* and *Windsor*, the two headmost ships in the British order of battle, "hauled dead to the wind," after they had received two or three broadsides from the enemy, and withdrew from the line of fire. This dastardly desertion of the "flag," enabled the two sternmost ships of the French squadron to bring upon the *Breda* a destructive fire, which ceased only with the fall of night. Incensed at the then unaccountable conduct of the majority of his treacherous and conspiring captains, the vice-admiral had already resolved to change his order of battle, and to *lead* himself on either tack.

On the 20th, with the break of day, Benbow, and Walton (the close and constant supporter of his chief) found themselves far in advance of their own squadron, the remaining ships of which, with light and variable winds, were severally seen in positions too distant astern to afford, in the event of attack, succour to their daring and gallant leaders. Although at this critical juncture the *Breda* and *Ruby* were each well within range of the enemy's guns, still, strange to say, at neither ship was directed a solitary shot. Either, apparently, it was not the enemy's policy to provoke a renewal of the fight, or he might disdain to take advantage of his adversary's unsupported position. It is at all events certain, that while Benbow and Walton were awaiting the junction of their *friends* astern, their enemies abreast, to cite the expression of an eye-witness, "civilly withheld their fire." At two P.M. the enemy taking advantage of the sea-breeze, and re-forming first his order of battle, crowded sail, and shaped a *retreating* course, the *Breda* and *Ruby* following the fugitives, and plying their rear, till dark, with a constant fire from their bow guns. During this retreat of Du Casse, (a *retreat* which, it may be here remarked, all the French chroniclers of naval events convert into "a steady preservation of his course,") the remaining ships of the British squadron were still a considerable distance astern, slowly and sluggishly closing with their incensed chief.

On the dawn of the 21st, the British admiral attacking the enemy's rear, a warm encounter ensued; one of the largest vessels in this division of the French line suffered severely, and eventually became unserviceable, and the *Ruby* was so much shattered in her hull, spars, and rigging, as to render it necessary to tow her clear of the concentrated fire of her two powerful opponents. During this encounter, which continued for upwards of two hours, the *Defiance* and *Windsor* never discharged from their batteries a single shot, although each vessel had taken up a commanding position on the beam of the sternmost ship of the French line.

On the 24th, about two in the morning, Benbow, favoured by a light wind, and reaching within hail of the enemy's sternmost ship, opened upon that vessel a destructive fire, which was warmly returned. At three A.M. a chain-shot shattered the right leg of the British chief. When the day dawned, a French seventy-gun ship was seen with her mainyard down, lying across the gunwale, her fore-topsail yard shot away, and her mizen-mast gone close by the board. In this affair the *Falmouth* took a prominent part; not so the *Greenwich*, *Defiance*, *Windsor*, and *Pendennis*. Passing ahead of the French line, each of these *non*-combatants bore up, and ran to leeward, for no more important object, it might seem, than to discharge a few straggling shot into the enemy's already disabled ships.

Seeing these four defaulters disposed so little to support their chief, the enemy's hopes revived, and he became the attacking force, bringing a concentrated fire on the British flag-ship. In this attack the *Breda* suffered much in her hull, spars, and rigging, and had two or three of her lower-deck guns dismounted. Still was seen waving in the wind the signal for close action; a signal Benbow directed to be kept flying both *night* and day.

The combatants had already hauled off to repair their respective damages; and now it was that the wounded chief directed his flag-captain to fire two shotted guns at those ships of his squadron which so glaringly and disgracefully disregarded his signal for battle. Seeing things in this confusion, the enemy remanned their disabled ship, took her in tow, and proceeded on their course for Carthagena.

When the *Breda* had repaired her damages, Benbow, who had been borne to the cock-pit for surgical assistance, now, placed in his "cradle," reappeared on the quarter-deck. After despatching a mission to those captains who had so misconducted themselves, desiring them to regain their stations, and "behave like men," and try to retrieve their characters, the admiral instructed his flag-captain to pursue the enemy, then about three miles on the lee-bow. But before this step was taken, the captain of the *Defiance* had arrived on board the *Breda*. Kirkby entreated his superior to desist from further attack; represented the enemy as extremely strong, and went so far as to tell the admiral that "from what had already *passed*, it was plain there was nothing *more* to be *done*." Desirous to ascertain the opinions of the other captains, the admiral instantly caused them, by signal, to be summoned on board the *Breda*. Upon their appearance in the presence of their maimed and mortified superior, whose mental sufferings even exceeded his bodily tortures, they one and all concurred in Kirkby's dastardly advice. Reluctantly yielding to this ignominious counsel, the vice-admiral relinquished his intention to renew action, and desired a course to be shaped direct for Port Royal, where he was soon after joined by rear-admiral Whetstone with the squadron under that officer's command.

Some French writers have given this affair a turn to their own advantage; but if dependence can be placed on the following generous epistle, said to have been addressed to Benbow upon his arrival at Carthagena, M. Du Casse, the admiral opposed to him, might seem to have been astonished at his escape:—

"*Sir,—I had little hopes, on Monday last, but to have supped in your cabin; but it pleased God to order it otherwise; I am thankful for it. As for those cowardly captains who deserted you, hang them up; for, by ——, they deserve it. Yours,*

"Du Casse."

On the 6th of October, Benbow, as commodore and chief on the station, issued an order to rear-admiral Whetstone to convene a court-martial for the trial of the following captains:—

Kirkby, commander of the	*Defiance*	of 64	guns.
Constable	*Windsor*	60	,,
Wade	*Greenwich*	54	,,
Hudson	*Pendennis*	48	,,

The charges exhibited against them were cowardice, breach of orders, and neglect of duty, in the fight with Du Casse, for six days off the coast of Carthagena. Kirkby was first brought to trial, and the crimes charged against him being fully proved by the evidence of the admiral, ten commissioned officers, and eleven warrant and inferior officers, he was sentenced to be shot, but the execution of his sentence was reserved for her majesty's sanction. Constable was acquitted of cowardice, but found guilty of the other charges, and sentenced to be cashiered, dismissed the service, and imprisoned during the queen's pleasure. Wade was the next tried, and convicted on the clearest evidence of the same charges that were proved against Kirkby, and also that he had been drunk during the entire period when the enemy was in sight. He received sentence to be shot. Hudson died a few days previous to his trial, and by that means probably escaped the fate of his companions.

On the 12th, captain Vincent, of the *Falmouth*, and captain Fogg, Benbow's flag-captain, were both tried for signing, at the persuasion of captain Kirkby, a paper, containing an obligation on themselves *not to fight the French*. The charge was proved, nor was it denied. All that the prisoners offered in extenuation, was, that being apprehensive of Kirkby's desertion to the enemy, their conduct was intended to prevent so great an evil. This tale would have carried little weight with the court had not the vice-admiral attested to their gallantry in action. Both officers were suspended until his royal highness's pleasure was known.

In the following spring, Kirkby and Wade were conveyed in the *Bristol* prisoners to England. Their death-warrants had been waiting at all the western ports, in order that the confirmed sentence of the court might be carried into execution on their arrival in the country; and that there might be no delay in punishing culprits who had so disgraced their sovereign's service, and brought such dishonour on the British flag. They arrived at Plymouth on the 4th of April, and on the 6th they were both shot on board the *Bristol*.

On his arrival at Port Royal it became manifest that Benbow's shattered leg was not to be saved; the limb was, therefore, amputated; and this operation, together with his mental suffering, producing a fatal fever, he died on the 4th of November, 1702, aged, it is thought, about fifty-two, regretting to his last moments the misconduct of his captains, which had robbed him of so fair an opportunity of rendering an eminent service to his king and country.

As to his character, the bitterest enemies admitted him to be a brave, active, and able commander; while no friend or admirer could overlook his deficiency in those conciliatory manners which usually secure to the superior regard and personal attachment from those whom he commands. Honesty, integrity, and blunt sincerity, were in Benbow the prominent features of his private character. In his public capacity, to employ a professional phrase, he was a "*taut* hand," and was wont to be rigidly strict, and often extremely severe with officers disposed to be dilatory or negligent in the discharge of their several duties.

BENBOW, (John,) son of the preceding, remarkable for a shipwreck, in 1701, on the coast of Madagascar. The whole crew being made prisoners, were marched into the interior, where they found other prisoners from England and Scotland. Though scarcely sixty in number, they seized the king, and pursued by thousands of the natives, all better armed than themselves, they bore him away in triumph. Notwithstanding, however, the remonstrances of Benbow, he was surrendered for six muskets. The natives now became the assailants. Some of the Europeans surrendered and were immediately put to death; the rest, with Benbow at their head, fought their way to Fort Dauphin. Many years elapsed, however, before a European ship appeared off the coast. This interval was employed by Benbow in writing his description of the southern part of Madagascar, but the MS. unfortunately perished by fire.

BENCI, or DE BENCIIS, an Italian physician, called Hugh de Siena, who died at Rome, in 1438, having translated from Greek and Arabic the most esteemed works of the ancient physicians, especially Hippocrates, Galen, and Avicenna.

A son of the preceding, *Francis Benci*, gave lectures on medicine at the university of Padua, where he died in 1487. (Biog. Univ.)

BENCI, (Francis, 1542 — 1594,) a Jesuit of Aquapendente, distinguished as an orator and Latin poet. Several of his works have been published. He was also editor of a poem by Stella, on the voyage of Columbus. (Biog. Univ.)

BENCI, (Thomas,) a noble Florentine, who flourished about 1470, and was a distinguished pupil of Marsilio Ficino. (Cenni Biographici.)

BENCIVENNI, (Ser Zucchero,) a Florentine, who lived in the fourteenth century, was a notary by profession, and in 1316 resided at Avignon. He became eminent by rendering works from other languages into Italian; one of the first of which was Rasis, translated in 1300.

BENCIVENNI, (Joseph,) a Florentine writer, who died in 1808, at the age of seventy-seven. His most esteemed work is a Life of Dante. (Biog. Univ.)

BENCOVICH, (Frederic,) a native of Dalmatia, educated as a painter, at Bologna, and frequently called Frederighetto di Dalmazia. His pictures are in the style of Cignani, but do not reach its amenity of colouring. Bencovich, however, was correct in design, powerful in execution, and thoroughly acquainted with the principles of his art. He resided in Germany some years, and died about 1760. His name is variously spelt, as Bencorich, Bendonich, Benconich, but by himself Bencovich. (Lànzi, Stor. Pitt. v. 165. Bryan's Dict.)

BENDA. The name of two eminent musicians.

1. *Francis*, (1709—1786,) a celebrated violinist, and master of the concerts to Frederic II. of Prussia, born at Altbenatka, in Bohemia. He died at Potsdam. In the compositions of Benda, which are almost wholly for the violin, there is scarcely a passage not within the power of the human voice to sing. He published,—Studies for the Violin, Progressive Exercises, and Solos for the Violin. (Mus. Biog. Dict. of Mus. Biog. Univ.)

2. *George*, (1721 or 1722—Nov. 6, 1795,) brother of the preceding, and born at the same place, one of the most eminent musicians of Germany. Called to Gotha in 1748, as chapel-master to the duke, he there composed a great number of pieces of sacred music, which gained him high reputation. Dr. Burney says, that the music of George Benda is new, profound, and worthy of a great master; the sole objection that can be made to it is an occasional affectation of too great novelty; but this observation can only apply to his earlier productions, before he went to Italy. There are several other musicians of this name enumerated. (Biog. Univ. Biog. des Contemporains. Dict. of Mus.)

BENDA, (John William Amádéus Otho,) son of Ernest Benda, musician to Frederic II., born on the 30th of October, 1775, at Berlin. His profession was the law, but he distinguished himself in general literature. He wrote—1. Erreurs de l'Amour. 2. Des Impôts. 3. De la Police à l'Egard des Charges. 4. Contes romantiques. 5. Agrippa, a tragedy. 6. Complete translation of Shakspeare. 7. A translation of the poetical works of Sir W. Scott, with some of Lord Byron's pieces. (Biog. Univ.)

BENDAVID, (L.) born at Berlin, of a Jewish family, in 1762, an able mathematician, and industrious author, whose philosophical principles were those of Kant. He died at Berlin in 1832.

BENDELER, (John Philip,) a German organ and piano player, who died in 1708. His works, still valuable, are,—Ærarium Melopoeticum, Nürnbergæ, 1688, fol.; Organopœia, Merseburg, 1690, 4to; the latter, an important work on the construction of organs, entering into the most minute detail, and which went through several editions. Directorium Musicum, Quedlinburg, 1706, 4to. Bendeler also firmly believed that he had solved the problem of the quadrature of the circle, concerning which he wrote, Planimetria Practica, Quedl. 1700, 4to; Quadratura Circuli, Lips. 1700.

BENDELER, (Solomon, 1683—1724,) a German singer, with a counter-tenor voice of such extraordinary compass, so fine, and so powerful, that at a concert at London, he drowned the sound of fifty instruments, and in the cathedral of St. Paul it predominated over that of the organ. (Biog. Univ.)

BENDINELLI, (Augustine,) a good contrapuntist, born at Lucca, about 1550, died at Rome in 1610. He published, from 1585 to 1604, several sacred pieces, reprinted at Frankfort-on-the-Maine. (Bononcini, Musico Prattico. Baini. Schilling.)

BENDLOWES, or BENLOWES, (Edward,) an English poet, born in 1602, of an ancient and opulent family, seated at Brent-hall, Finchingfield, Essex. He succeeded his grandfather in 1613, and much of his conduct in life was like that of a person spoiled by this early release from restraint and forethought. At sixteen, he was admitted a fellow-commoner of St. John's college, Cambridge, to which he subsequently became a benefactor. On leaving the university he went abroad with a tutor; and after visiting seven continental courts, he came home with a degree of information and refinement rather above the usual standard of his day. He now patronized poets, especially Quarles, Davenant, Payne, and Fisher, who returned his liberality by flattering him in dedications and verses. His very name suggested a complimentary anagram, being tortured into *Benevolus*. As habits of thoughtless liberality to literary men were accompanied by a like facility towards musicians, buffoons, and mere sycophants, as well as by a rage for collecting curiosities, Bendlowes, although unmarried, and possessing landed property worth seven hundred or a thousand pounds a year, then an excellent income, suffered a recovery about 1654, and alienated his family estates. He soon afterwards fixed his residence in Oxford, and gave a handsome fortune to his niece, Philippa, married to Walter Blount, a gentleman seated at Mapledurham, in that county. His resources were farther impaired by the good-natured weakness of making himself responsible for debts contracted by his needy and hungry parasites, so that he became at length seriously involved, and underwent the misery and degradation of a detention in prison. After his release, he spent eight years in Oxford, but in great poverty, having an insufficient supply even of the commonest necessaries. He died at Oxford, Dec. 18, 1676. In early life he had imbibed a disposition towards Romanism, but in his later days he often argued against it. He also took a strong dislike to the doctrines of Arminius and Socinus. He wrote Sphinx Theologica, seu Musica Templi, ubi discordia concors, Camb. 1626, 8vo; Theophila, or Love Sacrifice, a divine poem, Lond. 1652, fol., with his own portrait prefixed; also some other pieces, both in Latin and English, now wholly forgotten, and probably indebted largely for the notice that they ever received to the author's position in society at the time of their publication. (Biog. Brit. Wright's Hist. of Essex.)

BENDONSKY, (Symon Szymonowicz,) a Polish and Latin poet, born in Galicia, in 1557, styled by himself in his Latin works, Simonides. He died in 1629, greatly esteemed by many eminent scholars of the time, especially by Justus Lipsius, who compares him to some of the first writers in antiquity, and more especially to Catullus. By others he was styled the Sclavonian Pindar and the Polish Theocritus. But it is his Polish poems that now constitute his best title to literary fame, although they consist only of eclogues, and a few epitaphs. They are included in Bobrowicz's series of Classic Polish Poets, Leipzic, 1834, which publication has furnished the above particulars; but, as is there observed, they have for the modern reader one pervading defect, that of being studied imitations of his Grecian model, Theocritus.

BENE, (Sennuccio dal,) a native of Florence, who died in 1349. His *Rime*, partly printed, partly preserved in MS., are considered good specimens of the taste of his age. (Cenni Biographici.)

BENE, (Baccio, or Bartolommeo,) a native of Florence, much distinguished as a Greek and Latin scholar. He flourished about 1560, and his *Rime* are mentioned with applause in the Vocab. della Crusca. (Cenni Biographici.)

BENEDETTI, (Francis, about 1792—1821,) an Italian dramatic poet, born at Cortona, who took Alfieri as a model; and such pieces as he lived to complete, gave promise that he would have been an able successor of that poet. (Biog. Univ. Suppl.)

BENEDETTI, (Matthias,) a fresco painter of the Modenese school, born at

Reggio, and flourished about 1702. Lanzi says that he was a priest of Reggio, and that he was instructed in perspective by Talami, in which both he and his brother excelled. (Lanzi, Stor. Pitt. iv. 45.)

BENEDETTI, (Alexander,) a celebrated Italian physician, born at Legnano, near Verona, as his writings show, a learned man. Mazzuchelli places his death in 1525. Benedetti has the merit of attempting to relieve medicine of the barbarisms with which it was loaded; but his writings do not warrant the extravagant eulogiums passed upon them by Hensler. His works are worthy of being consulted, for they contain many remarkable cases. Haller says he is the first author to make mention of biliary calculi. His works are,—De Pestilenti Febre, sive Pestilentiæ Causis, Præservatione et Auxiliorum Materiâ Liber, Venet. 1493, 4to; Paviæ, 1516, fol.; Basil. 1531, 12mo. This work is also to be found in the collections of Bolognini, Almenar, Massaria, and others. Anatomiæ, sive Historiæ Corporis Humani Lib. v. Venet. 1493, 1498, 1502, 4to; Paris, 1514, 1519, 4to; Basil. 1517, 4to; Colon. 1527, 8vo; Strasb. 1528, 8vo. It is also to be found in the works of George Valla. De Medici et Ægri Officio Aphorismorum Libellus, Paris, 1514, 4to; this is likewise printed by Symphorien Champier, in his Libelli de Medicinæ claris Scriptoribus. De Re Medica, Venet. 1535, fol.; Basil. 1539, 4to, 1549, 1572, fol.

BENEDETTI, (Dominic,) an Italian physician of the eighteenth century, who cultivated letters as well as medicine; and besides several works on the latter science, chiefly in verse, he left,—Il Temistocle in Persia, Dramma Recitato da' Comici nel Teatro di S. Salvatore di Venezia l'anno 1732, Venez. 1732, 12mo. Illustrium Virorum Synopsis, qui de Sano D. D. Medicorum Physicorum Veneto Collegio extiterunt, &c. Venet. 1753, 4to. La Moda, Dramma giocoso per Musica, rappresentatio in Venezia nel Teatro di San Mose, l'anno 1754, Venez. 1754, 12mo.

BENEDETTIS, (Dominic de, 1610—1678,) a painter, born in Piedmont, who went to Rome, and became a scholar of Guido, whose graceful style he successfully imitated. (Bryan's Dict.)

BENEDETTO. See Castiglione-Marcello.

BENEDETTO DA MAJANO, a celebrated Florentine architect, in the middle of the fifteenth century. He had a brother named Julian, and they both excelled, not only in architecture, but also in sculpture. A monument of Benedetto's genius, all but imperishable, exists in the colossal and majestic Strozzi palace, at Florence, begun by him in 1450, but completed by Simon Polajolo, called Cronaca, about 1500. Before the rule of the Medici, this republic was liable to violent convulsions; the factions, into which the citizens were divided, obliging the chiefs, for their own defence, to erect palaces strong enough to withstand the desperate assault of an enraged and armed multitude; large enough to contain a numerous retinue of followers, with all the necessaries of war; and lofty enough to admit of no aggression from the adjoining buildings. These fortress-palaces generally occupy an imposing length of frontage; and although presenting only three floors in elevation, and those distinctly marked, yet rise to a prodigious height. The lower part of the Strozzi palace consists of a lofty rusticated basement, having a central arched gateway or portal, leading to the interior court; and the rough stone work is pierced on each side by a series of small openings, defended by strong barred gratings. The two upper stories, which are also channelled, and with the stones strongly indicated, are lighted by ranges of circular headed windows. A gigantic cornice, elaborately enriched, surmounts the noble pile, its projections throwing a deep shadow over the fronts, and giving a solemn effect to the edifice. There are several little subordinate details, which strikingly contribute to the character of the building. There is a broad stone bench, or seat, running all round the palace, on which it may be supposed the attendant soldiers or retainers of the prince usually sat in the day-time. There are large metal rings pendent from the front of the basement, to which warriors might attach their horses; on the angles project capacious iron lamps, capriciously designed, and which used to be filled with inflammable materials, that burned fiercely and diffused a broad glare to light the followers or partizans to the dwelling of the chief. Between the windows of the upper stories are also projecting bars, with circular orifices at the ends, in which were placed the poles of the banners displayed on festive days, or at times of assault, waving defiance to the assailants. The interior court consists of two colonnades, one over the other, less sombre in effect than the exterior, which, on the contrary, seems to challenge attack.

These buildings are the finest instances

of the power of architecture speaking to the imagination. They are like fragments torn from the pages of history; and as the traveller looks on them, they recall those times of intestine trouble, when Guelphs and Ghibellines were by turns possessed of power, or driven from their native country. They paint a terrible race, long since passed away, and now succeeded by people as effeminate as their ancestors were warlike, as indolent as they were energetic.

BENEDICT, (St.) the corner-stone of monachism as established in the west before mendicant friars began, born in 480, in or near Nursia, once an episcopal town in the duchy of Spoleto, a portion of the papal states. He sprang from rather a superior family, (*liberiori genere*, in the words of his biographer, Gregory the Great,) and was sent to Rome for education. He soon, however, became so shocked by the vices of his fellow-students, that he clandestinely withdrew to Subiago, (*Sublacus*, or *Sublacum*,) a place nearly forty miles from Rome, and concealed himself in a cave there, unknown to all the world, except a single hermit, named Romanus, who supplied the scanty fare on which he subsisted. After a seclusion of three years, his retreat was discovered by a clergyman residing at some distance, and subsequently it became frequented by the shepherds employed among the solitudes around. To them he dispensed religious instruction with great success. Every day making him better known and more respected, he was chosen abbot of a neighbouring monastery, and with great reluctance entered upon his new duties, foreseeing that his views of monastic obligation were likely to provoke resistance in the fraternity. He soon found himself to have judged rightly, the monks complaining, probably with sufficient reason, that his inexperience made him quite unfit for governing others, especially as he was harsh and merciless. Their dissatisfaction seems to have occasioned an attempt to poison him. At all events he withdrew very shortly from a charge to which he was most likely then quite unequal, whatever he might have subsequently become. His residence, however, among monks, appears to have turned his attention towards that class of persons who had originated in the east, but were then making their way into notice among the religious public of western Europe, though hitherto under little better regulation than some discretionary adhesion either to the rule of Basil, or that of Pachomius. Benedict quickly found occasion for his meditations upon monastic discipline, many devout spirits flocking to him for instruction, and being anxious to second any views that he might entertain. He now, therefore, established twelve monasteries around his retreat at Subiago, each containing twelve monks, with a superior, and the whole being under his own direction. This colony, however, at length excited a strong opposition, led by a neighbouring clergyman, whose conduct is naturally imputed to the worst motives by monastic writers, but is very likely to have really flowed from experience of the evils that must have been observable among a heterogeneous assemblage, universally of a complexion rather fanatical, and necessarily comprising persons of little discretion. But be the cause of Benedict's trouble what it might, it had the effect of dislodging him and his party from Subiago, about the year 528. He now transferred himself to Mount Cassino, about seventy miles from Rome, and nearly fifty from Naples, on which he found a temple and a grove of Apollo, devoutly cherished by a pagan population. This last he converted, and destroying all remnants of the former superstition, he founded on the mountain a monastery, with such regulations as rendered it eventually the prototype of all the establishments for monks in western Europe. The date of his death is differently given by ancient writers, but it appears to have occurred either in 542 or 543. One of the most celebrated establishments of his order in very early times, was that of Fleury, in France, and this laid claim to the possession of his remains, which had been removed thither, it was said, in 660, by Aigulf, a monk of the house, after the destruction of the monastery on Mount Cassino by the Lombards. Italy, however, treated this as an interested fiction, maintaining that Benedict's once mortal part was not removed from its original resting-place; an assertion stoutly denied in France, but which there is every reason to believe. (Mabillon. Annall. Ord. Bened. i.)

BENEDICT, of Aniane, the first reformer of the Benedictine system, hence called second father of the western monks, and head, as it were, of all the Frankish monasteries in his day, a native of Languedoc, highly esteemed by Lewis the Pious. He was son of the count of Maguelone, but of Gothic origin, and at one time a member of Charlemagne's army. In 774, however, he retired into a monastery in Burgundy; in 797 he became himself the builder and abbot of one on the banks of the Aniane, in Languedoc. He subsequently built the monastery of Indre, near Aix-la-Chapelle, and presided over it also. In 779, he was sent into Spain by Charlemagne, to reason Felix of Urgel out of his opinion that Christ's human sonship rested upon the Father's adoption. Benedict died in 821, at the age of 70. His exertions brought all the western monks, eventually, under the rule of his Nursian namesake, obliterating the diversities of usage which had hitherto rendered them a body very divided and far from generally respectable. He wrote, Codex Regularum, (which is a series of rules for the use of monks and nuns, compiled from the fathers,) printed at Rome, 1661, and at Paris, 1664; Concordia Regularum, (which harmonizes the Benedictine rule with others,) printed at Paris, 1648; also some smaller treatises, which have partly appeared in published collections, and partly remain in MS. (Cave. Hist. Lit. Du Pin. Eccl. Hist. Mabillon. Annall. Bened. iii.)

BENEDICT, (of Appenzell,) a great contrapuntist, about 1540, who wrote, according to Burney, in a more easy and correct manner than any before him. (Schilling.)

BENEDICT, (Biscop,) a distinguished Anglo-Saxon monk of the seventh century, called Baducing by Fridegod, in his metrical life of Wilfrid. He was of elevated birth, and received a competent estate from his native sovereign, Oswy of Northumbria, in whose service he was. In 653, however, being then about five-and-twenty, he relinquished a secular life, and made a pilgrimage to Rome. On his return, he exerted himself to spread a knowledge of the religious institutions that had fallen under his notice abroad. After two years, he went again to Rome, and in his way back he made a stay of two years in the monastery of Lerins. He joined the society there, took the tonsure, and was regularly initiated in all the requirements of conventual life. A trading vessel then touched at Lerins, and Benedict could not resist the opportunity for another visit to Rome. He reached it at an important juncture. The kings of Kent and Northumbria, weary of religious dissension between the British and the Roman parties, had concurred in sending Wighard, a native priest, for papal consecration to the see of Canterbury, hoping, probably, that such a recommendation might prove serviceable in securing the acquiescence of all Anglo-Saxon Christians. The metropolitan elect was at the pontifical court when Benedict arrived, but he died before consecration. Vitalian, then pope, now determined upon trying the success of a nomination by himself. His choice eventually fell upon Theodore, an elderly Cilician monk, of extraordinary merit. He was to be accompanied by Adrian, an African abbot, also recommended by unusual qualifications. Both, however, from all the habits and associations of their former lives, laboured under an obvious unfitness to make a favourable impression at first upon English society. To smooth a way for them, Vitalian persuaded Benedict that it was his duty to be their guide and interpreter. Arriving with them in Kent, he undertook the abbacy of St. Peter's, and retained it two years, when he went to Rome again. He returned with a considerable collection of books, and numerous relics. His original intention was to stop in Wessex; but Kenwalch, king of that country, on whose friendship he had reckoned, unexpectedly died, and he travelled onwards to his native Northumbria. Displaying his foreign acquisitions there to Egfrid, now upon the throne, and his conversation proving highly attractive, that prince gave him a tract of land at the mouth of the Wear in 674. There Benedict founded a monastery; but not contented with native workmen, he procured from Gaul both masons to build a church of stone, and manufacturers of glass to glaze its windows. He subsequently made two other journeys to Rome, bringing home a large addition to his library, and various pictures to ornament his church. In 682, he received a farther donation of land from Egfrid, and upon this new estate he built the monastery of Jarrow. He died in 690, after an illness borne in an admirable spirit, and was buried in his monastery of Wearmouth. As time rolled on, the remains of any man famed for sanctity became of great importance in monastic calculations, and in the tenth century, when this principle was in very active operation, a large sum of money procured the transfer of Benedict's bones to Thorney Abbey, in Cambridgeshire. His literary competence was attested by some pieces penned by him for monastic use; but his chief claims to the notice of posterity rest upon the library, works of art, and artificers, that he imported from the continent. He thus, undoubtedly, conferred a lasting benefit upon his native country. (Vita S. Bened. auctore Ven. Beda.)

BENEDICT, (of Gloucester,) a monk of the great abbey there, of whose time nothing is known. He has left a life of Dubricius, archbishop of Caerleon, printed by Wharton, (Anglia Sacra, ii. 654.) This relates the translation of Dubricius, in 1120; consequently the author must have lived after that year, and the MS. used is thought not much later. (Angl. Sacr. ii. Præf.)

BENEDICT, (of Norwich,) a learned monk, author of several works, one of which was entitled, Alphabetum Aristotelis. He died and was buried at Norwich in the year 1340.

BENEDICT, (of Peterborough,) an English historian, educated at Oxford, formerly prior of Christ church, Canterbury, but elected abbot of Peterborough in 1177, and keeper of the great seal from 1191 to 1193, in which latter year he died. He wrote a life of Becket, which has gained him, from the scurrilous pen of Bale, the character of a *vile impostor*, but seemingly for no good reason. He also wrote a history of Henry II. and Richard I., ranging from 1170 to 1192, a valuable work, published at Oxford, by Hearne, 1735, 2 vols, 8vo. (Chalmers' Biog. Brit.)

BENEDICT I. (pope,) a Roman, son of Boniface, elected in June 574, after a vacancy of more than ten months, occasioned, seemingly, by national troubles. He died July 30, 578, overcome with grief, it is thought, at the miseries then brought upon Italy by the Lombards. (Platina. Bower.)

BENEDICT II. a Roman, son of John, elected in July, 683, but not consecrated until July 26, 684, from the want of imperial confirmation, perhaps, accidentally delayed. The new pope represented such delays as prejudicial to religion, and Constantine Pogonatus, then upon the Byzantine throne, gave up the right of confirming papal elections; a concession that Justinian revoked. Benedict appears to have been personally worthy of any reasonable indulgence, from piety, morals, and professional information. He died May 7, 685, and his name appears among the saints in the Roman martyrology. (Bower. Platina.)

BENEDICT III. a Roman, son of Peter, unanimously elected by both clergy and laity, Sept. 1, 855, much against his own inclinations, as he preferred religious privacy. The messengers to notify his election at the imperial court, were intercepted by Arsenius, bishop of Eugubio, who desired the election of Anastasius, excommunicated by Leo. IV. the last pope, but favoured by the emperors Lothaire and Lewis, from whom officers quickly arrived in Rome, to force their candidate upon the church there. The attempt, however, was firmly resisted by Benedict's friends, a riot being made, in which he was shamefully used, and the emperors saw the policy of acquiescing in his election. An Englishman may think him worthy of notice as the pope to whom Ethelwulf of Wessex paid a visit, with his youngest son, the illustrious Alfred. More general interest attaches to his name from the senseless figment of a discreditable and surprising occupancy of the papal see by pope Joan, immediately after his predecessor Leo's death. Benedict died April 8, 858, leaving an excellent character in every respect, especially for amiable temper. (Bower. Platina. Mabillon. Annall. Bened.)

BENEDICT IV. a noble Roman, son of Mommolus, elected in August, 900, and consecrated without waiting for imperial approbation. The throne was then in dispute between Berenger and Lewis; hence a reference to either competitor might reasonably seem an unsafe recognition of his claims. Lewis eventually succeeded, and coming to Rome, was crowned there in 901. Benedict's character appears to have been quite worthy of his elevation, and altogether above the standard of that degenerate age, of which he saw the opening; but his pontificate afforded nothing remarkable. (Bower. Platina.)

BENEDICT V. a Roman, elected in 964, on the violent death of John XII. That infamous pontiff was, however, then under a formal sentence of deposition, and had only returned to Rome a short time before in a sedition. When he was driven away, Leo VIII. had been elected in his place. Leo fled to the emperor Otho, on John's forcible resumption of the papal chair, and that monarch soon marched an army to restore him. Benedict was now degraded as an intruder, and he died in exile at Hamburgh, in 965, leaving an excellent character for learning, abilities, and moral worth; so that if his election had occurred when there was a real vacancy, there is no doubt but it would have given general satisfaction. (Bower. Platina.)

BENEDICT VI. a Roman, son of Hildebrand, elected in November, 973, on the death of John XIII., occupied the papal chair only a few months. The death of the emperor Otho the Great rendered Italian faction wild, and Cynthius, as Platina calls him, a Roman citizen, or Cenci, in modern language, having made a violent party against the imperialists, assaulted the Lateran palace, and dragged Benedict to Hadrian's mole, now the castle of St. Angelo, as a favourer of them. In confinement there, he was either strangled or starved to death in 974. (Bower. Platina.)

BENEDICT VII. bishop of Sutri, a Roman, son of David, elected by imperial influence, in 975. His pontificate afforded nothing remarkable, and he died in 984. (Bower.)

BENEDICT VIII. son of Gregory, count of Tusculum, was, before his election to the papal chair in 1012, John, bishop of Porto. Family influence appears to have caused his elevation, and a competitor, named Gregory, immediately disputed it so successfully, that he was driven into Germany to seek protection from Henry, the religious king of Italy, eventually emperor, and admitted among the saints. His application being favourably received, and Henry moving upon Rome to seat him in the papal chair, the Romans expelled Gregory, and recognised his pretensions. Benedict is remarkable for a dicided movement in those fanatical and mischievous encroachments upon clerical discretion as to marriage, which ended in making the contraction of it a canonical offence. In a council, holden at Pavia, under him, it was decreed that a clergyman's children are slaves of their father's church. Benedict died in 1024, revered for liberality to the poor, and highly commended for zealous attempts to reform a dissolute clergy. Neither he nor his eulogists appear to have suspected that a removal of unnatural restrictions would have rendered some of this reforming zeal superfluous. (Bower.)

BENEDICT IX. son of Alberic, count of Tusculum, and named himself Theophylact, was, it is said, nephew of John XIX., the last pope. He was a mere boy, eighteen years old, or less, when family influence, aided largely, rumour maintained, by bribery, placed him on the papal throne, in 1033. His conduct in this post being marked by all the vices of unrestrained youth, the Romans, in 1045, were driven by the scandal of his morals, and the oppression of his government, to supersede him by John, bishop of Sabina, designated Sylvester III. That prelate, however, was not strong enough for Benedict's family faction, the Tusculans, and after three months, he was under the necessity of fleeing from Rome. Benedict now returned, but soon becoming weary of the restraints exacted by his station, he resigned it in favour of John Gratian, known as Gregory VI., and withdrew from public notice to lead a life of unobstructed profligacy. He was generally said to have resigned for a valuable consideration, and Gregory's possession of a dignity conferred for life, while two former possessors of it, Benedict and Sylvester, yet survived, was an additional reason for questioning his title. To remedy the evils arising from a settlement so unsatisfactory, the emperor Henry the Black's interference was urgently required, and that monarch held a council at Sutri, which declared Gregory's election irregular. The decision met with humble acquiescence from Gregory himself, and Suiger, bishop of Bamberg, being elected in his room, under the name of Clement II., at the close of 1046, he quietly surrended to him the ensigns of pontifical dignity. The new pope, however, died in October, 1047, and then Benedict IX., for the third time, took possession of the papal chair; but he retained it only until the following July, when he finally withdrew into private life, either from fear of the emperor, or from late compunction for the public scandals and personal pollutions of his unhappy course. Exactly what became of him afterwards is unknown, but he seems to have died in 1054, deeply penitent, in the monastery of Grotta Ferrata. (Bower. Biog. Univ.)

BENEDICT X. a Campanian, named John Mincio, bishop of Veletri, hastily chosen, by corrupt means, it was said, on the death of Stephen IX., in March, 1058. The emperor would not, however, recognise this election, and in the following October, Benedict's faction found itself unable to support him. He was, accordingly, under the necessity of giving place to Nicholas II., who had been raised under imperial recommendation to the papacy. Benedict bore his loss of dignity with great propriety, and lived afterwards in a sort of confinement, deprived even of the priesthood. He died in 1059. (Bower. Biog. Univ.)

BENEDICT XI. (Nicholas Bocasini,) succeeded Boniface VIII., in October 1303. He was a native of Trevigi, of obscure parentage, his father being a shepherd, or, according to some accounts, a notary. He had subsisted, at one time, by tuition, and taken great pains with his pupils; "for he agreed," says Ciaconius, ii. 347, "with Plato, that nothing makes such a difference to a state, as care or neglect in the education of its youth." He subsequently became a Dominican friar, and was general of his order in 1298, when his imperious predecessor, Boniface VIII., appointed him cardinal bishop of Sabina. For the healing of that pontiff's breach with Philip the Fair, Benedict's brief pontificate is principally remarkable. In the beginning of 1304, an embassy arrived from France, but charged with no request for absolution, only with instructions to receive it if offered; the king's letters too spoke of Boniface as a false shepherd and a robber; but expressed sincere respect for the church and the pope, and a desire that all grievances should be adjusted. A reconciliation was soon effected. In several successive bulls, the king and his nobles were absolved from excommunication, the French clergy pardoned for their resistance to Boniface, and the kingdom restored to all the ecclesiastical privileges which it had previously enjoyed. (Fleur. b. lxxx. s. 41, ed. 1836.) From this amnesty, two persons only were excepted, William of Nogaret and Sciarra Colonna, who had surprised Boniface in his palace at Anagni. They were summoned to take their trial within a certain time at Rome. On their non-appearance they were excommunicated.

Benedict was warmly attached to the mendicant orders: his only cardinals that he selected were from them; and he endeavoured to allay their differences with the regular parochial clergy. A bull of his allows them to preach everywhere publicly, except during the hour of service; to become confessors to all who preferred them to the ordinary clergy; and to bury in their own church any persons who desired. Nor were the bishops allowed to control or alter these privileges. (On the Mendicant Orders, see Fleury's Dissert. after b. xciv. of his Hist.)

The death of Benedict (6th July, 1304) was attributed to a dish of poisoned figs; and Ferretus of Vicenza, a contemporary historian, accuses Philip of the murder. Others charge it upon Boniface's family, provoked by the patronage now enjoyed by their enemies, the Colonnas; others, again, upon the Florentines, then under an interdict. Probably, the pontiff's death was natural, and it found his character unimpaired for that humility, simplicity, and piety, which had marked it before his accession to the papacy.

BENEDICT XII. (James Fournier, 1334—1342.) His peaceful and useful papacy was wholly spent at Avignon, and one of its earliest cares was to compose the strife with the emperor Lewis of Bavaria, left him by his predecessor, John XXII. He was willing to recall that monarch's excommunication, but the French cardinals were predominant at Avignon. This impelled the German diet not only to declare the pope's proceedings against the emperor null and void, but even to derive his power wholly from the electors (nec auctoritate sedis apostolicæ super administratione bonorum et juris imperii indiget: Olenschlager ap. Giesel. p. iii. d. iv. c. 1). Although this bold step was neutralized by the subsequent vacillation of Lewis, yet he was able to maintain his empire and his contest against the popes till his death, in 1347. Notwithstanding the goodness of Benedict's intentions, and the irreproachable character which he really seems to have borne, although there are not wanting allegations to the contrary, some of his public acts were founded upon those papal assumptions which are most injurious to society. He authorized the levy of a tenth of all benefices in France, under pretence of a holy war, an exaction which Philip turned into his own coffers. He absolved Leo, king of Armenia, from an oath made to the sultan of Egypt. "After such dispensations," says Fleury, "what trust could the infidels place in the promises of Christians?" The establishment of Frederic of Aragon in Sicily (in 1303) had been accompanied by an acknowledgment that his kingdom was held as a fief of the Roman see. On his death the succession was again disputed, and Benedict asserted his right to decide between the two rival claimants, Peter of Aragon, son of Frederic, and Robert of Naples. But his efforts to establish the latter were unsuccessful; Peter was already in possession, and defied his legates and his excommunication. In other cases, the pretended papal right of political interference was exercised in a manner less exceptionable. Magnus, king of Sweden, begged him to recognise his authority over a part of Norway which he had seized; but Benedict replied, that it was the rule of his predecessors never to give away property without first hearing all the claimants. The Teutonic order unjustly invaded Poland; it was universally laid under a heavy penalty, and the leaders were excommunicated. Among duties properly professional, Benedict was called upon to decide a dispute upon the beatific vision, and his decision, in effect, imputed heresy to his predecessor. That pontiff's liberal promises of preferment he revoked. He strove also to abolish pluralities and simony, to reform morals, extirpate heresy, and regulate the monastic bodies. By these exertions he naturally made enemies, who did not fail to seek revenge in calumny.

BENEDICT XIII. (Peter Francis Orsini, or Ursini,) eldest son of the duke of Gravina, born in 1649, a Dominican friar in 1667, cardinal in 1672, elected successor of Innocent XIII. in 1724. In the following year he held a council at Rome to confirm the bull *Unigenitus*, published by Clement XI. This measure had considerable success, the cardinal de Noailles, archbishop of Paris, now accepting that bull, but it was afterwards the cause of many persecutions in France. In 1729 he published a brief, authorizing and praising the pretensions of Gregory VII. on the temporal rights of sovereigns, which met with much opposition, and was rejected by most of the European churches, particularly in Sicily, where, by timely concession, he put an end to the quarrel. In the same manner he also settled the dispute with the king of Sardinia, concerning that island, by waiving the pretensions of the papal investiture put forth by Clement XI. He could not, however, succeed in settling the right of nomination to abbacies and benefices in Piedmont; nor the dispute with Austria, whether Parma and Piacenza were fiefs of the Roman see or of the empire. In some other things, he contributed to the preservation of peace between the several powers of Europe. Nor among his acts worthy of commendation, should it be forgotten that he increased the pension settled by former popes upon the pretender, James Stuart, then living at Bologna. He died on the 21st of February, 1730, at the age of eighty-one, after a pontificate of five years and eight months, with the reputation of being generous, charitable, simple in his habits and manners, strict in his morality, and though zealous in maintaining the prerogatives of his see, yet conciliating, and unwilling to resort to extremes. But among much real merit, he was so unfortunate and blamable as to bestow his confidence upon bad ministers, especially upon cardinal Coscia, whose abilities were overshadowed by his avarice. So great, accordingly, was his unpopularity, that on Benedict's death, he would have been torn in pieces, had he not been confined by Clement XII. in the castle of St. Angelo, whence he was relieved by Benedict XIV. who banished him to Naples, where he died in 1729.

BENEDICT XIV. (Prosper Laurence Lambertini,) born in 1675, of an illustrious family, at Bologna, cardinal in 1728, elected pope, after five months of discussion and intrigue, in 1740. He began his pontificate by a wise adjustment of the disputes long pending between the papal court and Sardinia, Portugal, and Naples. With Charles III. he concluded a concordat, which laid the foundation of the great ecclesiastical reform, begun by that monarch, and completed by his son, Ferdinand IV., in the kingdom of the Two Sicilies. By a brief also to cardinal Saldanha for the reformation of the Jesuits, he paved the way for the temporary suppression of their order.

During the Austrian war of succession he remained strictly neutral, though he could not prevent the Spanish and German armies from marching through the papal states. At the restoration of peace, he turned his attention to the improvement of his dominions, by protecting arts and sciences, and by a generosity towards the learned, who flocked around him; which his courtesy and delicacy rendered additionally valuable. He embellished Rome, repaired churches, constructed magnificent fountains, built vast granaries, and dug out the obelisk of the Campus Martius, wrongly called of Sesostris, afterwards raised by Pius VI. He sought besides, by founding professorships in his capital, to render its importance in the learned world not unworthy of that which it enjoys in the religious. With this view he added also to the collection of the Capitoline Museum, established a school of drawing, and an academy for the instruction of the prelates of his court in ecclesiastical history, canon law, and knowledge of the rites and discipline of the church. By his means, too, were translated into Italian the best French and English books; and he ordered the printing of a catalogue, with accounts of the MSS. in the Vatican library, to which, numerous as they were already, he added not less than 3300 more. Nor was he negligent of his native town of Bologna, to whose university and institute of sciences he contributed by donations; and though he found the treasury poor and in debt, and notwithstanding so much generosity, by reductions and economy he cleared all encumbrances, and re-established its credit, for he did nothing for his relations, whom he would not even allow to come to Rome.

Amidst so much care for the improvement of his own dominions, he was always alive to the welfare of other countries. Being no favourer of the Jesuits, or rather of their worldly policy, it has been said that he gave them hints which might have saved them from sinking, as they did after his death, under a general burst of indignation. Seeing France distracted by quarrels between them and the Jansenists, the court and the parliament, the priests and the philosophers, he carefully avoided every thing that could in the least encourage the fanatical party in reviving the persecutions against the protestants of Languedoc; he even abolished the patriarchate of Aquileja, at the instance of Maria Theresa, notwithstanding the opposition of the Venetians, and allowed her to grant a full toleration to the protestants in her dominions. He abolished likewise a number of holidays which working people were obliged to observe; in fact, he may be said to have introduced a new system of temperate and conciliatory policy in the court of Rome, especially in its transactions with foreign affairs, which has been in a great measure followed by his successors. He died on the 2d of May, 1758, at the age of eighty-three, after a painful illness, regretted and lamented by all the world; for during the eighteen years of his pontificate, Rome enjoyed peace and prosperity; and for a long time after his death the reign of Lambertini was still remembered, and spoken of by the Romans as a green oasis in the midst of the sandy desert of Africa, and the last period of happiness of their country. He was succeeded by Clement XIII. Benedict was learned, not only in theology, but also in history, canon law, in the classical writers, and in elegant literature, and had even a taste for the fine arts. He was of irreproachable morals, kind, generous, affable, and benevolent, and many of his humorous repartees, which he loved to utter in his own Bolognese dialect, are still familiar at Rome; whilst others may be found recorded by different travellers, and particularly by the abbé Richard, in his Voyage d'Italie. His works were published at Rome, in 12 vols, 4to.

BENEDICT, a learned Maronite, of a noble Syrian family, named Ambarach, born at Gusta, in Phœnicia, in 1663, and sent to Rome for education in the Maronite college, at nine years old. He remained there thirty years, when, leaving it deeply versed in oriental languages, and other branches of learning, he returned into the east as a Romish missionary. The patriarch of Antioch then charged him with the correction of some works that he had written upon the liturgy and origin of the Maronites. Benedict gave him full satisfaction, and translated, moreover, his pieces into Latin. He was then sent back to Rome on some business of the Maronite church, and having executed this, he was preparing for a second return, when Cosmo III., duke of Tuscany, invited him into his dominions, for various purposes connected with oriental literature. His reward was a Hebrew professorship in the university of Pisa. At four-and-forty he became a Jesuit. His last years were spent at Rome, whither Clement XI. had drawn him to assist in correcting the Greek text of Scripture. Cardinal Quirini induced him to undertake, when very far advanced in life, a share in a new and improved edition of the works of his venerable countryman, the father, known as St. Ephræm Syrus. He lived, however, only to go through about half of the second volume, dying at Rome, September 22, 1742, universally loved, admired, and regretted. Another honour to Syria, Assemani, completed this work. Benedict also translated part of the Greek *Menology*, which was printed at Urbino, by means of cardinal Albani. (Biog. Univ.)

BENEDICT, (z Kozmina, or Kozminski,) professor of theology at Cracow, who, according to Zaluski, made the first Polish translation of Lucan's Pharsalia, printed in 1533 at Cracow. (Zaluski, Bibl. Poetów. Bentkowski.)

BENEDICTIS, (Jacob, or Jacoponus de,) a Minorite friar, born in Umbria, who died in 1306. He wrote, Hymni et Prosæ Sacræ, published by F. Frisati, Rome, 1558. He is the reputed author of the canticle, *Stabat Mater Dolorosa*, highly and justly popular among Romanists. (Fabricius.)

BENEDICTUS, (Zacharias,) a native of Vicenza, and a Carthusian monk, about 1508. He wrote, Vita St. Brunonis in hexameter verses, printed in the Paris Ascension edition of Bruno's works, and some other pieces. (Fabricius.)

BENEDICTUS, bishop of Marseilles, in 1229. Some of his MSS. are preserved in continental libraries. His Epistola ad Innocentium IV. de Reb. Gestis in Terra Sancta, is published in Dacheri Spicel. (Fabricius.)

BENEDICTUS, (Angelus a St. Vincenzio,) a Carmelite friar, born at Palermo in 1654, died in 1725. He wrote, (under the name of Fabio Cavalleani,) Discorso Philosophico e Astronomico, 12mo; Autitheatro della Gloria Serafica, 1725, 4to. (Bibliotheca Carmelitorum Excaleatarum.)

BENEDICTUS, (John Baptist,) a native of Venice, and afterwards in the service of Octavius Farnese, duke of Parma, and then of the duke of Savoy. He could not write Latin, but used, in his works, which are arithmetical and mathematical, and written in that language, the pen of F. M. Vialardi. He died at Turin, in 1590. (Thuani Historiarum sui Temporis, London, 1733, fol.)

BENEDICTUS, (Levita,) deacon of Mentz, in the first half of the ninth century, and known as the author of a collection of capitularies in three books. Though it professes to be a supplement to the collection of Ansegisus, and does indeed contain parts of capitularies, yet it was in all probability designed especially for the clergy and the use of ecclesiastical courts, with which view passages from the Bible, the fathers, acts of councils, decretals, the Westgothic Breviary, the Theodosian Code, Julian's Epitome, and the ancient German laws, are collected indiscriminately, without any regard to method, or indication of the various sources from which they are derived. From the preface, we learn that the book was compiled at the instance of Otgar, archbishop of Mentz, between A.D. 840 and 847, though it was not published till some years later. At first it was quoted as a separate collection, but was afterwards joined to the four books of Ansegisus, as the fifth, sixth, and seventh books of Capitularies. They were published by Baluze, under the title of Capitularia Regum Francorum (Par. 1677, reprinted by Chiniac, Par. 1778, 2 vols, fol.); a new edition has been given by Pertz, in the Monumenta German. Histor. vol. iii. (Hanov. 1835, fol.) Although this is the only work of which Benedict is known to have been the author, others are also attributed to him:—1st, The Collection of Decretals bearing the name of Isidore, bishop of Seville. 2dly, The Collection of Decretals, to which Hincmar, bishop of Laon, appeals in his defence against his namesake of Rheims, and which is incorrectly said by the latter to have been brought from Rome by Angilramn, bishop of Metz.

BENEDICTUS, or BENEDICTI, an eminent French civilian, who died, it is supposed, in 1520; and was the author of a Commentary on the Chapter in the Decretals (De Testamentis), a work abounding with learning, but composed without regard to method or arrangement.

BENEDICTUS, (John,) a physician, on the recommendation of Isaac Casaubon, named professor of Greek at Saumur, where he died in 1664, having filled the chair with great reputation. He published an edition of Lucian, with a Latin translation, in 1619, 8vo; also an edition of Pindar, 1620, 4to; and he made a translation of Horace into Greek verse, which has never been printed.

Another John Benedictus, also a physician, published at Cracow, in 1530, a Latin treatise on the Treatment of the Sweating Sickness, recently introduced into Germany from England.

BENEFIAL, (Mark, 1684—1764,) a painter, born at Rome, of great talents, though unequal in his performances, which Lanzi attributes rather to negligence than deficiency of powers. Opinions in Rome vary as much at this day as they did when Benefial was alive regarding his merit. He is by some considered as a painter without genius or skill. He is buried in the Pantheon. (Lanzi, Stor. Pitt. ii. 196; Pilkington's Dictionary by Fuseli; Bryan's Dict.)

BENEFIELD, (Sebastian,) an English divine of the seventeenth century, born at Prestonbury, in Gloucestershire, in 1559; fellow of Corpus Christi college, Oxford, and Margaret professor of divinity in that university, in 1613. He held this appointment with great reputation until 1626, when he resigned it, and retired to his rectory of Meysey-Hampton in Gloucestershire. There he spent the remainder of his life in a pious and devout retreat from the world. He died there, August 24, 1630. He was a decided Calvinist, but his knowledge of the fathers and the schoolmen was unequalled in the university. In 1613 he published a Commentary or Exposition on the First Chapter of the Prophecy of Amos. This work was translated into Latin by the learned Henry Jackson, of Corpus, and printed at Oppenheim, in 1615. Subsequently Benefield published Expositions upon the two succeeding chapters of Amos, and other works of less importance.

BENEKENDORF, (Charles Frederic von,) descended from a noble family in Brandenburg, born in 1720, at the family estate of Blumenfeldt, where he died in 1788. He wrote on political and rural economy, with a practical knowledge that long gave his works a standard reputation; but want of precision and brevity, with other obvious defects, caused them gradually to be neglected. He wrote, also, Traits from the Life of King Frederic William I., with various anecdotes of important events and remarkable individuals during his reign, (German,) 8vo, Berlin (10 parts), 1787, 1791;—a work more worthy of credit than many, or most similar collections. (Baut. in Ersch und Gruber.)

BENELLI, (Anthony Peregrino, Sept. 5, 1771—August 26, 1830,) an Italian musician, born at Forli, much admired in London, in 1798, both as a composer and a singer. During a residence of some years at Berlin, he wrote his Letters on Music, published in the Musical Journal of Leipsic, which excited a controversy between him and Spontini, whose compositions he had attacked. The most excellent of his works are masses. He was also very successful in a *Pater Noster* for five voices, a *Salve Regina*, an *Ave Maria*, and a *Stabat Mater*. (Biog. Univ. Suppl.)

BENESCH, (Benedict,) a Bohemian ecclesiastic in the fourteenth century, famous for a history of his native country. (Born Abhandl. einer Privatges. ii. p 315.)

BENESE, (Richard,) a canon of Merton, in Surrey, before the dissolution of monasteries, then rector of All Saints, Honey-lane, London, and, subsequently, prebendary of Lincoln. He was author of a little work on mensuration, entitled, A Tretis of Measuring Land, as well Wood-land as Plow-land. There are several editions of this work, one in quarto, and the others in duodecimo, which last are abridgements. The quarto edition is very rare, but a copy of it is in the library of the Royal Society.

BENETTI, (John Dominic,) a physician of Ferrara, where he was born, Feb. 3, 1658. He printed a singular work, connecting medical precepts with Romish religious ceremonies, entitled, Corpus Medico-Morale, divisum in duas Partes. Prima continet Adnotationes in J. Bascarini Med. Ferr. Dispensationum Medico-Moralium Canones XII., totidemque Explanationes de Jejunio quadrigesimali. Secunda continet Append. de Missâ et de Horis Canonicis, Additionem ad Parochos Monialium, Confessores, et Medicos, ubi de Confessione viaticâ et extremâ Unctione, quantum ad Medicos attinet. Corollaria, Additiones, et Complementum de Penitentiis ac de Oratione, Mantuæ, 1718, 4to.

BENETUS, (Cyprian,) an Aragonese Dominican, who died in 1522, and left, among other works, De prima Orbis Sede, Romæ, 1522; Aculeus contra Judeos, *ib.* 1515, 4to; Oratio contra Dogmata D. Lutheri, cum ejus Imago et Scripta Romæ exurerentur, *ib.* 1521. (Fabricius.)

BENEVENT, (Jerome de,) a French official in the seventeenth century, who translated the Phœnix of Claudian, and wrote some pieces upon subjects of temporary interest. (Biog. Univ.)

BENEVOLI, (Horace,) a composer of the seventeenth century, who surpassed all the masters of his time in writing for four, and even six choirs. A mass of his, composed on the cessation of the plague at Rome, for six choirs, of four parts each, the score consisting of twenty-four different parts, was performed in St. Peter's. The singers, amounting to more than two hundred, were arranged in different circles round the dome, the sixth choir occupying the summit of the cupola. Benevoli seems to have died before the commencement of the eighteenth century. (Mus. Biog. Dict. of Mus.)

BENEVOLI, (Anthony,) a celebrated Italian surgeon, born in 1685, who devoted himself especially to the diseases of the eye, and to the treatment of hernia. He died May 7, 1756, having published:—Lettere sopra due Osservazioni fatte intorno alle Cattaratta, Flor. 1722, 8vo. Nuove Proposizioni intorno alle Caroncula dell' Urethra, volgarmente dettè Carnosità, Flor. 1724, 4to. Tre Dissertazioni dell' Origine dell' Ernia intestinale: intorno alle piu frequenti Cazione dell' Iscuria, sopra il Leucoma, aggiuntivi quaranta Osservazioni, Flor. 1747, 4to, translated into Dutch, with notes by J. B. Sandifort, La Haye, 1770, 8vo.

BENEZET, (Anthony,) born at St. Quentin's, in Picardy, on the 31st of January, 1713, of protestant parents, and removed, after two years, to London. In 1731 he and his family went over to America, and settled at Philadelphia, where they became quakers. In early life he was in business, but all his latter years were given up to charity. The negroes especially were objects of his pious care; and as a large body of them wept around his remains on their way to the grave, an officer exclaimed,—*I would rather be Benezet in his coffin, than Washington in his glory.* This excellent man died on the 8th of May, 1784, having published some tracts on Guinea and the Slave Trade, between 1762 and 1771; a short Account of the Religious Society of Friends, 1780; a Dissertation on the Plainness and Simplicity of the Christian Religion, 1782; also some tracts against the Use of Ardent Spirits, and Observations upon the Aboriginal Inhabitants of America. (Allen's American Biog. Dict.)

BENFATTO, (Lewis, 1551—1611,) a painter, known by the name of dal Friso, a sister's son, and for many years the guest, of Paul Veronese, by whom he was instructed in the art. At first he was a servile copyist of his great preceptor, but afterwards he assumed a more easy manner, yet never advanced beyond the rank of an expert imitator. (Lanzi, Stor. Pitt. iii. 149. Bryan's Dict.)

BENGEL, (John Albert,) a Lutheran theological critic, of the Pietist school, born in June 1687, at Winnenden, in Wirtemberg. He died 1752, respected as a great authority by contemporary theologians, and esteemed by all who knew him for a conscientious discharge of his public duties, and for a blameless private life. He published good editions of Cicero's Epistolæ ad Diversos, and of Chrysostom's books, De Sacerdotio, but he became celebrated from a critical edition of the New Testament, which appeared in 1734, and was founded upon very careful and extensive inquiries, both personally and by means of correspondence. This work, to which was appended an Apparatus Criticus, created a great sensation in the theological world, from its superiority to preceding German editions, but encountered considerable critical opposition from C. B. Michaelis, S. Baumgarten, and others. Later German critics have objected to him, that his system of criticism is too confined, and its spirit too practical. His translation of the New Testament into German is a failure, from his too great anxiety to be faithful, and from his often preserving even the order of the original words. A stiffness and poverty of style is to be remarked in all his writings in his native language.

Bengel also wrote upon the Apocalypse. In that book he sought the final development of prophecy, which he regarded as the principal object of revelation. He was betrayed, however, by this opinion, into speculations equally original and extravagant; he believed, for instance, that the world would exist for exactly 7777½ years, and that its end would be in the summer of 1836. Bengel's authority, as a critic, has been long eclipsed by subsequent writers: but it is to some of his religious ideas that the Pietists of Wirtemberg, and indeed of the south of Germany generally, owe their peculiar character.

BENGER, (Elizabeth Ogilvy,) a female of considerable genius, daughter of a purser in the navy, born at Wells in 1778, where her mother resided. Her literary tastes seem to have been early developed; and as, from the straitened resources of her parents, books were out of her reach, she used as a child to stand at the window of the only bookseller's shop in her native town, to read the open pages of the new publications there displayed, returning day after day to examine whether by good fortune a leaf of any of them might have been turned over. In 1802, she prevailed upon her mother to remove to London, her father having died in 1796, where, by the kindness of some literary friends, who fully appreciated her merits, she was brought forward and enabled to mix with persons of superior and congenial minds. Her first literary production was a poem on the abolition of the slave trade; she afterwards published two novels anonymously; but the works by which she will be hereafter known are her Memoirs of Mary Queen of Scots, the Queen of Bohemia, Mrs. Elizabeth Hamilton, and John Tobin; also a Life of Anne Boleyn. She died on the 9th of January, 1827. (Ann. Biog. 1828.)

BENGI, (Anthony,) a French lawyer, possessed of a manorial estate, born in 1569. At the age of six-and-twenty he succeeded the famous Cujas, professor of law at the university of Bourges, and had often two thousand scholars. He died in 1616, leaving unfinished the Traité des Bénéfices, which his grandson, an advocate in Paris, completed, and published in 1659. (Biog. Univ.)

BENGUAFIT, or more commonly, ABENGUEFIT, called by Choulant (Handbuch der Bücherkunde für die Aeltere Medicin) IBN GUEFIT, but said by Reiske (Add. to D'Herbelot, vol. iv. p. 590,) to be more correctly spelled IBN VAFID, an

Arabic physician of uncertain date, and of whose life no particulars are known. He is supposed by Sprengel (Hist. de la Méd.) to have lived in the time of Rhazes, viz. about the end of the ninth century A.D., or of the third century A.H., because he is quoted by the younger Serapion (cap. 120), who lived about the end of the eleventh century A.D., and of the fifth A.H.; but it would have been more correct, as Serapion lived two centuries after Rhazes, if he had merely said that he must have lived some time before the time of Serapion. (Kühn. Additam. ad Ind. Medicor. Arab. à J. A. Fabricio in Bibl. Græc. vol. xiii. Exhibitum, Manip. i.) He is the author of a little work, De Virtutibus Medicinarum et Ciborum, which has never been published in Arabic, but of which a Latin translation by Gerardus Cremonensis was appended to several editions of Mesue. It first appeared in a separate form, Argent. 1531, fol. ap. J. Schottum, and at the end is added the Tacui, Sanitatis, and Alkindi's treatise, De Medicam. Compos. It treats of the mode of ascertaining the properties of medicines by their various external qualities. Haller (Bibl. Med. Pract.) calls it of little worth. Mr. Adams speaks more favourably of it, (Append. to Barker's Lempriere, 1838,) and says it contains an useful outline of the principles of ancient pharmacy and the materia medica, but is mostly taken from the introductory books to Galen's work, De Simplicium Medicamentorum Temperamentis et Facultatibus. He adds that his account of the tastes is derived in a great measure from the Timæus of Plato, and Theophrastus De Causis Plantarum, lib. vi.

BENI, (Paul,) born in Candia, about 1552, but bred and educated at Gubio, in the dukedom of Urbino; hence he called himself *Eugubinus*. His first intention was to become a Jesuit, but being restrained from publishing a commentary, thought rather free, upon the banquet of Plato, he withdrew from the society. His reputation, however, obtained for him several appointments in succession, the last of which, that of professor of elegant literature at Padua, miserably frustrated the hopes conceived of him. His long flow of words, without meaning, displeased his auditors; they left him; and after having held the office for thirteen years, he resigned, retaining one half of the liberal salary. He died at Padua in 1625, leaving his library and fortune to the Theatines of that city. He was an able man, of great reading, and some genius, but of a disposition that led him into endless controversy and violent disputes. His works are numerous, some of which have never been published, and some are little known. Of those given to the public, a general collection appeared at Venice, in 5 vols, fol. 1622. Among them may be noticed, a Comparison between Homer, Virgil, and Tasso; a Defence of the last poet's *Jerusalem*, against the censures of the Academy *della Crusca;* a Defence of Guarini's *Pastor fido;* the *Anti-Crusca*, being an attack upon the famous philological Italian academy. This piece is not without foundation, but it elicited a very sharp reply from Orlando Pescetti; which, in its turn, received an answer from Beni, under the name of Michelangelo Fonte. Besides these Italian works, Beni left in Latin, a Discourse upon Plato's *Timæus;* an able apologetic disputation upon Baronius's *Annals;* an Enquiry into the Mode of Terminating Disputes upon Grace and Free-will; and a disputation to display the superiority of prose to verse in dramatic composition. The last two productions occasioned considerable commotion. The book upon grace and free-will was put into the *Index;* and Faustino Summo vigorously defended dramatic verse. Beni did not answer him. Another of Beni's Latin works was, A Discourse upon the Writing of History, which takes great liberties with Livy, a boldness thought unusually offensive, because occurring at Padua. Here, again, therefore, the critic found more assailants than admirers. His life, in fact, was one continued course of literary strife, and nature seems to have meant him for a soldier rather than a scholar. (Biog. Univ.)

BENIERE, (Thomas, 1663—1693,) a young sculptor, born in England, of French parents. His models and small works in marble are much commended. The anatomical figure, formerly exhibited in the generality of the shops of apothecaries, was taken from his original model. He carved portraits in marble from the life for two guineas. He lived and died near the Fleet Ditch. (Walpole's Anecdotes of Painting, by Dallaway, iii. 206.)

BENIGNO, or BENIGNUS, abbot of Vallombrosa, in Italy, who died in 1236, leaving some historical and devotional works. (Pocciantius Script. Florent.)

BENIGNUS, an Irish prelate, in the fifth century, the alleged successor to St. Patrick in the see of Armagh. Some accounts, however, make Benignus to have been the third prelate, Moctheus having been Patrick's immediate successor. Benignus appears to have been the son of a wealthy person in Meath, who gave Patrick a kind reception. The young man was probably baptized by the great Irish apostle by the name of Stephen, which, accordingly, is one of the appellations given to him. The Latin form of his name is thought to have come from the Irish word *Bin*, meaning *sweet*, a designation fixed upon him from his natural sweetness of disposition, and his great fondness for St. Patrick. His succession to the see of Armagh is placed in 455, but William of Malmesbury makes him to have relinquished it before the end of life, and to have died a hermit at Ferlingmore, near Glastonbury. (Usser. Brit. Eccl. Antiq. Biog. Brit.)

BENINCORI, (Angelo Maria, Mar. 1779—December 30, 1821,) an eminent musical composer, born in the north of Italy. (Biog. Univ. Suppl.)

BENINI, (Sigismond,) a Cremonese painter, born about 1675, who excelled in landscapes, but was very deficient in figures, which are never introduced into his pictures without lessening their value. (Lanzi, Stor. Pitt. iv. 132. Bryan's Dict.)

BENINI, (Vincent,) a physician, born at Bologna in 1713, who appears to have cultivated poetry rather than medicine, and published the poem of Fracastorius de Morbo Gallico, in Italian verse, La Sifilida, Padua, 1730, 4to, which has been preferred to many other translations.

BENISLAWSKI, (Constantine,) a Polish poet, who wrote in praise of Catherine II. of Russia, Vilna, 1780, 4to. (Bentkowski.)

BENITEZ, (John Montero,) a Spanish ecclesiastic, who became bishop of Gaeta, in the kingdom of Naples, and died in 1680, at Granada. During his stay at Madrid, on the business of his church, he published a work of considerable use in Spain, because upon questions hitherto little discussed there, entitled, Tratados Militares que contienen la Jurisdiccion Ecclesiastica que tienen los Vicarios generales de los Exercitos de Mar y Tierra, Madrid, 1679, 4to. (Antonio.)

BENITZKY, (Alexander Petrovitch,) a Russian writer of very considerable promise, born in 1780, who began in 1807, Thalia, a literary miscellany, of which, owing to his death, only one volume made its appearance. Great expectations were formed of him, but he was cut off either in 1808 or the following year.

BENIVIENI, (Anthony,) a physician of the fifteenth century, a native of Florence, where he died Nov. 11, 1502. Haller regards him as the best observer of his time. He abandoned speculative conjectures, and attentively watched the operations of nature. He describes diseases with precision, but is rather too laconic. He foresaw the advantages which would accrue from a cultivation of pathological anatomy. Only one work is known as his, and it contains one hundred and seventeen cases, many of which are of great interest. De abditis nonnullis ac Mirandis Morborum et Sanationum Causis, Flor. 1506 and 1507, 4to; Paris, 1528, fol.; Basil. 1529, 8vo.

BENIVIENI, (Jerome,) the youngest of three distinguished brothers, born at Florence in 1453, where he died in 1542, at the advanced age of eighty-nine. In conjunction with Lorenzo de' Medici, Poliziano, the brothers Pulci and others, he laboured to give Italian poetry that popularity which a preference for classical studies had hitherto denied it. His works are upon the divine love, treated after the fashion of the times, according to the imagination and ideas of Plato. They were collected in Florence in 1519, and in Venice, 1524, with the addition of his famous Canzone dell' Amor Celeste e Divino, and the commentary of Pico della Mirandola, both of which have been translated into French by Chappuis, and printed together with the Discorso dell' Amore Onesto, by Marsilio Ficino, also translated into French. They are in all sorts of metre, and of great merit.

Of the two elder brothers of Benivieni, *Dominic*, the eldest, was canon of the cathedral of Florence, very learned in theology, and a great friend of Savonarola, in defence of whose doctrine he wrote a treatise and a dialogue.

BENJAMIN of TUDELA, a Jewish rabbi of the twelfth century, a native of the town in Navarre from which he is usually named. Few personal details of his life have been preserved, but he is believed to have died at Saragossa about A.D. 1173, shortly after his return from the peregrinations, the written account of which has been principally instrumental in handing his name down to posterity as one of the earliest travellers of the more modern ages. Considerable diversity of opinion has existed respecting the value and authenticity of this narrative, some even maintaining that

Benjamin never travelled at all in the countries which he describes, but only drew up a compilation from the relation of others. This hypothesis, however, is clearly disproved by examination of the work, though the author does not at all times sufficiently distinguish those regions which he personally visited, from those which he notices apparently from hearsay. There can be no doubt that he visited Bagdad, and penetrated far into Persia, though it does not appear so clearly whether he reached India. Most of the parts of Europe, Asia, and Africa, then known, are mentioned in the course of the work, either from personal observation or from information imparted by others. His account of the imperial court of Constantinople under the emperor Manuel, is curious and interesting; and his description of the far-famed Bagdad, which, though greatly fallen from the high estate which it held under Haroon-al-Rasheed and his immediate successors, still displayed under the later Abbassides a spectacle of pomp and magnificence far surpassing the rude courts of western Europe, gives the only contemporary details now extant on the ceremonial and etiquette observed in the palaces of the last commanders of the faithful. But the principal objects of his attention and solicitude, in all the countries which he visited, were the Jews therein resident. Their numbers and quality are every where mentioned with tedious minuteness, and the power and state of the "Prince of the Captivity," a sort of subordinate Jewish monarch, who resided at Bagdad under the protection of the khalif, and exercised a limited authority over the Jews of the surrounding countries, are dwelt upon with all the pride and partiality of an Israelite, venerating this last relic of the former rule of the kings of Judah. The latest edition of the Itinerary of Benjamin of Tudela, is that of Asher, 8vo, London and Berlin, of which the first volume, containing the Hebrew text and an English translation, appeared in the year 1840; a second volume of notes is announced as in preparation. The preface to this edition enumerates twenty-two other editions or versions; the first in Hebrew only, printed at Constantinople in 1543; the second, and most accurate as to the Hebrew text, from which Asher's edition is principally taken, was printed at Ferrara in 1556, but is now exceedingly rare, only a single copy (that in the Oppenheim division of the Bodleian library at Oxford,) being known, according to Asher, to exist. The principal versions are the Latin ones of Arias Montanus (Antwerp, 1575,) and Constantine L'Empereur, (Leyden, 1633;) that of Baratier, in French, (1734;) and the English ones in Purchas's Pilgrims, vol. ii. (1625), and of Gerrans (1783), the last of which seems to have been undertaken principally with the view of confuting and weakening the authenticity of the author.

BENJAMIN has been the name of many Jewish writers.

Benjamin de Halia, (Rabbi,) wrote, or rather arranged a work, entitled, Hayerayin, (Of those who fear;) and wrote himself a treatise on judicial causes, entitled, Sepher Yediduth, (The Book of Delight.)

Benjamin, (Rabbi, de Ardono Germanus,) wrote in German a book entitled Mitzvoth Nashim, (Precepts of Women,) which was translated into Italian by Rabbi Jacob ben Rabbi Elchanan, and printed at Venice in 1652.

Benjamin, (Rabbi, Ashkenazi,) (German,) wrote a Makhzor (breviary) of prayers for the use of the German nation.

Benjamin, (Rabbi, Zeeb,) author of a work of questions and answers, to which he gave his own name, printed at Venice, 4to, 1534, the same year in which it was written.

Benjamin, (Rabbi, ben Rabbi Judæ Romanus,) whose name appears in the preface to the Commentary on the Grammar of Rabbi David Kimchi. The real author, however, was Rabbi Elias Levita, the German, who complains in another place of the theft of his servant. He had been entrusted to copy the book by his master, who was shut up by the prevalence of the plague in Padua, and took advantage of this circumstance to publish the book in his own name, 8vo, Venice, 1504. The work has several times been reprinted, with and without the text of Kimchi.

Benjamin, (Rabbi, Judæus,) a Greek, who wrote in his own language a Treatise on the Composition of Medicines and their Preparation. A fragment of this is given in the Bibliotheca Vaticana. No. 282, p. 437, with this title, *Σκευασιαι κεκκινων Ζουλαπιων εμωλαστρων συντεθεισαι εις την Ἑλλαθα παρα Ιουδαιου Βενιαμιν.*

Benjamin, (Rabbi, Judæus,) wrote Shaare et Hayyim, (Gatesi of the Tree of Life,) and Kiryath Oz (City of Strength).

Benjamin, (Rabbi, ben Rabbi Joseph

Arignano,) a printer in the house of Antonio Balada at Rome, in 1545, where he printed several Hebrew works.

Benjamin, (Rabbi, ben Mosis,) a Karaite, an Arab by nation, and wrote in Arabic. (Bartolocco.)

BENJEZLA, a christian physician of Bagdad, called by Abul-Pharaj (Hist. Dym. p. 240) YAHIA BEN ISA BEN JEZLA. Having a great desire to learn logic, and not being able to find any Christian learned enough to teach him, he applied to Abon Ali ben Al-Walid, chief of the sect of the Motazali, (see Pocock, Spec. Hist. Anb.) who at last converted him to Islam, A.H. 466, (A.D. 1073-4.) Upon this he wrote a treatise in favour of his new religion, in a letter addressed to Elias, a christian priest, which does not appear to be still extant. He was afterwards secretary to Abon Abdalla Al-Damagáni, chief judge to the khalif Moctadi, and died A.H. 473, (A.D. 1080-1.) It should be mentioned in his favour, that notwithstanding his apostasy he is not only said by Abul-Pharaj (*loco cit.*) to have given gratuitous advice to the sick, but also to have provided them with medicine for nothing. Among his more celebrated works, Abul-Pharaj mentions two by name, both of which are still extant in MS.; the first, called Menháj, (Methodus,) is a treatise in alphabetical order on different medicines, articles of food, &c. It has never been translated, but exists in MS. both in Paris and Oxford. Casiri mentions (tom. i. p. 297) a commentary on this work by an anonymous author. His other work is entitled Takwím-al-Abdan, (Rectificatio Corporum,) which was translated into Latin by Farraguth, a Jew, and published, Argent. 1532, folio, with the following title, Tacuini Ægritudinum et Morborum fere omnium Corporis Humani, cum Curis eorundem, Buhahylyha Byngezla Auctore. This also exists in MS. both at Paris and Oxford, and in the copy at Paris there are notes by Beitár. Some persons, as Freind and Astruc, have asserted this work to be the same, or nearly so, with that called Tacuini Sanitatis Elluchasem Elimithar, (see ELLUCHASEM;) but Haller says (Biblioth. Med. Pract.) that he compared the two works, and found them entirely different. It consists of tables, in which are ranged the different parts of the human body in order from head to foot, together with the diseases to which they are liable, and the remedies proper for each. It served as a model for Abulfeda in composing his geographical work, entitled Takwím-al-Boldán, (Rectificatio Provinciarum.) His life is found in Ibn Abi Baibia, Oioún al' Ambá fi Tabacát al-Atebbá, (Fontes Relationum de Classibus Medicorum.)

BENKOWITZ, (Charles Frederic,) a light miscellaneous German writer, formerly popular, but now almost forgotten, born in 1764, who committed suicide at Glogau, in 1807. His works consist of novels, stories, poems, a critical essay on Klopstock's Messiah, humorous pieces, Travels in Italy, the German Don Quixote, the New Westphalian Robinson, and a History of an African Ape, called Muley Assan, formerly Voltaire, Berlin, 1807. His narrative is lively and agreeable, but he had little originality or vigour, and has identified himself so completely with the maudlin sentimentality fashionable when he wrote, that a generation which has risen superior to this weakness has all but forgotten him.

BENN, (James,) whose name is variously written, *Benedicti*, *Bennet*, *Bene*, and *Biort*, a Scottish prelate, who having early taken orders, became archdeacon of St. Andrews. In 1328, while at Rome, he was elected by the canons of St. Andrews their bishop, but before information of this choice had reached him, he obtained collation to that see at the hands of pope John XXII. In 1329 he crowned king David II. and was shortly after created lord great chamberlain of Scotland. On the invasion of Edward Baliol he fled into Flanders, and died at Bruges on the 22d of September, 1332. (Keith's Scottish Bishops, by Russell. Crawford's Great Officers of State.)

BENN, (William,) a puritan minister, born in Cumberland in November, 1600, and settled at Dorchester, in the rectory of All Saints, from 1629 to 1662, when he was ejected under the Act of Uniformity. There is a treatise of his against Mr. Francis Bampfield in Defence of the Christian Sabbath against the Jewish, 8vo, 1672; and a volume of his Sermons on Soul Prosperity was published after his death, 1683.

BENNATI, (Francis,) an Italian physician, born in October 1798, who died March 10, 1834, and particularly studied the human voice. He published, Recherches sur le Mécanisme de la Voix Humaine, Paris, 1832, 8vo; Recherches sur les Maladies qui affectent les Organes de la Voix Humaine, Paris, 1832, 8vo; a second edition of this work, united to the preceding, was published as Etudes

Physiologiques et Pathologiques sur les Organes de la Voix Humaine, Paris, 1833, 8vo.

BENNET, (John,) an English composer, eminent in his line, who printed in 1599, Madrigals for Four Voices. (Mus. Biog.)

BENNET, (Christopher,) an English physician, born at Raynton, in the county of Somerset, in 1617, and educated at Lincoln college, Oxford. He made an extensive practice in London, and died there in 1655, of consumption, a disease to which he had paid particular attention. Besides some works, once popular, relating to it, he published Muffett's Health's Improvement, or the Nature, Method, and Manner of Preparing all Manner of Food used in this Nation, Lond. 1655, 1746, 8vo.

BENNET, (Benjamin,) a presbyterian minister, of great influence among the dissenters, born in 1674, at Temple-hall, in Leicestershire, and pastor of a large congregation at Newcastle-upon-Tyne. Here he continued till his death, on September 1, 1726, very popular in his own town; and by his treatise, entitled Irenicum, or a Review of some late Controversies about the Trinity, published in 1722, was instrumental in causing a general renunciation of that doctrine in the body of English nonconformists to which he belonged. His other works are, a Memorial of the Reformation, 8vo, 1721; a Defence of that work, 8vo, 1723; and his Christian Oratory, a book of which the title would mislead as to the nature of the contents, the word *oratory* being used in the sense of a plan for meditation and prayer. This was long a very favourite work in the English presbyterian body.

BENNET, (Henry, earl of Arlington,) a distinguished statesman in the reign of Charles the Second, born in 1618, son of Sir John Bennet, of Arlington in Middlesex, educated at Christchurch, Oxford, and while there distinguished by his poetical compositions. He entered public life at the beginning of the civil wars, when the king being at Oxford, he was appointed under-secretary to lord Digby, secretary of state. He fought also in the king's armies; and when the royal cause was hopeless, he went abroad, and was residing in Spain as agent to Charles II., when that monarch was restored. Being recalled soon afterwards, he was appointed keeper of the privy purse, and in 1662 principal secretary of state. In 1664 he was created baron Arlington, and in 1672 earl of the same place. He was one of that corrupt ministry called the *Cabal*, from the initials of the titles of those who composed it; and when this was broken up, he found himself under the necessity of retiring from a political situation, but was appointed lord-chamberlain. In 1679 he was named of the new council then formed, and on the accession of James II. was continued in his office of lord-chamberlain. He was then, however, near the end of his life, dying on July 28, 1685. He was haughty, timid, and slow, but penetrating, cautious, and specious, suspected of popery, but strict in all the outward observances of protestantism, and anxious to make the king equally so from a selfish fear of ruining his affairs. He was buried at Euston in Suffolk, an estate now enjoyed by the duke of Grafton, descended from his only child Isabella, who married the first duke of Grafton, one of the illegitimate children of king Charles the Second.

The eldest brother of the earl of Arlington, Sir John Bennet, was also advanced to the peerage by king Charles the Second, by the title of lord Ossulston; and the son of the first lord Ossulston was created earl of Tankerville by king George the First, soon after his accession.

BENNET, (Sir John,) an eminent civilian of the reigns of Elizabeth and James the First, grandfather of the two brothers, the earl of Arlington and lord Ossulston, judge of the prerogative court of Canterbury, and chancellor to the archbishop of York. His great professional success did not, however, secure to him an old age of ease and honour. He was charged with corrupt practices, and being convicted, he was deprived of his offices, imprisoned, and sentenced to pay a fine of 20,000*l.* He never recovered from this disgrace, dying, says Mr. Lodge, in the third volume of his valuable Illustrations of British History, in obscurity and indigence, in the parish of Christchurch, London, in 1627.

BENNET, (Robert, B.D.) a divine ejected under the Act of Uniformity, in 1662, from the rectory of Waddesden in Buckinghamshire, to which he had been presented by lord Wharton, a great patron of the puritan clergy. He died at Abingdon in 1687. A work of his has been much esteemed, entitled, A Theological Concordance of the Synonymous Words in Scripture, 8vo, 1657.

BENNET, (Thomas,) a controversial divine in the reigns of William and Anne, born at Salisbury, on May 7,

1673, and sent to St. John's college, Cambridge, in 1688. He applied himself particularly to Hebrew literature, and in 1695 wrote, in that language, a copy of verses on the death of queen Mary, which was printed. In 1699 he published an Answer to the Dissenters' Pleas for Separation. In the next year he became rector of St. James's, Colchester, and taking up his residence in that town, he became an assiduous parochial minister. He now published a Discourse on Schism, the object of which was to show the guilt of schism, and to fix that guilt on the dissenters. Replies being made to it, he published a Defence and an Answer to the objections against it. He also attacked the Roman catholics, in a book which he entitled a Confutation of Popery, and the Quakers, in a Confutation of Quakerism. He wrote besides, in quick succession, tracts on baptism, liturgies, and clerical rights. About 1714 he became D.D. and about the same time gave up his church at Colchester, and removed to London, where he was chosen lecturer at St. Olave's in the Borough, and morning preacher at St. Lawrence Jewry. In 1716 he attacked the principles of the nonjurors, in a pamphlet entitled, The Nonjurors' Separation from the Public Assemblies of the Church of England, examined and proved to be Schismatical on their own Principles. He was soon after presented to the vicarage of St. Giles's, Cripplegate, where he quickly became involved in disputes with his parishioners on the rights of his church. In 1718 he engaged in the Trinitarian controversy, in an examination of Dr. Clarke's Scripture Doctrine of the Trinity. In 1726 he published a Hebrew grammar. He died of apoplexy on October 9, 1728.

BENNIGSEN, or BENNINGSEN, (Bentlin Levin Augustine Theophilus,) Imperial Russian general of cavalry, born in Hanover, in 1745; who first distinguished himself under Catherine II. in the war against the Poles, in 1794. Being concerned, in 1801, with the party that murdered the emperor Paul, Alexander gave him the government of Lithuania, and the command of a regiment, which he led to Austria against Napoleon; but the battle of Austerlitz ended the campaign before his arrival, and he returned to Russia. He subsequently made a conspicuous figure in most of the operations against France, and in 1815 he followed general Barclay de Tolly towards the Rhine with 150,000 men, but was stopped at Berlin by the news of the battle of Waterloo. He now took an opportunity of returning to his native country, where he died in 1826. He wrote, Thoughts on some Points of Knowledge essential to an Officer of Light Cavalry, Riga, 1794, Wilna, 1805. (Militair Conversations Lexicon.)

BENNO, a cardinal and arch-presbyter of the Roman church in the eleventh century, famous among protestants for the biography of Hildebrand, or Gregory VII., and proportionably decried by Romanists. He was a German, a staunch partisan of Guibert, or Clement III. (ordinarily branded as an anti-pope,) and was one of the subscribers at the council, or, according to papal writers, schismatic *conciliabulum*, holden at Rome in 1098. No other particulars of his life are known, but 1085 is ordinarily named as the period in which he flourished. Being a contemporary, his Life of Gregory VII. (a Latin work, ill-written, and rather confused, occupying fifteen largely printed folio pages in the Frankfort edition of 1581,) is really very valuable, although some allowance must unquestionably be made for the bias under which it was written. Romanists, making the most of this advantage, treat Benno's life as a satire and a libel; but even if it were fairly deserving of such a character, there is no reason for slighting its testimony as to leading facts. The author may be fairly considered from his prominence and station as a person of integrity, though a warm partisan. Such men colour and conceal, but seldom invent. Their narratives, therefore, generally supply the truth to any discerning mind at the pains of sifting for it. Benno's Vita et Gesta Hildebrandi, was published in 1535, by Orthuinus Gratius, in the Fasciculus Rerum Expetendarum; by Flaccus Illyricus, in the Catalogus Testium Veritatis; by Reiner Reineccius, at Frankfort, in 1581, together with an ancient anonymous life of the emperor Henry IV.; and by Melchior Goldastus, among the Opuscula Anti-Gregoriana, at Hanover, in 1611. (Cave, Hist. Lit. Cent. Magdeb. Labb. et Coss. Concill. Biog. Univ. Du Pin. Eccl. Hist.)

BENO, or BENNO, bishop of Meissen, in the eleventh century, canonized in 1523, to the indignation of Luther, who then wrote his German tract, *The New Idol and Old Demon of Meissen.* During the quarrel of Henry IV. with Gregory VII., he sided at first with the emperor.

but he was afterwards reconciled to the pontiff. The Germans considered him as lord of rain and sunshine, hence they said of a promising field, *Bishop Beno has been this way.*

BENOIST, (P. V.) born in Anjou in 1758, known at the beginning of the French revolution by some articles on political economy, and subsequently employed by the imperial government in various national improvements. He published, Cléopâtre, Paris, 1789, 3 vols, 12mo; Le Cultivateur Anglais, *ib.* 1801, 18 vols, 8vo; and some more works. His wife, *Madame Benoist*, a pupil of David, the painter, exhibited some good pictures. (Biographie des Hommes Vivants.)

BENOIST, or BENOIT, (William Philip, 1725—1780,) a French engraver, who resided, during the latter part of his life, in London, where he died. Amongst his plates are portraits of Sir Isaac Newton and Alexander Pope. (Bryan's Dict.)

BENOIT, or BENOIST, (Elias,) historian of the Revocation of the Edict of Nantes, born of poor parents, at Paris, in 1640, and somewhat irregular in youth, but his habits quickly improved, and he became pastor of the protestant congregation at Alençon. While there, he had a controversy with a Jesuit named Larue, who garnished his Lent sermons with reflections on the Geneva Bible. When the edict of Nantes was revoked, Benoit left France, and became minister of the Walloon church at Delft, where he spent the rest of his life. Here availing himself of the MS. Memoirs of Tessereau, formerly secretary to Lewis XIV., he wrote his Histoire de l'Edit de Nantes, 5 vols in 2, 4to, Delft, 1693-95, a work which gives the history of the reformed church in France from the reign of Henry IV. to the year 1691, carefully and accurately written, but with a natural prejudice in favour of his persecuted brethren. He wrote also several controversial works, which appeared anonymously. In 1715 he retired from public life, and died in 1728. Some of his opinions in theology, criticism, and philosophy, were sufficiently singular, and have been preserved in an autobiographical memoir which he left behind him in MS. (Ersch und Gruber.)

BENOIT, or BENEDICT, (de Sainte Maure,) a troubadour of the time of Henry II., by whom, according to Robert Wace, he was engaged to write, in French verse, the History of the Dukes of Normandy. This work, consisting of 23,000 verses, begins from the first irruption of the Normans, under Hastings and De Bier, surnamed *Côte de fer*, and terminates with an account of the three children of William the Bastard. A copy of it is in the Harleian Collection (No. 1717). In Warton's Hist. Engl. Poetry (vol. ii. p. 235), this poem is treated as a mass of fables. But if we compare this author with the Norman historians who have preceded him, we shall find his statements to be in accordance with theirs. His work met with the greatest success, and preserved for a length of time a very high reputation. It was translated into prose in the fourteenth century, and afterwards dramatized. James Millet, in 1484, published it in folio, under the title of Destruction de Troyes la Grant. Tyrwhitt thinks Benoit the author of the life of Thomas à Becket, in the Harleian Collection, No. 3775. (De la Rue, Essais Historiques sur les Bardes. Hist. Lit. de France.)

BENOIT, (René,) a French divine, confessor to the unfortunate Mary Stuart, while resident in France, and her companion in returning to Scotland, but chiefly remarkable as a translator of the Bible into the vernacular tongue. He was born at Savernières, near Angers, in 1521, and published a French Bible, with marginal notes, chiefly taken from Vatablus, at Paris, in 1566, folio. He did not pretend to any skill in Hebrew or Greek, and his version was quickly decried as a mere copy of the Genevan, with some verbal changes. Another edition of it, however, appeared with an apology, in 2 vols, 4to, in 1588, when Benoit had already found his biblical labours no hindrance to his preferment, being appointed to the parochial benefice of St. Eustace's in Paris, in 1569, and to the royal professorship of theology in the college of Navarre, in 1587. His importance was augmented by such an extraordinary degree of popularity among his parishioners as gained him the title of *the market-people's pope*. Hence a censure, passed upon his version as a plagiarism from that of Geneva, in 1567, was rendered more severe in 1572, by his exclusion from the faculty, and this censure was ratified by Gregory XIII. While the faction of the *Seize* had possession of Paris, in 1591, Benoit took refuge in the camp of Henry IV., and he obtained considerable influence over that monarch's mind, being ultimately appointed his confessor. When, accordingly, Henry was thoroughly prepared for his politic conversion to Romanism, Benoit was one of the three parochial clergymen, employed with some ecclesiastics of superior degree, in the farcical *instruction* that was to throw an appearance of decency over this remarkable disavowal of protestantism. Benoit's various claims upon his royal master's favourable consideration were acknowledged in an appointment to the bishopric of Troyes; but the faction of the League exerted its influence successfully to prevent him from obtaining the usual bulls from Rome. The heterodoxies of his French Bible were alleged as the reason of this, but his zeal for the independence of the Gallican church has been considered as the real cause. But whatever might be the origin of Rome's hostility, it was found insurmountable; and accordingly, after enjoying the revenues of his bishopric during eleven years, Benoit found himself obliged, in 1604, to resign it. He lived until March, 1608, leaving a great character for eloquence and moral worth, and having occupied a large space in the public mind by his vernacular Bible, his connexion with Henry IV., his numerous publications upon questions of temporary interest, and his refusal to consider the Huguenots as heretics, before they had been formally proved such, or condemned by some better authority than the council of Trent, an assembly not recognised in France. (Biog. Univ. R. Simon. Hist. Crit. O. T. Smedley's Hist. Ref. Rel. in France.)

BENSEN, (Charles Daniel Henry,) professor of financial science at Würzburg, born in 1761, who lectured, with great applause, on criminal justice, police, and finance, and died at Würzburg in 1805. His works, which are chiefly on the subjects on which he gave lectures during his life, are highly valued. (Ersch und Gruber.)

BENSERADE, (Isaac de,) a French wit, remarkable for the skilful improvement of talents excellently fitted for amusing and flattering the great. His birth was at Lyons-la-Forêt, a small town of Normandy, in 1622, his father, apparently, being an attorney at Gisors, who then professed protestantism, but became a Romanist two years afterwards. Hence it was that the future poet was named after an Old Testament patriarch, instead of some saint, whom, according to Romish usage, he could adopt for a tutelary genius, and celebrate on the annual return of his festival, designated as his own name-day. The bishop, when young Benserade came for confirmation, shocked by his want of an enticement into this absurd superstition, asked him if he would not like to get rid of his Jewish name, and bear one fit for a Christian? "*Yes,*" replied the boy, "*if I could get anything by it.*" The prelate probably thought himself to have accidentally stumbled upon the key to the conversion of the Benserade family, and therefore prudently made no farther step towards providing the young candidate with a name-day. His father seems to have died early, leaving little or nothing behind him; but his mother claimed a relationship with cardinal Richelieu, which easily served as a passport to that minister's notice, probably on account of the family's conversion to Romanism, then a strong recommendation to patronage. From the cardinal, Benserade obtained a pension; and it might have been continued after his death by the duchess of Aiguillon, could the poet have prudently forborne from writing the following epigrammatic epitaph:—

> "*Cy gist, oui gist, par la mort bleu,*
> *Le cardinal de Richelieu,*
> *Et, ce qui cause mon ennui,*
> *Ma pension avec lui.*"

But one lady's condemnation of him as ungrateful and unfeeling, proved of no importance to Benserade. He was a perfect master of sycophancy, yet famous for plain dealing; that is to say, most likely, he never made any scruple of turning out less considerable members of a company for the amusement of those more considerable, and he did it admirably. He was inimitable also in making verses for court ballets, and in throwing an air of genius over other frivolous exertions of elevated station to kill time. Thus he became indispensable at court, and received as rewards a pension from the queen-mother, together with others from cardinal Mazarin, upon a bishopric and two abbeys. These various resources made him able to move among his elevated associates with a carriage of his own and suitable accompaniments, though he was always full of raillery on his poverty.

Among his sonnets, one to a young lady deserves notice, because it made a great noise. Benserade said that Job could reveal his grief, while *he* was obliged to suffer in silence. Voiture had written some such thing on Urania, and a comparison of the two divided all the court into Jobelins and Uranists. Benserade now fancied himself able to translate Ovid's Metamorphoses into rondeaux; a ridiculous undertaking, which proved a total failure, but he received 1000 louis from the king to have the work printed with proper vignettes and engravings. When he grew old, finding the taste for points and rondeaux gone by, he retired to Gentilly, where he passed his time in religious exercises, diversified by the writing of inscriptions to ornament his house and garden, which Voltaire thinks the best of his productions. He died in 1691.

Benserade was not a man of learning; but no one ever knew better how to cover his ignorance. "*Pray, sir,*" said a lady to him one night, in an opera-box, "*what is the difference between a dryad and a hamadryad?*" He was rather startled, but soon replied, "*Why, madam, the same that there is between a bishop and an archbishop.*" He had observed one of each waiting for her outside the door, being ashamed to show themselves in the house. He began early to print, and continued to do so till almost the end of his life. His works consist of five tragedies and one comedy; Paraphrase in verse on the Nine Lessons of Job; the Metamorphoses, in rondeaux; Æsop's Fables, in quatrains; the translation of almost all the Psalms; and fugitive pieces, collected in two vols, in 1697. (Bayle.)

BENSLEY, (Thomas,) an eminent printer, at the beginning of the nineteenth century, who "demonstrated to foreigners that the English press can rival and even excel the finest works that have graced the continental annals of typography." (Nichols. Lit. Anecd. Gent.'s Mag.)

BENSO, (Julius, 1601—1668,) a painter, born at Genoa, who excelled all his school in painting architecture and perspective. (Lanzi, Stor. Pitt. v. 267. Bryan's Dict.)

BENSON, (George, D.D.) a learned English dissenting minister, born at Great Salkeld, in Cumberland, in September 1699, originally a Calvinist, but eventually an Arian. He died in 1763. He wrote, besides three Discourses, published when he was a Calvinist, and which he was afterwards anxious to suppress, A Defence of the Reasonableness of Prayer; An Account of the Burning of Servetus at Geneva, and of the Concern of Calvin in that Act; An Account of Archbishop Laud's Treatment of Dr. Leighton; A Dissertation on 2 Thess. ii. 1—12, against the Church of Rome; A Paraphrase and Notes on the Epistle to Philemon, in the manner of Mr. Locke; which was followed by Paraphrases and Notes, on the same plan, on the Epistles to the Thessalonians, Timothy, and Titus, and the Catholic Epistles. In 1735 he published a History of the First Planting of Christianity, in two vols, 4to. He wrote also the Reasonableness of the Christian Religion as delivered in the Scriptures; a Collection of Tracts against Persecution; a volume of Sermons; and a History of the Life of Jesus Christ, a posthumous work, published in 1764. To this work a portrait of the author is prefixed, and also Memoirs of his Life. He was not only respected among the dissenters, but some prelates of the church likewise gave him marks of favour and regard, as Herring, Hoadly, Butler, Benson, and Conybeare.

BENSON, (William,) best known as Auditor Benson, born in 1682, son of Sir William Benson, who was sheriff of London in 1707. He received a liberal education, travelled abroad, and on his return served the office of sheriff for the county of Wilts, 1710. He subsequently published a Letter on the Miseries of Sweden after her submission to arbitrary power, an evil, according to him, then to be apprehended in England. For this he was brought before the privy council, but no prosecution seems to have followed, and his pamphlet had an immense sale. On the accession of George I. Benson came into parliament for the borough of Shaftesbury, and his politics being agreeable to the Whig party, now in power, and intent upon grasping every public employment, he was chosen to supersede, as surveyor-general, in 1718, Sir Christopher Wren. This infamous slight upon the greatest of English architects, then advanced, besides, beyond most men in the vale of years, was quickly put to shame by public proof of the new surveyor-general's incompetency. He had reported that the House of Lords, and the Painted Chamber adjoining, were in danger of falling. On examination, both were found secure. The ministers now saw that a continuance of their friend as national architect was impossible; and the earl of Sunderland stifled a petition from the lords for his removal, by informing the house that his majesty would anticipate their wishes. Benson, however, had either been too valuable, or he was now too importunate, to be left inconsolable. A considerable debt due to the crown in Ireland was assigned to him, with a reversion to the office of auditor of imprests. This he enjoyed by outliving Mr. Edward Harley.

Apart from architecture and politics, Benson deserves respectful remembrance. In 1724 he published Virgil's Husbandry, with Notes, Critical and Rustic; and in 1739, Letters concerning Poetical Translations, and Virgil's and Milton's Arts of Verse; and soon after an edition of the Psalms in a Latin version, by Arthur Johnston, whom he preferred to Buchanan, a critical judgment which exposed him to the severe censure of Ruddiman. About the same time he promoted a design for erecting a monument in Westminster Abbey to the memory of Milton. He thus found sufficient matter for the pointed couplet of Pope:—

"On two unequal crutches propt he came,
Milton's on this, on that our Johnston's name."

He gave Dobson 1000*l*. for a Latin translation of the Paradise Lost. He also paid a debt of 200*l*. and the charges upon it, for which Elisha Smith, author of The Cure of Deism, was confined in the Fleet, merely from the satisfaction given to him by a perusal of the work. He encouraged Pitt to translate the Æneid; and his own translation of the second book of the Georgics, though not very poetical, is faithful.

It is said, that in the latter part of his life he conceived an utter aversion to books; having very much retired from society to a house which he had at Wimbledon, where he died in February 1754. (Chalmers.)

BENT, (John Vander, 1650—1690,) a Dutch painter, born at Amsterdam, at first pupil to Peter Wouwermans, and afterwards to Adrian Vander Velde, but his works may easily be mistaken for those of Nicholas Berghem. (Bryan's Dict. Biog. Univ.)

BENTHAM, (Edward,) a very learned and exemplary English divine, born in the college at Ely, July 23, 1707, and son of Samuel Bentham, vicar of Witchford, a small living near that city. Being one of a very numerous family, Dr. Smalridge, dean of Christchurch, Oxford, placed him in the school of that college; and when sixteen, he was matriculated of Corpus Christi college in that university, seemingly as bible-clerk. Subsequently he became in succession, vice-principal of Magdalen hall, and fellow of Oriel college. Of this latter society he was tutor during more than twenty years, to the great benefit of those under his care. In 1743, his unquestionable merits were rewarded by a stall in the cathedral of Hereford, and the services which he rendered to the chapter there were in perfect keeping with all that he had done in the whole course of his meritorious life. In 1763 he was reluctantly induced by Abp. Secker, and others who knew his qualifications, to accept the canonry of Christchurch, Oxford, to which the regius professorship of divinity is annexed; and he discharged its duties in a manner worthy of his whole life, until he died, in August 1776.

His published writings, besides occasional sermons, are An Introduction to Moral Philosophy, 8vo, 1745; Advice to a Young Man of Rank upon coming to the University; Reflections on Logic; Funeral Eulogies upon Military Men, from Thucydides, Plato, Lycias, and Xenophon, in the original Greek, with notes; De Studiis Theologicis Prælectio, 1764; Reflections upon the Study of Divinity, 8vo, 1771; De Vitâ et Moribus Johannis Burton, S.T.P. Etonensis; An Introduction to Logic, 8vo, 1773; and De Tumultibus Americanis, deque eorum Concitatoribus Senilis Meditatio. (Chalmers.)

BENTHAM, (James,) brother to Edward, a divine and ecclesiastical antiquary of the eighteenth century, passed from the grammar school at Ely to Trinity college, Cambridge, where he was admitted March 26, 1727. In 1733 he was presented to the vicarage of Stapleford, in Cambridgeshire, which he resigned in 1736, on being made minor canon in the church of Ely. He also held, at various times, three parochial benefices in Norfolk, and the rectory of Bow-Brickhill, in Buckinghamshire. To this last he was presented in 1783, and four years before that time he was collated by bishop Keene to a prebend of Ely. He died, November 17, 1794, at the age of 85, famed for a History of the Church of Ely, which he commenced soon after he became an officer of that cathedral, and published in 1771; a work held in deserved esteem, but at the time of its publication chiefly valued for the ample remarks which it contained on the various styles of ecclesiastical architecture found in the churches of England. The remarks which Mr. Bentham made on this subject invited a closer attention to them than had been hitherto known. There was a second edition of his history in 1812. Mr. Bentham's other publications were tracts, published at different times, recommending improvement in the culture and in the roads in the Isle of Ely.

There were two other brothers of the Benthams who were clergymen, and a fifth brother who was for many years printer to the University of Cambridge.

BENTHAM, (Jeremy,) an English jurisprudential and political writer, born in London, February 15, O. S., 1748. Both his father and grandfather were attorneys. His own infancy, like that of most persons who make studious men, was remarkable for a love of books, that led him, at three years of age, to amuse himself with Rapin's History of England, a taste magnified by his friends into a perusal of the work. At seven, he is said to have read Telemachus in French; and at thirteen, he was admitted of Queen's college, Oxford. Proceeding regularly onwards, he took his master's degree, March 27, 1767, and he voted at the election of 1768, before he was of age. To this extraordinary speed in education, his own precocity, no doubt, contributed, but it must have chiefly arisen from the weak partiality of a father, who could fancy him a reader of English history, when he was hardly out of his cradle; a fondness that left, as usual, indelible marks upon him through life. He was intended for a lawyer, his father's well-frequented office rendering him pretty secure of practice, and about 1772 he was called to the bar. Young men very often, on entering upon a laborious profession, and at length aware that inferiority must long be their lot, so shrink from the prospect before them, that if they can decline the struggle, they gladly do so. Bentham could decline it, for his father was wealthy; and although he meant him to be wealther still, by rising at the bar, yet he could maintain him and be proud of him, without any profession at all. The first exception taken by young Bentham to his new profession was founded upon the exorbitant charges laid upon suitors before the masters in chancery. He determined, at once, that his honesty was too great for an employment which rendered him a party to such impositions; and instead of working his way up to a condition in which he might have the power of checking them, he took the easier course of travelling about, and resolving to reform mankind. Nearly twenty years elapsed between his majority and the French revolution, during which period of preparation for important changes he was thrice upon the continent, residing each time chiefly in Paris. In the second of these visits he formed an intimate acquaintance with Brissot de Warville; and his connexions appear always to have run in a revolutionary channel. Helvetius, he had, indeed, read when he was a boy, with great eagerness and satisfaction; hence his mind had grown to maturity with a strong bias towards those principles which, since the rise of Voltaire, have made war upon the existing institutions of Europe. In 1792, Bentham lost his father, and inheriting from him a handsome independence, he could devote all the rest of life to such pursuits as were most congenial to his taste. He now abandoned, accordingly, every thought of the law as a profession, and only so far made use of his initiation into it, as promoted his exertions to place it altogether on a new footing. For this purpose, he produced a constant succession of works, which excited considerable attention, as they appeared, among persons given to change, or on the watch to supplant the party in power, and which impartial judges, however unfavourable to the author's general principles, have always considered as worthy, on many accounts, of serious attention. But although he was a rigid economist of time, anxious for the success of his theories, and ever careful to commit his meditations to paper, his habits appear to have been too excursive and impatient of the finishing strokes for the regular business of authorship. Hence his compositions rarely made an advantageous impression upon any who were not prepossessed in their favour; and he had accumulated an immense mass of matter, written without skill or care, without connexion or method, when he became acquainted at Bowood with Dumont, the marquis of Lansdowne's Swiss librarian, who had been obliged to quit his own country for France, and the latter for England. To his labours upon Bentham's effusions the public is indebted for the Treatises on Legislation, in a readable shape. The author proceeded in his career of writing and publishing until very near his death, which took place at his house in Queen's-square, Westminster, June 6, 1832. He was then in the eighty-fifth year of his age. Of his real character, those who did not know him personally, cannot easily form an accurate estimate. He was best known to speculators upon happiness attainable by man without revelation, and upon advantages attainable by states under a total overthrow of their existing institutions. Such persons offer nothing respecting him to an inquirer's notice, but an indiscriminating mass of eulogy. This is echoed also by the political party that was in opposition during most of his life, and was eagerly bent upon finding means to force itself into power. Foreigners, too, more or less unfavourable to the social state at home, or anxious for the character of superior liberality and illumination, have usually treated Bentham's works and memory with profound respect; indeed, with far greater deference than they have received in his own country. The great bulk of his own countrymen really took no great notice either of him or his writings. But it may safely be said of him, that he was a man of patient thought and good intentions, whose exertions aided in the amelioration of civil institutions, and may still be useful for that purpose. Whether his practical knowledge of human nature was sufficient for the ends that he had in view, may be fairly doubted. He spent his long life chiefly in London, easy in circumstances, and without a profession. Few persons come less into contact with the great mass of mankind than those who are so situated. It was his habit also to surround himself with individuals of sentiments congenial with his own, and abstain from reading attacks made upon him. Thus he preserved, through every stage, the self-complacency which parental fondness originally founded; and by keeping himself unacquainted with other men's opinions upon his theories, he had some sort of excuse for considering every thing that he did not approve as a mark of ignorance, illiberality, and bigotry. Had he known more of others, it may be charitably hoped, that his utilitarian and felicitarian speculations would have been seen at once as utopian dreams, unless they could be founded upon religion.

The following is a list of this remarkable man's publications:—A Fragment on Government; being an Examination of what is delivered on the Subject in Blackstone's Commentaries, 1776. A View of the Hard-Labour Bill, 1778. An Essay on the Usefulness of Chemistry, translated from Bergman, 1783. Defence of Usury; shewing the Impolicy of the present legal Restraints on the Terms of pecuniary Bargains, 1787. Letter to a Member of the National Convention, 1787. An Introduction to the Principles of Morals and Legislation, 1789. Draught of a New Plan for the Organization of the Judicial Establishments in France, 1790, Panopticon, 1791. Essay on Political Tactics, 1791. Truth *versus* Ashurst; or Law as it is contrasted with what is said to be; written 1792, printed 1823. Supply without Burden, 1795. Traités de Législation Civile et Pénale, publiées en François d'après les MSS. par Dumont, 1802. Letters to Lord Pelham on Penal Colonization; A Plea for the Constitution, against the New South Wales Colony, 1803. Scotch Reform considered, 1808. Defence of Economy against Burke, 1810-17. Defence of Economy against Rose, 1810-17. Elements of the Art of Packing, as applied to Special Juries, 1810-21. Théorie des Peines et des Récompenses, redigée en François, par Dumont, 1812. On the Law of Evidence, 1813. Essai sur la Tactique des Assemblées Politiques, par Dumont, 1816. *Swear not at all;* containing an Exposure of the Needlessness and Mischievousness, as well as anti-Christianity, of the Ceremony of an Oath, with Proof of the Abuses of it, especially in the University of Oxford, printed 1813, published 1817. Table of Springs of Action, printed 1815, published 1817. Chrestomathia: Part I., explanatory of a proposed School for the Extension of the new System of Instruction to the higher Branches of Learning, for the Use of the Middling and Higher Ranks of Life; Part II., being an Essay on Nomenclature and Classification, including a Critical Examination of the Encyclopædiacal Table of Lord Bacon, as improved by d'Alembert, 1817. Plan of Parliamentary Reform, with Reasons for each Article; and an Introduction, shewing the Necessity of Radical, and the inadequacy of Moderate Reform, 1817. Papers relative to Codification and Public Instruction; including Correspondence with the Russian Emperor, and divers constituted Authorities in the American United States, 1817. The Rationale of Reward; translated by a Friend from M. Dumont's *Traité des Récompenses*, with the benefit of some parts of the original, which were in English, 1825. Church of Englandism and its Catechism examined; preceded by Strictures on the Exclusionary System, as pursued in the National Society's Schools, printed 1817, published 1818. Radical Reform Bill, 1819. Observations on the Restrictive and Prohibitory System, especially with reference to the Decree of the Spanish Cortes of July 1820, by Dr. Bowring, from Jeremy Bentham's MSS. Three Tracts on Spanish and Portuguese Affairs,

1821. Letters to Count Toreno on the Proposed Penal Code delivered in by the Legislative Committee of the Spanish Cortes, 1822. Codification Proposal, addressed to all Nations professing Liberal Opinions, 1822. Supplement, 1827. Preuves Judiciaires, par Dumont, 1823. Leading Principles of a Constitutional Code for any State, 1823. The Book of Fallacies, from unfinished Papers of Jeremy Bentham, by a Friend, 1824. Rationale of Judicial Evidence, especially applied to English Practice, 1827. Indications respecting Lord Eldon, 1827. Rationale of Punishment, 1829. Constitutional Code, Vol. I. 1830. Book of Church Reform, 1830. Dispatch—Court Proposal, 1830. Official Aptitude Maximized; Expense Minimized, 1830. Justice and Codification Petitions, 1830. Jeremy Bentham to his Fellow-citizens, on the Punishment of Death, 1831. Jeremy Bentham to the French Chamber of Peers, 1831. Parliamentary Candidates' Declaration of Principles, 1831. On the Bankruptcy Bill; or Lord Brougham Displayed, 1832. (Annual Obituary.)

BENTHAM, (Thomas,) an English divine, eminent in his day for a knowledge of Hebrew, and conspicuous in the settlement of protestantism under Elizabeth. He was born of respectable parentage at Sherborn, in Yorkshire; and having obtained a fellowship at Magdalen college, Oxford, he was a strenuous assertor there of reformed opinions. This rendered him one of the victims of the visitation undertaken by bishop Gardiner, in 1553. King Edward's laws as to religion were still in force, but every one reckoned upon their speedy abolition, and therefore Gardiner felt no hesitation in exerting the visitorial powers vested in him by the founder, to free the society of a college so important from that large infusion of protestantism which had lately distinguished it. In such a purgation, Bentham could not hope to escape, as his opinions were not only decidedly protestant, but also he had been formerly concerned in shaking the censer out of the hands of one ministering at mass, in the choir of the chapel, to prevent, as it was said, incense from being offered to an idol. This reprehensible indecency, of course, was not forgotten when the visitor came to Oxford, and Bentham was ejected from his fellowship. He then went abroad, and after living some time at Zurich, Basle, and Frankfort, he returned before the end of Mary's reign, and secretly officiated as minister of a protestant congregation in London. He was even bold enough, upon one occasion, to venture upon courting public notice. When seven martyrs were to be burnt in Smithfield, proclamation was made that none should speak to them, comfort them, or pray for them. Bentham, however, no sooner saw fire put to the pile, than he cried out, "We know that they are God's people; we must, therefore, wish them well, and pray him to strengthen them. Oh, may God Almighty, for Christ's sake, give them strength." Loud shouts of "Amen" arose immediately on every side, greatly to the confusion and amazement of those who were charged with this cruel execution. A clergyman so zealous on the protestant side as Bentham, and at the same time so well qualified for promotion, could not be overlooked when Elizabeth's government was established. He was accordingly selected, soon after her accession, for delivering reformed opinious from the influential pulpit of Paul's Cross, and on the 24th of March, 1559, he was consecrated to the see of Lichfield and Coventry. Like the other new bishops, he would have been glad to see the old habits and certain religious ceremonies altogether abolished in the church. But when the queen and the legislature, wisely bent upon conciliating Romish prejudice, and retaining some of the more venerable, yet harmless features of the old service, refused this concession, Bentham, with his brethren upon the bench, determined that opportunities of professional usefulness were not to be foregone on that account. He died at his episcopal residence, Eccleshall castle, in Staffordshire, on the 21st of February, 1578, and was buried in the chancel of the parish church there. (Godwin de Prœsull. Strype's Parker, Annals, Memorials.)

BENTHEM, or BENTHEIM, (Henry Ludolph,) a Lutheran theologian, born at Zell, in 1661, who, after a literary journey through England and Holland, was archdeacon at Dannenberg in 1689, superintendent at Bardewick in 1692, superintendent and provost at Ulzen in 1704, and in 1710 general superintendent and consistorial, and ecclesiastical counsellor at Haarburg, where he died in 1723. He wrote Statistics of the Churches and Schools in England and Holland; works which contain much valuable information on the state of institutions for religious and secular instruction in the two countries at the time of his acquaintance with them. His favourite object was the union of the reformed and Lutheran churches, which he imagined as easily feasible as the mixture of Calvinists and Arminians in the church of England. On this subject he wrote more than one work, which, with his sermons and translations from the English, have very much passed out of notice. (Ersch und Gruber.)

BENTINCK, (William,) founder of the English honours enjoyed by his descendant, the duke of Portland, born of a distinguished family in Guelderland, began life as page of honour to William, prince of Orange, to whose fortunes he attached himself through the remainder of his life. He was in England with the prince in 1670. In 1677 he was sent by him to solicit Charles II. for the hand of the princess Mary, daughter of the duke of York; and again, in 1685, to offer the prince's assistance to king James against the duke of Monmouth. His services, at the time of the revolution, were employed in negotiations with the elector of Brandenburg, who was prevailed upon to promise his assistance to the prince in his design, and, afterwards, in the secret preparation of the expedition. He came over in the same ship with William; who no sooner was declared king, than he made Bentinck groom of the stole, first lord of the bed-chamber, and a member of the privy council. Not satisfied with this, even before the coronation, he created him an English baron, viscount, and earl, the title of his earldom being Portland, which had formerly been enjoyed by the Weston family. He was also captain of the Dutch guards, and as lieutenant-general served with great success in Ireland. He was at the great congress at the Hague, in 1691, and in subsequent years attended king William in his campaigns in the Low Countries.

By way of rewarding Bentinck substantially for all these services, William granted him, in 1695, the lordships of Denbigh, Bromfield, and Yale, royal demesnes, intended for a prince of Wales. But the Commons remonstrated, and this bounty was retracted, with a promise that its place should be competently supplied. Other grants were accordingly made to him quite sufficient to support his honours. His temper does not, however, appear to have been mercenary, as he has the credit of refusing a bribe of 50,000*l.* offered him on behalf of the East India Company if he would use his interest to obtain the renewal of their charter.

In 1697 he was made knight of the garter, not without a manifestation of some disapproval on the part of the ancient nobility. After this he was in military and diplomatic employment, being the principal person at the negotiations for the treaty of Ryswick. He had also much to do with the unpopular Partition Treaty, and seems to have lost very much the respect of the people towards the close of the life of his royal patron. The king remained faithful to one who had been a principal means of saving him from the assassination plot, and had served him faithfully to the last. He expired in his arms. With the death of king William ended his connexion with public affairs. He went to Holland, and resided there for some time; and on his return to England, lived a private life at Bulstrode, in Buckinghamshire, where he died, November 23, 1709, being sixty years of age. He was buried in Henry the Seventh's Chapel, at Westminster.

A little of the jealousy natural on the promotion to such high dignities of a gentleman of foreign descent, was taken off by his marriage with a lady of a noble English family, who went to Holland as maid of honour to Mary, princess of Orange. This was Anne Villiers, daughter of Sir Edward Villiers, and sister to the first earl of Jersey. She was mother to the second earl of Portland, who was created duke of Portland in 1716. His fortunes were injured in the South Sea bubble, but the family was amply enriched, soon afterwards, by the marriage of his son, the second duke, with Margaret Cavendish, sole daughter and heir of Edward Harley, earl of Oxford, who married the only daughter and heir of John Cavendish Holles, duke of Newcastle. The former lady formed the curious museum at Bulstrode, and was owner of the celebrated Portland vase. Her son, the third duke, was an eminent political character in the reign of George III., holding several important offices, and being, for a short time, first lord of the treasurer. He died in 1809.

BENTINCK, (John,) a captain in the British navy, son of William, count Bentinck, and connected with the Portland family. He was inventor of many useful nautical improvements, particularly those relating to the construction of pumps for vessels of war; one of which, the chain-pump, in consequence of additions and alterations suggested by captain Bentinck, still bears his name. He died September 23d, 1775.

BENTIVOGLIO, (John,) of an ancient Bolognese family, who, heading the popular party against the pope, was proclaimed sovereign of Bologna, in 1401. He was, however, defeated and put to death; but his descendants, mindful of their ancestor's short-lived sovereignty, were in constant opposition to the popes, and hence looked upon as protectors of the people's rights.

BENTIVOGLIO, (Hercules,) son of Hannibal Bentivoglio, (the last of his family that strove to maintain Bologna against the popes,) one of the best Italian poets. He was scarcely six years old when his father was driven from Bologna, and he ultimately found a home at Ferrara, being protected and employed by the princes of Este, his near relations. He died on the 6th of November, 1573. His poetical works consist of sonnets, short poems, eclogues, six satires, equal in style to those of Ariosto, five capitoli, after the manner of Berni, which were all first published separately, and afterwards collected in one vol. 12mo, in 1719, at Paris; besides two comedies, in blank verse, entitled, Il Geloso, and I Fantasmi, which were translated into French.

BENTIVOGLIO, (Guy,) cardinal, a papal statesman of consummate address, and a valuable historian. He was of the same noble family as the preceding, and was born at Ferrara in 1579, his father being the marquis Cornelius Bentivoglio. After an education at Padua, he returned to his native city in 1597. Pope Clement VIII. was then taking possession of the duchy, regardless of the house of Este, and Guy Bentivoglio, though only nineteen, contrived to make up a quarrel, for an elder brother, with the pope's representative. This introduced him to Clement himself, who came next year to Ferrara, and who made him his private chamberlain. After that pontiff's death, in 1605, the next pope, Paul V., appointed Bentivoglio his referendary and nuncio to Flanders, where he arrived in 1607, and remained till the year 1617. He was then sent as nuncio to Lewis XIII. of France, and conducting himself with his habitual dexterity, that monarch appointed him protector of France at the court of Rome, in 1621, when he was made cardinal. In this new situation he became the intimate friend of pope Urban VIII., and at his death, in 1644, public opinion marked him out for the vacant tiara; but he had scarcely entered the conclave, when he was attacked by fever, which carried him off on the 7th of September in that year, at the age of sixty-five. He died in embarrassed circumstances, having indulged too freely that taste for pomp and grandeur, which was usual among the cardinals of his day. His morals, however, were irreproachable. The works of Bentivoglio are:—1. Della Guerra di Fiandra, in three parts, which he brings down to 1607, printed at various times, but all included in the edition of Cologne, 1639, 4to, which is the best. It is an excellent work, the best of the sort, and though written in the spirit of an advocate of the church of Rome, and of the Spanish authority, it is very fair, and much superior in this respect to that of his contemporary, the Jesuit Strada. 2. Relazioni in Tempo della Nunziatura di Fiandra e di Francia, Cologne, 1630; it is a remarkable work, full of information. 3. Memorie, Amsterdam, 1648, 8vo; it is a diary of his life, published after his death. 4. Lettere. In all these works Bentivoglio shows himself, as he was, a finished diplomatist and a consummate politician, who knew better than most men how to keep others, whether hearers or readers, in ignorance of every thing that he did not wish them to know; his language, however, is forcible and pure, his style grave and dignified. The first three have been translated into almost all the languages of Europe, and have passed through several editions.

BENTIVOGLIO, (Hippolytus,) distinguished by the surname of Aragona, born at Ferrara, and sprung from a collateral branch of the same family as the preceding; a dramatic and lyric poet. He died at Ferrara, February 1. 1685. (Biog. Univ.)

BENTIVOGLIO, (Cornelius d'Aragona,) son of the preceding, a Roman cardinal, of considerable poetical talent, employed much to the satisfaction of Lewis XIV. as nuncio to the court of Versailles, while the bull *Unigenitus* was in agitation. He died on the 30th of December, 1732, leaving several works, of which the Italian translation, in blank verse, of the Thebaid of Statius, under the assumed name of Selvaggio Porpora, is the best.

BENTLEY, (Richard,) born at Oulton, near Wakefield, in Yorkshire, on the 27th of January, 1661-2, eldest son of Thomas Bentley, owner of a small estate at Woodlesford, and Sarah, daughter of Richard Willie, a stone-mason at Oulton, from whom he derived his christian name. Bentley's mother was only nineteen years old when she married Thomas Bentley, then considerably advanced in life; and when Richard was thirteen, his father died, leaving the property at Woodlesford to a son by a former marriage. After his father's death, Richard was committed to the care of his maternal grandfather, who eventually bequeathed some property to him, and was happily the immediate cause of sending him to the university.

Many men who have attained great literary eminence, have been indebted largely for their earliest mental culture to a sensible and affectionate mother. Bentley had this advantage; his parent, in addition to general training, teaching him the rudiments of Latin. As his years advanced, he was sent, first to the neighbouring day-school at Methley, and subsequently to Wakefield grammar-school, whence he removed to Cambridge at the early age of fourteen, having been entered as subsizar of St. John's college on the 24th of May, 1676. The competition at the university of Cambridge was not great in those days; nor does it appear that any extraordinary distinction attached to a high place in the examination for the degree of B.A. When Bentley took that degree (23d of January, 1679-80), his name appeared as sixth on the first tripos; and as the second, third, and fourth places were filled by nominees of the vice-chancellor and proctors, he may be considered as having been third in his year. Bentley could not be elected a fellow of his college, because at that time there was a provision in the statutes of St. John's college, which did not allow of more than two fellows from the same county, and Bentley's county was already full. The fellows of the college, however, soon found an opportunity of giving the young scholar a proof of their favourable opinion, for the nomination to the head-mastership of Spalding grammar-school having lapsed to St. John's, Bentley was appointed to fill the vacant office, though he had only just completed his 20th year. Nor did their patronage stop with this; for before he had resided a twelvemonth at this school he was recommended by St. John's college as a proper person to fill the office of domestic tutor to the son of the eminent Dr. Edward Stillingfleet, then dean of St. Paul's, an office that held out obvious advantages to a young man of studious habits, whose views were directed to the church.

After taking the degree of M.A. at the usual period, (in July, 1683,) Bentley discontinued his connexion with Cambridge for about seventeen years. At first he resided in London, directing his attention mainly to theology, but also carrying on his classical studies in a regular and systematic manner. It was at this time, as he has told us himself, that he acquired a knowledge of the Hebrew language, by compiling a dictionary of all the Hebrew words which occur in the Bible, and subjoining interpretations from all the languages in the Polyglot, except Arabic, Persian, and Ethiopian.

Conscientious refusals to take new oaths, while old obligations appeared still in force, having made several sees vacant after the revolution of 1688, king William was naturally anxious to fill them with persons of piety and learning, well affected to his government. One of those thus recommended was Dr. Stillingfleet, consecrated bishop of Worcester soon after the abdication of king James. About this time, Bentley proceeded to Oxford, with his pupil, James Stillingfleet, who had entered as a student of Wadham college. The tutor also became a member of the same college, and was admitted to the degree of M.A. *ad eundem*, on the 4th of July, 1689.

During his residence at Oxford, Bentley employed himself, with his usual diligence, in ransacking the stores of the Bodleian library, and formed plans for the publication of extensive and laborious works; such, for instance, as a publication in parallel columns of the old Greek lexicographers, and a complete collection of the fragments of the Greek poets. He also formed intimacies with several persons then, or subsequently, well known in the literary and learned world; among others, with Mill, Bernard, and Hody. It was at Oxford that Bentley laid the first foundations of his fame as a classical scholar. The curators of the Sheldon press having determined to print, under the superintendence of Dr. Mill, an edition of a dull and useless chronicle, written by a Syrian, commonly known as Joannes Malelas, applied to Hody, after it was partly printed, to write the prolegomena to it. While the work was still in the press, Bentley was induced by Dr. Mill, and his friend, bishop Lloyd, to contribute some remarks on Malelas by way of appendix. These remarks were published in the form of an epistle to Mill, which was at once acknowledged by the scholars of Europe to be a master-piece of learning and criticism. There is, perhaps, no learned work of the same compass which can be compared with it for ingenuity, originality, and copious erudition. The observations on Hesychius are particularly valuable, and it is still a matter of regret with scholars that Bentley did not publish an edition of this lexicographer, as in his epistle to Mill, (p. 39,) he states that he had made above 5,000 emendations in Hesychius; and his copy of the lexicon, which is preserved in Trinity-college library, is full of MS. corrections. His plan of publishing a combined edition of all the Greek lexicographers was too extensive ever to have been realized, even had his subsequent occupations been less varied and distracting than they were. It was Bentley's misfortune, in this his first publication, to get himself involved in a controversy with his friend Hody, and that, too, about a question of no greater importance than the Latin orthography of the chronicler's name—Hody maintaining that it should be written *Malela*, and Bentley asserting that the proper form was *Malelas*.

Bentley was ordained on the 16th of March, 1689-90, and was soon after appointed chaplain to the bishop of Worcester. It was as a divine that he made his next appearance in print. The Hon. Robert Boyle, who died in December, 1691, left by his will a salary of 50*l*. a-year to found a lectureship for the defence of religion against infidels; and the four trustees, Dr. Tenison, Sir H. Ashurst, Sir J. Rotheram, and John Evelyn, immediately nominated Bentley first lecturer on this foundation. The selection was, no doubt, highly honourable to Bentley, a young man, and only in deacon's orders. The trustees, however, had no reason to repent of their choice; Bentley's sermons in confutation of atheism, produced a great sensation; the sixth edition was published at Cambridge in 1735, and they were translated into Latin by Dr. Ernest Jablonski. In these sermons the discoveries in Newton's Principia (published about six years before) were, for the first time, brought forward in a popular form, and rendered applicable to the confirmation of natural theology. Bentley was reappointed Boyle's lecturer in 1694, but his second series of sermons was never printed.

In 1692, he took priest's orders, and was made a prebendary of Worcester; in 1695, Stillingfleet gave him the rectory of Hartlebury to hold till his pupil, James, should be old enough to take it; and in 1696 he took the degree of D.D. at Cambridge.

In December, 1693, Bentley obtained the appointment of royal librarian by a compromise with Mr. Thynne. It was in this office that he became involved in a controversy, the issue of which raised him to the highest pinnacle of literary fame. The celebrated Sir William Temple, in An Essay on Ancient and Modern Learning, had mentioned as masterpieces of wit and genius the fables of Æsop and the epistles of Phalaris, which he supposed to be the oldest prose writings by profane authors. To this work, which made a great stir at the time, Wotton, a college contemporary of Bentley's, wrote an indirect reply, entitled, Reflections upon Ancient and Modern Learning; and Bentley having stated, in the course of conversation, that the epistles of Phalaris were forgeries, and that there are no genuine remains of Æsop, Wotton extorted from his friend a promise that he would contribute some remarks in proof of these assertions, to be published in his book then in the press. Circumstances prevented Bentley from fulfilling his promise at the time, though he had before avowed his sentiments on the subject in the Appendix to Malelas, and in a letter which he wrote to Joshua Barnes. In the mean time, Sir William Temple's eulogy had induced Dr. Aldrich, the dean of Christ Church, Oxford, to select the epistles of Phalaris for one of those republications which he entrusted to the promising young men of his college, and the task of editing this highly extolled work was committed to the Hon. Robert Boyle, brother of the earl of Orrery. In order to make the text of the proposed edition as correct as possible, Mr. Boyle was desirous of getting a collation of such MSS. as could be procured, and there was one, though neither old nor valuable, in the Royal Library, of which Bentley was keeper. Accordingly, Bennett, the publisher, was directed to get this MS. collated. This was early in 1694. Bennett executed his commission in such a tardy, procrastinating manner, that only a small portion of the MS. was collated when it was demanded back again by the librarian, who was about to leave town to keep his residence at Worcester. To conceal his own carelessness, the bookseller misstated the whole affair to Boyle, and attributed the failure of his attempt to get the book collated to the incivility of Bentley. When the new edition of Phalaris was published, in January 1695, the preface was found to contain the following sentence:—*Collatas etiam curavi usque ad Epist.* xl. *cum MS.to in Bibliotheca Regia, cujus mihi copiam ulteriorem Bibliothecarius, pro singulari sua humanitate, negavit.* On seeing this reflection on himself, Bentley wrote to the editor, explaining the real state of the case; but after two days' consideration, Boyle wrote back to him that it was too late to interpose, and that he might seek his redress in any manner that he pleased. In 1697 a new edition of Wotton's book was published, and appended to it was a dissertation by Bentley, completely proving the spuriousness and general worthlesness of the epistles attributed to Phalaris, and of the fables of Æsop; and also explaining the circumstances which had taken place between the bookseller, Bennett, and himself. To this essay, which made a great sensation in the literary world, the Christ-church scholars published a joint reply, under the name of Boyle, the principal part of which was written by Atterbury and Smalridge, afterwards bishops of Rochester and Bristol. This reply was not very remarkable for accurate learning, still less for fairness of argument; but it was at first thought to have effected its object, and Bentley was considered as discomfited. Many other attacks were also made upon him, of which the best known are those in Swift's Tale of a Tub, and Battle of the Books. Bentley did not immediately publish a rejoinder; at last, however, in the beginning of 1699, he gave to the world a greatly enlarged edition of his Dissertation on Phalaris, of which it may be said, with perfect truth, that, as a combination of profound learning and great originality, with lively wit and sound logic, it has never been paralleled. Although it came forth as an occasional and controversial work, such is the fulness with which every subject in it is discussed, that it is still used as a text book in our universities, and will always continue to be read even by those who have no interest in, or acquaintance with, the book to which it is professedly an answer. Bentley's victory over his opponents was as complete as it could be; and though they at first gave out that they intended to publish a further reply, they were too happy to drop a dispute in which they had lost so much; and from a continuance of which, could not hope to gain anything. In after life, Bentley lived on terms of courtesy and kindness with Atterbury, the leader of the Christ-church party.

The result of the controversy about Phalaris placed Bentley at the head of English scholarship, and he was soon after rewarded by an appointment well suited to his high position in the learned world. On the death of queen Mary, William had established a commission, consisting of six bishops, who were to recommend fit persons to fill all vacancies in the ecclesiastical or university preferments in the gift of the crown. The promotion of Dr. Montague to the deanery of Durham in the latter part of 1699, having made a vacancy in the mastership of Trinity college, Cambridge, Bentley was appointed his successor, on the unanimous recommendation of the commissioners. He was installed on the 1st of February in the following year; was elected vice-chancellor in the November of that year; and married, on the 4th of January, 1701, Joanna Bernard, daughter of Sir John Bernard, bart., a lady whom he had frequently met in Dr. Stillingfleet's house. In June, 1701, he was appointed archdeacon of Ely, and thus became a member of the lower house of convocation.

Being now placed at the head of the richest and most learned college in Europe, a society which reckoned among its members, before and during his time, some of the greatest names in the literary history of England—Bacon and Coke, Newton and Barrow—Bentley might, surely, have contented himself with a peaceful prosecution of his literary labours, or with a zealous discharge of his duties to the college and university. It would, indeed, have been happy, not only for his own reputation, but also, and still more so, for the advancement of classical learning, and the rational improvement of that academical system, with which he had become so prominently connected, could he have henceforth carefully avoided strife, as detracting from his usefulness, comfort, and credit. Unfortunately, however, natural disposition rendered him unfit for filling the high post to which he had so deservedly been raised. Obstinate and overbearing, of a grasping and uncompromising resoluteness of temper, and not gifted with much delicacy of feeling, or any nice perception of the limits which bound the right of self-aggrandizement, he was placed at the head of a corporation, governed by statutes, of which some are obsolete, or inapplicable to existing circumstances, and in which the master's authority is so clumsily defined, that an able and unscrupulous man might make it almost despotic. We cannot wonder, then, that such a man, possessing such facilities for abuse, should seek to forward his own interest, or, in some cases, what he imagined to be the interests of the college, at the expense of a body of resident fellows, with whom he had little either of intercourse or sympathy. It would be irksome to follow his disputes with them, through all their tedious details; nor can such an investigation be expected in a sketch like the present. The whole proceedings have been stated with most scrupulous accuracy by Bishop Monk; and it will be sufficient to refer for particulars to his elaborate work. The dissensions in Trinity college may be divided into three epochs. The first open rupture took place in 1709, and after a great many delays the cause was tried in Ely House, before Dr. Moore, bishop of Ely, the visitor of the master. The trial commenced in May 1714, and the charges of violating the statutes and wasting the property of the college were fully proved against the master; but before sentence could be pronounced, bishop Moore died, (on the 31st July, 1714, the day before the death of queen Anne), and this event nullified all the proceedings. The second epoch of the college dissensions began in the following year; but as bishop Fleetwood, Moore's successor, would not stir in the matter, Bentley remained unmolested until the year 1717, when, having been, by an unscrupulous and skilful stratagem, elected regius professor of divinity, he demanded an unusual fee of four guineas from the D.D.'s created on occasion of the king's visit to Cambridge. Dr. Conyers Middleton paid the fee with a proviso; and the vice-chancellor having afterwards, at his instance, issued a decree to arrest Bentley for that sum, an esquire-beadle was sent to serve the process, but was locked up for some hours in the lodge of Trinity college, and was obliged to return without effecting his commission. After a variety of proceedings in consequence of this disturbance, a grace was passed by the senate, on the 17th of October, 1718, stripping Bentley of all his degrees (ab omni gradu suscepto), and reducing him to the rank of an under-graduate. Against this violent measure he petitioned the king as supreme visitor of the college, but more than five years elapsed before he could get redress; at last he obtained a peremptory mandamus from the court of King's Bench, by which he was restored to his degrees and the other rights and privileges of which he had been deprived. In the mean time he had successfully prosecuted his enemies, Middleton and Coldbatch, for libels, and had compounded with his most active opponent, serjeant Miller, who appears to have been as unprincipled as Bentley himself. In 1723 bishop Fleetwood died, and was succeeded by Dr. Greene, who declared his willingness to act as visitor if his right was legally determined and his expenses guaranteed. This constitutes the third epoch in the Trinity quarrel. The right of the bishop of Ely to act as visitor having been fully confirmed, Bentley was again summoned to appear at Ely House, (1st April, 1729.) After a number of proceedings, Bentley was found guilty of the charges against him on the 27th April, 1734, and the bishop pronounced him to be deprived of the mastership of Trinity college. The vice-master Hachet was ordered to execute this sentence, but at first hesitated, and then resigned in favour of Bentley's friend, Richard Walker, who raising the quibble that he was not *the same* vice-master, refused to carry the bishop's decree into effect. This went on till the 28th May, 1738, when bishop Greene died, and the whole proceedings were nullified, and never again revived. And thus did Bentley, by his firmness and ingenuity, hold out for twenty-eight years against all right and law, despising alike ecclesiastical authority and the censures of the university.

During all this turmoil, this extraordinary man's literary energy never abated. It was in the midst of his first litigation with the fellows, that he contrived to finish one of the greatest of his works—an edition of Horace, on which he had been engaged for ten years. It was published on the 8th December, 1711. We cannot in our present limits enter upon any satisfactory review of the merits and defects of this celebrated work. There can be no doubt that Bentley really did a great deal for Horace: his scheme of the chronolgy of the poet's works is sound; he has collected a mass of illustrations such as had never before been brought to bear on the criticism of a classical author; and a great number of the emendations which he has introduced into the text are as certain as they are ingenious. On the other hand, the book is deformed by the greatest arrogance and presumption on the part of the editor; and in his boasting preface he admits great haste and some carelessness, and withdraws above twenty of his vaunted emendations. Its various faults brought upon him a number of attacks, of which the most severe and amusing was Johnson's Aristarchus anti-Bentleianus, which was not published, however, till the beginning of 1717. Bentley's next publication was his answer to Collins on Freethinking, which appeared in 1713, under the name of Phileleutherus Lipsiensis, and was a complete overthrow of the shallow but dangerous book against which it was directed; so much was it esteemed at the time, that the thanks of the university were voted to Bentley at the end of the following year for his able defence of the christian religion. On the 15th April, 1716, Bentley addressed a letter to archbishop Wake, proposing to restore the text of the Greek Testament to the same state in which it was at the time of the council of Nice. The plan which he had laid down was to emend the Greek text through the Latin Vulgate,' in the same way as the version of Plato by M. Ficino is made the basis for corrections of the Greek text of that philosopher. In 1720 he published a regular prospectus, together with the twenty-second chapter of the Apocalypse, as a specimen; but although great preparations were made, a number of MSS. collated, and 2000*l*. subscribed, the plan was never carried into effect; and perhaps it is fortunate that it was not, for it is to be feared that Bentley's love of change would have led him to introduce some mischievous alterations into the text of the sacred writings. In 1716 an abortive attempt was made to publish a set of classics *in usum Principis Friderici*, in imitation of the well-known French series *in usum Delphini*, and it was intended that Bentley should be the editor; in consequence, however, of some disagreement about the remuneration to be offered to him, the plan fell to the ground. In 1726 he published an edition of Terence, to supplant one by Dr. Hare, in which that scholar had used, without due acknowledgment, the hints given him by Bentley in private conversation with regard to the metrical systems of the Latin poets. Although the motive for publishing Terence was so occasional and temporary, this edition is one of the most careful of Bentley's works, and it is much less discursive than the Horace. The Schediasma on Latin metres, which is prefixed to it, is still the best treatise on the subject. Indeed Bentley may be considered as absolutely a discoverer in relation to Latin metres: he had given a proof of his originality in this field in 1709, in some notes on Cicero's Tusculanæ Disputationes, appended to Davies's edition, in which he had restored, in a most ingenious and satisfactory manner, the fragments of the Latin poets quoted in that work. Bentley subjoined to his Terence an edition of Phædrus and Publius Syrus, which was the most hasty and careless work that he ever published, and subjected him to a very acrimonious attack from Hare, whose intended edition of the fabulist it was designed to anticipate. But there was still another work of Bentley's, by which his reputation has more materially suffered than by anything which he has written. In an evil hour he undertook to publish a corrected edition of Milton's Paradise Lost, for which he was totally unqualified. Even in his treatment of the classical poets, he had given unquestionable proofs of a great deficiency of poetic taste; but the evils which might have resulted from this were in a great measure obviated by his perfect familiarity with the whole range of Greek and Roman poets, and by his unrivalled acquaintance with the languages in which they wrote. But Bentley had never read, so far as appears, the older English poets; he was utterly ignorant of the Italian and romantic writers from whom Milton had so largely borrowed; and, what was worst of all, his knowledge of his own language was very slight, in a literary point of view, as may be inferred from the crudities and Latinisms with which his style is infected. With these defects of outward preparation, added to his inherent disqualifications, it is quite wonderful that he should have undertaken a task by which he could hardly fail to lose credit. The only explanation of that which would otherwise appear like infatuation or dotage, is, that the work was suggested to him by queen Caroline. It had been hinted by Fenton, Pope's coadjutor in the translation of the Odyssey, that some apparent corruptions in the text of the Paradise Lost might have been occasioned by the carelessness or misapprehension of the amanuensis who wrote from the dictation of the blind poet. Bentley adopted this opinion, and also started the hypothesis, that some nameless friend of Milton's, who corrected the press for him, had wilfully altered and interpolated the poem. Acting on this supposition, the critic did not hesitate to make a complete *rifaccimento* of the poem according to his own unpoetical notions, and it need hardly be said that the attempt was as ludicrous as it was presumptuous. This new Paradise Lost, which appeared in January 1731-2, was received by the public with unqualified disapprobation; and no one has been found, among all the admirers of Bentley, who has been able up to this day to say one word in defence of this preposterous attempt, though it must be admitted, with Bishop Monk, that it contains, here and there, some acute and judicious remarks.

Not discouraged by the failure of this attempt to restore the text of one great epic poem, according to an hypothesis of its original state, Bentley applied himself, at the age of seventy-two, to a still harder task—the reproduction of the text of Homer in the state in which it existed under the old rhapsodists. This he intended to effect principally by the revival and insertion of an old letter, originally the sixth of the Greek alphabet, which, as the exigences of the metre showed, must have been in use at the time when the Homeric poems were composed. This letter, which is commonly called the *digamma*, has a significance even for the readers of our lighter literature. Most persons are familiar with the lines which Pope, in the fourth book of his Dunciad, puts into the mouth of Bentley:

> "Roman and Greek grammarian, know your better,
> Author of something yet more great than letter;
> While tow'ring o'er your alphabet, like Saul,
> Stands our digamma, and o'ertops them all."

The last line refers to the representation of the digamma by a capital F, in two quotations from Homer which appeared in the notes to Milton. Bentley's labours on Homer were stopped by a paralytic stroke, some time in the year 1739. He left, however, a corrected copy of Homer, which was lent to Heyne, and used by him in his edition of that poet, and a book of MS. notes, containing a collection of the passages of Homer in which the digamma might be introduced, and of the notices of this letter in the old grammarians. The most valuable parts of this document have been recently printed in Mr. Donaldson's New Cratylus. Bentley's last work was an edition of Manilius, published in 1739 under the superintendence of his nephew Richard, who wrote the preface to it.

In the early part of 1740, Bentley lost his wife, to whom he had been united for forty years. His grandson, Richard Cumberland, gives a very pleasing picture of his last years, though we may perhaps be justified in believing that the description is coloured by some not inexcusable partiality. Bentley died of a pleuritic fever on the 14th July, 1742, and was buried in the chapel of Trinity college. He left behind him a son, Richard, who inherited a large share of his father's abilities, but, owing to his want of application and desultory habits, failed to turn them to any profitable account. He also left two daughters; the elder, Elizabeth, was married first to Humphrey Ridge, esq., and again, after her father's death, to the Rev. James Favell, fellow of Trinity college; the other daughter, Joanna, who was celebrated for her beauty and talents, was married to Denison Cumberland, afterwards bishop of Dromore; his son Richard holds a high rank among our popular writers.

As a scholar, Bentley has perhaps no rival; the only man who can be placed in competition with him is Joseph Justus Scaliger; but, though we are far from wishing to underrate the merits of the latter, we confess that, in our opinion, Bentley has more valid claims on the gratitude of the learned. His name constitutes an epoch in the history of philology. He united in one person the copious erudition of the older scholars, and that peculiar felicity in verbal emendation, which is so remarkable in some modern critics, and especially in Porson. We may fairly consider him as the literary progenitor of the great and enlightened philologers of modern Germany; indeed, it would not be too much to say, that the Dissertation on Phalaris paved the way for Niebuhr's History of Rome. Considered, however, without reference to his scholarship, Bentley's character was not one of those which can be contemplated with any degree of pleasure or satisfaction. The texture of his mind was strong, but at the same time coarse and rude. He was gifted with great courage and an indomitable will; but unhappily he had no high moral principle to guide these mighty instruments of good or evil. Intellectually, Bentley was a giant, possessed of faculties which, when properly directed and exercised, always claim the respect and admiration of men; but morally he was conspicuous only for a littleness of character, which, if it fail to excite our indignation, cannot escape our pity and contempt.

Dr. Monk, bishop of Gloucester and Bristol, has written a Life of Bentley, which is a model for works of that kind. An abridgement of Dr. Monk's book is inserted in Mr. Hartley Coleridge's Biographia Borealis. The Rev. A. Dyce has commenced a complete edition of Bentley's works, of which three volumes have appeared, containing the Dissertation on Phalaris, the Epistle to Mill, and all the theological writings; and it is expected that a collection of Bentley's letters will shortly be published by the Rev. J. Wordsworth, fellow of Trinity college, Cambridge.

BENTLEY, (Thomas,) nephew of the great Richard, was brought up at St. Paul's school in London, from whence he went to Trinity college, Cambridge, where he became a fellow. While he was yet an A.B. he published an edition of Horace in 1713, which was merely the text of his uncle's edition, with a brief statement of the reasons for rejecting the old readings and substituting the new. In 1718 he printed an edition of Cicero de Finib. et Paradoxa, with a few emendations of his own and of John Walker, whom he describes as a young man of excellent genius and of surpassing erudition, and whose notes on Cicero de Nat. Deor. were published by Davies. Despite the neglect into which Bentley's work has fallen, it contains a few remarks that merit notice; and he has there shown himself a better Latin scholar than he did a Greek one, when he put forth his anonymous edition of Callimachus in 1741, which Davies attributed to the uncle, an error that might have been easily escaped, for the editor states that he had seen, and partly collated the Vatican MS. of the Septuagint at Rome, a place which Richard Bentley, whose travels did not extend beyond England, had never visited.

BENTLEY, (Sir John,) a British admiral, distinguished for his valour and professional ability. He entered the navy at an early age, and, according to Charnock, he served as second lieutenant of the *Namur*, the flag-ship of admiral Matthews, in that officer's ill-supported encounter with the French fleet in 1744. The conduct of Bentley, on this occasion, procured for him immediate promotion. After attaining his "post rank," we find him filling the onerous office of flag-captain to admiral Anson, and participating in the action which ended in the defeat of the French force under M. De la Jonquiere. Upon lord Anson's striking his flag, Bentley was appointed to the *Defiance* of sixty guns, and in this ship took a prominent part in the succeeding defeat of L'Entendiere's force by rear-admiral, afterwards lord Hawke. In 1756 he commanded the *Barfleur*, and in this command his name stands recorded as one of the members of the court-martial who sat in judgment upon the unfortunate admiral Byng.

Desirous to be employed on more active service, in 1758 he was appointed captain of the *Invincible*, one of the ships ordered to reinforce the squadron against Louisbourgh; but unfortunately this vessel, (an ill-fated name in the British navy,) was totally wrecked a few hours after departing Spithead. In Boscawen's action off Cape St. Vincent, with the French squadron under M. De la Clue, Bentley distinguished himself in an eminent degree. "Captain Bentley, of the *Warspite*," says the admiral, in his official relation of this gallant affair, "was ordered against the *Temeraire*, of seventy-four guns, and brought her off with little damage, the officers and men all on board." On his return home he was "knighted" by the king, "an honour well earned, and worthily deserved." "The *Warspite*," says Charnock, "was immediately after this ordered to join the fleet under Sir Edward Hawke, with whom he served at the time of the memorable defeat given to the last naval exertion, or, armament of France, during the war; so that Bentley had the fortune which very few, if any, commanders, himself excepted, could ever boast, of being present at every naval encounter of consequence, or that deserved the name of an action, from his *first* entrance into the sea service of his sovereign to the time of his death. In 1761, or, according to Beatson, in the ensuing year, he was appointed an extra-commissioner of the navy, an office that he resigned on being promoted, in 1763, to the rank of rear-admiral of the White. After attaining the grade of vice-admiral, he died on the 14th of December, 1772.

BENTLEY, (William,) an American, who died in 1819, having published some sermons, and a History of Salem, which appeared in the sixth volume of Historical Collections.

BENVENUTI, (Charles,) an Italian Jesuit and mathematician, born at Leghorn, in 1716, who succeeded Boscovich as mathematical professor at Rome. In 1751, he published an Italian translation of Clairaut's Geometry. In 1754 he published, in 4to, Synopsis Physicæ Generalis; and De Lumine Dissertatio Physica; two works that gained him much reputation, and are very serviceable in superseding the false principles received in the Roman college by the Newtonian system, which he had himself adopted. Illness, however, prevented him from finishing the latter work, and this was done by Boscovich. After the Jesuits were suppressed, an attack upon them appeared at Rome, entitled, Reflessioni sul Gesuitismo, 1772, to which Benvenuti made a sharp reply, entitled, Irreflessioni sul Gesuitismo. This gave so much offence that he was obliged to leave Rome and retire into Poland, where he was well received by Stanislaus Poniatowski, the king. He died at Warsaw, September 1789. (Biog. Univ.)

BENVRAS, (David,) a Welsh poet of the thirteenth century, who wrote Encomium Leolini principis Joroverthi Filii, and other poems, some of which were preserved in the Hengwrt library.

BENWELL, (J. H. 1764—1785,) an English artist, who executed a few small pictures in a way almost peculiar to himself, being painted with a combination of crayons and water-colours. (Edwards's Anec. of Painting, 114.)

BENYOWSKY, (Maurice Augustus,) an adventurer, of noble Hungarian birth, whose memoirs were much read, about the end of the eighteenth century, by those who use books chiefly for amusement. He was born in 1741, and his first conspicuous adventure was an attempt to gain forcible possession of a castle, which he claimed as his rightful inheritance, but his brothers-in-law persuaded the Austrian government to be of a different opinion, and he was banished. He then went into Poland, and after mingling himself in the convulsions of that country, he was exiled to Kamschatka. From this remote region he was helped away by means of a love affair with the governor's daughter, and assistance from his fellow-exiles. With these, and the young lady dressed as a sailor boy, he escaped in a corvette, prudently provided for the purpose beforehand, and after various other adventures, he arrived in France, and persuaded one of the ministry there to send him to Madagascar, to found a colony. When arrived in that island, an old negro woman came forward with a tale that he was last survivor of the royal family there, and he returned to Europe in 1776, in the hope of inducing some government to assist him in establishing himself as a Madagascar prince. As neither France, Germany, nor Britain, would enter into this scheme, Benyowski was under the necessity of returning to his pretended hereditary dominions as a sort of supercargo, a valuable shipment of articles thought suitable for Madagascar being placed under his care by some commercial speculators. He had, however, no sooner landed than he seized a French storehouse, and attempted to take a factory belonging to that nation. The governor of the Isle of France now thought it time to interfere, and sending a ship, with sixty regulars on board, Benyowsky was killed, May 23, 1786, in an attempt to defend himself. All these latter facts have the merit of unquestionable authenticity. The statements down to this adventurer's departure from Madagascar, in 1776, depend upon his Memoirs, published in 1700, in 2 vols, 4to.

BENZEL DE STERNAU, (Anselm Francis de,) born on the 28th of August, 1738, chancellor of state in the electorate of Mentz, in which office he applied himself as well to reform schools as to regulate and diminish convents. He was a principal mover in the union of German bishops against the court of Rome. He died May 7, 1784, leaving a remarkable tract, entitled, Nouvelle Organisation de l'Universite de Mayence. (Biog. Univ.)

BENZEL, a Swedish family, named from the little village of Benzebye, in Westgothland, and from which several of the first scholars of Sweden are descended. Of these, Erich Benzel, born in 1642, was employed by the royal chancellor, count de la Gardie, as tutor to his sons. He travelled with his pupils through Denmark, Germany, France, England, and Holland, and was proceeding to Italy, when he was called, in 1665, to the public professorship of history and morals at Upsal, an appointment which was followed by an advancement to the chair of theology in the following year. In 1675 he became doctor of theology; two years afterwards was raised, by Charles XI., to the bishopric of Strengenäs; in 1700 he was archbishop of Upsal, and died in 1709. He instructed Charles XII. in religion, and enjoyed the esteem of that monarch during the whole of his life. He wrote Breviarium Historiæ Ecclesiasticæ Veteris ac Novi Testamenti, 12mo, Upsaliæ, 1717; several dissertations on points of theology and church history; and a Latin translation, with notes, of some Homilies of St. Chrysostom, transcribed by him from MSS. at Oxford. The Swedish translation of the Bible, printed by Charles XII., and still known as his, appeared under Benzel's superintendence. He was twice married, and had by his first wife thirteen children; three of the sons were archbishops of Upsal; five, the most remarkable of the number, are mentioned below.

Benzel, (*Erich*,) the younger, was born in Upsal, in 1675. His father sent him on a literary journey, after the completion of his studies, from 1697 to 1700, during which he visited several German academies, and made acquaintance with some of the most eminent scholars of England and Holland. On his return to Sweden, he was appointed, in 1702, librarian at Upsal; in 1726 he was preferred to the see of Gothenburg; in 1731 to that of Lincöping, from which he was translated to the archbishopric of Upsal. He died in that city in 1743, with a high character for skill in northern and Jewish literature. Among his literary labours was the supply of an amended text, with a Latin version and annotations, to the Gothic Gospels, published by Lye, at Oxford, in 1750. He founded the Academy of Sciences in Upsal, in 1720; was the editor of the Acta Literaria Suecica, 4to, Upsal, 1720-33; and one of the first members of the Academy of Sciences at Stockholm, founded in 1739. He was also long employed on an edition of Philo, which, however, was never printed. He left behind him one son, Charles Jasper Benzel, born at Upsal in 1714. He devoted himself to theology, made his way through various grades in the church to the bishopric of Strengenäs in 1776; in 1786 was admitted a member of the order of the Northern Star; and died in 1793. He wrote a Commentatio de Johanne Duræo Pacificatore celeberrime, maxime de Actis ejus Suecanis, 4to. Helmstadt, 1744.

Benzel, (*Lars*,) born at Upsal in 1680; after studying there, he was auscultant in 1700 of the mining college, and disputed at Upsal, in 1703, De Re Metallica Sueo-Gothorum. In the following year he travelled through Denmark, Germany, France, Holland, and England, studying as he went the natural history, and especially the mineralogy of those countries; returned to Sweden in 1706; was vice-notarius in the Royal Mining College in 1708; and, in 1713, bergmaster of the mines in the Dales of Sweden. In 1719 he was ennobled, and his family name changed into Bengelstjerna, (pronounced Bengelsheerna.) After several further marks of the esteem in which his talents and services were held, he received, in 1748, the order of the North Star; in 1751 was treasurer of the three royal orders; and died in 1755. He left three sons, of whom Lars, born 1719, was professor of the Greek language at Upsal; Charles, born 1723, directed the new copper mines in Westmoorland; and Frederic, born 1729, was captain of a regiment in Stralsund.

Benzel, (*Jacob*,) born at Upsal in 1683; and after travelling through Denmark, Germany, France, and Holland, he returned to his native city. In 1731 he was bishop of Gothenburg; and in 1744, archbishop of Upsal. He died in 1747. He wrote, Repetitiones Theologicæ and Epitome Repetitionum, which were used by royal command as class books in the universities, and several dissertations, De Palæstina, De Fatis Palæstinæ, &c. He had a son, John Jacob von Bengelstjerna, who was born in 1720, studied at Upsal, taught jurisprudence in Greisswald, and was afterwards instructor of the duke Frederic Adolphus of Ostgothland. He died about 1766.

Benzel, (*Gustavus*,) born at Upsal in 1687; was first employed in the royal archives, then in the chancery of Sweden; was ennobled in 1719, appointed royal librarian in 1732, in 1737 received the additional appointment of *censor librorum*, and died in 1746. His great claim to reputation rests on his letters to his brother Eric, published long after his death, and containing critiques of new works, archæological inquiries, etymological disquisitions, bibliographical notices, &c.

Benzel, (*Henry*,) was born at Strengnäs in 1689, studied theology at Upsal, and in the course of his travels, undertaken on the completion of his studies, came to Charles XII. at Bender. Charles had then the idea of sending a deputation of learned men to Palestine, and his choice fell among others upon Benzel. This latter, after being taken by the Tartars, who, however, soon released him, came in 1714 to Constantinople, thence to the Archipelago, Syria, Palestine, and Egypt, visiting on his return Italy, Germany, and Holland. The results of this journey are still in MS., but many interesting notices from them are found in his Syntagma Dissertationum, 4to, Frankfort and Leipsic, 1745. After filling various university professorships, he was advanced to the see of Lund in 1740. When his brother Jacob, archbishop of Upsal, died in 1747, he succeeded him in this dignity, and died in 1758. (Baur in Ersch und Gruber.)

BENZI, (Hugo,) called sometimes Hugo of Sienna, his native place, one of the most celebrated physicians of the fifteenth century. It is said that he died at Rome in 1438, and that in 1448 his children erected a superb monument to his memory in Ferrara. A work of his on the Aphorisms of Hippocrates was printed at Venice in 1498, and others of his productions appeared early in the following century.

BEOLCO, or BIOLCO, (Angelo, about 1502—March 17, 1542,) a poet and dramatist, born at Padua, and known in Italian literature by the name of *Ruzzante*, from his imitations for the stage of inferior country life, in rustic poems and farces, in which he was considered to be without an equal. Riccoboni, in his History of the Italian Stage, attributes to him the introduction of the characters of the Venetian pantaloon, the Bolognese doctor, and the Bergamese harlequin. His works, consisting of comedies and other writings, were at first published separately at Venice, from 1548 to 1556, and were collected in one volume, under the title, Tutte l'Opere del famosissimo Ruzzante, Vicenza, 1584, and reprinted in 1598, and again in 1617. The collection contains five comedies; two dialogues in the provincial patois, or rustic dialect of Padua; and three discourses in the same; and a variety of other pieces, full of originality and fun. (Biog. Univ.)

BEORN, or BIORN, an Icelandic writer of the seventeenth century, whose work, De novitiis Groenlandorum Indiciis, gives intimations of a Norwegian colony in East Greenland, a country inaccessible to navigators from the early part of the fifteenth century. He also wrote, Annales, sive Collectanea Groenlandiæ, ab A. C. 1400, usque ad sua tempora; a piece which does not appear to have been ever published. (Gorton's Biog. Dict.)

BEOWULF, an individual commemorated in a romantic Anglo-Saxon poem, of high antiquity and great interest, as a specimen of poetic genius in a race commonly deemed unequal to such a production, and a record of various usages in some very distant age. The hero has been considered by Suhm, the Danish historian, to have fallen in Jutland, in 340; but he seems really to be a mythological personage, with whom, therefore, history and biography have little or no concern. The only known MS. of his poetical history, one thought to be of the tenth century, is preserved in the Cottonian collection in the British Museum; and the piece remained unpublished until 1815, when it appeared at Copenhagen, with a Latin version, preface, and two copious indices, by Thorkelin, already celebrated in northern literature. An edition, far more correct, was published in London, in 1833, by Mr. Kemble, who followed it in 1837, by a valuable translation and glossary. An able analysis of this curious poem may be seen in Mr. Turner's History of the Anglo-Saxons, iii. 286; and one still more copious and poetical, in the late Mr. W. D. Conybeare's Illustrations of Anglo-Saxon Poetry, p. 30.

BERAIN, (John,) a designer in the service of Lewis XIV., born in Lorrain, about 1630, and died at the age of seventy-seven years, at the gallery of the Louvre, where he had an apartment. There is by him a folio volume, without date, name of the printer, or place of publication, containing engravings of his principal designs, which consist chiefly of arabesques. They evince much facility, remarkable talent in perspective, and a rich and well-cultivated imagination. There are also sets of ornaments designed and engraved by him. He left a son named John, who was also a designer, and little known. The funeral ceremonies, at St. Denis, in honour of the dauphin and of Lewis XIV. were by the younger Berain. (Biog. Univ. Suppl. Bryan's Dict.)

BERARD, (Frederic,) a physician, born at Montpelier, in 1789, and engaged in some medical periodicals. He published, with Rouzet, an edition of professor Dumas's work, Sur les Maladies Chroniques, with notes, &c. in 2 vols, 8vo; and shortly after, Doctrine des Rapports du Physique et du Moral, Paris, 1823, 8vo; and also a letter, Sur les Causes Premieres, from the pen of the celebrated Cabanis. He died April 16, 1828. After his decease, in 1830, M. Petiot published one of his manuscripts, entitled, Esprit des Doctrines Medicales de Montpelier, accompanied by a notice of his life and writings.

BERARDI, (Angelo,) a canon of the collegiate church of St. Angelo di Viterbo, author of many musical tracts, printed towards the close of the seventeenth century and beginning of the eighteenth, when they were high authority. (Mus. Biog. Dict. of Mus.)

BERARDI, (Fabius,) an Italian engraver, born at Sienna in 1728. He went to Venice when young, and engraved chiefly after the works of modern Venetian painters. He also executed six views of Venice, in conjunction with Wagner, after pictures by Canaletti, dated 1742. (Bryan's Dict.)

BERARDIER DE BATAUT, (Francis Joseph,) grand master of the college of Louis le Grand, born at Paris in 1720. He was deputy from the clergy of Paris in the constituent assembly, and died at Paris in 1794. By means of his pupil, Camille Desmoulins, although a priest who had not taken the oaths, he escaped the massacre of September 2, 1792. He wrote, Precis de l'Histoire Universelle, an excellent introduction to the study of history, which has passed through several editions; Principes de la Foi sur le Gouvernment de l'Eglise, 8vo, of which fourteen editions were printed within six months, and which has also been published under the title, Vrais Principes de la Constitution du Clergé. (Biog. Univ.)

BERARDIER, (Peter,) an apothecary at Grenoble, about the middle of the seventeenth century, who wrote a valuable work on the botany of Dauphiny, in 7 vols, fol. This has never been published, but its able compiler's merits have been commemorated by Villars, in the name *Berardia*, given by him to a genus of plants. (Biog. Univ.)

BERAUD, (John James,) a French physician and naturalist, born February 5, 1753; and died February 1, 1794, having published three memoirs, which obtained prizes at the college of Marseilles, entitled, Sur la Culture du Câprier, sur l'Education des Abeilles, et sur une Machine propre à pêcher le Corail. In the Journal de Physique there are also some papers by Beraud, one of which is on the means of detecting the presence of alum in wine.

BERAUD, (Laurence,) a French Jesuit, eminent in mathematics and most branches of natural philosophy, born at Lyons, March 5, 1701. The suppression of his order gave him a shock that he never thoroughly recovered, and nothing could prevail upon him afterwards to take any public employment. He died June 26, 1777. Mathematics engaged his principal attention, and among his pupils were some who became the most brilliant ornaments of physical science—Lalande, Bossu, and Montucla. He published various papers, most of which are to be found in the Memoirs of the Academy of Sciences of Lyons, among which is an account of his discovery of the luminous ring around the planet Mercury, as observed by him in the passage of that planet over the sun, May 6, 1753, and which had previously been sought after in vain. His observations in physical astronomy are marked by great accuracy and enlightened research. He wrote on vegetation, the evaporation of liquids, light, the rotatory motion of the earth, the inclination of its axis, and other questions in physical science. He sustained, against Boyle, the imponderable nature of heat; and this memoir was crowned with a prize by the Academy of Sciences of Bourdeaux in 1747. He received another prize for his researches into the relation which exists between magnetism and electricity, which he looked upon as identical.

BERAULD, or BERAULT, (Nicholas,) born at Orleans in 1475, the learned host of Erasmus, in his way through Orleans, to Italy in 1500. He Latinized his name into *Beraldus Aurelius*. In 1516, appeared the works of William, bishop of Paris, edited by him; and in the same year, Pliny's Natural History, with many of his corrections; but, notwithstanding, Hardouin has not allowed him a place among the editors of Pliny. There are also some other works of his of less importance. (Biog. Univ.)

BERAULD, (Francis,) son of the preceding, an eminent Greek scholar, who became a protestant, and was employed by Henry Stephens to translate the two books of Appian, which contain the Spanish wars, and those of Hannibal. (Biog. Univ.)

BERAULT, (Christopher,) an advocate of the parliament of Rouen, published, in 1625, a volume, entitled, Sur les Droits de Tier et Danger. (Biog. Univ.)

BERAULT, (Josias,) an advocate of the parliament of Rouen, who was born in 1563, and who died in 1646, published Commentaire sur la Coutume de Normandie. (Biog. Univ.)

BERAULT-BERCASTEL, (Anthony Henry,) a French writer, born early in the eighteenth century, and originally a Jesuit, but afterwards beneficed as a secular priest, both parochially and in a cathedral. He died during the revolution. He first appeared before the world in 1754, as author of a small poem. This was succeeded by a romance from the Spanish, and a collection of Idylls. He then attempted poetry upon a larger scale, publishing a piece in twelve cantos, on the

Promised Land; but it was a mixture of sacred history and mythological imagery, that gained him any thing rather than credit. His next literary labour was more suitable to his profession, being an Ecclesiastical History, that extended over 24 vols, 12mo, the first of which appeared in 1778. It is a work that wants the gravity of Fleuri, who is often copied without acknowledgment, but written in an easy style, and in a spirit adverse to the Gallican liberties. Hence it had considerable success, and a second edition appeared at Toulouse in 1811. The author also left a MS. abridgement of his History, in 5 vols, 8vo. (Biog. Univ.)

BERAULT, (Michael,) pastor and professor of theology at Montauban, about the beginning of the seventeenth century; was chosen to enter into conference with cardinal du Perron at Mentz, in 1593, and in 1598, wrote against him, Briève et claire Defense de la Vocation des Ministres de l'Evangile, 8vo.

BERAULT, (Claude,) succeeded d' Herbelot as professor of Syriac in the royal college of Paris, best known by his edition of Statius, 1685, 2 vols, 4to. He died in 1705. (Biog. Univ.)

BERCH, (Charles Reinhold,) a Swedish writer, born early in the eighteenth century, who died in 1777. He was well versed in history, numismatics, and political economy. He published several works, in Swedish, on the medals, history, and remarkable persons of his native land. (Biog. Univ.)

BERCHELMAN, (John Philip,) a physician, born at Darmstadt, June 3, 1718, who died August 13, 1783. He published, Dissertatio de Liene, Giessen, 1750, 4to; Tractatus de Hydrope Ascite in Gravidâ cum Febre Quartanâ conjuncto, post Abortum funesto, Giessen, 1753, 4to, and some medical works in German.

BERCHEM, or BERCHEMIUS, (William de,) canon of the church of Nimwegen about 1466, having written, Compendium Chronicorum Geldriæ, reaching to that period. (Swertii Ath. Belg.)

BERCHEM, (James Ciachetto, or Jacket of Mantua,) a native of the Netherlands, who lived for a considerable time at Mantua. He composed many of the madrigals and motets to be found in collections published at Venice, between 1539 and 1561. Some of his compositions, published in 1543, are in the British Museum. They have a clearness, simplicity, and purity, rarely surpassed by the early composers. Berchem was living in the year 1580. (Mus. Biog. Dict. of Mus.)

BERCHEM, (Nicholas,) an eminent painter of landscape and cattle, born at Haerlem in 1624, first taught by his father, an indifferent painter of fish, vases, and objects of still life, but he afterwards studied under some distinguished masters. He painted the whole of his pictures with such admirable skill and care, that it was difficult to point out any particular as better than the rest. So anxious, accordingly, were collectors for his works, that their price was ordinarily paid before he began them; and such was his industry, that he commonly painted through an entire summer day, from four in the morning till twilight. He died in 1683. (Pilkington.)

BERCHENY, (Nicholas,) a Hungarian chief, of Transylvanian origin, born in 1664, who, in 1700, plotted with prince Ragotzky, a relative, the separation of his native country from Austria. The two having received a subsidy from France, then at war with Austria, assembled an army on the frontiers of Hungary, which quickly augmented to near sixty thousand men, and made its way almost to the gates of Vienna. Reverses, however, were at length undergone, and the confederation dwindled by degrees, so that in the winter of 1711, Bercheny, who had been made ducal lieutenant of Hungary, was under the necessity of fleeing into Poland. He died at Radosto, in Turkey, in 1725. One of his sons entered the French service, and rising in it to high commands, a regiment of Hussars went by his name until the year 1790. (Biog. Univ.)

BERCHETT, (Peter, 1659—1720,) a French painter, who came to England in 1681, and was employed in ornamenting houses for the nobility, under the direction of Rambour, a French painter of architecture, but he only remained in England a year, when he returned to Marly. He paid another visit to this country, and was again fully employed, until William the Third sent him to Loo to decorate his palace there, in which Berchett was engaged fifteen months; and then, a third time, repaired to England, where he painted the ceiling of Trinity-college chapel, Oxford, and executed some other works of the same kind, which are no longer in existence. His drawings of academic figures were much approved. Towards the close of his life he retired to Mary-le-bone, and painted only small pictures of fabulous history, the last of which was a bacchanalian, to which he put his name only the day before he died. He was also an engraver. (Walpole's Anecd. of Painting, by Dallaway, iii. 245. Strutt, Dict. of Eng.)

BERCHORIUS, (Peter,) a learned French Benedictine, whose vernacular name was Bercheure, born in the beginning of the fourteenth century in Poitou, and famed for such a knowledge of the Bible as enabled him to cite from it authorities upon any subject from memory. He died at Paris in 1362, prior of the monastery of St. Eloy, since occupied by the Barnabites. He wrote several works which are lost; those which remain are in 3 vols, fol, under the title of Reductorium, Repertorium et Dictionarium morale utriusque Testamenti, Strasburg, 1474; Nuremberg, 1499; and Cologne, 1631-1692; a species of Biblical Encyclopædia, displaying great knowledge and boundless imagination. Warton, in his History of Poetry, ascribes to him the Gesta Romanorum. Berchorius also wrote, Doctrinale Metricum, long used as a school book in France. Besides these works, he translated Livy, and his version was published at Paris in 1514, 3 vols, fol. (Biog. Univ. Chalmers.)

BERCHTOLD, (Leopold, count von,) an Austrian nobleman, worthy to be called the German Howard, born in 1758. He travelled for thirteen years in Europe, and for four in different parts of Asia and Africa, with the view of mitigating the sufferings of humanity; publishing, in several countries, the results of his inquiries, in the language of the country concerned, and distributing the greatest part of these publications gratis. In his Essay to Direct and Extend the Inquiries of Patriotic Travellers, he draws attention to the means adopted in various parts for the preservation of life, and succour of the poor; also to the captives made by African corsairs, and to the means of their liberation; and other similar subjects. Among his writings distributed gratis, are various publications, suggesting improvements in police regulations. By the prizes which he instituted, he called forth a number of useful works on the recovery of the drowned. In London, he became a member of the Humane Society, encouraged the writings of Fothergill and Poppe, and took steps to bring Struve's Tables into circulation. He founded a Humane Society in Moravia, and *Rettungsanstalten* at Prague and Brünn. In 1791 he published, at Vienna, an anonymous compilation from the best modern German physicians, on the restoration of the apparently dead, and on measures to prevent burial before death. This was also distributed gratis; and the author laid a French translation of it before the National Assembly. In 1792 we find him publishing, at Lisbon, a work on the preservation of life in different dangers; and in the following year, in the same capital, he gave to the Portuguese, an Essay towards extending the Boundaries of Beneficence to Men and Animals, which was reprinted from a Vienna edition. In 1795-7 he travelled in Turkey, to study, from actual observation, the plague and its remedies: in a work published at Vienna, in 1797, he strongly recommends its treatment by a simple oil liniment. He afterwards greatly exerted himself to render vaccination general. He collected nearly 65,000 florins for the unfortunate inhabitants of the *Riesengebirge* during the famine of 1805-6. In 1809 he converted his beautiful castle of Bucklowitz into an hospital for the Austrian soldiery; and he died here the same year, of an epidemic nervous fever.

BERCKMANN, BERKMANN, BARKMANN, or BERGMANN, (John,) author of the Chronicles of Stralsund, born between 1490 and 1500, probably at Stralsund; there at least he lived as an Augustinian friar. He embraced Lutheranism about 1527, and was a preacher of that doctrine, first in Brandenburg, and afterwards at Stralsund. He died in 1560. His work, written in low German, and very little known, though written often in a confused and inartificial manner, contains some important information not to be met with elsewhere, and is besides an interesting specimen of the low German dialect. It exists only in MS. (Ersch und Gruber.)

BERCKMANS, (Henry,) a Dutch painter, born in 1629. After receiving lessons from Philip Wouwermans, Thomas Willeborts, and James Jordaens, he took nature alone for his guide. He had made great progress as an historical painter, when he took to portraits, to which he chiefly confined himself. Such was the desire of possessing them, that he had great difficulty in fulfilling his engagements. The portraits of most of the distinguished contemporaries of his country were painted by him. (Biog. Univ. Bryan's Dict.)

BERCKRINGER, (Daniel,) tutor to the king of Bohemia's children, and in

1640, by the queen's interest, appointed professor of philosophy at Utrecht. He died in 1667, leaving several works, of which the principal were—Exercitationes Ethicæ, Æconomicæ, Politicæ, Utrecht, 1664; Dissertatio de Cometis, 1665; and Examen Elementorum Philosophicorum de bono Cive, which remains in MS., and was written against Hobbes. (Chalmers.)

BERDI, or BIRDI-BEK, the ninth of the Mogul khans of Kapchak, descended from Toushi, son of Jenghiz-khan, succeeded his father Jani-Bek, A.D. 1357, (A.H. 758.) He died from the effects of his excesses, A.D. 1360, (A.H. 761,) and as with him became extinct the direct descendants of Mangu-Timur, who had reigned for five generations from father to son, the throne was disputed by the collateral branches represented by Auruss-khan (see AURUSS-KHAN) and Tokatmish, till the irruption of Timour, who first favoured, and then attacked the latter pretender, gave a fatal blow to the power of the monarchy. (De Guignes.)

BERE, (Oswald,) a German physician, born in 1472; died at Basle in 1567. He became a protestant, and wrote a Commentary on the Apocalypse; a treatise, De Veteri et Novâ Fide; and a Catechism. (Biog. Univ.)

BERE, (Lewis,) born at Basle, towards the close of the fifteenth century, one of the four presidents in the religious conferences of Baden; he died at Friburg in 1554. He published, in 1551, at Basle, De Christianâ Preparatione ad Mortem; Quorundam Psalmorum Expositio; and an examination in Latin, of the question, "Whether a Christian may flee in time of pestilence?" (Biog. Univ.)

BEREGANI, (Nicolas, Feb. 21, 1627—Dec. 17, 1713,) an Italian poet and historian, born at Vicenza. His poems evince that he possessed considerable taste, but corrupted by the age in which he lived, and his characters are exaggerated and unnatural. His historical work is entitled, Istoria delle Guerre d'Europa dalla comparsa delle Armi Ottomane nell' Ungheria l'anno 1683. Three years after his death also appeared a translation of Claudian by him, with notes, which is a work in good estimation, and is to be found in the grand collection of Italian translations from the ancient Latin poets, printed at Milan, in the early part of the eighteenth century. (Biog. Univ.)

BERENDS, (Charles Augustus William,) a celebrated German physician, born in 1753, who was named to a special clinical and therapeutic professorship at Berlin. He was much esteemed as a professor, although the state of his health frequently interrupted the course of his lectures. He died in 1826, and his discourses were published by Sunderlin, who was his successor in the clinical chair: Vorlesungen ueber praktische Arzneiwissenschaft, herausgegeben von Karl Sunderlin, Berlin, 1827-29, 9 vols. 8vo. It is the most complete system of practical medicine ever published in Germany. His posthumous works in Latin were published by Stosch, Berlin, 1829-30, in 2 vols, 8vo.

BERENGARIO, (James,) a celebrated Italian physician and anatomist. He was a native of Carpi, near Modena, and is very frequently designated by the name of his birthplace. Albert Pio, lord of Carpi, a zealous protector of the sciences, entertaining a wish to revive the study of anatomy, proposed the public dissection of a pig, which office he entrusted to Berengario, who was the son of an able surgeon, named Faustino, and had already evinced his taste for anatomical research. His success stimulated him in his studies, and he went to Bologna, and there took the degree of doctor of medicine, after which he went to Pavia, and taught surgery, but returned to Bologna, where he was appointed to a chair in the university, which he occupied from 1502 to 1527. Berengario is to be regarded as one of the chief restorers of anatomy. He directed his researches to the human body itself, and abandoned the practice of merely commenting upon the works of Galen, which was the too general custom of his day. He boasts of having dissected more than one hundred bodies. His style of writing is rude, but he communicates many discoveries. He was the first to point out the true form of the uterus, and to prove that a peculiar arrangement of the blood-vessels common to quadrupeds does not exist in man. He treats with ability of the structure of the larynx; he also displays the true anatomy of the intestines, the kidneys, &c., which prior to his researches were but imperfectly understood. His work is accompanied by anatomical figures, offering the earliest specimens of the kind, and for the period in which they were executed of no mean excellence. They are said to have been engraved by Hugo de Carpi. He employed largely mercurial frictions in his practice; but he was not the first to introduce them, as is often erroneously reported. He carried the employment of mercury to a very dangerous extent. His works are.—Isagoge brevis in Anatomiam Corporis Humani, Bononiæ, 1514, 1522, 1523, 1525, 4to; Venetiis, 1525, 1535, 4to; Coloniæ, 1529, 8vo; Argent. 1530, 8vo. De Cranii Fracturâ Tractatus, Bonon. 1518, 4to; Venet. 1535; Lugd. Batav. 1629, 1651, 1715, 12mo. Commentaria cum amplissimis Additionibus super Anatomiam Mundini, Bonon. 1521, 1522, 4to; Venet. 1535, 4to; translated into English 1664, 12mo.

BERENGARIUS, or BERENGER, always written anciently, Mabillion says, Beringerius, one of the most conspicuous individuals in religious controversy; born about the close of the tenth century, of a superior family, at Tours, and educated under Fulbert of Chartres, greatly to the credit of both parties. Fulbert is, however, said to have entertained suspicions, divulged at the approach of death, that his promising pupil would prove eventually a dangerous man. Having completed his education at Chartres, Berenger returned to Tours, and was there appointed lecturer in the public schools attached to St. Martin's church. He was afterwards nominated archdeacon of Angers, by Eusebius, who bears the surname of Bruno, bishop of that see, a favourer of his opinions, and whom Mabillon considers likely to have been among his scholars. The number of these was very considerable, Tours enjoying, under his care, the highest credit as a place of education. Nevertheless, according to Guitmond, one of Berenger's bitterest opponents, formerly a monk in the monastery of St. Leufroy, in Normandy, and eventually archbishop of Aversa, in the Neapolitan territory, the famed Turonese doctor was really defective in depth of understanding, and hence, could never gain a sufficient insight into the whole range of philosophy. Lanfranc, then master of the monastic seminary at Bec, and eventually archbishop of Canterbury, was thus placed upon much higher ground by the majority that admired him, his competence in every known branch of learning being considered as indisputable. His credit is represented accordingly as eclipsing Berenger's, to the latter's great mortification; which was rendered more complete by some trial of skill in a logical disputation of no very abstruse character, in which the two were engaged, and Lanfranc was found altogether superior. Being thus humiliated, and finding his academical establishment losing ground, Guitmond proceeds to say, that Berenger turned his mind to Scripture, in hopes of wresting from it some novelty that might recover his reputation, *preferring men's admiration as a heretic, to a life merely under God's eye as a catholic.* These representations have been industriously circulated by modern Romish writers, and coming, as they do, from a contemporary, controversialists may be excused in making the best of them; but they are not countenanced by Lanfranc's own account of the first proceedings that arose from Berenger's opinions. Those upon the eucharistic presence were in unison with John Scot's tract upon that question, written in the ninth century, by desire of Charles the Bald. Lanfranc had adopted a different view, then unquestionably becoming every day more popular, but, as it seems, by no means firmly established, even upon the continent. Ingram of Chartres informed Berenger of Lanfranc's bias, and he wrote to that eminent man a friendly letter, yet extant, and unlike that of a mortified rival, inviting him to a conference upon the eucharistic question, and concluding by saying, that if he considered John Scot a heretic, he must give the same character to Ambrose, Jerome, Austin, and others. When Berenger's messenger brought this letter into Normandy, he found Lanfranc gone, and delivered it, accordingly, to some clergymen who might, perhaps, be charged with opening letters for him in his absence. They were so highly scandalized by the communication, that they put it into the hands of others, and an opinion got abroad, that Lanfranc himself must really be of Berenger's opinion, or otherwise he never would have been addressed by him in such a letter. An opportunity, however, occurred of sending it by a clergyman from Rheims to Rome, whither Lanfranc had gone to attend a council holden under Leo IX. after Easter, in 1050. To this council it was read, and being disapproved, Berenger was excommunicated. Lanfranc was then desired to purge himself of any participation in his opinions, which he did to the satisfaction of all present. As this whole proceeding was rather hasty and irregular, Berenger was now summoned to attend a council to be holden at Vercelli, in the September of that year. He did not come in person, but some friends appeared for him, alleging his authority. They seem, however, to have come forward only once, and he was condemned, as was John Scot's book; and thus the church of Rome formally committed herself to the doctrine of transubstantiation. Berenger himself had gone into Normandy, in hopes of protection from William the Bastard, eventually conqueror of England, but that prince detained him at Brionne, and calling an assembly there of the bishops in his duchy, he was condemned, together with a clergyman who accompanied him. This condemnation appears to have preceded that of Vercelli. France was, however, much agitated by this controversy, and to appease it, king Henry called a council at Paris, in the November of the same year, which again condemned Berenger, and imposed a recantation upon him and his adherents under pain of death. Still no progress was made by the partisans of transubstantiation, and hence Victor II., who succeeded Leo IX. in 1054, was urged into some effective notice of the controversy. This led to a council at Tours, in 1055, at which Hildebrand, afterwards the famous Gregory VII., was present as legate, and in which Berenger was said to have completely recanted, binding himself at the same time with an oath to keep in future the common faith of the church. He appears, however, merely to have admitted the real presence, a question perfectly distinct from the corporal presence. Hence the council was no sooner over, and his opponents talked of him to all the world as beaten into an acknowledgment of the divine presence in the eucharist, than he himself restricted his acknowledgment of this privilege to faithful communicants. He was, however, so much overborne by the arm of power, that instructions of a popular character were in a great measure intermitted of necessity, and he could only avail himself of private conversation and the composition of controversial treatises. He was very active in both ways, thus keeping his opponents continually on the defensive. Hence they exerted themselves to obtain another summons for him to Rome, from Nicholas II., then pope, in 1058. In the following year he answered personally this summons, and in a very full council, at first maintained his own views, but subsequently, either overcome by fear and importunity, or confused in argument, he signed a confession, that in the eucharist, Christ's body and blood are so present as to be sensibly handled and masticated. Even this concession, however, does not come up to transubstantiation, for the sensible presence is limited to the faithful; but it is conceived in terms from which Berenger recoiled when left to himself. He had no sooner, therefore, returned to France, than his old style of teaching was revived, and Nicholas appears to have taken no further notice of him. Nor did the next pope, Alexander II., move any otherwise in this business than to send him a friendly letter, exhorting him to alter his opinions. This, in a written answer, he positively declined, apparently trusting in the protection of some powerful men who would not forsake him. Thus the controversy continued with unabated violence, and Hildebrand, now Gregory VII., thought it advisable to try the effect of another summons to Rome. Berenger accordingly appeared again there in 1078, and made another profession, worded rather particularly, and containing no mention of the faithful, but really amounting to nothing more than an acknowledgment of the real presence. This gave great dissatisfaction to the anti-Berengarians, being reprobated as ambiguous, which it is, in truth; and as Gregory was known to think well of the Angevin archdeacon, he was charged with permitting him to sign such an evasive form, because he really had himself an inclination to his opinions. The pope was therefore driven into another attack upon him, in a council holden at Rome in 1079. Before this, Berenger signed another form, professing that Christ's presence is essential and substantial; but really, as upon every other occasion, leaving the doctrine of transubstantiation, under all circumstances, undecided. Hence, when returned to France, he remained an object of uneasiness with persons who believed in that doctrine, and in 1080 he was summoned to a legative council, holden at Bourdeaux, to give an account of his faith. This was his last public appearance; the remaining years of his life being spent in religious retirement, in the little isle of St. Cosmas, near Tours. He died there Jan. 6, 1088, aged about ninety. Some Romish writers represent him to have abandoned his opposition to transubstantiation during the latter years of his life, grounding their opinion, probably, upon religious services performed annually for ages over his tomb by the canons of Tours, and by the insertion of his name in the menology of the cathedral of Angers, honours deemed unlikely to be paid to one who died under the imputation of heresy. But his great religious and moral excellences are a sufficient reason for these tributes of respect to his memory, especially as the doctrine which has rendered his name so famous, really was not definitively settled until a later age. Romanists would make disputes upon it to have originated with him, and accordingly call ancient opponents of transubstantiation Berengarians; but it should be remembered that his text-book was written by John Scot two centuries before, and that he appealed for confirmations to the fathers. His principal work, the Reply to Lanfranc, was supposed, like John Scot's piece upon the eucharist, to have been destroyed under the general prevalence, eventually established, of opinions adverse to it; but it has been discovered in the library of Wolfenbutel, and a large part of it was published by Lessing, at Brunswick, in 1770. It hence appears that Berenger, as a careful consideration of his history sufficiently shows, did not believe the eucharist a rite merely commemorative, but admitted a real presence to faithful communicants, only excluding that substantial change, which is necessary to make the sacramental elements allowable objects of adoration. There is a short contemporary account of the leading particulars in this remarkable man's history, in Labbe and Cossart's Councils, ix. 1050. Lanfranc's account of the earlier movements may be seen in the next page; Guitmund's account of him may be seen in Mabillon's Annales Benedictini, iv. 477. That work also contains other particulars of him, but written in an unfriendly spirit. Cave's Historia Literaria treats him differently, and with sufficient fulness, as does Mosheim's Ecclesiastical History, ii. 379, new edit. Du Pin's Ecclesiastical History, ix. 6, is also full, and upon the whole fair, upon this important character in ecclesiastical biography.

BERENGER I. son of Everard, duke of Friuli, recognised as king of Italy by an assembly of the estates, assassinated in Verona in 924. (Biog. Univ.)

BERENGER II. king of Italy, grandson of the preceding, held the throne as a fief from Otho, by whom he was afterwards dethroned, and confined at Bamberg, where he died in 966. (Biog. Univ.)

BERENGER, (Raymond de,) a native of Dauphiny, and knight of St. John, elected twenty-ninth grand master of the order A.D. 1365. His arrival at Rhodes was signalized by the equipment of a formidable armament destined for the attack of Alexandria, the corsairs of which port scoured the Levant. The king of Cyprus joined the expedition with all his forces; but they failed in possessing themselves of the town, and were forced to retreat at the approach of the sultan of Egypt. The administration of Berenger was principally occupied by efforts to enforce the regulations of the order, which had fallen into desuetude, and to terminate the quarrels between the languages or divisions of the knights; but his unaided efforts were unsuccessful, and he was compelled to appeal to the pope, Gregory XI. who, in a general assembly holden at Avignon, 1373, succeeded in reconciling the differences, and establishing subordination among the tenants of commanderies; and from this period the decisions of Avignon were frequently referred to in the disputes of the order. Berenger died the next year, 1374, at an advanced age. (Boisgelin. Vertot.)

BERENGER, (Richard,) many years gentleman of the horse to George III. of Great Britain, who published in 1771, The History and Art of Horsemanship, 2 vols, 4to, plates. He died in 1782, aged 62.

BERENGER, (John Peter,) a French miscellaneous writer, born at Geneva, in 1740, died in 1807. He published a History of Geneva, in six vols, 12mo, 1775; Busching's Geography abridged, 12 vols, 8vo, 1776; a Collection of all the Voyages round the World, 1788, 9 vols, 8vo; and some other works. (Chalmers.)

BERENGER, (Peter,) a disciple of Abelard, in whose defence he wrote a work entitled Apologie d'Abelard, printed in 1616, in Duchesne's edition of the works of Abelard, and likewise the author of some pieces reflecting severely on the church, to be found in the same publication. (Hist. Lit. de la France.)

BERENGUELA, a beautiful and spirited queen of Castile, said to have shamed the Moors from prosecuting the siege of Toledo in 1139, by upbraiding them with the choice of a town entrusted to the care of a woman, rather than that of one where her husband was in the field, and where honour might be gained. (Vertot's Revolutions in Spain.)

BERENGUELA, eldest daughter of Alphonso III., king of Castile, married in 1201, Alphonso IX. king of Leon; divorced in 1209, on the ground of consanguinity, by pope Innocent III.; declared regent of Castile during the minority of her brother, Henry I.; on his death proclaimed queen, but immediately resigned in favour of her eldest son, Ferdinand. She died in 1244, universally regretted. (Vertot's Revolutions in Spain.)

BERENGUER, (Peter John Morales,) a Valencian clergyman, who wrote, Universal Explicacion de los Mysterios de nuestra Santa Fe, Valenzia, 1608, 3 vols, fol. (Antonio.)

BERENGUIDDUS, a theologian, of the Sorbonne, said by Dempster to have been from Scotland, author of a treatise upon the Apocalypse, about the year 1446, in some MS. copies of which he is styled archbishop of Turin.

BERENHORST, (G. H. v.) a natural son of prince Leopold of Anhalt-Dessau, and the forerunner of Bülow in a strenuous opposition to antiquated strategic rules, born in 1733, and placed when a boy in the Prussian army. He served in the seven years' war, but in 1761 he left it, and repaired to the court of Dessau, where he spent the greatest part of his remaining life, engaged in more congenial studious pursuits. From 1765 to 1768 he travelled in Italy, France, and England, with one of the princes of Dessau. After his return, he filled various offices at court. In 1785 he was made chief tutor to the crown prince, Frederic, (who died 1814,) for whose education a small academy of learned men, under Berenhorst's superintendence, was instituted. He died October 30, 1814. To all writers on strategy, he is known by his works on this subject. His Reflections on the art of war, written in 1795-6, excited great attention, as they sought scientifically to overthrow tactics previously esteemed.

BERENICE, or BERONICE, mentioned in Scripture as Bernice, (Acts xxv. 13,) daughter of Herod Agrippa, or Agrippa the Great, vassal king of Chalcis, and sister of Drusilla, the Jewish wife to Felix, whose name appears in the chapter immediately preceding. She was first married to her uncle Herod, then king of Chalcis; but losing him after four years, she went to live with her brother, Herod Agrippa the younger, now made, by the favour of Claudius, king of Chalcis. Her stay with him was publicly branded with an incestuous character, and hence Juvenal, (Sat. vi. 158,) lashing the female depravity of his day, makes a diamond ring, *given by the barbarian Agrippa to his incestuous sister*, to have been prized above its real value on that very account. At length Berenice was incited by these attacks upon her character into serious thoughts of a new marriage, and her great wealth, rendered additionally attractive by unusual beauty, enabled her to contract one with Polemon, king of Cilicia. But whatever might be the licentiousness of her morals, she appears to have been rather strict in the religious observances of Judaism; hence Polemon was constrained to profess himself regularly a convert to that faith. He did not, however, secure by this compliance any long connexion with his fascinating, but licentious wife. She soon left him, and her departure was the signal of his own return to paganism. Berenice herself continuing to alternate fits of devotion with moral obliquity, was duly engaged at Jerusalem in the religious exercises of one under a vow of purification, when the troubles which ended in the destruction of that unhappy city were beginning there. Vainly did she intercede with Florus, the Roman governor, for his merciful consideration of her miserable countrymen. His troops made sport of her penitential appearance, her appeals being made barefooted, as the vow obliged her, a peculiarity at which Juvenal glances in the next line to that cited above, which talks of the country *where royalty keeps solemn sabbaths with foot unshod*. As the war advanced, Berenice endeavoured to mitigate its horrors by liberal presents to Vespasian, and artful attacks upon the heart of Titus. Both had their weight, especially the latter, Titus being so fascinated, that he received her as an inmate in the imperial palace, and his marriage with her is said to have been only prevented by popular murmurs at the prospect of it. In deference, however, to public opinion thus expressed, he sent the seductive Jewess home. As Berenice was now between forty and fifty, some persons have supposed that it was her niece of whom Titus became enamoured; but it seems more likely to have been the aunt, who was unquestionably very handsome and very artful, and whose real hold upon the affections of Titus may be a good deal exaggerated. (Josephus. Bayle.)

BERENICE, wife to Ptolemy Lagus, or Soter, the first Macedonian king of Egypt, originally an attendant of Eurydice, a former wife, but being exceedingly handsome, he married her, and when over eighty (B.C. 285,) resigned the crown to Ptolemy Philadelphus, elder of his two sons by her, in prejudice to the admitted rights of Ptolemy Ceraunus, his eldest son, born of Eurydice. (Prideaux, Connect. ii. 7. Justin. xvi. 2.)

BERENICE, *the king's daughter of the south* of Daniel, (xi. 6,) daughter of Ptolemy Philadelphus, king of Egypt, married by him (B.C. 249) to Antiochus Theus, king of Syria, *the king of the north*, on condition of his divorcing Laodice, his former wife, and making the issue of his new marriage heirs to the throne. On Ptolemy's death, however, Antiochus dismissed Berenice, and recalled Laodice. The latter fearing some new arrangement, and stung by resentment for past injuries, poisoned him, a crime soon followed by the murder of Berenice, and an infant son that she had by him. (Prideaux. Justin. xxvii. 1.)

BERENICE, another daughter of Ptolemy Philadelphus, but adopted by Magas, king of Cyrene, married to her brother, Ptolemy III., king of Egypt, called *Euergetes, the Benefactor*, because he recovered in the Syrian wars many of the Egyptian gods. While absent in this expedition, Berenice vowed her beautiful hair as an offering to Venus, should he safely return. Being gratified in this, the hair was deposited in the temple of the Zephyrian Venus, from which, by accident or carelessness, it soon disappeared, to Ptolemy's great indignation. He was, however, appeased by Conon, a Samian astronomer, then at Alexandria, who assured him that the royal locks had been transferred to the skies, where he had discovered them, and he pointed out, accordingly, the constellation yet called *Coma Berenices*, or *Berenice's head of hair*, as proof that his mode of exculpating the Zephyrian priests was worthy of implicit reliance. Callimachus added lustre to this mode of soothing offended royalty by writing a poem on *Berenice's Hair*, now lost in the original Greek, but preserved in a Latin version of Catullus. Berenice was put to death by her own son, Ptolemy Philopator, early in the third century before Christ. (Prideaux. Lempriere.)

BERETTARI, (John,) a canonist, born at Modena, towards the very end of the fifteenth century, whose talents for Italian poetry acquired for him the friendship of the cardinals Bembo and Bibbiena. Abandoning poetry for theology, he made a great progress, but was summoned to Rome to give an account of his faith before the inquisition. Being absolved after some months, he returned to Modena, and passed tranquilly the rest of his life.

BERG. The name of two artists:—

1. *Mathias van den*, (1615—1647,) a Flemish painter, born at Ypres, son of the manager of the estates of Rubens, and best known by his excellent copies of the pictures of that master. (Biog. Univ. Bryan's Dict.)

2. *Nicholas Vander*, a Flemish engraver, supposed to be a native of Antwerp. He etched some plates after Rubens, which he marked N. V. D. Berg. (Bryan's Dict.)

BERG, (Joachim von,) the most celebrated member of a family still existing in Silesia, born in 1526, who devoted his whole property to the creation of a fund for the assistance of his poor countrymen in devoting themselves to a literary life. This fund, by the express words of the donor, was restricted to protestant youths, but the emperor Leopold, in 1679, appropriated it to Romanists, an injustice afterwards repaired by the Prussian government.

BERG, (Magnus,) born in Norway in 1666, in his youth a valet, but his talent for sculpture procured him a recommendation to king Christian V. who placed him under the court painter Anderson. He afterwards travelled at the king's expense to Italy. The rest of his time, till his death in 1739, was devoted to painting, and carving in ivory, an art in which he particularly excelled. (Worm. Forsög til et Lexicon, &c.)

BERG, (John Peter,) a German theologian and philologer, born at Bremen, in 1737, who in 1758 went to Leyden, and studied under Schultens, Alberti, and von Muschenbroek. In 1760, he published his first work, Specimen Animadversionum Philologicarum ad Selecta V. T. loca Lugdun. Bat. 1761. In 1762 he was made professor of Greek and of the oriental languages in his native town. In the following year, he was appointed professor of theology and the oriental languages at Duisburg; and also in 1777, of ecclesiastical history.

Berg was a man of great mental powers and indefatigable activity; a good philologer (especially versed in Arabic, as is shown by the numerous additions with which he enriched his copy of Golius, now at Bonn); a cautious critic, a sound and judicious commentator of the Bible, and an erudite historian of the church. In private life he was tolerant, modest, and generally estimable. He is the author, besides the work above-mentioned, of various articles in periodicals; of an unpublished History of the Reformation in the Lower Rhenish Provinces; and of commentaries on various parts of the Bible, which have also not been printed.

BERGA, (Peter,) a Spanish ecclesiastic, born in Catalonia, prebendary of Tarragona, conspicuous for inciting John Felton, an English Romanist of good family, to post the papal bull, pretending to dethrone queen Elizabeth, on the gates of the bishop of London's palace, on Corpus Christi day, 1570. This was the first of those offensive and dangerous acts that aroused Elizabeth into severities against her Romish subjects, and Felton, the party by whom the outrage was actually committed, was justly executed as a traitor. He seems to have been a violent fanatic, but he might, perhaps, have never ventured upon this defiance to his native sovereign, had he not fallen in the way of a man like Berga. That wily Spaniard showed, however, no disposition to share with his English dupe the glories of martyrdom, as Felton's punishment was termed by Romanists. Having lured this unhappy gentleman to toss the firebrand of sedition among his countrymen, he promptly fled, to boast upon the continent of the mischief that he had done in England, and of his own good management in shifting the whole penalty upon the shoulders of another. (Ribadeneyra. Scisma de Inglaterra, 267.)

BERGALLI, (Louisa,) an Italian dramatic poetess, born at Venice, April 15, 1703, daughter of a shoemaker in that city, and married at thirty to count Gaspard Gozzi, a noble Venetian, known in Italian literature for his comedies and other works. Her works are very numerous, many of them original plays, but among them are translations from Terence, Racine, and others. (Biog. Univ.)

BERGAMASCO, (William,) an architect, who flourished at Venice during the earlier part of the sixteenth century.

BERGAMO, (Henry de,) a Carmelite friar of Mantua, who published, about 1470, an heroic poem, addressed to Julianus Brixiensis, viceroy-general of his order. (Bibliotheca Carmelitana.)

BERGAMO, (Andrew,) an Italian poet and satirist, about 1546, who wrote, Satire alla Carlona. Venetia, 1566. (Calvi Scritt. Bergam.)

BERGAMO, (Damiano,) a Dominican friar, accomplished in inlaying woods of various colours. Of this art, Lanzi says that he can trace nothing of its inventors, though it is said to have taken its rise in an imitation of mosaic work and of works in stone. No other coloured woods besides black and white were at first in use; nor any other objects beyond large edifices, temples, colonnades, and ornaments with architectural views. Vasari says of Bergamo, that he succeeded in refining the art of colours and of shades to such a degree, as to make him the very first in this line. He died in 1549. (Lanzi, Stor. Pitt. iii. 56.)

BERGAMO, (Gerard da,) a learned theologian of the fourteenth century, elected bishop of Savona in 1342, who died in 1356, leaving many MS. works in divinity.

BERGASSE, (Nicholas,) a celebrated French political writer and barrister, born at Lyons in 1750, of a family originally Spanish. In 1784 he published, Considerations on Animal Magnetism, a work of some talent, but much like a general attack upon physicians, moralists, and legislators. About this time he came to Paris, and soon established a high reputation at the bar; but mixing politics with his pleadings, he augmented that growing dissatisfaction with existing institutions which made way for the revolution. In 1789, Bergasse was elected deputy from Lyons for the Tiers-état to the States-general, but he did not prove an active member. He seemed, indeed, inclinable to the court, and Lewis XVI. requested him to reduce into some form his thoughts upon the government most suited to the time, which he did, and though never published, his plan caused a great many pamphlets to be launched forth against him; and after the tragical end of Lewis, he wished to retreat into Spain, but he was arrested in July 1794, and sent back to Paris; managing, however, to delay his arrival there, he saved his life, and was only sentenced to imprisonment. He then lived in retirement, but occupied himself in the composition of metaphysical and political works. After the restoration, he published an admirable pamphlet, entitled, Réflexions sur l'Acte Constitutionnel du Sénat. In 1821 Bergasse published an Essay on the relation which ought to subsist between religious and political law; and also a work in 8vo, which went immediately into a second edition, on the propriety of restoring to the emigrants the possessions forfeited in the revolution. For this he was arraigned in the court of assize, but honourably acquitted. This was the last of his writings. He died in 1832, aged 82. (Biog. des Contemp.)

BERGASSE, (Alexander,) brother of the preceding. He gained an ample competency by commerce, and was noted among his fellow-citizens of Lyons for virtue and honesty. In 1816 he wrote and printed in 8vo, a work entitled, a Refutation of the false Principles and Calumnies advanced by the Jacobins to cry down the Administration of our Kings, and to justify the Usurpation of the Royal Authority and of the Throne, by an Old Frenchman; a curious and bold book, which the author was obliged to suppress, and a few copies only were distributed among his friends; it is therefore very rare. He died at Lyons in 1821. (Biog. Univ. Suppl.)

BERGE, (Ernest Gotlib von,) born in 1649, who, coming into England in 1678, made the acquaintance of several Englishmen of distinction; among others of Lloyd, then bishop of St. Asaph, afterwards of Worcester, and on his return to the continent, published a German translation of Milton's Paradise Lost. This work had been already in part translated by Theodore Haak, a German, resident in England; but it is doubtful, from the terms of Von Berge's preface, whether he began the work anew, or continued the imperfect translation of Haak. The translation is executed in a masterly manner, in the same measure as the original. The title of this work is Paradise Lost, from the incomparable poem of John Milton, composed in the English language during his blindness. 8vo, Zerbst. 1682.

BERGEN. The name of two painters, one born at Breda about 1670, died very young, after giving great promise. (Biog. Univ.)

2. *Dirk*, or *Theodore van*, born at Haarlem about 1645, and was the best pupil of Adrian van der Velde, and, like him, painted landscape and animals. Van Bergen passed many years in England, and then returned to his own country. His works are well composed and coloured, but some of them want firmness of touch. (Biog. Univ. Bryan's Dict.)

BERGEN, (Daniel,) an engraver, born at Berlin in 1744, who engraved several portraits of the royal family of Prussia, and other works. (Bryan's Dict.)

BERGEN, (Charles Augustus de,) a celebrated anatomist and botanist, born at Frankfort-on-the-Oder, Aug. 11, 1704, whose researches on the intercostal nerve were considered worthy of a place in the collection of Haller. He endeavoured to simplify the study of botany, and died October 7, 1760.

BERGER, (Albert Louis,) a lawyer, born at Oldenbourg in 1768, who having inherited a large fortune from his father, travelled, and lived subsequently as a wealthy man of letters. Taking a prominent part in the movements made by his country against the French in 1813, he was shot, after a mock trial. He wrote, 1. Studien. 2. Letters from Italy. (Biog. Univ.)

BERGER, (J. Henry de,) a learned lawyer, born January 1657, professor of law at Wittemberg, and counsellor at Dresden. In 1713 he was summoned as aulic counsellor to Vienna, where he died, 25th of Nov. 1732. His works, often reprinted, are—1. Electa Processûs Executivi, Processorii, Provocatorii et Matrimonialis. 2. Electa Disceptationum Forensium. 3. Electa Jurisprudentiæ Criminalis. 4. Responsa ex omni Jure. 5. Œconomia Juris. Berger left three sons, all distinguished in the same profession. (Biog. Univ.)

BERGER, (Theodore,) professor of law and history at Cobourg, born in 1683, and died in 1773. His great Universal History is a work much esteemed. (Biog. Univ.)

BERGER, (Christian John,) a Danish physician, born August 14, 1724, professor in ordinary of medicine, surgery, and midwifery, at the university of Kiel. He died April 2, 1789, leaving some professional publications.

BERGER, (John Gotfried de,) a celebrated German physician, born Nov. 11, 1659, professor at the university of Wittemberg. He died October 2, 1756, having been fifty years in the exercise of his academical functions. In medicine he embraced the opinions of the mechanical sect, with some few modifications. His writings are numerous, and some of them have been reprinted in the collection of Haller. Those which merit most notice are:—Physiologia Medica, sive de Naturâ Humanâ Liber bipartitus, Wittemb. 1702, 4to, Lipsiæ, 1708, 4to, Francof. ad Mæn. 1737, 4to; Dissertatio de Naturâ, Morborum Medico, Wittemb. 1702, 4to; De Thermis Carolinis Commentatio, qui omnium Origo Fontium Calidarum itemque Acidarum, ex Pyrito ostenditur, Wittemb. 1709, 4to.

BERGERAC, (Savinien Cyrano de,) a French writer, of dissipated habits, but successful in works of imagination, born in Perigord, about the year 1620. He died at the age of thirty-five. He has been considered as an author to whom Molière, Fontenelle, Voltaire, and our own Swift, have been a good deal obliged. (Biog. Univ.)

BERGERET, (John Peter,) a lecturer on botany at Paris, where he died in 1813. His principal works are, Observations on Extra-Uterine Conception, and Phytonomatotechnie Universelle, or the art of giving to plants names derived from their characters. (Biog. Univ. Suppl.)

BERGERON, (Nicolas,) an advocate of the parliament of Paris, born at Bathisy, in the duchy of Valois, towards the middle of the sixteenth century. He was a learned man, but not very brilliant as a speaker. He was the first author of the synchronic tables, which present history at one view. The date of his death is not known, but supposed to have been about 1584. (Biog. Univ.)

BERGERON, (Peter,) son of the above, died 1637, leaving a treatise on navigation and on modern conquests and discoveries, introduced by notices of Carthaginian discoveries, but really beginning with that of the Canaries, and coming down to his own time, Paris, 1629; a History of the First Discovery and Conquest of the Canaries in 1402, Paris, 1630; a Narrative of the Expeditions of several distinguished Travellers in Tartary, Paris, 1634, reprinted in 1729. (Biog. Univ. Suppl.)

BERGIER, (Nicholas,) a French antiquary, born at Rheims on the 1st of March, 1567, died on the 18th of August, 1623. He is best known by his work on the History of Roman Roads, in which he was assisted by his friend Peiresc. It appeared in 1622, but becoming scarce, was reprinted in 1728, with the *Carte Itinéraire* of Peutinger. A third (1736) soon followed, though the first is considered the best edition. The work is learned and curious, but the facts are ill arranged, a fault of the age in which he lived. It has been translated into Latin, with learned notes, by H. C. Henninius, professor of the university of Duisbourg. This translation may be found in Grævius's Antiquities. In 1712, the first book of it appeared in English, in London, entitled the General History of the Highways in all parts of the world, particularly in Great Britain. Bergier also began a history of Rheims, and his son published all that he accomplished of it. His other works are not of considerable importance. (Biog. Univ.)

BERGIER, (Nicholas Sylvester,) born at Darnay, in Lorraine, Dec. 31, 1718, an industrious, talented, and excellent ecclesiastic, who obtained deservedly great credit by strenuous endeavours to stem the pestilential torrent of pretended French philosophy. In early life he was incumbent of a little village church in Franche-Comté; but as years rolled on, his admirable qualities raised him to a professorship of theology, and afterwards the headship, in the college of Besançon; to a canonry in the cathedral of Paris, and to the post of confessor to the aunts of Lewis XVI. He might have had better preferment, but a spirit above all intrigue, a simplicity and modesty that sought retirement, and an indifference to every thing but prospects of serving mankind, rendered him perfectly contented with such a provision as was made for him. After obtaining youthful reputation by some academical pieces at Besançon, he secured notice of a more general kind in 1764, by the publication of a treatise on the primitive elements of languages. Three years afterwards, he published a translation of Hesiod, combined with a dissertation on pagan mythology. This work was well received, and maintains its character, many still preferring Bergier's version to subsequent attempts. He now felt himself, however, called away from any farther excursions in the seductive fields of philology and classical antiquity, by the louring aspect of the religious horizon. Most of the smartest, and some of the subtlest wits in France were tempted by their own corruption into attacks upon Christianity, persuading themselves and others that this impious folly was a revival of sound philosophy. Against this pernicious, but shallow school, Bergier published, in 1768, his Certitude des Preuves du Christianisme, in answer to the Examen critique des Apologistes de la Religion Chrétienne, falsely attributed to Freret. It is a work wise and moderate, logically argued, and ably written. Bergier never wrote anything that attracted so much attention; and three editions appeared within the year. Some extolled it as it deserved, others loaded it with unqualified censure. Even Voltaire found himself under the necessity of attempting a reply, and, accordingly, he sought to prop his miserable system by the Conseils Raisonables, a piece that proved, what wanted no proving, that he was witty and dexterous, but really left Bergier in possession of the field. Voltaire's talents and celebrity, however, procured him the honour of a reply; and it was the only compliment of the sort that any conceited, licentious scoffer ever extorted from Bergier. Another opponent, quite equal to Voltaire in infatuation upon all that is vitally important, but otherwise even ludicrously below him, the German baron Cloots, conspicuous during the worst paroxysms of the French revolution, under the adopted first name of Anacharsis, published in London, in 1780, an attempt to discredit Bergier's work, entitled, Certitude des Preuves du Mahometisme, par Ali Gier-Beer. These wretched attempts to discountenance principles that alone can raise and comfort man, were estimated at their real value in all quarters worthy of deference, and Bergier's services were acknowledged in a pension of 2,000 livres, settled upon him by the clergy of France. He next undertook a dissection of Rousseau's religious principles, in his Déisme refuté par lui-même, published first in 1765. Four years afterwards appeared an answer to baron Holbach, entitled, Apologie de la Religion Chrétienne contre l'auteur du Christianisme devoilé. He then applied himself to expose the fallacies of those who would convert an imperfect knowledge and artfully-coloured views of physics, into an engine for cheating mankind out of revelation; and this labour produced his Examen du Matérialisme, ou Réfutation du Système de la Nature, Paris, 1771. The following nine years were employed in a work of greater length than any of his preceding productions, in which Bergier recast all that he had previously written against infidelity, adding a great quantity of new matter, thought suitable to the times. This undertaking appeared in 1780, in 12 vols, 12mo, entitled, Traité historique et dogmatique de la vraie Religion, avec la Réfutation des Erreurs qui lui ont été opposées dans les différents Siècles. In 1787, this indefatigable writer put forth a discourse on the Marriage of Protestants; and in 1790, some observations on Divorce. Unfortunately he was persuaded into an appropriation of his later literary labours, which rendered them injurious to the cause that his invaluable services had so strenuously defended. The Encyclopédie Méthodique being undertaken, Bergier engaged to furnish a Dictionnaire Théologique, as a portion of it. He fulfilled his task as might be expected of him; and if he had refused any concern with the work except as editor, the object of his friends in urging him to take a share, namely, to prevent religious articles from falling into dangerous hands, would have been secured. But his consent to become a contributor merely, had a mischievous effect. The public was not quite ripe for that unblushing infidelity which soon polluted France, and therefore Bergier's respected name was eagerly brought forward as a security against the appearance of any thing that serious men must refuse to admit. But it only served as a blind. As a whole, the work proved more exceptionable than any one of the kind hitherto published. Bergier died at Paris, April 9, 1790, generally ranked among the best writers of his time for clear conception, lucid arrangement, and logical reasoning, though blemished by a style rather too diffuse. (Biog. Univ. Baruel, *apud* Chalmers.)

BERGIER, (Claudius Francis,) an advocate, brother of the preceding, born at the same place, about the year 1728. He translated Webb's work on painting, Porter's Turkey, Dow's Hindoostan, and Fergusson's Essay on Civil Society. He died in 1784. (Biog. Univ. Suppl.)

BERGIUS, (Peter Jonas,) a Swedish physician and botanist, who took the degree of doctor of medicine at Upsal in 1750. Linnæus named a genus of plants "Bergia," in compliment to his botanical knowledge. He died in 1790.

BERGIUS, (Benedict,) a learned Swedish writer of the eighteenth century, born at Stockholm in 1723, and died 1784. His most celebrated work is, On Luxuries, 8vo, Stockholm, 1785, 1787. In treating this apparently unpromising subject, he has introduced a mass of learned notes and of interesting quotations, such as are scarcely to be found in any other work. He wrote also a treatise on Vegetables used for Feeding Cattle, 8vo, Stockholm, 1769.

BERGLER, (Joseph, May 1, 1753—June 25, 1829,) a Bohemian painter, who passed the greater part of his life at Passau, where his father, statuary to the bishop, taught him the elements of design and painting. The talents that he displayed induced the bishop to send him to Italy in 1776. After five years' sojourn at Rome he returned home, and having settled himself at Passau, he became painter to cardinal Aversberg.

Having produced many important works, he died at Prague. Biog. Univ. Suppl.)

BERGLER, (Stephen,) born about 1680, at Cronstadt, and thought to have been the son of a baker. Leaving at an early age his native place, he went to Leipzig, where he was employed by Fritsche as a corrector of the press; and subsequently to Amsterdam, where he edited, for Wetstein, the Homer that appeared in 1707. From thence he migrated to Hamburg, where he assisted Fabricius in the compilation of his Bibliotheca Græca; and on his return to Leipzig he was a considerable contributor to the Acta Eruditorum; where he reviewed Kuster's Aristophanes, Bentley's Horace, Emendations on Menander, and Barnes's Homer. In 1715 he published his edition of Alciphron's Epistles, and prepared for the press his Notes on Aristophanes. These subsequently fell into the hands of Peter Burman, jun. who printed them at Leyden in 1760, 4to, and gave in the preface a full account of their author; and though the notes were held in little honour by Brunck, yet Reisig has not hesitated to consider them superior to those of the Strasburg editor. He translated likewise into Latin the Four Books of the Byzantine History, by Joseph Genesius, and which are to be found in the 23d volume of the Venice edition of that collection, but not in the Parisian. By his translation of a Greek work by Alexander Mavrocordato, published with the original at Leipsic, in 1722, under the title of Περι των Καθηκοντων, he so ingratiated himself with the hospodar of Wallachia, as to be taken in the employ of his son, and to obtain access to the prince's library, containing many Greek MSS.; and amongst them Bergler found the first three chapters, previously wanting, of the Demonstratio Evangelica of Eusebius, and sent them to Fabricius, who printed them in his Delectus Argumentorum, in 1725. On the death of his patron, Bergler went to Constantinople, where he died in 1746, having embraced Mahometanism. Such at least is the story circulated by his biographers, with the exception of Seivert; who, in his Ungar. Magazin. tom. ii. pars iv. p. 504,—quoted by Wagner, in the preface to the 2d volume of his Alciphron,—says that Bergler never became a Mahometan; and though he went to Constantinople to teach in a school established there, for Greek youths, yet he returned to Bucharest, where he died from drinking too freely his favourite wine of Hungary. The work by which he is best known is the edition of Alciphron; where he has exhibited an extensive and accurate knowledge of Greek, and no inconsiderable talents as a conjectural critic; and it is to be regretted that he never published his notes on Herodotus, where ample scope is still left for the exercise of a scholar's ingenuity.

BERGMAN, (Joseph,) a German physician, naturalist, and theologian, born at Aschaffenbourg, in 1736, early admitted into the society of the Jesuits, and devoted principally to natural history and the physical sciences. In 1773, upon the suppression of his order, he returned to his native place, and afterwards he was professor of physics and natural philosophy at Mentz. He died Sept. 20, 1803, at Aschaffenbourg, whither the university of Mentz had been transferred upon the union of that city with France. He published Anfangsgruende der Naturgeschichte, Mogunt. 1782, 1783, 3 vols, 8vo. Kurzer Unterricht in der Naturwissenschaft fuer Kinder in den Realscholen, *ib.* 1783, 1784, 8vo. Was die Thiere gewiss nicht, und was sie am wahrvcheintichsten seyen? *ib.* 1784, 8vo. Lehrsaetze mit Anwendungen aus der Experimental Physik. *ib.* 1684, 4to. He also translated from the German into Latin, Bruckhausen's Elements of Physic, Mentz, 1790, 3 vols, 8vo.

BERGMAN, (Tobern Orlof,) a celebrated Swedish chemist, born at Catharineberg, March 9, 1731, and at seventeen, sent to the university of Upsal. He devoted himself with such ardour to mathematics, physics, and philosophy, that his health became disordered. He was under the necessity of retiring from the university for fifteen months, and returning to his home, where, however, he engaged himself in the study of botany and entomology. In the latter branch of natural history he made for himself a system of classification, based upon the characters of the larvæ, to facilitate his inquiries. The plates representing the different classes of the larvæ are to be found in the first volume of the Memoirs of the Royal Society of Sciences of Upsal. Linnæus honoured him by naming a species of the genus Phalæna after him. His health being re-established, he returned to Upsal; and in 1755, defended with great ability a thesis in physics and mathematics on the Nature of Twilight. He furnished to the academy of Stockholm two papers, containing some curious researches relative to leeches; and showed the Coccus aquaticus to be nothing more than the eggs of the leech. Linnæus disputed the accuracy of this opinion, but afterwards admitted its truth, and wrote upon the Memoir, as it passed through the academy, *vidi et obstupui.* He defended another thesis on Astronomical Interpolations, in 1758; and then received the degree of doctor in philosophy. He produced another thesis on the subject of Attraction, which obliged him to make some experiments in electricity. He assisted in making observations at the observatory, and was recompensed by an appointment to a chair of mathematics; which he afterwards exchanged for that of algebra, upon the death of Meldercreutz. He made many researches, and presented to the academy memoirs upon the rainbow, aurora borealis, electricity, &c., which occupied his attention in an especial manner. Extracts from some of his papers were printed by Wilson, in the Philosophical Transactions. In 1763, he gained the prize offered by the academy for the best means of destroying caterpillars; and he obtained a second prize on a future occasion, for further suggestions on this subject, so important to rural economy. It is not within the limits of this sketch to enumerate the various papers furnished to the academy by Bergman; they amount in number to forty-one, and embrace the consideration of many subjects deeply interesting to the students of natural history and the physical sciences. His labours were so highly esteemed by the body to whom they were addressed, that they accorded to him an annual pension of six hundred francs in consideration of his services, and to encourage him in his pursuits.

In 1758 he had associated with some ingenious friends to establish a society for advancing a knowledge of the earth. To each of the members a certain division of the subject was allotted, and to Bergman was assigned that which related to physics. He was occupied in this labour during eight years; at the expiration of which time he put forth a work, (an edition of which was exhausted in six months,) which was translated into French, German, Danish, Russian, and English. In this work he displayed the extent of his knowledge of chemistry and mineralogy. A vacancy occurred in the chemical chair, by the resignation of Waller, and Bergman was anxious to obtain it; but envy had been excited in the breasts of some of his contemporaries, and it was contended that however general and extensive his knowledge might be, he had not yet published any work in this particular department of science. He therefore shut himself up in his laboratory, applied with extraordinary zeal to some operations, and soon produced a memoir on the subject of alumen; which has always been regarded as a most able composition. His enemies were enraged at this display of his ability; and had he not been so fortunate as to obtain the protection of the prince royal, afterwards Gustavus III., who was at that time chancellor of the university, very serious consequences might have arisen to him. This prince, himself able to estimate the merit of Bergman, took also the advice of those most conversant in the matter, and he warmly defended him in the senate, and he obtained the appointment. He ever manifested his gratitude for this noble conduct, and rejected, at a future period, the advantageous offers which were made to him by Frederic the Great, king of Prussia, to attract him to Berlin. Devoted now to chemical pursuits, he laboured with that zeal which he had already manifested in other departments of science; and his fame increased the reputation of the university, and drew to it a very large number of students. His incessant activity abridged his life; and he died July 8, 1784, at the baths of Medevi, whither he had resorted with the hope of improving his health.

The career of Bergman was altogether very brilliant, and as a chemist, he has always been considered unsurpassed in his day. His researches on the acids, on carbonic acid gas, and his analyses of mineral waters, are highly esteemed. He is the discoverer of the hydro-sulphuretted gas. On the subject of chemical affinities he has led the way to the most important discoveries. He is not entitled to less respect for his researches in crystallography, and the precision that he has introduced into chemistry by his mathematical knowledge. Besides many academical prizes, he published the following important works:—Physisk Beskryvnig cofver jordklolet, Upsaliæ, 1766, 1769, 1773, 1774, 2 vols, 8vo; translated into French, Paris, 1770, 1774, 8vo; into German, by L. H. Koehl, Gripswald, 1769, 1780, 8vo; and at Leipzig, by G. Grosse, 1781, 8vo. Afhandling om bitter Salzer-Spa-och Pyrmontn Watters raetta halt och tibredning gonom konst, Upsal. 1776, 8vo. Chemisk afhandling om jaernmalms proberande pac vactn vaegen, *ib.* 1777, 8vo. Tal om Chemiens nyasti framsteg, Stockholm, 1777, 8vo; translated into German by Wiegleb, Berlin and Stettin, 1790, 1791, 8vo. Dissertatio sistens Chemiæ Progressus à Medio Sæculi VII. ad Medium Sæculi XVI. Upsal, 1782, 4to; translated into German, by Wiegleb, Berlin and Stettin, 1792, 8vo. Sciagraphia Regni Mineralis secundùm Principia proxima digesti, Lips. et Dessau, 1782, 8vo; translated into French, by Mongez, Paris, 1784, 1792, 8vo; and, with additions, by H. de la Methrie, into English, London, 1783, 8vo; and into Italian, Florence, 1783, 8vo. Opuscula Physica et Chemica, plerumque antea seorsim edita, jam ab Auctore collecta et aucta, Stockholm, Upsal, et Abo, 1779, 1783, 3 vols, 8vo; translated into French, by Guyton de Morveau, Dijon, 1780, 1785, 2 vols, 8vo; into German, by H. Tabor, Francof. ad Mæn. 1790, 2 vols, 8vo; and into English, by Dr. Edmund Cullen, Lond. 1784, 1791, 3 vols, 8vo.

BERGMANN, (Michael Adam von,) burgomaster and chief magistrate of Munich, born in that city in 1733, and chiefly known as its historian. He died in 1783. (Ersch und Gruber.)

BERGMANN, (Gustavus,) born March 1744, died July 11, 1814; known by several published works on Livonian history and literature, besides a Lexicon of the Lettish tongue, left in MS.

BERGMULLER, (John George, 1687—1762,) a painter and engraver, born at Dirckheim in Bavaria, scholar of Andrew Wolf, and an enthusiastic imitator of Carlo Maratti, whose style he adopted both in his painting, and copied as exactly as he could in his engraving. His pictures and prints are mostly signed with his initials, J. G. B., but sometimes with a monogram peculiar to himself, and in a few instances with his name. (Biog. Univ. Suppl. Bryan's Dict.)

BERGONZONI, (Laurence,) an historical portrait painter, born at Bologna in 1646, and died in 1700.

BERGSTRASSER, (John Andrew Benignus,) born in 1732; appointed, in 1760, rector of the Evangelical Lutheran Lyceum of Hanover; died in 1812. He wrote many works for Latin students, and also for improving the system of instruction; a good catalogue and notice of them may be seen in Ersch und Gruber's Lexicon.

BERIGARD, or BEAUREGARD, (Claudius Guillermet Signor de,) born at Moulins, in 1578, and died in 1663, at Padua, where he taught philosophy. He published a work on ancient philosophy, entitled, Circulus Pisanus, Florence, 1641, and Dubitationes in Dialogum Galilæi pro Terræ Immobilitate, 1632, which latter subjected him to the charge of materialism. (Chalmers.)

BERING, (Vitus,) a Danish Latin writer, born in 1617, member of the council of finance, and royal historiographer. He published Florus Danicus, sive Danicarum Rerum, Breviarium, Odensee, 1698. The other editions, excepting that at Tirnaro, 1716, are merely the unsold copies of the first, with new title-pages. Bering's poems are printed in Deliciæ quorundam Danorum, Leyden, 1693, the smaller pieces being the best. He died in 1675. (Chalmers.)

BERING, or BEERING, (Vitus,) an eminent navigator, born at Horseus, in Jutland; chosen, in 1728, to command the Russian voyage of discovery in the north seas, particularly about Kamschatka. In 1741, he was sent out again to ascertain the northern boundary of America, and was cast on the island which bears his name, where he was taken ill and died. Fragments of his voyages have been published by Mullen, and also at Antwerp, in 1766, under the title, Voyages et Découvertes faites par les Russes. (Biog. Univ.)

BERINGER, (Michael,) born at Uhlbach, in Wirtemberg, in 1566; educated at Tübingen; appointed, in 1599, professor of Hebrew there, with a very small salary. His laborious life terminated in 1625. The celebrated William Schickard, his successor in the professorship of Hebrew, said of him: "Theologus erat, jurisperitus, philosophus, philologus, disputator, astronomus, orator, poeta, Græcus et Hebræus, imo et Gallicæ linguæ non ignarus." Besides different theological, juridical, and philosophical dissertations, orations, a Latin and Greek grammar for the use of the prince of Wirtemberg, a system of rhetoric, which was introduced into the neighbouring state of Baden; he also wrote, by command of the "visitators" of the university, Institutiones Linguæ Sanctæ, and a Vindication of the Vernacular Version of Luther against the Jesuit, Zanger.

There are two other German writers of this name; viz.

Beringer, (Erich,) a legist, who wrote a work, which still has its value, entitled, Discursus Hist. Polit. de Historici Officio, Hanov. 1614; and,

Beringer, (J. B. A.) chiefly known as victim of a learned imposture. He published, in 1726, a folio account, with 21 plates, of petrifactions discovered by him, as he thought, near Würzburg, but which really were manufactured and buried by the Jesuit Rodrik, to deceive him. When he discovered this, he sought to buy up all the copies in circulation, and the vexation is said to have accelerated his end. Göbhard, a bookseller of Bamberg, purchased the edition of his heirs, after his death, and republished it under another title.

BERINGER, (Diephold,) an ignorant peasant, who excited great attention about the time of the reformation by his sermons against popery. He is variously styled, Beringer, Peringer, and Schuster (shoemaker, probably from his trade); and also the Peasant of Wöhrd. At this last place (near Nuremberg) he appears first to have preached in 1524; afterwards, being banished from Nuremberg, at the complaint of the archduke Ferdinand to the council of that city, he fixed his residence at Kitzingen in Franconia. His sermons were taken down and printed, some of them going through several editions. Nothing is certainly known of his history after 1525, but there appears to be ground for supposing that he perished in the famous commotions known in the history of the reformation as the War of the Peasants. (Ersch und Gruber.)

BERINGTON, (Joseph,) an English ecclesiastic of the Romish church, conspicuous in his day for advocating moderate views of her peculiarities. He was born in Shropshire, and first appeared before the world in 1776, as author of A Letter on Materialism, and Hartley's Theory of the Human Mind. Three years afterwards he published, Immaterialism Delineated, or a View of the First Principles of Things. The progress of events, however, had now relieved English Romanists from the pressure under which they had long laboured from prevailing fears of a prince belonging to themselves, and hence they began to think of standing once more boldly before their countrymen. Berington was among the first that made the experiment. In 1779, he published A Letter to Fordyce, on his Sermon on the delusive and persecuting Spirit of Popery. In the next year appeared his State and Behaviour of English Catholics from the Reformation till 1780. In 1786, he came forward with An Address to the Protestant Dissenters who had lately petitioned for a Repeal of the Corporation and Test Acts. In the following year, he published The History of Abelard and Heloisa, with their genuine Letters. A second edition of this work appeared in 1789. In 1787, also, Berington published Reflections, with an Exposition of Roman Catholic Principles, in Reference to God and the Country; and other tracts followed closely upon this. In 1790, this industrious writer, published in 4to, a History of Henry II., and his two sons, vindicating the character of Becket from Lord Lyttleton's attacks. In 1793 appeared a more important work, entitled, Memoirs of Gregorio Panzani; giving an account of his agency in England, in the years 1634, 5, and 6, translated from the Italian original, and now first published. As Panzani's objects were both the reconcilement of differences between the Romish seculars and regulars in England, and to obtain permission for the settlement of a Romish bishop, his attention was much directed to the oaths required, and he was favourable to some middle course, offering a prospect of satisfying the existing government. Many Romanists were displeased at seeing evidence published of such a disposition in a papal agent; and Charles Plowden, a clerical member of their body, published Remarks on Berington's publication, in 1794, calling in question the authenticity of Panzani's Memoirs. Of that, however, there is no doubt; but Berington was never forgiven by some of his church for publishing matter so unpalatable. Still he was not to be deterred from public expressions of dislike to those proceedings within his church that most lower her in the eyes of opponents. He published, accordingly, in 1796, a tract on the base and senseless attempts to rouse the Italian populace by pretended miracles, recently adopted in Italy, instead of manly and rational courses, under the French invasion. In 1814, Berington published his largest work, A Literary History of the Middle Ages; comprehending an Account of the State of Learning, from the Close of the Reign of Augustus to its Revival in the Fifteenth Century. This industrious and enlightened clergyman died at Buckland, in Berkshire, December 1, 1827, aged 84. (Annual Biog. Butler's Hist. Mem. of the Engl. Ir. and Scot. Cath. iv. 52.)

BERKEL, (Abraham,) a Dutch philologist, who died about 1688. He was professor of Greek at Leyden, and edited with annotations Epictetus, Cebes, Antoninus Liberalis, and Stephanus Byzantinus. (Ersch und Gruber.)

BERKELEY, (Sir William,) a gallant British admiral, slain in battle. He was lineally descended from Robert Fitzharding, the fortunate grantee of Berkeley castle, in the reign of Stephen. Entering the sea service of his sovereign at an early age, his professional advancement appears to have been unusually rapid—*five* years having hardly elapsed ere he attained the rank of rear-admiral of the Red. After signalizing himself in the duke of York's first action with the Dutch, he was, in 1666, promoted to the rank of vice-admiral, and this, too, before he had attained the age of twenty-six.

The French had already declared war with England. The fleet of the former, which was intended to act in conjunction with that of the Dutch, lay at Toulon, under the command of the duke of Beaufort. Lewis XIV., immediately on the commencement of hostilities with England, ordered the duke to sail for this purpose. The fleet was composed of forty sail. It was naturally imagined that the French would enter the English Channel in order to execute the commands of their sovereign; the Dutch fleet, under the command of De Ruyter and Tromp, was already at sea, to the number of seventy-six sail. The English fleet, which did not exceed seventy-four sail, was under the joint command of prince Rupert and the duke of Albemarle.

The policy of the English, under the relative circumstances in which they and the enemy were placed, was sufficiently obvious; "they, (the British,) with all their force, should have attacked the Dutch separately, before they were joined by the French; of this opinion most decidedly was Sir George Ayscue, who was sufficiently well acquainted with the skill and bravery of the Dutch admirals, particularly of Tromp, but his advice and remonstrance unfortunately were of no effect. The duke resolved to detach prince Rupert, with twenty ships, for the purpose of attacking the French. (See Memoirs of Sir Thomas Allen.) No sooner had this resolution been carried into effect, than Albemarle determined to bring the Dutch to action. They, on their part, were not slow or averse to fight, but immediately cut their cables and prepared for battle under sail. The action had not continued long before Albemarle became sensible of the gross fault committed in weakening his fleet by sending prince Rupert against the French; however, he did all in his power to atone for his rashness by his valour." (Campbell.)

Nearly at the conclusion of the first day's action, the *Swiftsure,* Sir William Berkeley's flag-ship, was, with two others, cut off from the line, and surrounded by the enemy. In this perilous situation, that gallant officer displayed a courage worthy of him. He fought his ship, not only in the most heroic and determined manner, but with as much skill as could possibly be brought to bear under these circumstances; but neither courage nor skill could avail him; he saw his crew fall in great numbers on all sides of him; his vessel was a complete wreck, and totally unmanageable; the enemy poured in their men; obstinate contests took place on the deck; and Sir William at length perceived his own fate, and the *Swiftsure's,* to be fast approaching. Still he continued to fight, and though now left almost alone, with his own hand he killed several of the enemy. The Dutch, struck with awe and respect for his resolute bravery, offered him quarter; but this he proudly rejected. Hitherto he had almost miraculously escaped unhurt, but at last a musket-ball struck him in the throat. Being sensible that his wound was mortal, he retired into his own cabin, where he was found dead, extended at his full length, on a table, and almost covered with his own blood.

The Dutch, who had respected him while alive, embalmed his body, which, by the express orders of the states-general, was deposited in the chapel of the great church at the Hague. As Sir William Berkeley was well known to be a great favourite of his royal master, the Dutch sent a messenger to England, expressly to inquire of king Charles how he wished the corpse to be disposed of; at the same time, intimating that they were induced to show this attention and respect on account of the noble family of Sir William Berkeley, the high command which he held, and the valour that he had displayed during the action which terminated his life. (Campbell.)

Campbell's account of the respect paid by the Dutch to the "body" of Berkeley, is not borne out by that which, for the first time, appears in print in the recent publication of "The Life, Journals, and Correspondence of Samuel Pepys, Esq., Secretary to the Admiralty in the reigns of Charles II. and James II." According to the secretary's statement, the possession of the British admiral's remains was made by the Hollanders a matter of triumph. "Berkeley," says the man of memoranda, "lies dead in a *sugar-*

chest, for *every body to see*, with his flag standing up by him; and Sir George Ayscue is carried up and down the Hague, for the people to see."—Vol. i. p. 110. In the same work is brought to light a letter from the duke of Albemarle, addressed to Sir William Coventry, deprecating the conduct of many of his captains in this "desperate fight" with the Dutch. The letter is dated *Royal Charles*, Gun Fleet, June 6th, 1666.—"The captain of the *Sovereign gave up his ship without a shot*. The *Essex* fell foul of the *Bull*, *who* was foul *on* (of) a prize which we had taken. I presume the *Bull* and prize both sunk; but the *Essex*, they (the Dutch) carried away. If *Sir William Berkeley* be well, which I have not heard of since the first beginning, they have no more. Captains Bacon, Tearne, Wood, Moothan, and Whitty are slain. I assure you I never fought with *worse* officers than now in my life." Again,—"Sir William Clarke had his leg shot off, and died within two days. The *Loyal George*, *Seven Oaks*, and *Sir William Berkeley*, are still missing, which three never *engaged* with us. Captain Coppin is dead of his wounds. This is all at present." When we consider the number of captains killed and wounded in the English fleet, the noble duke's expression of never having fought with *worse* officers, would savour as something like an ill excuse for his own rash and unjustifiable proceeding in dividing his fleet and attacking that of the enemy with an inferior force. De Witte, however, who was no flatterer of the English, appears to entertain an opinion perfectly opposed to that expressed by the British chief. "If the English," says the Hollander, "were beaten, their defeat did them more *honour* than all their former *victories*. . . . . . All the Dutch had discovered was, that Englishmen might be killed, and English ships burnt; but that the English courage was *invincible*." (Wicquefort, Histoire des Provinces Unies, liv. xv.)

BERKELEY, (John, Lord Berkeley, of Stratton,) a British admiral. He was the second son of John Berkeley, the constant and loyal adherent of Charles I., and no less "faithful follower of Charles II. when in exile." On the death of his elder brother, Charles, who had attained the rank of captain in the royal navy, the title descended to John, the subject of our present sketch.

According to Charnock, he commanded the *Edgar* in 1688; and, though he had never manifested aught of disloyalty or disaffection towards king James while he continued his legal sovereign, yet, so high was the opinion entertained of his integrity and zeal for the well-being of the nation, that, at that time of general distrust and confusion which immediately preceded the settlement of government after the landing of the prince of Orange, he was appointed to act as rear-admiral of the fleet, then under the command of the lord Dartmouth.

In 1694 he commanded the unsuccessful and "rashly undertaken" attack on Brest. Russel was then chief of the channel fleet; but the execution of this daring and desperate service was entirely committed to lord Berkeley. The force, however, of the enemy, the strength of their fortifications, and, as Charnock asserts, evidently alluding to the future duke of Marlborough, "the treachery of some persons at home," rendered abortive the utmost efforts of gallantry on the part of the English; and by giving the French timely notice of the point where the meditated blow was to be struck, afforded them every opportunity of providing for their defence. No part, however, of that general discontent which ill success, particularly in an expedition of such magnitude, never fails to excite, fell on lord Berkeley. The voice of the populace, sometimes unable to distinguish between criminality and misfortune, on this occasion became compassionate, and divided its sorrows between the fate of the brave general, who fell a victim to the contest, and the disappointment of the no less gallant admiral who saw, but could not prevent it.

After this "misfortune," the fleet returned into port to refit, and again sailed on an expedition similar to the former, against Dieppe and Havre de Grace. Very considerable mischief was done to the enemy, who took all possible pains to represent his loss as trivial, insignificant, and by no means equal to the expense incurred by the English in making the attack.

It being determined to pursue a similar system of attacking the enemy's ports in the channel, lord Berkeley had now to proceed to London in order that the authorities might consult the admiral upon the immediate execution of their favourite project. Dunkirk was first mentioned, but was afterwards postponed in deference to the engineers and pilots, who thought the season too far advanced. An attempt on Calais was next proposed; and lord Berkeley repaired to the fleet about the middle of August to carry it into execution. He sailed on the 19th; but the wind being contrary, and increasing almost to a tempest, he was obliged to return to the Downs on the same evening. At a subsequent council of war, in which the pilots who were to conduct the ships in, and the engineers who were to *direct* the attack, were consulted, it was agreed to be impracticable at the advanced season of the year; so that the admiral seeing no prospect of any further enterprise during the remainder of that season, repaired to London on the 27th of the same month, resigning the command to Sir Cloudesly Shovel.

On the 12th of June, 1695, lord Berkeley hoisted his flag on board the *Shrewsbury*, at Portsmouth. The Dutch ships, under lieutenant-admiral Allemonde, together with the bomb-ketches and small vessels, joined him at Spithead on the 16th, and on the 29th, the whole fleet stood over to the coast of France, to renew the depredations of the former year. St. Maloes and Granville being the first objects of attack, he arrived before these ports on the 4th of July, and after "having completely executed his commission," he returned to Spithead on the 12th.

On the 18th he sailed for the Downs, being directed to make a second attempt against Dunkirk. Contrary winds and unfavourable weather prevented its being made till the beginning of August, when the same ill-success befel it that had attended the former. Foiled at Dunkirk, the vengeance of the English was next directed to Calais, where the mischief done to the enemy was much greater, and that sustained by the English and Dutch much lighter, than in the former attempt. The season being thought too far advanced to warrant an attack on any other of the enemy's ports, the fleet returned into the Downs on the 20th of August. Lord Berkeley struck his flag and went on shore at Dover on the 18th, leaving the command with Sir Cloudesly Shovel.

The French government having projected the invasion of England, made every preparation for carrying it into execution early in the spring. Twenty thousand soldiers were marched with the utmost secrecy from the nearest garrisons to the sea coast. At Dunkirk, Calais, and the adjacent ports, 500 transport vessels were collected to convey them, with their necessary stores and equipage, and a strong squadron of seventeen large ships of war, to be commanded by the marquis of Nesmond, and the celebrated Jean Bart had rendezvoused at Dunkirk to escort them. To counteract this "menaced ruin," a fleet of fifty ships of the line, English and Dutch, collected with the utmost expedition, under the command of admiral Russel, lord Berkeley, Sir Cloudesly Shovel, and vice-admiral Aylmer, put to sea the latter end of February, and extended itself in a line from Dunkirk to Boulogne, completely blocking up the intended armament, and totally frustrating the mighty preparations and threats of the French.

In May, 1695, Sir George Rook, on taking his seat at the Board of Admiralty, proposed the destruction of a considerable number (some say *seventy*) French ships of war, then moored in Camaret Bay. But this was opposed by the ministry; and, ultimately, by a council of war pronounced impracticable. At a subsequent debate as to the manner in which the fleet could be rendered most serviceable, it was agreed, in case intelligence was not received that the French were disarming their ships, to stretch over to the coast of France, and cruise for fourteen or fifteen days, because, though the combined fleet should even not be able to destroy them, yet the demonstration might create much alarm, and draw such detachments from the army in Flanders, as would give the allied troops a decided superiority.

In consequence of this resolution, lord Berkeley put to sea in the middle of June; and after one or two attempts to turn down channel against a strong adverse gale, succeeded in reaching Camaret Bay on the 30th of the month. On the following day, the marquis of Nesmond, with a squadron of five ships, was then standing out to sea with a fleet of merchant vessels under his immediate escort; but on the approach of the combined fleet, he returned with the utmost haste into port. On the 3d and 6th, two detachments were sent from the fleet, the first of which was ordered to attack the Island of Gronais, one of the Cardinals; the other to bombard St. Martins, in the Isle of Rhe. Both these little enterprises were successful; but want of provisions, added to a diminution of force occasioned by the return of eight Dutch ships of the line to Holland, in consequence of positive orders from king William, "rendered the fleet incapable of attempting any thing farther." The larger ships of the line were now ordered into port for the winter, and before the time of their reengagement returned, a pleurisy and fever terminated the mortal career of this brave and noble seaman. He died on the 27th of July, 1696-7.

We have scarcely an instance in the annals of naval history of an officer attaining so high a rank at so early an age. At the time of his decease, he was not more than thirty-four years of age, during *eight* of which he had filled the office of admiral. The services in which he was chiefly employed were of a particular nature, new almost in practice, and, previous to this time, little understood. The first in which he was engaged was the most unfortunate; yet the ill-success damped not his ardour, nor made him diffident of future victories. (Charnock, Campbell, Hervey, and others.)

BERKELEY, (George,) an Irish prelate, of distinguished learning and abilities, but still more conspicuous for the solid excellences of a character truly christian. He was born at Kilcrin, in the county of Kilkenny; his father, whose name was William, being son of an Englishman whose family had suffered for its loyalty to Charles I., and who personally was rewarded, after the restoration, by the collectorship of Belfast. George's birth was on the 12th of March, 1684, and his earlier education was received at Kilkenny school. At fifteen he was admitted of Trinity college, Dublin, and he became fellow of that noble establishment in 1707, after an examination of great strictness, in which he acquitted himself admirably. That very year made him known to the world by the publication of his Arithmetica absque Algebra, aut Euclide demonstrata; a little work, actually written, as appears from the preface, before the author was twenty, and showing the powerful hold which Locke and Newton had already gained over the young author's mind. In 1709, Berkeley made a secure advance towards reputation by publishing the Theory of Vision, a treatise which rendered his depth of discernment unquestionable, it being the first attempt ever brought forward to distinguish perceptions drawn from sight only, from those in which that sense is aided by other senses. Inquiring minds were taught by this work to remark, that ideas for which men seem indebted to the eye alone, really need the touch, or other faculties, and that a person who reached some considerable age in blindness, would for a time be unable to judge how far he could trust his eyes as to the properties of objects placed before them. Berkeley's sagacity in conducting these arguments was strikingly confirmed in 1728, by the case of a boy, born blind, couched at fourteen, by the celebrated surgeon Cheselden. In 1733, he published a vindication of his Theory.

In 1710, Berkeley deserted the region of fact for that of theory, in his Principles of Human Knowledge; and in 1713, appeared his Dialogues between Hylas and Philonous. Ever since the Restoration, English society had been infected in its upper portions by a poisonous infusion of irreligious and immoral conceit, maintaining its delusions with considerable subtlety, and parading them under the seductive name of philosophy. Hence the divines of those days, together with such clerical scholars as directed public opinion during much of the eighteenth century, were injuriously diverted from attention to questions purely religious or ecclesiastical, into investigations of a philosophical character. Berkeley felt a call for his talents in this direction, but he had not his usual felicity in answering it. The two pieces intended for the purpose, attack received notions as to the existence of matter, arguing that it is not without the mind, but within it, being really an impression divinely made upon it, by means of certain rules, invariably observed, known as the laws of nature; the steady adherence to which by the Deity is the true ground of human apprehensions as to material objects. These principles are developed in the shape of an inquiry into the chief causes of such error and difficulty in the sciences, as freethinkers and infidels may find useful for the exercise of their own perverted ingenuity. The object of these treatises, accordingly, was to detect and expose the fallacies of enemies to revelation, by such argumentative weapons as they all professed to respect, and as might really act beneficially upon the more ingenuous and less corrupt members of their party. But such nice and thorny speculations are seldom conducted without affording advantages to acute opponents. Hence Berkeley, by these two works, has been considered as a forger of arms more useful to the enemies of revelation than its friends. Hume represented them as the very best lessons in scepticism to be found in any author, whether ancient or modern; and although the anxiety of such a man to make the best of an advantage given by one who eventually became a bishop, may have pushed his language rather too far, yet Beattie considers these treatises of Berkeley's to have a sceptical tendency.

It may be a sufficient excuse for them, as it certainly is for denying them any authority, that their author was under twenty-seven years of age when his unguarded theory first made its appearance. It is no illiberal disparagement of any man to consider his opportunities of reading, thought, observation, and reflection, as insufficient for the safe conduct of new and abstruse theories, involving important practical consequences, at such a time of life.

Berkeley's next appearance before the world was also such as to injure his memory. The overthrow of monarchical and ecclesiastical institutions in the middle of the seventeenth century, and the revolution of 1688, being followed by a selfishness that rendered the triumphant parties odious, those who felt themselves aggrieved by this exclusive spirit were tempted into injudicious measures of opposition to the men actuated by it. Hence the prevalence and popularity of unsound and pernicious endeavours to fill the public mind with principles of passive obedience and non-resistance. Berkeley was carried away by this ill-directed stream. In 1712, he published three sermons in favour of those political principles which the Stuarts were so desirous of seeing inculcated as religious duties. At first, he had reason to be satisfied with this employment of his time, his pulpit-advocacy of passive obedience and non-resistance reaching at least a third edition. But queen Anne's early death sent all such doctrines out of fashion, and any who had been conspicuous in embracing them were not unfairly treated as Jacobites, of whom the house of Hanover must be suspicious in justice to itself. Berkeley soon found himself labouring under this disadvantage, and it was not until after a lapse of several years, that a kind friend took off the impression by recommending him to queen Caroline, a princess eminent for the sense to value the society and support of literary men. In the meanwhile, however, Berkeley went abroad as travelling tutor to the son of St. George Aste, bishop of Clogher, and in his way through Paris, he paid a visit to his brother metaphysician, Father Malebranche. He found him preparing over the fire a medicine for an attack upon the lungs, under which he was then suffering. There was no want of topics for conversation, Malebranche having recently read a French version of Berkeley's system. So energetic, however, were his comments upon it, that an augmentation of his disorder followed, which carried him off in a few days. After this unfortunate exercise of his metaphysical powers, Berkeley went onwards with his pupil, and remained four years abroad, visiting all the usual points of attraction in France and Italy, together with some places which ordinary tourists overlooked. To Sicily he paid so much attention that he collected materials for its natural history, but they were unfortunately lost in his passage to Naples. He arrived in London, in 1721, at a time when nearly all classes were suffering from the gambling cupidity which had recently decoyed them into the South Sea scheme. Such general distress took full possession of his feeling mind, and he lost no time in suggesting a remedy, in An Essay towards Preventing the Ruin of Great Britain.

He was now favourably received in every quarter, but his only independence appears to have been his fellowship of Trinity college, Dublin, until Mrs. Vanhomrigh, the lady who obtained celebrity as Swift's Vanessa, made him one of her two executors, a trust requited by a legacy of 4,000*l.* In the course of his duties under this lady's will, he destroyed as much of her correspondence as he could find. In 1724, his position in society was farther improved by promotion to the rich deanery of Derry, which caused him to resign his fellowship. He now thought, however, of any thing rather than a life of dignified and luxurious repose. He could not remember the vast and important acquisitions which England had made in North America, without placing her gains and responsibilities by the side of each other, with a sorrowful conviction, too, that the latter had been inexcusably overlooked. Being now, therefore, in a situation to command attention even from persons in authority, he published, in 1725, A Proposal for Converting the Savage Americans to Christianity, by a College to be erected in the Summer Islands, otherwise called the Isles of Bermuda. As plans of this kind can rarely be executed without considerable personal sacrifices, Berkeley's truly christian spirit would not allow him to do no more than point out arduous duties. He was anxious to take the lead in a personal devotion to them. He made, accordingly, overtures for the resignation of his valuable preferment, and his settlement for the rest of life as principal instructor of young American Indians in the proposed Bermuda college, upon a stipend of 100*l.* a-year. As coadjutors in this generous undertaking, he persuaded three junior fellows of Trinity college, Dublin, to accompany him, upon stipends of 40*l.* a year each. The plan being approved by George I. and the ministry, a grant of 10,000*l.* was promised, under parliamentary sanction, and Berkeley set sail for America in 1728. His destination was Rhode Island, as the point most convenient for the Bermudas, and at Newport, in that settlement, he resided about two years and a half. The time was spent in a manner most useful and exemplary, securing to Berkeley the sincere love and respect of all within his reach; but every endeavour to realize the object which took him across the Atlantic utterly failed. Walpole, then minister, had, indeed, acceded to the proposed assistance from the public purse, but he never made a move towards a remittance of the money, and privately discouraged the plan altogether. Berkeley, therefore, found himself at length driven to return; but his departure, which took place at Boston, in September 1731, was preceded by demonstrations of his usual liberality. He gave his house, called Whitehall, with a hundred acres of cultivated land around it, to Yale and Harvard colleges; and he gave books, out of his own property, worth five hundred pounds, between one of those establishments and the clergy of Rhode Island. To the other college he transmitted a large number of books, entrusted by others to his disposal.

Having arrived in Europe, his attention was again turned to those philosophical speculations which had, with assistance from their own corruption, beguiled so many people out of solid happiness and trustworthy hopes. The fruits of his benevolent and pious application appeared in 1732, in a work in 2 vols, 8vo, entitled, The Minute Philosopher, a masterly series of dialogues, on Plato's model, which displayed the free-thinker under the various garbs of atheist, libertine, enthusiast, scorner, critic, metaphysician, fatalist, and sceptic. About the time of this publication, Berkeley was a frequent and prominent guest at those memorable parties which Caroline, queen to George II., gave, one evening in the week, to persons of established intellectual celebrity. Many questions were debated among the illustrious men thus brought together, and Berkeley had the honour of taking the lead in advocating those comprehensive and generous views which had shed an enviable brilliancy over every portion of his life, and which the cold and calculating Hoadly could not hear him pouring into the royal ears without characterising as visionary and extravagant. It was, however, impossible to prejudice the queen against him, and, by her means, he had an offer of the wealthy deanery of Down; but the duke of Dorset, then lord lieutenant of Ireland, was displeased at the manner in which the appointment was made, and it was thought unadvisable to press the completion of it. In a short time afterwards, the see of Cloyne became vacant, and to this Berkeley was consecrated, in Dublin, on the 19th of May, 1733. He took possession immediately of his episcopal residence, and lived in it constantly, unremittingly engaged upon the duties of his diocese, except one winter, when parliamentary business detained him in Dublin. He was never, indeed, inattentive to the interests of religion in the world at large, and the next proof that he publicly gave of this, was in the shape of a rebuke to those who would fain cover unbelief under a specious, but flimsy veil, woven by mathematics. Addison, visiting Garth, the poetical physician, then on his deathbed, some years before, was said to have spoken seriously to him on religion, and to have been shocked by this reply, "I have good reason for disbelieving it, for Dr. Halley, whose time has been spent so much in demonstration, assures me that it is quite incapable of standing a sufficient scrutiny." Berkeley took occasion from this to address "an infidel mathematician," in a discourse, entitled the Analyst, which argues that mathematical knowledge makes far larger demands than Christianity does upon the implicit acquiescence of mankind. One evidence of this was drawn from the doctrine of fluxions, and a controversy arose in consequence. Berkeley's principal antagonist appeared under the designation of *Philalethes Cantabrigiensis*, with a tract, in 1734, entitled, Geometry no Friend to Infidelity. The author was said to be Dr. Jurin; and when Berkeley published, in reply, A Defence of Free-thinking in Mathematics, he rejoined by The Minute Mathematician, or the Free-thinker no Just Thinker. The controversy went no farther, but it caused the doctrine of fluxions to be examined with unwonted care, and Maclaurin's able work was the eventual result.

Subsequently, Berkeley, though writing occasional pieces upon subjects of public utility, attracted no particular attention by any thing from his pen, except some treatises, upon which he bestowed a great deal of time, to recommend the medical use of tar-water; from which he fancied himself to have derived important benefit. He now thought, indeed, of retiring from a public station, and passing the remainder of his days in Oxford, partly for the sake of pious and learned meditation, partly for that of superintending the education of his son. He had, however, no wish to retain his Irish bishopric, under this alteration in his views, but sought to exchange it for a canonry of Christchurch, or a headship of a house. But the king would hear nothing of these disinterested proposals, and declared that Berkeley should die a bishop, in spite of himself, with full liberty to reside wherever he pleased. Upon the strength of this permission, he made a series of liberal arrangements at Cloyne, and then took up his abode in Oxford, but, as it proved, only for a few months. He settled in that venerable and beautiful city in July, 1752, and he died there on Sunday evening, January 14, 1753. He was placidly listening, while his wife read the lesson in the burial-service, when palsy at the heart set his pious and gentle spirit free, but in a manner so peaceful and easy, that his death was not discovered by those around, until he had become stiff and cold. He seemed asleep upon the couch, when really his nobler part had fled into another world. His remains were interred in Christchurch cathedral; and a monument, erected to his memory in that venerable and massive pile, is inscribed with an epitaph from the classic pen of William Markham, then master of Westminster school, subsequently tutor to George IV., when prince of Wales, and eventually archbishop of York.

Bishop Berkeley married, immediately before his voyage to America, a daughter of John Forster, speaker of the Irish House of Commons, a lady who seems to have possessed a disinterestedness of spirit like his own. He had an offer of the bishopric of Clogher, a far better preferment than Cloyne, and then rendered additionally eligible by an immediate prospect of ten thousand pounds from fines. He consulted his wife upon this offer, thinking that her wishes, as he had a family, were fairly entitled to consideration. She did not, however, counsel acceptance, and, with her full approbation, the tempting offer was declined. He had afterwards an opportunity of obtaining the primacy, but he would not avail himself of it, saying to Mrs. Berkeley, "I desire to add one more to the list of churchmen who are dead to avarice and ambition." Bishop Berkeley, though long little known in the literature of England, was a writer that deservedly attained a great reputation in his day, and rendered important aid in the diffusion of sound principles. It was, however, his admirable personal qualities that made the deepest, though not the widest, impression upon contemporaries. Bishop Atterbury said of him, "So much understanding, knowledge, innocence, and humility, I should have thought confined to angels, had I never seen this gentleman." Pope, too, ascribes

"To Berkeley every virtue under heaven."

He was, indeed, a prelate of whom Ireland may well be proud, and whose character it is almost impossible to contemplate without improvement. (Chalmers. Allen's American Biographical Dict.)

BERKELEY, (George,) son of the preceding, born in London, in 1733, but removed to Ireland early, and educated in the elementary branches of learning by his father. At nineteen he was admitted of Christchurch, Oxford, of which college he accepted a studentship from Bishop Conybeare, then dean. His first preferment, the vicarage of East Garston, Berks, came from that society, but archbishop Secker proving a warm friend and kind patron, he obtained by his means several other preferments in succession. He died in 1795, prebendary of Canterbury, rector of St. Clement's Danes, London, vicar of Ticehurst, Sussex, and chancellor of Brecknock, leaving the highest character for christian spirit and scholarly attainments. In 1785, he published a sermon, preached on the 30th of January, on the Danger of violent Innovations in the State, how specious soever the Pretence, exemplified from the Reigns of the two first Stuarts. This went through six editions. In 1799, his widow published a volume of his sermons, with a biographical preface. She was Eliza, daughter of the Rev. Henry Finsham, and died in 1800, having published, besides her late husband's sermons, a magnificent quarto volume of poems by her son, George Monck Berkeley, with a long rambling preface of her own. Her attainments were considerable, but she was liable to be led away by warmth of imagination, and irritability of temper. Her son, George Monck Berkeley, also published himself, in 1789, an amusing volume of anecdote and biography, entitled Literary Relics. (Chalmers.)

BERKELEY, (George, baron,) lineally descended from Robert Fitz-Harding, of the Danish blood-royal, to whom the castle and barony of Berkeley, in Gloucestershire, were granted under king Stephen, and who subsequently married into the family of the Berkeleys, possessors of these properties since the conquest. The Fitz-Hardings assumed the name of Berkeley, and their representative, George, thirteenth baron Berkeley by writ, distinguished himself in the House of Lords, in behalf of Charles I. For this he was impeached of high treason, with six other peers, by the Commons; but the impeachment was abandoned in June 1648, and the objects of it were restored to liberty and their seats. Lord Berkeley does not seem, however, to have been intimidated by the sense of his recent danger. Within a few months afterwards, his name honourably appeared among the twelve peers who rejected the ordinance for the unfortunate king's trial. He died in 1658. (Parl. Hist. Banks's Baronage. Nicolas's Peerage.)

BERKELEY, (George,) son of the preceding, entrusted, together with his nephew, Charles Berkeley, with the principal management of the duke of York's family. In 1679, he was advanced to the titles of viscount Dursley, and earl of Berkeley. He died in 1698, aged seventy-one, having bestowed a valuable collection of books, made by Sir Robert Coke, upon Sion college, and published, as there is every reason to believe, Historical Applications and Occasional Meditations upon several Subjects, written by a Person of Honour, 1670, 12mo. A third edition of this work appeared in 1680; the author's object was the admirable one of stemming the destructive torrent of licentious infidelity which swept over superior station in his day, by presenting some conspicuous instances of the testimony borne by distinguished persons to the great importance of religion, and to the absurdity of expecting a happy death without it. Lord Berkeley also published, in 1680, A Speech to the Levant Company, at their Annual Election. He passed through life with the highest reputation for piety and moral worth, being remarkable for such plain and courteous manners to people of every class, that Wycherley is supposed to have taken him as the original of his Lord Plausible, in the Plain Dealer, a piece of injustice equally natural and pardonable in a dramatic author who could attain popularity during the latter years of the seventeenth century. (Chalmers.)

BERKELEY, (Sir Robert,) one of the justices of the court of King's Bench, under Charles I., born in 1584, being second son of Rowland Berkeley, of Spetchley, in Worcestershire, where the family is seated still. He is indebted for a place in English history to his unfortunate concurrence with the other judges in maintaining the legality of Charles's levy of ship-money. For this he was impeached by the House of Commons, and long detained in custody. Being brought to the bar of the House of Lords, in October, 1641, he made a long speech, of which the purport was, that he was not guilty in manner or form as laid against him. After an interval of two days, his trial was deferred *sine die*, at the instance of the House of Commons, for want of witnesses. He was, however, put upon his trial before the Lords, September 9, 1643, three charges only being pressed against him, namely, the fourth, fifth, and sixth, which concerned ship-money. By the first of these three, he was accused of subscribing an opinion, November 30, 1635, in favour of the legality of ship-money; by the second, of subscribing an extra-judicial opinion, February 6, 1636, to the same effect, in answer to a case proposed by the crown; by the third, of delivering an opinion against Hampden, in the exchequer chamber, February 13, 1637. He admitted all these charges, but pleaded, in extenuation, that he thought himself, at the specified times, in strict conformity with law; an opinion that, since both houses of parliament had now decided another way, he absolutely abandoned. He was then fined in a sum of 20,000*l.*, disabled from all public employments in future, and sentenced to imprisonment in the Tower, during the pleasure of the house. He was eventually excused from the payment of half his fine, and the rest of his days were spent in retirement; but he continued to practise as a chamber-counsel, and with very considerable success; so that he left at last a good fortune to his family. The Presbyterians, however, continued a violent feeling of animosity towards him, and, a little before the battle of Worcester, they burnt his house at Spetchley to the ground. He then fitted up the stables for a residence. He died August 5, 1656. Whitlocke says that he "was a very learned man in our laws, a good orator and judge, and moderate in his ways, except his desires of the court favour." (Parl. Hist. Chalmers.)

BERKELEY, (Thomas, baron de,) remarkable in English history as the owner and occupant of Berkeley castle, in which the deposed Edward II. was murdered. The unfortunate prince was committed to his care, and to that of Sir John Maltravers, in 1327, and lodged in Berkeley castle. At the time of the murder, however, Berkeley was sick at Bradley, and neither knew anything of the transaction, nor was a consenting party to it, as he pleaded, when arraigned for the crime. He was accordingly pronounced *not guilty* of the murder, but since he had been concerned in placing about Edward those by whom the crime was actually committed, he was not allowed to remain at large, but was to await judgment from the next parliament. When this was assembled, in 1331, he petitioned for the discharge of his manuprisors, which petition was granted, and he thus escaped from farther molestation. (Parl Hist. Knyghton. x. Scriptt.)

BERKELEY, (William,) governor of Virginia, born of an ancient family near London, and educated at Merton college, Oxford, of which he became a fellow. In 1630 he travelled over various parts of Europe, and in 1641 succeeded Sir James Wyatt in the government of Virginia. In 1644, the Indians, irritated by encroachments on their territory, massacred about 500 of the colonists. On this, Berkeley, with a party of horse, surprised their aged chief, and took him prisoner to James Town, after which peace was concluded. During the civil war in England, governor Berkeley took the side of the king, and Virginia was the last of the Anglo-American colonies to acknowledge the authority of Cromwell. In 1651 the parliament sent a fleet to reduce Barbadoes, from whence a small squadron was detached, under the command of captain Dennis, to take possession of Virginia, which he was unable to accomplish by force, but succeeded by a manœuvre, when Berkeley and his friends were obliged to submit. Upon the death of governor Matthews, who was appointed by Cromwell, he received an application from the people to resume the government, which he only did on condition that they would submit themselves to the king's authority. Consenting to this, Charles II. was proclaimed in Virginia, before his restoration to the throne in England. Towards the end of his administration, which lasted nearly forty years, Berkeley appears to have become less popular. In 1667 he returned to England, and he died in 1677. He was the author of A Discourse and View of Virginia, 1663, and the Lost Lady, a tragi-comedy, 1639. (Carter's Amer. Biog. Dict.

BERKELEY, (Hon. G. Cranfield,) a British admiral. This officer, brother of the fifth earl of Berkeley, signalized himself in an eminent degree in the celebrated battle between the Revolutionary fleet of France and that of the British under earl Howe, June 1, 1794. On that occasion captain Berkeley commanded the *Marlborough* (74), one of the British ships which daringly "broke the enemy's line." On obtaining the rank of admiral, our officer was entrusted with onerous and responsible commands on the coast of America, as well as in the River Tagus. In the last-mentioned command he cooperated with the British army in Portugal, under Sir Arthur Wellesley.

BERKELEY, (John le Francq van,) a Dutch naturalist, born in 1729. He obtained great reputation by his Natuurlijke Historie von Holland, 6 vols, 1769. In 1803, he published, also in his own language, a History of Horned Cattle in the Low Countries. He was likewise a poet of considerable originality and energy. He died in 1812, at the age of 83; and in the following year a collection of his posthumous pieces was published by Loosjes.

BERKENHOUT, (John,) a physician and naturalist, born at Leeds in 1730, and descended from a Dutch family. His father was a merchant, and he was also intended for commerce; and, after a slight education at a school in his native place, he was sent to Germany to learn foreign languages. At Berlin, however, he gained a taste for military life, and joining a regiment of infantry, he rose to the rank of captain. In 1756 he quitted the Prussian service, intending to enter into the army of his own country; but peace having been concluded between France and England, he went to Edinburgh in 1763, and there studied medicine. He took the degree of doctor in 1765, and then settled in practice at Isleworth, in Middlesex, where he was much esteemed. In 1778 the English government employed him to proceed to Philadelphia, to assist in the negotiations with the American congress; and for these diplomatic services, as also to recompense him for an imprisonment that he had undergone, from a suspicion entertained against him of having entered into some political intrigues, he received a pension. He died on April 3, 1791, at Besselsleigh, near Oxford, to which place he had retired. He published, Clavis Anglica Linguæ Botanicæ Linnæi, Lond. 1764, 1768, 8vo; Disputatio de Podagrâ, Edinb. 1765, 4to; Pharmacopœia Medica, Lond. 1766, 1782, 8vo; Outlines of the Natural History of Great Britain and Ireland, Lond. 1769-70, 3 vols, 12mo; Symptomatologia, Lond. 1784, 8vo; Letters on Education, to his Son at Oxford, London, 1791, 2 vols, 8vo.

BERKH, (Vassili Nikolaevitch,) born at Moscow, May 18 (30), 1781; died at St. Petersburg, Dec. 21, 1834, (Jan 2, 1835;) distinguished himself by a variety of publications, chiefly of an historical kind. On leaving the college of Naval Cadets, in 1799, he entered the service as midshipman in the Baltic fleet, and was sent with the Russian squadron that joined the English, under Sir Home Popham, for the purpose of liberating Holland from the French, and he afterwards passed some time in England. Having returned to his own country, he received an appointment upon a circumnavigating expedition, a service for which he was eminently qualified, both by his general intelligence and abilities, and by his passion for voyage and adventure. Ill health, however, obliged him to quit the sea service altogether in 1809. From that period, whatever time he could spare from his official duties, in the admiralty department, was devoted entirely to literary pursuits; and one of the earliest productions of his pen was a journal of the voyage of the *Neva*, after that vessel was separated from the commander's in the expedition, containing a particular account of the settlements of the Russo-American Company, where he resided for fourteen months. Among his numerous productions the following may be mentioned: A Chronological Account of North Polar Voyages, 2 vols, 1821-3; Chronological History of the Discoveries of the Aleutian Islands, 1823; The First Russian Voyage of Discovery, 1823; History of all the Inundations at St. Petersburg, 1826; The Reigns of the three first Sovereigns of the Romanof Family, 5 vols, 1831-4; Lives of the Earliest Russian Admirals, or Materials for a History of the Russian Fleet, &c. 5 vols.

Berkh was well acquainted with the French, German, and English languages, from which last he translated the Life of Nelson, Mackenzie's Travels in North America, &c. (Entz. Leks.)

BERKHEYDEN, the name of two Dutch painters.

1. *Job*, (1628—1698,) born at Haerlem; originally placed with a bookbinder, but cultivating a natural taste for painting, he became a capital artist, and his success excited the emulation of his brother Gerard. Job Berkheyden, very industrious, and always consulting nature, acquired a great facility in painting the landscapes on the borders of the Rhine. He was also very successful in portraits, and in village fêtes, in the style of Teniers. The merit of this artist consists in neatness of touch and minuteness of delineation; but he is deficient in the management of light and shade, and has a vulgarity of design. (Biog. Univ.)

2. *Gerard*, (1645—1693,) also born at Haerlem. He worked almost constantly with his brother; and such was their affectionate attachment, that they seem to have tried which should most aid the celebrity of the other. The pictures which Gerard executed alone are generally faithful representations of views in the towns of Holland and Germany; but there are few of his works into which Job did not introduce figures. (Biog. Univ. Bryan's Dict.)

BERLEPSCH, (Emilia von,) wife of Hofrichter von Berlepsch, of Hanover. Her maiden name was Appel, and she was born at Gotha, in 1757. This lady became one of the most distinguished female writers of her day in Germany. Her first publication, consisting of a collection of miscellaneous pieces in prose and verse, appeared at Gottingen in 1787. In 1802 was published Caledonia, a work suggested by a tour which she made through Scotland.

BERLEPSCH, (Frederic Lewis von,) born at Stade, 1749, of affluent parents, first rendered conspicuous, 1794, by proposing to the Hanoverian States to negotiate with France. This was regarded as treasonable, and he was dismissed from the public service. He appealed to the imperial court at Wetzlar, which decreed that he should be restored to all his offices, dignities, and rights, and entrusted the execution of the decree to the king of Prussia. The government of George III. refused to obey this decree; addressed the German diet on the subject, and banished Berlepsch. When the French took possession of Hanover, he was restored, and subsequently employed. He became, however, eventually sensible of the injuries inflicted upon Germany by Napoleon's domination. He died at Erfurt, December 22, 1818. In judgment he was evidently defective; but his German biographers give him credit for purity of motive, though the facts relating to him, detailed by the Hanoverian ambassador before the diet, show him rather as a factious demagogue than a true patriot. It would certainly have been more to his credit, had his opposition to the enemies of his country been equal to that which he carried on against its native rulers. His numerous controversial and other writings are important documents in the history of his time, being, in a great measure, the genuine expression of a man who was an active partizan in a remarkable and interesting period.

BERLICHINGEN, (Goetz or Godfrey von,) a brave German knight, who accompanied his cousin Conrad, in 1495, to the diet of Worms. Losing his hand in war, and having an iron one made in its place, he acquired the surname of Iron-hand. He died in 1562, leaving the history of his own life, of which a second edition was published at Nuremberg in 1775, with notes. It has formed the subject for one of Goethe's plays. (Biog. Univ.)

BERLIN, (John Daniel, 1710—1775,) an eminent musician, inventor of the modern monochord, born at Memel, and organist at Drontheim in Norway. Besides other works, he published at Leipsic, in 1767, one upon Tonometry, and the Monochord, invented in 1752. The monochord has the advantage of scarcely any variation in tone from change of temperature. (Biog. Univ.)

BERLINGHIERI, (Andrew Vacca,) a celebrated surgeon, born at Pisa in 1772, who studied at Paris under Desault. In 1795 he came into this island, and attended the lectures of Hunter in London, and Bell in Edinburgh. Upon his return to Pisa he took a doctor's degree in medicine, but confined himself to surgery, in which he became a very expert and scientific operator. He retired to Paris in 1799, to attend more particularly to the practice of the hospitals. Towards the conclusion of 1799 he was united with his father in the professorship of surgery at Pisa; and, upon the establishment of a new clinical school, he was, three years afterwards, placed at the head of it. In this theatre he justly acquired renown, and he remained in the active exercise of his duties until his death, September 6, 1826. He introduced some improvements in various surgical instruments, and published several professional memoirs, in Italian, of which those upon lithotomy have been translated into French.

BERLINGHIERI, (Francis Vacca,) father of the preceding, born near Pisa, in 1732. Being professor of surgery there, he refused the situation of physician to the king of Poland, from reluctance to quit his father, then eighty years of age. He became a most popular professor, and was extensively engaged in practice. He had an offer from the government of Lombardy of the clinical chair at the university of Pavia, when the celebrated Frank was called to Vienna; but he chose to remain in his native place, surrounded by his family. He died October 6, 1812, having published, in his own language, several professional treatises, one of them against the theory of medicine introduced by John Brown.

BERLINGHIERI, (Camillus,) known as Il Ferraresino, an historical painter, born in 1585 at Ferrara, where he died in 1625.

BERLINGHIERI, (Francis,) a noble Florentine poet, who published a geographical poem in *terza rima*, entitled, Geografia di Francesco Berlinghieri Fiorentino, &c., in folio, at Florence, without date, but dedicated to Frederic of Urbino, who died in 1482. (Biog. Univ.)

BERMUDEZ, (Francis de Pedraza), a Spanish lawyer, born at Granada, eventually canon and treasurer of the cathedral there. He died in 1655, aged seventy, in his native city. His partiality for it was attested by a work upon its history, published in his youth. This, after many years, appeared again, under the title of, Historia Eclesiastica Principios y Progresos de la Ciudad y Religion Catolica de Grenada, 1638, fol. He also wrote, Historia Eucharistica, and some other works. (Antonio.)

BERMUDEZ, (Jerome,) a Spanish poet of the sixteenth century; really the author of two tragedies, which have been placed among the very first productions of his country's tragic muse. Of his history, little more is known than that he was a native of Galicia, a Dominican friar, a professor of theology at Salamanca, and a resident for some time in Portugal. His tragedies turn upon the romantic history of Ines de Castro, and are entitled, Nise lastimosa; y Nise laureada, Doña Ines de Castro y Valla-dares, Princesa de Portugal, Madrid, 1577, 8vo. Nise, it will be observed, is an anagram of Ines. The two pieces are closely formed upon the model of Greek tragedy, and are characterised as rather specimens of majestic dialogue, than compositions fitted for the stage. Their author, however, seems to have doubted as to the propriety of his appearance at all as a dramatic poet. Hence his tragedies were published under the name of Antonio de Silva, but he permitted a sonnet from a friend to precede them, which proves them to be his. Antonio, overlooking this, has assigned them to Silva. Bermudez afterwards wrote Hesperoida, a Latin poem, in praise of Ferdinand Alvarez de Toledo, the duke of Alva, whose administration of the Netherlands appeared so judicious to many Romanists, and so infamous to the whole body of Protestants. This piece he subsequently translated into Spanish. (Antonio. Biog. Univ.)

BERMUDEZ, (John,) a Spaniard, born in Galicia, conspicuous in the religious history of Abyssinia. He first proceeded to that country, in 1520, as physician to an embassy despatched thither from Portugal. The ambassador was not favourably received, and failed of accomplishing the objects of his mission, or of obtaining leave to return, until after a delay of five years. This interval was improved by Bermudez to ingratiate himself with the Abyssinian monarch, and in the course of years hostile neighbours gave rise to a desire for succour from the Portuguese court. Bermudez was, accordingly, sent to request this, having been previously appointed *abuna*, or patriarch of Abyssinia. In his way through Rome, in 1538, he sued for permission from pope Paul III. to undertake this office; a petition very gladly accorded, as it was an indirect mode of submitting the church of Abyssinia to that of Rome, and this, too, at a time when the papacy was reeling under the shock of rising protestantism. Bermudez was, accordingly, received with much distinction at the papal court, and consecrated patriarch. He then proceeded onwards to Lisbon, where John III. was found equally gracious, despatching him to India with authority to demand succours for the king of Abyssinia, from the Portuguese viceroy. Bermudez arrived at Goa in 1539, but he did not sail for Abyssinia until 1541. On penetrating into that country, he found that the king who sent him to Europe was dead, and that the new sovereign would hear nothing of dependence upon the Roman see. As he came, however, attended by a military escort, he could not be summarily dismissed. But his means of resistance were soon exhausted, and he was driven out of the country. After a series of difficulties and hardships he reached Goa once more in 1556. Thence he sailed to Lisbon, where he was well received by Sebastian, then on the throne, and where he died in 1575. He spent, upon the whole, about thirty years in Abyssinia, displaying a degree of address, firmness, and ability, which proved him to be a man of superior powers; and a degree of attachment to the religious principles of his youth, which entitles him to the respectful remembrance of all who value Romanism. As an author, Bermudez is known by an account of his observations on Abyssinia, addressed to his royal patron, Sebastian. (Biog. Univ. Antonio. Rees's Cyclop, *in voc.* Abyssinia.)

BERMUDO, or BERMONDO, sometimes written Weremond, called also, according to Spanish usage, Vermudo, and Vermondo, surnamed the Deacon, raised by the Asturian nobility, in 789, to the throne of that country, the cradle of Spanish royalty. He was son of Froila, brother to Alphonso the Catholic, and was made king of Oviedo, as the style then ran, in prejudice to the rights of Alphonso II., eventually known as the Chaste, son of his father's nephew, Froila I. The party that made him king stipulated for his marriage, which, as he had taken deacon's orders, was repugnant to the ascetic notions then strongly prevalent, and is represented by modern Romish writers as positively inconsistent with his ecclesiastical character. After no long interval, he became seriously ill, and then mournfully charging himself with injustice to his relative, Alphonso, he recalled that prince to Oviedo, and, disregarding the claims of his own infant family, made him his associate on the throne. During this conjoint sovereignty, many important advantages were gained over the Moors, but it was of brief continuance, Bermudo dying in 797. (Vertot.)

BERMUDO II., or the Gouty, king of Leon and the Asturias, descended from Ramiro I., son of Bermudo I. His father was Ordoño III.; his mother, Elvira, daughter of a Galician nobleman, but she became queen while Ordoño's former wife, daughter to Gonzalez, the powerful count of Castile, who had grievously offended him, was yet alive. Thus, in addition to his infancy, Bermudo could be not unfairly treated as illegitimate, and accordingly, his uncle Sancho had little difficulty in placing himself upon the throne, and in transmitting it to his son, Ramiro III. That prince, however, became extremely obnoxious to his nobility, who took up arms, in consequence, to support the pretensions of Bermudo. An obstinate battle ensued, in which Ramiro was defeated, and shortly afterwards he died, leaving Bermudo undisputed master of the throne. This was in 982. The successful prince, however, found himself to have made a very uneasy acquisition. While his habits, and perhaps his health also, made him anxious for repose, a rebellion broke out among his own people, and the Moors of southern Spain eagerly availed themselves of such an opening to break the rising power of Leon. Almanzor, one of the ablest and most successful of the Hispano-Mahometan captains, moved upon Bermudo's territories, and after a desperate encounter, entirely defeated him. The Moor was not, however, left in any immediate condition to make the most of his victory. He found himself under the necessity of returning to Cordova, merely threatening that in the following year Leon should be destroyed. As the dreaded time approached, Bermudo saw little prospect of resistance. He therefore withdrew, with the relics and other objects deemed important, into the mountain-fastnesses of the Asturias, which had heretofore enabled his ancestor, Pelagius, to lay the foundations of a renovated christian monarchy in Spain. Almanzor now fulfilled his threats against Leon, although that city did not fall until after a brave resistance. At length the Moorish captain's progress alarmed so much the count of Castile and the king of Navarre, that, burying all differences in oblivion, they made common cause with Bermudo, and the three Christians met Almanzor on the plains of Osma, in Old Castile, in 998. Spain never saw a more sanguinary battle, but its termination, though this was not known when night closed in, was completely in favour of the Christians. Bermudo died in the following year. (Vertot.)

BERMUDO III., succeeded Alphonso V. on the throne of Leon, in 1027. He was a brave, generous, and prudent prince, but met with an untimely death, and was the last male descendant of Pelagius, or Pelayo, upon the Asturian throne. His sister, Sancha, was married to Ferdinand, son of Sancho the Great, king of Navarre, in whose favour Castile, originally governed by counts dependent upon Leon, was erected into a kingdom. Bermudo, however, made war upon his brother-in-law, to recover some portions of his former dominions which had been wrested from him during the lifetime of that prince's father, Sancho, king of Navarre. During about twelve months, the new king of Castile was compelled, by the posture of his affairs, to dissemble his resentment at the successful activity of Bermudo, but having then placed himself in a condition to commence hostilities, a desperate battle ensued in 1037, in which the king of Leon was killed. Ferdinand now caused himself to be crowned king of Leon, in right of his wife, and thus an important christian monarchy was consolidated in Spain. (Vertot. Moreri.)

BERNABEI. The name of two musicians.

1. *Hercules*, a Roman by birth, pupil of Benevoli, chapel-master to the elector of Bavaria, and eventually so employed in the pontifical chapel. He died about the year 1690, and may be ranked amongst the greatest masters of harmony in the ancient ecclesiastical style. A specimen of his works is inserted in Stevens's Sacred Music. (Mus. Biog. Dict. of Mus.)

2. *Joseph Anthony*, (1643—1732,) son of the preceding, but greatly superior to him, both in melody and modulation. He succeeded his father as chapel-master to the elector of Bavaria, by whom he was made an aulic counsellor. There are extant several of his compositions, replete with musical science. The modification of the vigour of the old style afforded him an opportunity, of which he amply availed himself, of infusing into his church music that melody and modulation for which his works are so remarkable, especially as compared with the compositions of his father and the other followers of the elder school. (Mus. Biog. Article in Rees's Cyclop.)

BERNAERTS, (John,) in Latin, Bernartius, born, in 1568, at Mechlin, where he practised as an advocate. He died in 1601. His knowledge was extensive, but Justus Lipsius and others injured him by their compliments. He wrote, in Flemish, the Life and Martyrdom of Mary Queen of Scots. But his most valuable contribution to literature is an edition of Statius, with learned annotations, first printed at Antwerp, in 1595, and since reprinted several times. He also undertook an edition of Boethius, which, with his notes, was published in 1607. (Biog. Univ. Suppl. Fabric. Bibl. Lat.)

BERNALDO, (Anthony de Quiros,) a Spanish Jesuit, who died in 1668, leaving, in Latin, some Commentaries upon Aquinas, a Treatise upon Predestination, which has been printed, and a course of philosophy, comprising logic, physics, and metaphysics, published in 1656. (Antonio Bibl. Hisp. Nova.)

BERNARD, king of Italy, son of Pepin, and grandson of Charlemagne. His father died July 8, 810, but he was not placed as his successor on the Italian throne, until after a lapse of about two years, when the country being menaced by the Saracens, a domestic government appeared essential for its safety. Bernard was then not more than twelve or thirteen years old, but a council was assigned to him of sufficient experience for the exigences of the times. On Charlemagne's death, in 814, Bernard conceived himself injured, as representative of that emperor's eldest son, by the advancement of his uncle Lewis, surnamed *le Debonnaire*, to the imperial dignity. He was, however, but a young boy, and, accordingly, Lewis found himself able to bring him for a reprimand to Aix-la-Chapelle, and to deprive him of the two counsellors on whom he chiefly relied. Still Bernard built upon some improvement of his condition; but when Lewis associated his own son, Lothaire, with himself on the imperial throne, he saw no prospect of regaining what he considered his hereditary right, unless in the field. He assembled, accordingly, an army, but even now, being nothing more than a mere lad, his uncle no sooner approached, than his own troops fled. He saw, therefore, no resource but in the emperor's pity, and his appeal to it was made at Chalons-on-the-Marne. He was, however, taken to Aix, put upon his defence, and capitally condemned. Lewis commuted the sentence for the loss of his eyes, a penalty that was inflicted upon him with such barbarity that he died three days afterwards, namely, April 17, 818. (Moreri.)

BERNARD, duke of Septimania and Toulouse. The former country comprised a large portion of Languedoc, and took its name from seven great cities which it contained. Charlemagne united it to the kingdom of Aquitain, from which Lewis *le Debonnaire* separated it, in 817, and joining it with the Marches of Spain, made of the two a duchy, having Barcelona for the capital. This duchy was conferred, in 820, upon Bernard, son of William, duke of Toulouse. The new duke soon distinguished himself against the Spanish Moors; but in 828 he was called to the imperial court, and invested with the highest offices there, chiefly through the influence of Judith, Lewis *le Debonnaire's* second wife, who sought his aid against the emperor's first family, and who soon fell under suspicion of a criminal intercourse with him. Driven from court by the prevalence of this report, joined to other accusations less credible, Bernard retired to Barcelona, the principal city of his government. In the following year, however, he presented himself at the diet of Thionville, offering battle, according to the usage of the times, to any who chose to accuse him, and, no one accepting the defiance, he purged himself by oath. But although he thus satisfied the law, he did not find his former influence restored. Hence he connected himself with Pepin, king of Aquitain, and thus became obnoxious to the vengeance of the emperor, who deprived him of his duchy of Septimania, in the diet of Joac, in the Limousin, in 832. Bernard managed so as to recover this dignity in the following year, and in 835 he succeeded Berenger in the duchy of Toulouse. Being thus at the head of two great provinces, he laboured to render himself independent; but, in 844, he appears to have been condemned as a traitor, in a diet holden by Charles the Bald, in Aquitain, and executed accordingly. There are accounts, however, which make him to have concluded a peace with Charles, and to have been treacherously assassinated afterwards by that emperor's own hands; a crime designated as both murder and parricide, Charles's likeness to him being sufficient evidence that common fame was perfectly correct in calling Bernard the paramour of Judith. (Moreri. Biog. Univ.)

BERNARD, or BERN-HART, a Romish saint, archbishop of Vienne, in Dauphiny, in which country he was born, of a noble family, in 778. Being educated by an exemplary ecclesiastic, he seems to have imbibed a desire to follow his profession, but parental authority compelled him to become a soldier. On his father's death, however, he determined upon founding a monastery, and retiring into it. As he was a married man, the latter design could not be realized without his wife's consent; but that he obtained, and became a monk. He was soon afterwards elected abbot of his house, and in 810 archbishop of Vienne, an election in which he was constrained to acquiesce by pope Leo III. to whom Charlemagne had announced it. He died Jan. 10, 842, or, according to some authorities, 852. (Moreri.)

BERNARD, of Menthon, a Romish saint, celebrated as the originator of the *Great* and *Little St. Bernard*, two religious establishments yet remaining among the most inhospitable passages of the Alps. He was born near Annecy, in Savoy, in 923, of noble parents, and consecrated, in opposition to their wishes, after a suitable education, to the ecclesiastical profession. Becoming archdeacon of Aosta, in Piedmont, he engaged himself in laborious missions among the neighbouring mountaineers, who were still, to a great extent, pagans. Two principal places of resort for their worship were a temple of Jupiter, on Montjoux, as the French called the height, or Mountjoy, as the English, and a column dedicated to Jupiter, at a pass in the mountains. Having reclaimed the people from their heathen prejudices, Bernard destroyed the temple of Jupiter, and reared on its site a conventual pile, to serve for the double purpose of containing a religious fraternity, and of rendering hospitality to pilgrims crossing the Alps on their way to Rome. Another such establishment he placed by the idol's column, and both are still known by his name, having rendered, during their long existence in those dreary solitudes, innumerable services to travellers. The self-devoted monks who tenant these frozen abodes, perhaps the highest European habitations, train sagacious dogs to scour the neighbouring wilderness, and return on discovering any individual unable to help himself. He then receives such attentions and hospitality from the kind brethren as his case requires. Bernard having thus substantiated an enduring claim to the respectful remembrance of mankind, resumed his missionary labours in the neighbouring regions. He died at Novara, in the Milanese, May 28, 1008, but his festival is the 15th of June, being the day of his interment. His relics were greatly venerated at Novara. Treves, however, boasted of possessing his head, although no satisfactory account could be given of its transfer to such a distant resting-place. (Moreri. Biog. Univ.)

BERNARD, abbot of Tiron, a Romish saint, born at Abbeville, in Picardy, who gained a high reputation in the eleventh and twelfth centuries by a life of self-denial, and a supposed possession of miraculous powers. After preaching zealously in many parts of France, he founded, in 1109, a Benedictine monastery, upon the strictest principles of the order, in the wood of Tiron, between Chartres and Nogent-le-Rotrou. It was a wild spot, but the founder's fame for sanctity quickly drew a society to it, from all parts of the kingdom. Bernard died April 14, 1116, aged upwards of 70. (Moreri.)

BERNARD, (Uberti,) a Romish saint, a cardinal, and bishop of Parma, a member of the noble Tuscan family named Uberti. He was at one time abbot of Val-Ombrosa, and afterwards general of the order designated from that famous Tuscan monastery; but his chief reputation was gained by exertions made in Lombardy against opponents, treated as schismatical, to the dominant papal party. He died in 1133. (Moreri.)

BERNARD, of Clairvaux, a Romish saint, from whom the Cistercians in France were called Bernardins, one of the most conspicuous personages in the twelfth century. He was third son of Tescelin, the knightly proprietor of Fontaine, in Burgundy, where he was born either in 1090, or the following year. His mother, Aletha, or Adelaide, a lady of great piety, daughter of the count of Montbar, died when he was about fifteen, having brought him to that age under a strong sense of her own religious impressions, and destined him for a monk. As Bernard, however, grew up, his own inclinations were strongly tempted into a contrary direction. He became a very fine young man, with a pleasing countenance, insinuating manners, powerful intellect, and agreeable address. Hence he found inducements on every side to take that station in the gay and busy world for which he had so many promising qualifications. He seems besides to have been susceptible of an amorous passion, and accordingly he once caught himself gazing with considerable interest upon a handsome female face. Perhaps that maternal destination of him to a cloister, with which he had been haunted in his dreams, then crossed his mind, for he rushed into a pond, and persisted in standing there, up to his neck in water, until he had nearly fainted. Still he felt considerable difficulty in finally relinquishing secular pursuits. But his reluctance at length yielding, he resolved upon embracing the monastic life in its utmost rigour. This was to be found in the new Cistercian rule, which had hitherto failed of any extensive popularity, from the weight of its repulsive obligations. Here was, however, a strong recommendation to the ardent and inflexible temperament of Bernard. Hence he not only made up his own mind to the Cistercian profession, but would not rest until he had won over four of his brothers to the same determination. The fifth was not old enough. At first this pious family, with some friends influenced by their example, lived retired at their own houses; but in 1113 they transferred themselves to Cîteaux, a monastery built fifteen years before, about five leagues from Dijon. The society there had long lived in apprehension of gradual extinction; for although every body admired the ascetic virtues which it displayed, most people, notwithstanding, considered such mortifications entirely above the ordinary strength of man. From the prevalence of this opinion, the choice of Bernard and his friends occasioned extreme surprise, and, by a common revulsion in the human mind, extensive emulation. Devotees of every age, country, and condition, became eager for admission at Cîteaux, or for the establishment of its rigorous discipline in places fitted for their own adoption of it. Thus a monastic system, admired, indeed, but thought impracticable for a continuance, owed popularity and permanence to Bernard's adoption of it. After a year's noviciate, that celebrated man bound himself by the irrevocable vows; and in the following year, or 1115, he was sent by the abbot, with twelve associates, to found a new establishment upon the Cistercian system. A spot was assigned for his occupation by Hugh, count of Champagne, in a rugged vale, a customary harbour for banditti, near the river Aube, and known as the valley of Absynthe. It is about five leagues from Langres, and its name was now changed to Clairvaux. Bernard, young as he was, became the first abbot. In that situation, by his extraordinary energy, talents, and self-denial, he not only rendered the Cistercian order popular throughout Europe, but also his opinion, advice, and mediation were more highly valued than those of any contemporary, however superior to him in station.

One of the first evidences of this European reputation was a request made to him in 1128, by the grand master of the Templars, to consider a body of statutes for that order. Two years afterwards, he had the honour of a call to an episcopal council assembled by Lewis VI. or the Gross, king of France, at Estampes, to decide upon the rival pretensions of Innocent II. and Anacletus II. The case was left entirely in his hands; and when he decided that Innocent was legitimate possessor of the papal chair, his decision was unanimously deemed conclusive of the question by the prelates present. France being thus brought over to Innocent's party, Bernard became anxious to render him a similar service in other regions of the west, and after great exertions he succeeded. During the years that were consumed in healing this unhappy schism, the abbot of Clairvaux was absent from his monastery, upon various negotiations both at home and abroad; and he had not resumed his former habits more than about two years, when, in 1140, he was called to the council of Sens, to confront the famous Abelard. His own treatment of theological questions was the reverse of that which this acute, but half-principled and unfortunate scholar adopted, being like that of the fathers, and he has been considered as the last of them; whereas Abelard had become illustrious by teaching divinity with those refinements, and that methodical subtlety, upon which the scholastic system was erected. Bernard's views were entirely practical, and hence his mind was unfitted for the examination of Abelard's system, perhaps also for an accurate comprehension of it. He charged it, accordingly, with dangerous errors; and since the philosopher's influence, great as it was, fell immeasurably below the abbot's, the council of Sens condemned his opinions, and he had not courage to maintain them. Bernard's next triumph was of a character still more conspicuous, although its issue was sufficient to undermine the credit of an ordinary man. Lewis VII. or the Younger, the first European sovereign that resolved upon becoming a crusader, was driven into that senseless determination by remorse for an act of barbarity perpetrated by his troops at Vitry-le-brulé, in 1143. More than thirteen hundred persons had taken refuge in a church, at the sack of that town, during Lewis's war with his vassal, Theobald, count of Champagne. The church was fired, and they were inhumanly burnt, to the king's extreme concern, when a fit of sickness drove him into serious thought. He now offered to make any atonement within his power; and Bernard represented that none could be so meritorious as an expedition for the firm establishment of a christian power in Palestine. Hence the second crusade. Eugenius III. no sooner heard of Lewis's determination to embark in this new enterprise, than he applauded it highly, and Bernard was commissioned to travel through France and Germany for the purpose of raising another army of crusaders. His first great effort was at Vezelai, at Easter, 1146, where Lewis, after receiving the sacrament, joined the preacher in imploring the assembled nobles to strain every nerve for the rescue of Zion's holy hill from all future danger of infidel pollution. The hearers were deeply moved by this appeal; and Bernard's fervid eloquence quickly rendered all around mad for a religious expedition into Palestine. No building could contain his hearers; he therefore fixed a lofty pulpit in the fields, and from it thundered such appeals as agitated every hearer. He came provided with crosses for the marking of those whom his eloquence should engage as holy volunteers. But these were soon exhausted; and as the hearers crowded round him to receive the badge, he could only answer their importunities by tearing his monkish dress into very shreds, and making crosses of it for the shoulders eagerly submitted to his hands. A like success attended him in other places, not in France alone, but in Germany besides. The emperor, however, Conrad III. was not so easily persuaded. Yet even he, at last, could not resist the French preacher's uncommon powers. Bernard painted such a picture of the day of judgment, with its frightful penalties for slothful servants, and inconceivable delights for those who did their duty, that Conrad's caution was effectually stormed, and his adhesion given to the new crusade. Bernard's great success in preaching this, must not, however, be attributed wholly to the soul-inspiring powers of his pulpit oratory. He was considered so eminent for working miracles, that some of his credulous admirers called him the *thaumaturgus of the west;* and his great reputation betrayed him into the weakness of displaying himself as a prophet. His hearers were buoyed up by assurances that success was reserved for a new crusade. Of these rash pretensions to a knowledge of the future, he soon saw the fallacy, and he then accounted for a disappointment so mortifying, by declaring that the crusaders, by their sins, had defeated Heaven's original intentions in their favour. Before Bernard was driven to the necessity of making this ridiculous apology, he came before the world as an active persecutor of the religious party in southern France, known as Petrobrusians, from Peter Bruis, burnt at St. Gilles, in 1126. An eminent disciple of this martyr, however, kept his opinions alive, in all their former popularity, and Bernard was filled with disgust and indignation in observing deserted churches, and a general abhorrence of those Romish peculiarities which are nearly akin to paganism, and from which the Reformation so wisely and piously delivered a large section of the catholic church. Bernard himself, though undoubtedly touched by a spirit of vital religion, had an unhappy leaning towards this miserable superstition, having imbibed early some unauthorized sort of veneration for the blessed Virgin. He therefore gladly interfered, at the solicitation of pope Eugenius II., in the religious concerns of southern France; and it was chiefly by his means that Henry was burnt at Toulouse, in 1147. Yet the famous abbot of Clairvaux, although the severest of ascetics in his own person, and the sternest and most unsparing of opponents in every case where he thought principle or practice defective, was not naturally cruel. He exerted himself, accordingly, during the fever that raged from his preaching of the crusade, to disabuse the public mind from the sanguinary illusions introduced by a fanatic monk, who advised a general massacre of the Jews. He had also the sense to refuse an offer, made to him at Chartres, to undertake the conduct of his favourite expedition to Palestine. An air of ridicule may easily be thrown over this refusal, as dictated by consideration of Peter the Hermit's recent failure, and by a keen perception of the difference between running others into danger, and sharing it with them. But Bernard really seemed altogether above personal considerations of any kind, at the same time that his vigorous understanding could not overlook the necessity of military talents for the successful conduct of a warlike expedition. A mind so active and energetic as his was likely to wear out, before its time, even a strong frame sufficiently regarded; but Bernard's life was one of the strictest mortification, and it was brought to a close in 1153, when he had only attained the age of sixty-three. During his many conspicuous appearances in some of the most elevated, busy, and spirit-stirring scenes that the age afforded, he had repeated offers of the episcopal dignity; but he would hear nothing of a final separation from Clairvaux. He was at all times ready to leave it, as a mediator between states, an assistant at councils, a preacher of religious truth, or that which he considered such; and he was ever diligently employed in it, in regulating its affairs, extending the bounds of his order, correspondence, and literary labour with religious views; but the part of a mere great man upon the stage of life was below his ambition. Still Bernard cannot be ranked among the very brightest characters that biography records. Conscious of his own self-denial, pure intentions, and brilliant parts, he measured all mankind by a narrow standard, formed within himself, and he had no consideration or mercy for any that it did not suit. Hence he has laid himself open to objections from those who entertain different sentiments from his. He had notoriously but little respect for human learning; and in this weakness has been found a reason for some of the heat with which he pursued Abelard, of whose excellences he was really but little judge, and of whose reputation he has been considered as rather jealous. He could make no allowances for human weakness, the force of circumstances, or motives that he might not understand. He could set no bounds to his disapprobation and invective, whenever, according to his own apprehensions, the case called for censure. Hence Bayle rallies his whole history as a complete exemplification of his mother's dream, when pregnant with him. She thought herself likely to produce a dog; and the lively biographer observes that she did really produce a being that barked unmercifully at every thing which he did not like or understand. But in spite of these just objections to his character, St. Bernard was really one of the greatest men that his age produced, and was inferior in substantial excellence to very few that have been known. Some of his influence undoubtedly arose from a cast of thought in perfect unison with that which prevailed in his time; still enough will remain to command respectful deference and extensive admiration from any race of men. His canonization took place under circumstances of unexampled solemnity, twenty years after his death; and the 20th of August was set apart as his commemorative festival.

St. Bernard's great abilities and popularity have occasioned more editions of his works, than of those left by any other father. One of these mounts up to a high date in the art of European printing; his Sermons on the Times and Saints, together with his book dedicated to the Knights Templars, having been printed at Mentz in 1475. But the best edition of his works is that by the learned father Mabillon, printed at Paris, in 1690, in two volumes folio. The first volume contains his letters, and all his undoubted works. Of the letters, which are 440 in number, a particular account may be seen in Du Pin's Ecclesiastical History, (x. 44.) They are followed by a Treatise on Consideration, addressed to Eugenius II., and intended for that pontiff's instruction; a similar treatise, addressed to Henry, archbishop of Sens, on episcopal duties; a Discourse upon Conversion, addressed to the clergy of Paris, containing exhortations to repentance and amendment, with reflections upon ambitious and incontinent ecclesiastics; a piece upon Commands and Dispensations, treating of monastic questions, and maintaining, among other things, that the Benedictine rule is proposed to all mankind, but not to be forced upon any; an Apology to William, abbot of St. Thierry, denying imputations cast upon him and others of his own order, of having defamed all Benedictines who had not embraced the Cistercian reform, but notwithstanding speaking severely of the Cluniac monks; a Treatise in commendation of the New Militia, that is, of the Templars. These are followed by treatises upon pride; the love of God; some theological opinions of an anonymous author; and the errors of Abelard. After these come a life of St. Malachy; a tract on singing; sermons for a year, and upon the Canticles. These latter sermons, though 86 in number, are only upon the first two chapters of that book, and the first verse of the third chapter; yet, by means of mystical and allegorical excursions over a field so very limited, they contain a vast number of moral and spiritual ideas, strikingly displaying the wonderful fertility of the author's mind, and his great command of language. Of the second volume, published under Bernard's name, it is the less necessary to speak particularly, because all the pieces in it are not certainly known to be his.

St. Bernard was master of a happy style, being lively, noble, and concise. His genius often takes a lofty flight, but an agreeable diction ever waits upon it. Sweetness and violence come upon the reader by turns; now stealing upon his affections, then agitating his breast. He meets with exhortations that admit of no evasion; of admonitions and rebukes that defy indifference, and provoke no offence. Even Bernard's raillery seldom causes irritation, being so tempered with good nature, that it seems merely used as the best instrument to confer a service. Bernard's mind was deeply stored with Scripture; hence he scarcely writes a period without words or thoughts suggested by the Bible. Of the fathers, Austin and Ambrose were his great favourites and authorities. He considered them as models that he was bound to imitate; but although most of his thoughts really come from these and others of the ancients, yet he has managed them all with so much address, and impressed his own genius upon them so decidedly, that they seem to have originated with himself. In thus writing from Scripture and antiquity, Bernard placed himself in strong contrast with those scholastic theologians who were beginning to engross the regards of learned men, and who, after his decease, were long almost the only divines that appeared in western Europe. To this cause, Bernard probably owed some portion of his popularity. Subtle and ingenious as was, undoubtedly, the scholastic theology, it soared so much above the ordinary range of thought, that religious reading more suited for minds of every order, and for acting upon the heart, could not fail to command considerable attention. Hence Bernard, merely as *the last of the fathers*, the most recent example of a venerable class that had disappeared, was secure, especially with such solid claims as his, to be deeply venerated and constantly perused.

Although Bernard was a zealous adherent of the papal see, and tinctured with Rome's present superstitions, his authority has been alleged against some of the theology to which she now stands committed. As might be expected, he evidently did not hold those refinements, or perversions, of the doctrine of justification, which school-divinity unfolds, and the Reformers denounced as dangerous Romish errors. But he also bears testimony against transubstantiation, the vital doctrine of Romanism; a fact which shows that, in spite of the persecution undergone by Berenger, the papal church really had not as yet adopted a view of the sacramental presence which makes an officiating priest call down the Deity to be present sensibly, though veiled, into the midst of a congregation. Bernard also seems to have been grounded but imperfectly in the modern Romish purgatorial doctrines. He teaches that the souls of the blessed are admitted into heaven, and into the society of angels, immediately on their separation from the body, but not to the enjoyment of the beatific vision in full perfection, only to that of our Lord's human body.

St. Bernard's life was written by contemporaries. The most ancient biography of him is in five books, of which the first was written by William, abbot of St. Thierry; the second by Arnold, abbot of Bonneval; and the last three by Geoffrey, secretary and disciple to the great abbot of Clairvaux himself. This life is in Mabillon's second volume, and it is followed by two ancient books, detailing Bernard's fancied miracles; another life, written by Alan, bishop of Auxerre, who retired to Clairvaux, in 1161, and died there in 1181; some fragments of a third ancient life; and a fourth life, written about 1180, by John the Hermit, who had lived with Bernard's disciples. There are also extant about fifty-five letters written by Nicholas of Clairvaux, secretary to St. Bernard, which have been published in the *Bibliotheca Patrum*, but contain nothing of much importance either as to doctrine or discipline. (Mabillon. Annall. Bened, v. 267, 268, 497, 547, 572, 582, 594, 605. Moreri. Bayle. Chalmers. Biog. Univ. Mills's Hist. of the Crusades, i. 364. Du Pin, Eccl. Hist. x. 42. Allix's Albigenses, 146. Cosin. Hist. Transubst. Papal. 143.)

BERNARD, (Andrew,) an Austin friar, born at Toulouse, upon whom was conferred a salary of ten marks a-year, as *poeta laureatus*, by Henry VII. of England, until he could obtain some equivalent employment. He also appears to have been royal historiographer, and grammar-master to prince Arthur. Some poems of his are extant, and several prose pieces; among the latter, a History of Henry VII. to the capture of Perkin Warbeck. All these are in Latin, and in MS. Bernard was living in 1522, and seems to have been as much in favour with Henry VIII. as he was with his father. (Chalmers.)

BERNARD, (Bartholomew,) curate of Kemburg, worthy of record as the first clergyman in Saxony, who, in an early stage of the Reformation, namely, in 1521, dared to marry. For this he was cited to appear at Halle, by cardinal Albert, archbishop of Magdeburg, who requested the elector (Frederic) of Saxony to enjoin episcopal obedience on his subject. But the elector contrived to protract the business until Melancthon had composed for Bernard a learned defence, addressed to the officials of the court; and the matter does not appear to have been carried further.

BERNARD, (Catharine,) a French poetess and novelist, born at Rouen. In 1689, she produced her tragedy of Laodamie, and in 1690, that of Brutus, from the latter of which Voltaire has imitated some passages. She was the writer of three romances and some poems, the former entitled, Les Malheurs de l'Amour, 1684; Le Comte d'Amboise, 1689; and Inès de Cordoue, 1696. Some biographers have attributed to her La Relation de l'Ile de Borneo, a work thought by others to be by Fontenelle. Mademoiselle Bernard died at Paris, in 1712. (Biog. Univ.)

BERNARD, (Charles,) historiographer of France, born at Paris on the 25th of December, 1571, and died in 1640. He wrote:—1. La Conjonction des Mers. 2. Discours sur l'Etat des Finances. 3. Histoire des Guerres de Louis XIII., of which about three dozen copies were printed. 4. Carte généalogique de la Maison de Bourbon. (Biog. Univ.)

BERNARD, (Edward,) a distinguished astronomer, critic, and linguist, born at Perry St. Paul, near Towcester, on the 2d of May, 1638. He received his education at Merchant Taylors' School, and St. John's college, Oxford, where he laid the foundation of his philological knowledge, and made himself acquainted with the mathematical sciences, and with several of the oriental languages, besides all the usual branches of a classical education. After taking his degrees at the university, and passing through the office of proctor, he made a journey, in 1668, to Leyden, in order to consult some oriental manuscripts in the public library there, but more especially the 5th, 6th, and 7th books of the Conics of Apollonius, the Greek text of which has been lost. This Arabic version having been brought from the east by the celebrated Golius, a transcript was thence taken of it by Bernard, and brought by him to Oxford, with an intent to publish it there with a Latin translation; but he was unfortunately compelled to relinquish that project for want of encouragement. It appears from some letters published by the Historical Society of Science, that it was originally the intention of Golius to publish this Arabic version, and that afterwards Dr. Pell undertook the same task. (Letters on Scientific Subjects, edited by Halliwell, p. 88.) The glory of completing it was reserved for Dr. Halley, who printed Dr. Bernard's edition of these books in 1710, in his complete version of the Conics of Apollonius. In 1669 he was appointed deputy to the celebrated Christopher Wren, professor of astronomy at Oxford, when the latter became surveyor-general of his majesty's works; and in 1673, on the resignation of Wren, Bernard was appointed to the vacant professorship. He had, in the mean time, been presented to a living, and made chaplain to the bishop of Bath and Wells. In 1676 he was sent to France, as tutor to the dukes of Grafton and Northumberland, sons to king Charles the Second by the duchess of Cleveland, who then lived with their mother at Paris; but the simplicity of his manners not suiting the gaiety of the duchess's family, he returned about a year afterwards to Oxford, and resumed his studies. In 1691 he was presented to the rectory of Brightwell, in Berkshire, resigning, at the same time, his professorship in favour of Dr. David Gregory. Towards the latter end of his life he was much afflicted with the stone; yet, notwithstanding this and other infirmities, he undertook a voyage to Holland, to attend the sale of Golius's MSS. On his return to England he fell into a languishing consumption, which put an end to his life on the 12th of January, 1696, in the 58th year of his age.

His literary projects were more numerous than those that he actually presented to the world. About 1670, a scheme was set on foot at Oxford of collecting and publishing the works of the ancient mathematicians, and he took a most active part in the execution of the preliminaries of the project, which was but very imperfectly carried out. He left, however, a very valuable synopsis of the writers selected for publication, which will be found in the biography of him published by Dr. Smith. He also superintended the publication of the Catalogus Manuscriptorum Angliæ et Hiberniæ, fol. Oxon. 1697; a work in use at the present day. Bernard was likewise the author of some papers in the Philosophical Transactions, and a few philological tracts. He left behind him many pieces in MS., and a large collection, all of which are now deposited in the Bodleian Library.

BERNARD, (Sir Francis, Bart.,) an English barrister, educated at Westminster and Christchurch, governor of New Jersey in 1758, in which province his administration received the highest applause. He was removed to Massachusetts in 1760, where at first he was greatly liked—the general court voting him a grant of land and a salary of 1,300*l.* a-year; but the spread of disaffection soon terminated this friendly understanding, and drew down upon Bernard the indignation of those whom Dr. Allen designates as "the sons of liberty." The home government appears, however, to have entertained a high opinion of his conduct, and on the 5th of April, 1769, he was created a baronet. He was at length recalled, in consequence of an address to the crown from the general court, and embarked on the 1st of August, 1769. He died in England in 1779. His select letters on the trade and government of America, written in Boston, from 1763 to 1768, were published in London in 1774. Others of his letters appeared in 1768-9. Some Greek and Latin poems of his composition were printed in the Pietas et Gratulatio, Cambridge, 1761.

BERNARD, (Sir Thomas,) third son of the preceding, an English baronet of great public spirit, and considerable literary talent. His father was immediately succeeded by John, the second son; an elder one, named after himself, having died before him. Thomas was born at Lincoln, in 1750, but as his father went over to America, about eight years afterwards, his education was chiefly conducted at Harvard college, in New England. He was, however, still a youth when Sir Francis came home, and he then entered himself of Lincoln's Inn. He was called to the bar in 1780, but he practised entirely as a conveyancer, and with considerable success. In 1782, he married Margaret Adair, who ultimately became, by the death of an only sister, her father's sole heiress. This rendered her husband wealthy, and gradually retiring from practice, he devoted all his later years to objects of public utility. He succeeded to the baronetcy conferred upon his father, by the unexpected death of his brother, Sir John, in the West Indies, in 1809. One of his first public undertakings was the improvement, both in property and management, of the Foundling Hospital, in London. His good success here led him into a general consideration of some plan for benefiting the poor, and a society for that purpose was founded by his means in 1796; his admirable relative, Shute Barrington, bishop of Durham, with some other individuals of like beneficence, cordially seconding his views. The society thus formed was largely instrumental in calling the attention of opulence to the most pressing wants of poverty, and in pointing out means to remedy the evils disclosed. Among these, undoubtedly, one of the most serious was the insufficiency of a religious provision for the poor of great towns. In these, churches had long been much less numerous than the population required, and, in consequence, the accommodation which they afforded was, to a great extent, engrossed by the wealthier parishioners. Sir Thomas Bernard set an example of relieving humbler life from these injuries, by procuring the erection of a free chapel in St. Giles's, one of the poorest and most densely-peopled quarters of London. He next cooperated actively with Sir Benjamin Thomson, more generally known as Count Rumford, in providing the English metropolis with a literary and scientific institution upon the plan of the French National Institute. Hence arose the Royal Institution, chartered in 1800, and rendered famous throughout Europe, as the theatre on which Davy took his place among the greatest of chemists. To Sir Thomas Bernard, also, principally, London was indebted for the British Institution, which has assembled, from scattered collections, some of the finest specimens of art, much to the benefit of native artists. His benevolent spirit was likewise actively engaged in behalf of indigent children, by directing attention to their treatment in cotton-mills, and as chimney-sweepers; to their education when blind; and to the extension of vaccination. His beneficent life was closed July 1, 1818. Sir Thomas Bernard left the following works:—Observations on the Proceedings of the Friends of the Liberty of the Press, 1793. A Letter to the Lord Bishop of Durham, on the Measures now under Consideration of Parliament for Promoting Industry, and the Relief of the Poor, 1807. The New School, being an Attempt to illustrate its Principles and Advantages, 1810. The

Barrington School, being an Account of that established by the Bishop of Durham, at Bishop's Auckland, 1812. An Account of the Supply of Fish for the Manufacturing Poor, 1813. Spurinna, or the Comforts of Old Age, 1813, reprinted 1816, and 1817. Case of the Salt-Duties, 1817. The Cottager's Meditations. Dialogue between Monsieur François and John English. The entire Prefaces, and most of the Reports, of the Society for bettering the Condition of the Poor.

As Sir Thomas Bernard died without issue, the baronetcy devolved upon his brother, Scrope, who, marrying the daughter and heiress of a London banker, named Morland, assumed that name in addition to his own. (Ann. Biog.)

BERNARD, abbot of Fontchaud, in Languedoc, in the latter half of the 12th century, known as the author of a work against the Vaudois, published by Gretser, in 1614, and abridged by Bossuet. (Hist. Lit. de France.)

BERNARD, (John, 1756—1828,) an actor and theatrical historian, born at Portsmouth, who played fops and fine gentlemen with considerable success, both in London and the country. He afterwards became a provincial manager, but failing about 1797, he embarked for America, where he continued upon the stage until 1820. In 1830 his son published a work written by him, under the title of Retrospections of the Stage, from which the foregoing facts are collected.

BERNARD, (John Stephen,) a learned German physician, of French origin, son of Gabriel Bernard, a protestant minister at Berlin, where he was born in 1718. He went to Holland to study medicine, and settled himself in that country. All the leisure time that he could snatch from the duties of his profession, he devoted to the study of Greek literature, to which he rendered important services, not only by republishing several of the minor Greek medical writers, whose works had become extremely rare, but also by editing anonymously the Daphnis et Chloe of Longus, Gr. and Lat. 1754, (an edition really printed at Amsterdam, though Paris appears in the title-page,) 4to, and Thomas Magister De Vocibus Atticis, Lugd. Bat. 1757, 8vo, to which Oudendorp wrote the preface, and which continued to be till within the last ten years the *editio optima*. After this he gave up writing, and retired to Arnheim, where he was so completely forgotten, that in the seventh volume of Saxii Onomasticon Literarium his death was said to have taken place in 1790. In order to prove that he was still alive, (as he tells us himself,) he published a short anonymous fragment, De Hydrophobia, Gr. and Lat. Arnhem. 1791, 8vo, which was afterwards inserted, with a preface and additional notes, in his Reliq. Medico-Crit. He also began to edit Theophanes Nonnus, which, however, he did not live to finish, but died at Arnheim in 1793. The following is a list of the medical works edited by him:—1. Demetrius Pepagomenus, Περι Ποδαγρας, De Podagra, Gr. and Lat. Lugd. Bat. 1743, 8vo, and again, with a new title-page, Arnhem. 1753. 2. Ανωνυμου Εισαγωγη Ανατομικη, Anonymi Introductio Anatomica, Gr. and Lat. Lugd. Bat. 1744, 8vo, containing also Sanguinaticii Ἑρμηνεια των του Σωματος Μερων, Nomenclatura Partium Corporis, Gr. and Lat., with anatomical plates, taken from an ancient MS. 3. Michael Psellus, Περι Λιθων Αρετης, De Lapidum Virtutibus, Gr. and Lat. Lugd. Bat. 1745, 8vo, containing also a fragment De Colore Sanguinis ex Doctrina Medica Persarum. 4. Palladius, Περι Πυρετων Συντομος Συνοψις, De Febribus concisa Synopsis, Gr. and Lat. Lugd. Bat. et Trajecti ad Rhen. 1745, 8vo, containing also Lexicon Alphabeticum Chemicum, et Excerpta ex Scriptoribus Chemicis, Græce. 5. Synesius, Περι Πυρετων, De Febribus, Gr. and Lat. Amstel. et Lugd. Bat. 1749, 8vo, containing also part of the seventh book of the Viaticum Peregrinantium of Constantinus Africanus. 6. Theophanes Nonnus, Επιτομη της Ιατρικης Ἁπασης Τεχνης, Compendium totius Artis Medicæ, Gr. and Lat. Gothæ et Amstel. 1794-5, 8vo. This edition, which is the most learned of any of his works, was finished after his death by C. G. Gumpert and J. G. A. Sparr. Besides these works, he was the author of the remarks on some Greek authors, in the Acta Litteraria Societatis Rheno-Trajectinæ, tom. i. § 7, and of several learned letters to J. J. Reiske, inserted by him in the second part of his Memoirs, Leipzig, 1783, 8vo. He also contributed to the Miscellaneæ Observationes Criticæ Novæ of Dorville the various readings of a MS. of the Lexicons to Hippocrates of Erotianus and Galen, tom. ix.; Amstel. 8vo, 1749; and C. G. Gruner published after his death, Jenæ, 1795, 8vo, various letters and opuscula, with the title, Jo. Steph. Bernardi Reliquiæ Medico-Criticæ.

BERNARD, (John,) an English divine, born at Castor, in Lincolnshire, and originally of Queen's college, Cambridge, whence he transferred himself to Oxford, in hopes of promotion from the parliamentarian visitors. By them he was made fellow of Lincoln college, in 1648, and about three years afterwards he became a preacher in Oxford and its vicinity. He formed, however, a matrimonial connexion in a family that entertained views very different from his, that of the celebrated Dr. Peter Heylin, then living in retirement at Abingdon. While the republican party remained in the ascendant, Bernard showed no appearance of any change of conviction derived from his wife's relations, and he held valuable preferment in his native county. Even so late as the latter end of 1659, or beginning of the following year, he published a pamphlet against the unfortunate incumbents who had been ejected by Cromwell's triers, appointed in 1654, entitled, Censura Cleri, or Against scandalous Ministers; not fit to be restored to the Churches Livings, in point of Prudence, Piety, and Fame. This piece was anonymous, and the author, when both the times and himself were decidedly changed, wished anything rather than to acknowledge it. On the restoration, he conformed, retained his excellent living in Lincolnshire, accepted, besides, a prebend in the cathedral there, took a doctor's degree, and published two vindications of his father-in-law, Heylin. The former of these is entitled, Theologo-Historicus; or the true Life of the most Rev. Divine, and excellent Historian, Peter Heylin, D.D., Sub-Dean of Westminster, Lond. 1683, 8vo. It is professedly an answer to a life, treated as defective and calumnious, of that eminent party writer, by Vernon. Bernard's other vindication is printed with this, and is entitled, An Answer to Mr. Baxter's false Accusations of Dr. Heylin. His death occurred in 1683. (Wood's Athenæ.)

BERNARD, or BARNARD, (John,) son of the preceding, by Letice, daughter of Dr. Heylin, elected fellow of Brazennose college, Oxford, in 1682, he being then 20 years of age. On king James's accession, about three years afterwards, he made himself conspicuous by arguments in favour of popery, and he soon professed himself a convert to that religion. This movement was quickly noticed at court. In 1686, Bernard received a royal protection against any consequences of his acts or omissions; in other words, a dispensation to hold protestant preferment with an open profession of Romish opinions. In the following January, came down a *mandamus* from the king to make him lecturer in moral philosophy. But before another year was expired, the good sense of protestant England was effectually roused, and Bernard, like many others, became apprehensive that the prince of Orange was far from unlikely, within a short space of time, to protect from the insidious encroachments of prerogative those inestimable privileges which had been so gloriously won at the Reformation. Hence in October, 1688, he withdrew from Oxford, and soon afterwards resigned his fellowship of Brazennose. By the following January, his worst anticipations were realized, and he then resigned his lectureship in moral philosophy. When James II. landed in Ireland, Bernard went thither to him, and received some of his notice. He made besides an attempt to serve him by the writing of some small pieces, which were printed. But in September, 1690, he made his way to Chester, in such distress, that he seems to have depended for some time upon relief from the bishop. He appears also now to have been reconciled to the church of England. Being, probably, in want of subsistence, Bernard, who added Augustine to his name, on professing himself a Romanist, undertook to continue, correct, and enlarge the great Geographical Dictionary of Edm. Bohun, Lond. 1693, fol. To this he prefixed a Reflection upon *le Grand Dictionary Historique*, or the Great Historical Dictionary, of Lewis Morery, D.D. printed at Utrecht, 1692. (Wood's Athenæ.)

BERNARD, (John Frederic,) an eminent and learned bookseller of Amsterdam, where he carried on business from the year 1711 to that of his death, 1752. He supplied a preliminary dissertation, two other dissertations, and an account of Great Tartary, to the Recueil des Voyages au Nord, contenant divers Mémoires très utiles au Commerce, et à la Navigation, Amst. 1715-38, 10 vols, 12mo. He edited, Mémoires du Comte de Brienne, Ministre d'Etat sous Louis XIV. avec des Notes, 1719, 3 vols, 12mo; Picart's Cérémonies et Coûtumes religieuses, 9 vols. fol. 1723-43; Superstitions Anciennes et Modernes, 2 vols, fol. 1733-36; besides several works of less importance. (Biog. Univ.)

BERNARD, (James,) a native of

Geneva, originally a Franciscan friar, and a zealous Romanist. When, however, the three reformed ministers, Farel, Viret, and Froment, after the attempt to poison them, were lodged for safety in his convent, Bernard's intercourse with them, especially with Farel, shook his faith in Romanism, and led him to meditate a renunciation of the monastic life. But he first wisely adopted a measure which issued in the establishment of the reformation at Geneva. He proposed a public discussion, and in it to maintain, against all opponents, a series of theses, declarative of the chief protestant doctrines, as distinguished from those of Rome. The council of Geneva approved, and by every means promoted the discussion; on the other hand, the bishop obstructed the meeting all in his power, forbidding his clergy to attend. However, it took place in the great hall of the Franciscans, June 1535, and lasted 25 days, Bernard himself taking the lead on the one side, and on the other, Peter Caroli, a doctor of the Sorbonne, and John Chapuis, a Dominican of Geneva. In the end, the latter acknowledged themselves beaten, and professed to embrace the protestant creed. The general effect was extraordinary: nearly the whole city went over to the reformed; among them many monks and priests, and soon afterwards the Reformation was established in that city by public edict.

BERNARD, (James,) a French protestant minister, much valued in his day as a man of letters. He was born at Nions, in Dauphiny, Sept. 1, 1658, and partly educated at Geneva. In his native province he was pastor of two congregations, successively, but having preached in places interdicted by the king, he withdrew to Geneva in 1683, from fear of an arrest. Even there, however, he did not feel himself secure; and accordingly he transferred his residence to Lausanne, where he continued until the revocation of the edict of Nantes. He then settled in Holland, where his relative, Le Clerc, rendered him various services. He gained a subsistence by preaching, giving lessons in literature and mathematics, and writing for the press. As a minister of religion, his politics were at one time found an obstacle to his advancement; king William having twice refused to confirm his appointment to the Walloon church at Leyden, because he considered him a republican, and had himself been offended by some free language that he had heard him preach; although it has been observed, Bernard's avowed opinions did not really differ from those of the parties to whom William owed his English throne. Bernard was a good Hebraist, well skilled in polite literature, and an able teacher of the mathematics, although possessed of no extraordinary knowledge of them. As a literary man, he was most laborious; but his style is incorrect, diffuse, and blemished by words and phrases that authors of taste avoid. He died of an inflammation of the chest, brought on by too much application, April 27, 1718. He left behind him, Recueil des Traités de Paix, depuis l'an de J. C. 536, jusqu'à l'année 1700, 4 vols, fol.; Histoire abrégée de l'Europe, 5 vols, 12mo. Lettres Historiques, containing accounts of the principal European transactions, with remarks, begun in 1692, and published monthly until 1698, when, indeed, it did not cease, but passed into other hands. Actes et Négociations de la Paix de Ryswic, 4 vols, 8vo, published first in 1699, reprinted in 1707, in 5 vols, 12mo. A continuation of Bayle's Nouvelles de la République des Lettres, begun in 1698, and continued until December, 1710. A continuation of Le Clerc's Bibliothèque Universelle, being the greatest part of the twentieth volume, and all the five next, but thought unequal to Le Clerc's own portion of the work. Théâtre des Etats de S. A. R. le Duc de Savoye, traduit du Latin de Blaen, 1700. Traité de la Repentance tardive, 1712. De l'Excellence de la Religion Chrétienne, 1714. Of this last a translation was published in England, in 1793, by the author's grandson, Mr. Bernard of Doncaster, with his life, and notes. (Moreri. Biog. Univ. Chalmers.)

BERNARD DE MORLAS, monk of Cluny, in the twelfth century, author of a dactylic poem, De Contemptu Mundi, in three books, each of which contains a thousand verses. It was published in 1483, at Paris. Many editions have since appeared. (Hist. Lit. de France.)

BERNARD, (Nicholas,) a learned English divine, chiefly remembered in connexion with the great archbishop Ussher. He was originally of Cambridge, but incorporated M.A. of Oxford in 1628, being then chaplain to the learned primate of Ireland. He had been ordained by him two years before, at Drogheda, where he had the care of his invaluable library. By his interest he was preferred to the deanery of Ardagh, and he was employed in making collections for some of his literary undertakings, especially for his Britannicarum Ecclesiarum Antiquitates. When the Irish troubles broke out, Bernard, who had now a doctor's degree, was, like other conspicuous protestants, stripped of every thing, and he took refuge in England. He was able to bring with him his patron's magnificent collection of books, which eventually found its way back to Ireland, and is now in Trinity college, Dublin. Dr. Bernard was quickly more than recompensed for his Irish losses, by John Egerton, first earl of Bridgewater of that family, who presented him to the great rectory of Whitchurch, in Shropshire. Upon this preferment he spent all the rest of his life, in spite of the church's temporary downfal, being probably like his early patron, archbishop Ussher, a Calvinist in doctrine, and inclined for no very high ground in questions of discipline, otherwise he could hardly have become chaplain to Cromwell, as he did, when protector, and preacher to the society of Gray's Inn. Upon the Restoration, he would not return to Ireland, being doubtful, it has been thought, as to the permanency of any ecclesiastical settlement that might be made there. Whitchurch, however, was, probably, a more lucrative appointment than the deanery of Ardagh, as it certainly was more eligible to a protestant in point of situation. Even if its rector were tempted by the prospect of an Irish bishopric, which is thought to have been Bernard's case, he would commonly be found to hesitate, at least. Dr. Bernard died at Whitchurch, in the winter of 1661. His first publication gave offence, being a detailed account of an unhappy criminal of the episcopal order, executed in Dublin, in 1640, whom he attended before his death. He details the wretched offender's penitence; but he was considered blamable for doing any thing likely to prevent the whole case from sinking into oblivion. Bernard next published the whole proceedings of the siege of Drogheda, in Ireland. He was an eye-witness, and several times in danger of his life. He also published a farewell sermon preached at Drogheda; but his more important works relate to archbishop Ussher. They are—The Life and Death of Dr. James Ussher, Primate and Metropolitan of all Ireland, in a Sermon preached at his Funeral, in the Abbey of Westminster, April 17, 1656, with Enlargements. The Judgment of the late Archbishop of Armagh, concerning, first, the Extent of Christ's Death and Satisfaction; secondly, of the Sabbath, and Observation of the Lord's Day, Lond. 1657. This drew a reply from Dr. Peter Heylin, entitled *Respondet Petrus*. Letters between himself and Heylin. Some works of Archbishop Ussher, with enlargements. *Clavi Trabales*, or Nails fastened by some great Masters of Assemblies; as Archbishop Ussher, and others, concerning the Royal Supremacy and Episcopacy, Lond. 1661. (Wood's Fasti.)

BERNARD, (Richard,) a celebrated puritan divine, who first published a complete translation of Terence, in English. In the inscription on his portrait, engraven by Holler, it is said that he was aged 74, at the time of his death, in 1641, so that his birth may be referred to 1566 or 1567. He was probably a native of Lincolnshire, as his first patrons were two ladies of the family of Wray, of that county, daughters of the Lord Chief Justice, and the wives of Sir George St. Paul, and Sir William Brown, both afterwards peeresses; the former as countess of Warwick, and the latter as lady Darcy. To these ladies, in the dedication to his translation of Terence to their nephew, Christopher Wray, he acknowledges that he owes all he has. They sent him to Cambridge, where he was of Christ's college, and is named by Fuller as one of the eminent persons belonging to that society. When he left Cambridge he does not appear to have taken upon him immediately the cure of souls, and he was living at Epworth, in the isle of Axholm, in 1598, probably as an instructor of youth, when he published his Terence in English. However, he took holy orders, which was, no doubt, the intention of the two ladies, his patronesses, who were remarkably devout and pious; and from that time he seems to have renounced all other subjects, and to have devoted himself, exclusively and zealously, to his ministerial studies and duties. In 1601, on June 19, he was instituted to the vicarage of Worksop, in Nottinghamshire, which he held twelve years, displaying great concern for the spiritual welfare of the parish; although he probably was so injudicious as to raise or feed within it a party spirit upon mere externals. This may be inferred from a piece that he published there against the imposition of ceremonies, and upon the liberty of ministers respecting them. But although a puritan, he was anxious to preserve the unity of the English Protestant Church, as appears by his Dissuasion from the Way of Separation, 1605. While at Worksop he published his Faithful Shepherd, or the Shepherd's Faithfulness, 4to, 1607, which is a treatise on the duty of ministers. This he dedicated to Dr. Montague, dean of the Chapel Royal, from whom he had received favours.

In 1612, or 1613, he ceded the living of Worksop, having been presented to the rectory of Batcombe, in Somersetshire, where the remainder of his days were spent in the laborious exercise of his ministry.

But beside the discharge of his ministerial duties, he prepared and published various works connected with his calling. The following are the chief of them:— Key of Knowledge for the opening of the Secret Mysteries of St. John's Mystical Revelation, 1617. Look beyond Luther; or, an Answer to that Question, Where this our Religion was before Luther's Time? 1623. The Isle of Man, or the Legal Proceedings in Man-shire against Sin, 1627. This has been frequently reprinted, and has been thought by some the origin of Bunyan's Pilgrim's Progress. Thesaurus Biblicus, sive Promptuarium Sacrum, formerly used as a sort of concordance. (Lives of the Puritans, by Benjamin Brooke, 8vo, 1813, vol. i. p. 462.)

BERNARD, (Samuel,) an opulent French capitalist, son of a painter and engraver of the same name, who died in 1687. He was in the habit of lending money to Lewis XIV., who always condescended to ask for it in person. Lewis XV. sent a message to him for the same accommodation, but Bernard answered, that "when one wanted people, the least that could be done was to tell them so one's self." The king was in no condition to resent this liberty; hence he desired to have Bernard presented, and gave orders for treating him with every distinction. He was accordingly flattered and feasted among the great to his heart's content, in spite of witty remarks upon his admirable fitness for a counting-house; and as he lent the money, all his grand acquaintances greeted him as the saviour of the state. He was, however, a man of real generosity, being found at his death, in 1712, at the age of 88, to have lent large sums, which remained wholly unpaid. (Biog. Univ.)

BERNARDES, (Diego), considered one of the best bucolic poets of Portugal. Having accompanied king Sebastian into Africa, at the unfortunate battle of Alcacer he was made prisoner, and retained in captivity during a considerable time. On returning to Portugal he obtained some situation at court, which he held until his death, in 1596. He wrote, O Lima, em o qual se contém Eglogas e Cantas, Lisboa, 1596, 4to. Rimas varias Flores do Lima, ibid. 1597, 8vo. His misfortunes are beautifully painted in the elegy beginning—

> "Alpunto que naci, luego fortuna
> Estendió sobre mi su mano fiera."

(Machado. Moreri.)

BERNARDI DEL CASTEL BOLOGNESE, (John,) so named from the place of his birth; born about 1495, and chiefly remembered for two masterly engravings on crystal, both after Michael Angelo; one, the fall of Phaeton, the other, Tityus, with the vulture gnawing his heart. He died at Faenza, in 1555. (Biog. Univ.)

BERNARDI, (Francis, commonly called Senesino, 1680—about 1750,) a soprano singer, born at Siena, who came to London in 1721, at the invitation of Handel, and appeared at the Opera. In 1726 he returned to Italy, on account of ill health, but two or three years afterwards he again came to London. He retired to Florence in 1739. Senesino's voice was penetrating, clear, equal, and flexible. His intonation was pure, his shake perfect, and he was peculiarly admired for the delivery of recitative. (Dict. of Mus.)

BERNARDI, (John,) an English officer, conspicuous for his sufferings as an adherent of James II. His family was Genoese, and his grandfather, Philip de Bernardi, created in 1629, for services to the house of Austria, count of the holy Roman empire, lived for twenty-eight years in England in some public capacity. Marrying an English woman, of an ancient Romish family, he had by her two sons; of whom Francis, the younger, the father of major Bernardi, was resident, at one time, in England, from the republic of Genoa. Being disgusted with something that occurred in his intercourse with that state, he determined upon ending his days in England, the country of his nativity, and retired into Worcestershire. He is represented by his son, John, the future major, as a man of austere temper, who made no scruple of treating him with great severity for very insufficient reasons. The boy, accordingly, ran away from his paternal roof, at the age of thirteen; and meeting with persons who felt for his case, he was enabled to avoid the necessity of a return. His friends first attached him to the garrison at

Portsmouth, where he learnt the duties of a military life, and afterwards sent him over to Holland, as a private in one of the English companies employed by the States. During a residence of several years abroad in this service, he was repeatedly in action, and received some severe wounds; but his course otherwise was prosperous, as he rose in his profession, and in 1677 married a Dutch lady of good family and fortune. In 1687, however, James II. demanded from the States the six British regiments, although they had been in their service for fifteen years. The demand was refused; but permission was given to any of the officers that chose it, to withdraw. Only about sixty did so, out of two hundred and forty, and major Bernardi was among them. King James received the sixty with great distinction, and declared those of their late comrades who remained, rebels. Obedience to the royal summons was, however, soon shown to have been highly impolitic; but Bernardi honourably stood by his choice, following James into France and Ireland, and endeavouring to serve him also in Scotland. When the deposed monarch's cause was irretrievably ruined, Bernardi, after some difficulties and dangers, fixed himself in retirement near London. Subsequently he took up his abode in the city itself; but in 1696 he was taken into custody, as an accomplice in the plot for assassinating king William. There was not sufficient evidence to convict him, and, according to his own account, he was wholly guiltless. But six successive parliaments passed acts to detain him and some others in prison; a plain proof that he was considered a dangerous person. He died in Newgate, in 1736, after a confinement of nearly forty years; having, in the course of it, married a second wife, by whom he had ten children. (Biog. Brit.)

BERNARDI, (Stephen,) an Italian composer, of whom Dr. Burney speaks as a learned theorist, as well as a composer of masses and madrigals of a most elaborate and correct kind. He flourished from 1611 to about 1634, and was, in 1623, *Maestro di Capella* of the *Duomo*, at Verona. He published a didactic work, entitled Porta Musicale, the first part of which was printed at Verona in 1615, which, as an elementary tract, has the merit of clearness and brevity. (Mus. Biog.)

BERNARDIN, of Siena, a Romish saint, whose family, named Albizeschi, came from that city, but he was born at Massa Carrara, where his father was then chief magistrate, September 8, 1380. At three years old he lost his mother; at seven, his father, and an aunt then took charge of him. After a sufficient education, he displayed a disposition highly religious, and entered into the confraternity of the disciplinators of the hospital of *la Scala* in Siena, proving himself a very effective member during a raging pestilence, and practising, besides, numerous austerities. In 1405, he became a Franciscan friar in an Observantine convent, near Siena. Being ordained priest, his talents for the pulpit soon rendered him highly popular, but he could not resist the excitement of a pilgrimage to Jerusalem, and had the satisfaction of receiving an appointment as guardian of the Holy Land. Having returned to Italy, his qualities as a preacher were found as popular as ever, and he heightened their effect by displaying a picture of Jesus surrounded by the sun, of which he sold numerous copies. His exhibitions in the pulpit were, however, offensive to some, and he was denounced to Martin V. as a disseminator of heretical opinions. An examination proved this charge unfounded, but he, probably, did infect ignorant and excitable hearers with fanatical delusions. There being, however, many to whom such indiscretion is not objectionable, if accompanied by real piety, Bernardin was urged by three cities in succession to become their bishop. But he would undertake no superior appointment, except that of general of his order: an office which he accepted with a view to extend the Observantine rule. He died at Aquila, in Abruzzo, May 20, 1444, and was canonized by Nicholas V. in 1450. His works were printed at Venice, in 1591, by the care of Rodulfi, bishop of Sinigaglia, in 4 vols, 4to; again at Paris, in 1636, by the care of Peter de la Haye, in 2 vols, fol. They consist of sermons, religious tracts, and a commentary on the Revelations. Bernardin's sermons are not altogether unworthy of the popularity that they once enjoyed, being well arranged, and inculcating a solid morality; but the style is not striking. They are, however, free from those unsound and puerile reflections which some of the more ancient preachers have left in writing. (Du Pin. Eccl. Hist. xiii. 81.)

BERNARDIN, (Theophilus,) of Sedan, a Jesuit, who taught theology, ethics, and controversial divinity. He died at Arras, in 1625, aged 56, having been a member of his order thirty-two years. His works are:—De Perseverantia. Speculum Perfectionis Religiosæ. Institutio Vitæ. De SS. Florentio, ejusque Socio, Martyribus. De l'Acquisition des Vertus. Cynosura Christiana, sive de eligendo Vitæ Statu. (Moreri.)

BERNARDINO, (Fr. Gaspar de S.) a native of Lisbon, ordained a priest in 1593, who embarked as a missionary to the East in 1604. After various perils in the Indian ocean, he landed at Ormus, and made his way to Jerusalem, where he arrived in 1606. He published an account of his travels in Portuguese, Lisbon, 1611, 4to. (Machado.)

BERNARDINUS, (de Caravajal,) a native of Placenzia in Portugal, (or, according to Antonio, of Spain,) made a cardinal by Alexander VI., but deprived of that dignity by Julius II., for taking part in the council assembled at Pisa to curb his excesses. Bernardinus was reinstated by Leo X. He wrote, De eligendo S. Pont. Romano, Romæ, 1492; with some other pieces, less likely to be noticed by posterity. He died at Rome in 1523, after a life spent very much in the eye of the world. (Fabricius. Antonio.)

BERNARDONI, (Peter Anthony, June 30, 1672—January 19, 1714,) an Italian poet, born at Vignola, in the duchy of Modena, who lived a long time at Bologna, and is hence sometimes called at the head of his works, a Bolognese. He was named, in 1701, *Poeta Cesareo*, or Imperial poet to the court of Vienna, which he enjoyed under the emperors Leopold and Joseph I. He died at Bologna. He published two collections of poems, I Fiori, primizie poetiche, &c. Bologna, 1694; and Rime varie, Vienna, 1705; besides some dramatic works. In 1706 and 1707 his collected works were published at Bologna in 3 vols, 8vo. (Biog. Univ.)

BERNATOWICZ, (Felix,) a Polish writer of novels, of whose earlier life little is known. In 1805, however, he was taken into the establishment of prince Czartoryiski, by whom he was afterwards employed in the capacity of private secretary and reader. After his patron's death he took up his residence at Pulawy, where he made his first essay in novel writing, greatly to the surprise of his friends, who for some time doubted whether he was really the author of a production so little to be expected from one of his habits and disposition. His best performance of the kind is his Pogata, an historical romance, founded on the conversion of Lithuania to Christianity. He died in a state of mental imbecility, September 5, 1836.

BERNAZZANO, (Martin,) a Milanese painter, who flourished about the year 1536. He painted landscapes, animals, and fruit, and was excellent as a colourist, but deficient in the drawing of the human figure. Cesare da Sesto introduced groups into his landscapes. It is doubtful whether Bernazzano was instructed by Leonardo da Vinci, but he certainly availed himself of his models. (Lanzi. Stor. Pitt. iv. 162. Byron's Dict.)

BERNERS, (Juliana,) an early English authoress, daughter, as it is believed, of Sir James Berners, of Berners' Roding, vulgarly *Barnish*, a small parish near Chelmsford, in Essex. The Berners family has been considered and treated as baronial, although its title to that distinction has embarrassed competent inquirers. Sir James Berners, Juliana's reputed father, was beheaded in 1388, as one of Richard the Second's evil counsellors. This fact is a corroboration of the received opinion as to the authoress's parentage; nothing being more likely than that the orphan child of a ruined man should seek shelter and provision in a convent. It is, accordingly, known of this lady that she was prioress of Sopewell nunnery, near St. Alban's, about the middle of the fifteenth century. She seems, however, to have been rather fitted for a mistress of some such country mansion as her father's, than for presiding over a body of religious female recluses. Such, at least, is the inference that may not unfairly be drawn from a book written by the prioress of Sopewell, the authorship of which is really all that indisputably attaches to the name, so highly venerated among bibliomaniacs, of Juliana Berners. It was once a very favourite work, as is testified by the frequent reprints of it which appeared before the seventeenth century. It is believed to have been first printed at St. Alban's, in 1481. Undoubtedly there was an impression of it there in 1486, in a small folio. In 1496, a 4to edition of it came forth from Wynkyn de Worde's press in Westminster. An imperfect copy of this fetched, at the duke of Roxburgh's sale, ever memorable in the history of scarce books, 147*l*. The last impression of it was in 4to, in London, in 1595, with the following title,—The Gentleman's Academie, or the Book of St. Alban's; containing three most exact and excellent books; the first of Hawking, the second of all the Terms of Hunting, and the last of Armory; all compiled by Juliana Barnes, in the year from the incarnation of Christ 1486; and now reduced into better method by G. M. The owner of these initials appears to have been led into this date, by finding it affixed to the third or concluding book in the St. Alban's edition, which relates to heraldic blazonry, and which is there said to have been translated and compiled at St. Alban's, in 1486. This really, however, seems to have been an addition to the work of Juliana Berners, who could hardly have been alive at the time when it was made. It is, in fact, made up of nothing more than extracts from a work of Nicholas Upton, written about 1441. (Chalmers. Wright's Essex. Nicholas's Synopsis of the Peerage.)

BERNHARD, count of Anhalt and duke of Saxony, youngest, or one of the younger sons of Albert the Bear, born about 1140. At the death of his father, in 1170, he received Anhalt and the county of Plotzkau, which the emperor in vain contested with him. In 1175 he was involved in war with Henry the Lion, his father's adversary, and this was carried on very destructively, till the emperor, who remembered Henry's desertion of him in his Italian expedition of 1174, put him under the ban, and divided his dominions amongst the other princes. Bernhard received Saxony and part of Eastphalia and Engern, and called himself henceforward duke of Saxony, augmenting his family arms with the ducal crown of Saxony. Henry had recourse to arms again in 1180, defeated Bernhard, and wasted his territory; but on the approach of the emperor, he retired upon Erfurt, in 1182. In 1189, Henry the Lion again took the field against the emperor, and also against Bernhard, and the contending parties were not reconciled till five years afterwards, during which the fortune of war was often against Bernhard. The latter successfully opposed the design of the emperor Henry to make the imperial dignity hereditary, and persuaded him to forego it. At his death, in 1197, the imperial crown was offered to Bernhard, but he refused it, and persuaded the electors to choose Philip of Suabia, first as guardian of the kingdom, and afterwards as king of Rome. He died in 1212, leaving behind him two sons, of whom the elder, Henry, received the family government of Anhalt, and Albert the duchy of Saxony. (Ersch und Gruber.)

BERNHARD, duke of Saxe-Weimar, and one of the greatest generals in the thirty years' war, born at Weimar in 1604, being the youngest of eleven sons of duke John of Weimar, who died in 1605. At the breaking out of the thirty years' war, he took part with the elector Frederic, king of Bohemia, against the emperor, and in 1621 took a command of cavalry under his brother William, to join count Ernest of Mansfeld, who was defending the upper palatinate against Maximilian of Bavaria and general Tilly. On the retreat of count Ernest, the brothers sided with the margrave of Baden, George Frederic, against the emperor, and Bernhard took part in a bloody action near Wimppen, in 1622, in which Tilly was totally routed. In the autumn of 1623, Bernhard entered the Dutch service; in 1625, that of Christian, king of Denmark, and assisted in the war in Westphalia. The fortune of war was unfavourable to the Danes; one after another of the brothers of Bernhard died, or submitted to the emperor; and he himself, in 1628, followed the example of the latter, after which he travelled through Holland, France, and England, examining the fortifications of every place on his travels worthy of note. He was one of the first German princes who joined the party of Gustavus Adolphus on his landing in Germany. This appears to have been in the middle of 1631, and it was the beginning of the most brilliant period of his life. He accompanied this monarch in most of his expeditions, and after Horn and Baner, enjoyed more of his friendship than any other general. From the time just mentioned till the death of Gustavus, he distinguished himself in the storm of Marienberg and Mannheim, took several strong places on the Rhine in 1632, entered Bavaria with the victorious army of Gustavus, commanded a separate division of the army with the greatest honour and good fortune, and joined his royal master for the attack on the camp of Wallenstein at Nuremberg in August 1632, a bold but fruitless attempt. He remained behind with an army to cover Franconia while the king returned to Bavaria, and joined him again in his march to Saxony against Wallenstein. At the battle of Lutzen, in which Gustavus was killed, he commanded the left wing, took the command after the king's death, and by his unexampled efforts, contributed mainly to the victory. His severe exertions, however, injured his health, and he retired to Weimar during a part of the winter. On the reopening of the campaign, the chancellor Oxenstierna, on whom the conduct of the war had devolved, placed under his direction the smaller division of the army in Upper Germany, where his talents for command were put to the proof by a mutinous spirit among the officers of the Swedish army, discontented at the non-fulfilment of the promises made to them by their monarch. This was quieted for a time by the influence of Bernhard; but ultimately Oxenstierna found himself obliged to divide among the claimants the greater part of the conquests which had been made in Germany. Bernhard himself claimed the command of the army and the dukedom of Franconia. The latter claim was allowed, and in 1633 he was solemnly installed in this dignity, with the possession of Bamberg and Würsburg. Leaving his brother Ernest as his lieutenant in the government, he returned to his military command, and in 1633 took Regensburg, penetrated into Bavaria, and attempted an entrance into Austria, when he was checked by Wallenstein, and eventually obliged by the season, for it was now the depth of winter, to suspend his operations. Wallenstein, who had long paid but a suspicious obedience to the emperor, now made treasonable proposals to Bernhard, who was preparing to take advantage of them, when the negotiation was brought to an end by the death of Wallenstein in the February of 1634. On hearing of this, the duke hastened to the frontiers of Bohemia, but was compelled to return with little advantage and much personal risk. In May of 1634 the king of Hungary, afterwards the emperor Ferdinand III. who had taken the command on the death of Wallenstein, besieged Regensburg, and took it in July, after an ineffectual attempt of Bernhard and Horn to relieve it, and a brave defence by the Swedish general Kagge. This success of the imperialists was followed by others; and at length, at the battle of Nordlingen, fought to relieve that town in 1634, the Swedish army was totally routed, some of the most distinguished generals taken prisoners, and Bernhard himself saved only by the fortunate substitution of a dragoon's horse for his own. The extinction of his duchy of Franconia, and the dissolution of the league of Heilbronn, followed this defeat; and after a fruitless call upon the German protestant princes on the part of Oxenstierna, Bernhard had recourse to France. During the year 1635, the imperial army pursued its successes, and recovered nearly all the territory conquered by the Swedes, the greater number of the German princes accepted the terms of the peace of Prague between Saxony and the empire, and Bernhard, unwilling to accede to this, and separated from the Swedish army, took the resolution of making a treaty on his own account with France. By the terms of this treaty he was to receive a yearly payment of four million livres, on condition of keeping on foot a German army of 12,000 foot and 6,000 cavalry, and of making no peace with the emperor or his allies without the consent of the French king. The latter, on the other hand, promised in any future peace to regard Bernhard's interests as his own, and those of the German prisoners as those of his own people. By a secret article of the treaty also, the king of France guaranteed to Bernhard a considerable additional pension, the possession of the county of Elsasz, and all the rights he had enjoyed from the Swedish administration. A delay in the payment of the subsidies took the general in person to Paris, where, conceiving himself slighted by the preference given to the duke of Parma, who was allowed to be covered in the royal presence, he put on his hat at the same time as the king: the court was in confusion; the king hastily took off his own hat, and dissolved the assembly. He obtained, however, the supplies which were the object of his journey. In 1637, after a second visit to Paris, in which he obtained fresh supplies of money, and was appointed commander-in-chief of the French auxiliaries, as well as of the German troops, he pursued his conquests in Elsasz, after an ineffectual attempt to penetrate into Suabia and Bavaria; in the latter part of 1638 he took Breisach, after an obstinate defence, in which several prisoners of his own army had died of famine in the prisons of the town, and the defenders had been driven by hunger to eat corpses, and even, it was said, stolen children. He received the capitulation of this place in his own name, garrisoned it with German troops, and it has been supposed that he intended to make it a centre for future conquest, and to create an independent power in Germany, as the head of which he might hold the balance between the emperor and his opponents. Richelieu, attempting in vain to procure the surrender of Breisach, as a capture made with French soldiers and money, stopped the supplies from the court of Paris. It is said that Bernhard contemplated a marriage with the landgravine of Hesse, widow of the landgrave William the Steadfast, when his projects were interrupted by death, in July 1639. In his will he provided that his conquests should belong to Germany, under the government of such of his brothers as chose to undertake it; in the event of their declining this, the choice was left to the king of France, but they were to revert to the empire in the event of a general peace. There were some suspicions that his death was caused by poison. Marshal Turenne fought under him in the early part of his career. (Rese in Ersch und Gruber.)

BERNHARD I., founder of the Meiningen line of the principality of Gotha, born in 1649. By the will of his father, he and his six brothers were to rule in common in the name of the eldest brother, and to share one residence until the falling in of fiefs and other circumstances should increase the paternal inheritance sufficiently to allow its division into seven parts, each sufficient to place its possessor in a respectable position among the princes of Germany. In 1681, accordingly, Bernhard received Meiningen with its appurtenances. He died in 1706, much respected for his piety, and a genuine protestant spirit, but noted for dreams of becoming rich by means of alchymy, and other marks of a credulous disposition. (Ersch und Gruber.)

BERNHARD, (John Adam,) a German historian, born at Hanover in 1688, who, after following theology, rather from necessity than inclination, became superintendent of the Hanoverian Archives in 1736. He died in 1771, leaving some treatises on the antiquities of Hanover, Wetterau, and the adjacent country; a new edition of the Exegesis Historiæ Germaniæ of Franciscus Irenicus, fol. Hannov. 1728; and a continuation of Winkelmann's Hessian Chronicle. (Baur in Ersch und Gruber.)

BERNHARD, a German organist, who, so early as the year 1470, invented pedals for the organ at Venice. (Dict. of Mus.)

BERNHARDI, (Augustus Frederic,) born at Berlin, 1768. He studied at Halle under the celebrated philologer Wolf, and at an early age his attention was given to the study of language, its philosophy and history. The first public evidences of this taste were his Latin and Greek grammars, which bear unquestionable marks of a systematic and philosophic spirit. He was shortly afterwards diverted from such studies by a connexion with Tieck, the Schlegels, and other members of the romantic school, then rising into note. Bernhardi was for a time violently smitten by this class of literature, and contributions to it from him were admitted into various periodicals of the day. He showed, besides, considerable critical ability in a dissertation on the Philoctetes of Sophocles, published in Berlin, in 1811; and although he did not attempt much of original production, he did enough to establish a character for lively writing and successful satire of the lighter order. Bernhardi married Sophia Tieck, sister of the poet, but separated from her in the course of a few years; and he seems then to have taken a decided aversion to the romantic school. At all events he went back to cultivate with renewed vigour his youthful studies. He cannot, indeed, in the interim have quite deserted them, for so early as 1801 appeared the first volume of his System of Language, which was followed by a second in 1803. In 1805, was published his Elements of the Science of Language; an excellent work, treating that scientifically which had previously been handled empirically by almost all writers on the subject. It displays great philosophic acuteness, with other rare qualities and acquirements; but, of course, is not free from defects, nor are all the improvements which it presents the results of the author's own inquiries. His works on language might be said to form a philosophy of vocal expression in its entire extent; they commence with its simplest elements, and treat it finally, as style, in its most refined and cultivated state. In the consideration of its various bearings, he did not neglect its relation to music. (See his review of Herrmann's Handbuch der Metrik, in the Jena A. L. 3, in the year 1804.) Although the more profound grammatical labours of subsequent philologers have deprived some of the writings of Bernhardi of much of their value, the merit is still his of having been one of the first to open a new and better path in the study of language. He died at Berlin, June 2, 1820.

BERNHOLD, (John Michael,) a German physician, born in 1736, and died, January 12, 1797. He published:—Dionysii Catonis Distichorum de Moribus ad Filium, libri iv. Augsburg, 1784, 4to. Sintonii Largi Compositiones Medicamentorum, Argent. 1786, 8vo. Cœlii Apicii de Opsoniis et Condimentis, sive Arte coquinariâ, libri x. (Norimb.) 1789, 8vo. Theodori Prisciani, Archiatri, quæ exstant tomus i. (Norimb.) 1791, 8vo.

BERNI, (Francis,) called also Bernia, and Berna, an Italian poet of high celebrity. He was born towards the close of the fifteenth century, at Lamporecchio, in Tuscany, of a Florentine family, noble, but poor. At nineteen he went to Rome, in hopes of patronage from cardinal Bibbiena, his relation, but, according to his own account, got neither good nor harm from him. To obtain a subsistence, he became secretary to Giberti, bishop of Verona, datary to pope Leo X., and, with a view to make the most of this introduction, he entered into orders. Nothing could, however, be more unsuitable to such a disposition as Berni's than the dull routine of official correspondence, and the restraints of clerical life. He joined, accordingly, a party of kindred spirits, young ecclesiastics too, like himself, who called themselves *Vigna-juoli*, (vine-dressers,) both from their fondness for wine, and from their indulgence in such merry humours, as are conspicuous in the vintage. These gay young men were not, however, mere unintellectual sensualists. At their jovial meetings, verses were produced which extracted mirth from every thing, whether serious or jocose. Of these effusions Berni's were incomparably the best; having all that caustic drollery embodied under a natural appearance of the nakedest simplicity, which gradually rendered him so famous, and caused such poetry to be called *la Poesia Bernesca*, or *Berniesca*.

When the constable Bourbon sacked Rome, in 1527, Berni lost his little all, and he soon afterwards went with his patron, Giberti, to Verona, Venice, and Padua. But he grew tired of wandering about in the grave and humble capacity of attendant upon a bishop. Hence he determined upon retiring to Florence, and living as well as he could upon a canonry which he had in the cathedral there. He soon raised himself by his uncommon talents and inexhaustible pleasantry, to an intimacy with the ducal family. To this has been attributed his death, which is ordinarily fixed on the 26th of July, 1536. Alexander de' Medici, the duke, was upon ill terms with his relative, the cardinal Hippolytus de' Medici, and each of the two is said to have been intent upon poisoning the other; one of them being anxious to make Berni an accomplice. He refused, and his own life by poison paid the forfeit. If this account be true, Berni must have received the infamous proposal from Alexander, the duke, as Hippolytus, the cardinal, died in 1535, as it was thought, by poison. Berni did not die until the following year, and a man capable of committing a murder, must, undoubtedly, have been also capable of committing another to conceal it.

Berni has been chiefly noticed out of Italy for a reform and re-modelling of Boiardo's great poem, the Orlando Inamorato. His labours upon it greatly added to its merit and popularity. He did not, however, only make a new arrangement of the whole, nor did he merely insert such ludicrous appendages as a genius like his would be tempted irresistibly to supply. Some of his additions are fully worthy of the epic muse; and the whole poem, under his masterly management, has acquired additional value of every kind. This work was printed at Venice, in 1541, 4to; Milan, 1542, 8vo; Venice, with additions, 1545, 4to. This last edition is the most esteemed and rare. There are also two good modern editions, that of Naples, but dated Florence, 1725; and that of Molini, Paris, 1768. Berni also left Rime Burlesche, often reprinted, some dramatic pieces in Italian, and some Latin poems. As an author, no one ever knew better than Berni, that *ars est celare artem*, and how to do so. He is, apparently, the most unstudied and natural of writers; but he was really indefatigable in recasting and reconsidering the products of his brain; thus giving another rebuke to the vain hope that ability without severe toil, can achieve great things. (Biog. Univ.)

BERNIER, (Francis,) a physician, born at Jouard, in Anjou, who, in 1654, left his native country for the East. In Syria and in Egypt he remained a considerable time. At Cairo he passed a whole year, and was attacked with the plague. He then embarked at Suez for India, where he dwelt for twelve years, eight of them spent as physician to the emperor Aurengzebe. He returned to his native country in 1670, and in 1685 visited England. He died at Paris, Sept. 22, 1688. He published an account of his travels, the events of which are narrated in an easy, simple style, and with great precision. They treat largely of the epidemic diseases that he had witnessed in India, and they give a very faithful picture of the countries that he visited; of which, in many places, no traveller had hitherto published any account. He was a warm advocate of the philosophy of Gassendi; and was, in consequence, involved in a controversy with J. B. Morin, whom he has ridiculed in two tracts—Anatomia ridiculi Muris, Paris, 1651, 4to; and Favilla ridiculi Muris, Paris, 1654, 4to; he having the bad taste to make allusion to the name of his antagonist as derivable from *mus, muris.* He wrote several pieces in the Journal des Savans, in the Histoire des Ouvrages des Savans, the Menagiana, and the Collection of Curious Pieces, by Bayle. His works on the East have gained him a lasting reputation; they are,—Histoire de la dernière Révolution des Etats du Grand Mogol, Paris, 1670, 2 vols, 12mo; Suite des Mémoires sur l'Empire du Grand Mogol, Paris, 1671, 2 vols, 12mo. These were combined and published as Voyages de François Bernier, contenant la Déscription des Etats du Grand Mogol, de l'Indostan, du Royaume de Cashemire, Amsterdam, 1699, 2 vols, 12mo; and again in 1710 and 1724. They were translated into English, London, 1671, 1675, in 8vo and 12mo. Bernier published besides, Abrégé de la Philosophie de Gassendi, Lyons, 1678, 8 vols, 12mo; Paris, 1684, 7 vols, 12mo. Doutes de M. Bernier sur quelques-uns des Principaux Chapitres de son Abrégé de la Philosophie de M. Gassendi, Paris, 1682, 12mo; Traité du Libre et du Volontaire, Amst. 1685, 12mo.

BERNIER, (John,) a physician, born at Blois, who was in practice at Paris in 1674. He was a sarcastic writer, and at one time warmly engaged in the celebrated controversy upon the use and abuse of Emetics. He died May 18, 1698, leaving, Histoire de Blois, Paris, 1682, 4to. Essais de Médecine, où il est traité l'Histoire de la Médecine et des Médecins; du Devoir des Médecins à l'Egard des Malades, et de celui des Malades à l'Egard des Médecins; de l'Utilité des Remèdes, et de l'Abus qu'on en peut faire, Paris, 1689, 4to; Supplement, Paris, 1691, 4to. Histoire Chronologique de la Médecine et des Médecins, Paris, 1695, 1714, 4to. Anti-Menagiana, Paris, 1693, 12mo. Jugemens et Nouvelles Observations sur les Œuvres Grècques, Latines, Toscanes, et Françaises de Maître François Rabelais, Docteur en Médecine; ou la véritable Rabelais Réformé, avec la Carte du Chinonois, les Médailles de Rabelais, celles de l'Auteur, et celles du Médecin de Chandray, Paris, 1697, 12mo.

BERNIGEROTH, (Martin, 1670—1733,) a German engraver, who resided at Leipsic, and engraved a great number of portraits in a creditable manner. He died in that city. (Heinecken, Dict. des Artistes. Bryan's Dict.)

BERNIGEROTH, (John Martin, 1713—1767,) son and pupil of the preceding, who also engraved portraits in a clear neat style, bearing some resemblance to that of Houbracken, though much inferior. (Heinecken, Dict. des Artistes. Strutt's and Bryan's Dictionaries.)

BERNINI, (John Lawrence, 1589—1680,) a distinguished Italian artist, son of a Florentine, who had married and settled at Naples, where John was born. He was educated by his father, a painter and sculptor of some repute; and having, when a mere child, evidenced surprising talents, his fame reached the ears of Paul V. The father, then employed at Rome, took him to the pontiff, who asked for some proof upon the spot of his reputed genius. "Model me a head," said the pope. "What head, holy father?" replied the boy, nothing daunted. "What!" exclaimed the pontiff, "art thou so dexterous and ready? Produce me a head of St. Paul;" and in half an hour a bust of the apostle, full of dignity and expression, excited the wonder and admiration of the whole court. He was then commended to the patronage of cardinal Maffeo Barberini, a judicious Mecænas of art and literature. His kindness and protection fostered the young artist, and subsequently afforded scope to his highest flights of imagination. When he became pope, under the title of Urban VIII., he sent for Bernini, and said to him, "It is peculiarly fortunate for you to see your friend Maffeo Barberini, pope; but much happier is it for him to have a Bernini under his pontificate." He was not eighteen when he produced the Apollo and Daphne of the Villa Borghese, which is gracefully grouped, and tells the story admirably; the elegant form of the nymph, partially converted into the willow, the proportions of the god, founded upon his studies of the one in the Belvedere of the Vatican, and the expression of the figures, denote an exquisite sensibility in the artist. But the Apollo is disfigured by the drapery, which cuts the figure completely in half, and destroys the outline of the form. The Rape of Proserpine is another early work, and forms a subject quite classical, evidencing the intention of the sculptor to treat it in that style; but the forced contortions of the figures, and extreme violence of the expression, form no advantageous contrast with the Greek school of Praxiteles. Bernini's group is principally valuable for the boldness and exquisite finish of the execution.

These works necessarily excited the highest admiration for his talents; so that even as he passed through the streets he was pointed at as a prodigy. But instead of allowing himself to be corrupted by these exaggerated marks of respect, he exerted himself the more, by unwearied study, to maintain and deserve the eminence that had rewarded former efforts. The powers which he displayed in execution, the vigour and variety of his imagination, the boldness of expression in some of his figures, and the deep feeling and tenderness in others, prove that if Bernini had lived in a less corrupt epoch, although he could hardly have acquired a greater renown among contemporaries, yet he would have ensured a more enduring reputation by the production of works that might have vied with the happiest and noblest periods of Greek, Roman, or Italian art. But the most remarkable circumstance in this extraordinary man, was the prodigious versatility of his talents; for he evidenced in architecture the same brilliancy of conception, the same daring felicity, and the same aberrations from correct taste, that prevailed in his sculptures. He lived during nine pontificates, and he had a share so important in all that was done in art in that long period, that what he did not execute himself he directed; or where he could not direct he influenced.

The grandest efforts of his genius in architecture were reserved for the Vatican; in which his creations were so surprising, that Lewis XIV. sent him urgent proposals to visit Paris, in order to give a design for the completion of the Louvre, which that magnificent monarch was anxious to complete in a style commensurate with his own enlarged ideas of architectural grandeur. The journey of Bernini was a triumphal pageant. Each city, as he passed, prepared him new honours, with extravagant displays of admiration and respect. The king sent a splendid equipage to convey the illustrious foreigner to Paris, who was met at some distance from the city by the papal nuncio, and escorted into the French metropolis as one who honoured France by his presence. The only fruits of all this pomp, and eight months' stay in Paris, were an indifferent design, that was luckily not adopted, a flattering portrait of the king, and the most profuse liberality towards the great artist and his companions. He had, indeed, some need of solace for his wounded spirit; since, from the moment that he entered Paris, he had been assailed by the petty malice of Perrault and the whole body of artists, who were envious of the patronage and distinction showered down upon him. Bernini was superior, but was not insensible to these attacks; for he was of a really generous disposition; of which no greater proof can be given than the eulogium which Voltaire represents him as having bestowed upon Perrault's façade of the Louvre; an anachronism, it is true, of the poet, as it was not then executed, but which derives value from the view entertained of the Italian's noble character:—

"A la voix de Colbert Bernini vint de Rome,
De Perrault dans le Louvre il admira la main.
Ah! dit-il, si Paris renferme dans son sein
Des travaux si parfaits d'un si rare génie,
Fallait-il m'appeller du fond de l'Italie?
Voilà le vrai merite. Il parle avec candeur,
L'envie est à ses pieds, la paix dans son cœur."

Our king Charles the First, who possessed a genuine taste for the fine arts, was desirous of having his bust carved by the chisel of Bernini. As the Italian was unwilling to visit England, the king caused his portrait to be painted by Vandyke, in three different positions. From these scanty materials Bernini produced a very fine bust, for which Charles sent him a ring, worth 6000 crowns, saying to his messenger, "Go and crown that hand which has wrought a work so splendid." In fact, such pecuniary benefits, together with lucrative commissions and appointments, were repeatedly showered down upon him; so that it is not extraordinary, that in a long life he amassed property to the amount of 100,000*l*. Queen Christina, of Sweden, is indeed reported to have thought this little for such a man, saying, "that if he had been in her service, she should have been ashamed at his leaving so moderate a property." His rival, Perrault, represents him as low in stature, but with a handsome countenance, and frank intelligent aspect; as being of a lively and brilliant spirit, and succeeding admirably in making the most of himself; a good speaker, ready wit, and full of *bons mots*, short stories, and apt illustrations in his discourse; by which he rendered his conversation so particularly amusing and instructive, that Innocent X. said, "he was born to live with princes." He was extremely charitable, of a liberal disposition, and averse from calumny and envy. While engaged in modelling, or carving, he never ceased working in order to speak to his visitors; and cardinals, lords, or persons of any rank whatever, sat silent observing his operations. He was the first to depart from the usual practice of giving a smiling affected air to portraits; and, on the contrary, threw into his busts great fire and expression, representing the individual character of the object. In order to give him an insight into the peculiar feelings of the individual, he required him to walk about while he was forming the model, and to converse in his usual natural manner. None of his portraits are free from a certain degree of affectation, but there are more of them wanting in dignity and character. He died Nov. 28, 1680. (Baldinucci, Vita del Bernini. Milizia, Memorie degli Architetti. Cicognara Storia della Scultura, vol. iii. Quatremère de Quincy, Dictionnaire d'Architecture.)

BERNIS, (Francis Joachim Peter de,) cardinal, a French statesman, born at St. Marcel de l'Ardêche, in May, 1715, of a noble but poor family; his parents in consequence brought him up to the church, and his birth soon procured him a canonry in the noble chapter of Brionde. Still he was in very narrow circumstances; but unexceptionable birth, good address, and talents to flatter or amuse, made him sanguine of pushing his way to opulence, if only well introduced at Paris. But although he had Richelieu's acquaintance, his morals stood in the way of his promotion, until some verses found him a friend in the royal mistress, Pompadour. She introduced him to Lewis XV., and found him an apartment, furnished by herself, in the Tuileries, adding to it a pension of 1500 livres (about 60*l.*) Bernis soon discovered abilities fit for something better than gay sycophancy to royal profligates and gilded courtezans. He went to Venice, as mediator between that republic and pope Benedict XIV. Both parties were satisfied by his intervention. On his return to Paris, he was admitted into the council of state. Soon after he was appointed secretary for foreign affairs, and in 1758 the cardinal's hat was conferred upon him by pope Clement XIII.; but the seven years' war, so disastrous to France, covered him with obloquy, and he resigned his office. He was then banished to Soissons, where he remained for six years. Being recalled in 1764, he was appointed to the archbishopric of Alby, and five years after he went to Rome, to assist at the conclave in which Clement XIV. was elected pope. The talent which he showed on that occasion procured him again the appointment of ambassador of France. In this capacity he took a share, against his own inclination, in the suppression of the Jesuits; and after the death of Clement, in 1774, the office of protector of the Gallican church was added to that of ambassador. He had now an income of about 16,000*l.* a-year, and lived in princely magnificence, his house being the general *rendezvous* of distinguished foreigners. He had, at length, the melancholy satisfaction of receiving in it the aunts of Lewis XVI., when driven by the revolution, in 1791, from their native land. But the storm soon overtook himself. The noble revenues that he had drawn from France were confiscated, and he was left in distress. The court of Spain, however, came to his relief with a generous pension, which he received until his death, on the 2d Nov. 1794. The works of Bernis have been printed several times. Didot published a complete edition of them in 8vo, in 1797. His poetry, although the making of his fortune, is in the main little to his credit; and he thought so when advanced in life, and living as a dignified ecclesiastic. After his death, however, was published a poem more suited to his profession, entitled, La Religion Vengée. But none of his poetry is of much account, although his letters maintain their reputation. (Biog. Univ.)

BERNOLDUS, BERNALDUS, BERNARDUS, BERTHOLDUS, a German monk, who died at Schaffhausen, in 1100. He left behind him a chronicle from the birth of Christ to the year 1100, some of the later events of which he describes as an eye-witness. The best edition is that of Usserman, in the first and second volumes of the Monumenta Res Alemannicas illustrantia. His other works are in the second volume of the same collection.

BERNON, (Abbot of Richenow,) was a native of France, and lived in the eleventh century. He had the reputation of being one of the most learned men of his age, and was equally distinguished as a poet, orator, musician, philosopher, and divine. Sigebert reckons him amongst those illustrious abbots under whom flourished the monasteries of France and Lorraine. He is the author of a treatise on the office of the Mass, published at Cologne, in 1568, by Melchior Hillorpius, and a life of S. Udalric, or Ulric, bishop of Augsburg, who died in 973, printed at Augsburg in 1595, and of several other minor productions. (Hist. Lit. de la France.)

BERNOULLI, (James,) the eldest of three brothers, of a family originally from Antwerp, known in the history of mathematics by the scientific productions of eight of its members, born at Basle, on the 27th December, 1654. His father destined him for the church, but nature made him a mathematician. In vain did his father oppose this inclination; his progress in geometry was so extensive and so rapid, that he soon turned his attention to astronomy, taking for his device Phaëton driving the chariot of the Sun, with the motto, "*Invito patre sidera verso*," in allusion to his father's opposition to his studies. At twenty-two he travelled to Geneva, and from thence to France, Holland, and England, and returning home in 1680, he began to study the philosophy of Descartes.

The comet which appeared in that year furnished him the subject of his Essay on a new System of Comets. His next production, in 1683, was his Dissertation on the Weight of the Air. In the following year, Leibnitz having published, in the Acts of Leipsic, his first essays on the differential calculus, which he had invented since the year 1674, without stating the art and method of it, Bernoulli, with his brother John, discovered the beauty and extent of it, and published two essays in 1691, which made Leibnitz say that this discovery was as much theirs as his own. In the mean time, in 1687, he was elected professor of mathematics at the university of Basle, whither his reputation drew a great number of foreigners. In 1699 he was admitted foreign member of the Academy of Sciences at Paris, and in 1701, with his brother John, was chosen member of the Academy of Berlin. He died at Basle, of a slow fever, August 16, 1705. He married at the age of thirty, and left one son and one daughter. His works are many, but by far the greater part consists of pieces, dissertations, and treatises, on all branches of mathematics, on the promotion of the new analysis, infinite series, the quadrature of the parabola, the geometry of curve lines, of spirals, cycloids, epicycloids, &c. &c. Of these, forty-seven were published at various times in the Acta Eruditorum of Leipsic, seven or eight in the Journal des Savants, and nearly as many in the Histoire de l'Académie. Besides these, he wrote a letter to his brother, Cum annexa Solutione Problematis Isoperimetrici, which caused a violent misunderstanding between them, and the Ars Conjectandi, which was published after his death, with a Tractatus de Seriebus infinitis, et Epistola Gallica de Ludo Pilæ Reticularis, in which he has inserted Mr. Huygen's treatise, De Ratiociniis in Ludo Aleæ, on the different fortune of those who play at dice.

BERNOULLI, (John,) second brother of the preceding, like him professor of mathematics at Basle, member of the French, English, Berlin, and Petersburg academies, was born in August, 1667, at Basle. After having finished his education, he was sent to Neufchatel, to learn the French language and commerce; but, like his brother, he would only apply to the mathematics. He worked with his brother to discover the method used by Leibnitz in his essays on the differential calculus, gave the first principles of the integral calculus, and with Huygens and Leibnitz was the first to give the solution of the problem proposed by his brother of the catenary, that is, the curve formed by a chain, supposing it perfectly flexible every where, and suspended by both its extremities. In 1690, being in France, he made the acquaintance of several eminent mathematicians, among them the marquis de l'Hôpital, who took him to his country-seat, where they solved together several of the most difficult problems of geometry. In 1693 he was elected professor of mathematics at Wolfenbuttel; but in March of the following year, having married Dorothea Falckner, a lady of Basle, he returned thither, received the degree of doctor of medicine, and employed some of his time in tuition. In 1695 he was elected professor at Groningen, where he continued till the year 1705, when he succeeded his brother James in the mathematical professorship at Basle. He died in that city, on the 1st of January, 1748, leaving three sons, Nicholas II., Daniel, and John II., who all distinguished themselves.

In private life, John Bernoulli was not sufficiently careful of his temper. The quarrel which he had with his own brother James really appears to have arisen from envy of talents superior to his own. There was, indeed, an instance in which John Bernoulli showed himself above any such unhappy feeling, namely, in giving private lessons to Euler, while his pupil at Basle, in addition to those delivered to the public. His works contain an immense mass of discovery. They all consist of memoirs, published in the transactions of the day, and were collected and printed at Lausanne and Geneva in 1742, in 4 vols, 4to.

BERNOULLI, (Nicholas,) eldest son of the preceding, born January 27, 1695, at Groningen. He came to Basle with his father, where he first studied law, and took his degree, but afterwards attended the mathematical lectures of his father, together with Euler, with whom he formed an intimate friendship. After travelling through France and Italy, where he became a member of the Institute of Bologna, he was appointed professor of law at Berne; but in 1705 he was invited, with his brother Daniel, to Petersburg, by the empress Catherine, and died there in the July following. We must not confuse the above with his cousin of the same name, who edited the Ars Conjectandi of his uncle James, and solved many of the problems which were proposed by his other uncle, John Bernoulli, and was at first professor of mathematics at Padua, then of logic, and at last of law at Basle, and also a member of the Academy of Berlin, of the Royal Society of London, and of the Institute of Bologna, and died 29 November, 1759, leaving many memoirs, which have been published in the Acta Eruditorum of Leipsic, and in the Giornale dei Letterati d'Italia.

BERNOULLI, (Daniel,) brother to the preceding, and second son of John Bernoulli, born at Groningen, February the 9th, 1700. His father at first intended him for trade, but allowed him afterwards to study medicine, at the same time that he instructed him in mathematics. He passed some time in Italy, studying medicine and mathematics, under the celebrated Morgagni and Michelotti; and though scarcely twenty-four years old, he refused the presidency of the Academy of Science at Genoa. In the following year he went, not with his father, as it is asserted in the Biog. Univ., but with his brother Nicholas, as professor of mathematics to Petersburg, where he remained for six years after the death of the latter. He returned to Basle in 1733, where he obtained at first a chair of medicine, and afterwards of natural philosophy, to which was added one of metaphysics, or speculative philosophy. In the mean time his numerous publications had raised his reputation so high as to have procured him admission into the Academies of Petersburg and Berlin, the Royal Society of London, and the French Academy of Sciences, where he succeeded his father in 1748. He was found dead in his bed on the 17th of March, 1782.

The works of Daniel Bernoulli are many; amongst them, those which have been printed separately, are:—1. Dissertatio Inaugur. Phys. Med. de Respiratione, Bas. 1721, 4to; in which he calculates the quantity of air which enters the lungs at each breathing; republished by Haller in his fourth vol. of the Select. Dissert. Anatom. 2. Positiones Anatomico-botanicæ, *ibid.* 1721, 4to. 3. Exercitationes Mathematicæ, Venetiis, 1724: in which he styled himself "Son of John Bernoulli," which he continued ever after. 4. Hydrodynamica, &c. 1738, 4to. It is the first work in which the motions of fluids are reduced to a question of mathematics. In one point, it is like the subsequent work of the Mécanique Analytique, by La Grange, in which the question is reduced to the result of one principle, called the conservation of the *vis viva*, by Bernoulli. Besides these there is, in the different Transactions of the several academies of which he was a member, a great number of memoirs upon all sorts of mathematical as well as physical subjects, such as on the effects of inoculation—on the means of ascertaining the hour at sea—on the means of supplying the action of the wind to set large vessels in motion—on the ebbing and flowing of the sea, on which he divided the prize with Euler, Maclaurin, and the writer of a fourth piece, who explained it according to the principles of Des Cartes, and was the last time in which the French academy did so.

BERNOULLI, (John,) youngest son of John I., and brother of the two preceding, born at Basle on the 18th of May, 1710, where he died on the 17th of July, 1790. He studied law and mathematics; travelled in France; in 1743 he was elected professor of eloquence, and five years after of mathematics at Basle. He succeeded his brother Daniel in the French Academy, from which his memoirs obtained twice the prize on the propagation of light, and on the loadstone, in which last his brother Daniel had a share; so that, in point of fact, from the year 1699 to 1790, for the space of ninety years, there was always a Bernoulli in the list of the foreign members of the French Academy of Sciences. He was also a member of the academy of Berlin. He left two sons, John III. and James II.

John III., his eldest son, born at Basle, May 18, 1744, and died at Berlin, July 13, 1807. He studied at Basle and Neufchatel law and mathematics. At nineteen years of age he became a member of the Academy, and Astronomer Royal at Berlin; the memoirs and ephemerides of which contain a great number of his numerous observations. He travelled through Germany, England, France, Italy, Switzerland, Russia, and Poland; was a member of the Academy of Petersburg, Stockholm, and the Royal Society of London. His works are many. Amongst them he gave an edition of the Algebra of Euler. His Lettres sur différents Sujets, &c., in 1774-5-7, and 9, contain much information on the state of observatories at Greenwich, Oxford, Cambridge, London, Paris, Gottingen, Cassel, and other places in Germany. His Historical and Geographical Description of India, is a valuable production, which contains the works of Thiessenthales, d'Anquetil du Perron, and of G. Reussel, with many notes and additions, Berlin, 1786, 3 vols, 4to; besides a vol. De la Réforme Politique des Juifs. A collection of voyages in German; Description d'un Voyage en Prusse, en Russie, et en Pologne; another, par l'Allemagne, la Suisse, la France Méridionale, et l'Italie. Lettres Astronomiques. Archives of History and Geography, &c. &c.

James II., second son of John Bernoulli, a younger brother of the preceding, born at Basle, October 17, 1759; was the pupil and the deputy of his uncle Daniel, during the infirmity of the latter, in the professorship of natural philosophy, without, however, succeeding him, because both academical and civic offices were filled up by lot. He was afterwards professor of mathematics at Petersburg, where he married a grand-daughter of Euler. He was also a member of the Academies of Petersburg and Basle, and correspondent of the Royal Society of Turin. The memoir which he published in the New Transactions of Petersburg, evidently proves that he intended to follow the footsteps of his uncle Daniel; but he died at the early age of thirty, of an apoplectic fit, whilst bathing in the Neva, on the 3d of July, 1789.

BERNSTORF, (John Hartwig Ernest, count of,) an eminent Danish statesman, born at Hanover, May 13, 1712. Being connected with Denmark, he passed into that country, and his talents eventually conducted him, under Frederic V., to the head of the foreign department there. In 1761, Peter III. of Russia marched an army towards Holstein, and Bernstorf made very judicious preparations for defence. Peter's death rendered their efficacy untried, and the Danish foreign minister immediately took advantage of it to exchange ducal Holstein, which the grand-duke Paul now inherited, for Oldenburg, which belonged to the king of Denmark. This exchange, effected in 1773, was highly advantageous in a territorial point of view to Denmark. Subsequently, Bernstorf was able to conclude a series of discussions upon the right of sovereignty over Hamburg belonging to the house of Holstein. The town was declared independent, on condition of abandoning its claims for loans made both to the kings of Denmark, and the dukes of Holstein. Bernstorf's reputation was next extended by an act of enlightened liberality towards the serfs attached to a large estate which he possessed near Copenhagen. He enfranchised them, and gave them long leases of their lands; a substantial service that was gratefully commemorated by an obelisk which they raised by the side of the high Copenhagen road. In other instances, Bernstorf displayed a spirit fully worthy of his fame and reputation. He was the zealous patron of manufactures, commerce, and the arts. To him principally the world was indebted for Niebuhr's Travels in Arabia, he having warmly encouraged the scheme of sending some competent observers into the East. By his means, too, Frederic V. settled a pension upon the poet Klopstock. When that monarch died, Bernstorf continued minister, during a few years, but in 1770, Struensee became head of the council, and Bernstorf received his dismissal, with a retiring pension. He lived at Hamburg until Struensee's fall; when he was greeted by a summons to Copenhagen. Before he could, however, take advantage of it, death overtook him, February 19, 1772. (Biog. Univ.)

BERNSTORF, (Andrew Peter, count of,) nephew of the preceding, and, like him, a famous Danish minister. He was born at Hanover, August 28, 1735, and became one of the king of Denmark's council in 1769, but Struensee reduced him to a private station. After that minister's disgrace, he was reinstated, and took a prominent part in the national affairs. To him was owing, in 1778, the accession of Denmark to the armed neutrality, but his influence subsequently declined, and the public lost sight of him again. When the prince royal, however, in 1784, took the chief direction of affairs, Bernstorf more than regained his ground, being henceforth the leading minister of Denmark. Under his direction that country steadily entered into the views of France as to the rights of neutral flags. Upon the soundness of this policy there may be differences of opinion, but it is otherwise with Bernstorf's exertions for the internal amelioration of Denmark. From these, the serfs obtained emancipation, criminal justice was placed on a better footing, monopolies were abolished, and financial evils were effectually redressed. This great minister died, highly respected both at home and abroad, January 21, 1797. (Biog. Univ.)

BERNULF, or BEORNWULPH, king of Mercia, the throne of which country he seized, although no member of the royal family, on the expulsion of Ceolwulf, in 823. He was wealthy, but as it is represented, far from wise. A powerful neighbouring state in such hands tempted the ambition of Egbert, king of Wessex, and a desperate battle was fought between him and Bernulf, in 824, at Ellandune, supposed by some to be Wilton, by others, to be Allington, near Amesbury. The contest, although terminating in Egbert's favour, crippled him so severely that he did not venture to follow it up by an invasion of Mercia. It improved, however, his position so materially, that he entered at once upon a series of attempts to establish the superiority of Wessex on every side. In the course of these, he determined upon assisting East Anglia to shake off the yoke of Mercia. Bernulf made an effort to retain his authority over this state, but it proved fatal to him, as he was slain by the East Anglians before the termination of 824. (Sax. Chr. Malmesb. Gest. RR. Angl. i. 132.)

BERNWARD, a Romish saint, of noble birth, who became bishop of Hildesheim in 993, having been chaplain to the emperor Otho III. He died in 1024, and was canonized about the end of the thirteenth century. (Moreri.)

BEROALD, or BEROALDE, (Matthew,) born at St. Denis, near Paris, in the beginning of the sixteenth century, and educated at the college of cardinal Lemoine, where he attained great proficiency in theology, history, and literature. Together with Scaliger, he embraced the protestant religion in 1550, for which he was arrested at Coutances, and would have been burnt alive, had it not been for an officer who favoured his escape. He then went to Orleans, where he taught Hebrew. The time of his death is unknown, though it must have been before the year 1584. He published a book of chronology in 1575, under the title of Chronicon Sacræ Scripturæ Auctoritate Constitutum, in which he maintains that no other guide is to be followed, in arranging events connected with Scripture, than the sacred volume itself; in consequence of which, he struck Cambyses and Darius Hystaspes out of the catalogue of Persian kings, their names never appearing in Scripture. It is not true that Vossius and Scaliger speak highly of this work, as it is asserted in the Biographie Universelle, for, in fact, they censure both the matter and manner; and we cannot likewise help observing, that the accusation brought by Bayle against Moreri, of having said that there appeared many other works of Beroald besides his Latin Chronology, is unfounded.

BEROALD, (Francis,) of Verville, son of the preceding, born at Paris, April 28th, 1558; a man of learning, who turned Romanist after the death of his father, and, taking orders, became a canon of St. Gatien, at Tours. He published several works, some of which were collected and published under the title of Apprehensions Spirituelles, Paris, 1583, 12mo; among them is a poem in imitation of Sir Thomas More's Utopia. He died about the year 1612.

BEROALDO, (Philip, the elder,) born at Bologna, Dec. 7th, 1453, of an ancient and noble family; and pursuing his studies, rather well than wisely, he fell into a dangerous disorder at 18; from this he had scarcely recovered, when he opened a school in his native city, and subsequently he did this at Parma and Milan. He then went to Paris, where his lectures were attended by a very large auditory, and where he would have remained longer had he not been recalled home to become professor of belles-lettres, and to be invested with civic honours. The early part of his life was devoted alternately to letters and dissipation; but after his marriage with Camilla de Vicenza, which took place when he was in his 44th year, his habits were irreproachable. He died July 17th, 1505; and at his funeral, which was uncommonly splendid, his body clothed in silk, and his head crowned with laurel, all persons of literary or civic distinction at Bologna assisted. At the age of 19 he commenced his notes on Pliny, a portion of which was published at Parma, in 1476; but the remainder, and especially those that he had collected in after-life, were written on a copy which was stolen from him, and for the loss of which he expressed a regret at his dying hour. A full account of his works, which are very numerous, and chiefly conversant with Latin authors, is given by Niceron, in Mémoires, &c. t. 25; and a few of his notes have been reprinted in the Lampas sive Fax Artium of Gruter. His Declamatio Ebriosi, Scortatoris, et Aleatoris, for which his early life furnished ample materials, was paraphrased by Calvi de la Fontaine, Par. 1556, and put into French verse by Gilbert Damalis, Lyons, 1558.

BEROALDO, (Vincent,) son of the preceding, known by his explanation of all the words employed by his half-brother, Bolognetti, in his poem, Il Constante. A portion of it was published by his friend, Maltacheti, under the title of Dichiarazioni di Tutte le Voci proprie del Constanti, Bologn. 1570.

BEROALDO, (Philip, the younger,) born at Bologna, Oct. 1st, 1472, nephew and favourite pupil of the elder. At the age of 24 he was appointed professor of belles-lettres in his native town; but he went afterwards to Rome, where he was made president of the academy. He was one of the admirers of Imperiali, a celebrated courtesan, and a rival of Sadoleti, afterwards the cardinal, as stated in one of his Latin odes, printed at Rome in 1530, and translated, amongst others, by Clement Marot. During his residence at Rome he attracted the attention of cardinal John de' Medici, by whom, when he became pope, he was appointed librarian to the Vatican; but an estrangement that subsequently took place between the two, is said to have so affected Beroaldo that he died of a broken heart, in 1518. The story, however, seems at variance with the assertion of Bembo, the secretary of Leo X., who says, in the epitaph on Beroaldo, that—

"E'en the Medici's cheeks were wet with tears."

Although scarcely less learned than his uncle, his fame as a scholar rests entirely on his edition of the Annals of Tacitus, Rom. 1515, which was dedicated to Leo X., at whose request it was undertaken, and who gave a considerable sum for the MS. from which it was copied to an individual, who brought it from the abbey of Corvey, in Westphalia.

BEROLDINGEN, (Francis von,) a distinguished mineralogist, born at St. Gall, Oct. 11th, 1740, canon of Hildesheim and Osnabruck. He made many extensive journeys for the purpose of investigating agricultural, mineralogical, and geological facts. The result was an immense accumulation of interesting and important matter, which he communicated to the public in several German works, of great value, though somewhat injured by his hypothetical and prejudiced turn of mind. He died March 8th, 1798. He published, anonymously, at Hanover, in 1778, Doubts and Questions on Mineralogy. This was reprinted, with great additions, and with his name, at Hanover and Osnabruck, in 1792, and a second volume appeared in the following year. He afterwards published upon the quicksilver mines in the Palatinate, upon ancient and modern volcanoes, a new theory of basalt, in the supplements to the Annals of Chymistry, and a Description of the Well at Driburg. (Biog. Univ.)

BEROSUS, a celebrated Babylonian historian, who has been sometimes treated as a contemporary of Moses. Tatian, however, who says that he was a priest of Belus, at Babylon, also informs us that he "lived in the time of Alexander," and "dedicated to Antiochus, who was the third after him, his history, which he wrote in three books, of the affairs of the Chaldeans, and the actions of their kings." The third Antiochus after Alexander the Great, was Antiochus Theus, who came to the Syrian throne, B.C. 261. To this period, therefore, or very soon after it, must the history of Berosus be referred. It must have been written early in the reign of Theus, because Alexander, with whom the author is said to have lived, died sixty-four years before his accession. Prideaux, accordingly, supposes that he might be then 84 years old, estimating his age at 20 when the Macedonian conqueror died. After Alexander became master of Babylon, Berosus appears to have acquired the Greek language from his followers. He subsequently opened a school for the teaching of astronomy and astrology, at Cos, in the Ægean, famed as the birth-place of Hippocrates and Apelles. From this place he removed to Athens, where, according to Pliny, his predictions, or, at all events, a popular belief in them, gained him such applause, that the city erected a statue of him, with a gilded tongue, in the *gymnasium*, or public place of their exercises. Although Pliny terms the Chaldean astrologer's prophecies *divine*, posterity can be well contented under their disappearance. Not so with respect to the historical productions of Berosus. Of these, unfortunately, fragments alone remain in the works of Josephus and Eusebius, who had the advantage of using the important work, from which they made such valuable selections. Even these quotations have rendered essential service in making out the series of Babylonian kings. The learned world has, therefore, great reason to regret the irreparable loss that it has sustained in the history of Berosus. If Europe, however, had, like China, remained in a state of intellectual stagnation, her scholars would say little of their deficiencies in Chaldean history. Annius, or Nanni, of Viterbo, a Dominican friar, published at Rome, on the revival of literature, a collection, under the names of authors whose works had been given up as lost. Among these were Manetho, *Berosus*, and Megasthenes. The last author he calls Metasthenes, an error into which he was betrayed by Rufinus's Latin version of Josephus. This led to suspicion, after some time, and the progress of sound criticism soon reduced learned men to the fragments merely of Berosus that survive in other authors. It should be added, that some have considered the historian Berosus, as a different person from the astrologer. (Prideaux. Connect. ii. 55, i. 445. Plin. vii. 37.)

BERQUEN, (Lewis,) a Fleming, of noble birth, who accidentally discovered, in 1476, the art of cutting diamonds. He was then young, and one day amused himself in rubbing two diamonds against each other. He was discerning enough, however, to remark that incisions were made, a discovery that kept his active mind upon the stretch, until by the invention of a wheel, and by means of powder from two rough diamonds, he succeeded in giving to them a perfect polish. Subsequent improvements were needed for bringing the art to its present state, but its inventor was the Flemish noble. (Biog. Univ.)

BERQUIN, (Arnold,) a French writer, well known for the skilful composition of children's books, born at Bordeaux, about 1749. He first appeared before the world, in 1774, as author of some Idylls, which were much admired for gracefulness and sensibility. In 1775, he published his Tableaux Anglais, which are translations from various English pieces. He produced, besides, some romances and a poem; but his fame rests upon the Ami des Enfans, translations of Mrs. Trimmer's Familiar Introduction to the Knowledge of Nature, of Day's Sandford and Merton, with other works of the same kind. He was at one time editor of the Moniteur, and he died at Paris, Dec. 21, 1791. (Biog. Univ.)

BERQUIN, (Lewis de,) an early French martyr, connected with protestantism. He took his name from a village in Artois, of which he was lord, and had made a proficiency in learning far above the usual standard of persons born to independence. He was also remarkable for strict morality, although, in addition to hereditary fortune, he obtained an introduction to the court of Francis I. and was appointed one of his counsellors. Nor had he imbibed any admiration of Luther's proceedings; on the contrary, he expressed an abhorrence of Lutheranism, and was a regular attendant upon the religious duties of the established church. But his dislike of the great Saxon reformer did not extend to all his publications, and still less to those of Erasmus, which really prepared the way for them. Nor did it lead him into the politic course of supporting generally the clerical opposition to Luther's defection from Rome. So far was Berquin from upholding the established system in this way, that he disliked school-divines, charged monks and friars with brutality and ignorance, and took a violent antipathy to some of the more unconciliating and morose among the clergy. He was also warm in condemning preachers for invoking the Virgin, instead of the Holy Ghost; and as he never concealed anything which he thought it his duty to utter, his freedoms in talking of ecclesiastics whom he disapproved gave them deadly offence. To their personal anger, accordingly, his troubles have been ascribed. He was prosecuted as a heretic in 1523, on the strength of certain works by Luther and Melancthon, among them that De Abroganda Missa, found in his study, seven or eight pieces by himself, tending towards the Reformation, and some French translations of Latin treatises advocating its principles. Nothing, however, to which he stood committed would

Berquin retract; and it seems that he would then have been burnt, had it not been for the interference of powerful friends. Erasmus had hopes of persuading him to keep clear of such dangers, but he resolutely persisted in obeying the dictates of his own conscience, wholly regardless of any dangers upon which he might thus be rushing. He was in consequence arrested a second time, and would have been sacrificed, apparently, had not Margaret, queen of Navarre, made such urgent representations to her brother Francis, then a prisoner at Madrid, as preserved him again. But the parliament was violently prejudiced against him, and detained him in prison until Francis returned from Spain, and insisted upon his release. When the king was afterwards wholly absorbed by Italian politics, Berquin's enemies were able to wreak that vengeance upon him for which his own perfect contempt for danger, when he thought it involved any compromise of principle, always laid him open. He was accordingly thrown in prison for the third time, and condemned to a public acknowledgment of his errors, the burning of his books by the common executioner, the boring of his tongue, and imprisonment for life. He seems to have been surprised by such a sentence, and appealed both to the king and the pope. The twelve commissioners who tried him were enraged by this appeal, apprehending, probably, that Francis would again befriend their intended victim. They told him, accordingly, with all the bitter parade of inquisitorial mercy, that having *thus* received the prospect given to him of longer life, he should suffer as an obstinate heretic on the following day. This was April 17, 1529, when Berquin, then about forty years of age, was taken to the Place de Grève, and strangled, after which his remains were burnt. He met his fate with perfect equanimity; but such was the popular prejudice against him, that not a single bystander appears to have recommended his soul to God at the moment of its departure, although that sort of commiseration had been customarily shown for every criminal, however atrocious, when deprived of life. Berquin's French translations of two pieces by Erasmus, the one entitled Le Vrai Moyen de bien et catholiquement se confesser, the other, Le Chevalier Chrétien, were published at Lyons in 1542. The latter is a version, with alterations, of the celebrated Enchiridion Militis Christiani. (Smedley's History of the Reformed Religion in France, i. 18. Bayle. Biog. Univ.)

BERRETINI, (Nicholas,) an eminent historical painter, pupil of Carlo Maratti, born at Montefeltro in 1627, died in 1682. His style was that of Guido.

BERRETTINI, (Peter,) born at Cortona, in Tuscany, in 1596, deceased at Rome, 1669. This celebrated artist is one of many instances of men, who, having distinguished themselves in one art, persuade themselves and others that they are endowed with equal powers of excellence in all. Pietro da Cortona is the name by which this artist is generally known, rather than by his family one of Berrettini. His talents as a painter acquired him a deserved celebrity, for he had a fruitful and bold imagination, and great facility of execution; natural endowments, which too frequently betray the possessor to neglect those severe studies and strict mental discipline, without which none have ever arrived at that eminence which has procured such men the reverence of future ages, and raised their productions to the distinction of being the models of after times. Pietro da Cortona appeared to attain without effort those results which to a Domenichino were the fruits of painful labour; but nature at the same time seems to produce a compensation in this apparently unequal distribution of her gifts, for excellence is only attained by an unwearied struggle with difficulties to be overcome, while the very ease with which a naturally gifted man passes through the primary elements of his art, too often unfits him for more intense application in a later stage, leaving him in a brilliant mediocrity. The Italian nobility have ever taken a pride in encouraging rising genius, feeling, perhaps, that the halo which surrounds gifted men sheds also a ray of glory upon those who aided them through early difficulties. The marquis Sacchetti, seeing young Pietro in a gilder's shop, painting some small figures, was surprised with the ability of the youth, and afforded him the opportunities of study and improvement, so that he soon surpassed the expectations of his patron. Pope Urban VIII. employed him upon some great pictures, and being satisfied with them, engaged him to paint the ceiling of the Barberini palace, a work of great talent. In this he evidenced that freedom and facility of drawing, that feeling for colour, and bold handling of the brush, which fitted him eminently for grand decorative compositions, of which he has left numerous examples in Italy. But his pictures are crowded with images, and thus one does not at first remark their deficiency in the higher qualities of art. As an architect, he executed several works of importance, in which he incurs less the reproach of impure detail than of a certain decorative license in the general composition, displaying a systematic independence of approved precedents. He died at the age of seventy-three, after having for a long time suffered a very painful illness. He was a handsome man, majestic in his deportment, of a good height, and pleasing demeanour, quick at reply, but circumspect and even-tempered. He was fond of application, and always ready with his pencil: but he also enjoyed relaxation and amusement. He was frugal, generous, and devoid of pride; qualities which won the love and respect of all.

BERRI, (John, duke of,) third son of John, king of France, and of Bonne of Luxemburg, born at the castle of Vincennes, Nov. 30, 1340, originally called count of Poitou, but created duke of Berri in 1360. He was at the great battle, so glorious to England, fought Sept. 19, 1356, in the fields of Beauvoir and Maupertuis, near Poitiers, and designated from that city. At the treaty of Bretigny, in 1360, the young prince, styled in the English version of its conditions, *Monsieur* John, earl of Poictiers, was delivered as a hostage to Edward III. and he subsequently spent nine years in England. He was then allowed to return, for the avowed object of raising a sum to ransom himself. He had only a year's leave, but when it expired, he continued, by a series of excuses and evasions, to prolong his absence, until the war between France and England broke out again. He then, in 1372, commanded in Guienne, against the Black Prince, and with considerable success. He subsequently played a conspicuous part, upon several occasions, in the domestic politics of France; a distinction apparently owing solely to the accident of his birth, as he was rash, dissipated, and indolent. He died at his house in Paris, the Hôtel de Nesle, June 15, 1416. (Biog. Univ. Moreri. Barnes's Edward III. 513, 587.)

BERRI, (Charles, duke of,) third son of Lewis, dauphin of France, called the *Great Dauphin*, son of Lewis XIV. by Maria Christina, of Bavaria. He was born Aug. 31, 1686, and named, in 1700, by Charles II. of Spain, successor to the throne of that country, in case of his brother, the duke of Anjou's, death before the vacancy should happen. As this contingency did not happen, Anjou, under the name of Philip V., becoming king of Spain, the duke of Berri passed through life in that real insignificance for which nature formed him. All were captivated by his gentleness of disposition, but none could say much in favour of his capacity or spirit. It is probable that his grandfather, Lewis XIV. observed impatiently these deficiencies, for the young prince could never approach him without trembling. He died at Marly, May 4, 1714. (Biog. Univ.)

BERRI, (Charles Ferdinand, duke of,) younger son of the count of Artois, subsequently known as *Monsieur*, and Charles X., by Maria Theresa of Savoy. He was born at Versailles, Jan. 24, 1778. Being very young when his father escaped from the horrors of the French revolution, in 1789, his education was subsequently conducted at Turin, among his maternal relatives. As his age advanced, he was initiated in the duties of a soldier, under the prince of Condé, then making a vain struggle on the banks of the Rhine to support the cause of royalty in France. He commanded a little troop of cavalry, and with considerable credit, from 1794 to 1797. In the next year his troop went into the Russian service, and he took the opportunity of paying a visit to his father at Edinburgh. Subsequently he spent some time in Italy, and then again joined the Condean army, with which he remained until its dispersion. When at length a Bourbon of the elder race had no hope of safety out of Great Britain, he took refuge there, in common with other members of his family, and lived very much as an ordinary man of fashion. On the 13th of April, 1814, he landed at Cherbourg, amidst loud acclamations, manifesting all that emotion, on touching again his paternal soil, and possessing the realities of princely station, which a change that long seemed so hopeless could not fail to excite. He arrived at Paris on the 21st of April. As his elder brother, the duke of Angoulême, was married, but childless, it became desirable that the duke of Berri should marry, and it was proposed that he should make choice of a Russian princess; but difference of religion broke off the project. In 1816, however, he espoused the princess Caroline of Naples, then very young. The first issue of this marriage were two children, who soon died, one of them a son; the third survived, but she was a daughter. After these repeated disappointments, it became known that the duchess was pregnant again, and hopes, eventually realized, revived of an heir qualified by sex for the throne of France. The duke himself, however, was cut off before the occurrence of an event so joyful to his family. He had striven with considerable assiduity and address to render himself popular; but great pains were taken to make him the reverse, by assailing his character with calumnies and exaggerations. There stalked abroad, indeed, a sullen spirit of republicanism, which rendered all royalty odious to a large portion of the inferior French, and a particular antipathy to the Bourbon family extensively prevailed among persons of better feelings and condition. To an hostility thus widely spread, the duke of Berri fell a victim. As he was leaving the opera, on the 14th of February, 1820, the last Sunday of the carnival, a saddler's servant, named Louvel, formerly a soldier in the old imperial guard, stabbed him under the right breast. He was immediately conveyed to one of the saloons of the house, and every attention that Paris could afford was promptly rendered. But the assassin had done his work too well; the wound was deep and mortal. Before six on the following morning the duke expired, having first humanely pleaded in favour of his wretched murderer, who seems to have been one of those infuriate political fanatics that France has produced in such fearful abundance ever since her ancient institutions were overthrown. In the following September, the duchess of Berri gave birth to a son, immediately created duke of Bordeaux, the city which had been among the first and most energetic in demonstrations of loyalty to the ancient but exiled royal race; but after his grandfather's abdication in 1830, himself became an exile, and mocked among a handful of unyielding partizans by the vain title of Henry V. (Gent.'s Mag. Biog. Univ. Suppl.)

BERRIMAN, (John,) brother to Dr. William Berriman, born in 1689, and educated academically at St. Edmund's hall, Oxford. Having taken orders, his ministerial life was spent in the city of London, first as curate and lecturer, eventually as rector of St. Alban's, Wood-street. He died upon that benefice, December 8, 1768. In literature, he is known as author of eight sermons, preached at Lady Moyer's lecture, and published in 1741; exhibiting a critical view of more than 100 Greek MSS. of St. Paul's Epistles, many of them not hitherto collated. He was also editor of two volumes of his brother's sermons, published in 1750. (Chalmers.)

BERRIMAN, (William,) an English divine, born in London, September 24, 1688, son of an apothecary there, and grandson of a clergyman, beneficed in Surrey. His earlier education was partly received at Merchant Tailors' school, and at seventeen he was entered of Oriel college, Oxford. He applied himself with great assiduity to the oriental languages, so that he acquired a critical knowledge of Scripture, far from usual, especially among the younger clergy. His first professional employments were of a subordinate nature in the city of London, but Whiston's erratic genius gave him an opportunity, which he judiciously embraced, of emerging into general notice. In 1719, he published A Seasonable Review of Mr. Whiston's Account of the Primitive Doxologies; and before the year was out, a second Review. By these well-timed proofs of professional competence, Dr. Robinson, then bishop of London, was so much pleased, that he appointed Berriman his domestic chaplain, and found him highly serviceable in most of the concerns that required his attention; assistance which he requited by collating him, in 1722, to the rectory of St. Andrew Undershaft, London. In 1723, this generous and discerning patron died, but his will gave a new proof of the estimation that he had entertained for Berriman, a fifth part of his valuable library being bequeathed to him. He had now taken his doctor's degree, and he established abundantly his title to that distinction by An Historical Account of the Trinitarian Controversy, in eight sermons, delivered at Lady Moyer's lecture, in the years 1723 and 1724, and published in 1725. This publication induced Dr. Godolphin, the provost of Eton, to procure his election, in 1727, to a fellowship of that noble institution. But although one class of divines hailed Berriman's exertions with cordial approbation, those who were impatient of established restraints upon opinion, became anxious to lower his credit with inquiring minds. Among these restless spirits was Conyers Middleton, who, at first, treated Berriman with respectful courtesy, but subsequently spoke of him contemptuously. To meet these attacks upon him, he published, in 1731, A Defence of some Passages in the Historical Account. In 1733 were printed his Brief Remarks on Mr. Chandler's Introduction to the History of the Inquisition; which was succeeded by A Review of the Remarks. Berriman next appeared as author of a course of sermons preached at Boyle's lecture, in the years 1730, 1731, and 1732, and published in two volumes, in 1733. This work states the evidences of Christianity from the Old Testament, and vindicates the inspiration of Moses. Besides these productions, Dr. Berriman printed several occasional sermons; and after his death, which occurred February 5, 1750, three volumes of his sermons were published, but at two several times. Their excellent author passed through life with a high character for learning, practical good sense, integrity, and strict regard for his professional obligations of every kind. (Chalmers.)

BERROYER, (Claudius,) an advocate in the parliament of Paris, who gained great professional reputation; but as an author, is more known by publishing and commenting upon the works of others, than by any thing original. His publications were once highly esteemed among lawyers, but changes in jurisprudence have rendered them of little value. He died March 7, 1735. (Biog. Univ.)

BERRUGUETE, (Alonso,) a distinguished Spanish artist, born at Paredes de Naba, near Valladolid, in what year is not certainly known, but he died at the advanced age of about 80 years at Toledo, in the year 1545. In 1500 he went to Italy, the great and then only school of the fine arts; and, inspired by the illustrious example of Michael Angelo and Leonardo da Vinci, who were then in the full splendour of their fame, he devoted himself with the utmost energy to perfect himself in his studies. The paucity of artists in his native country, no less than the practice of the most celebrated masters of that period in Italy, led him to acquire the rudiments of architecture, and to study painting as well as his favourite art of sculpture, in which he chiefly excelled, so as to acquire the title of Prince of Spanish Sculptors. Toledo is full of his productions, the last of which was the marble sepulchre of the Cardinal di Tabera, in the church of his great hospital in that city. Charles V. employed him extensively in great works as an architect. He designed the principal gate of Toledo, called that of S. Martin; a simple and graceful composition. He is supposed to have been the architect of the palace of Alcalà, opposite the archbishop's palace, as also of a great part of the cathedral of Cuença. He was tolerably correct in the details of his orders, but in their application, not sufficiently dignified. He excelled in architectural decoration, then much in vogue for altars and in pictures. When he died he left a considerable property. (Milizia, Memorie degli Architetti.)

BERRY, (Sir John,) an eminent English naval commander, born in Devonshire, in 1635. He first came conspicuously forward at the battle of Southwold Bay, for his conduct at which he was knighted. In 1682, he commanded the *Gloucester* frigate, in which James, duke of York, was proceeding to Scotland, and when that vessel was wrecked at the mouth of the Humber, by his presence of mind he saved the prince, with many about him. When that infatuated personage was trembling for his crown, on the prince of Orange's approach, Berry was entrusted with a command under lord Dartmouth, and on the noble admiral's retirement from his post, he became sole commander of the fleet. He nevertheless attached himself to king William's government, when that monarch was established; and hence he not only retained his employments, but his influence also, being frequently consulted by the new government. He was poisoned, as it seems, accidentally, on board a king's ship, which he was paying off at Portsmouth, in February, 1691. (Chalmers.)

BERRY, (William,) a Scottish artist, born about 1730, and apprenticed to an Edinburgh seal-engraver; which he became himself in due time, although he displayed a power in the execution of intaglios, approached by one artist only in all Europe, Piccler of Rome. Berry's first attempt of this kind was a head of Sir Isaac Newton, which astonished every judge. Ten or twelve heads besides, of equal, if not superior excellence, were subsequently executed by him; but although every one of them was warmly and extensively admired, yet, unfortunately, such works were not in such demand as would encourage the ingenious artist to undertake them. Hence he was always anxious to decline an engagement of this kind, and confine himself to the drudgery of seal-engraving, as the surest mode of providing for his numerous family. He died June 3, 1783, in circumstances far from affluent. (Chalmers.)

BERRY, (Sir Edward, Bart.) a British naval officer, distinguished for intrepidity, son of Edward Berry, of London, by Elizabeth, daughter of a clergyman. He was born April 17, 1768, and went to sea at an early age, under Lord Mulgrave. The first recorded circumstance of his life afloat, appears to have been the boarding of a French ship of war, for which he was rewarded with a lieutenant's commission. His subsequent conduct in the glorious battle of June 1, 1794, appears also to have obtained for him the approbation of his superiors. In 1796, he was recommended by Sir John Jervis to the especial notice of commodore Nelson; and in the capacity of first lieutenant, sailed with that officer, who at that period was "laying the foundation of his future fame." Following the commodore from the *Agamemnon* into the *Captain* (74), (the ship which bore the broad pendant of Nelson, his heroic patron, in Sir John Jervis's memorable defeat of the Spanish superior force off Cape St. Vincent,) Berry's daring and extraordinary activity in boarding from the low channels of the "little *Captain*," two of the enemy's largest ships, procured for him the honest eulogium of every officer in the British fleet. "The first man," says Nelson, in his narration of the daring attack, "who jumped into the enemy's mizen-chains, was captain Berry, late my first lieutenant."

Berry's post-commission bears date March 6, 1797. In the course of the same year he appeared at court with Sir Horatio Nelson; and it has been said, that after George III. had complimented the illustrious admiral on his exploits, and condoled with him on the loss of an arm at the attack of Santa Cruz, he pointed to his companion, remarking kindly, "I have had really no great loss, since *my right hand* here has been saved."

At the close of the same year, captain Berry commissioned the *Vanguard* of 74 guns for the flag of his friend Nelson, with whom he soon after returned to the Mediterranean station. The prominent part taken by Berry in the battle of the Nile, stands recorded in the rear-admiral's public letter, addressed to the commander-in-chief of the British forces then employed on the Mediterranean station. The passage in Sir Horatio's despatch runs as follows:—"The support and assistance I have received from captain Berry, cannot be sufficiently expressed. I was wounded in the head, and obliged to be carried off the deck, but the service suffered no loss by that event. Captain Berry was fully equal to the important service then going on, and to him I must beg leave to refer you for every information relative to this victory. He will present you with the flag of the second in command, that of the commander-in-chief being burnt in *L'Orient*."

On his passage down the Mediterranean, in the *Leander* of 50 guns, then commanded by the late Sir T. B. Thompson, captain Berry, the bearer of Nelson's despatches, had the misfortune to be taken prisoner by *Le Généreux*, a French 74-gun ship, of the largest class. In the desperate action that ensued, the subject of this sketch was severely wounded in the head. "The enemy," says Marshall, "on taking possession of their prize, not only plundered the officers and crew of every thing they possessed, but afterwards, by their cruelty and neglect, exposed the sick and wounded to almost certain death." But captains Thompson and Berry were permitted to return, on their parole of honour, to England, where they were welcomed with marked manifestations of popular applause. Captain Berry, after his exchange, was knighted, received a gold medal in common with the other officers who had shared in the late triumph, and was presented with the freedom of the metropolis, in a gold box, value 100 guineas.

In the autumn of 1799, Sir Edward repaired once more to the Mediterranean, as captain of lord Nelson's flag-ship, the *Foudroyant*; and early in the following year had the satisfaction of assisting at the capture of his old opponent, *Le Généreux*, and of *Le Guillaume Tell*, a French 80, the only remaining ship which had escaped from the battle in Aboukir Bay. A more heroic defence than that made by the latter vessel is not on record. Her colours were kept flying until she had become an ungovernable log, and sustained a loss of 200 men, killed and wounded. In this encounter Sir Edward Berry was hurt in the foot. The *Foudroyant* had eight men killed, and sixty-one wounded.

In the month of June following, Sir Edward conveyed the queen of Naples, her family, and attendants, from Palermo to Leghorn, at which anchorage, on the ship's arrival, her Sicilian majesty presented our subject with a gold box, set with diamonds, and a diamond ring. (Marshall.)

In the summer of 1805 Sir Edward was appointed to the command of his old ship, *Agamemnon;* in which vessel, after having, by the most masterly manœuvres, escaped from a French squadron, consisting of five sail of the line, two frigates, and a brig, he joined lord Nelson's fleet in time to participate in the glorious battle of Trafalgar. On the 6th of July, 1806, we find him in the same ship, taking part in Sir John Duckworth's defeat of the French squadron off the island of St. Domingo. This we believe to be the last occasion in which the services of this distinguished officer were called into active operation. In June, 1815, he was nominated a K.C.B. At the general promotion, August 12, 1819, he obtained one of the vacant colonelcies of royal marines; and in July 1821, was advanced to the rank of rear-admiral of the blue. His patent of baronetage bears date December 12th, 1806. He expired at Bath, on the 13th of July, 1831, aged 63. Sir Edward died without issue, and the baronetcy has consequently become extinct.

BERSEO, (Gonsalvo de,) a Spanish Benedictine, in the eleventh century, as it has been said, who wrote in a measure then usual, consisting of thirteen feet, (*endecha doblada*,) some lives of saints, and other poems. There is, however, a doubt, both as to this author's age, and his profession; there being good reason to believe him really to have lived in the earlier part of the thirteenth century, and to have been a secular priest. His poetical works are to be found in Syllog. Poet. Hisp. ante ann. 1500, Matriti, 1779, 3 vols, 8vo. (Antonii Bibl. Hisp. vetus.)

BERSMANUS, (Gregory,) born in 1538, at Annaberg, in Saxony; who, after the best education that his own country could afford, visited Strasburg, Paris, Lyons, Geneva, Padua, Ferrara, and Bologna, to perfect himself in medicine. In 1571 he went to Leipsic, as professor of poetry, and in 1575 followed his former teacher, Joachim Camerarius, as professor of the Greek and Latin languages. The religious troubles of Saxony obliged him to leave that country in 1580, and he found refuge in Anhalt. Joachim Ernest, prince of Anhalt, made him rector of the united schools, and of the newly-founded Gymnasium illustre. This office he entered upon in 1582, and discharged the duties of it honourably and successfully for thirty years, dying in 1611. He edited Virgil, Ovid, Lucan, Horace, Cicero in part, &c.; translated the Psalms into Latin metre, &c. (Ersch und Gruber.)

BERTANA, BERTANI, or BERTANO, (Lucia.) The family name and birth-place of this learned Italian lady have been subjects of great dispute. Some pretend that she was born at Bologna, and that her family name was *Oro*. Others insist on her being a native of Modena, and of the noble family of the Erri; and though no one has been able to ascertain the exact time of her birth or of her death, yet it is certain that she lived in Modena during the middle of the sixteenth century, and was the wife of Giurone Bertano, or Bertani. Tiraboschi calls her husband Bertana, a Modenese gentleman, brother of Peter, cardinal Bertani. She is represented as noble-minded and generous. Her husband died in October, 1561, and it is believed that she survived him. She wrote several elegant poems and fugitive pieces, very properly admitted into various collections.

She had a son called Julius, who was also a poet, and whose MS. works have been added to the edition of Sannazaro's Arcadia, published during the sixteenth century.

BERTANO, (John Baptist,) a celebrated architect, at Mantua, towards the middle of the sixteenth century. He was well grounded in the study of the edifices of ancient Rome, then more numerous and less dilapidated than at present, and was expert in perspective, at that period a new science. He also distinguished himself as a writer in certain remarks upon the cathedral of Milan, and in observations upon obscure and difficult passages in Vitruvius, particularly on the Ionic order. (Milizia Memorie degli Architetti.)

BERTAUT, (John,) a French poet, born at Caen, in 1552, who rose to eminence, both professional and secular, it is said, chiefly by means of a power to charm in verse. Undoubtedly, if he had no better claim to patronage, a poet has rarely been so well requited; for he was secretary and reader to the king, counsellor to the parliament of Grenoble, abbot of Aunay, and first almoner to queen Mary de' Medici. His Œuvres Poétiques were printed at Pâris, in 1602, 8vo, and reprinted afterwards with additions. The most complete editions are those of 1620 and 1623. He also left some translations, controversial pieces, sermons, and a funeral oration over Henry IV., to whose conversion, or apostasy, he had the credit of contributing. He died in 1611. (Biog. Univ.)

BERTELIUS, (John,) a Flemish Benedictine, who wrote, Historia Luxemburgeusis, Coloniæ, 1605, 4to; De Diis Deorumque Gentilium Sacrificiis, *ibid.*; and some more works. (Athenæ Belgicæ.)

BERTELLI, the name of three engravers.

1. *Cristofano*, a native of Rimini, in the duchy of Modena. There are a few plates by him, executed with the graver in rather a stiff manner. He flourished about 1525. Many of his plates are inscribed, Per me, Cristofano Bertelli. (Bryan's Dict.)

2. *Ferrando*, born at Venice about the year 1525, and engraved some plates after the Venetian painters. (*Id.*)

3. *Lucas*, probably a relation of the preceding artist. He engraved several plates after the Italian painters, and is said to have been a printseller. Some of his prints are very scarce. (*Id.*)

BERTHA, only daughter of Charibert, king of Paris, a christian princess, married to Ethelbert, king of Kent, then a pagan, about A.D. 570, on condition that she should be allowed the free exercise of her religion. Luidhart, bishop of Soissons, accompanied her to England, and Ethelbert assigned for her use a small British church at Canterbury, long desecrated. It was dedicated to St. Martin; and by this little establishment an opening was made for the eventual conversion of Ethelbert himself.

BERTHAULD, (Peter,) a French historian, born at Sens, about the year 1600, and by profession an ecclesiastic. His Florus Gallicus, and Florus Francicus, were long used in education among the French, as the best abridgments of their national history. The latter has gained considerable credit from the excellence of its style. Berthauld's reputation, however, of a higher kind, rests chiefly upon his treatise, De Ara, a work full of erudition and research, printed at Nantes, in 1635. There are also some poetical publications of his, upon subjects of temporary interest. His death, at a very advanced age, occurred Oct. 19th, 1681. (Biog. Univ.)

BERTHEAU, (Charles,) a French protestant, born in 1660, at Montpelier, but driven from his native land by the revocation of the edict of Nantes. In 1686 he was appointed a minister of the French church in Threadneedle-street, London, and he filled that situation most satisfactorily during a long course of years. He died Dec. 25th, 1732, leaving two volumes of French sermons; the first printed in 1712, the second in 1730. (Chalmers.)

BERTHELOT, (John Francis,) a French advocate, born at Paris, in June, 1749, best known in conjunction with the Roman law. He published, in 1785, Reflexions sur la Loi du Digeste. In 1802 he undertook to translate six books of the Digest, to complete the forty-four which had been published by Hulot. He died on the 13th of February, 1814. (Biog. Univ. Suppl.)

BERTHET, (John,) a Jesuit, born at Tarascon, in Provence, Feb. 24th, 1622, and chiefly worthy of mention as author of Traité de la Présence Réelle, followed by a series of testimonies from all the ancient fathers, against modern controversialists. He wrote also some works of national interest, and died among the Benedictines, in 1692. (Biog. Univ.)

BERTHIER, (William Francis,) born at Issoudun, in the province of Berri, on the 7th of April, 1704, entered the society of the Jesuits in 1722, where he soon distinguished himself by his great erudition and superior talents. In 1745 they entrusted to him the care of publishing the Journal de Trevoux, which he did for seventeen years, with great credit for his impartial and learned criticism, but which procured him the enmity of many writers, amongst whom was Voltaire, then very young, but notwithstanding violent and vain, who not being able to answer the strictures which Berthier had published on some of his works; and last of all, on his Essay, Sur l'Histoire Générale, had recourse to ridicule, and published, in 1760, a Relation of the Malady, Confession, and Death, of the Jesuit Berthier. By him, however, this ebullition of malicious wit was left unnoticed. For a short time he was assistant tutor to the future Lewis XVI. and *Monsieur*; but some circumstances relative to the society of the Jesuits obliged him to leave the court, and retire to Offenburg, where he resided for ten years, and wrote a translation of the Psalms, with notes and reflections; these he published in Paris, in 8 vols, 12mo, when he returned to France, spending the remainder of his life in the study and exercises of religion. He died of a fall, at Bourges, 15th December, 1782. A little before, the assembly of the clergy had given him a pension, as a reward for his continuation of the History of the Gallican Church; a learned work, in six volumes, in which he had cleared up many obscure and controverted points.

BERTHIER, (Peter Alexander,) one of the French revolutionary marshals, born at Versailles, Nov. 20, 1755, and brought up to the army. When the national troubles commenced, he displayed fidelity to the unfortunate house of Bourbon, and he favoured the escape of Lewis the Sixteenth's aunts; but when royalty was overthrown, he sedulously pushed his fortune under the republic. His first appearance in a position of importance was in Buonaparte's famous Italian campaign of 1796. Being a far older man than his commanding officer, many thought him really the cause of much that then occurred, so greatly to the advantage of France. Berthier no sooner found himself thus coming into collision with Buonaparte's rising fame, than he took pains to occupy decidedly a second place, with all that instinctive perception of his own interest for which he was so remarkable through life. The fruit of this judicious policy was a constant and overflowing stream of prosperity. He commanded at Rome, in 1798, when the pope was deposed, and pronounced the childish harangue, heard by the Romans as people generally hear a school-boy, who is no relation, in which the manes of Brutus and Cato were invoked, and a republic was proclaimed. Afterwards he went to Egypt with Buonaparte, but sorely against his will, as he wished to remain at home with an Italian lady, who had won his heart. When the great captain became the first man in France, perhaps in Europe, Berthier continued as necessary to him as ever; and his important services, both in the cabinet and the field, were requited in 1806, by the principality of Neufchâtel. Buonaparte then insisted upon his marriage with a princess of Bavaria Birkenfeld, an honour which he would gladly have declined, from the continuance of his old Italian attachment, and which marred his domestic peace. In 1809 his arrangements were infinitely useful in securing the victory of France over Austria, and these services were acknowledged in the title of prince of Wagram. In the Russian campaign Berthier followed Buonaparte, but unwillingly; and on the fall of that celebrated personage, he seems to have found no great difficulty in returning to the feelings of his youth, and welcoming the Bourbons, even before the abdication of his benefactor. In this he found his account again; but on Napoleon's return, he followed Lewis XVIII. to Ghent, whence he retired to Bamberg, and there, either throwing himself, or being pushed out of a window, he was killed. (Biog. Univ. Suppl.)

BERTHELEMY, (John Simon, March 5th, 1743—March 1st, 1811,) an historical painter, born at Laon, who especially excelled in ceilings, of which he executed many at Fontainebleau, at the Museum, and at the Luxembourg. (Biog. Univ.)

BERTHOLDT, (Dr. Leonhard,) a German theologian of the so-called rational school, was born in 1774, at Ernskirchen, in Baireuth, and received his education at Erlangen, where he was master in 1795, in 1803 adjunct of the philosophical faculty, in 1805 extraordinary, and in 1808 ordinary professor of theology, and afterwards combined with this office that of a university chaplain and director of the Homiletic Seminary. His first important work was a Commentary on the Prophet Daniel, highly spoken of by Gesenius, from whom this account is taken, who finds no great fault with the doctor's supposition, that this part of the Old Testament was written by various hands, and part of it as late as the time of Antiochus Epiphanes. He wrote, also, an Introduction to the Old and New Testaments, 6 vols, 8vo, 1812—1819, and edited the Critical Journal for Theology, at first jointly with Ammon, and afterwards, from 1813, alone. He died in 1822. (Gesenius in Erach und Gruber.)

BERTHOLLET, (Claudius Lewis,) a celebrated chemist, born at Talloire, near Annecy, in Savoy, Nov. 9, 1748, who, after studying nearer home, finished his education at Turin, where he took the degree of doctor of medicine, in 1770. Transferring his residence to Paris, in 1772, he was elected member of the Royal Academy of Sciences, and ultimately appointed professor of chemistry in the Normal School and the Polytechnic School. In 1795 he was chosen a member of the National Institute, and a corresponding member of the Royal Society of London. He accompanied the French expedition to Egypt, being nominated one of a commission for the transport of objects of art from that country, as he had previously been for those obtained by the French by conquest in Italy, in 1796. Upon his return to Paris he was made a senator, a count of the empire in 1804, and a grand officer of the Legion of Honour. In June 1814, he was advanced to the chamber of peers. He died Nov. 6, 1822.

Berthollet was a most able chemist, and applied his science particularly to the arts. His investigation of chemical affinities has placed him in a high rank among chemists; and he lent his assistance to reform the chemical nomenclature, with Lavoisier, Guyton de Morveau, and Fourcroy. He may be considered as the discoverer of the art of bleaching cloth by the aid of chlorine, and of fixing the colour of the dyes. He published a great number of papers, upwards of eighty of which are scattered through various Transactions of the day; also some separate works. They were written between the years 1776 and 1817, and consist, principally, of Expériences sur l'Acide Tartareux. Mémoire sur l'Acide Sulfureux. Observations sur l'Air. Mémoire sur les Combinaisons des Huiles avec les Terres, l'Alcali Volatil, et les Substances Métalliques, (1776—1779.) Prospectus d'un Cours de Matière Médicale, Paris, 1779, 8vo. Recherches sur la Nature des Substances Animales, et sur leur Rapport avec les Substances Végétales. Observations sur la Combinaison de l'Alcali Fixé avec l'Acide Crayeux. Observations sur l'Acide Phosphorique de l'Urine. Essai sur la Causticité des Sels Métalliques, (1780.) Observatious sur la Décomposition de l'Acide Nitreux, (1781.) Recherches sur l'Augmentation de Poids qu'éprouvent le Soufre, le Phosphore, et l'Arsenic, lorsqu'ils sont changés en Acides. Observations sur la Causticité des Alcalis et de la Chaux. Observations sur la Disposition Spontanée de quelques Acides Végétaux. Sur la Différence du Vinaigre Radical et de l'Acide Acéteux. Sur la Préparation de l'Alcali Caustique, sa Cristallisation et son Action sur l'Esprit de Vin, (1782.) Mémoire sur l'Acide Marin Déphlogistique. Mémoire sur l'Analyse de l'Alcali Volatil. Suite des Recherches sur la Nature des Substances Animales, et sur leur Rapport avec les Substances Végétales, ou Recherches sur l'Acide du Sucre. Observations sur l'Eau Régale, et sur quelques Affinités de l'Acide Marin. Sur la Combinaison de l'Air Vital avec les Huiles. Mémoire sur la Décomposition de l'Esprit de Vin et de l'Ether par l'Air Vital, (1785.) Mémoire sur le Fer, considéré dans ses différents Etats Métalliques. De l'Influence de la Lumière. Lettre à M. de la Métheric sur la Décomposition de l'Eau. Notes sur l'Analyse du Sable Vert Cuivreux du Pérou, rapporté par Dombey, (1786.) Mémoire sur l'Acide Prussique, (1787.) Observations sur quelques Combinaisons de l'Acide Marin Déphlogistique. Sur un Procédé pour rendre la Chaux d'Argent fulminante, (1788.) Sur les Combinaisons des Oxides Métalliques avec les Alcalis et la Chaux. Sur la Combinaison des Oxides Métalliques avec les Parties Astringentes et les Parties Colorantes des Végétaux. Suites d'Expériences sur l'Acide Sulfureux. Considérations sur les Expériences de Priestley, relatives à la Décomposition de l'Eau, (1789.) Précis d'une Théorie sur la Nature de l'Acier et ses Préparations, Paris, 1789, 8vo. 1. Observations sur la Décomposition du Tartrate de Potasse Antimonié, et du Muriate Mercurial Corrosif par quelques Substances Végétales. Observations sur quelques Faits que l'on a opposés à la Doctrine Antiphlogistique, (1791.) Eléments de l'Art de la Teinture, Paris, 1791, 2 vols, 8vo, second edition, 1804, translated into German by W. F. Gœhler, Berlin, 1806, 2 vols, 8vo. 2. Description de l'Art du Blanchiment des Toiles par l'Acide Muriatique Oxigéné, (1795.) Observations sur quelques Combinaisons de l'Acide Muriatique Oxigéné, (1798.) Recherches sur les Lois de l'Affinité, Paris, 1801, 1806, 8vo, translated into German by E. G. Fischer, Berlin, 1802, 8vo; and into English by Farrell, London, 1804, 8vo. Essai de Statique Chimique, Paris, 1803, 2 vols, 8vo; translated into English by Lambert, London, 1804, 2 vols, 8vo; into Italian by Dandolo, Rome, 1804, 8vo; and into German by G. G. Bartholdy and Fischer, Berlin, 1805 and 1811, 8vo. Faits sur les Effets de la Vaccination, (with MM. Percy and Hallé,) Paris, 1812, 4to. Mémoires sur l'Emploi des Fumigations Sulfureuses, Paris, 1817, 8vo.

BERTHOLON DE ST. LAZARE, so named from the community of which he was a member from a very early age, was professor of physics at Montpelier, and afterwards of history at Lyons. He held the opinion that earthquakes were attributable to the disturbance of the equilibrium between atmospheric and terrestrial electricity, and suggested a means which, in his opinion, would effectually prevent the recurrence of such events, namely, by carrying as far as possible into the earth long bars of iron, furnished at each end with a crown of many points, the lower one being provided with many branches. This wild and impracticable speculation found a defender in Wiedebourg, a German, who proposed the erection of pyramids to aid the object in view. Bertholon was the friend of Benjamin Franklin, and he paid great attention to electrical phenomena. He directed his studies to the subject of medical electricity. He collected together a number of interesting facts, but the application of them has been productive of little advantage to science. He died at Lyons in 1799, leaving several works, now forgotten.

BERTI, (Alexander Pompey,) born at Lucca, 23d December, 1686, entered very young the congregation of the Madre di Dio, at Naples, in pursuance of a vow which his parents had made, and returned to Lucca in 1704, to study philosophy and theology, sacred and profane history, belles-lettres, poetry, and above all, pulpit eloquence. In 1739 he went to Rome, where he remained till his death, 23d March, 1752. During his life, Berti acquired great reputation as a scholar and a preacher. His works, twenty-four of which are published, amount to not less than forty-five, most of them of historical or biographical character, but some are religious.

BERTI, (John Laurence,) a learned monk of the order of St. Augustine, born May 28, 1696, at Serravezza, a small village in Tuscany, celebrated for a work entitled De Disciplinis Theologicis, printed at Rome, in 8 vols, 4to, in 1739. In this he adopted the opinions of St. Augustine in their utmost rigour, after the example of Bellelli, his brother monk, and he thus exposed himself to the attacks of Saleon, bishop of Rhodes and archbishop of Vienna, who not only published works against him, but accused him to pope Benedict XIV. as a disciple of Baius and Jansenius. The prudent pontiff, without noticing the accusation, advised Berti to defend himself, which he did in a work exposing the many contradictions of his opponents. In gratitude to the pope, who had thus protected him, Berti published a Latin ecclesiastical history, in 7 vols, 4to, in which he enlarges upon what he had asserted before in some other of his works, and speaks of the pope as the absolute monarch of kingdoms and empires, whose sovereigns are but his lieutenants. He afterwards published an abridgement of this work, in 2 vols, 8vo, which is not worth much, besides dissertations, dialogues, panegyrics, academical speeches, and very indifferent Italian poems. He died on the 26th of May, 1766, at Pisa, where the emperor Francis I., then grand duke of Tuscany, had appointed him professor at the university, with a considerable pension, and the title of imperial theologian.

BERTI, (Peter,) a learned Jesuit, born at Venice in 1741, and died at Padua in 1818. At the dissolution of his order he became a tutor in noblemen's families, and a collector of valuable books. He wrote, in Latin, a funeral oration for the doge Luigi Moncenico, and another in Italian, for the *solenne ingresso* of Pietro Moncenico in Venice, besides a small poem on the fishery of Comacchio, and a learned preface to a, not very exact, Italian translation of Æsop.

BERTIE, (Richard,) an English gentleman in the sixteenth century, married to Catharine, baroness Willoughby, of Eresby, and duchess dowager of Suffolk, relict of Charles Brandon, who was, like himself, a zealous protestant. In queen Mary's reign, bishop Gardiner charged him to persuade his wife to turn, but he declared that to be quite hopeless, except by the truth; reminding him that "religion went not by age but by truth;" and that "one by judgment reformed is worth more than a thousand transformed temporizers." Bertie and the duchess soon saw the prudence of consulting their safety by quitting the kingdom; and he, under pretence of business abroad, went first; the duchess followed by stealth, in disguise, with much difficulty and risk, and joined her husband in Brabant. They resided first at Santon, a town of Cleves, whence they were soon obliged to flee by night: after enduring great hardships and fatigues, they reached Wesel, where on their arrival they could find no shelter, and were about to lodge all night in the church porch, starved with both cold and hunger, when, through means of Francis de Rivers, minister of the refugee Walloons there, they were discovered, and soon comfortably settled in a hired house of their own. Here was born to them a son and heir, Peregrine Bertie, (so called from his birth abroad,) who afterwards claimed and obtained the barony of Willoughby of Eresby. Finding themselves insecure here, they removed to Weinheim, in the palatinate of the Rhine, where they remained until they began to be in want, and almost in despair. At this juncture they received a very opportune and kind invitation from the king of Poland, and in April 1557 left Weinheim. Before they reached Frankfort they narrowly escaped murder, and with much trouble and danger arrived in Poland, where they were well received by the king, and generously placed by him in the earldom of Kroze in Samogitia, in which they continued in honour, peace, and plenty, until the death of Mary. The singular and severe troubles that they endured were afterwards commemorated in a curious old ballad, entitled The most rare and excellent History of the Duchess of Suffolk and her Husband's, Richard Bertie's, Calamities, to the tune of Queen Dido, published in the reign of queen Elizabeth, reprinted in 1738, and again in 1806.

BERTIE, (Peregrine,) so called from his birth, *in terra peregrina*, during the exile of his parents, son of the preceding, born October 12, 1555. He was made a free denizen by royal patent, dated August 2, 1559; and on his mother's death, in 1580, he was admitted to her barony of Willoughby of Eresby. He was much noticed by queen Elizabeth, and entrusted by her with several honourable employments, of which the most important was, the command of the English auxiliary force in the Low Countries, on Leicester's recall. He died in 1601, highly respected as an excellent officer and a generous man. (Biog. Brit.)

BERTIE, (Robert,) eldest son of the preceding, godson of queen Elizabeth, born in London, December 16, 1582, a distinguished officer, and loyal adherent of Charles I. Being early inured to arms, he was a sharer in many of the most conspicuous warlike movements of his country, both by sea and land, during the latter part of Elizabeth's reign. He succeeded to the barony of Willoughby of Eresby, on his father's death in 1601; and from his mother, who represented a branch of the De Veres, earls of Oxford, he inherited the office of lord great chamberlain. In 1626, he was created earl of Lindsey; and in 1628, on the duke of Buckingham's assassination by Felton, he was made admiral. On this he sailed with a large fleet to the relief of Rochelle, but although great bravery was displayed in the attempt, it failed. In 1635, he was made lord high admiral, having had the command of an English fleet upon several expeditions. When the civil war broke out, he came actively forward in his unfortunate sovereign's defence, and he received a wound at the battle of Edgehill, October 23, 1642, which, a loss of blood, that, apparently, might have been prevented by timely care, rendered mortal. (Biog. Brit.)

BERTIE, (Montague,) son of the preceding, and his successor in the earldom of Lindsey, taken prisoner at Edgehill, in attempting to rescue his father, but afterwards exchanged. He then became one of the king's most zealous officers, and in the battle of Naseby he was wounded. Charles appears to have entertained a very high opinion of him, and he was one of the four peers who attended the remains of that ill-used sovereign to the tomb at Windsor. Subsequently, the earl compounded, and lived in privacy until the restoration, when he was appointed one of the judges for the trial of the regicides, and a knight of the garter. He died July 25, 1666, with a great reputation for military talent, consistent loyalty, a judicious economy, that extricated him from considerable difficulties, and an enlightened patronage of learning. (Biog. Brit.)

BERTIE, (Willoughby,) fourth earl of Abingdon, descended from the preceding by his second wife, Bridget Wray, in her own right, baroness Norris of Rycote. The elder son of this marriage, James, was summoned to parliament, upon his maternal barony, in 1679; and in 1682, he was created earl of Abingdon. Willoughby, the fourth earl, was educated at Geneva, a circumstance to which has been attributed something of the violent democratic bias that rendered him conspicuous in after life. In the House of Peers he had scarcely any weight, his intemperate harangues being characterised by an eccentricity that made them little else than interruptions and interludes in the debate; but Wilkes very naturally said of the noble speaker, whatever he might have thought of him, that he was one of the most steady and intrepid assertors of public liberty that the age could boast. Lord Abingdon certainly thought of his exertions himself at least equally well, as he took great pains, and spent some money, to procure the insertion of his speeches in the newspapers, with a degree of fulness and prominence that many thought them likely to have missed, if left to struggle into notice with no better recommendation than their own intrinsic importance. He was also the author of some political pamphlets; one of which, Thoughts on the Letter of Edmund Burke, Esq., to the Sheriffs of Bristol, passed through six editions. To him, likewise, was attributed, A Letter to Lady Loughborough, on her Presentation of Colours to the Bloomsbury and Inns of Court Association. This passed through eight or nine editions. The earl died in 1799. (Chalmers. Biog. Brit. Nicolas's Synopsis of the Peerage.)

BERTIE, (Sir Thomas,) an eminent British admiral, who originally bore the surname of Hoar, born in London, of a family from the bishopric of Durham, July 3, 1758. He first went to sea at the latter end of 1773, in the *Sea-horse* frigate, commanded by the gallant captain Farmer, eventually killed in the *Quebec*, and with him he went to the East Indies. On board the *Sea-horse*, young Hoar was messmate with lord Nelson and sir Thomas Trowbridge, and he continued an intimate friend of both as long as life allowed. In 1777 he was removed from the *Sea-horse* to the *Salisbury*, by desire of his patron, lord Mulgrave, and subsequently, being then lieutenant, he was appointed to the *Monarch*. While belonging to this ship he introduced the life-buoy, which soon became general in the channel fleet. After considerable services in the West Indies, he married, May 20, 1788, Dorothy, daughter of Peregrine Bertie, of Low Layton, Essex, a descendant of the ennobled Berties, and agreeably to that gentleman's will, he assumed the name of Bertie, wholly dropping that of his family. In November 1790, he was advanced to post rank, and at the same time appointed to the *Leda*. That frigate was, however, soon afterwards put out of commission, and captain Bertie was not employed again till 1795, when he commanded the *Hindostan*, a 54-gun ship, under orders for the West Indies. In this service he caught the yellow fever, and was obliged to return home in October 1796. Having recovered his health, he was appointed to the *Braakel*, and in October 1797 he succeeded to the command of the *Ardent*, a 64, vacant by the death of captain Burgess, killed in the glorious action of Camperdown. While in this command he made an improvement in his vessel's 42-pounder carronades, which was eventually adopted in all ships of war furnished with that kind of ordnance. In the various naval expeditions which rendered the first revolutionary war with France so glorious to Britain, Bertie was generally employed, and always greatly to his credit. In 1808 he was made a rear-admiral, but his long and meritorious services were terminated in 1810, by the failure of his health. In 1813 he was knighted, and about the close of that year, he was advanced to the rank of vice-admiral. He died June 13, 1825. (Ann. Biog.)

BERTIER, (Joseph Stephen,) member of the Academy of Sciences at Paris, and the Royal Society of London; born at Aix in Provence, in 1710; entered, very young, the Congregation of the Oratory; and died at Paris on the 5th of November, 1783. He was such a zealous defender of the doctrine of Des Cartes, even after it had been exploded, that Louis XV. called him *l'Homme aux Tourbillons*. He seems to have been a very kind, excellent man, ready to oblige every body, so that strangers were most eager to be recommended to him as a sure means of being introduced to the most celebrated men, and assisted in all their pursuits.

He published some books that made a great noise at the time; these are, La Physique des Comètes, 1760, 12mo; a fantastic work, in which he defends the opinion that the comets are not planets, but a sort of apparition produced by the action of the vortices. Physique des Corps Animés, 1755; in which he asserts that not animal spirits, but heat is the principal agent which sets the body in motion; and that the peristaltic motion of the intestines does not exist during life, but begins after the death of the animals. Principes Physiques; in which he relates the proofs in favour of, and the objection against, the system of Newton. Histoire des Premiers Temps du Monde, 1778:—a very foolish work, in which he pretends that for the proper understanding of Genesis, it must be read backward.

BERTIN, a Romish saint, related to St. Omer, and appointed second abbot of Sithieu in 695. He resigned that appointment in the following year, and died in 709. (Moreri.)

BERTIN, (Exuperius Joseph,) a celebrated anatomist, born at Tremblay, near Rennes, September 21, 1712. His father was a physician, and descended from one of the best families in Britany. At an early age he evinced great disposition to study, and great attachment to the physical sciences. His predilection to medicine appears to have been excited by accidentally meeting with Verhagen's celebrated work on Anatomy, which he studied with such extraordinary eagerness, that he acquired a knowledge of every part of it by heart. Going to Paris, he was particularly noticed by Hanauld, and made considerable progress in medical science; taking the degree of doctor of medicine there in 1741. His studies having exhausted his pecuniary resources, he accepted the office of phy.i:ian to the hospodar of Wallachia and Moldavia. After some time he returned to his native country, and then travelled in Germany. In 1744 he was named an associate anatomist by the Royal Academy of Sciences, as a reward for his honourable labours on the nerves of the heart, and the important anastomosis of the mammary and epigastric arteries. In 1746 he printed a Memoir on the Structure and Functions of the Kidneys; and another on the Stomach of the Horse. He was engaged in a controversy with baron Haller on the anatomy of this organ in the human species. His health suffered much from the intensity of his application, and from chagrin at the want of success, in a worldly point of view, by which he was oppressed. He laboured under a singular disease during three years, which was marked by occasional accessions of fever, accompanied by violent delirium, terminating in a lethargic condition, after which he was left in the entire possession of his faculties. He published three memoirs, of distinguished ability, on the circulation of the blood through the liver of the foetus. He contemplated the publication of a large work on anatomy, the execution of which proceeded only as far as the bones, when a return of his delirium occurred, and put a stop to the progress of his undertaking. Geoffroy St. Hilaire, and other anatomists, have eulogized the performance of Bertin; and this celebrated anatomist considered his researches, in reference to the sphænoid bone, as so truly original and perfect, that he has called the bone after him the *os bertinal*. Bertin withdrew, in 1750, to Gahard, near Rennes, where he devoted himself to the education of his children, and died there February 1, 1781. He must be considered as one of the best anatomists that France has produced; and Condorcet has done justice to his memory in the *Eloge* delivered on occasion of his death, at the Royal Academy of Sciences. He published:—Ergò Causa Motûs alterni Cordis Multiplex, Paris, 1740, 4to. This is also to be found in the collection of Haller. Ergò non datur Imaginationis Maternæ in Fœtum Actio, Paris, 1741, 4to. Lettre sur le Nouveau Système de la Voix, La Haye, 1745, 8vo; written in opposition to the theory of Ferrein. Lettres sur le Nouveau Système de la Voix et sur les Artères Lymphatiques, Paris, 1748, 12mo. Ergò Specificum Morsûs Viperæ Antidotum Alcali Volatile, Paris, 1749, 4to. Traité d'Ostéologie, Paris, 1754, 12mo. This was translated into German by J. P. G. Pflug, Copenh. 1777-78. The most perfect edition is that of Paris, 1783, in 4 vols, 12mo, accompanied by three memoirs by M. Herissant. Consultation sur la Légitimité des Naissances Tardives, Paris, 1764, 8vo. There are also many pieces by Bertin in the Memoirs of the Royal Academy of Sciences and in the Journal de Médecine.

BERTIN, (Nicholas, 1667—1736,) an eminent French painter, born in Paris, the son of a sculptor, from whom he learned the rudiments of design; and having displayed considerable talent at an early age, he was sent to Rome at the king's expense. Being driven from that city by fears of a lady's relations, whose heart he had gained, he returned to Paris, where he died. Bertin had a correct taste for design, not unlike that of the Caraccis; his compositions were learned, and his expression admirable. There are but few of his works in public collections. (Biog. Univ.)

BERTIN, (Réné Joseph Hyacinth,) son of Exuperius, born at Gahard, near Rennes, April 10, 1767, studied medicine at Paris, and entered the medical department of the army. In 1798 he was deputed inspector-general of the French prisoners in England, whence after a year he returned, and was named principal physician to the hospital Cochin. In 1807 he was employed with the French and Prussian armies in Poland; and in 1822 he occupied a chair of Hygiène, vacant by the death of Hallé, at the Faculty of Medicine of Paris. He died in 1827, having published Quelques Observations Critiques, Philosophiques et Médicales, sur l'Angleterre, les Anglais, et les Français detenus dans les Prisons de Plymouth, Paris 1801, 12mo. Dissertation sur l'Emploi des Incisions dans les Plaies d'Armes à Feu, Paris, 1802, 8vo. Traité de la Maladie Vénérienne chez les Nouveau-nés, les Femmes et les Nourrices, Paris, 1810, 8vo. Traité des Maladies du Cœur et des Gros Vaisseaux, Paris, 1824, 8vo. He also translated Brown's Elements of Medicine from the Latin, Paris, 1805, 8vo, with the notes and commentary of Beddoes; and he made likewise a French translation from the Italian translation of the Entwurf-einer einfachen Arzneykunst, oder Erlaeuterung und Bestaetigung der Brownischen Arzneylehre, of M. A. Weickhard, by J. P. Frank, with a Preliminary Discourse, containing a life of

Brown, and an analysis of, and criticism upon, his doctrine.

BERTINI, (Salvator, 1721—1794,) a composer, born at Palermo, who composed both for theatres and churches, being successful in both styles. His melodies are sweet and simple in his dramatic pieces; in his ecclesiastical compositions they are pathetic and sublime. He died at his native place. (Dict. of Mus.)

BERTIUS, (Peter,) a geographer, once in good repute, born at Beveren, in Flanders, November 14, 1565. His father had become a Protestant, and this rendering a continuance in the Netherlands insecure, he took refuge in England, when Peter was about three months old. In the suburbs of London, accordingly, the young Bertius received the rudiments of his education; but when twelve years old he went over to Holland, his father having been appointed minister at Rotterdam. When only seventeen he began to live by teaching, but he subsequently travelled for improvement into Germany, with Lipsius, and afterwards into some of the neighbouring countries. On his return to Holland, he obtained some employments in the university of Leyden, but becoming active on the Arminian side, he was dismissed from all that he held, and refused any compensation, although burthened with a numerous family. He had already been honoured by Lewis XIII. with the title of his cosmographer, and he now took refuge in France, where he professed himself a Romanist, to the great disgust of the Protestants. He was requited by the professorship of rhetoric in the college of Boncourt, the office of royal historiographer, and an assistant regius professorship of mathematics. He died October 3, 1629, leaving several geographical works, of which the Theatrum Geographiæ Veteris, 2 vols, fol, 1618 and 1619, is most known. Bertius was, however, only editor of it, and seems to have discharged his duties as such, with no very exemplary care. (Chaufepié. Chalmers.)

BERTOLOTTI, (John Laurence, 1640—1721,) a painter, born at Genoa, a scholar of Castiglione, who painted history with considerable reputation, being chiefly employed upon altar-pieces. (Lanzi, Stor. Pitt. v. 280. Bryan's Dict.)

BERTON, (William,) one of Wickliffe's opponents, fellow of Merton college, and afterwards chancellor of the university of Oxford. He became conspicuous about the year 1381, and is the author of three tracts, all of which relate to the great reformer of Lutterworth:—1. Determinationes contra Wiclevum. 2. Sententia super justa ejus Condemnatione. 3. Contra ejus Articulos.

BERTRAM THE PRIEST, the most ordinary designation of an author who lived in the ninth century, and wrote a tract, On the Body and Blood of our Lord, which excited extraordinary notice about the time of the Reformation. It was originally published at Cologne, in 1532, and has been frequently translated and reprinted. By it archbishop Cranmer and many others were first brought to see the fallacy of believing that the Romish doctrine of transubstantiation is of high antiquity in the catholic church. The author, however, was evidently not called *Bertram*, but *Ratramn*, and it seems likely that his name was corrupted from the affix of *Be*, the first syllable of *Beatus*, not unusually placed before names of persons holden in high estimation for piety and learning. Such was, undoubtedly, the case with this remarkable ancient divine, who was a monk of Corbey, in the diocese of Amiens. A description of him as *Be-Ratramn* would easily be formed, from a cursory inspection of an ancient MS., in which words are very much run together, into *Bertram*, that being a well-known name. As there is, however, no reason for believing it the proper name of this important writer, any farther notice of him is unsuitable to this place. (Historical Dissertation prefixed to the Book of Bertram. Claude's Answer to Arnaud, 286.)

BERTRAM, (Augustus William,) a German physician, born Aug. 18, 1752, who died March 25, 1788, having published a German translation of Elliott's Elements of Physics applied to Medicine, Leipsic, 1784, 8vo.

BERTRAM, (Charles,) an English antiquary, of whose personal history little is known, and who is remarkable for having been the means of bringing into public notice the Treatise de Situ Britanniæ, attributed to Richard of Cirencester. He spent the greater part of his life in Copenhagen, where he was living in 1746, and was then professor of the English language in the Royal Marine Academy. In 1751 he printed at Copenhagen a work entitled Ethics, or Select Thoughts from several Authors, the words accented, to render the English pronunciation easy to foreigners. He was then, and had been for some time, in correspondence with Dr. Stukeley, to whom he communicated a copy of an important manuscript, which he alleged to be in his possession, which contained, together with a description of Britain, which purported to be by a monk of the fifteenth century, an ancient map of Roman Britain, and divers Itinera, apparently the work of the Roman period, some of which coincide with the Itinera in Antonine, and others are peculiar to this manuscript. Stukeley and the antiquaries of the time hailed the discovery as one of the most important which had been made for the Roman topography of Britain. Stukeley published the work at home, and there was an edition of it in the same year, 1757, by Bertram himself, published at Copenhagen, in a small volume, which contained two other early English writers. The title of the work was this:—Britannicarum Gentium Historiæ Antiquæ, Scriptures tres,—Ricardus Corinensis—Gildas Badonicus—Nennius Banchorensis—recensuit Notisque et Indice auxit Car. Bertramus. Doubts have been, however, from time to time expressed of the genuineness of this treatise; and though it has still many firm believers, the opinion that it is a fabrication appears rather to be gaining ground. It is a subject which well deserves a thorough examination. Bertram, we believe, continued to reside at Copenhagen till his death, but no search has hitherto brought to light the manuscript which he transcribed.

BERTRAM, (Cornelius Bonaventure,) a learned orientalist and critic, born at Thouars, in Poitou, in 1531. He studied at Paris, under Tunnebus, learned Hebrew there from D'Ange Caninius, and afterwards attended lectures on jurisprudence at Cahors. In 1568 he fled to Geneva, to escape the danger of being murdered for his religious opinions, received there the rights of citizenship, and an appointment as pastor; in 1566, the professorship of oriental languages; and in 1572 that of theology. In 1586 he removed to Frankenthal, and thence to Lausanne, where he was professor of theology. He died in 1594. He was one of the first translators of the Bible from the Hebrew; laboured with Beza and others at the French translation, published by the clergy of Geneva in 1588; had a share in the commentary of Mercerus on the book of Job; and contributed almost all the additions to the folio edition of Pagnini Thesaurus Linguæ Sanctæ, in 1575. He also wrote several works on the Jewish polity, and some elucidatory of obscure passages in the Old Testament. (Baur in Ersch und Gruber.)

BERTRAM, (John Frederic,) a distinguished theologian of his time, and a successful investigator of the history of East Friesland, born at Ulm in 1699. He died in 1741. Besides his many contributions to the history of East Friesland, he wrote several introductions to the belles-lettres and philosophical sciences, some sacred poems, and many philosophical and theological works. (Ersch und Gruber.)

BERTRAND, (John Baptist,) a physician, born at Martignes, July 12, 1670. He was originally destined for the church, and therefore commenced his studies in theology; but feeling much greater inclination for medicine, he went to Montpelier, and there took the degree of doctor of medicine. He then returned to his native place, exerted himself most laudably during the plague at Marseilles, in 1720, for which he was granted a pension by the government. He was an experienced physician. He died Sept. 10, 1752, having published, Reflexions sur la Système de la Trituration, Trevaux, 1714, 8vo. Observations sur la Maladie Contagieuse de Marseille, which was printed, together with the Relation Historique de la Peste de Marseille, Cologne, 1720, Lyons, 1723, 8vo. It is unquestionably one of the best records of this celebrated pestilence. It was translated into English by Miss Plumptre, Lond. 1805, 8vo. Dissertation sur l'Air Maritime, 1724, 4to. Lettres à M. Dirdier sur le Mouvement des Muscles, 1732, 12mo.

BERTRAND, (Thomas Bernard,) a French physician, born at Paris, Oct. 22, 1682. He took the degree of doctor of medicine in 1710, was made professor of surgery in 1724, of pharmacy in 1738, became dean of the faculty in 1740, and professor of materia medica in 1741. He was, for many years, one of the physicians of the Hôtel Dieu, and he died April 19, 1751. He wrote,—Ergò Catamenia à Plethorâ, Paris, 1711, 4to. Ergò in Ascite paracentesin tardare Malum, Paris, 1730, 4to. Ergò Aquæ potus omnium saluberrimus, Paris, 1739, 4to. Ergò Venæsectio Operationum frequentior, simul periculosior, Paris, 1744, 4to. Ergò Alvis Astrictioribus Medicina in

Alimento, et blandâ Catharsi, Paris, 1747, 4to. He left many manuscripts, one of which only has been printed:—Notice des Hommes les plus Célèbres de la Faculté de Médecine en l'Université de Paris, depuis 1110 jusqu'en 1750, extraité du Manuscrit de feu T. B. Bernard, communiquée par son fils, et redigée par J. A. Hazon, Paris, 1778, 4to.

BERTRANDI, (John Ambrose Maria,) a celebrated surgeon, born at Turin, Oct. 17, 1723, the son of an ignorant barber and phlebotomist. His mother was of superior talent, and promoted the education of her son, who displayed great aptitude for learning, and acquired a great knowledge of Greek and Latin, logic, geometry, mathematics, and physics. Finding his progress in learning impeded by narrow circumstances, he would have entered into the order of the Minorites, but his parents were averse to his taking the habit, and urged him, by prayers and entreaties, to abandon all thoughts of an ecclesiastical life. While thus embarrassed, he attracted the notice of Sebastian Klingher, the professor of surgery, a very able man, and surgeon to the king, who possessed, of right, the power of selecting a student for education in the Royal College of the Provinces. He made choice of Bertrandi, who thus became destined to the study of surgery. In this pursuit he showed no less zeal than he had previously exercised in other branches of learning. He was deeply interested in dissection, and in three years was named reader in anatomy. In another year he was appointed reader in practical medicine; and being familiar with the Latin language, he was soon after made reader of the Institutes of Medicine, which office had never before been entrusted to a surgeon, but to the most able physicians. The king, Charles Emanuel, aware of his ability, prevailed upon him to travel in France and England. He arrived at Paris in 1752, and was presented to Lewis XV. by the ambassador, who took him into his house, and honoured him with his friendship. He studied with great zeal, and read to the Academy of Surgery a memoir upon Hydrocele, in October, 1753, and in 1754 another, on the Cause of Abscess of the Liver supervening in cases of Injuries of the Head. He was shortly after named foreign associate of the Academy, and the king confirmed the nomination. He then visited London, resided with Mr. Bromfield, the surgeon of St. George's Hospital, and made himself acquainted with the practice of the English, as he had previously done that of the French surgeons. He now determined upon returning to Turin. At Piedmont he was well received by the court, his reputation being known; and the king was induced to create for him an extraordinary chair of practical surgery. He acquitted himself, as a professor, with great distinction. He instructed many able pupils, and gained such renown, that the king determined upon establishing an amphitheatre of anatomy, a school for midwifery, and a veterinary school, upon the model of those instituted at Lyons, in 1761. Bertrandi was appointed chief surgeon to the king, and professor in ordinary of practical surgery. These distinctions served only to increase a zeal for his profession, that was only subdued by an attack of dropsy of the chest, which terminated his life, Dec. 6, 1765. Bertrandi must be considered as one of the most distinguished anatomists and surgeons that Italy has produced, and his writings are remarkable for their order and precision. The most considerable of them are,—Dissertationes Anatomicæ de Hepate et Oculo, Torini, 1748, 4to. Trattato delle Operazioni di Chirurgia, Niza, 1763, 2 vols, 8vo. This was translated into German, Vienna, 1769, 8vo; and into French, by Salier de la Romillais, Paris, 1769, 8vo. The best edition is that of Penchienati and Brugnona, Torino, 1802, 3 vols, 8vo.

BERTRIC, king of Wessex, like all those who filled the throne of that country, a descendant of Cerdic, but, it seems, not in a direct line, or, perhaps, even so near in the strict order of succession as Alkmund, vassal king of Kent. Why he was preferred to that prince does not appear; but advanced age, or some other unfitness, might have weighed with the West-Saxon legislature in its choice of Bertric. He came to the throne, according to the Saxon Chronicle, in 784; but his accession has been referred upon other authorities to 783, 785, and 786. He had no sooner established himself than he became exceedingly jealous of Egbert, Alkmund's son, eventually founder of a consolidated Anglo-Saxon monarchy, and heir of claims to the kingdom of Wessex, quite as good as his own, if not better. Egbert became, accordingly, apprehensive of safety unless he could find a refuge out of Bertric's reach; and he sought the court of Offa, king of Mercia, the most powerful of contemporary Anglo-Saxon kings. Bertric then lost no time in making overtures of marriage to Edburga, Offa's daughter, and these being accepted, Egbert fled out of England, and found an asylum with Charlemagne, a most fortunate preparation for the distinguished part which he eventually played in his own country. Bertric's marriage with Edburga, which was solemnized in 787, secured his political position at the price of his domestic happiness. The lady proved violent and imperious, with all the ill qualities of her father, Offa, but without his experience and knowledge of the world to mitigate them. Her husband appears to have been a religious and good-natured man, but easily led away by favourites. He had, however, no sooner fixed his affections upon any one, than Edburga did all in her power to turn them in an opposite direction; and if her artifices failed, poison removed the obnoxious individual. She had endeavoured vainly to shake her husband's predilection for Worr, a young alderman, or earl, and hence made no scruple of resorting to her usual policy; but the drugged bowl did more execution than she desired. Bertric himself tasted of it, and to both him and Worr it proved fatal. This appears to have been in the year 800, although there are reasons for placing it two years later. Early in this reign, the Northmen, or Danes, made their first descent upon England, on the Dorsetshire coast, but only with three ships, back to which they were driven, leaving their plunder behind. Bertric is not known to have left any family, and thus a way was opened for the succession of Egbert, who hastened home from his continental exile, trained for war and policy under Charlemagne, one of the ablest monarchs that history records. (Sax. Chr. Malmesb. i. 59, 127.)

BERTRICH, (F. J.) a German miscellaneous writer, born at Weimar, 1747, who, after studying first theology and then law, became, in 1769, tutor to the sons of the baron von Echt, who had been Danish ambassador in Spain, and who inspired him with that love for Spanish and Portuguese literature which afterwards led to such useful results. He appeared on the field of literature under the patronage of Wieland. His too free translation of Don Quixote was published 1775. He had already, in 1773, become the coadjutor of Wieland in the publication of the German Mercury, and subsequently editorial business largely occupied his time. In the production of many of the works which bear his name, he had doubtless but a very slight share: he laboured principally in planning and projecting; in encouraging and directing others. He was intended by Nature for a man of business rather than for a man of letters, his talents being chiefly of a practical order; and in creative or original power as a writer he was altogether deficient. Hence his bookish friends at Weimar, during its celebrated period, made very light of his pretensions to literary fame; and his good-tempered officiousness appears to have rendered him sometimes an object of their ridicule. (See Böttiger's Lit. Zustände und Zeitgenossen, 1838.) The more important works bearing his name, not enumerated above, are his Magazine of Spanish Literature, 1780-3, 3 vols; his Allgemeine Geograp. Ephemered, Weimar, 1806-22; and his Neue Bibliothek der Reisebeschreibungen, Weimar, 1815-22.

BERTULF, king of Mercia, brother of Wiglaf, who consented to hold his throne under Egbert, king of Wessex. Bertulf became king in 839, and was dethroned by the Danes in 851. He died shortly afterwards. (Sim. Dunelm. 120. Bromton, 778. Hardy's Note to Malmesbury, i. 133.)

BERTUSIO, (John Baptist,) a painter of the Bolognese school, formerly pupil of Denys Calvart, but he abandoned his master's style, and endeavoured, though with little success, to imitate that of Guido. He left a variety of paintings at Bologna, his native city, and in the surrounding villages, "displaying," says Lanzi, "beauties more apparent than real." Bertusio died in 1644. (Lanzi, Stor. Pitt. v. 49. Bryan's Dict.)

BERULLE, (Peter de,) an illustrious French controversialist and cardinal, born February 4, 1575, at the manor-house of Serilly, in the neighbourhood of Troyes, of a family known in Champagne from the beginning of the fourteenth century. He became early conspicuous for piety, learning, and a winning address. His zeal first showed itself in disputation with the protestants, who were then numerous in France, and with whom he argued at great advantage from the sweetness of his manners. A man of family at once so able, conciliating, and exemplary, was naturally regarded as extremely fit for reviving that monastic taste in France, which might find a vent for some of her gloomier or more ascetic spirits, but which the gradual subsidence of ancient fanaticism, and protestant exposures of the conventual system, had rendered an instrument of little practical utility

Berulle's first exertions in this way were directed to the naturalization among his countrymen of a Spanish Carmelite society; in which he succeeded, after a journey to Spain in 1603, and after much opposition from those of that order on both sides of the Pyrenees. Those in Spain did not like the departure of a detachment from their body into a foreign country; those in France were displeased at seeing any of their affairs in the hands of an individual not commissioned by themselves. Afterwards, Berulle grappled with still more serious difficulties as founder of a French congregation of priests of the Oratory, a society of seculars recently established in Italy by Philip Neri. He was urged into this undertaking by the pressing solicitations of Francis de Sales, and others. Feeling satisfied that such a body as that of the Oratory was likely to serve the Romish cause in France, he would not rest until, in 1613, he had overcome all opposition to it; and that of the Jesuits, who felt the institution of this new society as an attack upon their own, proved extremely embarrassing. An Englishman, however, chiefly feels an interest in Berulle, because he solicited at Rome the dispensation under which Henrietta Maria was married to Charles I., and he accompanied that princess into England. In his application to the papal court, he argued against objections by charging what he called the English schism upon want of a conciliatory spirit towards Henry VIII.; and when he came over with the princess, his amiable manners gained him universal respect. His character was also perfectly disinterested. He made a vow in early life to accept of no ecclesiastical dignity; and in obedience to it refused several tempting offers. At length, Urban VIII. took upon himself to dispense with this vow, and Berulle was made cardinal, in 1627, to the great disgust of several bishops, who thought such a dignity proper only for a Frenchman of their own order. To sustain it he accepted of two abbacies. He died while saying mass, October 12, 1629. During his life he was the patron of letters, and smoothed obstacles at Rome to the printing of Lejay's Polyglott. His own works, which were chiefly controversial, had great popularity in their day. They were collected, in 1644, in two folio volumes. (Moreri. Biog. Univ.)

BERURIA, a Hebrew female, mentioned in several places of the Talmud as uncommonly learned. She lectured on the 300 lessons of the wise men, and ridiculed the saying of the Hebrew sages, "That the knowledge of women was small," unless it had this qualification, "except that of Beruria." Her husband, jealous, perhaps, of her superior learning, is said to have laid a trap to secure evidence warranting a jealousy of a more ordinary kind; the stratagem was successful, say the Hebrew historians: Beruria strangled herself for shame, and her husband fled to Babylon. (Bartoloccius.)

BERWICK, (Marshal,) a celebrated commander, illegitimate son of James II., when duke of York, by Arabella Churchill, sister to John Churchill, originally his page, but eventually the renowned duke of Marlborough. The offspring of this amour was named James, after his father, and the surname given him was Fitz-James. He was born August 21, 1670, and at seven years of age sent over to France for education. On his father's accession in 1685, he went into the imperial army, to be trained for a military life under Charles, the famous duke of Lorraine, and he was present at most of the great operations which occurred about that time in Hungary. In 1687 he was created duke of Berwick; and before the next year closed, he became an exile with his father in France. He passed over with that misguided prince into Ireland, was present at the battle of the Boyne, and witnessed with him the final ruin of his hopes in the naval engagement of La Hogue. He then entered the French service, was made a marshal in 1706, and in the war of succession, acquired great reputation in Spain. His first efforts were not particularly fortunate; but in 1707 he struck a blow that established Philip V. on the Spanish throne. The associated English and Portuguese generals entertained hopes of crushing his forces, which were posted along the frontiers of Aragon and Valencia, in detail, before he could receive fresh succours from France. Hence they suddenly collected their troops to the amount of 30,000 men, and endeavoured to break into his quarters. Berwick, however, detained them by throwing garrisons into Villena and Chinchilla, until he had reunited his army on the *Vega*, or plain of Almanza, in New Castile, where he was opportunely joined by a part of the expected reinforcements. Of this the allied commanders were unaware, and they imprudently ventured into action, April 25, 1707. At first, their boldness appeared likely to succeed; but the skill and firmness of Berwick eventually triumphed over every obstacle, and rendered the defeat of Almanza almost as disastrous to the allies, as that of Bleuheim had been to the French. The victorious marshal, in recompense of this great service, was created a Spanish grandee, and duke of Liria and Xerica. He was subsequently entrusted by the French government with a series of important commands, and showed himself upon all occasions worthy of the confidence reposed in him. He was killed by a cannon-ball, June 12, 1734, before the walls of Philipsburg on the Rhine, a strong place, of which the siege was undertaken by his advice. Berwick's manners were cold, thoughtful, and rather severe; but his habits were correct, and his whole career was that of a great man. His English honours were forfeited by an attainder passed against him in 1695; but French and Spanish titles conferred upon him descended to his posterity. In 1695, he married an Irish lady, daughter of Burke, earl of Clanricard. From this marriage came the dukes of Liria, in Spain. In 1699 he married a second wife, named Bulkeley, and by her he was father to the first marshal de Fitz-James. In 1700, Lewis XIV. erected the estate of Warthi, near Clermont, in Beauvoisis, into a dukedom, with a peerage for marshal Berwick, and his heirs by the second marriage. The name of Warthi was afterwards changed for that of Fitz-James. In 1770, the duke of Fitz-James published the memoirs of the marshal, with a continuation to his death, in 2 vols, 12mo. (Coxe's Memoirs of the Kings of Spain, i. 408, iii. 268. Biog. Univ. Banks's Dormant and Extinct Baronage, iii. 80.)

BERYLLUS, bishop of Bostra, in Arabia, about the year 244, remarkable for broaching one among the speculative opinions upon our Saviour's divinity, which distracted the religious world in his time. Until the appearance of this new theory, Beryllus was universally respected as a pious and learned man, who had long discharged his duties in a most satisfactory manner. The doctrine which lowered his credit, was, that Jesus Christ, before living among men, had no distinct essence of his own; and hence had no divinity proper to himself, but only the Father's divinity dwelling in him. He is, therefore, considered as a sort of Sabellian; but some have not ranked him among heretics, because he would not stand by his judgment, when its unsoundness was pointed out. A council was assembled for this purpose, at Bostra, in 244, and Origen then exerted himself to convince the bishop that he was mistaken. He succeeded completely, Beryllus professing himself convinced of his rashness in declining from the established faith. Beryllus wrote some small treatises, and some epistles to Origen, thanking him for the pains that he took in confuting his errors. In St. Jerome's time, the particulars of the conference were extant, by which the bishop of Bostra was brought to abandon his hasty speculations; but at present nothing remains written by him. (Chaufepié. Cave, Hist. Lit. Mosheim, i. 268. Du Pin. i. 116.)

BESECKE, (J. Melchior Gottlieb,) professor of law at Mittau, born in 1746. His great claim on the gratitude of the Courlanders was the share he took in the foundation of a poor-house in Mittau, which was finished, with very slender means, in 1795. Besides a principal share in the Thesaurus juris Cambialis, he wrote Contributions to the Natural History of the Birds of Courland, 8vo, Mittau, 1789. Attempt to sketch a Complete Plan of Laws for Crimes and Punishments, 8vo, Dessau, 1783. Sketch of a System of Transcendental Chemistry, 8vo, Leipsic, 1787. Specimen of a Critical Commentary on Kant's Critique of Pure Reason, 8vo, Mittau, 1789. Attempt at a History of Hypotheses on the Generation of Animals, 8vo, Mittau, 1797. Attempt at a History of Natural History, 8vo, *ib.* 1802, (reaching from the creation of the world to 1791.) He died in 1802. (Ersch und Gruber.)

BESLER, (Basil,) an eminent botanist, born at Nuremberg in 1561. He had but little education, and practised pharmacy, but his great pursuit was botany; hence he established a botanic garden, and entered into correspondence with the chief botanists of his day. Plumier named a genus of plants (Besleria) in honour of his labours. His chief work, however, was revised, if not in a great measure composed, by Inngermann, professor at the university of Altdorf, and the synonyms supplied by his brother Jerome Besler. The education Basil had received was insufficient for such a work, which is altogether very magnificent, and has 356 folio plates, containing 1086 figures, engraved on copper.

BESLER, (Jerome,) brother to the preceding, born at Nuremberg, September 29, 1566. He took the degree of doctor of medicine at Basle, in 1592; and died

November 22, 1632, having printed:—Dissertatio de Hydrope, Basil, 1592, 4to. Epistola Medica, inserted in the Cista Medica of J. Hornung; and the preface and synonyms of his brother's Hortus Egstettensis, Norimb. 1613, 1640, 1750.

BESLER, (Michael Robert,) born at Nuremberg, July 5, 1607, doctor of medicine at Altdorf. He was well versed in natural history and antiquities. He died in 1661, leaving, besides some medical works, Gazophylacium Rerum naturalium è Regno Vegetabili, Animali, et Minerali, &c. Norimb. 1642, folio. Mantissa ad viretum Stirpium, Fruticum et Plantarum, *ib.* 1646, 1648, folio.

BESLY, (John,) king's advocate at Fontenay-le-comte, born in 1572, an active opponent to the reception of the council of Trent, and deeply skilled in the history and antiquities of his native province. He died in 1644. His principal work is, Histoires des Comtes de Poitou et Ducs de Guienne; the fruit of forty years' study. (Biog. Univ.)

BESMI, the name of three Turkish poets. The first, born at Aidin, in Roumelia, died towards the end of the reign of Selim I. The second, Mustafa Besmi, a descendant of Mohammed Efendi, who built the college of Merlevis, at the New Gate of Constantinople, accompanied Mustafa Pasha of Rodosto to the siege of Vienna in 1682, and was killed by the bursting of a bomb. The third died in 1708, at Chios. (Ersch und Gruber.)

BESNARD, (Francis Joseph,) a physician, born at Buschsweiler, in Alsace, May 20, 1748. He was educated at Hagenau, in the Society of the Jesuits, and afterwards sent to Strasburg to study medicine. In 1775 he took the degree of doctor of medicine, and exercised his profession and was appointed physician-in-chief to Maximilian, the count palatine. In 1783 he proposed to the Academy of Sciences a plan to supersede the employment of mercury as a remedy in certain diseases, and a committee was appointed to take the subject into consideration; the Revolution, however, suspended its labours. In 1790 Besnard returned to the palatinate, practised at Manheim, and was afterwards placed at the head of the hospitals of Munich. He successfully laboured to introduce vaccination into Bavaria. He died June 16, 1814, having printed some professional works.

BESODUN, or BESTON, (John,) prior of the Carmelites at Lynn, highly distinguished as a learned man in his day. He graduated as doctor of divinity at the universities of Cambridge and Paris; he died at Lynn in the year 1428. He is the author of—1. Super Universalia Holcothi. 2. Compendium Theologiæ. 3. Determinationum Liber. This book is not mentioned by either Bale or Pits, but is recorded by Leland; and Tanner thinks that it may be the same as the Ord. Quest. Liber, mentioned by Bale. 4. Sacrarum Concionum Liber. 5. Sermones in Evangelia. 6. Sermones in Epistolas. 7. Lecturæ Sacræ Scripturæ. 8. Rudimenta Logices. 9. De Virtutibus et Vitiis oppositis. 10. Epistolarum Libri Duo. 11. De Trinitate: and another set of sermons. Some of these titles are given here for the first time from catalogues of manuscripts; several of them are preserved in the public library of the university of Cambridge.

BESOLD, (Christophe,) an historical writer, born at Tubingen in 1577; who, becoming a Romanist, just before his death in 1638, received an offer from the pope of a professorship at Bologna, and a pension of 4000 ducats. His principal work is Historia Imperii Constantinopolitani et Turcici. (Biog. Univ.)

BESOZZI, (Ambrose,) an architectural painter of Milan, born in 1648, and died in 1706.

BESSARION, (John), a cardinal, eminent for scholarship, patronage of learning, and an abandonment of the Greek church for the Roman. This last circumstance has led his literary painters to use very different colours. Romanists bring him upon the scene, prejudiced against papal peculiarities and prerogatives, but constrained by the light which gradually broke in upon his ingenuous mind to admit himself hitherto mistaken. Protestants represent an ecclesiastic of consummate art, who, seeing the approaching ruin of his own country, eagerly embraced an opportunity of establishing himself handsomely in Italy. This remarkable man was born at Trebizond, as it might seem from an epitaph written by himself, in 1389; but copies of this inscription are not uniform, and Bandini, who wrote Bessarion's life, places his birth in 1395. One of his masters was Gemistius Pletho, celebrated for introducing the study of Plato among scholars in the west: hence, probably, his mind was prepared for a belief in purgatory, that being a doctrine which Platonics have inculcated. As Bessarion's age advanced, he became a monk of the order of St. Basil, and he spent one-and-twenty years in a monastery in the Peloponnese. His employments there, however, were so scholarly and intellectual, that people naturally thought him fit for great emergencies. Hence John Paleologus, the Greek emperor, was glad of his assistance in an attempt to gain relief from the Christians of the west. It was growing every day more clear that nothing but effectual aid on the European side could long save the throne of Constantinople from falling a prey to Turkish ambition, and it was well known, that western sympathy was hopeless without concessions to the Latin church. The emperor was, therefore, driven to the necessity of expressing a disposition for such, and he came to the council of Ferrara, in 1438, attended by some of his principal divines, ostensibly for that purpose. Bessarion was one of his clerical attendants, having previously been decorated with the title of archbishop of Nice, for the sake of appearing with suitable dignity. In other respects his appearance was that of an able and scholarly disputant, quite equal to meet any advocate on the papal side. After gaining, however, great applause by this display of eloquence and information, he began to show signs of an alteration in his opinion; and before the council, which removed from Ferrara to Florence for fear of a pestilence, finished its deliberations, Bessarion was a declared Romanist. Interested motives were assigned upon plausible grounds for his conversion; and Mark, archbishop of Ephesus, who would not give way, branded him as a bastard Greek, false to his country and his church. Romanists attribute Mark's pertinacity to envy of Bessarion. The two were able and admired above any of their national deputation; but at length, Mark is considered as discerning, with deep mortification, a general disposition to prefer his former friend. Hence the reproaches with which he assailed him, and his own immovable determination to stand by the religious principles that he had ever entertained. Bessarion having gone over himself, was employed by the pope to gain the other Greeks; and as their country's cause was nearly desperate, rewards, persuasions, threats, and promises, induced most of them to comply. They admitted a double procession of the Holy Ghost, a purgation of disembodied souls by fire, and the papal supremacy. On Bessarion's return to Greece, his distressed sovereign, and such as were willing to purchase Latin help almost on any terms, would have raised him to the patriarchate of Constantinople. But the people generally abhorred him as an apostate; and the seeming reconciliation with Rome, of which he and a few others said so much, was denounced as an unprincipled compromise, accomplished by fraud and artifice. Bessarion, therefore, found himself under the necessity of taking refuge in Italy, and he occupied a splendid station there during all the rest of his life. He had been made cardinal, in 1439, by Eugenius IV. as an immediate acknowledgment of his adhesion to the papal church, and he subsequently became archbishop of Siponto. Pius II. also pretended to confer upon him the patriarchate of Constantinople. Of substantial distinctions he had an ample share, being much employed by successive popes, and more than once rather likely to be elected pope himself. Whatever may be thought of the road by which he found his way to so much worldly prosperity, he showed himself worthy of it. His private habits never departed greatly from those of a Peloponesian monk; but his ample revenues found generous hospitality for men of genius, and for the collection of a noble library. Bessarion died at Ravenna, on his way from France, whither he had gone as ambassador from Sixtus IV., Nov. 19, 1472. His body was taken to Rome for interment, and the pope attended his funeral, an honour not hitherto paid to the memory of any cardinal. His library he left to the senate of Venice; a legacy of considerable importance, as he had procured manuscripts, regardless of expense, from all parts of Greece. Bessarion left numerous literary remains; but most of those that are strictly theological, except such portions as are in the collections of the councils, have never been printed. A treatise of his, De Sacramento Eucharistiæ, was, however, published at Paris, in the 26th vol. of the Bibliotheca Patrum; and four small treatises were published at Rome, in 1634, in a collection of Opuscula Theologica. Bessarion's most celebrated works are Latin translations of Xenophon's Memorabilia, and Aristotle's Metaphysics, together with a treatise Adversus Calumniatorem Platonis. This calumniator was George of Trebizond, who had been incited to the offensive attack by Gemistius Pletho, Bessarion's tutor, a violent Platonist, and hence led into an invidious comparison of him with Aristotle. It was but a diminutive production, but garnished with such reflections upon Aristotle as gave his admirers great offence. Three of them accordingly, Gennadius, George of Trebizond, and Theodore Gaza, came forward in the great Peripatetic's vindication. Bessarion received an appeal from the contending parties during the heat of their dispute, and counselled moderation, arguing that the two philosophers, rightly understood, were not really so far apart in sentiment as a hasty consideration might lead one to suppose. George of Trebizond, however, was irritated instead of convinced, and he lost no time in writing the Comparatio Platonis et Aristotelis, a long piece to prove Aristotle's inconceivable superiority to Plato, and treating the latter's admirers with contempt. It was this work which brought forth Bessarion's from the press of Sweynheim and Pannartz, Adversus Calumniatorem. The book is without date, but it is unquestionably very early, and is of extreme rarity: the conjectural date is 1469. There are also editions of 1503 and 1516, which too are very rare. Another of Bessarion's works has a value of the same kind. His Orationes de gravissimis Periculis, quæ Reipublicæ Christianæ à Turcâ jam tum impendere providebat, printed at Rome in 1543, have likewise become very scarce. (Cave, Hist. Lit. Mosheim, iii. 27. Clement. Bibliothèque Curieux, iii. 250.)

BESSE, (John,) a physician, born at Peyrouse, who took the degree of doctor of medicine in 1713 at Paris, and was afterwards appointed physician to the queen dowager of Spain. He died at Paris at an advanced age, having published several works. It is sufficient to enumerate, Des Passions de l'Homme, où, suivant les Règles de l'Analyse, l'on recherche leurs Natures, leurs Causes, et leurs Effets. Toulouse, 1699, 8vo. Recherches Analytiques sur la Structure des Parties du Corps Humain, où l'on explique leur Ressort, leur Jeu, et leur Usage, *ib.* 1701, 2 vols, 8vo, Paris, 1702. Lettre à l'Auteur (J. C. A. Helvetius) du Nouveau Livre de l'Economie Animale, et des Observations sur les Petites Véroles, Paris, 1723, 8vo. Replique aux Lettres de M. Helvetius, &c. Amst. (Paris) 1726, 12mo.

BESSE, or BESSET, (Henry de,) a French gentleman, employed under the Marquess de Villacerf, inspector of royal buildings. He published, Relations des Campagnes de Rocroy et de Fribourg, en 1643 et 1644, Paris, 1673, 12mo. This has been attributed to the Marquess de la Moussaye; and, being in good credit, has been reprinted both in the Recueil de Pièces, by La Monnoye, and at the conclusion of the Mémoires pour servir à l'Histoire de M. le Prince (de Condé), 1693, 2 vols. 12mo. (Biog. Univ.)

BESSEL, (Godfrey von,) a German Benedictine, born in the electorate of Mentz, Sept. 5, 1672, and employed by the archbishop-elector in various diplomatic missions, but eventually elected abbot of Gottwich, in Austria, in 1720. He died Jan. 20, 1749, having published St. Austin's Letters to Optatus on the Punishments of Unbaptized Infants; and being long thought author of the Chronicon Gottwicense, a work really written by Francis Joseph de Hahn, afterwards bishop of Bamberg, and so admirably illustrated by documents that it has thrown great light upon German affairs, and has been even reckoned comparable to the De Re Diplomaticâ of Mabillon. (Biog. Univ.)

BESSENYEI, (George,) a Hungarian writer of the eighteenth century, once in the Hungarian guard at Vienna, and on his retirement from it, creditably distinguished in the literature of his country. He wrote some tragedies, a discourse on the truth of Christianity, and a translation of Pope's Essay on Man. (Biog. Univ.)

BESSER, (John von,) a German poet, born in Courland in 1654, and long employed, in ceremonial capacities, at the courts of Berlin and Dresden. He died at the latter place in 1729, leaving poems published in a collected form at Leipsic in 1752, and an account of Frederic the First's coronation, twice printed at Berlin. (Biog. Univ.)

BESSIÈRES, (John Baptist,) one of the revolutionary French marshals, born at Preissac, in Languedoc, Aug. 6, 1768, of a needy and obscure family. He had, consequently, very little education, and his original calling was the humble one of a wig-maker; undoubtedly at that time of rather more importance than alterations in fashion have since rendered it. In 1792, however, the lowering aspect of French politics rendered a military life a general object of attention to enterprising youth, and young Bessières entered as a private in the constitutional guard of Lewis XVI. He proved so faithful to his unfortunate master's cause, that concealment at one time was necessary to shield him from republican vengeance. When royalty was finally overthrown, he returned to the army, and rose gradually to the rank of captain. In 1795, he was in Italy with

Buonaparte, and distinguished himself upon several occasions, particularly at Roveredo and Rivoli. He was accordingly sent to Paris, to present the captured colours to the Directory; and thenceforth he became connected indissolubly with Napoleon. He was with him in Egypt, returned with him to France, and was highly serviceable to him when arrived at Paris. Being subsequently with him in Italy, he contributed materially to the victory of Marengo, and his fortune was now completely made. He was appointed general of division, Sept. 13, 1802; marshal of the empire, May 19, 1804; and finally, duke of Istria. He subsequently made a conspicuous figure at the great battles of Austerlitz, Jena, and Eylau; accompanied Napoleon to the interview of Tilsit; and receiving a command in Spain, gained a decisive victory over Cuesta. He was then summoned into Germany, to grapple with Austria; and he commanded the imperial guard at Landshut, Elsberg, and Wagram. At the last great battle, his horse was shot under him, to the extreme concern of his men, who set up a shout of grief, supposing him killed. When the campaign was over, Bessières was despatched into Holland, which England had invaded, and his exertions were soon crowned with complete success. He subsequently figured at the marriage of Napoleon, and he was then sent into Spain again, but he found such difficulties there as made him speedily solicit his recall. Being gratified, he shared in Buonaparte's disastrous Russian expedition, and when the emperor decamped, Bessières remained in Germany, to save all that could be saved of his imperial friend's once boasted army. At the beginning of 1813, he made a hasty visit to Paris, but he soon returned to Germany, to command again the imperial guard in the approaching Saxon campaign. He was killed, however, by a cannon-ball, May 1, the evening before the battle of Lutzen, when making observations of the enemy's position, near the place where Gustavus Adolphus fell. (Biog. Univ. Suppl.)

BESSIN, (William,) a learned French Benedictine, born in Normandy, March 27, 1654. He died at Rouen, Oct. 18, 1726, leaving Réflexions sur le Nouveau Système du R. P. Lami, 1697; Concilia Rotomagensis Provinciæ, 1717. (Biog. Univ.)

BESSON, (James,) an ingenious French mechanician, professor of mathematics at Orleans in 1569, author of some scientific works highly esteemed in their day; one of which, Theatrum Instrumentorum et Machinarum, Lyons, 1578, fol. subsequently augmented by Paschalis, was translated into French, Italian, and German. (Biog. Univ.)

BESSON, (Joseph,) a Jesuit missionary, born at Carpentras, in Provence, in 1607. He died at Aleppo in 1691, leaving several works, of which the most curious is, La Sainte Syrie, ou des Missions des Pères de la Compagnie de Jésus en Syrie, Paris, 1660, 8vo. (Biog. Univ.)

BESSUS, governor or satrap of Bactria, notorious in the history of Alexander the Great for the murder of Darius. That unfortunate prince, finding his affairs all but ruined by the battle of Gaugamela, could see no hope of retrieving them, or hardly of personal safety, unless in Bactria, where mountains might protect him from the conqueror's advance. But while on his way thither he became apprehensive of being overtaken; and hence resolved upon making a stand with such forces as were then with him, these falling little or nothing short of forty thousand men. Bessus, however, and Nabarzanes, another Persian of distinction, disapproved of this determination, and finding the king unwilling to proceed, made him their prisoner. They then placed him in a close carriage, and carried him on with them towards Bactria; intending, it is thought, in case of Alexander's pursuit, to make terms by delivering him into his hands, or in case of no pursuit to kill him, and seize, if possible, his kingdom, or as much of it as might prove attainable. After some delay, the Macedonian conqueror overtook them, and then they would have persuaded Darius to mount a horse for greater expedition, and flee with them. He refused, and after giving him some desperate wounds, they left him dying in his carriage. After he was dead, Alexander came up, and was deeply moved at seeing the mangled corpse of one who had so lately been esteemed the greatest and most fortunate of men. He would have then pursued Bessus, but found him beyond reach at such an advanced season of the year. Early, however, in the following spring, that of 329 B.C., Alexander marched into Bactria, and driving Bessus out of the country, he marched after him into Sogdiana, whither the traitor had retired, in hopes that the river Oxus might be found impassable by the Macedonians.

In this he was deceived, and his followers, despairing of safety unless from unqualified submission, delivered him into Alexander's hands. By that conqueror he was delivered for punishment to Oxatres, brother of Darius, and under his direction Bessus was executed as a traitor with ingenious cruelty. (Prideaux, Connect. i. 398.)

BESTUZHEV-RUMIN, (Count Alexei Petrovitch,) a Russian statesman, born at Moscow, May 22, 1692, and educated at Berlin. Travelling subsequently through part of Germany, at Hanover he was greatly noticed by the elector (afterwards George I. of England), who made him one of his pages, and in 1714 sent him as envoy to St. Petersburg, to announce his accession to the British throne. When he quitted his service, he entered that of the dowager duchess of Courland; and in 1720 he was appointed Russian resident at the court of Denmark. When Anne became empress, he was removed from Copenhagen to Hamburg, in capacity of envoy extraordinary for Lower Saxony; but in 1734 he was sent again to Denmark, where he remained till 1740, when he was recalled to St. Petersburg, and made one of the cabinet ministers. For this advancement he was indebted to the favourite Biron, who hoped to find in him a counterpoise to the abilities and influence of Ostermann. The fall of the favourite, however, involved Bestuzhev; he was put under arrest, and though shortly after liberated, did not regain any office or employment till after the accession of Elizabeth. The empress herself was by no means disposed to favour him, but motives of policy prevailed over her personal dislike; for Russia had just lost two of its ablest ministers in Ostermann and Golovkin, (both of whom had been disgraced and banished;) therefore, at the urgent recommendation of her chief adviser and favourite, Lestocq, Elizabeth restored Bestuzhev to office.

A new course was now opened to him, and his advance in it was rapid. Honours and emoluments poured in upon him; and for fourteen years he virtually directed the state-machinery of a vast empire. His policy was once, according to Malinovsky, crossed by a very trifling incident. He had prevailed upon the empress to break with Prussia, and she had not only taken up her pen to sign the manifesto, but had written the letter E, when a fly happened to light upon it and smear the paper. This was regarded as a bad omen, and she refused her signature! Thus was delayed the rupture with Prussia for two years; yet, although when hostilities took place, some splendid successes were obtained by the Russians, they did not contribute to the minister's security. The immediate cause of his disgrace is variously related; according to some, he incurred Elizabeth's resentment by ordering the return of the army after the battle of Gross Jagersdorf, when she was rendered incapable of attending to business, by an illness expected to terminate mortally, in order to conciliate the heir to the throne (Peter III.), who was an admirer of Frederic II.; while others say, that he had prevailed upon the empress to exclude Peter from the succession, and transfer his rights to his infant son Paul, under the sole guardianship of Catharine; on which the other parties in the cabinet turned his schemes against him, representing him as guilty of misleading his sovereign, and inducing her to sanction a piece of treasonable injustice. Certain it is that he was arrested (Feb. 1758), tried by a special commission, deprived of all his offices and emoluments, declared infamous, and banished to Goretovo, a village 120 versts from Moscow, where he had no other dwelling than an ordinary peasant's cottage. The sole indulgence granted him was that of having his wife and son as the partners of his exile; but he lost the former in 1761, and her death was severely felt by him. Nevertheless his firmness of mind enabled him to bear up against all his trials, and he sought for comfort in religion. It was in this season of adversity that he composed his *Utæshenie*, or Christian Consolation, published at Moscow in 1763, after his recall from exile, which work was translated into French, German, and Swedish. Immediately after Catharine ascended the throne, the exile was not only recalled, but taken into favour; the injustice of the former sentence against him was officially declared; and fresh honours and pensions were bestowed upon him; although, on account of his advanced age, no place was assigned him in the administration. He passed the remainder of his life in tranquillity, and died, after an illness of only three days, at St. Petersburg, April 10 (22), 1766, at the age of 74.

Bestuzhev was a man of great talents, and of practical knowledge confirmed by experience, indefatigable and persevering, daring and intrepid as a statesman, and when overtaken by adversity, unshaken.

But the reverse of the medal is not so creditable to his character; for if his enemies are to be believed, he was also no less ambitious, perfidious, ungrateful, revengeful, and rapacious. He is said to have discovered the medicine once so celebrated under the name of "Bestuzhev's Drops," or "Tinctura Tonica Bestuschevil." (Entz. Leks.)

BESTUZHEV, (Alexander Alexandrovitch,) a Russian author, of whose origin and education no particulars have transpired. He was first known as editor of the *Poliarnaya Zvæsdá* (Polar Star), in conjunction with Riliæv, in 1822. That publication was at the time quite a novelty, being the very first Russian literary annual upon the plan of the German *Almanache;* and it preceded by about a year the earliest English one of the kind. In its plan it was rather an improvement upon its models, because, in addition to articles of the usual kind, it gave a general report of the chief literary productions of the preceding season. Yet, although it was the parent of a very numerous race, it was dropped after the second year. Both Bestuzhev and Riliæv were implicated in the conspiracy at St. Petersburg, in December 1825; when the latter was sentenced to death and executed, while the former was only deprived of his commission in the guards, and banished to Siberia. Afterwards he was removed to a regiment stationed on the Persian frontiers, where he served for some time in the garrison of Derbent. It was about this period that Bestuzhev resumed his pen under the fictitious name of Marlinsky, by which he is now very generally known. The productions which earned for him considerable popularity under that *nom de guerre,* consist chiefly of romantic tales and sketches, chiefly turning upon military adventure. Though they display some talent, they also betray great carelessness, and want of skill in the construction of a story. By far the best as well as the longest of them is Amalet Bek; the hero of which is a wild and daring young Circassian, of noble lineage. But, perhaps, the most striking of all Marlinsky's compositions is his Letter to professor Ermann of Berlin, with whom he became acquainted while the latter was in Siberia, for the purpose of making meteorological and magnetic observations. It was originally written in French, but translated into Russian by Marlinsky himself, and has been allowed to be one of the most brilliant specimens of style in the language. It is both poetical and elegant; and never were the characteristics of Siberia and Persia more vividly portrayed or more forcibly contrasted.

Bestuzhev died in 1837. There are a few posthumous pieces of his in the first volume of the Sto Russkikh Literatorov, or Century of Russian Literateurs, St. Petersb. 1839; but there is no portrait of him, although one is given of each of the other writers.

BETHENCOURT, (James de,) a French physician of the sixteenth century. He is said to have been descended from the family celebrated by the discovery of the Canaries. He is the first to have substituted the appellation of venereal to those diseases previously known as French. His work on the subject bears the following singular title: Nova pœnitentialis quadragesima et purgatorium in Morbum Gallicum sive Venereum, unà cum Dialogo Aquæ Argenti ac Ligni Guiaci colluctantium super dicti Morbi Curationis prolaturâ, opus fructiferum, Paris, 1527, 8vo.

BETHENCOURT, (John,) baron of St. Martin-le-Galliard, in Normandy, called sometimes king of the Canaries, and undoubtedly the first European that esablished himself in them; they had hitherto been merely visited by merchants or Spanish pirates. But Bethencourt, rendered uneasy at home by the quarrels between the houses of Orleans and Burgundy, which agitated all the provinces of France, and especially Normandy, determined upon making a settlement in them. He left his own country with several other adventurers, May 1, 1402; and after a short stay in Spain, he landed in Lancerota, and built a fort. Want of provisions, however, and disagreements among his own people, soon obliged him to sail for Spain, and seek aid from Henry III. of Castile. He obtained what he asked, and was invested with the lordship of the Canaries as a fief of the Castilian crown. He was thus able to overcome some of the difficulties that had hitherto baffled him; but still he found his position very uncertain, and to strengthen it, he sailed for Harfleur, Jan. 3, 1405. Having arrived there, he collected a fresh body of adventurers in Normandy, and by their assistance he so confirmed his hold upon the Canaries, that, about the close of 1405, he sailed for Europe with the double view of touching in Spain, and soliciting a bishop for his new colony from the pope in a personal visit to Rome. He returned in the beginning of 1406, and died nine years afterwards a widower, but without children. (Moreri. Biog. Univ.)

BETHISY DE MÉZIERES, (Henry Benedict Julius de,) a French prelate of considerable note during the revolution and the ecclesiastical movements consequent upon it. He was born July 28, 1744, in the diocese of Amiens, at Mézières, the seat of his family, known among the nobles of Picardy from the eleventh century. Being brought up to the church, his birth early secured him promotion, and he was consecrated bishop of Uzès, in Languedoc, Jan. 16, 1780. In 1789 he was deputed to the ever-memorable states-general, and he silently disapproved of the foolish abandonment of their tithes, by which the deputies of the clergy disgraced themselves, and betrayed their order, in the sessions of Aug. 4 and 18. When, however, Talleyrand, soon notorious as the apostate bishop of Autun, and eventually as a selfish, crafty, lay statesman, declared clerical endowments applicable to public wants—in other words, the legitimate prey of politicians, the bishop of Uzès made a creditable stand against this iniquitous view, and exposed its folly as any thing beyond a temporary expedient. Having thus honourably come forward, Bethisy continued his opposition to the various movements for revolutionizing the national church; and when those of his party were wholly overpowered, he found himself obliged to retire from France. His first refuge was Brussels; afterwards he passed into Germany. But, 1793, four days after the death of Lewis XVI. he came to Paris, and was shocked at finding it just as peaceful, gay, and dissipated as he had ever known it. A long stay there must have cost him his life, and accordingly he went again to Brussels, and thence to England, the protestant but kind asylum of the French clergy. On the application which reached him there, and others of the exiled bishops, from Pius VII., to resign their sees for the convenience of Buonaparte's government, then negotiating with the papacy, Bethisy was among those prelates who protested against the concordat, in an instrument published at London, April 6, 1803. He subsequently, on the bishop of Leon's death, was principally concerned in distributing the bounty of the English government to the French emigrant clergy. On the restoration of the Bourbons in 1814, the bishop of Uzès went over to Paris, and the people of his diocese offered to repair and furnish for him his ancient episcopal palace; but Lewis XVIII. was in no condition to restore sufficiently former institutions, and the mortified prelate soon returned to London. He received there, in common with others of his order, in the beginning of 1816, a letter from the king, requiring the resignations of their several sees. All of them complied conditionally, Bethisy alone adding that he must judge for himself as to the advantages involved. He died in London, at the close of 1817, having published there, in 1800, upon the oath exacted by the consular government of the clergy desirous of returning to France, Véritable Etat de la Question de la Promesse de la Fidélité. (Biog. Univ. Suppl.)

BETHLEHEM GABOR, so called after the Hungarian fashion, which places the family after the christian name, a celebrated Transylvanian prince, really named Gabriel Bethlehem. He was the son of a Transylvanian Calvinist, well-born, but poor, and at one time supported Gabriel Bathori, prince of Transylvania, but on his fall he ingratiated himself with the Turks, and, by their aid, became his successor on the throne of Transylvania, to which he was chosen by the states of that country, Oct. 27, 1613. He was during many years a formidable enemy to the house of Austria, and in 1619 he was proclaimed king of Hungary. He was, however, so closely allied with the Turks, that a prejudice arose against him as an enemy to Christendom; and the Austrians, improving the advantage given by this, and by the refusal of his oriental allies to face a winter campaign, he renounced his pretensions to the Hungarian throne. He retained that of Transylvania to his death, which took place Nov. 15, 1629. (Coxe's House of Austria, ii. 437, iii. 18. Moreri.)

BETHLEN, (Wolfgang, count of,) chancellor of Transylvania, died in 1679, aged 31, leaving a Latin history of his country, which was printed at the family seat, by the care of a younger brother, in 1690, and of which a new edition was published by Hochmeister, about 1796, with a continuation and notes left by Sewarz in the library of Gottingen. The original work is in ten books, and although not free from errors, contains a valuable account of Transylvanian affairs, and of those of the neighbouring countries, between the years 1526 and 1601. Another count of Bethlen, named John, also chancellor of Transylvania, who died in 1678, wrote a short account of his country's history from 1629 to 1663, entitled Rerum Transylvaniæ, libri iv. printed at Amsterdam in 1664, 12mo. This was reprinted at Hermanstadt in 1782, and a second part, down to the year 1673, in the following year, at Vienna. (Biog. Univ.)

BETHUNE, (Philip de,) count of Selles and Charost, younger brother of the celebrated Maximilian de Bethune, duke of Sully, and sixth son of Francis de Bethune, baron of Rosny. He was gentleman of the chamber to Henry III., and after that monarch's death, he attached himself to Henry IV., in whose wars he rendered considerable service. In 1599, he was sent into Scotland as ambassador extraordinary to James VI., and subsequently he filled several similar situations in different countries. He was also governor to Gaston, duke of Orleans, second son of Henry IV., who died in 1611. Towards the close of life the count retired to his seat, Selles in Berri, and he died there in 1649, at the age of eighty-eight, leaving a work of good repute, entitled, Diverses Observations et Maximes Politiques, pouvant utilement servir au Maniement des Affaires publiques, which is to be found at the conclusion of l'Ambassade de M. le Duc d'Angoulême. (Moreri. Biog. Univ.)

BETIS, famed in the history of Alexander's great Asiatic expedition for the defence of Gaza, and an act of cruelty said to have been perpetrated upon him, B.C. 332. He was an eunuch, but a soldier of invincible courage and exemplary fidelity to Darius. Gaza, of which he was governor, was fortified in a manner suitable to its importance, being the last place in Phœnicia, on the edge of the desert, and hence the key of Egypt. The Macedonian conqueror was thus unable to pass it by. But its acquisition cost him very dear. He was two months before it, and received a severe wound himself in the course of the siege. On its capture, he is reported by Quintus Curtius to have ordered the heels of Betis, the gallant governor, to be bored, and to have dragged him behind his chariot round the walls: a childish imitation of the ungenerous treatment of Hector, assigned by Homer to Achilles. But Alexander's reported act was far more inexcusable, because Betis appears to have been alive when he was fastened behind the conqueror's car; whereas Achilles offered his brutal insult to a corpse. For the honour, however, of Alexander and human nature, there is reason for believing this account of the treatment received by Betis, one of the embellishments that abound in Curtius. The people of Gaza generally fell by the sword; and in all probability this was also the fate of their governor. The other account really appears to have been taken from a ridiculous history of Alexander's exploits, now lost. (Quint. Curt. iv. 6. Prideaux, Connect. i. 387. Biog. Univ.)

BETTELLINI, (Peter,) an Italian engraver, born at Lugano in 1748, pupil to Gandolfi at Bologna, and coming to England he was instructed by Bartolozzi. Among his prints executed in the dot manner is, The Queen of Edward IV. after Rigaud. (Bryan's Dict.)

BETTERTON, (Thomas,) an eminent English actor, born in Westminster, in 1635, his father being under-cook to Charles I. He was well educated, and his habits proving studious, there were thoughts at one time of bringing him up to some learned profession. The unsettled condition of public affairs, however, was an obstacle to this design, and at his own desire he was bound apprentice to a bookseller. He had scarcely attained manhood when he came upon the stage, and the Restoration soon afterwards not only removing all restrictions upon a dramatic life, but also rendering it highly popular, he long enjoyed a degree of public favour hitherto unknown to any of his profession. He seems to have been fully deserving of this distinction, being described as both an admirable actor and a virtuous man. In his declining age, he was tried severely by disappointment, a sum of two thousand pounds, which he had saved, being embarked in a venture to the East Indies, which miscarried; the ship in which he and others had invested their money being captured by the French, when all but arrived at home. Betterton bore this misfortune with exemplary magnanimity, although it plunged his declining years in poverty. He died in 1710, universally respected, and was buried with much solemnity in Westminster Abbey. (Biog. Brit.)

BETTES, the name of two artists in the reign of queen Elizabeth. They were brothers, and named Thomas and John. Thomas was a painter, and is mentioned by Meres in his second part of Wit's Commonwealth, published in London in 1598. John was both a painter and engraver, and is mentioned in the same book. Foxe, in his Ecclesiastical History, says that John Bettes executed a pedigree and some vineats (vignettes) for Hall's Chronicle, and speaks of him in 1576 as then dead. Richard Heydock speaks of one of them in his translation of Lomazzo on Painting, published in 1598, as a painter of miniatures. (Walpole's Anecd. of Painting, by Dallaway, i. 287, 306-7; v. 21.)

BETTESWORTH, (George Edmund Byron,) a captain in the British navy. The short but brilliant career of this brave and intrepid youth commenced under the immediate auspices of the present Sir Robert Barlow, then in command of the *Phœbe* frigate. In this famous and ever favourite vessel, whose achievements had won for her the proud prefix of the "*fighting Phœbe*," our subject, as a midshipman, participated in two triumphant actions, singly contested; each contest terminating in the capture of a French frigate. These conquests, as severally achieved, are placed in the following chronological order :—

Captured by the Phœbe.
Néréide (36) French frigate, December 1797.
Africaine (36) ditto February 1801.

Although in the latter combat the *Phœbe*, in her spars, sails, and rigging, sustained considerable damage, still it would seem from her official return, that she suffered little in killed and wounded, having but one among the former, and twelve among the latter; whilst the carnage on board of her over-peopled opponent may be pronounced as unprecedented in any similarly-contested case. On going into action the *Africaine* mustered at quarters 715 seamen and soldiers, and out of that number, *two hundred* were *killed*, and one hundred and forty-three wounded,—the greater part mortally. And three medical officers were actually slain in the cockpit while ministering surgical aid to the mutilated mass which crowded that lower and confined compartment.

When subsequently serving as lieutenant of the *Centaur*, on the West India station, (a volunteer ever, on detached and daring service,) his lion-hearted courage was conspicuously let loose in the celebrated boat-attack, which achieved the conquest of the *Curieux*,—a French corvette of formidable force.

This vessel was moored in Fort-Royal harbour, and placed purposely in a position of supposed security, under cover of a strong and commanding battery. In this situation did the boats of the *Centaur*, (four in number,) after a long and harassing "pull" of *twenty* miles, assail her at midnight, on the 3d of July, 1804. The triced-up boarding-netting around the vessel, rendered it extremely difficult for the boarders, on grappling with the foe, to find a footing on deck. But led by the brave Reynolds, who commanded the enterprise, and who severed with his sabre the after extremity of the netting, the assailants at length gained the stern of the vessel. A sanguinary combat now ensued. Handspikes and the butt ends of muskets became annihilating weapons in the hands of the British. The French officers displayed their accustomed valour, falling in close combat at the foot of their opponents. But the foremast men fled to the forecastle. Here, for a time, they made a strong stand, opposing to the British a formidable array of pikes. But all was unavailable; and despite of the batteries, which opened upon the brig a tremendous fire upon cutting her cable and making sail, the *Curieux*, long before daylight, dropped her anchor beside the outer position in which the *Centaur* was riding—presenting with the dawn a proud trophy of British valour and daring intrepidity.

Upon this occasion, young Bettesworth received several bodily wounds, of which, however, none proved of a serious nature; and upon the death of his gallant leader, who but a few months survived the several pike-thrusts and sabre-cuts which had disabled him on the *Curieux's* deck, he succeeded to the command of that beautiful brig—for she had been purchased for the service of the crown, and expressly commissioned for the brave and lamented Reynolds. In this vessel he became the bearer of Nelson's despatches, apprising the British government of Villeneuve's homeward flight from the West India Isles. The celerity with which he executed this important mission procured for him his post rank.

In the early part of 1808, he became captain of the *Tartar* (32), and on the 16th of May, 1808, he fell on the battle-deck, gallantly defending that inferior frigate from the joint attack of a squadron of Danish gun-boats, in the vicinity of Bergem, on the coast of Norway. In James's Naval History, vol. iv. will be found a full account of the *Tartar's* perilous position, the contest that ensued, and the nature of the daring enterprise which led to the death of her gallant and universally revered commander.

Captain Bettesworth had been but recently married to lady Hannah Grey, sister of earl Grey; and, according to a statement which appeared in the Naval Chronicle of 1808, "he was but twenty-three years of age, and had been wounded *twenty-four* times before (stricken by) the shot which produced his death." In person, he was eminently handsome; in disposition, kind, frank, and friendly, carrying with him an amenity of manner which ensured for him the respect and esteem of all who had the happiness to live under his immediate command.

BETTI, (Zachary,) an Italian poet, born at Verona, July 16, 1732, chiefly celebrated for a vernacular poem on the silk-worm, published in his native town in 1756. He thus trod, and successfully, in the steps of Tesauro, whose Séreide appeared in the sixteenth century. Betti died at Verona in 1788. (Biog. Univ.)

BETTINELLI, (Xavier,) an Italian writer of some repute, born at Mantua, July 18, 1718, who, after studying in the schools of the Jesuits at Bologna, entered that order in 1736. From 1739 to 1744 he taught the *belles-lettres* at their college at Brescia; then returned for awhile to Bologna to complete his theological studies there; and in 1748 proceeded to Venice, where he became acquainted with the most eminent literary characters of that city, whom he has celebrated in his Parnaso Veneto, one of his earliest poetical productions. In 1751 he became director of the college of Nobles at Parma, and it was about that time that he planned his best and most useful work, one which, although of no great extent, manifests considerable diligence, namely, his Risorgimento d'Italia, or History of Literature and the Arts of Social Institutions, Manners, &c. in Italy, from the close of the tenth century, with a sketch of the period immediately preceding. In the course of the eight years during which he continued to hold his situation at Parma, he availed himself of the vacations to travel and visit not only many parts of Italy, but also Switzerland, France, and Germany. When in the last mentioned country, in 1755, he returned with the two sons of prince Hohenlohe, who had requested him to undertake their education. It was with the elder of these pupils that two years afterwards he visited Paris, during which journey he composed the Lettere di Virgilio, a work that made a very great noise at the time, on account of the freedom and hardihood with which Dante and Petrarch are there censured. It obtained for him the compliments of Voltaire, but occasioned great coolness towards him on the part of his friend Algarotti, and drew forth a no less severe than able reply from Gasparo Gozzi. Having resigned his situation in the college at Parma, he obtained another at Verona, where he continued till 1767; after which he became professor of eloquence at Modena. On the suppression of the order of Jesuits in 1773, he retired to his native city, devoting himself thenceforth entirely to literary occupation. There he remained until the French advanced upon the place, when he sought an asylum at Verona, but returned again to Mantua in 1797. Two years afterwards he brought out a complete edition of all his writings, in 24 vols, 12mo, Venezia, 1799—1801. He still, however, continued to take up his pen occasionally, and one of the best of his sonnets is that to Zambeccari, written by him at the age of eighty-six. He died, after a very short illness, September 13, 1808, in his ninety-first year. As a poet, Bettinelli never stood very high; and the productions of his muse, including his three tragedies, are now forgotten. His best work—that by which he still continues to be known, is his Risorgimento; while that entitled l'Entusiasmo, or a philosophical essay on Enthusiasm, though much applauded on its first appearance, is now generally acknowledged to be very unsatisfactory and superficial.

BETTINI, (Anthony,) an Italian author, celebrated for producing the first known book with copper-plate engravings. He was born at Siena, in 1396, and drawn from a convent in 1461, to fill the see of Foligno. He discharged his episcopal duties in a most exemplary manner, but resigned his bishopric, when oppressed by age, and retired to a monastery in his native place, where he died October 22, 1487. His bibliographical fame rests upon Il Monte Santo di Dio, Florence, 1477, 4to, which contains three copper-plates, attributed to the same artist that engraved for the Dante of 1481. This is a famous book, that has abundantly employed bibliomaniacs. It was reprinted at Florence in 1491, but with wood-cuts instead of copper-plates. Bettini also left, De Divina Præordinatione Vitæ et Mortis Humanæ, 1480, 4to, of which there is said to be another edition, without date: Esposizione della Dominicale Orazione, Brescia, 1586, Genoa, 1690, 12mo. (Biog. Univ. Suppl.)

BETTINI, (Marius,) a learned Italian

Jesuit, born at Bologna, February 6, 1582, professor of ethics, mathematics, and philosophy at Parma. He died at Bologna, November 7, 1657. He published at Parma, in 1614, a Latin pastoral satire, entitled Rubenus, frequently reprinted, and translated into several languages. In 1622 he published, also at Parma, a drama dedicated to Lewis XIII. of France, entitled, Chlodoveus, sive Lodovicus, Tragicum Sylviludium. This was reprinted at Paris in 1624. He published, also, some other works of the imaginative kind, but his reputation really rests upon the Apiaria Universæ Philosophiæ Mathematicæ, in quibus Paradoxa et nova pleraque Machinamenta ad Usus eximios traducta et facillimis Demonstrationibus confirmata exhibentur, fol. Bologna, 1641. Other volumes of this work were afterwards published, and among its contents is an explanation of Euclid, Euclides Explicatus. (Biog. Univ.)

BETTS, (John,) an English physician, born at Winchester, at which place he received his earlier education, and in 1642 was elected scholar of Corpus Christi college, Oxford. He took the degree of bachelor of arts in 1646, and that of doctor of medicine in 1654. Previously to this, however, in 1648, he was ejected by the parliamentary visitors, being suspected of attachment to the royal cause. It was this circumstance which led him to the study of medicine. He practised in London with great success, principally among Roman Catholics, being one himself, and was ultimately promoted to the rank of physician to Charles II. He published, De Medicinæ cum Philosophiâ naturali Consensu, Lond. 1662, 4to. De Ortu et Naturâ Sanguiis, Lond. 1669, 8vo. Anatomia Thomæ Parri, &c., inserted in the Opera Omnia of Dr. Wm. Harvey. (Wood's Athenæ.)

BETULEJUS, (Sixtus, or Xystus,) born at Augsburg in 1500, and eventually principal of the college there, with great reputation, during sixteen years. His family name was Birk, (*Birch*,) but he translated it into Latin, after the fashion of that age. He wrote the dramas of Judith, Susanna, and Sapientia Salomonis, in Latin; and Zorababel, Eva, Joseph, Bel, and Herodes, in German; besides editing the Sibylline Oracles, and supplying notes to the Lactantius, published at Basle, in 1563, and Commentaries on Cicero de Naturâ Deorum, Basle, 1550. These last are valuable, but rare and little known. They are, however, to be found in the Humanitas Theologica, Paris, 1660. (Erhard in Ersch und Gruber.)

BETUSSI, (Joseph,) an eminent Italian scholar, born at Bassano, in the *Marca Trivigiana*, in the beginning of the sixteenth century. From an early age he showed great talents for literature, especially for poetry, but unfortunately took for his guide the famous Peter Aretino, whose example he followed, in all sorts of irregularities, to the great prejudice of his advancement in life. For some time he earned his bread in Venice by directing the printing office of Giolito, and afterwards wandered through Italy, and went even to France, finding everywhere opportunities of dissipation, but none of employment. Through the protection of Luca Contile he obtained at last the situation of secretary to a nobleman, whom he accompanied to Spain; but on his return to Italy he resumed his dissipated life, which he seems to have continued till his death, which took place after the year 1565, though the precise time of it cannot be ascertained. He wrote several works, in prose and in verse, amongst which are two dialogues on the nature of love—an Italian translation of the seventh book of the Æneid—another of the three Latin works of Boccaccio—a *raggionamento* on beauty—and many letters. Tiraboschi also mentions a History of all the Illustrious Houses of Italy, the MS. of which has been lost, not without some well-grounded suspicion of having fallen into the hands of Sansovino, who availed himself of it to compile his own work on the same subject.

BETZKII, (Ivan Ivanovitch,) born at Stockholm, February 3, 1704, president of the Academy of Fine Arts at St. Petersburg, and chief director of the imperial buildings and gardens. Some mystery hangs over his birth; but he is reported to have been the son of the Russian general, prince Trubetskoi, who having been made prisoner by the Swedes at Narva, was ordered by Charles XII. to be sent to Stockholm. When there, the prince captivated the affections of a lady of some rank, and he being married, they formed an illicit connexion, the fruit of which was the subject of this notice. The most romantic part of the story is, that shortly afterwards the princess arrived at Stockholm for the purpose of seeing her husband, and having learnt what had occurred, generously resolved to adopt the infant, and treat him as one of her own children. According to some accounts, he was first of all placed in the cadet school at Copenhagen, and afterwards sent to finish his education at the university of Leipsic; while others say, that he completed it either in France or Italy. Which of these statements is the correct one, is of little moment, since they so far agree as to the main point, namely, that care was bestowed upon his education. Towards the end of 1718 the prince and his family proceeded to St. Petersburg, and a year or two afterwards Betzkii was placed in the college for Foreign Affairs, at first in a subordinate situation. In the course of time his abilities attracted the notice of count Ostermann, and his further advancement was greatly facilitated by prince Galitzin, who had married one of Trubetskoi's daughters. He did not, however, rise to any very great distinction until the reign of Catharine, to whom he had been especially recommended by her mother, the princess of Anhalt-Zerbst, who knew him when he was travelling in Germany. The first appointment he received from Catharine was that of inspector of the palaces and other imperial buildings. He was next commissioned to plan various institutions connected with public instruction and education. One of the chief of these was that for the Academy of Fine Arts; another, that for the Cadet Corps. The academy had in fact been provisionally established in 1758; consequently Betzkii cannot be considered as the originator of it, but merely its improver, when appointed president in 1764, at the time that the first stone of the present edifice (by the architect Kakorinov) was laid by the empress. He certainly did very much towards rendering it effective, since it was primarily owing to him that the collection of original paintings, of engravings, and casts from the antique, was formed; also a library of works on the fine arts,—in short, that all the materials for study were amply provided. After 1789, Betzkii being then very advanced in years, did not often visit the academy, but he continued to take an interest in its prosperity to the very last. It was also in 1764 that he projected the plan of what is termed the Smolnoi Monastery at St. Petersburg, an establishment for the education of young ladies of respectable families. A similar institution was likewise founded, about the same time, at Moscow. Besides other rewards and honours, his public services of this kind obtained for him, in 1772, the high compliment from the senate, of a gold medal, having on its obverse his portrait, and on the reverse a figure representing "Public Gratitude." He died at St. Petersburg, August 31 (September 11), 1795, was buried in the Alexandrovsky monastery, and honoured with a funeral oration by the archimandrite (afterwards archbishop) Anastasius Bratinovsky. A collection of Memoirs and Documents by Betzkii, relative to seminaries, &c. for education, was published in 1789-91. (Entz. Leks.)

BEUCKELAER, or BUCELTRAR, (Joachim,) a painter, born at Antwerp in 1530, and died in 1610. Excelled in kitchens, still life, &c.

BEUCKELS, (William,) a Dutch fisherman, celebrated for discovering, at the beginning of the fifteenth century, the art of curing herrings. He was born at Bieruliet, in Dutch Flanders, and he died there in 1449. A statue was raised in commemoration of him, and Charles V., with his sister, the queen of Hungary, visited his tomb in 1536, as that of a national benefactor. (Biog. Univ.)

BEUGHEM, (Cornelius van,) a bookseller at Emmerich, in the latter half of the seventeenth century, known for the publication of several bibliographical works, which, from haste and inaccuracy, have proved of little value. The earliest of these is, Bibliotheca Juridica et Politica, Amst. 1680, 12mo. Another is, Incunabula Typographiæ, sive Catalogus Librorum proximis ab Inventione Typographiæ Annis ad Annum 1500 editorum. Amst. 1688, 12mo. (Biog. Univ.)

BEUGHEM, (Charles Anthony Francis de Paule, van,) a Flemish ecclesiastic, born at Brussels, in 1763; first employed in education, but rendered generally known by attention to mendicity, on which he published a treatise at Ghent, in 1775. In 1790 he became secretary to cardinal van Frankenberg, archbishop of Mechlin, an appointment which he held until 1792, when the prelate fled before the French army. Van Beughem had shown himself, in the revolutionary movements of his own country, very far from a believer in the indefeasible rights of sovereigns, but he was not prepared for swearing hatred to royalty; and hence he was arrested at Mechlin, imprisoned there seven months, then taken to Versailles, and subsequently condemned to be transported to the Isle of Oleron. This, however, his health forbade; and after a detention of two years in the prison of Versailles, he was allowed to live in the town, under observation of the mayor. On Buonaparte's fall he returned to his own country, and entered, with all the heat of his earlier days, into an opposition to the union of Belgium with Holland; a question which he did not view as a politician anxious to benefit the land of his fathers, but as a Romish priest, bent upon upholding the peculiarities of his creed, and apprehensive of their stability if placed upon an equality with protestantism. He wrote, accordingly, various tracts advocating his opinions, which, with his piece upon mendicity, and some poems in Latin, Flemish, and French, will occasionally be found in libraries; but his talents were not such as to render any thing that he wrote likely to be sought, unless for the illustration of contemporary politics. (Biog. Univ. Sup.)

BEULANIUS, the name of two British writers, a father and a son, the latter of whom was named Samuel. The father was the instructor of Nennius, and is referred to about the year 600: he wrote a work, De Genealogiis Gentium; probably a scholarly form of those family histories which were habitually produced by the bards.

The son appears to have been born in Northumberland; and as it is presumed that the father was a priest, his case has been cited by protestants as a proof that the British clergy of that day were allowed to marry; a conclusion which Romanists would fain deny; but really with very little reason, because it is indisputable that learning, in that day, was confined almost wholly to ecclesiastics. Samuel Beulanius was educated chiefly in the Isle of Wight, and he wrote a description of it from his own observation, combined with accounts by Ptolemy and Pliny. He was very studious of his nation's history, upon which he wrote some works, together with an historical itinerary. (Nicolson's Eng. Hist. Library, 31, 33. Chalmers.)

BEUMLER, (Mark,) born in 1555, at Volketswyl, a village in the canton of Zurich. He died in that town of the plague, in 1611. After studying at Geneva and Heidelberg, he spent several years in Germany. In 1594 he became professor of theology at Zurich, and was generally regarded as one of the ablest defenders of the Swiss Reformers. To general literature he contributed a grammar, printed in 1593, and a work on rhetoric, printed in 1629, both often reprinted, with some treatises on education, illustrated by his own comments from Cicero, Demosthenes, and Plutarch. As a religious teacher, he compiled a catechism, in Latin and German, long used by the youth of Zurich. As a divine, he wrote various pieces long since forgotten. The following one of them, however, may be mentioned, because it bears upon an interesting controversy of the day, and shows the ridiculous taste then prevalent: Falco emissus ad capiendum, deplumandum, et dilacerandum audaciorem illum cuculum ubiquitarium, qui nuper ex Jac Andreæ, mali corvi, malo ovo, ab Holdero simplicissimâ curucâ exclusus, et à dæmoniaco Bavio Fescenio varii coloris plumis instructus, impetum in philomelas innocentes facere cœperat. Neustadt. 1585, 4to. (Biog. Univ.)

BEUNINGEN, (Conrad van,) one of the most distinguished statesmen of the seventeenth century, born at Amsterdam in 1622. Till his 39th year he entered but little, and almost by constraint, into public life; and his own habits were more those of an ascetic than of a statesman. In 1650 he was appointed syndic of his native town. As a member of the Assembly of the States, he was sent, with others, into Friesland, to invite that province to a union for founding a government without a stadtholder. In 1652 he was sent ambassador to Sweden, to gain that country as an ally in the Dutch war with England. His character for learning it was thought would recommend him to queen Christina; but Sweden preferred a neutrality to a partisanship which might hinder her trade; and the Hanse Towns, which Beuningen also attempted on his journey, were moved by similar considerations to the same line of conduct. He was afterwards ambassador to Denmark and France. The designs of the latter upon the Netherlands were frustrated by his patriotism and influence in the Dutch council, but he was obliged to agree to the restoration of the prince of Orange, William III., in 1672. The same jealousy of the liberties of his country which had led him to oppose the designs of aggrandizement of Lewis XIV., induced him to oppose a levy attempted by William III. as a defence against France—an opposition which at first threatened to produce fatal consequences for its author, and for which the offended prince never fully forgave him. In 1686 Beuningen laid down his official employments, and occupied his time and money in speculations, the failure of which appears to have unsettled his reason. He died in 1693. (V. Kampen in Ersch und Gruber.)

BEURER, (John Ambrose,) a celebrated botanist. He was the son of an apothecary, and born at Nuremberg, March 2, 1716. He was desirous of studying medicine, but his father determined that he should pay attention to pharmacy, and sent him to an apothecary at Ratisbon, with whom he passed three years. He made considerable progress in chemistry, and studied, with great assiduity, botany and natural history. In 1735 he repaired to Berlin to pursue his studies, and afterwards travelled in Germany, Holland, England, France, and Switzerland. He returned in 1739 to his native city, succeeded to the business of his father, and was, in 1750, admitted a member of the Imperial Academy of the Curious in Nature. He died June 27, 1754. He published no separate work, but he contributed largely to the Opera Botanica of Conrad Gesner, published at Nuremberg in 1753, fol.; and there are several of his papers inserted in the Acta Academiæ Naturæ Curiosorum; Commercium Litterarium Noribergense, and in the Hamburgischer Briefwechsler. Three Letters, addressed by him to baron Haller, were printed in the Einiger Gelehrten Teutschen Briefe an den Hrn. von Haller, Berne, 1777, 8vo; and he also furnished to the Royal Society of London, through P. Collinson, the naturalist, two papers, which were printed in the Philosophical Transactions, vols. xlii. and xliii., on the Nature of Amber, and an Inquiry concerning the Stone Osteocolla.

BEURNONVILLE, (Peter Riel, marquess of,) a conspicuous French officer during the revolutionary period, born at Champignoles, near Bar-on-Aube, May 10, 1752, of a trading family. He was originally meant for the church, but at an early age entered the army, and went into the east. Being evidently conceited and quarrelsome, he was sent away from the Isle of Bourbon by the governor, in 1789, and came home to make his complaints. Nothing could be more opportune; the revolution was then beginning, and Beurnonville appealed to the National Assembly. He entered immediately, with great violence, into the revolutionary projects that agitated society; and unwilling to be left behind in the crowd of political speculators, he published a project of a constitution for the eastern colonies. When war broke out in 1792, he became aide-de-camp to marshal Luckner, with the rank of colonel, and was employed upon several occasions with great credit to himself. Dumourier even thought so highly of him, that he called him the French Ajax; but perhaps his great height was one reason for paying him this compliment. He was also a finished adept in that art of concealing things unfit for general knowledge, and in throwing a thick coating of bombast over every public transaction in the least capable of it, which served so much to inflate the French, and make other nations laugh, during the revolutionary times. But, nevertheless, he could not satisfy Buonaparte. That wonderful man had, indeed, a high value for talents to blind mankind, but he was not very anxious to engage them, unless they were accompanied by qualifications of a higher order. In these he thought Beurnonville deficient; and hence, although a public man that had been employed in various ways, and made a count, he would not confide any thing of importance to him, or make him a marshal, like other generals who had commanded in chief. He did, indeed, at the beginning of 1814, when pressed by the near aspect of ruin, seek his assistance; but it soon became out of any royalist's power to render any, and Beurnonville entered readily into Talleyrand's projects for the restoration of the Bourbons. They requited him by making him a peer; and as he followed them to Ghent, he was eventually made a marquess, minister, privy counsellor, and marshal. He died April 23, 1821; being unquestionably one of the persons most benefited by the restoration. (Biog. Univ.)

BEURS, (William,) born at Dort in 1656, displayed a natural genius for drawing and designing. He was a pupil of William Drillenburg, whom he soon equalled in landscapes, flowers, and portraits. He died in 1690.

BEUSEKOM, (F. van,) a Dutch engraver, who flourished from about 1640 to 1650, and was principally employed by the booksellers in engraving portraits. Among others he engraved a portrait of Ant. le Brun, after a picture painted by A. V. Hulle. (Bryan's Dict.)

BEUTER, (Peter Anthony,) a Spanish theologian and historian, born in Valencia, favourably noticed by pope Paul III. Besides some theological works, he published Primera Parte de la Coronica general de España, especialmente del Regno de Valencia, Valent. 1546; and again 1604, fol.; Segunda Parte donde se tratan las Cobranzas del las Tierras de

Poder de Moros, par los Reyes de Aragon, y Condes de Barcelona, *ibid.* 1546, fol. (Antonio.)

BEUTHER, (Michael,) professor of history at Strasburg; born at Karlstadt, in Franconia, in 1522, studied at Wurzburg, Coburg, and Marburg, and was teacher of ancient literature at the monastery of Saalmünster, in his 17th year. After a short stay here he removed to Wittenberg, where he studied under Luther and Melancthon; entered the army of the elector, John Frederic, against Maurice, of Saxony, in 1542; returned afterwards to Wittenberg, where he gave juridical and mathematical lectures; and in 1546 was appointed professor of history, mathematics, and poetry, at Griefswald. In 1548 he entered the service of the bishop of Wurzburg as counsellor, visited the chief academies in France in 1549, returned to the bishop's service, and in 1552 was sent on a diplomatic mission to the imperial court. The two following years were spent chiefly in Italy, and in the study of medicine; but in 1555 he attended the Imperial Assembly at Augsburg, on the bishop's part. His leaning towards the protestants exposed him to much enmity, and was the proximate cause of his entering the service of the elector palatine, Otho Henry, as spiritual counsellor and librarian; on his patron's death, however, a year after, he laid down his office, and refused many offers of further employment. In 1567 he accepted the professorship of history at Strasburg, and held this till his death in 1587. His works consist of historical essays and commentaries on ancient authors; among the first class are a Continuation of Sleidan's History of the Reformation, and a Commentary on the Exploits of Chas. V. (Baur in Ersch und Gruber.)

BEUTLER, (James,) a German engraver, who flourished about 1593. From the smallness of his prints he is ranked amongst the little masters. He used the same mark as was sometimes adopted by James Buicke, John Burgkmair, and other German engravers, namely, I. B., which renders it necessary to pay attention to the style to distinguish his works from theirs. (Bryan's and Strutt's Dictionaries.)

BEVER, or BEVENUS, (John Siriacope,) a native of Belgium, and teacher of philosophy at Louvain, who died in 1563, called the Aristotle of his age. Cosmo, duke of Florence, invited him to his court, but he declined the offer. He wrote, Commentarii in libb. Aristot. de Physica Auscultatione; De Cœlo, de Anima, de Generatione et Corruptione, Louanii, 1567, fol. (Sweertii Ath. Belg.)

BEVER, (Thomas,) a scholarly English civilian, born at Stratfield Mortimer, in Berkshire, in 1725, fellow of All Souls college, Oxford, LL.D., April 5, 1758. In 1762 he gave lectures in civil law, the regius professor of that faculty being then prevented, by ill health, from doing so. The introduction to his course he published in 1766, under the title of A Discourse on the Study of Jurisprudence and the Civil Law. In 1781 he published, The History of the Legal Polity of the Roman State; and of the Rise, Progress, and Extent of the Roman Laws; a work displaying deep research and extensive information upon the subject of which it treats; but not complete according to his plan, and hopelessly left in that state, although his papers might have carried it farther, because he gave directions for the destruction of his MSS. after his death; and it is said that he himself destroyed those relating to this history in his last illness. Dr. Bever died in Doctors' Commons, London, Nov. 8, 1781, remembered as "a better scholar than writer, and a better writer than pleader;" but universally respected for private worth, and a disposition to befriend rising genius. (Chalmers.)

BEVERIDGE, (William,) generally known among foreigners by the latinized name of Beveregius, an exemplary and learned English divine, born early in 1637, at Barrow, in Leicestershire, of which his grandfather, father, and brother, were successively vicars. He was educated in grammar learning, first by his father, and afterwards at Okeham school, in Rutland. In 1653 he was admitted a sizar of St. John's college, Cambridge. He there distinguished himself, both by an exemplary life and a diligent study of the oriental languages. His proficiency in these was attested by a treatise on their utility, followed by a Syriac grammar, composed when he was only 18, and actually published two years afterwards, with this title; De Linguarum Orientalium, præsertim Hebraicæ, Chaldaicæ, Syriacæ, Arabicæ, et Samaritanæ, Præstantiâ et Usu, cum Grammaticâ Syriacâ, tribus Libris traditâ, per G. Beveridgium, Lond. 1658, 8vo. It was expressly compiled for the use of those who should study Walton's Polyglott, then the general object of attention with scholars, and a conspicuous glory of the depressed Church of England, under the republican government. Although superseded by the later labours of Michaelis, Jahn, and others, Beveridge's Syriac Grammar was found of considerable use in its day, as is attested by a second edition of it, which appeared in 1664. At the same time was printed a second edition of the Dissertation on the Excellency, Necessity, and Use of the Oriental Tongues, which ought always to be bound up with the Grammar, although separately paged, and was intended as an answer to some philosophers of the day, who decried application to the eastern languages as a needless waste of time. Beveridge employed himself simultaneously with the composition of his Grammar upon a Syriac Lexicon, but did not mean to publish it unless the design of completing a lexicon to accompany the London Polyglott should fail. As it happily proceeded, he communicated his collection to Dr. Castell, whose great Heptapolyglott Lexicon appeared in 1669, in two volumes, fol. Two years before the publication of his Syriac Grammar, that is, in 1656, Beveridge took his bachelor's degree, and in 1660, his master's. This was the year of the Restoration, an event which he was prepared by his studies to appreciate highly upon rational grounds, being deeply smitten by a reverential regard for antiquity. Hence he was not of a temper to relish the crude novelties of those who would indolently comprise theological knowledge within the limits of Scripture interpreted by themselves and a few moderns. His fitness for the times appears to have been discerned by Gilbert Sheldon, then bishop of London, who collated him to the vicarage of Ealing, in Middlesex, Jan. 4, 1661. For this preferment he seems to have been especially ordained, as he was admitted deacon on the day before his collation, and priest on the 31st of the same month; a departure from the canonical interval between the inferior and superior orders, which, although discretionary with the bishop, is unusual, except for especial reasons. Beveridge remained at Ealing nearly twelve years, diligently and conscientiously employed, as he was wherever Providence placed him, in his professional duties. He did not, however, intermit that learned appropriation of a large portion of his leisure, which is essential among clergymen, to maintain the respectability and substantial usefulness of their order. In 1669, accordingly, appeared his Institutionum Chronologicarum Libri duo, una cum totidem Arithmetices Chronologicæ Libellis, which is professedly no more than a manual of the science of which it treats, but is extremely useful to those who wish to understand its technical part, being clear of those obscurities by which Scaliger and Petau had embarrassed it. In the second part is a short system of chronological arithmetic, which he calls characteristic, as distinguished from practical, intended for aiding students to a thorough understanding of dates, and this was a new feature in such works. The whole was very favourably received; but works of this kind seldom find a rapid sale. A second edition of it, however, was printed in 1705, in 4to, and a third in 1721, in 8vo. Considerable use, in fact, has been made of it, by English chronologers especially. In 1672 appeared Beveridge's most important work, entitled Συνοδικον, sive Pandectæ Canonum SS. Apostolorum et Conciliorum ab Ecclesiâ Græcâ receptorum; nec non Canonicarum SS. Patrum Epistolarum; una cum Scholiis Antiquorum singulis eorum annexis, et Scriptis aliis huc spectantibus; quorum plurima e Bibliothecæ Bodleianæ, aliarumque MSS. Codicibus nunc primum edita: reliqua cum iisdem MSS. summâ Fide et Diligentiâ collata. Totum Opus, in duos Tomos divisum, Gulielmus Beveregius, Ecclesiæ Anglicanæ Presbyter, recensuit, Prolegomenis et Annotationibus auxit, 2 vols, fol. This important work was dedicated to Beveridge's original patron, Sheldon, now become archbishop of Canterbury, the munificent builder of the noble theatre at Oxford, in which a printing press was placed, first used, as the publisher says, in a dedication to the archbishop, for the printing of this very work. It is a collection that excited very considerable notice, both among natives and foreigners; but being rare abroad, erroneous opinions were afloat about it, some bibliographers mentioning three editions of it; whereas, in fact, there never was but one. The first of Beveridge's two admirable volumes contains the canons that have been assigned to the apostles, those of the two Nicene councils, of four Constantinopolitan councils, and of other Asiatic councils, together with the arguments and Arabic paraphrase of Joseph, surnamed the Egyptian, on the canons of the first four general councils; the whole being prefaced by the learned editor's Prolegomena. The second volume contains the canons of Dionysius and Peter, both of

Alexandria; various monuments of oriental episcopacy; the *Syntagma*, or alphabetical index, compiled by Michael Blastaris; the acts of the synod, which restored Photius to the patriarchate of Constantinople, and those of the eighth council holden there. The work has Greek in one column, a Latin translation in the other, and comprises the *Scholia* of learned orientals on most of the canons, together with copious notes by Beveridge himself. He did not, however, gain fame alone from this work. He had given in it a higher antiquity to the canons, called apostolical, than scholars of the reformed church would generally concede. The Jesuit, Francis Turriano, had maintained, in an answer to the Centuriators of Magdeburg, printed in 1573, that these canons were really enacted by the apostles in council at Jerusalem, and put in their existing form by Clemens Romanus. John Daillé, on the other hand, the glory of French protestantism, had argued in his treatise, De Pseudepigraphis Apostolicis, Paris, 1652, that they came from some anonymous heretic, who forged them about the end of the fifth century. The Jesuit's hypothesis was easy to demolish, for the canons have been overlooked by writers of the first three centuries, which is impossible if they had been genuine, and are besides convicted of imposture by many anachronisms and improprieties. Beveridge took the earliest date that they could anywise support, assigning them to the commencement of the third century, or a little before. In taking this ground, he does not content himself with assigning reasons for it, but also assails Daillé's arguments for giving them a lower date, speaking at the same time of that learned Frenchman as a man of admirable erudition, deeply versed in antiquity. This testimony did not, however, keep that excellent scholar's countrymen from displaying a becoming jealousy of his well-earned fame. One of them published anonymously at Rouen, in 1674, Observationes in Ignatianas Pearsonii Vindicias, et in Adnotationes Beveregii in Canones Apostolorum. This author, subsequently known to be Matthew de l'Arroque, not only defends Daillé, but also maintains that episcopal authority is chiefly supported by means of these canons and the Ignatian epistles. Beveridge did not allow his positions to pass uncensured and unexamined. In 1679, he published at London, Codex Canonum Ecclesiæ Primitivæ Vindicatus et Illustratus, in which use is made of admissions by opponents of episcopacy as to its actual establishment at an earlier date than suits their hypothesis, and his own opinion as to the antiquity of the contested canons is maintained more fully than before. His vindication has, however, failed in several respects of giving satisfaction to the learned world. Beveridge was now no longer in the retirement of a country village, for such was Ealing then. In November, 1672, he was instituted to the rectory of St. Peter's, Cornhill, London, to which he had been presented by the city corporation, patrons of it, and he very soon afterwards resigned his vicarage of Ealing, another vicar being instituted there in April 1673. On the 22d of December of the following year, he was collated by Humphrey Henchman, then bishop of London, to the prebend of Chiswick, in St. Paul's cathedral; and 1679 he proceeded to the degree of doctor of divinity. As his conduct at St. Peter's, Cornhill, was quite in unison with that which he had constantly pursued at Ealing, and fully worthy of his high reputation among scholars, Henry Compton, then bishop of London, did equal honour to his own discrimination, and to the excellent object of it, by collating him, Nov. 3, 1681, to the archdeaconry of Colchester. In discharging the duties of this new office, he did not content himself with mere meetings of the clergy at certain places, and receiving there presentations from churchwardens; he made a personal visitation of every parish within his archdeaconry, a practice now as usual as it is desirable, but probably then rare, as it is noticed among Beveridge's claims to the respectful remembrance of posterity. His merits were farther acknowledged in his promotion to the fourth stall in Canterbury cathedral, vacated by the death of Peter du Moulin the younger, in which he was installed Nov. 5, 1684. He was shortly afterwards associated with the learned and pious Horneck in projects for establishing some religious societies within the church of England. Hitherto there had been little of cooperation among her members; but James the Second's infatuated exertions to rob his country of an unadulterated scriptural faith, awakened all such as knew the value of that privilege to the necessity of combining to preserve it in the land. From the protestant zeal of that agitated period eventually sprang the Societies for Promoting Christian Knowledge and for Propagating the Gospel. On James's constrained withdrawal, the scheme, agitated repeatedly before, since the Restoration, of comprehending dissenters within the establishment, by making concessions to them, was again brought forward. It had been desired by some politicians to have such questions considered by a committee of laymen and clergymen combined; but even Tillotson and Burnet, although little partial to high-church opinions, opposed a plan so likely to offend many moderate friends of the establishment, and so certain to furnish Romanists with a new pretence for branding the national religion as a mere emanation of the secular power. The scheme in that form was in consequence abandoned, and in its place a committee of thirty divines, ten of whom were bishops, was appointed to prepare a plan of comprehension to lay before convocation. Among the thirty thus commissioned, Beveridge was included. The whole body comprised the most eminent of their profession; but a disposition to concede might certainly seem to have had some considerable influence in the selection of names. Beveridge, however, is considered from his Concio ad Clerum, then preached, and subsequently published, as in a great degree unfavourable to the proposed concessions; his knowledge of antiquity might make him view them as improper, and his knowledge of men might make him view them as hopeless. His colleagues generally were in favour of them, and accordingly a number of alterations was contemplated, which it was clear the convocation would reject, and would probably be applauded by the country generally for doing so. The violence, indeed, then displayed by the triumphant presbyterians in Scotland gave a warning that could not be lost upon cautious minds. Men must have seen that nothing short of an unconditional surrender was likely long to content the complainants, if once encouraged by success. The scheme of comprehension was consequently abandoned as impracticable. Whatever might have been Beveridge's conduct while it was in agitation, he does not appear to have offended the court, as he had an offer of the see of Bath and Wells, on bishop Ken's refusal to swear allegiance to the new government. He took three weeks to consider this offer; a delay that really did give offence at court, where there was naturally a great anxiety to fill sees vacated in a manner so honourable to the actual possessors, by individuals who stood high in public estimation. At length, however, Beveridge declined the invidious appointment, much, apparently, to the dissatisfaction of William's government, as he never had another offer of a mitre during that monarch's life. In 1701 Beveridge failed in a lower object of ambition. It was proposed to elect him prolocutor of convocation; but Atterbury's influence prevailed, and he was rejected, the numbers being thirty-seven against twenty-nine. In 1704 he had an offer of the see of St. Asaph, from queen Anne's government, and he not unwillingly accepted it, being consecrated July 16. He began immediately upon his new duties with all that conscientious diligence which had attended him through life, and soon gave an evidence of this to the public at large, by the publication in London, before the year 1704 expired, of the Church Catechism explained, for the use of the Diocese of St. Asaph, 4to. Long services to the church in an episcopal character were, however, now precluded by age. Bishop Beveridge died at his apartments in the cloisters of Westminster Abbey, March 5, 1708, and was buried in St. Paul's cathedral. He was a widower, without issue; and his wife had been connected, either as sister or sister-in-law, with a gentleman of Hinckley, in Leicestershire, named Stanley. His library was left to St. Paul's, as the foundation of one for the use of the London clergy, and a portion of his other property was bequeathed to pious and charitable uses. He was universally regarded as one of the best men of his time. Unquestionably modest, erudite, pious, and conscientious, he never showed himself without winning love and admiration.

Besides the works already mentioned, bishop Beveridge also published four sermons, delivered on special occasions, and afterwards published by request. These Sermons, and the Catechism explained, are the only English works that he printed; every thing else put forth by himself was in Latin: he was, indeed, averse from printing in English. His executor, however, printed at different times, large quantities of his MSS. These posthumous works consist of Sermons, Thesaurus Theologicus, Private Thoughts, Treatises on the Necessity and Advantages of Public Prayer, and of Frequent Communion; a Defence of Sternhold and Hopkins's Version of the Book of Psalms; and an Exposition of the Thirty-Nine Articles. All these, together with the English works published by the bishop himself, were collected by the Rev. Thomas Hartwell Horne, in 1824, in 9 vols, 8vo, prefaced by a memoir of the author. Of this whole collection, the Private Thoughts have enjoyed the greatest popularity. Perhaps, indeed, they are the chief reason of Beveridge's hold upon the majority of minds. They were first published in two volumes in 1709, and have been often reprinted. A German translation of them appeared at Leipsic, in 1716; and a French translation, made from the *eleventh* English edition, appeared at Amsterdam, in two volumes, in 1731. They are, however, a very juvenile production, being written before the author had completed his twenty-third year, and evidently never meant for publication, but merely for his own private use. Hence they rather display a good heart and a pious disposition, than a sound judgment. Beveridge's Thesaurus Theologicus is a sort of skeleton system of divinity, the various branches of religious knowledge being arranged in regular order, under various heads, introduced by texts of Scripture, and illustrated by references properly disposed. It was probably used by the author in the preparation of his own sermons, and for this purpose it has been advantageously used by others ever since its publication. Beveridge's Exposition of the Thirty-Nine Articles was first published in 1710, and reprinted in 1716, fol. As a specimen, the first article was published separately, and its favourable reception brought out all the rest, so far as they could be procured, which was not beyond the thirtieth, although it appears that the bishop had gone through the whole thirty-nine. Like the rest of his posthumous works, this discovers a want of final correction and revision. It occasioned a severe anonymous attack upon the bishop's literary character, published in 1711, under the title of A Short View of Dr. Beveridge's Writings, which may serve as a preliminary discourse to an examination of his Articles. He is there treated as a tasteless writer, an unsound reasoner, a Calvinist who went beyond the more sober of his party, and an advocate whose indiscretion gives advantage to enemies of the truth. Such remarks cannot be more favourably characterised than as ill-natured exaggerations. That Beveridge's English works are open to exception, is, indeed, undeniable; but it should be recollected that a very small portion of them was published by himself, although they extend over nine octavo volumes. He would probably have agreed with any objector who might pronounce them unfit for publication. He must have considered them as little else than sketches; and for such, subjected to public scrutiny by others, no man is fairly answerable. It is, however, plain that he was not equal as a writer to Tillotson, and some others of his more illustrious contemporaries; but still his works are an important acquisition to the serious literature of England. (Memoir prefixed to Mr. Hartwell Horne's edition of Bishop Beveridge's English works. Chaufepié. Newcourt's Repertorium. Le Neve's Fasti. Cardwell's Hist. of Conferences, 411. Additions to Mosheim, iv. 308. Clement. Bibl. Cur.)

BEVERIDGE, (John,) a native of Scotland, in 1758 appointed professor of languages in the college and academy of Philadelphia. He published a volume of Latin poems, called Epistolæ Familiares et alia quædam Miscellanea. (Carter's Amer. Biog. Dict.)

BEVERINI, (Bartholomew,) a distinguished Italian scholar, born at Lucca, May 3, 1629. So precocious were his talents, and so exemplary was his application, that he made notes, which even scholars thought worthy of attention, upon the principal poets of the Augustan age, by the time that he was fifteen. In the following year, he went to Rome, and entered a congregation of regular clerks, in which he took the vows in 1647. He finally fixed himself at Lucca as a teacher of rhetoric, and remained there to the end of life, highly respected, and in correspondence with many of his more illustrious contemporaries; among them with Christina, the abdicated queen of Sweden. He died Oct. 24, 1686, leaving numerous works, both in Latin and Italian. Among them is a vernacular translation of the Æneid, originally the fruit of only thirteen months' application, but subsequently corrected with care. It first appeared at Lucca, in 1680, 12mo, and has been reprinted several times; the last edition is that of Rome, 1700, 4to. Beverini's chief claim, however, upon the notice of general scholars, is founded upon a learned posthumous work, first printed at Lucca in 1711, 8vo, and often reprinted in collections, entitled, Syntagma de Ponderibus et Mensuris, in quo veterum Nummorum Pretium, ac Mensurarum Quantitas demonstratur. This is followed by a treatise on the Comitia of the Romans. Beverini left also many MSS., among them a Latin history of Lucca, preserved at that place, and said to be valuable. (Biog. Univ.)

BEVERLAND, (Adrian,) a Dutch philologist and writer of the seventeenth and beginning of the eighteenth centuries, born at Middelburg, in Zealand, about the middle of the former century. He first studied jurisprudence, but by no means confined himself to this; theology and classical literature occupied much of his attention—and in the latter department, deserved the reproach too often and justly incurred by his learned countrymen, of exhibiting a preference for the most obscene classical authors. The same depraved taste showed itself in his dissertations, and more than once drew upon him the judicial reprimands, and even punishment, of the authorities of his native country. He enjoyed much favour with Isaac Vossius, his maternal uncle, by whose advice, it is supposed, he visited England in 1672. In 1677 he was again in Holland—was expelled from Utrecht and Leyden for the licentiousness of his life and writings, and in 1680 was in England, under the patronage of his uncle Vossius, himself a canon of Windsor. Here his mode of life, however, was as scandalous as in his own country; his writings against many of the dignified English clergy gained him no good will; and after the death of his uncle he sank into such poverty that he was obliged to sell his library and collection of antiquities. In 1710 he was living at Fulham, and that (says his German biographer), in such company, that his countryman, Offenbach, travelling in England, was loth to visit him. After 1712 we find no further account of him, and it is probable that he died about this time.

BEVERLEY, (John of,) so called from the place of his burial, a celebrated English prelate in the eighth century, and a Romish saint, born of noble parentage, at Harpham, a small village in Northumbria, and educated under Theodore of Tarsus, the archbishop of Canterbury, to whom the Anglo-Saxons owed so much of their literary culture. John acquired a degree of learning unusual in that age, and had himself the honour of instructing Bede. He proved extremely pious, and was at one time an inmate in the monastery of Whitby. But he afterwards occupied a hermitage on the Tyne, from which he evangelized the neighbouring country. In 685 he was placed in the see of Hagulstald, the modern Hexham, during the troubles of Wilfrid, but he held it only one year. In 687 he undertook the see of York, and occupied it with extraordinary credit until within four years of his death, which took place in 721. These four years were spent in a monastery for secular priests that he had founded at Beverley, in Yorkshire. His memory was highly venerated in the north of England; and besides having the credit of numerous miracles, he seems to have left some religious works, and some epistles. In 1416, a synod, holden in London, consecrated the day of his death, May 7. His body had long before been placed in a shrine adorned in the most costly manner. (Stubbs. apud x. Scriptt. 1691. Godwin. de Præsull. Anglia Sacra.)

John of Beverley is also the name of a learned Carmelite, professor of divinity at Oxford about 1390, who wrote some questions on the Master of the Sentences, and some disputations. (Biog. Brit.)

BEVERLY, (Robert,) a native of Virginia, clerk of the council, about 1697, author of a History of the Province, including notices of its natural productions and advantages, Lond. 1705; with Gribelin's cuts, 8vo, 1722; or in French, Amsterd. 1705. It is even yet worthy of perusal, though its historical portions are concise and unsatisfactory. The author died in 1716. (Carter's Amer. Biog. Dict. Allen's Amer. Biog. Dict.)

BEVERN, (Augustus William, Duke of Brunswick-Luneburg,) a celebrated Prussian general, born at Brunswick, in 1715. He entered the Prussian service in 1731, and was appointed, in the same year, captain in the regiment of Kalkskin; in this same regiment he attained the rank of commander in 1739, having accompanied the king, Frederic William I., during the intermediate period, in his campaign on the Rhine. In 1740 he took part in the first Silesian war, was wounded in the battle of Mollwitz, received the command of the regiment of fusileers, formed out of a Wirtemberg corps which had entered the Prussian service, and in 1741 exchanged this for the regiment of Bredon, the command of which he retained till his death, a period of forty years. In the second Silesian war he distinguished himself in the battle of Hohenfriedberg (1745); was named, in

1747, governor of the fortress of Stettin; and in 1750, lieutenant-general and knight of the Black Eagle. In the seven years' war he commanded a part of the Prussian army in the expedition into Bohemia; routed the Austrians in the battle of Reichenberg and Prague; and in the battle of Kollin, after a desperate but unsuccessful struggle, in which his division suffered more than any other part of the Prussian army, he was left with an army of defence, while the king opposed the French troops. The fatal battle of Breslau, in which the Prussian army lost, in killed and wounded, more than 6,000 men, and 3,600 prisoners, stopped his military career for a time. Riding out to reconnoitre by night, two days after the battle, he was taken by the Austrians, and detained a prisoner till the next year (1758), when the dispute between the Prussian and Austrian monarchs, as to the terms of his ransom, was decided by his liberation unconditionally. Frederic, "who loved not beaten generals," suffered him to retire to his command of Stettin; but in 1762 he recovered his reputation by a signal victory over the Austrians at Reichenbach, who had attacked him on all four sides of his army at once. After this he commanded the Prussian army in Silesia and Lusatia, till the peace of Hubertsburg. He died at Stettin in 1782.

BEVERNINK, (Jerome,) a celebrated Dutch statesman, born at Tergouw, in Holland, April 25, 1614. His grandfather, John, was of a noble Prussian family, who entered the military service of the States in 1575, and marrying the daughter of a burgomaster of Tergouw, who was also treasurer-general of the province of Holland, he settled in the country, and founded a family there. Jerome Bevernink first showed himself advantageously in public affairs at home, and his capacity for political undertakings being thus established, he was sent over to England as ambassador extraordinary to Cromwell, the protector. In this employment he had the honour of concluding the peace between England and Holland, April 28, 1654. During this embassy, the office of treasurer-general of the United Provinces was conferred upon him, and he held it until 1665, when his resignation was reluctantly accepted, after an ineffectual trial of both reasons and entreaties to retain him in place. After this time he appeared repeatedly as a distinguished diplomatist in several parts of Europe. He was twice at Cleves in 1666, concluding, on his first visit, a strict alliance with the elector of Brandenburg; on his second, making peace with the bishop of Munster. In the following year he concluded, as ambassador, the treaty of Breda with England. In 1668 he was sent as ambassador extraordinary to Aix-la-Chapelle, on account of the treaty of peace between France and Spain, and this treaty was concluded May 2. In 1671 he went into Spain as ambassador extraordinary, to make up the differences between that country. His masters here were fully satisfied with his conduct. After several other successful displays of diplomatic talent, and when retired, as he hoped for life, he was urged to take an active part in the treaty of Nimeguen, which made peace between France and Holland, and which was signed August 10, 1678. Even then his countrymen would not dispense with his services. His last appearance, however, as a politician, was towards the close of 1679, when he concluded a treaty of peace and commerce between Sweden and the States. He lived afterwards in retirement, at a handsome seat near Leyden, finding employment for his active mind in promoting the academical utility of that celebrated town, and in botanical pursuits at home. It was a chill that he caught in inspecting the MSS. of Isaac Vossius, then lately bought for the university of Leyden, which brought on his last illness. He died October 30, 1690. To Bevernink's botanical taste, Europe owes the introduction of the *Tropæolum majus;* and to it also Paul Hermann's researches in the East Indies. (Bayle. Biog. Univ.)

BEVERWYCK, (John van,) a celebrated physician, better known by his Latinized name, *Beverovicius*, born at Dort, in Holland, November 17, 1594. At the age of twenty he went to Caen, thence to Paris, Montpelier, and Padua; taking at the last place the degree of doctor of medicine. In the course of these travels, he availed himself of the instructions of Pineau and Riolan at Paris, of Varandal and Ranchin at Montpelier, and of Fonseca Sanctorius and Sylvaticus at Padua. The acquisition of his degree did not lessen his thirst for knowledge; and excited by the reputation of Bartoletti he went to Bologna; whence, after a time devoted to practical medicine, he returned to Dort, passing through Basle and Louvain, where he became acquainted with Felix Plater, and other persons of considerable eminence. He now devoted himself to practice, was named physician to his native city, made professor of medicine in 1625, and honoured, besides, with several civil appointments. He was, indeed, much engaged in public affairs, and was, on several occasions, sent to the Dutch States by his fellow-citizens. He died January 19, 1647, deeply regretted; and an inscription, composed by Heinsius, was engraved on his tomb in the principal church of Dort. His writings are distinguished by their purity of style, and their relation of facts. His practical knowledge was not of the highest order; and this is readily to be accounted for by the diversity of subjects foreign to his profession, which occupied his attention. He, however, successfully refuted the opinions advanced by the celebrated Montaigne against physic and physicians; and he was in correspondence with the extraordinary Anne Schurrmann, in whose works some of his writings are to be found. He exposed the quackery of the urinoscopists, and laboured to simplify the methods of prescribing for the cure of diseases. Of his productions it is sufficient here to notice, Idea Medicinæ Veterum, Lugd. Bat. 1633, 1637, 12mo and 8vo; De Excellentiâ Fœminei Sexus, Dord. 1636, 1639, 8vo; Epistolica Quæstio de Vitæ Termino, Lugd. Bat. 1637, 1639, 1652, 4to; De Calculo Renum et Vesicâ: cum Epistolis et Consultationibus magnorum Virorum, Lugd. Bat. 1638, 1641, 12mo; In Hippocratis Aphorismorum de Calculo, Lugd. Bat. 1641, 1642, 12mo. Epistolicæ Quæstiones cum Doct. Responsis. Accedit ejusdem necnon Erasmi, Cardani, Melancthonis, Medicinæ Encomium, Roterd. 1644, 1665, 12mo; Introductio ad Medicinam Indigenam, Lugd. Bat. 1644, 12mo. The entire works of Beverwyck were published, Amst. 1651, 1664, 1672, 1680, 4to and 8vo; and an edition in Flemish. Amst. 1656, 4to.

BEVILACQUA, (Ambrose,) an Italian artist, known by a picture at St. Stephen's, in Milan, representing St. Ambrose, with Saints Gervasius and Protasius standing at his side. Other works obtained him the character of a fine draughtsman of perspective, though in this he has violated its rules. The design is good, excepting that it has some traces of dryness of style. Memorials of him are found as early as the year 1486. (Lanzi, Stor. Pitt. iv. 144.)

BEVILLE, (Charles,) an artist, born at Paris in 1651, and died in 1716.

BEVIN, (Elway,) an eminent English musician, who flourished about the end of the reign of queen Elizabeth, and during that of king James. He was of Welsh extraction, and studied under Tallis, upon whose recommendation he was sworn gentleman extraordinary of the Chapel Royal, in 1589. His service in D minor, printed in Boyce's collection, has the true ancient cast of modulation, the *ferrugo pretiosa* upon it, which gives a dignity to its effects for which we can now hardly account. The accents, as usual with old masters, are often erroneously placed; but if that imperfection be removed, or regarded with indulgence, the composition must be allowed, in point of harmony and modulation, to be admirable. There are also some grand effects produced by pauses and long notes, without changing or infringing the original measure, which afford very pleasing sensations. Before the time of Bevin the precepts for the composition of canons were known to few. Tallis, Bird, Waterhouse, and Farmer, were eminently skilled in this most abstruse part of musical practice. Every canon, as given to the public, was a kind of enigma, and was considered as one of the greatest triumphs of intellect, whilst its solution was as difficult as the most abstruse and complicated problem in Euclid. Compositions of this class were sometimes exhibited in the form of a cross, sometimes in that of a circle; and there is one now extant resembling a horizontal sundial. The resolution, as it was termed, of a canon, that is, the resolving it into its elements, and reducing it into score, was deemed a work of almost as great difficulty as the original composition. Besides his appointment in the Chapel Royal, Bevin was organist of Bristol Cathedral, and preceptor of Dr. Child. In 1636 or 1637 he was dismissed from all his employments, on being found an adherent of the Romish communion. He composed some church services, and a few anthems; and in 1631 published a work entitled, A Briefe and Short Instruction of the Art of Musicke, to teach how to make discant of all proportions that are in use, &c., by Elway Bevin, thin quarto of 52 pages; a work that is replete with harmonic erudition. The rules contained in it for composition are in general very brief; but for the composition of canons there is in it a great variety of examples, of almost all the possible forms in which they are capable of being constructed, even to the extent of sixty parts. (Hawkins's Hist. of Music, iii. 373. Rees's Cyclopædia.)

BEWICK, (Thomas,) an English artist, eminent for reviving the art of engraving on wood; or, more properly, for inventing a mode of carrying it to much greater perfection than it had ever attained before. Although known in Europe even before printing, properly so called, and used with great skill in ornamenting books in the fifteenth and sixteenth centuries, wood-engraving had sunk almost below contempt, when Bewick's genius gained it general admiration. In the earlier specimens of the art, little more is attempted than a bold outline, with cross-hatching introduced in the larger blocks. But Bewick's burin produced a more complete and finished effect, by displaying a variety of tints, and effecting a perspective. This improvement was accomplished by slightly lowering the surface of the block where the distance or lighter parts of the engraving were to be shown to perfection. It was first suggested to Bewick by Mr. Bulmer, the spirited and enlightened printer, who was a Newcastle man, of his own time of life, and an intimate acquaintance during the time that they were both apprentices in that town. Bewick was born at Cherry Burn, in the parish of Ovingham, Northumberland, Aug. 12, 1753, and early showing a great talent for drawing, he was apprenticed to an engraver at Newcastle. While serving his time, Charles Hutton, then a schoolmaster in the town, afterwards eminent as Dr. Hutton of Woolwich, applied to Bewick's master for engravings to illustrate his great work on mensuration. Wood-cuts were recommended as giving an opportunity to place each proposition, with its figure, on the same page; and young Bewick was employed in executing many of the cuts. He did his work so admirably, that his master advised him to turn his attention chiefly to this branch of engraving. Judiciously taking this advice, he made a short visit to London, but his eye was so formed for rural objects, that he soon returned into the north, and fixed himself in Newcastle, as his former master's partner, but constantly indulged himself with rambles into the country. The first important work by which his talents became known to the world, was the General History of Quadrupeds, with his wood-cuts, which appeared in 1790; and subsequently a succession of publications came forth, adapted for displaying Bewick's abilities as a wood-engraver and an accurate observer of nature. He died at his residence, near the Windmill-hills, Gateshead, Nov. 8, 1828. His brother John, who was seven years younger than himself, and had been his apprentice, became also an eminent wood-engraver, but he died consumptive, in 1795. (Ann. Biog.)

BEXARANO, (Francis Matthew Fernandes,) a Spanish physician, said to have been from Estremadura, author of La Noticia Intuitiva de Todas las Artis y Ciencias, 1625, which appeared also in Latin; likewise of De Facultatibus natural. Disput. Medic. et Philosoph. Granatæ, 1619, 4to. (Antonio.)

BEXON, (Gabriel Leopold Charles Aimé,) a French naturalist and miscellaneous writer, especially distinguished as assistant of the celebrated Buffon. He was born at Remiremont, in Lorraine, in March, 1748, and died at Paris, February 15, 1784, being chantor of St. Chapelle there. He owed his advancement to the first volume of a History of Lorraine, published in 1777, 8vo. No other volume ever appeared; but in the Conservateur were published, Matériaux pour l'Histoire naturelle des Salines de Lorraine, a clear proof that Bexon really meditated at one time the prosecution of his historical work. He had really published before it, namely, in 1773, Système de la Fermentation, but to this he put his brother Scipio's name. In 1775 he printed Catechisme d'Agriculture, ou Bibliothèque des Gens de la Campagne. (Biog. Univ.)

BEXON, (Scipio Jerome,) brother of the preceding, and born at the same place in 1753. His profession was the law, and he became by that means connected with the abbey of Remiremont. When he saw this foundation likely to be sacrificed by the revolutionists in 1790, he published his Cri de l'Humanité et de la Raison, in the vain hope of saving it, and thus, as he thought, protecting the country from ruin. He afterwards transferred his residence to Paris, and obtained a succession of professional appointments, among them the honourable charges of remodelling the criminal codes of Bavaria and of the kingdom of Italy. Upon theoretic jurisprudence he published several works, highly esteemed, as he was well versed in the subject, wise, methodical, and clear. (Biog. des Contemps.)

BEYER, (John de,) a painter, born at Arau, in Switzerland, in 1705, went to Holland at an early age, and there settled. He was more occupied in designing than painting, and executed with remarkable ability various views of towns, castles, &c. Some of his pictures and designs have been engraved. The date of his death is unknown. (Biog. Univ.)

BEYER. There are several German writers of minor note who bear this name.

Beyer, (*G.*) professor of law, born at Leipsic, 1665; studied there, and afterwards at Frankfort-on-the-Oder; elected, in 1706, to the professorship of law at Wittemberg, where he died 1714. What will preserve his memory is the fact, that he was the first who separated German law from the Roman, and wrote a particular work upon it, which appeared after his death, under the title, Specimen Juris Germanici, Hal. Magd. 1718, 4to, edited and completed by Griebner. It afterwards went through numerous editions, and is remarkable as the first attempt of the kind. Besides this, he is the author of a work on juridical bibliography, and of a few other productions now forgotten.

Beyer, (*A.*) a German writer, chiefly of bibliography, born at Bertholsdorf, near Freiberg, in 1707; studied at Leipsic and Wittemberg; librarian successively to J. D. von Schönberg, and to the count von Bünau, at Dresden; filled, in this capital, various clerical and scholastic offices, and died there 1741. His two chief works are, Memoriæ Historicocriticæ Libror. rarior. &c. Dresden, 1734, 8vo; and the Arcana Bibliothecar. Dresdensium, with two continuations, Dresd. 1738-40, 8vo. Beyer wrote the life of the noted linguist, George Gentius. He is said to have assisted the Swede, von Strahlenberg, in his Description of the North and East of Europe, Asia, &c.

Beyer, (*J. R. G.*) preacher at Sömmerda, near Erfurt, born 1756, and educated at the latter place, and at Jena; filled, in the course of his life, various scholastic and clerical offices at Erfurt, and in the neighbourhood. He suffered considerably by the war between France and Prussia, in 1805, and the subsequent change of government. Three years before his death, the French appointed him superintendent of the villages of the Kameraldiöces, and Oberschulrath at Erfurt. Especially unfortunate were the last weeks of his life, in which his parsonage had to be turned into a military hospital. An epidemic disease, which broke out in it, and defied medical control, put a period to his active career in Dec. 1813. He was a popular preacher, an esteemed writer in the catechetical form, and on all clerical subjects wrote with uncommon facility; and possessed, in a remarkable degree, the talent of developing his ideas in a perspicuous, generally comprehensible, and popular manner. In this respect his Handbook for Children and Teachers of the Young on the Catechism of Luther, received and deserved general approbation, and has continued to be very widely used in Germany. His General Magazine for Clergymen, according to the Requisitions of our Time, and its continuation, Museum for Clergymen, though inferior to the works of the same class by Teller, Löffler, and Ammon, contains a great quantity of useful practical matter. In his popular sermons, of which he published a considerable number, his style is often too diffuse and negligent; arrangement is wanting; and no approach made to true eloquence.

BEYERLINK, (Laurence,) a learned ecclesiastic, of a family from Bergen-op-Zoom, but born, in 1578, at Antwerp, where his father was an apothecary. His education was received partly among the Jesuits, partly in the university of Louvain. In the neighbourhood of that city he afterwards became a parochial incumbent, joining with his clerical duties the professorship of philosophy in a house of canons regular within a short distance. He was eventually called to situations of greater importance, both educational and professional, at Antwerp, where he died, June 7, 1627. Literature owes to him, Apophthegmata Christianorum, Ant. 1608, 8vo. Biblia Sacra variarum Translationum, *ib.* 1616, 3 vols, fol. Promptuarium Morale super Evangelia Communia, et particularia quædam Festorum totius Anni, 8vo, three parts, often reprinted. Magnum Theatrum Vitæ Humanæ, a work founded on materials left by Conrad Lycosthenes, arranged and augmented by the elder Swinger; farther augmented, with some alterations, by the younger Swinger; and completed by the great additions and corrections of Beyerlink. It did not, however, appear until after his death, being printed at Cologne, in 1631, in 8 vols, fol. It was reprinted at Lyons in 1678, and at Venice in 1707. It is a collection of theology, history, politics, and philosophy, but full of worthless matter. (Biog. Univ.)

BEYGTACH, (Hadji,) a famous Turkish dervise, founder of an order in that class of Mahometan devotees, called after him *Bertachys*. This is not, however, his principal claim upon the notice of Europeans. That is founded upon his connexion with the Janissaries, long the prætorian bands of Turkey. Having raised this body, destined for such a long continuance, and to become so famous, Amurath I., in 1362, called Hadji Beygtach, considered from celebrity, both for prophecy and miracle, as Mahomet's especial friend, to bless its colours. The dervise, holding his sleeve over the first soldier's head, thus addressed him, "Be thy face fierce, and thine arm victorious: keep thy scimitar ever drawn: may your foes find in all of you their deaths, and may ye return safe and sound from every encounter with them: let your name be *yeny chery*," (the new soldiers.) From this combination the word *Janissary* was formed, and the cap worn by a member of that body never lost the form of Hadji Beygtach's sleeve. His death occurred in 1368, and his memory, even yet respected, causes many a visit to his tomb, at the village of Beygtach, near Galata. (Biog. Univ.)

BEYLBROUCK, (M.) a Flemish engraver, who resided in England about 1713. He engraved a plate of the death of Dido, after Sebastian Bourdon, which is neatly executed, but in a stiff formal style, and without much effect. Mr. Strutt thinks he may have been a pupil of Gerard Scotin, from the similarity of their styles. (Bryan's and Strutt's Dictionaries.)

BEYMA, (Julius,) was born at Dorkum, in Holland, in the year 1539. Having taken the degree of law licentiate at Orleans, he practised as an advocate at Leward, in Friseland; but becoming suspected by the Spanish government on account of his Lutheranism, he was soon obliged to quit that town. He retired into Germany, and practised at Wittemberg. The times becoming more calm, he returned to his native land, and obtained a professorship of law at Leyden. After having taught with success at this university during fifteen years, he went in 1596 to Franeker in the same capacity. He died in 1598, leaving several dissertations upon law, which were published at Louvain, in one volume 4to, in 1645. (Biog. Univ.)

BEYS, (Charles de,) a French poet, born about 1610, and early conspicuous as a versifier, both in Latin and French. When, however, mature in age, his fondness for convivial pleasures prevented him from making any great figure as a literary man, and his productions are now only valued as book rarities. But he lay under the suspicion, at one time, of engaging in party politics, being sent to the Bastile, as the author of the Miliad, one of the most violent of the satires levelled at cardinal Richelieu. He soon proved his innocence; and when at liberty again, returned to his old habits of dissipation. These undermined his health, and he died Sept. 26, 1639, leaving three tragi-comedies, a comedy, and some poems. (Biog. Univ.)

BEYS, (Giles,) a Parisian printer in the sixteenth century, who first made a distinction in printing between *i* and *j*, *u* and *v*. He was indebted for this to Ramus, who made use of it in his Latin grammar of 1537, but seems to have discontinued it afterwards. Beys adopted it first in Mignaut's Commentary on Horace. He died at Paris, April 19, 1593.

BEYZOVI, a Persian judge, or cadi, who died in 1299, leaving an historical work that treats of most of the Asiatic sovereigns, particularly of the ancient Moguls. (Moreri.)

BEZA, (Theodore de,) or, as he ordinarily signed his name himself, Bes-ze. By the French generally his surname is written De Bèze. He was born June 24, 1519, at Vezelai, a small town of the Nivernois, formerly a member of the duchy of Burgundy; hence he styled himself in Latin, *Theodorus Beza Vezelius*. His family had long been wealthy, and his father, whose name was Peter, was bailiff (*præfectus, bailli*,) of Vezelai. His mother was Mary Bourdelot, also from among the gentry. While still extremely young, Theodore was sent to Paris to an uncle, counsellor to the parliament there; and he dying within a short time, another uncle, abbot of Froidmond, gladly took charge of him. In December, 1528, he was sent for education to Orleans, under Melchior Wolmar, a German of distinguished scholarship, especially in Greek, but a convert to protestantism, who afterwards removed to Bourges, where, by the queen of Navarre's means, he was appointed Greek professor. Young Beza followed him thither, continuing under his tuition about six years altogether, and making a progress highly creditable to both parties, but imbibing all the time an antipathy, which such an instructor would undoubtedly place upon solid grounds, to Romish corruptions. Wolmar was, in fact, one of the first introducers into France of the light recently thrown in Germany upon religion. His promising pupil Beza was, however, soon placed under such temptations as rendered religious information rather a treasure of the mind than an active influence of the heart. Wolmar, besides grounding him thoroughly in all branches of elegant literature and philosophy, taught him something of law, to which it was wished that he should apply himself, after the learned German's departure from France for his own country in 1535; and he did actually take the degree of licentiate in law, at Orleans, in 1539. But he had no taste for the study, and returned immediately to Paris, where a good introduction, easy circumstances, a fascinating address, and fine parts, caused him to be generally caressed. He had, besides, acquired, before his departure from Orleans, the sort of reputation to serve him with persons of cultivated minds in the upper circles. While ostensibly studying law, he was really occupied with Latin poetry more than any thing else, and he made himself no contemptible rival of his classical models. Unhappily, however, with their spirit and diction, he suffered himself to imbibe some of their baser qualities; and his own Latin poems, accordingly, have an alloy of gay licentiousness which, from different causes, rendered them immensely popular. He collected them himself under the title of Juvenilia; and their intrinsic merit, joined to an exceptionable tone, secured them at once a large degree of notice: eventually, their hold upon the public mind was increased enormously. They were invidiously reprinted by the Romish party, as specimens of a great religious reformer's real character, and vainly did their humiliated author strive to suppress them. While of an age to think of them with pride and pleasure, he was living on the revenues of the priory of Lonjumeau, and of another benefice, procured for him by interest, although only meant for orders, and probably himself with little serious intention of taking them: a sort of abuse then common, and undoubtedly a preparative for the Reformation; although this, with a few other irregularities, were not, as Romanists would fain believe, the only solid grounds for quitting their communion. Besides his two benefices, Beza succeeded, when young, to a considerable income from the death of an elder brother; so that, at the time of life when temptations to gaiety are most irresistible, he was more than usually beset by them. It is, however, as little necessary, as it is charitable, to suppose him entangled in them to any very culpable excess. It is probable that he was convivial, thoughtless, and lively, rather than dissipated; such really being the character of many whom misinformation or ill-nature paints in far blacker colours. Beza's final escape from this period of temptation was effected, as it has often been, by a fit of sickness. One reason of his indisposition for orders was love for Claudia Denosse, a young female, of whose original condition nothing farther is known than that it was inferior. A marriage with her would have vacated his ecclesiastical preferments, and he had great difficulty in making up his mind to such a sacrifice. Illness, however, terminated his vacillation, and on recovery, he resigned his benefices, with prospects of much better, determined upon fulfilling a vow long since made to embrace protestantism, to marry the female to whom he had been four years engaged, and to retire from France. Accordingly, on the 24th of October, 1548, he arrived at Geneva, and married the object of his affections. He lived happily with her forty years. Having now no definite object, he soon went to Tubingen to see his old tutor, Melchior Wolmar. In the following year he became professor of Greek at Lausanne, and he so continued nearly ten years. While there he published his tragi-comedy, in French verse, entitled, Le Sacrifice d'Abraham, which was considered, rather to the surprise of unfriendly critics in later times, as an admirable piece of pathetic writing, and was translated into Latin towards the close of the century by two several authors. During his vacations he commonly visited Geneva, where Calvin urged him to become a minister, and to complete the version of the Psalms which Marot had begun. He took immediately the latter advice, and produced one hundred psalms, in French verse, but not so happily, it is said, as the fifty which his predecessor had left. In 1556 appeared his Latin version of the New Testament, of which he published subsequently numerous editions, commonly with many alterations. The literary labour, however, of his residence at Lausanne, which has been most noticed in after ages, is a small tract, entitled, De Hæreticis à Civili Magistratu Puniendis, in answer to one by Sebastian Castalio, published soon after the burning of Servetus, Oct. 17, 1553, and entitled, Quo Jure, quove Fructu, Hæretici Gladio puniendi? Beza's tract is triumphantly cited by Romanists as a full vindication of their own church's contemporary proceedings against attacks upon her peculiarities, which she boldly branded as heretical. Her adversaries are thus exhibited as equally intolerant; proving, therefore, such intolerance really to have been the fault of the age, not of any particular party then existing. These representations, however, are only true in a great measure. The reformers lighted a few fires to consume persons whose opinions had been solemnly condemned in the church as damnable heresies, by the first four general councils; and it might be argued upon plausible grounds, that no such fires would ever have been lighted at all, had not reproaches been cast upon the party by its opponents; that it had artfully or blindly opened the flood-gates of heterodoxy and of error in every form. The Romanists, on the other hand, burnt great numbers for a denial of their own sectarian distinctions, principally for that of transubstantiation; although none of them could appeal to any authority of high antiquity, or generally respected by the catholic church. Bad, accordingly, as are both cases, they are not equally so.

In 1558, Beza, and two others, were employed to take letters from Calvin into Germany, soliciting some of the protestant princes of that country for their influence with the court of France, in favour of the persecuted witnesses against Romanism immemorially seated in the valleys of Piedmont, then subject to the French, and in favour also of some protestants recently apprehended in Paris. The object was gained so far as to obtain a promise of the intervention sought, but it proved of little value at the French court. During this journey he had the pleasure of some personal intercourse with Melancthon. In 1559, he quitted Lausanne, and established himself at Geneva, where he became closely connected with Calvin, not only entering into his ideas, but also, in a short time, sharing his duties, both clerical and educational. The latter were important: as the little republic of Geneva was bent upon establishing a college, which, in addition to the inculcation of protestant opinions, might attract students by superior opportunities of improvement. Calvin refused the office of rector, but recommended Beza for it, engaging himself to teach theology. Beza's next conspicuous employment was a journey to convert Anthony de Bourbon, duke of Vendôme, father of Henry IV., become by means of his wife, Jane d'Albret, heiress of that throne, king of Navarre. He was a weak, vacillating prince, who cared much more for his ease and pleasure than for serious things of any kind. But his birth and expectations gave him an importance that mere nature and habit would have placed immeasurably above his reach. Such of the French nobility, accordingly, as had embraced protestantism, or were jealous of the grasping house of Guise, anxiously desired his total alienation from the Romish party; and Beza was thought likely to gratify them in this. He was, therefore, invited to Nerac, in Guienne, then the residence of Anthony and his royal wife, being the capital of the duchy of Albret. No step could be more judicious. Protestantism was soon preached openly in the place, a church for that purpose was built there, and in the following year, 1560, the monasteries and Romish churches were destroyed by queen Jane's orders. Beza stayed in Nerac until the commencement of 1561, when he was called, by the king of Navarre's desire, to attend the famous colloquy between the Romanists and the Reformed, which was opened at Poissy on the 30th of July, in that year. When the colloquy really began, on the 9th of September, he was chosen their spokesman by the protestant ministers, and in his opening address gave violent offence. Touching upon the great eucharistic question, he disclaimed both transubstantiation and consubstantiation, proceeding to say,—"Should any one ask whether we assert Christ's absence from the sacrament, we answer unhesitatingly, No. But if we look to the distinction of places, as we must, when this doctrine is narrowly examined, we then pronounce, that our Lord's body is as remote from the bread and wine, as the highest heaven is from the surface of the earth." Hitherto profound attention had been bestowed upon his oratory, but this attack upon the vital principle of Romanism immediately excited indignant murmurs, which soon passed into loud cries of "Blasphemy." Beza has been much blamed by Romanists for thus assaulting the prejudices of his auditory, and to him has been attributed, in a great degree, the disappointment of hopes entertained from the colloquy at Poissy, and the bitterness infused into the theological dissensions of France. But although distinguished ecclesiastics, who ring a bell at their communion-service, to announce the sensible presence of an incarnate Deity, claiming the bended knee from his worshippers, could do no less than cry "Blasphemy" when they heard that doctrine publicly denied before such an assembly as that of Poissy; yet it was hardly possible for a divine who thought them entangled there in a capital error, to speak otherwise than Beza did. The turn, therefore, given to the colloquy by his opening speech is fairly chargeable, neither upon his indiscretion, nor upon the intolerance of his opponents, but upon the necessity of handling a doctrine unequivocally, which was really at the bottom of the whole dispute. After this remarkable assembly dispersed, Beza did not immediately return to Geneva. He was retained in France by the king of Navarre, and the prince of Conde, aided by the queen mother herself, who said, that as a Frenchman, he ought to remain in his own country. Being, indeed, at liberty to exercise his ministerial talents publicly by the edict of January 1562, which allowed that privilege, under certain restrictions, to the reformed, he preached often in the suburbs of Paris, and rendered himself conspicuous upon every occasion that offered, by a zealous advocacy of reformed opinions. During this residence in his native land, he was engaged in a conference, holden in the council-chamber, at St. Germain's, upon the religious use of images. This had been suggested by queen Catharine de' Medici, either from a real hope of effecting some agreement, or with a view to amuse and deceive the protestant ministers. It was, in fact, a point upon which many of the more moderate Romanists were disposed to make considerable concessions, very great abuses having, undeniably, flowed from figures in places of worship. Beza's ready wit served him upon this occasion, some of the more dogged champions of images making use of arguments and assertions, which only needed a lively exposure to make admirable subjects of merriment. One of them felt sure that in the time of St. Denis, whom he described as a disciple of St. Paul, these helps to worship were used in Paris, as might be seen from the windows of St. Benedict's church. This amazing stretch of folly Beza pronounced an argument fragile as glass, and his mode of shivering it to atoms drew down peals of laughter on every side. His more serious displays of argument were chiefly reserved for a long written disquisition, presented to the queen, in which the unlawfulness of using images in religion was maintained from the second commandment, so infamously kept out of sight by the church of Rome, by various dishonest artifices, during many ages. But although proofs of this concealment, which may be found in abundance, are enough to convict iconolaters of upholding an unlawful system, the conference left both parties, as is usually the case, with a fixed resolution to maintain their own opinions. Nevertheless, the tolerant edict of January 1562, might have secured religious peace for some considerable time, had not a tumult unexpectedly occurred on Sunday, the 1st of March next following, at Vassy, on the borders of Champagne, from the intolerant insolence and anxiety for pillage of an armed troop in personal attendance upon the duke of Guise. A large protestant congregation, then assembled for worship, was brutally assaulted by these licentious troopers, and sixty of its members butchered, more than two hundred besides being wounded. This was the first outrage upon a large scale upon the protestant party that France had witnessed; and the reformed congregations lost no time in presenting a memorial, inculpating the duke of Guise, to the queen-mother, Beza being selected by the ministers as their representative upon this occasion. Catharine gave a gracious, but evasive answer, and the audience would hardly deserve mention had it not been rendered famous by a conversation that took place between Beza and Anthony de Bourbon, king of Navarre. That weak and licentious prince had relapsed into Romanism, and was now out of town with the court, attracted by one of Catharine's handsome maids of honour, who had been ordered into waiting, because it was known that Anthony would follow her, and his absence from Paris was then thought desirable. The foolish king, however, considered himself bound to show his importance and newly-born religious zeal before the protestant deputation. Sternly regarding Beza, he said, "So, then, places of worship are now attended by the Huguenots with arms." He was answered, "Arms discreetly borne are the surest guarantees of peace, and are shown to be necessary by the massacre at Vassy, until the church shall be sufficiently protected." The cardinal of Ferrara then interposed with some incorrect representation of the collision between Romanists and Protestants which had occurred at the church of

St. Medard, by Paris, in the preceding December. But Beza was an eye-witness of this, and he soon silenced him. The king of Navarre now came forward again, and with considerable warmth. Beza replied with mingled dignity and gentleness, reminding him of their former intercourse, and of the invitation from himself that brought him again into France. In conclusion, he said, "It belongs to God's church, in the name of which I now address you, to suffer blows, not to strike them. But pray remember, sir, that the church is an anvil which has worn out many a hammer." Such warnings are generally given in vain at the outset of an agitated period, and mutual exasperations, accompanied by inexcusable violence on both sides, rendered a formal trial of strength inevitable. Beza was with his friends as their spiritual adviser when they contested the hardly-fought battle of Dreux, December 19, 1562, in which they were defeated, although likely, at one time, to be victorious. When the duke of Guise was assassinated before Orleans, in the following February, Poltrot, his wretched murderer, at first named Beza as the instigator, but he soon retracted the accusation, and persisted until death in clearing the calumniated minister from any participation in the deed; nor have Romanists of any credit gone farther in connecting him with it than by the utterance of inflammatory denunciations against the duke as an enemy to religious truth. Beza's own protestations in this case were equally decisive and ingenuous. He admitted his full participation in the odium that had generally fallen upon the duke of Guise from the massacre of Vassy, but denied any wish for his punishment, unless by ordinary forms of law. It was to array these against him that he had joined in the memorial to the queen and the late king of Navarre. He admitted also exhortations to the reformed to use their arms, and take especial care to keep themselves from circumvention, since war was now begun; but protested himself to have been always an earnest counsellor of peace, if it could be had without compromising God's honour. With Poltrot, he declared himself to have been wholly unacquainted, and entirely without communication, either direct or indirect; but he did not deny that the fate which by that miserable man's crime had overtaken the duke, appeared to him a just judgment of God, well fitted for an awful warning to all the enemies of sound religion. As for certain expressions attributed to him by the assassin, he pointed out their inconsistency with his doctrine, which was very far from promising paradise to any man as the reward of his works. He did not remain much longer in France; the treaty of Amboise, promulgated by the crown, March 19, 1563, having secured a qualified toleration to the reformed, his services appeared less necessary among his own countrymen, and he returned to Geneva. On Calvin's death, May 27, 1564, Beza took the place that had been occupied by that illustrious reformer, and hence became really the head of presbyterianism. In the little town of his residence he was, perhaps, the most important personage, and his influence extended over his whole party in France. Personally, he was very little in that country any more. In 1568 he visited Vezelai, on some family business; in 1571 he was summoned to Rochelle, to attend the synod holden there under royal authority, and he was unanimously elected its moderator. He was also engaged in other important affairs at a distance from his home, thus giving proofs to all Europe of a fitness for business as well as literature and preaching, and of the high estimation in which his party held him. In April 1588, he lost his wife, and although now seventy, he married again within the year, to Catharine de la Plane, a widow, who survived him, and whom he called his Shunammite, alluding to the history of David. He fortunately found a person who took great care of him in his old age, and to her he left all that he possessed at Geneva. He died in that place October 13, 1605, in full possession of his faculties, though in the 87th year of his age. During the last eight years of his life he had been compelled to spare himself more than had been usual with him, venturing but rarely to speak in public, and from this he abstained altogether at the beginning of 1600; but his zeal for the principles that he had embraced, and the society of which he had so long been the head and centre, never left him. When, accordingly, declining nature forbade him active services, he was always ready with advice and information. He was, unquestionably, among the greatest men of his age, and has been surpassed by few of any age; but his controversial prominence raised a host of enemies. The Romanists abhorred him; and Protestants, averse from the doctrine or discipline of Geneva, often thought his conduct and opinions open to censure or suspicion. Romish hostility went, indeed, so far as to assail his memory with the grossest calumnies; his retirement from France, where he resigned an important professional income, enjoyed without exertion, and went to earn a subsistence as a scholar among foreigners, having drawn down the most odious imputations. This extravagance, the natural fruit of party-rancour in a period imperfectly civilized and uncontrolled by periodical literature, has now wholly vanished; all sides acknowledging that Calvin's successor, though not equal to that great man himself, was really worthy of the position that he so long occupied in the theological world.

In English religious affairs Beza was a good deal involved, partly from his intrinsic importance, but chiefly from his influence over that party which long laboured to introduce presbyterianism. He did not, however, approve of all that was done by his English admirers. He witnessed with concern Knox and Goodman's attacks upon female government in queen Mary's reign; and in the beginning of her successor's, he answered with considerable moderation an appeal to him as to the use of those ecclesiastical habits which were then occasioning a violent clamour among a section of the English clergy. He thought it injudicious to impose them again, as having been formerly employed for superstitious purposes; but he would not admit any real impiety in them, or even the propriety of throwing up ministerial charges rather than wear them. Still his opinions upon political questions were rather free for that age; evidently inclining to the propriety of resisting civil authorities that stood in the way of his opinions, but stopping short of inflammatory language. He did, however, go so far, in a letter to some great man in England, probably Elizabeth's favourite, Leicester, as to maintain that pure doctrine is of little use without pure discipline; in plain words, that England must be studded all over with petty democratic oligarchies, like Geneva, or her reformation would be found of no great value. Such an assertion was so agreeable to the puritanical party, that Beza received many appeals from it, and some of his answers were characterised, not unfairly, on the other side, as written in a strain of assumption equal to that displayed in papal epistles. Archbishop Whitgift naturally felt displeased at the countenance given by him, either directly or indirectly, to the party that was then striving earnestly to force presbyterianism upon England, and wrote to expostulate. Beza was, however, now far in the decline of life, and he made a very becoming answer to the rebuke, disclaiming all intention of interfering with foreign churches in which doctrine was unexceptionable, though discipline was not framed upon the Genevan model. He declared both himself and his brethren at Geneva, quite willing to ask themselves, when suspected of interference with others, "Who gave us authority over any church but our own?"

As a scholar and a man of letters, Beza was industrious in the highest degree. Being placed over the academy of Geneva, as its first rector, in 1559, he continued an indefatigable manager of its affairs and studies during forty years. It proved an institution to which learning was very much indebted; and such was Beza's anxiety for its efficiency, that when the council of Geneva was obliged to suppress two professorships from want of funds to maintain them, he filled the duties of both himself, without neglecting any other engagement, although more than seventy years of age. Besides his works already mentioned, it should be known that the editions of his *Juvenilia*, published in 1569, 1576, and 1597, contain only a part of these poems, exceptionable pieces being retrenched. His Confessio Christianæ Fidei was published in 1560. In the same year, was printed at Geneva, a French translation of his tract upon the Punishment of Heretics by the Civil Power, by Calladon. One of his works is extremely rare, entitled, De Peste, Quæstiones duæ Explicatæ; una, Sitne contagiosa? Altera, An et quatenus sit Christianis per secessionem vitanda? Genev. 1579; Leyd. 1636. Others of his works are, Histoire Ecclésiastique des Eglises Réformées du Royaume de France, depuis l'an 1521 jusqu'en 1563, 3 vols, 8vo, 1580. Icones Illustrium Virorum, 1580; translated into French by Goulet, under the title of Vrais Pourtraits des Hommes Illustres en Piété et en Doctrine, Genev. 1581. A Latin treatise on Divorce and Polygamy. Epistles. The best edition of his Testament is that of Cambridge, 1642, fol. He was also engaged, among the other ministers of Geneva, in the translation of the Bible, corrected by the aid of the Greek and Hebrew, published at Geneva, 1588, fol. (Bayle. Biog. Univ. Smedley's History of the Reformed Religion in France.

Strype's Whitgift. Soames's Elizabethan Religious History.)

BEZBORODKO, (Prince Alexander Andreevitch,) one of the most distinguished characters in the reign of Catharine II., as a statesman and diplomatist; born in 1742, at Stolny, a village belonging to his father's estate, about fifty versts from Tchernigov. Having distinguished himself by the progress that he made in his studies at the academy of Kiev, he obtained a situation in the chancery of Little Russia; but afterwards (1769) joined, at his own request, the troops then engaged in the campaign against the Turks, in the course of which he saw much service at Larga, Kaluga, and the storming of the Turkish entrenchments at Silistria. He was rewarded with the rank of colonel in the Kiev regiment; and after the peace, in 1775, became first secretary to the empress, who, discovering his abilities and integrity, soon began to place entire confidence in him. From this epoch may be dated his public career as a most influential and active member of the government; in which capacity he is deservedly entitled to the esteem of posterity. While his application was unremitted, his tact, his promptitude, his judgment, were no less conspicuous. Of his readiness and presence of mind a remarkable instance is related. When being once summoned to the empress, he was ordered by her to read an ukase that he had been instructed to draw up; he accordingly took out the paper from his portfolio, and instantly read it off-hand; which being done, Catharine took up a pen to sign it; but great was her astonishment at perceiving that the paper was a blank, and that what she had been listening to was merely an *impromptu* on the part of Bezborodko, who had not expected that the document would be required so speedily. This incident is said to have raised him still higher in the good opinion of his sovereign. Neither was he less valued by her successor, for it was Paul who conferred on him the title of prince, and advanced him to the post of chancellor of the empire. He did not, however, enjoy that dignity very long, for he died at St. Petersburg, April 6 (18), 1799; when, as he had never been married, all his immense property fell to his brother, count Ilyi Andreevitch, who, in conformity with the other's intentions, founded the college which bears the name of Prince Bezborodko's Lyceum.

The prince was an admirer of the fine arts, and formed a valuable collection of paintings. He particularly delighted in those of Vernet; and twenty-two productions of that master adorned his sleeping-room. Scarcely any diplomatic manuscripts were found among his papers after his death; which may be accounted for by its being his practice generally to write in pencil only for the sake of greater celerity, and with so many abbreviations, that his secretaries alone, and not every one of them, could decipher his handwriting, and make a fair transcript from it. (Entz. Leks.)

BEZE, a French Jesuit, missionary in India, about the end of the seventeenth century, eminent for numerous observations connected with natural history, inserted in the Mémoires de l'Académie, from 1666 to 1699. The remarks of Bèze upon botany have been put together under the title of Description de quelques Arbres, et de quelques Plantes de Malaque. (Biog. Univ.)

BEZONS, (James Banin de,) a distinguished French military officer, who served in Portugal under marshal Schomberg, in 1667, he being then 22 years old. He subsequently distinguished himself in the various French wars which occurred during his years of activity, and he was one of the council of regency during the minority of Lewis XV. He finished his long and honourable career, May 22, 1733, at the age of 80. (Biog. Univ.)

BEZOUT, (Stephen,) an eminent French mathematician, born at Nemours, March 31, 1730. Being under the necessity of struggling for a subsistence, he devoted himself to the teaching of mathematics with such assiduity and success, that in 1763 he was entrusted by Choiseul at the head of the educational department for the royal navy. He died Sept. 27, 1785, leaving Cours de Mathématiques à l'Usage des Gardes du Pavillon, et de la Marine, Paris, 6 vols, 8vo, 1764-69, 1781-82; Cours de Mathématiques à l'Usage du Corps Royal de l'Artillerie, Paris, 4 vols, 1770-72; Théorie générale des Equations Algébriques, Paris, 1779, 1 vol. 4to. (Biog. Univ.)

BEZOZZI, (Ambrose,) a decorative painter and engraver, pupil of Danedi and Ferri, born at Milan in 1648, and died in 1706.

BHEILOL-LODI, a celebrated sultan of Delhi, and founder of the Affghan or Lodi dynasty, whose rule immediately preceded the establishment of the house of Timour in India. His family were chiefs of a noble tribe of Affghans, named

Lodi, who had established themselves in the Punjab about Sirhind and Lahore; the attempts made to reduce or expel them by the weak monarchs of the Saadat dynasty at Delhi were ineffectual; and Bheilol, after routing (A.D. 1436, A.H. 840) the last army sent against him, found himself undisputed master of all the country as far as Paniput. At this juncture, though the monarchs of Delhi were still titular sultans of India, their actual power was limited to a few miles round their capital, while six principalities were established close round the city, and thirteen independent Mohammedan kingdoms existed in different parts of the peninsula. (Ferishta.) Delhi itself was threatened with an attack, in 1440, from the sultan of Malwa, and Said-Mohammed Shah, unable to oppose any effectual resistance, implored the powerful aid of Bheilol, who advanced with 20,000 cavalry, and repulsed the Malwa army. He now began to aspire personally to the crown, but he failed in occupying Delhi during the life of Mohammed; Ala-ed-deen, however, the son of that prince, voluntarily abdicated in his favour, A.D. 1450, (A. H. 854,) on condition of being allowed to live in retirement at Budaoon. The first care of Bheilol, after assuming the crown, was to reduce the petty sovereignties in the neighbourhood of Delhi, which he effected without difficulty; but the war with the neighbouring kingdom of Joonpoor (the monarchs of which are usually styled Sherki-Shahi, or kings of the east) was a more arduous undertaking; and it was only after an almost continual struggle of twenty-eight years, through three reigns of Joonpoor kings, that Bheilol at last succeeded in completely subjugating the hostile territory, in consequence of three successive victories over the last king, Hoossein Shah, A.D. 1478, A. H. 883. The power of the Delhi kingdom was in a great measure re-established by this important conquest, and the rajah of Gualior, with other princes, paid tribute to Bheilol, whose remaining years were undistinguished by any remarkable achievements: he died in his camp, A.D. 1488, (A. H. 894,) at a great age, and was succeeded, after some competition among his sons, by Iskender, one of the younger. Bheilol is described as a just and merciful prince, cool and circumspect in deliberation, and prompt in action: to the native valour of an Affghan he united the talents of a commander, and retained, through life, the frank and martial habits of his early life, avoiding the pomp of royalty, and saying that it was sufficient for him that the world knew he was king: he is also said, though but slenderly acquainted with literature, to have been an encourager and patron of learned men. (Ferishta.)

BIACCA, (Francis Maria,) an Italian scholar, born at Parma, 12th of March, 1673. He addicted himself principally to the study of history, chronology, and antiquities. He entered into holy orders, and became, in 1702, domestic chaplain in the illustrious family of Sanvitali, as well as tutor to the two younger sons of that house. In one of his most elaborate works, Trattinemento Istorico e Chronologico, &c. Naples, 2 vols, 4to, written during the period of this engagement, he defended Josephus's Jewish Antiquities, maintaining that that historian's statements are neither false, nor contrary to Scripture. By this book, though published, possibly, without his consent, he very much offended the elder of his pupils, who had now succeeded to the estate of his father, and had become much attached to the Jesuits, one of whom, Cæsar Calino, had lately favoured views contrary to those put forth by Biacca. Notwithstanding this unfortunate and abrupt termination of his connexion with this powerful family, after it had continued during a period of twenty-six years, he was treated with much respect by several other considerable patrons; and having spent the rest of his life chiefly at Milan, he died at Parma, 15th of September, 1735.

In addition to the work above mentioned, he wrote, 1. L'Ortografia Manuale, o sia Arte facile di correttamento Scrivere e Parlare, Parma, 1714, 12mo. 2. Notizie Storiche di Rinuccio Cardinale Pallavicino, di Pompeo Sacco Parmigrano, &c., printed in vols. i. and ii. of the Notizie Istoriche degli Arcadi Morti; with other original works, besides translations of some of the Latin poets into Italian. Prefixed to several of these publications we find the assumed name of Parmindo Ibichense, which he took according to the rules of the society of Arcadians, a literary association for the cultivation of the belles-lettres, established at Rome A. D. 1690. (Moreri. Biog. Univ. Chalmers.)

BIAGI, (John Maria,) a learned Italian, born at Roveredo, in 1724, chiefly known out of Italy by a Latin preface to the works of Chrysostom, printed at Roveredo, in 1753, but not distinguished by his name. He died in 1777. (Biog. Univ.)

BIAGIOLI, (Josaphat, 1768—1831,) an Italian linguist, professor of Greek and Latin at Urbino, and afterwards, while residing at Paris, the author of Commentaries on the Poems of Dante, Michael Angelo, &c.; of several grammatical works, &c. It is said that having been compelled by his father to take orders, he renounced them during the revolution, obtained a degree of secularization, and married. He was much admired at Paris as a lecturer.

BIALOBOCKI, (John,) a Polish poet in the seventeenth century, who published some hymns translated from the Latin, Cracow, 1648, and some poems of national interest, published later in the century. (Biog. Univ.)

BIAMONTE, (Joseph Lewis, 1730—1824,) a distinguished philologist and poet; he was keeper of the private library of the prince Khevenhuller, which situation afforded him opportunities of pursuing the study of languages, especially the Latin, Greek, Hebrew, and Italian; afterwards he was chosen professor of eloquence in the university of Bologna; from whence he was shortly called to occupy the same station at Turin, where he continued till age and infirmities rendered his retirement necessary. His last years were spent at Milan. His works are,—1. Discourses delivered on various Occasions. 2. An Italian Grammar. 3. A Treatise on Oratory. 4. Iphigenia in Tauris, a tragedy. 5. Sophonisba, a tragedy. 6. Fragments, in prose and verse. He undertook a poetical translation of the Book of Job, but did not live to finish it.

BIANCANI, (Joseph,) an Italian Jesuit, born at Bologna, in 1566, who died at Parma in 1624, leaving several mathematical and astronomical works, now forgotten. The most interesting is, Aristotelis Loca Mathematica ex Universis ejus Operibus collecta et explicata. (Biog. Univ.)

BIANCHI, (Antonio,) a gondolier of Venice, who distinguished himself during the eighteenth century as a poet of no mean genius. It was not to be expected that his compositions should be exact, or his language correct; but, notwithstanding their defects, two of his works attracted much attention, and deserved great praise. These were, Il Davide Re d'Israele, 1751, fol.; and, Il Tempio ovvero il Salomone, 1753, 4to. (Biog. Univ.)

BIANCHI, (Francis Ferrari,) called also Il Frari, a painter of eminence; was born at Modena, A.D. 1447. He was distinguished for fineness of colouring, gracefulness of attitude, and grandeur of invention; but his figures are not always correct, especially in the eyes. According to Vidriani, he had the honour of being the instructor of Antonio Coreggio. (Pilkington. Bryan.)

BIANCHI, (Francis,) a musical composer of eminence, born at Cremona, about the middle of the eighteenth century. His Disertor Franchese, which afterwards became a very popular opera, was nearly condemned at its first representation, in consequence of the introduction for the first time upon the stage, of the dresses of ordinary life. Bianchi coming to England at a subsequent period, wrote, Castore e Polluce, for Signora Storace, and Inez di Castro, for Mrs. Billington; which productions, as well as his Semiramide, were much admired. (Biog. Dict. of Mus.)

BIANCHI, (John Antony, otherwise known by the name of Blanchini,) born Oct. 2, 1686. He was of the order of the Minorites, and became their provincial; and was also counsellor of the Inquisition of Rome. He employed himself in teaching theology and philosophy. His works are published under the name of Farnabio Gioachino Annuteni, being an anagram of Fra-Giovanni Antonio Bianchi. He wrote several tragedies, of one of which Sir Thomas More is the hero. He was also the author of a work in defence of the power of the pope, against the doctrines of Giannone and Bossuet, Rome, 1745—1751, 5 vols, 4to. He died Jan. 18, 1758. (Chalmers. Biog. Univ.)

BIANCHI, (John,) a learned Italian physician and naturalist, more generally known under the name of Blancus, or Plancus, born at Rimini, Jan. 3, 1693. In 1741 he was named professor of anatomy at the university of Siena, which office he held for three years, and then returned to Rimini, where he revived the Academy de' Lincei, which assembled at his house, and the members of which struck a medal to commemorate his services. He died Dec. 4, 1774. His principal works are, Lettera intorno alla Catteratta, Rimini, 1720, 4to. Lettera ad un Amico, intorno alla Magnesia Arsenicale, Pesaro, 1722, 4to. De Conchis minùs Notis, cui accessit Specimen Æstûs reciproci Maris superi ad Littus Portumque Arimini, Rimini, 1739, 1760, 4to.

Relazione dell' Esequie del Cardinal Giov. Ant. da Via, Venez. 1740, 4to. Fabii Columnæ Lyncei Phytobasamus, cui accessit Vita Fabii Columnæ, Florent. 1744, 4to. De' Vesicatori Dissertazione, Venez. 1746, 8vo. De Monstris ac Monstrosis quibusdam, *ib.* 1749, 8vo. Se il Vitto Pittagorico di Soli Vegetabili sia Giovevole per conservare la Canità, *ib.* 1752, 8vo. Lettera sopra un Pretesto Supplimento alla Storia d'un Apostoma del Lobo destro del Carvello, Rimini, 1755, 8vo. Epistola de Urinâ cum Sedimento Cæruleo, Venet. 1756, 12mo. Bianchi also published several letters and small pieces, under the assumed names of P. P. Lapi, M. Chillenio, P. Ghisi, and C. Stilita.

BIANCHI, (John Baptist,) a celebrated physician and anatomist, born at Turin, Sept. 12, 1681. He publicly defended theses on difficult points in philosophy before he had attained the age of fifteen, at which period he commenced the study of medicine, in which the same facility of learning was displayed; and he received the degree of doctor of medicine when only seventeen years of age. The confidence reposed in his extraordinary talents was such, that he was almost immediately entrusted with the care of the hospital of the city of Turin. Pathological anatomy, in an especial manner, claimed his attention, and he lost no opportunity of examining the bodies of all cases terminating fatally. The precocity displayed by Bianchi in so many branches of knowledge is a very remarkable feature in his character. He delivered no less than thirteen public courses of lectures, during the same time, on subjects of philosophy, chemistry, pharmacy, practice of medicine, &c. He was chosen a member of many foreign academies, who all recognised his merit, and filled the first chair of anatomy at Turin. As a practitioner, Bianchi does not appear to the greatest advantage; and a perfection in practice is hardly to be expected from one whose precocity of talents had led him to dogmatize at so early a period, and whose attention was divided among so many branches of professional learning. Notwithstanding these defects, Bianchi must be considered as one of the most distinguished medical men of his day, and the reputation he enjoyed was fully merited by his extensive and profound acquirements. He died at Turin, June 20, 1761. His works are numerous; it is sufficient to mention the principal ones. Historia Hepatica, seu de Hepatis Structurâ, Usibus et Morbis, Opus Anatomicum, Physiologicum et Pathologicum, Aug. Taur. 1710, 1716, 4to; Genev. 1725, 2 vols, 4to. Ductus Lachrymales Novi, eorum Anatoma, Usus, Morbi, Emotiones, Aug. Taur. 1715, 4to; Lugd. Bat. 1723, 8vo. Fabricæ Humanæ generalis Prospectus, Aug. Taur. 1716, fol. De Naturali in Humano Corpore, Vitiosâ, Morbosâque Generatione Historia, *ib.* 1741, 8vo. De Lacteorum Vasorum Positionibus et Fabricâ, *ib.* 1743, 4to. Storia del Monstro di due Corpi che nacque sul pavese in Gennaro 1748, *ib.* 1749, 4to. Lettera sulla' Insensibilita ed Irritabilita delle Parti nelli Uomini e nelle Bruti, *ib.* 1756, 8vo. This was written in opposition to the treatise of Haller, who replied to it with great severity. Bianchi, in 1757, published 54 plates of anatomy in 4to, which contain 270 figures, of much interest, both natural and morbid. Several of his treatises are to be found in the Bibliotheca Anatomica, and in the Theatrum Anatomicum of Mangetus.

BIANCHI, (Peter,) a painter of some reputation, born at Rome, 1694. He confined himself to no particular branch of his art, but painted various subjects in fresco and distemper, as well as oil. He was employed in some of the decorations of St. Peter's. In all probability he would have attained higher distinction as an artist, had he not fallen a victim to consumption in the vigour of life. He died at Rome, A. D. 1739.

BIANCHINI, (Francis,) a learned Italian philosopher and antiquary, born at Verona, 13th Dec. 1662. Having received the elements of education in his own country, he removed to Bologna; where, after a course of rhetoric and philosophy in the Jesuits' college, he studied, with great success, mathematics and design. At Padua, whither he removed in 1680, he took the degree of doctor in divinity. The learned Montanari, his master in natural philosophy, was much attached to him, and bequeathed to him all his mathematical instruments. With the purpose of entering the church he went to Rome, where Cardinal Peter Ottoboni made him his librarian, and he became distinguished as a member of the Physico-mathematical academy established there by Ciampini. Having returned in 1686 to his own country, he assisted in re-founding the Society of Aletophili; and, in order to encourage their mathematical studies, presented them with Montanari's instruments. Settled afterwards at Rome, he turned his attention to the learned languages and antiquities. His patron, Ottoboni, being now chosen pope, by the name of Alexander VIII., gave him a canonry, and would have promoted him farther; but Bianchini, not having made up his mind to take even deacon's orders until 1699, declined being ordained priest. Clement XI. was no less partial to Bianchini than Alexander had been, and in 1703 raised him to the rank of nobility. At this time, being employed about reforming the calendar, he constructed his celebrated gnomon; to commemorate which, the pope caused a medal to be struck. In 1712, being sent to Paris as the bearer of a cardinal's hat to Armand de Rohan-Soubise, he was introduced to the literati of France, and was constant in his attendance at the sittings of the Academy of Sciences; communicating to them a great improvement in the construction of long telescopes, by which their tendency to bend in the middle was obviated. Before returning to Rome, Bianchini visited the Low Countries and England, and appears to have received some special mark of respect at Oxford. His observations on the planet Venus attracted much attention among contemporary astronomers, but the use of better instruments seems to have led more recent observers to conclusions different from his. He died March 2, 1729; his memory being honoured by a monument erected in the cathedral of Verona, at the expense of the city. His works were numerous, of which the following are some of the principal:—1. Three astronomical papers in the "Acta Eruditorum" of Leipsic for 1685 and 1686. 2. Relazione della Linea Meridiana, &c., in the Journal "De Letterati d'Italia," vol. iv. 3. Hesperi et Phosphori Nova Phenomena, &c. Rome, 1728, fol. 4. De Kalendario et Cyclo Cæsaris, &c. Rome, 1703, 1704, fol. This contains an account of his gnomon, with many works on antiquities, as well as other subjects. (Biog. Univ. Chalmers.)

BIANCHINI, (Joseph,) born at Verona, Sept. 9, 1704, nephew of the celebrated Francis, under whose care he was educated at the college of Montefiascone. He took orders, and became priest of the oratory at Rome. His favourite study was ecclesiastical antiquities; and his publications consist of, 1. The 4th and last vol. of his uncle's edition of Anastasius Bibliothecarius, Rome, 1735, fol. 2. Vindiciæ Canonicarum Scripturarum Vulgatæ Latinæ Editionis, Rome, 1740, fol; being the first volume of a work which was never completed. 3. Evangeliarum Quadruplex Latinæ Versionis Antiquæ, &c. 1749, fol. 4. Demonstratio Historiæ Ecclesiasticæ Quadripartitæ Monumentis ad Fidem Temporum et Gestorum, 1752, fol. He also published a curious account of the death of the Countess Cornelia Zangari. This lady, as is said, died of spontaneous combustion, and the novelty of the circumstance attracted great attention. The time of his death is uncertain.

BIANCHINI, (Joseph Maria, November 18, 1685—February 17, 1749,) an eminent Italian scholar, a native of Prato, in Tuscany. He was educated at Florence, and at the early age of twenty years was classed among the principal literati of that city. He afterwards repaired to Pisa, where he received the degree of doctor of laws, and was admitted to priest's orders. There also the bishop of Prato appointed him lecturer upon the Fathers, to the study of whose works, especially those of St. Bernard, he was much attached. His literary fame procured him admission into the most celebrated academies of Italy; while his blameless life and exemplary performance of his duties as a parish priest rendered him an object of esteem to all who were acquainted with him. His principal works are, 1. De Gran Duchi di Toscana della real Casa de Medici, Venice, 1741, fol. 2. Della Satira Italiana Trattato, Massa, 1714. Besides these he translated the Song of Solomon into Italian verse, and was a contributor to many of the literary works of the time.

BIANCHINI, (John Fortunatus,) a celebrated physician, born at Chieti, in the kingdom of The Two Sicilies, in 1720; educated at Naples, where he took the degree of doctor of medicine, and practised physic for some years. He afterwards went to Venice, whence he was called to Udina, in 1759, to supply the place of the first physician of that city, where he remained until 1777. He was then chosen professor of practical medicine in the university of Padua, in which city he died, Sept. 2, 1779. He left, among others, the following works:—Saggio di Esperienze intorno la Medicina Elettrica fatte in Venezia da alcuni Amatori di Fisica, Venez. 1749, 4to. Lettere Medico-pratiche intorno all' Indole delle Febbri maligne, &c. colla Storia de' Vermi del Corpo Umano, e dell' Uso del Mercurio, *ib.* 1750, 8vo. Osservazioni intorno all' Uso del' Elettricita Celeste e sopra l'Origine del Fiume Timavo, *ib.* 1754, 4to. Bianchini also translated into Italian, Letters on the Power of the Imagination in Pregnant Women, under the anonymous designation of Isaac Bellet, at Venice, 1751, 8vo.

BIANCONI, (John Lewis,) a celebrated Italian physician and man of letters, born at Bologna, Sept. 30, 1717. He studied at the university of his native place, and became one of the members of the Institute. At the age of nineteen he was appointed assistant physician to the hospitals of Bologna, and he took the degree of doctor of medicine in 1742. He was appointed physician to the landgrave of Hesse Darmstadt, and subsequently to Augustus III. king of Poland, who created him a count. In 1760 he was induced to undertake a diplomatic engagement; but having no taste for state business, although he had manifested great ability while so employed, he finally relinquished it in 1764, devoting himself henceforward to literary pursuits. He died at Perugia, Jan. 1, 1781. He printed many papers in the Effemeridi Litterarie di Roma, which he was one of the first to establish. He published, Due Lettere di Fisica, al Signore Marchese Scipione Maffei, Venez. 1746, 4to. Lettere sopra alcune Particolarità della Baviera, e di altri paesi della Germania, Lucca, 1763, 4to; translated into German, Leipsic, 1764, 8vo; Munich, 1771, 8vo. With several other works, which were translated into German. He also translated into Italian, and published, in 6 vols, 8vo, Bologna, 1743-1744, Winslow's celebrated work on the Anatomy of the Human Body.

BIANCUCCI, (Paul,) of Lucca, pupil of Guido, noted for a picture of Purgatory, in a church at Lucca. He died in 1653, aged 70.

BIANOR, an illustrious Tuscan prince, otherwise called Ocnus, who fortified and improved Mantua, naming it after his mother, and accordingly he was commonly considered its founder. His father was said to be the river Tiber, his mother was Manto, the daughter of Tiresias, and a reputed inheritor of his prophetic powers; hence Virgil, (Æn. x. 198,)

"Ille enim patriis agmen ciet Ocnus ab oris,
Fatidicæ Mantûs et Tusci filius amnis,
Qui muros, matrisque dedit tibi, Mantua, nomen."

In the poet's days, the last resting-place of this ancient sovereign's remains, probably a lofty barrow, was yet visible in the neighbourhood of the city that he had founded.

——"sepulchrum
Incipit apparere Bianoris."
(Eccl. ix. 59.)

The annotators of Virgil usually explain this passage, by referring to the practice that prevailed eventually among the Romans, of placing tombs by the sides of highways, and inserting in the inscriptions upon them, accordingly, such phrases as *Sta viator*, *Abi viator*. But sepulchres of this description, however costly, were not likely to be seen from a distance, which seems to have been the case with this of Bianor. On the other hand, the barrows of an earlier race, for which, besides, conspicuous sites were commonly chosen, are, from their bulk, objects of attention to the surrounding country. That the ancient Etrurians buried their illustrious dead under such remarkable monuments is well known; but when classical commenting was at its height, little attention had been paid to such subjects.

BIARD, or BIART, (Peter,) a Jesuit, born at Grenoble, in Dauphiny, one of the first French missionaries to Canada, and remembered for an early account of that country, published at Lyons, in 1616, entitled, Relation de la Nouvelle France, et du Voyage que les Jesuites y ont fait. The last nine years of his life were spent as professor of theology at Lyons, where he died in 1622. (Moreri. Biog. Univ.)

BIAS, one of the seven wise men of Greece. His father's name was Teutamus, and he was born at Priene, in Ionia, in the sixth century before Christ. He seems to have been wealthy, and became famous both for unquestionable moral worth, and for a superior understanding, highly cultivated. When his native place was on the point of capture, and people were fleeing from it with every thing that seemed likely to be saved, somebody asked him, why he was carrying nothing away? He answered, "I am taking all that I have," meaning his learning, integrity, and wisdom Among his famous sayings was, "The really unhappy are those who cannot bear unhappiness." When asked, "What is difficult?" he answered, "To bear magnanimously a change for the worse." When sailing with several wicked men, who nevertheless loudly called upon the gods in a storm, he said, "Be quiet; I am afraid that they will know you to be at sea." Being once asked by an irreligious person, "What is piety?" he made no answer; but when the reason of his silence was inquired, he said, "It is because you are asking about that which does not concern you." Being asked, "Doing what is a man pleased?" "Getting money," was his answer. One of his sayings, worthy of a purer theology than that with which he was acquainted, was, "Whatever good you do, refer it to the gods." As an author, Bias was known by two thousand verses on the means of making Ionia happy. He died immediately after pleading for a friend, but so tranquilly, that it was not discovered until a decision in his favour was pronounced. His funeral was magnificent, at the public expense, and to his memory a sacred grove was dedicated, which bore the name of Teutamium. (Diog. Laert. 1570, i. 30. Lloyd. Biog. Univ.)

BIBAGO, (Abraham Ben Yrm Fou,) a Spanish Jew, born at Aragon, flourished towards the end of the fifteenth century. He wrote a treatise on the articles of the Jewish faith opposed to the christian belief, a volume of philosophical discourses, and other controversial and philosophical treatises. Several of his works have been printed, and others are preserved in MS. in the *Bibliothèque Royale* and the Vatican. (Hartmann in Ersch und Gruber.)

BIBARS, (Malek-al-Dhaher Rokn-ed-deen,) a celebrated sultan of Egypt, the fourth of the Baharite or Tartar dynasty of Mamlukes, mounted the throne A.D. 1260, (A.H. 658,) after the murder of his predecessor Kotouz. (See KOTOUZ.) He was originally a Mamluke of the Ayubite sultan Nodjem-ed-deen, by whom the Baharite corps was instituted, and received his early discipline under a *bondokdar*, or officer of crossbowmen, whence he is often known by the epithet of Al-Bondokdari, corrupted by Frank writers into Bendocar. At the battle of Mansooriyah against the forces of the sixth crusade, he rallied the Egyptians after the fall of their commander-in-chief, and finally contributed to the victory which led to the captivity of Lewis IX. and his army. He was afterwards a principal actor in the revolt in which Tooran-Shah (the last of the Egyptian Ayubites) was slaughtered; but on the accession of Aïbek he fled into Syria, where he remained till the reign of Kotouz, by whose assassination he at length opened himself a way to the throne of Egypt. The seventeen years of his reign present an uniform picture of incessant warfare against the Moguls of Persia, the Christians of Palestine, and the Moslem princes of Syria and Anatolia. The first, who had in 1261 a second time crossed the Euphrates, sustained near Emessa a signal defeat, which relieved the Syrians from their fears of subjugation by these barbarous invaders; and the establishment of a khalifate in Egypt by a junior branch of the Abbassides expelled from Bagdad, (see MOSTANSER, HAKEM,) gave the Mamluke sultan, as protector of the commander of the faithful, the first rank among Moslem princes.* By a treaty with the Greek emperor, he was enabled to import through Constantinople from the Euxine continual supplies of slaves to recruit the ranks of his Mamlukes; and the remains of the Latin dominion in Palestine rapidly crumbled away under his fierce and repeated attacks. Cæsarea was taken in 1264; Jaffa shared the same fate three years later; and in 1268 a still greater triumph was achieved in the capture of Antioch. "The first seat of the christian name was dispeopled," (in the words of Gibbon,) "by the slaughter of 17,000 and the captivity of 100,000 of her inhabitants. The maritime towns of Laodicea, Gabala, Tripoli, Berytus, Sidon, Tyre, and Jaffa, and the stronger castles of the Hospitallers and Templars, successively fell; and the whole existence of the Franks was confined to the city and colony of St. John of Acre." The truce which was procured in 1271,

* It will not be amiss here to notice an inadvertent error into which Mr. Marsden has fallen in the Numismata Orientalia, as the high authority of that valuable work gives importance to even a trivial inaccuracy. At p. 250, No. cclx., in describing a gold coin of Bibars, now in the British Museum, part of the inscription on which is "Kasim Emir-al-Mumenin," the following remark is made:—"The name of Kasim is that of a nominal khalif whom Bibars had set up, or whose pretensions he allowed, on the extermination by the Moguls of the Abbassite race in Bagdad. He bestowed on him the title of Al-Mostanser-billah Abu'l-Kasim Ahmed, and in return received from this pageant the investiture of his own dominions." Now, (exclusive of the fact that the *title* of a khalif, as in this case, Mostanser-billah, was always inscribed on the coin instead of the bare *name*, as Kasim,) the date of this coin is A.H. 667, (A.D. 1268,) whereas Al-Mostanser fell in battle against the Tartars A.H. 660, and was succeeded in the titular pontificate by Hakem-bemrillah Ahmed. But the true explanation is to be found in a well-known historical work, the Giauhar-al-athameen, where it is stated that among other titles lavished by Mostanser on his benefactor, he gave him the appellation of "Kasim," (or partner,) with the "Emir-al-Mumenin," (commander of the faithful;) an honour so great, says the Arabic author, as never to have been granted by preceding khalifs to any of the princes on whom they were virtually dependent: but this last statement is incorrect, as the same title appears to have been borne by the great Seljookian sultan Malek Shah.

by the valour of Edward, son of Henry III. of England, afforded a short respite to the Franks; but the restless activity of Bibars found sufficient employment in repelling the attacks of the Moguls under the son of Hulaku, and in subduing or reducing to vassalage the minor princes of the Ayubite family. In two destructive invasions he ravaged nearly all Armenia, then an independent kingdom, under a christian prince named Haiton; and even the Tsmailis of Mount Lebanon, the retainers of the famous Old Man of the Mountain, paid allegiance to the formidable sultan of Egypt and Syria, whose alliance was courted by the distant queen of Bulgaria, (Gibbon, ch. 62,) against her uncle, the emperor Michael Palæologus. But he was cut off in the midst of this career of war and bloodshed, by inadvertently partaking of the remains of a poisoned draught which he had administered to an Ayubite prince, and died at Damascus, A.D. 1277, (A.H. 676.) The martial exploits and indomitable courage of Bibars have earned him an enduring renown in the east, which he was far from meriting by his other qualities, for he was cruel, treacherous, and avaricious; still among the warlike series of the Mamluke sultans, his name alone appears to have been handed down as a hero of popular tradition. A romance, founded on his history and achievements, is said by Mr. Lane to be even now frequent among the professional story-tellers of Egypt. The son and successor of Bibars, Barkah-Khan, possessed neither the talents nor authority of his father, and was deposed in less than two years by the military chiefs, whom he had disgusted by his vacillating and arbitrary conduct. His brother Selamish, a boy seven years old, was then invested for a few months with the nominal dignity of sultan, till he was deposed and succeeded by the emir Kalaoon, A.D. 1280 (A.H. 679.) (Abulfeda. Abul-Faraj. Makrizi. Soyuti. Ibn-Shohnah. The Giauhar-al-athameen. The Maured-allatafet. D'Herbelot. De Guignes. Gibbon, ch. 59. Mills, Hist. of Crusades. Lane's Modern Egyptians, &c.)

Bibars was also the name of the twelfth Baharite sultan, who mounted the throne A.D. 1309, (A.H. 709,) on the second deposition of Nasr-Mohammed, the son of Kalaoon, on whose recovery of his authority the following year Bibars was put to death. He was the first Circassian by birth who attained the sovereignty of Egypt. Oriental historians generally distinguish him from his predecessor of the same name, by the epithet of Jashankir, or "the cupbearer."

BIBERACH, (Nicholas von,) a German divine, in the latter half of the thirteenth century. He spent some part of his time at Rome, and noted the then growing degeneracy of the papal court. Many passages in his writings paint this in bold and decided colours. His works are known chiefly from the quotations of later writers, and it is doubtful whether any part of them has yet been printed. (Ersch und Gruber.)

BIBERG, (Niels Frederic,) a Swedish professor, born at Hernos, in 1770. In 1797 he received a post as teacher in the academy at Upsal, and was called by the king to Stockholm, in 1805, to undertake the instruction of the crown prince. When the revolution put an end to this arrangement, he returned to Upsal, where in 1811 he was appointed professor of moral and political science. He had formed the project of writing a general system of jurisprudence, which was to be the fruit of a comparison of ancient and modern jurisprudence, and in which he followed the order of the Pandects; but he performed this task with so laborious a diligence, that ten years' labour brought him only to the doctrine of contracts. He died in 1827. Three volumes of his works were published, but their success was not such as to encourage the continuance of the publication. (Ersch und Gruber.)

BIBERSTEIN, (Francis A. baron von,) an eminent botanist and traveller, born in 1766, at Aarberg, in the Swiss canton of Bern. He was educated at Stutgard, and afterwards entered into the Russian military service; and his duties leading him into the Crimea, he there formed the acquaintance of the celebrated professor Pallas. He afterwards had the command of troops in the provinces bordering on the Caspian sea, and eventually the post of inspector of the establishments for rearing silk-worms there. He thus had great opportunities for prosecuting his favourite botanical pursuits, to which he devoted all his leisure time, the results of which were given to the world in his Flora Taurico-Caucasiaca, Charkov, tom. i. ii. 1808, tom. iii. Suppl. 1819, 8vo. He died at Merosa, near Charkov, Oct. 5, 1826. (New German Necrology. Goetons' Appendix. Biog. Univ. Suppl.)

BIBIANA, a Romish saint, called Vivienne by the French, daughter of a

Roman knight, named Flavius, and his wife Dofrosa. She, together with her parents, suffered martyrdom during a persecution of the Christians at Rome, under the emperor Julian, about the middle of the fourth century. Her body was afterwards secretly removed by a christian priest, and buried near the palace of Licinius, in the year 465. Pope Simplicius caused a noble church to be erected on the spot, which edifice was rebuilt in 1628 by Urban VIII.

BIBIENA, (Bernard,) called by Tiraboschi and others, Bernardo Dovizio, born in 1470, of an obscure family, at Bibiena, a small village, from which he took his name. After having completed his education at Florence, by the interest of his brother Peter, who was secretary to Laurence de' Medici, he entered the service of John de' Medici, afterwards cardinal, and eventually pope, under the name of Leo X., whom he followed in his banishment and travels, and with whom, having gone to Rome, he succeeded in obtaining the favour of pope Julius II.

In the conclave which took place after the death of Julius, he managed the affairs of his patron so well, that though he was only thirty-six years old, he made the cardinals believe him unlikely to live long, and by this means induced them to elect him. Grateful for these services, Leo immediately appointed Bibiena his treasurer, in 1513 created him cardinal, and two years after inspector of the building for the *holy house* of Lorete, one of the most impudent and ridiculous of papal impostures. Bibiena now showed a taste, worthy of his good fortune, for literature and the arts, attaching to his service men of talent, such as Paleotti, Sanga and Sadoleto; and great artists, among whom he chiefly protected Raphael, to whom he would have given one of his nieces as a wife if the premature death of that prince of painters had not prevented the marriage.

Continually employed by the pope in all important affairs, he was appointed legate to the emperor Maximilian, and president of the pontifical army during the war of Urbino, which he brought to the close as wished by his patron; and in 1518, legate to Francis I. of France, in order to form a league against Selim, the emperor of the Turks, whose victories and ambition threatened Europe. At the end of 1519 he returned to Rome, but on the 9th of November of the following year, 1520, though in excellent health, he died suddenly, as some have considered, from the effect of poison, given him by the order of Leo, in fresh eggs; though the reasons assigned for this alleged crime do not by any means agree. Bandini, who has written the life of Bibiena, and given an accurate catalogue of his works, seems to adopt the opinion, that, urged by ambition, he had conspired against Leo, for the sake of succeeding him in the papal chair, and was, therefore, poisoned by his injured patron. Moreri, on the other hand, pretends that offence given to the court of France was the cause of his death. But this is all fancy, as Mr. Roscoe observes, for he would not even enter into the details of it, notwithstanding what Grassi, in his *Diario*, relates, that the corpse of Bibiena being opened, there was no doubt of the appearance of poison; for if Leo had caused poison to be given to him, he would have prevented the body from being opened, as nothing could have been more easy to him, under pretence of paying honour to the remains of his faithful servant, to have his body immediately inclosed in a superb coffin.

BIBIENA, (Timothy,) a Camaldolese monk, who lived during the beginning of the sixteenth century, and wrote, in Italian heroic verses, the life of St. Benedict, which he left unfinished, in 1531, when he died.

BIBIENA, (Angelo Dovizio,) nephew of the cardinal of that name, who having resigned in his favour two of his benefices, induced him to take orders. He then became apostolical prothonotary, and secretary of Cosmo I., duke of Florence, during which, in 1557, he wrote a Sommario della Cose degne di Memoria Successe nella Guerra di Algieri dall' Anno 1541 fino al Giugno del 1553, &c. He wrote also a canto, entitled, Trionfo della Dea Minerva, printed in a collection, at Florence, in 1559. He seems to have been a patron of the learned, amongst whom we find the famed Francis Berni, whom he was obliged to expel from his court on account of a most violent love fit. The time of his death is not mentioned.

It is curious, however, that Quadrio, after having rightly attributed to cardinal Bibiena the comedy of Calandria, speaks of it soon after as if the work of his nephew.

BIBIENA, (Ferdinand,) son of John Maria Galli, a painter and architect, born at Bologna, in 1657. Exhibiting early signs of a lively imagination, he was encouraged and assisted by his able instructor, Cignani. Employed by the duke of Parma, and the emperor, Charles III., he was celebrated for his theatrical decorations, skill in perspective, and architectural designs, upon which subjects he left some treatises. He died blind, 1743, leaving three sons, who followed with success the profession of their father: Anthony, employed by the emperor Charles VI.; Joseph, who died at Berlin; and Alexander, who was in the service of the elector palatine. (Biog. Univ.)

BIBIENA, (Francis Galli,) brother of the preceding, and distinguished by similar talents in the same line of art. He died A.D. 1739, aged 80 years. (Biog. Univ.)

BIBLIANDER, or BUCHMANN, (Theodore,) a learned protestant divine, born at Bischoffzell, near St. Gall, in Switzerland, probably in 1504. He became at an early period of his life distinguished for his acquirements in theology and philology; and after Zwingle's death, was appointed, March 24, 1532, to the professorship of theology at Zürich. His lectures on the books of the Old Testament, which he treated *seriatim*, were not only attended by students, but also by numerous learned men then resident in Zurich. In the *Stifts bibliothek* of that city, are still preserved forty-five large *fasciculi* of notes from his lectures, which were taken by the celebrated Henry Bullinger, who used to say that he knew no one who excelled him in learning, understanding, and kindness. At a subsequent period his reputation diminished: he is said to have become vain and captious; a change which was attributed to his great labours and consequent exhaustion. Possibly we may find reason to doubt the perfect accuracy of this contemporaneous verdict, when we learn that he had arrived at opinions differing from the prevailing doctrines on predestination and free-will, having embraced the views put forth by Erasmus, in his tract, De Libero Arbitrio. His understanding, as was said by his opponents, was at length so much weakened that it became necessary to declare him unfit to occupy the professor's chair; though he was left in the receipt of his salary. He died four years afterwards, November 26, 1564, of the plague. His Machumetis Saracenorum Principis ejusque Successorum Vitæ, Doctrina ac ipse Alcoran, &c. Basil, 1543, fol., contains a Latin translation of the Koran, by Petrus Venerabilis, abbot of Cluni, with several minor dissertations refuting the doctrine and errors of the Koran. He added to it an apologetical preface, assigning reasons for its publication; and this, to use Bayle's expression, "raised a great outcry." The Spanish inquisitors condemned, in this edition, not only Bibliander's notes, but the Koran itself. Sanctarellus, however, says that the Index forbad the reading of it, "only because the editor's notes, with the prefaces of Luther and Melancthon, were adjudged to be impious." This was, of course, a prejudiced view. Bibliander published many other works, which it is not necessary to specify. (Moreri. Bayle. Rees.)

BIBLICANUS, (Theobald,) a preacher at Nordlingen, in Swabia, in 1522, of great eloquence, who caused the reformed doctrines to be so universally received, that in 1525 not a professed papist remained in the city, excepting some stewards of monastic estates. The very monks resigned their monasteries and revenues, stipulating only for life annuities for themselves; declaring they were convinced from the Scriptures of the erroneous and dangerous state in which they had lived, and desiring that henceforth nothing should be taught contrary to the Scriptures; though some popish observances were long retained. Having, however, succeeded thus far, Biblicanus, in 1536, retired from want of health.

BIBRA, (Philip Antony Sigmond von,) born at Bamberg in 1750, died at Fulda, on the 3d of March, 1803. He was educated as a noble at the court of Fulda, and received into the chapter there; he became afterwards president of both its spiritual and temporal government, mitred provost of the consistory and exchequer, electorate counsellor of Mentz, and after the secularization, privy counsellor to the prince of Nassau-Orange-Fulda. He acquired great reputation as a statesman and a learned man. (Ersch und Gruber.)

BIBULUS, (M. Calpurnius.) It was his singular destiny throughout life to be the colleague, the enemy, and the tool of C. Julius Cæsar. The name of his father is unknown. In the year 65 B.C., he was curule ædile; and contributed the larger share of the expenses of the magnificent shows with which the people were entertained. Cæsar, however, gained the credit for them; and Bibulus compared himself on this occasion to Pollux: for a temple had been dedicated to the Dioscûri Castor and Pollux; but was called by the name of the former alone. In

62, he was again associated with Cæsar in the prætorship; and again they were at variance. Cæsar proposed extraordinary honours to Cneius Pompey, who was now anxiously expected in Italy, on his return from his eastern conquests; and Bibulus, in common with the senate, regarded with suspicion the political connexions, the reputation, and the authority of that fortunate general. It was probably by Cæsar's contrivance that Bibulus was employed away from Rome in the Pelignine territory, against Cataline and his levies. In canvassing for the consulship, Bibulus sought a reconciliation with the notorious Piso, in hopes of dividing the office with him; but Cæsar's selfish arrangements for carrying the election alarmed the aristocracy; and even Cato subscribed to secure the return of Bibulus. Still further to disappoint the prospects of Cæsar, it was determined that at the expiration of their office, the consuls of 59 B.C. should not be appointed to provinces, but should hold a barren commission over highways and forests: a resolution which had merely the effect of depriving Bibulus of a provincial government of any value; since Cæsar managed to elude it, and secured to himself the rich and powerful province of Gaul. In 59, the year of his consulate, Bibulus was opposed singly to the most popular, the most wealthy, and the most powerful men of the age, who were bound together in the first triumvirate. His success in opposing them was answerable to the relative strength of the aristocracy and the coalition. His resistance to the Julian Agrarian laws, although three tribunes and L. Lucullus supported him, ended in a violent assault upon his person, and in his remaining, for the remainder of his magistracy, a voluntary prisoner in his own house. His efforts were now confined to the publication of violent edicts; which were rather libels upon the private characters of his principal opponent, than acts of office or state. From this source some of the most serious imputations on Cæsar have found their way into history. He was called the Bithynian Queen, an allusion to an alleged connexion of his early youth with Nicomedes, king of Bithynia; he was prohibited, on religious pretexts, to hold a public assembly during the whole term of his office, since Bibulus made no scruple of avowing that he held an observation of the heavens when Cæsar transacted business with the tribes; and he was denounced as the accomplice of Cataline. The edicts of Bibulus, although Cicero made his consulate the object of his ridicule, were read, copied, and circulated by the aristocratical party and its dependents; and their author was compared to Fabius Cunctator. It was a current pleasantry of the year to note the inefficiency of Bibulus by denominating the consulate as that of Julius and Cæsar, and even wills and contracts are said to have been so subscribed. The tribune P. Vatinius, a creature of Cæsar's, was however hardly withheld from sending Bibulus to prison; he was named by Vettius in the pretended conspiracy against Pompey, and on the expiration of his office was prohibited by P. Clodius to explain or defend his acts to the people. Bibulus remained at Rome during the year 58, since no province had been assigned him. His hatred to Cæsar made him seek the political support of Cicero; although the great consular had ridiculed his behaviour, and given him no aid in his recent difficulties. In 57, it was Bibulus who brought before the senate a bill respecting the validity of the consecration of Cicero's house. He was the steady opponent of the triumvirate on all occasions; for indiscriminate opposition was his only means of distinguishing himself. In 56, he withstood Pompey's project for the restoration of Ptolemy Auletes to his kingdom; the pretext assigned was, that the Sibylline books forbade the restitution of a king to Egypt by an armed force; and he proposed instead, that three *legati* of private condition should be commissioned to reinstate the exiled monarch. This amendment, however, was disapproved by the senate; and Gabinius, proconsul of Syria, was secretly instigated by the triumvirate to aid Auletes. The principle of action in Bibulus was personal hatred to Cæsar; and, therefore, when, after the death of Crassus and Julia, the relations between the two most powerful leaders in Rome were changed, Bibulus adhered to Pompey, and was the mover that he should be appointed consul without a colleague, to settle the disturbances which ensued upon Clodius's death. In 51, Bibulus was proconsul of Syria. If we may trust Cicero, whose views of men and of measures, in his epistles especially, must be taken with some reservation, the conduct of Bibulus, in his foreign administration, was as inefficient as his political life at home. He remained within the gates of Antioch, until the country was clear of the Parthians. But envying

Cicero's successes, and his acquired title of Imperator, he attempted to win for himself a similar distinction on the *Syrian*, that is, on the *safer* side, of Mount Amanus. He was, however, repulsed, with the loss of an entire cohort, of Asinius Dento, a centurion of the first rank, of Sextus Lucilius, a military tribune, and of several other officers of the same division. Notwithstanding his losses, Bibulus aspired to a triumph; and was honoured with a supplication (thanks-festival) of twenty days, which his father-in-law, Cato, was instrumental in obtaining for him. The civil wars which immediately broke out, prevented, however, the completion of either ceremony. Bibulus, after some hesitation whether Marcus Cato should not be preferred, was nominated by Pompey to the chief command of the fleet. He stationed the different divisions in the Ionian sea, and himself remained in Corcyra. Delay, sickness, and hollow negotiations, rendered the most formidable part of Pompey's forces inefficient. Bibulus did not even block up the passage of the Ionian sea; while Cæsar excluded him from the ports on its eastern coast. He died, before the actions at Dyracchium, in the neighbourhood of Corcyra. He would probably have left behind him a barren name in the Fasti, had it not been for his remarkable relations to the foremost man of the age.

BICAISE, (Honoré,) an eminent physician, born at Aix, in Provence, in 1590, where he studied, and took the degree of doctor of medicine. He was afterwards appointed professor of medicine; and particularly distinguished himself by his attention during the visitations of the plague at Aix, in 1629 and 1649. He published the result of his observations; and he also printed an excellent work, entitled, Manuale Medicorum, seu Promptuarium Aphorismorum Hippocratis, &c.

BICHAT, (Maria Francis Xavier,) a celebrated physiologist and physician; born at Thoirette, in the department of the Aix, Nov. 11, 1771. His father and first instructor, John Baptist, was a doctor of medicine of the university of Montpelier. Xavier displayed great aptitude for acquiring knowledge, excelled in mathematics, and was well skilled in the Latin language. He studied anatomy and surgery under M. A. Petit, principal surgeon of the Hôtel Dieu at Lyons. The revolution obliged him to quit that city; and wishing to enter the army, he repaired to Paris, to study military surgery, where he attended the lectures of the celebrated Desault. Here he distinguished himself, and laid the foundation of his future celebrity, by the manner in which he gave, when unexpectedly called upon to do so, an abstract of a lecture on the fractures of the clavicle, which he had just heard delivered by Desault. The latter invited him to reside in his house, and he became his assistant, as well in his public lectures as in his private practice. Of these excellent opportunities for improving himself he made the best use, until the unfortunate and almost sudden death of Desault, which took place in 1790. The works of that celebrated physiologist were subsequently arranged for publication by his grateful pupil.

Bichat commenced as a lecturer in 1797, and began to put forth those grand physiological views which were ultimately to effect so great a change in the prosecution of medical inquiries. His incessant application undermined his health, and brought on an attack of hœmoptysis, which threatened his life.

The novel method adopted by Bichat in the examination of the structure of the human body appears to have been suggested by an observation of M. Pinel, that disease consisted of an alteration in the tissue of an organ; and he therefore resolved to study anatomy by a separate consideration of the structures which enter into the formation of the different parts. He commenced with the membranes, and made an arrangement of them of the utmost importance in a physiological and in a pathological point of view.

After the publication of his Traité des Membranes, in 1800, he directed his attention to some interesting physiological inquiries, and published the result in his work, Recherches Physiologiques sur la Vie et la Mort, in which he gives a general exposition of his physiological views, and demonstrates the intimate connexion which exists between the three principal organs of life, the brain, heart, and lungs. These views rendered a new system of anatomy essential; and he commenced this in his Anatomie Générale, in which the whole of the human body is classed according to its tissues, embracing twenty-one divisions. This arrangement is not to be looked upon as yet perfect; but it is worthy of remark, that no system since offered, though based upon that of Bichat, has been so well received by physiologists in general. He accomplished this work in the short space of one year, printing chapter by chapter, as it was written. He then published a System of Descriptive Anatomy, two volumes of which were all that he printed; the remaining three volumes were left by him in an imperfect state, but completed and published, after his death, by MM. Buisson and Roux.

In 1800 Bichat was appointed one of the physicians of the Hôtel Dieu; and in affording clinical instruction he was pre-eminently distinguished. His attention to morbid anatomy led him to inspect the bodies of all those who died under his care in that extensive hospital; and he is reported to have examined no less than 600 during one winter. Modern pathology owes much to his indefatigable spirit and genius; for much of the precision now introduced into this science has arisen from the investigation of disease in the separate tissues of the human frame.

In 1802 Bichat sustained a fall in descending a staircase at the Hôtel Dieu; he suffered a slight concussion of the brain, and was otherwise injured; and not being in a good state of health, the result, possibly, of too close application to his professional pursuits, this accident, though at first not very alarming, was the cause of his death, which took place on the 22d of July, he being only 30 years of age. The death of Bichat was regarded as a national loss. Corvisart communicated his decease to the first consul, Napoleon Buonaparte, in the following words:—"Bichat has fallen on a field of battle which numbers many a victim; no one has done in the same time so much and so well." The French government caused his name, together with that of his teacher, Desault, to be inscribed on a memorial erected at the Hôtel Dieu.

In all the relations of life, Bichat, it appears, was most amiable. Kind, affable, modest, intelligent, and lively, he was a universal favourite. Besides the anatomical and physiological works already mentioned, Bichat printed several papers in the Mémoires de la Société Médicale d'Emulation; and also a complete edition of the surgical works of Desault, in 3 vols, 8vo, Paris, 1812. The best edition of the Anatomie Générale is that published by Beclard, in 1821. The Pathological Anatomy was printed from an autograph MS. of P. A. Beclard.

BICHENO, (James,) an anabaptist minister, who obtained some note in his day from works on the prophecies, now forgotten; he was also the author of several other works of no general interest. He died in 1831. (Gent.'s Mag.)

BICKER, (Andrew,) one of the heads of the anti-orange party in Holland, in the time of prince William II.; was counsellor under prince Maurice, and burgomaster of Amsterdam in the reign of Frederic Henry. To his interposition may be mainly attributed the milder spirit of the government towards the Remonstrant or Arminian party, who had been treated with great severity by prince Maurice. Bicker was ambassador to Poland and Sweden in 1627, 1635, and 1645, to procure that intervention of protestant Sweden in the affairs of Germany, which, by engaging the Spanish power in the empire, was so important to Holland. In the contention between the states of Holland and prince William II., in 1650, the former seeking to increase the naval power, and the latter to preserve the quota of the land forces, Bicker held stoutly to the part of the States. Amsterdam was surrounded by the troops of the prince, who consented to withdraw them only on condition that Andrew Bicker, and his brother Cornelius, should resign their offices, and retire from the city. Cornelius was restored at the death of William, in 1651, but Andrew died in private life. (Ersch und Gruber.)

BICKERSTAFF, (Isaac,) a dramatic writer, a native of Ireland, born at the latter end of the eighteenth century; author of Love in a Village, Lionel and Clarissa, &c. (Thesp. Dict. Gorton.)

BICKERTON, (Sir Richard Hussey,) a British admiral, born 11th of October, 1759; the son of rear-admiral Sir Richard Bickerton, bart., himself a very gallant officer. He entered the naval service as a midshipman, in December 1771; and having served on board several ships, he was made lieutenant, 16th of December, 1777, and appointed to the *Prince George;* but soon afterwards accompanied captain Middleton, afterwards lord Barham, into the *Jupiter*, of 50 guns. On 20th of October, 1778, the *Jupiter*, then commanded by captain Reynolds, afterwards lord Ducie, fought, in conjunction with the *Medea*, a small frigate, a very gallant action with the *Triton*, a French line-of-battle ship. The *Medea* being disabled at the commencement of the engagement, captain Reynolds maintained the unequal conflict until night, when the French ship bore away. Mr. Bickerton was immediately afterwards made master and commander; a sufficient proof of his good conduct.

In February 1782, captain Bickerton was present, in the *Swallow*, at the capture of St. Eustatia, by the united forces of Sir George Rodney and general Vaughan; and on the 8th of the same month was posted into the *Gibraltar*, of 80 guns. In the skirmish which took place on the 29th of the following April, between the British and French fleets, under the command, respectively, of Sir Samuel Hood and the count de Grasse, he was present in the *Invincible*, of 74 guns.

Upon the death of his father, February 1792, he succeeded to the baronetcy; but continued to exhibit his usual vigilance, activity, and gallantry, wherever he was employed. On the 13th of May, 1800, Sir Richard, being appointed to a command in the Mediterranean, under lord Keith, sailed for that station, having generals Abercrombie, Moore, and Hutchinson, with him as passengers. On his arrival, having hoisted his flag on board the *Swiftsure*, he proceeded to Cadiz, with four seventy-fours, and two frigates, to blockade that port. But the expedition against the French in Egypt being ready, he left Cadiz, and proceeded with lord Keith to Alexandria, which port he blockaded until it surrendered. Lord Keith, in his letter to the Admiralty, 2d of September, 1801, while bearing gratifying testimony to the merits of the officers on this service, makes special mention of the subject of this memoir, in the following terms:—"During my absence, the blockade has been conducted much to my satisfaction by rear-admiral Sir R. Bickerton." During his stay in Egypt, he had the honour of being invested, by the capitan pacha, with the insignia of the Turkish order of the crescent. Advanced to the rank of rear-admiral of the red in 1804, and to that of vice-admiral in November 1805, upon a change of administration taking place in April 1807, Sir Richard was nominated one of the lords commissioners of the admiralty, and was soon afterwards returned to parliament as one of the representatives for Poole; and in July 1810, was made admiral of the blue. He retained his seat at the admiralty until 1812, when he succeeded Sir Roger Curtis as commander-in-chief at Portsmouth. Sir Richard was created a knight commander of the Bath in 1815; and in 1818 was appointed lieutenant-general, and, subsequently, general of the royal marines. He died at Bath, 9th of February, 1832, in the 73d year of his age, having previously taken the name of Hussey, in addition to his own, in compliance with the will of his maternal uncle, lieutenant-general Vere Warner Hussey. (Ann. Biog.)

BICKLEY, (Thomas, D.D., born at Stow, in Bucks, 1519, died at Chichester, April 30, 1596,) an English prelate, educated in the free-school connected with Magdalen college, Oxford, of which college he was first made chorister, then demy, and ultimately fellow. In the beginning of the reign of king Edward VI. he was promoted to be one of the royal chaplains, and was subjected to the enmity of the Romanists by his decided advocacy of the principles of the Reformation. When Mary ascended the throne he was compelled to leave his college, and, like many other English divines, take refuge abroad; but on the accession of Elizabeth, he returned home, and was made chaplain to archbishop Parker; soon after he was preferred to the archdeaconry of Stafford, and to a residentiary canonry at Lichfield. In 1569 he was elected warden of Merton college, and in 1585 was made bishop of Chichester. He left land and money to Merton college, and other bequests to the university. (Wood, Ath. Ox.)

BIDDLE, (John,) born at Wootton-under-Edge, 1615, died in London, 22d of September, 1662, a Socinian writer, styled by Toulmin the father of the English Unitarians, was educated at the free-school of his native place. Before he had completed his 20th year, he published a translation of the Eclogues of Virgil, and the first two satires of Juvenal. In 1634 he was entered at Magdalen hall, Oxford; having proceeded to the degree of M.A.; he was appointed master of the free-school, Gloucester, where he was much esteemed as a diligent teacher. Here it was that his antitrinitarian opinions began to discover themselves. Relying, it appears, entirely on his own judgment, and discarding the voice of christian antiquity, he was led to deny the divinity of the Son and the Holy Spirit. "He gave," says Mr. Toulmin, "the Holy Scriptures a diligent reading, and made use of no other rule to determine controversies about religion than the Scriptures; and of no other authentic interpreter, if a scruple arose concerning the sense of the Scriptures, than *reason;*" in other words, than his own biassed opinion. The same biographer adds, "he afterwards carefully examined the Fathers, to ascertain their sentiments concerning the one God; but it likewise proves that he had a low opinion of their judgment, or of the weight of their testimony, which he used merely as an *argumentum ad hominem*." But however likely was the course that he took in seeking after truth to lead him into error, there is every reason for admitting fully the sincerity of spirit in which the search itself was conducted; he was so diligent a reader of the New Testament, that with the exception of a few chapters in the Revelations, he had the whole by heart, both in English and Greek; and the persecutions that he afterwards endured, sufficiently prove his firm belief in the doctrines which he advocated. His first publication upon this subject is entitled, "Twelve Arguments on Questions drawn out of the Scripture, wherein the commonly-received Opinion touching the Deity of the Holy Spirit is clearly and fully refuted. The publication of this work had been delayed about three years, in consequence of the prosecution of the magistracy of Gloucester; for having expressed his opinions with considerable freedom, he was called upon to make a formal confession of his error, which he after some hesitation consented to do, in order to avoid imprisonment. Having, however, by reading various authors, become more confirmed in his opinions, he drew up the work referred to, with the intention of printing it privately; but a professed friend having informed the magistrates, and also the parliamentary committee (then in the town) of this project, the unfortunate author, though suffering under a fever, was committed to the common gaol, till parliament should take cognizance of the matter (Dec. 2, 1645). He was soon after released upon bail, and in 1646 received a visit from archbishop Ussher, who was passing through Gloucester on his way to London; but all the efforts of that great scholar to convince him of his error were unavailing. Shortly afterwards he was summoned before the parliament at Westminster, by a committee of which he was examined, when he requested permission to dispute upon the subject with some learned theologian; but no prospect appearing of this request being complied with, he took the decisive step of publishing a declaration of his opinions in the work just spoken of. This work exciting considerable attention, the author was summoned to the bar of the House of Commons; and on the 6th of September, 1647, it was ordered "that the house being acquainted with a blasphemous pamphlet in print, entitled, &c., by John Biddle, Master of Arts, all printed copies should be seized and burned by the common hangman, in Cheapside and at Westminster." These measures only served to increase the sale of the work, of which a second edition appeared in the month of October. But the storm that he had hitherto raised, was trifling in comparison with that which followed his next production, in 1648, A Confession of Faith touching the Holy Trinity according to Scripture. In this the divinity of the Son is expressly denied. Upon the publication of this and another work, called the Testimony of the Fathers to these Doctrines, the Assembly of Divines petitioned parliament that the author might be punished with death, an ordinance to which effect was passed; but the dissensions by which the parliament was then torn, seem to have prevented its being carried into effect. Biddle was, however, kept in confinement, the severity of which was not long after mitigated, and he was even allowed to travel into Staffordshire, when he became chaplain to a justice of the peace, and preacher in a church; but this indulgence coming to the knowledge of Bradshaw, a closer degree of confinement was the consequence. He now languished for several years in prison, until he was reduced to the greatest indigence; he was fortunate enough, however, to obtain employment in correcting the press for Daniel's edition of the Septuagint, which kept him from absolute destitution. At length, in 1654, he obtained his liberty under the General Act of Oblivion, passed in that year, and immediately established a separate society of the converts to his doctrines, to whom he regularly preached every Sunday. This prosperous state of things was but of short continuance; a catechism which he published in 1654 caused his return to confinement, in which he continued for the next six months, when he was liberated by course of law. Undaunted by the persecutions he had suffered, he had no sooner obtained his liberty, than he engaged in a dispute with one Griffin, a baptist teacher, who feeling his inability to cope with an antagonist so talented, meanly took measures for procuring his apprehension on a charge of blasphemy. He was accordingly committed first to the Poultry Compter, and afterwards to Newgate, where he endured great privations. He was tried on the capital charge of blasphemy and heresy, at the Old Bailey, under the Act of May 2, 1648. By the interposition of the Protector the trial was stopped, and Biddle was again sent to prison. At length, in October 1655, Cromwell, wearied with the petitions for and against him, banished him to the castle at St. Mary's, one of the Scilly islands. Here he applied himself to the study of theology, and to the book of the Revelations in particular. In 1658 he was restored to liberty by writ of *habeas corpus;* and upon his return to London became pastor of an independent meeting: but fearing the presbyterian party, who came again into power upon the death of Oliver Cromwell, he retired to privacy in the country. Upon the dissolution of that parliament he came forward again; but on the restoration of Charles II. he was compelled to withdraw from public observation. Being, however, narrowly watched, he was detected in holding a conventicle in the house of a citizen. Both he and his congregation were then brought before the magistrate, and committed for trial. Each of the hearers was fined 20*l.*, and Biddle 100*l.*, and to lie in prison till paid. Here the severity of his confinement brought on a disease, which terminated his life, Sept. 22, 1662, in the 47th year of his age. His private character appears to have been unexceptionable. Anthony Wood allows that, "except his opinions, there was little or nothing blameworthy in him;" and adds, "he was accounted by those of his persuasion a sober man in his discourse, and to have nothing of impiety, folly, or scurrility to proceed from him; also so devout, that he never prayed without being prostrate or flat on the ground;" a posture, says Toulmin, which he was in the habit of recommending to his most intimate friends.

As Biddle has some claims to be considered the father of the modern Unitarians, it may be proper to append a brief statement of the doctrines that he taught. They are thus detailed in Toulmin's memoir:—

"The principle on which Mr. Biddle and his adherents first formed themselves into a distinct and separate society, was, that *the unity of God is a unity of person as well as of nature.* That the Holy Spirit is indeed a person, but not God, (a superior angel.) Mr. Biddle's society, emancipated from the restraints of an establishment, adopted some other discriminating notions, such as these: 'that the fathers, under the old covenant, had only temporal promises — that saving faith consisted in universal obedience performed to the commands of God and Christ—that Christ rose again only by the power of his Father, not his own—that justifying faith is not the pure gift of God, but may be acquired by men's natural abilities—that faith cannot believe any thing contrary to or above reason—that there is no original sin—that Christ hath not the same body now in glory in which he suffered and rose again—that the saints shall not have the same body in heaven which they had on earth—that Christ was not Lord, or King, before his resurrection, or Priest before his ascension—that the saints shall not, before the day of judgment, enjoy the bliss of heaven—that God certainly does not know future contingencies—that there is not any authority of fathers, or general councils, in determining matters of faith—that Christ, before his death, had not any dominion over the angels—and that Christ, by dying, made no satisfaction for us."

We further learn from the above writer, that the followers of Biddle at first called themselves Bidellians, but adopted shortly after the designation of Unitarians, by which they seem to insinuate a charge of polytheism against other Christians. Besides the works mentioned above, Mr. Biddle published some Notes on the Revelations, and two or three other theological treatises.

BIDDULPH, (Thomas Tregenna,) born at Claines, in Worcestershire, July 5, 1763, died at Bristol, May 19, 1838, an eminent English clergyman, in his day, among the party known as evangelical. He was of Queen's college, Oxford; B.A. 1784, M.A. 1787. On the 26th of September, 1785, he was ordained deacon by Dr. Ross, bishop of Exeter, and priest by Dr. Barrington, then bishop of Salisbury, May 18, 1788. After serving several country curacies in succession, he removed to Bristol, and ultimately became incumbent of St. James's there. For some time his preaching was by no means approved in Bristol; but he succeeded in gradually drawing round him a numerous body of attached friends; while the excellence of his private character gained for him the esteem and respect of those who differed from his theological opinions. His writings consist of Essays on the Liturgy, 1798; Search after Truth in Holy Scriptures, 1818; Pamphlets on Regeneration (in opposition to Dr. Mant), 1816; Letters in the Christian Guardian, in defence of the Hutchinsonian

Philosophy, under the signature of Physico-Theologus; the Theology of the Early Patriarchs, 2 vols, 8vo; Lectures on the Holy Spirit; on the Fifty-first Psalm; a tract on the Inconsistency of Conformity to the World, and several single sermons; he also commenced a periodical called Zion's Trumpet, which was the foundation of the magazine called the Christian Guardian. Mr. Biddulph was strongly attached to the Church of England, and held high opinions of her apostolical character and authority. He died at Bristol, and was buried in St. James's church, of which he had been the minister for forty years. (Gent. Mag. 1838. Christian Guardian, 1838.)

BIDERMANN, (John Gottlieb,) born at Naumburg in 1705, where he was rector of the academy in 1741, and was afterwards appointed to the same post at Freiberg, where he died in 1772. His works, chiefly consisting of occasional discourses, many of them on the Hebrew language, were partly collected by himself, under the title of Otia Literaria, 8vo, Leipsic, 1751; but the first part only was published. He also collected the Acta Scholastica, 8 vols, Leips., and Isenac. 1741, 8vo. He wrote also several works on Numismatology, the laborious amusements of a more laborious life; many of these are very interesting. (Ersch und Gruber.)

BIDLAKE, (John,) an English divine, born at Plymouth, in 1755, educated academically at Christchurch, Oxford, and subsequently master of the grammar school in his native town. Being Bampton lecturer three years before his death, he was seized with epilepsy, in the pulpit at St. Mary's, during the delivery of one of his sermons, and subsequently he became totally blind. He died in 1814, leaving some poetical and other works. (Gent. Mag.)

BIDLOO, (Godfrey,) a celebrated Dutch surgeon and anatomist, a native of Amsterdam, born March 12, 1649. At an early age he manifested considerable taste for letters, and he cultivated poetry with tolerable success. Destined, however, by the will of his parents, to the medical profession, he applied himself with eagerness to the study of anatomy. He soon acquired information in this branch sufficient to admit of his entering into practice as a surgeon, in which capacity he served in the army for some time, and afterwards took the degree of doctor of medicine. In 1688 he was appointed to a chair of anatomy at the Hague, and in 1694 he was called to the university of Leyden, and nominated to a professorship of anatomy and surgery, and gained a high reputation. He was made physician to William III. of England, and permitted to retain his professorship. He died at Leyden in April 1713. As a surgeon, by his writings he does not appear to have possessed any great merit; he is better known as a zealous cultivator of anatomical science. In his large work, many of the plates give excellent views of the parts they are intended to designate; but in the greater number the useful purpose is destroyed by the attempts of the artist to produce extraordinary effects. Cowper, the celebrated English anatomist, purchased of a bookseller at Amsterdam, 300 copies of the plates of Bidloo's work, and most unpardonably published them, with nine additional ones, as his own. The name of the real author of the work is even effaced on the engraved title-page, and that of Cowper substituted. This edition appeared in 1698, at Oxford. Bidloo warmly and justly published a statement relative to this disgraceful transaction. His chief works are, Variæ Anatomico-medicæ Positiones; Anatomia Corporis Humani; Antiq. Anatom. Oratio, Lugd. Bat. 1694, fol.; Vindiciæ quarundam Delineationum Anatomicarum, contra ineptas Animadversiones Frid. Ruyschii, Lugd. Bat. 1697, 4to. Guliel. Cowper Criminis Literarii citatus Coram Tribunali nob. ampl. Societatis Britanno-Regiæ.

BIDPAI, (commonly called Pilpay, through an error in transcription from the Persian, according to Sir Wm. Jones,) the author, or reputed author, of the celebrated collection of tales known as the Fables of Pilpay. In the Sanscrit original, translated by Sir Wm. Jones, the name of the author or narrator is called Vishnusarman; but as Cashafi states the word Bidpaï to imply in Sanscrit *beloved*, or *favourite physician*, Sir William conjectures the appellation to be a corruption of *baidyapriya*, which bears that meaning; "the author having been, it is supposed, of the *baidya*, or medical tribe, and a favourite of his rajah." No particulars relative to Bidpaï or Vishnusarman appear to be known, and even the precise period at which he lived is not ascertained. The fables attributed to him are generally considered as the germ of all more modern collections, and exist under different forms, according to Sir Wm. Jones, in more than twenty languages. A critical account of the Pancha Tantra, or Sanscrit original, (of which the Hitopadesa, translated by Sir Wm. Jones, is an abridgement,) and of its various oriental productions, is given in the Transactions of the Royal Asiatic Society, vol. i. pp. 155—200, from the pen of Mr. H. H. Wilson, now Sanscrit professor at Oxford.

BIE, (Jacob van,) an eminent engraver of coins, antiquities, &c., born at Antwerp, in 1581. He published Imperatorum Roman. Numismata, Numismata Græciæ, and La France Métallique. His prints rank with the best of the early Flemish engravers. (Pilk. Dict.)

BIE, (Adrian van,) a painter, born in 1594, at Liere, near Antwerp. He painted portraits and architectural ornaments. His most esteemed work is a picture of St. Eloi, in the church of his native town. On account of the delicacy of his style he was frequently employed to paint on jasper, agate, porphyry, &c. He died about 1640. (Pilk. Dict.)

BIEHL, (Charlotte Dorothea,) one of the few female Danish writers, born at Copenhagen in 1731, and died there in 1788. From her earliest years she showed extraordinary talent, reading Danish and German at five years of age; she subsequently made herself mistress of most of the languages of Europe, and read the best authors in all of them. Her parents appear neither to have estimated nor assisted this extraordinary propensity for literature, and the young lady pursued her studies under the most unfavourable circumstances, during hours stolen from sleep. With such tastes, it is remarkable that she combined a character perfectly domestic. The needle was as familiar to her as the pen; and after her mother's death, she not only superintended her father's household, but nursed him in his illness, refusing all offers of marriage, for the sake of devoting herself to this pious duty. Amongst her works, the best are, The Affectionate Daughter, a drama; Freedom and Fright, a prise poem; Moral Stories, in four parts; and Correspondence between Intimate Friends, in three parts. She also translated from the Italian the work of the abate Bianchi on Happiness, and Don Quixote from the Spanish. (Ersch und Gruber.)

BIEL, (Gabriel,) born at Spire, died in 1495, one of the ablest scholastic divines of his age, in great reputation as a preacher at Mentz, till appointed to the theological chair of the new university of Wittemberg, in 1477. He died at an advanced age, in a college of regular canons, to which he had retired a few years before. His principal works are one upon the Canon of the Mass, and another expository of the same ritual.

BIEL, (John Christian,) born at Brunswick in 1687, died in 1745, a Lutheran divine, author of many theological dissertations, printed in Ugolin's Thesaurus Antiq. Soc.; also of a Lexicon for the Septuagint, which has since been augmented by Schleusner.

BIELER, (Charles Ambrose,) a physician, born at Ratisbon in 1693. He studied at the university of Jena, and took the degree of doctor of medicine in 1719, after which he practised at his native place, where he died Sept. 14, 1747. He was well versed in natural history, and wrote the part relating to Champignons in Weinman's work, Sur la Botanique; and he also published, Dissertatio de Amore Insano, Jenæ, 1717, 4to; Dissertatio de Paralysi, *ib.* 1719, 4to.

BIELFELD, (Jacob Frederic, baron of,) born at Hamburg, 31st March, 1711, died at Treben, 5th April, 1770. He studied at Leyden, and afterwards travelled through the Netherlands, France, and England, and in 1738 came to Brunswick, where the Prussian court was then resident. Here he was made known to the then crown prince, afterwards Frederic II., whose favour he acquired by his talents, and in whose society he lived for some time at Reinsberg. On Frederic's accession, in 1740, he entered entirely into his service, and went in the same year as secretary of legation to Hanover and London, and was appointed in the following year counsellor of embassy in the department for foreign affairs. In 1745 he was made second tutor to the king's youngest brother, prince Ferdinand; and in 1747 inspector of all Prussian universities, and director of the hospitals at Berlin. In 1748 he was ennobled, and in the same year he married, at Halle, a lady named de Reich, by which marriage he acquired the territories of Treben and Hasselbach, in the duchy of Altenberg. A few years afterwards he left the Prussian court, and retired to his estates, from whence he fled in 1757, on account of the war, to Hamburg. When peace was concluded he lived again at Treben, and continued there in the enjoyment of the king's favour till his death. Nearly all his writings are in the French language. His first work, Progrès des Allemands dans les Sciences, les Belles Lettres et les Arts, particulièrement dans la Poésie et l'Eloquence, Berlin, 1752, 12mo, was a very imperfect production, for Bielfeld was but ill acquainted with the subject of which he treated, and was almost an entire stranger to the modern literature of his fatherland. Even when, in 1767, a third edition of this work, revised and considerably augmented, appeared at Leyden, in two 8vo volumes, he was utterly ignorant of Wieland, Ramler, Winkelmann, even of Klopstock; in a word, of all those who may be considered the heroes of German literature. Likewise his encyclopædian work, Les Premiers Traits de l'Erudition Universelle, ou Analyse abrégée de toutes les Sciences, des Beaux Arts et des Belles Lettres, Leyden, 1767, 3 vols, 8vo, is defective and superficial. And his dramatic works, Comédies Nouvelles, 1753; Amusemens Dramatiques, Leyden, 1768, 2 vols, 8vo, are but indifferent productions. His Lettres Familières et autres, are interesting from the many anecdotes they contain, particularly from those which relate to the court during his time, Hague, 1763, 8vo; seconde édition, revue, augmentée et corrigée, Leyden, 1767, 2 vols, 8vo. A miserable German translation appeared at Dantzic, 1765, and a second edition 1770. The ablest and the best known of his works are the Institutions Politiques, Hague, 1760, 2 vols, 4to. Nouvelle édition, revue, corrigée et augmentée, à Leide, 1767, 2 vols. 8vo. The celebrated philosopher and jurist, Darjes, wrote an introduction to this work. During the latter years of his life, he published weekly, in German, a work named the Hermit, Leipsic, 1767-9, 12 vols, 8vo. (Ersch und Gruber.)

BIELKE, (Stenon Charles, baron von,) a liberal patron of science, born at Stockholm in 1709, and became a useful member of the academy of sciences in that city. It was at his expense that professor Kalm, an accurate observer, travelled in Sweden and Russia, to acquire a better knowledge of the natural history of those countries, where the baron himself had made a collection of manuscript works on botany; among which was the Flora of the Volga, with those of Tartary and Moscow. He died in 1754.

BIELKE, (Nicholas, count von,) of the same family as the preceding, lived during the latter half of the eighteenth century, and was a member of the senate at Stockholm. Placed at the head of the department for the management of the mines, his zeal and activity were manifested by many useful reforms; especially in the manner of working the vast porphyry quarries of Elfdale, in Dalecarlia.

BIELSKI, (Martin,) a Polish historian, who wrote in the sixteenth century a work entitled Chronicon Rerum Polonicarum ab Origine Gentis ad Annum 1587, cum iconibus Regum. These annals were continued by his son Joachim to the reign of Sigismund III. The work is highly esteemed, not only for its authenticity, but also for the elegance of the style. (Biog. Univ. Ap. to Gorton.)

BIENAISE, (John,) a celebrated French surgeon, born in 1601. He distinguished himself as an operator, and invented a bistoury, which has long since fallen into disuse, but which probably suggested to Frère Côme the idea of his Lithotome Cachout. Being consulted in the case of Anne of Austria, who was afflicted with a cancer, he had the honesty to declare to her son, Lewis XIV., the incurable nature of the malady. He attended that monarch in two campaigns in Flanders. Having acquired a large fortune, he bequeathed it to the poor and to the establishment of two professorships, one of anatomy, the other of surgery, at the school of St. Côme. He died Dec. 25, 1681. The following work, which was published after his death, has been much esteemed:—Les Opérations de Chirurgie par une Méthode courte et facile, Paris, 1688, 12mo; *ib.* 1693, 12mo.

BIENER, (Christian Gottlob,) born in 1748, at Zörbig; entered in 1768 the university of Wittemberg. In 1777 he was created doctor of laws, and on this occasion wrote his Discourse de Jurisdictione Ordinaria et Exemta. In 1778 he greatly extended his reputation by his observations on the disputed Bavarian succession. He died in 1828, whilst he was still in full activity, leaving behind him numerous works, chiefly on legal subjects. (Conversations-Lexicon der Neuesten Zeit und Literatur.)

BIENNE, (John,) in Latin, Benenatus, a French printer, distinguished for the beauty and correctness of his editions, especially of works in the Greek language. He died in 1588. (Biog. Univ.)

BIENVENU, (James,) a satirical

writer, born at Geneva in the sixteenth century, where he translated into French verse, and published in 4to, 1562, John Foxe's Triumph of Jesus Christ, an apocalyptic comedy, in six acts. This piece is of extreme rarity. His satires were sufficiently biting, if we may judge from the number of enemies they appear to have raised up against him. (Biog. Univ.)

BIENVILLE, (J. D. T.) a celebrated French physician of the eighteenth century. Little is recorded of his education or life, but he is well known by his work La Nymphomanie. He is said to have graduated at Leyden, practised at Rotterdam, and afterwards at the Hague. He published, La Nymphomanie, Amst. 1771, 8vo; 1788, 12mo; translated into German, Amst. 1772, and again in 1782, by Anthony Hildebrand, and into English by Dr. E. Sloane Wilmot, London 1775, 8vo. Le Pour et le Contre de l'Inoculation de la Petite Vérole, Rotterdam, 1771, 8vo. Recherches théoriques et pratiques sur la Petite Vérole, Amst. 1772, 8vo. Traité des Erreurs Populaires sur la Santé, La Haye, 1775, 8vo; translated into German by Kirtzinger, Leipsic, 1776, 8vo.

BIERKANDER, (Claude,) a botanist and entomologist, born in 1735. He became pastor of Grefback, in West-Gothland. He published several works, chiefly on the physiology and habits of plants. He died in 1795. (Biog. Univ.)

BIERLING, (Frederic William,) professor of divinity at Rinteln, born at Magdeburg in 1676. He was distinguished by much acumen and extensive erudition. He was the correspondent of most of the literary men of his day; and his letters to Leibnitz are preserved in the fourth volume of the letters of that illustrious man. He died in 1728. He published, among other works:—1. De Pyrrhonismo Historico, Leips. 1724, 8vo. 2. Observationum in Genesim Specimina vi., Rinteln, 1722 and 1728, 4to. (Biog. Univ.)

BIERLING, (Gaspar Theophilus,) a celebrated physician, born at Leipsic, who, having received his education at Padua, practised with great success at Magdeburg about the end of the seventeenth century. Contemporary with the illustrious Sydenham, he adopted his views as to the erroneous method, then prevailing, of treating the small-pox and other kindred diseases with stimulants; but he was not so successful in emancipating himself from other errors of his age, such as a persuasion of the efficacy of medicines compounded of a variety of ingredients. He died in 1693. He published, among other works—1. Thesaurus Theoretico-practicus, Magd. 1693, 4to. 2. Consilium Pestifugum, Magd. 1680, 8vo. 3. De Diarrhœâ Chylosâ, de Febre Tertianâ Purâ Intermittente, &c. (Biog. Univ.)

BIERMANN, (Martin,) a German physician of the sixteenth century. He filled a chair of medicine at Helmstadt, from which he retired in 1593, having maintained a great reputation in his profession, and wrote a work, Disquisitio de Magnis Actionibus, Helmst. 1590, 4to. This was in answer to John Bodin, on the subject of demoniacal possessions, which attracted much notice at this time, and was inserted in the Dissertationes Physico-Medicæ de Spectris et Incantationibus of Tobias Tandlor. (Wittemburg, 1613, 8vo.) He also printed, De Principiis Generationis Rerum Naturalium internis, Helmst. 1589, 8vo.

BIERON, or BIHERON, an ingenious Parisian lady, celebrated for anatomical models in wax, born in 1719, died in 1795.

BIESIUS, (Nicholas,) a Flemish physician, born in 1516, who published several works, two of which, namely, De Methodo Medicinæ, and De Naturâ, have been reprinted several times. (Rees.)

BIESTER, (John Eric,) chief librarian of the Royal Library at Berlin, and member of the Berlin Academy of Sciences, born at Lubeck in 1749, one of the secretaries of the baron von Zedlitz, the Prussian minister. In 1784, Frederic II. appointed him his librarian. He died Feb. 20, 1816. He is best known by his miscellaneous periodical, the Berlines Monatschrift, continued in various series from 1796 to 1811. Its pages were an arena in which he proved himself one of the most zealous champions of such innovating notions as prevailed among the Prussians in his day; and he was especially active in denouncing the Jesuits, who, according to him, were the authors of all possible mischief. It was a great affliction to this claimant of superior liberality, that his own son went over to Romanism. The Transactions of the Berlin Academy contain numerous dissertations and memoirs by Biester. An excellent specimen of historical criticism is a paper by him, proving, in opposition to Thunman, that all that is related of inhabitants of the Prussian territories on the Baltic, before they were colonized by Sclavonians, rests on very uncertain data. He was an industrious contributor to the old and new Allgem. Deutsche Biblioth. and also to various critical periodicals. He wrote a sketch of the life and reign of Catharine II. of Russia, Berlin, 1797. His elegant translation of Barthelemy's Anacharsis is enriched with learned notes, and an Appendix on the geography, chronology, history, and also on the measures, weights, and coins of ancient Greece. Biester was censor at a period prolific of controversy, and is praised for the liberality and moderation with which he performed the duties of that office. He was the personal friend and literary ally of the noted Nicolai, and was his coadjutor in the production of various works.

BIET, (Antony,) born in 1620, a native of Senlis, in which town he afterwards held the living of St. Geneviève, which he resigned for the purpose of going as a missionary to Cayenne in 1652. A company had been formed by whom a number of emigrants and several ecclesiastics were sent out to colonize Cayenne, but owing to the divisions and jealousies which took place, they were unable to establish themselves. A pestilential fever carried off many of them, and Biet was the only one spared of the medical and clerical members of the colony. The survivors quitted Cayenne, December 1653. Biet, however, wished to return thither, but was unable. Having returned to France, he published an account of his voyage in 1664. (Biog. Univ.)

BIEVRE, (N. Maréchal, marquis of,) grandson of George Maréchal, first surgeon of Lewis XIV., born in 1774, and brought up to the army. His claim to notice rests on a talent for puns, and other such nonsense, a collection of which was made and published in the tenth year of the Republic, under the title of Bievriana. It was quite suited to the wretched taste and abominable morals of that unhappy time. Biévre wrote also for the stage, but his health being undermined by dissipation, he went to Spa in 1789, where he died, preserving to the last his gaiety and love of puns. The theatre of the Troubadours at Paris has celebrated this mania in a farce, entitled, M. de Biévre, ou l'Abus de l'Esprit.

BIEZELINGEN, (Christian Jans van,) a Dutch painter, born at Delft in 1558. It is said that he painted a portrait of the prince of Orange, after his assassination, which was considered a better likeness than any taken during his life-time. Biezelingen died in 1600.

BIFFI, (John,) an Italian poet, born in 1464 at Mezega, in the dukedom of Milan. He wrote in Latin verse only, and is best known by a work on the miracles of the Virgin Mary. He also describes in his poems most of the principal cities of Italy through which he travelled. The time of his death is uncertain.

BIFFI, (Ambrose,) an Italian poet, born at Milan in the beginning of the seventeenth century. From his earliest age he showed a decided inclination for literature, but to please his father he was obliged to pass a great part of his youth in the shop of a woollen-draper; and it was not till late in life that he dedicated himself to his favourite pursuit, particularly to poetry. The date of his death is unknown. He wrote several works, both in poetry and prose.

BIGG, (William Redmore, R.A.) an eminent English artist. His paintings are chiefly upon domestic and familiar subjects, and have the merit of great feeling and truth. He died Feb. 6, 1828. (Gent. Mag.)

BIGLAND, (John,) an industrious English author, born at Skirlaugh, in Holderness, and engaged until over fifty, as a village-schoolmaster. In 1803 he published Reflections on the Resurrection and Ascension of Christ, a subject which he had studied for the removal of his own doubts, and upon which he now ventured to reason publicly in print for the admirable purpose of benefiting any who might be entangled in similar misgivings. The success of this piece encouraged its author to exchange the ill-paid drudgery of a little school for a literary life; and he published a series of popular works, beginning with Letters on the Study and Use of Ancient and Modern History. He contributed the 16th vol. to the Beauties of England and Wales, being an account of his native county, Yorkshire. Other subjects were afforded to his pen from history, geography, and natural history. He died at Finningley, near Doncaster, Feb. 22, 1832, universally respected for moral worth, and literary perseverance. (Ann. Biog.)

BIGLAND, (Ralph,) garter king at arms, born at Kendal, in Westmoreland, in 1711, of a family originally from Bigland, in Lancashire. After passing through various inferior situations in the Herald's Office, he was appointed garter in 1780; but he died in 1784, in London, leaving a considerable character for antiquarian knowledge, and collections for a history of Gloucestershire, which he did not live to publish, but which have been since partly published by his son. (Chalmers.)

BIGLIA, (Andrew,) a nobleman of Milan, born at the end of the 14th century. He entered very young the order of the Hermits of St. Augustine, in the convent of St. Mark, of that city; and, by his great knowledge of the classical languages, as well as of the Hebrew tongue, and by his proficiency in all the departments of science, and particularly in theology, he was elected professor of rhetoric, and soon after, of natural and moral philosophy at Bologna, an office which he held from 1423 to 1429, and acquired, like Thomas Aquinas, the surname of *Dottore Angelico;* and, on account of his many virtues, he obtained after his death the title of *Beato*, that is, deserving canonization. His works are very numerous, but only two have been published; one, a history from the year 1402 to 1431, is considered very faithful, besides having the merit of being the first of the kind. He died at Vienna in 1435.

BIGNE, (Gace de la,) born about 1428, often mentioned by the name of *La Vigne*, but he himself gives his name Bigne, of the noble family of Bigne, or Vigne, in the diocese of Bayeux. Having taken orders, he became chaplain to Philip of Valois, and subsequently to King John, with whom he came to England, as a fellow-prisoner, after the battle of Poictiers. In 1459 he commenced the poem called Roman des Oiseaux, which he finished in the reign of Charles V., to whom also he was chaplain. The poem represents certain allegorical personages disputing on the different departments of the chase; copies of it are very scarce, and it is considered a favourable specimen of early French poetry. Bigne was alive in 1473, but the date of his death is unknown. (Chalmers. Biog. Univ.)

BIGNE, (Marguerin de la,) of the same noble Norman family as the preceding, born about 1546, and supposed to have died at Paris in 1589. He had been promoted to dignities in the cathedrals of Bayeux and Mans. His title to such patronage was abundantly established by A Library of the Fathers, undertaken, as it has been supposed, in opposition to the Centuriators of Magdeburg, whose great historical work was doing much mischief to Romanism, by weakening a belief in the antiquity of its peculiarities. There seems, however, some difficulty in discovering any particular opposition between their Centuries and Bigne's Library. The latter work was printed in folio at Paris, the first volume in 1575, under this title, Bibliotheca Veterum Patrum et Antiquorum Scriptorum Ecclesiasticorum, Latine, per Margarinum de la Bigne. In 1579 the collection reached a ninth volume. It was the first attempt at a complete library of the fathers, and hence it answered extremely well; so that, in 1589, the industrious editor was enabled to bring out a new impression, also in nine folio volumes. De la Bigne appears to have been an excellent preacher as well as an industrious man of letters. In the latter capacity he also published, in 1580, an edition of Isidore of Seville, fol. In 1578 he published a Collection of Synodal Statutes, 8vo. (Chaufepié.)

BIGNELL, (Henry,) born in Oxford July 11, 1611, an English clergyman, admitted servitor of Brazennose college, Oxford, in 1629, but afterwards removed to St. Mary Hall. He published, The Son's Portion, containing Moral Instructions for the Education of Youth in Knowledge, 8vo, London, 1640; English Proverbs; also a few other small tracts. He afterwards went to the West Indies as a colonial clergyman, where he died, about 1660. (A. Wood, Ath. Oxon.)

BIGNON, (Jerome,) a learned French writer, born Aug. 24, 1590, of an ancient family, originally from Anjou. His father, Rowland, was a very learned lawyer, who instructed him in languages, philosophy, mathematics, history, and other branches of erudition. Both tutor and pupil being of the first order, young Jerome made a surprising progress at a very early age. At ten years' old, accordingly, he published Chorographie, ou Description de la Terre Sainte, a much better work upon the subject than had hitherto appeared. In 1604 appeared his Discours de la Ville de Rome, principales antiquitéz et singularitéz d'icelle. In the following year was printed his Traité sommaire de l'Election des Papes. Both these works, now extremely rare, made a great noise at the time, and scholars were extremely desirous of an acquaintance with a boy who could produce such proofs of learning. It must, however, be supposed not only that the young author had been extremely fortunate in having a learned father for his tutor, but also that his books were not without great advantages of a more direct kind from the same source. When Bignon arrived at manhood he maintained his early reputation, which is more than can be said of many precocious geniuses. He became eventually advocate-general of the parliament of Paris, counsellor of state, and royal librarian. Such situations necessarily allowed him no great time for literature, but he published, in 1610, his work, De l'Excellence des Rois et du Royaume de France, in reply to a treatise by Diego Valdez, claiming precedence over other sovereigns for the kings of Spain. This production Bignon was considered to have refuted most completely. In 1613 he published an edition of the formulary of Marculfus, with very learned notes. A second edition was published by his family in 1666. Besides his regular official labours, Bignon was distinguished as an able diplomatist upon several occasions; and in short, he was one of the greatest men of his time. He died April 7, 1656. (Moreri. Clement. Bibl. Cur.)

BIGOT, (Emeric, or Emery,) a liberal patron of literature of the 17th century; was the son of John Bigot, dean of the court of aides, in Normandy. The love that he had for letters determined, as his easy circumstances enabled him to devote all his time to their cultivation and encouragement; and more especially to the collection of curious and valuable books, by which he augmented very greatly a library of 6000 volumes, left to him by his father. He numbered among his friends the most celebrated learned men of his day, in England, Holland, and Germany, as well as in his native country; but, although he liberally assisted others in the publication of many valuable works, thereby benefiting the public in the most disinterested manner, he printed nothing under his own name except the Greek text of a life of St. Chrysostom by Palladius, which he found in the library of the grand duke at Florence, and published at Paris in 1680. In this volume he inserted the Latin translation of the celebrated Epistle of St. Chrysostom to Cæsarius; but this proving to be too direct a confutation of the doctrine of transubstantiation, was condemned by the censors and suppressed. Mr. Wake (afterwards Archbishop of Canterbury) having obtained a copy of the leaves which had been thus cut out of Bigot's book, published it in his Defence of the Exposition of the Doctrine of the Church of England against the Exceptions of M. de Meaux, &c. London, 1686, 4to, embracing the opportunity of giving an account, which is both curious and instructive, not only of the suppression of this letter, but of the controversy to which it gave rise in Archbishop Cranmer's time. At his death, Bigot, being desirous of preventing the dispersion of his library, the value of which was estimated at more than 40,000 francs, entailed it on his family, together with a legacy for its preservation and annual augmentation; but so far was he from succeeding in this design, that the whole collection was sold by auction in Paris in 1706, scarcely seventeen years after his death, which took place October 18, 1689. (Moreri. Biog. Univ. Chalmers.)

BIKRA, (Sultan Hussein Mirza Bikra,) a prince of the lineage of Timour, (from whom he was descended in the fourth degree,) who attained considerable power in Eastern Persia, towards the end of the 15th century. He inherited but little territory from his father Mansoor, but by skilfully availing himself of the dissensions among the numerous princes of his family, he made himself master of Asterabad and Mazanderan, A.D. 1458 (A.H. 863.) In attempting, however, to gain a footing in Khorassan, then governed by Abu-Said, (head of the race of Timour, and grandfather of the famous Baber,) he was not only defeated, but, after some vicissitudes of fortune, stripped of his previous dominions. But the defeat and death of Abu-Said by the Turkmans of the White Sheep, (1468,) in the celebrated expedition called "the disaster of Irak," left the field again open; Hussein-Bikra occupied the throne of Khorassan by the invitation of the people, and by the defeat and death (A.D. 1470, A.H. 875) of Yadijar-Mirza, a great-grandson of Shah-Rokh, the famous son of Timour, who had attempted to supplant him, he established himself in possession of all the remaining territories of the house of Timour west of the Oxus. His long and prosperous reign presents from this period little worthy note: it was disturbed only by occasional petty hostilities with the Timouride sovereigns of Transoxiana, and by the rebellions of his own sons, which, however, he always succeeded in easily quelling. He died A.D. 1505 (A.H. 911) in the 67th year of his age, and was succeeded in great part of his dominions by his son Badi-el-Zeman, (see BADI-AL-ZEMAN,) who was expelled a few years later by the Uzbebs. Sultan Hussein-Bikra was a brave and politic prince, though in his latter years he became, according to Baber, indolent and luxurious. He was fond of pomp and state, and the splendid court which he maintained at Herat was the closing scene of the glories of Khorassan, a country which before that period had almost always been the residence of a sovereign, but has since sunk into a province of Persia. He was a munificent patron of learning, and was himself no contemptible poet. The Persian historian Khondemir was his subject, and commemorates the great qualities of his sovereign at the close of his work; and his taste for music became so proverbial in the East, that the Turkish annalist Eoliya Effendi, writing in the middle of the seventeenth century, compares the musical parties of Sultan Mourad IV. by way of eulogium, to those of Hussein-Bikra. His relative, Sultan Baber, describes him as robust and well made, with straight and narrow eyes; lively and convivial in disposition, but quick-tempered, and addicted to wine, and to wearing gay clothes, even when advanced in life. He also gives a long account of his family. (Autobiography of Sultan Baber. Khondemir. D'Herbelot. De Guignes. Malcolm.)

BILDE, (Ove,) a Danish bishop, who lived in the sixteenth century, to whom the crown prince Frederic, step-brother of Christian VII., erected a monument on his estate of Jägersprüs, in Zealand. He resisted the introduction of the reformed religion into Denmark, and even opposed the succession of Christian III. who had openly professed it; yet he gave up his opposition when he saw that no other disposition of the crown was likely to save his country from ruin, though the almost immediate consequence of Christian's accession was his own imprisonment. He was liberated, however, after a confinement of a few months, and received a gift of the estate of Skous Kloster, where he lived eighteen years in tranquillity, enjoying the full confidence of the king, and died in 1555, after embracing the Lutheran religion. (Ersch und Gruber.)

BILDERDIJK, (William,) a modern Dutch writer of eminence, whose poetry is highly esteemed in his own country, was born at Amsterdam in 1756. At the university of Leyden, where he devoted himself to the study of jurisprudence, he had the advantage of being pupil to Van der Keessel, who formed his character as a sound jurist—a character which he maintained in a practice of many years at the Hague, in his lectures and as a writer. An acknowledged adherent of the hereditary stadtholder, he left his native country on the deposition of the latter by the French, and repaired first to Brunswick, and afterwards to London, in which latter city he gave lectures on jurisprudence, poetry, and literature. In 1806 he returned to his native country, when order seemed restored and a durable form of government established, and was named by Lewis Buonaparte, then king of Holland, his instructor in the Dutch language, and one of the first members of the newly formed National Institute. He died in 1831 at Haarlem, where he had lived since 1827. His poetry was marked by great richness of imagery, warmth and purity of style, and elegance of expression; and with that of Bellamy, Feith, De Lannoy, and Merken, seemed to recall the best ages of Dutch literature. His works were as voluminous as various; for he left behind him 90 vols, including imitations of Pope's Essay on Man, and Delille's Homme des Champs, as well as original poems in Italian, French, and English. He left also an almost completed history of his native country, of which the first volume only has as yet been published, by his friend, professor Tydeman, in Leyden. (Conversations-Lexicon. Brockhaus.)

BILFINGER, (George Bernhard,) an original and acute philosophical writer, of the school of Leibnitz and Wolf, born at Kannstadt, in Wirtemberg, in 1693, was educated in the theological school at Tubingen, where he devoted himself to the mathematics. He left this place to study immediately under Wolf, at Halle, for whom he had conceived the greatest admiration. A strong attachment was formed between master and scholar; and the former admitted that he was not a little indebted to the latter for the revision and better definition of his ideas. In 1721, Bilfinger was appointed extraordinary professor of philosophy at Tubingen, with which office, in 1724, he combined that of teacher of mathematics at the Collegium Illustre. In 1723 he published a work, De Harmoniâ Animi et Corporis Humani maxime præstabilitâ, Francof. 8vo; in which he developed the doctrine of Leibnitz, and refuted the objections to it raised by Foucher, Bayle, Newton, Clarke, and others. In 1725 appeared his most important work, Dilucidationes de Deo, Anima Humana, Mundo, et generalioribus Rerum Affectionibus, (the last edition, c. præfat. A. F. Böckii, is that of 1768, Tub.) His opinions not being favourably received at Tubingen, Wolf procured for him an invitation from Peter the Great, to fill the office of professor of philosophy and physics at St. Petersburg, which was gladly accepted by him; and he repaired thither in 1725. His scientific writings now increased his fame, and attracted the attention of the duke of Wirtemberg, who, in 1731, recalled him to Tubingen as professor of theology. He enjoyed also the particular esteem of the next duke, Charles Alexander, who made him a privy-counsellor in 1735, and during whose minority and reign he took an active and beneficial part in the administration of public affairs. He studied the science of fortification so successfully, that the system he invented was long followed, and still retains his name. He died at Stuttgard in 1750.

BILGUER, (John Ulric de,) a celebrated surgeon, born at Coire, in the Grisons, in Switzerland, May 1, 1720. In 1742 he was employed in the Prussian army, of which he eventually became surgeon-general. He thus had most extensive practice, which was increased by the battles of Kunnersdorf and Torgau. He acquired much reputation by his great ability and skill. In 1761 he took the degree of doctor of medicine at Halle, and his thesis on this occasion was translated into various languages: in it he maintained the inutility of amputation in cases of gunshot wounds and fractures, a doctrine which, opposed by Pott and other men of eminence, and supported by Kirkland, has been productive of great improvements in the practice in that branch of surgery. He died April 6, 1796. His famous inaugural dissertation, De Amputatione rarissime administrandâ, aut quasi abrogandâ, has been translated into most of the languages of Europe; and various other works on the practice of surgery. See Haller's Bib. Chirurg. (Rees. Biog. Univ.)

BILLARD, (Charles Michael,) a celebrated physician, born at Pelonaille, near Angers, June 16, 1800. He was educated at Loval, and afterwards at Angus, at which place, in 1819, he obtained a situation in the hospital. His attention was especially directed to pathological anatomy, and he went to Paris to complete his researches, which were given to the public as Traité de la Membrane Mucueuse Gastro-intestinale dans l'Etat Morbide, Paris, 1825, 8vo. In the same year he published a translation of Thomson's Principles of Chemistry, Paris, 8vo, 2 vols; and in 1826 an edition of the Précis de l'Art des Accouchements, by M. Chevreul. He graduated in 1828, and then returned to Angers, where he became extensively engaged in practice, and published a translation of Lawrence's work on the Diseases of the Eye, Paris, 1830, 8vo; to which he added a Précis of the Pathological Anatomy of the Eye. He likewise published several papers on Croup and other medical subjects. He died of a consumption, January 31, 1832.

BILLAUD-VARENNE, (J. Nicholas,) one of the principal actors in the most sanguinary scenes of the French Revolution, born at Rochelle in 1762. The son of an attorney in very small practice, he had nevertheless some education; but was early distinguished by a rebellious and licentious character. When yet a mere lad, he seduced a young woman from her parents, and joined a company of players; but not being fitted for the stage, either by person, or by mental qualifications, he soon relinquished it, and entered the congregation of the Oratory, but without taking orders. Here, however, he could not long conceal his innate depravity; and having given just cause of offence to his superiors by some verses that he wrote, he was obliged to quit that establishment. Having mended his fortune by a marriage with a natural daughter of Verdun, farmer-general, he might have recovered, by good conduct, his position in society; but just at this time the Revolution burst forth, and it suited well with Billaud's temper and views to connect himself with the popular cause. He now (1789) published a vehement attack upon the ancient system of government in France, in 3 vols, 8vo, under the title of Le Despotisme des Ministres de France. Become conspicuous, he was named, in 1791, one of the judges of the fourth arrondissement of Paris; but he had no taste for quiet and regular occupation. Allied from the first with Danton, Marat, and Robespierre, he was most active in the Jacobin club; was among the loudest of the advocates for putting the king to death; and in the horrible massacres of September, he was the person who, with one foot in a pool of blood and another planted on the corpse of one of the victims, encouraged and promised rewards to those who were becoming tired of their murderous employment. At length, having taken part in all the atrocities of the period, and having been one of the most violent accusers of his colleague Robespierre, he was himself the object of attack; and, together with Barère, Vadier, and Collot d'Herbois, he was condemned, April 1, 1795, to be transported to Guiana. In the unhealthy forests of that noxious climate the energy of Billaud's mind, and the strength of his bodily constitution, supported him for nearly twenty years; and, after having seen many of his former associates, and some of his former opponents, sent to share his punishment, he escaped, in 1816, to St. Domingo, where he offered his services to the negro government. The Mulatto Petion, who was at that time in power there, under the title of President, gave Billaud a small pension, which he enjoyed until his death, which took place at Port au Prince, in 1819. (Biog. Univ. Suppl. Biog. Nouv.)

BILLAUT, (Adam, commonly called, apparently jocosely, Master Adam,) a joiner at Nevers, but distinguished by some poetical pieces, which were celebrated in their day. Though by no means a writer of distinguished genius, he was not without considerable vigour of imagination. His Chevilles, Vilebrequin, and Rabot,—thus he humorously named his poetical works, after the implements of his trade,—were the principal favourites. He flourished at the end of the reign of Lewis XIII., and the beginning of that of Lewis XIV., and was patronized by cardinal Richelieu. (Moreri. Chalmers.)

BILLBERG, (John,) an eminent Swedish astronomer and mathematician of the latter part of the seventeenth century. He was patronized by Charles XI., through whose influence he was promoted, after he had studied divinity, to the see of Strengnes. He also attended as astronomer in an expedition of geographical discovery fitted out by that sovereign. He died in 1717, leaving behind him several scientific and theological tracts; he was also one of the best Latin poets in Sweden. (Gezelius.)

BILLECOQ, (John Baptist L. J.) a French lawyer and writer of eminence, born in Paris, January 31, 1765. He distinguished himself at the bar on various occasions; among others, on the trial of Georges Cadoudal, when he defended the marquis de Rivière from the charge of attempting the life of the first consul. Billecoq employed himself in translating many valuable foreign works into the French language; among which may be mentioned, The English Farmer, 18 vols, 8vo, in which undertaking he had Lamare and Benoît as his coadjutors. He also wrote, together with several others on political subjects, a pamphlet under the following title: Un Français à sa Grace Lord Wellington, sur sa Lettre du 23 Septembre dernier à Lord Castlereagh. This letter, which was on the occasion of the spoliation of the Museum, was truly French. (Biog. Nouv.)

BILLERCY, (Claude Nicholas,) a physician, born at Besançon about 1667, distinguished by his knowledge of mathematics, astronomy, and medicine: of the latter he was a professor in the university of his native place. He died in 1759. He wrote several works, two only of which were printed:—Traité sur la Maladie pestilentielle qui dépeuplait la Franche-Comté, en 1707, Besançon, 1721, 12mo; Traité du Régime, *ib.* 1748, 12mo. Also a work in MS. which is now in the public library of Besançon.

BILLI, or BILLY, (James de,) born in 1535, died in 1581, abbot of St. Michel-en-l'Erin, distinguished for his erudition, particularly in the Greek and Hebrew languages. He translated St. Gregory of Nazianzen, St. Isidore, and other of the Greek fathers, into Latin, and published several smaller works in other departments of literature.

BILLI, (James de,) born in Compeigne in 1602, died at Dijon in 1679. A French Jesuit, author of a great number of mathematical works, of which it will be sufficient to mention, Nova Geometriæ Clavis Algebra, Paris, 1643, 4to; Doctrinæ Analyticæ Inventum Novum, Toulouse, fol. (Moreri.)

BILLIDRIUS, (Anthony G.) a German chemist, son-in-law and pupil of Angelo Sala, and the first clear and accurate writer upon chemistry. He lived in the beginning of the seventeenth century. He published, Exercitium Chimicum Ultimum, Brunæ, 1625. Dissertatio de Thessalo in Chimicis redivivo, seu de unitate Medicinæ Chemico-hermeticæ, Francof. 1649 and 1653. With other works upon similar subjects.

BILLINGSLEY, (Sir Henry,) a mathematician of some note, the son of Roger Billingsley, of Canterbury. He was born before the middle of the sixteenth century. Having spent about three years at Oxford, he was removed from the university, and bound apprentice to a haberdasher in London; a circumstance, as Wood says, not altogether unusual in those days. Turning his attention vigorously to his new pursuit, he acquired in process of time a very large fortune; and became successively sheriff, alderman, a commissioner of customs, and, at length, in 1596, Lord Mayor, when he received the honour of knighthood. Having become acquainted with an eminent mathematician of the name of Whitehead, an Augustine friar at Oxford, he had the opportunity, when, at the dissolution of his house by Henry VIII., his friend was reduced to poverty, of showing at once the generosity of his nature and his love of learning by taking Whitehead into his house as one of his family. He, in his turn, became the benefactor, by instructing Billingsley in mathematics; who, though now not very young, proved to be so apt a pupil that he soon made great progress in that science; in which, at length, he became no mean proficient. Whitehead, at his death, bequeathed to him his papers; and, among the rest, some valuable manuscript notes on Euclid's Elements; which induced Billingsley to translate that author, illustrating the text with these notes, together with Scholia, and learned observations of his own, and prefixing an introductory preface by Dr. John Dee. This work was published under the following title: The Elements of Geometry of the most Ancient Philosopher, Euclid of Megara, faithfully translated into the English Tongue; whereunto are added certain Scholias, Annotations, &c., London, 1570, fol. Billingsley died 22d of November, 1606. (Wood's Athenæ.)

BILLINGSLEY, (John,) educated at St. John's college, Cambridge, but being in Oxford at the time of the parliamentary visitation, he was, by the commissioners, placed in a Kentish fellowship in Corpus Christi college at that university. He had already taken his degree of bachelor of arts at Cambridge, and after his incorporation, proceeded to that at Oxford. Having obtained presbyterian orders, he became minister of Chesterfield, in Derbyshire, where he had many followers and admirers; but he experienced great annoyance from the Quakers. He published—1. Strong Comforts for Weak Christians, with due Cautions against Presumption; the Substance of several Sermons at Chesterfield, 4to, Lond. 1656. 2. The Grand Quaker proved a gross Liar. These two works were answered by George Fox, in a book entitled, The Great Mystery of the Great Whore, &c. unfolded. 3. The Believer's Daily Exercise, in Four Sermons, 8vo, Lond. 1690. (Wood, Ath. Oxon.)

BILLINGTON, (Elizabeth.) This celebrated singer was born about 1769, of German parents, of the name of Weicschell, who made music their profession. Her mother was known in London as a concert and Vauxhall singer, and was a favourite pupil of J. C. Bach's. The daughter very early showed marks of extraordinary musical genius, and when only seven years old performed a *concerto* at the theatre in the Haymarket. She married, when only sixteen, Mr. S. Billington, one of the band at Drury-lane; and, accompanied by him, went to Ireland, where she met with great applause as an actress and singer. This procured her an engagement at Covent Garden theatre, where she came out in 1785 as Rosetta, in Love in a Village, with unprecedented success, and from that time was considered as one of the first singers of her day. The following summer she repaired to Paris, and received great benefit from the instructions of the celebrated Sacchini. On her return, her fame continued to increase, and she was of essential benefit to the funds of the theatre by the crowded houses that she drew. In 1794 she went to Italy, where she fully sustained her reputation, and was perhaps the first singer who received as large sums for the exercise of her talents in foreign countries, as others had done in England. Her husband died in 1796, of apoplexy, at Naples, where they were staying, and she afterwards, in 1799, married a M. de Felessent, a Frenchman, attached to the army of Buonaparte, in his invasion of Italy. She then purchased a small estate near Venice, upon which they resided for about two years, when, after repeated invitations from the managers of the English theatres, she returned alone to her native country, and reappeared at Covent Garden theatre in Oct. 1801, and was received by crowded houses with all that rapturous applause which her superior talents commanded. She acted at both theatres and the Opera House, besides singing at concerts, so that she is said to have realized 10,000*l.* in one year, 1801-2, by her various engagements. In 1817 she again returned to Italy, and died of apoplexy on the 25th of August, 1818. She may be said to have been not only the first singer of her country, but of her age, whether as regards science or sweetness and compass of voice. (Ann. Biog.)

BILLUART, (Charles René,) a learned Dominican, born Jan. 18, 1685, at Revin, in the diocese of Liege. In 1710 he became professor of theology in the college of Douai, and in 1725, he was raised to the first professorship in that institution. In 1728 he was elected provincial of the province of St. Rose. He had been appointed prior of the convent of Revin, in 1721, and he died in that house, Jan. 21, 1757. Of his numerous works, the following are the most important—De Mente Ecclesiæ Catholicæ circà Accidentia Eucharistiæ, contra D. Lengrand, Liege, 1715, 12mo. Le Thomisme vengé de sa prétendue Condamnation par la Constitution *Unigenitus*, 1720, 12mo. Summa S. Thomæ hodiernis Academiarum Moribus accommodata, sive Cursus Theologiæ juxta Mentem D. Thomæ, Liege, 1746-51, 29 vols, 8vo. This theological course, having gained a great reputation in Romish colleges, has been twice reprinted. (Biog. Univ. Suppl.)

BILNEY, (Thomas,) an English martyr, born in Norfolk. He was fellow of Trinity hall, Cambridge, and early conspicuous for an extreme anxiety to prepare himself for another world. Perhaps there might be something of bodily unhealthiness connected with his eager aspirations after spiritual excellence, as his stature was diminutive, his constitution far from robust, and his mind inclining to melancholy. His approaches towards a thorough change of heart and life were, accordingly, far too slow for giving satisfaction to himself. He was constantly haunted by self-condemnation, pouring out his griefs in confession, and praying for such advice as his case might seem to require. He was directed to fast, purchase indulgences, and adopt other means usual among Romanists for subduing remorse or religious melancholy. He did these things, but notwithstanding, his troubled spirit found no rest. At length, a friend mentioned to him the New Testament, lately published by Erasmus, highly commending the manner in which the work was executed. Bilney bought the book, but chiefly with an expectation of seeing matter delightful to him rendered additionally so by the enlivening graces of composition. This purchase gave an impulse to his thoughts equally new and irresistible. He pondered with absorbing attention the words of eternal life, and now discerned in the sacrifice of the cross a refuge from the misery by which he had been so long haunted. Ascetic exercises, hitherto used as medicines for his wounded spirit, he now spurned as delusive palliatives. It became his firm conviction that he, with all around him, had been deceived in points vitally important, and he felt constrained to raise a warning voice, that might apprize others of a precipice, down which he believed himself to have all but fallen. His zeal, it may even be his enthusiasm, emboldened him to set all hazard at defiance. He laboured to disseminate his opinions among members of the university, and Latimer with others became his converts. He preached also earnestly in the neighbourhood of London against pilgrimages, penances, the invocation of saints, and perhaps every other peculiarity of popery, except transubstantiation, a doctrine which he held firmly to the last. As might have been expected, his conduct exposed him to a prosecution for heresy. He was convicted, but sentence was purposely delayed, in the hope, probably, that his own fears and the importunity of friends would overcome his resolution. Any such expectation was gratified: he recanted.

After this escape from imminent danger, Bilney returned to Cambridge, but to misery there, far more intense than any undergone in former times. His constitutional melancholy seized him with greater violence than ever. The cheerfulness once infused into his mind by the contemplation of scriptural Christianity, the excitement arising from the communication to others of the knowledge acquired by himself, were exchanged for the intolerable gloom of a corroding indolent despair. His meals were taken without appetite or relish; the kind attentions of his friends were received with stagnant apathy; even religious topics no longer gave him consolation. He viewed himself as an apostate and a reprobate, who, for the sake of lingering upon earth during a few years of iniquity and misery, had basely denied his Saviour, stupidly bartered away the inestimable prize which had been lately the anchor of his hope, and perfidiously lured others to destruction. Such were the horrors engendered by the constant attrition of these gloomy thoughts, that such as loved him, apprehensive of some suicidal act, anxiously watched over him both night and day. For more than a year he continued to struggle with despair. At last he came, one night, into the college hall, bade farewell to certain of his friends, and told them that he had set his face to go to Jerusalem. His meaning was soon apparent. When next heard of, he was in Norfolk, where, first among his family connexions, afterwards openly in the fields, he boldly preached the doctrines that he had once abjured, and exhorted his hearers, as they valued their own salvation, to renounce the principles in which they had been reared. As he had probably both anticipated and desired, these exertions in discharge of his conscience led to his apprehension, and being again convicted of heresy, he was sentenced to the stake. His martyrdom took place Sept. 6, 1531, on a low spot of ground without the walls of Norwich, called the Lollards' pit. He met his fate with invincible constancy and cheerfulness, joined with such a bright display of christian charity, that when some of the friars, apprehensive lest the people, imputing to the malice of their class the guilt of his death, should contract their liberality towards them, entreated him to exculpate them from the charge, Bilney promptly complied, and begged of the spectators not to intermit towards these mendicants their accustomed kindness. After light was communicated to the pyre, his sufferings appear to have been of no long duration. The wind, indeed, raged violently, and twice or thrice blew from his scorched and blackened form the blazing mass in which he was at first enveloped. He was then observed to beat his breast, being heard at intervals ejaculating, "Jesus," or "I believe;" but his head soon dropped, and it was evident that he had ceased to breathe. Anxious to relieve the eyes of those around from dwelling on the slow combustion of his withered corpse, an officer with his halberd loosed the staple by which the chain about it had been secured, and the martyr's body fell. Fresh fuel was then expeditiously supplied, and ere long a heap of ashes only marked the spot where lately stood the willing victim, anxious to atone for injuries inflicted by him in an evil hour upon the cause he loved. His memory was aspersed by a report, carefully circulated upon no less authority than that of Sir Thomas More, that he brought a scroll to the stake, containing his recantation, which he read there. But archbishop Parker, then a young man, and a great admirer of Bilney, went from Cambridge to Norwich, as a witness of his martyrdom, and he declared him neither to have had any writing or scroll in his hand, nor to have read any recantation. (Soames's Hist. Ref. i. 285. Strype's Memorials, i. 311. Parker, i. 12.)

BILON, (Hyppolitus,) a distinguished physician, born at Grenoble, in 1780. He was educated at Paris, and was a pupil of the celebrated Bichât. He took the degree of doctor of medicine at Montpelier, and on his return to Grenoble, was made secretary of the faculty and professor of the physical sciences, and gained much reputation. He died of consumption, Oct. 29, 1824, having published Eloge Historique de Bichât, Paris, 1802, 8vo. Dissertation sur la Douleur, Paris, 1803, 4to. He wrote several articles for the Dictionnaire des Sciences Médicales, and many papers which were read before the Academy of Grenoble.

BILON, or PILON, a native of Armenia, of the seventh century, who translated into his native language the Ecclesiastical History of Socrates, to which he made some additions. He also wrote a history of the Patriarchs of Armenia. (Biog. Univ.)

BILS, (Lewis de,) a celebrated Dutch anatomist, who lived about the middle of the seventeenth century. He resided for a long time at Rotterdam, and afterwards at Louvain. In 1658 he announced a discovery for the preservation of anatomical preparations by a process of embalming, which, however, he kept secret; declaring that he had found out a means of drying bodies dissected, at the same time preserving the muscles, vessels, viscera, and other parts all in their natural situation. De Bils professed that his dried specimens possessed the flexibility and appearance of moist preparations, and offered to communicate his secret, provided a sufficient remuneration was given to him, which he fixed at the sum of 120,000 florins. The States of Brabant purchased five of his preserved bodies, but after a time they began to manifest symptoms of putrefaction. De Bils pretended that the professors of Louvain had purposely effected this condition by improper means, and he quitted Louvain in 1669, and went to Bois-le-Duc, where he continued his operations with better success. His secret, however, was never developed; and although it has been much overrated, it must not be denied to him that he had made many improvements in the mode of preserving anatomical subjects. De Bils proposed also a new theory in relation to the lymphatic system, which was criticised by Bartholin, Barbetti, Van Horne, and Sylvius, and has now passed into oblivion, principally by the researches of the celebrated Ruysch. De Bils exhausted his fortune in his experiments, and died of a consumption, greatly accelerated, according to the testimony of Clauderus, by his constant occupation amidst putrid exhalations. His writings, which were numerous, and excited much interest at the time, were collected and published in 1692, in 4to, under the title of De Bils Inventa Anatomica antiquo-nova cum Clarissimorum Virorum Epistolis, et Testimoniis, ubi Annotationes Joannis ab Hoorne et Pauli Barbette, refutantur, interprete Gederne Buenio, Amst.

BILSCH, (Caspar,) born at Strasburg, in 1606, and died there in 1636, professor of jurisprudence in his native town. It is considered that he deserves as much credit for his exposition of the Lombard feudal law, as Cujas acquired for himself with respect to Roman jurisprudence. His Commentarius in Consuetudines Feudorum, appeared at Strasburg in 1673, 4to. It is likewise more than probable that he had a great share in the getting up of Mayer's Collegium Juris Argentoratense, a work of very great reputation in matters pertaining to civil law. (Ersch und Gruber.)

BILSON, (Thomas,) born at Winchester, 1536, died at Westminster, 1616, a learned prelate of the English church, successively fellow of New College, Oxford, master of Winchester school, prebendary of the cathedral, and warden of the college in the same city. In 1585 he published, The True Difference between Christian Subjection and Unchristian Rebellion, dedicated to Queen Elizabeth. This work was intended, on the one hand, to confute the Romish party, who were plotting against the throne; and on the other, to defend the queen's interference in the Low Countries to save the protestant population from sinking under the vindictive power of its old master, the king of Spain. How well soever the work may have fulfilled the immediate purposes of the writer, the doctrines laid down in it were urged with fatal success against the unfortunate Charles I., it being the book most frequently quoted by his puritanical opponents in justification of their treasonable practices. In 1593 Bilson published The Perpetual Government of Christ's Church, one of the most able treatises in favour of episcopacy ever written. In 1596 he was made bishop of Worcester, and the next year was translated to Winchester. About this time he preached some sermons which gave great offence to the puritans, inasmuch as he opposed the Calvinistic doctrine of particular election, and asserted that the descent into hell mentioned in the Creed was to be understood of an actual descent into the place of torment. A stop was put to the discussion by the authoritative command of the queen. At the commencement of the reign of James I. bishop Bilson was one of the managers of the conference at Hampton Court, and he was the colleague of Dr. Smith in the revision of the new edition of the Bible; he was likewise one of the delegates who pronounced the sentence of divorce between the earl and countess of Essex. At length, says Anthony Wood, when he had gone through many employments, and had lived in continual drudgery, as it were, for the public good, he surrendered up his pious soul to God on the 18th June, 1616, and was buried on the south side of Westminster Abbey.

BINET, (Réné,) a translator of Virgil, born near Beauvais, in France, in 1732. He was a professor at the military school, and afterwards at the college of Plessis, and taught rhetoric there until the suppression of that establishment in 1792. He was at that time also rector of that ancient university. After the revolution, when the central schools were set up, he found himself obliged to accept the humble situation of Latin master at the school of the Pantheon: he had subsequently a superior appointment at the Lyceum, which was named after Buonaparte, and during his few hours of leisure employed himself in translating Virgil, Horace, and other Latin classics. He died at Paris in 1812.

BINET, (Stephen,) a French surgeon born at St. Quentin, in Picardy. He studied at Paris, and entered the army, in which he rose to be surgeon-major of the military hospitals. He died at the siege of Rochelle, in 1628. He published, Les Œuvres Anatomiques et Chirurgicales de Germain Courtin, traduites du Latin, Paris, 1612, folio; Rouen, 1656, folio.

BING, (J. B.) a German, of the Jewish persuasion, born at Metz, in 1759. He acquired a considerable reputation by his knowledge of the Hebrew language and the theology of his nation, and appears to have been a man of enlarged views on general subjects. His translation of the celebrated Phædo of Mendelsohn, published at Berlin, attracted much attention. Coming to Paris to obtain the means of supporting a numerous family, he became acquainted with many distinguished persons there, who honoured him with their friendship. He died at no advanced age. (Biog. Univ.)

BINGHAM, (Sir George Ridout,) born in 1777, a gallant British officer, who served with distinction in the Peninsular war, and was in consequence nominated knight commander of the Bath in 1815. He also had the charge of Buonaparte from England to St. Helena, where he remained several years, as lieutenant-colonel of the 53d regiment. He was descended from an ancient Dorsetshire family, and died January 3, 1833. (Ann. Biog.)

BINGHAM, (George,) born at Melcomb-Bingham, Dorset, 1715, died at Pimpern, 1800, an English divine, educated at Westminster and Christchurch, Oxford, from whence he was elected fellow of All Souls, where he formed an intimacy with Sir W. Blackstone. He was afterwards rector of Pimpern, Dorset, and also of More Critchel, in the same county. He wrote, A Vindication of the Doctrine and Liturgy of the Church of England, in answer to Mr. Lindsey's Apology for Quitting his Living, 1774; an Essay on the Millennium; Dissertationes Apocalypticæ; Paul at Athens; a Commentary on Solomon's Song; and some Sermons: but the work by which he is more generally known, is the History and Antiquities of Dorset. In his theological opinions he was more liberal towards the church of Rome than was common at that time; he held that church to be part of Christ's visible church. He denied that the pope was antichrist, or that any of the predictions of Daniel or St. John referred to the papal power. He was much beloved and regretted by his parishioners.

BINGHAM, (Joseph,) one of the most illustrious scholars produced by the English church; born in September 1668, of respectable parentage, at Wakefield, in Yorkshire. His early education having been received in that town, on May 26, 1684, he was admitted of University college, Oxford. He proved a most laborious student; but ecclesiastical antiquity had more attractions for him than classical. He was, indeed, far from inattentive to the literature of Greece and Rome; only he considered its importance inferior to that of seeking satisfactory explanations or confirmations of scriptural doctrines from the fathers. He took the degree of B. A. in 1688, and on the 1st of July 1689, he was elected fellow of his college. His degree of M. A. was taken June 23, 1691, and he became one of the college tutors. In that situation he had the good fortune to be concerned in the education of a young fellow-townsman, brought by his means into the university, to whom he paid great attention, discerning in him, probably, the seeds of future excellence. This was John Potter, eventually archbishop of Canterbury, and rendered worthy of that exalted situation by unusual erudition, and unquestionable moral worth. Bingham's happiness and usefulness in the university were abruptly terminated by his appearance in the Trinitarian controversy. Much discussion was afloat as to the precise view of it exhibited by the fathers, and especially as to their exact meaning in using the terms *οὐσία* and *substantia*. Some very erroneous representations of these matters, according to Bingham's opinion, had recently been delivered from the university pulpit in St. Mary's; and his own turn to preach there coming shortly afterwards, he thought himself qualified, by the peculiar direction of his studies, to give a sounder view. The other side, however, had been advocated by a preacher of considerable influence in the university, and accordingly, Bingham's exposure of its weakness raised a violent party against him. He had really contented himself with exhibiting an elaborate account and vindication of the sense given to the term *person* by ecclesiastical antiquity, which he contended was at variance with representations recently heard in that place. Indignant at this attack, the late preacher exerted himself successfully to obtain from the leading members of the university a censure upon Bingham's discourse, as containing false and impious doctrine, upon which the catholic church had fixed the brand of heterodoxy. His character was now at the mercy of every thoughtless or envious tongue, and charges against him of arianism, tritheism, and the heresy of Valentine Gentilis, resounded on all sides. He had preached his obnoxious sermon on the 28th of October, 1695; but such were the activity and violence of his opponents, that on the 23d of the following month, he found himself under the necessity of resigning his fellowship, and of retiring from Oxford. He was not, however, allowed to languish in destitution. Dr. Radcliffe, the greatest of contemporary physicians, and eventually famous for extraordinary liberality to the university of Oxford, presented him immediately, but without solicitation, on the resignation of his fellowship, to the rectory of Headbourn-Worthy, in Hampshire, then valued at about 100*l.* a year. Having settled himself upon this preferment, Bingham was called to preach, on the 12th of May, 1696, a visitation sermon in Winchester cathedral, and he then pursued the subject which had occasioned so much clamour at Oxford. He introduced a vindication of himself, admitting that if truth had been at the bottom of the charges brought against him, they were "enough to give all wise and sober men a just abhorrence" of his opinions. A third sermon was preached upon the same subject, Sept. 16, 1697, also at a visitation; and this concluding his argument, he made arrangements for committing the whole series to the press, as a full vindication of himself. This design, from unknown reasons, he never executed; and his three remarkable sermons remained in MS. until they were published in the complete edition of his works, for which the world has been indebted recently to his great-grandson, the Rev. Richard Bingham. After a residence of about six years at Headbourn-Worthy, Bingham married a daughter of Richard Pococke, then rector of Colmere, in Hampshire, and grandfather of the bishop of Ossory of the same name, known as author of the Description of the East. This marriage produced two sons and eight daughters. Burthens of this kind, with their attendant cares, would have disposed most men, in narrow circumstances, even of scholarly tastes and habits, to consider deep research as impossible. Bingham himself, however sorely against his will, might have been driven to this conclusion, had not his residence been placed within about a mile of Winchester. To clergymen of small incomes in the country, books to any sufficient extent for learned purposes, are usually quite inaccessible. They can neither buy what is wanted, nor afford the time and expense required by a competent use of it in public libraries. Bingham had observed a great deficiency in ecclesiastical literature. There were esteemed and well-known books which gave connected views of Greek and Roman antiquities. The Church, taking that term in its widest extent, could boast of no such book. Many writers, both Romish and Protestant, had learnedly treated of various points in christian antiquity; a general arrangement of the whole subject was reserved for Bingham, a country clergyman, with a large family, and no means worth naming of buying books, or visiting public libraries. Nothing can be more striking than the account given by himself in the preface to his Antiquities, both of the difficulties under which he laboured, and of the happy circumstance that rendered them unequal to stifle his anxieties for the production of that learned work. "I confess," he says, "that this work will suffer something in my hands for want of several books, which I have no opportunity to see, nor ability to purchase. The chief assistance I have hitherto had, is from the noble benefaction of one, who *being dead, yet speaketh*, I mean the renowned bishop Morley," (who filled the see of Winchester from 1662 to 1684,) "whose memory will ever remain fresh in the hearts of the learned and the good; who, among other works of charity and generosity becoming his great soul and high station in the church, such as the augmentation of several small benefices, and provision of a decent habitation and maintenance for the widows of poor clergymen in his diocese, has also bequeathed a very valuable collection of books to the church of Winchester, for the advancement of learning among the parochial clergy; and I reckon it none of the least parts of my happiness, that Providence, removing me so early from the university, where the best supplies of learning are to be had, placed me by the hands of a generous benefactor (Dr. Radcliffe), without any importunity or seeking of my own, in such a station as gives me liberty and opportunity to make use of so good a library, though not so perfect as I could wish." Profiting by the advantage of a residence near bishop Morley's library, Bingham produced the first volume of his immortal work, the Origines Ecclesiasticæ, or Antiquities of the Christian Church, in 8vo, in 1708. He regularly proceeded with it, until, in 1722, he printed the tenth and last volume, thus securing to the English church the glory of supplying an important deficiency in ecclesiastical literature. But independently of the gratification which this may fairly give an Englishman, it may be added as a circumstance eminently fortunate, that learning owes this inestimable appliance to a member of the Anglican communion. Had it fallen into Romish hands, even a writer of considerable candour could scarcely have escaped a disposition to colour and conceal, so as to make every thing papal carry an air of the most venerable antiquity. Protestant dissenters have rarely either taste or qualification for such works, their body generally caring little for serious books which are not either devotional, or expository of Scripture in their own way. Such a work as Bingham's Origines could not, accordingly, be undertaken more safely by a member of any communion than of the Anglican, and it could not have fallen into more competent hands than his. It soon attracted that notice abroad which its extraordinary intrinsic excellence must have eventually commanded. In 1724, the first volume of it in Latin, by Grischovius, appeared at Halle, and Romish scholars were driven to confess that it was a most important addition to theological libraries, though much less so than a similar production would have been from one of their own body. It is not a pleasant consideration that the author of a compilation so celebrated and useful, was to the last but moderately requited by preferment. When posterity thinks of the numerous men of that day, now wholly forgotten, and who never could have been thought likely to pass through a professional career with more than average respectability, but who, notwithstanding, reaped a golden harvest from the smiles of ministers and prelates, it is hardly possible to view Bingham's narrow circumstances without imputing to contemporary patrons no very nice perceptions of a public trust. The only excuse for these dispensers of the church's patrimony that readily presents itself, is that learned person's death at an age which may be considered as rather early. His constitution had never been robust, and constant labour must have aggravated its defects. He died, accordingly, Aug. 17, 1723, in the 55th year of his age, and was buried in the churchyard of Headbourn-Worthy. He did not, however, spend his latter years with no better provision than could be supplied by that benefice. In 1712, Sir Jonathan Trelawney, then bishop of Winchester, collated him to the rectory of Havant. Charles Trimnell, also, Trelawney's immediate successor in the see of Winchester, expressed an intention to confer upon him the first prebend in the cathedral there that should fall vacant. The prelate, however, only held Winchester two years, and his death occurred on the very same day as Bingham's. That learned person's latter years might have passed somewhat more easily than they did, by means of the income derived from Havant, and some small sums occasionally received from his works, had he not imprudently been duped by the South Sea bubble, as it was eventually called; and when it burst, in 1720, he, like multitudes of others, was reduced to the brink of ruin. His widow spent her declining age in bishop Warner's eleemosynary foundation for persons like herself, at Bromley, in Kent. She sold the copyright of her late husband's writings to the booksellers, who published, in 1726, an edition of them in two folio volumes. This publication is chiefly occupied by the Origines Ecclesiasticæ; but it also contains, A Scholastical History of Lay Baptism; A Dissertation on the Eighth Canon of the Council of Nice; The French Church's Apology for the Church of England; and a Discourse concerning the Mercy of God to Penitent Sinners. This was a reprint of the works exactly as they had appeared before, although Bingham had left materials for various improvements; but his son, who undertook the charge of correcting the press, was then under twenty years of age, and hence might be thought scarcely qualified for venturing upon alterations. That son reaped some of the reward earned by his father's extraordinary merits, the rectory of Havant being holden for him until he could take it himself. A grandson also was preferred by bishop Lowth, expressly on the ground of the neglect experienced by his great ancestor, whose "great and inestimable merits," that able prelate truly said, "were not rewarded as they ought to have been." Bingham's corrections, and other additions, were published in the recent edition of his works. (Life of the Rev. Joseph Bingham, M.A., written by his Great-Grandson, the Rev. Richard Bingham, B.C.L., published in 1829 by him in his edition of his learned ancestor's Works.)

BINGHAM, (Joseph,) the second son and youngest child of the preceding, educated at the Charterhouse, and Corpus Christi college, Oxford; who died at the early age of 22 years. He was an exemplary and persevering student, who had prepared for publication a valuable edition of the Theban Story, which was published after his death by a gentleman who had lent a sum of money upon it to facilitate the publication. (Life of the Rev. J. Bingham, by the Rev. R. Bingham.)

BINGLEY, (William,) an English clergyman and naturalist, a native of Yorkshire. Being left an orphan at a very early age, his friends designed him for the law, but his own inclination led him to prefer the church. He graduated at Cambridge in 1799, being a member of St. Peter's college. While an undergraduate he made two tours in Wales, which furnished the subject of his first publication. His great work was Animal Biography, or Anecdotes of the Lives, Manners, and Economy of the Animal Creation, published in 1802, in 3 vols, 8vo; and which has since been translated into the French and German languages. He also edited the Correspondence between the Countesses of Pomfret and Hertford. He likewise wrote The Economy of a Christian Life, 2 vols, 8vo. Memoirs of British Quadrupeds, 1 vol. 8vo. Biographical Dictionary of Musical Composers, 2 vols, 1813. For many years he was engaged upon a history of Hampshire, which he did not live to publish. He died March 11, 1823. (Gent. Mag. 1823.)

BINI, (Severinus,) generally known by the Latin form of his name, *Binius*, noted as a collector of the Councils; a work by which he meant to serve materially the church of Rome, but which he so conducted as rather to lower her credit. He was born at Randelraidt, in the duchy of Juliers, and eventually became canon and professor of theology at Cologne, where he died in 1641. His Collection of the Councils was first published at Cologne, in 1606, in four volumes, folio, being entirely Latin. The second edition, that of 1618, printed also at Cologne, is in nine volumes, folio, and contains, besides many other great additions, all such Greek originals as could be found. A third edition was published at Paris, in 1636, in ten volumes, folio, but it is merely a reprint of the second Cologne edition. Binius has not ventured upon retaining all the errors, misrepresentations, and absurdities of the preceding collectors of the Councils, but he has clung to as many of them as possible, and he has rendered his work, perhaps, more exceptionable than any former one of the kind, by selecting for it a body of notes from those violent papal partizans, Bellarmine, Baronius, and Suarez. He has, besides, taken a great number of liberties with the text, without authority from MSS. Ussher, accordingly, called him, *Conciliorum Contaminator*, and he certainly has earned the ignominious designation. (Labb. et Coss. Conc. Comber's Roman Forgeries. Biog. Univ.)

BINK, (James,) a German engraver, born either at Nüremberg or Cologne, about the year 1504. He was a pupil of Albert Durer, and afterwards went to Rome and placed himself under Marc Antonio, the celebrated engraver. Subsequently he resided for a considerable time in Königsberg, at the court of the king of Prussia, and was, in 1549, sent by that prince into the Netherlands, to erect a monument to the memory of Albert's wife. In the year 1550 he was employed by the king of Denmark in the erection of a fortress at Holstein; but in the following year he entered again into the service of the king of Prussia, and died at Königsberg in 1560. The works of this master are generally marked either with the letters I. B. or the cipher ICB. (Ersch und Gruber.)

BINNING, (Hugh,) a Scotch presbyterian minister, born in Ayrshire, in 1627. He graduated at Glasgow, where, when only 19 years of age, he was appointed professor of moral philosophy. He was one of the ministers on the presbyterian side who were admitted to dispute with the independents in the presence of Cromwell; on which occasion he was so successful in baffling his opponents as to attract the particular notice, and arouse the angry feelings, of Oliver. Unwearied in his labours in the sacred cause to which his life was dedicated, he undermined a constitution naturally weak, and died of consumption at Govan, near Glasgow, of which place he was minister, in 1654, being only 27 years old. His commentaries on the Epistle to the Romans, with some sermons and tracts, were collected and published in 4to, Edinburgh, 1735. (Chalmers.)

BINOS, (l'abbé de,) born in 1730, canon in the cathedral church of Comminges, but more celebrated as a traveller than a divine. He travelled by Italy into Egypt, where he investigated with great care the ancient method of embalming; he then, in the dress of an Armenian priest, traversed Palestine and Libanus, and returned to Italy in 1777. The next year he settled himself at his native place, St. Bertrand de Comminges, of which he was afterwards appointed incumbent. Here he continued till his death, which took place in 1803. He published an account of his travels in

Italy, Egypt, and Palestine, at Paris, 1786, 2 vols, 12mo.

BION, a celebrated Greek pastoral poet, of whose writings there still remain some idylls of exquisite taste. He was born at Smyrna, and lived during the reign of Ptolemy Philadelphus, king of Egypt, about the time of the 123d Olympiad, and 288 years before the christian era. He passed part of his life in Sicily, and was poisoned, according to the account of Moschus, who is supposed to have been his disciple, and whose idylls are now always annexed to those of Bion.

BION, a Greek philosopher, born at Borysthenes, in Scythia, and lived in the reign of Antigonus Gonatas, king of Macedonia, about 126 years before the christian era. Beginning life as a disciple of Crates, he turned cynic; then listened to the demoralizing lectures of Theodorus, the atheist; and at last became a follower of Theophrastus, the peripatetic. Though Bion succeeded in clothing his philosophical lessons in the attractive garb of elegant language, yet such was his unpopularity, in consequence of the causticity of his satire, at which he principally aimed, that no one chose to be called his disciple. Professing to be a teacher of morals, his own habits were, nevertheless, extremely vicious, and his vanity excessive. He is said, however, to have borne testimony to the superiority of virtue, by the distress of mind that he exhibited before his death, on the recollection of his crimes. (Diog. Laert.)

BION, (John,) was born at Dijon, 1668, and appointed to a parochial benefice in Burgundy. Being desirous of obtaining a more public sphere of duty, he was made almoner to the *Superb*, a vessel in which the protestants were imprisoned. It was his duty to endeavour to bring back those prisoners to the Roman church; but the patience and resignation which they displayed under their sufferings made such an impression upon his mind, that he himself was led to adopt the faith of the captives. Dismissal from his office of course followed, and Bion betook himself to Geneva, where he embraced the views of Calvin. He afterwards kept a school in England, until he was appointed to an English congregation in Holland. The date of his death is not known. He wrote several works, among which the following were the most considerable:—1. Relation des Tourments que l'on fait souffrir aux Protestants qui sont sur les Galères de France, Londres, 1708. 2. Essais sur la Providence et sur la Possibilité de la Resurrection.

BIONDI, (John Francis,) an Italian writer, of great elegance, born in Liesena, a Dalmatian isle, in 1572. Introduced to James I. by Sir H. Wotton, he was employed by that monarch on a secret mission to the duke of Savoy, and received the honour of knighthood. He wrote, in Italian, A History of the Civil Wars between the Houses of York and Lancaster, which gained him great reputation, and was thought worthy of a translation into English, by Henry Carey, earl of Monmouth. He married a daughter of Sir Theodore Mayerne, and died in the canton of Berne, in 1644. His history was printed at Venice, 1637, 3 vols, 4to, and the English translation appeared in 1641; or in folio, London, 1724. (Biog. Univ. Chalmers.)

BIONDO, or BLONDUS, (Michael Angelo,) a physician of the sixteenth century, born at Venice, May 4, 1497, and practised at Rome and Naples. He was one of the first practitioners who demonstrated the errors of the method of treating wounds then prevalent, preferring the application of simple water to remedies of a heating nature. Gesner deemed him worthy of a place in his list of the best writers on surgery. He published, on the subject above mentioned, De Partibus-ictu-sectis citissime sanandis, &c. Venice, 1542, 8vo; with many other works.

BIORN. Of the four kings of this name who ruled Sweden in the ninth and tenth centuries, was Biörn Järnsida, (Ironside,) one of the four sons of the famous Ragnar Lodbrog. During his youth he visited, with his brothers, France, Italy, Spain, and England; conquered Bordeaux, Nantes, and Barcelona; and took London and Canterbury in 852. After the cruel death of Ragnar, his sons divided his immense dominions amongst them; and Sweden, with East and West Gothland, fell to the share of Biörn. The most important event of his reign was the introduction of Christianity into Sweden, though the virtual conversion of Sweden did not take place till two centuries later. He died in 870, and was succeeded by his son, Erik Biörnson, (V. Gehren in Ersch und Gruber.)

BIRAGO, (John Baptist,) surnamed the Advocate, was a lawyer of Genoa, who lived during the seventeenth century. He is known from his works on history and jurisprudence. The time of his birth and his death are, however, uncertain. He left many works, the most important of which are,—1. Mercurio Veridico, ovvero Annali Universali d'Europa, Venezia, 1648, 4to; which seems to be a criticism upon the Mercurio published by Vittorio Siri. 2. Storia Africana della Divisione dell' Imperio degli Arabi d'all' Anno 770 fin al 1007, Venezia, 1650; a very good work, which has been translated into French by the Abbé Pure, under the title of Histoire Africaine, Paris, 1666.

BIRCH, (Peter, D.D.) born in 1652, an English clergyman, descended from the Birches of Lancashire, and educated in presbyterian principles. He first matriculated at Cambridge, but in 1673 he was admitted of Christ Church, Oxford, having conformed to the church of England, and taken a doctor's degree. He filled successively several clerical appointments in Oxford, and eventually became a prebendary of Westminster. He published several sermons preached before the House of Commons, one in 1689, and another, January 30, 1693. Some passages in this latter sermon gave great offence; *e.g.* "Our boasted freedom is now only a liberty to bite and devour one another; our long cried up liberty of conscience proves one of impiety, licentiousness, error, &c." In reply to this appeared, A Birchen Rod for Dr. Birch, 4to, 1694. "This answer, wherein are many vile things against king Charles the Martyr," was supposed to "be penned by the anonymous author of a letter from major-general Ludlow to Sir E. S. (Seymour), on the alledged tyranny of Charles I." (Wood, Ath. Oxon.)

BIRCH, (Thomas, D.D.) a laborious and voluminous writer of the last century; born in Clerkenwell, 23d of November, 1705, of Quaker parents, and received his education at several schools kept by persons of that persuasion. It was the wish of the father to bring up his son a coffee-mill maker, which was his own business; but the youth feeling a decided attachment to literature, was at length permitted to follow his own inclination; the father declining, however, to afford him any maintenance or assistance. For some years he filled the situation of usher in various schools; and during this period he attended very assiduously to his own improvement. Having separated himself from the Quakers, he sought orders in the church of England, and was ordained deacon Jan. 17, 1730, and priest, Dec. 21, 1731, by Dr. Hoadly, then bishop of Salisbury. About two years before his ordination he had married the daughter of Mr. Cox, a clergyman, whom he afterwards served as curate; his wife died, however, within a twelvemonth of her marriage. It is most likely that he was in some degree indebted to his father-in-law for his success in obtaining orders. From this period, however, preferment flowed in upon him more rapidly than might have been expected. In 1732 he was presented to the vicarage of Ulting, in Essex; in 1734 he was appointed chaplain to the earl of Kilmarnock (who was executed in 1745); in 1735 he was elected fellow of the Royal Society, and also of the Society of Antiquaries; in 1743 he received from the crown the sinecure rectory of Landdewy Welfry, in Pembrokeshire; in 1744 (Chalmers says in 1731, immediately on his being ordained priest) he was presented to the rectory of Liddington St. Mary's, and the vicarage of Liddington St. Peter, Gloucestershire; but this living he appears shortly after to have resigned for the united rectories of St. Michael, Wood-street, with St. Mary Staining, London; in 1746 he became rector of St. Margaret Pattens, with St. Gabriel, Fenchurch-street; in 1752 he became one of the secretaries of the Royal Society; in 1753 he received the degree of D.D. from the Marischal college, Aberdeen, the same body having, in 1735, conferred upon him that of A.M.; in this same year (1753) he also received the degree of D.D. from Dr. Herring, then archbishop of Canterbury; about this time he was made a trustee of the British Museum; and in 1761 he was presented to the rectory of Depden (or Deepden), in Essex, which he held, together with his living in Fenchurch-street, till his decease, in 1766, which was caused by a fall from his horse, or perhaps by a fit of apoplexy, while riding between Hampstead and London.

The literary labours of Dr. Birch might have given him a good title to some of his later preferments; but we must look, perhaps, for some other cause for those of an earlier date, since, at that time, he could not have established any literary reputation. His success may, however, be accounted for from the circumstance acknowledged by his biographers, that his religious sentiments coincided with those of bishop Hoadly; and in these sentiments the lord chancellor Hardwicke, Dr. Birch's firm friend and patron, was supposed to participate. A complete enumeration of Dr. Birch's works would occupy more space than can here be devoted to them. The most valuable of them is, perhaps, The General Dictionary, in 10 vols, fol.; the first of which was published in 1734, the last in 1741. Messrs. Bernard and Lockman were associated with him in this undertaking; and it cannot now be ascertained which articles were written by Birch, and which by his colleagues. The work professes to be a translation of Bayle, purged of its scepticism, and augmented by a great quantity of original matter. 2. Another voluminous and important work is, an edition of the State Papers of Thurloe, Secretary of State during the Usurpation of Cromwell, in 7 vols, fol, 1732. 3. An Historical View of the Negotiations between the Courts of England, France, and Brussels, from 1592 to 1617, 8vo, 1749. 4. Memoirs of Queen Elizabeth, from 1581 to her Death, 1754. Dr. Birch also published memoirs of several distinguished persons:—Tillotson, 8vo, 1752; R. Boyle, Esq., 1744; Dr. Ward, 1766; Hervey; the Memoirs annexed to Houbraken and Vertu's Heads of Illustrious Persons, in numbers, from 1747 to 1752; Life of Henry, Son of King James I., 1760, 8vo; The Papers and Speeches of Lord Bacon, 1763, 8vo; The History of the Royal Society, 4 vols, 1756-7. He also edited Sir Walter Raleigh's Miscellaneous Works; Mrs. Cockburn's Works, 2 vols, 8vo, 1751; Professor Greave's Miscellaneous Works, 1737, 2 vols, 8vo; Dr. Cudworth's Intellectual System, 1743, 2 vols, 4to; Spenser's Faery Queene, 1751; Letters between Col. Hammond, Fairfax, and Cromwell, respecting Charles I.; besides which he left a great quantity of valuable MS. researches to the British Museum.

That Dr. Birch was an indefatigable collector of facts, his numerous publications evince; but this is nearly the extent of praise to which he is entitled. His friends admit that he had no talents for selection or arrangement; nor did he possess any great store of theological or classical learning.

BIRCHINGTON, (Stephen,) or, as his name is spelled in an obituary of the time, Brychington, an historical writer of the fourteenth century, born in the village of Birchington, in the isle of Thanet, and became, in 1382, a monk of the metropolitical church of Canterbury. He wrote a history of the archbishops of Canterbury to the year 1368, which Wharton published, as the first article in his Anglia Sacra, from a manuscript in the archbishop's library at Lambeth. In the same volume are contained, histories of the kings of England to 1367; of the Roman pontiffs to 1378; and of the Roman emperors to about the same time; which Wharton says are certainly by the same author. These, however, have never been published. The time of his death is not known. (Ang. Sacr. Whart.)

BIRCK. See Betuleus.

BIRCKBECK, (Simon,) an English divine, fellow of Queen's college, Oxford, born at Hornby, in Westmoreland, in 1584. He acquired considerable reputation as a preacher, and also for his acquaintance with the works of the fathers. He was afterwards vicar of Gilling, near Richmond, in Yorkshire, which living he continued to hold during the Usurpation. His principal work is called, The Protestant's Evidence, showing that for 1500 years next after Christ, divers Guides of God's Church have, on sundry Points of Religion, taught as the Church of England now doth. He died in 1656. (Wood's Ath. vol. ii.)

BIRD, (Edward,) an English painter, a member of the Royal Academy, and historical painter to the princess Charlotte of Wales, born at Bristol, in 1772. Several of his pictures were very popular at the time, and as he generally drew from nature, they abound in portraits. He died in his native city, in 1819, after an illness of several years' continuance, which prevented his attaining to that eminence in his profession of which his early productions gave promise.

BIRD, (Francis,) an English sculptor, born in 1667. He is known principally from the monument that he executed in Westminster Abbey of Dr. Busby, though the statue of queen Anne, in the front of St. Paul's cathedral, the conversion of St. Paul, on the pediment, and the bas-reliefs under the portico, were also sculptured by him. He died in 1731.

BIRD, (John,) an eminent mathematical instrument maker, who executed, among other things, a mural quadrant on the west side of the pier in the observatory at Greenwich, for the purpose of taking observations towards the north. Of this instrument Bird gave a description in a pamphlet published in 1768, in 4to. He is also the author of a piece entitled, The Method of dividing Astronomical Instruments, 4to, London, 1767. He died on the 24th of March, 1776.

BIRD, (William,) an eminent composer of sacred music, born in 1543, and supposed to have been the son of Thomas Bird, one of the gentlemen of Edward VI.'s chapel, in which he himself was a singing boy. He was chosen organist of Lincoln cathedral in 1563, in 1569 one of the gentlemen of the Chapel Royal, and subsequently organist to queen Elizabeth. His compositions, which are very numerous, were mostly set to parts of the Romish service, but many of them have since had English words adapted to them by Dr. Aldrich, who collected his works. The celebrated canon, *Non nobis Domine*, has been generally ascribed to him. Although it does not appear in any of his works published by himself, in 1652 it was inserted in a collection of canons with his name prefixed to it, and was not claimed for any other composer until a hundred years afterwards, when it was attributed to Palestrina, without, however, sufficient authority. He died in 1623. (Rees' Cycl.)

BIRÉ, (Peter,) a French writer of the sixteenth century, who wrote a history of the origin, antiquity, and nobility of the ancient Armorica, or the Lesser Brittany, under the title of Gazette d'Aletin le Martyr. This work, which contains much curious information, was published at Nantes, in 4to, in 1580. (Biog. Univ.)

BIREN, (John Ernest,) duke of Courland, born in 1687 of humble parents, his grandfather, as is said, having been a groom. Being taken into the employment of Anne, duchess of Courland, he became such a favourite, that, when that princess ascended the throne of Russia, in 1730, she placed in his hands the entire management of the government, which his vast energy enabled him to conduct with great success. Upon the death of Anne, she entrusted to him the regency during the minority of her nephew, Yvan; but, entering into an intrigue to marry his son to the princess Elizabeth, and his daughter to the duke of Holstein, afterwards Peter III., he was arrested by the influence of his former associate, marshal Munich, and sent as an exile into Siberia. When Elizabeth ascended the throne, she banished Munich, and permitted Biren to retire to Yaroslaw. Disgusted with Peter III., who had recalled him, for not restoring to him his duchy of Courland, which had been conferred on him by Anne, Biren joined the party which placed Catharine II. on the throne; who, as a reward, bestowed on him the prize that he so much coveted, and he was reinstated in the dukedom. He died October 28, 1772, leaving his son Peter as his successor; who was, however, despoiled of his possessions by Russia within the period of four years. (Biog. Univ.)

BIRGER, (de Bielbo,) a distinguished Swedish general, of the thirteenth century. He completed the conquest of Finland, begun by Eric, the reigning sovereign of Sweden, whose sister, Ingeborg, he had married. During Birger's absence on this expedition Eric died, and being the last of his family, Waldemar, the son of Birger, then only thirteen years of age, was elected king. The father upon his return to Sweden assembled the senate, and expressing great dissatisfaction at their election of a minor, he was appointed regent, and held the reins of government until his death. Stockholm owes its origin to him; and he it was who laid the foundation of the cathedral of Upsal. His wise enactments also for the regulation of the internal affairs of his country mark a new epoch in the history of Sweden. His plans for the promotion of social order, however, would have been more permanently beneficial if he had not, a short time before his death, sowed the seeds of future dissension, by dividing the kingdom between his four sons; the eldest to have the title of king, and the others to have duchies. This impolitic arrangement introduced anew the anarchy and bloodshed in which Sweden had been involved during the preceding age. He died in 1266. (Biog. Univ.)

BIRINGUCCIO, (Vanuccio,) a mathematician, born at Siena about the end of the fifteenth century. Turning his attention to the practical details of the arts connected with war, he distinguished himself by a book upon the composition of gunpowder, and on the best method of casting ordnance. His work, entitled, Pirotecnia, treating upon subjects of great interest, though very little understood at that time, has been frequently reprinted, and translated into different languages. (Biog. Univ.)

BIRINUS, a Roman Benedictine, sent by pope Honorius upon a mission into Wessex, where he seems to have arrived in 634. Kynegils, king of Wessex, appears to have been baptized in the following year. A see was founded for Birinus at Dorcic, as Bede says the place was called, now Dorchester, in Oxfordshire. After considerable success in his undertaking, he died about the year 650; being buried at Dorchester, from whence his remains were removed to Winchester. (Bede, H. E. iii. 7. Sax. Chr. 36. Rudborne. Hist. Maj. Wint. Angl. Sacr. i. 190.)

BIRKBECK, (George,) an English physician, born January 10, 1776, at Settle, in Yorkshire, where his father was a merchant and banker of considerable eminence. A strong inclination for mechanical pursuits, to which he was all his life devoted, is said to have manifested itself at the village school to which he was first sent. It was, however, determined that he should be educated for the medical profession; with which view he went first to Leeds, and from thence to London, where he was fortunate enough to become the pupil of the deservedly celebrated Dr. Baillie, whose friendship he retained until the death of the latter. Having gone to Edinburgh to complete his education, he became acquainted with some of the principal scientific and literary persons of Scotland, and was appointed, before his twenty-second year, professor of natural philosophy in the Andersonian Institution at Glasgow. Here it was that Birkbeck, witnessing no doubt with pain the vices and misery of the crowded population of that great manufacturing district, conceived the idea of bettering their condition by affording them the opportunity of intellectual improvement. For this purpose he established a mechanic's class; the members of which had, besides the use of books, the advantage of attending lectures upon such branches of science and the arts as were likely to be useful or interesting to them. Encouraged by the success which attended this first attempt, he founded, in 1822, on a larger scale, a similar association in London. By his exertions, and pecuniary assistance, a building, with a theatre suitable for the delivery of lectures, was built in Chancery-lane; and here, the London Mechanic's Institute, of which Dr. Birkbeck was president until his death, hold their meetings and transact their business. From this, the parent society, other similar institutions have been established, with more or less success, in almost every considerable town in Great Britain. Dr. Birkbeck followed his profession for many years in the metropolis, where he enjoyed a considerable share of reputation. He died at his house in Finsbury-square, Dec. 1, 1841, in the 66th year of his age. (Gent. Mag.)

BIRKENHEAD, (John,) one of the earliest English journalists, born of poor parents, at Northwich, in Cheshire, about the year 1615. He was entered a servitor of Oriel college, Oxford, in 1632, under Humphrey Lloyd, afterwards bishop of Bangor. Having taken his degree, he became secretary to the celebrated and unfortunate archbishop Laud. When the civil war broke out, and Charles took up his residence at Oxford, Birkenhead was chosen to keep up a spirit of loyalty in the nation, by conducting a species of gazette, or newspaper, to circulate intelligence of the king's proceedings over all parts of his dominions. This journal, entitled, Mercurius Aulicus, or the Court Mercury, first appeared January 1, 1642, and the publication of it continued every week, in one or more quarto leaves, until the end of 1645. Birkenhead proved extremely well fitted for the conducting of it, having a talent for raillery, which rendered his writing highly agreeable to all that were not violently prejudiced against the royal cause, and which was stigmatized as buffoonery by the more decided parliamentarians. As an acknowledgment of his services, the king recommended him for the professorship of moral philosophy; an office rather honourable than profitable, of which he was deprived by the parliamentary visitors in 1648. He then took refuge in London, but suffered frequent imprisonments as a royalist, and was reduced to the necessity of seeking a precarious subsistence by writing songs, love-letters for people incapable of such compositions themselves, and, in short, any thing that offered a prospect of immediate gain. At the restoration, Birkenhead became doctor of laws, member for Wilton, a knight, and a member of the Royal Society. Besides these barren honours, he was appointed master of requests, and the archbishop of Canterbury's master of the faculties. Thus his latter years were passed in opulence; but apparently, he was not highly respected. Some people never forgave the liberties that he had taken with themselves, their friends, or their party; others accused him of forgetting in prosperity services that he had received in adversity. He died at Westminster, December 4, 1679, leaving, besides the Mercury, a few literary pieces, suggested by passing events, and now forgotten.

BIRKHEAD, (Henry,) born in London, in 1617, and educated at Trinity college, Oxford, but persuaded to join the Jesuits at St. Omer's: afterwards he returned to the church of England, and was elected fellow of All Souls, by means of archbishop Laud. This fellowship he retained during the usurpation. He called himself Bircheadus, and was particularly distinguished for his Latin poetry, of which he published several volumes, and was the founder of a poetical lectureship in 1707. The date of his death is not precisely known. (Wood's Athenæ.)

There was also a Henry Birkhead, who wrote a tragedy, called Cola's Fury, or Lirenda's Misery, Lond. 1646; the subject of which is the Irish Rebellion, that broke out in October, 1641; but he was a Bristol merchant. (*Ibid.*)

BIROLI, (John,) an Italian botanist, born at Novara, in 1772, and educated at Pavia, where he became professor of agriculture. He was subsequently appointed to the botanical chair at Turin. He died January 1, 1825. He left several works on botany and agriculture, among which may be mentioned, 1. Flora Agoniensis, seu Plantarum in Novariensi Provinciâ Sponte nascentium Descriptio, Vigevano, 1808, 2 vols, 8vo. 2. Trattato d'Agricoltura, Novara, 1809, 4 vols, 4to. (Biog. Univ. Suppl.)

BIRON, (Armand of Gontault,) an eminent French commander, lord and baron of Biron, a small town in the Perigord, originally page to Margaret, queen of Navarre. In the civil wars occasioned by the religious dissensions of his country, Biron took a prominent part, being at the battles of Dreux, St. Denis, and Moncontour, besides several sieges, on the court side, although secretly partial to the Huguenots. In 1577 he was made a marshal of France. On the accession of Henry IV. he declared for him immediately, a service of great value, which was requited by every thing that the monarch could bestow. Biron was killed by a cannon ball, July 27, 1592, while making observations on the outworks of Epernay, in Champagne, at the age of 68. He was a finished soldier, who owed his rise, not to favouritism, but merit. He had commanded in chief in seven battles, and bore away from them as many wounds. Nor was he without literary talent, having written Commentaries on his own Times, and a Treatise on the Duties of a Field-Marshal, works not extant, as de Thou thinks, greatly to the public loss. (Smedley's Ref. Rel. in France, ii. 326. Moreri. Biog. Univ.)

BIRON, (Charles of Gontault,) created duke of Biron by Henry IV., and advanced by him besides to the dignities of admiral and marshal of France, with other distinguished marks of favour. He was a person of great intrepidity; but all the good in him had so powerful an alloy of evil, that made it really of little value. He was vain, fickle, and treacherous. In 1601 he was sent over with a formal announcement to queen Elizabeth, of his royal master's marriage with Mary of Medicis, and he was received with extraordinary distinction. In the following year, however, Henry was under the necessity of ordering his arrest, proofs having been obtained of a treasonable correspondence with the court of Spain, which had flattered him with hopes of an independent sovereignty in Burgundy, as a dowry with a princess either from Spain or Savoy. Being found guilty of thus compromising the interests of his country, he was beheaded in the court of the Bastile, at Paris, July 31, 1602, in the fortieth year of his age. (Moreri.)

BIRR, (Anthony,) a learned German physician, born at Basle, April 20, 1693. He studied at the university of his native place, and took the degree of doctor of medicine in 1748. He was more celebrated for his acquirements in classical literature than in medicine, and he filled a chair for teaching the Greek language. He died March 29, 1762, having published several works on ancient literature and anatomy; he also edited the Thesaurus Linguæ Latinæ, of Robert Stephens, Basle, 1741, 4 vols, fol.

BISACCIONE, or BISACCIONI, (Masolino, count of,) born in 1582, at Ferrara, of noble ancestry, in the state of the Church, but settled at Ferrara, where he became professor of rhetoric and poetry. He wrote, I Falsi Pastori, a comedy in verse, printed at Verona, in 1605, and several lyric poems, published in different collections.

His son, also called Masolino, educated at Bologna, was known during many years as a quarrelsome military man, continually fighting duels, but he seems never to have neglected literature. He died in June 1663, leaving not less than twenty-nine works, of which Mazzucchelli has given a catalogue; amongst them, the most important are—Statuti e Privilegi della Sacra Religione Constantiniana, Trento, 1624. It is an interesting account of the knighthood under that name, still in existence at the court of Naples. Several histories of the wars of Germany, England, Catalonia, France, and Savoy, &c., published at Venice, amongst which is a continuation of the history of Zilioli, from 1636 to the peace of Munster in 1650; five dramas for music; and some novels.

BISBIE, (Nathaniel, D.D.) rector of Long Melford, near Sudbury, Suffolk, and highly esteemed as a preacher and a zealous churchman. He was deprived of his living on account of his refusing to take the oaths of allegiance to William III., and died September, 1695. He published—Sermons; The Modern Pharisee; Prosecution no Persecution, preached at Bury; Two Sermons on the Evils of Anarchy and Conventicles; The Bishop Visiting; A Visitation Sermon. (Wood's Athenæ.)

BISCAINO, (Bartholomew,) an Italian painter, born at Genoa, in 1632. He gave early indications of genius, and had finished several considerable paintings before he was 25 years old, when he died of the plague. There are three of his pictures in the gallery at Dresden. He also etched several plates in a good style. (Bryan.)

BISCHOF, (Melchior, or Episcopus,) the son of a shoemaker, born at Pösneck, 1754, and employed both as an instructor of youth and a preacher. He died in 1614. His writings are extremely rare, and for the most part forgotten; with the exception, however, of his hymns, one of which, Das Leben, is particularly beautiful.

BISCHOF, (Charles Augustus,) rector of the school at Fürth, was born at Neuhausen, in the Erzgebirge, 1762. He was a man of considerable attainments, and a useful writer on subjects of natural history, astronomy, and physics. For a list of his works see Menzel's Gelehrtes Teutschland. He died in 1814.

BISCHOFFBERGER, (Bartholomew,) a Protestant theologian, born in 1622, in the Swiss canton of Appenzell, the author of some theological writings; but is chiefly known by his Chronicle of Appenzell, from the earliest period to his own time, St. Gall, 1662, 8vo, valuable as the first history of the canton by a native, but not free from inaccuracies, and also too diffuse, and since superseded by that of Welser.

BISCHOP, (Cornelius,) a Flemish painter, born in 1630, a pupil of Ferdinand Bol, whose style he imitated so successfully, that his paintings have been considered not inferior to his master's. A picture of his of some figures by candle-light, was so much admired by Lewis XIV., that he purchased it at a high price; and the king of Denmark admitted his works among those of the best masters. He died in 1674, leaving a son, Abraham, who, although instructed by his father in designing historical subjects, preferred painting birds, particularly domestic fowls, which he represented so faithfully, that his pictures were highly valued. The time of his death is unknown. (Pilkington.)

BISCHOP, (John van,) a designer and engraver, born at the Hague in 1646. Though following with success the profession of an advocate, he found time to execute a great number of prints; but his most considerable work is a set of plates for the Paradigmata Graphices variorum Artificum, tabulis æneis, Pars i. et ii. Hagæ, 1671, fol. He died at Amsterdam in 1686. (Bryan.)

BISCHOP, (Nicholas, in Latin, Episcopius,) a celebrated printer of Basle, born towards the end of the fifteenth century. In conjunction with Jerome Froben, he undertook a collection of the Greek fathers. A great number of works, to which the learned world accorded the merit of beauty and correctness, issued from his press. He used as his device an episcopal cross, surmounted by a crane. (Biog. Univ.)

BISCIONI, (Anthony Maria,) born at Florence, in 1674, an Italian priest, celebrated as a preacher and scholar. After being for some time engaged in tuition, he was, in 1741, made royal librarian and canon of Florence. His writings consist chiefly of notes, commentaries, prefaces, dissertations, &c., appended to the works of others; *e. g.* those of Dante, Boccacio, Menzini, R. Borghini, &c. He has considerable reputation as a critic. He died in 1756.

BISCOE, (Richard,) an English divine, born about the end of the seventeenth century; probably the son of the nonconformist, John Biscoe, of New Inn hall, Oxford. Originally the minister of a dissenting congregation, he subsequently conformed to the church of England, and, in 1727, was presented to the living of St. Martin Outwich, in London, holding with it a prebend of St. Paul's. He was the author of the well-known work, The History of the Acts of the Apostles, confirmed from other Authors, &c.; being the substance of his sermons preached at Boyle's lecture in 1736, 1737, and 1738, and published in 2 vols, 8vo, 1742. It is of this work that Doddridge has recorded his opinion, that "it demonstrates incontestibly the truth of Christianity." (Chalmers.)

BISHOP, (Samuel,) an English divine and poet, born in London, in 1731, and educated at Merchant Tailors' school, of which he afterwards became head master. The company of Merchant Tailors, in 1789, presented him to the living of St. Martin Outwich, which, together with the rectory of Ditton, in Kent, he held until his death, which happened in 1795. His poetical works were published after his death, with a memoir of the author, by the Rev. T. Clare; also a volume of his sermons. His poems are of a miscellaneous description, and are generally of no higher character than the amusements of a man of learning; but he has passed for the author of the well-known farce, High Life below Stairs, introduced by Garrick as his own, the real author thinking such a piece unsuitable to the gravity of his character. When this first came among the players, all were surprised at Garrick's extreme facility in admitting the propriety of various alterations, a subject on which dramatic authors had been usually found extremely sensitive. When, however, people saw good reason for doubting Garrick's authorship, they could completely understand his candour.

BISHOP, (William,) born at Brayles, Warwickshire, 1553, vicar apostolical, and the first Romish bishop in England after the Reformation, educated at Oxford, either at Gloucester hall (now Worcester college,) or Lincoln college. Wood thinks at the former, the master of which was at least a favourer of the Romish doctrine, if not a Romanist himself. He left Oxford in 1573, or 1574, and completed his education in the seminaries at Rheims and Rome. He was then sent as a missionary to England, but was arrested at Dover, and confined in London till the end of the year 1584. Being released, he went to Paris, and having taken his degree of licentiate, he returned to England in 1591. In February 1623, Dr. Bishop was declared bishop elect of Chalcedon (a titular prelacy to qualify him for episcopal consecration): in the following month a bull issued for his admission to that important rite. It was followed almost immediately by a brief, conferring on him episcopal jurisdiction over the Romanists of England and Scotland, but so worded as to render his official powers revocable at pleasure; and he thus became, in the language of the curialists, vicar apostolic, with ordinary jurisdiction. In the exercise of his powers, he instituted a dean and chapter, as a standing council for his own assistanee, with power, during a vacancy of the see, to exercise episcopal ordinary jurisdiction, professing, at the same time, that "what defect might be in his own power, he would supplicate his holiness to make good from the plenitude of his own." He died universally respected and beloved among those of his communion, in 1624. His writings, which are chiefly controversial, have ceased to attract notice; but as an editor he deserves respectful remembrance, from the publication of Pitts's useful work, De Illustribus Angliæ Scriptoribus, 1623, with a learned preface of his own. (Butler's Memoirs of the Engl. Ir. and Sc. Cath. iii. 415.)

BISSAT, BISSET, or BISSART, (Patrick, 1500—1568,) was descended from the earls of Fife, and was born in Scotland, in the reign of James V. From the university of St. Andrew's he removed to that of Paris, and from thence to Bologna, where he was appointed professor of canon law, which office he filled with great reputation for several years. He was also distinguished as a poet, an orator, and philosopher. His works were published at Venice, 1565, in 1 vol, 4to. (Chalmers.)

BISSE, (Thomas, April 22, 1731,) an English divine, educated at Corpus Christi college, Oxford. In 1715 he was chosen preacher of the rolls, and in 1716 he was made chancellor of Hereford, by his brother, Dr. Philip Bisse, bishop of that diocese. He was much esteemed as a preacher, and published several volumes of sermons. (Chalmers.)

BISSEL, or BISSELIUS, (John,) a German writer of the seventeenth century, born at Babenhausen in Swabia. He early joined the Jesuits, and was professor of philosophy and rhetoric in several colleges. In his native country he had the reputation of a good poet, and elegant prose writer. He published, 1. Icaria, Ingoldstadt, 1638, 16mo. This contains a description of that province, and a recital of the events of which it had been the theatre. 2. Argonauticon Americanorum, Munich, 1647, 12mo; Medulla Historica, Amberg, 1675, 5 vols, 8vo; and other works. (Biog. Univ. Suppl.)

BISSENDORF, (John,) pastor of the church at Gödingen, near Hildesheim; author of several scarce works in German, chiefly of a controversial nature, and especially opposed to the Jesuits, whose enmity he excited to such a degree that they procured his imprisonment, and ultimately his death. He was burnt at Cologne in 1629, after having been in prison two years. (Biog. Univ.)

BISSET, (Charles,) a physician, born at Dunkeld, in Perthshire, in 1717. He studied medicine at Edinburgh, entered into the marines, and visited America, the West Indies, &c. He afterwards practised at Knayton, near Thirsk, in Yorkshire, where he died, Jan. 14, 1791. He had paid great attention to mathematical studies, and was a good engineer, as well as an able physician. He published an Essay on the Theory and Construction of Fortifications, Lond. 1751, 8vo; A Treatise on the Scurvy, *ibid.* 1755, 8vo; An Essay on the Medical Constitution of Great Britain, *ibid.* 1762, 8vo, translated into German by J. G. Moellor, Breslau, 1779, 8vo; Medical Essays and Observations, Newcastle, 1766, 8vo; London, 1767, 8vo; translated into German by Moellor, Breslau, 1781, 8vo. An interesting medical correspondence between Drs. Bisset and Lettsom, was printed in Pettigrew's Memoirs and Correspondence of Lettsom; and there is in the library of the Medical Society of London, a copy of Dr. Cullen's First Lines of the Practice of Physic, with numerous manuscript annotations, by Dr. Bisset.

BISSET, (Robert, LL.D.) a native of Scotland, intended for the pulpit, but at one time a schoolmaster at Chelsea, near London; subsequently an author by profession. His chief works are, A History of George III. 6 vols, 8vo; and a Life of Edmund Burke, 2 vols, 8vo. He died in 1805, aged 46. (Gent. Mag.)

BISSET, (William,) rector of Whiston, Northamptonshire, and elder brother of St. Katharine's hospital, gained some reputation, in the early part of the last century, as a pamphleteer. He was most violently opposed to Sacheverell and his principles, religious and political, and attacked him with great severity and injustice, in a work called The Modern Fanatic, which was replied to in the same strain by the friends of Sacheverell. This caused a rejoinder by Bisset. Four parts of the above-named publication appeared at intervals. The dispute seems to have been entirely personal; and the coarseness with which it was carried on is disgraceful to both parties. Bisset was a great advocate for the Society for the Reformation of Manners, which met with some opposition. He preached a long sermon on this subject, at Bow church, which gave great offence to the rector and many of the parishioners; in fact, whatever he said or did, however well-intentioned, was marred by the coarseness and flippancy of his manner, though it is very probable that his contemporaries did not consider his style so offensive as it appears to us; nor was it more virulent than that of his opponents.

The death of queen Anne, and the change in the succession, afforded other subjects of interesting discussion, and the petty quarrel of Bisset and Sacheverell no longer engaged the attention of the public. Bisset lived for many years after, but how long cannot easily be ascertained. (Biog. Univ. Suppl. Nichols's Literary Anecdotes, vol. i.)

BISSO, (Francis,) a physician of Palermo, where, in 1581, he was appointed by Philip II. his first physician in the kingdom of Sicily. He was an excellent writer, both in prose and verse. He died at Palermo, 20th of January, 1598, having published, among other works, Epistola Medica de Eresypelate, Messina, 1589, 8vo.

BISSO, (Francis,) a Sicilian divine, son of the preceding. Well skilled in all kinds of learning, he became a most celebrated preacher, and was esteemed for his eloquence, not less in Italy, than in his native country. Having filled several important offices, among which was that of judge of the kingdom of Sicily, and having obtained equal honour in them all, he was preferred, by Philip III., at the request of the magistrates of Palermo, to the bishopric of Patri. He died at Careni, August 14, 1623; having published some sermons and funeral discourses. (Moreri.)

BISSON, (Count P. F. J. G.) a French general, the son of a common soldier, born at Montpelier in 1767. He had obtained no advancement until the revolution, but he then received a commission. Exhibiting, on several occasions, a great deal of personal courage, he was raised by Napoleon to the rank of general of division, and on the 7th of January, 1806, was created a count, and admitted grand officer of the Legion of Honour. The following year he was made governor of Brunswick. He died at Mantua, 11th of July, 1811.

BISSON, (Lewis Charles, October 10, 1742,) bishop of Bayeux. At the period of the revolution he was *curé* of St. Louet-sur-Lozon, and though he took the oath required by the constituent assembly, he refused to renounce his orders. His firmness cost him six months' imprisonment. In 1799 he succeeded Fauchel as bishop of Bayeux. He assisted at the council of Paris in 1801, and the same year resigned his bishopric into the hands of cardinal Caprara. As honorary canon of Bayeux he passed the last years of his life in study and devotion. His writings, which are not numerous, are chiefly devotional; but he also published a History of the Diocese of Bayeux during the Revolution, and a Biographical Dictionary of the Departments of La Manche, Calvados, and l'Orne. He died in 1820. (Biog. Univ. Suppl.)

BISTAC, (Francis,) a French grammarian, born at Langres in 1667. He is known as the editor of Garnier's Latin grammar, called the Rudiments of Langres, which, having gone through many editions, is used very generally in the colleges of that province, and being translated into Italian, was published at Perugia in 1813. He died in 1752.

BISTERFELD, (John Henry,) a native of Germany, professor of theology and philosophy at Weissenburg or Karlsburg, in Transylvania, to which appointment he was invited in 1629. Here he met with great success, and displayed such knowledge in mathematics and physics, that he was considered by the common people to be a necromancer. He warmly opposed Stephen Catona, chaplain of the royal household, who brought with him puritanical doctrines from England, and wished to introduce them into the reformed church of Transylvania and Hungary. He succeeded so far, that prince Raksczy decreed that none professing the puritanical faith should sit in the synod of Sakmar. However, after Catona's death the puritan became the prevailing faith amongst the reformers of Transylvania. Bisterfeld died on the 6th Feb. 1655, leaving various writings of no interest to English readers. (Ersch und Gruber.)

BITAUBÉ, (Paul Jeremiah,) born at Koningsberg, Nov. 24, 1732, a French protestant minister and miscellaneous writer. He published a translation of the Iliad, Berlin, 1762; and the Odyssey, 1785; Joseph (1767), a poem much esteemed in France, but too inflated for English tastes; Les Bataves, a poem, 1773; also in the same year, Examen de la Confession de Foi du Vicaire Savoyard, a work directed against the scepticism of Rousseau. He died November 22, 1808. (Biog. Univ.)

BITON, a Greek mathematician, who flourished in the fourth century before Christ. He is known as the author of a treatise on the machines used in war, which is inserted in the Paris edition of the Mathematici Veteres, folio, 1693. This work is mentioned by Pappus in the 8th book of his Mathematical Collections.

BITZLEER, (Liwa,) a Jewish rabbi, who flourished in Bohemia about the close of the sixteenth century. He was chosen superintendent of all the synagogues in Poland; having rendered himself famous by establishing, in 1592, an academy called Klause, in which he instructed a vast number of disciples. (Rees.)

BIUMI, (Paul Jerome,) an Italian physician. Having received his education at Pavia, he became, in 1699, professor of anatomy at Milan, where he died in 1731. He published, besides several other works on anatomy, Esamina di alcuni Canaletti Chiliferi che dal Fondo del Ventricolo per le Tonache del Omento sembrano penetrare nel Fegato, &c. Milan, 1717, 8vo. This treatise was much noticed at the time on account of its containing certain new views on the process of digestion. (Biog. Univ.)

BIVAR, (Francis,) a Spanish Cistercian monk, of the seventeenth century, professor of philosophy and theology at Madrid. Besides other works, he published, with a commentary, The Chronicle of Flavius Lucius Dexter; but this piece, notwithstanding his defence, is thought to be a forgery.

BIVERO, (Peter de,) a Spanish Jesuit, born at Madrid in 1572. His talents for public teaching, which he had exhibited as professor of theology in several colleges, procured him, in 1616, the appointment of preacher to Albert and Isabella at Brussels. He published, besides sermons in Spanish, several practical works in Latin, which are valued on account of the prints with which they are illustrated. The titles of these are as follows—1. Emblemata in Psalmum Miserere. 2. Sacrum Sanctuarium Crucis, &c. 3. Sacrum Oratorium piarum Imaginum Immaculatæ Mariæ. (Biog. Univ. Suppl.)

BIVERONI, or TUTSCHET, (James,) a divine of Upper Engadina, in the Grisons. He was the first person who, in 1524, preached the reformed doctrines in the League of God's house, one of the three states of the Rhetian republic. Before this time the vernacular language of that country, divided into two dialects, the Romansh and Ladin, had never been written. But Biveroni translated into the latter, Comander's German Catechism, the New Testament, and the Psalms of

David; printing them at Puschiavo, and publishing them respectively in 1552, 1560, and 1562. To the Reformation, it has been said, several people owe their literature, but the Rhetians are indebted to it for their alphabet; and Biveroni was one of the principal means of their enjoying this advantage. When his first book was published, his countrymen stood in the utmost astonishment, an opinion having prevailed among them that their language was not capable of being committed to writing. (M'Crie's Hist. Ref. in Italy, 314, 325, 326.)

BIZARDIERE, (Michael David,) a French writer of the seventeenth century. He was the author of several clever and well-written works on historical and political subjects connected with Poland. He published also—1. Historia Gestorum in Ecclesiâ Memorabilium ab Anno 1517 ad Annum 1546; 1701, 12mo. 2. Histoire d'Erasme, sa Vie, &c. Paris, 1721, 12mo; with other works. (Biog. Univ.)

BIZARRI, (Peter,) a distinguished Italian historian, born about the year 1530, at Perugia. Having spent some years, and published more than one work, at Venice, he came, in 1565, into England, expecting to be noticed by queen Elizabeth, whose fame he had celebrated in several poems. Archbishop Parker, who valued him as well for his learning as for his profession of the protestant religion, preferred him to a prebend in his gift in the church of Salisbury, of 20*l*. value. Bizarri, discontented with what he thought an insufficient reward for his merits, returned to Italy, having previously applied for permission to retain his prebend. He spent much of the remainder of his life in Germany and the Low Countries, having been already encouraged and patronized by the celebrated Hubert Languet, who introduced him to the notice of his master, Augustus, the elector of Saxony, and obtained some favours for him. The time of his death is unknown. He published many voluminous works, some of them of great value, of which we may mention—1. Bellum Cyprium inter Venetos et Solimanum, &c. Basle, 1573. 2. Descriptio Belli Pannonici sub Maximiliano II. 3. Varia Opuscula, Venice, 1565, 8vo. This last is one of the rarest of those which issued from the press of Paolo Aldo. (Strype. Moreri. Biog. Univ. Suppl.)

BIZET, (Martin John Baptist,) a French clergyman, who took refuge in England at the time of the French Revolution, but returned after the concordat in 1801, and was first employed as curate of a parish in Paris, of which he became incumbent on his principal's death. He died, regretted by his parishioners, July 8, 1821, leaving, Discussion Epistolaire entre G. W. Protestant de l'Eglise Anglicane, et M. J. B. B. Catholique Romain, Paris, 1801. (Biog. Univ. Suppl.)

BIZOT, (Peter,) canon of St. Saviour d'Herisson, in the diocese of Bourges. He died in 1696, aged 66, leaving, besides some Latin translations from Boileau, Histoire Métallique de la République de Hollande, Paris, 1687, fol. reprinted at Amsterdam, 1688, 2 vols, 8vo. A supplement was published at Amsterdam in 1690. This work, though curious, has been superseded by that of Van Loon, on the same subject, of which a French translation was printed at the Hague, in 1752. (Biog. Univ.)

BJERKEN, (Peter de,) a celebrated Swedish surgeon, born at Stockholm, January 2, 1765, who, after an education at Upsal, came to London in 1793, and studied under Mr. Cline at St. Thomas's Hospital. Here he remained three years, and then returned to Sweden, and found his way there to the head of his profession. He died at the age of 53, February 2, 1818, leaving but little written; but he published in the Annals of the Medical Society of Stockholm, a paper on a Prolapsus of the Tongue, and another on the effects of Arsenic upon Chancres. (Biog. Univ. Suppl.)

BJOERNSTAHL, (James Jonas,) a Swedish traveller, of some celebrity, was born in Sudermania, in 1731, and educated at Upsal. He travelled through great part of Europe; and during his stay in Paris, devoted himself to the study of the Oriental languages. Thus qualified for such an undertaking, he was sent by Gustavus III. to travel in the East; but having caught the plague, he died at Salonichi, 12th of July, 1779. His writings, which contain many valuable observations on the medals, manuscripts, and rare books, which he had met with, were collected from the periodical publications in which they first appeared, and printed separately under the title of Letters of Bjoernstahl, 3 vols, 8vo, Stockholm, 1778. (Biog. Univ.)

BLACHE, (Anthony,) a native of Grenoble, born of respectable parentage, Aug. 28, 1633, and originally a soldier, but being maimed in the Italian wars, he took orders. To show his competence for this new profession, he held several conferences with the famous minister Claude, and he published Réfutation de l'Hérésie de Calvin, par la seule Doctrine des prétendus Réformés, with a view of confirming recent converts to Romanism. He was also a good astronomer, and Lewis XIV. saw the eclipse of 1684 through a telescope of his. His intellects were, however, liable to disorder, and the Jesuits were the principal objects of their morbid action. Against this body he wrote a MS. of a thousand folio pages, which was discovered in 1763, and brought forward as evidence against the fraternity of Loyola, then highly unpopular in France. Thus Blache became a person of historical importance. But he had been long since dead. Being found very troublesome, he was shut up in the Bastille, where he ended his days, Jan. 29, 1714. (Biog. Univ. Suppl.)

BLACK, (Joseph,) an eminent chemist and physician, born in France, on the banks of the Garonne, in 1728. His father, John Black, was a native of Belfast, in Ireland, but descended of a Scottish family, and resided chiefly at Bordeaux, where he carried on the trade of a wine-merchant, was much respected, and lived on terms of intimacy with the celebrated baron Montesquieu. In 1740 Joseph Black, who was one of thirteen children, was sent to Belfast, to obtain a British education; and after attending the grammar-school, and applying to various branches of study for six years, he went to the university of Glasgow, to acquire a knowledge of medicine and the collateral sciences. He attended Dr. Cullen's lectures on chemistry, besides the other usual courses of professional instruction. In 1752 he visited Edinburgh to complete his medical studies, and resided with a relation on his mother's side, Mr. Russel, the celebrated professor of natural philosophy in the university of Edinburgh. He took the degree of doctor of medicine in 1754, and printed an inaugural thesis on a subject which at that time was one of an active controversy at Edinburgh, involving an inquiry into the nature and operation of various lithontriptics, particularly lime water. This thesis, which was entitled Dissertatio Medica de Humore Acido a Cibis orto, et Magnesiâ Albâ, was revised and corrected by Dr. Cullen, to whom it was inscribed as a particular mark of respect to his preceptor. It contains the original account of Black's discovery respecting the cause of the mildness and causticity of earths and alkalies, and points out several of the properties belonging to carbonic acid gas. The experiments contained in this thesis were translated and printed in the second volume of the Edinburgh Essays and Observations, Physical and Literary, and afterwards formed the basis of a distinct work, entitled, Experiments upon Magnesia Alba, Quicklime, and other Alkaline Substances, Edinb. 1777, 12mo; and again in 1782, accompanied by an Essay on the Cold produced by Evaporating Fluids, and of some other means of producing cold, by Dr. Cullen. The thesis of Black procured for him a great reputation; his views were new, ingenious, and satisfactory, and appeared to solve the difficulties in which the subject had been hitherto involved. The researches relating to fixed air or carbonic acid gas may fairly be esteemed as having led to the discoveries of Cavendish, Priestley, Lavoisier, and others of the pneumatic school, the importance of which is now justly admitted.

The modesty and reserve of Black, united to the predilection that he manifested for chemical pursuits, and the accuracy and diligence that he displayed in executing the operations and experiments entrusted to him, secured for him the friendship and affection of Cullen, with whom he had enjoyed daily intercourse, and with whom he maintained a correspondence during his residence in Edinburgh, which exhibits the unreserved confidence that existed between the teacher and pupil upon all chemical subjects. Upon the removal of Dr. Cullen to Edinburgh, in 1756, Dr. Black was, upon the strong recommendation of Dr. Cullen, appointed his successor, and made professor of anatomy and chemistry. The former of these appointments was, however, ill-suited to Black's taste or abilities, and he succeeded in making an exchange of it for a chair of medicine. He therefore delivered lectures on the Institutes of Medicine, and was much liked in that capacity, and also as a practitioner in Glasgow.

As early as 1756, as appears from his note-books, Dr. Black entered upon an investigation of the subject of heat, and in this research he was particularly engaged for several years. It forms, perhaps, the most important of his philosophical investigations, and has justly placed his name high in the records of chemical science. The results of his researches were laid before a society, which consisted of many members of the university and several gentlemen of the city having a taste for philosophical and literary pursuits, the meetings of which were held in the faculty room of the college in 1762. Black discovered and developed the general law that connects and explains the phenomena of the production of heat and cold which occur in the combination, liquefaction, and evaporation of bodies, several of which, it must, however, be admitted, had been previously attended to by Dr. Cullen. The doctrine of latent heat, to the discovery of which Dr. Black's claims are indisputable, was applied to the explanation of numerous natural phenomena, and he was assisted in his experiments by two of his pupils, afterwards well known to the scientific world — Mr. James Watt and Dr. Irvine. Mr. Watt always professed to have been indebted to the instruction and information received from Dr. Black for the improvements that he made in the steam-engine. It is much to be regretted that Black did not publish a particular account of his researches, since it served to deprive him of much credit to which he was justly entitled. Many philosophers put forth various opinions concerning heat, evidently founded upon those of Dr. Black, without acknowledging their obligations to him; and in several instances, even the experiments, by means of which he had arrived at his conclusions, were published as belonging to others. The claims of Black are now universally admitted, and it is therefore unnecessary to particularize those who ungenerously endeavoured to appropriate that merit to themselves which fairly belongs to another. Dr. Black's lectures served as the vehicle by which his information was transmitted; and by means of the notes taken by his pupils his opinions were made known, though necessarily in an imperfect manner, in different parts of the world.

Dr. Black remained at Glasgow until 1766, at which time Dr. Cullen was advanced to the chair of medicine in the university of Edinburgh. He therefore vacated the professorship of chemistry which he had previously held, and Dr. Black was unanimously appointed his successor. Professor Robison, upon the recommendation of Dr. Black, succeeded him at Glasgow. In his capacity as a lecturer, no professor ever gave more satisfaction than Dr. Black. It was his incessant endeavour to simplify his subject, and to render himself intelligible to the meanest capacity of his auditors. His exertions in this respect were so successful, that he absolutely made the study of chemistry fashionable among the better class of society. The celebrated Dr. Adam Ferguson has described him as a lecturer. His style, he says, was characterised by the most elegant simplicity. His address in performing experiments was remarkable; and in the impression that he made, subjects perplexed or intricate became conspicuous and clear of superfluous or questionable matter. To the last, and under symptoms of declining health, his mind gave proofs of strength undiminished. In speaking, his voice, though low, had an articulation which made him to be distinctly heard through every corner of a spacious hall, crowded with some hundreds of his pupils; and the simplicity of his expression, if not eloquence, had, to those who listened for information, something more engaging and powerful than any ornament of speech could produce.

Dr. Black was remarkable for moderation and sobriety of thought; his researches were therefore never made in haste, nor conducted with any peculiar pertinacity; his progress was slow and sure, sound and well established. As an illustration of this it may be stated, upon the authority of professor Robison, that he was led to caution his pupils earnestly to check the first incitements of high expectations, and never to allow their fancy to be warmed with the brilliant appearance of some general view, which promised at the first glance to explain a multitude of phenomena. Adam Smith said of Black, that no man had less nonsense in his head, and he often acknowledged himself obliged to him for setting him right in his judgment of character. Professor Robison considered him to possess in an uncommon degree the judgment of human character, and a talent of expressing his opinion in a single short phrase, which fixed it in the mind, never to be forgotten. He was of a constitution naturally delicate, and liable to frequent attacks of spitting of blood. He could not endure vicissitudes of temperature; and any little irregularity in his diet would immediately produce disorder. Intense application would frequently induce illness; and he was under the necessity of abstaining from great exertion or mental solicitude. He was a most amiable man, of manners gentle and pleasing, of a very cultivated taste and kindly spirit. By his circle, from the circumstances mentioned necessarily select, he was much beloved for the extent of his knowledge, his high talents, and his accomplished manners. His principal friends, omitting his professional ones, Cullen, Monro, &c., were James Watt, James Hutton, David Hume, John Home, Adam Smith, Adam Ferguson, John Clerk, Sir Geo. Clerk, &c. In 1770 a society was formed upon a principle of zeal for the militia, and a conviction that there would be no lasting security for the freedom and independence of these islands but in the valour and patriotism of an armed people. Of this society Dr. Black was many years a member. It became known by some whimsical accident as the Poker Club. Many men of the highest rank, judges, lawyers, military men, citizens, and men of letters, belonged to this body. Dr. Black died suddenly, November 26, 1799, in the seventy-first year of his age. His death was remarkable; he expired without any convulsion, shock, or stupor, to announce or retard the approach of dissolution. Being at table, it is said, with his usual fare, some bread, a few prunes, and a measured quantity of milk, diluted with water, and having the cup in his hand, when the last stroke of his pulse was to be given, he had set it down on his knees, which were joined together, and kept it steady with his hand, in the manner of a person perfectly at ease, and in this attitude expired, without spilling a drop, and without a writhe in his countenance; as if an experiment had been required to show to his friends the facility with which he departed. His abstemious habits and frugal manners enabled him to amass a considerable fortune, far beyond the expectations of any of his friends. He never married, and therefore left his property to his numerous relations, having divided the whole into 10,000 shares, and appropriated them in numbers or fractions, in the manner he thought most equitable and proper. He was in 1790, upon the death of Dr. Cullen, appointed by the king first physician to his majesty in Scotland. He was a fellow of the College of Physicians and of the Royal Society of Edinburgh. He was also a foreign associate of the Royal Academy of Sciences of Paris, and a member of the Imperial Academy of Sciences of St. Petersburg. In addition to the works already noticed, he furnished a paper to the Royal Society of London, through Sir John Pringle, bart. which was printed in the Philosophical Transactions for 1775, on the supposed effect of boiling water in disposing it to freeze more readily, ascertained by experiments; and another to the Royal Society of Edinburgh, printed in the third volume of the Transactions, on an Analysis of the Waters of some Hot Springs in Iceland. He also wrote Two Letters, one published by professor Crell in 1784, in the tenth volume of his Collections; the other addressed to M. Lavoisier, and published in the Annales de Chimie. The publication of his chemical lectures took place after his decease by his friend, pupil, and successor, professor Robison, in 2 vols, 4to, Edinb. 1803. This work was translated into German by Crell, and published at Hamburgh, 1804—1815, again in 1818, in 4 vols, 8vo.

BLACKBOURNE, (John,) a nonjuring English divine, born in 1683, and educated at Trinity college, Cambridge, where he took the degree of M.A. It is not known whether the revolution found him with any preferment, but he then refused the oath of allegiance to William, and subsequently lived in very great privacy, though in such estimation among his friends, that he was made a bishop by the nonjuring prelates.

In order to obtain a livelihood, he became corrector of the press to the celebrated Bowyer. "Here," says Nichols, "that *opprobrium historiæ*, Burnet's Memoirs, were first put into his hand to be corrected for Bowyer's press...... As he was himself too honest to deal with such as have no honesty, he advised Mr. Bowyer to be concerned no farther in the impression, so it was taken out of his hands. This good man for several years past has been a nonjuring bishop, equal to most of our bench. I waited on him often in Little Britain, where he lived, almost lost to the world, and hid amongst old books. He afterwards showed me the commission for his consecration; upon this I begged his blessing, which he gave me with the fervent zeal and devotion of a primitive bishop. I asked him if I was so happy as to belong to his diocese. His answer was, I thought, very remarkable,—Dear friend, said he, we leave the sees open, that the gentlemen who now unjustly possess them, upon the *restoration* may, if they please, return to their duty, and be continued. We content ourselves with full episcopal power as suffragans." (Nichols's Bowyer, vol. i. 253.)

Mr. Blackbourne also edited Bales' Chronycle concernynge Syr Johan Oldecastell, 1729; likewise Holinshed's Chronicle. He died Nov. 17, 1741, having passed a life of hostility both to Romish and Low-church theology; hence his epitaph, in Islington churchyard, describes him as, "Ecclesiæ Anglicanæ Presbyter, Pontificiorum æque ac Novatorum Malleus," without any reference to his episcopal character.

BLACKBURN, (William,) an architect, born in Southwark, in 1750, who obtained considerable eminence in his day by skilful plans for the erection of penitentiary houses. He died in 1790. (Rees, Cycl.)

BLACKBURNE, (John,) a Lancashire gentleman, who died in 1786, at the patriarchal age of 96. He had a celebrated garden, a catalogue of the plants in which was printed by his gardener, Neal, in 1779. He is considered the second gentleman in England who cultivated the pine-apple. (Chalmers.)

BLACKBURNE, (Francis,) an English divine, who made a considerable noise in his day as author of the Confessional, born at Richmond, in Yorkshire, June 9, 1705. His father, who bore the same name, was alderman of his native town, and his mother was descended from the learned Dr. Comber, dean of Durham. After an education at some provincial schools, he entered at Catharine hall, Cambridge. The principles that he adopted there, those of Locke and Hoadly, having disappointed him of a fellowship, he went to reside with a clerical relative in his own county, where he remained, till he was presented, in 1739, to the rectory of Richmond. He proceeded B.A. 1726, M.A. 1733. On the 18th of July, 1750, he was collated to the archdeaconry of Cleveland, and on the 1st of August following to the prebend of Bilton, by Matthew Hutton, archbishop of York, which preferments he held till his decease, which occurred in 1787, while on his thirty-eighth annual visitation.

The writings of archdeacon Blackburne consist chiefly of short pieces; and the object which most of them have in view is the propriety of throwing open the Church to all protestants by the removal of subscription to the Articles, and a remodelling of the service-book. His first publication, in 1749, entitled, An Apology for the Free and Candid Disquisitions relating to the Church of England, was a pamphlet in defence of a work written by the Rev. John Jones, vicar of Alconbury, suggesting certain alterations in the Liturgy. His great work, however, published anonymously in 1766, was The Confessional, or a full and free Inquiry into the Right, Utility, Edification, and Success of establishing systematical Confessions of Faith and Doctrine. This work, which had lain by him some years in MS. contains a well-digested course of arguments and quotations in favour of the author's views. Archbishop Secker considered it of so much importance, that he took pains to procure suitable answers to it. The controversy thus raised continued for several years. A "summary view" of it may be seen in the Gentleman's Mag. vol. xli. 405, and vol. xlii. 263. The work was soon ascertained to be archdeacon Blackburne's, who indeed took so little care to conceal his disapprobation of some things prescribed by his preferment, that many expected him to follow Mr. Lindsey's example, and secede from the church. He received accordingly an invitation from a body of dissenters in London to become their pastor. This, however, he did not accept, but continued until death an archdeacon and a parochial incumbent, little to the credit of his consistency, it must be owned, although otherwise in a manner that gave general satisfaction. From his connexion with Priestley, Lindsey, and others of similar opinions, he was, not without some reason, suspected of holding Socinian doctrines, especially as his preaching and writings gave no indications of contrary sentiments. It appears, however, that shortly before his death he made an explicit avowal to one of his relatives, that he did believe in the divinity of Christ; and after his decease a small tract was found among his papers, consisting of answers to the question, Why are you not a Socinian? which had been written many years before, but for some reason not published. The fact is, he had made a resolution early in life to have as little to do with the Trinitarian controversy as possible; but his biographers do not intimate that he entertained on this subject any opinions at variance with the catholic doctrine. His grand desire was to unite every description of protestants against the papists, for whose tenets he has no respect whatever. Hence it may be supposed his opinions respecting episcopacy were rather low; and the most that his son can say for him on this point is, that the archdeacon thought episcopacy lawful. On the subjects of grace and predestination he appears to have had some leaning to Calvinism. Archdeacon Blackburne was much beloved in private, and his habits bespoke a religious frame of mind. The following is a list of his works, besides the two before mentioned. 1. A Letter to Dr. Butler, bishop of Durham, in opposition to his celebrated Charge in 1751. 2. A Sermon preached to a large Congregation in the Country, on Friday, January 5, 1753, being the Day distinguished in the Almanacks for this present year by the Title of Old Christmas-Day. This sermon is curious, as being written just after the alteration of the style, which gave great offence, especially in the country. The object of the discourse is to disparage the observance of Christmas and all other festivals except the weekly Sunday, and it contains many decided expressions of disapprobation of the English ritual. Its style is very plain and agreeable, and gives us a favourable impression of the author's talents for addressing a country congregation. It has, however, been doubted whether the sermon really was ever preached, from fears that it might occasion some disturbance. 3. A Letter containing Remarks on Archdeacon Sharp's Charges. 4. A Commentary on Archbishop Secker's Letter to Walpole on the Subject of Bishops for America. 5. No Proof of an Intermediate State of Happiness or Misery between Death and the Resurrection. 6. Remarks on Dr. Warburton's Account of the Sentiments of the Early Jews concerning the Soul. 7. A Review of some Passages in the Divine Legation. 8. An Historical View of the Controversy concerning an Intermediate State. 9. A Consideration of the Present State of the Controversy between the Protestants and Papists in England, and how far the latter are entitled to Toleration. 10. Four Charges, an Assize Sermon, and other small tracts. His works, with a life prefixed, were edited by his son, and published in 7 vols, 8vo, 1805. (Life by his Son. Nichols' Literary Anecdotes, vol. iii. 14.)

BLACKBURNE, (Thomas,) son of the preceding, a physician, sent to Cambridge for education, but he would not graduate there, from objections to the Thirty-nine Articles. He took his doctor's degree at Edinburgh, and settled at Durham, to practise his profession. He died there in 1782, when only thirty-three, and is chiefly worthy of notice from a communication which appeared in a work upon Tænia, by Dr. F. S. Simmons. (Gorton.)

BLACKET, (Joseph,) an English poet, born in Yorkshire, in 1786, son of a day-labourer, who, after a very moderate education, was apprenticed, at eleven years of age, to his brother, a shoemaker in London. He devoted every leisure hour to such books as he could procure; and at the age of fifteen, having conceived an enthusiastic admiration of Shakspeare, from witnessing Kemble's performance of Richard III., he began to write poetry. About the year 1809 a small volume was printed for private circulation, under the title of Specimens of the Poetry of Joseph Blacket; which is thought to exhibit marks of a higher genius than that displayed by Bloomfield in the Farmer's Boy. Very shortly after this time, Blacket, still employed at his trade of a shoemaker, and in very poor circumstances, was seized with consumption, of which complaint he died at Senham, near Sunderland, 18th of August, 1810. After his death his various pieces were collected, and published as The Remains of Joseph Blacket. (Gent. Mag.)

BLACKHALL, (Offspring,) an eminent English prelate, born in London in 1654, and educated academically at Catharine hall, Cambridge. In 1690 he became rector of South Ockenden, Essex, and in 1694, rector of St. Mary Aldermary, London. He also held successively two lectureships in the city. It is to the credit of both parties, that he was appointed chaplain to king William, though notoriously so unfriendly to the revolution that he was charged in an anonymous pamphlet, published in 1705, with continuing a nonjuror for two years. In 1698, Toland, in his life of Milton, after maintaining that Charles I. did not write the Icon Basilike, insinuated, from the prevalence of a contrary belief, that the multitude of spurious christian writings in the early ages of the Church was any thing rather than surprising, but might fairly engender a suspicion against some of the received Scriptures. Upon this infidel insinuation Blackhall passed a severe censure, in a sermon preached before the House of Commons, Jan. 30, 1699. To this Toland replied in his Amyntor; and Blackhall published a rejoinder in a 12mo pamphlet, which is now scarce. This controversy bringing him into considerable notice, in 1700 he was chosen Boyle's Lecturer, and in 1707 was consecrated bishop of Exeter. This preferment was owing to the recommendation of archbishop Sharp, and gave great offence to the Whig party; Burnet says, "These divines (Blackhall of Exeter, and Sir W. Dawes, appointed at the same time to Chester) were in themselves men of value and worth, but their notions were all on the other side; they had submitted to the government, but they, at least Blackhall, seemed to condemn the Revolution and all that had been done pursuant to it." (Life and Times, ed. 1734, p. 487.) Blackhall, though not a violent politician, had not hesitated to utter from the pulpit some sentiments not quite agreeable to the party in power, in a sermon on the Queen's accession, preached at St. Dunstan's, in 1704, and in another, preached on a similar occasion, at St. James's, in 1708. He argued for the divine origin of civil government, and asserted that, even when the magistrate was elected by the people, his authority was not derived from man, but directly from God; that his decrees were to be obeyed even if contrary to the laws of God; or in cases where obedience might become a crime, the punishment for disobedience was to be cheerfully submitted to. These sermons gave rise to a long and angry controversy, in which Hoadly, eventually the well-known bishop, bore a conspicuous part. Blackhall died at Exeter, November 29, 1716, and was buried in the cathedral. Archbishop Dawes, who had been long and intimately acquainted with him, says that he never met with a more perfect pattern of christian life than that which he exhibited; he was also much admired both as a preacher and a writer. His works were published by archbishop Dawes, in 2 vols, fol. 1723; they consist of practical discourses on the Lord's Prayer, and the Sermon on the Mount; the Boyle's Lectures; his pamphlets on the controversy above mentioned, and other occasional sermons and tracts. (Biog. Brit. Brit. Mag.)

BLACKLOCK, (Thomas,) born of English parents at Annan, in the county of Dumfries, in 1721, a Scottish poet and divine, remarkable for having attained a respectable rank in literature under total want of sight. This misfortune happened to him at the early age of six months, from the small-pox. To amuse him as he grew up, his friends, who were poor, but well-informed, read various books to him; among others, the works of Spenser, Milton, Prior, and Addison. By these he was highly delighted, and before the age of twelve years he made several attempts to imitate them. When only nineteen he lost his excellent father, but was happy enough to attract the attention of Dr. Stephenson, an eminent physician of Edinburgh, who, forming a favourable opinion of his talents, invited him to the Scottish metropolis, and procured his admission to the University, where he studied several years. During that period he published a collection of poems, which procured for him several influential friends. In 1759 he was licensed to preach by the Presbytery of Dumfries; and the warmth, piety, and elegance of his compositions soon procured him a great degree of celebrity among the higher classes of society. In the year 1762 the earl of Selkirk obtained for him, from the crown, a presentation to the church of Kirkcudbright, but his admission was violently opposed by the congregation. His blindness was undoubtedly a disqualification, but fault appears also to have been found with his preaching, as too elevated and refined. After two years' litigation he was induced to resign the living, and accept of a small annuity, with which he retired to Edinburgh, and spent the remainder of his days in the tuition of a few young men, and in those literary pursuits to which he was so ardently attached. He married in 1762, and in 1767 the degree of D.D. was conferred upon him by the Marischal college, Aberdeen. He died July 7, 1791. That a person blind, almost from birth, should attain a knowledge of Greek, Latin, French, and Italian, besides a competent degree of theological learning, does seem extraordinary; and it is impossible that so much could have been acquired without the most persevering industry, aided by uncommon powers of memory.

BLACKLOE, (Thomas,) an English Romanist, first professor of theology in the college at Douay, afterwards canon of the London Chapter, formed by Bishop. He was a man of considerable learning, but of an unquiet and turbulent disposition. He formed a party in the chapter against Smith, (who succeeded Bishop as vicar apostolic in England,) as neither a member of the body, nor nominated by it. Having succeeded in forcing the attention of government to this dispute, Smith was banished from the kingdom in 1628. Blackloe was equally opposed to Gage, Smith's successor, and obliged him to abandon his office of vicar apostolic. Blackloe published several pieces, which were condemned by the inquisition.

Among his works are :—Institutiones Ethicæ, 1660, in which an attack is made upon the Jesuits, and they procured a censure upon it from the faculty of theology at Douay. De Medio Animarum Statu, in which he denies that the prayers of the faithful can have any effect in releasing souls from purgatory. This treatise made a good deal of noise, and its purgatorial and other doctrines were branded in print as the *Blackloan heresy.* De Obedientiæ et Gubernationis Fundamentis, a work written in favour of Cromwell, and condemned by parliament, 1660. (Biog. Univ.)

BLACKMORE, (John,) an English mezzotinto engraver, born in London about the year 1740. He executed some clever plates, chiefly portraits after Sir Joshua Reynolds. (Bryan.)

BLACKMORE, (Sir Richard,) an English poet, born in Wiltshire, of respectable parentage, sent to Westminster school at the age of thirteen, removed to St. Edmund's hall, Oxford, in 1668, and graduated as master of arts in that university, June 3, 1676. Upon the whole, he seems to have resided in Oxford about thirteen years, but evidently with no very close attention to his studies, because, when he afterwards became a voluminous author, he showed his learning to be far from exact. In early life he was compelled to seek a subsistence by teaching in a school, a circumstance which pointed many an acrimonious line against him, when professional wealth and some degree of literary reputation brought a swarm of envious hornets about his ears. He was not, however, long under this depression. On the contrary, his circumstances appear to have soon taken a turn decidedly favourable, as he was enabled to travel into Italy, and take the degree of doctor of medicine at Padua. On his return to England he practised as a physician, and became fellow of the college, April 12, 1687, being one of the thirty added under the new charter of James II. to that learned body. His residence was at Saddler's hall, in Cheapside, and his practice lay chiefly in the city. But it became considerable, and hence Blackmore was appointed one of the royal physicians by king William III., from whom he received also the honour of knighthood. But numerous as were his professional avocations, they did not prevent him from appearing continually as an author. In 1695 he published Prince Arthur, an heroic poem, in ten books, now forgotten, but popular at the time of its publication, there being a demand for a third edition before the end of two years. Such success excited no very pleasurable feelings among needy men of letters, who had neither found so ready a way to the reward of their own labours, nor possessed, like Blackmore, a handsome income from sources independent of the press. Hence the successful poet was formally attacked by Dennis, in a criticism replete with acrimony. Blackmore imprudently manifested his contempt for such attacks by publishing, in 1700, A Satire upon Wit, which not only brought upon him all the small fry of literature, but also some superior minds, that ought to have been above such company. In the same year Blackmore published a Paraphrase on Job, and other parts of Scripture. In 1705 he published Eliza, an heroic poem, in ten books, which seems to have attracted little or no notice. In 1706 he wrote a poem on the Kit Cat Club, in which several living characters were commemorated. In the next year he followed up this subject by his Instructions to Vanberbank, an eminent painter. Blackmore's principal work, however, was reserved for 1712, when appeared his Creation, a philosophical poem, in seven books, intended to demonstrate God's existence, from the design evident in his works. This has been admitted into collections of English poetry, and is a work of the best intention, and no contemptible execution, but too dull and deficient in striking passages for lasting popularity. In 1723, Blackmore produced King Alfred, an heroic poem, in twelve books, but it proved, like his Eliza, a total failure. He published also other works, both in verse and prose, some being medical, and others historical. But every thing that he wrote has long been forgotten, except his Creation. He died October 8, 1729, manifesting to the last that fervent piety which had really been the chief glory of his life. (Life of Blackmore, prefixed to his Creation.)

BLACKRIE, (Alexander,) a Scottish apothecary, who published, in 1766, A Disquisition on Medicines that Dissolve the Stone, 12mo; reprinted with additions in 1771. (Rees, Cycl.)

BLACKSTONE, (J.) an apothecary, of whom little is known, except that he published some interesting and useful works on botany; one in 1737, entitled, Fasciculus Plantarum, circa Harefield, Sponte nascentium, cum Appendice ad Loci Naturam spectante, 8vo, London;

and another in 1746, Specimen Botanicum, quo Plantarum plurium Angliæ indigenarum, Loci naturales illustrantur, 8vo, London. (Rees, Cycl.)

BLACKSTONE, (Sir William,) the most popular of English legal writers, and one of the most illustrious, born in Cheapside, London, July 10, 1723. His father, named Charles, was a silkman, and his grandfather a city apothecary, who came of a family resident in Salisbury, or its neighbourhood. His mother was Mary, daughter of Lovelace Bigg, a gentleman seated at Chilton Foliot, in Wiltshire. He had two elder brothers, both educated at Winchester school, under the eye of their uncle, Dr. Bigg, warden of the college, and both eventually beneficed clergymen, although the elder of them had previously practised as a physician. Their father died before William was born, and their mother did not see him twelve years old. His guardian was Thomas Bigg, a maternal uncle, an eminent London surgeon, who, surviving elder brothers, died proprietor of the family estate at Chilton, and by whose judicious care the young Blackstones received such educations as compensated greatly for early loss of parents and deficiency of fortune. William, the youngest of these orphans, was placed in the Charterhouse school, in 1730, and five years afterwards, a maternal relative obtained for him, from Sir Robert Walpole, an appointment upon the foundation there. He proved every way worthy of the minister's patronage, so exerting and distinguishing himself that he became head-scholar at fifteen, and by his promising qualities, a general favourite with the masters. On November 30, 1738, he was entered of Pembroke college, Oxford, but he spoke, on the 12th of the following month, the oration commemorative of the liberal founder of the Charterhouse; and this valedictory appearance at the place of his early education proved fully answerable to the reputation that had hitherto attended him within its venerable precincts. At Oxford, Blackstone was a hard student, being especially attentive to logic and the mathematics, which were of essential service to him in after life by forming those habits of close reasoning and systematic investigation that rendered him eventually so remarkable. His mathematical knowledge he applied with no contemptible success to architecture, a treatise on the elements of that fascinating subject having been compiled by him at the age of twenty, but with no view to publication, although very favourably estimated by some who had opportunities of seeing it.

Among his intellectual pleasures was poetry. He wrote several very pleasing pieces, which were circulated privately among his friends; and he made various annotations upon Shakspeare, evincing a deep insight into that prince of dramatists, which, shortly before his death, were communicated to Malone, and thus obtained admission into the supplement to Johnson and Steevens's edition. But Blackstone was not a man to dream of gaining an eligible position through the muses, or to overlook the necessity of restraining mere amusement, however intellectual, from frittering away that application which is indispensable for professional success. Having determined, accordingly, upon following the law, he tore himself away from poetry, but not without considerable reluctance, which he painted with great felicity in The Lawyer's Farewell to his Muse, eventually inserted in Dodsley's poems. He entered in the Middle Temple, November 20, 1741; and in the November of 1743, he was elected fellow of All Souls college, Oxford, a noble and venerable establishment, which thus afforded him a moderate independence, and by so doing, made good another claim to the gratitude and respect of Englishmen. His time was now divided between Oxford and London. In the former place he rendered considerable service to his college by arranging its muniments, and improving the mode of keeping its accounts, while he filled the office of bursar. In London he applied himself with great assiduity to his legal studies, and he was called to the bar November 28, 1746. On June 12, in the preceding year, he had taken the degree of B.C.L. The early years of a barrister's life are seldom very gratifying either to himself or his friends, and Blackstone had neither those oratorical recommendations, nor influential connexions, which occasionally render it otherwise. He found himself, therefore, under the usual necessity of passing through a season of professional obscurity; but he wisely availed himself of the opportunity to lay up such a store of legal knowledge as rendered him secure of eminence when he came fairly before the world. In 1749, an uncle resigned the recordership of Wallingford, and Blackstone was chosen to succeed him. On the 26th of April, 1750, he proceeded D.C.L., and in the course of that year he published An Essay on Collateral Consanguinity, a subject of peculiar interest to members of All Souls college, from the multitude of claims to fellowships brought forward by real or supposed connexions of the founder, Archbishop Chicheley. This work was highly creditable to the author, although its practical results were not immediately answerable to his expectations. When, however, subsequently, Archbishop Cornwallis was called, as visitor, to review the question of founder's kin, at All Souls, he chose Blackstone as his common law assessor, and some limitations were framed for those claims of consanguinity for which the college statutes expressly provided, but which were fast outstepping every reasonable bound.

In 1753, Blackstone became weary of the neglect and fruitless expense that had hitherto met his exertions to establish himself in Westminster hall. He determined, accordingly, to reside upon his fellowship, meaning to read lectures upon law in Oxford, and to practise as a provincial counsel. He had previously planned a course of lectures on the laws of England, and it was generally thought in the university that he would be found admirably qualified for carrying the design into execution. Hence when he began to lecture, a most flattering attendance, comprising many young men of family, greeted him. To facilitate the studies of his hearers, he published An Analysis of the Laws of England, which was found highly serviceable in smoothing the approaches to legal erudition. He was not, however, so completely engrossed by his lectures as to be rendered incapable of serving the university in other ways. On the contrary, he made himself extremely useful in regulating the Clarendon press, of which he was chosen a delegate in 1755, and for the more effectual management of which he acquired an insight into the mechanical part of printing. Having also become connected with Queen's college, in 1757, by means of the foundation, originating from Mr. Michel's bequest in 1739, his exertions rendered that important benefaction available for completing the beautiful erections towards the High-street, and likewise terminated the difficulties, hitherto found insurmountable, of connecting the new and old establishments in a satisfactory manner.

In March, 1758, Blackstone again appeared as a legal author, by publishing Considerations on Copyholders, a work which originated in his employment as counsel in the great contest for Oxfordshire, that occurred in 1754; when it was debatrd whether copyholders of a certain nature were not entitled to vote for counties. On the 20th of October, 1758, he was unanimously elected to the Vinerian professorship of common law, an office created by means of a legacy of 12,000*l.* left by Charles Viner, in 1755, for that and other purposes. Within a few days of his election, Blackstone read an introductory lecture, which gave so much satisfaction, both from style and matter, that the vice-chancellor and heads of houses requested him to publish it. He subsequently prefixed it to his immortal Commentaries. These were the lectures that he delivered as Vinerian professor; and such was the applause gained by them, that he was requested to read them to George III., then prince of Wales. But his engagements in the university did not allow him to accept the flattering invitation. He sent, however, such of these admirable pieces as appeared most interesting, to the young prince, and received in return a handsome gratuity; so far was the future king from taking offence at a refusal which he was taught by his own good sense to consider reasonable. In 1759, Blackstone published two small professional pieces upon questions then agitated in the university, one of them, Reflections on the Opinions of Messrs. Pratt, Morton, and Wilbraham, relative to the Disqualification of Lord Lichfield, then a Candidate for the Chancellorship; the other, A Case for the Opinion of Counsel on the Right of the University to make new Statutes. In the same year he published a new edition of the Great Charter and Charter of the Forest, an appearance before the world which confirmed his character as a lawyer, besides exhibiting him advantageously as an antiquary and historian. About the same time he published a small treatise on the Law of Descents in Fee Simple. His reputation was now fully established, and, in June 1759, he bought chambers in the Temple, with a view to attendance at Westminster hall, which he resumed in the following Michaelmas term. He did not, however, withdraw wholly from Oxford, but continued to read his lectures there at such times as his professional avocations in London would allow. These now became considerable, so that he thought of parliament, and in March, 1761, he was returned for the borough of Hindon. In the following May he had a patent of precedence as king's counsel. Some months before, he had declined the office of chief justice of the Irish court of Common Pleas. His condition was now such as to allow of a marriage with prudence, and on May 5, 1761, he was united to Sarah, eldest surviving daughter of James Clitherow, esq., deceased, of Boston house, Middlesex. This union lasted nineteen years, greatly to Blackstone's happiness, and was productive of nine children, seven of whom survived him. It necessarily vacated his fellowship of All Souls; but the earl of Westmoreland, then chancellor of the university, made him principal of New Inn hall, so that he still had a residence in Oxford, with a rank as head of a house that he had not previously possessed.

In 1762, Blackstone collected several of his pieces, and re-published them under the title of Law Tracts. But such attention as he could spare for authorship soon became necessarily engrossed by his lectures. Many incorrect copies of them were abroad, and an unauthorized edition of them was either expected from Ireland, or had actually appeared there. In justice, therefore, to himself, the learned and admirable lecturer was compelled to print his immortal course. The first volume of it, under the title of Commentaries on the Laws of England, appeared in Nov. 1765; and within the four succeeding years, three other volumes were published; the whole making a work which has ever since maintained a rank as an English classic of the highest order. To the legal profession it has rendered most important services; and eminent lawyers observed, on its appearance, that such a book would have spared them in their youth a great deal of labour. Blackstone's knowledge, experience, and connexions having given him a warm attachment to the venerable institutions of England, he expressed himself in some points rather unguardedly in their favour, and this gave an advantage to such as longed for political changes. The dissenting doctors, accordingly, Priestley and Furneaux, attacked some of his positions, the latter at considerable length, in his Letters to the honourable Mr. Justice Blackstone, concerning his Exposition of the Act of Toleration, and some positions relative to Religious Liberty, in his celebrated Commentaries on the Laws of England. Blackstone never took any particular notice of these letters, but he tacitly allowed them a degree of weight by altering some things in subsequent editions of his work that were treated by them as exceptionable and unsound. To Dr. Priestley, however, he did publish an answer. In 1776, also, some of the political principles in his Commentaries were assailed by Jeremy Bentham in his Fragment on Government. It was a severe attack, but the great jurist felt himself quite strong enough to bear it with equanimity. Hence, when he became afterwards personally acquainted with Bentham, he treated him with perfect kindness.

Blackstone's long connexion with Oxford was terminated in 1766, by his resignation both of the Vinerian professorship, and the headship of New Inn hall. He had endeavoured to render that house an establishment for the study of law, and Mr. Viner's will offered facilities for such a purpose; but the house of convocation proved unfavourable, and the scheme consequently miscarried. Blackstone now fixed himself in London; and had his constitution been equal to his reputation, he must have made a great and rapid fortune. He had, indeed, an offer of the solicitor-generalship, on Dunning's resignation, in January, 1770; but he could not venture to undertake the complicated duties, both legal and political, which that office required. In the following month he was appointed one of the justices in the court of Common Pleas, and in this honourable post he continued until his death, February 14, 1780. He was then only in the fifty-sixth year of his age, and he left a character as a Christian, a lawyer, and a man, that all might envy, but very few could hope to reach. He was buried, according to his own desire, under the chancel of St. Peter's, Wallingford, a church rebuilt by his exertions, and the spire of which was raised at his expense. (Chalmers. Rees. Lysons.)

BLACKWALL, (Anthony,) a native of Derbyshire, born in 1674, who became a critic of some distinction. In 1690 he was admitted a sizar of Emmanuel college, Cambridge; and soon after he had taken his degree of M.A. in 1698, he was appointed head-master to the free school at Derby, and lecturer of All Hallows in the same town. In 1722 he was appointed head-master of the free school at Market Bosworth, Leicestershire; and in 1725 appeared his principal work, The Sacred Classics Defended and Illustrated, a second volume of which was published in 1731, a few weeks after the death of the author. The object of this work is to vindicate the sacred penmen of the New Testament from the charge of inelegance in respect of style, and to show that passages which have been adduced as instances of incorrect composition may be justified by the usage of classical authority. In 1726 Sir H. Atkins, who had been a pupil of Blackwall, presented him to the rectory of Clapham, Surrey, which, however, he resigned in 1729, and returned to Bosworth, where he died April 8, 1730. His other writings are, Theognidis Megarensis Sententiæ Morales Novâ Latinâ versione, &c. 1706; an Introduction to the Classics, 1718, 12mo; and a Latin Grammar, which he used in both his schools. (Chalmers. Aikin. Nichols.)

BLACKWELL, (George,) an English divine of the Roman church, born in Middlesex, in 1545, admitted scholar of Trinity college, Oxford, May 27, 1562, probationer in 1565, actual fellow in the following year, and M.A. in 1567. Having imbibed a partiality for Romanism, he did not long retain his fellowship, but first retired to Gloucester-hall, and subsequently to a Romish seminary abroad. He resided several years at Rome, where, by his learning and good conduct, he gained the esteem of many eminent persons, among them of cardinal Bellarmine and Robert Persons, the famous Jesuit, so conspicuous in the religious and political movements of Elizabeth's reign. At length the expediency of an episcopate for the English Romanists came under discussion. So long as there was any survivor of the old hierarchy, displaced soon after the queen's accession, the question was not raised. But Thomas Watson, the deprived bishop of Lincoln, who was the last of that body, died in 1584. Even then the want of a Romish episcopacy was not greatly felt. William Allen, made cardinal in 1587, was considered as the cardinal of England; and being resident in the Low Countries, he was sufficiently within reach for any appeal from his native country. But after his death, in 1594, the body of English Romanists found itself wholly without a leader. It was, however, urgently in want of one from dissensions among its members. The Jesuits had, for several years, obtained an ascendency in recusant families, which the secular clergy viewed with jealousy and indignation. One of their order even went so far as to claim a superiority over his fellow-prisoners in Wisbeach castle; and the disputes between the two rival bodies ran so high as to threaten English Romanism with injurious consequences. To avert such, projects for the establishment of a Romish hierarchy in England were seriously entertained. It was proposed that the kingdom should be parcelled into two divisions, a northern and a southern, and various arrangements devised by which a compact religious body might be formed. But when the scheme came to be considered in detail, the regulars objected to it as likely to interfere with their special privileges, and place them under the control of the seculars. Hence the design miscarried, and Persons, who had originally approved of an episcopate, retracted his opinion. Another plan was now proposed,—that of commissioning an archpriest, who should exercise a general superintendence over the clergy, and the spiritual concerns of laymen in communion with Rome, as bishops ordinarily do over flocks confided to them, but who should be no more authorized to consecrate chrism and confer orders and confirmation, than others merely of sacerdotal rank. This plan was thought most expedient; and accordingly, March 7, 1598, cardinal Cajetan, who was recognised at Rome as protector of the English nation, directed letters to Blackwell, mentioning the disagreements among English Romanists, with their general wish for an ecclesiastical superior, and announcing the pope's wish that he should act as archpriest over the secular clergy. Blackwell was also furnished with private instructions, forbidding him to determine any matter of importance without consulting Garnet, provincial of the Jesuits, and some others of that order. When the new archpriest entered upon his functions, a violent spirit of resistance to him arose among the seculars. They treated him as a mere creature of the Jesuits, and rationally objected to his credentials, as bearing upon their face no higher authority than that of an individual cardinal, who might have acted without sufficient powers, and made arrangements which the pope would not sanction. Blackwell was tempted by this opposition into considerable intemperance, branding his antagonists as schismatics, and menacing them with ecclesiastical censures. They determined, accordingly, upon an appeal to the pope, Clement VIII.; and two of their body, delegated by the rest, arrived in Rome, in December 1598. Persons received them in the English college there with great incivility, and soon drove them from it in a manner equally offensive. They then took up their quarters at an inn, but a company of soldiers, attended by him, removed them, and they were confined, under his personal direction, with extreme severity, until a fortnight after the promulgation of a bull, dated April 6, 1599, in which the pope sanctioned cardinal Cajetan's letter, together with the archpriest's appointment and acts. Even this, however, did not allay the ferment in England. An appeal was now made to the faculty of divines in the university of Paris, as to the imputations of schism and sin laid by Blackwell upon the refractory seculars. That learned body unanimously determined that there was neither schism nor sin in the case. Blackwell then forbade every one, whether lay or clerical, to defend in any manner the judgment received from Paris, under pain of interdiction. As if to make this arbitrary decree appear more odious and indefensible, the pope's bull, confirmatory of Blackwell's appointment and proceedings, was no sooner received, than the dissatisfied seculars paid unqualified submission to it. But the archpriest, refusing to admit present acquiescence as any acquittal of former opposition, persisted in treating them as schismatics. This was more than they could bear, and accordingly, Nov. 17, 1600, they served him with a formal notice of appeal to the pontiff. This was kindly received at Rome, and produced a letter from the pope to Blackwell, dated Aug. 17, 1601, in which he was admonished to milder courses; but the appeal was very feelingly rejected, with a view to prevent farther irritation. Still the contending parties proved irreconcilable, and a third appeal was made to the pope. This produced a papal brief to the archpriest, dated Oct. 6, 1602, in which that indiscreet functionary was charged with an occasional excess of his powers, and commanded to abstain from consulting either the provincial of the Jesuits, or any of that order, in the discharge of his official duties, and in which the appellants were pronounced free from the loss of any of their faculties by their proceedings. This made peace, though certainly very little to the advantage of Blackwell's character for discretion and independence. Had he been a man of more address or temper, and less likely to be found a servile tool of Jesuitism, his difficulties in establishing himself at the head of his clerical brethren must have quickly vanished. In other points, Blackwell's character shows advantageously. When a few desperate Romanists were detected in contriving the Powder Plot, he wrote a circular, dated Nov. 28, 1605, condemning that nefarious conspiracy as *detestable and damnable, a most grievous offence to God, scandalous to the world, utterly unlawful in itself, and against God's express commandments.* Afterwards, on receiving the pope's *mandatum*, disapproving of such devices, he sent it abroad, July 22, 1606, with a short note of his own, declaring himself to have *never allowed any such attempts.* In a like spirit he received eventually the oath of allegiance, enacted in consequence of this conspiracy, and branding the deposing power assumed by popes as *impious and heretical.* It appears really to have been framed with the wise and humane view of diverting popular odium from English Romanists, by enabling them to disclaim solemnly upon oath such extravagant political principles as have been advocated by some of their body, and may justly throw upon occasions a suspicion over all those members of it who refuse to make a manly disavowal of them. Factious or fanatical men, however, would admit neither wisdom nor humanity in the oath, but branded it as an ambiguous form, offensive to tender consciences, drawn up chiefly by archbishop Bancroft, and Perkins, a renegade Jesuit, to divide the Romish body, and afford pretences for new persecutions. It is much to the credit of Blackwell that, after due consideration, he took no such improbable, uncharitable, and unsound views of this document. On the contrary, though opposed strongly to the oath before it was published, he subsequently addressed a letter to the English members of his church, maintaining its lawfulness, and advising them to take it. His old friend, cardinal Bellarmine, no sooner heard of an approbation so distasteful to the more violent papal partizans, than he wrote to the archpriest, condemning his conduct, and recommending him to retract. Paul V., too, now pope, issued a brief to the English Romanists, condemnatory of the oath. It was, however, supposed by some in England, that the storm thus raised at Rome really rested upon a confusion of the oath of allegiance prescribed under James with that of supremacy prescribed under Elizabeth; and many represented the pope's disapproving brief as dictated by no deliberate judgment, but extorted by importunity, and hence not binding upon English Romanists. To remove this impression, Paul issued another brief, dated Aug. 22, 1607, declaring the former to have been framed by his especial direction, after a full deliberation, and hence to be binding upon all who owned his authority. But before this instrument was even drawn up, Blackwell had again, and in a most particular manner, expressed his approbation of the oath. He was apprehended June 24, 1607, apparently for corresponding with cardinal Bellarmine without permission from the government. He was detained in close custody twelve days, during eight of which he underwent very rigorous examinations at Lambeth, before a board of commissioners. They examined him at great length, and elicited from him a series of judgments adverse to the political pretensions of Rome, which do great honour to his christian principles, theological knowledge, and good sense. The particulars of this examination were immediately published, under the following title,— The Large Examination taken at Lambeth, according to his Majesty's direction, Point by Point, of Mr. George Blackwell, made Archpriest of England by Pope Clement VIII., upon occasion of an Answer of his, without the Privity of the State, to a Letter lately sent to him by Cardinal Bellarmine, blaming him for taking the Oath of Allegiance, together with the Cardinal's Letter, and Mr. Blackwell's Letter to the Romish Catholics in England, as well Ecclesiastical as Lay. Imprinted at London, by Robert Barker, printer to the King's most excellent Majesty, 1607. Afterwards Blackwell addressed a second letter to the English Romanists, repeating his approbation of the oath, and advising them to take it, even to the neglect of papal briefs. This was too much for the endurance of Rome; and in 1608 he was superseded, George Birket, a clergyman of more conciliatory manners, being appointed archpriest. Blackwell died suddenly, Jan. 12, 1612. The oath which he had the manliness to approve was also approved, in 1682, by no less an authority than Bossuet, although that celebrated controversialist stigmatized as *captious* the clause which pronounced papal pretensions to depose princes *impious and heretical*. (Butler's Hist. Mem. i. 303; iii. 395. Wood's Athenæ. Collier, ii. 694. Tierney's Additions to Dodd, iv. 73.)

BLACKWELL, (Alexander,) a native of Scotland, noticed in his day as author of A New Method of Improving Cold, Wet, and Clayey Grounds, Lond. 1741. This rejects manure, and recommends repeated ploughing, or other modes of turning the soil. The author, educated for a physician, after attempts to get into practice, both in Scotland and London, first became corrector of the press, and subsequently set up for a printer himself, but failed. Eventually his agricultural piece recommended him for employment in Sweden, where he both superintended various rural operations and practised physic. He was, however, involved in a plot for changing the succession to the Swedish throne, for which, after undergoing torture, he was beheaded, Aug. 9, 1747. He denied the crime imputed to him. (Chalmers.)

BLACKWELL, (Elizabeth,) wife of the preceding, conspicuous for the services that she rendered to botany, when her husband's failure plunged them in pecuniary distress. She was daughter of a merchant of Aberdeen, and having a good taste for drawing, she applied herself to the preparation of a herbal of medicinal plants, then greatly wanted. Some specimens of her fitness for this task having been submitted to Sir Hans Sloane, and other eminent physicians, she received such encouragement as induced her to take up her residence by the botanical garden at Chelsea, where, by drawing plants as they came fresh to hand, engraving her draughts on copper, and colouring them herself, she produced a work that received extensive patronage, and afforded such effectual relief to her husband under his difficulties, that it enabled him, it is said, to regain his liberty after a confinement of two years. The first volume of this ingenious and industrious lady's production was published in 1737, the second in 1739, fol. It is entitled, A Curious Herbal, containing 500 cuts of the most useful Plants which are now used in the Practice of Physic, engraved on folio Copper-plates, after Drawings taken from the Life, by Elizabeth Blackwell. To which is added, a short description of the plants, and their common uses in physic. Most of the delineations are faithful, but necessarily wanting in that strict accuracy which the botanical knowledge of later years has rendered indispensable. That this work, though bulky and expensive, was intrinsically valuable, is shown by repeated editions of it. Trew made a

German translation of it, which, with a Latin text besides, was published at Nuremberg, with large additions of his own, between the years 1750 and 1760, in six volumes, under the title of Herbarium Blackwellianum. A supplemental volume was printed by other botanists in 1773. Subsequently was published at Leipsic, in 1794, 8vo, Nomenclator Linnæanus in Blackwellio-Herbarium, per C. G. Groening. Mrs. Blackwell's services to botany were commemorated by Commerson, in the name Blackwellia, given by him to a race of plants. The date of her death is not known. (Chalmers. Rees. Biog. Univ.)

BLACKWELL, (Thomas,) brother-in-law of the preceding, born Aug. 4, 1701, at Aberdeen, where his father had been settled as minister in the preceding year, but became eventually professor of divinity and principal of the Marischal college, offices which he held until his death, in 1728. In that college Thomas Blackwell took the degree of master of arts in 1718, which is considered, as he was only seventeen, a proof of extraordinary proficiency. In this establishment he was appointed Greek professor by the crown, Nov. 28, 1723, and he subsequently gained great reputation as a teacher of that language. He was appointed principal of the college by George II. Oct. 7, 1748, being the only layman so distinguished since the patronage came to the crown, by the forfeiture of the Marischal family, in 1716; but he did not resign the Greek professorship, although several years before his death a consumptive habit obliged him to employ an assistant in teaching his class. He became LL.D. in 1752. At length his health became so seriously impaired, that he was advised to travel, and accordingly he left home in February, 1757, but he was not able to go any farther than Edinburgh. He died there on the 8th of the next month. Dr. Blackwell produced several works connected with classical literature, the first of which, printed in 1735, An Inquiry into the Life and Writings of Homer, was anonymous. This is thought to be his best work, and a second edition of it was published in 1736. Soon afterwards he published, Proofs of the Inquiry into Homer's Life and Writings, translated into English. This was a translation of the notes in various languages appended to the original work. In 1748 Blackwell published Letters concerning Mythology, in a large 8vo. In 1753 appeared the first volume of his Memoirs of the Court of Augustus, 4to. A second volume was published in 1755; and a third, left incomplete at his death, was prepared for the press by John Mills, and published in 1764, together with a third edition of the two former volumes. It is therefore evident that Blackwell's literary talents found many admirers; but others, and among them no less a man than Dr. Johnson, treated them with ridicule, and even with severity. His taste, in fact, was defective. He displays a pompous pedantry, and affects a knowledge of the world, which offend such as are best qualified to judge both of books and men. (Chalmers.)

BLACKWOOD, (Adam,) a Scottish writer, born at Dumferling, in 1539, of an ancient family. His great uncle, Robert Reid, bishop of Orkney, and an eminent statesman, sent him for education to Paris, where he studied under Turnebus and Dorat. On bishop Reid's death, in 1558, he paid a short visit to Scotland; but he soon returned to Paris, where the liberality of his native sovereign, recently married to the dauphin, enabled him to pursue his studies. The unfortunate Mary continuing to patronize him, appointed him member of the presidial of Poictiers, her dowry town. He died there in 1613, and is known to posterity as a warm advocate of the unhappy queen, to whom he had lain under so many obligations, and in whose behalf he had been actively engaged upon several occasions. His first publication is entitled, Caroli IX. Pompa funebris Versibus expressa: per A. B. J. C. 1574. The initials mean Adamus Blackwood, Juris Consultus. In the following year he published, but without even initials, De Vinculo seu Conjunctione Religionis et Imperii, et de Conjuratorum Insidiis Religionis Fuco adumbratis. In 1580, or the following year, was published with his name, Adversus Georgii Buchanani Dialogum de Jure Regni apud Scotos, pro Regibus Apologia. He also revised and corrected the Relation du Martyre de Marie Stuart, Reine d'Ecosse, printed at Antwerp in 1588, a violent piece, denouncing the sovereigns of Europe, if they should not avenge Mary's death. His concern with it fairly entitles it to a place among Blackwood's works, which were published in a collected form at Paris, in 1644, 4to, under the following title,—Adami Blackuodæi, in Curiâ Pictonum Præsidis et Consiliarii Regii, Opera omnia: de Jure Regni adversus Buchananum, de Vinculo Religionis et Imperii, Meditationes in Psalmum 50. Carmina, le Martyre de la Reine Marie Stuart d'Ecosse. It is a very rare volume. (Chalmers. Clement. Bibl. Curieuse.)

BLACKWOOD, (Henry,) nephew of the preceding, born at Paris, professor of medicine and surgery, died at Rouen, Oct. 17, 1634, admired for his talents, but notorious for a fickleness and a spirit of intrigue that marred his fortune. He published several works, and among them a Latin translation of the Prognostics of Hippocrates. (Biog. Univ.)

His father, also named Henry, first taught philosophy at Paris, and afterwards practised medicine. He is thought to have died in 1613 or 1614. (Chalmers.)

BLACKWOOD, (Sir Henry, bart. K.C.B.) a brave and distinguished British admiral, sixth surviving son of Sir John Blackwood, bart., of Balliliedy, in the county of Down, by Dorcas, daughter of James Stevenson, Esq., created in the peerage of Ireland baroness Dufferin and Clanboyle, in 1800. He entered the navy in April 1781, being then eleven years old; officiated as senior lieutenant of the *Invincible*, (74,) in Howe's memorable defeat of the French revolutionary fleet; and upon the return into port of the victorious forces, received his commander's commission. In 1798, when captain of the *Brilliant*, (28,) he sustained for several hours a running fight, ably and resolutely conducted, with two formidable French frigates. His movements were no less ably executed, than boldly conceived and promptly adopted. Hence he finally escaped capture, after crippling his nearest and warmest pursuer, and coming off in the conflict the least sufferer. After this gallant and masterly defence, Blackwood removed into the *Penelope*, (36,) a frigate celebrated in the best days of naval discipline for her incomparable order, fighting efficiency, and the wondrous celerity with which she was wont to execute the heavy evolutions incidental to vessels of war. In this ship was assigned to Blackwood the special service of watching the French movements at Malta, particularly those of the *Guillaume Tell*, (86,) bearing the flag of admiral Decrés, who, after his timely flight from the battle of the Nile, found refuge in the port of Valetta. On the night of the 30th of March, 1800, the *Guillaume Tell*, taking advantage of a strong southerly wind, and the darkness that succeeded the setting of the moon, weighed and departed port. But the vigilance of Blackwood was not to be eluded. To his skill and daring in assailing singly and crippling, when far in advance of the pursuing force, the enemy's towering two-decker, may in a great measure be ascribed the capture of the finest battle-ship of her class afloat, and unquestionably the best fought, and, if we may be permitted the phrase, the most desperately defended vessel of war that ever bore the flag of France, whether under the royal or revolutionary banner.

After the short peace of Amiens, and the renewal of war with France, Blackwood became captain of the *Euryalus*, a new frigate of 36 guns. The signal service that he subsequently rendered to his country in that active and vigilant vessel, Nelson's *confiding* frigate, will be found fully recorded in the detailed accounts descriptive of the battle of Trafalgar. Still, as a matter unobserved by the chroniclers of that great and glorious achievement, it may be here stated, as a fact familiar to all serving in the British fleet, that on Blackwood's vigilance, his able and judicious guidance in leading the British force to the direct locality in which would be found that of the enemy awaiting battle, Nelson founded his fondest hope of fulfilling his anticipated triumph. "I rely on captain Blackwood," telegraphed the confiding chief, in the full face of the fleet, "to keep sight of the enemy during the night." This public declaration of reliance was seen flying in symbolic combinations at the mast head of the *Victory*, the flag-ship of the British chief, as the sun was sinking in the horizon on the eve preceding the eventful day which lost to the conjoined enemies of England a formidable force, and to England herself the greatest and most revered of her host of heroes.

In Marshall's Naval Biography, will be found, vol. i. part ii., Blackwood's recorded account of a conversation, highly interesting, that he had held with the heroic Nelson during the protracted period which had been occupied in closing with the Franco-Spanish force; an approach which had been rendered, by the lightness of the wind and the heaviness of the swell, annoyingly slow and sluggish. For four hours and upwards Blackwood and his brother officer Prowse, captain of the *Syrius* frigate, paced the poop of the *Victory*, holding occasional converse with the all-observing and inquiring chief on subjects connected with the coming fight. "I mean today," said Nelson, in a playful tone, "to bleed the captains of the frigates, as I shall keep you both on board until the very last minute." As soon, however, as the *Victory* came within range of the enemy's raking fire, and that straggling shot gave token of impending mischief, Blackwood and Prowse were directed to take to their respective boats, and to proceed along the column led by the commander-in-chief, more strenuously to impress upon the mind of those captains who were seen crowding canvas on their several vessels, that, if they found it impracticable to follow the prescribed order of battle, they were to adopt whatever method they thought best, provided that it led them quickly and closely alongside of the enemy. This injunction was no sooner delivered than Blackwood, taking the hand of his revered friend, expressed a hope "that on his return to the *Victory*, which would be as soon as he could possibly effect, he would find his lordship well, and in the possession of *twenty* prizes." To this heartfelt expression of hope was responded Nelson's unequivocal prediction of his own death, "*God bless you, Blackwood; I shall never speak to you again!*" Long before the action had terminated Blackwood proceeded in his boat, through the fire of both fleets, to obtain intelligence of Nelson's safety, and arrived in the cockpit of the *Victory* as the suffering and mutilated hero yielded his last breath.

The *Euryalus* soon after returned to England, and her commander had the melancholy satisfaction of taking a part in the procession at the public funeral of his late noble friend. On this occasion he acted as train-bearer to the chief mourner, Sir Peter Parker, admiral of the fleet. (Marshall.)

At the commencement of the ensuing year, our subject took command of the *Ajax*, of 80 guns, in which ship he accompanied Sir John T. Duckworth on the expedition against Constantinople; but unfortunately, at nine on the night of the 14th of July, 1807, that noble and efficient vessel was discovered to be on fire; and despite of the most energetic and daring efforts to stifle the conflagration, the destruction of the ship became inevitable. On the flames bursting up the main hatchway, thereby dividing the fore from the after part of the ship, Blackwood called to the people to go forward "and save themselves as fast as they could." No sooner had he reached the forecastle himself, than all parts of the vessel, abaft the centre of the booms, appeared in a raging flame. After exhorting the officers and men, to the number of 400, who were crowded around him, to be cool and collected, and to depend upon the boats of the squadron; and feeling that he could no longer render them the least possible service, he jumped overboard from the spritsail-yard. After struggling in the water for half an hour, he was picked up by one of the boats of the *Canopus*, and taken on board that ship in a state of great exhaustion. The *Ajax* burnt all night, and drifted on the island of Tenedos, where on the following morning, at five o'clock, she "blew up," producing a terrific explosion. Many lives were lost, and of those who escaped, some were so dreadfully scorched that they died after they had been brought on board the different ships attached to the squadron.

At the close of 1807, Blackwood was appointed to the *Warspite*, a new third-rate, fitting at Chatham; and in the summer of 1810 we find him, when in command of the inshore-squadron off Toulon, again contending with a powerfully superior force; and by his bold and spirited conduct, frustrating the designs of a French squadron, in their endeavour to cut off his old and favourite frigate (the *Euryalus*), together with the *Sheerwater* brig.

In 1814, Blackwood was appointed captain of the fleet assembled at Spithead, under the duke of Clarence, who hoisted his flag in the *Impregnable*, of 98 guns, in honour of the visit paid by the allied sovereigns to England. On the fourth of the following month, captain Blackwood was advanced to the rank of rear-admiral, and shortly after to the dignity of a baronet of Great Britain. In August 1819, he was nominated a K.C.B., and, about the same time, appointed commander-in-chief on the East India station. In December 1822, he returned to England. Sir Henry Blackwood was thrice married, and left a family; his eldest son being, like himself, a naval officer. He died at Balliliedy, his brother's paternal seat, in the north of Ireland, of typhus fever, December 17, 1832.

BLACKWOOD, (William,) an eminent Scottish publisher, remarkable for the Edinburgh magazine that bears his name. He was born in Edinburgh, November 20, 1776, of parents in a humbler station than that which he attained himself, but highly respectable, and careful to give him a good education. He early showed such a decided fondness for literature, that it was determined to bring him up for a bookseller. After passing through an apprenticeship in his native city, eagerly reading much that fell in his way, especially Scottish history and antiquities, he was employed both in Glasgow and London, and thus gained a knowledge of old books not often surpassed by persons of his class. In 1804 he settled himself in Edinburgh as a dealer in old books, but in 1816 he disposed of his stock, and undertook the business of a publisher. In 1817 he brought out his magazine, an excellent miscellany, which has been the vehicle for much agreeable writing, and for political principles at variance with those advocated in the great Whig periodical, the Edinburgh Review. Blackwood was firmly attached to the politics that were maintained in his magazine. He lost no opportunity of resisting the progress of such alleged reforms as he thought pernicious or deceptive, nor any of promoting the correction of practical evils. In his magazine he scarcely ever wrote himself, but it was conducted by him, and occupied so much of his time, that any other than a man of highly energetic character would have been found unequal to the task. Blackwood's private character was exemplary, and he was generally respected. After an illness of four months, attended with much severe suffering, he died at his house in Edinburgh, September 16, 1834. (Ann. Biog.)

BLADEN, (Martin,) known as an English translator of Cæsar. In his youth he served under the duke of Marlborough, and he became a lieutenant-colonel. In 1714 he was appointed comptroller of the Mint, and in 1717 a lord of trade, which he continued to be until his death, Feb. 14, 1746. He sate in nine parliaments. He married Frances Fouch, niece to a half-proprietor of the Aldborough Hatch estate, in the parish of Barking, Essex; and coming, by her, into possession of that property, he built upon it, in 1730, a capital mansion, at a great expense. He wrote two very indifferent dramas, Orpheus and Euridice, and Solon, which were printed in 1705 without his consent. His principal work, dedicated to the duke of Marlborough, was the Commentaries of C. Julius Cæsar made English from the original Latin, by Martin Bladen, Gent.; with the Life of Cæsar, Notes, and Sculptures from the Designs of Palladio, 8vo, Lond. 1705. Reprinted in the same form, 1712-15-19-26-32. A new edition was printed by Bowyer, the learned printer, in 1750, with notes of his own, marked *Typogr.* In 1753, this translation of Cæsar was superseded by that of Duncan. (Chalmers. Wright's Essex, ii. 483. Adam Clarke's Bibliog. Miscell.)

BLAEU, or BLAEUW, BLAUW, (William,) born at Alcmaer, in 1571; died at Amsterdam, 21st of October, 1638; a celebrated mathematician, surveyor, and publisher in that city. In astronomy he was the pupil of Tycho de Brahe; and as early as 1599 was employed in making terrestrial and celestial globes, and likewise large quadrants for the observatory at Leyden. About the year 1606 he discovered a star in the breast of the Swan. His claim, however, to this discovery has been partly disputed. In 1628 he surveyed the entire coast between the Texel and the Meuse, with a Rheinland rod of twelve feet in length, and took the latitudes with an instrument, having a diameter of twenty-eight feet, and a bend of twelve degrees. When Galileo, in 1637, undertook to prove the longitude of Jupiter's satellites, he was one of the four commissioners engaged by the states-general to inquire into it. The other three were Lawrence Reael, Martin Hortensius, and one Beckman. His principal employment consisted, however, in the construction of globes and publication of charts. We find him, as early as 1612, a printer and bookseller at Amsterdam; from his having commenced business under the name of Guiliemus Janssonius, he was confounded with the members of another printer's family at Amsterdam of the same name. This confusion might very well have been avoided, since none of those Jansons bore the name of William, which was always attached to his publications. The titles of his works are:—1. Zeespiegel, inhoudende een Rorte Onderwysinghe in de Konst der Zeevaart, en Beschryvinghe der Seen en Kusten van de Oostersche, Nordsche en Westersche Schipvaert, Amst. 1627, fol. 3 parts in one volume. Another similar edition was published in 1643. 2. Appendix Theatri Abr. Ortelii et Atlantis Ger. Mercatoris, continens Tabulas Geographicas diversarum Orbis Regionum, nunc primum editus cum Descriptionibus, Amst. 1631, fol. 3. Tweevondigh Onderwys van de Hemlesche en Aerdischen Globen, Amst. 1655, 4to. There are earlier editions of this work both in French and Latin. 4. Novus Atlas, in 6 vols, fol.

5. Tafilen van de Declinatie des Sons ende der vornaemste vaste Sterren, Amst. 1625, 8vo. 6. Theatrium Urbium et Munimentorum, Amst. 1619. 7. Four Letters to Professor Schichard, of Tubingen, during the years 1633 and 1634, printed in Ch. F. Schnurrer's Account of the Old Masters of Hebraic Literature, Ulm, 1792, 8vo, p. 256. (Ersch und Gruber.)

BLAEU, (John,) son of the preceding, born at Amsterdam, in the beginning of the seventeenth century. He applied himself to the study of law, in which he obtained a doctor's degree, without, however, abandoning the business of his father. After he finished his studies he went to Italy, and on his return to Amsterdam, established a printing house, in which we find him actively engaged as early as 1637. His business, like that of his father, consisted chiefly in the printing and publishing of geographical and topographical works and charts, by which he acquired great reputation. He quickly took precedence of the rival establishment of the Jansons. His first publications were the first and second volumes of his father's Atlases, (mentioned in the foregoing article.) After his death he brought out the third volume, in connexion with his brother Cornelius, whom, in 1640, he had taken into partnership; and his brother dying in 1642, he published alone the remainder of the work. Afterwards he immediately engaged in the production of a far more numerous and beautiful collection of charts, which appeared in 1662 with a Latin text, under the title of Atlas Major. This work assisted greatly in the diffusion of geographical knowledge. About the same time he projected a series of topographical engravings, on a most extensive plan, the first of which was entitled, Theatrum Urbium Belgicæ. Like most of the Dutch publishers of that period, he was very extensively engaged in foreign business, and from 1663 he possessed an establishment at Vienna. On the night of the 22d of February, 1672, his printing-house, the greater part of his publications, and nearly all the plates belonging to his geographical and topographical works, were destroyed by fire. The old man did not long survive this calamity; he died in 1680. His works are as follows:—1. Novum ac Magnum Theatrum Urbium Belgicæ Regiæ et Fœderatæ, Amst. 1649, fol. 2 vols. 2. Atlas Major, seu Cosmographia Blaeuiana, qua Solum, Cœlum accuratissime describuntur, Amst. 1662, fol. 11 vols. 3. Le Grand Atlas, ou Cosmographie Blaviance, en laquelle est exactement descritte la Terre, la Mer, et le Ciel, Amst. 1663, fol. 12 vols. 4. Atlas Mayor, Geographia Blaviana que contiene las Cartas y Descripciones de todas las Partes del Mondo, Amst. 1659-72, fol. 10 vols. 5. Theatrum Civitatum et Admirandorum Italiæ, Amst. 1663, fol. 2 vols. 6. Theatrum Civitatum et Admirandorum Neapolis et Siciliæ Regnorum, Amst. no date, fol. 7. Theatrum Statuum Sabaudiæ Ducis, Pedemontii Principis, Cypri Regis, Amst. 1682, fol. 2 vols. 8. Nouveau Théâtre d'Italie, Amst. 1704, fol. 4 vols. 9. Théâtre des Etats de Savoye et du Piémont, (traduit par Jac. Bernard,) Haye, 1700, fol. 2 vols. (Ersch und Gruber.)

BLAGDEN, (Sir Charles,) a celebrated English physician and chemist, born April 17, 1748. He lived on terms of intimacy with the chief scientific men of his day, and particularly with Sir Joseph Banks, bart., for nearly half a century, and was for many years one of the secretaries of the Royal Society. His inclination led him to the study of medicine; and having attended the usual lectures and practice, he took his doctor's degree at Edinburgh in 1768, and afterwards printed his thesis on this occasion, De Causis Apoplexiæ. He then entered the army, in which he served as a physician for many years, rose to a high situation, and acquired a considerable fortune, which was greatly increased by a legacy, amounting, it is said, to 16,000*l*., bequeathed to him by his friend, the celebrated chemist, Cavendish. He travelled a good deal in America, Italy, and Germany, and towards the latter part of his life he usually passed some months in each year at Paris, where he rendered much service to science by cultivating the offices of good fellowship, by letters of introduction, and by his advice to the *savans* of the two nations. He died suddenly from an effusion in the brain, March 26, 1820, at Arceuil, in the residence of the renowned chemist, count Berthollet.

Sir Charles Blagden's writings are to be found in various volumes of the Philosophical Transactions, and they treat of subjects of considerable interest, relating to the animal economy and to the physical sciences. His experiments in a heated room were made with Dr. George Fordyce, the Hon. Capt. Phipps, Sir Joseph Banks, and Dr. Solander. These gentlemen breathed an atmosphere of a temperature from 150 to 210 degrees of Fahrenheit without much inconvenience. His papers are as follow:—Experiments and Observations in a Heated Room; On the Heat of the Water in the Gulph Stream; History of the Congelation of Quicksilver; Proceedings relating to the Accident by Lightning at Heckingham; An Account of some Fiery Meteors, and Observations; Some Observations on Ancient Inks, with the Proposal of a New Method of Recovering the Legibility of Decayed Writings; Experiments on the Cooling of Water below its Freezing Point; Experiments on the Effects of various Substances in Lowering the Point of Congelation in Water; Report on the best Method of Proportioning the Excise upon Spirituous Liquors; Supplementary ditto; Some Account of the Tide at Naples; Appendix to Mr. Ware's Paper on Vision, relative to the Near and Distant Sight of different Persons.

BLAGRAVE, (John,) an early English mathematician, of considerable eminence, second son of John Blagrave, of Bulmarsh-court, Sunning, Berks, educated at Reading school, and St. John's college, Oxford, where he applied himself chiefly to the mathematics. Hence he retired to Southcote, in the parish of St. Mary's, Reading, where he built a manor-house, and spent the rest of his days. After a life of study and seclusion, but of active benevolence, he died in August 1611, and was buried at Reading, in the church of St. Lawrence, where a sumptuous monument was erected to his memory. His works are:—1. The Mathematical Jewel, fol. Lond. 1585; a very curious work. 2. Of the Making and Use of the Familiar Staffe, 4to, Lond. 1590. 3. Astrolabium Uranicum Generale, 4to, Lond. 1596. From this work it appears that Blagrave was a convert to the heliocentric theory of Copernicus. 4. The Art of Dialling, 4to, Lond. 1609. Besides these works, a large MS. volume in his autograph, on mathematical subjects, is preserved in the archiepiscopal library at Lambeth. (Wood's Athenæ. Hutton's Dictionary. Halliwell's Collection of Scientific Letters. Lysons's Berkshire.)

BLAGRAVE, (Sir John,) thought to be of the same family, a learned lawyer, who wrote upon the stat. 32 Hen. VIII., concerning jointures, a work that has been published. (Biog. Brit.)

BLAGRAVE, (Joseph,) an astrological writer, born in the parish of St. Giles's, Reading, in 1610, but not, it is thought, of the celebrated mathematician's family, there having been another of that name in Berkshire. He published The Astrological Practice of Physic, 1682, a large supplement to Culpepper's Herbal, and some other works. He died in 1679. (Biog. Brit. Chalmers. Lysons's Berkshire, 345.)

BLAINVILLE, (Charles H.) a Parisian musical performer and teacher, who died about 1768, after publishing the following compilations, which are but little esteemed:—Essai sur un Troisième Mode, 1750. Harmonie Theorico-pratique, 1751. Esprit de l'Art Musical, 1754. Hist. Générale, Critique et Philologique de la Musique, 1761. (Biog. Univ. Suppl.)

BLAIR, (John,) a Latin poet, born in Scotland, in the thirteenth century, educated at the school of Dundee with Sir William Wallace, whose death has cast an everlasting stain on the memory of Edward I., king of England. On leaving school, Blair went to Paris to study theology, became a monk of the order of St. Benedict, and changed his name of John into that of Arnold. On his return to Scotland, he went to reside at the monastery of Dumferling, where he remained till the year 1294, when Wallace having been appointed governor of the kingdom, Blair became his chaplain. He wrote the History of his Life, in 1327, in Latin verse; a fragment only of this poem remains in the Cottonian library, which was published in 1705, by Sir Robert Sibbald, the celebrated botanist. It is translated in Hume's History of the Douglases. The time of this author's death is unknown.

BLAIR, (James,) a Scottish divine, ordained and beneficed in the episcopal church of his own country, but he quitted it for England about the end of Charles the Second's reign. Becoming known to Compton, bishop of London, he was by him, in 1685, sent to Virginia as a missionary, and four years after appointed his commissary. In this character he formed the project of establishing a college at Williamsburgh, for the propagation of the gospel; for this purpose, in 1693, he returned to England to solicit assistance from the government. Having succeeded, his institution was called William and Mary college, and he was appointed its president. This office he retained nearly fifty years. He died in 1743, leaving four volumes of discourses explanatory of our Saviour's Sermon on the Mount, Lond. 1742; to a second edition of which Dr. Waterland wrote an eulogetic preface.

BLAIR, (Patrick,) originally a medical practitioner at Dundee, in Scotland, first known by an account of the dissection of an elephant which died there in 1706, published in the Philosophical Transactions in 1710. It contains an accurate description of the proboscis, and confirms, Haller says, the opinion already entertained, that the elephant has no gall-bladder. The intelligent anatomist was a nonjuror; and in the rebellion of 1715, he was imprisoned as an adherent to the Stuarts. He afterwards came to London, where he republished his Anatomy of the Elephant, 4to; and in 1718 he produced Miscellaneous Observations on the Practice of Physic, Surgery, and Botany, 8vo. In 1720 he published Botanical Essays, 8vo, in which he treats of the sexes of plants, confirming his arguments in proof of them by sound reasoning and some new experiments. It is a work yet valued by botanists. Blair eventually settled at Boston, in Lincolnshire, and there published his Pharmaco-Botanologia, an alphabetical and classical dissertation on all the British indigenous and garden plants of the London dispensatory, 4to, 1723-28. This work, which only reached the letter H, introduces some plants discovered by the author near Boston. There are also some other papers of his in the Philosophical Transactions. The time of his death is unknown. (Rees.)

BLAIR, (Robert,) a Scottish poet and divine, born in 1699, who died at Athelstaneford, East Lothian, where he was settled as minister, Feb. 4, 1747. He was descended from a namesake, chaplain to king Charles the First, from whom also Dr. H. Blair was descended in a different line. Robert Blair, one of his sons, president of the Court of Session, died in 1811. The minister is known to the public by his poem called the Grave, which at first attracted no great notice, but having become popular, has been often reprinted. Its numerous defects render it, however, a piece in no high estimation with the more discerning readers. It was first printed in 1743, at London.

BLAIR, (John,) a learned Scotch chronologer, born in the beginning of the eighteenth century, at Edinburgh, which he soon left for London, where he became usher at a school. In 1754 he published, by subscription, his celebrated work, dedicated to the lord chancellor Hardwick, entitled the Chronology and History of the World, from the Creation to the year of Christ 1753, illustrated by 56 tables, &c. &c.; in which he follows the disputed reckoning of the Hebrew text. This work was partly projected by his relative, Hugh Blair. The applause with which it was received, procured to Blair, in 1755, the honour of being elected fellow of the Royal Society; two years after of being appointed chaplain to the dowager princess of Wales, and mathematical tutor to the duke of York; and in 1761, fellow of the Antiquarian Society. He was also advanced to a prebendal stall at Westminster, with other preferments. In 1763 he attended his royal pupil on a continental tour, and on his return to England, published a second edition of his Chronology. The death of his brother, captain Blair, who fell in battle, at sea, in 1782, seems to have accelerated his death, which took place on the following June. A course of lectures on the Canon of the Old Testament was published after his death.

BLAIR, (Hugh, D.D.) a Scottish divine, born April 7, 1718, at Edinburgh, where his father was a merchant, educated at the university of that city, A.M. 1739, but his degree of D.D. was conferred upon him by the university of St. Andrew's. He was licensed to preach in 1741, and his first living was the parish of Colessie, in Fife. In 1743 he was appointed second minister of the Canongate church; in 1754 he was removed to Lady Yester's, one of the city churches; and in 1758 to the High Church (or ancient cathedral) of Edinburgh, which appointment he held till his death, December 27, 1800. In 1759 he read a course of lectures on the art and graces of composition, in the college at Edinburgh, which gave great satisfaction, insomuch that George III. was persuaded to institute and endow a professorship of rhetoric and the belles-lettres, and to appoint Dr. Blair the first professor. These lectures were afterwards published, are still in considerable repute, and will no doubt be the work by which the author will be known in aftertimes. The works, however, from which he, during his lifetime, derived the greatest fame and profit, were his Sermons, which it was the fashion to admire in the last century. On the composition of these celebrated productions the author had unquestionably expended much labour; every sentence is evidently elaborated with the most patient care, as may be perceived by comparing the successive editions of them. Polished, indeed, as marble, but also as lifeless and as cold, they had this very extraordinary (some will think very undesirable) recommendation, that they were alike acceptable to persons of every shade of religious opinion or doctrine. They are, in fact, principally discourses on moral subjects, with but few allusions to the peculiar doctrines of Christianity. They passed through four editions in the lifetime of the author, and have been republished since.

BLAIR, (William,) an English surgeon, born in Essex in 1765, and originally educated for the church; but feeling inclined towards medical science, he studied under Mr. John Pearson, and by him was made house-surgeon to the Lock Hospital. He had considerable attainments, was a good surgeon, and a benevolent man. Hence he took an active part in organizing several of the London charitable institutions. He was a zealous promoter of vaccination, and a warm supporter of the Bible Society. This led him into a correspondence, which he published, on the formation, objects, and plan of the Roman-Catholic Bible Society, with Mr. Charles Butler. He died suddenly, Dec. 6, 1822, at his house in Bloomsbury, of an affection of the heart, of the nature of which he had long been fully cognizant, and the knowledge of which he bore with great piety and resignation. Besides furnishing many papers to the Memoirs of the Medical Society of London, in the well-known engraving of which he is represented, he published several works, among which may be enumerated, The Soldier's Friend, or the Means of Preserving the Health of Military Men, Lond. 1798, 12mo. Essays on the Venereal Disease, Lond. 1798—1800, 8vo. This was translated into German by C. A. Struve, Altemb. 1799; Glogau, 1801. Anthropology, Lond. 1803, 8vo. The Vaccine Contest, Lond. 1806, 8vo. Letter to Dr. Jenner on the Supposed Failures of Vaccination, Lond. 1808, 8vo. Essays on the Venereal Disease and its Treatment, intended to ascertain the Effects of Nitrous Acid and other analogous Remedies, lately proposed as Substitutes for Mercury, Lond. 1808, 8vo. Prostitutes reclaimed and Penitents protected, being an Answer to some Objections against the Female Penitentiary, Lond. 1809, 8vo. Strictures on Mr. Hale's Reply to the Pamphlets lately published in Defence of the Female Penitentiary, Lond. 1810, 8vo. The Pastor and Deacon examined, or Remarks on the Rev. J. Thomas's Appeal in Vindication of Mr. Hale's Character, Lond. 1810, 8vo.

BLAISE, a Romish saint, bishop of Sebaste, in Armenia, martyred by Agricola, governor of Cappadocia and of the Lesser Armenia, about the year 316. His fame is of long standing in the East; but the West cared little or nothing for him until an importation of his relics by the crusaders. These acquired a high character for miraculous cures, especially of children and cattle. His acts, written in Greek, have a very slender authority. (Moreri. Biog. Univ.)

BLAISE, a Romish saint, bishop of Oreto, in Spain, a town no longer to be found, martyred at Cifuentes under Nero. Lovers of relics might see his head both at Lerma and Toledo. (Moreri.)

BLAISE, (Bartholomew,) a French sculptor, born at Lyons in 1718, and educated for his profession there and in Italy. He went subsequently to Paris, and established a high reputation. In 1787 he was employed by the family of the count de Vergennes to execute a monument to his memory. It was scarcely finished when the revolution broke out, and it was not erected until 1818. While public terror was at its height, Blaise lived retired at Poissy. Afterwards he was employed by the government upon many important works. He died at Paris, in April 1819. (Biog. Univ. Suppl.)

BLAKE, (Robert,) a famous naval chieftain in the time of Oliver Cromwell, born at Bridgewater, in Somersetshire, A.D. 1594, the eldest son of Humphry Blake, of an ancient family, who having acquired a considerable fortune as a Spanish merchant, purchased a small estate in that neighbourhood. Robert having received the rudiments of his education at a free-school in Bridgewater, entered at St. Alban's hall, Oxford, in 1615, and removed subsequently to Wadham college. He proceeded B.A. Feb. 10, 1617. In 1619 he stood unsuccessfully for a fellowship at Merton college. He had failed of obtaining a studentship of Christchurch, while an undergraduate. In 1623 he wrote a copy of verses on the death of Camden; and soon afterwards leaving the university, he returned to his native town, where for a considerable time he quietly resided on his paternal estate. His temper was naturally severe, his politics inclining to republicanism, and his religion to puritanism. In 1640 accordingly the discontented party in Bridgewater returned him to represent that borough in parliament; but a speedy dissolution afforded him no opportunity of trying his oratorical powers; and when the Long Parliament was elected, he was not returned.

On the breaking out of the civil war, he entered the parliamentary army, and rapidly became a captain of dragoons. When prince Rupert laid siege to Bristol, a fort within the line of defence had been entrusted to Blake. This redoubt he bravely and unflinchingly defended, and held for a considerable time after the town had capitulated. This "act of obstinacy," as designated by the victor, produced a threat to hang the commander of the fort; but friends interposed, and pleaded in excuse Blake's total inexperience in the recognised rules of war. Attaining the rank of lieutenant-colonel, he subsequently served in Somersetshire; and for his bold defence of Taunton against two successive sieges in 1645, obtained a parliamentary grant of 500*l*. In February 1649, colonel Blake, in conjunction with two officers of the same rank, Deane and Popham, was appointed to command the parliamentary fleet, for few of the small number of sea officers who had been employed in the royal service were then retained in stations afloat involving responsibility and trust; and upon this subject it may be here mentioned that all historians, early and modern, have observed a silence highly reprehensible in public chroniclers,—"blinking," as it were, a matter calculated so materially to affect the guidance and governance of vessels of war. True it is, (though few are possessed of the fact,) that when the progress of naval warfare rendered necessary an improved manifestation of nautical skill, a class of mariner sprung up, designated "the sea captain," a sort of *quasi* officer in war, and a trader or private adventurer in peace. Still did the principal command afloat devolve upon a land officer, whose pretensions to sustain the station of a naval chief were usually founded upon his experience in courts and camps, or sometimes, as in the case of Blake, his aptitude for field tactics, and dexterity in executing cavalry evolutions, as if squadrons of horse and squadrons of ships were to be moved by similar means. In short, the sea officer, from the circumstance of his holding no commission, nor enjoying aught of military rank, was merely looked upon in the light of a subordinate drudge, a sort of *driver* "driver," to move and direct the massive machine. Nevertheless, it must be said of Blake, that of all the "sailor-soldiers" who for so many years had contrived to reap laurels afloat, he unquestionably evinced the quickest capacity in the acquirement of nautical knowledge: and certes, to him is due the credit of being the first to bring artillery afloat to face fortresses and contend with batteries ashore.

Passing over the several services Blake had rendered to the parliamentary cause, in subduing the royalists and defeating them in their different strongholds, and his persevering pursuit of prince Rupert,—services already recorded in our memoir of Sir George Ayscough,—we shall trace him to the period in which he was about to follow a more glorious career, namely, to battle with the legitimate enemies of his country. This was preparatory to an expected rupture with Holland. In March, 1652, he received an appointment, limiting him for "nine months" as chief in command of the force employed in the narrow seas. In the following May hostilities with Holland commenced, arising out of an act of aggression on the part of Van Tromp, who thought proper to return shotted broadsides to single unshotted guns, fired with a view of reminding the Dutch admiral of the tribute of respect usually observed to the English flag. The action that ensued took place in the straits of Dover; and though Tromp sought to annihilate Blake's ship, still, by the timely succour of a squadron under major Bourne, the British chief defeated the Dutch admiral, capturing one vessel of war, and sinking another. On the news of this action arriving in Holland, the States were thrown into a violent consternation, and immediately despatched Pensionary de Paauw as their ambassador-extraordinary to the commonwealth of England, directing him to lay before the council the narrative which Tromp had sent of the battle. They entreated the English, by all the bonds of their common religion and common liberties, not to precipitate themselves into hostile measures, but to appoint commissioners, who should examine every circumstance of the action, and point out the aggressor. But the demands of the English parliament were not of a nature calculated to lead to satisfactory results; consequently negotiation ceased, and on the June following, war was declared by Holland. Meanwhile Blake amply avenged the premature aggression of Tromp, for in a few weeks he had made capture of some forty sail of Hollanders, homeward bound and richly laden. On the 28th of September, the hostile fleets again met; that of the Dutch under Cornelius De Witt, for popular clamour in Holland had already compelled Tromp to throw up his command. Judging dispassionately from the undisputed facts established by the principals engaged on both sides, and rejecting, as conflicting, confused, and in some instances unintelligible, much of the *detailed* matter which Heath, Burchett, Campbell, and others of the older chroniclers have severally put forth descriptive of this struggle in the "narrow seas," it is manifest to every mariner competent to pronounce an opinion upon the subject, that from the incautious and *blind* manner in which many of Blake's vessels bore up to attack the Dutch force in its sheltered position under the lee of the Goodwin Sands, there must have been a sad deficiency of nautical experience in the English fleet, as well as a deplorable unacquaintance with the shoals and shallows in the vicinity of the Kentish coast. Nevertheless British valour prevailed. The Dutch, in addition to the capture of a rear-admiral, had three ships sunk and one blown up. After pursuing the defeated fleet to the very mouth of their own harbour (Goree), where it eventually found refuge, Blake returned in triumph to the Downs, and from thence to the river, "having had about 300 men killed, and as many wounded." For this service, he, together with his officers, received from the republican parliament a vote of thanks. After this battle, the necessity of detaching small squadrons on different services of a pressing nature reduced the main fleet under Blake to about thirty-seven sail; and with this force he resumed his station in the Downs. Apprized of the reduced force of his late opponent, Van Tromp, who was again invested with the command of the Dutch fleet, put to sea, for the express purpose of annihilating the force under the brave Blake. On the 29th of November the Dutch fleet approached the English coast in the vicinity of Dover. Blake, after holding a council of war, resolved not to refuse battle, notwithstanding the great inequalities of the two fleets; but a fresh gale and a tossing sea, induced both belligerents "to defer fighting till the next day." In the morning both fleets (doubtless to gain something of sea-room) worked to the westward, that of the British maintaining the weather-gauge. About eleven in the forenoon the battle began with great fury. Blake, in the *Triumph*, with his seconds, the *Victory* and *Vanguard*, was for a long time assailed by an overpowering division of the Dutch fleet; but the seasonable intervention of friends rescued the British chief and his gallant supporters from their perilous plight. In this encounter the English had two ships taken and four destroyed, and the rest were so shattered in their hulls, and cut up in their spars and rigging, that they were compelled to take shelter in the Thames. This advantage over Blake, small as it was, when his opponent's vast superiority of force is taken into account, produced throughout Holland a feeling of proud exultation; and such was the idle bravado of Van Tromp, that he is said to have sailed down Channel with a broom at his mast-head, insinuating, by the exhibition of a symbol at once vulgar and vaunting, that he had swept the seas of the vessels of the English. But this insult, as it will presently appear, was not long unresented.

All the homeward-bound trade of Holland was appointed to rendezvous at the Isle of Rhe, in the Bay of Biscay; thither Van Tromp and De Ruyter, who was now the second in command, with their formidable and victorious fleet, repaired to escort them home. Impatient to "wipe off the disgrace" which their arms had sustained, the English parliament exerted every endeavour to collect their naval force from all quarters. At the request of Blake, general Monk was sent for from Scotland to join in the command; and Deane was to act as rear-admiral of a formidable fleet, fitted and assembled with unusual celerity. This force sailed from the Downs before Van Tromp had time to "return from the bay," (Biscay.) The Dutch admiral was not a little surprised to see so powerful a navy drawn up to receive him off Portland, for the British force was now equal to that which was led by Van Tromp. The latter had seventy-six vessels of war, and was escorting about three hundred sail of merchantmen. As the day dawned, on the 18th of Feb. 1653, the English descried the Dutch fleet to leeward, steering along the coast of France, in the vicinity of Cape la Hogue, and immediately bore up, shaping a course to bring the enemy to battle.

The fight which ensued was the most curious that had been fought between the naval forces of the rival republics. Almost at the first onset, Blake received a wound in the thigh, and his captain (Ball,) and his secretary (Sparrow,) were both slain by his side. In this long and obstinate contest, for it occupied an interval of three days, the English had sunk one ship of war, the *Samson*; and the Dutch lost eleven fighting vessels, and had taken from them thirty sail of merchantmen. The number slain on each side is said to have amounted to fifteen hundred; a loss of life of most unusual amount in naval battles. In this action Blake for the first time made use of small arms, having embarked a considerable number of troops, who acted in the capacity of marines, and whose fire from musketry is said to have done great execution. On the 2d and 3d of June another great battle ensued between Van Tromp and generals Monk and Deane. On the first day the Dutch had the advantage; on the second, the timely arrival of Blake, with a reinforcement of eighteen sail, turned the scale in favour of the English. When Cromwell dissolved the Long Parliament and assumed the office of Protector, Blake, though in principles a staunch republican, readily recognised the new government. "It is not *our* business," said he, addressing his officers, "to mind state affairs, but to keep *foreigners from fooling us*." He sat in the first two parliaments summoned by the Protector, who always treated him with great respect. Nor in his selection of able and efficient men was Cromwell's penetration at all at fault, when, in 1655, he despatched Blake to the Mediterranean, with a commanding force to uphold the honour of the English flag, and demand reparation for injuries done to the English trade. The duke of Tuscany yielded to the demands of the British chief; and the piratical states of Algiers and Tripoli, terrified into submission, promised to abstain from further depredations. The dey of Tunis alone resisted, and, in answer to Blake's demand of satisfaction for the depredations committed on the commerce of England, replied, "Look at our castles of Goletta and Porto Ferino, we do not fear you; you may do your worst." Blake immediately entered the bay of Porto Ferino, and brought his squadron within musket-shot abreast of the fort, which by the fire of his ships was soon reduced to a defenceless state, following up the blow by the despatching of his boats manned and armed to board and burn the pirate's "capital ships," nine in number.

On the breaking out of the war between Spain and England, in 1656, Blake was sent with a fleet of forty sail to blockade Cadiz, and to "intercept the galleons" on their return home. The latter, however, was performed, in his absence, by a squadron under the orders of commodore Stayner. In the same year, having obtained intelligence that another "plate fleet" had put into the harbour of Santa Cruz, in the island of Teneriff, he immediately proceeded thither, and on his arrival discovered the galleons, six in number, with ten other vessels, lying in the harbour. The galleons' draught of water prevented them being moored *within* the boom which had been placed across the entrance of the port in its narrowest part. The entire anchorage was well fortified, being defended by a strong castle, well supplied with artillery, and seven formidable forts, united by a line of communication, "manned with musqueteers." The Spanish governor considered his dispositions so well made, and the vessels in the port so well secured, that when the master of a Dutch ship desired permission to put to sea, in order to avoid the assault of Blake, the Spaniard made answer, in a confident tone, "Get you gone, if you please, and let Blake come, if he dare." The English chief, after reconnoitring the position of the enemy's vessels, and their means of defence, and seeing the impracticability of bringing them *out*, called a council of war, at which it was resolved to attempt their destruction. Stayner, who had been so successful in the preceding year, was entrusted to lead this daring enterprise. With a small squadron he forced his passage into the bay, while another division of vessels kept up a cannonade on the forts and castle. Stayner's squadron was quickly supported by Blake, with the main portion of the fleet; "the wind seconded his courage," and blowing full into the bay, in a moment brought them among the thickest of the enemy. After a brave resistance of four hours, the Spaniards yielded to the intrepidity of the assailants, and abandoned their ships, which were set on fire, and consumed with all their treasure. "It is here necessary to mention a circumstance which has exposed this celebrated affair to much professional remark, both at the time it occurred, and ever since. It is stated that the direction of the wind, which prevented Blake from bringing his prizes out, would have prevented him from getting out himself, but for its sudden veering to the south-west; a change of very rare occurrence at that time of the year. Should this latter assertion be true, it must be confessed that this daring attack wears the appearance of a trusting to contingency, or bare possibility, which must be deemed rash in the extreme; and so it has been frequently termed by authors of considerable reputation. Unhappily the gallant performer of the exploit died before he reached his native land, which deprived the world of his own explanation of the affair; but as the bay of Santa Cruz is open, without any difficulty in the egress, we cannot help suspecting that the land breeze, which so timely carried him out, was not so unusual as here represented; and that he rested upon a feasible exertion of skill and seamanship, and not upon an interference in his favour so apparently special, that it might almost be deemed miraculous. The writer of the account whence we gather this narration, (Heath's Chronicles,) directly attributes this change of wind to Providence, which leaves Blake's professional prudence in great jeopardy, as he could have scarcely looked forward to such an interposition. Is it not more probable, that a man who united so much coolness and judgment to undaunted resolution saw many things possible which were invisible to less gifted eyes? When a man of invention and enterprise ventures boldly, and is uniformly successful, it is both more generous and more just to attribute the success to his superior capacity, than to dwell invidiously upon apparent temerity, or surprising good fortune. Every case no doubt is, strictly speaking, individual, and must rest upon its own merits; but the naval annals of Britain would have been very different from what they are, had a too calculating spirit of caution been prevalent in those whose deeds they record." When the news of this success reached the Protector, he caused the parliament, then sitting, to appoint a day of general thanksgiving—a ring of five hundred pounds value was voted to the commander-in-chief—a present of one hundred pounds to the captain that brought the news,—and also to be transmitted a public expression of thanks "to all the officers and seamen concerned in the action." This was the last, and, as having to contend with batteries, was the cherished achievement of the renowned Blake. Shortly after he again cruised before the harbour of Cadiz, when "finding his ships become foul," and that his own health and spirits wore away, he resolved to sail for England. By this time he was languishing under an inveterate scurvy, attended with dropsy. In his passage home he became worse; and as he perceived his end approaching, his inquiries touching the probable time of "making the land" were frequent, and, indeed, anxious in the extreme, it being his most ardent desire "to breathe out his last in his native country." But the great Disposer of all events ruled it otherwise. He died, as his ship (the *St. George*) entered Plymouth Sound, on the 17th of August, 1657, in the 59th year of his age. "The next day after his death his body was embalmed, and wrapped in lead; his bowels taken out and buried in the great church at Plymouth; and his corpse, by order of the Protector, was conveyed by water to Greenwich, and from thence carried, with great funeral pomp, to Westminster Abbey, where it was interred. It is melancholy to be obliged to add, that at the Restoration the shadowy honour of an interment in the Abbey was no longer to be allowed to this great commander, whose body was dug up, with those of Cromwell, Ireton, and many more. Some distinction was, however, made; the remains of Blake were decently reinterred in St. Margaret's churchyard, while the bones of the others were treated with the greatest ignominy. The propriety of this transaction as regards Blake was questioned at the time, even among the friends to the Restoration; at present it will be regarded with unmixed disgust. The naval services of this valiant man were so truly national,—he had done so much to render the power and character of his country respected, and in such strict accordance with the ideas entertained of public duty on all sides,—that any manifestation of disrespect to the remains of so illustrious a patriot was as revolting to good feeling as to good policy."

BLAKE, (Thomas,) an English puritan divine, born in Staffordshire, 1597; died June 1657; he took orders, and (Wood states) had some clerical duty, but of what description does not appear. In 1648 he sided with the parliament, and subscribed the covenant, after which he was minister of St. Alcmonds, Shrewsbury, and from thence "received a call" to Tamworth, Staffordshire, where he continued till his decease. He was one of the committee for the ejection of ignorant and scandalous ministers and schoolmasters. He wrote several controversial treatises on Infant Baptism; Vindiciæ Fœderis, a Treatise of the Covenant of God with Mankind, 1653, 4to; The Covenant Sealed; Living Truth in Dying Times, and other Sermons.

BLAKE, (Joachim,) a Spanish general, celebrated in Bonaparte's war upon the Peninsula. His family was Irish, originally from Galway; his father was a merchant, and he was himself born at Velez Malaga. Having served from his youth with credit in the army, he became commander-in-chief of the Galician forces in 1808; and if his counsels had prevailed with Cuesta, he would have prevented the loss of the battle of Medina del Rio Seco, July 14 in that year, which Napoleon considered as important to the interests of his brother Joseph, as the victory of Almanza had been to those of Philip V. Blake, after this disastrous engagement, which really did make the Spaniards doubt their ability to cope with French tactics in the field, withdrew to the mountains in front of Galicia, where he maintained himself and reorganized his forces. In the various events which agitated Spain in consequence of Napoleon's unprincipled invasion, he subsequently played a conspicuous part; but it was his misfortune to be in command at Valencia, when Suchet besieged that city at the close of 1811, and he was under the necessity of surrendering at discretion, Jan. 9, 1812, thus yielding to the French arms various acquisitions of the highest importance. He was then sent into France, and confined in the castle of Vincennes until the imperial government was overthrown. After receiving some marks of esteem from the emperor Alexander, he returned into Spain, and was appointed director-general of the engineers. This post he held until 1820, when he exchanged it for one in the council of state. The political changes brought about by the French army in 1823, proved highly disadvantageous to him. He was obnoxious to the absolute party, then dominant, and had much difficulty in obtaining his *purification*. He died at Valladolid, in 1827. He had much military knowledge, and was quite equal to discern beforehand the best modes of conducting a campaign, but he wanted quickness under the difficulties of an action, and the art of gaining a powerful hold upon the mental organization of his men. (Alison's Hist. Fr. Rev. vi. 707; viii. 257. Biog. Univ. Suppl.)

BLAKE, (William,) an English engraver, who died August 13, 1827, aged 68. His works, which are chiefly book-plates, gained him great credit; but his habits, though strongly marked by piety and intelligence, were eccentric: hence he lived and died in deep poverty. (Ann. Biog.)

BLAKENEY, (Lord,) an illustrious English general, born, 1672, at Mount Blakeney, in the county of Limerick, the ancient seat of his family. He entered the military service of his sovereign in the beginning of queen Anne's reign, and served as a subaltern at the siege of Venlo. Though admitted by all his superiors to be an officer of no ordinary merit, his professional advancement was long retarded; and, but for the duke of Richmond's influence, it seems probable that his services would not have procured for him the command of a regiment. He subsequently served in the capacity of brigadier-general at Carthagena, and gallantly led the assault of Boca-Chica. In 1745, his conduct and courage in the defence of Stirling Castle against the rebels "and their French auxiliaries, won for him general applause; yet," says Entick, "his great merit and unblemished character could obtain for him nothing better in the decline of life, when old age had borne hard upon him, than a command on the island of Minorca, where he was compelled to reside several years as lieutenant-governor." This post he filled when a French army, in April 1756, under marshal Richelieu, with a fleet commanded by de la Galissonnière, commenced operations against that island. But the British ministry, though warned of its danger, were regardless of its defence. Blakeney himself thus addresses Mr. Fox:—"I can't be too early in acquainting you, sir, that by different informations from France and Spain, there is great reason to believe the French intend very shortly to make an attack upon this island. In consequence I've called a council of war, and we were unanimously of opinion, that considering who these informations came from, and the reports every where about, which seemed to tally with them, this island ought, with the greatest speed, to be put in the best state of defence it can; and I am accordingly applying myself to every measure I think for the safety and defence of this place."

Such advices proving fruitless, a force fifteen thousand strong was able to debark upon the island before even the unfortunate Byng had been despatched from Spithead. After the French had spent twenty days upon the siege of fort St. Philip, and the garrison had been reduced to two thousand five hundred men, Richelieu, pushing matters with the utmost vigour, determined to carry the castle by assault.

The besieged behaved like heroes, disputing the ground inch by inch; but after much execution, by the fire on both sides, one redoubt was taken by assault, another by escalade. British resistance was, however, spiritedly continued, until the besiegers obtained a cessation of arms, under colour of burying their dead, which, indeed, lay in heaps about the place of action. But their chief object was, to snatch an opportunity to secure the lodgments that they had made, by introducing into them a considerable number of troops, through a subterranean passage, which had been opened by a shell, and not discovered by the besieged till the day had cleared up, and then it was too late to dispute its possession with the enemy.

By this passage the enemy might proceed to all the other "subterraneous" communications with the out-works, which, for want of numbers, the garrison was not in a condition to defend. The governor, therefore, during the cessation of arms, held a council of war; the majority of which, having duly considered all circumstances, declared for a capitulation. The minority argued that, as the garrison was very little diminished, was still in high spirits, and in want of nothing,—that, as there was no breach made by the enemy in the *body* of the castle, nor a single cannon erected to batter in breach,—that, as the loss of an outwork was never deemed a sufficient reason for surrendering a fortress of such strength and importance,—that, as the counterscarp was so well secured, by its rocky foundation, as not to be taken otherwise than by assault, which would cost the enemy more men than in their last attempt,—that, as the counterscarp must be taken before the enemy could attack the ditch, or batter in breach, and they must have recourse to galleries before they could pass the fosse, which was furnished with mines and counter-mines,—and that, as they might hope for relief from the English fleet when properly reinforced,—they could not see the necessity of capitulating.

By this capitulation, the aged governor, then in his eighty-second year, was considered, even by the enemy, to have in no way compromised the honour of the British arms. The duke of Richelieu declared, in his answer to the second article, that he had been induced, by the brave defence made by the governor and garrison, "to grant them such generous terms, as would entitle them to march out with all the honours of war, and to be conveyed by sea to Gibraltar. And his majesty (George II.) approving of general Blakeney's gallant defence of St. Philip, ennobled him, on his arrival in England, by the title of Baron Blakeney, of Mount Blakeney, in the kingdom of Ireland. (Entick, and others.)

BLAKEWAY, (John Brickdale,) an English antiquary, born at Shrewsbury, June 24, 1765, educated at Westminster School, and Oriel college, Oxford. In 1786 he left the university, and entered at Lincoln's Inn. He was called to the bar in 1789, and had actually begun to travel the Oxford circuit, with fair prospects of success, when a disappointment in his hereditary expectations induced him to decline a profession which might involve him in considerable expense without an adequate return for several years, and to think of holy orders. He was ordained in 1793; and in the following year, by means of an arrangement with his uncle, then possessed of that preferment, he succeeded to the perpetual curacy of St. Mary's, Shrewsbury. He subsequently obtained preferment in the country, where he resided half the year, passing the other half upon his town cure, which afforded him the sort of society that was most congenial to his tastes. He had an excellent memory, a striking talent for the acquisition of languages, and a general love for literature; but his chief partiality was for the study of antiquities. This led him to make large collections for a history of his native county, but he left them unarranged at his death. He lived, however, to complete a History of Shrewsbury, which he began, with assistance from archdeacon Owen, in 1822, and of which the last number was printed, though not actually delivered to the subscribers, when his decease occurred. He died March 10, 1826, in consequence of a tumour in his side, which had troubled him some years, and for relief from which he at length underwent an operation. Besides his History of Shrewsbury, he published three single sermons, and two pamphlets on the authorship of Junius, which he ascribed to Horne Tooke. (Ann. Biog.)

BLAMPIN, (Thomas,) a learned French Benedictine, of the congregation of St. Maur, born at Noyon, in 1640, chosen by his superiors to continue the edition of St. Augustine, begun by Francis Delfau. This important work was completed in 11 volumes, published between the years 1679 and 1700. It gave occasion to an attack from the Jesuits, charging the editors with Jansenism. Blampin took no public notice of this, but some learned men of his order wrote several replies to it. Blampin's editorial services were no less highly than justly appreciated by the learned world; and although he sought only retirement, it was found out of his power to decline public and dignified employments. He died visitor of the province of Burgundy, Feb. 17, 1710. (Moreri. Biog. Univ.)

BLANC, (Vincent le,) born at Marseilles, about the year 1553, a traveller in Asia, Africa, and America, who wrote a work called, Les Voyages Fameux, &c. 1648. It is not without value, but it is confused, careless as to dates, and credulous. (Carter's Amer. Biog. Dict. Moreri.)

BLANC, (Thomas le,) a French Jesuit of Vitry, in Champagne, who governed several houses of his order, and became provincial of Champagne. He died at Rheims, August 25, 1669, leaving several religious works, the most considerable of which is, a Commentary on the Psalms, in six folio volumes, printed at Lyons in 1665, and some subsequent years. (Moreri.)

BLANC, (Francis le,) a French numismatist, born in Dauphiny, and incited to extend his reseaches into the coins of his country, by a remark in the little treatise of Marquardus Freherus upon Ancient Moneys, that scarcely any thing was known about those of France. Le Blanc having conceived the design of supplying this void in his country's history, communicated it to Du Cange, who approved it highly. He was then fortunately called to Versailles to arrange and catalogue the coins in the royal cabinet. Making his design known there, Lewis XIV. commanded him to execute it. His publications upon the subject are two, Traité Historique des Monnoyes de France depuis la Commencement de la Monarchie jusqu'à present, Paris, 1690, 4to; and a work published at Paris, in the preceding year, entitled, Dissertation Historique sur quelques Monnoyes de Charlemagne, de Louis le Débonnaire, de Lothaire, et de ses Successeurs, frappées dans Rome, par lesquelles on refute l'Opinion de ceux qui prétendent que ces Princes n'ont jamais eu aucune Authorité dans cette Ville, que du Consentement des Papes. These two pieces are commonly bound together; and when it is otherwise, though both are rare, Le Blanc's Traité Historique fetches a lower price. A second edition of them both was printed at Amsterdam, in 1692; also in 4to, and this may be the safer purchase, though less valued than the first edition, because the Dissertation forms part of the volume. Le Blanc died suddenly at Versailles, in June 1698. (Moreri. Clement. Bibl. Cur. De Bure. Bibl. Instr.)

BLANC, (Anthony le,) called le Blanc de Guillet, a French novellist and poet, born at Marseilles, March 2, 1730. After some education at Avignon, he entered into the congregation of the Oratory, and remained attached to it ten years. He then went to Paris, and was employed upon the *Conservateur*, a periodical in some credit. In 1761 he published Mémoires du Comte de Guines, a romance, that was favourably received. In 1763 he produced the tragedy of Manco Capac, which made considerable noise, by the freedom of its language against arbitrary government, and gained for its author the designation of *le poète citoyen*. In 1772, Le Blanc produced Les Druides, but this tragedy was prohibited, after twelve representations, by means of the archbishop of Paris. It seems creditable to the royal government, that it offered a pension to this democratic politician, when without resources, in 1788; but he acted with a consistency far from universal among such persons, and declined the proffered aid as contrary to his principles. The revolution was rather slow in rewarding an adherent so creditable upon some accounts, but in 1795, the convention made him a grant of 2,000 livres. In 1798 he became a member of the Institute; and July 2, 1799, he died. Besides the works already mentioned, and some others, Le Blanc published a translation of Lucretius, 1788 and 1791, with a preliminary dissertation and notes of some value; and two tragedies, which mark the man and his times, Le Clergé devoilé, ou les Etats-Généraux de 1303, 1791; Tarquin, ou la Royauté abolie, 1794. (Biog. des Contemp.)

BLANC, (Lewis le,) a celebrated

French lithotomist, of the eighteenth century. He was a native of Pontoise, but exercised his profession at Orleans, and was surgeon-in-chief to the hospital of that city, being esteemed an able and ingenious surgeon. He printed many papers in the Memoirs of the Academy of Surgery, and in the Journal de Médecine. He also published, Discours sur l'Utilité de l'Anatomie, Paris, 1764, 8vo. Nouvelle Méthode d'opérer les Hernies, *ib.* 1768, 8vo. Réfutation de quelques Réflexions sur l'Opération de la Hernie, *ib.* 1768, 8vo. Précis d'Opérations de Chirurgie, *ib.* 1775, 8vo, 2 vols. This is a work of considerable merit.

BLANCARD, or BLANCKAERT, (Nicholas,) a classical critic, born at Leyden, of a noble family, Dec. 11, 1625. At one time he practised medicine, but in November 1669, he was chosen Greek professor at Franeker. He published Quintus Curtius, with notes, Leyden, 1649, 8vo. Florus, with his own and *variorum* notes, *ibid.* 1650, 8vo; reprinted at Franeker, 1690, 4to. Arrian's History of Alexander, Amst. 1668, 8vo; an edition little esteemed. Arriani Tactica, &c., Amst. 1683, 8vo. Harpocration, Leyden, 1683, 4to. Philippi Cyprii Chronicon Ecclesiæ Grecæ, Fran. 1679, 4to; a work hitherto inedited, but now given with a Latin translation from a MS. obtained at Constantinople. Thomæ Magistri Dictionum Atticarum Eclogæ, Fran. 1690, 8vo; reprinted 1698, with the notes of Lambert Bos. Bernard's valuable edition of this work, in 1757, follows Blancard's text, and gives Bos's notes. Blancard had begun to labour on Thucydides, and on the Glossary of Cyril, when the infirmities which had been gathering upon him ever since 1690 forced him to give up literary labour. He died May 15, 1703. (Biog. Univ.)

BLANCARD, (Stephen,) son of the preceding, a voluminous medical writer, now little esteemed. He graduated doctor of medicine at Franeker about 1678. Among his works, Anatomy Reformed, published in Dutch, in 1686, was translated into Latin, German, French, and English; the last being published in 1690. His Lexicon Medicum Græco-Latinum, Amst. 1679, 8vo, was frequently reprinted, and an English translation of it was published, Lond. 1708, 1715, 1726, 8vo. This work long maintained a great popularity; and an edition of it published in 1777 was increased to nearly treble its original bulk, filling two large volumes, 8vo. Blancard's most valuable work is, however, said by Haller to be his Anatomia Practica Rationalis, sive variorum Cadaverum Morbis denatorum Anatomica Inspectio, Amst. 1688, 12mo. But he has introduced many observations from other writers without acknowledgment. This work, which contains two hundred cases, generally worthy of notice, was published in German, at Hanover, 1692, 8vo. Some of Blancard's contemporaries not only blamed him as a plagiary, but also as untrue to his own profession, by writing so much in the vernacular tongue, and thereby rendering its secrets accessible to people without a liberal education. (Rees. Biog. Univ.)

BLANCARD, (Peter,) an eminent French navigator, born at Marseilles, April 21, 1741. He was early initiated in the mercantile marine, and had gained considerable nautical and commercial experience when the exclusive privilege of the old East India Company was suppressed in 1769. He was in the following year sent to India in charge of the trading speculations of a frigate granted by the government to a house at Marseilles. Upon this and other occasions his conduct was highly satisfactory and advantageous to the interests of France generally. He died March 16, 1826, having published a valuable work, entitled Manuel du Commerce des Indes Orientales et de la Chine, Paris, 1806, fol. (Biog. Univ. Suppl.)

BLANCAS, (Jerome de,) a celebrated Spanish historian, son of a notary at Saragossa, where he was born. He was educated at Valencia, and the early development of superior talents, joined to an especial taste for history, pointed him out as worthy to succeed the famous Zurita, as historiographer of Spain. Blancas died in his native city, Dec. 2, 1590, without issue, although he had married. He first published a collection of inscriptions for the royal portraits at Saragossa, then the chronology of the *Justizas* of Aragon; both Latin pieces, printed at Saragossa, in 1587; and both reprinted in Schott's Hispania Illustrata. In 1588, Blancas produced his Aragonensium Rerum Commentarii, fol. a very rare book, which supplies what Zurita had left, and is highly valued, both for authenticity and style. It was originally written in Spanish, and translated by the author into Latin; but this original, which Uztarroz, the biographer of Blancas, saw, has never been printed. The following is a very rare posthumous work by the Aragonese historian, which John Francis

Andrew de Uztarroz, historiographer of Spain, published at the national expense, with additions by John Matthew Stephanus, a treatise on the same subject by Jerome Martel, and a life of Blancas, by himself—Coronaciones de los Reyes de Aragon, escritas por Geronimo de Blancas, Cronista del Reyno, con dos Tratados del Modo de tener Cortes en Aragon, del mismo Autor, y de Geronimo Martel; con algunas Notas, Zaragoça, 1641, 4to. (Antonio. Clement. Bibl. Cur.)

BLANCHARD, (James,) a French painter of considerable eminence, born in Paris in 1600, sometimes called the French Titian, from the success with which he imitated that great master's style. He introduced into his own country a more true and natural manner of colouring than had hitherto obtained there. He died in 1638. (Biog. Univ. Bryan's Dict.)

BLANCHARD, (Francis,) a Parisian advocate, who died in 1660, having published, Eloges de tous les Premiers Présidents du Parlement de Paris, depuis qu'il a été sédentaire jusqu'à présent, 1645, fol. Les Présidents à Mortier du Parlement de Paris, depuis 1631 jusqu'à présent, 1647, fol. L'Histoire des Maîtres des Requêtes depuis 1260 jusqu'en 1575, 1670, fol. (Biog. Univ.)

BLANCHARD, (William,) son of the preceding, and also an advocate, author of Une Table Chronologique, contenant en Abrégé un Recueil des Ordonnances, Edits, Declarations, et Lettres Patentes des Rois de France, depuis l'an 1115 jusqu'en 1688. A second edition of this work, carrying it upwards to 987, and downwards to the actual time, was published in 1715, 2 vols. fol. It is said to be a very defective compilation, in spite of the author's facilities for making it otherwise. He was probably aware of this himself, and was employed upon a third edition when death overtook him, Sept. 24, 1724. (Moreri. Biog. Univ.)

BLANCHARD, (John Baptist,) a French writer, formerly a Jesuit, born in 1731. He died June 15, 1797, leaving Le Temple des Muses, ou Recueil des plus Belles Fables des Fabulistes Français, with remarks, critical and historical. Ecole des Mœurs, often reprinted, a collection of historical sketches, with suitable reflections. (Biog. Univ.)

BLANCHE, of Castile, a celebrated queen and regent of France, daughter of Alphonso IX., king of Castile. She came into France in 1200, when scarcely fourteen, as wife to a prince about the same age, eventually Lewis VIII., surnamed the Lion. On that sovereign's death, in 1226, Blanche succeeded, under his will, to the regency, during the minority of her son, Lewis IX. or *Saint* Lewis. Her authority was immediately threatened by a formidable conspiracy among some of the principal vassals of the crown; but qualities of a very superior order enabled her to overcome every difficulty. When her son, the sainted king, departed upon his expedition to Palestine, Blanche was again regent. She had earnestly dissuaded him from entering upon this unwise undertaking, arguing against the vow that he thereby fulfilled, as merely extorted by the tyranny of sickness over his brain. But her disinterested representations proving ineffectual, she once more took possession of supreme authority in her adopted country. As before, her administration was admirable; but Lewis's absence and dangers occasioned her serious and constant uneasiness. She never saw him more, dying Dec. 1, 1253, with a reputation for beauty, piety, and wisdom, that no one of her sex has ever surpassed. (Gifford's Hist. Fr. Moreri. Biog. Univ.)

BLANCHE, of Bourbon, queen of Castile, daughter of Peter, duke of Bourbon, married at fifteen, in 1353, to Peter the Cruel, king of Castile. On her way towards Spain, Peter's natural brother, who had gone to receive her, was reported to have gained her affections; and Peter met her at Valladolid, with a strong prejudice against her. Immediately afterwards he left her, and lived with his mistress, Mary de Padilla. Blanche's indignation tempted her into a confederacy that menaced her faithless husband's throne. Peter's hatred now became boundless, and he ordered the queen's committal to the castle of Toledo. In her way thither, Blanche escaped, and took refuge in the cathedral. The citizens rose in her defence, but Peter took the town by assault, and imprisoned Blanche in the castle of Medina Sidonia. There she died in 1361, as it was said, of poison, given by Peter's orders. Vengeance for the sufferings undergone by this unfortunate princess was one of the causes alleged for Du Guesclin's invasion of Spain at the head of the companies, or disbanded soldiers, harboured in southern France. (Biog. Univ. Gifford's Hist. Fr.)

BLANCHEROSE, (Claude,) a French physician, settled at Lausanne, who "was the chief speaker" on the part of the Romanists in the Disputation of Lausanne, held in 1536. He contended for some time against Farel's statement of justification; but when satisfied that the Scriptures which Farel had cited were really a part of the sacred text, which he had questioned, he closed with the exclamation, "It is true, then, that we are justified by faith, and the Thesis is right." None of the clergy of the place, secular or regular, took any part in the discussion; which led Farel pleasantly to remark, that "the priests certainly felt their cause to be in a *sickly* state, seeing they had given it up into the hands of the doctor."

BLANCHET, (Peter,) a French poet, of considerable merit, born at Poitiers, in 1459. After studying law in his youth, he became an ecclesiastic at forty, and he died in 1519. When young, he prepared some dramatic pieces for representation by himself and his fellow-students, which satirized vice with a boldness that must have recoiled severely upon himself, had he not been conspicuous for purity of morals and goodness of heart. To him is attributed the Farce de Pathelin, first published in black letter in 1490, and often reprinted. It was translated into Latin, with the following title-page, Comœdia nova quæ Veterator inscribitur, alias Pathelinus, ex peculiari Linguâ in Romanum trad. Eloquium per Alex. Connibertum, Paris, 1512, 12mo. (Biog. Univ.)

BLANCHET, (Thomas,) a French painter, born at Paris in 1617, originally intended for sculpture, and resident some years in Italy. He became eventually one of the ablest historical painters that his country could boast. He died at Lyons in 1689. (Bryan.)

BLANCHET, (Francis,) a French writer, of cultivated taste, and conspicuous benevolence, born January 26, 1707, and originally meant for a Jesuit, but early detached from that order. He died Jan. 29, 1784, leaving Variétés morales et amusantes; Apologues et Contes Orientaux; and Vues sur l'Education d'un Prince. (Biog. Univ.)

BLANCHET, (John,) a French writer, born September 10, 1724, sent by the Jesuits, who were among his earliest instructors, to La Flêche, in contemplation of his entrance into their order. But he left them after a trial of some years, and settled in Paris, where his attention was chiefly fixed on the sciences, especially on medicine. In this faculty he took a doctor's degree, but an advantageous marriage relieved him from the necessity of practising. He left, L'Art, ou les Principes Philosophiques du Chant; Idée du Siècle littéraire présent, reduit à six vrais Auteurs; L'Homme éclairé par ses Besoins; Logique de l'Esprit et du Cœur. (Biog. Univ.)

BLAND, (John,) one of the Marian martyrs. He was for some time engaged in tuition, and had among his pupils Edwin Sandys, eventually archbishop of York. At Mary's accession, he was rector of Adisham, Kent, in which he was superseded by Richard Thorneden, suffragan bishop of Dover, who had turned with the times. Before him, assisted by Collins, acting as commissary for cardinal Pole, and Harpsfield, archdeacon of Canterbury, articles were exhibited against Bland, charging him with denying, 1. The corporal presence; 2. That the sacraments should be administered in an unknown tongue; 3. That the eucharist should be administered only in one kind. These charges he nobly admitted; and on the 12th July, 1555, was burned to death at Canterbury, together with another clergyman and two laymen. (Foxe, 1518. Strype, Mem. iii. 211, 213, 356.)

BLAND, (Robert,) born in London in 1779, son of Robert Bland, M.D., author of some medical works, and of Proverbs, chiefly taken from the Adagia of Erasmus, 2 vols, 1814. He was educated at Harrow school and Pembroke college, Cambridge, whence, after taking his degree, he returned to Harrow as an under-master. While there he printed Edwin and Elgiva, with other poems, in 1805. In the following year he published the first edition of his Translations from the Greek Anthology, in which he was assisted by his friend, J. H. Merrivale, and hence they were hailed as "associate bards" by lord Byron in his English Bards, &c. In 1809 appeared The Four Slaves of Cythera; and in 1813 he translated, in conjunction with Miss Plumtree, the Memoirs of De Grimm and Diderot. After quitting Harrow he became minister of the English church at Amsterdam, and on his return he married. His eldest son has trodden in the steps of his father as a translator of some pieces from the Greek, to be found in the third edition of the Collections from the Anthology, published in 1833. Mr. Bland died, after a short illness, at his curacy of Kenilworth, in 1825, leaving, besides the publications already mentioned, an excellent elementary work on Latin versification, which has been frequently reprinted.

BLANDINA, one of the martyrs who perished in the persecution at Lyons, A.D. 177. She was a christian slave, remarkable even among her heroic fellow-sufferers for the bold avowal of her principles, and the perfect resignation with which she underwent a succession of tortures. (Euseb. Eccl. Hist. v. i. Mosheim, new ed. i. 137.)

BLANDRATA, (John George,) a physician, born in the environs of Saluzzo, who studied medicine at Montpelier, and took the degree of doctor in that faculty in 1533. Partaking of the religious excitement then prevalent, he abandoned Romanism for the doctrines of Luther, which he afterwards abandoned for those of Calvin. About 1545 he is reported, but on doubtful authority, to have embraced antitrinitarian opinions, in company with several other professed free-thinkers associated at Vicenza, in the Venetian states. His medical reputation obtained for him an invitation from Sigismund Augustus, king of Poland, and repairing to that country, he was appointed physician to the queen. The natural love of home led him to quit Poland for Italy, where the promulgation of his opinions excited the attention of the inquisition at Padua, and he was thrown into prison. He made, however, his escape, and passed on to Geneva, where Calvin, after endeavours to reclaim him, procured his arrest as an abettor of the opinions of Servetus. To save his life he again professed Calvinism, and returned to Poland in 1558; but letters from Calvin pursued him, and he became glad of a retreat at the court of John Sigismund, prince of Transylvania, who placed him about his person, in 1563. This enabled him to disseminate his Socinian opinions, with which the prince accorded. Upon the death of John Sigismund, which occurred in 1570, he was appointed chief physician to Stephen Battori, whom he afterwards accompanied into Poland. Another change in his opinions here manifested itself: he abandoned Socinianism, and connected himself with the Jesuits, who were then in great favour with the king. He had made a will in favour of his nephew, who is reported to have smothered him in his bed; but the date of this event has not been stated. He wrote several letters and unimportant tracts relating to the Socinian doctrines, of which it is unnecessary to quote the titles, as they may be found in the Bibliotheca Anti-Trinitariana of Sandius. (Mosheim, new ed. iii. 601. M'Crie's Ref. in Italy, 154. Biog. Univ. Chalmers.)

BLANE, (Sir Gilbert, bart.) a distinguished physiologist and physician, fourth son of an opulent Scottish merchant, and born at Blanefield, in the county of Ayr, August 29 (O.S.), 1749. Having studied medicine and surgery, he entered into the navy as an assistant-surgeon, and was present at the celebrated engagement between the British and French fleets in the West Indies, April 12, 1782. He published an account of this in a Letter addressed to Lord Dalrymple, Lond. 8vo, 1782. He speedily rose in the service, took the degree of doctor of medicine, was enrolled a licentiate of the Royal College of Physicians, and at the time of his death, stood at the head of the list. He was elected physician to St. Thomas's Hospital, and appointed physician-extraordinary to George IV., and physician to the household. He was subsequently made physician to the Fleet, and also physician in ordinary to William IV. He was created a baronet, December 26, 1812. He was a fellow of the Royal Societies of London and Edinburgh, and a member of the Imperial Society of Sciences of St. Petersburgh, and many other foreign literary and scientific institutions. He died June 27, 1834, at his house in Sackville-street, aged 84, leaving issue to continue his title, his wife having been Elizabeth, only daughter of Abraham Gardner, merchant. His zeal for his profession, particularly as relating to the department of the naval service, was not only evinced by his various publications, but also by a proposition made in November 1829, and sanctioned by the lords of the Admiralty, to found a prize medal for the best journal kept by the surgeons of the navy. This medal is awarded every second year, the commissioners selecting four journals, from which Sir Gilbert, during his life, and afterwards the presidents of the Colleges of Physicians and Surgeons, were to decide which was best entitled to the reward.

His publications are numerous; the earliest appears to have been An Address to the Medical Society of Students at Edinburgh, upon laying the foundation of their Hall, April 21, 1775, 8vo. This was followed by A Short Account of the most effectual Means of Preserving the Health of Seamen, Lond. 1780, 4to. An Account of the Hurricane at Barbadoes, on the 10th of October, 1780, in which he states the extraordinary fact, that the tempest had a visible good effect on the diseases of the climate, fevers and fluxes. Some recent cases of phthisis, and even the acute state of pleurisy, were cured by it; and many chronic diseases much alleviated or removed. This was published in the first volume of the Trans. of the Royal Society of Edinburgh, 1784. Observations on the Diseases incident to Seamen, Lond. 1785, 8vo; second edition, 1799; third ditto, 1803. A Lecture on Muscular Motion, read at the Royal Society, 1788, Lond. 1790, 4to. This is a publication of considerable ability, and is frequently referred to by the most eminent physiologists; an enlarged edition was published in 1791. Letters on the subject of Quarantine, Lond. 1799, 4to. A Serious Address to the Public on the Practice of Vaccination, Lond. 1811, 8vo. Elements of Medical Logic, including a statement respecting the contagious nature of the Yellow Fever, Lond. 1818, 8vo; second edition, 1819; third ditto, 1825. Select Dissertations on several Subjects of Medical Science, Lond. 1822, 8vo. A Brief Statement of the Progressive Improvement of the Health of the Royal Navy at the end of the Eighteenth and beginning of the Nineteenth Century, Lond. 1830, 8vo. Narrative of Facts connected with the Manœuvre of Breaking the Enemy's Line on the 12th of April, Lond, 1830, 8vo. Reflections on the Present Crisis of Public Affairs, Lond. 1831, 8vo. Warning and Admonition to the British Public on the Introduction of the Cholera of India, Lond. 1832, 8vo. Sir G. Blane was president of the Royal Medico-Chirurgical Society, and contributed several papers to the Transactions, the most important of which are, A Case in which Death was brought on by a Hemorrhage from the Liver, ii. 18. On the Effect of the Pure Fixed Alkalies and of Lime Water in several Complaints, *ib.* p. 132. History of Cases of Disease of the Brain, *ib.* p. 192. Facts and Observations respecting Intermittent Fevers, iii. 1. Observations on the Comparative Prevalence, Mortality, and Treatment of Different Diseases, iv. p. 89.

BLANKENBURG, (Christian Frederick von,) born 1744, at Kolberg, in Pomerania, educated in the royal military school at Berlin. Having entered the Prussian army at an early age, he served in the seven years' war; but after rising to the rank of captain, was obliged to retire on account of ill health. He then lived at Leipsic, engaged in literary pursuits, till his death in 1796. He translated Johnson's Lives of the Poets and other works from the English. He published also an edition of Sulzer's Theory of the Fine Arts and Sciences, in 4 vols, which has been often reprinted; also the same author's Miscellaneous Writings, and Zollikofer's Sermons, in 7 vols. Blankenburg was a tasteful, perspicuous writer, a good critic of the school of Sulzer, but without original powers. He did some service to literature in his time, but is now little known. His character appears to have been modest and amiable.

BLANKENSTEIN, (Ernest, count of,) an illustrious Austrian general, of a very ancient family, born at Reinsdorff, in Thuringia, in 1733. Entering early into the Austrian service, he took a distinguished part in most of the wars upon which the imperial family entered during the middle and latter end of the eighteenth century. In 1793 he was engaged, with great honour and considerable success, against revolutionary France, in covering the Moselle; but in the following year, notwithstanding great and able exertions, he was eventually foiled, and in 1795, his advanced age gave him an admonition, which he did not neglect, to retire from the fatigues of active service. He died June 12, 1816, at Battelau, in Moravia. Blankenstein's hussars were highly celebrated in Germany. (Biog. Univ. Suppl.)

BLANKHOF, (John Teunisz,) born at Alkmaer, 1628, died 1670, an eminent landscape painter, first instructed by two obscure artists; but he soon became a pupil of Cäsar of Everdingen, acting on whose advice he went to Rome, where he became a member of the Society of Painting: he received from it the name of Maat, (*mate* or *comrade*,) by which he is best known. His restless spirit allowed him no repose. He travelled three times from Holland to Rome, and finally joined a fleet bound for Candia. This last voyage completed his education as an artist. He observed the agitation of the sea, sketched the coasts and adjacent countries, the motions of the ship, the sailors, the storm; nothing, in fact, escaped his attention. All these operations of nature may be seen in his paintings, represented in beautiful colours, and with the happiest effect, as he combined the truth and nature of the Dutch school, with the grand scenery of Italy. (Ersch und Gruber. Bryan.)

BLANPAIN, (John,) a French eccle

siastical writer, born October 21, 1704, early distinguished for learning and abilities. Having entered the Premonstratensian order, he was chosen by Hugo, abbot of Estival, his own house, to assist him in his Sacræ Antiquitatis Monumenta. Being disappointed, however, of the post of coadjutor of the monastery, Blanpain broke with Hugo, and retired to Nancy, where he entered upon an unfriendly examination of his late abbot's works. The fruit of this was entitled, Jugement des Ecrits de M. Hugo, Evêque de Ptolémaide, abbé d'Estival en Lorraine, Historiographe de l'Ordre de Premontré, Nancy, 1736, 8vo. This work, which bears only upon Premonstratensian history, being written by one who both knew well the subject, and Hugo's weak points in treating it, is judicious and solid. Blanpain afterwards laboured upon the annals of his order, but did not complete the work. After Hugo's death, he returned to Estival, and he died there about 1765, having written besides the works mentioned above, some other pieces connected with his order. (Bibl. Univ. Suppl.)

BLANQUET, (Samuel,) a French physician and naturalist, born in the diocese of Mende, in which he settled, after taking the degree of doctor of medicine at Montpelier. A pestilence at Gévaudan, in 1722, called forth his exertions, and they have been honourably noticed in the Journal des Savans of that year. He was well versed in natural history, and he furnished to the Academy of Béziers several interesting papers. He is reported to have died at Mende in 1750. He published, Examen de la Nature et Vertu des Eaux Minérales de Gévaudan, Mende, 1728, 8vo. Discours pour servir de Plan à l'Histoire Naturelle du Gévaudan, 1730, 4to. Epistola de Aquâ quæ in Saxa obrigescit, Mende, 1731, 4to.

BLANQUET, (du Chayla, Armand Simon Maria de,) a rear-admiral of France. He served as second in command under vice-admiral Brueys at the battle of the Nile. It would appear, that when the French arrived in Aboukir Bay, the commander-in-chief held a council of flag-officers and captains to determine "whether, in case of attack, the fleet should engage at anchor or under sail." All the officers assembled, with the exception of the rear-admiral, approved of the fleet's remaining at anchor; but Blanquet maintained, that it was only when a fleet could be supported by strong forts crossing each other in their fire, that any advantage was gained by a stationary position. However, finding the majority against him, he requested that the *Franklin*, his flag-ship, might be placed as one of the "seconds" to the commander-in-chief. His request was granted. Blanquet was wounded in the action, but he escaped not the censures of Bonaparte, who, for some inexplicable reason, sought to inculpate the brave Blanquet; and on the 24th of August, the following passage appeared in a "general order," addressed to the army—"the *Franklin* struck her flag without being dismasted or having sustained any damage." Rear-admiral Gantheaume, who served in the capacity of captain of the fleet, immediately hastened to the camp to defend the character of his wounded brother officer, and pleaded his cause with so much effect, that Bonaparte, yielding a little, issued a second order, stating that rear-admiral Blanquet had been wounded in the action; but which left uncontradicted the false assertion that the *Franklin* surrendered when in a perfect state. At the instance of the vice-admiral Brueys, the minister of marine, justice was at length done by the Directory to the character of Blanquet, but he was never afterward employed, although on the first restoration he sought to gain from the Bourbons, by protestations of loyalty, that notice which he had found hopeless under Bonaparte. They merely made him knight of St. Lewis, officer of the legion of honour, and honorary vice-admiral. He died at Versailles, August 29, 1826. (Victoires et Conquêtes, tom. ix. p. 107. Biog. Univ. Suppl.)

BLARRU, (Peter,) an historical poet, born in 1427, who died in 1505, canon of St. Diez, in Lorraine, sometimes considered a native of Paris, because he added *Parhisianus* to his name; but this merely denotes his birth at, or near a Cistercian abbey, in the diocese of Bâle, called *Paris* or *Peris*. He wrote a Latin poem commemorating the siege of Nancy by Charles the Rash, duke of Burgundy, killed before that town in 1476. Though but an indifferent piece, it is of some value as a monument of contemporary history. Among bibliomaniacs it is also valuable from its extreme rarity. The poem being left in MS. by its author, came after his death into the possession of John Basin de Sandancourt, who caused it to be printed in a handsome style, in small folio, in 1518, with the following title, Petri de Blarrorivo, Parisiani, insigne Nanceidos Opus, de Bello Nanceiano, hac primum exaratura elimatissime nuperrime in lucem emissum. At the end is, "Finit feliciter egregium ac insigne Nanceidos Opus Petri de Blarrorivo, Parisiani, de Bello Nanceiano, impressum in celebri Lotharingiæ Pago per Petrum Jacobi Presbyterum Loci Paganum, Anno Christianæ Incarnationis MDXVIII. Nonas Januarii, quo Die ipsum quoque Bellum Nanceianum peractum, Anno Incarnationis MCCCCLXXVI." Blarru passed several years in blindness, a calamity which caused him to be compared with Homer; but modern readers of his poety have failed of discovering the smallest resemblance in any other particular. (Clement. Bibl. Cur. Biog. Univ.)

BLASIUS, or BLAES, (Gerard,) a celebrated physician of the seventeenth century, born at Oostvliet, in the island of Cadsandt, near Bruges. He first studied medicine at Copenhagen, whence he repaired to Leyden, where he took the degree of doctor of medicine in 1646, and afterwards settled at Amsterdam. He practised in this city for some years, and in 1660 was appointed to a chair of medicine in the university, and named physician to the hospital and librarian to the city. He was held in great esteem, chosen one of the members of the Academy of the Curious in Nature in 1682, and admitted into it under the name of Podalirius II. In the same year he died. Blaes was a successful cultivator of anatomy, both human and comparative. He made many discoveries, and his name, in conjunction with that of Steno, in the demonstration of the parotid duct, and with that of Swammerdam of the valves in the lacteal vessels, is well known. He was the first to prove that the chyle was uniform in its character, however different the materials from which it had been derived. He gave a good description of the spinal marrow, and he entertained clear views with respect to the arachnoid membrane of the brain. He was also an observant pathologist, and his writings contain many important facts and relations in morbid anatomy. He published, Commentarius in Syntagma Anatomicum Veslingii, atque Appendix ex veterum, recentiorum, propriisque Observationibus, Amst. 1659, 1666, 4to, Utrecht, 1669, 4to. Oratio de iis quæ Homo Naturæ, quæ Arti debet, Amst. 1660, fol. Medicina Generalis, novâ accuratâque Methodo Fundamenta exhibens, *ib.* 1661, 12mo. This was afterwards published as Medicina Universa Hygieines et Therapeutices Fundamenta, &c. Amst. 1665, 4to. Dissertatio Anatomica de Structurâ et Usu Renum, Amst. 1665, 12mo. Anatome contracta in Gratiam Discipulorum conscripta et edit. *ib.* 1666, 12mo. In Dutch, *ib.* 1675, 8vo. Anatome Medullæ Spinalis et Nervorum inde provenientium, *ib.* 1666, 12mo. Institutionum Medicarum Compendium, Disputationes XII. *ib.* 1667, 12mo. Miscellanea Anatomica, Hominis et Brutorum variorum Fabricam exhibentia, *ib.* 1673, 12mo. Observata Anatomica in Homine, Simiâ, Equo, Vitulo, Testudine, Echino, Glire, Serpente, Ardeâ, variisque Animalibus aliis; accedunt extraordinaria in Homine reperta, Praxim Medicam æque ac Anatomen illustrantia, Lugd. et Amst. 1674, 8vo. Zootomia seu Anatomes variorum Animalium, Amst. 1676, 12mo. This was again published, with additions, as Anatome compilata Animalium Terrestrium, Volatilium, Aquatilium, &c. *ib.* 1681, 4to. Observationes Medicæ rariores, *ib.* 1677, 12mo. Medicina Curatoria, Methodo novâ, in Gratiam Discipulorum conscripta, *ib.* 1680, 8vo.

BLASTARES, (Matthew,) a Greek monk, of the order of St. Basil, who lived about the year 1330, and acquired a considerable knowledge of divinity and canon law. He is author of an Alphabetical Collection of Canons, Councils, Decisions of the Fathers, and Laws of the Greek Emperors, concerning Ecclesiastical Affairs, printed in Greek and Latin in Beveridge's Συνοδικον; of Questions upon Marriage, printed in the Jus Græco-Romanum of Leunclavius; and of a piece on the Offices of the Court, and of the Great Church of Constantinople, printed in Greek and Latin by Goar, in his edition of Codinus. Blastares also wrote some other pieces, which are extant in MS. (Biog. Univ. Moreri.)

BLAU, (Felix Anthony,) a German Romish theologian, born 1754, professor at Mentz, and author of several anonymous works, written with unusual freedom; viz. On the Worship of Images, Mentz, 1788. On the Efficacy of the Ritual Usages in the Catholic Church, Frankf. 1792; and (conjointly with Dorsch) Contributions to the Improvement of External Divine Service in the Catholic Church, Frankf. 1789. Blau censures in a bold but modest and rational manner the liturgical abuses which have crept into the Romish service. His History of Ecclesiastical Infallibility with a view to promote a Free Examination of Romanism, Frankf. 1791, is a book of great care and research, and has been stated to be one of the most important modern polemical works, to have shaken the system of the Roman-catholic religion at its foundation, and to have demonstrated its untenability. Soon after the French revolution, Blau resigned his offices at Mentz, and went to France, in expectation of the great benefits which, in common with many others, he expected from that event to the whole human race. He was not only deceived, but had the misfortune, in 1793, to be captured by the Prussians, who imprisoned him at Königstein, where he suffered great inconveniences. On his liberation thence, he returned to Mentz, where he was made a judge of the criminal court, and where he died, 1798. His last work was a Critical Essay, founded on Pure Principles of Common and Ecclesiastical Law, respecting the Religious Ordinances which had been passed in France since the Revolution. Strasb. 1798.

BLAURER, (Andrew,) a native of Constance, of a noble family, born in 1492. He early entered a monastery at Alberspach, in the duchy of Würtemberg; but being converted by reading Luther's writings, he quitted his convent, returned to Constance, and taught the reformed doctrines. Being driven away with other reformed ministers of the place by the Interim in 1548, he retired to Brienne, and died there in 1568. His character being assailed, he drew up, in 1524, An Apology, or Defence of Himself against his Accusers; but was advised by Œcolampadius, to whom he submitted his MS., not to print it, as inexpedient at that time, but "to employ his excellent abilities, and the talent for writing evidently possessed by him, on some work of a more general character."

BLAVET, (John Lewis,) a French writer, son of an eminent musician, who has the credit of saying of Frederic II. of Prussia, in whose dominions he made a temporary stay by invitation: "You think that he likes music. You are mistaken; he likes nothing but the flute, or rather, his own flute." The younger Blavet was born at Besançon, July 6, 1719. His father took him to Paris, and he entered a convent of Benedictines, but, becoming impatient of it, he obtained his secularization. He took, however, the title of *abbé*, and dressed as an ecclesiastic. He was librarian to the prince of Conti, and by his means one of the royal censors. Blavet published at Paris, in 1755, in conjunction with Melin, Essai sur l'Agriculture Moderne. The abbé Blavet subsequently was most known as a translator from the English. In 1775 appeared his French version of Adam Smith's Theory of Moral Sentiments; in the following year his translation of Dalrymple's Historical and Political Memoirs; in the years 1779 and 1780, his translation of Adam Smith's Wealth of Nations. This work was published separately in 1781, and again in 1800. It has now been superseded by a translation from the pen of M. Garnier. The abbé Blavet died at Paris when verging upon ninety, about the year 1810. (Biog. des Contemp.)

BLAYNEY, (Benjamin, D.D.) an eminent English Hebraist, entered first of Worcester college, Oxford, where he took the degree of M.A. 1753. He subsequently became fellow of Hertford college (since dissolved), and was admitted B.D. 1768, D.D. 1787. In the December of that year he was appointed canon of Christchurch and regius professor of Hebrew. He was also rector of Polshot, Wilts, where he died, Sept. 20, 1801, distinguished as a biblical critic of the first order. He published dissertations on Dan. ix. 20; a new translation of Jeremiah and the Lamentations; a discourse on Isa. vii. 14—16; a new translation of Zechariah; and several occasional sermons. He also took great pains in correcting the text of the Authorized Version of the Bible, which was printed at the Clarendon Press, 1769, 4to, and to which he added a great number of marginal references. He likewise left behind him many valuable papers, which he directed by his will to be deposited in the archiepiscopal library of Lambeth, after submission to his patron and friend, Shute Barrington, long known as the munificent bishop of Durham, and the persevering encourager of clerical erudition.

BLAYNEY, (Andrew Thos.) eleventh baron Blayney of Monaghan, an eminent British military officer in the French revolutionary wars, born Nov. 30, 1770. He succeeded to the family title on the death of an elder brother, April 2, 1784. In 1789 he entered the army, and he saw a great deal of active service in the Low Countries, whither he went with the earl of Moira, in 1794, as attached to the expedition under Frederic, duke of York. In 1798, he was employed in

Ireland; and although, from the violence of party, it was difficult to execute his duties in a satisfactory manner, yet he received thanks from the grand juries of three counties, and was greeted with full approbation from the commander-in-chief. He was subsequently employed in Sicily, where the king, then driven from his continental dominions, had taken refuge, and important services were rendered by the British forces in preventing that island from falling under the power of France. Lord Blayney was then successively employed in the siege of Malta, and in the Egyptian campaign under Sir Ralph Abercrombie. On the resumption of hostilities after the short peace of Amiens, he had the misfortune to join the expedition so disgracefully foiled under general Whitelock, at Buenos Ayres. On the termination of this mortifying service, he proceeded with the 89th to the Cape, and thence to India. He subsequently served in the Peninsula, but was taken prisoner at Fingerole. He died at Dublin, April 8, 1834, regretted as an excellent officer and a most good-natured man. (Ann. Biog.)

BLEBEL, (Frederic,) an eminent mathematician, born in Normandy, and sent at an early age to the university at Paris, where he made such progress in the exact sciences, that he was chosen as private tutor to the son of a French nobleman of high rank. He died at Bruges in 1562, leaving behind him an elaborate treatise on astronomy, which is still preserved in MS. in the royal library at Paris. A treatise of his, De Sphærâ, was published at Antwerp in 1573.

BLECK, or BLEECK, (Peter van,) a Flemish engraver, of no very superior merit, but who executed his work neatly, and has left some pieces worthy of notice. He came to England about 1730, and is thought to have been the son of Richard Bleeck, a portrait painter. (Bryan.)

BLECKER, (J. G.) a Dutch designer and engraver, born, it is said, about 1600. He etched several plates, both from his own designs and from those of others. They are slight and spirited. (Bryan.)

BLEDA, (James,) a Spanish writer, born at Algemese, in Valencia, in early life rector of Corbera, in that province. His parish contained a number of unhappy Moriscoes, outwardly conformists to Romanism, but, as he soon saw, with deep indignation, really Mahometans. After brooding over their dissimulation for some time, he bent all his energies to reclaim or punish the whole race of Spanish Moors. He resigned accordingly his benefice, and took the habit of St. Dominic, in the friary of that order, at Valencia, May 24, 1586, thinking his favourite object likely to be secured in no way so well as by joining himself to a body which wrote *Defensio Fidei* over the portals of its convents. After about three years Bleda took a journey to Rome, but apparently his fiery zeal did not easily kindle a corresponding enthusiasm there, as he made subsequently two other journeys thither, and memorialized altogether three popes, Gregory XIV., Clement VIII., and Paul V. He made also many journeys to Madrid, painting to all who would listen to him the perfidy of the Moriscoes, and the duty of persons in power to extirpate them. Unfortunately for their interests, a much more influential person than Bleda was brought over to that zealous friar's views, namely, John de Ribera, archbishop of Valencia, by whom Philip III. was besought to decree their expulsion from Spain. The grandees, however, opposed this project, fearing that their estates would suffer severely if suddenly stripped of the industrious Moorish tenantry. But at length all considerations were overpowered in an insane and unfeeling anxiety to purge the land of Mahometan dissimulation; and in 1609 the royal decree was passed which drove from Spain about a million of her most industrious inhabitants. Bleda lived several years to witness the results of his successful importunities, dying December 3, 1624, in a Dominican convent founded by himself, in his native village, Algemese. As an author, he is chiefly known out of Spain by two very scarce Latin tracts upon his favourite subject, entitled Jacobi Bledæ Defensio Fidei in Causâ Neophytorum, sive Moriscorum Regni Valentiæ, totiusque Hispaniæ: Tractatus de justa Moriscorum ab Hispaniâ Expulsione. Valentia, per Joan. Chrysost. Garriz, 1610, 4to. He also published in Spanish, Chronologia de los Moros de España, in 8 books, fol. 1618, Valent., a valuable work; likewise three tracts upon some fancied or pretended miracles. (Clement. Bibl. Cur. Antonio.)

BLEFKEN, (Dithmar,) an early navigator, author of a Latin account of Iceland, of seventy-one 8vo pages, which Du Fresnoy, in his Méthode pour Etudier l'Histoire, highly commends, and which at one time excited a good deal of notice. The writer is thought to have been a native of Lower Saxony, and to have embarked for Iceland in 1563. In 1565 he made a voyage to Lisbon, and thence passed into Africa. After visiting various countries, he became attached to the counts of Schaumburg, and he subsequently accepted an invitation from the elector of Cologne. In his way to that prince at Bonn, he was attacked by robbers, who wounded him severely, and went away with all his effects, including his notes upon Iceland. The MS. was, however, at length recovered, and after a lapse of forty years from the visit which it commemorates, the substance of it was published under the following title,—Dithmari Blefkenii Islandia, sive Populorum et Mirabilium quæ in eâ Insulâ reperiuntur, accuratior Descriptio: cui de Gronlandia sub Finem quædam adjecta, Lugd. Bat. 1607, 8vo. This little piece professes to supply the omissions of former writers, as Olaus Magnus, Munster, and others, relates many marvellous things, and paints an offensive picture of Icelandic morality. Arngrim Jonaŝ, pastor of Mestland, in Iceland, published at Hola, in that island, in 1612, a powerful exposure of Blefken, reprinted at Hamburg, in 1617, under this title,—Anatome Blefkeniana, quâ Ditmari Blefkenii Viscera, magis præcipua, in Libello de Islandia, Anno MDCVII. per manifestam Exenterationem retexuntur. This work convicts Blefken of using Olaus Magnus and Munster without acknowledgment, exposes his ignorance of Icelandic topography and history, both natural and civil, vindicates the morality of the country, and concludes that the navigator had either never been there at all, or had visited it in the most transient manner. Probably the work of Jonas did not immediately reach Germany, as Blefken's piece appeared in German, in the Northern World of Megiserus, in 1613. (Clement. Bibl. Cur. Biog. Univ.)

BLEGBOROUGH, (Ralph,) an English physician, born April 5, 1769, at Richmond, in Yorkshire. After an education at the grammar-school of his native place, he acquired the rudiments of medicine under his father, a general practitioner there, who, by an extensive practice and the inheritance of a paternal estate, had amassed a considerable fortune. Having passed some time in this manner, young Blegborough departed for the university of Edinburgh, where he resided during two years; afterwards he repaired to London, and studied under Mr. Cline and Mr. (afterwards Sir Astley) Cooper, at Guy's and St. Thomas's hospitals. In 1793, having become a member of the corporation of surgeons, he commenced as a general practitioner in London, and continued in this career ten years, at which time he determined upon taking his degree; and having complied with the conditions imposed by the Royal College of Physicians by attendance for two years at an university, he became a member of that learned body. Dr. Blegborough had not confined his attention simply to the attainment of that knowledge which was immediately necessary to his profession, but had also cultivated natural and experimental philosophy. In 1802 Mr. Smith, of Brighton, had put forth an invention of considerable merit in the construction of an air pump vapour bath, an instrument of great power, and which has proved of remarkable efficacy in certain chronic cases. On this subject Dr. Blegborough addressed two letters to Dr. Bradley, the editor of the Medical and Physical Journal, and in 1803 he published a work, entitled Facts and Observations respecting the Air Pump Vapour Bath in Gout, Rheumatism, Palsy, and other Diseases. Soon after this, Dr. Walshman, a practitioner in midwifery of great celebrity, invited Dr. Blegborough to join him in the exercise of that department of the profession. This was accepted, and the remainder of his life devoted to it. He gave a large portion of his time to the most difficult cases that occurred among the poor, and he died literally worn out by his benevolent exertions at the age of 57, in the month of January, 1827. His opinion on subjects connected with midwifery was much valued, and he was one of the medical profession examined before the committee of the House of Peers upon the question of the Gardiner Peerage. He printed several cases in various periodical medical works, which display considerable practical ability. He was ardent in his advocacy of the benefits of vaccination. In private life he was universally esteemed as a most amiable and benevolent man.

BLEGNY, (Nicholas de,) an eminent French surgeon, who practised at Paris, and delivered lectures on surgery and pharmacy. In 1678 he was appointed surgeon in ordinary to the queen, and in 1679 commenced the publication of a periodical work, which professed to be written by an association of learned men, under the title of Journal des Nouvelles Découvertes concernant les Sciences et les Arts qui font Parties de la Médecine. This monthly journal was suppressed by an order of council in 1682, on the ground of its insignificance; but it appeared again in the following year, under the title of Mercure Savant, without the name of Blegny, who associated himself with Gautier, a physician of Niort, then living at Amsterdam, and the collection was again put forth in 1684. This work would scarcely be deserving of notice, were there not reasons for believing that its publication gave rise to the celebrated Nouvelles de la République des Lettres of Bayle, which commenced in the same year. In 1683 Blegny was named surgeon in ordinary to the duke of Orleans, and in 1687 physician in ordinary to the king, to the great astonishment of every one, for his habits were debauched. He assumed to himself the title of *chevalier*, appertaining to an order which had no real existence, but which he pretended to revive, and he went so far as to establish an hospital at Pincourt, which only formed a convenient place for the pursuit of his immoralities. These being made known, he was imprisoned in the Fort l'Evêque, June 4, 1693, whence he was conducted to the castle of Angers, where he remained during eight years, at the expiration of which period he repaired to Avignon, and there exercised his profession with much success. He died in 1722, at the age of 70 years. He may fairly be considered as the inventor of elastic bandages as applied to surgical purposes.

He published, L'Art de Guérir les Maladies Vénériennes, expliqué par les Principes de la Nature et de la Méchanique, Paris, 1673, 12mo; La Haye, 1683, 8vo; Lyon, 1692, 12mo; Amst. 1696, 8vo; translated into English, Lond. 1676, 1707, 8vo. L'Art de Guérir les Hernies de toutes Espèces dans les deux Sexes, avec le Remède du Roi, &c. Paris, 1676, 1693, 12mo. Nouvelles Découvertes sur toutes les Parties de la Médecine, Paris, 1679, 1680, 1681, and 1682, 12mo; translated into Latin by Theophilus Bonetus, under the title of Zodiacus Medico-Gallicus (Genevæ), 1679 to 1683, 5 vols, 4to. Mercure Savant, Amst. 1684, 12mo. Histoire Anatomique d'un Enfant qui a demeuré Vingt-cinq Ans dans le Ventre de sa Mère, Paris, 1679, 12mo. Le Remède Anglais pour la Guérison des Fièvres, Paris, 1681, 1683, 12mo; Bruxelles, 1682, 12mo. La Doctrine des Rapports de Chirurgie, Paris, 1684, 12mo, a curious work on legal surgery. Secrets concernant la Beauté et la Santé, Paris, 1688, 1689, 2 vols, 8vo.

BLEISWICK, (John van,) a member of the ancient family of that name, seated at Delft, in Holland, and spread into Brabant. He was born at Delft, Nov. 8, 1483, and after travelling in France and Spain, he settled himself in his native town as its priest. He died Aug. 25, 1565, very highly respected, leaving a treatise on the contempt of temporal riches. (Moreri.)

BLEISWICK, (Nicholas van,) of the same noble family as the last, a learned canonist in the 14th century, who wrote a life of St. Pancras. (Moreri.)

BLEISWICK, (Peter van,) great pensionary of Holland, born at Delft, in 1724, and educated at the university of Leyden, where he became doctor of philosophy in 1745. He published in that year an excellent dissertation on dykes, a subject of great interest in his country, entitled De Aggeribus, Leyd. 1745, 4to; a Dutch translation of it by Esdré appeared in 1778. Bleiswick was named great pensionary of the States-general in 1772, and he filled that office until 1787, having generally shown himself highly qualified for the public service; but he has been thought wanting in the decision necessary for circumstances of particular difficulty. (Biog. Univ.)

BLEKERS, (N.) a Dutch painter of history and landscape, born at Haerlem about 1635, patronized by the prince of Orange, and celebrated by Vondel, one of his country's poets. (Bryan. Pilkington.)

BLES, (Henry van,) a Flemish painter, born at Bovines, near Dinant, in 1480, and instructed merely by diligent study of Patenier's works. He was most successful in landscapes, but these are generally crowded with figures neatly drawn. His works are known as the Owl pictures, that bird being usually painted in the corner instead of his name, and are valued, even in Italy, from their delicate pencilling, skilful designing, variety, and good execution, notwithstanding that his manner, like that of contemporary artists, was dry and stiff. Bles died in 1550. (Bryan. Pilkington.)

BLESENSIS, or of Blois, from the place of his birth, (Peter,) an eminent statesman and divine, once keeper of the seals, under William II., king of Sicily, greatly valued by pope Alexander III., and much in the confidence of Henry II. of England. By that monarch's means he was appointed, in 1175, to the archdeaconry of Bath. He subsequently became archdeacon of London, and was present, in that capacity, at the making of a statute, in 1192, by Ralph de Diceto, dean of St. Paul's. He was afterwards deprived of this archdeaconry, but the certain time does not appear. He was also the archbishop of Canterbury's chancellor, and seems to have died about the year 1200, or soon after. He was not more distinguished for great abilities and acquirements, than for an ingenuous freedom, which never spared either prince or prelate when there appeared occasion for plain speaking. The chief of his works were published at Paris, in 1667. His letters contain admirable rules, both doctrinal and religious; and the 140th of them has been noted for the word transubstantiation, thought to be found in no earlier author. His continuation of Ingulph was first published with that author, at Oxford, in 1684. (Blount, Censura celebr. Author. Le Neve. Fasti.)

BLESSENDORF, the surname of two Prussian artists, both born at Berlin, Samuel in 1670, and Constantine Frederic in 1675. The elder was an enamel painter and engraver. His plates are very neatly finished. The younger was a miniature painter and engraver, who chiefly worked for the booksellers. (Bryan.)

BLETTERIE, (John Philip René de la,) an eminent French writer, born at Rennes, Feb. 25, 1696. After passing through the first stages of education with striking success, he entered into the congregation of the Oratory, in which he became professor of rhetoric, and to which he remained greatly attached through life, although he was led to quit it by a regulation against wigs. Desiring to acquire Hebrew, he adopted the system of Masclef, and published, in good Latin, a defence of it, entitled, Vindiciæ Methodi Masclefianæ, which is to be found in the second impression of Masclef's Hebrew Grammar, edited by La Bletterie, in 1731. This would not have rescued the editor from oblivion, but he published various works, connected with classical literature, which rendered him celebrated in his day, and make him still an object of attention. The most conspicuous of these is a Life of Julian the Apostate, a well-written, impartial, and accurate performance, published in French, at Paris, in 1735, and reprinted there, with additions and corrections, in 1746. In this latter year appeared an English translation of it. La Bletterie next produced his Histoire de Jovien, et la Traduction de quelques Ouvrages de l'Empereur Julien, Paris, 1748. This is also an excellent work, but Jovian was an ordinary man, who could not make, in spite of his Christianity, a striking picture; whereas Julian, powerfully drawn, was sure to interest even those who reprobated his principles. La Bletterie, accordingly, did not find his Jovian's popularity keep pace with that of his Julian. Subsequently he published French translations from Tacitus, with a life of that powerful historian, to whose writings he was ardently attached. His Manners of the Germans and Life of Agricola were published in 1755; his Annals in 1768. The last work was considered as very much of a failure. Great expectations of it were entertained beforehand; but when it appeared, although its correctness was admitted, it was blamed as inelegant and stiff. The abbé de la Bletterie died June 1, 1772, justly respected for morality, scholarship, and industry. In religious opinions he inclined to Jansenism, and one of his publications was a pamphlet on Quietism, containing a defence of Madame Guyon. To this cast of opinions he owed his exclusion from the French Academy. (Biog. Univ.)

BLEUL, (John Henry von,) born at Coblentz, in 1765, a German statesman, first in the service of the elector of Treves, and afterwards, about 1791, director of the Austrian war chancery. He died in 1807, leaving behind him the reputation of a patriotic statesman and sagacious diplomatist. He is the author of several valuable contributions, chiefly statistical, to different journals, a number of which was collected and published under his name, in 1806, at Salzburg, where he was long employed.

BLIGH, (Sir Richard Rodney, G.C.B.) a British admiral, descended from an ancient family in Cornwall, where he was born in the year 1737. He was the godson of the celebrated lord Rodney, under whose auspices he was early sent to sea. In 1777 he attained the rank of post-captain, and for a series of years continued employed on active and stirring service. In 1794, when in command of the *Alexander* (74), and in company with the *Canada*, captain Charles Hamilton, he encountered a French squadron, consisting of five line-of-battle-ships, three frigates, and a brig corvette, under rear-admiral Neilly. The enemy's squadron descried the *Alexander* and *Canada* at 2 A.M., November 6. The British battle-ships were steering to the northward and eastward with a free wind at west; but on perceiving a strange squadron, both ships immediately "hauled upon a bow-line," in order to close with it, and ascertain its national character. Before daylight, Bligh had felt well assured that the approaching strangers were enemies, and consequently had to resume his former course, and press sail, to avoid coming in collision with a force so powerfully superior to that of his own. But the French admiral, outsailing the *Alexander*, approached that vessel sufficiently near to open upon her a fire from her "bow-chasers." This was at about 9 A.M. The *Canada's* signal was now made to form ahead for mutual support; a signal which captain Hamilton promptly sought to obey, but the enemy frustrating his intention, the *Canada* was directed to resume her course. The *Alexander* had kept up an unceasing fire with her stern guns until 11 A.M., when the advanced ship of the three in chase of her, (supposed to be the *Jean Bart*,) ran up abreast of the British ship, and brought her to close action. So well directed a fire in return was opened by the *Alexander*, that, in half-an-hour, the French 74 was compelled to sheer off and call a frigate to her assistance. The French commodore, in the *Tiger*, next advanced, but would not come fairly alongside; notwithstanding which, the *Alexander*, in about half an hour, shot away her essential spars, and completely crippled her. A third ship now took the latter's place, and used her endeavours to bring the contest to a close. This unequal conflict the *Alexander* sustained until "some minutes past one P.M.," by which time she had all her serviceable spars shot away—her running-rigging cut to pieces—her sails torn into ribands—her hull shattered, and on fire in several places, and her hold nearly filled with water. The other ship, also, which had quitted her consort, was rapidy advancing, and the French admiral already threw his shot over her. Captain Bligh, therefore, justly deemed any further efforts as a heedless waste of lives, and ordered the colours of the *Alexander* to be hauled down.

As far as could be ascertained, the *Alexander's* loss amounted to about 40 men in killed and wounded; including among the latter, one lieutenant of marines, the boatswain and pilot. The *Canada*, owing to the high firing of the French, sustained very little damage and no loss, and reached a home-port in safety. According to the French papers, the *Alexander's* two principal opponents were very much disabled, and sustained between them a loss in killed and wounded amounting to 450, officers and men. When captured by the enemy, though not aware of it himself, Bligh had attained the rank of rear-admiral. In the early part of the year 1795, he arrived in England from France, where he had been a prisoner, we believe on parole; and on the 27th of May was tried by a court-martial for the loss of the *Alexander*, and, to use the words of a naval historian, "was, as may be well supposed, honourably acquitted." After attaining the rank of full admiral of the red, he died near Southampton, April 30, 1821.

BLIGH, (William,) an English navigator, recommended by serving as master, under Cook, in sailing round the world, for an expedition that had very remarkable consequences. The bread fruit, with other vegetable productions of importance, grown in the islands of the great Pacific, were thought likely to prove highly useful in the West Indies, and George the Third's government fitted out a vessel, the *Bounty*, to make the transfer. Bligh, being appointed to command her, after a prosperous and interesting voyage through the southern hemisphere, sailed from Otaheite, where he had remained upwards of five months, with his vegetable cargo, April 4, 1789. Within a few days afterwards a mutiny broke out among the crew, and Bligh, with eighteen officers and seamen, were turned adrift in the launch belonging to the ship. After a difficult and anxious voyage, this little band succeeded in reaching Timor. They were almost exhausted, but the governor of Coupang rendering them every necessary aid, they soon recovered strength, and proceeded to Batavia, whence they sailed for England. The intelligence furnished by Bligh was deemed so important by the government, that a vessel was speedily despatched in search of the mutineers, and fourteen of them were seized at Otaheite, whither they had returned. Ten arrived in England, and three were executed. Fletcher Christian, the chief mate, or first lieutenant, a young man of talents, who commanded the whole body, did not remain with them, but sailed away with others of the mutineers, and nothing was known of his fate, although many reports respecting him were in circulation, until his son, one of the actual mutineers, and descendants of several more by Otaheitan women, were found on Pitcairn's Island in 1814. Bligh, soon after his return to England, published A Narrative of the Mutiny on board H. M. Ship Bounty, and this was immediately translated into French. He subsequently incorporated his account of the mutiny in a detailed relation of the voyage, published in 1792. As his own historian, he naturally threw all the blame upon an unruly crew, and thus awakened in his favour the sympathies of all Europe. Being appointed, however, to the government of New South Wales, his want of judgment armed the whole colony against him, and he was ignominiously sent back to England. It is now known that his own harshness and indiscretion caused the mutiny in the *Bounty*, but his foresight and coolness, when turned adrift, were admirable. An inferior man would, probably, have been found unequal to conduct an open boat, without losing a single life, from the mutinous *Bounty* to the shores of Timor.

BLIN DE SAINMORE, (Adrian Michael Hyacinth,) a French poet and historian, born Feb. 15, 1733. Among his poems is La Mort de l'Amiral Byng, published in 1752. In 1798 and 1799, appeared his Histoire de Russie depuis l'An 862 jusqu'au Règne de Paul I., 2 vols, 4to. In 1800 he was appointed, by the first consul, conservator of the library of the Arsenal. He died September 26, 1807. (Biog. de Contemp.)

BLISSEM, (Henry,) a learned Austrian Jesuit, eminent for public speaking and close application to theology. He died provincial of his order, at Gratz, in 1586, having published at Ingolstadt, De Communione sub unâ Specie; and De Ecclesiâ Militante, contra Herbrandum Tubingensem. (Moreri.)

BLITTERSWYCK, (John van,) a Flemish devotional writer, who produced many pieces now forgotten. He became connected with the Carthusians in 1605, and died in 1661. His works are chiefly translations into Flemish, either from Latin, French, or Spanish; but he also published three original pieces, two of them connected with the worship of the Virgin, and of saints. (Biog. Univ. Suppl.)

BLITTERSWYCK, (Willian van,) a learned Flemish functionary under the Spanish rule, thought to be brother of the preceding. He translated from Spanish into Latin, a work by Saavedra, which he published anonymously at Brussels in 1649, and again at Amsterdam, in 1652, with the following title, Symbola Politica Christiana. In 1666, he published Dissertatio de Rebus Publicis, and Ruremunda vigens, ardens, renascens. He died at Mechlin, in 1680, with the character of a learned lawyer, an orator, and poet. (Biog. Univ. Suppl.)

BLIZARD, (Sir William, knt.,) an eminent English surgeon, born in 1743, son of an auctioneer. Having studied anatomy and medicine according to the superficial method of his time, he was, in 1780, appointed surgeon to the London Hospital; and he has the merit of having united with Dr. Robert Maclaurin to form the first regular school of medical science in connexion with the hospital in 1785. Here he educated many who afterwards distinguished themselves in medicine and surgery, among whom it is sufficient to mention John Abernethy, who frequently took occasion in his lectures at St. Bartholomew's Hospital, and at the College of Surgeons, to acknowledge the obligations he was under to his teacher. For a long series of years Sir William Blizard delivered lectures on anatomy, physiology, and surgery. He was esteemed a good anatomist, an able practical surgeon, a bold and skilful operator. He was the first surgeon to tie the superior thyroideal artery in cases of bronchocele, and one of the earliest to secure the subclavian artery in cases of aneurism. He continued to operate until the year 1827. On the eighty-fourth anniversary of his birth he amputated an arm with considerable ability and steadiness, and having completed this, he resigned his situation at the London Hospital, of which he was a most zealous supporter, liberal benefactor, and active friend. He took great interest in the prosperity of the Royal College of Surgeons, and was one of the petitioners for the charter, having been admitted a member of the previous Corporation of Surgeons in 1796. Of the college he was twice president; and he delivered the first public course of lectures at the building in Lincoln's-inn Fields on anatomy and surgery. He presented to the College Museum, upon his retirement from teaching at the London Hospital, in 1811, his collection of preparations illustrative of human and comparative anatomy in healthy and in morbid conditions of organs, animal monstrosities, calculi, &c., amounting to nearly 900 specimens, of which the college published a catalogue in 1832. He was chosen an examiner at the college in 1810, and continued to perform the duties of that office until the time of his death. Towards the close of his life he became blind from cataract; and at the age of 91 submitted to an operation by Mr. Lawrence, which was completely successful in restoring him to sight, which event he commemorated by an ode. He died August 28, 1835, aged 92 years. He received the honour of knighthood from George III., in 1810, upon the presentation of an address of condolence from the Medico-Chirurgical Society, on the death of the princess Amelia. His publications are not numerous, but they were useful in their day, particularly the one which relates to the economy of hospitals, and which was translated into German. Among the others are, A New Method of Treating the Fistula Lachrymalis, Lond. 1780, 4to. Of the Expediency and Utility of Teaching the several Branches of Physic and Surgery by Lectures at the London Hospital, Lond. 1783, 4to. On the Danger of Copper and Bell-Metal in Pharmaceutical and Chemical Preparations, Lond. 1786, 8vo. A Lecture on the Situation of the Large Blood Vessels of the Extremities, &c. Lond. 1798, 8vo, third edition.

BLIZARD, (Thomas,) a celebrated English surgeon, born in 1772, educated professionally under his cousin, Sir William Blizard. Being a most excellent operator as well as medical surgeon, he formed an extensive practice in the city of London, and acquired a large fortune. After a retirement of several years from the labours of his profession, he died on the 7th of May, 1838. In the performance of operations he was perhaps never excelled, yet he displayed no eagerness for them. His knowledge of anatomy was minute and accurate. He invented a long slender-backed knife for the operation of lithotomy, which is still used by many surgeons, and is known by the name of the inventor. Finding himself, however, then in very easy circumstances, he retired from the practice of his profession at the early age of forty-six. He wrote but little. There is, however, by him an excellent Description of an Extra-Uterine Fœtus, in the fifth volume of the Transactions of the Royal Society of Edinburgh, of which institution he was a fellow; and also a paper in the first volume of the Transactions of the Medico-Chirurgical Society, on a Case of Intussusception of the Bowels.

BLOCH, (John Erasmus,) a Danish gardener, who published at Copenhagen a work on the practice of his profession, entitled Horticultura Danica, 1647, 4to. (Chalmers.)

BLOCH, (George Castaneus,) bishop of Ripen, in Denmark, born in 1717, died in 1773, eminent for applying botany to the illustration of Scripture. In 1767 he published at Copenhagen, Tentamen Phœnicologices, 8vo, a work containing much curious information on the palm tree, or *phœnix dactylifera* of modern botanists, and explaining passages in the Bible which mention it. (Chalmers.)

BLOCH, (Mark Eliezer,) a German naturalist, born at Anspach, of very poor Jewish parents, in 1723, and brought up in such ignorance that he knew neither German nor Latin at nineteen. Being then employed by a surgeon of his nation at Hamburgh, he there acquired German, and a poor Bohemian gave him some instructions in Latin. He now became a hard student, addicting himself particularly to anatomy and natural history. Having taken the degree of doctor of medicine at Frankfort on the Oder, he settled at Berlin as a physician. He died Aug. 6, 1799, leaving three German treatises upon fishes, united, in 1785, under the title of Icthyology, which is one of the most splendid works upon natural history that had then appeared. It would, indeed, have been found impossible to complete it, had not the wealthier Prussians, considering it a national honour, come forward with assistance. A French translation of this work by Laveaux was twice printed. Bloch also published a tract upon intestinal worms, and the medical treatment of them, which was well received. (Biog. Univ.)

BLOCHIUS, (Cornelius,) prior of the canons regular at Utrecht, where he died, Dec. 5, 1553, leaving Tractatus de Simoniâ Religiosorum: Sermo de Proprietatibus Religiosorum. (Moreri.)

BLOCHWITZ, (Martin,) a German physician, who wrote a work on the elder and its medical uses, published after his death by his brother, at Leipsic, in 1631, under the title of Anatomia Sambuci. This appeared in London, but merely with a new title-page, in 1650. In 1655, an English version by Shirley was published, entitled The

Anatomie of Elder. A German translation of it with additions was published at Königsberg, 1642, and Leipsic, 1685. (Biog. Univ.)

BLOCK, (Benjamin,) a painter of history and portraits, born at Lubeck, in 1631, and sent into Italy for improvement by Frederic Adolphus, duke of Mecklenburg. His historical works, which are respectable, consist chiefly of German and Hungarian altar-pieces. (Bryan. Pilkington.)

BLOCK, (Daniel,) father and original instructor of the preceding, an eminent portrait-painter, born at Stettin, in Pomerania, in 1580. He died in 1661, deeply mortified at losing, by the irruption of a plundering party, the very considerable gains which his talents and parsimony had enabled him to amass. (Bryan. Pilkington.)

BLOCK, (J. R.) a Dutch painter of architectural subjects, born at Gouda in 1580, said to have been complimented by Rubens as the ablest artist that his country could boast in his particular line. He was drowned by means of a fall from his horse in 1632, when crossing a brook with a reconnoitring party. (Bryan. Pilkington.)

BLOCK, (Joanna Koerten,) a Dutch female artist, born in 1650, whose talents for executing with scissors what others effected by a graver, long excited admiration in almost all the courts of Europe. She died in 1715. (Biog. Univ.)

BLOCK, (Magnus Gabriel,) an intelligent Swedish writer, who, after extensive travels in different parts of Europe, became member of the medical board at Stockholm, and was ennobled. He died in 1722, leaving in his own tongue a valuable treatise respecting the river Motala and the Wetter lake; also two treatises upon predictions and prodigies, one of them translated from the English. (Biog. Univ.)

BLOCKLANDT, (Anthony de Montfort,) an eminent Dutch painter, of noble family, born at Montfort, in 1532, and chiefly employed upon portraits, but with a genius excellently fitted for historical compositions. He was a thorough master of perspective, skilful in grouping figures, and had an agreeable style of colouring. He died in 1583. (Bryan. Pilkington.)

BLOEMAERT, (Abraham,) a Dutch painter and engraver, born at Gorcum, about 1564, but mostly resident at Utrecht. He painted history and landscapes, of which the colouring is excellent, but the drawing defective, and his figures appear to have been designed without sufficient attention to real life. His most esteemed prints are spiritedly executed in *chiar-oscuro*, with outlines, not cut on the blocks of wood, but etched on copper. (Bryan. Pilkington.)

BLOEMART, (Adrian,) second son of the preceding, a painter of history and portraits of some merit, who, after some instructions from his father, travelled into Italy, and eventually settled at Salzburg. He was killed in a duel. An elder brother, named Henry, painted portraits, but with little success, his colouring being bad and his pencilling stiff. Frederic, the third brother, born at Utrecht about 1600, became a distinguished engraver. He was, however, surpassed by Cornelius, the fourth brother, born at Utrecht in 1603, but resident at Rome the greater part of his life. He made great improvements in the art of engraving, and left numerous specimens of his talents behind him, which are universally admired, but several of them are very scarce. He is thought to have died at Rome in 1680. (Bryan. Pilkington.)

BLOEMEN, (John Francis van,) called Orizonti, or Orizzonte, from a peculiarity in his style, an eminent painter, born at Antwerp, in 1656, and considered as an Italian master, because he went to that country when very young, and remained all the rest of his life there. He painted landscapes with great success, in the manner of Gaspar Poussin, but not so ably. He died in 1740, leaving pictures that are highly prized in every part of Europe. (Bryan. Pilkington.)

BLOEMEN, (Peter van,) called Standard, from some of his pictures representing attacks of cavalry. He was brother of the preceding, and born at Antwerp, where he fixed his residence after a stay of some years at Rome. His composition is rich, and his pictures well filled with figures correctly and spiritedly drawn. Some of his pictures are, however, considered stiff and laboured. (Bryan. Pilkington.)

BLOEMEN, (Norbert van,) youngest brother of the preceding, born at Antwerp, in 1672. He spent some time at Rome, but eventually settled at Amsterdam, where he died. He painted portraits and conversations, but with no remarkable success. (Bryan. Pilkington. Biog. Univ.)

BLOM, (Charles Magnus,) a Swedish physician, born at Kafsvik, in Smolandia, March 1, 1737, originally intended for the church, but preferring medicine, he embraced it as a profession, and devoted his leisure time to the study of natural history. This he pursued under Linnæus, and took a voyage into Holland in 1760 to acquire information in his favourite branch of science. Returning home, he wrote a Thesis de Ligno Quassiæ, in 1763, when he took his doctor's degree at the university of Upsal. In 1774 he went to Dalecarlia, and there entered into practice. He introduced vaccine inoculation into Sweden. He died April 4, 1815, having published many papers in the Transactions of the societies to which he belonged; among these are, Descriptiones quorundam Insectorum nondum cognitorum ad Aquisgranum anno 1761 detectorum. Essays on Aconite, Remedies for and Preservatives against Dysentery, Putrid and Bilious Fevers.

BLOMBERG, (Alexander von,) a German dramatist, born 1788, at Jagenhausen, in Lippe. He entered the Prussian army in his thirteenth year, was present at the battle of Jena, and was dismissed by the French on parole, after that fatal day; lived then for some time at Berlin, which he left to take part in Schill's heroic revolt, for his share in which he was imprisoned for three months. He afterwards entered the Russian army, and fought for the liberation of his country from foreign oppression till 1813, when he fell by a French bullet before the Schönhäuser gate at Berlin. La Motte Fouqué published his Conradin of Swabia, Waldemar of Denmark, and minor poems, in 1820. As literary productions they are but indifferent, but the sentiments that they contain are those of an ardent, noble, and patriotic spirit.

BLOMENVENNA, (Peter,) a Carthusian, born at Liege, and hence often designated Leodiensis. He died in 1536, much venerated for piety, and left several religious works behind him. (Moreri.)

BLOMFIELD, (Edward Valentine,) son of C. Blomfield, of Bury St. Edmund's, where he was born Feb. 14, 1788. After an education at the grammar-school there, he went to Caius college, Cambridge, and was subsequently chosen fellow and tutor of Emmanuel, where he died Oct. 9, 1816, almost immediately on his return from the continent, which he had visited as one of the travelling bachelors of the university. His academical career, to use the language of his biographer in the Gent.'s Mag., was distinguished by every honour that could adorn the brow of youth, or give an earnest of future excellence. To a critical knowledge of Greek and Latin, he added an extensive familiarity with the languages of modern Europe; and while his eminent attainments were even surpassed by the qualities of the heart, the accomplishments of the scholar were heightened by the graces of a christian life. To him England is indebted for the translation of Matthiæ's Greek Grammar, which was published after his death by his brother, C. J. Blomfield, the editor of Æschylus, subsequently bishop of Chester and of London in succession. From the preface of this distinguished prelate, we learn that had his brother's life been spared we should have had the first Greek and English lexicon, and doubtless something more than the mere translation, of the German works by Schneider and Passow. The only original specimens of his scholarship are to be found in some papers of the Museum Criticum. We have heard, moreover, that he had a great talent for drawing; but his career was unfortunately too short to enable the world to witness more than the blossoms of hope.

BLOND, (Michael le,) a German engraver, born at Frankfort about 1580, and chiefly resident at Amsterdam, where he seems to have been ordinarily engaged upon ornaments for the goldsmiths. His prints are very small, and executed entirely with the graver, in the manner of Theodore de Bry. (Bryan.)

BLOND, (James Christopher le,) an artist, born at Frankfort in 1670, and resident for some time at Amsterdam as miniature painter. His productions had a good reputation, but being chiefly for bracelets and other small ornaments, they injured his sight. Hence he attempted portraits upon a larger scale, and again with success. He was, however, too fickle and scheming for a long continuance in any one course. He came accordingly to England with a project, not, it seems, originally his own, but taken from Lastman and others, of printing mezzotinto plates in colour, so as to imitate the pictures from which they were copied. The specimens which he produced astonished all who viewed them from a proper distance, but they would not bear a close inspection. Hence when he disposed of them by lottery, the winners were not particularly pleased with their prizes. Le Blond explained his art in a book published in 1730, entitled, Il Colorito, or the Harmony of Colouring in Painting reduced to Mechanical Practice under easy Precepts and infallible Rules. Afterwards Le Blond embarked in a scheme for copying the Cartoons of Raphael in tapestry; and having made some fine drawings for the purpose, considerable expense was incurred. Matters had not, however, gone very far before it was found impossible to raise the requisite funds, and Le Blond suddenly disappeared, greatly to the dissatisfaction of those who were engaged with him. He died in an hospital at Paris, in 1740. Besides the work already mentioned, he published in 1732 a French treatise on Ideal Beauty, afterwards translated into English. (Pilkington. Bryan. Chalmers.)

BLONDE, (Andrew,) a French advocate, born at Auxerre, in 1734, who published at Amsterdam, in 1774, being then obliged to retire from France, a translation of Pestel's Foundations of Natural Jurisprudence. On the accession of Lewis XVI. Blonde returned into his own country; and when the revolution broke out he came forward in the question as to the competence of the civil power to erect and suppress episcopal sees. He died April 3, 1794. (Biog. Univ. Suppl.)

BLONDEAU, (James,) a French engraver, born at Langres, about 1639, and employed in Italy in engraving from some of the painters of that country. He seems to have imitated Cornelius Bloemaert, but with no remarkable success. (Bryan.)

BLONDEAU, (Claudius,) a French advocate, who commenced with Guéret, in 1672, the Journal du Palais, and published in 1689 the Bibliothèque Canonique. (Biog. Univ.)

BLONDEAU, (Charles,) an advocate at Mans, where he died Dec. 31, 1680, having published, Portraits des Hommes Illustres de la Province du Maine, 1666, 4to. (Biog. Univ.)

BLONDEAU, (Anthony Francis Raymond,) a French general, born in Franche-Comté, Jan. 7, 1747, and in early life a private soldier. In the revolutionary wars he served with distinction, especially during the Italian campaign of 1799. He died May 8, 1825, after a retirement of several years. (Biog. Univ. Suppl.)

BLONDEAU DE CHARNAGE, (Claudius Francis,) a French writer, born in 1710, and died 1776, who spent his latter years at Paris upon a pension, and wrote a great number of pieces, chiefly collected in two volumes 12mo, under the title of Œuvres du Chevalier Blondeau, Avignon, 1745. Among these is a bad imitation of La Bruyère, and a sort of ill-written romance, without invention, entitled, Mémoires du Chevalier Blondeau. (Biog. Univ.)

BLONDEEL, (Lansloot,) a Flemish painter, born at Bruges, in 1500, originally a mason. While following this trade he amused himself with drawing architectural designs, and thus he educated himself for a successful painter in this line. He died in his native town in 1559. (Pilkington.)

BLONDEL, or BLONDIAUX. There are two French minstrels of this name, who are often confounded with each other. The first was the favourite of Richard I. king of England; the second, surnamed de Nesle, lived much later, and is reckoned by M. de Fauchet as the eighteenth in the series that he gives of the French poets, whose works he records. Unfortunately, of him he affords no other notice than a few specimens of his poetry; but of the former he relates, on the authority of an old French chronicle, the current story, which is, however, considered by Mr. Berington, in the History of the Life of King Richard, "as possibly a fiction," that when that monarch, on his return from Palestine, was made prisoner by Leopold, duke of Austria, and confined in an unknown fortress, Blondel, wandering through Germany in search of him, having arrived at the castle of Lowenstein, and being informed that a great personage was there confined, thinking that he might possibly be Richard, began to sing under the window of that fortress the first stanza of a song which they had composed together, and to his joy he heard Richard, who had recognised his voice, sing the remaining part. On this Blondel returned immediately to England, and by relating the discovery that he had made, procured the liberty of Richard.

BLONDEL, (David,) a protestant minister, of distinguished learning, born at Chalons, in Champagne, in 1591, admitted to the ministry in a synod of the isle of France in 1614. He officiated at Houdan, near Paris, for five years, during which he wrote a book in defence of Protestantism, under the title of Modeste Déclaration de la Sincérité et Vérité des Eglises Reformées de France, printed at Sedan in 1619; an answer to some of the Romish party, and particularly to the bishop of Lusson, so well known afterwards as the cardinal Richelieu. The reputation which this book procured him, aided by his beautiful hand-writing, caused him to be twenty times appointed secretary in the synods of the isle of France, four times in the national synods, of which he collected and drew up the acts; and there is reason to suppose that by that of Castres, he was deputed, in 1626, to return thanks to the king in the name of the assembly, and ordered to write in defence of the protestants, and particularly against the Annals of Baronius, towards which he did no more than insert a great number of marginal notes on his copy of that work. This copy, after his death, was bought and given by the magistrates of Amsterdam to the public library of that city; and many years before the revocation of the Edict of Nantes, when the burgomaster desired a refugee minister of Bearn to confute Baronius, were by him published, with a little addition of his own, under the title of Anti-Baronius Magenelis, a very poor work. In 1631 the province of Anjou applied to the national synod at Charenton, to elect him professor of divinity at Saumur; but although this request was not then granted, because he was thought to have no talent for the pulpit, he was by the same synod, in 1645, made titular professor, with a suitable pension, which had never been done before, in order that he might dedicate his talent to writing in favour of the protestants. This he did by several publications, such as the Explications on the Eucharist; de la Primauté de l'Eglise; the Pseudo-Isidorus, et Turrianus Vapulantes; a work against the decretal epistles; a treatise on the Sibyls, in which he refutes the practice of praying for the dead; another, De Formula Regnante Christe; a third, about the liberty of conscience, opposed to the Bull of Innocent X. against the peace of Munster, which he published under the assumed name of Amand Flavien; a fourth, De Episcopis et Presbyteris, which very much pleased the protestants, though he displeased them much more by another publication, in which he showed that what is reported of Pope Joan is a ridiculous fable, for he was accused of having compiled the book for the sake of favouring the Roman catholics.

After the death of Vossius, he was, in 1650, appointed to succeed him in the professorship of history by the curators of the college at Amsterdam. But there his intense application, and the damp atmosphere, soon affected his health and his sight; and it is said that in this condition he dictated two folio volumes on the genealogy of the kings of France against Chifflet, at the request of the chancellor Seguier. Some persons suspected him of Arminianism, on account of the Considerations Religieuses et Politiques, which he published during the war of Cromwell and the Dutch. He died in 1655. It is said that he had a singular way of studying, which was, to lie flat on the ground, and to have round him all the books that he wanted for the work he was about.

He had two elder brothers, both ministers; the name of the eldest was Moses, minister at Meaux, and afterwards in London, and the author of a book of Controversies, whose learning was not useless to David, and it was he who gave the MS. from which the explanation about pope Joan was printed.

BLONDEL, (Francis,) born at Liege, in 1613, physician to the elector archbishop of Treves, and after the death of that prince established at Aix-la-Chapelle. He was made superintendent of the baths there, and upon them he published some works. He died May 9, 1703.

BLONDEL, (Francis,) an eminent architect, born at Ribemont, in Picardy, in 1617. He died at Paris in 1686. Being appointed tutor and governor to Henry Lewis de Lomenie, son of the count of Brienne, minister of state, to whom Lewis XIV. had given the reversion of his father's office, he accompanied him in his travels through the north of Europe, from 1652 to 1655, of which he published a Latin account in 1660; a second edition of which, enlarged and corrected, appeared two years after. He was also employed in several military and diplomatic affairs; and particularly in 1659, when he was sent to Egypt and Constantinople as a special ambassador of Lewis XIV., on account of the imprisonment of the French minister by the Porte. The success of this negotiation procured him the diploma of minister of state, and the situation of teacher of mathematics and literature to the dauphin; and in 1669, he had also the satisfaction of seeing that all the public works in Paris were by a royal order to be executed according to his designs, which were afterwards published in 1671, in his lectures on architecture. His principal works are:—Comparaison de Pindar et Horace, 1675. Histoire du Calendrier Romain, 1676. Cours de Mathematiques, 1683. L'Art de jetter les Bombes, 1685. Manière de fortifier les Places; this work, though long written, was not allowed by Lewis XIV. to be published until the fortifications that he had ordered to be made to different places were finished.

BLONDEL, (Francis,) doctor of medicine at Paris in 1632, distinguished by his opposition to the chemical sect of physicians. He contended violently against the introduction of antimony into medicine, and fell under the severe criticism of Guy Patin, who, however, failed not to acknowledge his great and profound erudition. He died September 5, 1682. He edited the latter three volumes of the Commentaries of Réné Chartier on the works of Hippocrates, and he also published, among other works, the following:—Ergò Jejuno Vomitus, Paris, 1631, 4to. Ergò Primipartus Vivaciores, *ib.* 1632, 4to. Statuta Facultatis Medicinæ Parisiensis, *ib.* 1660, 12mo. Epistola ad Alliotum de curâ Carcinomatis absque Ferro et Igne, *ib.* 1666, 4to. Non ergò Monstra Formatricis Peccata, *ib.* 1669, 4to. Elogium Ludovici Savot, *ib.* 1673, 4to.

BLONDEL, (Peter James,) born at Paris, and author of La Vérité de la Religion Chrétienne, and of a Mémoire contre les Imprimeurs et leurs Gains excessifs. He died in 1730.

BLONDEL, (Laurence,) cousin to the preceding, also born at Paris, and attached to the Solitaires of Port Royal, who induced him to turn his talents to works on religion. His early occupation was to keep a school, but soon after he became the corrector of Desprez's and Desessart's press, an employment which he kept for seventeen years, during which he published a new Vie des Saints, and other religious works. He died at Paris in 1740.

BLONDEL, (James Francis,) born at Rouen, in 1705, and nephew of Francis Blondel. Though not instructed in architecture by him, as some biographers have asserted, he showed so much talent in the pursuit as to be able to be the first to open a public school at Paris, and give public lectures, at the age of thirty-five. Being elected in 1755 a member of the Academy of Architecture, and soon after regius professor, he was employed to write all the articles of the Encyclopédie on that subject; and by his public, as well as by his private lectures, which he continued for thirty years, he produced a new era in architecture, and died in 1774. He erected the episcopal palace at Cambray; the portal of the cathedral, the casernes, and the Hôtel de la Ville at Metz, with other monuments of his taste elsewhere. His principal works are—Cours d'Architecture, ou Traité de la Decoration, Distribution et Construction des Batimens, 6 vols, 8vo, 1771 and 1773, of which he only published the first four, with engravings. De la Decoration des Édifices. Discours sur l'Architecture.

BLONDEL, (James Augustus,) a physician of French origin, but born in England. He was a member of the London Royal College of Physicians, and died in London in 1734. He is known by an ingenious and able work, entitled, The Strength of the Imagination of Pregnant Women examined, and the Opinion that Marks and Deformities are from them, demonstrated to be a vulgar Error, Lond. 1727, 8vo. This was published in French by Albert Bruno, Leyd. 1737, 8vo; in Dutch, Rotterdam, 1737, 8vo; and in German, Strasburg, 1756, 8vo. He also published, The Power of the Mother's Imagination over the Fœtus examined, in Answer to Dr. Daniel Turner, Lond. 1729, 8vo; and he is also the author of Dissertatio de Crisibus, Lugd. Batav. 1692, 4to, where it is probable he graduated.

BLONDIN, (Peter,) a French botanist, born in Picardy, December 18, 1682. He came to Paris in 1700, to finish his studies, and attached himself particularly to the famous botanist Tournefort, who had the highest opinion of him. To his zeal for botanical knowledge, the world owed accounts of many plants hitherto unnoticed, but he left nothing written behind him besides a correction of Tournefort's Classification in some particulars. He died of a fever at Paris, April 15, 1713. (Moreri.)

BLONDIN, (John Noel,) an excellent and industrious French grammarian, born at Paris in 1753, once member of the order of Feuillans, and secretary interpreter in the king's library. When the revolutionary fury had closed all the colleges, Blondin, in pity to his maddened countrymen, gratuitously gave courses of grammatical instruction at the Louvre and the Oratory. He died at Paris, May 13, 1832, not only respected for this proof of an enlightened public spirit, but also with claims upon the gratitude of posterity for several grammatical works of merit. One of these, Grammaire Française demonstrative, often reprinted, received the prize, in 1796, awarded to elementary books of the greatest utility. Other works of Blondin's requiring notice are, a French Grammar for the English, 1788; an English Grammar, 1790; an Italian Grammar, 1791; a Collection of English Extracts, 1798; a Polyglott Grammar, French, Latin, Italian, Spanish, Portuguese, and English, 1811, second edition 1825; and a Demonstrative Latin Grammar, analogically compared with the French. (Biog. Univ. Suppl.)

BLONDUS, (Flavius,) an Italian historian, whose vernacular name really seems to have been Flavio di Biondo Ravaldini. He was born at Forli, in the Romagna, in 1388, and died at Rome, June 4, 1463, having been secretary to Eugenius IV. and some other popes. As an author, he is exact, but his style retains something of the barbarism which Italy was then beginning to repudiate. His Roma Triumphans appears from Mattaire to have been first printed at Brescia, in 1482; but editions of it, even in the following century, are very uncommon, though the last-named is least so. The first of them was printed at Brescia, in folio, in 1503; another at Paris, 1533, 8vo; another at Bâle, by Froben, 1531, fol.; a fourth, esteemed the best, by the same printer, 1559, fol., bears the following title,—Blondi Flavii de Roma Triumphante Lib. x. Romæ instauratæ Libri iii. de Origine ac Gestis Venetorum Liber. Italia Illustrata, sive Lustrata, in Regiones seu Provincias divisa xviii. Historiarum ab inclinato Romano Imperio Decades iii. There are also Italian translations of this author's works printed at Venice in the sixteenth century. (Clement. Moreri.)

BLOOD, (Thomas,) a ruffianly adventurer, known as Colonel Blood, whose cunning, boldness, and strange escapes, made considerable noise in the time of Charles II. He was born in Ireland, and said to be the son of a blacksmith, but his father seems really to have been an ironmaster, who realized a fortune, and obtained a grant of lands at Sarney, and other places, in the county of Meath, from Charles I.; hence his notorious son was sometimes called Blood of Sarney. The young man was in England about the close of Charles the First's reign, but returning soon after to his own country, he sided with the prevailing party, and became a lieutenant in the parliament's army, having an estate assigned him for his pay. This he might have lost at the Restoration, as he then became involved in circumstances, and described himself as an injured man. His desperation drove him, in 1663, upon a scheme to surprise Dublin castle, and seize the duke of Ormond, then lord-lieutenant. He had many confederates, some of them persons of consideration; and had not the plot been discovered, when on the very eve of execution, it seems likely to have proved, if not absolutely successful, at least productive of serious mischief. His brother-in-law was executed as an accomplice in this conspiracy; but although he was himself esteemed a principal, and great exertions were made for apprehending him, he escaped. After various adventures in Ireland, Scotland, and Holland, he came to England, assumed the name of Ayliffe, and passed for a physician. While thus out of observation, he entered upon a vindictive scheme to seize, and probably to murder his old object of antipathy, Ormond. As the duke was returning in his coach down St. James's-street, December 6, 1670, from a dinner given to the young prince of Orange, six horsemen stopped him, and one of them dragging him from the carriage, fastened him by a leathern belt behind another. The object was said to be to carry him to Tyburn, and hang him there. In the way, however, Ormond regained his liberty, but not without personal injury; and although pursuers were at hand, the darkness of the night enabled his captors to escape. A reward of a thousand pounds was offered, but no arrest ensued. Unwarned by this new escape, Blood's desperate circumstances next impelled him upon a plan to seize the crown jewels in the Tower. As a preliminary, he dressed himself in a gown and cassock, then worn by clergymen at ordinary times, and professing himself to be of their order, formed an acquaintance with Edwards, who had the care of the regalia. One morning the pretended ecclesiastic called upon that officer, with two companions, under pretence of a visit to the jewel room. Having been admitted, they threw a cloak over the head of Edwards, gagged him, and because he struggled, wounded him. Blood then put the crown under his cassock, and his two companions took away the globe and sceptre. Before they got clear from the

Tower, an alarm was given, and two of them were apprehended. The third was taken on horseback, two hours afterwards. When Blood was examined, the king was foolish enough to be present. The prisoner now saw his advantage. He avowed his crimes, justified his attempt upon Ormond as an act of vengeance to which he was driven by necessity, because the duke had robbed him of his estate; declared himself to have been engaged in a plot for shooting Charles himself while bathing at Battersea, as an oppressor of the godly, and to have been actually secreted in the reeds for that purpose; but when taking aim at the royal person, to have been restrained by an indescribable sense of awe from accomplishing the traitorous design. The fathomless depths of human vanity will generally find ample room for the vigorous operation of language like this. Blood, however, did not rest without working upon the monarch's fears. He expressed such an extreme indifference to life as would not allow him to betray a single friend; and added that hundreds were engaged in the conspiracy with himself, who might be conciliated by lenity, but would infallibly avenge with frightful severity any confederate who should be sacrificed. The strange results were, that Blood was not only pardoned, but also presented with a pension of 500*l.* a year, probably as a compensation for the lands to which he laid claim in Ireland. He subsequently was a good deal about the court, and had at one time some political influence. But at last he was under the necessity of giving bail to answer for a scandalous imputation on the duke of Buckingham, and before the trial came on, he died at his house in Westminster, Aug. 24, 1680. (Biog. Brit. Kennet's Hist. Engl. iii. 280, 283.)

BLOOMFIELD, (Robert,) an English pastoral poet, the youngest of six children, born in 1766, at Honington, a village near Bury St. Edmund's, in Suffolk, where his father was a poor tailor, and brought up by his widowed mother, who supported herself and family by keeping a little school, where Robert was taught to read. At eleven years of age he was hired as a farmer's boy, but could not continue in that situation, from weakness of constitution. He was then sent to London to a relative, to learn the trade of a shoemaker. Fond of reading, and borrowing when he could from his friends books of poetry, amongst which his favourite was Thomson's Seasons, whilst at work with six or seven other young men, who paid each a shilling a week for their lodgings, in a poor garret, he composed his beautiful poem, The Farmer's Boy, which was printed by means of Mr. Capel Lofft, after it had been refused by several London booksellers. So great was the admiration excited by a piece of so much merit from a poor untaught youth, originally a peasant, now a journeyman mechanic, that in the course of three years 26,000 copies were sold. Foreign nations were not behind in sharing with the English this feeling, for in the following year a new edition was published at Leipsic; a French translation, entitled, Le Valet du Fermier, was printed at Paris; another appeared in Italian, at Milan; and in 1805 a very clever effort, in imitation of the Georgics, was made by Mr. W. Club, in Latin verse, under the title of Agricolæ Puer.

Animated by so extraordinary a success, Bloomfield continued to write, and increased his reputation by the publication of his ballads and songs, and particularly his Good Tidings, or News from the Forest, Wild Flowers, Banks of the Wye, &c. The duke of Grafton appointed him to a situation in the Seal Office, with a pension of a shilling a day, which he retained through life; but from ill health he was obliged to resign the office, and return to his trade of ladies' shoemaker. Unable, however, to support his family, for he had now a wife and four children, though he had begun to employ his leisure hours in making Æolian harps, he became involved in difficulties, and retired to Shefford, in Bedfordshire, where he died in 1816, in a condition little short of insanity, caused by losses, ill health, and incessant headaches, leaving debts to the amount of 200*l.*, notwithstanding a subscription promoted by the duke of Bedford for his benefit when he first went to Shefford. His works have been published in 2 vols, 12mo; and some of them deserve praise from the ablest critics for simplicity and moral excellence, though perhaps they are hardly equal to the expectations of modern times, and never would have attained the popularity that they once enjoyed without aid from the author's interesting history.

BLOOT, (Hugh,) in Latin, *Hugo Blotius*, first librarian of the imperial library at Vienna. He was appointed by the emperor Maximilian to the care of the collection then recently formed, and continued in that situation by Rodolph II.

in 1575. He continued to give satisfaction in it until his death, in 1608. He was a native of Delft, in Holland; eloquent, but libertine. His literary remains are only some orations. (Moreri.)

BLOOT, (Peter,) a Flemish painter, who died in 1667, remarkable for depicting scenes of low life with extreme fidelity, a good knowledge of chiar-oscuro and perspective, delicate pencilling, and mellow colouring, but without elegance. Nevertheless his pictures are much valued; and really their faults appear more imputable to the taste of his country than to any want of genius in himself. (Pilkington.)

BLOOTELING, or BLOTELING, (Abraham,) a very eminent Dutch designer and engraver, born at Amsterdam in 1634, and thought to have been a pupil of the Visschers. When the French invaded Holland in 1672, he came to England, and resided there two or three years, meeting with good employment. Being no less laborious than able, he produced a great number of etchings, some plates executed with the graver, and several in mezzotinto. His plates are sometimes marked with his name at length, at others with a cypher composed of A. and B. Several of his portraits are of English personages. (Bryan.)

BLOSIUS, or DE BLOIS, (Francis Lewis,) a devotional writer, of the illustrious family with his name, to which several crowned heads are allied. He was born in 1506, at the seat of Donstienne, in the territory of Liege, and educated with prince Charles, eventually the emperor Charles V. At fourteen he took the Benedictine habit in the monastery of Liesses, in Hainault, of which he became abbot in 1530. Charles V. urgently pressed upon him the archbishopric of Cambray, but nothing could move him from his abbey. He died either in 1563 or 1566, highly respected. In a more limited way he was known to posterity by a body of statutes provided for his house, and approved by the pope. As an author he was more generally known; his works, which are in a strain highly devotional, being printed by Frojus, his disciple, at Cologne, in 1571, in one volume folio. They have been subsequently reprinted three times. The most famous of them is the Speculum Religiosorum, or Dacryanus, the *Weeper*, a designation adopted from the author's tears over the relaxation of monastic discipline. A good translation of this was published at Paris in 1726, by the Jesuit de la Nauze, entitled Directeur des Ames Religieuses. (Moreri. Biog. Univ.)

BLOT, baron of Chauvigny, gentleman to Gaston, duke of Orleans, brother of Lewis XIII. He contributed to the elevation of cardinal Mazarin, by recommending him to Richelieu as fit for his purposes. When Mazarin, however, became minister he overlooked Blot, who took that vengeance by means of epigrams and satires for which an inexhaustible gaiety peculiarly qualified him. Not content with assaults of this lighter kind, Blot ranged himself against the cardinal in the war of *la fronde*, and at length it was deemed advisable to disarm him by a pension. He died at Blois, March 13, 1655. (Biog. Univ.)

BLOT, (Maurice,) an engraver of portraits and fancy subjects, born at Paris in 1754. His style is characterised as neat. (Bryan.)

BLOUNT, (John,) in Latin *Blondus*, or *Blundus*, an ancient English divine, who read divinity at Oxford with great applause, and was elected, in 1232, archbishop of Canterbury by the monks there. Two of their former elections had been set aside at Rome; one, that of Ralph Neville, bishop of Chichester, and chancellor of England, because he was a courtier, slenderly learned, and hasty in temper; the other, that of John, their own subprior, had fallen by his voluntary act, he being persuaded by the pope that he was a man too far advanced in life. The monks were not more fortunate in their election of Blount. Intelligence reached Rome, that, immediately after his election, Peter des Roches, bishop of Winchester, had given him a thousand marks, and lent him another thousand. Corrupt objects were assumed from these transactions, and Blount was spoken of as a Simoniac. He was also charged with holding two benefices with cure of souls without a dispensation, contrary to conciliar authority. It was pleaded that no such authority had forbidden him when he took them. But the plea was ineffectual, and upon this ground chiefly, as it seems from Matthew of Westminster, the pope declared his election void. Bale surmises, in his usual spirit towards Rome, that Blount's learning and abilities were greater than the papal court desired in such a see as Canterbury, and the conjecture may not be wholly unworthy of attention. Westminster assigns no other reason for the rejection of Blount than a letter soliciting interference in his favour from the bishop of Winchester to the emperor. The pope did not like that sovereign. Whatever was the real reason of Blount's rejection, contemporaries treated that assigned for it as a pretence. By Abp. Parker, or Joscelyn, who worked under him in compiling the Antiq. Brit. Eccl., it is referred to a fear that an able man, like the elect, might imitate Langton, in taking a more patriotic and independent position than was consistent with papal interests, and the hopes that king John's disreputable submission had encouraged. Nor does this view of the case want probability. After Blount's disappointment he returned to Oxford, and passed his declining age in those learned habits which had all but raised him to the summit of his country's church establishment. He died in 1248, respected as a prodigy of erudition, and leaving some literary works, which appear to be no longer extant. (Matt. Paris, 377, 385. Matt. Westm. 293. De Antiq. Brit. Eccl. 250.)

BLOUNT, (Charles,) an English officer and statesman, eventually baron Montjoy and earl of Devon, descended from a son of le Blound, lord of Guisnes, who came into England with William the Conqueror. Charles Blount was second son of James, sixth lord Montjoy, of Thurveston co. Derby, and was born in 1563. His education was received at Oxford and the Inner Temple; but when about twenty he made his appearance at court, where his tall stature, pleasing manners, and handsome face, recommended him to the notice of queen Elizabeth. Although a younger brother, and provided for like one, he came early into parliament, and at twenty-three was knighted. In 1588 he was among the young noblemen and gentlemen who fitted out ships at their own expense to join in pursuit of the Spanish Armada. In 1594 he was appointed governor of Portsmouth; and in the same year he succeeded his brother William, and became eighth lord Montjoy. He now lived in a manner suitable to his rank, although he possessed not more than a thousand marks a year, amusing himself with literature, especially such branches of it as are connected with military affairs. He was not, however, merely a speculative warrior, but had a company in the Low Countries; and in the expedition to the Azores, he was lieutenant-general of the land forces under Essex, and commanded the ship *Defiance*. Under the earl of Essex, too, lord Montjoy served in Ireland as second in command, and upon that unfortunate peer's disgrace, he was appointed lord-lieutenant. Queen Elizabeth considered him the only person fit for conducting to a successful issue those Irish troubles by which she had been so long harassed. His would be the fortune and honour, she said, to cut the thread of that fatal Irish rebellion, and bring her peacefully to the grave. Montjoy embarked at Beaumaris for Ireland, Feb. 23, 1600, and his judicious management soon put a new face upon the war. At length, Dec. 24, 1601, he gained a decisive victory over the rebels and their Spanish auxiliaries, near Kinsale. This blow disarmed farther opposition; and when James I. succeeded, he found Ireland in a state that had mocked his predecessor's hopes until the very end of her honourable career. The successful general, who had been made knight of the garter in 1597, was requited by an advancement in the peerage, being created earl of Devon July 21, 1603, and by more substantial marks of royal favour in pecuniary means to support his new dignity. He subsequently took a prominent part in public affairs, but his credit was undermined at last by a marriage with Penelope, daughter to Walter Devreux, first earl of Essex of that family, and sister to queen Elizabeth's unhappy favourite. This female was the divorced wife of Robert lord Rich, eventually earl of Warwick; and her infamy resulted from a criminal connexion with Montjoy, to whom she had been attached in early life, when he was a younger brother, and thought an unfit match for her. Laud, afterwards the famous and unfortunate archbishop, then Montjoy's chaplain, married the guilty parties at Wanstead, Dec. 26, 1605, to the great subsequent disquietude both of himself and them. He was strongly blamed for the act; and Montjoy received such mortifications both at court and elsewhere, that his constitution materially suffered, and he died of a fever, April 3, 1606, having lived, people commonly said, too long for his credit, public services being thrown into the shade by the scandal of private immorality. With him the hereditary honours of his family expired; but the eldest son, born of his miserable connexion, Montjoy Blount, received from him a very liberal provision, and after obtaining an Irish peerage from James I., was created by Charles I. baron Montjoy, of Thurveston, in 1627, and earl of Newport in the next year. These honours became extinct in 1681 by the death of Henry, his third son, and the fourth who had enjoyed them, his two elder sons having before successively inherited them. (Lloyd's State Worthies, i. 554. Banks's Baronage, i. 36; iii. 535.)

BLOUNT, (Sir Henry, knight,) an English country gentleman, of considerable note in the seventeenth century, descended from the ancient family of his name at Sodington, in Worcestershire, born Dec. 15, 1602, at his father's seat, Tittenhanger, in the parish of Ridge, near St. Alban's, Hertfordshire. He was third son; and his father, also knighted, was named Thomas Pope, the latter name being assumed to keep up the remembrance of the family's connexion with Sir Thomas Pope, founder of Trinity college, Oxford. To this institution Henry Blount was sent after a preliminary education in the grammar-school of St. Alban's; and having passed through his under-graduate's course with reputation, he took his bachelor's degree in 1618, and then entered at Gray's Inn to study the law. In 1634 he went abroad, and after visiting countries nearer home, he spent some time in Turkey and Egypt. In 1636 he printed an account of these eastern travels, in quarto. It proved a gratifying venture, three quarto editions being rapidly sold, and subsequently several in duodecimo. The title is long, beginning with A Voyage to the Levant, and then explaining particulars. The work was honoured by translations into French and Dutch; but nevertheless it has been characterised as a very superficial and unsatisfactory performance, detailing brief observations of the writer's own, and much at second hand, in a very indifferent style, and with but slender marks of accuracy. Charles I. then desirous of surrounding himself with men of ability, was, however, induced by it to notice the author, and he appointed him one of the band of pensioners. In 1638 his father, Sir Thomas Pope Blount, died, and left him the ancient seat of Blount's Hall, in Staffordshire, with a considerable fortune. In the following year he was knighted; and when the civil war broke out, like the elder branches of his family, he espoused the royal cause, and was with the unfortunate Charles at several places. At the battle of Edge-hill he was present, and, as there is reason to believe, had the young princes under his care. Subsequently he withdrew to London, and was there questioned as an adherent to the falling monarch. He excused himself as chargeable only with such acts as the place demanded which he had filled in the royal establishment, and his exculpation was allowed. He came, in fact, very much into the views of the prevailing party, and might accordingly escape censure, without any extraordinary degree of that wariness and dexterity in answering to which his deliverance has been attributed. He was a great enemy to tythes, and wished no minister of religion to have more than a hundred a year. Such proofs of liberality, as the phrase runs now, were then enough to push any influential man into public confidence; whatever might be said by the plundered and oppressed minority to show that selfish landowners must long for the tythes, and proud spirits desire to keep every neighbour immeasurably below themselves. While, however, selfishness and insolence are in a condition to trample down all opposition, none but fine names for them can be heard. Sir Henry Blount accordingly became a prominent personage during the whole period intervening between his desertion of the royal cause and the restoration. Nor were his services unimportant to the country, especially as a member of the board of trade and navigation. When Charles II. came into possession of the throne, Sir Henry Blount was more than usually wealthy, even among persons of his class, an elder brother having died about six years before, and left him the estate of Tittenhanger, where he rebuilt the mansion. He now had no difficulty in returning to his allegiance, and accordingly he was appointed, in 1661, high sheriff of Hertfordshire. The remainder of his life he spent in the dignified privacy that a large estate allowed him. He died at Tittenhanger, October 9, 1682, having lived until forty in the free indulgence of convivial pleasures, and with every mark of exuberant animal spirits. He passed another forty years very nearly, but as a water drinker of serious habits. He seems to have been possessed of good natural abilities, but his imagination was often an overmatch for his judgment, so that he gave way to some strange opinions. Besides his travels, he published six comedies, written by John Lilly, under the title of Court Comedies, by the care of Mr. Henry Blount, Lond. 1632, 8vo; The Exchange Walk, a satire, 1647; an epistle in praise of tobacco and coffee, prefixed to a little treatise by Walter Rumsey, entitled Organon Salutis, 1657. The satire was declared to be his by some of his friends, though his sons disclaimed all knowledge of it. His style is represented as manly, flowing, and less affected than the fashions of his age and the subjects of his pen would lead one to suspect. A Latin fragment, published by his son, is thought to throw more light upon his real character than any thing put forth by himself. It exhibits him as a deep but irregular thinker, who could colour the most paradoxical opinions in such a way as to make them pass for truth with ordinary minds. (Biog. Brit. Chauncey's Hertfordshire.)

BLOUNT, (Sir Thomas Pope,) eldest son of the preceding, made a baronet by Charles II., January 27, 1679, in his father's lifetime, born at Upper Holloway, Middlesex, September 12, 1649. His father had married the co-heiress of a gentleman named Wase, seated there. After a careful education, suited in all respects to the expectant of an ample fortune, he came into public life as member for St. Alban's in two parliaments, and for Hertfordshire in three. He filled also, during the last three years of his life, the office of commissioner of accounts, to which he was elected by the House of Commons. As a politician, he professed an ardent love of liberty, and appears to have kept steadily with his party, but he abstained from violence towards the other side. It was, however, as a literary man that he chiefly shone; for although he was but little of an original author, he published enough to prove himself a very careful, discerning, and industrious reader. The most valuable of his works is the Censura celebriorum Authorum, rather a small folio, published in London, in 1690, and twice reprinted, as it seems, at Geneva, in 4to, first in 1694, and secondly, in 1710. But it has been doubted whether the second of these is any thing else than unsold portions of the first, with a new title-page. In these continental editions the quotations from modern languages are translated into Latin, so as to give the whole work one uniform appearance. It is a compilation perfectly unambitious, containing nothing by Blount himself, except a preface and a few dates, but bringing diligently together the judgments of various able critics, in their own words, to bear upon the several authors, who are almost six hundred. No class or age is omitted; and the arrangement is nearly chronological, carrying literature downwards from the earliest remains of it to the compiler's own time. There are, however, deficiencies as to science and polite literature; but upon the whole, the volume is well worthy of a place in any library. It originated in *memoranda* for private use, which grew so fast, and became so valuable, under the habits of an industrious literary life, that judicious friends naturally suggested the propriety of publication. It has been compared with Baillet's Jugemens des Savans; but Baillet reports other men's opinions in language of his own, and hence may misrepresent them. Besides the Censura, Sir Thomas Pope Blount published seven essays in an octavo volume, which are placed upon a level as to learning, judgment, and freedom of thought, with those of Montaigne; a third edition of them appeared in 1697. He also published, in 1693, a Natural History, selected from various authors; and in 1694, a work of the same kind upon poetry, entitled, De Re Poeticâ, or Remarks upon Poetry. He died at Tittenhanger, married and leaving issue, June 9, 1697. (Biog. Brit. Pref. to Hallam's Literature of Europe. Chauncey's Hertfordshire. Pref. to the Censura. Clement. Chaufepié.)

BLOUNT, (Charles,) brother of the preceding, and, like him, born at his grandfather's residence at Upper Holloway. This was April 27, 1654. He was chiefly educated under the eye of his father, a species of intellectual nurture that ordinarily feeds conceit; and in this case the fond instructor was himself a person far from conspicuous for sobriety of judgment. Young Blount, accordingly, although possessed undoubtedly of considerable abilities, did not prove discreet in the employment of them. His first appearance before the world was an anonymous vindication of Dryden as a dramatic writer, which was printed when he was under twenty. From a subject so congenial to his age, he passed over to another, unhappily also agreeable to the contemplation of youth. In 1679 appeared Anima Mundi, or an Historical relation of the Opinions of the Ancients concerning Man's Soul after this life, according to unenlightened nature, by Charles Blount, Gent. The tendency of this piece is deistical, and its original tone appears to have been far more decided than that which it ultimately bore, passages which had been seen when it was handed about in MS. having lost much of their strength in the subsequent impression. The young author was thought to have been assisted in this work by his clever but wrong-headed father, who was extremely fond of him, and early settled him in handsome circumstances. The piece was duly licensed by Sir Roger l'Estrange, upon whom then rested the responsibility of overlooking issues from the press; but in this case, he was quickly taxed with neglecting his duty, complaints being made to Henry Compton, bishop of London, that a dangerous book had been suffered to appear. The prelate, on perusal, thought it unfit for ordinary readers, and desired its suppression. Some other person burnt it. Blount next published a broad sheet, entitled Mr. Hobbes's last Words and dying Legacy, being passages from the Leviathan, intended to expose the philosopher of Malmesbury; but the compiler appears to have, at one time, thought highly of him, and he never could have been a very formidable opponent. Blount's connexions were decidedly averse from the politics most in favour at court, and he produced a strong expression of their opinions in An Appeal from the Country to the City, a pamphlet in which popery and a Romanist successor are most roughly handled; and the duke of Monmouth is indicated for the throne in such a manner as to make the tract chargeable with sedition at least, if not with treason, according to the expositions of the law then generally received. Junius Brutus were the names put to this publication. In 1680, Blount published, with his name, the work, a thin folio, by which his notoriety was chiefly gained, under the following title, The two first Books of Philostratus concerning the Life of Apollonius Tyaneus, written originally in Greek, with Philological Notes upon each Chapter. It was these notes that chiefly gave offence. They brought before the reader's eye a multitude of facts and reasonings, which wore a very plausible appearance, and were well fitted for prejudicing the weak and superficial against revelation. The book was, accordingly, soon suppressed; and as the copies first sent into circulation were neither numerous, nor the national taste favourable to such attempts, it made far less noise in England than abroad. In the same year, Blount again courted notice in his Great is Diana of the Ephesians, a work professedly levelled against the priestcraft of ancient paganism; and speaking highly of Christianity, but evidently levelled also against priests of a more modern date. A new clamour now assailed him, and not undeservedly, as in addition to the obvious tendency of his writings, he took great pains to propagate deistical opinions in private, and came to be considered as the leader of persons who held such; yet he admitted them to be less satisfactory than Christianity. After so many attempts of this unhappy kind, it is pleasing to observe that Blount's attention could be turned to the improvement of men's minds when he could escape from an anxiety to unsettle their faith. In 1684 appeared his Janua Scientiarum, or Introduction to Geography, Chronology, Government, History, Philosophy, and all genteel sorts of Learning. On the overthrow of James the Second's government, Blount made a very unfortunate literary and political calculation, having published, in his zeal for king William, a pamphlet which placed that monarch's claims to the throne on the footing of a conquest. This gave such offence that both branches of the legislature concurred in ordering it to be publicly burnt by the common hangman. The termination of this clever and industrious, but misguided, and probably conceited man's course, was most miserable. He had married, at eighteen, a daughter of Sir Timothy Tyrrel, of Shotover, in Oxfordshire, and on her premature decease, he made offers of marriage to her sister. These were received not unfavourably, but objections were started to such a connexion as illegal and improper. Divines, among them, it is said, the archbishop of Canterbury, having pronounced such objections valid, the lady would not consent to the union. On this Blount shot himself through the head in August 1693, and lingering two or three days afterwards, refused to take any thing from other hands than those of the lady whose conscientious refusal had occasioned his guilty rashness. In the earlier part of that very year, Blount had published a collection of small tracts, entitled The Oracles of Reason, with a preface by Gildon, one of which advocates the successive marriages of sisters; and this, probably, was the real reason of the publication, the author being anxious to fix public attention favourably upon a question most tenderly concerning himself. This was reprinted, with most of Blount's other works, but omitting his unlucky political pamphlet, in a collection edited by Gildon, in 1695, entitled, The Miscellaneous Works of Charles Blount, Esq., with his life and a vindication of his death. In this Gildon talks of following his example; but he proved either too cowardly or too wise. One of the best pieces penned by Blount, is a Just Vindication of Learning and of the Liberty of the Press, a treatise written when the act for suffering no books or pamphlets to be printed without authority from a licenser was upon the point of expiring. Blount uses arguments against the renewal of this act, which have generally been adopted by succeeding writers upon the same subject, all tending to prove that liberty of every kind may be safe, while that of the press remains; but let it go, and all else that is valuable is very likely to follow. The tract was addressed to the two houses of parliament, and public opinion going with it, the act for fettering the press was allowed to expire. (Biog. Brit. Clement. Chaufepié.)

BLOUNT, (Thomas,) a valuable miscellaneous English writer, born, in 1618, at Bardesley, in Worcestershire, son of Miles Blount of Orleton, in Herefordshire. He was a diligent student, but never at the university, although he entered of the Inner Temple, and was duly called to the bar. Being, however, a Roman Catholic, he never pleaded, but after a time resided chiefly at Orleton. Sedentary habits having much impaired his health, he was unable to bear the hurrying about from place to place, which was either necessary, or thought so by him, when the popish plot was in the mouths of all men. His fatigues, accordingly, brought on palsy, of which he died at Orleton, December 26, 1679. He published, The Academy of Eloquence, or Complete English Rhetoric, 1654, 12mo, often reprinted. Glossographia, or a Dictionary of Hard Words, 1656, 8vo, also reprinted several times. The Lamps of the Law, and the Lights of the Gospel, 1658, 8vo. Boscobel, or the History of his Majesty's Escape after the Battle of Worcester, 1660. Boscobel, the second part, with the *Claustrum Regale reseratum*, or the King's Concealment at Trent, in Somersetshire, published by Mrs. Anne Windham of Trent, 1681. The Catholic Almanac for 1661-2-3. Booker Rebuked; or Animadversions on Booker's Almanac. A Law Dictionary, 1671, fol., reprinted with additions. Animadversions on Sir Richard Baker's Chronicle, Oxford, 1672, 8vo. A World of Errors discovered in Mr. Edmund Philip's World of Worlds, Lond. 1673, fol. Fragmenta Antiquitatis. Ancient Tenures of Land, and Jocular Customs of some Manors, 1679, 8vo, reprinted in 1784. A Catalogue of the Catholics who lost their Lives in the King's Cause during the Civil War, printed at the end of lord Castlemaine's Catholic Apology. A pedigree of the Blounts, printed in Peacham's Complete Gentleman, 1661. Blount, besides, translated from the French, The Art of making Devises, treating of Hieroglyphics, &c., and left some works in MS. (Chalmers.)

BLOW, (John,) an English musical composer, born at North Collingham, Nottinghamshire, in 1648, and one of the first set of children of the Chapel Royal after the restoration, made doctor of music by archbishop Sancroft, without performing any exercise for it in the university. He died in 1708, and was then considered at the summit of his profession. Being composer to the Chapel Royal, he produced many pieces of sacred music, which have never been collected, but some of them were printed by Boyce, and many more remain in MS. They are commonly in a bold and grand style, but, notwithstanding unequal, and often unhappy when attempts are made at new harmony and modulation. His secular compositions were published in 1700, under the title of Amphion Anglicus, but such a designation is considered altogether out of keeping with their merits. (Rees.)

BLUCHER, (Gebhardt Lebrecht von,) prince of Wahlstadt, one of the most illustrious of military veterans, born at Rostock, in the duchy of Mecklenburg Schwerin, December 16, 1742, of an ancient family seated at Gross Renzow. His father, a cavalry officer in the service of Hesse Cassel, sent him, in 1756, with his brother, to an aunt's in the Isle of Rugen. The two boys had been educated hitherto most imperfectly, and this evil was not now repaired, but they lost no opportunity of invigorating their frames by bodily exertions of all sorts, both by sea and land. While thus unconsciously fitting themselves for the physical exactions of a campaign, a regiment of Swedish hussars fired their imaginations, and no representations of their aunt's husband, Krakwitz, availed to prevent them from joining it. As if to punish his wilfulness, Gebhardt Blucher was taken prisoner by the Prussians in his first campaign, and he was then pressed by the colonel who had captured him to enter their service. During a year he resisted, but in December, 1760, a Swedish officer having been exchanged for him, he entered into the Prussian regiment of black hussars, and distinguished himself in the seven years' war. In private life he does not appear to have been very discreet at that period, being prone to duelling, and to the dissipation by which youth is commonly tempted, and especially that of an officer. He thus naturally became rather obnoxious to elder men; and having misconducted himself on being disappointed of promotion, he was dismissed the service. He then retired into the country, and devoted himself to agriculture, but not so exclusively as to prevent him from acquiring a great fund of military knowledge. It was during his retreat from the army that he married, and as his wife's family was wealthy, while his own energies made the best of every advantage that it afforded him, he rapidly made money himself during the fourteen years that he spent in the country. Nevertheless, he constantly regretted his old profession; and Frederic the Great, who had dismissed him, being now dead, he repaired to Berlin, in 1786, and solicited his restoration to the army, much against the wishes of his wife, who died in the following year. His application being successful, he entered as a major the very regiment which he had left as captain. In 1788 he obtained the rank of lieutenant-colonel; and after being decorated by the order of merit, he became colonel of the black hussars in 1790. Two years afterwards he was engaged in the hostilities undertaken by Prussia against France; but as nothing of much importance was attempted, he had merely an opportunity of displaying considerable valour and activity. He had, however, amply established a title to promotion, and in 1794 he was appointed major-general. He soon afterwards married again. In 1801 he became lieutenant-general. In 1802 he took possession for Prussia of some territories ceded to her as indemnities; and in the following year he was named governor of Munster. The times immediately succeeding present nothing remarkable in Blucher's history beyond his undisguised contempt for the temporizing policy which generally prevailed in the Prussian councils, and a firm expression of belief that spirited resistance to France would soon effectually stop her encroachments. These representations of his have been considered as far from unimportant in impelling Prussia upon those decisive steps which prostrated her in 1806. He then commanded a detached *corps* of 12,000 men in Westphalia. Of the two battles of Jena and Auerstadt, which made the 14th of October in that year so ruinous to Prussia, Blucher was present at the latter, and his conduct there has been censured; but nothing could exceed his retreat, with the force that he led from the fatal field. With this he reached Lubeck, and there made a stand under circumstances that would have deterred almost any man from the attempt. At length, however, stern necessity compelled him to sign a capitulation at Ratkau, near Lubeck, which he did with tears in his eyes, and he became a prisoner of war. Soon afterwards he was exchanged for the French marshal Victor; and he was then sent off by the king of Prussia with a small force to Swedish Pomerania, which he evacuated at the peace of Tilsit. Subsequently he was employed in the war department, and as commanding officer at Kolberg, where he so busied himself, apparently without orders, in strengthening the fortifications, that Napoleon became suspicious, and the prostrate Prussian government could do nothing else than disavow and dismiss him. He then indignantly withdrew once more into private life, full of undisguised bitterness towards France, and of sanguine expectation, that, notwithstanding so many appearances to the contrary, her day of reckoning was at hand.

Blucher had long foreseen that French rapacity would eventually prove an overmatch for German indolence and leaning towards revolutionary politics. "I reckon much," said he to Bourrienne, when at Hamburgh, on *parole*, "upon the public spirit of my country. Our universities are aroused; our very defeats have nurtured honourable feelings, and a passion for national glory. Be assured, that a whole people, bent upon emancipation, will accomplish it. We are steadily upon the way for such an universal military organization as France never had the spirit to produce. In our struggles against you, at the beginning of the revolution, we fought for the rights of kings, in which, for my part, I felt but little interest. Now we are fighting for our homes; and the spirit of those who feel this will not be destroyed, however armies may. The time is coming, when Europe, ground to the earth by your emperor's exactions, will rise up as one man against him, and proportioned to the numbers that he enslaves will be the explosion when they break their fetters." When Buonaparte's mighty armament miserably crumbled away in the snows of Russia, these prophetic words were speedily made good. Simultaneously whole nations rose to crush the spoiler who proclaimed unblushingly that war must support war; or, in other words, that every man's possessions, great or small, must pass for a lawful prize wherever the French eagles could force an entrance. In 1813, when this truth, emboldened by Napoleon's tottering state, had at length sufficiently acted on the public mind, Blucher was seventy-one years of age, but his energies were unimpaired, and he pressed emulously to the field. At Lutzen and at Bautzen, he showed himself more than equal to the arduous duties undertaken by him; but it was in the great battle of the Katzbach, August 26, 1813, that he permanently won a place among the greatest of military chiefs. This engagement annihilated the army of Macdonald, and was glorious above most conflicts recorded in the annals of European warfare. Its trophies were immense; eighteen thousand prisoners, a hundred and three pieces of cannon, besides other military appliances in proportion, and a loss to the enemy of twenty-five thousand men altogether. When Macdonald reformed his broken bands behind the Queisse, he could scarcely muster around him fifty-five thousand broken-spirited soldiers. Eighty thousand followed his standard when he received the command from Napoleon. On the other hand, the allies purchased this incalculable advantage at a loss comparatively trifling—it did not exceed four thousand men. There was, indeed, but little serious fighting. Blucher surprised the French when wholly unprepared; and the weather, bringing destruction by floods, of bridges in their rear, prevented them subsequently from re-uniting their broken bands, or forming any regular mass to resist their foe.

In most of the warlike movements that succeeded, Blucher's name appears, fully maintaining its previous renown; and being now, from his great services, made field-marshal, he had the satisfaction of pursuing his fleeing enemy to the Rhine. He crossed that noble stream, January 1, 1814, and planted his hostile foot on the territory of France. A series of severe actions, with alternate success, leading to the decisive victory at Laon, February 9, opened the way to Paris; a consummation which opponents of French revolutionary aggression had scarcely thought, in their most sanguine moments, within the verge of possibility. Blucher commanded the centre of the allies in their attack upon that capital, at the close of March, and he was much displeased by the capitulation, thinking that a forcible entry would exact a just retaliation for some of the innumerable wrongs that Prussia had suffered under Buonaparte's iron gripe. To this displeasure of the heroic veteran was ascribed his absence when the allied sovereigns entered Paris, March 31. He remained on the heights of Montmartre, while the splendid procession was moving through the streets of the captured city. He did not enter it until the following day. His absence, however, when the sovereigns made their entrance, may be very reasonably ascribed to indisposition. He was then suffering under fever and an attack in the eyes, and had on the day before vainly attempted to mount his horse. On the 2d of April, he resigned his command under plea of the necessity to re-establish his health. He was then created by the king of Prussia, Prince of Wahlstadt, a title peculiarly appropriate, as it was drawn from a convent near the Katzbach, the scene of his most illustrious exploit. At Paris, Blucher lived wholly without pretension, often walking about in an ordinary frock-coat, undistinguished by any decoration, and dining at a *restaurateur's*, where, if incommoded by heat, he dispensed with superfluous articles of dress without the least ceremony, greatly to the astonishment of the waiters, but eliciting favourable remarks from English observers upon the honest simplicity of his habits. Passing over to England with the allied sovereigns, he was received with a degree of popular enthusiasm that thrust the reception of his imperial and royal companions, gratifying as it was, entirely into the shade. On his return to Germany he was similarly greeted; but political arrangements caused him deep dissatisfaction. He declared that France must not be treated with a thoughtless liberality, but according to her own mode of treating Prussia, if the peace now concluded were meant for any thing better than a hollow truce. When Buonaparte's arrival from Elba, in the following spring, convinced him that his anticipations had been prophetic, aged as he was, he thought only of the battle-field again; and being appointed general-in-chief of the army destined for operation between the Rhine and the Moselle, he set out from Berlin on the 10th of April, and reached Liege within a few days afterwards. At the end of May he was on the Sambre, having under his command a force of 80,000 men. His first active operations against the French were not successful, although neither his own powers of any kind appeared in the least impaired, nor did his enemy gain any decisive advantage over him, and in the battle of Ligny, on the 16th of June, he narrowly escaped, by the fall of his horse, being taken prisoner. On the following day he was engaged in concentrating his forces at Wavre; and on the 18th, which gave to Europe a long respite from revolutionary rapacity on the glorious field of Waterloo, his timely arrival in the evening broke the spirits of the French. They did, however, still make a desperate stand, but in spite of all their gallantry, the Prussians gained upon them. The duke of Wellington now ordered a charge of the whole British line, and this proved irresistible. Blucher was, therefore, greatly instrumental in securing to pillaged and insulted Europe the victory at Waterloo, although it may well be doubted whether the French are justified in attributing Napoleon's final discomfiture, almost entirely, to his arrival, and representing it as a lucky accident. Blucher, under his new triumph, displayed all those vindictive feelings towards the French that had burst from him a year before; and he would have blown up the bridge of Jena, as a monument of his country's disgrace, had not the Prussian engineers been rather tardy in their operations, and a ransom of 300,000 francs, offered by the city, made him send counter orders. In accepting this sum, he was only retaliating upon the French, one of whose plans for extorting money from an exhausted neighbourhood, was to lay a train to some bridge of importance to it, and to spare the explosion on the receipt of a stipulated sum. As a farther concession to Prussia, orders were given that the bridge should no longer be called that of Jena, but the *Pont des Invalides*, being near the hospital similarly named. Among the distinctions justly showered down upon Blucher from most of the great European powers, was a cross of iron, surrounded by golden rays, presented to him by his own sovereign, who said, in giving it, "I know that no golden rays can heighten the splendour of your services, but I cannot deny myself the pleasure of thus marking my own sense of them."

After Blucher's retirement from active life, advanced age, and extraordinary exertions, were found to have fully done their ordinary work upon him. He gradually declined, and no change of air or other treatment gave him any substantial relief. He died at Krieblowitz, in Silesia, September 12, 1819, having been fully aware, for some time, that his end was near. The physicians were inclined to a different opinion, but he declared himself to know better, and expressed a willingness to go, as being no longer of any use. On his death-bed, he was visited by the king, and received from him those kind and warm expressions of affection and sympathy, which services like his to the Prussian monarchy had richly earned. His extreme hatred of the French naturally has drawn from them a very low estimate of his military character; but they freely admit his rare intrepidity, indomitable energy, extraordinary decision of character, a fitness, both natural and acquired, for a military life, and inexhaustible resources within himself for making the best of all its obstacles, reverses, and fatigues. Buonaparte affected, at one time, to despise him, and called him the *general of hussars*. By the troops who admired him he was often called marshal *Forwards*, from the rapidity of his marches it was said; but he really seems to have acquired the name at Leipsic, when pressed by the inhabitants to suspend hostilities. Wearied by their importunities, he impatiently cried *Vorwärts*, a word of the same import as the corresponding one in English; and it seemed so characteristic of the man, that it found a designation for him ever afterwards. (Alison. Ann. Biog. Gent. Mag. Biog. Univ. Suppl.)

BLUFF, (Mathias Joseph,) a learned physician, born at Cologne, of poor parents, Feb. 5, 1805, but enabled by kind assistance to study at the university of Bonn, where he remained from 1822 to 1825. In the latter year, in conjunction with Dr. Fingerhuth, he published the first part of his Compendium Floræ Germanicæ, which work has since been completed by Nees von Esenbeck and Schauer. Bluff took the degree of doctor of medicine at Berlin in 1826, and eventually practised with great success at Aix-la-Chapelle, but fell a victim to typhus fever, June 5, 1837, having, besides various communications to medical journals, published the following works, which are monuments of his taste, learning, and industry: — Entwicklungs-Combinationen Organischer Wesen. Cöln. 1827 Pastoral-Medizin, Aachen, 1827. Ueber die Heilkrafte der Küchengewasche, Nürenberg, 1828. Ueber die Krankheiten als Krankheits-ursachen, Aachen, 1829. Synonymia Medicaminum, Lipsiæ, 1831. Esquirol's Mordmomanie (translation) mit Zusatzen, 1831. Helkologie, Berlin, 1832. Velpeau, die Convulsionem (translation) mit Zusatzen Aachen, 1835. Leistungen und Fortschritte der Medicin in Deutschland, 4 vols, 1832-36. Reform der Medicin, 2 vols, Leipzig, 1836-37.

BLUM, (Joachim Christian,) a German poet, born at Rathenau, in the Mittlemark, in 1739, educated first at Brandenburg, then at Berlin, where he secured the esteem of the poet Ramler, and finally at Frankfort on the Oder, where he studied under Alexander Baumgarten. General literature and the ancient and modern languages were his chief studies, and, devoted exclusively to literary pursuits, he settled, on leaving the university, in his native town. The works which he afterwards published were well received, and honoured even by the notice of the Prussian court. He died Aug. 28, 1790.

The writings of Blum bear the impress of a correct understanding, and a mild, benevolent character; his style is ornate, but easy and natural. He disappoints those who look for originality, or profundity of thought, or learning. His Walks, a collection of moral essays, in three vols, which have passed through three regular editions, and also a pirated one, belong to a class of writings once in great request with the public, but which the present generation altogether neglects as weak and insipid. It must be confessed that they lack force and fire, and can only have been very popular when quite novel. Blum also published a useful collection of proverbs. His lyrical poems are imitations of the methodical Ramlet, but without his energy. In philosophical, didactic, and descriptive verses, he was as successful as most of his numerous competitors. His tedious drama, The Conquest of Rathenau, by the great Prince Elector in 1675, was applauded in representation by the patient and patriotic citizens of Berlin.

BLUMAUER, (Aloys,) a celebrated German burlesque poet, born at Steyer, 1755, educated in his native town. He entered at Vienna, in 1772, the order of the Jesuits, which was suppressed the next year. He afterwards gained a livelihood as a tutor and by literary pursuits, until he obtained the appointment of censor of the press. In 1793 he resigned this office, and went into a book business. He died of consumption, March 16, 1798. He was tall and thin. his complexion very yellow, and he was often afflicted with a complaint of the eyes. During the latter part of the last century, he was one of the most popular poets of Germany, and was not without influence on the intellectual and religious culture of the Austrians. Of those writers who were encouraged to indulge in a liberal spirit by the example and measures of Joseph II., he was certainly one of the least objectionable. Some of his serious poems are in a tone of manly independence, which reminds the reader of Burns or Bürger; and in his Confession of Faith of a Catholic searching for Truth, the reaction of the time is expressed in a noble and harmonious strain. His literary fame was first established by a collection of poems on various subjects, and by the travestied Æneid. In all his works his understanding was more taxed than his imagination, which was neither very strong, nor very extensive in its range. Blumauer's most noted production is his travestie of the Æneid, which for several years after its publication was extremely popular. The Germans welcomed it the more eagerly, as it belonged to a branch of literature which had been hitherto much neglected amongst them, or cultivated with but indifferent success. Besides a good stock of wit and satire, it also displayed a bold opposition to the pope, and this may partly account for its success. On the other hand, it is sometimes coarse without being pointed, and passages are not wanting in which the humour is laboured and artificial. The travestie only extends to the end of the ninth book of Virgil. It was translated into Russian by Ossipof, St. Petersburg, 1791-93. Like all other successful writers, Blumauer was followed by a crowd of imitators, whose miserable copies were calculated rather to disgrace than reflect credit on their original. All the feeble and witless scribblers of the day were seized with the mania of burlesque. Travesties appeared of the Iliad, of Ovid, and one of Blumauer's officious disciples had even the impudence to assume his name. Blumauer's prose is more perspicuous and compact than that of most of his contemporaries. The didactic style was that which he cultivated with least success. It is singular that the first production of this writer was a tragedy, Erwine von Skruheim, full of bombastic pathos, and aiming only at effect. The journey of pope Pius VI. to Vienna, in 1782, he celebrated in a prophetic prologue, of which a second edition was soon called for, and also in an epilogue. He wrote a satirical prologue to Nicolai's noted Travels; and Nicolai was also the cause of his publishing Considerations on Austria's Enlightenment and Literature, Vienna, 1783. In 1785, he published Songs of a Freemason, which were well received: he was a member of the order. In 1786 appeared his Art of Printing, a poem. Besides several other minor works and single articles, he furnished a number of poems to the Vienna Muses' Almenach, which, from 1781 to 1791, he edited in conjunction with Ratschky. From Oct. 1782 to Oct. 1784, he managed the Vienna Realzeitung, and had also some share in the management of the Allgem. Literat. Zeitung. His collected works were published at Leipsic, in 8 vols, 1801, (this edition was edited by Kistenfeger); at Munich, 1827, in 4 vols; and at Königsberg, 1827, in 4 volumes.

BLUMBERG, (Christian Gotthelf,) a learned German Lutheran divine, born in 1664, and engaged, after serving as an army chaplain, in serving different pastoral cures in the electorate of Saxony. He died at Zwickau, in 1735, leaving Fundamenta Linguæ Copticæ, 1716, and other works, chiefly philological, some of which have not been published. (Biog. Univ.)

BLUMENBACH, (John Frederic,) an eminent naturalist and physiologist, born at Gotha, May 11, 1752, who studied at Jena and Göttingen, and took the degree of doctor of medicine in 1775. He was particularly noticed by Heyne, Michaelis and Büttner; the last of whom, a man of very extraordinary acquirements, formed a collection of medals and natural history, which was purchased by the university, and Blumenbach was engaged to arrange it. The manner in which he performed this office procured for him the appointments of conservator of the Museum of Natural History and extraordinary professor of medicine in 1776; and two years afterwards of professor in ordinary, an appointment held by him for nearly sixty years. During this period he maintained a correspondence with the most eminent philosophers of all countries, received all scientific persons who visited Göttingen, was justly esteemed as the "patriarch of the university," held the most distinguished reputation, and was universally beloved for the suavity of his manners and the kindness of his disposition, as well as for his varied and extensive learning. In 1788 he was made an honorary counsellor of state, and in 1812 secretary of the Royal Society of Sciences, to the Transactions of which he contributed largely. He was one of the Foreign Fellows of the Royal Society of London, and a member of the chief literary and scientific institutions in this and other countries. He died, Jan. 22, 1840, at the advanced age of eighty-eight years, maintaining his faculties and cheerfulness to the last. The lectures delivered by him related not only to medicine, but also to natural history, comparative anatomy, physiology, and pathology; and his publications in these departments of science have received their due meed of approbation, and been translated into various languages. This will appear from the following enumeration, embracing those most likely to be useful in this country:—Diss. Inaug. de Generis Humani Varietate Nativâ, Götting. 1775, 4to. Of this several editions have been printed, and it has been translated into French by Chardel, Paris, 1806, 8vo. Handbuch der Naturgeschichte, Gött. 1779-80, 2 vols, 8vo. Of this also various editions have been published, and it was translated into French by Soulange Artaud, Paris, 1803, 2 vols, 8vo. Into English, by Gore, Lond. 1825, 8vo. The 11th German edition is of 1825. Nuperæ Observationes de Nisu Formativo et Generationis Negotio, Gött. 1787, 4to. This essay originally appeared in 1785, and was translated into English by Sir A. Crichton, in 1792, Lond. 12mo. Institutiones Physiologicæ, Gott. 1787, 8vo. A variety of editions of this work were published, and it was translated into German by Joseph Eyerel, Vienne, 1789, 8vo; into French by Pugnet, Lyon, 1797, 12mo; and into English by J. Elliotson, Lond. 1817, 8vo. Of the translations, various editions have also appeared. Observations on some Egyptian Mummies contained in the British Museum, Lond. 1794, in the Phil. Trans.; translated into French by Chardel, Paris, 1806, 8vo. Handbuch der Vergleichenden Anatomie, Gött. 1805, 8vo. A third edition was published in 1824; it has been translated into English by William Lawrence, Lond. 1807, 8vo; also by W. Coulson, Lond. 1827, 8vo. Besides the above-named works, and many others less noticed out of his own country, there is a variety of papers by Blumenbach contributed to German periodicals.

BLUNDEVILLE, (Thomas,) an English mathematician, about the year 1600, principally known by his Exercises in navigation, cosmography, and the kindred sciences. This book obtained great popularity, passed through many editions, and continued to be reprinted till nearly the end of the seventeenth century. He is mentioned with commendation by John Davis, in his Seaman's Secrets, 4to, Lond. 1594.

BLUNTHLI, (John Henry,) a Swiss topographer, born at Zurich, in 1656, where he died in 1722. He published in German a history of his native town, which is valuable. The best edition is that of 1740. (Biog. Univ.)

BLUTEAU, (Raphael,) a Theatine, born in London, of French parents, Dec. 4, 1638. Having gone to Portugal, he died at Lisbon, Feb. 13, 1734, very highly esteemed, panegyrics pronounced on his death inquiring whether England was more honoured by his birth or Portugal by his death? His great work is a dictionary, Latin and Portuguese, 10 vols, fol. of which the publication began at Coimbra in 1712. Moraes de Silva made with corrections a good dictionary out of this, Lisbon, 1789, 2 vols, 4to. Bluteau also published some other works, of less general importance. (Biog. Univ.)

BLYENBURG, (Damasus van,) born at Dordrecht, in 1558, of a very good family. It is thought that he died about 1616. He published, Cento Ethicus ex Ducentis Poetis hic inde Contextus, Leyd. 1599. Veneres Blyenburgicæ, sive Amorum Hortus, Dord. 1600. These rare volumes bring together some of the most pleasing passages in various modern Latin poets. A third publication by Blyenburg is B. Fulgentii Sententiæ Sacræ, Amst. 1612. (Biog. Univ. Suppl.)

BOABDIL, last Moorish king of Granada, of the race of the Beni Alhamar, properly named Mohammed *Abu Abdallah*, but universally known by the Spanish term corrupted from the last two words. He was son of the king Abul-Hassan, by his principal wife Zoraya, sometimes called Ayxa, or Ayesha; and was placed in opposition to his father, at an early age, by the influence of his mother, who was indignant at the ascendant obtained over the mind of her husband by a younger rival in the harem. In the year after the commencement of the last war with Castile, A.D. 1482, (A.H. 887,) Abul-Hassan, returning to Granada from an unsuccessful expedition, found that his son had been proclaimed king by the populace, and was forced, after a fruitless conflict, to retire to Malaga, leaving Boabdil in possession of the capital, and the royal palace of Alhambra, (*Beit-al-Hamr*, the Red House.) The youth and princely qualities of the new king made him highly popular; but the following year, in heading his forces against the Spaniards, he was defeated and taken prisoner at Lucena. His father re-entered Granada; but a third party had now risen in favour of Abdallah Al-Zagal, brother of the old monarch, and a redoubted warrior, in whose favour Abul-Hassan was ere long persuaded or compelled to abdicate his pretensions. In the mean time Boabdil had been released from captivity on acknowledging himself a vassal of Spain, and engaging to pay an annual tribute; and a fresh civil war commenced between the younger king and his uncle: the former, by the aid of Spanish troops, continued to reign in the capital, but great part of the kingdom espoused the cause of Al-Zagal, who sustained for several years a gallant but fruitless struggle against the power of Spain, till A.D. 1490, (A.H. 895,) he ceded to Ferdinand the towns which remained to him, and shortly afterwards passed over into Africa. Boabdil was now sole monarch; but his weak and vacillating conduct during the war with Al-Zagal had alienated the Moors, without gaining for him the confidence of Ferdinand, who now called upon him, in pursuance of an alleged secret article in the treaty, to surrender Granada and the remainder of his dominions. The unfortunate prince endeavoured to evade compliance, and prepared for resistance; but in the campaign of 1491, the despairing valour of the Moors, who defended with unavailing bravery the last relic of their Spanish dominions, was overborne by the numbers of the Castilians; and the capital, after a blockade of some months, capitulated January 4, A.D. 1492, (A.H. 897,) thus extinguishing for ever the Moslem sway in Spain, after a duration of 781 years. Boabdil had domains allotted to him in the Alpuxarras, as a compensation for his loss of sovereignty; but his situation was irksome, and in 1496 he disposed of his territory to Ferdinand, and repaired to the court of his relative, the king of Fez, where he resided many years, and eventually perished in battle against the founders of the Shereef dynasty, now reigning in Morocco, about A.D. 1526. Such are the historical facts of the life of a prince whose adventures and misfortunes have furnished the theme of many a romance. The surname of *Al-Zogoybi*, or "the Unlucky," which was affixed to his name from his birth, in consequence of the prediction of an astrologer, was amply justified by the events of his life; and his mild and unsteady temperament was peculiarly unfitted to cope with the wily policy of the perfidious Ferdinand. In personal courage he was not deficient, and his name is not stained by any act of cruelty; for the massacre of the Abencerrages, which is familiarly associated with his reign, does not appear to have any historical foundation. A portrait in the gallery of the Generalife is said to represent Boabdil; the features are handsome, and the hair and complexion extremely fair: two suits of his armour are also preserved in the armoury of the Escurial. The Spaniards called him *El Chico*, or *The Little*, to distinguish him from an uncle of the same name. (Mariana. Abarca. Cura de los Palacios. Garibay. Conde. Prescott.)

BOADICEA, according to Tacitus, or BOUD-OUIKA, to Xiphilinus, wife of Prasutagus, famous for his treasures, king of the Iceni, inhabitants of the modern Norfolk, Suffolk, and some adjoining counties. To disarm Roman cupidity, Prasutagus left his daughters coheirs with Nero. This proved, however, little or no protection to the property of his orphans; while all the remonstrances of his widow were met only by blows and the violation of her daughters. Exasperated by this ill treatment, she covertly fomented a rebellion, to which the other parts of the island were instigated by the extortions practised on the people by the Roman officers; and taking advantage of the absence of the enemy's forces, she headed a large body of troops, that attacked and carried the Roman quarters at Camalodunum, (Colchester, or Maldon,) and subsequently massacred about 70,000 of the Romans and their allies. The whole country now would have been probably delivered from a foreign yoke, had not Suetonius Paulinus quickly returned from Mona, the modern Anglesey, whither he had gone on a warlike expedition, and marching against the Britons with only 10,000 troops, overthrown them. They were commanded by Boadicea in person, and accompanied by their wives and daughters, to witness their expected victory. But the skill of a few well-disciplined troops prevailed, as usual, over numerous and irregular masses; and the slaughter, it is said, of 70,000 Britons, was completed by the death of Boadicea, who destroyed herself by poison. The site of the battle, which took place A.D. 61, is placed by some on Salisbury Plain. According to Xiphilinus, Boadicea, after bidding the men of Britain to show that the Romans, like hares and foxes, were attempting to be the masters of dogs and wolves, took a hare from her bosom, and letting it loose, drew from the running away of the frightened animal an omen favourable to the cause of her country. This anecdote is omitted by Tacitus, who has, however, preserved a portion of the speeches supposed to be spoken by the leaders on each side; but where the language of Suetonius Paulinus is only the counterpart of that put by Thucydides into the mouth of Brasidas. ;

BOAISTUAU, or BOISTUAU, (Peter,) called Launay, a French writer, born at Nantes, who died at Paris, in 1566. A work of his, originally written in Latin, was published at Paris in 1584, entitled, Theatre du Monde, containing a number of singular accounts. It is said to have passed through more than twenty editions. He also left Histoires tragiques Extraites des Œuvres Italiennes de Bandel, which were continued by Belleforest, but not so well; and also Histoires prodigieuses Extraites de divers Auteurs, continued by the same writer. (Biog. Univ.)

BOARETTI, (Francis,) an Italian man of letters, born near Padua, in 1748, and professor of sacred eloquence at Venice, during ten years. He acquired great reputation in this office; and grief on its suppression, in 1795, was thought to have brought on the fit of apoplexy, which seized him a few days afterwards. He never was himself again, although he did not die until May 15, 1799. He was an excellent linguist, theologian, mathematician, and natural philosopher. Among his numerous works, which are able, but written too hastily, besides translations from Homer and the Greek tragedians, is a version of the Psalms, published in 1788, and favourably received; Dottrina de' Padri Greci relativa alle Circostanze della Chiesa nel Secolo 18, tratta de' Testi originali, 1791; Pensieri sulla Trisezione dell' Angolo, 1793. (Biog. Univ. Suppl.)

BOATE, (Gerard,) a Dutch physician and naturalist, whose name is more correctly spelt Boot, born at Gorcum, in 1604. After studying medicine in his native country, and taking his doctor's degree, he passed to London in 1630, where he was appointed physician to Charles I. Upon the death of the sovereign he repaired to Dublin, where he died in 1650. He is not known as a medical writer, but he first led the way in detailing the natural history of Ireland. His productions are, Philosophia naturalis reformata, id est, Philosophiæ Aristotelicæ accurata Examinatio, ac solida Confutatio, et novæ et verioris Introductio, Dublin, 1641, 4to. Ireland's Natural History, being a true and ample Description of its Situation, Greatness, Shape, and Nature of its Hills, Woods, &c., London, 1652, 1657, 8vo; Dublin, 1726, 1753, 4to; translated into French by P. Briot, Paris, 1666, 2 vols, 12mo. This work comprises a geographical description of the country, and a slight sketch of the diseases peculiar to the soil and climate. The edition of 1657 is the same as that of 1652, the preface and dedicatory epistle being suppressed, and a frontispiece added. A sequel to the work, relating to the vegetable kingdom, was promised by the author, but never appeared.

BOATON, (Peter Francis,) a man of letters, born in the Pays de Vaud, in 1734, of good family, and originally in the Sardinian army. His health failing, he was obliged to quit the service, and he became governor at the military school at Berlin. Some disagreement made him quit this post, and he opened a boarding-school in the Prussian capital. Although his undertaking succeeded, he was glad to relinquish it for the charge of a rich banker's only son. This found him an easy independence for the rest of his days. He died at Berlin, in June 1794, having published translations, in French verse, of Gessner's Idylls, and Death of Abel; also of Wieland's Oberon. The last, although not perfect, is considered very superior to Borch's version. Boaton likewise published Essais en Vers et en Prose, Berlin, 1782. (Biog. Univ. Suppl.)

BOBART, (Jacob,) a German botanist, born at Brunswick, superintendent of the botanic garden at Oxford, founded in 1632, by Henry Danvers, earl of Danby. The first gardener appointed was John Tradescant the elder, but it is not certain that he accepted the office. Bobart held it until his death, Feb. 4, 1680, at the age of eighty-one. He published, Catalogus Plantarum Horti Medici Oxoniensis, Oxoniæ, 1648, 8vo, of which a second edition, with considerable additions and many corrections, was put forth in 1658, by the care of his son and Dr. William Browne. It appears from this work, that about 2,000 species were then in the garden, of which 600 were English. Linnæus consecrated a genus of plants (Bobartia) to the memory of this venerable horticulturist, and to that of his son.

BOBART, (Jacob,) son of the preceding, botanical professor at Oxford, on the death of Morison, in 1683. He continued the labours of his predecessor, by the publication of the third part of the Oxford History of Plants, 1696, folio. He died in 1719, at the age of 79. (Ingram's Oxford.)

BOBRUN, (Henry and Charles,) two French portrait painters, born at Amboise, one in 1603, the other in 1604. They were highly esteemed at court, having the art of making their subjects look extremely well, without losing the likeness, and of using skilfully dress and ornaments in painting ladies. Their pictures, often executed between the two without showing any diversity, are now but little sought, or even known. Henry died in 1667, Charles in 1692. (Biog. Univ.)

BOCANEGRA, (Peter Athanasius,) a Spanish painter, born at Granada in 1638, a pupil of Alonzo Cano, but improved, it is said, by studying the works of de Moya and Vandyck. He died at Granada in 1688. (Bryan.)

BOCANGEL, (Gabriel y Unzueta,) a native of Madrid, son of a celebrated physician. He was employed as librarian, and in other situations about the Spanish court. He died Dec. 8, 1658, leaving considerable reputation both as a prose writer and a poet. His principal publication is, La Lira de las Musas de Humanas y sagradas Voces, Madrid, 1635, 4to. Some others of his published works are of a devotional and courtly character. (Antonio.)

BOCCA DI FERRO, (Lewis,) a learned Bolognese philosopher, often mentioned as Buccaferri and Buccaferra, born about 1482. He took doctor's degrees in philosophy and medicine at his native place, studying the latter under the celebrated Alexander Achillini. Being appointed to a chair of logic in the university, he had for his pupils Julius Cæsar Scaliger, Francis Piccolomini, and Benedict Varchi. The cardinal Gonzaga was also one of his disciples, and became his intimate friend. By him he was persuaded to quit the university of Bologna and repair to Rome, where he taught with equal success during five years the Aristotelian philosophy in the College della Sapienza. Upon the sacking of Rome by the Imperial troops, he returned to Bologna, and entered into orders. He died May 3, 1545. He was generally considered as the first philosopher of his day, and eminent in the development of the principles of his great master in philosophy. His works are various commentaries:—In Librum Primum Physicorum Aristotelis, Venet. 1558, 1570, 1613, folio. In Quatuor Libros Meteororum Aristotelis, Venet. 1563, 1565, 1570, folio. Lectiones in Parva Naturalia Aristotelis, Venet. 1570, folio. In Duos Libros Aristotelis de Generatione et Corruptione Commentaria, Venet. 1571, folio. Diatribe de Principatu partium Corporis, which is to be found in the Apologia pro Galeno contra Vesalium of Francis Puteus, Venet. 1562. 8vo.

BOCCACCIO, or BOCCACCI, (John,) an Italian writer, of great celebrity, whose history, notwithstanding, labours under considerable uncertainty. Bayle, Moreri, Betussi, and others, represent him as the son of a poor peasant, and born at the village of Certaldo; Salvini and Manni assert that he was born at Florence, of respectable parents; Villani makes him born at Paris. There are also many other gratuitous assertions, contradictions, and mistakes to be found in the biographies of this celebrated man. The following, collected from the best authorities, Manni, Mazzuchelli, Crescimbeni, and, above all, Tiraboschi, may be considered as the most faithful account of his life.

He was of a respectable family, possessed of a small estate at Certaldo, a village in the Val d'Elsa, about twenty miles from Florence. Hence the addition made by Boccaccio to his name. He was the natural son of Boccaccio di Chellino di Buonajuto, a merchant, who had filled "the most remarkable offices" at Florence. His mother was a French girl, with whom the father became acquainted, when on commercial business at Paris, and whom he married after his birth; this took place at Paris, in 1313. He was placed for education at Florence, under Zanobi da Strada, father of the celebrated poet of that name, and soon gave promise of talent; but his father, who wished him to follow trade, at ten years of age took him from school, and placed him with a merchant, with whom, after visiting Paris, and spending six years, very much against his inclination, he returned to Florence. His father then, still persisting in his former views, sent him to different places to acquire the necessary knowledge for commercial life. In the course of these travels, being now twenty years old, he arrived at Naples, and visiting the tomb of Virgil, his ardour for literature and poetry became so strong, that he obtained, at last, his father's permission to follow his inclination, under the condition of studying the canon law. Here, it is said, he became acquainted with Petrarch, which is not true, and to have fallen in love, in the church of St. Laurence, with a beautiful young married lady, called Maria, who is represented as a natural daughter of the king Robert. This is doubted by Mazzuchelli, and considered as a poetical fiction by Tiraboschi; though there can be no doubt that he was a great favourite with ladies, and among them, with some of high rank, whom he might have seen at church, as he relates in his Fiammetta. Hence also the Filocopo, a poor novel, in which he gives the history of his love; and soon after the Teseide, a poem in twelve books, on the fabulous adventures of Theseus, the only merit of which is, that of being the first romantic poem in the Italian language written in *ottava rima*, a metre which he had taken from the Sicilians, and improved by adding a third rhyme, and making the seventh verse rhyme with the eighth, as it is at present. From this poem Chaucer borrowed his Knighte's Tale, afterwards remodelled by Dryden under the title of Palamon and Arcite.

In 1342 Boccaccio was recalled to Florence; and it seems that he applied himself to the study of astronomy and Greek. Some say that he returned to Naples in 1344, remained there for several years, wrote some of his works, and appeared frequently at court; others, quoted by Mazzuchelli, assert that he went to Sicily to improve his knowledge of the Greek language; no one, however, mentions that he was sent in 1346 by the Florentines, who began to appreciate his merits, in the character of an ambassador to Romagna, and to Ostasio, lord of Ravenna, where he did not remain much more than a year; for in 1348 he lost his father, and returned to Florence to take possession of his inheritance, a great part of which he spent in travelling and purchasing MSS. both in the Greek and Latin languages, and copying those which he could not purchase.

Very little after this time, or not later than 1350, he seems to have made the acquaintance of Petrarch, who passed through Florence on his way to Rome for the jubilee, an acquaintance which soon ripened into friendship, which Villani describes as having "un' anima in due corpi." In 1351 he was sent by the Florentines to Padua, to carry to Petrarch the decree which restored to him his paternal inheritance, and invited him to come and honour their university with his presence. From that a regular correspondence was kept up between them, and all uncertainty about the events of their lives is at an end. On his return to Florence, at the end of the same year, he was sent ambassador to Lewis of Bavaria, marquis of Brandenburg, to invite him to come to Italy, to lower the pride of the Visconti; and in 1353 to pope Innocent VI., at Avignon, to settle the mode by which they were to receive the emperor Charles IV. on his visit to Italy.

In 1359 he went to Milan, to visit Petrarch, with whom he passed several days; and in 1360, having persuaded the Florentines to establish a professorship of Greek literature, he went to Venice for Leontius Pilatus, his old master, whom he entertained in his own house, and induced to make a Latin translation of Homer, of which Petrarch asked, and received as a present, a copy. Of this translation a copy, by Niccolo Nicoli, still exists in the Benedictine library at Florence. It has been said that there was an older translation, of a part at least, of Homer's poem; of which, however, there is no proof.

In the following year, Peter Petroni, a Carthusian monk, remarkable for piety, on his death-bed, 29th May, 1361, appears to have charged Ciani, another monk of the same order, to tell Boccaccio that he had but few years more to live, and therefore ought to abandon poetry. This communication being made effective by the mention of several circumstances, known, as he thought, only to him and Petrarch, Boccaccio became so frightened, that he resolved not only to give up poetry and every profane study, but also to get rid of all his books. Petrarch, however, exhorted him to take the warning without forswearing literature, but simply to make a good use of it, as so many pious men had done. Mazzuchelli asserts, that in consequence of his advice, Boccaccio, in 1362, assumed the clerical habit, and changed entirely the tenour of his life, which hitherto had been far from correct. Tiraboschi imagines that to this epoch must belong what Boccaccio relates of himself of having, at an advanced age, undertaken the pursuit of sacred studies; but that the difficulty he found, and the shame of having so late in life to learn the elements of a new science, had dissuaded him from it.

In the following year, 1363, being invited by Niccolo Acciojoli, high steward of the kingdom of Naples, Boccaccio visited that court; but, vexed at the manner of his reception, he left it in disgust, and went to Venice (which was the cause of the report then circulated, that he had become a Carthusian monk), where he passed three months in the society of Petrarch. The Abbé de Sade, however, says that he had gone to Naples from Florence on account of the plague, and on his return, for the same reason, went straight to Venice. In 1365 he was sent by the Florentines to pope Urban V., at Avignon, who seemed ill pleased with them. On his return to Florence he was appointed one of the magistrates, an office which he retained till the month of November, 1367, when he was again sent to the same pope Urban, though not to Avignon, as it is generally thought, upon the authority of Mazzuchelli, but to Rome. He returned in 1368, and went to Venice to meet Petrarch, but found him gone to Pavia.

In 1373 the Florentines having resolved to establish a professorship to lecture upon and explain Dante, they appointed Boccaccio to the office, with a salary of 100 florins; and on the 3d of October of that year he began his lectures at the church of St. Stephen, and wrote a commentary on the Inferno, which has been printed, and is much esteemed, with the life of the author, written more in the style of a romance than a history. In the mean time a malady by which he had been previously attacked, having left him in a state of great debility, aggravated by intense application, obliged him to retire to the small paternal estate which he had at Certaldo, where he made his will in 1374, leaving his property to his two nephews, and his valuable library, *vita durante*, to his confessor, father Martino di Signa; and after his death to the convent of the Spirito Santo, at Florence, for the use of the students, where it was destroyed by fire a century after.

Early in 1375 the sad news of the death of his dear friend Petrarch, who in his will had left him fifty golden florins to purchase a warm gown to protect him in his studies during the winter nights, hastened his dissolution, which took place December 21st, 1375. He was buried in the church of San Giacomo, at Certaldo, with a modest inscription, written by himself; in the last verse of which the words "Patria Certaldum," have been the cause of misleading the greatest part of his biographers in regard to his native place. In 1503 a cenotaph, with his bust in marble, was raised to his memory, which still exists. His grave was opened in 1783, not through fanaticism, as Lord Byron says, in Childe Harolde, but through a misinterpretation of the ordinance of the grand duke Leopold against burials within churches.

Boccaccio no doubt was a man of great talents and very extensive knowledge; like Dante and Petrarch he may be justly considered as highly instrumental in the revival of learning; but though, like the latter, he reckoned upon his Latin works to immortalize his name, yet, like him too, his reputation rests upon those written by him in Italian, which he valued but little. These, however, made him father of his country's prose, as Petrarch became by his the father of her poetry. Boccaccio's works are many, both in Latin and Italian; of the former we have De Genealogia Deorum, libri xv., which have passed through numberless editions and translations, both in Italy and elsewhere. It was a very useful work at the time, showing immense reading, but rather suspiciously quoting authors not now to be found. De Montium, Sylvarum Lacuum, Fluviorum stagnorum, et Marium Nominibus, Liber; which also was translated into Italian, and has been two or three times published. De Casibus Virorum et Fœminarum Illustrium, lib. ix., beginning with Adam, translated and published several times in all the languages of Europe. The same must be said of his next work, De Claris Mulieribus, which has had an immense circulation. Egloga xvi., in which he alludes, allegorically, to the events of his time; he gave the Key to the real names of the persons and places to his confessor, father Martino da Signa, of which Manni published an abridgment. They are all not worth much. Of his Italian works, five are in poetry and eight in prose; of the former, the Teseide, already mentioned, was twice published in Italy, and once at Paris, translated into French. L'Amorosa Visione, in fifty cantos, containing five *trionfi*, of wisdom, glory, riches, love, and fortune, written in *terza rima*, in which the first letter of each stanza being put together, form the name of Maria, the pretended daughter of king Robert, his mistress, the only occasion in which he ventured to do so, and which it would be impossible to find out without the key. Filostrato, a romantic poem, in *ottava rima*, in which he describes the loves of Troilus, son of Priam, and Chryseis, whom he represents as the daughter of Calchas, also often published, and translated into French. Poesie Diverse; they are not many, and such as they are, they seem to have escaped the general conflagration to which he condemned all his works after his interview with father Ciani. In favour of any of these pieces, very little can be said; though no doubt they deserve great credit, if we consider the time in which they were written, and the state of the Italian language.

Of his prose works we have already mentioned the Filocopo, a novel, extremely long and fatiguing, deficient in style, and in no way resembling that which he adopted afterwards; it has passed through several editions both in Italy and France, and has been twice translated into French. L'Amorosa Fiammetta, another such novel, no better than the first; translated into French and Spanish, and published several times in Italy and elsewhere. Il Ninfale d'Ameto, written both in prose and verse, in which he relates an event of his life, under the name of Ameto, a young sportsman in the midst of seven nymphs; it has passed through a good many editions. Il Corbaccio, o sia Laberinto d'Amore, a bitter invective, not only against a widow who had offended him, but an abominable satire against the whole sex, written in good style, though extremely indecent; it has passed through numberless editions, and been translated into French, first by Belleforest, and republished by Premont, under the t tle of Sogno di Boccaccio o il Larebinto d'Amore, with so many additions as to make it a new and desirable work. Vita di Dante Alighieri, a very indifferent work, which has more the air of a romance than a history. Commento sopra la Commedia di Dante Alighieri, an excellent work, consisting of the public lectures which he gave at Florence, and containing many anecdotes, which cannot be found elsewhere; it does not extend beyond the seventeenth chapter of the Inferno. Lastly, the Decamerone, consisting of one hundred novels, almost all founded on real facts, which he has embellished and altered, told during ten days by seven ladies and three young men, in a villa not far from Florence, where they had retired in the year 1348, at the time that the dreadful plague, of which he gives the most eloquent and pathetic description, ravaged that city. It is a work which has immortalized the name of Boccaccio, notwithstanding the two faults which some over nice critics have urged against it, of which we think it necessary to take notice. The fact that the greatest part of his novels are taken from the Provençal poets, is much exaggerated, and shows that they who advance it know nothing of the Fabliaux or of the Decamerone; for at most nine or ten stories are *imitated* from the Troubadours, if indeed they be not taken from more remote writers, from which these poets themselves have taken the subjects of their tales. Unfortunately, another accusation brought against this collection is partially true. It is licentious; which is, however, a fault of the times, and affects Boccaccio less than writers of other nations in Europe. He has, however, done much to redeem this fault, by depicting, in the language of his biographers, on a vast canvass, men of all conditions, of all characters, and all ages, representing events of every kind, comic and serious, and exhibiting models of eloquence and purity of expression, and elegance of style, to a degree of perfection unknown before his time. The numberless editions through which this work has passed, may well silence those who call its merit, with regard to language, exaggerated. Two popes, Paul IV. and Pius IV., more scrupulous than their twenty-six predecessors, forbade this book; and several academicians, by order of Pius V. and Gregory XIII., published reformed editions of it. But nothing could stifle the general consent of the nation, which has so much multiplied republications of the original text for the last two hundred years, as to nullify the prohibition. The original editions are become extremely scarce; and at the sale of the duke of Roxburgh's library, a copy of that in 1471, by Valdafer, was bought by the marquess of Blandford for the immense sum of 2,260*l*. Another copy, of the Giunti edition of 1527, 4to, at the same sale fetched 29*l*.

Boccaccio's Italian works were collected from the best MSS., and published at Florence, in 1827-34, in 4 vols, 8vo; and in regard to the Decamerone, the MS. by Manelli, written in 1384, and preserved in the Laurentian library, has been the text to the best editions.

BOCCACINO, (Boccacio,) a painter, born at Cremona, in 1460, and said to have been a scholar of Peter Vanucci, called *Pietro Perugino*. Lanzi observes of this painter, that he was the best modern among the ancients, and the best ancient among the moderns. He is considered inferior to Perugino in composition, less beautiful in the airs of his heads, less vigorous in light and shadow; but richer in his drapery, more varied in colour, more spirited in attitudes, and probably equal in architecture and landscape. He died in 1518. (Bryan.)

BOCCACCINO, (Camillus,) son of the preceding, born at Cremona, in 1511, and educated under his father. Although this instruction was far from the best for a genius like his, he succeeded pretty completely in overcoming its disadvantages, and formed a style of his own, alike pleasing and grand. Hence he has been placed at the head of the Cremonese school. Yet he died in 1546, at the early age of 35. (Bryan.)

BOCCACINO, (Francis,) a painter, born at Cremona, about 1680, who died in 1750. His style was chiefly formed at Rome, in the school of Carlo Maratti; and although he executed few of the larger works for churches, he produced many very pleasing historical and mythological pieces, which are valued in private collections. (Bryan.)

BOCCAGE, (Mary Anne le Page, du,) a French writer, so highly complimented in her day, that Voltaire, at Ferney, placing a laurel-wreath on her head, declared her dress wanted only *that* to render it quite complete. She was born at Rouen, Oct. 22, 1710, educated in a convent at Paris, and married to a placeman at Dieppe, whom she long survived. She attempted a translation of Milton's Paradise Lost, but with little success, even failing in those pictures of Adam and Eve which seem best fitted for a female pen. She was more fortunate in a poem on the Death of Abel; but her principal work, the Columbiad, an epic, although not without good passages, which contemporaries applauded, appears of little value to posterity. She also produced the Amazons, a tragedy, which was acted eleven nights, and soon after forgotten. It is, indeed, remarkable that this lady's fame, which once rested chiefly upon her poetry, has long had no other dependence than her prose. As a letter-writer she is still valued; the results of her travels in England, Holland, and Italy, upon which she set out in 1750, being given in a correspondence, which Voltaire, with more gallantry than truth, pronounced superior to that of lady Mary Wortley Montague. Madame du Boccage reached an extraordinary age, dying August 8, 1802, after a life of compliments, gained partly by superior talents, but also from the deference justly due to an amiable, talented, and agreeable person of her sex. Her works were several times reprinted, and translated into various languages. An indifferent English translation of her letters concerning England, Holland, and Italy, was published in 1770. (Biog. Univ. Chalmers.)

BOCCAGE, (Peter Joseph Fiquet, du,) husband of the preceding, born at Rouen, in 1700, and early employed in the finance department. His leisure time was chiefly spent upon English dramatic poetry, and he published in 1751, Melange de Differentes Pièces traduites de l'Anglais, containing, among other things, a version of Southern's Oroonoko; and in 1752, Lettres sur le Théâtre Anglais, which introduce a translation of Wycherley's Country Wife. Boccage died at Rouen, in August, 1767. (Biog. Univ. Suppl.)

BOCCAGE, (Manuel Maria Barbosa, du,) a Portuguese poet, of the same family as the preceding, born at Setuval, in 1771, and chiefly remarkable for an extraordinary talent in improvisation. As this often displayed itself in satirical effusions, under which persons of some importance were doomed to smart, it marred Boccage's fortune, and placed him in several disagreeable situations. In addition to the evils brought on him by these indiscretions, he wrote, about 1797, a philosophical epistle, after the manner of Voltaire, in which he denied the soul's immortality. This was extensively circulated in MS., and occasioned the author's confinement in the prison of the Inquisition. Being liberated by the influence of some of the principal Portuguese nobility, he published, between 1798 and 1805, five volumes of his poems, which have had great success. He died of aneurism of the heart, in 1806. (Biog. Univ. Suppl.)

BOCCALINI, (Trajan,) an eminent Italian satirical writer, born at Loretto, in 1556; said by Mazzuchelli and others to have been of a Roman family, but really a native of Carpi. His profession was architecture, and he was employed upon the *holy house* of Loretto, as the ridiculous imposition, so well known there, is called, during the pontificate of Pius IV. This has been fully proved by Tiraboschi, from the parochial register of that place, and from the records of the noble family of Pii, then living at Carpi. It is said that Boccalini's early education being neglected, he began rather late in life to study seriously. He read philosophy and law at Rome, where he lived for a long time, and acquired the friendship and protection of several influential persons, by whose patronage he became teacher of geography to cardinal Bentivoglio, and governor of different places in the state of the Church. He might also have been counsellor to the king of Spain, but he refused, from hatred of the Spanish domination. His conduct being far from correct, many complaints against him were forwarded to the pope, which produced his recall to Rome, where he continued his studies, and wrote his celebrated Ragguagli di Parnaso. Either now despairing to advance his fortune in that capital, or perhaps the desire of printing his works in a free country, at a safe distance from those whom he had abused, made him go to Venice in 1612. There he published the first *centuria*, or part, of the Ragguagli, and, in the year following, the second. He died on the 16th of November of the same year, by an attack of colic and a fever, as it appears from the entry of the parochial church of St. Mary's. It has, however, been absurdly reported that he was murdered by four or six assassins employed by the court of Spain, who entered his house when alone, threw him on his bed, and struck him with small bags full of sand, till they left him for dead. In the abuse which Boccalini had bestowed upon the ambitious views and tyrannical government of Spain, in his Pietra del Paragone Politico, a reason is found for this outrage; but this work was not published until two years after his death.

Of Boccalini's works, the most celebrated is the Ragguagli di Parnaso, or News from Parnassus, in which relations, complaints, and accusations are brought to Apollo, that he may pass judgment upon them. Boccalini uses this vehicle to censure the lives, actions, and writings of princes, warriors, and learned men. Its great success arose from the satirical reflections with which it abounds, for its judgments are capricious, and often incorrect. It has passed through several editions, and has been translated into several languages. It has been even asserted, though unjustly, that cardinal

Bonifacio Gaetani had a great share in the compilation of it. Boccalini also produced La Pietra del Paragone Politico, which is a sort of continuation, or a third part of the Ragguagli, but principally directed against the court of Spain. It was first published in 1615, at Cosmopoli (Amsterdam) and Venice; it has passed through many editions. This, too, has been translated into Latin, French, Spanish, German, and English. Cardinal Gaetani has also been accused, and equally unjustly, of having here likewise had a great share in the composition. Boccalini's Italian Commentaries on Tacitus were published at Geneva, in 1669, at Cosmopoli (Amsterdam), 1677, 4to, and in 1677, in three volumes, with illustrations by Du May, whose freedom sometimes outstrips that of Boccalini himself, especially as to religion. The first two volumes of this Commentary, and the Parnassus, too, are forbidden in the Roman Index of 1681. The Lettere Politiche ed Istoriche and la Segretaria di Apollo che Segue i Ragguagli di Parnasso, which by some have been ascribed to Boccalini, by the best informed critics and Mazzucchelli are denied to be his works.

BOCCANERA, (William,) a democratic leader at Genoa. There are in that city two sorts of noble families, the ancient and the new. The former, twenty-eight in number, alone administered the government, and amongst them the oldest and most influential were the houses of Doria, Fieschi, Grimaldi, and Spinola. The latter, to the number of 437, had been ennobled from time to time, but had no share whatever in the administration of state affairs. The Boccaneras being, although noble, among the excluded families, William, ardent and ambitious, became impatient, and joined the democratic party. The old nobility he accused of peculation and injustice, and his inflammatory language, joined with seductive promises, wrought so upon the people, that they abolished the existing government, and elected him in 1257 *capitano* for ten years, with all the power and attributes of the supreme power. The new government, however, was quickly found to have promised more than could be accomplished. Hence popular disappointment soon rose to an ungovernable height; and Boccanera, being overpowered in 1262, would have been put to death, had it not been for the archbishop's intercession.

BOCCANERA, (Simon,) grandson of the preceding, born in the beginning of the fourteenth century. After the failure of his grandfather, the government of Genoa became again vested in the nobility; but the people insisted on a magistrate of their own, called *Abate del Popolo*, who, like the tribunes of ancient Rome, should protect them against aristocratical encroachments. The city then was distracted, like other parts of Italy, between the Guelphs and Ghibellines. The four principal Genoese families being ranged two and two, on different sides, were powerless; for these disputes often ended in bloodshed, banishment, and confiscation of property, which gave to the government the appearance of tyranny. Simon Boccanera, whose connexions were with the democratic party, was in 1339 elected abbot of the people. A nobleman was not, however, eligible to this office; hence the people proclaimed him their doge for life, after the example of Venice. There was, however, this difference, that in Genoa the doge might be chosen either from among the new nobility, or from among the private citizens, but not from any of the twenty-eight ancient noble families, as it was in Venice. Boccanera justified for several years the expectation of the people, notwithstanding great opposition from the four great families, who, for the sake of recovering their power, forgot party, and acted in concert. He was able, however, to deprive them all of employment and authority, he banished those whose influence he thought most dangerous, routed the army of the marquess of Finale, and having obliged him to come to Genoa to sue for pardon, he shut him up in a wooden cage, and did not restore him to liberty until he had yielded to the republic the greatest part of his estates. But notwithstanding this and other acts which he did to keep down the nobles, their party was much too strong, and he was at last obliged, in 1344, to give up his office, and retire to Pisa, where he remained in banishment till after the Genoese submitted themselves, in 1353, to John Visconti, archbishop of Milan, who gave the government of their city to William, marquess of Pallavicini. In 1356, this latter being expelled, Boccanera was reinstated in the ducal office, which he held for seven years more, when he was poisoned at a dinner that he gave to Peter Lusignan, king of Cyprus, then on his way to that island.

BOCCANERA, (Julius, or Gilles,) brother of the preceding, whom he assisted with his prudence and valour in his elevation to the office of doge, and was by him raised to the command of the Genoese fleet. In this capacity, being sent with fifteen galleys in 1340 to the succour of Alfonso XI., king of Castile, against the allied Moors of Andalusia and Africa, he had an important share in the great victory of Tariffa, and in the taking of Algeziras in 1344 : indeed his services were of so much value to Alfonso, as to induce him to entrust Boccanera with the office of admiral of the Spanish fleet, and present him besides with the earldom of Palma. At the death of Alfonso, which took place in 1350, during the reign of Peter the Cruel, and the civil war which issued between him and his natural brother, Henry earl of Trastamare, to whom Alfonso had left the crown, we find no particular record of Boccanera, though there is reason to suppose him to have followed the fortune of Henry; for when in 1369 Peter was murdered, and Henry succeeded to the throne of Castile, and was crowned by the name of Henry II., we find Boccanera still holding the office of Castilian admiral. In 1372 he gained a great victory over the English fleet under the earl of Pembroke, who was made prisoner, while attempting to land at Rochelle, to enforce the claim of John of Ghent, son to Edward III., king of England, to the crown of Castile, as having married a daughter of Peter the Cruel. Boccanera seems to have died shortly afterwards.

BOCCHERINI, (Lewis,) a celebrated musical composer, born at Lucca, Jan. 14, 1740, who died at Madrid in 1806, after establishing a great reputation, especially for sacred pieces. (Biog. Univ.)

BOCCHI, (Dorothy,) a female scholar, daughter of doctor John Bocchi, said by Ribera, in his excellent work of Le Glorie Immortali delle Donne Illustri, to have lived in 1417. Masini, however, in his Bologna Perlustrata, and Orlandi, in the Notizie degli Scrittori Bolognesi, place her in 1350; but Mazzucchelli fixes on the year 1433, which appears the most probable. She seems to have excelled in philosophy and medicine, on which she read public lectures to the pupils of her father, with the salary of a hundred livres per annum, and to have written and spoken several orations and prælections.

BOCCHI, (Achilles,) born of a noble *family* at Bologna, in 1488, a classical *scholar*, who published, at the early age of twenty, in his native town, his Apologia in Plautum. This was followed in 1509 by his verses in praise of John Baptista Pius; and other specimens of his poetical powers are to be found in Gruter's Deliciæ Poetarum Italiorum, and in the second volume of the Poetæ Latini. But his principal work is Symbolicarum Quæstionum quas serio ludebat, libri v. printed at Bologna in 1555, and subsequently in 1574. Of these Symbols, the plates for the first edition were engraven by Julius Bonasoni, and retouched for the second by Augustine Caracci. The Symbols are accompanied by copies of Latin verses in different measures, and to the whole is prefixed a portrait of Bocchi, which bears a marked resemblance to the head which is usually given to Æsop and Socrates. Attaching himself, according to the practice of that period, to different princes, Bocchi so ingratiated himself with them by his talents and business-like habits as to obtain various situations of trust and emolument, and thus acquired an ample fortune, with which he built a palace and a printing-office, and founded the Academia Bocchiana, or, as it was also called in Italian, Ermatena, from its seals exhibiting the union of Hermes and Athena. At the age of twenty-four he was appointed professor of Greek and Latin at Bologna, and was subsequently employed by the senate to write in Latin the history of his native town. This, though never printed, is still preserved in the library of the Institute there, and in the royal library at Paris, and runs through seventeen books. There is likewise in the Laurentian library at Florence a MS. collection of poems, under the title of Achillis Philerotis Bocchii Lusuum Libellus ad Leon. X., where the name of Phileros is supposed to refer to the friendship which existed between himself and Lilius Gyraldus. He died at Bologna, in 1562.

BOCCHI, (Francis,) a very prolific author, born at Florence, in 1548. He died there in 1618, leaving numerous works, some in Latin, others in Italian, but chiefly of an interest merely local. (Biog. Univ.)

BOCCHI, (Faustinus,) a painter, born, it is thought, at Brescia, in 1659, a scholar of Everardi, called *il Fiammingo*. He chiefly shone in battle-pieces, and his figures, though small, have considerable merit, as also have his landscapes. (Bryan.)

BOCCHI, (Octavius,) an eminent literary man, born in 1697, at Venice, where his father, who was of a noble family, originally from Adria, had gone to exercise the legal profession. After a good education, he followed the legal profession; but his leisure was largely devoted to history and antiquities, particularly of Adria and the Polesine, on which he wrote three quarto volumes. In 1739 he also published another quarto, under the title of Osservazioni sopra un Antico Teatro Scoperto in Adria, on which he was elected member of the Academy of the Etruschi at Tortona; he also in 1747 and 1748 published the Istoria delle Origini, &c. del Polesine. He died in 1749.

BOCCHUS I., king of Mauritania, who sided at first with his son-in-law, Jugurtha, on the promise of his obtaining a third part of Numidia; but after the defeat of Jugurtha by Marius, he offered to betray Sylla, who had succeeded Marius, into the hands of his son-in-law. The fear, however, of the conquerors prevailed over affection for his countrymen, for which sacrifice he obtained the kingdom called, subsequently, Mauritania Cæsariensis, of which Fez is at present the principal portion.

BOCCHUS, BOGUS, or BOGUD, for the same person is found with these three names, a Mauritanian chieftain, who, through hostility to Juba, took the side of Julius Cæsar. That illustrious Roman, Suetonius says, lavished no little money on his wife, Eunoe, and this too without giving offence to the husband, whose timely assistance turned the day in his favour, when he was on the point of being beaten by the son of Pompey, in Spain. Disappointed, however, in his desire to be recognised as the sovereign of his country, he attached himself, after the death of Cæsar, to the standard of Antony, and was present at the battle of Actium; but driven from power by his people, who refused to side with the declining fortune of Antony, he sought an asylum in the camp of Octavius, and was subsequently murdered by Agrippa at Methone, about 29 B.C.

BOCCIARDO, (Clement,) called Clementone, from his great size, a painter, born at Genoa, in 1620, pupil of Strozzi, whom he surpasses in composition and design, but he is inferior to him in truth and purity of tint. He died in 1658. (Bryan.)

BOCCIARDO, (Dominic,) a painter, born at Finale, near Genoa, about the year 1686, pupil of Morandi. He had no great invention, but was a correct designer, and an agreeable colourist (Bryan.)

BOCCONI, (Paul,) a botanist, born at Palermo, in 1633, of a noble family, originally from Savona, in the Genoese territory. Having finished his studies, he took orders, and for the sake of improving his knowledge in natural history, particularly in botany, he visited most attentively the whole of Sicily, and then, with the same minute diligence, Malta, Corsica, and most parts of Europe, observing and collecting every thing that deserved attention, and becoming every where acquainted with the most eminent men in literature and science, with whom he afterwards kept a regular correspondence. On his return to Italy he received, at Padua, the degree of doctor of medicine, and was in Florence, botanist to the grand dukes of Tuscany, Ferdinand II., and Cosimo III. In 1682 he entered the order of the Cistercian monks of Florence, in the convent of Cistello, where he took the name of Silvio, and having performed the noviciate in that of Roccamadura, at Messina, without neglecting his favourite pursuit, was elected, in 1696, a member of the Academ. Curiosor. Naturæ in Germany, from which he was styled the Modern Pliny; and on the following year, going to Venice, was, by the botanist Sherard, persuaded to publish his Museo di Piante rare del'a Silicia, Malta, Corsica, Italia, Piemonte, e Germania, 4to, with 309 figures, which is a sort of a continuation of another work, published at Oxford in 1674, under the title of Icones et Descriptiones rariorum Plantarum Siciliæ, Melitæ, Galliæ, et Italiæ. Not long after, he returned to his native country, and settled in the monastery of Santa Maria d'Altifonte, near Palermo, where he died in 1704. Of the many writers who have made mention of him, some pretend that he was made professor of botany at Padua, and others have accused him of plagiarism. Both assertions have been most fully denied by several of his biographers, and most particularly by Mazzucchelli and Tiraboschi. His works are many; some published under his baptismal name of Paulo, and others under that of Silvio, which he assumed when he became a monk. Amongst them, the principal are, 1. Monitum de Abrotano Marino. 2. Elegantissimarum Plantarum Semina, &c. 3. Manifestum Botanicum de Plantis Siculis, &c. Catana, 1668. 4. Recherches et Observations naturelles touchant le Corail, Pierre étoilée, &c. Paris,

1672. It is a collection of letters written during his travels, to one of which, that treats of the eruption of Mount Etna, in 1669, the abbé Bourdelot replied in 1672, endeavouring to prove that the large caverns, full of sulphur, minerals, and bitumen, which are under the waters of the Mediterranean, and communicate with the mountain, are the only cause of its conflagrations and eruptions. 5. Della Pietra Belzuar, minerale Siciliano, Monteleone, 1669. 6. Osservazioni naturali ove si tengono Materie Medico-fisiche, e di Botanica, Bologna, 1689, much criticized by Haller, &c. &c. &c.

BOCCONI, (Alfonso,) brother of the preceding, and a friar of the order of St. Dominic, an eminent scholar and celebrated preacher, died at Forli, in 1681, leaving several religious works in prose, and some in verse, amongst which a collection of facetious sonnets on the Difesa del Tabacco, printed at Modena, in 1679.

BOCER, (Henry,) professor of law at Tübingen, from the year 1584 till his death, in 1630, born 1561. In 1604, he declined the proffered appointment of a vice-chancellorship at Stuttgard. As he had no family, he boarded students in his house, amongst whom were most of the princes who then studied at Tübingen, including the duke Augustus of Brunswick. His numerous writings are principally in explanation of the feudal and criminal laws of that time, and his "Disputations" were intended to form a kind of system. They were very well received, and were some of them frequently reprinted, but are now forgotten. For a more particular account of them, see Jugler's Beiträge zur Jur. Biog. 6 vols. 57—71.

BOCERUS, (John,) vernacularly surnamed Boedeker, syncopated into Bocker, an historical Latin poet, born at Hausberge, near Minden, in Westphalia, in 1525. He received a learned education, and gave early promise of high talent, but, probably, neither his abilities nor his pursuits were of a practical kind. Hence he fell at one time into great misery, wandering about in want of the commonest necessaries; a wretched state of destitution, which he pathetically paints in his elegies. He died of the plague, October 6, 1565, leaving, Fribergum, in Misnia, Lips. 1553, a Description of Freiberg, this edition of which is extremely rare, but the poem was reprinted in 1677. Elegiarum Liber Primus, Lips. 1554. De Origine et Gestis Ducum Megalopolensium, Lips. 1556; an historical poem, dedicated to the dukes of Mecklenburg, John Albert, and Gerard William, tracing the history of their country from Anthyrius, first king of the Heruli and Vandals, down to their own times. De Origine et Gestis Regum Daniæ, et Ducum Holsatiæ, Comitumque Schonnenburgensium, Lips. 1557. Brevis Illustratio Urbis Hagensis sitæ in Ditione illustrium Comitum Schonnenburgensium, cum Catalogo Clarorum aliquot Virorum in ea Urbe Natorum, Rostoch. 1560. De Origine, Antiquitate, et Celebritate Urbis Mindæ. Rostoch. 1563. Joannis Boceri Sacrorum Carminum, et Piarum Precationum, Libri quatuor, Rostoch. 1565. This last work is thought to have been reprinted the same year, there being some copies of it, with additions. The probability, however, is, that as Bocerus died that year, his friends made some additions to copies that remained unsold. When carried off, he was employed upon a poem, entitled, Francias, in which he meant to sing the exploits of the French kings. (Clement. Bibl. Cur.)

BOCH, (John,) the Virgil, as he has been called, of Belgium, born at Brussels, July 27, 1555. Attaching himself to cardinal Radzivil, he studied theology under Bellarmine, subsequently the celebrated cardinal; but preferring the life of a traveller to that of a priest, he visited different parts of Europe; and it was during his journey to Moscow, that his feet having been frost-bitten, and when he was about to undergo amputation, the place, where he then was, was surprised by a detachment of the army under the grand duke Basilides; and compelled thus to run for his life, he recovered the use of his feet. On his return home he amused himself with writing Latin poetry, which was printed at Cologne in 1615, together with some pieces by his son, who died at an early age in Italy. A specimen of his verses is found under the prints in Verstegan's Theatrum Crudelitatum Hereticorum, written against queen Elizabeth; while by his panegyric on the duke of Parma, upon the taking of Antwerp, he was appointed by the conqueror the town-secretary. He died January 13, 1609.

BOCHART, (Samuel,) a French protestant minister, eminent for erudition, especially as an orientalist, born at Rouen, in 1599, of an ancient family, son of a Huguenot minister, and nephew to Peter du Moulin. His philological talents were developed so very early, that in his fourteenth year, Thomas Dempster, a learned Scot, under whom he studied at Paris, prefixed forty-four eulogetic Greek verses, written by him, to his Roman Antiquities. He went through a course of philosophy at Sedan, and there is reason for believing that he studied theology at Saumur, under Cameron, whom he is known to have followed into England, when the academy at Saumur was broken up by the civil war. While over in this country, he laid a solid foundation, in the Bodleian library, for that immense knowledge of the eastern tongues which eventually rendered him so famous; but he soon returned to the continent, and became an enthusiastic student of Arabic under Erpenius, at Leyden. On his return to France, he was appointed minister of the protestant church at Caen. He there soon made himself the general talk of France, by a public discussion that he held with Francis du Veron, a Jesuit, entrusted by the court with a special mission to dispute in favour of Romanism. This applauded controversialist arrived in Caen towards the end of August, 1628, and soon singled out the young Bochart as an antagonist, from his rising fame, worthy of him, and as one, probably, whose youth was likely to expose points in which the trained acuteness of an elder mind would find an easy victory. He sent him, accordingly, a challenge on the 4th of September, and Bochart accepted it, at the same time stipulating for certain conditions. Veron made sure of a glorious result, and wrote, on the 11th of September, to his opponent, that he meant to teach him both Greek and Hebrew. But when the two parties were pitted against each other, on the 22d of the month, in the castle of Caen, before the duke of Longueville, governor of the province, and many competent observers of both religions, Veron soon found himself to have most egregiously under-calculated his difficulties. He did, however, no doubt, acquit himself with considerable dexterity and show of knowledge, for De Bincourt, a Romanist, but a wag, describing to a protestant the two principals in the dispute, and their two seconds, who were far inferior men, said, "I do not think your learned man more learned than ours, but our ignoramus is ten times more ignorant than yours." The disputation, after a continuance of ten days, was suddenly broken off by a serious illness that seized Bochart. Veron, who had found himself very little fit for instructing his opponent in Greek or Hebrew, or anything else, was now in high spirits, and reports flew about that the young Huguenot saw no chance of escape from complete discomfiture, unless in a convenient fit of sickness. But Bochart seemed not unlikely to recover, and the anxious Jesuit became apprehensive that he might soon propose a renewal of the disputation. While still in bed, he was sounded as to his intentions, and expressed himself determined upon continuance. He might, however, not prove able to appear again in public; and while this remained in suspense, Veron staid at Caen, but when Bochart's convalescence was established, he found some uncontrollable necessity for leaving the place. The particulars of this famous disputation were taken down by scribes on both sides, and published by the principals, Veron's appearing in 1629, Bochart's in 1630. Within that year, Bochart published a second part, in which he treated rather more fully than he had done orally, of some controverted points which had been insufficiently discussed when the conference was broken off. This occasioned Veron to publish, in 1631, a second piece, relating to the mass. In 1646, Bochart published his Geographia Sacra, a work of prodigious erudition and sagacity, which threw a flood of light upon the antiquities of nations, and was warmly applauded by the learned world. In modern times its credit has rather fallen, from the author's necessary ignorance of many facts which later books of travels, and other facilities for understanding Asiatic questions, have placed within reach of inquiring minds. This great work is divided into two parts; Phaleg, which treats of the dispersion of nations, and Chanaan, which discusses the colonies and language of the Phoenicians. Another famous work of Bochart's is the Hierozoicon, in which he treats of the animals mentioned in Scripture; but this, like the Geographia, labours under the disadvantage of composition, when the means of research were incomparably smaller than they are at present. These pieces, with some others, were collected, in 1675, in two folio volumes; and between 1692 and 1712, in three such volumes. In 1711 were published some sermons by Bochart, in 3 vols, 12mo. His great reputation procured him an invitation from Christina, queen of Sweden, to whose court he repaired in 1652, and he was received in a manner worthy of his intellectual eminence. He returned to Caen in the following year, and resumed his former duties. He died suddenly, while speaking in the academy there, May 16, 1667, leaving a reputation for scholarship surpassed nowhere in Europe, and yet no man of his day was more conspicuous for modesty. He was wealthy, and had an only daughter, whose declining health affected him so deeply, that it was considered one cause of his own unexpected death. At that time he was meditating publications upon the terrestrial paradise, upon the minerals and plants of Scripture, with other interesting subjects, and had already gone a considerable way towards the completion of his designs. In the last century, Bochart's great services to learning were made far more available by the labours of two German scholars. Rosenmüller reprinted his Hierozoican, at Leipsic, in 1793-96, in three volumes, 4to, with notes and additions. Michaelis published at Göttingen, in 1780, a supplement to his Geographia Sacra, filling up his omissions, and correcting his mistakes. (Clement. Blount. Chalmers. Biog. Univ. Moreri. Hallam's Literature of Europe, iv. 76.)

BOCHART DE SARON, (John Baptist Gaspard,) of the same family as the preceding, born at Paris, January 16, 1730, and first president of the parliament there. He was particularly eminent as an arithmetician, but all scientific pursuits excited in him the deepest interest. Such was his fondness for calculation, that astronomers made no scruple in calling upon him for assistance of this kind; and he was the first to discern that Herschell's newly-discovered heavenly body did not move in an orbit suitable to a comet. Hence the suspicion, subsequently verified, that it might really be a planet. Having ample pecuniary means, Bochart de Saron collected the best philosophical instruments, and astronomers, who could not command such facilities from their own resources, had freely the use of his. He also printed at his own cost, Laplace's Théorie du Mouvement Elliptique et de la Figure de la Terre. But no elevation of mind or public spirit could propitiate the sanguinary levellers whom the French revolution raised into power. Bochart retired from public life when these monsters began upon their atrocious course. They sent him, notwithstanding, to the scaffold, April 20, 1794. (Biog. Univ.)

BOCHAT, (Charles William Loys de,) a Swiss historical writer, born at Lausanne, of a good family, in 1695, and originally intended for the church. His health being thought unequal to its duties, he was allowed by his relatives to study law; and besides holding an university professorship, he filled some civil offices. He died April 4, 1753, universally respected as an excellent citizen and a learned man. His principal work, which is rather diffuse, bears the following title, Mémoires Critiques pour servir d'Eclaircissements sur divers Points de l'Histoire Ancienne de la Suisse, Lausanne, 1747-49, 3 vols, 4to. (Biog. Univ. Suppl.)

BOCK, (Jerome,) called sometimes Le Boucq, but more usually *Tragus*, the one being a French, the other a Greek translation of his name, which means *Buck* in English. He was born at Heidesbach in 1498, and after profiting by a good education, he became first a schoolmaster, then a physician, and eventually a Lutheran minister. In this last capacity he lived sixteen years at Hornbach, and he died there of phthisis in 1554. He is one of the fathers of modern botany. His taste for plants induced him to explore the country in every direction, and his discernment forbade an implicit acquiescence in received habits of arranging the vegetable world. Hence he forsook the practice of describing plants alphabetically for a classification of them according to their several properties. This innovation was necessarily conducted upon very imperfect principles, but it was an important stride towards real botanical knowledge. Bock published, in his own language, a new herbal in 1539, without figures, which he afterwards reprinted with them once or twice. Eventually his information was communicated to Europe generally, by means of a Latin version, published by David Kyber, in 1552, with a preface by Conrad Gessner, giving a history of botany to the actual time, under the following title,—Hieronymi Tragi, de Stirpium, maximè earum quæ in Germania nostra nascuntur, Libri tres. In commemoration of Bock's services to botany, Plumier named a genus of plants Tragia. (Biog. Univ. Rees.)

BOCK, (Frederic Samuel,) a consistorial counsellor, and professor of Greek at Königsberg, born there of an old noble Transylvanian family, in 1716, left a poor and neglected orphan at the age of 12. Having obtained at the Friedericianum and theological lectures of his native town considerable information, he became, in 1737, assistant to a country clergyman in the neighbourhood. In 1740 and 1741, he published a moral periodical, The Hermit, which was much read. In 1742 he delivered lectures on philosophy at the university of Königsberg. In 1748 he was chaplain to a Prussian regiment of dragoons in the same town. In 1753 he was appointed professor of Greek there, and also chief librarian to the university. Bock was a useful teacher and a learned writer, but deficient in method and arrangement. He left some very valuable works, though unfortunately not finished. Among them are, Historia Socinianismi Prussici, maximam partem ex Documentis MSStis. Regiom. 1753, (two dissertations, which in the following year were reprinted,) and his Historia Antitrinatariorum, maxime Socinianismi et Socinianorum, t. i. p. ii.; *ib.* 1774-76, t. ii. 1784, 8vo. He was also a useful writer on education, and during the latter part of his life, which was spent in the country, turned his attention to natural history, and wrote a lengthy Œconomical Natural History of East and West Prussia, &c. He died in Sept. 1786.

BOCK, (John Nicholas Stéphen, baron de,) a man of letters, born at Thionville, January 14, 1747, and impelled to the assiduous cultivation of literature by the hope of thus partially forgetting some severe domestic bereavements. His productions are of a miscellaneous nature, and perhaps that one of them which has been most popular is, La Vie de Frédéric, Baron de Trenck, écrite par luimême, traduite de l'Allemand, Metz, 1787. Bock at first hailed enthusiastically the French revolution, but he soon became alarmed and disgusted by its selfish and sanguinary character. After a time he saw no safety but in flight, and remained ten years away from his native land. He died at Arlon, in 1809. (Biog. Univ. Suppl))

BOCKELIUS, (John,) a medical writer, born at Antwerp, in 1535, who took a doctor's degree at Bourges, and was for a time professor of anatomy at Helmstadt. Eventually he settled as a physician at Hamburgh, and he died there in 1605, having published a Latin treatise in 1599 upon philters; another in 1577, on the plague, or some other epidemic so called, that prevailed in Hamburgh in 1565; and a third upon the disease apparently now called *influenza*, entitled, Synopsis Novi Morbi, quem plerique Catarrhum Febrilem, vel Febrem Catarrhosum vocant, qui non solum Germaniam, sed pene universam Europam gravissimè afflixit. Helmstadt, 1580, 8vo. (Biog. Univ.)

BOCKELMANN, (John Frederic,) professor of law at Leyden, born 1633, at Steinfurt, in the county of Bentheim, where his father was a *gograve* (country magistrate). He distinguished himself as a student at Heidelberg, and the prince elector, Charles Lewis, having signified to him his wish that he should write on the power of the sovereign in ecclesiastical affairs, he published on that subject, in 1661, an Epistol. Apologet., in which he broached doctrines very acceptable to the prince, but highly obnoxious to the theologians, who did not fail to resent them. One of his opponents translated his name into Hircander. The prince rewarded him with a professorship, and Böckelmann was soon termed his right hand. His distinguished fortune, however—for in course of time he was raised to the vice-presidency of the highest tribunal in the country—so excited the envy of his colleagues, that he was induced to accept a professorship at Leyden, where he died unmarried, in 1681. Böckelmann was one of the most esteemed jurists of his time. His Compend. Institut. Justinian, Lugd. Bat. 1679, 12mo, was for half a century a very favourite text-book, and was often reprinted. His numerous and profound disputations in all the departments of law, are correctly enumerated and reviewed by Juggler, in his Beit. zur Jurist. Biog. b. iv. 274—301.

BOCKENBERG, (Peter Cornelisson,) an historian and antiquary, born at Gouda, in Holland, in 1548. He went at first into the church; and after being a Jesuit, a professor of theology, and a parish priest, he became a protestant, and married a schoolmaster's daughter. His conversion drew from Dousa and Baudius several caustic epigrams. The states of Holland and West Friesland appointed him their historiographer in 1591. He died Jan. 17, 1617, at Leyden. He was an industrious inquirer into Dutch antiquity, a methodical writer, but devoid of taste. For a list of his writings, which are of local interest, see Swertii Athenæ Belg. 609; Foppens Bibl. Belg. t. i. 966; Saxii Onomast. t. iii. 559.

BOCKH, (Christian Gottfried,) born 1732, at a village near Nördlingen, educated in the latter place and at Jena, appointed in 1759 con-rector at Wertheim, and at the same time clergyman at Waldburghausen. In 1762 he became rector in the imperial town, Esslingen, and in 1772 deacon in the principal church at Nördlingen, at which town he died, Jan. 31, 1792. Böckh deserves honourable mention among those who, in the last century, exerted themselves for the improvement of education. With this view he published a weekly journal; and he was the chief contributor to the Allg. Biblioth. für das Schul u. Erziehungswesen. Nördlingen, 11 vols, 1774-86, a work containing thorough criticisms of educational writings, well considered propositions, &c. His writings for the young also met with great approbation. For instance, his Journal for Children, 14 vols, Nuremberg, 1780-83; Chronicle for Youth, Augsb. 4 vols, 1785-88; Sermons for Youth, Nuremb. 1783; The Counsellor of Young People, Leips. 2 vols, 1791, &c. Böckh was well versed in ancient German literature, but the greater part of his writings on this subject has never been published; a few, however, are found in the first volume of the Bragur, which he edited in conjunction with Gräter.

BOCKHORST, (John van,) an eminent painter, born at Munster, in 1610, of a respectable family, which settled at Antwerp when he was very young. He was a pupil of Jacob Jordaens, and gained from his stature the appellation of *Langen Jan*. His colouring occasionally resembles that of Rubens, but more frequently that of Vandyck, to whose portraits those of Bockhorst are scarcely inferior. (Bryan. Pilkington.)

BOCKHORST, (John van,) an artist, born at Deutekom, in Holland, in 1661, who studied in London under Kneller. He subsequently went to Germany, but finally settled in his own country, where he died in 1724. His best pictures are portraits and battles. (Pilkington.)

BOCKSHAMMER, (John Christian,) born at Teschen, in Austrian Silesia, May 27, 1733, in 1764, appointed chief preacher at Festenberg, in Prussian Silesia, where he died in 1804. He was a man of powerful memory, strong imagination, and extensive erudition, but especially most worthy of record for his exertions towards the religious and moral improvement of the Polish Lutheran congregations in Upper Silesia and in the neighbouring part of Poland itself. Being quite master of their language, he translated, and in some instances partially composed, for their use many valuable religious works.

BOCLER, (John Henry,) born at Cronheim, in Franconia, in 1611, and at the age of twenty appointed professor of eloquence at Strasburg; in 1648 invited by queen Christina of Sweden to hold a similar situation at Upsal, and in the following year made her historiographer, with a salary of 800 crowns, which she generously continued, when his health obliged him to return to Strasburg, where he was elected professor of history. In 1663 he was created a count palatine by the emperor Ferdinand III.; and such was his reputation, not only as a Hebrew, Greek, and Latin scholar, but also for his profound knowledge of history, politics, and law, that Lewis XIV. offered him a pension of 2,000 livres if he would settle in France; the court of Vienna, however, unwilling to part with a person of such talents, induced him to decline the invitation, and, to make up the pecuniary loss he suffered by his refusal, granted him another pension of 600 rix dollars, and thus enabled him to pursue his studies with unremitting ardour, until death put a finish to them, in 1692. During his lengthened life he published editions of or notes upon Herodian and Polybius in Greek; but his acquaintance was rather with Latin literature, as is shown by his labours on Terence, Virgil, Ovid, Manilius, Cornelius Nepos, Velleius Paterculus, and Tacitus. His dissertations on different points of history, together with his smaller pieces, were published under the superintendence of J. A. Fabricius, in 4 vols, 4to, at Strasburg, in 1712, while his Bibliographia Critica was reprinted at Leipsic by Krause, in 1715, 4to, who has added corrections of some mistakes into which Böcler had fallen. Of his other works, a list is given in the Biog. Universelle; and it is probably from his treatise on the Amphictyonic Council, that more modern authors have derived, directly or indirectly, some portion of their knowledge.

BOCMANN, or BOCKMANN, (John Laurence,) born at Lübeck, May 8, 1741, and first intended for the church; but his great love of mathematics and physics inducing him to quit theology in 1764, he was appointed professor of his favourite sciences at Carlsruhe. He afterwards filled successively various offices under the government of Baden. He died Dec. 15, 1802. His talents earned him the esteem of the margrave Charles Frederic, whom he accompanied on some of his travels, whose court he ornamented, and whose generosity was of great service to him in the formation of a museum. He instructed in physics the other members of the ruling family. Adopting with enthusiasm every foreign invention which promised to be of service to mankind, he availed himself of the confidence of his sovereign to introduce lightning-conductors throughout the country; and on the establishment of telegraphs in France, he proposed a simplification of the plan, and also other methods. The titles of most of his numerous writings will be found in Mensel's Gelehrt. Deutschl. and Gradmann's Gelehrte Schweiz.

BOCKMANN, (C. W.) eldest son of the above, born at Carlsruhe, 1773; from his youth a great lover of mathematics and physics, but diverted from his studies by the French war of 1792, in which he served as an under officer in the Baden army. In 1795, he and his father were appointed by the Austrians to establish a line of telegraphs. He wrote on the phosphorus contained in various gases, (Erlangen, 1800,) and translated Chaptal on the Preparation, &c. of Wine. In 1801 he quitted the army altogether, and became assistant to his father, whom he succeeded at his death as professor, though count Rumford urgently invited him to quit Baden for some place where he might be better known. Other offers of promotion abroad were equally unsuccessful. In 1805 was published his Sketch of a Guide for Use at Lectures on Physics, Carlsruhe, 8vo. In 1813 he was appointed a member of the commission of health, having previously published a work on the mineral springs of Baden. He was a member of no less than one-and-twenty learned societies at home and abroad, and various sovereigns to whom he had sent his writings honoured him with decorations or other marks of distinction. His works on the practical and useful applications of physics are very numerous, but modern theories did not engage his attention. He died June 18, 1821.

BOCQUILLOT, (Lazarus Andrew,) a French writer, chiefly on religious subjects, born at Avallon, April 1, 1649, of parents who were very poor, but contrived to give him a good education. He tried for admittance among the royal guards, but failing of success, he thought of the church. Being soon weary of the necessary preparation, he next went to Constantinople, in the train of De Nointel, the French ambassador. On returning, he repaired to Bourges as a law student; and having obtained the requisite qualification, he entered upon practice at Avallon. He found good encouragement, but his habits became dissipated. A fit of melancholy caused him to reflect upon them with shame and sorrow. His brother, who was himself of a religious order, now advised temporary retirement in a Capuchin convent. The advice was taken, and he determined, after a time, upon taking orders. He held, until deafness disqualified him for its duties, a parochial benefice, and subsequently a canonry, on which he died, September 22, 1728. He was a very prolific author, leaving some pieces on antiquities and history, together with many works of a professional character, of which the most valuable is, Traité Historique de la Liturgie Sacrée, ou de la Messe, Paris, 1701, 8vo. (Biog. Univ.)

BOCTHOR, (Ellious,) a learned Copt, born at Syout, in Upper Egypt, April 12, 1784, and engaged, when barely fifteen, as interpreter to the French army under Buonaparte, then occupying his country. When the troops returned home, Bocthor accompanied them, and rapidly acquired a complete mastery of French. In 1812 he was employed by the government in translating the Arabic portion of the correspondence which had originated in the Egyptian expedition; and he was afterwards attached as interpreter, with a regular salary, to the military department. In 1814 this place was suppressed, as it was again, and finally, in 1817, after a re-establishment of two years, at the instances of some academicians. In 1818, however, his salary was restored, for the purpose of enabling him to continue the French and Arabic dictionary, upon which he was engaged, and which oriental scholars were very desirous of seeing completed. In 1819 he was allowed to deliver a course on colloquial Arabic in the school of eastern languages, and he was appointed professor of that tongue in January 1821. He had now a prospect of respectable station and easy circumstances, but liver-disease carried him off, September 26, in that very year. He had published his discourse on the opening of his lectures upon colloquial Arabic, the Arabic alphabet, and an abridgment of the Arabic conjugations. The MS. of his French and Arabic dictionary was purchased by the marquis Amadeus, of Clermont-Tonnerre, and consigned for publication to Caussin de Perceval, his successor in the Arabic professorship. Having augmented Bocthor's work by numerous materials collected by himself for a similar purpose during a residence in Syria, the editor published it at Paris, in two volumes, 4to, in 1828. (Biog. Univ. Suppl.)

BOCZKAI, (Stephen,) a Transylvanian nobleman, who headed the revolt by which, in 1604, the Protestants of his own country, in conjunction with a strong party among the Hungarians, sought to throw off their subjection to the intolerant rule of Austria. Since the last cession of Sigismond Batthori, (see BATTHORI,) Transylvania had been annexed to the hereditary dominions, and an attempt to regain independence, in 1603, had been unsuccessful; but Boczkai, after concluding a league with the Turks, and placing the protestant interest under their protection, gave battle to the imperial commander, Belgiojoso, who was utterly routed and driven from Transylvania; and the states of the principality, assembling under the direction of the grand-vizir, elected Boczkai to the throne. In the ensuing campaign, his partizans, every day augmenting, overran Upper Hungary almost without opposition; and so highly was he esteemed by the Turks, that the sultan sent him a firman, creating him king of Hungary, to be held as a fief of the Ottoman empire; promising, at the same time, that, after the expulsion of the Germans, he would place him in possession of all the towns held by the Turks in Hungary, excepting those in which mosques had been founded, and he was accordingly crowned in the camp, on the plains of Rakosch, near Buda, in the presence of the vizir and the pashas of Buda and Temeswaer. Before the end of the year he was in peaceable possession of all Upper Hungary; and his popularity was such, that the towns were surrendered to him by their inhabitants in defiance of the German garrisons. Overtures of accommodation were made by the court of Vienna, but Boczkai refused to admit the envoys to his presence, declaring his intention to establish the independence of Hungary and the protestant religion; the conclusion of peace, however, between the Porte and Austria put an end to these ambitious projects, and he concluded a separate treaty with the emperor, by which the liberties of Hungary, and the free exercise of the protestant faith in that kingdom, were guaranteed, and Boczkai recognised as independent hereditary prince of Transylvania, with reversion to the house of Austria in failure of his male line. He did not survive this pacification more than six months, dying December 30, 1606, according to Istuanfi, of dropsy, though some accounts attribute his death to poison, in the fifty-first year of his age. "He was buried by his infatuated adherents," (says Istuanfi, who is unfavourable to him,) "with truly regal magnificence; and two crowns—one, that which he had received from the Turks, the other, one which had belonged to a despot of Moldavia—were laid on his coffin." His character is thus summed up by old Knolles, in his quaint but expressive language; "He died to the great sorrow and griefe of all the people in generall, who had him in great honor and regard. He was honorably descended, and a man of a great spirit; ambitious, wise, and politicke; a great lover of his countrey, but an extreame enemie unto the Germans, and their government in Hungarie." He had married a daughter of Count Hagorassi, but died issueless. (Istuanfi de Rebus Hungaricis. Von Hammer. Knolles. Naima, &c.)

BOD, (Peter,) born 1712, at the village of Felschö-Czernaton, in Transylvania; educated at a protestant seminary, to which he was afterwards professor of Hebrew, and librarian. He resigned these appointments in 1740; studied theology three years at Leyden, and was appointed, on his return home, cabinet preacher to the dowager-countess Teleki. He died at Magyar-Igen, 1768. His numerous writings, in Latin and Magyar, testify his learning, spirit of research, and literary industry; among them may be enumerated an Hungarian Dictionary, as a Guide to the Understanding of the Scriptures; his History of the Bible, and of the Saints (all in Magyar); his Synopsis Juris Connubialis, 1763; Magyar Athenas, &c., Herrmanist. 1766, 8vo, (confiscated by the court on account of too free expressions on the prevailing belief); Francisci Parizpapai Dictionarium Latino-Hungaricum locupletatum, *ib.* 1767, vol. ii. 8vo. From his History of the Unitarians in Transylvania, Lugd. Bat., 1776, 8vo, Walch gives extracts in his Modern History of Religion, vol. vii. pp. 464—480.

BODARD DE TEZAY, (Nicholas Maria Felix,) a French poet, born at Bayeux, in 1757, and originally intended for the bar. A desultory taste for letters preventing the accomplishment of this object, he became a placeman in 1792; but in the Reign of Terror he was denounced as a moderate, and underwent imprisonment. On recovering his liberty, he went as vice-consul to Smyrna, and after filling that situation in a very satisfactory manner, he did not return to France before paying a visit to Greece. He subsequently was consul-general at Genoa, where he remained until that place was incorporated with France, in 1805. He never was employed by the government again; but although his future amusements were literary, he does not appear to have produced any new publication. His known works are chiefly plays, which came forth anonymously; and the last of them, a comic opera, in one act, performed in 1790, was never printed. He died at Paris, Jan. 13, 1823. (Biog. Univ. Suppl.)

BODDAERT, (Peter,) a Dutch poet, born at Middelburg, in Zealand, in 1694, died in 1760; first known by a translation of Crebillon's Atreus and Thyestes. In 1717 he joined Steengracht and De la Rue in publishing a collection of Poetical Recreations, reprinted in 1728, though very moderate productions. Boddaert also published some religious poetry, which was very successful on its appearance, but has little to gain the notice of posterity. (Biog. Univ. Suppl.)

BODDAERT, (Peter,) a celebrated physician and naturalist, born in Zealand about 1730. He studied in Holland, took a doctor's degree at Leyden, and settled at Flushing, where he not only practised his profession, but devoted himself also to the study of natural history. He was named a counsellor of the city, and he visited the principal cities in Holland, making acquaintance with the most learned men of his time. Besides various papers printed in the Memoirs of the Academy of the Curious in Nature of Haarlem and Zealand, he published many works, both original and translations, of which may be named, Planches Anatomiques de Daubenton, with a translation of the text into Dutch. Pallas Elenchus Zoophitorum, Utrecht, 1768, 8vo. Pallas Mélanges de Zoologie, *ib.* 1770, 4to. De Chætodonte Argo, Amst. 1770, 4to. De Testitudine Cartilagineâ, *ib.* 1770, 4to. De Chætodonte Diacantho, *ib.* 1772, 4to. Hunter on the Natural History of the Teeth, translated into Latin and Dutch, Dordrecht, 1773, 4to. Elenchus Animalium, Roterod. 1785, 8vo. Zimmerman Hist. Geograph. Utrecht, 1787, 8vo.

BODE, (Christopher Augustus,) professor of the oriental languages at Helmstadt; born, 1722, at Wernigerode; educated at Klosterbergen, where he was a favourite of the abbot, Steinmetz, at Halle university, especially under Michaelis, and at Leipsic, where he studied under Hebenstreit. He began to lecture in 1747, at Halle, on Hebrew grammar. In 1749 he continued these lectures at Helmstadt, where he afterwards became ordinary professor, with the very scanty stipend of 300 dollars. To obtain the most accurate and extensive grammatical knowledge of the oriental languages, was the grand object of his life. He compared the old translations of the Bible in various languages, and translated them again into Latin. Amongst his labours of this class were, the Ethiopic version of St. Matthew, Halle, 1749, 4to; and the Persian version of the same evangelist, Helms. 1750. In subsequent years he published several books or portions of the New Testament, translated from the Arabic, Turkish, and Armenian. The prefaces to these publications contain many learned inquiries and valuable remarks. The collected results of his grammatico-critical labours he gave to the world in his Pseudo-Critica Millio-Bengeliana, Halæ, 1767, vol. ii. 8vo. His Latin and German styles were inelegant, and some of his learning was more tedious and laborious than useful or profitable. His comments on some of the books of the Old Testament are neither original nor valuable. He died March 7, 1796.

BODE, (John Joachim Christopher,) a noted German writer, son of a poor soldier, who was afterwards a day-labourer in the duchy of Brunswick. He was born in the city of Brunswick, January 16, 1730; and from his clumsiness at manual labour, nicknamed by his family, when a child, "Stupid Christopher." For some time his grandfather, a peasant in the village of Barum, employed him to tend his sheep. He showed early a passionate love of music; and in his fourteenth year his mother prevailed on her husband's brother to defray the expense of his apprenticeship to Kroll, the town-musician at Brunswick. He suffered much from the tyranny of his mistress, but succeeded in learning to play on most instruments with facility, if not with taste. His leisure was devoted to reading; and the Adventures of Simplecissimus, which he devoured at night in his garret, made a lasting impression upon him. Scarcely was his apprenticeship completed, when he was made hautboy-player to a regiment at Brunswick, and married a poor but pretty girl of sixteen. About 1750, having obtained leave of absence from his regiment, he went to Helmstadt, to take lessons in playing the bassoon of Stolze, a celebrated performer on that instrument. To support himself, meanwhile, he gave musical lessons to others. One of his pupils, a rich student of the name of Schluber, took him to live with him, and instructed him in French. Both studied Italian together, and Bode took Latin in hand, besides attending Stockhausen's lectures, and receiving instructions from him in German and English. His future career was now decided, and he determined upon devoting himself to literature; but his circumstances were for a long time unfavourable. Disappointed, on his return to Brunswick, of an office as musician to the court-chapel, he left the duchy for Hanover, where his hautboy was engaged for the Freudenmann regiment at Zell, at which place he remained four years, ardent and industrious as ever. To support his family, his day was spent in giving lessons; but all his leisure hours, and a part of his nights, were devoted to the study of music, the languages, and literature. A schoolmaster whom he instructed in music, corrected his first attempts in prose and verse, and threw open to him his library, which Bode eagerly rifled. His knowledge of English and Italian he now perfected; but Latin, notwithstanding that his new friend proffered him his professional assistance, he appears to have despaired of mastering. He had already published several musical compositions, when, in in 1754 and 1756, two collections of songs, which he had set to music, appeared at Leipsic, under the title of Odes and Songs, Serious and Comic, fol. He was as yet so young a critic, that the selection of these poems had devolved upon his friend Stockhausen, who also furnished the dedication. His talents and attainments procured for him the patronage of some people of the higher classes at Zell, whose society rendered him still more averse to his uncongenial position. At this period, his circumstances were peculiarly unfavourable. The arbitrary spirit of military discipline galled him; he was involved in quarrels by his nice feeling of honour, and even incurred a sentence of punishment, which, however, was not executed. His marriage was not happy; and his wife's mismanagement and extravagance were the source of violent recrimination between them. In 1756 his wife died of an acute disease, and his three children, whom he tenderly loved, soon followed her to the grave. He now took his leave of the army, flew to his friend Stockhausen, then at Luneburg, as co-rector of the Johanneum; and in 1757 set out with a small box, containing music, his linen, and a few letters of recommendation, given him by Stockhausen, for Hamburg, where he hoped to live by his talents. From the day of his arrival in this city fortune smiled on him. He had the children of wealthy parents for pupils in French and music; and he became a great favourite, from his attractive method of instruction, and his conversational powers. He now learned Spanish, taking lessons for a month from a shoemaker, who had worked at his trade in Spain. In 1759 he began to publish translations from the French and English, and for Koch's theatre adapted various plays from the French, Italian, and English. In 1761 he began his labours as a freemason, which, in after years, formed his principal business. He entered the great lodge, Absalom, afterwards reached very high grades, and was several times "Meister von Stuhl" of this lodge, with most of the members of which, at the end of 1764, he went over to the system of strict observance. In 1762 and 1763 he edited, with talent and success, the noted Hamburg paper, The Impartial Correspondent! In 1765, fortune, by a singular freak, proclaimed her peculiar affection for him: at the very moment when he was about to sue for the hand of Simonetta Tam, one of his rich and lovely scholars, on behalf of a friend, the lady suddenly offered it to himself. For a year Bode was the happiest of husbands, and was also rich, independent, and free from care; but at the expiration of that time he unfortunately lost his wife, from an accident, caused by the fall of a horse. She had left him her sole heir; but to escape the unjust complaints of her relations, he only retained a small part of her property (about 16,000 dollars it was said). To drown his grief, he made, in 1766, together with the privy-counsellor, Schubert von Kleefeld, a masonic journey to the superiors of the *Strict Observance* in Lusatia. On his return to Hamburg he established himself as a publisher, and married the daughter of Bohn, a man of experience in that line. The first work that he published was Lessing's admirable Dramaturgie. When Seyler's theatrical undertaking, in which he was interested, failed, he, together with his friend Lessing, formed a literary publishing company, by which works were to be published for the benefit of their authors. Notwithstanding Bode's advantageous connexion with Klopstock, Gerslenberg, Basedow, Zacharia, and other writers, this plan failed, from Lessing's habits, and Bode's ignorance of the details of the business. His career as a translator of English humorous works he commenced with Sterne's Sentimental Journey, which Lessing had recommended to him. This translation gave birth to the sentimental style in Germany, which soon became very fashionable, and was cultivated to a ridiculous excess. He also gave to the German public excellent versions of Humphrey Clinker, The Vicar of Wakefield, Yorick's Letters to Eliza, &c. From 1776 to 1780, inclusive, he published a Freemasons' Annual. After the loss of his third wife, and of four of her children, at Hamburg, he left that city, and settled at Weimar, as secretary to the widow of the celebrated minister von Bernstorf. Here he continued to translate from the English, French, and Spanish. His most successful production of this order was his version of Montaigne, which he executed *con amore*, and with the most scrupulous exactness. His translation of Tom Jones was more hastily performed and less creditable. Bode, from the time of his joining the freemasons, had begun to form a masonic library, which in time reached eight hundred volumes; and by stating the results of his inquiries and studies on the origin and tendency of masonry, he created a great sensation at the celebrated congress at Wilhelmsbad, in 1782, which he attended as a deputy. To the Jesuits' he ascribed great influence in the institution and propagation of masonry in Germany and England. At this same congress, the baron von Knigge enrolled him in the order of Illuminati, where he figured under the name of Amelius. The baron, (called Philo amongst the Illuminati,) conferred on him in rapid succession the dignities of the order of the Illuminati, and Scottish knighthood, or the rank of the directing Illuminati. Bode had promised the order his ardent support, if worthy of it, but had announced that deception, and especially Jesuitism, would find in him an uncompromising foe. He afterwards advanced to a point whence the whole machinery of the order lay exposed to his view, and corresponded with its founder, Weishaupt (Spartacus). The proceedings of neither Bode nor Knigge were exactly those best calculated to promote "the higher literary and moral objects of illuminatism." Disputes arose between the superiors; the order was persecuted and abolished in Bavaria, its home; and in Saxony, where Bode was one of the commanders, it was shortly compelled to suspend its activity, and indeed, as it proved, to terminate its career. In 1787, Bode went to Paris, where he was chiefly occupied in examining the rituals and tapestry of the French masons, who form an infinitely complicated institution. In 1788 he published a translation, with annotations, of Bonneville's remarkable work, The Jesuits driven from Freemasonry, and their Sword broken by the Freemasons, Leipzic, 2 vols, 8vo. Till the day of his death he continued to exert himself to improve the general arrangements, as well as the internal organization, of German masonry. Shortly after a visit, with Hufeland and Böttiger, to Brunswick and Zell, in which he showed himself far from ashamed of the humble capacity in which in bye-gone days he had figured there, Bode died (unexpectedly to himself, as he had always wished) at Weimar, December 13, 1793. He was buried between Lucas Cranach and Musaeus — a fanciful juxta-position. Herder and Wieland lamented him in their writings; and Böttiger wrote a memoir of him. The proportions of Bode were colossal; his head was extraordinarily large: his eyes, and almost every feature, displayed humour and originality. Though his appearance was far from prepossessing, he presented decided traits of good nature and humanity. He was vehement in his gesticulations; sensitive, and easily roused to anger, but as easily pacified; jovial and witty in society, but sarcastic. The incongruity between his education and subsequent position, between his susceptible temperament and rough exterior, furnished him with abundance of subjects for the humour with which nature had so richly endowed him. In his dress, which was never elegant, something was usually wanting or mismatched. In his manners and expressions, there was a certain *Lower-Saxon* roughness and simplicity. He was honest, benevolent, plain-spoken; a favourite with all classes, and even with the fair sex, in spite of his unpleasing person. His letters to some ladies with whom he was intimate, contain his happiest thoughts, and would form, if published, his best original work. His love of secret societies, and his faith in their efficacy, were weaknesses which may be pardoned him; especially when the activity of his nature is considered, and the little public scope which could be afforded to it in such a country as Germany. He was no disturber, however, of public order; he wished to keep politics and masonry quite apart; but he was a constant stickler for all the tedious ceremonies of the latter. He was the friend of the neglected, the oppressed, the mistaken, and especially of the young. He exerted his influence with different princes for the benefit of the necessitous. He supported his mother and sister till their death. Bode is scarcely known as an original writer; but his translations produced, and deservedly, a far greater effect than the original works of many more noted authors. In point of style, they may be regarded as quite original. He created a number of new words; and had such a thorough relish for, and appreciation of, his authors, which he never undertook to translate merely for profit, but, on the contrary, from inclination, that in his versions none of their spirit was lost. Style has since his time made such progress in Germany, that his writings appear now somewhat antiquated; but gratitude is not the less due to him for the service which he rendered to the literature of his day.

BODE, (John Elert,) a celebrated astronomer, son of the master of a commercial school at Hamburg, where he was born, January 19, 1747. Until seventeen years of age he acted as assistant to his father, who gave him his first instructions. He imbibed early a decided fondness for astronomy, made a telescope for himself, and eagerly observed the stars from a garret under his paternal roof. He thus acquired, at eighteen, an uncommon degree of astronomical knowledge, and Dr. Reimarus, who was called in to consult upon the case of his father, then dangerously ill, in 1765, saw with astonishment a youth, who had scarcely ever had anything like effectual assistance, occupied in calculating an eclipse of the sun. He communicated immediately what he had seen to professor Busch, who invited young Bode to his house, warmly encouraged him, and gave him free use of all his books and instruments. In the following year, Bode made his acquirements more generally known by the publication of a small work upon an eclipse of the sun, which was to happen before the end of summer. Soon afterwards, Busch persuaded him to undertake an Introduction to the Knowledge of the Starry Heaven, which was published in 1768, with a preface by the professor himself, and became highly popular in Germany. Bode next engaged himself upon an astronomical periodical. But his most celebrated publication is the Uranographia, or Great Celestial Atlas, a Latin work, published at Berlin, in 1801, containing a notice of 12,000 more stars than are to be found in older works of the same kind. Bode's extraordinary talents were justly appreciated by the illustrious Frederic II., king of Prussia, who appointed him director of the observatory at Berlin. As his age advanced, compliments and distinctions flowed in upon him from various quarters, and he has undoubtedly the glory of diffusing a taste for astronomy in Germany. He died Nov. 23, 1826. (Biog. Univ. Suppl.)

BODEKKER, (John Francis,) a painter, born in the duchy of Cleves, in 1660, and intended for his father's profession of music. He preferred, however, painting, and after some instruction from John de Baan, he painted portraits with success in several Dutch towns. He died at Amsterdam, in 1727. (Pilkington.)

BODENSCHATZ, (John Christopher George,) an orientalist, born at Rof, March 25, 1717; died October 4, 1797. His attention was given almost exclusively to subjects connected with Hebrew literature. In the years 1748 and 1749, he published, at Erlangen and Coburg, a work upon the Ecclesiastical Constitution of the Modern Jews. In 1756 he published, at Hanover, an Explanation of the New Testament by means of Jewish Antiquities, a work which has been considered of great importance in illustrating Scripture. (Biog. des Contemp.)

BODENSTEIN, (Adam,) son of Andrew Bodenstein, well known in the history of the Reformation, under the name of Carlostadt. Adam Bodenstein, a physician, or, perhaps, more properly, a quack, was born at Wittemberg, in 1528, and became a disciple of Paracelsus. Hence he talked of himself as both a transmuter of inferior substances into gold, and able to prolong human life. He lived, however, in poverty, and died at forty-nine, in February 1577, at Bâle, of a contagious fever, which he had professedly a specific to cure. He translated some treatises by Paracelsus, and wrote some works of his own upon alchemy and the like. (Moreri.)

BODIKER, (John,) rector of the Kölln Gymnasium, at Berlin, where he was educated; born 1641, of poor but nobly-descended parents. On the completion of his academical studies, he became pastor of Parstein in the Mark. He was appointed to his rectorship in 1675. He died in 1695. He was the author, amongst other works now forgotten, of Elements of the German Language, &c., Kölln auf der Spree, 1690, 8vo, which, in the value and richness of its contents and its clearness of style, far surpassed all previous works of the kind, was hence often reprinted, and still retains some value.

BODIN, (Henry,) a German professor of law at Rinteln and Halle. He died at the latter place, leaving many dissertations, and among them one, De Statu Reipublicæ Germanicæ Feudali, et Feudis Regalibus. (Biog. Univ.)

BODIN, (John,) an eminent political writer, born at Angers, about 1530, and positively said by some, according to Thuanus, to have entered into a society of Carmelites, but to have obtained a release from his vow, as made at an immature age. Whatever may be the truth of this report, it is known that he studied law, and made an effort to practise as an advocate at Paris; but although recommended by superior talents and acquirements, his prospects of success appeared either too uncertain, or too remote, for his satisfaction, and he withdrew from the legal profession to live a life of literature. His first appearance before the public in this capacity was in 1555, with a Latin verse translation of Oppian's Cynegetica, illustrated by notes. This has gained him the appellation of plagiary, unfair use having been made in it, as was reasonably objected, of an edition recently published by Turnebus. This work was followed by several others, and Bodin's reputation recommended him to Henry III., who was fond of literary society. His connexion with a throne did not, however, prove of much duration; either the envy of courtiers, as many thought, having made a breach, or what is more probable, political opposition to the king's views offered by Bodin. Still he did not lose his hold upon the royal family, the duke of Alençon now becoming his patron, and with that prince he visited both England and Flanders. In 1576 he retired to Laon and married; and in the same year, he was deputed by the *tiers état* of Vermandois to the states-general. In this charge he acquitted himself with great spirit and propriety, making strenuous, but unsuccessful exertions against those intolerant councils, which refused liberty of conscience, even at the risk of civil war. By this, and some other acts of opposition to the court, Bodin finally estranged the king, and he could not even obtain a place actually promised to him. He continued, accordingly, to reside at Laon, and by his influence there, caused that town to declare for the League. The same influence he subsequently exerted to make the inhabitants declare for Henry IV. He died at Laon, of the plague, in 1596. Among his works, one published in 1566, entitled, Methodus ad Facilem Historiarum Cognitionem, has been blamed as really anything but that which the reader might anticipate, being most unmethodical. Another, the Demonomanie des Sorciers, published in 1581, and soon translated into Latin by Francis Junius, is characterised as a most wretched production, sustaining popular prejudice, and denouncing, as a confederate of Satan, Wierus, a physician of the Netherlands, who had produced, in 1564, a treatise De Præstigiis, exposing the cruelty of burning for witchcraft. If Bodin, therefore, had not otherwise established a claim upon the notice of posterity, his name would now be merely mentioned as author of some few pieces prized by the curious in books, but neither known, nor deserving to be known, generally. He did, however, by the publication of a political work at Paris, in 1577, make a noise in the world, which long brought his name prominently forward, and still shields it from oblivion. This famous treatise, entitled De la Republique, is in six books, and was originally published in French, but, in 1586, Bodin himself published a Latin version of it, with many additions. Objections are made to it, though less than to his work upon the Knowledge of History, as deficient in method; and it is full of digressions and citations, which are neither so apposite nor correct as the several cases require. The truth is, Bodin was well acquainted with the political circumstances of his own country, but he lived before the diffusion of much exact information upon foreign states. Hence his inquisitive mind was driven to judge of other countries more by common fame, and loose accounts, than by such accurate statements as a work like his required. He appears also to have been a man of violent passions, and quite ready to flatter the prejudices of his countrymen. He thus raised a storm of indignation against himself in Germany, scholars there being indignant, and branding him as utterly unworthy of belief, from his representations of their country, as little else properly than a province of France. But in spite of all objections, Bodin really very far outstripped the political writers of his day, showing an extraordinary degree of learning and reflection. He brings to bear upon his subject a vast mass of various and discriminating reading, which facilitated and guided most importantly the labours of his successors; and he placed under their eyes numerous references to ancient learning, which they have evidently often used, but not so frequently acknowledged. In the first chapter of his fifth book, Bodin has attracted considerable notice in modern times, because La Harpe found there the model, or, as he calls it, *the germ* of Montesquieu's observations on the influence of climate, in his Esprit des Lois. But it has been remarked on the other hand, that if Montesquieu must be considered here as no original thinker, he might at least have taken the hint from authors far older than Bodin, who really has done no more in the matter than develop, with greater fulness than before, a principle that might have been suggested to him by Cicero or Hippocrates. Of this work, formerly so celebrated, a luminous general analysis is to be found in Mr. Hallam's Introduction to the Literature of Europe, (ii. 205.) It was quickly translated into several languages: the Italian version has neither date nor place. A spirited English version was published by Knolles, more generally known afterwards by a history of the Turks, which appeared in 1610. In 1633, Werden Hagen published, at Amsterdam, an abridgment of it, entitled Synopsis, sive Medulla J. Bodini de Republica; and in the eighteenth century, two French abridgments of it appeared by different authors, who have made new arrangements of the author's matter, and added much of their own. Bodin's reputation did not lag until death had rendered him unconscious of it. When he came to England, as attendant upon the duke of Alençon, then suitor to queen Elizabeth, he found his work made a text-book for lectures upon political science, both in London and Cambridge; a fact which has induced some continental scholars to believe that it was actually admitted among the established authorities in conducting an English university education. But such was not the truth. The book was merely used by some private individuals in giving instruction upon questions treated in it. Bodin was, however, stimulated by the gratifying discovery that a foreign people made even this use of his labours, to undertake the Latin version of it with improvements, by which he extended at once its European reputation. Besides the works already mentioned, he published Juris Universi Distributio, in 1580. In the year of his death, but it seems after that event, appeared his Universæ Naturæ Theatrum, which has been considered by some as a specimen of disguised pantheism; but others have failed to discover any such tendency in it. He left also a MS., of which there are said to be several copies in France and Germany, entitled, Colloquium Heptaplomeron de Abditis Rerum Sublimium Arcanis, but it has never been printed. Its religious principles appear to be unsound, the author introducing debates upon different religions, and giving an advantage either to deism or Judaism, for it seems not to be determined which of the two has his good opinion. In early life, Bodin appears to have been inclined to protestantism; but his latter convictions ran evidently in favour of Judaism. Hence his Republic quotes the Old Testament continually and deferentially, but seldom or never the New. Boccalini, in the Ragguagli di Parnasso, makes Apollo condemn him to the flames for maintaining liberty of conscience. (Hallam. Bayle. Blount.)

BODIN, (Laurence,) a French physician, born at St. Paterne (Sarthe), in 1762. Being a good scholar, and well versed in the literature as well as the practice of his profession, he established a periodical medical journal, which at first consisted simply of extracts from the Recueil Périodique de la Société de Médecine, but afterwards assumed a more useful form, as Bibliographie Analytique de Médecine, Paris, 1799, &c. In this, all medical works upon publication were noticed and regularly reviewed. He also published Le Médecin des Goutteux, Paris, 1796, 8vo. Réflexions sur les Absurdités du Système de M. Gall, Paris, 1813; and some other works.

BODIN, (John Francis,) born at Angers, September 26, 1766, and bred for an architect. The revolution rendered his art of little value, but he was, notwithstanding, an ardent revolutionist. This recommended him to patronage, though not in his own profession, and he continued very much of a politician until his death, in 1829. He is worthy of notice as author of several works upon Angevin history, antiquities, and biography. (Biog. Univ. Suppl.)

BODLEY, (Sir Thomas,) justly called by Wood, *another Ptolemy*, for his noble services to literature, in founding a library that may well bear comparison with that illustrious collection founded by Soter at Alexandria. His family was ancient, and resided at Dunscomb, near Crediton, in Devonshire; but his father, John, was of Exeter, where Thomas was born, March 2, 1545. His mother was Joan, daughter and heiress of Robert Hone, of Ottery St. Mary's, in the same county, esquire. John Bodley was a known enemy to popery, and hence, early in queen Mary's reign, he became obnoxious to professors of that religion, who watched him narrowly, and menaced him with vengeance. Apprehensive that an occasion would be found for carrying their threats into execution, he withdrew into Germany, where he was soon joined by his wife, whose religious opinions were the same as his own, and who came accompanied by their children. He first fixed himself at Wesel, in the duchy of Cleves, where there was a congregation of English exiles. Hence he removed to Frankfort, but he made no more than a short stay in either of these places, his object being a residence at Geneva. He arrived in that city, in May 1557, with his wife, three sons, Thomas, John, and Laurence, a daughter, three servants, two male and one female, and his brother Nicholas. He spelt his name *Bodleigh*, which was, no doubt, the habit anciently with his family; and besides being a member of the English church, he was one of the six individuals from that congregation received into the *bourgeoisie* of Geneva. His son Thomas had already been grounded in grammatical knowledge at Exeter, and he had now the best farther instruction that Geneva, then a town of scholars, could afford. He attended the lectures of Anthony Rodolph Chevalier on Hebrew, those of Matthew Beroald on Greek, together with those of Calvin and Beza on divinity. He boarded at the house of a learned physician, and there he also received private instructions in Homer, from Robert Constantin, whose Greek Lexicon appeared in 1562. These great advantages of education being bestowed upon a mind excellently fitted for improving them, young Bodley became thoroughly fond of learning, and was thus trained for the design that has immortalized him, of aiding future scholars by supplying them abundantly with literary appliances.

Very soon after queen Mary's death, in November 1558, the Bodleys appear to have left Geneva, as Thomas was entered at Magdalen college, Oxford, in 1559, under the tuition of Laurence Humphrey, who became president in December 1561, and rendered himself conspicuous as a leader in the vesture controversy. Young Bodley seems to have shown at Oxford, as elsewhere, a great aptitude for education, and soon after he took his bachelor's degree in arts, in July 1563, he was elected fellow of Merton college. Within a short time of his incorporation into that venerable society, he remarked with pain the little attention that was paid to Greek, and some of his brother-fellows persuaded him to lecture upon that language in the college hall. He undertook this task with no expectation of any other payment for his pains than his own improvement, but the society soon became sensible of its obligations to him, in thus giving it a new claim to public respect, and he was requited by an unexpected annual allowance of four marks. In 1566 he became master of arts, and he then read for a year natural philosophy, in the public schools. In 1569 he served the office of junior proctor with great applause. Being the eldest son of a man of fortune, Bodley seems to have thought rather of settling himself in the public service, than of confining his attention to any particular profession. He determined, accordingly, upon travelling, for his improvement in the modern tongues, and in the general knowledge of mankind. His plans being matured, and leave of absence from his college obtained, he left England in 1576, and remained nearly four years abroad; visiting, in the time, France, Germany, and Italy. On returning to his college, he applied himself to historical and political studies. In 1583 he was appointed esquire of the body to queen Elizabeth; and in little more than twelve months afterwards, he married Anne Ball, a wealthy widow, whose father, named Carew, was of Bristol. With her he spent happily four-and-twenty years. In 1585, Bodley's political life began, many important services to the state being henceforth rendered by him both at home and abroad. His first mission was in 1585, and took him to the king of Denmark, and the duke of Brunswick, with some other German princes. He was next sent, with extreme secrecy, to Henry III.

of France, when driven from Paris by the duke of Guise, and he acquitted himself both to the queen's satisfaction, and to the advantage of the French protestant party. He subsequently spent five years at the Hague, in charge of English interests with the United Provinces. He was there admitted into the council of state, took place in public assemblies immediately after count Maurice, and voted upon all questions proposed. In 1593 he returned to England upon his private affairs, but the queen soon sent him back again; and he remained almost another year, when he came over for a short time with some secret overtures. His royal mistress highly applauded him, and commanded his return to accomplish the business which he had proposed; nor did he obtain his recall from Holland until 1597. Having finally retired from foreign diplomacy, Burghley recommended him for secretary of state, in conjunction with his own son, Robert Cecil, afterwards earl of Salisbury. It happened, however, that the unfortunate earl of Essex gave the same recommendation, and with a warmth which made the old treasurer suspect some design of introducing a counterpoise to his own influence. He now, therefore, treated Bodley's appointment to the secretaryship with coldness, and soon found means to divert Elizabeth from thinking any more about it. Bodley was, probably, mortified and disappointed, as he determined immediately to bid a final farewell to politics. Foreign missions were offered to him several times afterwards, but nothing could shake his resolution to spend what might remain of life in a private station. Having thought of various plans to render himself useful, he says, "I concluded at the last to set up my staff at the library-door in Oxon, being thoroughly persuaded, that in my solitude and surcease from the commonwealth affairs, I could not busy myself to better purpose, than by reducing that place, which then in every part lay ruined and waste, to the public use of students. For the effecting whereof I found myself furnished, in a competent proportion, of such four kinds of aids, as, unless I had them all, there was no hope of good success. For, without some kind of knowledge, as well in the learned and modern tongues, as in sundry other sorts of scholastical literature; without some purse-ability to go through with the charge; without great store of honourable friends to further the design; and without special good leisure to follow such a work, it could but have proved a vain attempt, and inconsiderate."

Bodley was probably set upon this new and most enlightened object of ambition, not only by the regrets which he brought from Oxford, that although there was once there a public library, important at the time of its formation, its appearance had long been a reproach to the university, but also by observations that he had made abroad. Italy had excellent public libraries at Rome, Ferrara, and Florence: so had Germany at Vienna and Heidelberg. Sixtus V. had recently begun the noble collection at the Vatican. Philip II. founded the magnificent Escurial library about the year 1580. An older library still was at Salamanca; and cardinal Ximenes had, at the very beginning of the century, established one at Alcalà. France possessed, in the royal library, long carefully cherished by her kings, and transferred from Fontainebleau to Paris in 1595, a collection worthy of a great nation. The first prince of Orange founded the public library of Leyden, which rapidly became one of the best in Europe. The catalogue was published in 1597, the very year in which Bodley returned home from Holland; and amidst his political cares, he could not fail to remark how great and solid a distinction a struggling country, like the United Provinces, had thus gained above the peaceful and thriving land of his own nativity. There was, indeed, something of a public library at Cambridge, chiefly by means of archbishop Parker's recent liberality. But Oxford had no such advantage; and this deficiency was the more inexcusable, because it anciently was very differently circumstanced. A present of books had been made to that university very early in the thirteenth century by Roger Lisle, or *de Insula*, dean of York; and about 1320, Thomas Cobham, bishop of Worcester, laid the foundation of a regular library. About the year 1445, however, Humphrey, duke of Gloucester, enabled the university to form a collection, and build a receptacle for it, worthy of a seat of learning so venerable and useful, over the beautiful divinity school. Duke Humphrey gave besides 129 volumes, procured from Italy at a great expense; afterwards he made farther contributions of the same kind; and on his death, in 1447, he left to the university 100*l.*, then a sum of considerable importance, with many valuable MSS. A public library might have been thus formed at Oxford at a period not behind other parts of Europe in making such acquisitions; but the struggles of the rival houses of York and Lancaster, which desolated England immediately afterwards, were highly unfavourable to any design of a humanizing character; and the reformation which distinguished the following century, proved, it must be owned with grief and shame, highly adverse to the accumulation of literary treasures. A bigoted prejudice, often eagerly echoed by selfishness and stupidity, set in against a large proportion of books then extant, as not merely useless, but even also the pernicious monuments and appliances of a base and impious superstition. Hence great opportunities were given for destroying and embezzling books by individuals, and authorized visitors occasionally carried on the Vandalic business of destruction on an extensive scale. Thus it happened, when Bodley's attention was turned to the subject, that although private colleges had libraries, the university was without one; and duke Humphrey's noble room over the divinity school was little or nothing else than a conspicuous reproof to the times that had succeeded its erection, it being, Camden says, "through the iniquity of the times in the reign of Edward VI. stript of all the books."

It was in the year 1598, when Bodley seriously applied his time and money towards a remedy for evils so little creditable both to his own loved university, and to his country generally; "a task," as his friend Camden justly says, "that would have suited the character of a crowned head." In 1602 this generous and enlightened "task" had so far advanced towards maturity, that more than 2,000 choice volumes having been deposited in the library, and regularly catalogued, a solemn procession, on the 8th of November in that year, going from St. Mary's church to the library, opened it, and dedicated it to the use of the university. So rapidly now did the collection increase, that both the shelves and the room itself were soon found quite unequal to contain it. Sir Thomas Bodley, therefore, as he was now called, having been knighted after king James's accession, determined upon enlarging the building. The first stone of his intended addition was laid with great solemnity, July 19, 1610. He had not, however, the satisfaction of living to see it completed. His latter years were chiefly spent at Parson's Green, Fulham; but he also had a house in London, where he died, Jan. 28, 1613. His body was brought down to Oxford, and interred, according to his own desire, but with a degree of ceremony justly due to his character and services, in the upper end of the choir of Merton college chapel. By his will sufficient provision was made for the completion of the works that he had begun; and his whole estate, after debts, legacies, and funeral charges were defrayed, was settled upon the foundation, for which a charter of mortmain had been obtained in the second of James I. The first important addition from extraneous quarters made to the Bodleian library, was in 1629, when William Herbert, third earl of Pembroke of that family, and chancellor of the university, presented it with several hundreds of valuable Greek manuscripts, purchased by him from Francis Baroccio, a learned Venetian gentleman. It was only four years afterwards, when a valuable addition was made by the liberality of Sir Kenelm Digby, and this benefaction was quickly followed by another still more important from archbishop Laud, who sent to the university, at different times, 1,300 manuscript volumes, of inestimable value, in various languages, particularly of the oriental class. The next considerable addition was the magnificent library of Selden, amounting to 8,000 volumes, or more, and originally intended for the university of Oxford, but left by him on account of some offence, to his executors, who liberally sent it to its former destination, the Bodleian. At no long distance of time came the Anglo-Saxon MSS. of Francis Junius, which, though of no great bulk, are inestimably valuable, as being precious remains of a language, literature, and theology, dear to the best feelings of Englishmen, and casting considerable light upon several important questions. Thus, the seventeenth century did not close without seeing Oxford possessed, by Bodley's means, of such a library as might well bear comparison with the proudest in continental Europe, and which, by enormous accessions since, has fully maintained its honourable rank. The services that this all but unrivalled collection have rendered to learning are immense, and claim for Bodley a distinguished place among the benefactors of mankind. In 1609 Sir Thomas wrote his own life, which was deposited in the library, and published by Hearne, in

1703, 8vo, together with the first draught of his statutes, and some of his letters, under the title of Reliquiæ Bodleianæ, or some genuine Remains of Sir Thomas Bodley. From the letters, it appears that Sir Thomas was of the Calvinistical party in the university, as might, indeed, be expected from his education at Geneva. They are of no great historical value, containing but little information in that line, and that little generally rendered the more unserviceable from the omission of dates. They relate, in fact, to the buying and sorting of books, building the library, and other matters of the same kind. (Wood's Athenæ. Ingram's Memorials of Oxford. Livre des Anglois à Genève. Hallam's Literature, ii. 498. Camden. Britannia, Elizabeth. Biog. Univ.)

BODMER, (John Jacob,) a celebrated German poet and critic, professor of Swiss history at Zürich, born July 19, 1698, at Greifensee, where his father was pastor. The romantic scenery of the district in which he passed his early years impressed itself so forcibly on his memory, that in a letter written at the age of eighty, he paints it circumstantially and in lively colours. His imagination in childhood was nourished by the Bible alone, especially by the history of the pastoral patriarchs, of the fortunes of the Israelites in Egypt, the conquest of Canaan, and the deeds of the Judges and Kings. He was afterwards fascinated by Wikram's Ovid, and various works of fiction. He conceived a great aversion to the theological profession, for which his father intended hjm, and devoted himself to the classics, together with such authors as Le Clerc, Locke, and Bayle. His father, despairing of making him a clergyman, sent him, in 1718, to Geneva, and afterwards to Lugano, to learn the manufacture of silk. He now travelled to various parts of Italy, studied its poets, wrote sonnets, and convinced his employers that he would never make a merchant. In the latter part of 1719 he returned home, and spent the chief portion of his time in literary pursuits. General literature was then at a very low ebb in Germany; the learned wrote in Latin; and the public were contented with spiritless, servile imitations of foreign models. Bodmer, though unequal to the task, became ambitious of developing the national genius and taste. In 1720 he writes to a friend, "I should like to improve the German taste, if possible;" and accordingly, in conjunction with Hagenbuch and Breitinger, he established a weekly periodical, The Painter of Manners, a youthful imitation of the English Spectator, but without its polish. In 1727 he and Breitinger published at Leipsic and Frankfort their noted work On the Influence and Use of the Imagination towards the Improvement of Taste, in which they distinguished the then fashionable bombast from sublimity, censured the prevalent artificial and laboured style, condemned the pedantic and ridiculous use of foreign words, and recommended the classics and English writers as models, instead of the affected Italian poets, who were then in favour with the Germans. Their own style was as yet far from perfect; but the good sense of this appeal from affectation to nature was evident at once, and productive of excellent results. Gottsched was their competitor in the reformation of German taste; but the spirit in which he entered upon the work was anything but national or natural. In 1725, Bodmer was appointed to the chair of history at Zürich; and he became, too, a partner in a printing and bookselling business, in which great projects were contemplated. He wrote also as well as lectured on Swiss history. About this time he translated Paradise Lost and Hudibras, and also published a Character of German Poems, and Correspondence on the Nature of Taste, works which contributed to excite a grand controversy (into which combatants rushed in course of time from all parts of Germany,) between the critical school of Saxony, (where Gottsched ruled without a rival,) and that of Switzerland. Bodmer's cause was by far the better, but he was not the man to do it full justice. From 1740 to 1750 he supported it to the best of his ability in his Critical Dissertation on the Marvellous in Poetry, 1740; Critical Considerations on the Poetical Pictures of the Poets, 1741; Critical Considerations towards the reception of the German Drama, 1743; Critical Letters, 1746 and 1749; Translation of Pope's Dunciad, &c. &c. These works produced the decline of Gottsched's influence. When the first specimens of Klopstock's Messiah appeared, they, together with Bodmer's hexameters, attracted all eyes; for Bodmer, at the age of fifty, did not think it too late to make his first appearance as a poet, and had chosen Noah for the subject of an epic. This singular production raised him in his own esteem as far as it must sink him in the estimation of the critic. It contains a considerable quantity of heterogeneous matter; anticipations of post-diluvian events; exaggerated imagery in place of warmth or true sublimity; and is written in a stiff and tumid style. W. A. von Schlegel has compared the sensations produced by a perusal of it, to those felt by a person travelling on a very rough road in a carriage without springs. Other poetical works followed, chiefly on biblical subjects; they were all highly moral in their tendency, but all equally deficient in the elements of poetry. On the publication of the Messiah, Bodmer had hailed Klopstock as a disciple, and he afterwards invited him to Switzerland; but from the disparity in their ages and habits, they were disappointed in each other's society; mutual esteem, however, survived their disappointment. Bodmer's hospitality was afterwards extended in like manner to Wieland, whose first productions were written in his style, and whose subsequent adoption of a very different strain he of course lamented. Bodmer's reputation increased with his years. His integrity, independence, and republican simplicity, had the happiest effect on the rising generation. His political principles he incorporated in plays, the excellence of the sentiments in which compensated, he thought, for their deficiency in dramatic force. But his poems, both epic and dramatic, incurred abundant censure from contemporary critics, much to the annoyance of the veteran who in his youth had reigned over criticism as a conqueror, but who could not now even command its respect. In his eightieth year he published translations of the Iliad and Odyssey; a year later, a version of the Argonauts of Apollonius; and in his eighty-second year, translations of Ossian and of English ballads. Bodmer devoted considerable attention to the history of the German language. It was he who, on a journey to Hohen-Ems, discovered the Niebelungenlied; he copied a portion of it himself, and in 1757 published "Chriemhildens Rache," and the "Klage" appended to it. The edition of the whole poem, which appeared in the Berlin collection of Müller, was from a copy which Bodmer himself had made from the St. Gall manuscript. Amongst other labours in this department of German literature, Bodmer published, in 1757, an edition of Boner, under the title of Fables of the Times of the Minnesingers; and in 1758 and 1759 appeared a collection of Swabian poems which had been made by Manesse, a Zürich patrician of the fourteenth century, entitled Minnesingers of the Swabian Epoch, (containing 140 poets,) Zürich, 2 vols, 4to. In his later years Bodmer occupied himself with German grammar, and wrote a book on this subject for the Zürich schools, for which he also composed a history of his canton. His Swiss Stories, 1769, and Moral Stories, were written with the patriotic view of leading, in an attractive manner, the rising generation to the exercise of manly virtues. In 1775 he resigned the professorship of history, which he had held for fifty years, and was succeeded in it by one of his most beloved scholars, Henry Fuessli. In spite of a weak constitution, he lived to a very advanced age, with but trifling derangements of his health, and retained all the force of his faculties to the last. He was extremely temperate, and never drank either wine or coffee, but lived chiefly on milk, eggs, and vegetables. He died, possessing the highest esteem of his fellow-citizens, January 2, 1783. Bodmer, both as author and editor, occupied a conspicuous place in the literary history and controversies of his day, but partly for that very reason is become a comparatively unimportant person with posterity. He wrote not for all time, but for his own. He could not, however, resist the impression that he had put a finishing hand on German literature. It is not without a smile that we read the following passage from one of his letters to Gleim, written in his seventy-eighth year:—"In the bloom of my years poetry was not yet in existence. Then she stood on the isthmus of the Saturnian age. Hagedorn, Gleim, Klopstock came, and with them the silver times; then the spring of a golden period. No summer follows this spring. We are falling back into iron days, in which, however, it is true, mild and gently powerful rays break forth, like sunbeams in winter." Bodmer's chief merits consist in having pointed out to the Germans their forgotten treasures of national poetry, and in the zeal with which he vindicated English taste against the French frigidity of Gottsched. The history of this widely extending controversy between the Saxon and Swiss school is highly amusing. Bodmer delighted to assume the style and importance of a military chief; and both parties could scarcely find in words a sufficiently expressive medium for their feelings. After the death of his faithful ally, Pyra, in 1745, Bodmer writes to Gleim: "Your friendship is nothing less than indifferent to me, especially as we are not so warlike, but that we grow tired of this running fight with stupidity, if we are not encouraged by the shouts and swords of other friends of taste. Pyra has died in the midst of victories; Liscow is a sleeping lion; Rost is fighting in the war chancery; Hagedorn holds back; we are therefore impatiently expecting you and your friends to put on your armour." His friend and countryman, Hirzel, who visited Potsdam for some time, called the ambassador from the Zürich critics to the Brandenburg muses. Bodmer's correspondence with Zellweger, Sulzer, and Schinz, is a rich store of materials for the literary history of the time, and especially for that of the progress of science and theology in Zürich. Of the controversy with Gottsched, an account has been written by G. Schlegel. Amongst writers on German literature, Küttner and Meister may be enumerated as eulogists of Bodmer, and F. Horn as his most adverse critic.

BODONI, (John Baptist,) a celebrated Italian printer, born at Saluces, in the Sardinian states, February 16, 1740. His father, a printer there in humble circumstances, had him well instructed in design, for which his native place afforded facilities, and he early amused himself in making wood-cut vignettes, that are still sought by the curious. At eighteen, he became anxious to push his fortune at Rome, and he set out for that celebrated city with another youth, who had an uncle there, secretary to a prelate, upon whom they reckoned for subsistence until employment could be found for them. Long, however, before they reached Rome, the two lads were pennyless, and Bodoni sold some of his wood-cuts to the printers to raise funds for the continuance of their journey. On its termination, his friend's uncle declared himself unable to render them the smallest service, and advised an immediate return to Saluces. Before taking this mortifying step, Bodoni went to see the printing office of the *Propaganda*, which his father had often mentioned with extraordinary commendation. His manners, on this visit, were so attractive, that he was immediately engaged as a workman. He soon showed himself an important acquisition, and was recommended for farther improvement, to go through a course of oriental instruction in the college of Sapienza. There he acquired a facility in reading Hebrew and Arabic, which qualified him for a compositor in those languages; and some oriental works, which he conducted through the press, established his reputation. He thought soon afterwards of accepting some overtures made to him from England, and was visiting his friends at Saluces, on his way thither, when seized with illness. On his recovery, he was offered the superintendence of a press at Parma, then to be established on the model of that of the Louvre. Accepting this offer, he soon rendered Parma famous throughout Europe for beautiful printing; but he was not always fortunate in his editors, hence his classical books have no very high reputation among scholars. As a printer, however, the success and admiration that attended him were unbounded. He died November 20, 1813, leaving the Manuale Tipografico, on which he had long been employed, incomplete. It was finished by Lewis Orsi, and published in 1818. (Biog. Univ. Suppl.)

BOE, (Francis Dubois de la,) much better known under his Latinized name of Sylvius, a physician of great celebrity, born, in 1614, at Hanau, near Frankfort on the Maine. He received his education at the universities of Sedan and of Basle, at the latter of which he took the degree of doctor of medicine, March 16, 1637. He afterwards travelled, according to the custom of his day among the most highly educated members of his profession, and visited the universities and most illustrious men in Holland and Germany. At Leyden he formed a friendship with the professors Adolphus Vorstius and Otto Heurnius. He returned to Hanau, and commenced the exercise of his profession, but after two years he quitted it for France. Ultimately he fixed himself at Amsterdam. Although but twenty-eight years of age, he had acquired considerable reputation, and his assistance was eagerly sought after; and in 1658 he was selected to succeed Albert Kyper in the first chair of practical medicine in the university of Leyden. In his system of medicine, De la Boe espoused the cause of the chemical sect, although he did not neglect an attentive observation of the symptoms and character of disease at the bed-side of the patient. He urged also the necessity, and encouraged the practice of examining the bodies of the dead. He was highly esteemed as a teacher, and promoted the reputation of the medical school of his university. He advocated the doctrine of Harvey on the circulation of the blood, and was the principal means of its adoption at the Leyden school; yet he unquestionably impeded the progress of medical science, by his genius and eloquence, in espousing the chemical opinions, and by the introduction of an hypothesis, that had for its foundation the system of Van Helmont, which endeavoured to account for every morbid action that might occur in the animal economy upon the supposition of its being the result of chemical changes, produced in the system by the preponderance of an acid or an alkali, and the removal or cure of which was necessarily to be effected by the neutralization of the principle conjectured to be most active in operation. The errors consequent upon the propagation of these opinions were not successfully corrected until the labours of Sydenham dispelled the mist with which the subject had been obscured, and led the way to the observation of disease according to the true laws of nature, as established by careful inquiry and rational induction. De la Boe successfully cultivated anatomy, and made some discoveries which merit notice. He first described the os orbiculare of the tympanum of the ear; and he says that he once saw a sesamoid bone connected with the ligament of the stapes of that organ. He demonstrated that what had been described as the lacteals of the liver, were, in fact, the ordinary lymphatic vessels of the organ; and he successfully refuted the opinions of Lewis de Bils on the course of the lymph. He established the distinction still maintained in the arrangement of the glands of conglobate and conglomerate. His description of the brain and its membranes, and of the sinuses of the dura mater, are superior to those generally of his time. He was elected rector of the Leyden university, February 8, 1669; and upon resigning this office, in 1670, he delivered a discourse on the epidemic which had proved so fatal at that time, and had deprived him of his second wife. From this time his health succumbed under long continued and laborious application, and he died November 14, 1672, at the age of 58 years. He was buried in the choir of the church of St. Peter, where, in 1665, he had caused a tomb to be built for the reception of his remains, and to which he had attached the following inscription:—"Franciscus de la Boe, Sylvius, Medicinæ Practicæ Professor, tàm humanæ fragilitatis, quam obrepentis plerisque mortis memor, de comparando tranquillo instanti cadaveri sepulchro, ac de constituenda commodâ ruenti corpori domô, æquè cogitabat seriò. Lugduni Batavorum, 1665." He published various works, of which the following are most deserving of notice:—De Motu Animali ejusque læsione, Lugd. Bat. 1637, 4to. Dictata ad C. Bartholini Institutiones Anatomicas, *ib.* 1641, 4to. Disputationum Medicarum Duas, primarias Corporis Humani Functiones naturales ex Anatomicis Practicis, et Chymicis Experimentis deductas complectans: quarum, 1. agit de Alimentorum Fermentatione in Ventriculo; 2. de Chyli è Fœcibus Alvinibus Secretione, atque in Lacteas Venas Propulsione in Intestinis perfectâ; 3. de Chyli Mutatione in Sanguinem, circulari Sanguinis Motu, et Cordis, Arteriarumque Pulsu; 4. de Spirituum Animalium in Cerebro Cerebelloque Confectione, per Nervos Distributione atque Usu vario; 5. de Lienis et Glandularum Usu; 6. de Bilis et Hepatis Usu; 7. de Respiratione Usuque Pulmonum; 8. de Vasis Lymphaticis et Lymphâ; 9. de Febribus Prima; 10. de Febribus Altera: Amstelod. 1663, 16mo; Lugd. Bat. 1670, 16mo; Jenæ, 1673, 12mo; Francof. 1676, 12mo. Opuscula Varia, Lugd. Bat. 1664, 12mo; Amst. 1668, 12mo. Oratio de Affectûs Epidemici Leidensis Causis naturalibus dicta, Lugd. Bat. 1670, 12mo. De Cordis Palpitatione, *ib.* 1667, 4to. Praxeos Medicæ Idea Nova, Lib. iii. et Append. Lugd. Bat. 1667, 1671, 12mo; Francof. 1671, 12mo; Parisiis, 1672, 12mo; Venet. 1672, 12mo; Amst. 1674, 12mo; Hanau, 1675, 8vo. De Opio ejusque Usu Medico, Lugd. Bat. 1670, 4to. Index Materiæ Medicæ, *ib.* 1671, 12mo. De Inflammatione, *ib.* 1671, 4to. Opera Medica, Amst. 1679, 1695, 4to; Genevæ, 1680, folio; Utrechti, 1691, 4to; Venet. 1708, 1736, folio; Paris, 1671, 2 vols, 8vo. In the Ephemerides of the Academy of the Curious in Nature, vols. v. and vi., there are relations of several pathological examinations by De la Boe.

BOECKMANN, (Jonas,) a Swedish physician, born at Windberg, near Falkenburg, in the province of Halland, Dec. 16, 1716. At the age of seventeen he went to the university of Lund, being intended for the church, and he took the degree of M.A. in May, 1738. Having selected, however, the profession of medicine, after studying at Berlin and Halle, he established himself at Stockholm, took a degree of M.D. at Upsal, in 1743, and in 1747 was appointed to the second chair of medicine at the university of Greifswald, and made physician to the city. The king of Sweden named him his physician in 1753. He died in 1760, having published, Diss. de Cardine Novatorum, sive de Erroribus Stoicorum Fundamentalibus, Lund, 1737, 4to. Diss. de Fanaticismo Stoicorum per Novatores Recocto, Lund, 1738, 4to. De Consciencià sui ut unico Simplicium Fundamento, Lund, 1739, 4to. De Venæsectione corroborante, Upsal, 1744, 4to. Specimen Medicum de Sudore corroborante, Greifswald, 1752, 4to. Diss. Epist. contrà inepta Judicia de Arthritide Laxantibus Balsamicis retropulsa, Greifswald, 1753, 4to. Exercitium Academicum, Dejectionem corroborantem, et simul nexum Purgationis Alvinæ cum Sudore, Cutisque cum Ventriculo exhibens, Greifswald, 1755, 4to.

BOECLER, (John,) a physician, born at Strasburg in 1681; in 1708, appointed professor of medicine in the university there, and, in 1719, also professor of chemistry and botany. He died in 1733, having published, besides several academical pieces, Historia Instrumentorum Deglutitioni præprimis veræ Chylificationi inservientium, Argent. 1705, 4to. Dissert. de Sp. Vini atque Aceti Examine, *ib.* 1708, 4to. De Poris Corporum Effluviis et Odorum Historià, *ib.* 1711, 4to. Diss. de Cataracta, *ib.* 1711, 4to. Diss. de Vino, *ib.* 1716, 4to. De Irà, *ib.* 1716, 4to. De Morbillis, *ib.* 1720, 4to. Recueil des Observations qui ont été Faites sur la Maladie de Marseille, *ib.* 1721, 8vo. Theses Medicæ Miscellaneæ, *ib.* 1726, 4to. Pauli Hermanni Cynosura Materiæ Medicæ. &c., curante J. B., *ib.* 1726-31, 3 vols, 4to.

BOECLER, (John Philip,) a physician, born at Strasburg, September 21, 1710, who, in 1738, succeeded John Salzmann as professor of chemistry, botany, and Materia Medica. He died May 19, 1759, having published, De Coriandro, Argent. 4to; An Nitrum Sanguinem resolvet aut coagulat? *ib.* 1741, 4to; Diss. de Cinnabari Factitià, *ib.* 1749, 4to; and some other professional works.

BOECLER, (Philip Henry,) a physician, born at Strasburg, December 15, 1718. At an early age he displayed great aptitude for learning, and made such progress in philosophy and the mathematics, that at the age of seventeen he was received as a master of arts, having sustained, with great ability, a thesis, De Aurora Boreali. He, however, devoted himself to medicine, and took the degree of doctor of medicine, April 19, 1742; after which he went to Paris, and attended the lectures of Winslow and Ferrein. He then travelled to Aix, studied under the celebrated Lieutaud, and passed on to Montpelier. In 1744 he returned to his native country, and there distinguished himself by his practice in medicine and surgery, particularly in midwifery. In 1748 he was named professor extraordinary; and in 1756, professor in ordinary of anatomy and surgery, which office he held until his decease, June 7, 1759. He contributed much to the reputation of the university of Strasburg by the extent of his acquirements; his writings, however, are neither numerous nor important. It is sufficient to notice, Diss. sistens Decades Thesium Medicarum Controversarum, Argent. 1741, 4to. De Somni Meridiani Salubritate, *ib.* 1742, 4to. De Medicinâ Virgilii, Æn. xii. 397, *ib.* 1742, 4to. De Glandularum Thyroideæ Thymi et Supra-renalium Naturâ et Functionibus, *ib.* 1753, 4to. De Statu Animarum Hominum ferorum, *ib.* 1756, 4to.

BOEHM, (Jacob,) often called Behmen, and designated by his admirers as the German *theosophist;* a chemical mystic, born near Gorlitz, in Upper Lusatia, in 1575, and eventually a shoemaker in that town. He seems to have had always very strong religious impressions, and evidently also an imagination highly susceptible. As his education was merely suitable to the station intended for him, he was capable of reading little besides the Bible, from which, like other fanatics, he contrived to extract any confirmations needed by his views. He is thought also to have read Paracelsus, and he obtained, partly from intercourse with some physicians, an insight into the doctrines of the English medical mystic, Robert Fludd. From him, accordingly, Mosheim considers Boehm to have derived all his philosophy, which was the Rosicrucian, or a notion that fire was as useful in theology and the like, as it is in chemistry. By its agency, these visionaries reasoned, all bodies must be analyzed, and a sufficient attention to the results must end in a knowledge of the first principles of all things. Hence they taught a sort of coincidence and agreement between religion and external objects, insisting that God works in the same way both in the kingdom of grace and in the kingdom of nature. Having thus provided means for rendering mystical religion more unintelligible than ever, by propounding it with a mixture of chemical terms, they paved for themselves a highway to popularity with religious minds liable to be heated by the fumes of a riotous imagination. Boehm was exactly the man to take a lead among persons of this cast, being really respectable for piety and morals, but of a dreamy and excitable temperament, a fancy morbidly prolific, and restrained by ignorance from comparing his visions with those of earlier enthusiasts, and thus detecting their absurdity. The first announcement of his visions and supposed illumination was in a book entitled Aurora, which he put forth in 1612, and of which the neighbouring clergy complained to the magistrates as a mischievous vehicle for the errors of Paracelsus. The author was reprimanded, and the book suppressed as much as possible, but its circulation was already secured, and others of the same kind followed. Having thus rendered himself abundantly conspicuous, Boehm went to Dresden, and was examined there by some divines, who did not pass any censure upon him, probably from the blameless tenor of his life and his unquestionable piety. He died at Gorlitz, in 1623, leaving a great number of mystical pieces, with admirers in proportion. All his works were printed together at Amsterdam, in 1730, under the title of Theosophia Revelata. A new edition and English translation of them was for many years the employment of the well-meaning but gloomy visionary, William Law, and it appeared after his death in 2 vols, 4to. St. Martin translated three of Boehm's works into French; and a fourth was translated into that language by another. (Mosheim, iv. 48, 212. Biog. Univ.)

BOEHM, (Anthony William,) minister of the German chapel at St. James's, born 1673, fifth son of Anthony Boehm, minister of Oestoiff, in the county of Pyrmont, who died when he was six years old, but left him a pious parent's blessing. In his twentieth year he went to the university of Halle, in Saxony, where his attention was deeply fixed upon the holy Scriptures, and he would not enter into general society. He subsequently employed himself in teaching; and in 1698 was engaged by the count de Waldeck, as chaplain and religious instructor of his children. Opposition from some of the clergy, on account of his principles, induced him, after two years, to return to Halle, where he assisted professor Frank at the Orphan House until 1701, when, at the instance of some German families in London, he went thither to establish a school. This did not succeed, and he would probably have wanted bread, but for the aid of Mr. Ludolf, secretary to Prince George of Denmark, whose acquaintance he had made during the voyage to England, and who introduced him to many pious friends. He bore his disappointment like a Christian, saying, "that few become religious and learn to do good without stripes and chastisements." In 1705, Mr. Ludolf recommended him to assist Prince George of Denmark's chaplain. The solidity of his sermons gained a like appointment for himself, and henceforth he preached constantly before the prince until his death, in 1708. Queen Anne, however, commanded divine service to be continued by him at the chapel, gave him free access, and made him her private almoner; giving him considerable sums of money, which he dispensed with great fidelity, and seasonable exhortation. At his instance the queen persuaded the king of France to release many protestants who had been unjustly condemned to the galleys for their faith. On the accession of George I., he was continued in his appointment, and retained it the remainder of his life, which was terminated by a sudden attack of fever and ague, on the 27th of May, 1722. His age was 49 years, of which he had spent 21 in England.

His writings are numerous, consisting of German works translated into English, and about twenty original pieces, chiefly on points of christian practice. He had attained considerable fluency in the English language, and was a most effective preacher. Even those who were proof against his arguments could not but love him for his christian spirit. His counsels had considerable weight with the Society for Promoting Christian Knowledge; he first made that venerable body acquainted with the Tranquebar Mission, which it afterwards nurtured, and he translated into English the accounts transmitted from Hindoostan. Having known the trials of poverty, he had learned to sympathize with the poor and needy: he sought out the stranger and the friendless; spent one afternoon in the week in visiting asylums and prisons; devoted a large portion of his own income to the relief of the poor, and was constantly interceding with others for them. A charity-box was fixed in his rooms, with this motto, "He that hath pity upon the poor lendeth unto the Lord; and that which he hath given will he pay him again." (Prov. xix. 17.) It was often well replenished by the wealthy who visited him. The charitable society at the Savoy was instituted by him. Many rich persons, in and about London, made him their almoner. The distressed Germans and Palatines who went to America, were relieved by him; and he sent Bibles and other good books after them. He was eminent for genuine and deep humility, great contentment, and long patience. He was extremely methodical and exact in all his affairs; every day had its appointed work, which proceeded with the utmost regularity. An epitaph, descriptive of his rare character, is on a monument erected to his memory at Greenwich.

BOEHM, (Andrew,) privy-counsellor to the landgrave of Hesse, professor of philosophy and mathematics at Giessen, born at Darmstadt, November 17, 1720. In philosophy he did not deviate from his master, Wolf, but as a mathematician he was alive to the improvements of his age. He published, between 1777 and 1785, a useful work, known as the Magazine for Engineers and Artillery-men, Giessen, 12 vols, 8vo. He also left, Logica, Ordine Scientifico in Usum Auditorum conscripta, Frankfort, 1749-62-69. Metaphysica, Giessen, 1763, of which an improved edition appeared in 1767. He was also largely concerned in the Frankfort Encyclopædia; and he undertook, with Schleicter, the New Military Library, 4 vols, 1789-90. He died July 6, 1790. (Biog. Univ.)

BOEHM, (Wenzel Amadeus,) an excellent artist, born at Prague, in 1771, who died at Leipsic, May 1, 1803, and would have been one of the first engravers in Europe, had not his volatility prevented him from ever adhering steadily to any one pursuit. (Biog. Univ. Suppl.)

BOEHME, (John Eusebius,) born at Wurtzen, March 20, 1717, professor of history at Leipsic. He died Aug. 30, 1780, leaving a high reputation. His pursuits were chiefly illustrative of Saxon history, and he published in German, at Augsburg, 1782, materials for it. Other works of his are in elegant Latin; one of them, Diss. II. de Iside Suevis olim Culta, ad Locum Tac. de Mor. Germ., besides being printed at Leipsic, in 1749, is to be found in Wegelin's Thesaur. Rer. Suevicar. He published likewise, De Commerciorum apud Germanos Initiis; De Ortu Regiæ Dignitatis in Polonia; De Henrico nunquam Comite Palatino Saxoniæ; De Nationis Germaniæ in Curia Romana Protectione; Acta Pacis Olivensis inedita. (Biog. Univ.)

BOEHMER, (Justus Henning,) a learned writer upon German jurisprudence, born at Hanover, in 1674, professor of law at Halle, and one of the most distinguished men connected with that university. Canon law was his principal pursuit, but he has also written much upon civil law, every where displaying sound logic, excellent arrangement, and deep erudition. He died Aug. 11, 1749. His Corpus Juris Canonici, Notis atque Indicibus Instructum, Halle, 1747, 2 vols, 4to, was dedicated to Benedict XIV., who received it very graciously. Although the editor was a protestant, he executed his task with trustworthy moderation. Besides various other legal works, Boehmer left Duodecim Dissertationes Juris Ecclesiastici ad Plinium Secundum et Tertullianum; and some observations upon Fleury as to the institution of Ecclesiastical Law. (Biog. Univ.)

BOEHMER, (John Samuel,) son of the preceding, born at Halle, December 29, 1704, professor of law at Frankfort-on-the-Oder, where he died, May 20, 1772. He wrote with great applause upon criminal law; and a work of his, Meditationes in Constitutionem Criminalem Carolinam, Halle, 1770, was considered one of the most important pieces of the kind that Germany could boast. His Elementa Jurisprudentiæ Criminalis, Halle, 1732, has been reprinted several times; and his publications generally have the credit of solid erudition and great sagacity. (Biog. Univ.)

BOEHMER, (George Lewis,) brother of the preceding, born at Halle, Feb. 18, 1715, dean of the faculty of jurisprudence at Göttingen, where he died, Aug. 17, 1797. He fully supported his family's fame for legal erudition, producing some very valuable works upon canonical and feudal law. Among them his Principia Juris Canonici, Göttingen, 1762, has been four times reprinted, and his Principia Juris Feudalis, 1765, five times. (Biog. Univ.)

BOEHMER, (Philip Adolphus,) a physician, brother of the preceding, director of the university of Halle, and chancellor of the principality of Magdeburg, born at Halle in 1717. He was first educated at Glauca, in the neighbour hood of his native place, and in 1732 entered at the university of Halle, where he studied during six years under Hoffmann, Schultze, and Cassebohm. The former principally conducted his professional education, and it was under his presidency that he took the degree of M.D. Jan. 29, 1738. He quitted Halle for Strasburg to perfect his anatomy and to pay attention to midwifery. He then returned to Halle, was made physician to the city of Eisseleben, and first physician to the duke of Saxe-Weimar. He succeeded Cassebohm in the chair of anatomy upon his removal to Berlin. In 1769 he was elected first professor of medicine and dean of the faculty. In 1787 he was named counsellor to the king of Prussia, and made dean of the university. In this honourable office he remained until his death, Nov. 1, 1789. He was a member of the Imperial Academy of the Curious in Nature, and a foreign associate of the Royal Academy of Surgery of Paris. He published numerous works, among which most deserving of notice are,—Diss. de præcavendâ Polyporum Generatione, Halæ, 1736, 4to. De Numeri Septenarii felici augurio, *ib.* 1737, 4to. Præfamen Academicum quo Situs Uteri Gravidi Fœtûsque à Sede Placentæ in Utero per Regulas Mechanismi deducitur, &c. Lipsiæ, 1741, 4to. Haller thought this piece worthy of insertion in his Disputat. Anatom. Select. tom. v. p. 293. Observ. Binæ Anatomicæ de quatuor et quinque Ramis ex Arcus Arteriæ Magnæ adscendentibus, *ib.* 1741, 4to. De Ductibus Mammarum Lactiferis, *ib.* 1742, 4to. De Bronchiis et Vasis Bronchialibus, Halæ, 1748, 4to. Institutiones Osteologicæ, *ib.* 1751, 8vo. Observ. Anat. Rarior. *ib.* 1752, fol. 2 fascic. He also published an edition of Manningham's Manual, Artis Obstetricariæ Compendium, &c. Halæ, 1746, 4to.

BOEHMER, (George Rodolph,) a distinguished German physician and naturalist, born Oct. 1, 1723, at Liegnitz, in Silesia, where his father practised as an apothecary. After acquiring the ordinary elementary education at the school of his native place, he was sent in 1742 to Leyden, to study medicine. Philosophy and letters, however, were also cultivated by him, and he took the degree of master of philosophy, Feb. 20, 1749. He was much esteemed by the professors of the university, and Platner and Ludwig especially entertained for him a sincere friendship. They aided him in his studies, and in 1750 he took the degree of M.D. Natural history formed one of his most active pursuits, and he was ardently attached to the science of botany. In 1752 he was invited to accept a chair of anatomy and botany at the university of Wittemberg, which had lost much of its celebrity by the necessary consequences of the Seven Years' War, the small number of students within its walls, and the indolence of the professors. Boehmer, however, accepted the appointment, and taught with great diligence. He established, in a great measure at his own expense, the botanic garden, formed also a small museum of anatomical preparations, and collected together a variety of surgical instruments. He also encouraged the study of chemistry, by delivering a course of lectures on that science. Baron Haller recognised his merits, and upon the death of Zinn, in 1759, invited him to accept of his chair at the university of Göttingen. The war, however, prevented him from occupying this honourable situation, as well as another of a similar character, which was offered to him at Erlangen, in 1763. In 1766 he was appointed physician to the principality, and in 1792 to the city of Kemberg. He had also received the additional appointment of professor of therapeutics in 1783; and in 1799 and 1800, the jubilee of his double doctorate in philosophy and medicine was celebrated by the two faculties. He was elected dean of the faculty of medicine and of the university in general, and he died whilst in office, April 4, 1803. Jacquin named a genus of plants (Boehmeria) in honour to his memory. His works are very numerous, and distinguished by erudition and judgment. Many of his academical exercises are entitled to the highest commendation. Among the most important of his publications, we can only enumerate the following:—Diss. de Consensu Uteri cum Mammis, Lipsiæ, 1750, 4to. Flora Lipsiæ Indigena, *ib.* 1750, 8vo. Programma de Plantis fasciatis, Wittemb. 1752, 4to. Programma de Experimentis quæ Reaumur ad Digestionis Modum in variis Animalibus declarandum instituit, *ib.* 1757, 4to. Programma de Chirurgia Curtorum, *ib.* 1758, 4to. Planta, Res varia, *ib.* 1765, 4to. De Justa Medicarum Historiarum Estimatione, *ib.* 1765, 4to. Diss. duæ, Natura præstantior Arte in Re Medicâ et Economicâ, *ib.* 1770, 1774, 4to. Spermatologia Vegetabilis, *ib.* 1777, 1784, 7 parts, 4to. Comment. Physico-Botanica de Plantarum Semine, &c. *ib.* 1785, 8vo. Systematisch-Literarisches Handbuch der Naturgeschichte, Œkonomie, &c. Leipzig, 1785—1789, 9 vols, 8vo. Comment. Œconomico-Medico-Botanicæ, Wittemb. 1792, 4to. Technische Geschichte der Pflanzen, Leip. 1794, 2 vols, 8vo. Programmata duo de Rebus Naturalibus, Vermibus præcipue Intestinalibus, &c. Wittemb. 1796, 4to. Comment. Botan. Literat. de Plantis, Lipsiæ, 1799, 8vo. He published also a variety of translations, and assisted in other publications; the Definitiones Generum, of Ludwig; Botanisches Handbuch of Skuhr; the Herbal of Blackwell Theatrum Florum of Knorr, &c.

BOEHMER, (John Benjamin,) elder brother of the preceding, born at Liegnitz, May 14, 1719. He studied medicine under Walther, Platner, Hebenstreit, Quelmaly, Hartranft, Ludwig, and Kramer. Platner in particular directed his studies, and entrusted him with the care of many of his patients, whom he attended with great assiduity and skill. He took the degree of philosophy, Feb. 13, 1744, and that of medicine, Sept. 3 1745. In 1748 the king appointed him to an extraordinary chair of anatomy and surgery; and in 1750, upon Guntz accompanying the elector to Dresden in the capacity of first physician, Boehmer took his place, and became ordinary professor at the university. His health was bad, and his career but of short duration. He died March 11, 1754, having, besides some academical pieces, published the following works,—Diss. de Psyllorum, Marsorum et Ophiogenum adversùs Serpentes eorumque ictus Virtute, Lipsiæ, 1745, 4to. De Hydrocele, *ib.* 1745, 4to. De Ossium Callo, *ib.* 1748, 4to. Panegyricus Memoriæ J. Z. Platneri dictus, *ib.* 1748, 4to. Bibliotheca Medico-Philosophica, *ib.* 1755, 8vo. He also published an edition of Platner's work, Gruendliche Einleitung in die Chirurgie, *ib.* 1749, 2 vols, 8vo.

BOEL, (Cornelius,) an engraver, born at Antwerp, about 1580; he seems to have been instructed in the school of the Sadelers, and to have been in England in 1611. (Bryan.)

BOEL, (Peter,) an excellent painter of animals, fruit, and flowers, born at Antwerp, in 1625. After instruction by Francis Snyders and Cornelius de Waal, he went to Rome for improvement, and he subsequently spent some time at Genoa, where he met with good encouragement. He seems to have settled finally at Paris. He died in 1680. (Pilkington.)

BOERHAAVE, (Herman,) a celebrated physician, born at Voorhout, near Leyden, December 31, 1668. His father, a clergyman, gave to him an excellent education, and at the age of eleven years he was able not only to translate, but also to compose in Latin. At fourteen he was admitted into the public school of Leyden, and at sixteen into the university. He studied under Gronovius, Ryckius, Trigland, Schaaf, and other masters equally celebrated, maintaining disputations in logic, natural philosophy, metaphysics, and ethics, with distinguished ability. At the age of twenty-one he received a gold medal, in approbation of an academic oration, De Summo Bono, intended to prove that the doctrine of Epicurus concerning the chief good was well understood by Cicero. Upon taking a degree in philosophy, in 1690, he attacked the doctrines of Epicurus, Hobbes, and Spinosa, in a thesis, De Distinctione Mentis à Corpore. His studies were directed with a view to the church, but upon the death of his father, he found himself in a situation which compelled him to seek support by teaching the mathematics. This fortunately procured for him an introduction to John Vandenberg, burgomaster of Leyden, who recommended him for the comparison with the sale-catalogue, of the MSS. of Isaac Vossius, purchased in England for the university; and he also, upon the same recommendation, joined the study of physic and philosophy to that of theology. He most assiduously directed his attention to anatomy, attending even slaughter-houses to remark upon the conformation of animals. He read the works of ancient and modern medical writers, and was particularly attached to those of Sydenham. He studied chemistry and botany, and then went to the university of Harderwick, in Guelderland, where he took the degree of M.D. in 1693, delivering for his thesis, De Utilitate inspiciendorum in Ægris Excrementorum ut Signorum.

Boerhaave had already distinguished himself in an especial manner by opposition to the doctrines of Spinosa; but his determination to abandon theology for physic arose from an indirect acknowledgment made by him of that sceptic's talents. It appears that a discussion in a passage-boat, when he was present, on the doctrine of Spinosa, drew from one of the passengers a violent attack upon it as subversive of all religion, its mathematical demonstrations being especially singled out. It being, however, obvious that mere blind zeal actuated the speaker, Boerhaave coolly inquired of him, whether he had ever read the book that he so loudly abused? He was silenced by the question; but Boerhaave's name was inquired, minuted down, and at Leyden he was maliciously denounced as a Spinosist. Hence he saw reason to fear that it might be found out of his power to enter the ministry. Having, therefore, taken his degree, Boerhaave entered into medical practice, and upon the death of Drelincourt, in 1701, he commenced as a lecturer upon the institutes of physic, upon which occasion he pronounced an oration, extolling Hippocrates as the model for students of medicine. His success as a teacher was such as to produce a solicitation that he would also treat of chemistry. He now began rapidly to rise into estimation; the curators of the Leyden university voted an augmentation of his salary; and in order to secure his services, which had been sought after by the university of Groningen, he was to have the chief professorship of medicine when it should become vacant. In 1703 he appears first to have publicly contended for the use of mechanical reasoning in physic by the delivery of a discourse, Oratio de Usu Ratiocinii in Medicinâ; and he is to be regarded as one of the chief supporters of the mechanical sect, the doctrines of which were principally based on the views and opinions of Borelli. Boerhaave described the body as consisting of a conic inflected canal, which divided into lesser ones of the same description, derived from the original trunk; and being ultimately connected into a retiform contexture, mutually opening into each other, he conceived to send off the lymphatics and the veins, the former of which terminated in various cavities of the body, the latter in the heart itself. These tubes or canals he admitted to be for the conveyance of the animal fluids, on whose free and perfect action health was held to be dependent. *Obstruction*, therefore, in his view, formed the proximate cause of disease. To support this system, he drew from all the sources to which his learning gave him access; but so fallacious and so defective did it appear, that it maintained an existence for a period but little beyond that of its founder. The errors into which the mathematicians ran in their estimate of the powers of the various organs of the human body, are calculated to excite astonishment, not unmingled with contempt. The mechanical hypothesis is as insufficient to account for the operations of the animal economy in health as it is inadequate to the explanation of the phenomena of the various diseases to which the frame is subject. Boerhaave, however, attempted to explain the functions of the body in health, the phenomena of disease, their causes, symptoms, and even the action of medicines for their relief, according to the laws of statics and hydraulics, and also by the operations of chemistry. Happily for mankind, (it has been observed by Pettigrew, in his Life of Boerhaave,) his practice was little in conformity to those views; an observation of nature, and an extensive experience, taught him the means of subduing disease, and enabled him to meet the exigencies which occur in practice. His Aphorisms would be almost unintelligible but for the Commentary of Van Swieten, and would long since have been consigned to the "tomb of all the Capulets." They are formed upon gratuitous suppositions, for which no proofs can be offered. They were the product of great reading and patient research; but they wanted the experience and judgment only to be obtained at the bedside of the patient. Boerhaave altogether appears on the field of medicine rather as a lecturer or teacher than a practitioner: his comprehensive mind, his acute discrimination, his order and precision, his erudition, all combined to render him most popular as an instructor; and his renown must be considered as based upon the duties of his professorships at Leyden, rather than upon any practical acumen.

Upon succeeding Dr. Hotton as professor of medicine and botany in 1709, Boerhaave delivered a discourse, Oratio quâ repurgatæ Medicinæ facilis asseritur Simplicitas, to expose the fallacies of the alchemists and metaphysicians, and endeavoured, notwithstanding his predilection for the mechanical and chemical theories, to fix the science of medicine upon the basis of observation, experiment, and the inferences naturally deducible from such a method. He at one time contemplated giving a chronological history of the alchemists, intending to show that from Geber to Stahl they had all been misled by one and the same error; and it is much to be regretted that he never completed this undertaking, for which he was well qualified, for he had read over most diligently the works of Paracelsus four times, and those of Van Helmont seven times.

Boerhaave's appointment to the chair of botany drew his attention to the wants of the university in a more extensive collection of medicinal plants, and the possession of a more extended garden. These he supplied, and his labours gained for him so much respect, that in 1714 he was appointed rector of the university. In this year also he succeeded Bidloo as professor of physic, and attended the university hospital. He was likewise chosen president of the Chirurgical College, for at this time medicine and surgery were not separated from each other. In 1718 he succeeded to the chair of chemistry by the death of Le Mort, and delivered an oration, De Chemiâ suos Errores expurgante, which may be looked upon as the foundation of his celebrated Elements of Chemistry. In 1725 he resigned the rectorship of the university, and delivered a discourse on the method of obtaining certainty in physics,—Oratio de comparando certo in Physicis,—which again subjected him to a charge of favouring scepticism and Spinosism, for having attacked the Cartesian doctrines. The charge against him was put forth by Mr. Andala, of Franeker, who, upon being called on by the governors of the university to substantiate his charge, retracted it in the most ample manner, and thus further established the reputation of the professor. He resigned his chair of chemistry and botany in 1729, from ill-health, and in the following year was again elected rector of the university, which, however, he was compelled by his infirmities to relinquish in 1731, when he delivered an oration, De Honore Medici Servitute. He died of water in the chest, Sept. 23, 1738, aged 70 years. The city of Leyden erected a splendid monument in the church of St. Peter to his memory, with the inscription, SALUTIFERO BOERHAAVII GENIO SACRUM. He enjoyed the friendship of a very numerous and a very learned circle.

Boerhaave contributed by his lectures, beyond any other professor, to raise the celebrity of the university. Students flocked from all parts to attend his discourses. No foreigner of distinction passed through Leyden without visiting him. The czar Peter is reported to have lain all night in his pleasure barge against Boerhaave's house, to have the advantage of two hours' conversation with him on various points of learning the next morning before college time. He could converse in Latin, English, French, German, and Dutch. He was also acquainted with the Spanish and Italian languages. He married at the age of forty-two, and left to his surviving daughter a fortune of two millions of florins. His MSS. and his anatomical and chemical preparations he bequeathed to his nephews, Drs. Herman and Abraham Kan. He was benevolent, and used to say that the poor were his best patients, because God was their paymaster; but he was discriminate in the distribution of his charities. He was an early riser, and regularly devoted many hours to study. He was fond of music, and relieved himself from severer duties by playing on the violin, and singing also. He had a knowledge of music as a science, and had read the principal ancient and modern authors on the subject, as appears from the lectures that he delivered on sound and hearing; and he had a concert once a week during the winter at his residence. Towards the latter part of his life he frequently retired to his country seat, and there regaled himself in an extensive garden, planted with many choice exotics and other treasures of the vegetable kingdom. His memory was remarkably retentive, a circumstance of great importance to him as a lecturer. He could quote not merely the authors on various topics, but even pages and sections from their works. He enriched his botanical discourses with references to the poets, Ovid, Virgil, and others. He was elected into the Royal Academy of Sciences of Paris in 1728, and into the Royal Society of London in 1730. He was also a member of many other learned societies. He published a great many works, among which, in addition to those noticed in the course of this article, may be enumerated,—Institutiones Medicæ, Lugd. Batav. 1708, 8vo; several editions of this work were published, and it has been translated into various foreign languages, even into Arabic, by command of the mufti, and it formed one of the first works printed at the press erected by the grand vizier at Constantinople. Aphorismi de Cognoscendis et Curandis Morbis, *ib.* 1709, 8vo. This was the text-book of Boerhaave's lectures, and it has been commented upon by almost innumerable writers. Index Plantarum quæ in Horto, Lugd. Batav. reperiuntur, *ib.* 1710, 8vo. Index Alter, *ib.* 1720, 8vo. Libellus de Materia Medicâ et Remediorum Formulis, *ib.* 1719, 12mo. This was printed in consequence of a spurious edition being published in London in

1718. Epist. ad Ruyschium pro Sententiâ Malpighianâ de Fabricâ Glandularum in Corpore Humano, Amst. 1722. The author herein advocates the claim of Malpighi against Rudbeck in this well known controversy. Atrocis nec descripti priùs Morbi Historia, Lugd. Bat. 1724, 12mo. Atrocis rarissimique Morbi Historia altera, *ib.* 1728, 8vo. Elementa Chemiæ, *ib.* 1732, 2 vols, 4to. At the time of its publication this was unquestionably the best work on the subject, and the historical part will continue to interest all who are attached to this science. The connexion between chemistry and mathematics and natural philosophy is most happily demonstrated.

The lectures of Boerhaave in MS. taken by various pupils, are to be found in almost every public library. There are also two papers on the Transmutation of Metals in the Phil. Trans. vols. xxxviii. and xxxix. He assisted to publish and to edit various important works :—Bart. Eustachii Opuscula Anatomica, Lugd. Bat. 1707, 8vo. Prosper Alpinus de Præsagiendâ Vitâ et Morte Ægrotantium, *ib.* 1710, 4to. Prosp. Alpinus Hist. Nat. Ægypti Pars II. sive de Plantis Ægypti, *ib.* 1735, 4to. C. Pisonis Selectæ Observationes et Consilia, *ib.* 1718, 4to. N. Piso de Cognoscendis et Curandis Morbis, *ib.* 1733, 4to. Marsigli Histoire Physique de la Mer, Amst. 1725, folio. Vesalii Opera Anatomica et Chirurgica, Lugd. Bat. 1725, 2 vols, folio. Vaillant Botanicon Parisiense, Leyd. 1727, folio. C. Drelincurtii Opuscula Medica, Hag. Com. 1727, 4to. L. Bellinus de Urinis, Pulsibus, &c. Lugd. Bat. 1730, 4to. Aretæus de Causis, Signis, et Curatione Morb. Acut. &c. Gr. et Lat. *ib.* 1735, 2 vols, folio. Aphrodisiacus sive de Lue Venereâ, *ib.* 1728, 2 vols, folio. Swammerdami, Historia Insectorum sive Bibliæ Naturæ, *ib.* 1737, folio.

BOERIO, (Joseph,) an Italian lawyer and linguist, born at Lendinara, in 1754, and educated for the law at Padua, under the celebrated professor Bragolino. At twenty-two the Venetian senate constituted him coadjutor to his father, a distinguished magistrate, and he subsequently filled several judicial situations under the republic. When Bonaparte made over the Venetian states to Austria, in 1797, Boerio was appointed assessor of the criminal court at Venice. After the battle of Marengo, in 1800, he was nominated, by the French, judge of the Adriatic court of justice; and when the Austrians recovered Venice, in 1814, he had still the good fortune to be employed in various posts. He retired after thirty years of service, and died February 25, 1832, leaving several Italian works of considerable importance on Venetian jurisprudence, and a valuable dictionary of the Venetian dialect, undertaken in 1797, and published in 1827. (Biog. Univ. Suppl.)

BOERIUS, (Nicholas,) a French lawyer, of distinguished ability, born at Montpelier, who died in 1539, at the age of seventy. After lecturing upon the Pandects at Bourges, and subsequently practising as an advocate with great success, he filled the office of president at Bordeaux, nearly twenty years. He left several professional works relative to the national and provincial institutions of France. (Moreri.)

BOERNER, (Christian Frederic,) a German divine, of prodigious erudition, born at Dresden, November 6, 1683. After travelling through England and Holland, he became professor of theology at Leipsic, where he died, November 19, 1753. His principal works are, De Exulibus Græcis iisdemque Litterarum in Italia Instauratoribus, Leips. 1750, 8vo, a valuable production. De Socrate, *ib.* 1707. De Ortu atque Progressu Philosophiæ Moralis, *ib.* 1707. De Lutheri Actis, anno 1520, *ib.* 1720. De Actis Lutheri Vormaciensibus, anno 1521, *ib.* 1721. Institutiones Theologicæ Symbolicæ, *ib.* 1751. Dissertationes Sacræ, *ib.* 1752. The Journal des Savans for 1725 mentions also a dissertation of Boerner's on the Lycaonians, which adopts the hypothesis of those who deny the language of that people to have been a dialect of the Greek. Between the years 1728 and 1734, this very learned and laborious divine published a complete edition of Luther's works, in 22 volumes folio. He undertook, likewise, a new edition of Le Long's Bibliotheca Sacra, with additions and corrections, which appeared at Antwerp, in 1709, in two large octavos. It is his name which has found a distinction for an ancient MS. of part of the New Testament, called the *Codex Boernerianus.* It once belonged to him, and contains the epistles of St. Paul, but not that to the Hebrews. There is an interlinear Latin version, accompanying the Greek text, from one of those translations which were in use before Jerome's time. This has been thought of a later age than the Greek; but Matthei, who published it at Meissen, in 1791, argues that both are of the same date, from uniformity of handwriting, and similarity of colour in the ink. The antiquity of this MS. is proved by the form of the characters, and the absence of accents and of marks of aspiration. It seems to have been written during the period of transition from uncial to small letters; and from resemblances to the Anglo-Saxon alphabet, it is thought to have been written in the west between the eighth and twelfth centuries. It is now in the royal library at Dresden, but a copy of it is in that of Trinity college, Cambridge, among the books and MSS. left by Dr. Bentley. (Biog. Univ. Rees.)

BOERNER, (Christian Frederic,) a physician, son of the preceding, born at Leipsic, February 16, 1736. He studied at the university of his native place, took the degree of doctor of philosophy in 1756, and that of medicine in 1760. He entered the army as a physician, and died February 7, 1800, having published, Diss. de Nisu et Renisu ut Caussâ Vitæ Sanæ, Lips. 1756, 4to. Diss. de Nisu et Renisu Adversæ Valetudinis, *ib.* 1760, 4to. Die in den ueblen Folgen der Selbstbefleckung sicher rathende Ärzt. Leips. 1769, 1775, 1776, 1780, 4to. He contributed many pieces to the Allgemeine Deutsche Bibliothek.

BOERNER, (Frederic,) a physician, brother of the preceding, born at Leipsic, June 17, 1723. Being originally intended by his father for the church, great attention was paid to his education, and he acquired a very competent knowledge of the Hebrew language. The botanical discourses of Plaz, however, excited in him a love of the natural sciences, and in 1744 he went to Wittemberg, where he relinquished the study of theology, and devoted himself to medicine. He studied under Stengel, Vater, Langguth, and Bose; and at the expiration of two years, went to Brunswick, where he practised under the direction of J. J. Schläger. He was admitted into the college of Medicine in 1747, when he pronounced an oration De Adorandâ Dei Majestate ex mirabili Narium Structurâ; and in 1748, he took the degree of M.D. at Helmstadt, upon which occasion he sustained a thesis, distinguished by the extent of its learning and the elegance of its composition, De Arte Gymnasticâ Novâ. In 1750 he was admitted a member of the Imperial Academy of the Curious in Nature, under the name of Cineas II.; and in 1756 he was made a master in philosophy at Wittemberg. Upon receiving his degree at Helmstadt, he withdrew to Wolfenbuttel, where he entered into practice, and also married the daughter of the burgomaster. In 1754 he was appointed to an extraordinary chair of medicine at Wittemberg; but the war breaking out, he was obliged to leave the city and repair to Leipsic, where he died June 30, 1761. He was a man of great learning and judgment, well versed in literary history, and his premature death prevented the accomplishment of several important works that he had devised. He, however, published some which are highly esteemed, and composed many academical pieces of considerable merit. It is sufficient here to specify, De Alexandro Benedicto Veronensi, Medicinæ post Litteras Renatas Restauratore, commentatio. Bruns. 1751, 4to. De Vitâ, Moribus, et Scriptis Hieron. Mercurialis, *ib. ib.* 4to. De Cosmâ et Damiano, Helmst. 1751, 4to. Biblioth. Libr. Rarior. Physico-Med. Hist. Crit. *ib.* 1751-52. De Æmilio Macro, ejusque rariore hodiè Opusculo de Virtutibus Herbarum Diatribe, Lips. 1754, 4to. Diss. Epist. de Medico, Reipublicæ Conservatore, Legumque Custode, *ib.* 1754, 4to. Memoriæ Prof. Med. in Acad. Vitemberg, *ib.* 1755-56, 4to. Noctes Guelphicæ, Leips. et Weimar. 1755, 4to. Antiquitates Medicinæ Egyptiacæ, Wittemb. 1756, 4to. Institutiones Medicinæ Legalis, *ib.* 1756, 4to.

BOERNER, (Nicholas,) a physician, born at Schmieritz, a village in the neighbourhood of Neustadt on the Orla, in Thuringia, January 27, 1693. He lost his father in his infancy; and his mother being unable to defray the expenses attendant on a good education, apprenticed him to Bernhardi, an apothecary at Frankenhausen. After some years he went to Jena, where he remained three years in the laboratory of Voigt. He paid great attention to pharmacy, and visited the principal establishments of that kind at Frankfort, Strasburg, Landau, Spire, and Worms. He afterwards resided with a celebrated apothecary at Coblentz, but hearing of the death of his mother, he visited his native place, arranged his affairs, and determined upon retiring to Jena and studying medicine. He assiduously attended the lectures of the Wedels, Slevogt, Teichmeyer, and Wucherer; he then retired to Frankenthal, and afterwards to Griessen, where he entered into practice, and in 1725 took the degree of doctor of medicine. He then settled at Neustadt, where he died in 1770. He was admitted a member of the Imperial Academy of the Curious in Nature, under the name of Asterion II., and he published the following works:—Diss. Inaug. exhibens Rorem Marinum, Jenæ, 1725, 4to. Physic, oder Gründliche und Verunftmässige Abhandlung Natürlicher Wissenschaften, &c., Leips. 1735, 1741, 8vo. Medicus sui Ipsius, *ib.* 1744-48, 2 vols, 8vo. Kinderarzt, oder Unterricht von Kinderkrankheiten, &c. Fr. et Leips. 1752, 2 vols, 8vo. He has also some papers in the Acts of the Imperial Academy.

BOESCHENSTEIN, (John,) a German linguist, born towards the close of the fifteenth century, and deserving of notice as a principal restorer of Hebrew learning in his country. He was appointed as professor of that language at the university of Wittemberg, in 1518, by the elector Frederic, and in the same year he published there a small Hebrew grammar, entitled, Hebraicæ Grammaticæ Institutiones Studiosis sanctæ Linguæ à D. Jo. Boeschenstein, C. M. C. collectæ. He had previously published a collection of pieces, valued for their extreme rarity, entitled, Contenta in hoc Libello, nuper à Johanne Boeschenstein, Eslingensi edita. Elementale Introductorium in Hebraicas Literas Teutonice et Hebraice legendas. Decem Præcepta Exodi xx. Oratio Dominica, Matth. vi. Luc. xi. Salutatio Angelica, Luc. i. Symbolum Apostolorum. Canticum Mariæ, Luc. i. Canticum Simeonis, Luc. ii. Ann. Veni Sancte. Ann. Salve Regina. Canticum Zachariæ, Luc i. Augustæ, ex Officinâ Erhardi Oegelin, Mense Maio, anno 1514, 4to. In 1520, he published the grammar of Moses Kimchi; in 1526, the Seven Penitential Psalms, with literal Latin and German versions; and he also published several German pieces. He had the honour of instructing Melancthon. (Clement.)

BOETHIUS, (Anicius Manlius Torquatus Severinus,) the last of the Romans, whom Cicero, says Gibbon, would have acknowledged for his countryman, descended from an old patrician family, and born at Rome, A.D. 455, in the very year when his father, Severinus, who had been prefect of the palace to Valentinian III., was put to death by the emperor. The loss of his parent was, however, supplied by some of his relations, who sent him to Athens, where he resided eighteen years, and made himself master of all that was preserved in the literature of Greece relating to poetry, philosophy, and the abstruser sciences. Nor was he less distinguished for goodness of heart and correctness of conduct, than for genius and learning. Hence on his return to Rome his alliance was naturally courted by many families of distinction; but his choice fell upon Elpis of Messina, who was at once virtuous, learned, and accomplished, especially in poetry, and to whom have been attributed two hymns, Aurea Lux, and Felix per Omnes, still sung in the Romish church. At the age of thirty-two, Boethius was created consul by Odoacer; who, after putting to death Orestes, and deposing his son Augustulus, assumed the title of the King of the West. But his brief reign was terminated by his death, when two years afterwards Theodoric, king of the Goths, invaded Italy, and fixed the seat of his government at Ravenna. From thence, in the eighth year of his reign, he repaired to Rome, having previously conferred the consulship upon Patritius and Hypation, the two sons of Boethius; by whom a panegyric was pronounced on the conqueror in the senate, to which he not only returned a gracious answer, but also gratified the populace by distributing largesses even beyond their expectations. Ten years afterwards, Boethius was appointed consul again. Public affairs, however, did not engross his whole attention, for it was during this period that he wrote various commentaries on different portions of Aristotle; and, as it is said, actually translated also the whole of Plato, with the view of reconciling the conflicting doctrines of those two schools of philosophy; and, as the writings of Plato cannot be thoroughly understood without some knowledge of arithmetic, geometry, and music, he put into Latin such portions of the works of Greek authors as bore upon those subjects; and to elucidate the Aristotelian method of reasoning, wrote a commentary on the Topica of Cicero. But of all these numerous works, only a portion has been preserved. His time and talents were not, however, devoted to literature alone, for, like some of the earlier philosophers of Greece, he paid attention to practical mechanics; and was thus enabled to amuse, not a little, Gondobald, king of the Burgundians, by showing the son-in-law of Theodoric, when he visited Rome, various specimens of his mechanical inventions, and amongst the rest, two kinds of chronometers, one of which marked the hours of the day, and the other the apparent diurnal and annual motion of the sun along the ecliptic; and with which Gondobald was so delighted as to send an embassy to Theodoric, to procure the instruments for him, as we learn from Cassiodorus.

In 522, Boethius was appointed consul for the third time, together with Symmachus, whose daughter, Rusticiana, he had married after the death of his first wife, who was buried in the portico of St. Peter's at Rome. The year, however, which saw Boethius thus raised, like Pompey, to the pinnacle of honour, was destined to witness his fall, and to be the precursor of his destruction. Theodoric was an Arian, and Boethius a Catholic; when, therefore, he wrote a work on the Unity in Trinity, he opposed equally the Arians, Nestorians, and Eutychians; and as his opponents naturally possessed the greater influence with the emperor, they led him to believe that Boethius wanted to destroy not only Arianism, but also to deliver Italy from the dominion of the Goths; and the better to effect the ruin of their adversary, they forged letters in the name of Boethius, and on the evidence of three unprincipled villains, he was condemned to death, without being even allowed to be heard in his own defence. Unwilling, however, to put the sentence into immediate execution, the emperor contented himself with confiscating his property, and throwing him into prison at Pavia. Here he lay during the time that an embassy was sent to Constantinople; whither Theodoric had ordered pope John I. to repair, together with four of the principal senators of Rome, one of whom was Symmachus, to threaten Justin, the Catholic emperor of the East, that if he did not immediately revoke the edict he had published against the Arians, he would abolish the Catholic religion in Italy; but as the ambassadors were unable to effect the object of their mission, they were, on their return, thrown into prison, where the pope died of starvation, and the others were beaten to death; and scarcely had Boethius finished the work that has thrown such lustre on himself and his incarceration equally, when he was put to death, October 23, A.D. 526. His body was interred by the inhabitants of Pavia in the church of St. Augustine, where a monument was erected to his memory by the emperor Otho III., who, in A.D. 996, ordered the bones of Boethius to be taken up and placed in a shrine of marble upon the top of the monument, and which was to be seen until the church itself was destroyed, in the seventeenth century. After his death, Amalasuntha, the daughter of Theodoric, and the guardian of her son Athalaric, did all in her power to atone for the injuries inflicted by her father on one whose memory and fate she revered and lamented, by restoring to the family of Boethius the property that had been forfeited by his alleged treason.

Of the entire works of Boethius, which have come down to us, the only complete edition was published at Basle, in 2 vols, fol. 1570, and which was probably the basis of Histoire de Boèce, Sénateur Romain, avec l'Analyse de tous ses Ouvrages, that appeared at Paris in 1715, in 3 vols, 12mo. But of his Consolatio Philosophiæ, the editions have been extremely numerous; the first was printed at Nuremberg, in 1473, fol. and the last at Paris, in 1783, in 3 vols. 12mo, and was edited by Johan Eremita, *i.e.* Jos. Dufresne de Francheville; of which the British Museum has a copy in vellum, and likewise a copy of the Antwerp edition of 1607, containing a few of Bentley's corrections, together with the various readings of an unknown MS. At the revival of learning, the Consolation was considered equal to any production of the Augustan age, and was made the subject of various commentaries, detailed at length in Fabricius Biblioth. Latin. t. iii.; and it has been translated not only into almost every spoken language of Europe, but even into Anglo-Saxon, by Alfred, who seems to have had a fuller MS. of the work than any at present known to be in existence; while Maximus Planudes, who gave a Greek version of it, has, in the poetical parts, adopted the very measures of the original, as seen in the Carmina A. M. T. S. Boethii Græce Conversa, published by Wiber, at Darmstadt, 1833, 4to, from a Vienna MS., formerly in the possession of Jo. Sambrecci; and from whence it has been conjectured that the last of the Romans was indebted himself, in part, to a Greek original, written by the first of the Athenian philosophers, who converted a prison into the temple of the muses, and whose example has been followed by Grotius and a long list of literary prisoners, whose names are to be found in Fabricius, l. c.

BOETHIUS, BOECE, or BOEIS, (Hector,) a Scottish historian, born at Dundee, in Angus, about 1470, and, after a course of preliminary instruction in his own country, educated at Paris. Thence he was invited back into Scotland, about 1500, by William Elphinston, bishop of Aberdeen, who had lately founded King's college in that city, and wished to make him its principal. On reaching Aberdeen, Boethius found several scholarly persons among the canons regular there, and he became a member of that order himself. Having entered upon his functions as head of the college, he secured for coadjutor, William Hay, his fellow-student both in Scotland and France; and by the united exertions of these two accomplished friends, their native country made advances in learning to which it had hitherto been a stranger. In 1514, bishop Elphinston died, and Boethius wrote his life, preceded by the lives of his predecessors. The book was published at Paris, in 1522, 4to, with this title, Vitæ Episcoporum Murthlacensium et Aberdonensium. Elphinston's biography occupies one-third of it. The see was originally placed at Mortlich, or Murthlack, in the shire of Banff, about thirty-six miles from Aberdeen, and its foundation there originated in a victory over the Danes in 1010. Its first bishop was Beanus, appointed in 1015, with whom, accordingly, Boethius begins. It was removed to Old Aberdeen, when Nectanus was bishop, appointed about 1106. The bishops of Mortlich and Aberdeen form, therefore, one series. Boethius carries down their history to Gavin Dunbar, appointed in 1518, who held the see when he wrote, there having been another since his friend Elphinston died. He is not thought to have executed his task with any great success, the work being described as lame and imperfect. His contemporaries, however, were not qualified for a critical judgment upon literary productions; therefore, as Boethius was a man of talent, and of extraordinary acquirements for his time, it is no wonder that he felt himself encouraged to venture next upon a bolder undertaking. This was no other than a Latin history of Scotland, in seventeen books, beginning with times of which neither he nor any one else knew any thing, and ending with the death of James I. It was published in folio, at Paris, though no place is mentioned, by Badius Ascensius, as it seems in 1527, under the title of Scotorum Historia ab illius Gentis Origine. This work he continued and improved to the time of his death, which is thought to have happened about 1550, when two learned men of the continent are found lamenting his loss. His continuation amounts to one entire book, the eighteenth, with part of another. These additions appeared at Paris in 1574, in a new edition of the work, by John Ferrier, a Piedmontese, who made some new arrangements in the text of his author, and added a continuation of his own, bringing down the history to James III. As a historian, Boethius has been justly blamed for the admission of much fabulous matter, which has caused him to be compared with Geoffrey of Monmouth. He also displays that credulity and want of correct information as to matters connected relatively with his subject, that might be expected from his age, and imperfect means of information. But his taste and knowledge were greatly in advance of his time and country. Hence Johnson was fully justified in reverencing him as one of the revivers of elegant literature. (Biog. Brit. Clement. Keith's Scottish Bishops.)

BOETHIUS, (Jacob,) a Swedish archdeacon, pastor of Mora, in Dalecarlia, born in 1647. He was placed in his benefice in 1693; and when Charles XII. was declared major at fifteen, although the late king's will had denied him that privilege until the expiration of another three years, Boethius preached a sermon on the text of Ecclesiastes, *Woe to thee, O land, when thy king is a child.* Not contented even with this political display, the archdeacon soon after sent a memorial to one of the senate against the absolute government introduced under Charles XI. He was now arrested, tried, and capitally condemned; a sentence commuted for perpetual imprisonment. In 1710 he was, however, allowed to join his wife and family. He died in 1718, not only known for his indiscreet and unseemly political effusions, but also for the philological treatises, De Orthographiâ Linguæ Suecanæ, Mercurius Bilinguis, and some other pieces. (Biog. Univ.)

BOETHUS, (Flavius,) a Peripatetic philosopher, pupil of Alexander of Damascus. His name is mentioned oftener than once by Galen.—Of Sidon, a pupil of Andronicus of Rhodes, and contemporary with Strabo, and the person against whom Porphyry wrote his five books on the Soul. According to Fabricius, he was the author of the Platonic Lexicon, and the treatise on the doubtful passages of Plato, mentioned by Photius. The Epicurean and Geometrician is known only by two allusions in Plutarch. The Stoic is said by Diogen. Laert., to have been written before Chrysippus, a work on Nature and Fate. Of the Sculptor of Carthage, only the name has been preserved by Pliny. The writer of epigrams, mentioned by Strabo, was a native of Tarsus, and the contemporary of Pylades, the celebrated pantomime in the time of Augustus.

BOETIE, (Stephen de la,) one of the earliest French writers with republican principles. He was born at Sarlat, in Perigord, Nov. 1, 1530, and becoming counsellor to the parliament of Bordeaux, he was regarded as one of its brightest luminaries. His genius, indeed, seems to have been precocious in an extraordinary degree. He was an excellent poet, both in French and Latin, his verses having a delicacy and elegance which could not easily be surpassed. He acquired such a skill in languages as enabled him to translate, from the Greek, some pieces of Plutarch and Xenophon, which were highly valued about his time. As, in addition to these accomplishments, Boetie gained a deep insight into jurisprudence and philosophy, especially into ethics, it is no wonder that his contemporaries rated him very highly. He had also another advantage for the gaining of an ephemeral reputation: his death was premature, a dysentery having carried him off, in the neighbourhood of Bordeaux, when he was barely thirty-three. He was besides the friend of Montaigne, who loved and admired him, to whom he left his writings, and who published them after his death, he having published nothing himself. An editor and panegyrist so popular as Montaigne, would preserve any name from absolute oblivion, though he might not be able to secure lasting reputation for one without claims to it of his own. These are to be found in a political tract, entitled Le Contr'Un, ou de la Servitude Volontaire, penned by Boetie, in his nineteenth year, and published with great effect in 1578, after the horrors of the Bartholomew massacre had spread extensively over France a detestation of the court. The youthful author's indignant eloquence was poured forth on occasion of the constable de Montmorenci's great severity in punishing a sedition at Bordeaux, in 1548. It breathes all that fierce and indiscriminating abhorrence of tyranny, which a one-sided, superficial knowledge of history, and an ignorance of the world naturally produce in impetuous, ingenuous youth. Boetie upbraids the many for submission to a single one, as equally the basest and the greatest of follies. The individual, he strongly urges, before whom a multitude lies prostrate, has neither more hands, nor eyes, nor natural advantages of any kind, than the humblest of his dependents. He could not employ, therefore, so many hands to strike, did not the oppressed raise them at his bidding. He could not rob, did not the very parties that he pillages find him accomplices among themselves. This language, with much of the same sort, renders the Contr' Un of De la Boetie, one of the most remarkable among the political pieces of an early date, and in many quarters it has been denounced as a seditious libel. It is to be found at the end of some editions of Montaigne, and has given occasion to remark, that although the author's talents were evidently sufficient for the government of a state, he was fitter for a republic than a monarchy, and would have chosen to be born at Venice, rather than Sarlat. (Moreri. Hallam's Literature of Europe, ii. 184.)

BOETIUS EPO, the names of two learned men in the Netherlands, father and son, the former of whom was born in 1529, and died in 1599, a professor in the new university of Douay. He was a civilian, and had at one time been a protestant, but soon returned to his original profession of Romanism. His son, a professor of canon law, died in 1642, leaving many Latin works upon professional and other subjects, highly valued in their day, but now generally forgotten. (Moreri.)

BOETIUS, or BOECE, (Christian Frederic,) an engraver, born at Leipsic in 1706, pupil of C. A. Wartman, and chiefly resident at Dresden, where he became professor of the electoral academy in 1764. (Bryan.)

BOETTCHER, (John Frederic,) inventor of the Dresden china, born at Schlein, in the Voigtland, in the latter half of the seventeenth century, and originally placed with an apothecary at Berlin. He there turned his mind to alchemy, and a report that he had actually found the philosopher's stone, obliged him to take refuge in Saxony. The elector, Frederic Augustus II., king of Poland, soon, however, sent for him, and inquired whether the current rumours of his discovery were true. Boettcher disowned them; and the king, perhaps disappointed, ordered him to make further experiments in the fortress of Königstein, to which he sent him. The imprisoned alchemist, in seeking to obey this order, discovered the secret of making china, either in 1702, or the following year. The ware was first manufactured at Dresden, afterwards upon a larger scale at Meissen, and Boettcher was continualy making improvements in it until his death, in March 1719. His great discovery procured for him letters of nobility. (Biog. Univ.)

BOETTGER, (Christopher Henry,) born at Cassel, June 12, 1737, in 1761, M.D. at Rinteln, much celebrated both in medicine and as an accoucheur. In 1763 he was appointed physician to the Foundling hospital, also professor of botany, and elected a member of the College of Physicians of Cassel. In 1764 he was named physician to the French hospital, and in 1780 he occupied a chair of midwifery. He died Sept. 3, 1781, having published several works:—De Inflammatione Uteri, Rint. 1761, 4to. Beschreibung des Botanischen Gartens zu Cassel, als ein Beytrag zur Geschichte der Botanik, Cassel, 1777, 4to. Fortsetzung dieses Verzeichnisses, *ib.* 1777, 4to.

BOETTICHER, (Andrew Julius,) born at Wolfenbuttel, July 7, 1672, M.D. at Leyden. After holding medical professorships in the universities of Giessen and Helmstadt, he died July 26, 1719, having published,—Diss. de Vocis Organo, Lugd. Bat. 1697, 4to. De Ossibus, Giessen, 1698-1700, 4to. De Respiratione Fœtûs in Utero, Helmst. 1702, 4to. De Diabete, *ib.* 1704, 4to. De Peste, *ib.* 1712, 4to. De Cranii Ossibus, *ib.* 1718, 4to.

BOETTO, (Giovanile,) a painter and engraver, born at Turin, who died there about 1680. His pictures are frescoes, generally upon fabulous or allegorical subjects, but executed with great skill and spirit. (Pilkington.)

BOFFRAND, (Germain,) a French architect, born at Nantes, May 7, 1667. His father was a sculptor of no note, and his mother, sister to the poet Quinault. He came to Paris at fourteen, and at first gave his attention to sculpture and architecture conjointly, mingling with these more serious pursuits, the composition of some light dramatic pieces, which were both played and printed. Eventually he applied himself exclusively to architecture, and became celebrated, his chief works being splendid town mansions for the nobility. In 1745, he published, Livre d'Architecture, contenant les Principes généraux de cet Art, et les Plans, Elevations, et Profils de quelques-uns des Bâtimens faits en France, et dans les Pays étrangers, fol. with seventy plates. He died at Paris, March 18, 1754, far from rich, in spite of his great professional success, having suffered severely from Law's famous financial bubble. (Biog. Univ.)

BOGAN, (Zachary,) a learned English puritan, born at Little Hempston, Devon, in 1625, admitted commoner of St. Alban's hall, Oxford, in Michaelmas term, 1640, and scholar of Corpus Christi college, November 26, 1641. He left the university when Oxford became the king's garrison, but returned after the surrender of it to the parliament. Having taken the degree of B.A. A.D. 1646, he was elected fellow of his college, and proceeded M.A. in 1650. After this he gave himself up entirely to the study of languages and theology, his close application to which caused his premature death at the age of thirty-four years. He wrote additions to the Archæologiæ Atticæ of Francis Rous. 2. An Alphabetical View of Scripture Threats and Punishments. 3. Meditations on the Mirth of a Christian's Life. 4. Help to Prayer, both Extempore and of a Set Form; together with several smaller pieces. He was buried in the middle of the north cloister of his college, and his portrait may be seen in the Guildhall of Oxford, he having benefited that city by his will. (Chalmers.)

BOGATZKY, (Charles Henry,) born at Jankowa, in Silesia, 1690. He studied theology at Halle, and afterwards lived there as a private gentleman till his decease in 1774. He was of a weak constitution, and was encouraged when a child by his mother and grandmother in the reading of pietistical works, by the doctrines and tone of which the whole tenor of his subsequent life was influenced. His writings treat, in a crude and literal style, after the fashion of the pietists of his day, of atonement and grace, of the misery of sin, and of the accepting of the blood of Christ in faith. His private character was mild and actively benevolent. He is the author of a great number of religious works, amongst others, of The Golden Treasury of the Children of God, (often reprinted, and translated into several other languages); Versified Sighs on the principal Parts of the Christian Doctrine; A Daily House-book of the Children of God, (of which a fourth edition appeared in 1771, in small 4to); of various writings on the Life of Christ on Earth and in Heaven, &c. His Religious Poems, (Halle, 1749,) of which some will be found in modern hymn-books, are in a style of antiquated imagery not easily intelligible.

BOGDAN, (Martin,) a German physician of the seventeenth century, born at Driesen. He studied under the celebrated Thomas Bartholin, at the university of Copenhagen, afterwards travelled through England and France, and then took the degree of M.D. at Basle, in 1660. He practised in this city for several years, and then removed to Berne, where he was appointed physician to the city and the canton. He entered into the controversy respecting the discovery of the lymphatic vessels, so violently waged between Bartholin and Rudbeck, and espoused the cause of his master. He published, Rudbeckii Insidiæ structæ Vasis Lymphaticis, Th. Bartholini, Fr. et Copenh. 1654, 12mo. Apologia pro Vasis Lymphaticis Bartholini adversus O. Rudbeck, Copenh. 1654, 12mo. Simeonis Sethi Volumen de Alimentorum Facultatibus, Gr. et Lat. Paris, 1658, 8vo. Theses Medicæ Inaugurales, Basil. 1659, 4to. Tractatus de Recidivâ Morborum ex Hippocrate, ad Hippocratis Mentem, *ib.* 1660, 4to. Observ. Medicæ ad Th. Bartholinum. These have been published by Lyser at Copenhagen, 1665 and 1679, 8vo.

BOGDANE, (James,) a painter, born in Hungary, but not regularly educated for an artist. He came to England under queen Anne, and painted birds, fruit, and flowers with considerable success, but without a sufficient knowledge of perspective. He died about 1720. (Pilkington.)

BOGDANOVITSCH, (Hippolytus Feodorovitsch,) called the Russian Anacreon, born in 1743, in Little Russia, educated in the university of Moscow, then recently founded by the empress Elizabeth, where he showed great talent. He was originally intended for the army, but became so captivated by some dramatic representations, that mathematics, with other studies fit for training a tactician, were cast aside for poetry; and in 1765, The Isle of Felicity, a poem in three cantos, extended his fame to Petersburg. Some lyric pieces had already laid foundations for it elsewhere. He now was attached to the Russian embassy at Dresden, and he there acquired a great fund of information. French became familiar to him, and he translated into Russian, Vertot's Revolutions of Rome. His Douchenka, however, a poem in imitation of La Fontaine's Psyche, published in 1775, was the corner-stone of his reputation. About 1776 he returned to Russia, and edited during two years the Petersburg Courier. In 1796 his connexion with diplomacy ceased, and he was named president of the imperial archives. In 1777 he published one volume of an historical picture of Russia. He likewise published Dramatic Proverbs, and a collection of lyric poems. Some specimens of his talents are accessible to English readers, in Bowring's Russian Anthology. Bogdanovitsch died at Koursk, Jan. 6, 1803. (Biog. Univ. Suppl.)

BOGRA KHAN, surnamed Ilek, a powerful sovereign, of Turkish race, who reigned in the latter part of the tenth century of our ĕra, over Kashgar, Khoten, and the other countries intervening between Transoxiana and the Chinese frontier. Of the dynasty to which he belonged, and the extensive and formidable empire over which they ruled, we derive only occasional glimpses from the Mohammedan historians, who appear to consider the Turks as beyond the sphere of their researches till the establishment of the Seljookians in Persia; but these scattered notices have been diligently collected by M. de Guignes, (Hist. des Huns, i. 233, iii. 29, 157,) who has also succeeded in identifying them with the race called *Hoei-ke* by the Chinese annalists. The present race had been converted to Islam two reigns before the accession of Bogra Khan, whose Moslem name was Shahab-ed-Doulah Haroun; and their appearance in Mohammedan history is principally in connexion with the frequent wars which they waged with the *Samani* dynasty in Transoxiana and Khorassan, who themselves had originally issued from the same regions. In A.D. 993, (A.H. 383,) when the power of the Samaides was verging to its fall, Bogra Khan invaded their territories at the head of a mighty host, routed the reigning monarch, Nouh-Ebn-Mansoor, and drove him from his capital of Bokhara, which was occupied by the victor. The ill health of the khan, however, compelled him to abandon his conquest, and he died the same year, on his return to his own country. Abulfeda describes him as "a prince pious, just, and of praiseworthy life and manners." His successor is called Ilek Khan, which seems, however, to have been the common appellation of the family. (Novairi. Abulfeda. De Guignes.)

BOGROS, (John Armet,) a distinguished French anatomist, born June 14, 1786, at Bogros, a village in the mountains of Auvergne, near the baths of the Mont d'Or. He was designed for the church, and studied accordingly at the college of Billom; but his taste leading him to prefer medicine, he passed to

Clermont in 1808, and there made great progress in his professional researches. He quitted Clermont for Paris, and was particularly esteemed by the celebrated professor of anatomy, Beclard. Bogros was ardent in the pursuit of anatomy, and not only demonstrated with great ability the parts of the human body, when presented to the Faculty of Medicine, but also devised means for preserving the organs most susceptible of decay. The museum of the Faculty of Medicine contains many ingenious specimens of his art applied to the brain, liver, muscles, &c., which are perfectly dry, and notwithstanding preserve their flexibility and natural appearance. In 1823 he took the degree of M.D., and delivered an inaugural thesis, having for its title, Essai sur l'Anatomie Chirurgicale de la Région Iliaque, et Description d'un Nouveau Procédé pour faire la Ligature des Artères Epigastriques et Iliaque Externe, which was afterwards reprinted, with some modifications and with plates, in the Archives Générales de Médecine, tom. iii. In 1825 Bogros was attacked with a hæmorrhage from the lungs, which proved fatal in the month of September. His mode of preserving anatomical preparations is detailed in the Bulletins de la Faculté et de la Société de Médecine, tom. vi. He published a Mémoire sur la Structure des Nerfs, in which he endeavoured to prove by mercurial injections the existence of tubes in those parts. His experiments have, however, been shown to be fallacious by MM. Breschet and Raspail; but his researches have done much towards correcting various errors which had been common in the examination of the nervous system.

BOGUE, (David, D.D.) an eminent dissenting minister, born at Halydown, Berwickshire, in 1750, and educated at the university of Edinburgh, whence he came to England, and obtained employment in a school at Camberwell, and in a London meeting-house. He was afterwards invited to Gosport, where he continued pastor of an independent congregation during fifty years. An academy for the preparation of young men for the ministry was established at Gosport in the year 1788, by the late Mr. Welch, the banker. Of this seminary Mr. Bogue was placed at the head, and in the conduct of it displayed great ability. He was one of the originators of the (London) Missionary Society, and was on all occasions one of its most zealous agents and advocates. He died of ischuria, at a friend's house at Brighton, October 25, 1825, in the seventy-sixth year of his age. His principal work is the History of Dissenters, which he wrote in conjunction with his friend Dr. Bennett, of which a second edition appeared in 1833, 2 vols, 8vo. (Evan. Mag. Jan. 1826.)

BOGUET, (Henry,) a judge in Burgundy, born in Franche Comté, and famous for his zeal against sorcery. Upon this favourite subject he published, in 1602, Discours Execrables des Sorciers, ensemble leurs Procès faits depuis Deux Années en ça, en divers Endroits de la France, avec une Instruction pour un Juge en faits de Sorcellerie. This work, which discovers an extreme credulity, joined with a savage hostility towards unfortunate creatures suspected of witchcraft, was reprinted several times, but all the editions are extremely rare, Boguet's family having carefully suppressed it. Boguet afterwards published, Les Actions de la Vie et de la Mort de S. Claude, Lyons, 1609 and 1627, a work refuted by Lectius, a magistrate of Geneva. Another of his productions was professional, and obtained him lasting credit, being the first publication on the legal usages of Franche Comté. It is entitled, In Consuetudines Generales Comitatus Burgundiæ Observationes. Boguet died Feb. 23, 1619. (Clement. Biog. Univ.)

BOGUPHAL, bishop of Posnania, a Polish historian, who died in 1253, leaving an ill-written Latin chronicle, tracing the history of his country from the earliest times to the year 1252. It was continued to 1271, by Bacsko, and published at Warsaw by Zaluski, in 1752. It had already appeared in 1729, in Sommerberg's Scriptores Rerum Silesiac. (Biog. Univ.)

BOGYSLAWSKI, (Albert,) a Polish dramatic author, born of a good family in 1752, and well educated, being acquainted with several languages. By his exertions, both as author and actor, Poland became possessed of a respectable stage. In 1782 he brought out an original Polish opera. He wrote altogether eighty dramatic pieces, but printed only sixty of them in his works, published at Warsaw between 1819 and 1821, the remainder being translations of Italian operas. The first volume of his works is occupied by a history of the Polish theatre. After a life of admiration and considerable success, but, notwithstanding, chequered by many difficulties, Bogyslawski died at Warsaw in 1829. (Biog. Univ.)

BOHADIN, (Cadhi Yusuf Abu'l-Mahasen Boha-ed-Deen Ebn Rafi,) a Moslem jurist and divine of no inconsiderable reputation, though principally known in Europe as the biographer of his patron, the sultan Saladin, born in Moossul, A.D. 1144, (A.H. 539.) Having lost both his parents at an early age, he derived his education from the bounty of his maternal uncle, Sheddad, whence he is sometimes, but erroneously, spoken of by oriental writers as *Ebn Sheddad*. His proficiency in the study of the Moslem law brought him early into notice, and in the twenty-seventh year of his age he quitted his native city for Bagdad, where he remained some years in the college founded by Nizam-al-Mulk, the famous vizier of Malek Shah the Seljookian. He afterwards returned to Moossul, where he continued to reside, enjoying a high reputation as a jurisconsult, till 1186, when he performed the pilgrimage to Mekka; and on his return, the following year, diverged from the direct route in order to visit Jerusalem and the holy places in its vicinity. When thus employed, he received a summons to the camp of Saladin, (then engaged in the siege of the fortress of Kaukab,) who had been attracted by the fame of his legal and theological acquirements, and now conferred on him the lucrative appointments of judge of Jerusalem, and cadhi-asker, or judge of the army. During the remaining years of the life of his patron, Bohadin was almost constantly resident at his court; and the death of Saladin, in 1193, produced no diminution in his prosperity. He was appointed by his son, Malek-al-Dhaher, who succeeded to the throne of Aleppo, to the high office of chief judge in that city, which he continued to hold during all his reign; and during this period, his lectures were attended by a concourse of pupils, many of whom afterwards attained celebrity: among the number was the well-known biographical writer, Ebn-Khalekan, whom Bohadin, being himself childless, is said to have adopted as his son. On the death of Malek-al-Dhaher, he became, in conjunction with the *atabek* Togrul, tutor and guardian to his youthful son and successor, Malek-al-Azeez, whose education he tended with sedulous diligence; but the excesses to which the prince gave way at the conclusion of his minority so mortified his aged preceptor, that he is said never again to have left his house. He died A.D. 1235, (A.H. 633,) aged 91 solar, or 93 lunar years, and was buried in a college which he himself had founded. He was the author of various treatises on points of Mohammedan law and morals; but his great work was the Life of Saladin, which was edited by Albert Schultens, from a MS. believed to be the autograph of the author, and printed at Leyden in 1755, with a Latin version in parallel columns, and a valuable geographical appendix. The style and diction of this well-known work are generally easy and fluent; and it is only rarely that the author falls into the hyperbolical bombast of language which so frequently disfigures oriental composition; and as a history, its fidelity and authenticity are guaranteed by the almost constant attendance of the writer on the person of the sultan, and the unvarying confidence and friendship with which he was honoured by his sovereign. The early career of Saladin, and the history of his ingratitude to the family of his patron Noor-ed-Deen, are passed over with comparatively little detail: it is on the later exploits of his hero, and the scenes in which the narrator himself personally assisted, that Bohadin has expended his powers of description; and the minuteness and accuracy of his relation give a high value to this part of the work, which comprehends the warfare of the sultan against the crusaders, the famous siege of Acre, &c. But these momentous incidents are viewed by Bohadin with the eye rather of a Moslem divine, than of a statesman or soldier; and he delights to enlarge on the merits of Saladin, rather as a strenuous champion of Islam against the Nazarene invaders, than as the sagacious monarch or consummate general. This display of zeal, however, while it attests the sincerity of the author, detracts little from the importance of his work, which is deservedly valued as the most faithful record existing of the mighty monarch who furnishes its theme.

BOHA-ED-DEEN ABU'L-HASAN ALI SEMOOKI, also surnamed **MOKTANA**, a celebrated doctor of the Druses, whose works are quoted by De Sacy, Chrest. Arabe,. vols. i. ii. He appears to have lived in the fifth century of the Hejira.

BOHADSCH, (John Baptist,) professor of natural history at Prague, in 1753, where he died in 1772. He travelled to Naples, and dissected many mollusca and zoophytes, of which he has given an account in his work, De quibusdam Animalibus Marinis, eorumque Proprietatibus, vel nondùm, vel minùs Notis,

Liber. cum xii. tab. æneis. Dresd. 1761, 4to. He also published, De Utilitate Electrisationis in Arte Medicâ, Prag. 1751, 4to. Disputatio de veris Sepiarum Ovis, *ib.* 1752, 4to. Experimenta quibus constitit, eas Partes esse Sensu præditas, quibus Hallerus sentiendi Facultatem denegat, *ib.* 1756, 4to. Dienst-und nutzbarer Vorschlag, &c. *ib.* 1758, 8vo. De Synocho Putridâ Epidemica, *ib.* 1758, 4to.

BOHAN, (Francis Philip Loubat, baron of,) a French tactician, of noble family, born at Bourg en Bresse, in 1751, and educated for the army, which he entered at seventeen. In 1781 he published the fruits of his meditation and experience, under the title of Examen Critique du Militaire Français, 3 vols, 8vo; a work treating of all that concerns the organization of an army, displays the inconveniences of existing French usages, and proposes remedies for them. The third volume, which relates to cavalry, was reprinted, with extracts from the two former volumes, in 1821. Bohan was a moderate advocate of the French revolution, but he had a very narrow escape from the scaffold during its excesses. He died in his native place, after a retirement of several years, chiefly occupied in rural pursuits, March 12, 1804. (Biog. Univ. Suppl.)

BOHEMOND, one of the leading heroes of the first crusade, son of Robert Guiscard, first Norman duke of Apulia. His first essay in arms was made at an early age in the war which his father waged against the Greek empire. At the famous battle of Durazzo (Oct. 1081) his valour was signalized under the eye of Guiscard, who left the army under his command when he returned to Italy; but Bohemond, after defeating the emperor and ravaging Thessaly, was compelled, by the diminution of his forces, to abandon his conquests, and embark for Apulia. Four years later, he shared in the second Greek expedition of his father, and was present at the naval victory gained off Corfu, over the Greeks and Venetians. But at the death of Guiscard, Bohemond inherited from his father only the principality of Tarentum, the duchy of Apulia being bequeathed to his younger brother Roger. This unequal division excited the murmurs of Bohemond, and the public peace was frequently disturbed by his ambition, till the preaching of the first crusade, in 1095, presented to him an opening for fresh enterprise. He embraced the cross with an affectation of fanatic zeal, and, accompanied by his cousin, the famous Tancred, set forward with a force of 30,000 men for Constantinople, where he visited his ancient opponent, the emperor Alexius, and was converted, by a dexterous largess of gold and jewels, into a firm supporter of that politic and crafty monarch in his negotiations with his barbarous allies. At the battle of Dorylæum, and the painful campaigns of Asia Minor and Syria, (1097-8,) Bohemond maintained his ancient reputation for valour; and when Antioch fell into the power of the crusaders, he succeeded in securing that important conquest to himself, and made it the capital of an independent principality, which extended from Cilicia to Tripoli; but his usual selfish policy displayed itself in the means which he took to deprive the count of Toulouse of his share of the acquisition, and still more in his refusal to accompany the crusaders against Jerusalem, on the plea of his presence being necessary in his new dominions. In 1101 he was defeated and taken prisoner by the Turks, and only recovered his liberty, after two years' captivity, by a ransom of 130,000 bezants. The difficulties of his position were now increased by the hostilities of the Greek emperor, who claimed, in virtue of a convention concluded at Constantinople, the surrender of Antioch and its territory. Unable to maintain himself against the numbers of the Greeks, he resolved to return to Europe in search of aid; and evading the Greek fleet, according to Anna Comnena, by concealing himself in a coffin, he reached France in safety, where he married a daughter of king Philip I., and levied an army with which he invaded the Greek dominions in 1107; but he was repulsed from before Durazzo, and a peace was concluded in the following year. Its conditions, however, were only observed till he procured the means of breaking them, and he was on the eve of a fresh expedition when he died, in 1111, at Canosa, in Apulia, thus releasing the Greeks from "an adversary (as Gibbon describes him) whom neither oaths could bind, nor dangers could appal, nor prosperity could satiate;" a sentence which requires no addition to complete the delineation of his character. He was succeeded at Antioch by his son,

BOHEMOND II., then only four years old, who was educated at Tarentum, under the tutelage of his mother, till 1126, when he repaired to Palestine to claim his patrimonial sovereignty of Antioch, which had in the mean time been reunited to the kingdom of Jerusalem. His claims were admitted by Baldwin II., who gave him his daughter Alice in marriage; but his reign was neither long nor prosperous. In 1130 he was defeated in an attempt to surprise Damascus; and in February of the following year, he was overpowered and killed in an encounter with the Turks of Aleppo, at the age of 24.

BOHEMOND III., succeeded his mother, Constance, at Antioch, in 1163, and was in the same year defeated and taken prisoner by Noor-ed-Deen at the castle of Harenc. He recovered his liberty the following year by the interference of the king of Jerusalem, but the remainder of his long reign was undistinguished by any warlike achievement of note. In his disputes with the princes of Armenia, he used craft and treachery rather than arms; and his inhospitable reception of the fugitives from Jerusalem, after its capture by Saladin, has been deservedly reprobated by historians. He was thrice married, and was succeeded, at his death, in 1201, by his son by his first consort, Orgueilleuse, daughter of the lord of Harenc.

BOHEMOND IV., surnamed *le Borgne*, usurped the principality, at the death of his father, in violation of the rights of Raymond Rupin, son of his elder brother Raymond, who had succeeded his godfather Raymond, as count of Tripoli, during the life of Bohemond III. He also deprived Raymond of Tripoli, but this double act of rapacity drew on him the hostility of Livon, or Leo, king of Armenia, and uncle of Raymond Rupin. Bohemond was twice driven from Antioch, which each time remained several years in the possession of Raymond; but the death of his rival, in 1222, left him master both of Antioch and Tripoli till his death, in 1233.

BOHEMOND V., son and successor of the preceding, is known only by his wars with the Kharizmians who invaded Syria, and with the Armenians, in both which he was unsuccessful; he died 1251 or 1253, and was succeeded by his son,

BOHEMOND VI., under whom Antioch was taken by the Mamluke sultan Bibars, May 29, 1268. (See BIBARS.) Bohemond retired to Tripoli, where he died 1274.

BOHEMOND VII., son of the preceding, succeeded as count of Tripoli, but died childless 1287. The succession to Tripoli was disputed by his mother and sister; but the capture of the city in the following year, by Calaoun, sultan of Egypt and Syria, terminated the claims of both parties.

BOHIER, (Nicholas,) in Latin *Boerius*, a learned French lawyer, who died at Bordeaux, May 10, 1579, leaving some Latin works written in the barbarous style of his age, but valuable for their contents. The most important of them to literature generally is, Tractatus de Officio et Potestate Legati à latere in Regno Francorum, Lyons, 1509, 8vo. But others of his works, upon subjects more strictly professional, have obtained the greatest notice in France. (Biog. Univ.)

BOHL, (John Christian,) a celebrated physician, born at Koenigsberg, Nov. 19, 1703. Having begun his education there, he then passed to Leipsic and Leyden, at the latter of which places he became M.D. in 1726. Upon his return to Koenigsberg, he was chosen professor of medicine in the university, an appointment which he retained during life. He was made physician to the court in 1734, and to the king of Prussia in 1742. He died December 29, 1785, having published, Diss. de Morsu, Lugd. Bat. 1726, 4to. Diss. Epist. ad Ruyschium de Usu novarum Cavæ propaginum in Systemate Chylopœo, Amst. 1727, 4to. Diss. sistens Hist. Nat. Viæ Lacteæ Corporis Humani, Koenigsb. 1741, 4to. Diss. super Nervorum Actione et Collisione, *ib.* 1762, 4to. Programma de Insensibilitate Tendinum. *ib.* 1764, 4to. De Virium Corporis Humani Scrutinio Medico, *ib.* 1766, 4to. Programma de Lacte Aberrante, *ib.* 1772, 4to. Bohl also published a Latin translation of one of the works of Ruysch, under the title of Fr. Ruyschii Observationes Anatomicæ de Musculo in Fundo Uteri detecto, Amst. 1726, 4to.

BOHN, (John,) a celebrated physician and physiologist, born at Leipsic, July 20, 1640. After acquiring the rudiments of his general education in his native city, he removed to Jena to study medicine, whence he returned in 1659 to attend the professors at Leipsic. In 1663 he travelled, and visited the most celebrated universities in Denmark, Holland, England, France, and Switzerland. In 1666 he took the degree of M.D. at Leipsic, and in 1668 he was appointed professor of anatomy. In 1690 he was made physician to the city, and in the following year professor of therapeutics, and in 1700 he was elected dean of his faculty. He is well known in the history of medicine, from being the first to oppose the chemical doctrines of Francis de la Boe, and to demonstrate by experiment the fallacy of his system and statements. He proved that the bile did not contain any free alkali, and that the pancreatic juice was not of an acid nature. In his physiological opinions he principally followed Borelli, but ventured to differ from him on several points. He distinctly marked the difference of voluntary and involuntary muscles. He advocated the Harveian doctrine of the circulation of the blood, and demonstrated its course at Pavia by the machine invented by Boyle. He supported the opinions of Regnier de Graaf with regard to the pre-existence of germs in the ovaria; but his notions with respect to the nutrition of the fœtus appear to have been very imperfect. His reputation is greatest on the subject of medico-legal investigations, and he was frequently consulted on questions of medical jurisprudence by the tribunals of Germany. He was held in much esteem, and he died deeply regretted, December 19, 1718. He published a great number of works, of which the following are the most important:—Exercitationes Physiologicæ xxvi. Lips. 1668, 1677, 4to. Circulus Anatomico-Physiologicus, seu Œconomia Corporis Animalis, *ib.* 1680, 1686, 1697, 1710, 4to. Diss. de Alcali et Acidi insufficientiâ pro principiorum, &c. *ib.* 1681, 1696, 8vo. Observationes quædam Anatomicæ circa Structuram Vasorum Biliarorum, &c. *ib.* 1682, 1683, 4to. Diss. Chymico-Physicæ, *ib.* 1685, 1696, 4to. De Renunciatione Vulnerum, *ib.* 1689, 1711, 1755, 8vo, Amst. 1710, 12mo, shewing what wounds are necessarily fatal. Diss. de Duumviratu Hypochondriarum, Lips. 1689, 4to. De Rationis et Experientiæ Connubio in Praxi Medica, *ib.* 1689, 4to. De Motu Cordis, *ib.* 1690, 4to. Medicinæ Forensis Specimina iii. *ib.* 1690, 1691, 1692, 4to. Diss. de Anat. et Therap. Studii Conspiratione, &c. *ib.* 1691, 4to. De Utilitate Anatomes subtilioris in Praxi Medicâ, *ib.* 1691, 4to. De Officio Medici Duplici, Clinico nimirum et forensi, *ib.* 1704, 4to. He also printed several papers in the Acta Eruditorum, and published editions of the works of Fabricius de Aquapendente and Bellini.

BOHN, (John Sylvester,) a professor of theology, and a clergyman at Erfurt, born there 1712, and educated at Erfurt and Leipsic. He filled successively various educational and clerical offices in his native town. He was a member of the Erfurt Academy of Useful Sciences. He was the first who established periodicals of a miscellaneous character at Erfurt, and some of his journals obtained considerable circulation in other parts of Germany. He was the editor of Pleasant Evening Hours, Erfurt, 1748-50; The Bachelor, 1751, 1752, 8vo; The World, a weekly journal, Erf. 1753; Religion, 3 vols, Erf. 1755-57. He also wrote, Considerations on the Discourses of Jesus, 4 vols, Erf. 1757-59; some sermons and other religious works. In the pulpit he distinguished himself by his eloquence and taste, and in private life by his mild and tolerant character. He died of consumption, April 24, 1762.

BOHNENBERGER, (Gottlieb Christopher,) a clergyman at Altburg, near Kalw, in Wirtemberg, born at Neuenbürg, 1732, and educated at Tubingen, a man of general talent, and a good mechanician. He discovered a modification of the electric machine, of which he published an account, Stutt. 1784. He was also the author of Contributions to Theoretical and Practical Electricity, Stutt. 1793-95. These works are enriched with the results of many difficult and ingenious experiments. His work on Turning, Nuremb. 1799, 8vo, recommends itself, as indeed do all his writings, by its perspicuity, practical character, and by the cheapness of the apparatus which it describes. The treatises of this author can make no pretensions to systematic completeness, for he seldom draws general conclusions; they are also too diffuse, but have a certain value from the industry and ingenuity of the author in experimentalizing, and from their lively style. He died at Altburg, 1807.

BOHSE, (Augustus,) known as a writer under the name of Talander, born at Halle, 1661, studied law at Leipsic and Jena, and repaired, in 1685, to Hamburg, where for three years he gave to young people of the higher orders lectures on the elements of law, on eloquence, and the German epistolary style. He afterwards gave similar instruction for two years at Dresden, and then for a short time at Halle. After the death of his father, in 1691, he returned to Leipsic, where his lectures on rhetoric met with distinguished applause. But he only remained here half a year, till he received the appointment of secretary to the duke of Saxe-Weissenfels, who maintained at his court an excellent theatre, for which it was Bohse's principal occupation to write operettas. He subsequently lectured on rhetoric, &c. at Erfurt; took, in

1700, the degree of doctor of laws at Jena, and became a successful teacher at that university. He was finally appointed professor at the Ritterakademie, at Lieguitz, where he died, at an advanced age, between the thirtieth and fortieth years of the last century. Bohse, under the name of Talander, was one of the most noted writers of his day, and, according to Jördens, F. Horn, and others, was the first German who made literature his profession; but Reese, in Ersch's Encyclopædia, remarks that this had been previously done by Happel, who, in 1648, published a novel, called the Asiatic Onogambo. Bohse was the author of a great number of wretched, diffuse novels, somewhat in the style of those of duke Anthony Ulrick of Brunswick and Lohenstein. He published also a translation of Guarini's Pastor Fido, and several insipid Guides to German Correspondence, and other works, which appear to have suited the childish taste of the time. For a list of them, see Koch's Hist. of the Language and Literature of the Germans, vol. ii. pp. 251, 253; and Adelung, continuation of Jöcher, vol. i.

BOHUN, (Edmund,) a voluminous English writer, born at Ringsfield, in Suffolk, only son of Baxter Bohun, who, with his ancestors, had been lords of the manor of Westhall, in that county, from 25 Hen. VIII. Edmund was admitted fellow-commoner of Queen's college, Cambridge, in 1663, but driven from the university by the plague in 1666, considerably to his disadvantage as a scholar. In 1675 he was put into the commission of the peace for his native county, but in the second of James II. he was dismissed. On the establishment of William and Mary, the county members, without any application from himself, recommended his restoration, and this was done. He was alive in 1700, but the date of his death does not appear. Wood calls him "a worthy person;" and he certainly was a most industrious writer. He published An Address to the Freeholders and Freemen of the Nation, being the history of three sessions of parliament, the first of which began Oct. 21, 1678, and the last of them ended Jan. 10, 1680. A Defence of the Declaration of King Charles II. against a pamphlet, entitled, *A Just and Modest Vindication of the Proceedings of the two last Parliaments.* A Defence of Sir Rob. Filmer against the Mistakes and Representations of Algernon Sidney, Esq. in a Paper delivered by him to the Sheriffs on the Scaffold on Tower-hill, on Friday, December 7, 1683, before his Execution there. The Justice of Peace, his Calling, a moral essay. A Preface and Conclusion to Sir Rob. Filmer's *Patriarcha*, or the *Natural Law of Kings*, added to the second and perfect edition of that book. A Geographical Dictionary, representing the present and ancient Names of all the Countries, Provinces, remarkable Cities, &c. of the whole World, with a short Historical Account of the same and their present state, Lond. 1688, 8vo. The History of the Desertion, or an Account of all the Public Affairs in England, from the beginning of Sept. 1688, to the 12th of February following. An Answer to a piece called *The Desertion Discussed.* The Doctrine of Passive Obedience, or Non-resistance no way concerned in the Controversies now depending between the Williamites and Jacobites. The Life of Bishop Jewel, prefixed to a translation of his *Apology.* Three Charges delivered at the Quarter-Sessions for Suffolk. The great Historical, Geographical, and Poetical Dictionary, Lond. 1694, fol. wherein are inserted, The last Five Years' Historical and Geographical Collections, which the said Edm. Bohun, esq. designed for his own Geographical Dictionary, and never extant till in this work. Besides these original works, and the translation above mentioned, Bohun produced English versions of several books, among them of Sleidan's History of the Reformation. (Wood's Athenæ, iii. 217.)

BOHUSZ, (Xavier,) a Polish historian, born in Lithuania, January 1, 1746, and educated in the university of Wilna. He travelled over most parts of Europe, and collected an immense mass of information, which he preserved in three large volumes. Being involved in the troubles of his unfortunate country, the Russians banished him to Siberia, and he did not return home until after a long exile. He died at Warsaw, in 1825, permanently established in a high position among historical writers by his Researches on the History and Language of the Lithuanians, published in 1808. This work was reprinted in 1828. (Biog. Univ. Suppl.)

BOIARDO, (Matthew Maria,) count of Scandiano, of a noble and opulent family, settled at Ferrara, but originally from Reggio; according to Mazzuchelli, on the authority of Foscarini, in his Annot. to the Museum Illust. Poet., born at Fratta, a family estate, not far from

Ferrara, in June, 1430, of Gaspar Boiardo and Cornelia degli Api. Tiraboschi, in the text of his Istoria della Letteratura Ital. adopted this statement; but in a subsequent note to the same work, on the authority of Dr. Barotti, changed his opinion, and mentioned count John Boiardo and Lucia Strozzi, sister to the celebrated poet, Titus Vespasian to have been his parents; and afterwards, in his Biblioteca Modenese, endeavoured to prove the year 1434 as the date, and Scandiano as the probable place of the birth of our author, where his family held a sort of court. At Ferrara, where he received his education under Socino Benzi, a celebrated philosopher, he took his degree in philosophy and law, obtained the protection of Borso d'Este, duke of Modena and Reggio, accompanied him to Rome, where that prince went in 1471, to receive from pope Paul III. the investiture of the dukedom of Ferrara, and in the following year was sent by Hercules I., his successor, to receive and accompany to Ferrara his bride, Eleonora of Aragon, daughter of Ferdinand, king of Naples. Boiardo was honoured by that prince with knighthood, employed in affairs of importance, appointed in 1478 governor of Reggio, translated in 1481 to Modena, and not long after reinstated at Reggio, where he died, according to Mazzuchelli, on the 20th of February, and according to Tiraboschi, on the 20th December, 1494. He was buried in the cathedral of Ferrara, which circumstance has induced other writers to believe that he died in that city. Boiardo has left many works, both in verse and in prose; but the one to which he principally owes his celebrity, is Orlando Innamorato, a romantic poem, which gave to Ariosto the first idea of his Furioso. By Crescimbeni it is wrongly considered as the very first of the sort: it is generally and justly reckoned one of the four best. It seems to have been written for the amusement of the court of the duke Hercules, before whom Boiardo was in the habit of reading what he wrote; and notwithstanding the great faults of style, many of which would probably have been corrected, had he not been prevented by death from revising; it is an admirable work, from richness of imagination, truth of character, and pictures of that chivalric life, with which by his rank he was well acquainted. He left it unfinished, having reached only to the ninth canto of the third book, owing, as he says in the last stanza, to the invasion of the French under Charles III., who entered Florence a few months before Boiardo's death, on his way to the conquest of Naples. The poem was published for the first time in 1495, in Scandiano, by means of his son count Camillus, and several times afterwards republished at Venice. Nicholas Agostini, a Venetian, wrote a very inferior continuation of it, in three books, divided into thirty-three cantos, which, together with the original of Boiardo, passed through several editions, the first of which was in 1545. But before him, Lewis Domenico, his countryman, and Francis Berni, went farther, the former in correcting and improving, the latter in remaking the whole poem, which he published in 1541; and through the applause with which his work was received he has rendered the editions of Boiardo's original extremely rare. As, however, Berni's work, although highly meritorious, is in his peculiar style, many other poets attempted to remodel Boiardo after his own sober and grave manner; but no one has carried the undertaking through, so that Berni's alteration is the form in which the work of our author is now generally seen. Being a scholar, and well versed in the classical languages, Boiardo has left many translations of the Greek and Latin writers. They are, Apulejo dell' Asino d'Oro, Venezia, 1516—1518, 8vo, and 1519, 12mo. L'Asino d'Oro di Luciano, &c. Venezia, 1525. Erodote Alicarnasseo, &c., Venezia, 1533—1538, 8vo. A Chronicle of the Roman Emperors, from Charlemagne to Otho IV. &c., which he calls a translation of Ricobaldo of Ferrara, but which Tiraboschi and Muratori, who has published it, have thought Boiardo's own. Timone, Comedia, (in five acts, considered by the best critics the most ancient of the Italian comedies, and by Crescimbeni a farce,) a translation in *terza rima*, from Lucian's Timon. It was written and represented on the occasion of the magnificent spectacles given by the duke Hercules I., and published at Scandiano in 1500, and several times afterwards at Venice. Sonetti e Canzoni, Reggio, 1499, divided into three books, highly and deservedly esteemed, and such as to show, that if Boiardo had written the Innamorato in the same style that appears in the composition of these lyric poems, no one would have ever dared to alter even a syllable of it.

BOIELDIEU, (Francis Adrian,) an eminent musical composer, born at

Rouen, December 16, 1775, where his father was secretary to the archbishop. At seven he had begun to play upon the harpsichord, and in two years more to *improvise* upon the organ. His instructor was Broche, organist of the cathedral, whose severity drove him, when very young, to run away and go on foot to Paris, but who treated him with greater kindness when brought back to his family. Under this master Boieldieu made a rapid progress, and in 1795 he resolved, but now with his family's approbation, to try his fortune in the capital. His first efforts there as a composer were deemed extremely feeble; the fierce and tumultuous passions of a revolutionary public requiring energy rather than grace, even in a theatre. But his unquestionable talents, which gradually made their way into notice, and his great success as a music-master, caused him to be named professor of the piano at the Conservatory. It was while fully occupied, it was said, with his class, that he chiefly wrote the melodies of the Calif of Bagdad, which appeared in 1799, and had immense success. In 1802 Boieldieu married a famous opera dancer; but finding his domestic happiness ruined, instead of secured by this connexion, he suddenly determined, in 1803, upon settling in Russia. He was there made master of the imperial chapel, and lived several years with great distinction, producing various works, of which Telemachus, an opera, in three acts, was considered by himself his master-piece; and it gained him great applause. He became, however, impatient of his Russian exile, in spite of its various gratifications and advantages. Hence he solicited permission to revisit his country in 1811, and on returning to Paris he regained immediately all his former popularity. But residence in Russia had injured his constitution, and after some years of suffering he died at Jarcy, near Grosbois, October 8, 1834. His obsequies were celebrated in the Church of the Invalids, the archbishop of Paris having forbidden them in that of St. Roch. As a composer, Boieldieu is characterised by a sweet and natural melody, accompaniments simple, but agreeable, an expressive gaiety, and a great variety in imagination. (Biog. Univ. Suppl. Biog. des Contemp.)

BOIGNE, (Benedict, Count,) a military officer, first known in the wars of Hindostan, and subsequently as a distinguished benefactor of Chambery, in Savoy. He was born there, March 8, 1741, of a tradesman's family, and educated for the law. Disliking this vocation, he left his family, gave up his real name, *Le Borgne*, the *One-eyed*, and entered an Irish regiment, in the French service, for which strong, tall, and good-looking men like him, were particularly sought. His duty now took him to the Isle of France, where he remained eighteen months, but when he returned to Europe, there appeared so little hope of promotion, in spite of all his endeavours to deserve it, that he solicited permission to withdraw, and entered the Russian service. While thus employed, he was taken prisoner by the Turks, in 1780, and remained in captivity until peace was made; when again finding his prospects unsatisfactory, he left the empress Catharine's army, and made his way to India, after undergoing several difficulties. When arrived in the country, he was first obliged to gain a subsistence by teaching fencing, for which he was excellently qualified. At length he obtained a commission in a battalion of native infantry, but it was inferior to that which he had recently resigned in the Russian service. The troop, however, to which he was attached, perished almost entirely under an attack by Hyder Ally; and Boigne himself would most probably have been killed, had he not been sent in another direction just before the disaster. He now became dissatisfied once more, demanded his discharge, and resolved upon returning to Europe by land. Before he set out upon this journey, then very difficult and hazardous, he was presented to the English governor, the ill-used Warren Hastings, to whom his talents and services procured him recommendations, and who evidently sent him upon some secret errands among the native powers, for which his ostensible object of returning home overland might afford facilities. New introductions were thus placed in his way, and profiting by them skilfully, Boigne became general to a Hindostanee prince, and he proved a most successful one. His exertions being liberally rewarded, and some commercial speculations adding to his facilities for accumulating a fortune, when Boigne found his health fail, and counsel an immediate return to Europe, he was very wealthy. His Indian career is detailed in Mémoires sur la Carrière Politique et Militaire du Général Boigne, published at Chambéry, in 1828, by the Academical Society of Savoy, and reprinted in 1830.

When the successful officer first came to Europe, he thought of establishing himself in London, and he married a daughter of the marquis of Osmond, formerly French ambassador at the court of St. James's; but this young lady's age was most unsuitable, and his union with her, he quickly saw, could give him nothing but uneasiness. He determined, accordingly, upon a final retreat from the gay world to his native mountains. His latter days were spent at a beautiful villa close to Chambéry, upon which town he conferred a series of the most important benefits. He died there, June 21, 1830, and his funeral was conducted with all those marks of public respect which his abilities, and still more his patriotic liberality, had so richly earned. Like other successful men, Boigne did not escape obloquy. When on his way for Europe, he brought with him to Calcutta a regiment of Persian horse, which he commanded, and made over its services to the East India Company for a large sum of money. This transaction was mixed up with other circumstances, and the ruin of Tippoo Saib was attributed to Boigne's sordid treachery. (Biog. Univ. Suppl.)

BOILEAU, (Gilles,) eldest brother, by the whole blood, of the celebrated French poet; originally an advocate, but for the last four months of his life an officer in the royal household. His father, also named Gilles, highly respected for probity and habits of business, was registrar of the great chamber of the parliament of Paris. His family was ancient and noble, dating its importance from Stephen Boileau, provost of Paris under St. Lewis. The registrar was born at Paris, in 1584, and married twice, his talented sons being by the second wife. He died at his official residence, in the *Palais*, in 1637. The younger Gilles was also a Parisian, born in 1631; and as his age advanced, he discovered literary talents of some value. He published, in 1653, a translation of the Picture of Cebes, and two years afterwards another of the Enchiridion of Epictetus, with his life, and a sketch of his philosophy. This latter production gained him great credit, the Greek text being well rendered, and the account of Epictetus ably compiled. The translator, however, was not equally successful in a version of Diogenes Laertius, which appeared in 1668. He died in the following year, having besides published some small original pieces. In 1670, his illustrious brother, Nicholas, published some pieces of poetry that he left, with some letters, a translation of the fourth Æneid, and other things of less note, under the title of Œuvres Posthumes, 12mo. The two brothers had not been upon good terms, the elder being charged, in after times, with ill using the younger from jealousy of his rising talents; but before separated by death they had happily become reconciled. Gilles, though a man of learning and talent, was without sufficient industry for doing full justice to himself. He would not consume time upon the finishing of his literary works, and hence they really have less value than he might have given them. He even found fault with Nicholas for wisely pursuing a very different course; and when he remarked his care to retouch and supply, pronounced him deficient in genius, and consequently hopeless of distinction unless by dint of extraordinary labour. Nor was he even cured of this rash and illiberal impression by the success which attended his first satires. He would allow them no other charm than that of novelty, and foretold their oblivion when this should be gone. (Biog. Univ.)

BOILEAU, (James,) next brother of the preceding, born at Paris, March 16, 1633, a doctor of the Sorbonne, and a theologian of considerable eminence. He died in 1716, possessed of a canonry at Paris, and after acting for twenty-five years as dean and official of the diocese of Sens. His long life having been spent in scholarly pursuits, he left many evidences of the great erudition that it had amassed; but they were not individually of any considerable bulk, were generally of the class that may be designated as curious; and most of them appeared either anonymously, or with fictitious names. Among them are, De Antiquo Jure Presbyterorum in Regimine Ecclesiastico, published in 1676, under the name of Claudius Fonteius, and maintaining the association of presbyters in the government of the primitive church. Historia Confessionis Auricularis, 1683, a work of great research, intended to establish, against Daillé, that auricular confession had ever been esteemed necessary in the church. Historia Flagellantium, 1700, a work that made a great noise, proving that voluntary flagellations were unknown to primitive Christianity, had given rise to great errors and abuses, were injurious to health, and had never been tolerated in the Church without repugnance. This piece gave a variety of particulars respecting the fanatical sect of Flagellants, with other matters, having a mixture of indecency, over which Latin threw a veil. But an anonymous writer thought it likely to sell in French, and accordingly published a translation of it, in which all the passages unfit for indiscriminate perusal were made common to every reader. Boileau published a remonstrance against this unauthorized use of his labours, complaining that he was brought forward as author, softening down some things that incautiously trenched upon decency, and correcting various oversights. A new edition of this translation was published in 1732, with an historical preface, in which the exceptionable passages have been either suppressed, or made less offensive. Historica Disquisitio de Re Vestiaria Hominis Sacri, Vitam Communem More Civili traducentis, 1704, a piece levelled at the restriction of clergymen to a peculiar style of dress in ordinary life, maintaining its total want of authority in primitive times. Disquisitio Theologica de Sanguine Corporis Christi post Resurrectionem, ad Epistolam 146 S. Augustini, 1681, one of Boileau's most learned works, written against Allix, minister at Charenton; against whom he also published a new edition of Ratramn, with a French translation, preface, and notes. Notwithstanding his learned industry, James Boileau had an inexhaustible fund of playful gaiety, that contrasted rather oddly with his erudition, and liked bishops very little, but Jesuits still less; describing them as "gentry that lengthen the creed and shorten the commandments." (Biog. Univ.)

BOILEAU, (Nicholas,) sieur Despréaux, hence commonly called Despréaux by the French, youngest brother of the preceding, and one of the greatest poetical geniuses produced by their country; born at Paris, or in its immediate neighbourhood, November 1, 1636. His birth has been referred to the following year, apparently from a slip of memory, or piece of court flattery, once addressed to Lewis XIV. "When were you born, Despréaux?" he once asked. "At the most glorious of all periods for me," was the reply; "just one year before your majesty, as if on purpose to celebrate the wonders of your reign." As a young boy he seems to have shown that inattention to ordinary things which enables intellectual children to lay a solid foundation for their own intellectual stores, but which ordinary observers commonly consider very unpromising. Hence his own father said, comparing him with his brothers, considering him, apparently, a kind-hearted child, of slender capacity, "As for Colin, he is a good boy, that will never speak ill of any body." One of his instructors did, however, detect rudiments of excellence in his verses, and predicted his future eminence as a poet. His original destination was the bar, and he not only studied for it, and with considerable success, but was even admitted as an advocate. He was then twenty, and might probably, with his legal connexions, and superior abilities, have soon made his way to practice, had he not fancied himself quite unequal to an everlasting hunt for quibbles, and to representing falsehood as the truth. He determined, accordingly, upon giving up the law, to the great scandal of his family, who sought unanimously to change his purpose, and *turned pale*, he says, when all their words were evidently wasted. His next movement was upon theology, but a trial of the Sorbonne only filled him with a new disgust. He could not endure the thorny mazes of school-divinity, and expressed extreme surprise in seeing endless arguments upon vital truths, just as if they were airy speculations. He soon, therefore, quitted the Sorbonne *to stray upon Parnassus*. His father, in fact, had been dead some years, and had left him a small independence, about one-third of which he sank in the purchase of an annuity. Hence he could indulge his own inclinations; an opportunity to which he was, no doubt, much indebted for discerning the dishonesty of lawyers, and the crabbed sophistry of divines. His first appearance in the poetical world was as a satirist. He wrote some pungent pieces, exposing the bad taste and other evils of his day, with all the fire of youth, and the personal liberties that it is prone to take; but with far greater skill and care in composition than had hitherto been known in France. He was naturally willing that effusions of so much merit should circulate among his friends, but manuscript copies of them rapidly gained more extensive notice. Many of their best passages found a way into most cultivated societies; with verses, however, that were really his, Boileau found others often associated which he never penned, and which were altogether unworthy of his rising fame. They were even printed in this manner, what he wrote most incorrectly, and joined with pieces of which he knew nothing, but which were thus put abroad under sanction of his name. He therefore determined upon printing himself; and the royal privilege having been obtained, he published in 1666 his first seven satires. They are greatly inferior to his later productions; but La Harpe has pronounced them the first poetry in the French language, which displayed a thorough acquaintance with the mechanism of its verse, which attained a style ever elegant and pure, and which uniformly charmed the ear. Their success, accordingly, was prodigious; but although undoubtedly owing, in some degree, to the ill-nature of mankind, which delights in the exposure and ridicule of others, it arose much more from such a development of poetical powers as French literature had never hitherto been able to boast. Individuals brought under Boileau's lash were necessarily offended by his publication, and lost no opportunity of depreciating talents which they found so formidable. This gave rise to the young poet's eighth satire, composed in 1667, and published in the following year; which, under colour of censuring his own faults, or rather those of his genius, makes his opponents look more ridiculous than ever. This is considered unquestionably the best of his satires, and has been preferred to all that antiquity has left in that line. Boileau having thus founded for his country a new style of poetry, thought himself qualified for giving law upon the subject to others; and in 1673 appeared his Art of Poetry, a work preferred by his countrymen to Horace's poem of the same name, as being more regular in plan, more happy in its transitions, and superior in style. It greatly augmented his popularity, and foreigners gladly made it their own by means of translations. This service was rendered to England about 1680, by a Suffolk gentleman, named Soame, subsequently Sir William, by a patent of baronetcy from Charles II., Feb. 5, 1684. He died without issue male on his way to Constantinople, whither he was proceeding as ambassador, under James II., and had been intimately acquainted with Dryden, to whom he showed his version, desiring him to revise it. The poet kept it more than six months, and made very considerable alterations in it, particularly at the beginning of the fourth canto. He also thought it better to substitute English names for the French; and the translator coming into his opinion, he undertook to make the change. In this state the English version of Boileau's Art of Poetry appeared in 1683; and as Dryden so largely aided in bringing it satisfactorily before his countrymen, it may commonly be seen among that great poet's works.

Boileau, having hitherto trodden in the steps of Horace, appeared, in 1674, as a follower of Alexander Tassoni, who published at Paris, in 1622, a mock heroic, entitled, La Secchia Rapita, or Rape of the Bucket, which throws a merited air of ridicule over a hostile incursion, made long before, of the Bolognese to recover a bucket, carried off in a recent petty war by the people of Modena. A similar display of ill-will occurred in Paris; a violent quarrel having arisen there among the members of a chapter, from the placing and displacing of a reading-desk. Much as this had become the talk of the town, the president Lamoignon, defied Boileau to make anything of it as a subject for poetry. But it was really a subject germane to the poet's taste. Like his brother James, he hated Jesuits, and he had very little affection for any clerical fraternities; hence he was well pleased with an opportunity for turning out a body of canons to ridicule, as men given up to sleep and eating. He produced, accordingly, upon a theme, apparently so very unpromising, and really far more trifling than that which elicited Tassoni's pleasantry, Le Lutrin, the most popular of his poems. Its fame, indeed, is richly earned by a poignancy of wit and satire, by an elegance and superiority of numberless couplets, and by an ingenious adaptation of classical passages, which none but a master-spirit could approach. The Rape of the Lock, a similar piece, published in 1712, by Pope, has naturally been compared with Boileau's Lutrin. The English poet could hardly have undertaken his task without thinking of his French predecessor, any more than the latter could without remembering Tassoni; but plagiarism is wholly out of the question in either case. Pulci had, in fact, found a precedent for Tassoni; and all these eminent men really did nothing more than throw the charm of their genius around a style of writing, already existing in burlesque romances, and in numberless effusions of gaiety, which aim at teaching truth with a laughing face instead of a sad one. The French critics greatly prefer Le Lutrin to The Rape of the Lock; maintaining that its first four cantos have nothing comparable of their kind in any language; the powers of invention, painting, and language, displayed in them, being pronounced altogether superior to those displayed by Pope in the corresponding poem.

Boileau having thus challenged a comparison with Tassoni, returned subsequently to his original association with Horace, by publishing, at various times, a series of epistles. These have obtained more applause from posterity than his satires, although their popularity has naturally suffered from the number of later versifiers whom Boileau himself taught to write poetry. While he was really the only Frenchman who had attained a mastery over versification, the equable and elaborate strain of his Epistles excited universal admiration: now that the writers, whose credit he destroyed, have sunk into oblivion, his own great superiority is overlooked. Men are more prone to compare him with first-rate geniuses like himself, and especially with Horace, who had evidently fired him with emulation. He has not, however, the great Roman's colloquial ease. Marks of labour everywhere force themselves upon a discerning reader, and occasionally make him feel that his own pleasure must have been purchased at the price of his author's pain. In the more serious walks of literature, Boileau was not particularly successful. His ode on the taking of Namur, laid him open to bitter criticism; but it was translated into Latin by Rollin. His epigrams are of acknowledged inferiority; and his prose, though clear and correct, has few other claims to consideration. He seems, indeed, himself to have been aware of the difficulties that awaited him on any other than poetic ground. In 1677 he was appointed joint-historiographer of France, with Racine, and the two poets attended the king sometimes in his military movements to chronicle his exploits. But neither of them left any historical detail of the least importance. Boileau, indeed, made a joke of his unfitness for such a purpose. "When I was," he said, "at my old trade of satirist, which I understood pretty well, I got hardly any thing but menaces and insults; I have now taken up the trade of history, which I know nothing about, and am capitally paid for it." In private life, Boileau was an amiable man. "He is never cruel," said Madame de Sevigné, "but in verse." He did, however, by his wit and severity, arm a host of tongues and pens against him. Hence many represented him as an envious calumniator, who thought of nothing but raising his own reputation by ruining that of other men. He does, indeed, give way to a bitter scorn, which probably outstepped sometimes the bounds of justice; but false taste was so rampant in the literature of France when first he started into eminence, that nothing short of unsparing hostilities against it had any prospect of raising the poetic standard. For such a warfare Boileau had all the requisite boldness and ability. The sufferers under it, however, naturally complained, and endeavoured to retaliate; but bystanders laughed at their distress, and posterity has pronounced their treatment quite as good as they deserved. It was not, besides, their assailant's nature to consider others when the pen was in his hand. His great deficiency as an author, is insensibility; and here he falls greatly below Pope, with whom, in subjects, and in the kind of service rendered to literature, he has commonly been compared, as he must ever be. Seldom treading any other paths than those of reason and raillery, his moral tone is firm and severe, but very rarely noble; few authors having discovered less of pity or consideration for the weaknesses and hardships of mankind. Yet when Boileau came into personal contact with other men, he was capable of a generous self-devotion for their sakes. He found Patru on the point of parting with his library, the great pride and comfort of his life, to meet the demand of a clamorous creditor. He advanced him a sum more than sufficient to save the books, only stipulating that he should have them after his decease. When Colbert died, Corneille, then old, infirm, and declining, lost his pension. Boileau went to the king, and offered to transfer his own to the poverty-stricken poet, saying, that he should be ashamed of receiving the royal bounty when such a man as Corneille stood so much more in need of it. He was also liberal to his servants; and highly charitable, both living and dying, to the poor. His life was closed by dropsy in the chest, March 13, 1711, he having often said, not long before, "It is a great comfort to a dying poet, that he has written nothing injurious to morality." (Hallam's Literature of Europe, iv. 410. Dryden's Works. Biog. Univ. Chaufepié.)

Boileau's life has been written by Desmaizeaux, Amst. 1712, 12mo. Of his works, numerous impressions have appeared, but the edition of 1747 has been most valued. He left behind him the Satires, Epistles, Art of Poetry, Le Lutrin, Epigrams, and some other poetical pieces, both French and Latin; together with a Dialogue on Poetry and Music; another on the Heroes of Romance, a translation of Longinus on the Sublime, and some remarks of his own upon that author. Boileau was also one of the authors employed upon the great work in folio, entitled, Médailles sur les Principaux Evénemens du Règne de Louis le Grand, Paris, 1723; so that his appointment of royal historiographer was not wholly without fruit. He has, indeed, been thought also to have produced, in conjunction with his coadjutor Racine, the Campagne de Louis XIV., published under the name of Pelisson, in 1730, and again with the names of Boileau and Racine affixed, in 1784 with this title, Eloge Historique de Louis XIV., sur ses Conquêtes, depuis 1672, Jusqu'en 1678. These two associated poets were charged likewise to correct the style of the Constitutions de la Maison de St. Cyr, printed at Paris, in 1700.

BOILEAU, (Charles,) preacher to Lewis XIV. He died at Paris in 1704, and left some Lent sermons, and panegyrics, published after his death.—Another Boileau, named John James, also a religious French writer, died at Paris, March 10, 1735.—Another, named James René, director of the Sevres porcelaine manufactory, which he much improved, died in 1772. (Biog. Univ.)—Another, named Maria Lewis Joseph, descended, like the famous poet, from the ancient provost of Paris, was born at Dunkirk in 1741, and died at Paris, in 1817. He was a lawyer and literary man, but of little distinction, and the only one of his works likely to interest a foreigner, is, Histoire Ancienne et Moderne des Départemens Belgiques.—Another Boileau, Esmé Francis Maria, born at Auxerre, December 21, 1759, descended also from the provost of Paris, was a French country gentleman, whose amusement was the study of antiquities, and who died September 25, 1826, while engaged upon the publication of a curious work by Stephen Boyleaux, Sur les Métiers du 13 Siècle. He had already produced some small pieces on French antiquities. (Biog. Univ. Suppl.)

BOILLOT, the surname of some persons who have obtained a certain degree of celebrity in France. Henry, a Jesuit, born in Franche Comté, September 29, 1698, died at Dôle, rector of the college there, July 3, 1733, leaving an explication, Latin and French, on the second book of Horace's Satires, with other works, partly religious, partly educational.—John, a friar, who died in 1728, published some French religious books.—Philibert, a priest of the Oratory, who died in 1729, left a Latin poem, entitled, Passeres, and another in French, both inserted in the Mémoires de Littérature.—Joseph, an architect, alive in 1603, but how much longer is unknown, engineer to Henry IV.; published, in 1592, Nouveaux Portraits et Figures de Termes pour user en l'Architecture; and in 1598, Modèles d'Artifices de Feu, et de divers Instrumens de Guerre, avec les Moyens de s'en prevaloir pour assiéger, battre et defendre toutes Sortes de Places. (Biog. Univ.)

BOINDIN, (Nicholas,) a French writer, born in 1676, son of a placeman under government, and eventually one himself. He was a very sickly child, and hence unable to enter into the sports that interest early years; a peculiarity that forced him inwards upon himself, and nurtured both inquisitive habits and conceit. In 1696 he entered the army, but weakness of constitution obliged him to quit it at the end of a year. In after life he occupied himself very much with literature; and in 1706 he was admitted into the Academy of Inscriptions and Elegant Literature, for which he wrote some dissertations on classical subjects. He might also, from other claims to notice as a man of information, have been a member of the French Academy, had not just exception been taken to him as a professed atheist. He died in 1751; and his collected works were published in 2 vols, 12mo, two years afterwards, one of the most important of them being a dissertation, Sur les Sons de la Langue Française. This collection is headed by an autobiographical account of the author, which displays all the conceit and arrogance that any good judge of human nature would expect to find in a man like Boindin. (Biog. Univ.)

BOINVILLIERS, (John Stephen Judith Forestier de,) a laborious grammarian, born at Versailles, July 3, 1764, who died May 1, 1830. When the revolution broke out, he was among the most ardent of its admirers; but he bitterly deplored, afterwards, the enormities that it produced. His works are numerous, but chiefly connected with education, which formed the business of his life, and they are likely to be little known or valued out of France. (Biog. Univ.)

BOIREL, the surname of two French surgeons, in the seventeenth century, brothers, of whom Anthony published, in 1677, a Treatise on Wounds in the Head, of some value, from a number of exact observations.—The other, Nicholas, wrote upon Syphilis, but with little success. (Biog. Univ.)

BOIS, (Andrew du,) or Sylvius, prior of the abbey of Marchiennes, in the diocese of Arras, a writer of the twelfth century, who compiled, by the persuasion of Peter, bishop of Arras, a history of the kings of France of the first race, entitled, De Rebus Gestis, et Successione Regum Francorum ex Familia Merovingica. This is the work that was published in 1633, by Dom Raphael de Beauchamp, with annotations, under the title of Synopsis Franco-Merovingica. Andrew du Bois, who left also some other pieces, died in 1194. (Moreri.)

BOIS, (Francis du,) more known by the Latin form of his name, Sylvius, born in Hainault, in 1581, canon of Douay, and professor of theology there. He died in 1649, leaving some commentaries upon Genesis, and upon the Summa of Aquinas, with other works of a similar character. (Moreri.)

BOIS, (Gerard du,) priest of the congregation of the Oratory, born at Orleans, and early distinguished by a discriminating taste for history. Hence he was employed upon the last volume of Le Cointe's Ecclesiastical History, and was chosen by Harlai, archbishop of Paris, to write the history of that church. He completed a folio volume of it, finishing with the eleventh century, printed in 1690. Another volume, which goes down to the year 1364, was left unpublished at his death. Father Ripe was charged with the revisal and publication of it, and it appeared in 1710. The whole work is considered valuable, but readers of such books are far from numerous, and hence it is not much in request. Du Bois died at Paris, July 15, 1696. (Moreri. De Bure.)

BOIS, (Godfrey de,) a physician, born at Cruning, in Zealand, at the close of the seventeenth century. He practised medicine at Haarlem, and in 1729 was named professor of philosophy at Franeker. He was also made professor of anatomy and medicine in 1738, and of botany in 1744. He was highly esteemed and praised by Haller. He died Jan. 18, 1747, having written several pieces in physics and mathematics, and a dissertation, De Sono et Auditu, published at Leyden, in 1725, 4to, which has much merit, and is worthy of perusal at the present day.

BOIS, (John du,) a physician of the sixteenth century, born at Lille. He studied at Louvain; and after taking the degree of M.D., practised at Valenciennes, and became the principal of the college of St. John. Upon the establishment of the university of Douay, by Philip II. in 1562, he was named professor of medicine, which office he held until his death, April 6, 1576. Besides some professional works, he published, Acad. Nascentis Duacensis, et Professorum ejus, Encomium. Duac. 1563, 4to. This production is in verse.

BOIS, (John Baptist du,) a physician, born at St. Lô, towards the close of the seventeenth century. He studied at the college of Harcourt, at Paris, engaged himself to an advocate for four years in his native place, and then returned to study medicine at Paris. The year following his reception into the Faculty of Medicine, he was appointed chief physician to the dowager princess of Conti, then Latin and also French professor of surgery, and in 1730, professor at the Royal College of France. Upon the death of the princess, he declined to follow the prince of Wallachia, and preferred remaining in France, where he amassed a fortune. The state of his health obliged him, in 1744, to retire to his native place, where he devoted himself to literature. He died in April, 1759. He published,—An gracilibus Pomaceum Vino salubris? Affirm. An Fœtus extrà Uterum genitus, salvâ Matre, possit excludi? Affirm. Paris, 1727, 4to. An Vulneri moderatè suppuranti rara curatio? *ib.* 1734, 4to. An curtæ Nares ex Brachio reficiendæ? *ib.* 1742, 4to. An Colicis Figulis Venæsectio? *ib.* 1751, 4to.

BOIS, (James du,) better known by his Latinized name, Sylvius, an eminent physician and anatomist, born at the village of Louville, near Amiens, in 1478, the seventh of a family of fifteen children of a poor camlet maker. His education in the first instance came from his elder brother, principal and professor of eloquence in the college of Tournay. He soon acquired considerable knowledge of the Latin tongue, and was able not only to write in that language with elegance, but also to converse in it with facility. He was likewise well acquainted with Greek and Hebrew and Mathematics, and for a considerable time assisted his brother in instructing his pupils. Having, however, determined upon the profession of medicine, he studied anatomy under Tagault. His familiarity with ancient authors being such, that even before taking his degree he was able to teach the doctrines of Hippocrates and Galen, the Faculty of Medicine interdicted his exertions until he had been received as a doctor. To obtain this, he studied under Astruc, at Montpelier, and there matriculated in November, 1529. In the same month, it is said, he was received as bachelor of medicine, probably on account of his age, and in the following year admitted to the doctorate. He returned to Paris, was there received as a bachelor, June 28, 1531, and obtained permission to renew his lectures. In 1535 he delivered lectures at the college of Trégueir, where the number of his pupils amounted to five hundred. He is spoken of as an excellent orator, and a clear and able demonstrator. In 1550 he was appointed to the Royal College of France, upon the nomination of Henry II., as the successor of Vidus Vidius, and he continued to teach until his death, Jan. 13, 1555, being then in the seventy-seventh year of his age. He was, in accordance with his own request, buried at the cemetery for poor scholars, and was accompanied to the grave by the university in a body.

Du Bois exercised considerable influence on the progress of anatomical and medical studies in France. He was the first to put aside the dissection of the bodies of pigs for those of the human species; and in the making of anatomical preparations he has the reputation of being the inventor of the useful process of injection of the vessels. It is no mean honour to have been the master of so distinguished an anatomist as Vesalius. His great attachment to the doctrines of Galen, which were opposed by Vesalius, however, occasioned him, perhaps, to be unjust in acknowledgment of the great merits of his pupil; and in the controversy maintained between them respecting the merits of the ancients in anatomical discoveries, he unfortunately indulged too freely in observations of a nature grossly personal. He made many anatomical discoveries, among which must be mentioned the digastric muscles of the jaw, and the semilunar valve of the descending vena cava. He described with great precision the lobes of the liver and the cæcal appendix; and, considering the small number of human bodies to be obtained for dissection, and the prejudices that he had to encounter at the time in which he lived, he displayed great powers of well-directed observation. His name is associated with several parts of the human body, which he was the first accurately to describe, and his statements have universally been admitted to be most faithful.

In his ordinary habits and moral qualities, he does not appear to so much advantage as in his professional character. He was avaricious and sordid, dressing meanly, using exercise in cold weather to avoid the expense of fire, and acting very parsimoniously towards his domestics. His lectures were delivered only for a large fee, and he was rigorous in exacting the payment from his pupils. Many of his peculiarities have been recorded; amongst others, that he constantly wore his boots, and that he would not suffer them to be removed from his limbs whilst living. Henry Stephens is reported to have written, under the assumed name of Ludovicus Arrivabenus, a satirical dialogue, entitled, Sylvius Ocreatus, in which Du Bois is represented as being booted, in order to avoid payment to the ferryman Charon for the passing over the river Styx. It was replied to by John Melet, under the name of Claudius Burggensis, and the reply is inserted in the collection of the works of Sylvius by René Moreau. Upon the pulling down of his house after the decease of Du Bois, many pieces of gold were found secreted in various places; and the following distich from Buchanan is said to have been placed by one of the pupils on the door of the church upon the day of his interment:—

"Sylvius hic situs est, gratis qui nil dedit unquàm,
Mortuus, et gratis quod legis ista, dolet."

Among his works may be mentioned, In Linguam Gallicam Isagoge, una cum ejusdem Grammatica Latino-Gallica ex Hebræis, Græcis, et Latinis Auctoribus, Paris, 1531, 4to. Methodus sex Librorum Galeni de Differentiis et Causis Morborum et Symptomatum, *ib.* 1539, fol.; 1561, 8vo; Venet. 1554, 1561, 8vo. Liber de Ordine et Ordinis Ratione in legendis Hippocratis et Galeni Libris, Paris, 1539, 1561, 8vo. Isagoge brevissima in Libros Galeni de Usu Partium, &c. *ib.* 1555, 8vo, translated into French by Guillemin. De Medicamentorum Simplicium Præparatione, &c. *ib.* 1542, fol.; Lyons, 1548, 12mo; translated into French by And. Caille, Lyons, 1574, 8vo. J. Mesue de Re Medicâ, lib. iii. Sylvio interprete,

Paris, 1542, fol. In Hippocratis Elementa Comment. *ib.* 1542, fol. Vesani cujusdam Calumniarum in Hippocratis Galenique Rem Anatomicam Depulsio, Paris, 1551, 8vo; Venet. 1555, 8vo. This is the attack upon Vesalius, who is referred to under the name of Vesanus. In Hipp. et Galeni Physiologiæ Partem Anatomicam Isagoge, &c. Paris, 1555, fol.; translated by Guillemin, Paris, 1555, 8vo. De Mensibus Mulierum, &c. *ib.* 1556, 8vo; translated into French by Christian. De Salubri Francisci Primi vivendi Ratione, Paris, 1557, 1577, 12mo. Comment. in Galeni Lib. de Ossibus, *ib.* 1561, 8vo. Opera Omnia curante René Moreau, Genev. 1630, 1635, fol.

BOISEGLIN, (John de Dieu-Raymond de Cucé,) a French cardinal, born at Rennes, Feb. 27, 1732, of a very ancient Breton family, and intended, being a younger brother, for the church. Becoming the head of his house by an elder brother's death, he renounced his hereditary rights, and continued a professional career. In 1770 he became archbishop of Aix, and displayed in that dignified station a liberality which long caused his name to be respectfully remembered. On the breaking out of the revolution, he alleviated the popular ferment that arose from a scarcity of provisions, by great pecuniary sacrifices, and by pastoral advice. In 1789 he sat in the states-general, and conducted himself with great propriety; but he was obliged to take refuge in England, and remained there until the reconstruction of a religious establishment in France, in 1802, when he was appointed archbishop of Tours. He was soon after made a cardinal, and he died Aug. 22, 1804. He published, while in England, a French verse translation of the Psalms, entitled, Le Psalmiste, as a means of raising money for the relief of some emigrant families. He also published, Discours à la Cérémonie de la Prestation du Serment des Archevêques et Evêques, 1802. (Biog. Univ.)

BOISEGLIN DE KERDU, (Peter Maria Lewis de,) cousin of the preceding, born in 1758, and originally meant for the church, but his destination was changed for the army. Being a knight of Malta, he was in that isle, in 1793, when the English occupied Toulon in the name of Lewis XVII. He repaired thither, and commanded a regiment raised for the king's service. He did not return to Malta, but passed over into England; nor did he visit France again until the Bourbons returned in 1814. He died Sept. 10, 1816. He published, Ancient and Modern Malta, Lond. 1804, 3 vols, 8vo, a work detailing the condition and history of the isle, and advocating the restoration of its knights. Travels through Denmark and Sweden, Lond. 1810, 2 vols, 4to. Vertot's Revolutions de Portugal, with a continuation and additions. Boiseglin's Malta was translated into French in 1809. (Biog. Univ. Suppl.)

BOISLEVE, (Peter,) a French civilian, born in 1745, who lost his ecclesiastical preferment in the revolution from refusing to take the oath, but was named honorary canon of Nôtre Dame when the *concordat* was concluded. In order to obtain a divorce from Josephine, without appealing to the pope, then a prisoner, Bonaparte re-established the ecclesiastical court of Paris, and made Boislève the official. He did as the emperor wished, pronouncing the sentence of divorce, January 9, 1810. He died December 3, 1830. (Biog. Univ. Suppl.)

BOISROBERT, (Francis Metel de,) a French ecclesiastic, born about 1592, who died in 1662, and obtained, by means of cardinal Richelieu, to whom he made himself indispensable by an unceasing flow of gaiety, several rich benefices. The minister found him so important to his spirits, that a physician once said, "All our prescriptions will be useless without a drachm or two of Boisrobert." That witty person was, however, a dissipated sensualist, very little worthy of notice. But he has the credit of suggesting the French academy to Richelieu, and he was one of its earliest members. He died in March, 1662, having published some poems and plays, now forgotten. (Biog. Univ.)

BOISSARD, (John James,) a French classical antiquary and Latin poet, born 1528, who carefully travelled over Italy and parts of Greece, taking views of the most interesting remains then found there. On returning home he became tutor to the sons of a nobleman, with whom he travelled in France, Italy, and Germany. His large collections were, however, chiefly destroyed at Montbéliard, when the Lorrainers ravaged Franche Comté, a few only being with himself at Metz, whither he had retired. His intentions of publishing upon Roman antiquities would thus have ruinously suffered had not learned men, who were aware of them, sent him drawings from a variety of quarters. These contributions enabled him to bring out a work, in 4 volumes, folio, that was of great use in spreading a knowledge of Roman antiquities, entitled, De Romanæ Urbis Topographiâ et Antiquitate. He published, also, some other works, now very scarce, of which particulars are to be seen in Clement's Bibliothèque Curieuse. (Moreri.)

BOISSAT, (Peter de,) vice-bailiff of Vienne, in Dauphiny. He died in the early part of the seventeenth century, and is best known from a History of the Knights of Malta, partly translated from the Italian of Bosio, published in 1612. It was twice reprinted in the same century, with additions by Baudouin and Naberat. Boissat was also author of Le Brillant de la Royne, a genealogy of the house of Medicis, printed in 1613, and reprinted in 1620. He was father of another author, bearing both his names, lord of Licien and Avernay, born in 1603; in early life a man of pleasure, as age advanced, a devotee. Among the fruits of his earlier habits engrafted upon literature, was a romance founded upon materials furnished by Octavius Finelli, entitled, Histoire Négrépontique, contenant la Vie et les Amours d'Alexandre Castriot. This work was very freely used by Calprenède, in the composition of his once famous Cassandra, that appeared in 1642, and fills 10 vols, 8vo. When Boissat's feelings were all religious, he published in French and Latin upon the Virgin, and some fancied miracles connected with her name. (Moreri. Biog. Univ.)

BOISSEAU, (Francis Gabriel,) a physician, born at Brest, Oct. 12, 1791, who attended the French army, serving in Spain and Germany, from 1810 to 1813. At the time of Bonaparte's first abdication, he was a prisoner at Dresden, and he again joined the army upon his return from Elba. After the battle of Waterloo, being made assistant to the military establishment at Val de Grâce, he resumed his medical studies. He took the degree of M.D. in 1817. After the revolution of July, 1830, he was appointed physician to the military hospital for education at Metz, where he died, January 2, 1836. He was for twelve years the principal editor of the Journal Universel des Sciences Médicales. He wrote the medical articles in the Dictionnaire Abrégé des Sciences Médicales, many articles in the Biographie Médicale, the Encyclopédie Moderne, the Journal Hebdomadaire, &c. He edited, with notes, the works of Pujol; Thomson on Inflammation; Rolando's Physiological Inductions; Tissot's Treatise on the Health of Literary Persons; and he also published the following original works, — Pyrétologie Physiologique, ou Traité des Fièvres, Paris, 1826, 4 vols, 8vo, 3d ed.; and Nosographie Organique, ou Traité de Médecine Pratique, Paris, 1828, 1829, 4 vols, 8vo.

BOISSIERE, or BOISSIERES, (Claudius,) a French mathematician, much celebrated in his day, who lived in the middle of the sixteenth century, and left several works. Among them was an Art of Arithmetic, in French, printed in 1554, and a curious production, entitled Nobilissimus et Antiquissimus Ludus Pythagoricus, qui *Rhythmomachia* nominatur, in Utilitatem et Relaxationem Studiorum comparatus, Paris, 1556.—Another Boissières, named John, born in Auvergne, who lived about the same time, published a history of the crusades, and some poetical works. (Moreri.)

BOISSIEU, (Bartholomew Camillus de,) a physician, born at Lyons, Aug. 6, 1734, who took his degree in 1755, and after attending at Paris the most eminent professors of that day, settled in his native city. He was selected to direct the treatment of two epidemics that raged at Mâcon in 1762, and at Chazelle in 1769. He died of an acute pleurisy in December, 1777, having been affiliated to many learned societies, but leaving only two published memoirs, which obtained prizes from the Academy of Dijon.

BOISSIEU, (Denis Salvaing de,) a French writer, who drew the name by which he is most generally known from his lordship of Boissieu. He was born April 21, 1600, at Vourey, a manorial residence in Dauphiny, and received a legal education, but was at one time in the army. He devoted himself, however, to civil employments, and acquitted himself creditably both as a magistrate and a diplomatist. In the latter capacity he accompanied M. de Créqui to Rome, and being charged there, in 1633, to harangue Urban VIII., he made use of a freedom far from agreeable to the papal court; but he printed a faithful report of his speech soon after at Paris, in spite of a demand for the suppression of unpalatable passages. He died at the seat in which he was born, April 11, 1683, having published a Latin commentary on the Ibis of Ovid, with some works of local interest, being partly useful to the lawyers of Dauphiny, and partly displaying what a partial native excusably considered as its wonders. (Moreri.)

BOISSIEU, (John James,) also written Boissieux, a French artist, born of a good family, at Lyons, in 1736, and originally intended for the magistracy, but educated eventually for the fine arts, in compliance with his own taste and wishes. He painted successfully both portraits and landscapes; but a delicate constitution obliged him to discontinue this branch of his profession, and he latterly was known only as an engraver. After thus establishing a very high reputation, he died May 1, 1810. (Bryan. Pilkington. Biog. Univ.)

BOISSY D'ANGLAS, (Francis Anthony,) count, a French statesman and man of letters, born of a protestant family, in Languedoc, Dec. 8, 1756, and originally at the bar, but soon attached, by purchase, to the household of *Monsieur*, afterwards Lewis XVIII. He became, however, a decided partizan of the revolution, but kept himself aloof from its worst excesses. He seems to have been, indeed, a well-intentioned man, with a great fund of practical good sense, but indisposed for an obstinate adherence to any political theory that appeared likely to injure the interests of his country, or perhaps also those of himself. His aid was accordingly given in the downfal of the monarchy, in that of the republic, and in that of the empire. This last assistance procured his nomination as a peer of France, in June, 1814; but when his old master, Bonaparte, appeared at the Tuilleries in the following spring, Boissy d'Anglas re-organized his administration in the south of France, and obtained a place in the new chamber of peers. Notwithstanding, he combated the proposition to proclaim Napoleon II. after the battle of Waterloo; and although excluded at first from the upper house on the second restoration, he was re-established within a month, a favour attributed by the public generally to the sterling qualities which undoubtedly were his. Others thought it occasioned by the king's desire to conciliate the protestants. He died at Paris, October 20, 1826, much respected, upon the whole, as a statesman, and to be remembered in the literary world by some political pieces, an essay on the life, writings, and opinions of Malesherbes, with whom he had been well acquainted, and Etudes Littéraires et Poétiques d'un Vieillard, Paris, 1828, 6 vols, 12mo. (Biog. Univ. Suppl.)

BOISSY, (John Baptist Thibaudière de,) who died June 27, 1729, in his sixty-third year, a French scholar, who received a monastic education, and left two dissertations, one of no great depth, upon the expiations in use among the ancients, and a second upon the human sacrifices of antiquity.—Another Boissy, named Lewis, who died in 1758, was originally meant for the church, but became a dramatic author, and produced plays, now generally forgotten, enough to fill nine 8vo volumes. He suffered, however, at times very severe pecuniary distress.—A third Boissy, (Charles Desprez de,) who died at Paris, in 1787, was a successful barrister, known as author of Lettres sur les Spectacles, in two volumes, of which the second is an account of works both for and against plays. A seventh edition of this work appeared in 1780, but it is not very exact, nor are the opinions given sufficiently impartial. (Biog. Univ.)

BOISTE, (Peter Claudius Victor,) an eminent French philologer, born at Paris, in 1763. He died at Ivri-sur-Seine, April 24, 1824, worn out by literary labour, in spite of his very regular habits. To him, aided by Bastien, France owes the best dictionary of her language, and the work has accordingly been often reprinted, notwithstanding its omissions, abbreviations, and placing scientific words by themselves at the end. When the second edition of this dictionary was printing in 1803, the police, it is said, found that *Bonaparte* had been written against *spoliateur*, it being the author's practice to place an instance by every word. He was required to cancel this, and *Frédéric-le-Grand* filled up the vacancy thus created. Boiste also published a French grammar, a dictionary of literature, and another of geography. Unfortunately for his credit, he fancied himself likely to shine as a poet, and produced, in 1801, L'Univers, thrice reprinted afterwards, which, in twelve cantos of poetical prose, affords numerous occasions for notes on the Newtonian system, and the theory of the earth. But his physics, it is said, are a poet's, and his poetry is a philosopher's. (Biog. Univ. Suppl.)

BOISVILLE, (John Francis Martin de,) born at Rouen, in 1755, and canon of the cathedral there at the revolution. He was then driven into exile, but returned on the first opportunity, and in 1822, though his health was delicate, he found himself unable to decline the bishopric of Dijon. He died in that city, May 27, 1829, having published, in 1818, a verse translation of the Imitation of Christ, feebly executed, but with a good preliminary discourse. (Biog. Univ. Suppl.)

BOIT, (Charles,) a successful Swedish enamel-painter, both in France and England, who died in 1726. (Pilkington.)

BOITARD, (L.) a French engraver, known about 1760, who lived chiefly in England, and died in London. His productions, though neat, are deficient in taste and in correctness of drawing. (Bryan.)

BOITEL, (Peter,) sieur de Gaubertin, a French author, who published, in 1616, Les Tragiques Accidens des Hommes Illustres. The first of these *illustrious* unfortunates is Abel, the last the chevalier de Guise. He also published, besides some other works, Histoire des Choses plus mémorables de ce qui s'est passé en France depuis la Mort de Henri-le-Grand, jusqu'à l'Assemblée des Notables en 1617 et 1618. This work really goes no farther than December 29, 1617. A new edition, however, was published at Rouen in 1647, with a continuation to 1642.—Another Boitel, named Claudius, of Frauville, an advocate, born in 1570, who died in 1625, published French translations of Nonnus and the Odyssey, a history of French affairs between 1620 and 1623, and a worthless treatise on the education of princes. (Biog. Univ.)

BOIVIN, (Francis de,) baron du Villars, bailiff of Gex, and attached to the household of two dowager-queens of France, known as author of an historical work, which details French military movements in the north of Italy in the middle of the sixteenth century. Boivin relates facts from his own knowledge, having accompanied, as private secretary, during almost nine years, marshal de Brissac, who commanded the French army in Piedmont. He accumulated, in the course of his campaigns, a great mass of materials, which he did not reduce into order until a long time afterwards, when he was very far advanced in life. His work is in twelve books, containing much curious matter, and bearing an impress of frankness and truth, but faulty in style, and blemished by some anachronisms. It is entitled, Mémoires sur les Guerres Démelées tant dans le Piémont qu'au Montferrat et Duché de Milan, par Charles de Cossé, Comte de Brissac, Maréchal de France, Lieutenant-Général de-là les Monts, depuis 1550 jusqu'en 1559, et ce qui se passa les Années suivantes pour l'Exécution de la Paix, jusqu'en 1561. The first edition of this work was published in 1607, without the author's privity, and he complains of it in the second edition, published at Lyons, in 1610. A third edition, with a continuation to 1629, by Claudius Malingre, was published in 1630. The author died, very old, in 1618. (Biog. Univ.)

BOIVIN, (Lewis,) a celebrated French academician, born at Montreuil-l'Argilé, in Upper Normandy, March 20, 1649. After an education at home, under a clergyman, he was sent for further improvement to the Jesuits' college at Rouen. He subsequently studied at Paris, where, making great progress in various branches of learning, he settled down eventually into a general scholar, and became pensionary of the academy. He died April 22, 1724, leaving no proofs of his great erudition, beyond some dissertations, chiefly chronological, printed in the first four volumes of the academy's Transactions. He was a well-disposed man at bottom, but with a reserved, ill-humoured exterior, and a repulsive pertinacity in enforcing whatever he considered his right. This unhappy disposition rendered him extremely litigious, and, among other suits of less importance, once involved him, during twelve years, at a ruinous expense, in a legal contest with the abbey of La Trappe, to free a small estate purchased by him from a trifling rent-charge. To the very last, he felt sure of success; and when he found himself disappointed, he coolly said, "I gained my cause for twelve years, and lost it only one day." (Chaufepié.)

BOIVIN, (John de Villeneuve,) brother of the preceding, and chiefly brought up by him, their parents having died when he was very young. He was born March 28, 1663, and sent for education to his brother's house in Paris. Lewis himself undertook to teach him, and a boy was very unlikely to find a more competent instructor; but having been taught orally the principles of Greek and Latin, he was then shut up alone in a garret, with a Homer, all Greek, a dictionary and a grammar, until he was thoroughly master of his lessons. This mode of education was completely successful, the younger Boivin not only performing admirably all that was prescribed, but even also beginning every day upon the task intended for the morrow. He thus rapidly became learned far beyond his years, and when a young man, he had acquired such a knowledge of the classics, that every scholar in Paris was glad of an acquaintance with him. In 1692 he was placed in the royal library, a situation for which he was excellently fitted; and in that very year he discovered a palimpsest MS. containing a large portion of Scripture, apparently written about twelve or thirteen hundred years, and veiled by a body of homilies written in the fourteenth century. In the following year, Boivin published the Mathematici Veteres, left imperfect by Thevenot. He then employed himself upon the History of Nicephorus Gregoras, which was published at Paris in 1702, in 2 vols, fol., with this title, Nicephori Gregoræ Historiæ Byzantinæ, libri xxiv. ab Andronico Seniore, ad Joannem Palæologum, Gr. et Lat. ex Interpretatione Hieronymi Wolphii, et cum Notis et Appendicibus Joannis Boivin. This was a considerable gratification to the learned world. The history of Nicephorus is contained in thirty-eight books, of which the first eleven, with a Latin version, were published by Wolf, in 1562. These were now republished by Boivin, but with great improvements, both in text and version, and with an addition of thirteen more, hitherto inedited, and accompanied by a Latin version of his own. It was his intention to have edited the remaining books of this Constantinopolitan history, and thus to have extended the work over four volumes. The two promised volumes, however, did not appear, to the great regret of scholars, as Boivin showed himself, in those parts of the work that he published, qualified above most men for completing it. His reasons for leaving it unfinished are unknown, but those who are aware of the very slow sale that awaits such works, however excellent, will be at no loss to conjecture them. Boivin also published some French translations from the Greek, several learned dissertations, Latin lives of Pithou and Le Pelletier, and some Greek anacreontic poems. He sometimes Latinized his names Junius Biberiusmero; and he playfully called himself in Greek, Œnopion. He died October 29, 1726. (Chaufepié. Fabricius. Bibl. Gr. vii. 654.)

BOIVIN, (René,) a French engraver, born at Angers, about 1530, whose drawing is not equal to his engraving. Some of his plates are signed with his Latin baptismal name alone, *Renatus*, others with a cypher made up of his two initials combined. (Bryan.)

BOIZARD, (John,) author of a French numismatic treatise. It originated in information collected by him, under commission, as officer of the mint at Paris, and is entitled, Traité de Monnaies, de leurs Circonstances, et Dependances. He died about the beginning of the eighteenth century, and his work was deemed so unfit for indiscriminate perusal, from the particulars given of coinage and alloys, that a prohibition was issued against the reprinting of it. (Biog. Univ.)

BOIZOT, the name of some French artists. Lewis Simon, born in 1743, was a sculptor, son of an Anthony, a painter. He died in 1809, having executed several well-known busts and statues, but an insufficient study of nature and ancient models has betrayed him into some improprieties.—Another of his surname, Maria Louisa Adelaide, born in Paris, in 1748, was an engraver, whose works are very neatly executed. (Biog. Univ. Bryan.)

BOJANI, (Wenceslaus,) an Italian civilian, architect, and poet, born at Cividad del Friuli, of a noble family, and educated at Padua, where he applied himself to jurisprudence, mathematics, and architecture. He died in 1560, leaving a great number of Latin epigrams and other poems, which were after his death published by Francis Giusti, a monk of Cividad.

BOJE, (Henry Christian,) born July 19, 1744, at Meldorp, in Holstein, where his father was a clergyman, studied law at Göttingen, became, 1775, staff-secretary at Hamburg, held afterwards legal appointments in Ditmarsh, and died at Meldorp, 1806. He was a modest, zealous, and meritorious labourer in the field of literature. At Göttingen he enjoyed the society of Bürger, Höltz, the Counts von Stolberg, Voss, Miller, and the other members of that school of poetry which was formed there towards the latter end of the last century; and, as their senior, his influence amongst them was considerable. In 1770 appeared, under his and Gotter's editorship, the first German Musenalmanach. Köstner, the mathematician and epigrammist, had encouraged them to set it on foot, in imitation of the Almanach des Muses, which had appeared in Paris since 1761. From 1771 to 1775, Boje was the sole editor of the new annual; Göckingh, Bürger, and K. Reinhard afterwards succeeded him in the office, until, in its thirty-fifth year, this parent of a progeny so numerous expired.

The early fruits of Boje's own muse were published without his name, under the title of Poems, Bremen and Leipsic, 1770, 8vo. They are for the most part imitations of the classics, especially of Horace, then the favourite model of German versifiers. His later poems were published in his almanack. They are not equal in variety or originality to those of some of his Göttingen friends. His lyrical productions lack feeling, and his epigrams have none of the pungency of those of Köstner. From 1776 to 1788 Boje edited the German Museum, an excellent monthly periodical, combining literature and science, and presenting one of the best collections of the miscellaneous writings of that day.

BOKHARI, (Imam Abu-Abdallah Mohammed Ebn Ismail Al-Jaafi Al-Bokhari,) one of the most celebrated doctors of the Moslem law in the early ages of Islam, and the one on whose authority principally depends the great body of the traditions which govern the decisions of the judges. He was born in Arabia, of the tribe of Jaafa, under the khalifate of Al-Amîor, the son of Haroon, A.D. 810, (A.H. 194;) and "even from the age of ten years" (to quote his own words, as cited by Abulfeda) "felt himself smitten with so deep a love for the study of traditions, that he could entertain no doubt that the impulse resulted from heavenly inspiration!" The unwearied zeal and diligence with which he accordingly applied himself to the investigation of the traditions on record of the Prophet, his companions, and his immediate successors, raised him to fame and honours at an age unusually early. He is said to have been only eighteen when he repaired to Mekka, in which city, and in Medinah, he was occupied for sixteen years in the compilation and arrangement of the great work on which his enduring celebrity is based, and to which we shall hereafter recur. It was apparently after the completion of this task that he visited Bagdad, where his celebrity had preceded him, and a vain attempt was made by ten of the most skilful traditionists of the university to perplex him by repeating a hundred traditions, which they purposely misquoted, or ascribed to erroneous sources; the unaided memory of Abu-Abdallah enabled him easily to triumph over the snares laid for him, and his victory was hailed with applause by his antagonists themselves. It does not precisely appear at what date he migrated to Transoxiana, but most of his latter years appear to have been spent at Bokhara, a city which was then the resort of the learned from all parts of the Moslem world: but his residence here (whence he derived the surname by which he is generally designated) was disquieted both by the enmity of Khaled, the khalif's governor of the province, and by the jealousy of Ahmed Abu-Hafss, the cadhi of the city, (sometimes also entitled Al-Bokhari,) who was himself a legist of high reputation, and could ill endure to see his own fame eclipsed by the arrival of the most renowned jurisconsult of the age. By this personage Abu-Abdallah was taxed with entertaining heterodox opinions on the subjects of predestination and the creation of the Koran, two weighty points on which the Moslem world was then at variance: and though he repelled the charge with indignation, the controversy continued till Abu-Hafss was driven from Bokhara by the inhabitants, who were unable to endure his strictness in matters of discipline. Notwithstanding the removal of his rival, Abu-Abdallah seems still to have found his residence in Bokhara irksome, as he quitted that city for Samarkand shortly before his death, which took place on the last night of the Ramazan, A.D. 870, (A.H. 256.)—Gibbon (ch. 50, note) erroneously places his death in A.H. 224, though he quotes Abulfeda and D'Herbelot, both of whom give the date correctly, as his authorities.—Al-Bokhari was a voluminous writer on traditions and jurisprudence, and several of his works on these subjects exist in the European libraries: but his *magnum opus*, which for more than a thousand years has been held by the *Soonite* or orthodox sect of the Moslems, as the most indefeasible of authorities, next to the Koran itself, on all questions of divinity, and consequently of jurisprudence, is his great collection of the Traditions of the Prophet, above referred to, entitled, *Musnad-al-Ssahih*, or more frequently *Ssahih*, the Sincere or Undoubted. This consists of a selection of 3,275 traditions, decisions, and other sayings of Mohammed, which the author distinguished as bearing the stamp of authenticity, out of a mass whose number has been variously stated at 100,000, 300,000, and even 600,000. In this choice the preference was given to those which had been approved and received by Ahmed Ebn Hanbal, the founder of one of the four orthodox divisions of the Soonis. While employed in the versification and transcription of these important sentences, the author resided at Mekka, and (as he himself informs us) never committed a paragraph to writing without previous purification by prayer and ablution at the well of Zemzem. He afterwards removed to Medinah, to arrange and divide the work into subjects and chapters, each of which, when completed, he reverently laid between the tomb and the pulpit of the prophet, while he offered up prayers for the success of his undertaking, which (as above mentioned) consumed sixteen years in its execution. The standard compilation thus achieved is characterised by Abulfeda as a work, "from the accuracy of which there can be no appeal—the supremacy of which is unquestioned—and from which, as from a fountain of sweet waters, doctors drink in security, while judges agree in regulating both their decisions and their conduct by its dicta!" The title of Saahih has been sometimes given also to a work on a similar subject by Moslem, who, with Termedhi, holds a rank among traditionists second only to that of Al-Bokhari; but the compilations of neither of these authors have ever attained the high authority enjoyed by Al-Bokhari, whose work has been made the subject of innumerable commentaries by legists of every part of the Moslem world. Copies of the Ssahih (sometimes called Djami-al-Ssahih) are found in most of the great public libraries of Europe.

The city of Bokhara has in all ages of Islam been a noted resort of the learned, and many distinguished scholars have consequently borne the surname of Al-Bokhari, of whom D'Herbelot has enumerated several. Among them are Imam-Zadah (son of the Imam) Al-Bokhari, son of the author of the Ssahih, and himself an eminent jurisconsult; Abu-Hafss, the opponent of the Imam; his son, Ebn-Abi-Hafss; Mohammed Ebn Mousa, the author of a singular poem, every line of which ends with the letter M; Mohiyed-deen, the author of a work of high character on Legal Decisions, &c.—Nearer our own times, the appellation was assumed as a name of authorship by the noted Beggi-Jan (see Beggi-Jan), who was a voluminous writer on doctrinal points, under the title of Derwish-Bokhari. (Abulfeda. D'Herbelot. De Sacy. Pocock. Gibbon, &c. &c.)

BOL, the surname of some artists in the Low Countries. The earliest of them, Hans, or John, was born at Mechlin, in 1534, and is chiefly known by views of Amsterdam, and other towns, in some of which, ships and reflections of them in the water are admirably executed. He also etched from his own designs in a slight, spirited style. He appears to have died in 1593.—Ferdinand, born at Dort, in 1611, was a pupil of Rembrandt, and he never forsook his manner; but although his pictures may be mistaken, on a hasty view, for that great master's, they really want the clearness of flesh and relief that distinguish them. Bol also often fails in grace and outline. Besides his pictures, he left many etchings tastefully and spiritedly executed, with lights and shadows very judiciously managed. He died in 1681.—Cornelius, also a Dutchman, was in London when it was burnt in 1666. Of that conflagration he painted several views, and likewise of different buildings in and about the English metropolis. (Bryan. Pilkington.)

BOLANGER, (John,) a painter, born in 1606, who studied under Guido, and imitated him successfully in composition and colouring. His subjects are historical, and are executed with great taste of composition and delicacy of colouring. He was principal painter to the duke of Modena, and died in 1660. (Pilkington.)

BOLD, (John,) an English clergyman, born at Leicester, in 1679, of an ancient family, and educated academically at St. John's college, Cambridge, where he was matriculated at fifteen, and took his degree of B.A. with great credit in 1698. When admitted into holy orders, the bishop, pleased with his proficiency, purposed to make him his chaplain. But the prelate's death rendered this kind intention unavailing, and Bold remained through life upon the curacy of Stony Stanton, Leicestershire, to which he was ordained, with a stipend of 30*l.* *per ann.*, never augmented during the fifty years of his service there, nor had he any private means. In the interval between his taking his degree and his ordination, he had, indeed, taught a small endowed school at Hinckley, at a salary of 10*l.* *per ann.*, but on taking possession of his curacy, all the property that he possessed was his chamber furniture, and a small but select library; nevertheless, not only did he support himself upon his stipend, but also was enabled to spend 5*l.* a-year in charity, and to save another 5*l.* as a reserve for contingencies. He boarded with a farmer in his parish, to whom, in the beginning of his time, he paid 8*l.* *per ann.*, but which was gradually raised to 16*l.* *per ann.* Let it not, however, be supposed that this life of seclusion, of labour, and of frugality, was one from which he had no power of escaping, either by the exercise of his talents, or the kindness and influence of his friends. Though contented to exercise his ministry for fifty years in an obscure village—he was a man of great reading, especially in the Fathers and in the early writers of his own church. He was an excellent general scholar, had great talents as a preacher, and was also a correct and elegant writer. Mr. Nichols says, it was agreed that he wrote better than most contemporary divines, and that his style bore a great resemblance to that of Addison. But although he had an offer of preferment, he chose voluntarily to devote his whole life to the spiritual welfare of this one poor parish, under the conviction that, by so doing, he should "make his example and doctrine the more striking and effective," and so best fulfil the solemn obligations that he had undertaken. In fulfilling them, never was a minister of religion more exemplary, diligent, and successful. By his great economy, he was enabled to requite the assistance of a neighbouring clergyman, when disabled by infirmity during the last four years of his life; and when he died, in 1757, his savings amounted to between two and three hundred pounds, of which he left 40*l.* to be put out at interest; one-half of such interest to be paid at Christmas to the poorer attendants at church, and the other half for a sermon in Lent, "upon the people's duty to attend to the instructions of the minister whom the bishop should set over them." His writings are—1. The Sin and Danger of Neglecting the Public Service of the Church, Lond. 1745, 8vo. 2. Religion the most Delightful Employment. 3. The Duty of Worthy Communicating. All these are (or were, in orthodox times) on the list of the Society for Promoting Christian Knowledge. He also left a considerable number of MS. sermons. (Nichols' Leicestershire, vol. iv. pp. 2, 975.)

BOLDETTI, (Marc Antony,) a learned antiquary, born at Rome, November 19, 1663, of a family originally from Lorraine, and carefully educated, but so decidedly fond of Plutarch in youth, that his fellow-scholars called him by that philosopher's name. As his age advanced, he became distinguished as a student of Hebrew and antiquities. In the former branch of learning, his progress was so conspicuous, that he was employed to write Hebrew in the Vatican library, to review all documents relating to it, and to assist in the Saturday sermons preached to the Jews. His taste for antiquities led him to decorate the church of St. Mary beyond the Tiber, of which he was long canon, with ancient inscriptions, and other monuments of elder times, a practice that once exposed him to a temporary degree of obloquy, because he had admitted some pagan remains among his collections. He died December 4, 1749, having published at Rome, in folio, 1720, Osservazioni sopra i Cimiterj de' Santi Martiri ed Antichi Cristiani di Roma. He had also written other works, but they all perished in a fire, in 1737. (Biog. Univ.)

BOLDINI, (Nicholas,) called *Vicentino,* from Vicenza, where he was born, about 1510. He was an engraver on wood, chiefly after Titian, under whom he is thought to have studied. His execution is bold and free, but his works are scarce. (Bryan.)

BOLDONI, (Sigismond,) a noble Milanese, born about 1597, who, after a youth of literary distinction, became professor of philosophy at Padua, at twenty-five, and died in 1630. He wrote a poem in Latin, on the death of Philip III. of Spain; another in Italian, on the fall of the Lombards, published after his death by his brother, also a poet; two volumes of Latin epistles; Larius, containing a charming description of the lake of Como, and some academical orations. (Biog. Univ.)

BOLDUC, (James,) a Capuchin friar, born at Paris, about 1580, a famous preacher in his day, and yet remembered from some strange theological works, that are occasionally sought by admirers of literary curiosities. One of these, De Orgio Christiano, professes to prove that Adam and Noah instituted the eucharist; the former having grown corn, the latter made wine. (Biog. Univ.)

BOLESLAS, or BOLESLAUS, the name of several Polish and Bohemian monarchs.

BOLESLAS I., duke or prince of Poland, succeeded his father, Micislas, A.D. 992. He was a brave and warlike ruler, and commenced his reign by retaking Cracow, which had fallen into the power of the Bohemians: he was also successful in his wars against the pagans of Prussia, from whom he conquered great part of Silesia; but he sullied his laurels by his treachery to Boleslas III., duke of Bohemia, who had implored his assistance, and whom he inveigled into his power and blinded, A.D. 1002, with the design of seizing his dominions. The execution of this project was, however, prevented by the arms of the emperor, Henry II. of Germany, who waged a long war with Poland; but Boleslas succeeded, at the conclusion of peace, in 1018, in procuring the release of his country from the homage hitherto paid to the empire. A war with the Russian prince of Kiow, whom he reduced to pay tribute, occupied the remainder of his reign. He died 1025, and was succeeded by his son, Micislas II. Some historians have represented Boleslas I. as assuming the royal title, from confounding him with his great grandson.

BOLESLAS II., surnamed *the Bold*, who succeeded his father, Casimir I., in 1058. The greater part of his reign was passed in wars with Hungary, Bohemia, and Russia, not for the purpose of conquest, but in order to restore exiled princes of those countries who had sought his protection; but the desertion of his army in an expedition against Kiow, (1077,) exasperated his temper, and he became bloodthirsty and tyrannical. In the same year he assumed the title of king, placing the crown on his own head: but his cruelty continued to increase, and the vigorous remonstrances of the archbishop of Cracow, who threatened to excommunicate him for his enormities, at length so enraged him, that he slew the prelate at the foot of the altar, May 1079. This sacrilegious murder was speedily avenged by the anathemas of pope Gregory VII., who absolved the Poles from their allegiance, suppressed the title of king, and laid the kingdom under an interdict. Boleslas, deserted by his subjects, fled, in 1081, into Russia, where he died two years later.

BOLESLAS III. (surnamed Krzywoosty, or Wrymouthed,) nephew of the preceding, succeeded his father, Ladislas, at the age of fourteen, A.D. 1102. His reign was one continued scene of warfare; for the first fourteen years, against his natural brother, Sbigniew, to whom Pomerania had been left as an appanage, and who was finally taken and put to death, and subsequently against the Russians, Bohemians, &c.; and such were the military talents and good fortune of Boleslas, that he is said to have lost only one of forty-seven battles which he fought. He did homage to the emperor Lothaire in 1135, not for Poland, but for Pomerania, into which he first introduced Christianity. He died in 1138, dividing his dominions among his four sons. Ladislas, the eldest, was considered the head of the family; but in attempting to despoil his younger brothers of their inheritance, he was himself expelled by their united arms in 1146, and the next in age mounted the throne as

BOLESLAS IV., a prince able in his domestic administration, but unfortunate in his wars. The cause of his deposed brother Ladislas had been espoused by the pope and the emperor, the former of whom laid Poland under an interdict, but the thunders of the church were disregarded by the Poles. The armies of the empire were less easily encountered, and in 1157 Poland was invaded and over-run by Frederic Barbarossa in person, who compelled Boleslas to purchase peace by the payment of a large sum of money, and the acknowledgment of the emperor as his suzerain. The claims of Ladislas seem to have been entirely passed over in this arrangement, though some historians assert that he received lands in Silesia as a compensation for the loss of Poland. A war in which Boleslas engaged, in 1163, for the subjugation or conversion (then nearly synonymous terms) of the idolatrous inhabitants of Prussia, had an equally disastrous issue: the Poles were entangled in a morass (1167), and their army entirely cut to pieces, the duke himself escaping with difficulty. He died 1173, and another brother, Micislas III., succeeded.

BOLESLAS V., surnamed *the Chaste*, became duke of Poland at the age of seven, on the death of his father, Lesko, A.D. 1227. The commencement of his reign was troubled by the attempts of the duke of Breslau, Henry the Bearded, to supplant him in his throne, and by the devastations of the Prussian pagans, to arrest whose progress Conrad, duke of Masovia, the cousin and guardian of Boleslas, called in the aid of the Teutonic knights, to whom he ceded Culm and the adjacent territories, the foundation of the great subsequent power of the order on the shores of the Baltic. Boleslas assumed the reins of government in 1238, but his weak and timid disposition was ill fitted to withstand the torrent which burst on the country two years later, in the irruption of the countless host of Moguls under Batu, (see Batu, and Bela IV. of Hungary.) He took refuge in Hungary, and the invaders, after devastating Poland, and burning Lublin and Cracow, defeated, in the great battle of Lignitz, the combined forces of Poland, Silesia, and the Teutonic knights, filling nine sacks with the right ears of the slain. On the retreat of the Moguls, Boleslas returned to his dominions, but his flight in the time of danger had excited the contempt of his subjects, and one of his uncles sought to drive him from the throne. Though this attempt was unsuccessful, his authority continued to be disregarded by his nobles, who made peace and war on each other. He died, after an eventful reign of fifty-two years, A.D. 1279, and, leaving no issue, was succeeded by his cousin, Lesko VI. The famous salt-works of Wiliezka (1237) and Bochnia (1251) were opened during this reign.

BOLESLAS I. became duke of Bohemia A.D. 936, by assassinating with his own hand his elder brother, Wratislas, at the instigation of his mother, by whose advice he also re-established paganism. But this double outrage drew on him the arms of the emperor Otho the Great, who compelled him, after long wars, to re-establish Christianity, and to become tributary to the empire, A.D. 950. He subsequently followed Otho in his Hungarian wars, and died in 967.

BOLESLAS II., son of the former, succeeded him. He was a pious and valiant prince, and gained considerable advantages over the Poles, from whom he took Cracow: but his principal achievement was the final suppression of paganism in his own dominions, which he did not succeed in effecting without long and often-renewed civil wars. He built numerous churches, and in 977 erected Prague into a bishopric, subject to the archbishop of Mentz; it was not till the reign of Charles IV. that it became an independent archbishopric. He also introduced the use of the Roman alphabet in Bavaria in place of the Russian characters. He died in 999, and was succeeded by his son,

BOLESLAS III., a weak prince, whose reign lasted only three years, when he was treacherously seized and blinded by his relative, Boleslas of Poland. He resigned his states to his brother Jaromir, but survived till 1037.

BOLEYN, (Anne,) an English queen, rendered prominent in history by her unhappy fate and connexion with the Reformation. Her family is known to have been seated at Sall, in Norfolk, so early as 1283, and Geoffrey Boleyn was buried in the church there in 1440. A son of his, also named Geoffrey, settled in London as a trader, and amassed a very large fortune. He was sheriff of London in 1446, and lord mayor in 1457. By his will, proved July 2, 1463, he left 1000*l*. to the poor in London, and 200*l*. to those of Norfolk; a plain proof, considering the actual value of money, of his enormous wealth, especially as he had three daughters married highly, and a son, to whom he bequeathed a good estate. His wife also was Anne, daughter and co-heiress of Thomas Hoo, lord Hoo and Hastings. His second son, Sir William, who was of Blickling, in Norfolk, one of the eighteen knights of the Bath created at the coronation of Richard III. married Margaret, one of the daughters and co-heiresses of Thomas Butler, earl of Ormond, the only Irish peer who then enjoyed a seat in the English House of Lords. Sir William Boleyn's eldest son, named Thomas, married Elizabeth, daughter to Thomas Howard, earl of Surrey, afterwards duke of Norfolk, by whom he had a son named George, and two daughters, named Mary and Anne respectively. Anne was born at Blickling, apparently in 1507, but the baptismal register of that parish does not begin until 1557. She was sent to France in the autumn of 1514, with Mary, younger sister to Henry VIII., then married to Lewis XII. When the queen returned after that monarch's death in the following year, Anne did not come over with her, but remained in France with Claudia of Britanny, wife to Francis I., popularly called the *good queen*, being religious, equal tempered, and kind-hearted in a remarkable degree. This excellent princess, who had a large number of well-born young persons under her care, and who really conducted Anne Boleyn's education, died in 1524. Up to that time it has been generally stated, Sir Thomas Boleyn's daughter remained with her, and also that she was then transferred to the family of Margaret, duchess of Alençon, the favourite sister of Francis I., who, after losing her first husband, married, in January 1527, Henry d'Albret, nominal king of Navarre. Anne is thought to have returned almost immediately, but lord Herbert brings her back in 1522, or thereabouts, when, a difference having arisen between Henry and Francis, the English students were called home from Paris. Her parents, he says, then "thought it not fit that she should stay there any longer." However this may be, there is every reason to believe that Anne was in England at the time when the earl of Northumberland's elder son was married to the earl of Shrewsbury's daughter, a marriage of which the exact date is unknown, but which appears to have taken place about the close of 1523, or beginning of the following year. Anne Boleyn's connexion with this event depends chiefly upon a statement by Cavendish, gentleman usher to cardinal Wolsey, who says that the king had conceived a secret passion for her, and was consequently much hurt and offended by seeing that lord Percy, being similarly smitten, intended to espouse her. The result was, that Wolsey, to whom Percy was attached as an attendant, received orders from Henry to interfere, and a marriage was hastily made up between the unconscious rival of his sovereign and lady Mary Talbot. Wolsey's interference and its known results are here probably stated correctly, but as much cannot be safely said of Henry's concealed affection for Anne at that time. Cavendish says that the cardinal told Percy, "his highness intendeth to prefer her (Anne) to another person, with whom he hath travailed already, and being almost at a point with the same person, although she knoweth it not, yet hath the king, most like a politic and prudent prince, conveyed the matter in such sort, that she, upon his royal motion, will be, I doubt not, right glad and agreeable to the same." Now, it is merely a gratuitous inference, that this "other person" was the king himself. The fact really is, that Anne had been intended as a wife for the son of Sir Piers Butler, in order to terminate a dispute between the Boleyns and the Butlers, and that Henry having been brought, after some hesitation, to approve this plan, had charged Wolsey to carry it into execution. The "other person," therefore, intended for Anne by the king, was in all probability the son of Sir Piers Butler, and Henry, for aught that certainly appears, might have had little or no personal acquaintance with the celebrated beauty, whose miserable end has blemished his reputation so irreparably, until the time when she came to court as an attendant upon queen Catharine, which lord Herbert says was "about the twentieth year of her age." This coincides with the year 1527, when Henry first became actively busied about a divorce from Catharine, and when, accordingly, Anne's arrival from France has been commonly dated, her father having then gone over with Sir Anthony Brown to take the French king's oath to a league concluded some time before between the two crowns. Sir Thomas Boleyn had long been prominent among statesmen and courtiers, having been employed upon several embassies, and being treasurer of the royal household. It was his great ability as a diplomatist which raised him in Henry's estimation, it being found safer to trust him in all questions of foreign politics than any other English adviser of the crown. As an acknowledgment for these services, he was made knight of the Garter in 1523, and June 18, 1525, he was created viscount Rochford, being grandson and coheir of Thomas Butler, earl of Ormond, summoned to parliament, in 1495, as Sir Thomas Ormond de Rochford. He was also proprietor of that nobleman's estate at Rochford in Essex. It is idle to account for Sir Thomas Boleyn's elevation to the peerage upon any other ground than his own services, descent, and property. His daughter's charms, which ordinarily find a reason for the whole of his prosperity, were not likely to have had any weight at all in 1523, and could have had next to none in 1525. In the former year, Anne was a girl of sixteen, and in the latter, her age was only eighteen. Her acquaintance with Henry, besides, really appears to have commenced about two years later. Then, indeed, namely, in 1527, she gained undoubtedly a powerful hold upon the king, and her father's elevation, Dec. 8, 1529, to the earldoms of Wiltshire and Ormond, both honours, however, to which he had hereditary pretensions, was probably very much of a compliment to herself. Henry appears to have given the first public intimation of Anne's conquest, on Sunday, May 5, 1527, when he gave a grand entertainment at Hampton Court to the French ambassadors, who came thither for an audience of leave, after the conclusion of a treaty for the marriage of his daughter, the princess Mary, to some member of their royal family. Towards midnight, the king and viscount de Turenne, with six other persons, retired, and soon re-appearing, dressed as Venetian gentlemen, chose partners for a ball. Henry offered his hand to Anne Boleyn, Turenne to the princess Mary, dowager queen of France, and duchess of Suffolk. Subsequently Anne's progress to the dangerous height which she ultimately attained found little interruption. As a preliminary step she was created, Sept. 1, 1532, marchioness of Pembroke, under the name of Anne Rochford. The title itself might be considered as royal, Jasper Tudor, ultimately duke of Bedford, great-uncle to the king, having been earl of Pembroke. It has been represented that Henry's original design was to make Anne his mistress, and that she spurned the proposal almost in the words put into Elizabeth Woodville's mouth on receiving a declaration of love from Edward IV. Cardinal Pole also, whose violence upon paper is quite as remarkable as any smoothness that might have distinguished his ordinary conversation, attributes Anne's refusal of royal concubinage to experience of its uncertainty in her sister Mary's case. That lady was married January 31, 1521, to William Carey, esquire of the body, and a great favourite with the king, who seems to have been present at the marriage; and Romanists would fain believe it arranged by him as a provision for his cast-off mistress. It proved fruitful, not only a daughter springing from it, but a son also, Henry, created by his cousin, queen Elizabeth, baron of Hunsdon, although Romish imputations upon Mary Boleyn's memory are not strengthened by any hint of progeny from the king. Such imputations do not rest, however, upon Pole's authority alone. Sanders, the great provider of Romish darts against the English reformation, bears testimony likewise to Mary Boleyn's infamy. But he renders his account more stimulant, by relating that Henry fell into this connexion in the course of visits paid to Mary's mother, lady Boleyn, who was also his mistress, and bore him Anne, his future wife. Rastal is the authority cited by Sanders for this tale, which is equally revolting and absurd, Henry being not more than sixteen at the time of Anne's birth.

Her unhappy marriage was private, and it occurred about the 25th of January, 1533, as we learn from Cranmer, who has been represented as present, if not actually officiating. He did not, however, in fact, know of it until a fortnight afterwards. The ceremony was performed, according to Sanders and Stowe, by Rowland Lee, eventually bishop of Lichfield and Coventry. Soon afterwards, Anne's pregnancy rendered an avowal of the marriage necessary, and her brother, George Boleyn, viscount Rochford, was sent early in April to inform the king of France of it. Not even then, however, was it published to the world, probably under some expectation that papal approbation might be obtained for it in sufficient time for the expected issue. As this prospect soon became hopeless, Anne received the honours of royalty at court, on Easter-eve, April 12. On the 10th of the following month, Cranmer, as archbishop of the province, opened a court at Dunstable, within six miles of Ampthill, where Catharine of Aragon was residing, to examine the validity of her marriage with Henry. She treated his proceedings, notwithstanding the service upon her of a formal citation, with dignified silence, and thus, without any opposition on her part, sentence was given, on the 23d of May, pronouncing Henry's marriage with her null and void from the beginning, as being contrary to God's law, and consequently such as no human authority could render valid. Five days afterwards, Cranmer confirmed, at Lambeth, the king's marriage with Anne Boleyn, and on Whit Sunday, June 1, he crowned her at Westminster. On the 13th of the following September she gave birth to a princess, eventually the illustrious queen Elizabeth, at the royal palace of Greenwich. Of Anne's domestic life upon the throne few particulars remain, but her opinions were favourable to the Reformation; and Foxe declares her to have been most conspicuous for liberality to the poor. He also says that she desired her chaplains to use a perfect freedom in admonishing her of anything that they might consider in want of amendment. The honest and unsparing Latimer was one of these chaplains. Amidst so much deserving of commendation, it may reasonably be doubted whether Anne's manners were sufficiently guarded for the situation to which she was raised, and for Henry's overbearing jealous temper. Her education in France, where manners are more free than in England, may probably account for this defect. By such want of judgment she might have unconsciously laid a train for her downfal. But it was accomplished by the aid of other incidents. In the beginning of 1536, Catharine of Aragon died, exhibiting at the last that deeply religious feeling, and that kind affection for Henry, which necessarily raised her character, high as it stood before, and which made a powerful impression upon the king's mind. Anne could not be expected to share in his mournful reflections; but she might, and even without hypocrisy, have shown a saddened respect for the memory of a princess so amiable and unfortunate.

She did, however, it is said, show unseemly levity and exultation, when informed of Catharine's decease. At least she gave ground among the thoughtless crowd for such a view of her conduct, by departing from the national fashion of wearing black on the loss of friends, and appearing in a suit of yellow, the colour used as a mourning for queens at the court of France. Henry's complete alienation from her is attributed by Romish writers to a new passion that he had conceived for Jane Seymour, one of her maids of honour, daughter of a knight seated at Wolf-hall, in Wiltshire. Sanders relates that she surprised this young woman sitting on the king's knee, four months after Catharine's death, and that her emotions immediately became so violent as to throw her into premature labour, when she produced a shapeless mass. A contemporary French poet, whose interesting *Histoire d'Anne Boleyn* has been lately published by M. Crapelet, from a MS. in the royal library at Paris, at the end of Henry's letters to this unfortunate queen, gives a far more probable account of her parturition. According to this authority, Henry received so severe a fall from his horse when going out for a day's hunting, that his immediate death was at first apprehended. Anne being hastily informed of the accident was quickly seized by the pains of childbirth, and produced a male child, well-formed, but still-born. Henry's cherished hopes of a son were thus again rudely dashed to the ground, and nothing is more likely than that superstition immediately suggested to a mind like his, that he had married a second time under circumstances which rendered him obnoxious to the wrath of Heaven. Under any such belief, there can be no doubt that a new beauty's charms would quicken his exertions to be released, as those of Anne herself had done while the famous divorce was lagging tediously before mankind. Let any one remark the senseless excesses upon which Romish partisans are even now driven by the name of Boleyn, and he will see at once that nothing could be more within the reach of an arbitrary sovereign than a revolting case against the obnoxious Anne. When accordingly, on May-day, 1536, this unhappy beauty was publicly disgraced, the charges brought forward against her were of the most improbable and revolting character. Incest with her own brother, and adultery with other men, were alleged in justification of Henry's unmanly cruelty. Yet from all the particulars upon record of Anne's unhappy case, it is impossible to fix upon her memory the stain of moral guilt. Her brief career of splendour was unquestionably shaded by vanity and indiscretion. She was delighted to observe that the generality of men paid homage to those charms which had raised her to a throne; and nature had not formed her for dissembling the satisfaction that she felt. Such venial faults do appear, however, to have been the sole blemishes of her character. But when arraigned, May 15, 1536, before a court selected from the upper house, consisting of twenty-seven peers, she was found guilty, in spite of such a defence, unaided by counsel as she was, that made every spectator anticipate an acquittal. Two days after this, Anne's marriage with the king was annulled in an especial court holden before Cranmer at Lambeth. The ground is unknown, but it was something *confessed*, probably a prior engagement. This decision really destroyed Anne's imputed crime, but nothing short of her blood would satisfy the king, and on the 19th of May she was beheaded with a sword within the Tower. To all appearance a baser legal murder never disgraced a christian country. (Sanders. Heylin. Selden. Turner. Lingard.)

BOLGENI, (John Vincent,) an Italian Jesuit, born at Bergamo, in 1733, and remarkable, after the suppression of his order, for the ardent maintenance of those papal principles that it had been so active in disseminating. As he fell upon revolutionary times, when the papacy was at its lowest ebb, his various publications in favour of it, which are all in Italian, provoked great opposition, even some of his brethren feeling themselves called upon to refute them. He died at Cremona, in 1816. (Biog. Univ. Suppl.)

BOLINGBROKE, (Henry St. John, viscount,) a distinguished English writer and politician, only son of Sir Henry St. John, of Lydiard Tregoze, in Wiltshire, baronet, by Mary, his first wife, second daughter and co-heiress of Robert Rich, third earl of Warwick of that family. He was born at Battersea, in Surrey October 1, 1678, and his tender years were chiefly spent under the care of his grandmother, a rigid presbyterian, who found a tutor for him in Daniel Burgess, a minister of her own persuasion. This instructor was, perhaps, as unfit for a pupil like young St. John, as any that could be found, for he intermingled nonconformist austerity with flashes of sportive humour, which might laugh it out of countenance. Thus a boy, whose parts were unusually lively, was, at one time, driven to read puritanical divinity, at another, was amused by his tutor's oddities. His father, too, was one of the last men to give good advice, or exercise a sound control, having not only plunged into various excesses, but even also committed a murder, of which he was convicted, although for some unknown reason he escaped its penalty. An early training of this kind will account for much that is exceptionable in St. John's after-life. As his age advanced he was sent to Eton, where he became acquainted with Walpole, afterwards the celebrated minister, who was two years older than himself; but the two boys appear to have disagreed, and thus a foundation of personal dislike was laid for that political rivalry which estranged them at a future period. From Eton, Bolingbroke removed to Christ Church, Oxford, and was noticed there for great natural abilities, though neither for steadiness of application, nor moral propriety. On leaving the university, he plunged into all the excesses of fashionable dissipation; but a friendship formed with Dryden, then aged and depressed, proved him far above the intellectual average of wild young men. After a brief interval of riotous extravagance, his father grew tired of supplying the necessary funds, and resolved upon sending him abroad, both to improve his mind, and to break his connexion with a circle of objectionable associates. Besides obtaining these advantages from his travels, he thus gained a knowledge of the French language, which served him essentially when become a leading politician. Soon after his return he was married, in 1700, to a daughter and co-heiress of Sir Henry Winchescomb, the descendant of that opulent clothier, who was familiarly known under Henry VIII. as Jack of Newbury. By this lady he gained a large fortune, but otherwise the connexion proved most unsatisfactory. St. John complained that his wife's temper was insufferable; she, that his infidelities were shameless and intolerable; and they soon formally separated. Being, however, now in circumstances for a seat in parliament, he was elected member for Wootton Bassett, a borough which his father had several times represented. In the house of commons he soon made his way, by a brilliancy and readiness which rendered him secure of official greatness. Both his father and grandfather had been of the Whig party, which was yet in power, and with little appearance of weakness either in the house or out of doors. Young St. John, however, formed an intimate connexion with Robert Harley, afterwards earl of Oxford, whose hopes of rising were built upon a coalition of parties, which he thought himself able to effect. With a view of doing this, Harley, though representative of a presbyterian family, was now courting the Tories, whose popularity was upon the increase, and who came into power at the beginning of queen Anne's reign. Neither Harley nor St. John, however, was admitted into the ministry until the year 1704, when the former was made secretary of state, and the latter secretary at war. Harley was removed in 1707, and St. John immediately resigned. He soon afterwards retired from parliament, and spent two years in the country, diligently employed upon that acquisition of knowledge which had formerly been prevented by his irregular habits, and latterly by official duties. These duties had shown him the extent of his deficiencies, and he now devoted himself to the removal of them, with all the eagerness of an aspiring spirit, and with all the success that great abilities could command.

In 1710, the Godolphin administration fell, and Harley became head of a new cabinet. He desired originally an infusion of Whigs, but found it impracticable, and accordingly sought colleagues entirely among the Tories. Jealous of St. John's brilliant parts and restless ambition, he would fain have merely restored his old appointment. But St. John knew the value of his aid, and would not give it on such terms. Harley was, therefore, under the necessity of making him secretary of state. In supporting themselves under the difficulties of a powerful Whig opposition, the new ministry sought literary aid, which was very much under St. John's direction, and Swift, and Atterbury, with other such geniuses, were guided by his instructions in advocating Tory politics. The chief engine employed for this purpose was a weekly paper called the Examiner. In this, one piece appeared, which engrossed for a time public attention, known as Mr. St. John's Letter to the Examiner: it contains a detailed attack upon the late ministry, displaying advantageously the writer's peculiar talents for influencing popular opinion. In this view, even St. John's abuse of the celebrated duchess of Marlborough might not have been ill-judged, for contemporaries commonly take a malicious pleasure in such attacks upon each other. But posterity sees with disgust a female possessed of many superior qualities, though violent in temper, and at one time a court minion, branded as "a fury broke loose to execute the vengeance of heaven on a sinful people." This particular sally, too, is more than usually offensive from St. John's unhappy prejudices against religion. It can hardly be acquitted of cant and hypocrisy. Such was, however, the sensation made by St. John's paper, that besides attacks from distinguished men of letters, even earl Cowper, who yet held the seals, intermitted his judicial tasks to answer it. St. John was thus exhibited as the first English political writer of his time, and people generally thought him to have established a triumphant case. In the house of commons he became equally celebrated, his eloquence having established a decided supremacy there, even before Harley's elevation to the peerage, as earl of Oxford and Mortimer. After that period, he was the regular ministerial leader. He was not, however, fortunate in an expedition against Quebec, undertaken chiefly by his means in 1711. On the contrary, the ships employed were found too large for sailing up the river, and some unlucky accidents concurring with ill-devised measures, an expedition which affected considerably St. John's reputation, ended in disaster and disgrace. During the party contests which preceded the peace of Utrecht, the secretary came into more than a common parliamentary conflict with Walpole, his old rival at school. That statesman was found to have been connected with some clandestine practices, while he held office under the late ministry, a sum of 500*l*. paid for a contract being treated, certainly with a great appearance of probability, as a bribe received by himself. In consequence, it was voted, that he had been guilty of a high breach of trust, and notorious corruption; he was expelled the house of commons, imprisoned in the Tower, and declared incapable of sitting in the present parliament. To soreness from all this disgrace, and a conviction that it was chiefly owing to St. John, has been attributed much of that personal hostility with which the future minister is thought to have perseveringly regarded his old schoolfellow. In 1712, St. John was raised to the peerage, and thus gained the appellation by which he is generally known. In the preceding year, Paulet St. John, a collateral relative, died without issue, and thus the earldom of Bolingbroke, which he had enjoyed, became extinct. His cousin, the secretary of state, wished for a revival of this honour in his own person, but importantly as he had served the ministry, he could not obtain gratification to this extent. His colleague, Oxford, had long been jealous of him, and by talking to the queen of his profligacy in private life, had rendered him an object of her aversion. He could not, accordingly, obtain a higher rank than that of viscount, greatly to his disgust and mortification. But although he charged his disappointment chiefly upon Oxford, he did not choose to break with him openly, party spirit, or love of power, retaining him as the colleague of a minister, whom henceforth he envied as more successful than himself in the race of ambition, and abhorred as the author of a check that galled his haughty spirit. He never forgave Oxford. Many years afterwards, when exile and misfortune would have taught a christian spirit something better, he recapitulated his great services to the ministry, and spoke of the elevation that acknowledged them, as "a punishment, not a reward." To put him into good humour, Oxford subsequently said, he was sent on an embassy to France, while the negotiations lingered at Utrecht. It has, however, been asserted on the other side, that important ends were contemplated from Bolingbroke's mission, and that his abilities secured them. Be these things as they may, his diplomatic visit to France brought a severe stain upon his reputation. He was accused of betraying, in the course of it, English secrets to the court of Versailles. Madame Tencin, famed for personal attractions, and skill in intrigue, became acquainted with him, by the contrivance, it was reported, of De Torcy, and managed so as to steal some papers which that minister wished to see. Whatever may be the truth of this tale, not only an opening will be always given for circulating successfully such accounts when dissipated men like Bolingbroke are placed in situations of trust, but also there is a real danger of unintentional evils from them. Their want of the best principles, and subjection to a tyrannical thirst of pleasure, neither allow them a thorough mastery of their own actions, nor that circumspection which confidential offices require. On the secretary's return from his embassy, a new mortification awaited him. Death had recently placed several blue ribands at the queen's disposal, and Oxford obtained one of them, but Bolingbroke was passed over, to his great indignation. He now renounced every friendly feeling towards the early partner of his ambitious policy, and determined within himself, that one or both must fall. But before measures could be securely taken for Oxford's ruin, by one whose party prospects lay all on the same side, it was necessary to establish a strong position against the Whig interest, by completing the pacification of Utrecht. This proved an arduous undertaking both at home and abroad. Nor when, at length, in May 1713, the peace was proclaimed, were ministerial difficulties over. In parliament, indeed, a majority approved, and Whig opposition was rather noisy than dangerous; but every article of the treaty was attacked with extreme rancour and intemperance out of doors. Thus the ministers found none of the ease and popularity upon which they had reckoned from the successful issue of their labours; on the contrary, their position appeared to grow more uncertain every day, and, as usual, under such circumstances, individuals among them began to speculate upon the expediency of seeking fresh connexions. A leading cause of disunion arose from divisions among the Tories themselves. A few of them were Jacobites, anxious to restore her brother on the queen's death; but the majority consisted of zealous Protestants, who disapproved of the Pretender on account of his religion, and consequently maintained a close correspondence with the Hanoverian court. It became the prevailing belief there, that the English ministry generally, but especially Bolingbroke, desired nothing so much as a revocation of the Stuarts. Another cause of Tory unpopularity at the electoral court was the indifference with which it was treated by that party. The Whigs were assiduous in their communications and professions, while their political antagonists appeared rather to think the new royal family expected from Germany interested in seeking their support, than themselves concerned in securing its favour. As Anne's health became more precarious, these causes rendered the ministry weaker almost every day. Its acts were interpreted as insidious expedients to favour the Pretender, and interested observers were anxious to stand clear of men whose day of power seemed rapidly upon the wane. While external forces were thus actively at work upon the cabinet, its weakness became incurable from the old grudge between Oxford and Bolingbroke. The latter stopped at nothing likely to ruin his hated rival; but among his movements, no one is more discreditable to his memory than the support given to the Schism Bill. The queen's conscientious love to the Church made her strongly averse from dissent, and many of her subjects naturally felt in a similar manner. To secure support from her and them, a bill was brought into the house of commons, May 12, 1714, for taking from dissenters the means of educating their own children in non-conforming principles. Having passed that house, it was advocated by Bolingbroke, its probable author, with all the energy and eloquence of which he was master. He has thus earned for himself from the intended sufferers a parallel with Julian the Apostate, whose writings, they say, are the delight of infidels, and who would fain have crushed Christianity by the very means which the Schism Bill provided against protestant non-conformity. This intolerant measure, having passed the lords by five votes only, was to come into operation on the 1st of August, 1714. But on that very day queen Anne died, and the act became a dead letter. Before the royal demise, Bolingbroke had succeeded in obtaining Oxford's dismissal; and he would undoubtedly have been appointed treasurer in his room, had not the sovereign's dangerous illness, and an unexpected movement at the council-board, disappointed him. He soon found himself virtually dismissed from the office which he actually held. When the new council of regency assembled on George the First's accession, letters were no longer brought to him, but to them, by whom they were opened and canvassed. He lost no time in writing to the new king, in such terms as were likely to give pleasure; but his only answer was a despatch, received August 31, to dismiss him from the secretaryship. The seals of office were immediately demanded of him by the duke of Shrewsbury, who took possession of his papers, locking and sealing the room in which they were. Mr. Hare, the under-secretary, had found means, however, to remove those which were most available against his principal; but Bolingbroke's lofty spirit would not take advantage of this foresight, and every thing was returned. When George came to England, he made many protestations of loyalty and submission, but these were probably disbelieved; and when he requested the honour of kissing the king's hand, he was mortified by a refusal. The most searching investigations were now made into documents of every description, to furnish materials for impeachment of the late ministers. Even private letters, sealed up by queen Anne, to be burnt after her death, were opened. Such illiberal industry rendered it hardly doubtful that both Oxford and Bolingbroke, with Anne's connivance, had entered into schemes, though very cautiously, for excluding the house of Hanover. But Oxford soon showed himself unwilling to go far enough, while Bolingbroke's ambition urged him to an appearance of completely meeting the sovereign's known wishes. On the discovery of evidence so injurious to their credit with Anne's successor, the two discarded ministers acted accordingly. Oxford remained, and boldly faced his enemies; Bolingbroke fled. He seems, indeed, to have been assured, that an impeachment and some degree of punishment were not to suffice with him; nothing short of the scaffold was intended. After appearing at the theatre with all his usual gaiety, he left London, disguised as valet to one of the French king's messengers, on the night of Friday, March 25, 1715, and landed at Calais in the evening of the following Sunday. A new parliament had met about a week before, and a great majority were Whigs, not without anxiety, of course, as to the continuance of a government so new, and supported by a party so obnoxious to large numbers of influential men. Hence Walpole had not the least difficulty in impeaching Bolingbroke of high treason, and of other high crimes and misdemeanors; a single speech, after a long pause, being made in his favour, and that merely contending that no charge had been made which could possibly amount to high treason. An attempt was, indeed, made by another member to defend him; but the speaker's utterance was choked by his emotion, and he could only declare himself to have much in store for his friend's defence, which must be reserved until a future opportunity. The resolution for impeachment then passed without a division. When this matter came into the house of lords, an order was issued for arresting the accused; and a formal report of his flight being received, a message to that effect was transmitted to the commons. They passed a bill, summoning him to appear on a certain day, and in default, attainting him of high treason. This bill passed the lords, but not without a strong protest entered against it; and having received the royal assent, Bolingbroke, at the time specified, became degraded from his rank, attainted in blood, unable to inherit his family estates, and liable to suffer death if he should return to his native country. Fortunately for him, he had invested in foreign securities a sum of money, while yet in office; and he was now, therefore, above want, about 13,000*l.* being in his possession. Such resources, however, were miserably unequal to the cravings of a spirit greedy of dissipation and parade, like his. Still he would not link himself with the Pretender, until, in his own words, "the smart of a bill of attainder tingled in every vein." He had received overtures from the exiled prince immediately on his landing in France; but not contented with an absolute rejection of them, he even removed from Paris into Dauphiny, that he might be farther from the mimic English court. Proscription and confiscation at length overcame every scruple, and repairing to the titular monarch of Great Britain, he publicly avowed himself his adherent. He was made his secretary of state, and would have prevented his ill-concerted expedition to Scotland in the autumn of 1715; being well aware, that without powerful continental help, which was unattainable, the hostility of most people in England, and the apathy of others, would render the partial enthusiasm of Scotland perfectly useless to the Stuarts. Soon after, the event confirmed Bolingbroke's worst anticipations; the Pretender, from some sudden disgust, hastily dismissed him, undoubtedly, to his own very great satisfaction; as he had now gained a thorough insight into the personal weakness of his new master, the sanguine delusions prevailing among those about him, and the little interest taken in his cause by persons worthy of reliance. He saw himself, besides, second in his counsels to Ormond; and having borne impatiently a superior in the cabinet of England, his proud spirit was deeply wounded by finding one in a position so much less commanding. The queen-dowager felt immediately her son's folly in contemptuously discarding the ablest man connected with him, and begging Bolingbroke to retain the seals, promised a satisfactory arrangement. "No," he haughtily replied, "tell them that I am now a free man; and may this arm rot off, if, in their service, it ever direct a sword or pen again." The Pretender's little court was now all on fire, and charging Bolingbroke with treachery, and want of due exertion, it ridiculously took recent proceedings in England for a model, and impeached him. When this folly was known in England, a sense of Bolingbroke's importance with the Tories immediately made the ministry desirous of gaining him, and the earl of Stair received instructions to ascertain what could be done. With that nobleman the exile held a conversation during an hour and a half, in which he declared himself bound as a man of honour to keep inviolate all secrets learnt as the Pretender's adviser, but wholly discharged by his insults from taking any farther interest in his affairs; while his own duty as an Englishman both inclined and obliged him to render any service to king George that might be the means of healing those divisions which prevailed among his countrymen. As the ministers obtained no new information from this interview, they were probably disappointed and rendered careless of a more intimate connexion with Bolingbroke. They did, however, go so far as to ennoble his father, who reached an extreme old age, in July, 1716; but the son's attainder was left in force. During the exile that it inflicted on him, his first wife died. She and her husband had never been reconciled after their separation, and she adopted a line of politics the reverse of his, being highly loyal to the house of Hanover. Perhaps, this feeling might have earned her some indulgence, as she obtained from the wreck of his property a sufficiency to support her like a person of rank and fortune. The amount of Bolingbroke's forfeited resources appears from a return to parliament, made immediately after the rebellion of 1715, which states his estate at 2,552*l.* 15*s.* Before his wife died, he had become a favoured admirer of Madame Maintenon's niece, the widowed marchioness de Villette, a lady of considerable fortune, and greater expectations. To her he was married in May, 1720, and she immediately professed herself a protestant; an union with a papist being probably thought injurious to the bridegroom's political prospects. He did not, however, for some time publicly avow his marriage, as it seems, from a fear that it might confiscate about 50,000*l.* which his new wife possessed in the English funds. The interest of this sum was regularly received through an agent, who refused in 1722, when her marriage with Bolingbroke became known, to continue his remittances, alleging, very fairly, that he could not safely act otherwise to the wife of one under an attainder. To remedy this evil, the lady again appeared as a widow, and calling herself the marquise de Villette, set out for England, where, after some difficulty, she regained possession of her property. She was largely indebted for this to the influence of Simon, viscount Harcourt, who had been chancellor when Bolingbroke was secretary of state, and who now gladly befriended him. By his means the lady was next introduced to the king's left-handed wife, the duchess of Kendal, whose venality and influence over George I. were unbounded, and who was bribed by 11,000*l.* to press the exiled statesman's case upon him. Walpole, however, vehemently opposed indulgence, and at length, nothing farther was granted than restoration in blood, which passed the great seal in May 1723. Bolingbroke could now live in England, but he recovered neither his forfeited estate, nor his seat in the upper house. He hastened, however, back to his native land, and, it is said, came to Calais, in his way thither, when bishop Atterbury had just arrived in the same town on his way to exile for life. At all events, it seems, that the prelate heard there of his old friend's pardon, and remarked, "Ah! then, I see we are exchanged." Bolingbroke did not long remain in England, but he continued indefatigable in seeking a complete restoration. Towards this another step was made in 1725, by an act to reverse the forfeiture, which passed the legislature after a strong opposition. Bolingbroke was now enabled to take the family inheritance when it should fall to him, and to enjoy whatever other property he had acquired, or might acquire; but his attainder remained, and excluded him from parliament. With such a measure of mercy he was bitterly disappointed; and imputing its scantiness to Walpole, who really fell under great unpopularity for doing so much, he returned to England, settling himself at Dawley, near Uxbridge, where he bent all his energies to oppose the government. Being precluded from making his voice heard in parliament, he became a political journalist, and by a series of papers in the Occasional Writer, and in the Craftsman, he caused considerable uneasiness to the ministry. In the latter publication appeared his letters upon English history, written under the signature of Humphrey Oldcastle, which display great acuteness and an intimate acquaintance with the subject. These letters procured for the Craftsman, during their appearance, an immense sale, even exceeding that of the Spectator. All these efforts, however, proved unequal to shake Walpole's power, and by consequence to gratify Bolingbroke by a complete restoration. Hence he gradually became weary of the contest, and after publishing a Dissertation on Parties, he determined upon withdrawing to the continent. His masterly treatise, which is in nineteen letters, appeared in a complete state in 1736, furnished, like others of his works, with an ironical dedication to Walpole. He had, however, some months before, left England for Chanteloup, in Touraine, where he intended to pass the remainder of his days. He there soon employed himself upon his Letters on the Study and Use of History, which were privately printed and dispersed among his more intimate acquaintances. They are striking proofs of his memory and extent of reading; but his necessary reliance on the former, at a place where he had few books within reach, has betrayed him into some mistakes. Bolingbroke now contemplated a History of Europe, from the Pyrenean treaty to the conclusion of the negotiations at Utrecht; but although he meant it as a solid foundation for his literary fame, he never did more than prepare materials for the work. His attention was, indeed, continually turned away to productions of a less imposing character, among which, the Idea of a Patriot King attracted most notice. It was written with a view to the succession of Frederic, prince of Wales, who had made advances to the author, and become intimately acquainted with him. In drawing his picture, experience has not been taken as a guide, but brilliant political romances, like Xenophon's Cyropædia, and Fenelon's Telemachus. Hence his positions rest on unlimited pretensions to candour, liberality of sentiment, universal philanthropy, and a tender concern for the happiness of posterity. Perhaps Bolingbroke himself had occasional suspicions that some of these flights of imagination bordered upon romance. He did not, accordingly, wish his essay to be immediately published; but upon this, as upon some other occasions, he meant a few copies only to be first printed for circulation among the most intimate of his friends, intending to render the work fit for general reading at some future period. For this preliminary printing, the essay was handed over to Pope, and on his death, in 1744, it was found that 1,500 copies of it had been printed; nearly all of them had never seen the light, but more were in circulation than Bolingbroke intended. He was highly enraged, Pope not only having thus exceeded his commission, but also having taken the liberty, which was still more offensive, of making various alterations. Having obtained from the warehouse all the printed sheets remaining there, Bolingbroke now burnt them in one pile upon his terrace at Battersea. This was excusable; not so his employment of Mallet, as editor of a new and correct edition, and ostensible author of an Advertisement appended to it, severely reflecting upon Pope. Thus Bolingbroke, whom posterity chiefly knows as the St. John that appears in the first line of Pope's Essay on Man, did all in his power to blacken the memory of that immortal genius, whose acquaintance was one of the greatest real distinctions of his life. It cannot be urged in extenuation, that Mallet is responsible for this want of feeling and foresight. The original MS. of the Advertisement is preserved in the British Museum, exhibiting frequent alterations in Bolingbroke's own handwriting, and these are by no means the least bitter of its passages.

In 1742, Bolingbroke's father died, at the age of ninety, and as his capability of succeeding to the family estate had been restored, he determined upon removing finally from France, and fixing himself at Battersea, where the St. Johns had long possessed a seat. His old rival, Walpole, was driven from the helm of state in the very same year, and he owed, undoubtedly, that mortification very largely to Bolingbroke's exertions as a party writer. The latter was not, however, benefited by his downfal, a nominal coalition, but a ministry really Whig, succeeding. In 1750, Bolingbroke lost his wife, an accomplished woman to whom he was much attached; and on Dec. 15, 1751, he followed her to the tomb, a family vault in Battersea church. His mortal disease was cancer in the face, under which he sank rather sooner than had been expected, from the injudicious treatment of an empiric, to whom he had submitted himself. It was only latterly that he had avowed himself a deist; and he closed his eyes upon the world in awful consistency with that character, unhesitatingly rejecting the proffered services of a clergyman. He had, however, through life, been conspicuous for irreligion, licentious habits, naturally suggesting cavils at that by which he stood condemned. Yet his learning did not qualify him for any sufficient inquiry into the evidences of revelation. Of Greek he seems to have known little or nothing, authors in that language being used by him invariably through a Latin translation. Nor was he critically acquainted with either history or chronology. He was not sufficiently patient and laborious. His real strength lay in brilliancy of imagination, force of character, mastery of language, readiness of application, qualities for shining in society, and general information. As a writer, he ranks with Addison and Swift, and the three infused into English composition an elegance unknown before. Contemporaries considered him superior to the two others. Addison was, indeed, equally elegant, but not more correct, and his diction is less vivid and striking. Bolingbroke left the copyright of his works to David Mallet, with the liberty of reprinting them; and in 1754, a complete edition of them appeared. His public correspondence and state papers, written while he was secretary of state, have since been added, swelling the whole collection of his works to seven quartos. At the time when this remarkable man's productions were first fairly brought together before the world, they occasioned considerable disgust and some uneasiness. Many of the clergy preached against them, and the grand jury of Westminster presented them as a nuisance. Their importance now is gone. The elegance of style that characterises them has been long far from uncommon, the politics upon which they bear are little regarded, and their superficial, heartless treatment of vital questions, provokes pity, contempt, or indignation. (Cooke's Memoirs of Lord Bolingbroke. Coxe's Memoirs of Sir Robert Walpole. Horace Walpole's Memoirs of the last Ten Years of George II. Bogue and Bennett's Hist. of Dissenters.)

BOLIVAR, (Gregory de,) a Spanish observantine friar, who spent twenty-five years as a missionary in America, exploring completely both Mexico and Peru, hitherto little known and quite undescribed. The latter deficiency he undertook to supply, and accordingly a work for this purpose was prepared by him; but although nearly completed, it does not appear to have been published. As a missionary, Bolivar is said to have been very successful, his labours in that way having extended to the Moluccas and other parts of the East. To his literary talents the only published testimony appears to be, Memorial de Arbitrios para la Reparacion de España, Madrid, 1626. (Antonio.)

BOLIVAR, Y PONTE, (Simon de,) celebrated as the South American *liberator*, born at Caracas, July 24, 1783, and early deprived of his parents, who were opulent. At fourteen, he was sent to an uncle at Madrid for education, and great aptness for the exact sciences was displayed by him. After contracting a very early marriage with a cousin, whom he took over to South America, and soon lost there by a fever, he paid another visit to Europe, and was at Paris when Bonaparte was crowned. This extraordinary rise fired his imagination, already heated by dwelling upon the glories of Washington and Franklin. He thus became haunted with visions of accomplishing in America something similar to that which the able and seemingly-fortunate Corsican had accomplished in Europe. That ever memorable man found an opening for his patriotic ambition by the attempt to seize upon Spain, which at once dissolved the bands of government in Mexico and South America. Bolivar was not, however, very prompt in struggling for the independence of his country, treating some of the earliest movements for that purpose as very injudicious, and filling then no higher station than that of colonel in the militia. Notwithstanding, when the revolutionary parties succeeded, he was one of the envoys chosen for soliciting assistance from Great Britain. His mission proving little satisfactory, he left his colleague in England, and returned to America, where he rapidly rose to distinction as a commander and politician. He had many reverses to undergo, and at one time his fortunes were so low, after great previous successes, that he embarked for Jamaica, with a view to arrange new expeditions at a distance from his enemies. Hence he passed over to St. Domingo, where Petion promised him aid on condition of his emancipating the blacks in countries under his authority. While in that island, he was re-elected captain-general of Venezuela and New Grenada. Returning to the continent, he succeeded in forming these two provinces into a new state, to which was given the name of Columbia; and in 1821, he was chosen president of the republic established there. He took subsequently a prominent part in the distractions of Peru, a portion of which was formed into a new republic, named Bolivia, in honour of him. His object was to form all South America into one immense republic, not doubting that he would be able to become its chief. But jealousies and difficulties of various kinds were found insurmountable, and in May, 1830, he resigned even the presidency of Columbia, being quite worn out by the labours and misrepresentations that he had to undergo. He died on the 17th of December in that same year. (Biog. Univ. Suppl. Biog. des Contemp.)

BOLLAN, (William,) an American political writer, and agent from Massachusetts to Great Britain, who died in 1776, having published, Importance of Cape Breton, Lond. 1746; Coloniæ Anglicanæ Illustratæ, 1762, besides many political and other pamphlets. (Carter's Univ. Biog. Dict.)

BOLLANDUS, (John,) a learned Jesuit, born at Tirlemont, in the Low Countries, August 13, 1596, and celebrated as the first in a series of writers, called from him *Bollandists*, who have laboured upon the hagiology of papal Rome. He was chosen by his superiors to execute a design formed by Rosweide, one of his order, who died in 1629, to collect such information as could be found relating to the canonized dead, and publish it under the title of Acta Sanctorum quotquot toto Orbe coluntur. With him was associated Godfrey Henschen, and the two published at Antwerp, in 1643, the first two volumes of their laborious undertaking, folios, containing the saints whose days occur in January. February occupies three volumes, which appeared in 1658. Bollandus died Sept. 12, 1665, leaving March incomplete. Henschen now demanded a coadjutor, as Bollandus had done before, and Daniel Papebroch was assigned him. By their joint care the unfinished month was published in 1668, in three volumes, with an eulogium of Bollandus prefixed. April also, in three volumes, appeared in 1675, comprising an essay by Papebroch upon the mode of distinguishing the supposititious from the genuine in chartularies. May was not published all together, the first sixteen days appearing in 1680, the year in which Henschen died. Other labourers were, however, found by the society of Jesuits, and the collection ultimately filled fifty-three folio volumes, but it only reaches to the 14th of October. The fifty-third volume was printed at Tongerloo, in 1794. This voluminous work contains a vast mass of interesting matter, and is purged from much of the offensive absurdities that are found in ancient lives of saints. The forty-two volumes of it which go down to September 15, have been reprinted at Venice, but the new edition fails in correctness. Besides giving a beginning and a name to this famous collection, Bollandus wrote notes upon Eginhart's Life of Charlemagne, which Schminck printed in his edition of that work. (Moreri. Biog. Univ.)

BOLLANDUS, or VAN BOLLANDT, (Sebastian,) a Franciscan friar, born at Maestricht, who died at Antwerp, Oct. 13, 1645. He edited the Historica, Theologica, et Moralis Terræ Sanctæ Elucidatio of Quaresmius, and the Sermones Aurei of Peter Aux-Bœufs, a Franciscan, born at Paris, who was professor of theology in the fifteenth century. (Biog. Univ.)

BOLLIOUD-MERMET, (Lewis,) secretary to the academy of Lyons. He was born in that city in 1709, and he died in 1793, leaving De la Bibliomanie, 1761, and some other works, published anonymously, besides a discourse spoken before the academy. (Biog. Univ.)

BOLOGNA, (Lattanzio,) an Italian painter, pupil of the Caracci, much employed at Rome, and highly talented. He died about 1597, aged only 27. (Bryan.)

BOLOGNE, (John de,) an eminent statuary, born at Douay in 1524. He died in 1608, leaving many memorials of his genius.—(Peter de,) a French lyric poet, born in 1706, of a family long settled in Provence. He died about 1789, leaving some excellent sacred odes. (Biog. Univ. Biog. Univ. Suppl.)

BOLOGNESE, (Charles,) a good fresco painter, born at Bologna in 1665. His subjects were architecture and perspective. He died in 1718.—*Bolognese, il;* the eminent painter, John Francis Grimaldi, born at Bologna, in 1606, is commonly so styled. (Bryan. Pilkington.)

BOLOGNETTI, (Francis,) gonfalonier of Bologna in 1555, chiefly remarkable as author of Il Costante, an epic poem on the ancient model, highly applauded by Italian writers on the epopee, and by Tasso among them.—(Pompey,) doctor of philosophy and medicine, born at Bologna, of a noble family, towards the end of the sixteenth century, remarkable for two medical works, even yet worthy of notice, one entitled Consilium de Præcautione, Occasione Mercium, ab Insultibus imminentis Contagii; the other, Remora Senectutis. (Biog. Univ.)

BOLOGNI, (Jerome,) a Latin poet, born at Trevigio, in 1454. He died there in 1517, after a most uneasy life, having been successively a notary, an advocate, and a clergyman. He was long employed in superintending the editions brought out by Michael Manzolo, the celebrated printer of Trevigio. A Latin epic by him, entitled Mediolanum, suggested by a journey that he undertook to Milan about 1480, was published in 1626. (Biog. Univ.)

BOLOGNINI, (Angelo,) an Italian surgeon, who taught surgery at Padua from 1508 to 1517, and employed mercurial frictions in his practice, of the utility of which he appears to have been the discoverer. A work of his is inserted in the collection of Gesner and Uffenbach, entitled, De Cura Ulcerum exteriorum et de Unguentis communibus in Solutione continui.

BOLOGNINI, (Lewis,) a celebrated Italian civilian, who died in 1508. He had been sent as envoy from the papal court to that of France, but his claims upon the notice of posterity rest chiefly upon corrections of the text of the Pandects. These he entitled Emendationes Juris Civilis, and they were published at Lyons in 1516, in the Corpus Legum. In his lifetime he published also some legal works and some poems. He had a son named Bartholomew, who followed his own profession, and left some works concerning it, besides an epitome of Ovid's Metamorphoses in elegiac verse. (Biog. Univ.)

BOLOGNINI, the name of three artists, all born at Bologna. (John Baptist,) a painter and engraver, who died in 1688, was one of the ablest scholars of Guido Reni. His nephew and pupil, Giacomo, born in 1664, became a reputable painter of history. (Charles,) born in 1678, an architectural painter, was much employed at Vienna, where he resided some years. (Bryan.)

BOLSEC, (Jerome Hermas,) a Carmelite friar of Paris, who having given offence by his preaching, threw up the monastic habit, and fled to Ferrara, the duchess Renée of France then affording an asylum to persecuted protestants. Here with slender qualifications he practised medicine, but he was banished in disgrace. Thence he went to Geneva, as a physician, and acquired notoriety there by attacking the doctrine of predestination. After some private conferences with Calvin, in October, 1551, he objected publicly, 1. that predestination makes God the author of sin; 2, that election is the *consequence*, not the *source*, of our faith; 3, that it was not, as alleged by its advocates, the doctrine of Augustine or other ancient fathers, but of recent origin, and he warned the people to beware of assertions to the contrary, as false and pernicious. Calvin immediately defended his doctrine in a speech of more than an hour's duration, and Bolsec was committed to prison by a magistrate present, "for turbulently warning the people against their pastors." Conferences were held with him in prison by Calvin and others, of which regular reports were submitted to the churches of Zurich, Berne, and Basle. Their replies, especially that from Basle, are admirable for their wisdom and moderation. "We must guard (say they) against too much severity towards those who are in error, lest, while with excessive eagerness we seek purity of doctrine, we violate the rules of the spirit of Christ. Truth is dear to Christ; but so also are the souls of his sheep. Remember how much more easily men are led back to order by mildness, than dragged back by severity." Bolsec offered to subscribe the answer from Basle, but, being suspected of insincerity and equivocation to gain his release, his offer was little accounted of. At last, he was banished from Geneva by the senate for seditious conduct and Pelagian doctrine,—some add, for immoralities also. Berne likewise discarded him, on which he retired to France, and applied to the protestants there. In 1562 he recanted what was deemed objectionable in a full synod at Orleans, and was admitted, some say, to minister among the protestants; but the next year, in a synod at Lyons, he was deposed and branded as "a most infamous liar and apostate." He then returned to popery, and published in French, in 1577, what he called "A Life of Calvin," but in truth, "a satire and continued invective," full of foul charges and malicious falsehoods. In 1582, he produced a similar biography of Beza; and such was the violence of theological animosity in that age, that both these libels were speedily translated into Latin. The attack upon Calvin was also translated into German. Bolsec has been said to have written likewise biographies of this kind of Zuingle, Luther, and Œcolampadius.

BOLSWERT, the name of two brothers, eminent engravers at Antwerp towards the end of the sixteenth century. The younger, Scheltius, has left admirable prints after some of the finest pictures of Rubens and Vandyck. The elder, Boetius Adam, seems to have adopted the free open manner of Cornelius Bloemart. There was also another person of some celebrity, named from the same town in Friesland, which gave names to the two engravers. He was a lay brother in a monastery of canons regular of St. Austin, and wrote a history of Friesland down to the year 1550, which is the time when he lived. (Bryan. Moreri.)

BOLTIN, (John,) son of Nikita, a Russian historical writer, born at Petersburg, in 1735, and distinguished from most authors of that kind in his nation by a sound spirit of criticism and excellence of method. His profession was the military, but he published, so early as 1782, in Russ, a chorographical description of the mineral waters of Sarepta. In 1787, he published, at the expense of the imperial government, critical remarks upon the Russian history of the French physician Leclerc. It is a bitter but just exposure, and contains much valuable information. The French author, however, had followed prince Stcherbatow in many of his errors, and the latter felt so sore under Boltin's caustic, that he could not rest without attempting a defence. This produced Boltin's critical reflections upon the Russian history of prince Stcherbatow. But in spite of his ability in unfolding the national annals, Boltin shows his original deficiency of an enlarged education in adhering to some popular prejudices and fables. He died Oct. 6, 1792. (Biog. Univ. Suppl.)

BOLTON, or BOULTON, (Edmund,) an English historical and antiquarian writer, who was attached to the establishment of George Villiers, duke of Buckingham, James the First's great favourite. Of Bolton's history little else is known, than that he was a Romanist, which caused a life of Henry II. written by him for Speed's Chronicle, to be set aside as too favourable to archbishop Becket, and one by Dr. Barcham inserted in its room. He also wrote, The Elements of Armories, Lond. 1610; a poem on the removal of the remains of Mary, queen of Scots, from Peterborough to Westminster, entitled, Prosopopœia Basilica, extant in the Cottonian collection, but never printed; an English translation of Florus; Nero Cæsar, or Monarchie Depraved, an historicall worke, dedicated with leave to the duke of Buckingham, lord admiral, Lond. 1624, fol. This book is handsomely printed, and besides its value from several curious medals that adorn it, is worth notice from a mass of antiquarian matter. Among other things that make it useful is a particular account of the British revolt under Boadicea. Another of Bolton's works, entitled Hypercritica, or a Rule of Judgment for Writing or Reading our Histories, was published by Dr. Hall, in 1722, at the end of Nicholas Trivet's Annals. In his preface, the doctor styles Bolton "a considerable person," and "a very learned man." He was also author of an unpublished work upon the ancient state of London, entitled Vindiciæ Britannicæ, or London righted by Rescues and Recoveries of Antiquities of Britain in general and of London in particular. Bolton also made preparations for other historical and antiquarian works. Of the time and place of his death nothing is known. (Biog. Brit.)

BOLTON, (Robert,) an eminent puritan divine, born in 1572, at Blackburn, Lancashire, in the free school of which place, and at the colleges of Lincoln and Brazennose at Oxford, he received his education. Being an excellent scholar he was chosen to dispute before James I. when that monarch visited Oxford in 1605. He is said to have lived a very immoral life till his thirty-fourth year, when he reformed, and in 1609 entered into holy orders, becoming rector of Broughton, in Northamptonshire. Wood describes him as a painful and constant preacher, and a good casuist. He died in 1631, leaving a Discourse on Happiness, 4to, 1611, Lond., a number of Sermons, and The Four Last Things, Death, Judgment, Hell, and Heaven, published after his death. (Chalmers.)

BOLTON, (Robert, LL.D.) an English divine, born in 1697, son of a London merchant, educated at Kensington and Wadham college, Oxford, ordained in 1719, and in 1722 chosen senior fellow of Dulwich college. He afterwards lived at Kensington, and formed an intimacy with Whiston. On the resignation of Dr. Butler, afterwards bishop of Durham, he was appointed preacher at the Rolls chapel; by this means he became acquainted with lord Hardwicke, and his religious opinions agreeing to some extent with those of the chancellor, he was preferred to the deanery of Carlisle and the vicarage of St. Mary, Reading. He wrote several tracts against card playing and travelling on Sundays, three essays on the employment of time, and some other tracts, now forgotten. Dr. Bolton entertained objections to the articles of the church, which he was long reluctant to subscribe to. He seems to have been slightly infected with his friend Whiston's socinian notions, though his writings do not contain any allusion to the subject. He was very tall, thin, and dark complexioned; a good scholar, an active parish priest, and an amiable man. He died in London, November 26, 1763, but was buried in the church porch of St. Mary, Reading. (Chalmers.)

BOLTS, (William,) a native of Holland, who came into England at fifteen, and thence passed into Portugal, where he was in 1755, at the time of the earthquake at Lisbon. He subsequently went to Bengal, and was made, in 1765, a commissioner of revenue for the province of Benares recently ceded to the English East India Company. He afterwards embarked in commerce with great success, but engaging in a dispute with the company, he was sent prisoner to England. He there brought an action for false imprisonment against the Indian authorities, which occasioned a litigation of seven years, and ruined him. While it was in progress, he published Considerations on Indian Affairs, 2 vols, 4to, containing much valuable matter. He was afterwards appointed by Maria Theresa to form establishments in India for the Austrian government. This afforded him the means of making another fortune, which he subsequently lost by a speculation in the neighbourhood of Paris. He died in that city, poor, April 28, 1808. Having great acuteness and application, he acquired a most extensive acquaintance with languages. A work of his upon Bengal was translated into French. (Biog. Univ.)

BOLZANIO, (Urban Valerian,) an Italian Franciscan, born in 1440, the Greek preceptor of Leo X. He was a hard student, extensive traveller, and disinterested man. His grammar, entitled Urbani Grammatica Græca, Venice, 1497, the first attempt to explain in Latin the grammatical construction of Greek, was received so eagerly that Erasmus could not find an unsold copy of it in 1499. He died in 1524. (Chalmers.)

BOM, (Peter,) an excellent painter of landscape in distemper. He was born at Antwerp, in 1530, and died in 1572. (Pilkington.)

BOMBARDINI, (Anthony,) a noble Paduan, professor of canon law in his native place. He died in 1726, distinguished for a treatise, De Carcere, et antiquo ejus Usu ad hæc usque Tempora deducto. This piece, originally printed in 1713, was inserted, with remarks and corrections, in Poleni's collection of Greek and Roman antiquities. (Biog. Univ.)

BOMBELLES, (Henry Francis, count of,) born in 1681, a French tactician, descended from an ancient Portuguese family, and actively engaged in the wars of the earlier years of the eighteenth century. He was chosen by the regent Orleans, in 1718, to instruct his son, the duke of Chartres, in the military art, and this employment rendered him a writer upon tactics. But his works, though valued in their day, are now of little use. He died in 1760, much regretted by the army. (Biog. Univ.)

BOMBELLES, (Mark Maria, marquess of,) born October 8, 1744, educated with the duke of Burgundy, elder brother of Lewis XVI., who died in 1761, and originally in the army. He subsequently was entrusted with several diplomatic missions, but a refusal to take the oath imposed by the national assembly, reduced him to private life in December 1790. He was then at Venice, and he long afterwards endeavoured to serve the unfortunate royal family of France in various parts of Europe, first as a negotiator, afterwards as an officer in the Condéan army. Having lost his wife, the friend of madame Elizabeth, the excellent sister of Lewis XVI., he was quite overwhelmed with grief, and withdrew into a convent at Brunn, in Moravia. After filling some ecclesiastical offices in the Austrian states, he re-entered France with the Bourbons, in 1814, left it again on Napoleon's return, and finally settled there on the second restoration. He was consecrated bishop of Amiens in 1819, and died in 1822, having produced, while an exile in Switzerland, in 1795, Avis Raisonnable au Peuple Allemand, par un Suisse; and subsequently, in 1799, a small but remarkable piece, entitled La France, avant et depuis la Revolution. (Biog. Univ. Suppl.)

BOMBELLI, (Raphael,) a celebrated Italian algebraist in the sixteenth century, who saw better than Cardan the nature of the irreducible case in quadratic equations. His discoveries are embodied in a treatise on algebra in his own language, printed at Bologna in 1572, and subsequently reprinted. (Biog. Univ. Hallam's Literature of Europe, ii. 451.)

BOMBELLI, (Sebastian,) a painter,

born either at Udina or Bologna, in 1635. He was originally a pupil, and a most successful one, of Guercino, but he subsequently imitated Paul Veronese and Tintoretto. After producing some historical pictures of great promise, he transferred his attention to the more lucrative walk of portrait painting, in which his indisputable excellence gained him more commissions than he could execute. His death is ordinarily placed in 1685, but there is reason for believing him to have been alive so late as 1716. (Pilkington. Biog. Univ.)

BOMBERG, (Daniel,) an eminent Hebrew printer, born at Antwerp, but long settled at Venice, where he died in 1549. From his press issued various editions of the Hebrew Bible, in folio, quarto, and octavo. The earliest of them appears to have been a quarto, published in 1511. But Bomberg's most famous editions are his rabbinical Bibles, of which the first appeared in 1518, in four vols, fol. It has a dedication to Leo X. dated 1517, a circumstance which has made that pass for the year of its publication. The learned printer was assisted in bringing out this work by Felix del Prato, a converted Italian Jew, who taught him Hebrew, but who was deficient in Masoretic knowledge. Hence there is a confusion in the little Masora on the margin, which learned Jews immediately pointed out as a serious blemish. Bomberg accordingly undertook a second edition, under the care of rabbi Jacob Haiim, and it appeared also in four vols, folio, in 1525. It contains, besides the sacred text, the great and little Masora, Chaldee paraphrases, and commentaries of rabbins. Another edition of it appeared in 1548, a third in 1568, and a fourth in 1618. Of all the editions, the best are the second and third, both printed by Bomberg. The fourth, by Bragadini, also from the Venetian press, has traces of the inquisitors, who have expunged some things unfavourable to Christianity. It is besides less handsomely printed than the others. A fifth edition, published by Buxtorf, at Basle, is still less esteemed, various unauthorised liberties having been taken in it with the Chaldee paraphrases. Bomberg also began in 1520 to print the Babylonish Talmud. It occupied several years, and was at last completed in eleven folio volumes. He printed it twice afterwards, and every one of his three impressions cost him, they say, 100,000 crowns. (Moreri. Simon. Hist. Crit. V. T. 126.)

BOMBINO, the name of two Italian authors of a good family at Cosenza, apparently relations. Bernardin, who died in 1588, was a celebrated jurisconsult, author of some professional works, and of a book with a more general interest, entitled, Discorsi Intorno al Governo della Guerra, Governo domestico, Reggimento regio, il Tiranno, e l'Eccelenza dell' Uman Genere, Nap. 1566.—Peter Paul, who died in 1648, was a Jesuit, who left some Latin funeral orations, an Italian life of Loyola, a Latin work upon Spanish history, and an account of Campion, the celebrated Englishman of his order, executed for treason under Elizabeth. This curious book is entitled, Vita et Martyrium Edmundi Campiani, Martyris Angli, è Soc. Jesu. It first appeared at Antwerp in 1618, but not under the author's superintendence; and although he speaks kindly of the friend who published it, yet he will not own it as completely what he meant. In 1620, however, he produced himself at Mantua another edition, corrected and with many additions. (Biog. Univ. Clement. Bibl. Cur.)

BOMILCAR, a distinguished Carthaginian, styled *king* by Justin, who was preparing to pass over with the army to Agathocles, about the year 308, B.C. For this offence he was crucified in the forum of Carthage, the very seat of his former importance. He died with great spirit, upbraiding the people to the last. (Just. xxii. 7.) Another Bomilcar was at one time closely connected with Jugurtha, and provided by his desire an assassin to murder Massiva, Massinissa's grandson, then at Rome soliciting the kingdom of Numidia from the senate. He subsequently embarked in a plot against Jugurtha himself, which being detected, he was slain by him about 107, B.C. (Sallust. Jugurth. 35, 72.)

BOMMEL, the name of two authors in the Low Countries, of whom, John, living about 1471, a Dominican friar, left some Latin religious pieces. Henry, director of a convent at Utrecht, who died in 1542, wrote an historical work, entitled, Bellum Ultrajectinum inter Geldriæ Ducem, Carolum, et Henricum Bavarum. Episcopum Ultrajectinum. Marpurg, 1542, 8vo. (Moreri. Biog. Univ.)

BOMPART, the name of three French authors. Marcellinus Hercules, a physician at Clermont Ferrand in the former half of the seventeenth century, published several professional works, and among them particulars of a pestilence that raged in Auvergne, his native country.—N. de St. Victor wrote an account of the preceding, and some antiquarian information respecting Clermont.—John published in 1694 a Latin folio, containing an ample account of Provence, of which work seven other editions appeared in thirty-four years. (Biog. Univ.)

BOMPIANO, (Ignatius,) an Italian Jesuit, born at Frosinone in 1612, of a noble family from Ancona. He died in 1675, leaving, among other works, Historia Pontificatûs Gregorii XIII. Rom. 1655, 12mo. Seneca Christianus, Rom. 1658, 24mo. Historia Rerum Christianarum ab Ortu Christi, Rom. 1665, 12mo. (Biog. Univ.)

BON DE ST. HILAIRE, (Francis Xavier,) a wealthy French gentleman, eminent for literary and scientific tastes, born at Montpelier, October 15, 1678, and partly educated with the regent Orleans. He left several dissertations upon antiquities and natural history, of which the most remarkable was a dissertation on the spider, published at Paris in 1710, and translated into most European languages. An English translation appeared in volume xxvii. of the Philosophical Transactions. It contains particulars of spinning the spider's web into silk; and it was at one time thought so interesting, that a translation of it was made into Chinese, and read with great pleasure by the emperor of China. The ingenious author died January 18, 1761. (Biog. Univ.)

BONA, (John,) a learned Italian liturgist, born in 1609, at Mondovi, in Piedmont, of a family branching from that of Bonne de Lesdiguières, in Dauphiny. At fifteen he became a Cistercian monk, and in 1651, he was elected general of his order. Fabius Chigi, elected pope in 1655, under the name of Alexander VII., an intimate friend of his father's, drew him to Rome, and gave him several employments. Julius Rospigliosi, or Clement IX., the next pope, continued these, added others, and made him cardinal, November 29, 1669. He had no expectation of this dignity, and being then sixty, with habits germane to his taste, formed in a monastery, he shrank from the publicity upon which it cast him. He died at Rome, October 27, 1674, highly respected for piety, virtue, and erudition. In 1663, he published at Rome a work of considerable research, but pronounced very defective as to church music, entitled, De Divina Psalmodia, ejusque Causis, Mysteriis, et Disciplina; deque variis Ritibus omnium Ecclesiarum in psallendis divinis Officiis. From this work, Pallavicino, who wrote the history of the council of Trent, in opposition to Father Paul's, thought Bona excellently fitted for treating upon Romish liturgical matters. Being then upon intimate terms with him, he urged him, accordingly, to undertake this task. But Bona, for some time, was unwilling. At length he began upon it, and after an application of more than seven years, he published at Rome, in 1671, his well-known Rerum Liturgicarum Lib. II., which unfolds, with singular erudition, the various particulars that concern the Roman communion service, or mass. This book was reprinted at Paris in the following year. Bona wrote also several devotional pieces. The best edition of his works is that by Sala, Turin, 1747, 4 vols, fol. (Moreri. Rer. Liturg. Præf. Chalmers. Biog. Univ.)

BONA, (John Della,) an Italian physician, born September 8, 1712, appointed, in 1765, professor of medicine at Padua. He published, in Italian, upon the use and abuse of coffee, and in Latin, an account of some cures by corrosive sublimate, with other pieces, which mark the state of medical knowledge in his time.

BONAC, or BONNAC, (John Lewis d'Usson, marquis of,) an illustrious French statesman, descended from the ancient barons of Usson. He served in the army at the close of the seventeenth century, but subsequently his talents were given up to diplomacy. After conducting several other foreign negotiations in a satisfactory manner, he was despatched, in 1711, by Lewis XIV. to the court of Spain, where his talents, experience, and discretion were found very useful in persuading Philip V. to acquiesce in those terms of pacification, which settled him on his throne; and in prevailing upon that prince to abandon an impolitic journey into France, which he meditated on the deaths of his father, the Dauphin, and his brother, the duke of Burgundy. There being now only a sickly infant before him in the succession to the French crown, Philip thought his presence likely to secure him the reversion to that much-coveted prize. On returning from Spain, Bonac was sent ambassador into Turkey, and was as usual found excellently fitted for his duties. He died September 1, 1738. (Biog. Univ. Coxe, ii.)

BONACCIUOLI, (Alphonso,) a noble Ferrarese, attached to the ducal court of his native country, but too intellectual for a mere life of gaiety and parade. He translated, accordingly, into Italian from the Greek, Strabo and Pausanias, doing his work so ably, that his versions are considered more faithful and exact than those which had appeared in Latin. The Pausanias, published in 1593, was posthumous, which fact is the only known guide to the date of the translator's death. Bonacciuoli also translated from the Latin, Marcianus Capella's Nuptials of Mercury and Philology, printed at Mantua in 1578. (Biog. Univ.)

BONACCIUOLI, (Lewis,) physician to the duchess of Ferrara, remarkable for the publication of Enneas Muliebris, a work on generation, which appeared without place or date, but is referred to about 1480. Different portions of this treatise have been printed separately, and commonly pass for independent productions.

BONACINA, (Martin,) a Milanese canonist, who died in 1631, on his way to Vienna, whither he was going as nuncio to Urban VIII. He published a treatise on moral theology, which has been several times reprinted, with some ecclesiastical works of little use out of Italy.—(John Baptist,) a Milanese engraver, about 1620, whose style is neat, but rather dry and stiff. (Biog. Univ. Bryan.)

BONACOSSI, the name of a family that obtained the sovereignty of Mantua. The first of them so distinguished was Pinamonte, who died about 1293, and is mentioned in the Inferno of Dante. The last was Passerino, slain in 1328, when Lewis di Gonzaga was proclaimed lord of Mantua and Modena. (Biog. Univ.)

BONACOSSUS, or BUONACOSSA, (Hercules,) a Ferrarese, professor of medicine at Bologna, who died in 1578. His works, which are professional, and in Latin, make great use of the ancient Greek physicians, and may be advantageously used in illustrating their writings. (Biog. Univ.)

BONAFIDE, (Francis,) an Italian physician, appointed professor of botany at Padua, in 1533, and famous for suggesting the botanical garden, established there in 1540, which really began a new era in the knowledge of plants. The judicious projector withdrew from his duties as teacher of botany, in 1547, being then blind, and worn out by age. His only printed work is a Latin treatise advocating venesection in pleurisy. (Biog. Univ.)

BONAIR, (Henry Stuart, sieur de,) one of the twenty-five gentlemen of the Scottish guard, and historiographer to the king of France. Among other historical works, he published, in 1676, Sommaire Royal de l'Histoire de France, a translation of Berthault's Florus Francicus, with a continuation of twenty years. Even this has been thought no work of Bonair's, but of Cæsar, duke of Vendôme, natural son of Henry IV. Bonair was attached to the house of Vendôme, and wrote several pieces for its gratification; but his authorship is of an inferior cast. (Biog. Univ.)

BONAMI, (Francis,) a French physician, born at Nantes, May 10, 1710. He was descended from a Florentine family, studied medicine at Montpelier, and perfected his studies at Paris. In 1735 he took the degree of M.D. at Nantes, where he professed botany, to which science he was most passionately attached, and which he continued to teach until his death, in 1786. M. Du Petit-Thouars has consecrated a genus of plants (Bonamia) to his memory; and Vicq d'Azyr has eulogised his learning and science. Bonami assisted to form the first agricultural society in France. He published, Floræ Nannetensis Prodromus, Nantes, 1782, 12mo. Addenda ad Flor. Nannet. *ib.* 1785, 12mo. He also published, in the Journal de Médecine, an account of a very curious case in which a loss of the tongue was sustained by a young girl afflicted with small-pox. Loss of speech for several years was the consequence, but the faculty gradually returned to a degree sufficient to express her wants. It is the only one of the kind upon record.

BONAMY, (Peter Nicholas,) a French antiquary, born near Paris, towards the end of the seventeenth century, and educated for the church. He became, however, a professed man of letters, and eventually married. At an early period he was chosen under-librarian in the abbey of St. Victor; subsequently he became the first historiographer of Paris, and librarian of a collection founded at the town-hall of that city upon the basis of a large legacy of books left to the corporation by a public-spirited individual. Bonamy died in 1770, after leaving many interesting papers on French philology and antiquities, published in the Memoirs of the Academy of Inscriptions and Elegant Literature. (Biog. Univ.)

BONAMY, (Charles Augustus John Baptist Lewis Joseph,) a French general, born in 1764, and employed in many of the earlier military movements of revolutionary France, but unable to obtain a command after the battle of Marengo, in which his conduct was deemed unsatisfactory. He then retired into the country, and became a magistrate. In this capacity he appeared before Buonaparte, then emperor, in 1809, and being very kindly received, he entered again upon a military life. In the disastrous Russian expedition he distinguished himself greatly, but fell covered with wounds into the hands of the enemy, by whom he was detained 22 months a prisoner. Lewis XVIII. treated him with respect, but gave him no employment; and on the return of Napoleon from Elba, he came into public life once more. After the defeat of Waterloo, he was charged with the conducting of the magazines behind the Loire. Subsequently he lived in retirement. He died in 1830, having published, in 1803, Mémoires sur la Révolution de Naples. He had been an eye-witness of the events about which he wrote. (Biog. Univ. Suppl.)

BONANI, (Anthony and Vincent,) two brothers, pupils of father Cupani, and employed by him as assistants in the preparation of a great botanical work upon Sicily, to be called, Panphyton Siculum. He died in 1711, when the printing had actually begun. Anthony Bonani immediately stopped the press, and began the publication under his own name in 1713, an ungrateful injustice which Bernardi and Ucria properly exposed. (Biog. Univ.)

BONARDI, (John Baptist,) a French divine, who died in 1756, distinguished for his opposition to the bull Unigenitus. He printed some pieces upon theological subjects, and left three works in MS. upon the lives and productions of authors, chiefly suggested, probably, by his employment as librarian to cardinal de Noailles. (Biog. Univ.)

BONARELLI, the name of three literary Italians. Guidobald, born in 1563, and dead in 1608, was a man of quality, chiefly employed as a diplomatist, but acquired a title to the notice of posterity by writing the Filli di Sciro, (Phyllis of Sciros,) a pastoral drama, first printed at Ferrara, in 1607, which became hardly less famous, in spite of affectation, an ill-constructed fable, and ill-drawn characters, than the Aminta and the Pastor Fido. His brother Prosper, who died in 1659, was chiefly distinguished as a dramatic author. Prosper had a son, named Peter, also a dramatic writer. (Biog. Univ. Hallam's Literature, iii. 529.)

BONASONI, (Julius,) an Italian artist, chiefly celebrated as an engraver, but also known as an historical painter, born at Bologna about 1498. He studied painting under Sabbatini, and engraving under Marc Antonio. In the latter he never equalled his instructor, but the facility and elegance of his prints have gained them considerable estimation. He died about 1570. (Pilkington. Bryan.)

BONATI, (John,) an historical painter, born at Ferrara, in 1635, pupil successively of Guercino and Mola. He died in 1681, leaving some capital works in Rome. (Pilkington. Bryan.)

BONATI, (Theodore Maximus,) a Ferrarese mathematician, born in 1724, who gave his attention in a remarkable degree to questions concerned with water-courses, and furnished, among other things of the same kind, plans for the draining of the Pontine marshes. He died in 1820, having been consulted, even in his ninety-fifth year, by several governments, upon difficult points in engineering. He wrote some Italian papers upon the subjects that rendered him so famous, but no work of considerable extent. (Biog. Univ. Suppl.)

BONAVENTURA, (Frederic,) an Italian natural philosopher, born at Ancona, of a good family, in 1555, and most deserving the notice of posterity from a scarce and learned work, printed at Urbino in 1600, and at Frankfort in 1612, entitled, De Naturâ Partûs Octomestris, adversus vulgatam Opinionem. This book, of which the first edition is more esteemed, maintains the legitimacy of births at ten months. After publishing some other treatises connected with physical science, Bonaventura died in 1602. (Biog. Univ. Suppl.)

BONAVENTURE, (Brocard,) a native of Strasburg, who became a preaching friar, as some say, in 1218, and went into Palestine before 1227. Other accounts refer his travels to 1260, or 1280. He left, Descriptio Locorum Terræ Sanctæ, described as exact, and printed at Ingoldstadt, in 1604; at Cologne, in 1624; and elsewhere. (Cave. Du Pin.)

BONAVENTURE, a Romish saint, designated among schoolmen as the *seraphic doctor*, styled *Eustachius*, and *Eutychius*, by the Greeks. His surname was Fidenza, and he was baptized either John or Peter. He was born at Bagnarea, in Tuscany, in 1221, and being dangerously ill at four years old, his mother begged Francis of Assisi to pray for him. He consented, and the child recovering, he exclaimed, *O buona ventura!* (*what good luck!*) The name adhered to the object of his prayers, who became, in 1243, a friar of his order. The young Bonaventure studied at Paris, and took his doctor's degree with Aquinas, in 1255; his principal instructor being, it is said, Alexander Hales, the famous English schoolman, then settled at Paris, and dignified as the *irrefragable doctor*. Bonaventure soon showed himself worthy of such distinguished tuition, being chosen, after only seven years' application, public lecturer in the established text-book of school-divinity, Peter Lombard's *Sentences*. In 1256 he was chosen general of the Franciscans, upon the forced resignation of John of Parma, who had made himself a host of enemies by striving to reinstate that order in all its original rigour. Bonaventure took somewhat lower ground, but effected several reforms; and besides restoring peace to the fraternity by his prudence, he defended it by his erudition and acuteness. His great reputation, according to Wikes, procured for him from Clement IV., in 1265, a nomination, which he refused, to the see of York, vacant, in 1264, by the death of archbishop Kinton. Bonaventure's conduct upon this occasion has been represented as highly disinterested, and such, probably, was his real character. But if the nomination were ever made, it was not particularly tempting; Langton, dean of York, who had been elected to the archbishopric, being set aside by the pope, and it being obviously unlikely that the English government would both acquiesce in such a stretch of authority, and in the appointment besides of an Italian friar to a dignity of so much importance. It is more probable that Bonaventure might himself have been elected pope, had he been so disposed, on the death of Clement IV., and that he was the individual who recommended for election Theobald, archdeacon of Liege, then in the Holy Land. By this pontiff, known as Gregory X., he was made a cardinal, and by his desire he attended the council of Lyons in 1274. He died in that city, while the council sate, July 15, 1274. Sixtus V. canonized him in 1482; and Lyons, which venerated his relics until the Huguenots burnt them, and cast the ashes into the Saône, in the sixteenth century, took him for a patron saint. Bonaventure is a copious author, his works filling eight folio, or fourteen quarto volumes, and containing much to enlighten the mind and touch the heart. He united mystic with scholastic theology; and such is the genuine piety displayed in his writings, that Luther valued him highly. Many of his analogies, however, are visionary and absurd. He wrote commentaries on Scripture, and on the Sentences, a great number of tracts, either ascetic or practical, letters, and sermons. It must, however, be mentioned in derogation of his honest fame, that he did all in his power, which was a great deal, to betray Christians into the unauthorized, senseless, and pernicious worship of the Virgin Mary. (Cave. Du Pin. Mosheim. Moreri. Godwin de Præsull.)

BONAVENTURE, called BADUARIUS, from his family, which was noble, and seated at Peraga, a doctor of Paris, general of the Augustinian hermits in 1377, cardinal in the following year, murdered at Rome in 1388, or something later, by means of Carrara, governor of Padua, his native place. He was a man of conspicuous talent, especially in the diplomacy of Rome; and, besides other works, has been thought to have written the Speculum B. Mariæ, printed at Augsburg in 1476, which is really the production of his more celebrated namesake. (Cave. Du Pin. Moreri.)

There are also two antiquarian authors of southern France, named Bonaventure; one, distinguished as de St. Amable, published, towards the end of the seventeenth century, three volumes, folio, upon the history of the Limousin. The other, distinguished as de Sisteron, published, in 1741, a History of the Town and Principality of Orange. (Biog. Univ.)

BONAVIDIUS, or BONAVITI, (Mark,) a learned jurist of Padua, generally distinguished by the affix of *Mantua* to his baptismal name, his family having come from that city. He died either in 1582, or 1589, leaving several publications in Latin, of which the only one likely to be noticed by ordinary students, is the Dialogus de Concilio, Venice, 1541, placing a council above the pope in questions of faith, and in such as concern the general constitution of the church. (Biog. Univ.)

BONCERF, (Peter Francis,) a French advocate, who attained great notoriety by a piece printed in 1776, under the name of Francaleu, entitled, Les Inconvéniens des Droits Féodaux. This was denounced to the parliament by the prince of Conti, and condemned to be burnt. The author himself would have been prosecuted had not the king interfered. His work now became immensely popular, and besides numerous editions of it published in France, it was translated into several foreign languages. At the revolution its principles became law; but, notwithstanding, Boncerf had a very narrow escape from the scaffold. He died in 1794, leaving some other political tracts in addition to that which rendered him so famous. He had a brother, named Claudius Joseph, an ecclesiastic, who published some miscellaneous works of no great eminence, and died in 1811. (Biog. Univ. Biog. Univ. Suppl.)

BONCIARIO, (Marc Anthony,) an Italian scholar, of humble birth, born at Antria, near Perugia, in 1555, and placed for two years, by the liberality of a kind prelate, who became aware of his merit, under Mureto, at Rome. His patron then sent him back to Perugia, as director of a seminary that he had established there. Subsequently he became professor of elegant literature, and fulfilled his duties with great applause until 1590, when he became wholly blind. He died in 1616, leaving many works, all in Latin, but no one of much notoriety, except his Latin Grammar, which was used in schools, and several times reprinted. (Biog. Univ.)

BONCUORE, (John Baptist,) an Italian historical painter, born in 1643. He was a pupil of Albano, and painted with spirit, but he is more successful in design than in manner or colouring. He died at Rome in 1699. (Pilkington.)

BOND, (John,) born in Somersetshire, in 1550, educated at Winchester school, and at New college, Oxford, by which society he was appointed head-master of the free-school at Taunton. Here he continued many years; but tired at length of teaching, he turned his thoughts to physic, which he practised with considerable success in the town; where he died, August 3, 1612. He is best known by his edition of Horace, to which he gave short Latin notes, chiefly taken from Lambinus, first printed at London in 1606, and which has been frequently reprinted. His edition of Persius was a posthumous work, published by his son-in-law, and in consequence of his not living to revise it, is found to contain some errors in points of history and philosophy.

BOND, (John, LL.D.) a learned member of the Westminster Assembly of Divines, born at Dorchester, and educated at Catharine hall, Cambridge, where he obtained a fellowship. He held a lectureship at Exeter, and afterwards was preacher to the long parliament. In 1645 he was made minister of the Savoy; he was afterwards appointed master of Trinity hall, Cambridge, and professor of law at Gresham college. These two latter preferments he held till the restoration, when, being ejected from both, he retired to Dorsetshire, and died at Sandwich, in the isle of Purbeck, in 1676. His works are:—1. A Door of Hope, Lond. 1641, 4to. 2. Holy and Loyal Activity, Lond. 1641, 4to; and sundry sermons preached before the long parliament. (Chalmers.)

BONDAM, (Peter,) a Dutch jurist, born in 1727, appointed, in 1773, to a professorship at Utrecht. He died in 1800, chiefly known as author of, Specimen Animadv. Critic. ad Loca quædam Juris Civilis depravata, Fran. 1746; De Linguæ Græcæ Cognitione Jurisconsulto necessaria, Zutph. 1755; Pro Græcis Juris Interpretibus, 1763. (Biog. Univ.)

BONDE, (Gustavus, count of,) a Swedish scholar, born in 1682, of an illustrious family, and eminent for a great extent of knowledge, derived both from reading and foreign travel. He died in 1764, leaving several works in his own language, maintaining, among other singular opinions, that the Fins are descended from the ten lost tribes of Israel. (Biog. Univ.)

BONDI, (Clement,) an Italian poet, born in the Parmesan, in 1742, and originally a Jesuit. On the suppression of his order, he led a literary life, during many years, in the north of Italy; and rendering himself agreeable to the Austrian imperial family, he found an asylum at Vienna when his patron, the archduke Ferdinand, was driven home by the French successes in Lombardy. He died at Vienna, after a residence there of nearly twenty years, June 21, 1821. Besides various original Italian poems, Bondi published translations, in his own tongue, of Virgil, and of Ovid's Metamorphoses. His Georgics are the most esteemed of these, but his poetical reputation has latterly been rather on the wane. (Biog. Univ. Suppl.)

BONDIOLI, (Peter Anthony,) a distinguished physician, born at Corfu in 1765. He displayed an early attachment to letters, was educated in the university of Padua, and made such rapid progress, that before completing the usual period of academic study, he was permitted to read before the academy three memoirs, on the use of frictions in medicine, on medical electricity, and on sound. He received the degree of M.D. in 1789. He was an able practitioner, and settled in Venice, where he succeeded in curing the governor, Montana, of a severe epidemical attack. His success exciting the jealousy of his contemporaries, he availed himself of an opportunity to accompany the ambassador of Venice to the Porte, where he had abundant means of exercising his talents. From Constantinople he hastened to Corfu, hoping to assist his countrymen in the defence of their island against the attacks of the French, after which he went to Paris, and was honourably received. He became physician to the army in Italy from the battle of Marengo; and he was afterwards, in 1803, appointed to the chair of materia medica in the university of Bologna. He was very successful in his academical labours, and was elected one of the forty members of the Italian Academy of Sciences, and honoured with the order of the Iron Crown. Upon the reorganization of the university of Padua, in 1806, he was nominated to a clinical chair, which he filled during two years. In 1808 he returned to Bologna, took a part in the proceedings of the college of the Dotti, was attacked by an inflammatory disease, of which he predicted the fatal issue, and died, September 16, at the early age of forty-three years.

He directed that his MSS. should be destroyed, urging as his reason for such a decision, that he who leaves a manuscript, leaves only a moiety of his work, and this order was scrupulously fulfilled. He published, Sulle Vaginali del Testicolo, Vicenz. 1789; Padov. 1790, 8vo. In the Giornale Fisico-medico of Brugnatelli, tom. i., he has an admirable paper on the Aurora Borealis; and in the collection of the Italian Society, Ricerche sopra le Forme particolari delle Malattie Universali; and Memoria dell'Azione Irritativa.

BONDT, (Nicholas,) a Hollander, born in 1732, and chiefly known by a history of the confederation of the United Provinces, which appeared at Utrecht, in 1756. He died in 1792, with a high character for erudition. (Biog. Univ.)

BONELLI, (Francis Andrew,) a naturalist of eminence, especially in entomology, born in Piedmont, in 1784. In pursuit of the knowledge to which he was enthusiastically attached, he travelled over great portions not only of his own country, but also of France, England, and Sardinia. He died at Turin, exhausted by a life of labour, November 18, 1830. His publications chiefly consist of papers printed by the Academy of Sciences at Turin. His name has been given to several varieties of plants and insects. (Biog. Univ. Suppl.)

BONET, (Andrew,) a physician, son of Peter Bonet, born at Lyons, in 1556, who, by his second wife, Margaret Pinelli Borzoni, of an illustrious Genoese family, settled, like himself, at Geneva, had the two celebrated physicians, John and Theophilus, of whom John, the elder, was born at Geneva in 1615, and admitted doctor of medicine at the age of nineteen. He enjoyed great reputation, and contemplated a work, De Catarrhis, but upon reading Schneider's upon the same subject, he found his opinions so well pre-expressed, that he destroyed his MS. He has been reported to have published a work, entitled, Traité de la Circulation des Esprits Animaux, Paris, 1682, 12mo; but this is generally ascribed to a religious of the congregation of St. Maur.—Theophilus, the younger, a celebrated anatomist, was born at Geneva, March 5, 1620. He studied medicine with great ardour, and visited the principal universities of Europe. He took the degree of M.D. in 1643, and afterwards married the daughter of Spanheim, well known in the annals of literature. He was appointed physician to Henry of Orleans, duke of Longueville, but abandoned practice at the age of fifty, in consequence of a deafness which was so great as to disqualify him for the exercise of his profession. Then, applying himself to his library, he gave to the world a collection of cases illustrative of pathology, which, by their fidelity, have maintained a value to the present time. In this branch of professional research he is to be regarded as the precursor of Morgagni, distinguished by the originality of his observations, and the founder of the most important views in relation to medical science. Haller has said of him, that he was "Industrius collector neque propriis destitutus adnotationibus." He died of a dropsy at the age of 69, March 29, 1689. He published, Pharos Medicorum, id est, Cautelæ, Animadversiones, et Observationes Practicæ, Genev. 1668, 12mo; translated into English, Lond. 1684, fol. and reprinted in Latin under the title of Labyrinthus Medicus Extricatus, seu Methodus vitandorum Errorum qui in Praxi occurrunt, monstrantibus G. Ballonio et C. Septalio, Genev. 1687, 4to. Observations et Histoires Chirurgiques tirées des Œuvres Latines des plus renommés Praticiens, Genev. 1670, 4to. Corps de Médecine et de Chirurgie,

Genev. 1679, 2 vols, 4to. Prodromus Anatomiæ Practicæ, Genev. 1675, 8vo. Sepulchretum Anatomicum, Genev. 1679. 2 vols, fol.; *ib.* 1700, with additions by Mangetus, Lugd. 1700, 3 vols, fol. Mercurius Compilatitius, seu Index Medico-Practicus, Genev. 1682, fol. Medicina Septentrionalis Collectitia, Genev. 1684-86, 2 vols, fol. Polyalthes, seu Thesaurus Medico-practicus ex optimis Rei Medicæ Scriptoribus collectis, Genev. 1690-91-93, 2 vols. fol. Bonet also published translations of Mayerne de Arthritide, Genev. 1671, 1674, 12mo; Lond. 1674, 8vo. Rohaultii Tractatus Physicus, Genev. 1674, 8vo; and of the Journal of Nicolas Blegney.

BONFADIO, (James,) a distinguished Italian man of letters, born at Gazano, in the Brescian territory, about the beginning of the sixteenth century. The earlier years of his manhood were spent at Rome, in the service of two cardinals successively, as secretary, but becoming weary of such an occupation, he went into the Neapolitan territory, and thence into the north of Italy. There he first fixed his residence at Padua, whence he transferred it to Genoa, and read lectures on Aristotle's Politics. These gave so much satisfaction that he was engaged to lecture upon rhetoric, and the republic subsequently made him its historiographer; assigning him a good pension to continue its annals from the year 1528, where Folieta's history closes. Bonfadio's continuation reaches to 1550, being comprised in five books, written in very elegant Latin. Unhappily, the able author's infamous infatuation then abruptly terminated his labours. He was convicted of a hateful crime, and sentenced to be burnt. His punishment seems, however, to have been commuted for decapitation, although there is reason for believing his remains to have been eventually burnt. This miserable fate, which overtook him either in the summer of 1550, or in the following year, has been sometimes treated as unjust, certain powerful families which he had handled rather roughly in his history being eager to fasten upon any imputation to make him feel their vengeance in its extreme. But contemporary evidence preponderates against a view so favourable to this able scholar's memory. His Genoese history was published in 1586, by Paschetti, at Pavia, in a quarto of 206 pages, which is extremely rare. It was reprinted in the Thesaurus Antiquitatum Italiæ, but with several alterations. A better edition appeared at Brescia, in 1747, in 8vo. Paschetti also published, in 1586, an Italian translation of Bonfadio's history. Other works of this unfortunate author, comprising letters and some miscellaneous pieces, both in verse and prose, were published by Mazzuchelli, in a single 8vo volume, in 1746. They are all excellent, but the correspondence displays, to a discerning eye, a degree of labour scarcely suitable to that class of writings. (Bayle. Biog. Univ. Clement. De Bure. Hallam.)

BONFANTE, (Angelo Matthew,) a Sicilian poet and botanist, who died in 1676, leaving little in print besides poems, but also some MSS. upon botanical and other subjects. (Biog. Univ.)

BONFIGLIO, (Benedict,) an Italian painter, about the year 1503, equalled by no contemporary artist except Peter Perugino. (Bryan.)

BONFINI, (Anthony,) an Italian writer of the fifteenth century, born at Ascoli, in the marquisate of Ancona, and invited from his literary fame into Hungary, by the king, Matthias Corvinus. By this prince he was bidden to undertake the early history of Hungary, which the next sovereign, Uladislas, commanded him to continue. He died in 1502, having brought his history, which is in Latin, down to 1495. It was first published, but incompletely, in 1543. Subsequently the whole work appeared; and it has gone through five editions, the last being that of Cologne, in 1690. It is a well-arranged and well-written work; displaying generally great exactness, though not unmingled with credulity. Bonfini likewise produced some Latin translations from the Greek, of which the Philostratus is reproached with inexactitude, some commentaries upon Horace, which are of little value, and the Symposion Beatricis, which has been prohibited at Rome, highly eulogizing Matthias Corvinus, and his queen, Beatrice of Aragon. (Bayle. Moreri.)

BONFRERE, (James,) a learned Jesuit, born in 1573, at Dinant, in the territory of Liege, and justly celebrated as a Hebraist. He died in 1643, at Tournay, leaving excellent Latin commentaries upon the historical books of the O. T., accompanied by prefaces, which are especially valuable, and an Onomasticon, or account of places in Palestine, from Eusebius and Jerome, which is equally esteemed. The most complete edition of his works appeared in 1736. (Moreri. Chalmers.)

BONGARS, (James,) a learned French

protestant, attached to the household of Henry IV., and employed as his envoy in Germany, both before and after he was king of France. These employments, which extended over thirty years, never prevented Bongars from indulging those literary tastes to which his whole life was devoted, and of which he early allowed the world to judge by an excellent edition of Justin, printed at Paris in 1581. The religious troubles of his times allowed him opportunities, which he gladly embraced, of acquiring manuscripts formerly possessed by some ecclesiastical establishments. Of his fitness for such deposits, the learned world was allowed to judge by the publication at Hanau, in 1611, of a collection of contemporary history of the crusades, under the title of Gesta Dei per Francos. He had previously, in 1600, published a collection of Latin Hungarian historians. In 1641 was printed a collection of his letters, which contain much to illustrate German history in his time, and exhibit a correct Latin style, free from the affectation that once prevailed of rejecting every expression not to be found in Cicero. Bongars died at Paris, in 1612, aged 58. (Moreri. Bayle. Morhof.)

BONGIOVANNI, (Anthony,) in Latin, *Bonjoannes*, a learned Italian, born in 1712, and employed in St. Mark's library at Venice. In conjunction with Zanetti, he completed a catalogue of the Greek, Latin, and Italian MSS. in that famous collection. He also edited some Greek scholia upon Homer, some historical pieces of Leontius, a monk of Jerusalem, seventeen orations of Libanius, and two small works of Theodoret; satisfactory evidences of the diligence and ability with which he ransacked the forgotten treasures of the great Venetian library. (Biog. Univ.)

BONI, (James,) an Italian historical painter in fresco, born in 1688; he died in 1766. (Pilkington.)

BONI, (Mauro,) an Italian Jesuit, eminent in bibliography and antiquities, born November 3, 1746. After the suppression of his order, he lived in the various capacities of parish-priest, member of academic establishments, and private tutor. But he was keenly alive to literature, and on the restoration of Jesuitism, he joined it again. He died in the college of his order at Reggio, January 4, 1817, known as a principal compiler of the Italian dictionary of illustrious men, with several pieces in bibliography and antiquities; among them is an Italian translation, much augmented, of Harwood's View of the various Editions of the Greek and Roman Classics. (Biog. Univ. Suppl.)

BONICHON, (Francis,) a French priest of the oratory, who died in 1662, known from the Pompa Episcopalis, published in 1650, detailing the ceremonies anciently used when bishops first entered their dioceses; and a defence of episcopal authority against the mendicant orders. (Biog. Univ.)

BONIFACE, so named at Rome in 723, archbishop of Mentz, a Romish saint, designated as the *Apostle of Germany*. He was an Englishman, originally named Winifrid, born at Crediton, in Devonshire, in 670. His youth being spent in monasteries in his own country, he was ordained priest, about the year 700. Four years afterwards he passed over into Friesland, as a missionary, but meeting with little success, he returned in the following year. His affections, however, were left behind, and, in 715, he made a final emigration to the continent. He now was greeted with signal success both in Friesland and the neighbouring regions of Germany. Amidst his labours he found time for three journeys to Rome, where he was consecrated bishop of the Germans, by Gregory II, in 723, without any particular see. He now became an active partizan of the papacy, of which he was constituted vicar, and showed himself quite willing to raise its pretensions by the depression of the episcopal order. He was rewarded, with consent of the Frankish government, by the archiepiscopal dignity, in 738, the see of Mentz being made metropolitan for him, and henceforth he became, in every way, the leading ecclesiastic of his adopted country. He was not, however, to be seduced, by any degree of external importance, from a zealous anxiety to discharge his duties as an ordinary christian minister. Hence, in 754, he committed the care of his archiepiscopal duties at Mentz, to Lullus, one of his disciples, and hastened into Friesland, which was now relapsing into paganism. At first, his exertions were highly prosperous, but a violent pagan opposition was thus provoked, and he was killed in a tumult, raised by his enemies, in the June after his arrival. His correspondence was published by Serarius, at Mentz, in 1605, and it was reprinted in 1629. Some of his epistles are also to be found in the various editions of the Councils, and all of them in the Bibliotheca Patrum, tom. xiii. He wrote a treatise, De

Fidei Unitate, which pope Zachary commends, but it is not extant. It is otherwise with a life of St. Livinus, attributed to him. This, however, is thought not to be his. The style of his letters is harsh and barbarous, but they display a sensible mind, although such a degree of devotion to the papal see as even Romanists, favourable to the Gallican liberties, disapprove. (Cave. Hist. Lit. 481. Du Pin, vi. 96.)

BONIFACE I., bishop of Rome, A.D. 419 (Anastas. de Vitis Pontif.), until A.D. 423 (Prosper. and Marcellin. Chronica), dying consequently almost five years after his election, and not three, as is asserted by Anastasius. A schism arose upon his elevation, as was too commonly the case, one Eulalius being chosen in opposition to him by a portion of the Roman clergy; but his rival having presumed to enter Rome without permission, after the præfect of the city had banished both parties thence by order of Honorius, that emperor, who had at first opposed, now took the side of Boniface, and established him in the bishopric. (Anastas. as above, and Baron. Annal. ad Ann. 418, 419, from original letters in the Vatican.) A letter of this pontiff to the Gallican bishops, upon an accusation against Maximus, bishop of Valence, and another to Hilary, bishop of Narbonne, concerning the claim of the see of Arles to the primacy of Gaul, are still extant (Concil. as above); and while they show on the one hand the custom, then increasing, among bishops out of his jurisdiction of appealing to the bishop of Rome for the decision of ecclesiastical quarrels, prove, on the other, the consciousness of that bishop, that he had no canonical right to interfere in such cases. Five other letters of Boniface, addressed to Rufus, archbishop of Thessalonica, and to the other bishops of Illyricum, enforce the claim set up by the Roman pontiffs of the period to jurisdiction over that province, and are recorded in the Acts of a Council of Rome, held A.D. 531, which attempted a like usurpation. (Concil. tom. iv. pp. 170-2, *sq.*) The estimation in which this pontiff was held by his contemporaries, may be judged from St. Augustine's dedication to him of his treatise, Contra duas Epistt. Pelagian. Several letters also are preserved, (among the letters of St. Augustine Epistt. 182—197 inclusive,) which passed between them. (Tillemont, Mém. Eccl. Du Pin, Hist. Eccl. tom. iii. p. 210. Baron. Annal. Platina. Cave, Hist. Litt. Fabric. Bibl. Med. et Infim. Latinit. vol. i. p. 703.)

BONIFACE II., a Goth by birth, bishop of Rome, under the Gothic king Athalaric, from A.D. 529 to A.D. 532, the dates of Anastasius (De Vitis Pontif.) being in this instance a year wrong, according to Baronius and Du Pin. A schism, as was then too frequently the case at Rome, disgraced his election; but was arrested on the present occasion by the opportune death of the rival bishop Dioscorus. To prevent a recurrence of the evil, Boniface nominated a successor to himself in the person of the deacon Vigilius, but was speedily compelled to retract so unprecedented an invasion upon the claims of both king and clergy. (Anastas.) Two letters of his are extant (Concil. tom. iv. p. 1684), of which, however, that addressed to Eulalius of Alexandria is unanimously allowed to be spurious. The other relates to the Pelagian controversy, and is addressed to Cæsarius, bishop of Arles. A council was held at Rome by this pontiff, A.D. 531, ostensibly for the purpose of redressing the wrong done to Stephen, bishop of Larissa, who had been expelled from his see by the patriarch of Constantinople. (Concil. tom. iv. pp. 1690, *sq.*) In reality, however, it appears to have been one of the many instances, during this and the previous century, in which the bishops of Rome attempted to usurp, while the patriarchs of Constantinople as often refused to surrender, the jurisdiction of the Illyrian province. (Du Pin, Hist. Eccl. tom. v. p. 30. Baron. Annal. Platina. Cave, Hist. Litt.)

BONIFACE III. held the see of Rome no more than a few months, but has attracted great notice in the protestant controversy from a prevalent opinion, that in his person the papacy first assumed a character decidedly antichristian. He was a native of Rome, and had been sent by Gregory the Great, as papal resident, or *apocrisiary*, to the court of Constantinople. He there much ingratiated himself with Phocas, then on the imperial throne, which had been gained by crimes, and was still polluted by them. Boniface did not immediately succeed Gregory, Sabinian having filled the Roman see during an intervening period of about seventeen months. He was elected in February 606, a year, accordingly, which many writers have marked for the first in a great apostasy emanating from Rome. He lost no time in requesting Phocas to make a formal grant of precedence to the see of Rome, over that of Constantinople. The emperor was upon ill terms with Cyriacus, patriarch of the latter city, and consequently had no objection to gratify his rival by the desired precedence. Notwithstanding, it is said by Platina, that the grant was not made without *great contention*. The precedence of which Constantinople was thus deprived had merely rested upon the presence of the government, it being contended by the patriarchs, and having been synodically enacted in 589, that her prelates should be styled *œcumenical*, or universal, thus making ecclesiastical rank follow in the wake of imperial power. This principle, however, the Roman pontiffs resisted, contending that Constantinople was a mere colony from their own city, which remained, accordingly, the capital of the empire. Platina re-inforces this argument by others of his own, suggesting that Rome was the see of St. Peter, who left the keys of heaven to her bishops, not to those of Constantinople; and asserting that many princes, but especially Constantine, had given to the Roman see a paramount power over ecclesiastical synods. But the Magdeburg centuriators well observe, that such arguments are not easily found in writers, either contemporary with Boniface, or of the age that immediately followed him. The precise nature of Phocas's grant is unascertainable, the document not having been preserved, but Paul Warnefrid says it declared the Roman see the *head of all churches*. This decree Baronius represents as enacting that *universal* was a term applicable only to the Roman church and her pontiff, and consequently one to which the prelate of Constantinople was not entitled. This is, however, evidently an unauthorized amplification of the very scanty particulars that antiquity has left us upon the grant in question. Bellarmine represents this grant as merely declaratory, the pontifical power of Rome having been immemorially established, and an imperial recognition of it being now required merely from the encroaching pride of the Constantinopolitan patriarchs. So much importance given by the warmest and ablest papal advocates to the decree of Phocas, may excuse the use made of it by protestant controversialists. It really appears, however, little or nothing else, than the settlement of a warmly-contested question of precedence; the emperor having decided, chiefly, as as it seems, on personal grounds, that notwithstanding the presence of his court at another place, the ancient capital should undisputedly enjoy that ecclesiastical rank which had been hers in primitive times. The pope, to whom this grant has given such extraordinary prominence, lived little more than eight months after his elevation, dying in the November of 606. (Cent. Magd. vii. 243. Paul. Diacon. de Gest. Langobard, iv. 37. Baron. viii. 258. Mosheim, ii. 82. Bellarmin. de Pontif. Rom. ii. 17. Usser. de Christ. Eccl. Success. et Stat. 18. Cave's Gov. of the Anc. Ch. 323. Platina, 68.)

BONIFACE IV., elected successor to the preceding, was the son of a physician, and his pontificate is chiefly remarkable for a grant of the Pantheon, which he obtained from Phocas. It had been dedicated to Cybele and all the gods. Boniface dedicated it to the blessed Virgin and all the martyrs. He died in 614, and has been canonized, although no sufficient reasons for such a distinction have reached posterity. (Platina. Bower.)

BONIFACE V., a Campanian, was elected pope on the death of Deusdedit. He died October 22, 625. The course of his pontificate was marked by considerable success in the conversion of England, and a letter that he wrote to Edwin, king of Northumbria, has fallen under animadversion from the centuriators of Magdeburg, who represent it as teaching that we are freed by Christ *only* from original sin. Bellarmine retorts upon them, that *only* is an addition of their own; which, if it be not a gloss, is true. If meant as a gloss, the passage will bear it; Boniface's language being such as to warrant the Magdeburg construction, though not incapable of the view which Bellarmine, with some ingenuity, takes of it. (Platina. Cent. Magd. vii. 482. Bellarm. de Pontif. Rom. iv. 10. Bed. Eccl. Hist. ii. 10.)

BONIFACE VI., elected pope in 896, died in less than a month afterwards, and appears to have been a man of extremely bad character. (Platina. Bower.)

BONIFACE VII., originally named Franco, was elected pontiff by unlawful means in 974, and is usually considered as an antipope, though his name regularly appears in the papal series. After a very brief possession of the pontifical dignity, he was under the necessity of fleeing to Constantinople; but he took with him a vast quantity of altar plate, and other valuables, from the Roman churches. With this property he raised such a sum of money, as enabled him to bribe, after a time, the Roman authorities into acquiescence under his rule. But having holden it less than a year, he was suddenly carried off. The accounts of him are highly unfavourable, and he died in 985, universally detested. (Platina. Bower. Cent. Magd.)

BONIFACE VIII. (Benedict Cajetan, *i. e.* of Gaeta,) a pontiff, ranked from his pretensions to temporal authority with Gregory VII. and Innocent III. He lived, however, when papal influence was beginning to decline, and failing to see this, his pontificate gave a fatal blow to that ecclesiastical supremacy which rendered Rome still mistress of the world. He was born at Anagni, of a noble family, and followed the legal branch of the ecclesiastical profession; in which, as in other kinds of secular business, he became extremely eminent. Seeing Celestine V., recently raised from a hermitage to the popedom, fully realize the worst anticipations that might have been formed of his incompetence, he persuaded him into a resignation, and was unanimously elected in his room at Naples, December 24, 1294. He was crowned January 23, 1295. Celestine had resigned with a view of returning to his hermitage, but Boniface could not feel secure while he continued at large, many people maintaining that a pope's resignation was an invalid act. Hence he detained Celestine a prisoner in the castle of Fumone, in Campania, as some said, with rigorous cruelty, but probably, with every indulgence that safe custody would admit. His detention at all was, however, a foul blot upon Boniface; and although there is reason to believe it to have been borne with exemplary patience, common fame, naturally enough, made the pious prisoner say of the new pope, *He has risen like a fox, he will reign like a lion, and die like a dog.* The character thus given to his reign was abundantly confirmed by events. The two most powerful monarchs in Europe at that time, Edward I. of England, and Philip IV., or the Fair, of France, were at war, and Boniface undertook to reconcile them. His conduct was, however, so violent and imperious, that a mediation, which, in other hands, might have been effective, proved, in his, a source of new disorders. Even the soundest principles were maintained by Boniface in a manner so arrogant and excessive, that his vindication of them proved injurious. Philip had raised supplies for his wars by a partial and arbitrary tax upon property embarked in trade. This he soon found himself unable to continue, and he then, with equal injustice, transferred the burthen to the clergy. Under such oppressions, ecclesiastics had constantly sought papal interference, and Boniface answered their complaints on this occasion, by fulminating, in 1296, the famous bull known from its initial words as *Clericis laicos*, which forbade all clerical contributions to the civil power without sanction of the pontiff. France was not mentioned, but it was obviously included in the bull, and Philip felt sure that the blow was chiefly meant for him. He retaliated, accordingly, by prohibiting the exportation of any property whatever from France, without his own express permission; as in Boniface's bull, the prohibition wore a general appearance, no particular object being specified. But the pope knew that aim was taken at him, and followed up his former act by a declaration to the king, that no prince has any authority over the clergy. Philip found himself, however, so well supported by his people, that Boniface was quickly forced to modify this offensive principle; and in the following year, 1297, he made a sort of peace-offering to France, by canonizing her venerated monarch, Lewis IX. In Great Britain, Boniface exhibited his usual arrogance, by claiming for the Roman see a superiority over Scotland, at the instigation of some emissaries from that country. But Edward I. repudiated spiritedly the assumption, and his baronage, assembled in parliament at Lincoln, formally denied the papal right to temporal jurisdiction. Boniface being thus repulsed, both by Philip and Edward, found a temporary source of excitement in the establishment of a superstitious festival, which brought great pecuniary advantage to Rome. Some very aged man declared himself to have been at Rome with his father, in the year 1200, when Innocent III. was pope, and to have been then told that if he should live another 100 years, he might have in the same city a plenary indulgence. Reinforcing this tale by accounts of numbers whom he saw at that time in Rome from foreign parts, and other old people talking in the same strain, the evidence of a religious festival at the close of every century was deemed conclusive, although destitute of documentary confirmation. Hence Boniface, by a bull, dated Feb. 22, 1300, granted a plenary indulgence, or full exemption from purgatory, to all truly penitent, and confessing their sins, who should visit Rome, in honour of St. Peter and St. Paul, at that time, and again at the expiration of a century.

This institution proved so acceptable to the Romans, that Clement VI., in 1343, ordered its celebration every fiftieth year, in imitation of a similar Jewish usage, giving it also the name of *Jubilee*. Subsequently, the intervals of celebration were reduced to twenty-five years, which they still continue.

In 1301, Boniface's quarrel with Philip broke out anew. He had erected, in 1296, the abbey of Pamiers, in Foix, into a bishopric, and appointed Bernard Saissetti, a creature of his own, the first bishop of it. He now sent this prelate, although disagreeable to Philip, as legate to the court of France, charging him to urge the necessity of discontinuing wars among Christians, in order that their resources might be rendered available for crippling the infidels. In executing this commission, Saissetti displayed as much arrogance, and put forth pretensions as monstrous, as could be expected from Boniface himself in his worst moments. Philip, highly enraged, arrested the envoy, treating him, on account of his bishopric of Pamiers, merely as a subject of the French crown. Boniface was equally violent, and the two displayed an intemperance in their communications with each other, that is far from creditable to either of them. The pope's crowning folly in this dispute, was his issue of the famous bull, known as *Unam sanctam*, which asserts, that two swords, one spiritual, the other material, are in the power of the church, the latter being the superior, and that every human creature's subjection to the Roman pontiff is a necessary article of faith. As Philip, however, continued firmly supported at home, this extravagance merely brought obloquy upon the Roman see, and found means for embarrassing its cooler advocates ever since. But the king could not rest contented with exhibiting Boniface as contemptible and hateful. Determined upon making him feel the weight of his vengeance, he despatched William of Nogaret into Italy, under colour of publishing there an appeal from him, but really with a view of seizing him, to bring him before a council which he was endeavouring to assemble at Lyons, and which he calculated would vote his deposition. With Nogaret, returned into his own country Sciarra Colonna, latterly an exile in France, whose family had been proscribed by the pope as Ghibelines, or adherents of the imperial faction, and personal enemies. He entered the Roman territory in disguise, and easily, but secretly, made up a strong party among his friends for surprising Boniface, who was then at Anagni, in his family seat. Nogaret joined him with a small body of French mercenaries, and the two being aided by some of the pope's own household, whom they had gained, broke in upon him, September 7, 1303, plundered his property, of which he had a great abundance with him, and behaved with extreme indignity to himself. Boniface, at first, showed considerable address and self-possession, habiting himself in his pontifical robes as a martyr to sound ecclesiastical principles, and upbraiding Nogaret with the Albigensian opinions of his family; but at length he burst, under the fury of Colonna's revilings, into a flood of bitter tears. On the third day after this outrage, the people of Anagni rose upon the attacking party, and drove it out of the city. Boniface no sooner found himself at liberty, than, without waiting for the light of another day, he set out for Rome. His reception there was most satisfactory, but his haughty spirit had received a shock from which recovery was hopeless. He died October 11, 1303, leaving a high reputation for knowledge and abilities, but generally taxed for inordinate arrogance, insatiable cupidity, and intolerable nepotism. Boniface's quarrel with France has been treated at great length in a folio volume published by Peter du Puy, at Paris, in 1655, entitled, Histoire du Difference survenu entre le Pape Boniface VIII. et Philippe le Bel. There are, however, some deficiencies in this work, which are supplied in a 12mo vol. upon the same subject, published by Adrian Baillet, at Paris, in 1718. The correspondence relating to Scotland may be seen in Matthew of Westminster, Francf. ed. p. 435. A translation of the parliamentary letter sent to him by the barons from Lincoln, is in Collier's Eccl. Hist. i. 496. In another unwarrantable attempt upon England, Boniface received a mortifying check. The popes claimed a right of collating to all benefices technically described as vacant *in curia*, being such as fell void while the parties possessed of them were upon any business at Rome. John of St. German's resigned the see of Worcester under these circumstances, and Boniface immediately preferred to it William of Gainsborough, a Franciscan friar of considerable abilities, but an extravagant abettor of papal pretensions. In making this appointment he took upon himself to convey the temporalities with the spiritualities. Edward I., however, would not put the new prelate into possession until he had formally resigned the temporal portion of Boniface's grant, and he moreover fined him a thousand marks for accepting an instrument so prejudicial to the English crown. The record of his submission is printed by Collier, i. 726. The order to which William belonged appears to have suffered from Boniface's avaricious cunning. Minds tinged with remorse or fanaticism would receive spiritual aid from none but friars; a partiality which rendered orders, professing to live by mendicancy, richer every day. The regular clergy were naturally disgusted by the preference given to the mendicants, and strove against their constant interference in duties properly belonging to themselves. Boniface appears to have sanctioned such interference, but he is also charged with over-reaching the Franciscans. Westminster says that he was offered 40,000 gold florins, besides a great sum in silver, by that order for permission to deviate from the rule of St. Francis, by the purchase of real estates. The pope asked where the money was, and finding it lodged in the hands of certain merchants, he desired the applicants to come for their answer in three days. Meanwhile he released the merchants from their obligation to restore the money to the Franciscans, and desired them to keep it for his own necessities. When the friars came at the three days' end, he told them that a departure from their obligation to strict poverty was unadvisable. Thus, says the Benedictine historian of these rivals to his own wealthy order, they most fairly lost what they had unjustly gained. Among canonists, Boniface is memorable for adding a sixth book to the Decretals, hence generally known as the *Sext*, which is itself divided into five books, and is composed of decisions promulgated since Gregory IX. In this book he repeats, with his usual dogmatism, those papal pretensions to ecclesiastical patronage, which justly caused so much opposition in most parts of Europe, and which constituted really the only assumption in which he was tolerably successful. Upon the whole, his boundless claims, offensive insolence, and baffled performances, exercised a ruinous influence over the fabric of power which Gregory VII. had founded, and Innocent III. consolidated. (Hallam's Middle Ages. Collier. Mosheim. Bower. Platina. Matt. Westm. 436, 433. Gifford's France. De Bure. Moreri. Biog. Univ.)

BONIFACE IX., (Peter Tomacelli,) a Neapolitan, elected pope, November 2, 1389, by the Italian cardinals, then extremely anxious to draw the papal court away from Avignon. In that city was, however, enthroned another pope, known as Clement VII., supported by the power of France; and neither would he recede from his pretensions, nor would the cardinals who supported him abstain from electing a successor on his death. Thus Boniface occupied a contested throne, but he was acknowledged by Hungary, Germany, England, Portugal, Norway, and most of Italy. His pontificate was disgraced by a prodigal sale of indulgences, or exemption from purgatory, to all such as chose to buy them after the jubilee of 1390, under plea of inability to procure them by a personal journey to Rome. By this device a great deal of money was raised in many parts of Europe, but the collectors proved so shamelessly rapacious, that general disgust followed upon their mission; and thus the public mind was prepared for that explosion which burst eventually from Luther's vigorous hand. Boniface was not insensible to the evils which this exercise of a pretended power over another world brought upon mankind. But he was beset by rapacious relatives, whom he had not firmness to resist, and who had no tenderness for his character when it stood in the way of their own gain. Hence a brand of simony clings to his name, which in most respects is fair, as he seems to have been a good moral man. He died Oct. 1404. (Bower. Platina.)

BONIFACE, archbishop of Canterbury, son of a count of Savoy, and uncle to Eleanor of Provence, queen to Henry III. By the influence of this princess he was elected to the see of Canterbury in 1244, on the death of Edmund, afterwards canonized. He had a fine person, and many qualities befitting high birth, but neither the learning nor the peaceful habits required in a distinguished clergyman. Hence his promotion proved highly unsatisfactory to all parties in England, and eventually uncomfortable to himself. At length, accordingly, he withdrew to the continent in disgust, and died at the castle of St. Helen's, in Savoy, in 1270. (Antiq. Brit.)

BONIFACE, (Hyacinth,) a celebrated advocate at Aix, where he died in 1699. He is known by a professional work valued among French lawyers, entitled, Recueil des Arrêts notables du Parlement de Provence. (Biog. Univ.)

BONIFACCIO, (Francis,) an Italian artist, who died about 1700, the pupil of Peter of Cortona, whose manner he imitated successfully, becoming a respectable painter of history.—Another painter of the same surname, called *Veneziano*, born in 1491, studied under the elder Palma, but became an imitator of Titian. He died in 1553, leaving many capital pictures, that recall the memory of both his models. (Bryan. Pilkington.)

BONIFACIO, the surname of some Italian authors. John, born at Rovigo, in 1547, of a noble family, was a lawyer, who wrote some professional works, but is more generally known by a history of Treviso, where he settled, printed in 1591, and again, with improvements, in 1748. He also wrote various miscellaneous works, some of them betraying marks of his advanced age. He died in 1635. His nephew, Balthazar, was born at Crema, at the same birth with two other children, and the three were called by the names current among Romanists, as those of the magi, or "wise men," who were guided by a star from the east to the place of Christ's nativity, and who are known on the Rhine as the three kings of Cologne. Balthazar Bonifacio died bishop of Capo d'Istria, in 1659, leaving a variety of miscellaneous works in Italian and Latin, probably now forgotten even in his own country.—Gaspar, one of his twin brothers, obtained some notice as an Italian poet. (Biog. Univ.)

BONINGTON, (Richard Parkes,) an English painter, born at Arnold, near Nottingham, Oct. 25, 1801, who displayed such abilities as would, probably, have led him to the summit of his profession, had he lived long enough to gain adequate knowledge and experience. His father, who was a drawing-master, delighted with the artistical talent which he displayed almost in infancy, took him at fifteen to Paris for improvement. Afterwards he travelled extensively upon the continent, and viewing every object with a painter's eye, his imagination became crowded with interesting objects for the pencil. In marine pieces he excelled, and his best work is thought to be a view of the great canal at Venice; but although he reminds a spectator of Canaletti, he falls very short, as might be expected from his age, of that artist's exactness. He died of a rapid decline, consequent upon brain fever, September 23, 1828. (Ann. Biog. Biog. Univ. Suppl.)

BONJOUR, (Francis Joseph,) an eminent French chemist, born at La Grange de Combes, near Salins, December 12, 1754. Intended by his parents for the church, he commenced his studies in theology at Besançon, but selecting medicine for his profession, he removed to Paris, where, in 1781, he received a degree in that faculty at the university. He soon, however, withdrew from practice, having a sensibility too acute to attend the bedside of the sick, and he directed his attention to botany and chemistry. The progress that he made in the latter science attracted the attention of Berthollet, who engaged him, in 1784, in his researches in the art of bleaching cloth. He was at Valenciennes, carrying out the practical part of the research, when that city was besieged by the Austrians in 1793. In this siege he received a wound in the left arm. Being attached to the army as apothecary, he was of great service in the hospitals, in carrying into effect those measures which were necessary to check the progress of contagion and disinfect a polluted atmosphere. After these labours had terminated, he was named commissary of the district of Valenciennes by the board of administration of the saltpetre works, and he held this office during one year. He then returned to Paris, and was made professor of chemistry at the central school, and also connected with the normal school for the department of Paris. After this he was attached to the council of agriculture and the arts; and in 1797 made commissary of the government at the salt works of La Meurthe. He died at Dieuze, Feb. 24, 1811. He introduced several species of potatoe into France, and pointed out the best modes of cultivating them. He endeavoured also to naturalize several other useful plants. He translated Bergman's work on Chemical Affinities, or Elective Attractions, Paris, 1788, 8vo; and is said to have composed a complete treatise on botany, the manuscript of which is lost. He was sent into Germany, in 1801, upon business connected with the salt works, but his report has never been printed.

BONJOUR, (William,) sometimes written Bonjours, a learned Austin friar, born at Toulouse in 1670. Coming to Rome, by means of cardinal Noris, in 1695, he obtained the notice of Clement XI., who entrusted him with several affairs of some importance. He was afterwards director of the seminary at Montefiascone, but his literary tastes were decidedly oriental, and he became very desirous of going to China as a missionary. Being gratified in 1710, his mathematical knowledge soon introduced him to the emperor's notice, and he was employed, in conjunction with some Jesuit missionaries, upon a map of the empire. The labours, however, imposed upon him by this commission undermined his constitution, and he died in February, 1714. He had published at Rome, in 1696, Dissertatio de Nomine Patriarchæ Josephi à Pharaone imposito; a work which seeks, with very moderate success, for Hebrew etymologies in Egyptian words. In 1699 he published, Exercitatio in Monumenta Coptica, seu Ægyptiaca, Bibliothecæ Vaticanæ. He also published some works of less general interest, and left several MSS., among which a Coptic grammar appears to be valuable. (Biog. Univ.)

BONN, (Andrew,) a celebrated surgeon, son of an apothecary at Amsterdam, where he was born in 1738. After a good general education under the tuition of Burmann, Roellius, and Camper, he studied medicine at Leyden, where, having attended the lectures of Muschenbroek, Albinus, Royen, Boerhaave, and Gaubius, he took the degree of M.D. at the age of 25, delivering an able thesis, De Continuationibus Membranorum, Lugd. Bat. 1763, 4to, published in Sandifort's Thesaurus. This discourse has been conjectured by some anatomists to have given to Bichât some information put forth in his Traité des Membranes. Bonn, after taking his degree, proceeded to Paris, where he remained one year, and made acquaintance with Levret, Lorry, Sabatier, Petit, Louis, and several other most eminent men in his profession. He then returned to Amsterdam, engaged in practice, and in 1771 was named professor of anatomy and surgery. He performed the duties of his office for half a century, with great zeal and assiduity, and materially assisted to establish the society of surgeons in Amsterdam. To evince the regard in which his labours were held, the members of this body struck a medal in honour of his services. He died in 1819, having lived to the age of 81 years. Among his published works are, Commentatio de Humero Luxato, Lugd. Bat. et Amst. 1782, 4to. Descriptio Thesauri Ossium Morbosorum Hoviani, adnexa est Dissertatio de Callo, Amst. 1783, 4to. This is a description of a very valuable collection bequeathed by a celebrated physician of Amsterdam, James Hovius, in 1736, to the college of surgery.

BONNART, (John,) a French surgeon of the seventeenth century. He was provost of the ancient college of surgery of Paris, and he was also, according to the custom of his time, a barber. He died December 15, 1638, having published, Méthode pour bien Saigner, Paris, 1628, 4to. La Semaine de Médicamens, observés des Chef-d'œuvres des Maistres Barbiers de Paris, 1629, 8vo.

BONNEFONS, (John,) or Bonefonius, a French writer of Latin verse, born at Clermont, in Auvergne, in 1554, and bred to the law, under Cujas, in the university of Bourges. He practised for a time as an advocate at Paris, with good success, but his poetical talents found him some powerful friends, by whose interest he obtained a place at Bar-sur-Seine, where he died, in 1614. The most complete edition of his works was published at Amsterdam, in 1767, with this title, Joannis Bonefonii Patris, Opera omnia. The Pancharis, one of his pieces in praise of an imaginary mistress, in the style of Catullus, has been printed with Beza's Juvenilia. But his reputation is wholly gone, as he displays the very worst taste, and his Latinity is full of gross and obvious errors. His son, who bore both his names, succeeded him at Bar, and, like him, was a Latin poet, but of no account.—Another Bonnefons, (Elias Benedict,) was a learned Benedictine, of the congregation of St. Maur, who died in 1702, leaving two valuable MS. works, illustrative of the history of Normandy. (Biog. Univ. Hallam's Literature of Europe, ii. 340.)

BONNEFOY, (John Baptist,) a French surgeon, born at Lyons, in 1756. He was admitted into the college of surgery of his native place in 1783, and in the same year presented to the Royal Academy of Surgery a Memoir on the Influence of the Mind in Diseases appertaining to Surgery, which obtained the prize, and was inserted in the Prix de l'Académie de Chirurgie, tom. v. It contains upwards of fifty curious instances illustrative of the opinions of the author on a subject not yet sufficiently attended to. He also printed, De l'Application de l'Electricité à l'Art de Guérir, Lyons and Paris, 1783, 8vo. This was his inaugural discourse, in which he endeavours to assimilate the nature of the nervous fluid to that of electricity, and points out the various diseases in which the employment of this powerful agent has been attended with benefit. He also published Analyse raisonnée des Rapports des Commissaires chargés de l'Examen du Magnétisme Animal, Lyons and Paris, 1784, 8vo. He died in 1790.

BONNELL, (James,) a pious and learned person, whose good qualities attracted in their day considerable notice, descended from a Flemish refugee of ancient family, who settled at Norwich during the duke of Alva's persecution, and engaged in business. James Bonnell's father was in the Italian trade, and at Genoa the son was born, Nov. 14, 1653. The elder Bonnell was wealthy, and gave such large pecuniary assistance to Charles II. during his exile, that on the restoration he was appointed accountant-general of the Irish revenue, with a reversion to his son; the only return, as it appears, that ever he received for his advances. After the younger Bonnell had received a preliminary education in Ireland, he was sent to a sort of private academical establishment in Oxfordshire; but he soon found most of the moral disadvantages there, that he and his friends dreaded in an university, without the intellectual benefits which regular training in a college has to offer. He removed accordingly to Catharine hall, Cambridge. Subsequently he became tutor in a gentleman's family at Aspeden Hall, in Hertfordshire. He afterwards discharged in person the duties of his place in Ireland, but he disposed of it in 1693. He died in Dublin, April 28, 1699, quite remarkable for piety, morality, amiable temper, and liberality to the poor. It had been his intention to take orders, but he died a layman. Though an excellent scholar, nothing of his has been published, except some meditations and prayers inserted in his Life, and a Harmony of the Gospels, written by another, but reformed and improved by him for his own use. (Biog. Brit.)

BONNER, (Edmund,) otherwise written *Boner*, (which seems to be the true spelling, the double *n* being probably occasioned by the pronunciation,) the most unpopular of English prelates. He was born towards the end of the sixteenth century, and commonly passed for the natural son of George Savage, rector of Davenham, in Cheshire; but this was evidently a malicious aspersion, Strype being assured by Lechmere, a baron of the exchequer, that he was lawfully born of poor but reputable parentage, at Hanley, in Worcestershire. An ancestor of the baron's put him to school, and Bonner gratefully requited the obligation in after life, not only by personal friendship to the family, but also by helping it to some valuable leases of property vested in the see of London. The future prelate received his academical education at Broadgates hall, Oxford, since converted into Pembroke college. On June 12, 1519, he was admitted bachelor of canon law, and on the 13th of the next month he took the same degree in civil law. He seems never to have had much reputation for general scholarship, but he probably acquired a considerable insight into legal questions, and his talents for business quickly gained him notice. Of these, the bishop of Worcester availed himself in the management of his diocese. In 1525, Bonner took his doctor's degree, having been admitted into orders some time before. His first patron of importance was Wolsey, to whom he became master of the faculties and spiritual jurisdictions. He was with the cardinal at Cawood, at the time of his arrest, and sitting at table with him on the All Saints' day preceding, received a broken head, so as to draw blood, by the accidental fall of his cross, an unlucky incident, which the late favourite's declining spirits interpreted as an evil omen. By means of his early patrons, Bonner obtained four parochial benefices, and the prebend of Chiswick, in the church of St. Paul, London. The last preferment he resigned in 1539. He had long before that year paved his way to dignities of much more importance, having come over to Lutheran views on Wolsey's fall, and rendering himself conspicuous in advocating the king's divorce from Catharine of Aragon. This kind of prominence, being joined with boldness and knowledge of affairs, recommended him as companion to Sir Edward Carne in 1532, who was then sent to Rome as *excusator*, or apologist, for Henry's non-appearance in the papal court, to which he had been cited, either personally or by proxy. The first ground to be taken was founded on the canon law, and hence it was proper that the envoy should be attended by a professed canonist. But Bonner's learning was insufficient for the purpose, however he might otherwise have been qualified for it by a forward, confident, overbearing demeanour. It is evident, however, that he gave satisfaction at home, as he was despatched in the autumn of 1533 to Clement at Marseilles, that pontiff coming thither in October to meet Francis I. of France. Bonner was admitted into his presence on November 7, and gave him violent offence by closing ineffectual importunities for a favourable consideration of Henry's case, with an appeal from the papal authority to a general council. Clement is said to have talked of throwing his unwelcome English visitor into a cauldron of melted lead, or of burning him alive. Unquestionably he discovered great irritation; and Bonner's own account shows that he was pressed in a manner which few men would quietly bear. Hence Pallavicino is perhaps justified in saying that he was uncivilly treated, although Bonner's conduct might be taken as nothing more than proper firmness in the exercise of his commission. In 1535, Bonner was preferred to the archdeaconry of Leicester, on the promotion of Edward Fox to the see of Hereford. In the following year, he added a stringent preface to the second edition of Gardiner's famous treatise, *De vera Obedientia*, which eventually caused so much discredit and confusion to all the leading divines of the Romish party. In 1537 he was a member of the commission which prepared *Institution of a Christian Man*, an authoritative exposition of doctrine for popular use, mainly founded on the confession of Augsburg, but wearing, nevertheless, very much of a Romish complexion. His friend at court appears to have been Cromwell, who, like himself, had been in Wolsey's service, and probably thought him the man for many of those difficult undertakings which were then on foot. Bonner accordingly was entrusted with a series of diplomatic services abroad, although he really seems, from want of delicacy and discretion, to have been but little fit for making a favourable impression upon foreign courts. Thus Francis I. was so much offended in 1538, by his rude applications for the surrender of an Englishman, fled into France, that he would not rest satisfied without demanding his recall. Towards the close of that year, he was nominated to the see of Hereford, vacant by the death of Edward Fox, being confirmed December 17. He was still abroad, and had not taken possession, when John Stokesley, bishop of London, died. Cromwell we know had recommended him for the bishopric of Hereford, and he probably now procured his nomination to that of London. He was confirmed bishop of that important diocese, Nov. 11, 1539, and consecrated April 4, 1540, with Nicholas Heath, the new bishop of Rochester, under a commission from Cranmer, in St. Paul's cathedral. Gardiner was the principal officiating bishop; and it is conjectured by Strype, that Cranmer's absence upon this occasion was intentional, being caused by a dislike of Bonner, founded on experience of his insincerity, or other suspicious qualities. He was undoubtedly not without means of judging upon his character, having appointed him master of his faculties. To all appearance hitherto, however, Bonner was firm to reforming principles. He had exerted himself, when ambassador to the court of France, in 1538, to procure the printing of the English Bible at Paris; and when the sacred volume was authoritatively published in 1540, he placed six copies of it in St. Paul's, with admonitions for the proper reading of it. He had then just taken possession of the see of London, but nothing could be more base than the feeling which he showed immediately afterwards towards Cromwell, the kind friend to whom he really owed his splendid fortune. On that unhappy statesman's arrest, he expressed regret that it had been so long delayed, forgetful, apparently, that his ruin at an earlier period would probably have been fatal to the ambitious hopes which he had himself conceived. By thus implicitly accommodating himself to Henry's pleasure, he remained in favour with him to the last, being at the time of his death ambassador at the imperial court. On Edward's accession, he found himself obliged, in common with all other members of the prelacy, to take out a license, granted during pleasure, for the exercise of his episcopal functions. Nevertheless, he did not scruple to throw impediments in the way of the royal visitation, ordered soon afterwards. When summoned to St. Paul's before the visitors, Sept. 1, 1547, he took the oaths of abjuration and supremacy; but when called upon to receive the homilies and injunctions tendered to him, he formally protested against compliance, unless the matter contained in them should appear conformable with God's law and the church's ordinances. On the 12th of September he regularly retracted his protestation as unadvised, unbecoming a subject, and injurious in the way of example. He was, however, committed to the Fleet, and remained in custody until the middle of November. He then conformed outwardly to recent changes, but several connivances and other indications proved him a real enemy to them. When rebellious movements, accordingly, threatened Edward's policy, the bishop of London was ordered in council to correct some things that had occasioned animadversion, and to preach a sermon at St. Paul's Cross, inculcating the wickedness of rebellion, the superiority of practical holiness over ceremonial observances, and the competence of a minor king to make laws binding upon his subjects. On September 1, 1549, the prescribed sermon was delivered to a very numerous congregation; but although it touched upon rebellion and ceremonies, it passed over the question, then much litigated, of obedience to sovereigns under age. It contained, however, other matter, probably a defence of transubstantiation, likely to keep alive popular uneasiness. On these accounts the bishop was summoned by a commission under the great seal, dated Sept. 8, to appear at Lambeth. His judges opened their court on the 10th, and after seven sessions, in which he displayed a levity and insolence utterly below his age and station, he was deprived of his bishopric on the 1st of October. It does not seem that he was treated as a canonical offender, two lay statesmen being among his judges. He was, in fact, after an inquiry deemed sufficient, cashiered from the bishopric of London, an office which he had formally consented to hold during pleasure. After his dismissal, he was detained in prison, a severity to which the government probably was driven by fears that his liberty might endanger the public peace.

Queen Mary having overcome the opposition to her sovereignty, and entered London, August 3, 1553, gave a pardon to Bonner two days afterwards. On the 13th of that month, he attended a sermon preached by Bourn, his chaplain, at St. Paul's Cross, on the passage of scripture which he had himself discussed there four years before. In this discourse he was described as unjustly treated in the late reign; but some of the auditors exclaimed that he had preached abomination, and a tumult ensued, which is noticed in the histories of that period. On the 22d of the month, a commission was issued to certain civilians for considering his deprivation. They pronounced it void, but their sentence was not formally promulged until Sept. 5. He seems, however, to have already acted as diocesan, the Latin service being again used in St. Paul's, Aug. 27, most probably by his authority. By law it stood prohibited until the end of October, when an act was passed repealing king Edward's legislation, and restoring the old Romish liturgy, on the 20th of December. Bonner was equally prompt in depriving the married clergy of his diocese, taking upon himself to inflict this hardship upon them in February 1554, although the royal authority for his purpose was not issued until March 4. He showed subsequently a most revolting forwardness in the horrid proceedings which have rendered queen Mary's name, in spite of her personal good qualities, for ever infamous, and which have rendered his own name a by-word and a term of reproach to all succeeding generations. At one time he does undoubtedly appear to have become weary, and perhaps ashamed of the persecution. In common with other prelates, his energies in the hateful task relaxed. Upon him lay its chief weight. Gardiner did little more than set it on foot; and after him, Bonner was the most prominent of his order. The diocese of London, too, contained the principal seat of population, together with an extensive rural district, which, like the other eastern counties, had been largely imbued with protestantism. Prisoners from parts of England over which he had no jurisdiction, were likewise often sent to the metropolis, and thus considered as holding heretical opinions that came under his cognizance. Hence he was called upon to vindicate Romanism by fire and fagot, until some symptoms of reluctance were observed. The infatuated government saw them with displeasure, and by a circular, dated May 25, 1555, rebuked the prelacy for its abating zeal. Bonner immediately resumed his former activity, and it continued until Mary's death ended the persecution. In this hateful employment he displayed repeatedly a cruel, insolent demeanour, for which it is impossible to offer any excuse; but upon no occasion did he so conspicuously disgrace himself as when executing the commission to degrade archbishop Cranmer. His conduct was then so offensive, that, brutal as were the humours to which he was liable, it can scarcely be accounted for, without supposing a personal grudge. On Elizabeth's accession, he met her with others of his order at Highgate, in her way from Hatfield to London. The whole bench knelt and offered their allegiance. She accepted their courtesy with her usual grace, and gave to every one of them but Bonner her hand to kiss. His brief opposition to the restoration of protestantism was terminated May 30, 1559, by the tender of the oath of supremacy, he being the first individual thus called upon. He, like other distinguished churchmen, had taken that oath before; but a general resolution seems to have been formed among them, on Mary's death, to decline the ignominy of another recantation. Bonner, accordingly, refused the oath; and as his prominence in the late persecution had forfeited every claim to indulgence, proceedings were instituted on the 2d of June, for depriving him of his bishopric. This was effected on the 29th of that month. No personal restraint appears, however, to have been put upon him. But on the 4th of the following December, he signed, in common with four others of the deprived prelates, an insolent remonstrance to the queen, on the late alterations in religion. In an answer to this, returned on the spur of the moment, the subscribers were very fairly reminded of their several inconsistencies in former years, Bonner's notice being called to the time when he was archdeacon of Leicester, and wrote a preface to Gardiner's tract, De vera Obedientia. This rebuke did not reduce the dispossessed Romish clergy to silence. On the contrary, in the early part of 1560, there were several suspicious movements among them; the consequence of which were several committals. Bonner was placed in the Marshalsea, on the 20th of April, and he never seems to have regained his liberty. Of this, perhaps, he had no great reason to complain; the popular abhorrence with which he was justly viewed rather gaining strength by time. The atrocities with which he had been concerned, became, indeed, more accurately known every day. Hence, it is far from unlikely, that, if at large, an ebullition of popular vengeance might have sacrificed his life. But although secluded generally from the public eye, he sometimes walked abroad, and within his prison he lived in the free enjoyment of every personal indulgence. His last appearance before the world was caused by an injudicious tender to him of the oath of supremacy by Horne, bishop of Winchester, in whose diocese the Marshalsea lay. He refused it, and was indicted in the court of King's Bench. He employed very able counsel in his defence, who admitted his refusal of the oath, but started various legal objections to Horne's episcopal character, which, if substantiated, would have disqualified him for administering the oath. Parliament interposed to prevent the evils which legal subtlety might have caused from the agitation of this question. An act was passed affirming the validity of episcopal consecrations under the queen, and an indemnity was voted for such refusals of the oath as had already taken place. Thus Bonner escaped from further molestation. He died in the Marshalsea, Sept. 5, 1569, and was buried, among other prisoners, in St. George's church-yard, Southwark. Besides his preface to Gardiner's tract, he published, in 1554, a manual of religious instruction for the people of his diocese. (Burnet. Strype. Stowe. Newcourt. Harrington.)

BONNET, (Gisb.) born 1723, one of the most celebrated and influential Dutch theologians of the eighteenth century. He was first a preacher, and then, from 1761 to 1805, lecturer on theology at Utrecht. Voltaire's Traité sur la Tolerance called forth from him an academic discourse, De Tolerantia circa Religionem, in Vitium et Noxam vertente; and he pursued the subject in a dissertation On Ecclesiastical Tolerance, Utrecht, 1770. He wrote a Commentary on Ecclesiastes, which has been frequently reprinted; and also a Commentary on the Epistle to the Hebrews, in 10 parts. As a professor he was very popular; and several of the most distinguished Dutch preachers and professors of the present century, were among his scholars. The style of preaching in Holland was especially improved by his precepts and example. In spite of popular prejudices, he did not hesitate to receive instruction in oratory from the celebrated actor, Pünt. He published four collections of sermons: Leerredenen, Utrecht, 1774, 1776, 1788, 1792. In his latter years he was engaged in a controversy with Van Hemert, on the authority of reason in religion. He died at Utrecht, February 3, 1805.

BONNET, (Charles,) a celebrated philosophical writer, born at Geneva, of affluent parents, March 13, 1720, and destined for jurisprudence, but early devoted to natural history, from the delight with which he read Pluche's Spectacle de la Nature, and the works of Reaumur and Swammerdam. His discoveries, when no more than twenty years of age, on the propagation of the vine-fretter, earned him the praise of Trembley, his countryman, and procured for him, by means of Reaumur, the rank of a correspondent of the Paris Academy of Sciences. His zeal being thus stimulated, he instituted researches on the reproduction of fresh-water worms, on the respiration of insects, and on the economy of the tape-worm. In 1743 he became a doctor of law; but henceforth, it appears, legal studies were laid aside altogether for his favourite pursuits. In 1745 he published his Traité d'Insectologie, Paris, 2 parts in 8vo, which, from its philosophic tone, met with great applause. Bonnet's philosophy, as Sprengel truly observes, was the philosophy of his age; not a system of abstract truths, but a popular series of general positions based on experiments, which positions, though well connected and admitting of practical application, are still deficient in profundity and in any guiding principle. In Bonnet's next work, Recherches sur l'Usage des Feuilles, Leyden, 1754, he sought to extend the inquiries of Hales. It is a valuable contribution to vegetable physiology, showing the relation subsisting between the leaves and the various components of their atmospheric medium, and the manner in which the leaves, roots, and branches change their position, under various circumstances, in order to be duly accommodated with humidity, nourishment, and light. Bonnet's eyes having been injured by microscopic researches, he was compelled to exchange the more minute examination of particular departments of natural history for general observations. His constitution had been weak from childhood; and having found consolation in his sufferings from the doctrines of Christianity, he began, in consequence, to contemplate philosophical subjects from a more religious point of view, and from this period, a more obvious and systematic tendency is evident in his works. In his Essai de Psychologie, ou Considerations sur les Operations de l'Ame, he particularly endeavoured to explain the apparent incompatibility of the freedom of the human will with divine providence, in conformity with the principles of his own church, but without success, as he only treated the subject very incompletely. More excusable is the deficient acquaintance which this work betrays with the anatomy of the brain; a subject very much neglected at that time. His Essai Analytique sur les Facultés de l'Ame, 1760, is liable to similar objections; nor is it free from peculiar and rather fanciful hypotheses, by which its comparative failure with the public may be explained. In 1762 he published his Considerations sur les Corps organisés, in which, with many plausible arguments, he supported the doctrine of the preformation of germs, on grounds derived partly from the observations of Haller and Spallanzani. This work received high praise from the Berlin Academy, and was regarded as sufficiently important in France to be forbidden as dangerous; the interdict, however, was soon discovered to have been unnecessary, and was accordingly removed. His Contemplation de la Nature, Amsterdam, 1764, 1765, 2 vols, 8vo, is his most successful production. Its object is to demonstrate a regular scale of organization, rising from the most simple to the most complex of beings. It contains general contemplations in a popular and interesting style; communicates no new facts, but comprises a view of all nature, and demonstrates successfully the harmony of its several departments. As Bonnet's faculties for external observation diminished, and he was forcibly reminded by advanced age of another world, he concentrated his attention upon the nature of the soul, its hopes and prospects, especially upon its existence after death. In his Idées sur l'Etat futur des étres Vivans, ou Palingenesie Philosophique, Geneva, 1769-70, 2 vols, 8vo, he shows, from the ills of this world, and the irregularity of their distribution, the necessity for a compensation which can only be hoped for in another life. His Recherches Philosophiques sur les Preuves du Christianisme, is characterised by warmth of feeling, touching eloquence, and by the impress of truly pious sentiments. Lavater thought it so irresistibly convincing, that he hastened to translate it into German, with a dedication to Mendelsohn, the celebrated Jewish philosopher of Berlin, in which he called upon him either to refute the evidences of Christianity which it contained, or to become himself a Christian. Mendelsohn resented this appeal, and Bonnet, who was far from participating in the confidence of Lavater, distinctly assured him that he had taken no part in it. Bonnet's life was as tranquil and unruffled in respect to his circumstances, as a philosopher could desire; its only affliction was the ill health of himself and his beloved wife. He had no children, but met with a son's affection in his celebrated nephew, H. B. de Saussure, whom he brought up. His death took place from dropsy of the chest, May 20, 1793, at the age of 73. (A laudatory Memoir of Bonnet, published at Berne, 1794, and an excellent article by Sprengel, in Ersch's Encyclopædia, &c.)

BONNEVAL, (Claudius Alexander, count of,) a French military adventurer, born of an illustrious house in the Limousin, July 14, 1675. He was originally in the navy, but subsequently entering the army, he served with distinction. His fiery temper, however, drove him into exile, and pecuniary distress reconciled him to the acceptance of an Austrian commission, although it entailed upon him the necessity of fighting against France. In this new situation he again distinguished himself; and he might have gained an honourable provision had not his intolerable vices of temper driven him into a second exile. He now took refuge in Turkey, and renouncing the usages of Europe, became a leading officer in the Ottoman army, under the designation of Achmet Pacha. He introduced a knowledge of European tactics, instructed his new friends in the management of artillery, and in 1739, signalized himself in a campaign against the Austrians. As in every other place, he made himself, however, enemies in Turkey; and when death surprised him in 1747, he was meditating a return to Christendom. A work, purporting to be his autobiography, was published in 1755, but doubts are thrown upon its genuineness. (Biog. Univ.)

BONNIVARD, (Francis de,) honourably recorded in the annals of Geneva, born 1496, of an influential Savoyard family. Several of his ancestors had been priors of St. Victor, at Geneva, and he was elected to this dignity in 1513, on the renunciation of it by his uncle Amadeus. At this period, the bishop John attempted to cede his territory to the duke of Savoy, a step which was sanctioned by Leo X., but not unconditionally approved of by the college of cardinals, on account of the great opposition to it by the Genevese. In the course of this dispute, the bishop imprisoned a Genevese citizen, named Pecolat, for a biting witticism, and subjected him to torture. The archbishop of Vienne was prevailed upon to issue an order to bishop John in favour of the prisoner, which, however, no one dared to deliver, until, in 1516, Bonnivard, determined upon undertaking the liberation of Pecolat, delivered the order to the bishop, and thus incurred his enmity, as well as that of the duke of Savoy. The latter called him to account; but he justified himself with dauntless boldness. Shortly afterwards, two young Genevese were arrested at Turin, and conducted to Pignerol, where the bishop was staying. It was sought by torture to extort from them an avowal of a conspiracy in which Bonnivard was accused of being implicated. The latter was then on a journey to Rome, and had recommended the prisoners to an advocate; but a letter to them, which he entrusted to their gaoler, was betrayed by that person. The ill-fated youths were executed amidst protestations of innocence, then quartered, and their heads and limbs salted and sent to Geneva. Soon afterwards, Bonnivard, on his return, arrived at Turin. He braved the bishop, appeared boldly in public for eight days, though it was intended to arrest him, and then escaped secretly to Geneva. He was, however, delivered, by treachery, to the duke of Savoy, who imprisoned him for two years in the castle Grolée. When the Reformation began to make progress, Bonnivard was asked what he thought of the reform of the creed and of the clergy. "One of two things," was his answer; "if you abandon yourselves to wild courses as at present, you must not be surprised if others do the same. But if you wish to reform the clergy, you must first show them the way." Bonnivard appears to have been at this time a discreet friend of the protestant cause; and when some of his fellow-citizens wished to deter him from reading the excommunication of the Genevese by the archbishop of Vienne, saying, that from the moment he perused it, he must be regarded as excommunicated, he answered sportively, "If you have done wrong you are already excommunicated by God; but if the archbishop is in error, why then the pope Berchthold (by whom he meant the reformer Haller of Berne) will soon absolve you." In 1530, Bonnivard was allowed a safeguard by the duke, in order to go to Seyssel on a visit to his mother, who was old and infirm. Thence he repaired to Milden, where a diet was held. On his road from Milden to Lausanne, he was plundered by a band of marauders, with a couple of abandoned hirelings at their head, taken prisoner, and lodged in the castle of Chillon, where the duke kept him in confinement in spite of the intercession of Bern and Freiburg. For two years he was treated without great rigour, but was not brought to trial. The duke, at the expiration of that time, visited Chillon, and ordered him to be thrown into a rocky dungeon, which is below the surface of the neighbouring lake. Here he remained till 1536, when the Genevese conquered the Waatland.

He was then liberated, and returned to Geneva, where he avowed his adherence to protestantism, but dissuaded its supporters from introducing it rashly. Bonnivard died in 1570; he was twice married, but had no children. His mind was better cultivated than that of most of his contemporaries of the same rank. He was commissioned by the magistrates to write a chronicle of Geneva, and his manuscript history is now in the library of that city; it contains, in 4 books, a history of Geneva till 1530, written with research, in a simple but not unattractive style. There are other historical manuscripts of his in the same library. He also wrote a book on the nobility of Geneva. The captivity of Bonnivard is the subject of Byron's Prisoner of Chillon. (See an article by Meyer v. Kronan in Ersch's Encyclopædia.)

BONNYCASTLE, (John,) a valuable English writer of the mathematical class, born at Whitchurch, in Buckinghamshire, of parents in moderate circumstances. His education, though not classical, was far from neglected, and its deficiencies being in a great measure supplied by his own application, he went early to London, in the hope of advancing himself. He there married, when about nineteen; but his wife dying soon afterwards, he became tutor to the earl of Pomfret's two sons. He then became one of the mathematical masters at Woolwich, a situation which he filled more than forty years, and for which he was admirably qualified, an early taste, formed in him for the mathematics, having been assiduously cultivated. He died at Woolwich, May 15, 1821. He first published, in 1780, the Scholar's Guide to Arithmetic, which has passed through several editions. Afterwards appeared his Introduction to Mensuration and Practical Geometry, 1782; Introduction to Algebra, 1782; Introduction to Astronomy, which proved highly popular, 1786; Euclid's Elements, 1789; General History of Mathematics, from the French of Bossuet, 1803; A Treatise on Spherical Trigonometry, 1806; Introduction to Arithmetic, being the first part of a general course of mathematics, 1810; A Treatise on Algebra, 1813. (Ann. Biog.)

BONOMI, (Joseph,) an Italian architect, of considerable reputation, who lived long in England, and died in London, in 1808. (Gorton.)

BONONE, (Charles,) an Italian historical painter, pupil of Bastaruolo, but improved by study in the school of the Caracci. Of Lewis Caracci he became, indeed, a very successful imitator. His skill in foreshortening, and knowledge of *chiar' oscuro*, astonished the best painters of his time. Some of his most successful pieces, however, being professedly imitations, have added less to his reputation than might be expected from their intrinsic excellence. He died in 1632. (Pilkington.)

BONOSUS, probably bishop of Sardica, in Illyricum, near the end of the fourth century, occasionally mentioned in ecclesiastical history as an heresiarch. He seems to have maintained that the Virgin Mary bore other children besides our Saviour. Whether he also denied the divinity of Christ is doubtful. It is, however, certain that this was denied, in the fifth and sixth centuries, by some French and Spanish heretics called Bonosians; but their name might have been derived from another Bonosus. (Mosheim, i. 415.)

BONSTETTEN, (Charles Victor von,) a distinguished Swiss writer, born Sept. 3, 1745, at Berne, of a noble family, educated at Yverdun, where he became acquainted with Rousseau, and afterwards at Geneva, where he enjoyed the society of Bonnet, to whom he was indebted for the origin of many of his philosophical ideas. Whilst still a youth, he adopted a very original and useful method of studying a subject, which was also practised by Diderot: previously to reading a work, he copied the heads of the chapters, and committed to paper his own thoughts on the subject, which after its perusal he compared with those of the author. It was at Geneva that his religious impressions appear to have been formed. In a letter to Matthison he describes affectingly his first communion, "the happiest day of his life," and his having wept at the doubts which some raillery by Voltaire (to whose table he was often invited) had raised in his mind. After spending a year or two with Bonnet, he went to study at Leyden. He afterwards visited Cambridge, where he became known to Gray, passed a short time at Paris, and travelled into Italy, whither he often returned. In 1782, he published his first work, "Letters on a Pastoral Country of Switzerland," attributed at first to Ivon Müller, and depicting, in a charming and lively style, which the author never afterwards equalled, the manners, cultivation, and manufactures of the canton of Gessenay, in the Oberland valley. Though entrusted with some public appointments, his desultory and studious habits prevented him from distinguishing himself in them. He exerted himself, however, meritoriously to improve the educational institutions, and he published, in 1786, two memoirs on the education of the patrician families in Berne, which were penned in a style so severe, that it was long ere they were forgiven. At the fall of the republic of Berne, in 1798, Bonstetten quitted Switzerland for Germany, where he felt again at home, and then accepted an invitation from a Danish minister, and resided for three years at Copenhagen. Here he published, in four volumes 12mo, a collection of his writings on education, on the origin of language, the Scandinavian poets (with translations and historical details); also his travels, political observations, and remarks on other subjects, such as gardening, &c. On his return to Switzerland, in 1802, he resided chiefly at Geneva, where he had passed the happiest time of his youth, and where he found numerous and faithful friends. He afterwards, on different occasions, travelled in the south of France, as well as in Italy, always exercising a spirit of observation, and collecting materials for his writings. In the intervals of these journeys, he resumed and penned his meditations on various metaphysical subjects, to which his mind was naturally inclined. At the age of seventy his health received a shock from a malady which in the end proved fatal, but which on this occasion was arrested by the care of an expert physician. His intellectual faculties did not suffer from it; on the contrary, he seemed to acquire with age new ardour and a tendency to enthusiasm, which generally belongs only to youth. His Souvenirs, written at this period of his life, are an interesting proof of the liveliness and elasticity of his mental powers. He died February 3, 1832, of a fresh attack of his former illness, at the age of 86. His principal works, besides those enumerated above, are his Suisse Ameliorée, ou la Fête de la Reconnaissance, 1802, in 8vo, in which, in the character of a Swiss emigrant, he recounts, on his return to his native soil, the hospitable reception he had met with in a northern clime, and indulges in bright hopes for his country, now restored to independence, and calls for the regeneration of the people by the improvement of public education, and the reform of the political institutions. It is written in poetical prose, and was designed to inspire the youth of Switzerland with lofty and patriotic sentiments. His works, Uber National Beldung, Zurich, 1802, and Pensées sur divers Objêts de Bien Public, Genève, 1815, contain a number of general propositions for the improvement of political government. His Voyage sur la Scène des six derniers Livres de l'Enéide, suivi de quelques Observations sur le Latium moderne, Genève, 1804, will be found serviceable as a guide for travellers, though the style, as is frequently the case with this author, is too lofty and ornate. They may be read as containing numerous accurate and interesting observations both of the external world and of the author's own mind, but he must not be used as a guide or authority. Gray felt a warm friendship for Bonstetten, as is seen by some of his letters, published in the Notes to Matthison's Letters, translated into English by Anne Plumptre, 1799. To those interested in the biography of Bonstetten, the perusal of his Letters to Frederica Brun, 2 vols, Frankf. 1828, published by Matthison, may be recommended.

BONTEKOE, (Corrielius van,) a physician, the son of a burgher of Alcmaer, whose name was Gerard Decker, but who obtained the name of Bontekoë from having appended to his house the sign of a cow of many colours. He was born in 1647, and studied medicine at the university of Leyden. Having taken his degree, he visited the Hague, Amsterdam, and Hamburg. Frederic William, elector of Brandenburg, named him physician to the court; and he repaired to Berlin, where he died, February 13, 1685, from a fall, which fractured his skull. The elector honoured his memory by a pompous funeral. He was most zealous in recommending the use of tea to neutralize acidity, to which he attributed all fevers; in short, he regarded this beverage as an universal panacea. His enthusiasm on this subject is quite ludicrous, for he went so far as to endeavour to prove that both the physical and moral condition of man would be improved by the use of tea, as in its subtle elements and principles he conceived it to possess properties nearly allied to those of the animal spirits. He proposed the drinking of not less than 100 or 200 cups in the day; and he equally recommended the employment of the pipe, which, according to his doctrine, ought to be continually used during the twenty-four hours. These and other singular opinions entertained by him render his name of no celebrity in the annals of medical science, but rather present him as an example of grave error arising from speculative doctrines, to be avoided by all who desire to exercise their profession for the benefit of mankind. Of his writings, it is sufficient to mention, Alle die Philosophische, Medicinale en Chymische Worken, Amst. 1689, 2 vols, 4to, a part of which work has been translated into French by Devaux, Paris, 1698, 2 vols, 12mo.

BONTEMS, (Maria Jane de Chatillon,) a French lady of genius, born in Paris, January 14, 1718. She died Aug. 18, 1768, leaving, as a monument of her taste and accomplishments, a prose translation of Thomson's Seasons, published anonymously in 1759, and often reprinted. Garrick and Gibbon, when at Paris, were frequent visitors at the house of Madame Bontems, and entertained a high opinion of her. (Biog. Univ.)

BONTIUS, (Gerard,) a physician, born at Riswick, in 1538, esteemed an excellent scholar, particularly in Greek literature, professor of medicine at the university of Leyden, during twenty-four years, and in 1599 made rector. He died at the age of sixty-three, having composed many works, of which, after his decease, in conformity to his desire, the MSS. were destroyed.

BONTIUS, (James,) a physician and naturalist, son of the preceding, born at Leyden. He visited the East Indies in 1627, and for many years resided in Java, as physician to the governor of Batavia and the Dutch company. He was well skilled in his profession, and in natural history generally. Plumier has dedicated a genus of plants (Bontia) to his memory. He died in 1631. His work, De Medicinâ Indorum, Lugd. Batav. 1642, 12mo, 1719, 4to, (Paris, 1645, 1646, 4to; Amst. 1658, fol.; in English, Lond. 1769, 8vo; in Dutch, Amst. 1694, 8vo,) is very highly esteemed. After the death of Bontius, William Piso published partly from his MSS. De Indiæ utriusque Re Naturali et Medicinâ Lib. xiv. Amst. 1658, fol.

BONVICINO, (Alexander,) called *Il Moretto*, an Italian painter, born at Brescia, in 1514, and educated in the school of Titian, whose style he approached more nearly than any of his countrymen. He also caught something of Raphael's greatness, and thus painted most attractive pictures. His portraits have been compared to those of Titian; and his sacred subjects, by their grace, devotional expression, and freshness of colouring, have obtained a high rank among works of art. He died in 1564. (Bryan.)

BONWICKE, (Ambrose,) born April 29, 1652, educated at Merchant Taylors' school; elected to St. John's college, Oxford, 1668; appointed librarian there 1670; graduated B.A. 1673; M.A. 1675; ordained deacon, 1670; priest, 1680; proceeded B.D. 1682; chosen master of Merchant Taylors' school, 1686; and rector of Mickleham, in Surrey. At the Revolution he took the *non-juring* side. St. John's college, where are forty-six fellowships for scholars from this school, petitioned the Merchant Taylors' Company that he might, notwithstanding, continue the master for life, for the sake of his scholastic talents, but the request could not be granted; and at Christmas, 1691, he was removed for declining the oaths of allegiance. Upon this he established a school at Headley, near Leatherhead, in Surrey, which, from his great piety, learning, and talent for teaching, became very celebrated and prosperous. He there trained and sent out some distinguished characters; among others, the poet Fenton was his usher, and Bowyer, the learned printer, his scholar.

BOONE, (Daniel,) a colonel in the American service, and one of the earliest settlers in Kentucky, where he signalized himself by many daring exploits and adventures, of which he has given an account in Filson's Supplement to Imlay's Description of the Western Territory, 1793. He died 1820, at the age of nearly ninety. (Carter's Amer. Biog. Dict.)

BOONEN, (Arnold,) a Dutch portrait painter of great eminence, born at Dort, in 1669, the pupil, first, of Arnold Verbuis, afterwards of Godfrey Schalken. In the style of the latter, he painted a few pictures representing subjects by candle-light; but his growing reputation as a portrait painter soon confined him to that branch of the art. He was an excellent colourist, a faithful designer of his model, and had an uncommon facility in operation. He painted many of the most distinguished personages of his day, and among them, the great duke of Marlborough. He died in the year 1729. (Bryan.)

BOORHAN NIZAM SHAH I., the second king of Ahmednuggur in the Dekkan, succeeded his father Ahmed, the founder of the dynasty, (all of whom bore the title of *Nizam Shah*,) at the age of seven, A.D. 1508, (A.H. 914.) An attack on his dominions during his minority by the king of Berar, was signally repulsed by the valour and fidelity of the regent, Mookumil Khan; but the whole reign of Boorhan was a series of wars; and his infatuated love for a dancing girl, to whom he gave precedence over his queen, a sister of Ismail Adil Shah of Beejapoor (Viziapoor), involved him in a formidable contest with that monarch, who formed a league with other princes against him; but Boorhan was not deficient in valour, and defeated the confederates in 1527, with the loss of 300 elephants. The routed party, however, called in the aid of Bahadur Shah of Guzerat, one of the most warlike monarchs of India, (see BAHADUR SHAH,) who listened to their prayer, and (though Ismail Shah had in the meantime changed sides) overran the Ahmednuggur territory in a single campaign (1529), took the capital, and only retired on Boorham Shah submitting to hold his dominions as his vassal, and pay him tribute: the king of Ahmednuggur was even compelled to attend the court of the conqueror, and his artifices to evade the performance of homage are amusingly narrated by Ferishta. The death of Bahadur Shah, who was killed by the Portuguese in 1535, released him from this subjection; and the remainder of his life was consumed in continual petty hostilities against the monarchs of the Dekkan, whose hostility he had provoked by abandoning, in 1537, the Soonni, or orthodox sect of Islam, and embracing the Sheah heresy. He died of cholera, on his march against Beejapoor, A.D. 1553, (A.H. 961,) and was succeeded by his eldest son Hoossein. His body was sent for burial to Kerbela, in Persia; a spot holy in the eyes of the Sheahs as the scene of the martyrdom of Hoossein, the son of Ali and Fatima.

BOORHAN NIZAM SHAH II., grandson of the former, became king, as seventh of the dynasty, A.D. 1589, (A.H. 998.) He had previously lived many years in exile at the court of Delhi, and gained the throne by displacing his own son, Ismail, whom the nobles had made king;—a singular instance of the son preceding the father! He was at an advanced age when he attained the sovereignty, and the principal events of his reign are a war with Beejapoor, and an attempt which he made, in 1592, to wrest the fortress of Choul, or Reevadunda, from the Portuguese, in which he was unsuccessful, and sustained severe loss. He died A.D. 1594, (A.H. 1003,) leaving the crown to his son Ibrahim; but the civil wars which ensued among various pretenders, led to the overthrow of the kingdom, after no long intervals, by the Mogul emperors of Delhi. (Ferishta. Faria-e-Souza.)

BOORHAN-ED-DEEN AHMED, a petty prince of Siwas, or Sebaste, in Anatolia, in the latter part of the fourteenth century. He had been a cadhi, or judge, at Kaisariyah, whence the title cadhi is often prefixed to his name by historians; but at the extinction of a line of minor princes who had ruled there, and the division of their states by their emirs, he possessed himself of Siwas, where his cautious and wary conduct raised him to a considerable degree of political importance among the small states which surrounded him. He early conciliated, by embassies and presents, the favour of Timour, then pursuing his conquests in Persia; but the support which he gave to the revolted governor of Malatia, in 1387, drew on him the wrath of the powerful Mamluke Sultan Barkok, who, in the following year, sent an army to besiege Siwas; but though the Egyptians routed a Tartar corps sent by Timour to raise the siege, they failed to take the city. But in A.D. 1392, (A.H. 795,) the redoubted Ottoman sultan Bayezid, then employed in reducing the Anatolian principalities, made the shelter which the prince of Siwas had afforded to the deposed ruler of Kermian a pretext for attacking him. Boorhan-ed-Deen, dreading the result of this unequal contest, fled into the mountains, and was there overwhelmed and put to death, before the arrival of the Ottoman army, by another enemy, Kara Osman, the founder subsequently of the Ak-koinlu, or White Sheep dynasty of Turkmans in Persia. His territories fell into the power of Bayezid, but this acquisition was one of the principal causes which afterwards drew on the Turkish sultan the fatal hostility of Timour. (Sherif-ed-Deen. Arabshah. Makrizi. Phranzes. De Guignes. D'Herbelot. Van Hammer.)

BOORHAN-ED-DEEN, (Proof of the Faith.) D'Herbelot has also recorded several men of letters of this name, but none of any peculiar note.

BOOT, (Arnold,) an eminent Dutch physician, born at Gorcum, in 1606. He was an excellent scholar, and familiar with the oriental languages. His attention was principally directed to sacred history, philology, and criticism. He, however, practised medicine in London. Afterwards, being appointed principal physician to the earl of Leicester, lord-lieutenant of Ireland, he settled in Dublin, but political troubles obliging him to remove, he withdrew to Paris, and resided there during seven years, occupying himself chiefly in literary pursuits. He died in 1650, having published, Philosophia Naturalis Reformata, Dublin, 1641, 4to. Observationes Medicæ de Affectibus Omissis, Lond. 1649, 12mo; Helmst. 1664, 4to; Fr. et. Lips. 1676, 8vo. He assisted his younger brother, known as Gerard Boate, in his work on the Natural History of Ireland. (See BOATE.)

BOOTH, (Abraham,) an eminent Baptist minister, born May 20, 1734, at Blackwell, Derbyshire, of poor parents, who brought him up to farming and frame-work knitting. He was taught to read by his father; writing and arithmetic he acquired with scarcely any assistance. His parents belonged to the Church of England, but he himself formed an acquaintance which led him to become a general baptist when he was about the age of twenty-one. Having married in his twenty-third year, he sought a living as a schoolmaster and preacher, but he became, at length, a convert to the Calvinistic system, which obliged him to relinquish his charge in the country. He was then invited to become the pastor of a congregation of particular baptists in London. This charge he accepted in 1769, and retained it during the remainder of his life. Having by means of great exertion and perseverance acquired a creditable degree of classical and scientific knowledge, he wrote several works, which are much esteemed among holders of his opinions, and which were published in 3 vols, 8vo, in 1813. He was much opposed to the proposal of admitting pædobaptists to (even occasional) communion with baptist societies, and took a very prominent part in the controversy on that subject. (Memoir prefixed to Works, vol. ii.)

BOOTH, (Barton,) an eminent English tragedian, born in Lancashire, in 1681, of an ancient family. His father, whose circumstances were but moderate, removed to Westminster, when he was about three years old, and sent him, in due course of time, to the collegiate school there, still conducted by the famous Dr. Busby. Young Booth soon attracted notice from the masters, not only by his general diligence, but also by a peculiar talent for enunciating with harmony and force the best poetic passages that occurred in his lessons. He was thus pointed out as peculiarly fit for a prominent part in the Latin play, which then formed, as it still does, a most attractive exhibition in the annual exercises of Westminster school. Booth played his part inimitably, to the great delight of Busby, then very aged, whose praises made the young actor's father eventually say, that *the old man poisoned his son with his last breath*. The boy was intended for orders, but as the time approached for entering the university, he became so impatient of the prospect, that, at seventeen, he stole away from school, and joined a theatrical company at Dublin. He succeeded immediately as a tragic actor, and after three years, he returned to England, and was similarly successful there. The great distinction of his life was the part of Cato. The tragedy, named from it, and of which it forms the sole important feature, was brought upon the stage, in 1712, chiefly with a view to render Whig politics popular. But the Tories, aware of the object, applauded every sentence capable of a popular turn, quite as vociferously as their political opponents. Thus the two great English parties emulously joined in giving an enthusiastic reception to a piece, really but little fit for acting, being rather a poem than a play. It is true, that Booth was the hero of the night, and possessed such qualifications for his part in a stately declamation, and a tinge of classical acquirements, as the stage has very rarely been able to command. But the same advantages were possessed by John Kemble, when he gave a seeming popularity to Cato, about a century later. Yet shrewd observers of the drama then thought Addison's declamation quite as much indebted for an overflowing audience, to the horses that galloped over the stage in a noisy after-piece, as to the finished speaker who delivered it. As Booth's age advanced his health declined, and he was thus unable to appear upon the stage so much as the public wished, but he was always warmly greeted. He died May 10, 1733, and was buried at Cowley, in Middlesex, where he had regularly spent his summers. He was twice married; first to a daughter of Sir William Barkham, a Norfolk baronet; afterwards to an actress. In private life he was highly respectable; and having an advantage over his brethren, not in theatrical talent only, but also in family and education, he held a much higher rank in society than had been usually found attainable by members of his profession. By the world generally, his acting was compared with Betterton's; but he had profited greatly in early life by that eminent performer's precepts and example, and he never would allow himself to have become anything like an equal to him. (Biog. Brit.)

BOOTH, (George,) known in English history as a partizan of Charles II. while yet in exile, was of an ancient family, seated at Dunham Massey, in Cheshire. His grandfather was created a baronet, on the first institution of that order, in 1611, and he succeeded him, his father not having lived to inherit. His family was connected closely with the presbyterian party, but this became, on Cromwell's death, scarcely less desirous of Charles's restoration than the royalists. Booth, accordingly, placed himself in communication with the exiled king, and in the summer of 1659, appeared in arms against the parliament. Very extensive plans of insurrection had been prepared; but the treachery of Willis, an old cavalier, cognizant of the whole design, the reluctance of the royalists to coalesce with the presbyterians, and the fears engendered by a long series of depression, made the confederates generally disappoint each other. Sir George Booth was, however, true to his engagements. He headed a rising about the end of July, 1659, and being joined by some other gentlemen, took possession of Chester; not, indeed, openly as an adherent of the king, but merely under a profession of seeking deliverance for his country from the tyranny of an unrestrained soldiery, and an usurping legislature. Some of his friends appear to have been less cautious, as information arrived in London that Charles II. had actually been proclaimed at Wrexham, and other places near Chester. The rapid advance of Lambert, under orders from the parliament, soon rendered success all but hopeless; and a stand, made by the insurgents at Winnington bridge, near Northwich, proving abortive, nothing remained but to evacuate Chester, and seek safety in flight. Booth put on female attire, and riding on a pillion behind a servant, attempted to escape by way of London. In his journey, the suspicions of an innkeeper at Newport Pagnel were aroused, and he was arrested there, August 22. The house of commons immediately committed him close prisoner to the Tower, for levying war against the parliament and commonwealth, and forbade him the access of his friends, and the use of writing materials. Among his papers was found a letter from Brussels, dated May 16, 1659, directed to G. B., and subscribed *Charles R.* Great intercession was now made for him by some powerful friends; and as the adverse government grew weaker almost every day, it was resolved in parliament, February 22, 1660, that he should be released from the Tower, on giving bail for 5,000*l.* to answer any charge against him, and the sequestration of his estate was suspended until farther order. His political activity appears to have involved him in pecuniary difficulty, as a bill was brought into parliament, July 30, 1660, to enable him to sell part of his estate, for the discharge of his debts, and for the providing of his younger children with fortunes. This was, however, opposed as a needless sacrifice on the part of a man who had injured his own affairs by an endeavour to serve his country, and had actually, by his public-spirited appearance in arms, paved the way for the restoration. Hence, in spite of Sir George Booth's own opposition, instead of passing a bill to legalize the curtailment of his estate, 10,000*l.* were voted as a compensation for his services. As a farther reward, he was created, April 20, 1661, baron Delamere of Dunham Massey. He died at that place in 1684, aged 63, but his dislike of many measures in favour at court had long reduced him to political obscurity. (Parl. Hist. Kennet's Hist. Engl. Banks's Baronage.)

BOOTH, (Henry,) second, but eldest surviving son of the preceding by his second wife, Elizabeth, daughter of Henry Grey, first earl of Stamford. His father had been custos rotulorum of Cheshire, but he resigned that office to him in 1673. He sate also in parliament for that county several times during the reign of Charles II. His politics were, however, very obnoxious to the court. He zealously promoted the bill for excluding the duke of York from the throne; he insisted upon the necessity of frequent parliaments, denounced arbitrary imprisonment by the privy council, inveighed against senatorial corruption, and recommended a searching inquiry into the conduct of the judges, that such of them as took bribes for the perversion of law and evidence should be brought to condign punishment. He was also extremely zealous against popery. So much hostility to the royal will at length caused his removal from the commission of the peace, and from the office of custos rotulorum of Cheshire. Nor did Charles content himself even with these tokens of displeasure. About the time when Booth's father died, and he consequently became lord Delamere, he was committed close prisoner to the Tower. Of the particular charges against him nothing is known; but evidently little could be made of them, as after a few months he was restored to liberty without any trial. Soon after James's accession he was again taken into custody, as implicated in the duke of Monmouth's treason. According to his own account, presented to the house of peers, he was required by a royal proclamation, dated July 19, "to appear before the king in council, within ten days, not for any manner of treason, but for other matters therein contained." He obeyed within seven days, and found himself charged only with such offences as were bailable, and of which he did not admit himself to be guilty. He was, nevertheless, committed close prisoner to the Tower, under lord Sunderland's warrant, dated July 26, for high treason in levying war against the king. When parliament met, in November, Delamere made an application, detailing these circumstances, to the upper house, which voted an address to the king, inquiring why a member of their body was thus kept from attendance in his place. James replied, that "the lord Delamere stood committed for high treason testified upon oath, and that orders were already given for proceeding against him according to law. In the following January he was brought to trial before Jefferies, now chancellor, who sate as lord high steward, and a select body of peers, amounting to twenty-seven. He objected to this court, alleging, that, as parliament was not dissolved, but merely under a prorogation, he was entitled to a trial before the whole house. This objection, however, was overruled; but it was found impossible to produce any other positive evidence against him than that of a man named Saxton, who prevaricated so grossly, that Delamere was unanimously acquitted. James could not deny that he was fairly entitled to this verdict, and being violently disgusted with Saxton, he gave orders for his prosecution. The perjured witness now found his own turn come. He was convicted, thrice exposed in the pillory, twice publicly whipped, and then committed to prison until he should pay a fine of 300 marks.

After his acquittal, lord Delamere lived for a time in retirement at his seat at Dunham Massey; but when the revolution approached, he resumed his political activity. No sooner accordingly had a disposition shown itself in the army, after William's landing, to forsake the infatuated James, than he was enabled to appear in arms at the head of a considerable body, raised in Cheshire and Lancashire. When the king's flight rendered farther military operations unnecessary, he joined the prince of Orange, in the neighbourhood of London; and on James's unexpected return to Whitehall, he was sent with the marquess of Halifax and the earl of Shrewsbury to desire his immediate removal from the palace. The three peers bore a letter, dated from Windsor, Dec. 17, and subscribed by William, desiring the unhappy monarch to take up his residence at Ham, under plea that such a measure was necessary, both for his own safety and the tranquillity of London. The three commissioners reached Whitehall in the night of Monday, Dec. 17, and demanded an immediate audience of James. He was now in bed, where he received them about one o'clock in the morning of December 18. Finding resistance hopeless, he consented to quit the palace; but objecting to the dowager duchess of Lauderdale's house at Ham as uncomfortable, requested permission to retire to Rochester. After communicating with William, then at Sion house, the commissioners returned with an assent to his request. In executing this painful commission, Delamere behaved with so much propriety, that James afterwards declared himself to have been far better used by that one of the three to whom he had behaved ill, than by the other two, who had received kindnesses from him. Delamere's political hostility to the abdicated monarch continued, however, unabated, and he consequently received several marks of William's favour. Besides being reinstated in the office of custos rotulorum of his own county, he was appointed chancellor of the exchequer April 9, 1689; and by patent, dated April 17, 1690, he was created earl of Warrington. For the better support of this dignity, a pension of 2,000*l.* was conferred upon him. This was, however, only paid one half-year, and being then suffered to run into arrear, appears in the statement of king William's debts, drawn up by order of queen Anne. The earl only continued chancellor of the exchequer about twelve months. He appears to have been too intractable for a courtier, or even a minister of state, and hence his conduct upon several occasions was disagreeable to William. He died in London, Jan. 2, 1694, before the forty-second year of his age was completed, highly celebrated for such a love of civil and religious liberty as disdained servitude on any terms. The first earl of Warrington has a place among noble authors. In 1689, he published a vindication of his friend, William, lord Russell, who had perished upon the scaffold under Charles II. In 1694 was published an 8vo volume of his works. They consist of parliamentary speeches, family prayers, and political tracts. His wife was the daughter and heiress of Sir James Langham, of Cottesbrooke, in Northamptonshire, baronet, by whom he had four sons and two daughters. The eldest son died an infant, and George, the second, succeeded him in his titles and estates. This nobleman published anonymously, in 1739, "Considerations upon the Institution of Marriage, with some thoughts concerning the force and obligation of the marriage contract, wherein is considered how far divorces may or ought to be allowed. By a Gentleman. Humbly submitted to the judgment of the impartial." This is an argument for divorce from incompatibility of temper. George, earl of Warrington, also wrote a letter, in 1734, to the writer of the Present State of the Republic of Letters, vindicating his father from some reflections in Burnet's History of his Own Times. He died in 1758, without issue male, and consequently the earldom became extinct; but Mary, his only daughter, marrying in 1736 Henry Grey, earl of Stamford, her son by that nobleman was created earl of Warrington, in addition to his paternal earldom, in 1796. The barony of Delamere descended to a collateral relative, but has since become extinct. (Kennet's Hist. Engl. Bank's Baronage. Chalmers.)

BOOTHROYD, (Benjamin, D.D.) a protestant dissenting minister, born in 1768 at Warley, in the parish of Halifax, Yorkshire, of poor parents, who could merely send him to the village school during the fifth and sixth years of his life. After an early youth of immoral thoughtlessness, as he drew towards manhood he became more serious, and joined a society of nonconformists. He soon procured admission to a dissenting academy, and at Pontefract he was ordained an independent minister. The dissenters were not at all popular there at that time; and Boothroyd, finding himself without a sufficient maintenance, commenced the business of a printer and bookseller, at the same time continuing that of a preacher. In this capacity he published editions of several valuable religious works, and also a history of Pontefract, now scarce, written by himself. It was at this period that he began the study of Hebrew, in which, by dint of great industry, he made considerable proficiency. Whilst engaged in this pursuit, he formed the idea of publishing a correct text of the Old Testament without points, which he accomplished in the course of seven years. But his labours were not confined to editing this work: he also worked for six hours a day at the printing-press. Besides this, he corrected all the sheets, his wife, who knew nothing of Hebrew, reading over the proof *letter by letter*. Having accomplished this laborious undertaking, he proceeded to prepare an amended English translation. In 1818 he removed from Pontefract to Huddersfield, and, on the death of Mr. Moorhouse, was chosen pastor of Highfield chapel. In 1824 the university of Glasgow conferred upon him the degree of D.D., before which he had received that of LL.D. from the same quarter. After an illness of some weeks, he died September 8, 1836, having revised the last sheet of a second edition of his Bible at the commencement of his attack.—(Ev. Mag. 1837.) Dr. Boothroyd's edition of the Hebrew Bible is certainly a very valuable work, being, as Mr. Horne observes, the cheapest Bible with critical apparatus extant; and the judgment of the editor is no less apparent than his industry. The absence of the points, however, renders it less useful to the student who cannot procure more than one edition of the Hebrew Scriptures.

BOQUIN, (Peter,) otherwise written Bouquin, and Boquine, in Latin, *Boquinus*, a French Carmelite friar, who took the degree of doctor in divinity at Bourges, April 23, 1539, and after being prior of the convent in that city, became a protestant. He then left France, and wintered at Basle in 1541. Subsequently he went to Wittemberg, with an intention of passing into Pomerania, where he had a friend; but Melancthon persuaded him to go to Strasburg, as successor to Calvin, who had lately returned to Geneva. After lecturing at Strasburg upon the epistle to the Galatians, he returned to Bourges, lodging there with a brother, also D.D., and not unfriendly to the Reformation. Peter Boquin now gave public lectures at Bourges upon Hebrew grammar, and upon Scripture, but without any emolument. Having ingratiated himself, however, with Margaret of Valois, queen of Navarre, then passing near Bourges, he obtained a pension from her, and permission from the archbishop, by her means, to preach in the great church. His influence in high French society did not cease at the death of this princess; but at length it became insufficient for his protection, and after escaping various dangers, he returned to Strasburg, in 1555, and exercised his ministry during several months, in the French church there. In 1557, Otho Henry, elector Palatine, invited him to Heidelberg, as professor of divinity; but he was driven from that post in 1577, in company with some other professors, who, like himself, refused full satisfaction to the Lutheran party. Boquin now retired to Lausanne, where he taught theology until his death, in 1582. He published several Latin tracts upon the eucharistic presence, and a work entitled, Assertio veteris ac veri Christianismi adversus novum et fictum Jesuitismum, which was translated into English, under the following title: A Defence of the old and true Profession of Christianitie, against the new counterfeite Sect of Jesuites, by Peter Boquine, translated by T. G., Lond. 1581. (Bayle. Chalmers.)

BORCH, (M. J. Count von,) born of a distinguished family in the Polish province of Witepsk, educated at Warsaw, afterwards an officer in the Polish army. He made, in 1776, a journey to Sicily, and thence to Malta. The fruits of this excursion—Minéralogie Sicilienne Docimastique, and Lettres sur la Sicile et sur l'Ile de Malte—are still works of value. The latter were published as an appendix to Brydone, but contain original researches in natural history. On his return to his native country, he resided on his estates in White Russia, where he devoted himself to literature, and in 1798 published a French translation of Wieland's Oberon. In the latter part of his life the Jesuits succeeded in obtaining great influence over him. He died at his estate of Warkland, in the neighbourhood of Dünaburg, in December 1810. He was a member of various learned societies, and was governor of the province Witepsk, before its union with Russia.

BORCH, (Olaüs,) in Latin, *Borrichius*, a Danish physician, born April 26, 1626, son of a clergyman. He studied at Coldingen, Rypen, and Copenhagen, where, during six years, he applied himself to the study of medicine and the collateral sciences, under Worm, Pauli, and Bartholin. In 1650 he was named one of the professors at the school of Copenhagen, in which occupation he remained four years, when Frederic III. was desirous of conferring on him the prebend of Lund, as a reward for his merits. He wished, however, to attach himself to medicine, and had formed a design of visiting foreign countries, when he was engaged by Joachim Gersdorff, prime minister to the king of Denmark, as instructor of his children. Having devoted five years to this purpose, he received from the king, in 1660, the title of professor of philosophy, chemistry, and botany, accompanied by a permission to travel before entering upon the exercise of his professorship. He visited Holland, England, France, and Germany. He remained two years at Leyden and Paris, took the degree of M.D. at Angers, afterwards passed six months in Rome, and returned to Copenhagen in November 1666. He was then made physician to the king, appointed to the chair of medicine, commenced his lectures, and gained great reputation. For twelve years he was dean of the faculty of philosophy; and he was twice elected rector of the university, of which also he was made the librarian in 1680. In 1686 he was made an assessor of the sovereign council of justice, and afterwards counsellor of the royal chancery. He suffered greatly from stone in the bladder, for which he underwent an operation in 1690; but the calculus was of a very large size, and twenty days after undergoing the operation he died, at the age of sixty-four. By his will he bequeathed 50,000 crowns to his family, and 26,000 to form a college, in which sixteen persons, not having the means of education, should be enabled to cultivate the sciences. This establishment was to be supplied with a proper garden, laboratory, and library. Literature owes more than medicine to the learning of Borch. He was esteemed one of the most learned men of his time, and he has left numerous works; of these, his Docimaste Metallica, Copenh. 1677, 4to, was translated into German by Kuss; and a dissertation upon ancient Rome has been inserted in the Thesaurus of Grævius, (tom. iv.) His poems are printed in a collection entitled, Deliciæ quorundam Poetarum Danorum collectæ, Lugd. Bat. 1693, 12mo. This contains a life of Borch, written by himself.

BORCHOLTEN, or BORCHOLDUS, (John von,) professor of law at Helmstadt, born April 5, 1535, at Luneburg, educated in his native town, and also at Wittemberg, where he studied, under Melancthon and Wesenbeck, philology as well as jurisprudence. The fame of Cujas attracted him to Toulouse, where for five years he attended that illustrious professor. Immediately on his return to Germany, in 1566, he was appointed professor of law at Rostock, where he attained considerable reputation, so that in 1576 he was appointed, by the duke Julius of Brunswick, chief professor of law at the newly founded university of Helmstadt. Here several students of high rank resided in his house. His death took place prematurely, owing to excess of labour, October 9, 1593. He was distinguished, amongst the jurists of his time, especially by his philological acquirements; in Greek literature he was particularly versed. His learned Commentary on Justinian's Institutes passed through sixteen editions. He was modest, benevolent, and an active patron of merit. He left one son, who finally became chancellor of the province of Grubenhagen. For a list of his works, see Jugler's Beiträge z. Jurist. Biog. 2 B. 237.

BORCHT, (Henry van der,) a painter and engraver, born at Brussels, in 1583, but early taken to Frankfort, in consequence of the troubles of the Low Countries. There the earl of Arundel met with him, and seeing his qualifications for such a purpose, sent him into Italy to collect antiquities. He was afterwards employed for the same purpose by the prince of Wales, eventually Charles II. He died at Antwerp in 1660, leaving several good pictures of fruit and flowers. —Another of his surname, named Peter, a landscape painter and engraver, was born at Brussels, about 1540. His pictures are not much valued, and his engravings, which are numerous, are etched in a rough, careless style, displaying great fertility of invention, but a deficiency of judgment. (Bryan.)

BORCK, the name of an ancient family in Pomerania, which has produced two literary brothers, of whom Jasper William, ambassador at the court of London, and elsewhere, published, in 1741, a translation of Shakspeare's Julius Cæsar. He died, highly respected, in 1747.—His brother, a cavalry officer, published, in 1778, an excellent account of the agriculture of Stargardt, his family-place in Pomerania, where he spent the evening of his days. This work was reprinted in 1783. (Biog. Univ.)

BORDA, (John Charles,) an eminent French mathematician, born at Dax, chief town of the Landes, in Gascony, May 4, 1733. After a preliminary education there, he was sent to the Jesuits' college at La Flèche, and his instructors, delighted by his talents, made unsuccessful attempts to secure him as a member of their order. His father looked upon him differently, considesing a strong mathematical taste as little else than a temptation into an unprofitable consumption of time. At length, this opposition was overcome, and young Borda, entering the military service as an engineer, diligently prosecuted his favourite studies. While thus employed, he found himself likely to be called away from Paris, which could scarcely fail of proving injurious to his progress. He, therefore, entered the light horse, and in 1756, he read to the Academy of Sciences a paper upon the motion of projectiles, which obtained him very great credit. In 1757 he went upon active service, and was present at the battle of Hastembeck. But he found this life so great an interruption to the pursuit of knowledge which really interested him, that he soon returned to Paris, and sought employment as an engineer. His reputation immediately gained him a situation in the naval department, and this proved excellently fitted for developing his peculiar talents. He began with investigating the resistance of fluids, and the results of his experiments are given in the memoirs of the academy for 1763 and 1767. The apparatus which he used was not, however, his own invention, but that of Benjamin Robins, the celebrated English mathematician. In 1767, Borda published, in the memoirs of the academy, an excellent dissertation, entitled, Mémoire sur les Roues Hydrauliques, which accurately unfolded various properties of undershot wheels. This memoir was followed, in 1768, by another upon water-pumps. Borda's last publication, through the academy, was a dissertation on the theory of projectiles. A commission in the navy was now provided for him by the minister of the marine; and in 1771 he embarked with Pingré upon a voyage to discover the longitude at sea. The results of this expedition were published in two volumes, 4to, in 1778. In 1776,

Borda was sent to ascertain exactly the position of the Canary isles, then commonly used as the first meridian. The results of this voyage, though considered highly interesting, have not been given to the world. His chart, however, of those islands was used in the valuable map published in Spain, in 1778. In 1782, Borda commanded a ship with troops for Martinique. He landed his men, but subsequently, after a gallant resistance, he was captured by the English, who treated him with the distinction due to a person of so much eminence, and sent him home on *parole*. During his voyage with Pingré, Borda saw great room for improvement in Hadley's quadrant; and adding, by means of his own observations, to the improvements already made in it by Mayer, he produced a new circle, known by his name, but which Troughton eventually superseded by an instrument still more perfect. In addition to these great services rendered by Borda to France and science, he founded schools of naval architecture among his countrymen, and applied Euler's principles to the construction of ships, for the purpose of securing an uniform rate of sailing. The advantages which he thus obtained for the French navy have been acknowledged by experienced British officers. Borda was likewise actively engaged in reforming the weights and measures of France; and in 1792 he invented instruments and methods for determining, with a precision unknown before, the length of a pendulum swinging seconds at Paris. These various claims upon the national gratitude being fully admitted, he was candidate for the office of director of the French republic, in 1797. He died of dropsy in the chest, February 20, 1799. (Biog. Univ. Rees. Chalmers.)

BORDAZAR, (Anthony,) a learned Spanish printer, born at Valencia, in 1671. After a neglected education he taught himself Latin, and a strong taste for grammatical speculations being thus excited in him, he began to think upon the uncertain orthography of his own language, and the best mode of remedying that evil. The result was a system, generally approved by Spanish writers, and embodied in a work printed at Valencia, in 1728, entitled, Ortografia Española. This was reprinted in 1730, and abridged in the Practica de Ortografia Española, a work of which there have been several editions. Bordazar also published upon Latin orthography, and other subjects. Among his works is Reduccion de Monedas Antiguas y corientes de toda Europa. Val. 1736, 8vo. He made, likewise, an attempt, which was favourably received at court, to get church books printed in Spain; but some of the religious interested in importing them rendered his exertions abortive. Nor was be more fortunate in his endeavours to establish, at Valencia, an academy for the teaching of the mathematics; a branch of learning in which he was a considerable proficient himself. He died in 1744. (Biog. Univ.)

BORDE, or BOORDE, (Andrew,) styled by himself *Andreas Perforatus*, (as if his surname came from the verb to *bore*,) an English physician, born at Pevensey, in Sussex, about 1500. He was educated at Oxford, but before taking his degree, entered a Carthusian monastery in or near London. He soon, however, returned to Oxford, studied physic, and travelled through most parts of Europe and a portion of Africa. He settled at Winchester, and there practised his profession. He is supposed to have taken the degree of M.D. at Montpellier in 1541 or 1542, and to have been afterwards incorporated at Oxford. He maintained the austerities of his order, professed celibacy, and wrote vehemently against such ecclesiastics as disregarded canonical restraints, or broke their vows by marriage; yet he has been accused of many irregularities, and of violating his own pretensions to chastity by more illicit indulgences. He died insolvent in the Fleet Prison, in April 1549; and Bale has intimated that his death was occasioned by poison, in consequence of a discovery made that he kept a brothel for the brethren of his order. That he possessed wit and some learning is evident by his works, which are various in their character, and distinguished by a vein of singularity and eccentricity. The designation of "Merry Andrew" is said to be derived from him. Hearne says that he frequented markets and fairs, where a conflux of people used to get together, to whom he prescribed; and to induce them to flock thither the more readily, he would make humorous speeches. He offers a striking contrast to the grave persons practising physic in his day, yet he is reported to have been employed in his medical capacity by Henry VIII. As he was in practice a short time at Winchester, where stood a neglected royal residence, it is not unlikely that he may have had the title of physician to the king in that place. His works are:—Boke of the Introduction of Knowledge, the which doth teach a man to speak part of all manner of Languages, &c. Lond. 1542, 4to; Lond. 1814, 4to. Pryncyples of Astronomye, Lond. 1542, 16mo. Breviarie of Health, Lond. 1547, 1548, 1552, 1556, 1557, 1575, 1587, 4to. The second part of this book, under the title of The Extravagantes, was printed in the edition of 1575. Compendyous Regimente, or Dietary of Health, Lond. 1562, 16mo; 1567, 8vo; 1576, 8vo. Merie Tales of the Madmen of Gotham, (a well-known jest book,) without date, but probably 1565; also in 1630, 12mo. A Historie of the Mylner of Abyngton, 4to, and John Scogin's Jests, are also attributed to Boorde.

BORDE, (John Benjamin de la,) a voluminous French author, born in 1734, and at one time first *valet de chambre* to Lewis XV. At that monarch's death he was farmer general. During the revolution he sought an escape from public notice in Normandy, but the blood-thirsty men who then domineered in France, dragged him back to Paris, and guillotined him, July 22, 1794. Of his numerous works, the Essais sur la Musique Ancienne et Moderne, 1780, 4 vols, 4to, contain a vast mass of useful matter; but much is borrowed from Dr. Burney and others, without acknowledgment. De la Borde also translated Swinburne's travels in the two Sicilies, and wrote himself some letters on Switzerland, which exposed him to very severe criticism. (Biog. Univ.)

BORDELON, (Laurence,) a French doctor in divinity, and dramatic author, born at Bourges, in 1653. He died at Paris, in 1730, thus very truly characterising his numerous works and himself, "I know that I am a bad author, but, at all events, I am an honest man." (Biog. Univ.)

BORDENAVE, (Toussaint,) a celebrated French surgeon and physiologist, born at Paris, April 10, 1728. His father, Peter Bordenave, a surgeon, giving him a very liberal education, he acquired great knowledge of the classics, and could speak Latin with facility and elegance. He entered the army, and served in the campaign in Flanders, in 1746. In 1750 he was received at the College of Surgeons as a master in surgery. He was likewise a member of the municipal council of Paris, and a magistrate of that city. His civil services procured for him from the king the order of St. Michael. He was likewise director of the Royal Academy of Surgery, and professor of physiology in the school of St. Côme. In 1774 he was elected into the Royal Academy of Sciences. He died of apoplexy, March 12, 1782. His works are:—Essai sur la Physiologie ou Physique du Corps Humain, Paris, 1756, 12mo; 1764, 12mo; 1778, 2 vols, 12mo. Remarques sur l'Insensibilité de quelques Parties, 1757. This was printed in the Mercure de France, and by Haller in his Collections, 1758. Essai sur le Méchanisme de la Nature dans la Formation des Os, et Recherches sur la Façon dont se fait la Réunion des Os Fracturés, Paris, 1760, 8vo. Dissertation sur les Antiseptiques, Dijon et Paris, 1769, 8vo. Mémoire sur le Danger des Caustiques pour la Cure radicale des Hernies, Paris, 1774, 12mo. Discours prononcé à la première Séance de l'Academie Royale de Chirurgie, Nov. 16, 1775. He also translated Haller's Primæ Lineæ Physiologiæ, Paris, 1769, 12mo; and printed numerous papers in the Mémoires de l'Academie Royale de Chirurgie, (tom. ii. iv. v.) and in the Mémoires de l'Academie des Sciences, (tom. iv. vii.)

BORDEU, (Anthony de,) a French physician, of an ancient Béarnese family, born at Iseste, in the valley of Ossau, in 1693, and educated in the Barnabite college at Lescar. Having proceeded M.D. at Montpellier, in 1719, he practised at Pau, and had the superintendence of the mineral waters, upon which he published a Dissertation in 1749, Paris, 12mo. He was physician also to the military hospital of Barèges, and practised fifty-five years.

BORDEU, (Francis de,) son and pupil of the preceding, born at Pau in 1737, M.D. at Montpellier in 1758. He succeeded his father as inspector of the mineral waters, and as physician to the hospital of Barèges. He published, De Sensibilitate et Mobilitate Partium, Montp. 1757, 4to. Dissertation sur les Dragées antivéneriennes jointes aux Eaux de Barèges, et Précis d'Observations sur les Eaux de Barèges et autres du Bigorre et du Béarn, Paris, 1760, 12mo.

BORDEU, (Theophilus de,) an eminent physician, brother of the preceding, born February 22, 1722, who, after a general education in the Jesuits' college at Pau, studied medicine at Montpellier, where his academical exercises excited the astonishment of the professors by an unusual display of originality and genius. He took his degree in 1744, and returned to Pau, where, however, he remained only a short time, being desirous of obtaining further knowledge, for which he returned to Montpellier; and two years afterwards went to Paris, where he attended the Hôpital de la Charité and the Royal Infirmary of Versailles. In 1749 he was appointed superintendent of the mineral waters of Aquitaine, having, from 1746 to 1748, published several letters on their properties, and the mode of their administration. He also delivered lectures on anatomy and on midwifery. In 1752 he established himself in Paris, and put forth a work on the glandular system, which at once fixed his reputation. He soon greatly distinguished himself as a practitioner; but his uncommon success exciting jealousy and hatred, various atrocious calumnies were circulated to his prejudice. They were sufficiently credited to cause his name to be erased from the list of members of the faculty; but he obtained royal permission to practise, and he continued to labour in his vocation and to contribute to the advancement of medical knowledge. The controversies, however, in which he was necessarily engaged deranged his health, and he died of apoplexy, Nov. 23, 1776. The writings of Bordeu have done much towards the improvement of medical science; his application of physiological knowledge to practical objects entitles him to great respect; and he may fairly be looked upon as the precursor of Bichât, in some of his opinions relating to the organization of beings. His principal publications are:—Dissertatio Physiologica de Sensu genericè considerato, Montp. 1742, 4to; Paris, 1751, 12mo. Chylificationis Historia, Montp. 1742, 4to; Paris, 1751, 12mo. Lettres sur les Eaux Minérales du Béarn et de quelques-unes des Provinces voisines, Amst. 1746-48, 12mo. Observations sur l'Usage du Quinquina dans la Gangrène. These appeared in the work of Guisard on Wounds. Recherches Anatomiques sur les Articulations des Os de la Face. Printed in the Mém. de l'Acad. des Sciences, tom. ii. Recherches Anatomiques sur les différentes Positions des Glandes et sur leur Action, Paris, 1752, 12mo; *ib.* An. viii. 12mo, with notes by Hallé. Dissertation sur les Ecrouelles. A Prize Essay, printed in tom. iii. Prix de l'Académie de Chirurgie, 1757. An omnes organicæ Corporis Partes Digestioni opitulentur? Paris, 1753, 4to. An Venatio cæteris Exercitationibus salubrior? Paris, 1753, 4to. Utrum Aquitaniæ Minerales Aquæ Morbis Chronicis? in the Journal des Savans, 1754. Recherches sur les Crises; printed in the Encyclopédie, 1753. Recherches sur le Pouls par Rapport aux Crises, Paris, 1756, 1768, 1772, 12mo, 3 vols; in English, Lond. 1765. Recherches sur le Traitement de la Colique Métallique à l'Hôpital de la Charité, 1762-65; in the Journal de Médecine. Recherches sur quelques Points d'Historie de la Médecine, concernant l'Inoculation, Paris, 1764, 12mo, 2 vols. Recherches sur le Tissu Muqueux et l'Organe Cellulaire et sur quelques Maladies de la Poitrine, Paris, 1767, 12mo; in German, Vienn. and Leips. 1772, 8vo; Munster, 1800, 8vo. Recherches sur les Maladies Chroniques, &c. Paris, 1775, 8vo; An. vii., with notes by Roussel, and a life of the author. The works of Bordeu have also been collected together by Richerand, Paris, 1818, 8vo, 2 vols, accompanied by a life of the author. Bordeu likewise printed Hommage à la Vallée d'Ossau, in *patois basque*, and assisted La Caze in several works. He also established the Journal de Barèges.

BORDING, (James,) a physician, born at Antwerp, July 11, 1511. He studied at Louvain, Paris, and Montpellier, and took the degree of doctor of medicine at Bologna. The scantiness of his means obliged him to teach the Hebrew, Greek, and Latin languages, with which he was very conversant; and having embraced the reformed religion, he was necessitated frequently to change his residence. He practised medicine at Carpentras, where he was, in 1530, named principal of the college, afterwards at Hamburg, and then at Rostock, at which place the duke of Mecklenburg appointed him to be his physician, and gave him a chair of medicine. After this, Christian III., king of Denmark, invited him to Copenhagen, where, attached to the court and to the performance of academical exercises, he spent the remainder of his days. He died Sept. 5, 1560. He is the author of Physiologia, Hygiene, et Pathologia, tres Medicinæ Partes Rostochii et Hafniæ publicè enarratæ, et junctim editæ à Levino Batto, Rostoch. 1591, 8vo. Enarrationes in sex Libros Galeni de tuendâ Valetudine. Accessit Auctoris Consilia quædam illust. Principibus præscripta, *ib.* 1595, 1604, 4to.

BORDLEY, (John Beale,) an American writer on agriculture, died at Philadelphia, 1804. He published, Forsyth's Treatise on Fruit Trees, with notes; Sketches on Rotations of Crops, 1792; and several other agricultural works. (Carter's Amer. Biog. Dict.)

BORDONE, (Paris,) an eminent Italian painter, of noble family, born in 1513, and originally a pupil of Titian. He afterwards imitated Giorgione, but eventually formed a style of his own. Among his various excellences may be mentioned portrait painting, in which he was only surpassed by Titian. He died at Venice in 1588. (Bryan. Pilkington.)

BORDONI, (Benedict,) an Italian miniature painter and geographer, who died about 1530. His literary talents were first displayed as editor of a collection of Latin translations, by several hands, of some of Lucian's dialogues, published at Venice in 1494. He also produced a more exact account of Italy than any that had hitherto appeared, and dedicated it to cardinal Francis Cornaro. He is, however, most known among book-collectors, by his Isolario, first published at Venice, in 1528, containing an account of all known islands; a subject chosen, says the dedication, because islands were the only objects on which an abundance of writings, either ancient or modern, was not to be found. Of this book there was a reprint in 1534, and another in 1547. (Biog. Univ. Clement. Bibl. Cur.)

BORDONIO, (Joseph Anthony,) a learned Jesuit, born at Turin, in 1682, who went into England in 1712, as chaplain to the embassy from his native court. On returning home, he filled, during several years, the divinity chair. He died in 1742, highly respected for piety and erudition, leaving, besides some specimens of poetic talent, Discorsi per l'Esercizio della Buona Morte, a work of the ascetic class, highly prized. (Biog Univ.)

BORE, (Catharine,) celebrated as the wife of Luther. She was born 1499, of a good family, and early placed in the nunnery of Nimptschen, which she left with eight other nuns during the Holy Week in 1523. On the 13th of June, 1525, she was married to Luther, who had some time before resigned the habit of an Augustine friar. This marriage, at the time, created a great sensation. His *enemies* said—"He was an infamous hardened sensualist, who had neither command of his passions nor regard for his reputation; and his wife was worse." They exulted with bitter severity; and even Erasmus could not refrain from sarcasm. Luther *himself* said—"I have now stopped the mouths of our calumniators; in the opinion of some I have made myself contemptible; but I trust angels smile, and demons weep, at what I have done. I could not deny my father's earnest request. I judged it right to confirm, by my own example, the doctrine that I taught, and was desirous of showing my weaker brethren that I acted up to my principles." Never did he regret this decisive step: on his death-bed he affectionately expressed his satisfaction; and Catharine, almost broken-hearted, earnestly commended him to God. She spent the first year after his death at Wittemberg; which she left in 1547, when the town surrendered to Charles V., having previously received a present of fifty crowns from Christian III., king of Denmark, and other gratuities from the elector of Saxony and the counts of Mansfeldt, by which aids she maintained herself and her family in comfort. When the town was restored to the elector, she returned to Wittemberg, where she lived in a very pious manner until driven hence by the plague, in 1552. Retiring to Torgau, she met with an accident on her journey, which brought on her death within three months, on the 20th of Dec. 1552, aged 53 years, having borne to Luther five children. Her interment took place in the great church at Torgau, where her tomb and epitaph are yet to be seen.

BOREL, (Peter,) a French physician, antiquary, and linguist, born at Castres, in Languedoc, about 1620. He studied at Montpellier, took his doctor's degree in 1640, and then practised medicine in his native city, where he remained until 1653, when he was made physician to the king, and settled in Paris. In 1674 he was admitted into the Royal Academy of Sciences, in the department of chemistry, in which science, however, he appears to have had but little knowledge. He died in 1689, having published various works, of which the following retain a degree of interest:—Les Antiquités, Raretés, Plantes, Minéraux, &c. de la Ville et du Comte de Castres d'Albigeois, &c. 1649, 4to. Historiarum et Observationum Medico-physicarum Centuria, i. et ii. 1653, 8vo, Hagæ, 1656, 8vo; Paris, 1657, 8vo; Francof. 1670, 8vo, with a Life of Descartes, which has been translated into English. De Vero Telescopii Inventore, Hagæ, 1655, 4to. Trésor de Recherches et Antiquites Gauloises, Paris, 1655, 4to. This is a philological work upon the ancient French language, which was reprinted, with additions, and which has been partially incorporated with the Dictionnaire Etymologique of

Menage, Paris, 1750, fol. Discours prouvant la Pluralité des Mondes, Genev. 1657, 8vo; translated into English, Lond. 1658, 1660, 8vo.

BORELLI, (John Alphonso,) a celebrated physician, born at Naples, Jan. 28, 1608, founder of the Iatro-mathematical sect, whose doctrines divided empire with the chemists for a very considerable period. As a practical physician, Borelli is not entitled to much praise; but his learning and ingenuity are unquestionable. His peculiar doctrines, founded upon the application of statics and mathematics to the science of medicine, were espoused by Bellini, Pitcairn, Keil, and others of eminence; but the fallacies to which they led have long since consigned them to oblivion. It would be useless at this time to review the opinions of the mathematical physicians, or to expose their errors in the estimate which they formed of the powers of the various organs of the human body. It must, however, be admitted, that, notwithstanding the extravagant views entertained by these philosophers, Borelli did much to advance physiology, particularly in his account of the mechanism of the respiratory organs, and in his description of the bones and muscles, and their modes of action; and his work, De Motu Animalium, will always be consulted by the learned inquirer. Borelli taught mathematics at Florence, and afterwards at Pisa, where, in 1656, he accepted a chair of mathematics in the university, upon the nomination of the grand duke, Ferdinand II., with the approbation of the senate; and in 1657 he founded a society, the members of which were professed advocates of the philosophy of Galileo. This society, under the protection of Leopold of Tuscany, was regularly constituted as the Academy Del Cimento. This institution maintained an existence only during ten years, as upon the departure of Borelli for Messina it ceased altogether. He remained at Messina for a short time only, being, upon the restoration of that place by the French, banished from the states subject to the Spanish government, under a charge of having made some seditious discourses in favour of the revolt in 1674, when the citizens gave themselves up to France, and abandoned the Spanish interest. Borelli withdrew to Rome, composed his principal works, suffered a severe loss, being robbed of all he possessed by a domestic, and being thus reduced to indigence, he entered a religious house, where he for some time taught the mathematics. He was attacked with a pleurisy, of which he died, December 31, 1679. He is the author of Le Ragioni delle Febbri maligne di Sicilia, Naples, 1647, 1648, 12mo; Cosenza, 1649, 12mo; Pisa, 1658, 4to; Euclides Restitutus, seu prisca Geometriæ Elementa, Pisis, 1658, 4to; Romæ, 1679, 12mo. Apollonii Pergæi Conicorum Libri V. VI. et VII. paraphraste Abulphato Asphahanensi nunc primum editi. Florent. 1661, fol.; Antw. 1665, fol. De Renum Usu Judicium, Argentorat. 1664, 8vo. De Vi Percussionis Liber, Bonon. 1667, 4to. Osservazione intornò alle Virtù ineguali degli Occhi, Roma, 1669, 4to. Meteorologia Ætnea, sive Historia et Meteorologia Incendii Ætnæi, Anno 1669, Pisis, 1669, 4to; Reggio, 1670, 4to. Elementa Conica Apollonii Pergæi et Archimedis Opera, Romæ, 1679, 12mo. De Motu Animalium, Romæ, 1680, 4to; Pars Altera, 1681, 4to; Lugd. Batav. 1685, 1688, 1710, 4to; Neapoli, 1734, 2 vols, 4to; Hag. Com. 1743, 4to; printed also in the Bibliotheca Anatomica of Mangetus, tom. ii. p. 812. De Structurâ Nervi Optici, Amst. 1698, 4to; printed in the posthumous edition of the works of Malpighi. Relazione sopra lo Stagno di Pisa, &c. Flor. 1723, 4to.

BOREMAN, or BOURMAN, (Robert,) an English divine, fellow of Trinity college, Cambridge, D.D. by royal mandate, 1661, rector of St. Giles's in the Fields, Nov. 18, 1663, and brother to Sir William Boreman, clerk of the green cloth to Charles II. He died at Greenwich, unmarried, in the winter of 1675, known as author of The Churchman's Catechism, or the Church's Plea for Tythes, Lond. 1651; The Triumphs of Learning over Ignorance, being a defence of universities; with some occasional sermons, and other small pieces. (Chalmers. Newcourt.)

BORETIUS, (Mathew Ernest,) a German physician, born at Loetzen, in Prussia, May 18, 1694. His education was directed with a view to the church, but selecting the profession of medicine, he studied at Leyden, and took the degree of M.D. in 1720. He then visited England, where he dwelt for some years. He was afterwards appointed physician to the court at Königsberg, named assessor of the college of medicine, elected professor extraordinary, made physician to the city, and in 1738 to the king. He died October 4, 1738, having published, among other things of less interest, in 1722, a Latin account of the successful inoculation of six capital criminals in Newgate.

BORGARUCCI, (Prosper,) an Italian physician, born at Canziano, in the diocese of Gubbio, professor of anatomy in the university of Padua in January 1564. In 1567 the king of France invited him to Paris, and appointed him his physician; but he returned in the same year to Padua. He purchased at Paris a manuscript of the Chirurgia Magna of Vesalius, which he afterwards printed at Venice in 1569, 8vo. The year of his death is unknown. Besides other works, he also published, Della Contemplazione Anatomica sopra tutte le Parti del Corpo Umano, Vineg. 1564, 8vo. He afterwards produced a Latin version of this piece, as it was adopted in the schools as a text-book.

BORGHESE, (Camillus,) a Roman prince, conspicuous for his alliance with the Buonaparte family. His ancestors were of Siena, but Paul V. being of their house, and making himself eminent for nepotism, even among popes, the Borghesi acquired a most distinguished rank in the peerage of Rome. Camillus was born in that city, July 19, 1775; and although in view of a splendid inheritance, gained by aristocratic abuses, he adopted, as manhood approached, a line of politics diametrically opposite to his father's, and applauded the French revolution. True to his principles, he joined the populace in 1798, and welcomed into Rome the troops of revolutionary France. In 1803, he went to Paris, and was gladly accepted by Buonaparte, then eager for high alliances, as husband for his favourite sister Pauline, lately left a widow by general Le Clerc. This marriage, which first introduced the title of princess among the Buonapartes, took place Nov. 6, 1803. It proved a sterile, unhappy union, and the parties lived asunder. It led, however, the husband to the government of Piedmont, with a liberal salary. On Napoleon's fall, in 1814, the prince Borghese retired to Florence, where he died, April 10, 1832, issueless, leaving his immense fortune to his brother, prince Aldobrandini. He allowed his wife, who died June 9, 1825, and of whom Canova made an admirable statue in 1811, to inhabit his palace at Rome. The papal government would fain have drawn himself thither; but dislike, it was thought, of the Buonapartes, then living there, kept him steadily at Florence, where he refused to receive his wife. (Biog. Univ. Suppl.)

BORGHESE, (John Ventura,) an Italian painter in the seventeenth century, pupil to Peter of Cortona, and employed on that artist's death in finishing some of the pieces that he had left imperfect. (Bryan. Pilkington.)

BORGHESI, (Hippolytus,) a Neapolitan historical painter, of some reputation, pupil of Francis Curia. He lived about 1620. (Bryan. Pilkington.)

BORGHINI, (Raphael,) a Florentine poet and man of letters, towards the end of the sixteenth century. His most important work is entitled, Il Riposo, in cui si tratta della Pittura e della Scultura de' più illustri Professori antichi e moderni, Flor. 1584, 8vo. This was reprinted, with valuable additions, by Bottari, in 1730, and again in the collection of Italian classics, Milan, 1807. (Biog. Univ.)

BORGHINI, (Vincent,) a learned Benedictine, of a noble Florentine family, who might have been archbishop of Pisa, but chose to remain at the head of an hospital, which he had long administered with great advantage to the institution. He is chiefly known in literature as author of two scarce Italian works, on the history and antiquities of Florence and Tuscany. He was also employed, in conjunction with two others, by his sovereign, Cosmo I., upon the correction of Boccaccio's Decameron, according to the wishes of the Council of Trent. The reformed work appeared in 1573, and to Borghini its new form was chiefly due. He died in 1580. (Biog. Univ. Clement.)

BORGIA, (Cæsar,) second illegitimate son of Roderic Borgia, eventually pope Alexander VI., by Catharine Vanozza, daughter of a Roman lady, with whom the future pope became acquainted, it is said criminally, in Spain, his native country, and who dying, left her two daughters under his guardianship. One of these young ladies Roderic Borgia placed in a convent; by the other he had five children, four of them sons, and one a daughter, named Lucretia, who has come in for a full share of the infamy that attaches to her family. At the time of his father's elevation to the popedom, in 1492, Cæsar Borgia was under education at Pisa, but he proceeded immediately to Rome, where the new pontiff shocked him immeasurably by declaiming upon the evils of nepotism, and his own determination to patronize none of his family who could not substantiate pretensions of the most unquestionable kind. His mother is, however, said to have consoled him by declaring herself cognizant of very different intentions in the pope's breast, and by ascribing his unexpected speech to the necessity of keeping up appearances before observers. But whether words gave this consolation to Cæsar, or not, it is clear that he soon received it from realities. His elder brother, Francis, was however gratified first. Ferdinand the Catholic, king of Aragon, husband to Isabella of Castile, made him duke of Gandia, in Valencia. A sovereign of so much importance having thus ingratiated himself at Rome, the cardinals and sycophants about Alexander's court naturally thought of advancing their own interests by following so politic an example. They recommended, accordingly, for promotion to the rank of cardinal, both Cæsar Borgia and his cousin, John Borgia, archbishop of Montreal, in Sicily. As if to gratify them, Alexander conferred a red hat upon his nephew; but he declined that compliment to his son. He preferred him, however, to the archbishopric of Valencia, a see formerly holden by himself; and in the next year, 1493, being then in deacon's orders, he raised him to the cardinalate. Cæsar now became generally known as cardinal Valentine, a designation owing to his Spanish archbishopric. The politics of Italy soon becoming troubled, by the anxiety of Charles VIII. of France to seize the throne of Naples, as heir to the Angevin family, Alexander's influence became of great importance, and his family reaped abundantly the benefit of it. Their first advantages came from the king of Naples in possession, who married his daughter to the pope's youngest son, Geoffrey; promised great estates, with other lucrative gratification, to the duke of Gandia; and the best benefices, as they fell, to cardinal Valentine. A strong hold was thus gained by the Neapolitan family upon the Borgias; and accordingly, although Alexander could not help a formal alliance with Charles VIII., when that monarch was in Rome with his army on the way to Naples, and cardinal Valentine was under the necessity of accompanying him, ostensibly as legate, really as hostage, yet the young churchman took an early opportunity of escaping from him. At length, however, Alexander's parental fondness estranged him from the royal family of Naples. Cæsar Borgia's ecclesiastical grandeur neither suited his years nor his temper. He panted for magnificence of a kind more thoroughly secular, and hence looked with envy upon his elder brother, who, in addition to the Spanish dukedom of Gandia, was invested by his father, in 1497, with the dukedom of Benevento, in the ecclesiastical state; a single cardinal only, who eventually became Pius III., refusing assent to the alienation. The death of his brother, seemingly so fortunate, soon afterwards, rendered Cæsar still more impatient of his ecclesiastical character; and as Gandia fell by violence, he was charged with hiring assassins to murder him from envy. The duke disappeared one night, after leaving his brother on their way from their mother's, where they had been supping together; and on the third subsequent day his body was found in the Tiber, pierced by nine mortal wounds. But although Cæsar Borgia has commonly borne the infamy of this atrocious crime, there is no known evidence to convict him of it; and from the respectable contemporary evidence of Burchard, it is reasonable to suppose that the duke of Gandia was assassinated while pursuing some secret and licentious amour. The last conspicuous appearance of Cæsar Borgia in an ecclesiastical character, was August 10, 1497, when he crowned, as legate *à latère* specially commissioned, Frederic, king of Naples, at Capua, a solemnity performed in that place, because the plague then raged at Naples. The new monarch was disquieted shortly afterwards by the unexpected death, April 17, 1498, of Charles VIII., king of France, whose hasty abandonment of his Neapolitan advantages was a tolerably certain proof that little more of serious evil was to be expected from him. His crown had now descended, however, to the duke of Orleans, a distant relative, henceforth known as Lewis XII., who was some years older, and seemed likely to reign with greater ability. Hence both the usurping duke of Milan, and the king of Naples, each of them holding principalities to which France pretended, looked with great uneasiness upon this change in her crown. Alexander lost no time in seeking to profit by the Neapolitan sovereign's disquietude. Representing his son Cæsar's intention to renounce the ecclesiastical profession, he required Frederic to give him his daughter, with the principality of Tarento for her portion. The king clearly saw the danger of refusal, and the Milanese usurper pressed him to incur no such risk, but, notwithstanding, he respectfully declined compliance. As was apprehended, papal services were placed immediately within the grasp of France. Lewis was gratified by a divorce from Jane, the amiable but deformed daughter of Lewis XI., and by a dispensation to marry Anne of Britany; also by a treaty which bound the pope to assist him in his meditated wars upon the Milanese and Naples. On his part, he was to bestow some considerable estates, dignities, and titles, on cardinal Valentine, so soon as he should resume a secular character, obtain for him as a wife, the daughter of Alan d'Albret, and sister to the queen of Navarre, and likewise aid the pope in seizing the territories of certain petty princes, who had given no just cause of offence, in the Romagna, or ancient exarchate of Ravenna, styling themselves Vicars of the Church, and generally holding by legal titles of long standing under the Roman see. On the conclusion of this treaty, Cæsar made an application to the body of cardinals for leave to relinquish his ecclesiastical condition, declaring himself, probably with truth, to have entered it entirely against his own will, by desire of the pope. It was reserved for the year 1498, to see a man strip off the Roman purple and become a mere layman; but the cardinals knew it, in this case, to be the pontiff's wish, and they unanimously consented. On the following day, the late cardinal went in a rich lay habit to meet the French ambassador, who came with a ratification of the treaty between Lewis and Alexander. The stranger staid about a month in Rome, announcing, in the time, that his royal master had conferred upon Cæsar the dukedom of Valentinois, in Dauphiny, with an abundant provision for the support of this dignity. The date of this grant is 1499. In that year, the new duke accompanied the ambassador back into France, as bearer of the instruments required by Lewis for his matrimonial changes, and made a most extraordinary display of magnificence. Lewis met all this ostentation in a corresponding manner, however heartily he might despise his vain Italian guest. He had, however, considerable difficulty in bringing about his marriage with the Navarrese princess. He was now called upon to assist Alexander in subjugating the Romagna; and this enterprise was accomplished, but in a most inexcusable manner, under the command and management of Cæsar Borgia, generally called in his lay capacity, duke Valentine. As a recompense, he was made by a doting father, in 1501, duke of Romagna, and invested, in full consistory, with the whole province, to be holden by him and his heirs; Alexander thus making a war, waged under colour of recovering the church's patrimony, really appear nothing else than an unprincipled scheme for the aggrandizement of his own base progeny. Subsequently Cæsar, aided by the profligate old pope, was indefatigable in attempts to raise his own fortunes on the ruins of all within his reach who had anything to lose. But his career of reckless cupidity was unexpectedly brought to a close by Alexander's death. Upon the exact cause of this, there may be, perhaps, room for entertaining doubts, as Burchard attributes it to a fever, of which he details the progress. But Guicciardini, and other historians who might seem to have had opportunities of knowing the truth, attribute it to poison, prepared for their guests, and taken inadvertently both by father and son, Aug. 17, 1503. Alexander died on the following day. Cæsar is said to have been indebted for his recovery to youth and skilful medical treatment. His power was, however, gone, and he owed his life to the king of France's protection. After a time he fled to Naples, where Gonsalvo of Cordova arrested him, May 27, 1504, and sent him into Spain, considering apparently his talents for intrigue, knowledge of state secrets, and utter want of principle, dangerous to the peace of Italy. The Spanish court confined him two years in the castle of Medina del Campo, whence he escaped by a window, and took refuge with John, king of Navarre, his brother-in-law. He then strove to regain his hold upon Lewis XII.; but that prince would not receive him, confiscated his duchy of Valentinois, and withdrew the pensions that he had received from France. He was thus obliged for a subsistence to remain at the court of Navarre. The king of that little state was engaged in hostilities with Lewis of Beaumont, one of his subjects, and Cæsar Borgia, serving as a volunteer in his army, was killed under the walls of Viana, March 12, 1507. He was unquestionably a man of abilities, and was taken, some say ironically, by Machiavelli as a model in his Prince. Perhaps, indeed, few men have ever known better than Cæsar Borgia how to use opportunities for rising to sovereign power; and if his father had not unexpectedly been cut off before his position was firmly established, he might have founded a house among the petty princes of Italy. But then he let slip no opportunity, however infamous, for attaining his ends. He stopped not at fraud, or perfidy, or poisoning, or violence, or anything else, that bade fair for answering a temporary purpose. Hence the extreme infamy that attaches to the names of himself and his father, who was really his tool. His sister Lucretia, as if to leave nothing unsaid that can render the name of Borgia hateful, has been treated as a paramour both to his father and himself. But this female, after two previous marriages, made a third with Alphonso of Este, son of Hercules, duke of Ferrara, with whom she lived, as it seems, respected after all her family were dead. This is not favourable to current accounts of her profligacy. Nor is it likely that her father and brother, execrable as they undoubtedly were, are chargeable with all the crimes imputed to them. As one redeeming point in their revolting history, it may be mentioned that both of them were men of cultivated taste, and Cæsar Borgia produced specimens of poetic talent. (Chaufepié. Bower. Roscoe's Leo X.)

BORGIA, (Francis,) ordinarily written, according to the Spanish form, Borja, third general of the Jesuits, a descendant of Alexander VI., died 1572, leaving some devotional tracts. Another Francis Borgia, or Borja, commonly called Borja y Esquilache, descended from Geoffrey prince of Squillace, in Naples, youngest son of Alexander VI., was gentleman of the bed-chamber to Philip IV. of Spain, a knight of the golden fleece, and viceroy of Peru. He died at Madrid, far advanced in age, Sept. 26, 1658. Being a literary man, his high birth and station gained him the flattering title of *prince of Spanish poets*, a distinction that he long has lost, but he may be regarded as the last representative of the classic style of the sixteenth century. He published, Napoles recuperada por el Rey don Alonso, an epic, or rather historical, poem. Las Obras en Verso de Don Francisco de Borja, Principe de Esquilache, and a Spanish devotional work, chiefly drawn from Thomas à Kempis. With regard to cultivation, this noble writer may be placed on a level with Jauregui, but he deserves to rank no higher in poetic invention. The preface to his poems is in verse, and it explains the principles of his taste with so much modesty and elegance, that every reader is prepossessed in his favour. (Antonio Bouterwek.)

BORGIA, (Alexander,) of the same family as the preceding, born at Veletri, in Campania, in 1682. He was archbishop of Fermo, in the marquisate of Ancona, where he died, February 14, 1764. He published, in Italian, a life of St. Gerald, a history of Veletri, a life of Benedict XIII., and some letters and homilies. In Latin he published an account of a provincial council holden at Fermo, and upon the church there. His nephew, Stephen Borgia, eventually a cardinal, and chief of the congregation *de Propaganda*, born at Veletri, Dec. 3, 1731, was educated by him, and early became distinguished by an enlightened taste for antiquities. This attended him through life; and as he was willing to make almost any sacrifice, even to sell his plate or shoe-buckles, for the acquisition of valuable curiosities, he gradually accumulated a museum, rarely equalled even in Italy. He was not, however, a mere *virtuoso*, but a man who displayed great talents for business, and an ardent zeal for missionary enterprise. Benedict XIII. accordingly appointed him governor of Benevento, and he discharged his duties there in a most satisfactory manner. Hence, when revolutionary movements threatened Rome in 1797, Pius VI. confided to him and two associate cardinals the management of the city. Borgia soon showed himself worthy of the trust; but the French army, seconded by a party within the walls, rendered his exertions nugatory, and he was arrested, March 8, 1798. Before the month closed he was set at liberty, but ordered to quit the papal states. He took refuge in the north of Italy, and quickly organized, under the imprisoned pope's authority, a new *Propaganda*. When Pius VII. made his entry into Rome, cardinal Borgia was again called to arduous public duties, which he discharged with his wonted energy and ability. From these he was summoned to attend the pope on his journey to crown Buonaparte; but his age proved unequal to this new demand upon him, and he died at Lyons, November 23, 1804. Besides several Italian works of local interest, he published, Vaticana Confessio B. Petri, chronologicis Testimoniis illustrata, Rom. 1776, 4to. (Biog. Univ.)

BORGIANI, (Horace,) a painter and

engraver, born at Rome, in 1580, who spent several years in Spain, allured by the patronage bestowed upon the arts by Philip II. He returned, however, to his native city, and profited greatly by assiduous attention to the admirable works of art to be found there. He etched in a free, bold manner, with more finish than is usual in the works of a painter. (Bryan.)

BORGO, Lat. *Burgus*, (Peter Baptist,) a Genoese officer, who served under Gustavus Adolphus in the thirty years' war, of which he wrote a history to the death of Gustavus, entitled Commentarii de Bello Suecico, Liege, 1633, several times reprinted. He also published a Latin treatise, asserting the rights of Genoa over the Ligurian sea. (Biog. Univ.)

BORIS GODUNOF, a Russian noble, brother-in-law and prime minister to the czar Feodor Ivanovich. The imbecile character of the sovereign left almost unbounded power in the hands of Boris, who, on the death of Feodor, in 1598, and the consequent extinction of the male line of the house of Rurik, procured himself to be elected to the vacant throne by the nobles and clergy; having, as most accounts state, removed some years earlier the only impediment to his ultimate elevation, by the murder of Demetrius, sole brother of Feodor. During the first five years of his reign his administration was enlightened and equitable. He promoted commerce by the abolition of the exorbitant duties formerly levied; and during a famine, relieved the poor by the daily distribution of several thousand rubles. But he gradually became suspicious and cruel, alienating the nobles by arbitrary severity; and the appearance of a claimant to the crown, who represented himself as prince Demetrius, increased the difficulty of his situation. This pretender is said by most historians to have been a Polish monk, named Otrepief; while others have maintained, and apparently not without strong grounds, that he was really the person whose name he assumed. However this may be, his adherents gained repeated advantages over those of Boris; and the latter, on the approach of his rival to Moscow, terminated his own life by poison, A.D. 1605. Feodor, the only son of Boris, was declared czar for a few days by the nobles of his party, but was seized and strangled in prison, with his mother and sister, by order of Demetrius, who was himself dethroned and murdered, after a reign of only a year, by Basil Schuiskoi. See BASIL SCHUISKOI. (Tooke. Modern Universal History.)

BORKHAUSEN, (Maurice Balthazar,) born at Giessen 1760, began to study law in the university of his native town, but soon deserted this science for his favorite pursuit, natural history, occupying himself, under very inauspicious circumstances, especially with botany, zoology, physics, and mineralogy. He held successively various offices under the government of Hesse-Darmstadt; was finally appointed Kammerrath in the Oberforst collegium; and died November 30, 1806. His private character was estimable; and as a scientific man he was noted for his industry, observation, and powerful memory. His Natural History of European Butterflies in systematic order, Frankf. 5 vols, 1788-94, 8vo, is remarkable for its comprehensiveness and completeness, the succinctness of its descriptions, and its emendation of synonymes. Useful for beginners are his Botanical Dictionary, 2 vols, (the best edition 1816); his Teutsche Fauna, Frankf. 1 vol. 1797, 8vo, and his Handbuch der Forstbotanik. Together with some other men of science, he published an excellent German Ornithology, with plates, in sixteen numbers, fol. Darmstadt, 1800. He left behind him a collection of stuffed birds, including by far the greater part indigenous to Germany. His Tentamen Dispositionis Plantarum Germaniæ seminiferarum, secundum novam Methodum, a Staminorum Situ et Proportione, Darmst. 1792-1809, 8vo, appears to have attracted but little attention.

BORLACE, (Edmond,) a physician at Chester, where he died in 1682, son of Sir John Borlace. He was educated in the university of Dublin, and deserves mention as author of The Reduction of Ireland to the Crown of England, with the Governors since the conquest by Henry II. in 1172, and some passages in their Government; a Brief Account of the Rebellion of 1641; The Original of the University of Dublin and the College of Physicians, Lond. 1675, 8vo; The History of the Execrable Irish Rebellion traced from many preceding Acts to the grand Eruption, October 23, 1641, and thence pursued to the Act of Settlement in 1661, Lond. 1680, folio; Brief Reflections on the Earl of Castelhaven's Memoirs of his Engagement and Carriage in the War of Ireland, by which the Government of that Time and the Justice of the Crown since are vindicated from Aspersions cast upon both, Lond. 1682, 8vo.

BORLASE, (William,) an eminent antiquary and naturalist, born at Pendeen, in Cornwall, of an ancient family, February 2, 1696, educated at Exeter college, Oxford, where he proceeded to the degrees of B.A. and M.A. In 1722 he was instituted to the rectory of Ludgvan, Cornwall; and in 1732, to the vicarage of St. Just, of which parish he was a native. He published, in 1754, The History and Antiquities of Cornwall; a second edition appeared in 1769. In 1756 he printed his Observations on the Ancient and Present State of the Scilly Islands. In 1758, was given to the world, his Natural History of Cornwall, for which he had long been making collections. He also wrote, Paraphrases on Job, and the Books of Solomon, and a number of papers in the philosophical transactions. The fossils and antiquities collected for his works, he presented to the Ashmolean museum at Oxford, which procured him the thanks of the university, and the degree of LL.D. He died August 31, 1772. Two of his sons survived him; one, George Borlase, was professor of casuistry, and registrar of Cambridge; he died in 1809.

BORN, (Frederic Gottlieb,) a German philosophical writer, extraordinary professor of philosophy at Leipsic, from 1785 till 1802, born at Leipsic in 1743. He died at Dresden, December 8, 1807, and was one of the most zealous and active supporters of the philosophy of Kant, whose works he translated into excellent Latin—I Kantii Opera ad Philosophiam Criticam, Lips. vol. iv. 1796-8, 8vo. In conjunction with J. H. Abicht, he published a periodical, Das neue Philosophische Magazin, in which the Kantean system was expounded and defended. He also published original compositions of the same kind; translated Adelung's German Grammar, and Schroeck's Universal History, into Latin; and edited Anacreon and Sappho, though not in a very satisfactory manner.

BORN, (Ignatius Edler von,) born at Karlsburg, in Transylvania, December 26, 1742, of wealthy parents, whom he lost at an early age, was educated at Hermannstadt and Vienna; entered, in his seventeenth year, the society of Jesuits, but quitted it after sixteen months, and repaired to the university of Prague to study the law. After finishing his academic education, he travelled in Germany, Holland, the Netherlands, and France; and on his return home, devoted himself exclusively to mineralogy and natural history. In 1770 he was placed in the mining department and mint at Prague, and in the same year he made a mineralogical excursion to Lower Hungary, Transylvania, the Temeswar Banat, and Carniola. Its valuable results are contained in his letters on matters of mineralogy, (Briefe über Mineralog. Gegenstände,) addressed to the celebrated mineralogist, Ferber, by whom they were published. They have been translated into English, French, and Italian. A chronic disease, which originated in a descent he made into an Hungarian mine, compelled him to retire for four years to his estate, where he was carefully nursed by an affectionate wife, but he never quite recovered. In 1772-75, appeared his Lithophylacium Bornianum s. Index Fossilium, quæ collegit, in Classes et Ordines digessit Ign. de B. Pragæ, vol. ii. 8vo. He encouraged the production of works of general literature, and founded a society in Bohemia for the cultivation of the national history, mathematics, &c., the Transactions of which he edited, and enriched with several valuable papers. In 1776 his reputation induced Maria Theresa to invite him to Vienna, to arrange the imperial cabinet of natural history; and the first-fruits of his labours here was a splendid new edition of its catalogue, under the title, Testacea Musei Cæsar. Vindob. quæ jussu Mariæ Theresiæ disposuit et desc. Ign. a Born, Vien. fol. 1780, with 18 plates and numerous vignettes (price 36 dollars); one of the most valuable works on conchology, and of which the plates are especially faithful and well executed. In 1779 the empress gave him an appointment in the mining department; and he henceforth fixed his residence at Vienna, collecting round him a circle of individuals of merit. In 1784, after overcoming a vast number of difficulties, and performing a variety of experiments, he accomplished his famous discovery of the improvement of the amalgamation of minerals which contain precious metals; a discovery which places him amongst the benefactors to the human race. It effected a saving of wood; rendered it profitable to work mines in districts where they had hitherto been neglected for want of fuel; banished the fumes of lead from the operation, and thus greatly benefited the health of the workmen, and at the same time produced an increased quantity of metal at a diminished expense. For an account of it see Born's Uber das Anquicken der Gold und Silberhaltigen Erze, Rohsteine, Schwarzkupfer, and Hüttenspeise, Wien. 1786, gr. 4to, with 21 plates. A French edition of it was also published. The method was adopted, after considerable opposition at first, in all the Austrian states, and in Saxony, Bohemia, Sweden, and even in Mexico. Its discoverer was liberally rewarded by the emperor Joseph II. In 1789, Born, together with von Tebra, published a valuable Bergbaukunde, Leips. 2 vols, 4to. He also edited the Catalogue Méthodique et Raisonné de la Collection des Fossiles de Madem. E. de Raal, Vienne, 1790; a classical mineralogical work. His continued ill health prevented him from completing other literary undertakings. He died July 24, 1791, bequeathing the entire of his property to scientific purposes. Born was a man of powerful mind and active habits. He spoke and wrote with facility several modern languages. His wit, and talent for satire, are admirably evinced in his Monachology, (Joannis Physiophili Specimen Monachologiæ, Methodo Linnæana, Tabulis Tribus æneis illustratum, &c. Augustæ Vindelicorum, 1783,) in which, with admirable raillery, and in the most classic style, he applies the terminology of natural history to the description of the monks and nuns. In conversation, Born was cheerful, entertaining, and instructive.

BORNE, (Lewis,) a violent German political writer, of Jewish extraction, whose original name was Baruch, which he exchanged for Borne on going over, in 1818, to the protestant church, of which, however, he was only nominally a member, for he did not hesitate to ridicule his own admission into it. He was born at Frankfort on the Maine, May 13, 1786. He studied medicine at Berlin and Halle, but, in 1806, quitted this profession for political economy, to which he devoted himself at the universities of Heidelberg and Giessen. On the completion of his studies he became actuary of police in his native town; but after the old order of things had been restored, he was dismissed with a pension, which however he afterwards lost. He now devoted himself to literature and politics, resided in different parts of Germany until the revolution of 1830, when he rushed to Paris, in the confident expectation that all Europe would speedily be revolutionized after the French fashion, and where his writings rendered it necessary that he should remain until his death, which took place about 1839. No German writer of modern times has encountered, so remarkably as Borne, the extreme varieties of criticism;—the most extravagant praise from some; from others, the severest and most indignant censure. His early publications obtained for him the reputation of an acute, clever critic; and of an earnest, sanguine, benevolent character. He improved German prose in point of succinctness, vigour, and compression; rendered it more akin in these respects to French and English; and hence his merits as a writer are much better felt by his countrymen than by foreigners.

BOROWSKI, (Lewis Ernest von,) archbishop of the evangelical church, and general superintendent of East and West Prussia, born, in 1730, at Königsberg, where his father was sacristan to the castle-church. He was educated at the university of his native town; and during the residence of the royal family there, the king became acquainted with him. His rise was now rapid; in 1812 he was nominated general-superintendent of East Prussia, and in 1815, chief preacher to the court. In 1829, the dignity of archbishop was conferred upon him. As a theologian he was orthodox, but tolerant, and always disposed to inquiry. His sermons were attended by very numerous audiences. Though his frame was apparently weakly, his mental powers continued undiminished to a very advanced age. He died of a rheumatic complaint, November 10, 1831; and an imposing funeral, on the 22d, showed the respect which he had extensively inspired. Of his writings, the following two may be mentioned:—On the Authorship of the Writer of the Book on Marriage (Hippel), Königsberg, 1797; and a Sketch of the Life and Character of Immanuel Kant, Königsb. 1804; which latter work Kant himself is said to have seen, and corrected before it went to the press.

BORREKENS, (Matthew,) an engraver, born at Antwerp, about 1615, and chiefly employed in copying the works of more eminent professors of his art. He left, however, some original plates. (Bryan.)

BORRHAUS, (Martin,) originally called Cellarius, born at Stuttgard, in 1499, a disciple of Capnio, and at one time a friend of Melancthon. He became, however, a violent anabaptist, and in a conference with Luther, in 1522, displayed extreme fanaticism. He, notwithstanding, ultimately changed his opinions, and retiring to Bâle, in 1536, he dropped the name of Cellarius for that of Borrhaus, and taught for a living, first rhetoric, afterwards theology. He died of the plague in 1564, having published notes upon Aristotle's Politics, in 1545, a commentary upon his Rhetoric, in 1551, some commentaries upon Scripture, and other works of less importance. (Bayle.)

BORRI, (Joseph Francis,) in Latin, *Burrhus*, a chemist, quack, and heretic, born at Milan, May 4, 1627, who became notorious in his day. His education was partly conducted by the Jesuits at Rome, but he behaved himself eventually with such profligacy, that, in 1654, he could only escape from the officers of justice by seeking an asylum in a church. He then affected extreme piety, laid claim to heavenly revelations, grieved over the immoralities of Rome, and declared that shortly the pope would be acknowledged as the sole spiritual pastor of mankind. He did not, however, dissemble the necessity of military operations before this consummation should be effected, and he announced himself as the predestined leader of the papal armies which would overpower the opposition of wicked men. Having mingled with these absurdities some heretical positions upon the Trinity, he found himself obliged to quit Rome for Milan, from fear of the inquisition. A like fear made him quit the latter city, where he succeeded in drawing some dupes around him. He then successively appeared at Strasburg, Amsterdam, Hamburg, and Copenhagen, delighting and pillaging at all the three, wealthy subjects for imposition, by his talents for quackery, and pretensions to produce the philosopher's stone. By these last, he got very considerable sums from the king of Denmark, but on this monarch's death, Borri found himself under the necessity of quitting the country in haste. He now thought of Turkey as the most promising field for his impostures; but being arrested by mistake, on the Austrian frontier, he was claimed by the papal nuncio, and sent to Rome, under a promise that his life should be spared. He had been burnt in effigy there in 1661, a day on which he is said, like others punished in the same way, to have declared himself to have been colder than he almost ever remembered. He died a prisoner in the castle of St. Angelo, about the close of summer, in 1695. Some works, printed at Geneva, in 1681, are attributed to him. (Bayle.)

BORROMEO, (Charles,) a Romish saint, born in the Milanese, of an illustrious family, Oct. 2, 1538. Being nephew to Pius IV., he was made cardinal in his twenty-third year. Besides the archbishopric of Milan, he had several other preferments, which afforded ample means for indulging a taste for magnificence, and he freely availed himself of them, until the council of Trent, by bringing so much forward upon the necessity of clerical reformation, rendered him anxious to set an example of it in his own person. Henceforth he became one of the most exemplary of known prelates, and he died, worn out by austerities and pious labours, November 4, 1584, being only in his forty-seventh year. In 1610 he was canonized by Paul V.; and whatever may be thought of the alleged miracles by which this act was justified, there can be no doubt of the deceased prelate's pre-eminence in piety and morality. His works, which are chiefly doctrinal and practical, were published at Milan, with notes, in 1747, in 5 vols, fol. His instructions to confessors were printed as a manual for French ecclesiastics, in 1657, by the assembly general of the clergy of France. It is to him, in conjunction with Francis Foreiro, a Portuguese divine, Leonard Marini, archbishop of Lanciano, and Giles Foscariri, bishop of Modena, that the church of Rome owes her famous catechism, known differently as the *Catechismus Tridentinus*, *Catechismus Romanus*, and *Catechismus ad Parochos*. This compilation only wants the sanction of the council itself, which unfortunately it has not, having been produced after its termination, to render it worthy of the commendations commonly bestowed upon it. An undertaking, however, merely recommended by the council, but never submitted to it, has obviously no sufficient authority upon any point which the Trentine fathers have not accurately defined. (Biog. Univ.)

BORROMEO, (Frederic,) cousin-german of the preceding, and educated under his direction; like him, too, a cardinal and archbishop of Milan. He died in 1632, aged sixty-eight, leaving, Meditamenta Litteraria, published in 1633, and some religious works. Literature, however, is chiefly indebted to him as the founder of the famous Ambrosian library, at Milan, in which were placed nearly 10,000 MSS., many of them oriental. (Biog. Univ.)

BORROMINI, (Francis,) an architect, born in the Milanese, in 1599, who acquired great celebrity, but indulged a fantastic taste in design and ornament. He set himself up for a rival of Bernini; but his false estimate of his own talents exposed him to severe mortifications. These appear to have rendered him insane, and he destroyed himself in 1667. (Biog. Univ.)

BORRONI, (John Angelo,) an Italian painter, born at Cremona, in 1684, educated under Massarotti and Longo. He died in 1772. (Pilkington.)

BORSIERI DE KANIFELD, (John Baptist,) a celebrated Italian physician, better known under his Latinized name of *Burserius*, born of a good family, at Trent, in the Tyrol, March 25, 1725. At fourteen he evinced a desire to study medicine; and after attending various Italian schools for that purpose, when scarcely 20 he settled as a physician at Faenza, at which time a severe epidemic raged. His efforts to check its progress were eminently successful, and he acquired a reputation which spread into the neighbouring provinces. He declined an offer made to him of a chair at Ferrara; but the empress Maria Theresa nominated him in 1769 professor of materia medica, chemistry, and pharmacy, at the university of Pavia. In 1772 he was made professor of practical medicine, and this led him to establish a clinical school at the hospital attached to the university. When the great eminence to which this department afterwards arrived is considered, it is no mean praise to mention Borsieri as the first to lead the way to its establishment. He caused several beds, both for males and females, to be devoted to this branch of medical science, and he was highly successful in his mode of conveying instruction to the pupils. He continued in the performance of these duties until 1778, when he was chosen physician to the court of Milan. He died December 21, 1785, of a disease of the kidneys and bladder, which is supposed to have been much aggravated by his zealous application to study. His Institutiones Medicinæ Practicæ, Milan, 1781-88, 4 vols, 4to, is the work on which his reputation principally rests; the first two volumes, containing fevers and the exanthemata, are very superior to the following two, which treat of the diseases of the chest and abdomen, and which appearing after the author's death had not, therefore, the advantage of his revision. The work is esteemed classical in Italy. It has gone through many editions. It has also been published at Leipsic in 1787 and 1798, 4 vols, 8vo; at Berlin in 1823; and at Pavia in the same year by Brera, with many additions. It was translated into English by Dr. Wm. Cullen Brown, and printed at Edinburgh, 1800, in 5 vols, 8vo.

BORSUM, (Adam van,) a Dutch artist, who lived about 1666, and painted successfully animals with landscapes. (Pilkington.)

BORZONE, the surname of a family of Italian artists. *Lucian*, the father, born at Genoa, in 1590, at first was faulty and incorrect, but eventually painted both portrait and history, especially the former, in a grand and graceful style. While painting the ceiling of a church in Genoa, he fell from the scaffold, and was killed on the spot.—His son, *John Baptist*, who died in 1654, painted perspective and history in a good and correct style.—*Charles*, another son, has a high character as a portait-painter. —*Francis Maria*, a third son, who died at Genoa, in 1679, was a landscape and marine painter of great eminence. He resided several years at Paris, and was employed by Lewis XIV. (Pilkington.)

BOS, the surname of some Dutch artists. *Jerome*, called also Bosche, born at Bois-le-duc, about 1470, excelled in painting spectres and other supernatural subjects, which generally offend by their extravagance, in spite of a free touch and skilful colouring, that give them considerable value as works of art. He has, however, so painted some serious subjects as to avoid his faults, and yet exhibit the excellences really belonging to him. He was likewise an engraver, and died about 1530.—*Lewis Jansen*, also born at Bois-le-duc, but rather earlier than the preceding, became eminent for painting flowers, fruits, and plants, ordinarily grouped in glasses, or vases of crystal half filled with water. He died in 1507.—*Gasper vanden*, a marine painter, born at Hoorn, in 1634, is distinguished by a light free touch, a pleasing tint of colour, and an artful manner of handling. He died in 1666. (Pilkington.)

BOS, (Lambert,) born, November 23, 1670, at Worcum, in Friesland, where his father, who taught him Latin and Greek, was the head-master of the school. His mother, who was aunt to Vitringa, seeing her nephew raised at an early age to the professorship of oriental languages, expressed a hope that she might witness a similar honour conferred upon her son. She was, however, carried off by consumption before young Bos commenced his literary career. After living for some time as a tutor in a family, he went to Franeker, where his cousin Vitringa urged him to continue his classical studies, and especially Greek; and such was his progress, that he was appointed to succeed Blancard in the chair of the Greek professor in that university. He held the office, however, only thirteen years; for in 1716 he caught a malignant fever, which terminated in consumption, and carried him off on Jan. 6, 1717, five years after his marriage with the widow of a clergyman, by whom he left two sons. His first appearance as a scholar was in the notes appended to a reprint of his predecessor's, Blancard, edition of Thomas Magister, published at Franeker in 1698. This was succeeded by his Observationes Philogicæ, in 1700, and with considerable additions in 1713. But the work by which he is best known is the Ellipses Græcæ, which appeared in 1702, of which the fullest and latest edition is by Schœfer, Lips. 1809. In 1707 he gave his edition of the Septuagint, which was severely criticized by Breitinger in Le Journals Literaire. This was followed by his Antiquitatum Græcarum Descriptio, in 1713, of which an English translation by Percival Stockdale appeared in 1772, and again by George Barber, Camb. 1833. In 1715 he published his Animadversiones ad Scriptores Græcos, &c., and a new edition of Weller's Grammar. Like the generality of Dutch scholars, he was rather remarkable for the extent of his learning and the soundness of his judgment than his acuteness as an emendatory critic; and so devoted to his favourite pursuits as to consider all time as lost that was not passed in his study; and of modesty so rare, says Chaufepié, that he believed every one else superior to himself, and was the only person who seemed to be ignorant of his worth.

BOSC, (Claude du,) a French engraver, who came to England about 1712, and executed several works; but his manner is coarse and heavy, and his drawing incorrect. (Bryan.)

BOSC, (Lewis Augustine William,) a French naturalist, born at Paris, Jan. 29, 1759. His father, Paul Bosc d'Antic, who died in 1784, of an ancient protestant family in the south of France, was a physician, but is best known for researches and publications connected with the manufacture of glass. The younger Bosc, intended originally for the army, became conspicuous for acquirements in natural history, which he had great opportunities of studying both in Europe and America. He died July 10, 1828, leaving Histoire Naturelle de Coquilles, Paris, 1801; Histoire Naturelle des Vers, Paris, 1801; Histoire Naturelle des Crustacés, Paris, 1802. The aggregate of his observations he afterwards produced in the Nouveau Dictionnaire d'Histoire Naturelle, and in the Cours Complet d'Agriculture. (Biog. Univ. Biog. Univ. Suppl.)

BOSC, (Peter du,) a French protestant minister, particularly eminent as a preacher, born at Bayeux, Feb. 21, 1623. His father was an advocate, and his own talents recommended him for minister to the church at Caen, at an age unusually early for such an appointment. His prominence among the protestant body at one time procured a long audience from Lewis XIV., but eventually nothing could shield holders of his opinions in France, and in 1685 he was compelled to expatriate himself. He retired into Holland, and at the time of his death, January 2, 1692, was minister at Rotterdam. He published some sermons; and after his death, Le Gendre, his son-in-law, published his life, letters, and other pieces, together with some curious documents relating to the reformed churches in his time. (Chalmers.)

BOSCAN, (John Almogavèr,) a celebrated Spanish poet, who, in conjunction with his friend Garcilaso de la Vega, introduced the Italian style into Castilian poetry. He was born in Barcelona, towards the close of the fifteenth century, of one of the patrician families of that city, which bore equal rank with the nobility of the country. He received a good education, and had an independent fortune, but was at one time in the army. He also improved himself by foreign travel, but it is not known in what countries. If he went into Italy, which seems probable, he did not, at all events, discover on his return any desire to naturalize her versification among his countrymen; the first Castilian verses which he wrote being all in the ancient lyric style. It was not until 1526, after visiting the court of Charles V., and being well married in his native city, that he was induced by Navagero, the Venetian minister to the emperor, to think of imitating Italian poetry. When he ventured upon this innovation, he was assailed by a storm of remonstrances; but neither he nor his friend Garcilaso would give way, and their undertaking proved brilliantly successful. Of Boscan's maturer life little more is known than that it was chiefly spent in his native city of Barcelona, and that he was at one time governor to the young duke of Alva. Of his death the precise year is unascertainable, but it occurred before 1544. He was the first Spaniard who had an idea of classical perfection in works of imagination; and although he generally falls greatly below that standard, his poems are strikingly characterised by endeavours to reach it. He has thus amply earned for himself the distinction of being the first classical poet of Spain. Some of his expressions are now antiquated; but upon the whole, his language has continued a model for succeeding ages. Simplicity and dignity had never in the same degree, and under a form so correct, been united with poetic truth and feeling by any previous Spanish author. The first book of his works contains Boscan's early productions, which are much like other poems hitherto known in Spain. The second book contains *sonetos* and *canciones*, in the style of the Italian *sonetti* and *canzoni*. The greater part of the third book is filled by a paraphrastic translation of the Greek poem of Hero and Leander. Nothing of the kind had been previously known in the Spanish language. The first edition of Boscan's works appears to have been published at Lisbon, in 1543, 4to. (Bouterwek.)

BOSCAWEN, (Edward,) a British admiral, of considerable renown, third son of Hugh Boscawen, created viscount Falmouth in 1720, and Charlotte, daughter of Charles Godfrey, Esq., by Arabella Churchill, his wife, sister to the great duke of Marlborough. He was born April 19, 1711, entered the navy at an early age, and became, in the year 1737, captain of the *Leopard*, (50.) In 1739, he accompanied Vernon as a volunteer on the expedition against Porto-Bello; and subsequently (1741) he served under the same admiral at Carthagena. Here was afforded him the first opportunity of displaying that ardent spirit of enterprise and heroic contempt of danger, which so strongly marked his conduct in every future transaction of his life. In 1744, when in command of the *Dreadnought* (60), he captured the French frigate, *Medea*, commanded by M. de Hocquart. After acting with success as commodore of a squadron employed in the Channel, he served, in the year 1747, as a private captain in Anson's fleet, when the British admiral defeated the French force under Le Jonquiere. In this encounter he was severely wounded in the shoulder by a musket-ball. This was the last occasion on which he served in the capacity of captain, being, on the 15th of July following, promoted to the rank of rear-admiral of the blue. Immediately afterwards he was entrusted with a command of no ordinary nature—namely, that of the forces, naval and military, destined for the East Indies. No amphibious commission of the kind had been granted since the time of Charles II., except the earl of Peterborough's, it being deemed injudicious to place one person over the two services in conducting hostile operations of any extent. But Boscawen's appointment was received without any animadversion; and though his efforts were ultimately unsuccessful, his naval and *military* command excited neither murmurs nor reproach—a convincing proof, in a nation like ours, where popular discussions are carried on with such freedom, in what estimation his merits and abilities were held.

In 1751, Boscawen officiated as a lord of the admiralty; and in 1755, hostilities commencing with France, he was despatched with a squadron of eleven sail of the line to cruize on the banks of Newfoundland, for the purpose of intercepting a French force bound to the river St. Lawrence. By passing through the Straits of Belleisle, a course never before attempted by ships of the line, the French squadron, with the exception of two vessels pertaining to it, escaped capture. The ships of the enemy which fell into the hands of Boscawen, were called the *Alcide* (64), and the *Lys*, a vessel of similar class, but, when taken, only "armed en flute." It is worthy of remark, that by the capture of the *Alcide*, M. de Hocquart, who commanded her, became a third time Boscawen's prisoner. He had taken that officer first in the *Medea*, in 1744, when in command of the *Dreadnought*; secondly, in the *Diamond*, when in command of the *Namur*, in Anson's action with Le Jonquiere, May, 1747; and a third time, in the *Alcide*, as above stated.

In 1758 Boscawen was advanced to the rank of admiral of the blue, and appointed commander-in-chief of a formidable fleet equipped to cover the descent at the siege of Louisburgh. When the admiral arrived at Halifax, he was there joined by general Amherst and the army. The necessary arrangements being made, the fleet sailed from thence on the 28th of May. Including the transports, with the ships of war, it amounted to 157 sail: the military force that it conveyed consisted of upwards of 12,000 men. On the 2d of June, the fleet anchored in the bay of Gabarus, about seven miles to the westward of Louisburgh; and the siege was pressed with so much vigour, that on the 26th of July the officer who commanded in the fortress proposed to surrender. The terms of capitulation were readily settled, and the garrison, consisting of nearly six thousand men, became prisoners of war. In 1759 Boscawen resumed his seat at the Admiralty, but immediately afterwards was appointed to the command of a squadron, consisting of fourteen sail of the line and two frigates, ordered for the Mediterranean. He sailed from St. Helen's on the 14th of April, and proceeded direct for Toulon, off which port he cruized for a considerable time, in the hope of provoking De la Cue, who lay there with a squadron of twelve sail of the line and three frigates, to come out and engage him. Taking advantage of the absence of the British squadron, De la Cue, who being under orders to repair to Brest, departed port, thinking to elude the vigilance of the British admiral, who he knew by good information was refitting his squadron, and replenishing his water and provisions, at Gibraltar. But Boscawen's vigilance rendered the enemy's attempt abortive. Nearly half of the French squadron was captured or destroyed, and the foundation laid for the total subversion of the visionary schemes formed by the French court for the attack of the British dominions in their most vital part. Boscawen's last services were confined to the home station, dividing with lord Hawke the arduous duty of watching in the ports of the Bay of Biscay the remaining ships of Conflans' defeated fleet. The "Brave Boscawen," as he was usually styled, died at his seat at Hatchland, near Guilford, of a bilious fever, on the 10th of January, 1761, in the fiftieth year of his age, universally regretted. He was a seaman, in the fullest acceptation of the term; strongly attached to his profession, and always ready to quit a life of comparative ease at the admiralty (of which he continued till his death as one of the commissioners,) and to engage with alacrity in any service that his colleagues at the board might require him to undertake. He lies interred in the parish church of St. Michael, at Penkevel, in Cornwall, where a monument of exquisite workmanship was erected to his memory.

BOSCAWEN, (William,) the younger son of general Boscawen, was born Aug. 28, 1752, and sent to Eton before he was seven years old, whence he went to Exeter college, Oxford. Subsequently he became a barrister. In 1792 he published a Treatise on Convictions under the Penal Statutes, &c., which probably led to his appointment as a commissioner of bankrupts, an office which he held to his death, May 6, 1811, although he had quitted the bar after he was made a commissioner of the Victualling-office. As a literary character, he is best known by his translation of Horace, the first portion of which appeared in 1793, and the remainder in 1798. He was for several years a contributor to the British Critic, and is the supposed author of the Progress of Satire, and of A Supplement to the Progress, both written in verse, and accompanied with notes, occasioned by the liberties taken with some eminent characters in The Pursuits of Literature. By his marriage with Charlotte, daughter of archdeacon Ibbetson, he left five orphan children. He was one of the earliest and warmest supporters of that admirable institution, the Literary Fund, which he used to consider in the light of his child, and to aid it equally with his purse and pen.

BOSCH VAN DEN, the surname of two painters in the Low Countries.—*Balthasar*, born at Antwerp, in 1675, excelled in painting interiors of apartments, elegantly and curiously furnished. He also painted portraits of a small size with great success. His fame in this way induced the great duke of Marlborough, when at Antwerp, to employ him upon an equestrian picture of himself; but Van Bloemen painted the horse. Bosch died in 1715.—*Jacob*, born at Amsterdam, in 1636, painted fruit with extraordinary truth and neatness. He died in 1676. (Bryan. Pilkington.)

BOSCH, (Jerome van,) was the son of an apothecary at Amsterdam, where he was born, March 23, 1740. At an early age he distinguished himself as a writer of Latin poetry, and for a taste in literature, which Peter Burmann the younger encouraged and directed. Having formed when a boy an acquaintance with the son of Hooft, the burgomaster, he edited the posthumous poetry of his schoolfellow, and was by the interest of the father appointed to a lucrative situation, similar to that of town-clerk in England. In 1800 he was made curator of the university of Leyden, where he had the opportunity of repairing in part the injury done by the revolution. His library, which cost him sixty years to collect, was remarkable for the beauty of the copies; and so afraid was he of their being soiled, that he would never lend a book. He is best known by his edition, still imperfect, of the Anthologia Græca cum versione Latina H. Grotii, of which the first volume appeared in 1795, and the fourth and last in 1810, containing, with those of Huet, the unedited notes of Salmasius and his own, which do not, however, go beyond two of the seven books of the Anthologiæ; nor has the learned world much reason to lament the non-appearance of the remainder, for though they exhibit a considerable extent of reading, they rarely furnish the explanation of an obscure passage, or the correction of a corrupt one. Besides his Latin poems, printed at Utrecht in 1803 and 1808, he wrote a copy of Latin verses, which were translated, it seems, into Dutch, French, and German, under the title of Laudes Buonapartii, et Elogia ad Galliam, in 1801, on the occasion of the first consul's life being endangered by the blowing up of the infernal machine. He died Jan. 11, 1811.

BOSCHAERT, (Nicholas,) a painter of flowers and fruit, born at Antwerp, in 1696. His master was Crepu, but he soon surpassed him, and rose to great eminence in his line of art. He died about 1746. (Bryan. Pilkington.)

BOSCHI, the surname of two Florentine painters.—*Fabricius*, who died in 1642, was pupil of Passignano, and became eminent in history.—*Francis*, who died in 1675, was also of some note in historical composition, but his chief merit lay in portrait. (Pilkington.)

BOSCOVICH, (Roger Joseph,) a celebrated natural philosopher, born at Ragusa, on the Adriatic, in 1711, professor of mathematics successively at Rome, Pavia, and Milan. His youth was marked by no precocity of talent, though he was sent to study philosophy under the ablest masters of the day, the Jesuits. In his fifteenth year (1725) he was admitted into their body, and sent to Rome. Two years were here spent in learning the rules of his order, when he eagerly returned to the study of the classics, particularly Latin verse. Having completed his noviciate, he applied himself to mathematics and physics, which first brought out his great talents. He soon arrived at eminence, and was in consequence appointed mathematical professor in the Jesuits' college at Rome. In the public disputations in the schools it was his practice to advance, but very carefully, original ideas and opinions, which on the subject in hand had occurred to his own mind, with the view of testing the soundness of them, and of eliciting whatever light the ensuing debate might throw upon them. During his occupation of this chair, he published tracts on some of the most recondite subjects in the range of scientific inquiry, and in every one of them displayed great variety and depth of research, immense labour, and brilliant talent. He thus earned a high reputation throughout Europe, which made him much honoured and courted by the great and the learned. Pope Benedict XIV. and king John V. of Portugal consulted him on architecture, hydrodynamics, and like subjects. He was employed to correct the topography of the papal states, and to measure a degree of the meridian there. He was also sent by the senate of Ragusa to the court of London, to remove some unfavourable impressions from the British government. Scientific men paid him due honour while in England; and in return for attentions from the Royal Society, he addressed a Latin poem to them, De Solis ac Lunæ defectibus, elegant in its style, and a singular effort of rare talent in reducing matters of abstruse theory and calculation to harmonious verse. He declined, however, the invitation by the society to join some of their members in a voyage to America in 1762, to observe the transit of Venus. After filling the mathematical chair in the university of Pavia, and superintending the observatory at Brera, the empress queen promoted him to the chair of astronomy and optics at Milan. While here, the suppression of his order, in 1773, gave a blow to feelings which he never thoroughly recovered. He sought refuge in Paris, and by the interest of some patrons there, he obtained the appointment from the French government of director of the optical instruments of their marine, with an income of 8,000 livres. This enabled him to pursue his optical inquiries, but did not make him happy: he mourned for the ruin of his order. He beguiled much of his time at Paris in composition, and after ten years, in 1783, obtained leave to return to Italy on furlough, for the purpose of there printing his writings. Accordingly at Bassano he published a collection of them in five volumes 4to, of which a third part is occupied on one of the most difficult parts of optics, viz. the theory of achromatic glasses. Thence he visited Rome, to enjoy for a time the society of many eminent men who had been the companions of his former days. He then proceeded to Milan, and occupied himself there in revising some of his own works, and in preparing for the press the poems of the celebrated Benedict Stay. But his leave of absence from Paris, two years, was fast expiring, and he had to choose between resuming the duties of his appointment there and his resignation of it. He decided on the latter, for he could not bring himself again to exchange the society of tried friends, by whom he was held in high and affectionate estimation, for what seemed a state of vassallage in another land. But he did not long survive. Attacks of gout and other infirmities overpowered both body and mind, and he sank into a state of hopeless fatuity, which in five months more brought him to the grave, on the 13th of February, 1787, in the seventy-sixth year of his age.

Boscovich, we have seen, was a poet as well as a philosopher, and would frequently compose verses *impromptu*, and recite them to the no small amusement of his associates. He had travelled in all parts of Europe, and was a most agreeable, well-informed, lively companion. He published a work in 4to, on the result of the commission that he undertook, conjointly with father Maize, to measure degrees in Italy. It was translated into French, and printed at Paris in 1770. In his principal work, Theoria Philosophiæ Naturalis, he embraces partly the Leibnitzian and partly the Newtonian hypothesis, but goes beyond both in some points, especially in the attractive and repulsive forces. On light he agrees with Newton; on electricity with Franklin; and on sensation with Hartley.

BOSE, (Caspar,) a physician in the earlier part of the eighteenth century, senator of Leipsic, and also professor of botany there. He enriched the garden to such an extent as to render it the largest of its description in Germany. Linnæus consecrated a genus of plants (Bosea) to him, and he published Dissertatio de Motu Plantarum, Sensûs æmulo, Lips. 1728, 4to. Dissert. de Calyce Tournefortii, *ib.* 1733, 4to.

BOSE, (George Matthias,) a celebrated physician, son of a rich merchant of Leipsic, where he was born, Sept. 22, 1710. He was made M.D. 1729, and having devoted himself especially to the mathematical and physical sciences, he was chosen to succeed Martin Gottholf Lœscher in a chair at the academy of Wittemberg. He occupied this honourable position with great éclat for many years, and died at Magdeburg, whither the Prussians had conveyed him as a hostage, Sept. 17, 1761; highly esteemed by the learned of all Europe, to whom he was known by his researches into the nature of electricity. Among other works, he published, De Eclipsi Terræ, Lips. 1733, 4to. Schediasma Litterarium, quo contenta Elementorum Euclidis enunciat, et simul de variis Editionibus post Fabricium nonnulla disserit, *ib.* 1738, 4to. Oratio de Attractione ex Electricitate, Wittemb. 1738, 4to. Transitus Mercurii sub Sole observatus, *ib.* 1743, 4to; translated into French, 1745, 4to. De Electricitate, *ib.* 1743, 4to. Tentamina Electrica in Acad. Reg. Lond. et Paris, primum habita, &c. *ib.* 1744-47, 4to. Discours sur la Lumière des Diamans et de plusieurs autres Corps, Gotting. 1745, 4to; in German, Wittemb. 1745, 4to. De Sympathiâ, Attractione, et Gravitate substitutâ, Wittemb. 1756, 4to. He published also many papers in the Acta Eruditorum of Leipsic, and in the Philosophical Transactions.

BOSE, (John Andrew,) professor of history at Jena, born at Leipsic, June 17, 1626. He died August 29, 1674, highly respected among the best European scholars for talents and learning. He published a good edition of Cornelius Nepos, in 1657, and produced several valuable pieces of a limited size. In 1701 was published, Petronii Satyricon. puritate Donatum, è MS. Jo. And. Bosii. (Biog. Univ.)

BOSE, (Mag. John George,) born at Oschatz, in Saxony, in 1662, one of the most noted of the German pietists. He recommended domestic assemblies for pious exercises, declared himself for the doctrine of the millennium, and taught that God has appointed a certain period for repentance, after the expiration of which, the sinner must in vain look for grace or forgiveness. (See his Terminus Peremptorius Salutis Humanæ, 1698.) In consequence of this work, his brother clergy instituted public proceedings against him, and Böse was reprimanded by the consistory at Sorau. He did not seem, however, at all disposed to abandon his doctrine. His death took place in 1700; and the controversy to which he had given rise did not reach its height till afterwards. It spread throughout Germany, and employed a great number of learned pens. The opponents of the new doctrine by far outnumbered its friends; but Rechenbach, of Leipsic, its principal advocate, compensated for inferiority of numbers by industry and zeal. The dispute was most violent from 1700 to 1703; but did not terminate till 1709.

BOSQUET, (Francis du,) a learned French prelate, born at Narbonne, May 28, 1605, and originally in the law. He resigned, however, his legal appointments in 1650, for the bishopric of Lodeve, which he exchanged, in 1657, for that of Montpellier. He died June 24, 1676, universally respected for qualities highly becoming a christian prelate, and honourably commemorated in the literary world by some valuable publications. In 1632 he published, at Paris, the Synopsis Legum, written by Michael Psellus, junior, in Greek iambics, from a MS. in the archiepiscopal library at Narbonne, with a Latin version and notes. In the same year appeared the lives of eight French popes, who sate at Avignon from 1305 to 1394, by authors nearly contemporary, with Bosquet's notes. Much fault being found with these lives as incorrect, Baluze afterwards corrected them by the help of other MSS., and inserted them in his Vitæ Paparum Avenionensium, Par. 1693. Bosquet, in the year 1633, published an essay on the ecclesiastical history of France, entitled, Ecclesiæ Gallicanæ Historiarum Liber Primus. This contained a severe but just reflection upon the monkish credulity that has corrupted the fountains of medieval religious history. Archbishop Ussher extracted this passage in the beginning of his preface to the Brit. Eccl. Antiqu. A second edition, however, published in 1636, is without it. Bosquet subsequently published four books of Innocent the Third's epistles, with some other works of less importance. He was an able, candid, and learned man; but, perhaps, the important works that have been mentioned, require a greater degree of critical knowledge and acuteness than are usually found at the age when he undertook them. (Bayle. Clement. Fabr. Bibl. Gr.)

BOSQUILLON, (Edward Francis Maria,) a distinguished physician and Greek scholar, born at Montdidier, March 20th, 1744, of a noble family. His father, a physician at Rheims, sent him to the Jesuits' college at Paris in 1755, where he obtained many prizes for his knowledge of Greek. After proceeding M.A. in 1762, he devoted himself to medical science, for which his father had destined him. His profound knowledge of Greek led, however, to his appointment as professor of that language in the Royal College of France, in 1774. Some years afterwards he was made royal censor, and one of the physicians of the Hôtel Dieu. When chosen doctor-regent of the faculty of Paris, he delivered lectures in surgery and botany in the Latin language. The learning of Bosquillon has been displayed in various works, and his application was incessant, in spite of a disease of the pylorus, which he was conscious would prove fatal to him. Nevertheless, his friends vainly advised him to relax in his studies: he found in them a true consolation. He looked upon death, and contemplated every thing in relation to it, with the greatest tranquillity, and even composed his own epitaph, to be recorded in the cemetery of Père la Chaise. His death took place November 23, 1816. By his practice, and prudence in the management of his affairs, he acquired a very considerable and valuable library, consisting of upwards of 30,000 volumes, which contained all the best editions of the ancient classics. Among his publications, original and translated, are:—Hippocratis Aphorismi et Prænotionum Liber, Paris, 1784, 12mo; second edition, 1814. This work is the result of great application. Bosquillon examined a great number of MSS., corrected many errors, and established a variety of new readings. He added a Latin MS. version of the thirteenth century, from the Royal Library of Paris, (No. 1791,) accompanied, as he conjectured, with the Commentaries of Oribasius. Physiologie de Cullen, *ib.* 1785, 3 vols, 8vo. Élémens de Médecine Pratique de Cullen, *ib.* 1785-87, 2 vols, 8vo; 1819, 3 vols, 8vo. Traité Théorique et Pratique des Ulcères, par B. Bell, *ib.* 1788, 1803, 8vo. Traité de la Matière Médicale, par W. Cullen, *ib.* 1789-90, 8vo, 2 vols. Cours complet de Chirurgie, par B. Bell, *ib.* 1796, 6 vols, 8vo. Traité de la Gonorrhée Virulente de B. Bell, *ib.* 1802, 2 vols, 8vo. Mémoire sur les Causes de l'Hydrophobie, *ib.* 1802, in the Memoirs of the Medical Society of Emulation, (tom. v.) in which he maintains the absurd opinion, that this disease does not depend upon any specific virus. Bosquillon also published a letter condemning the edition of the Aphorisms of Hippocrates, put forth in 1779, in Greek and Latin, by Lefebvre, of Villebrune, and convicted this editor of several gross omissions and interpolations. He likewise translated Lawrence's Observations on a particular affection of the testis, Paris, 1808, 8vo. He also translated part for the Abrégé of the Transactions of the Royal Society of London. He furnished the terms in medicine and natural history to the Vocabulaire de Wailly; and revised the translation of Sprengel's History of Medicine. He had contemplated the publication of editions of various works, which death prevented him from accomplishing.

BOSSCHA, (Hermann,) a distinguished Dutch philosopher and antiquary, and one of the best Latin poets of modern times, born at Leeuwarden, 1755, educated first in his native town, and then in philology and jurisprudence at the university of Franeker, where, when scarcely twenty, he became rector of the Latin school. In 1780 he was appointed rector of the school at Deventer; but, in 1787, was dismissed from this office on account of his revolutionary principles, which he did not attempt to conceal, and was for two years without public employment. In 1795 he was appointed professor of history, antiquities, rhetoric, and Greek literature at Harderwyk. In 1798 he declined the situation of chief of the first office in the department of the ministry of the interior, offered him by the republican government. He was afterwards successively professor of history and antiquities at Gröningen, rector of the Latin school at Amsterdam, and professor of the history of the middle ages and of Holland to the Athenæum of that city. He died August 12, 1819. His Latin poems, Musa Daventriaca, 1786, and his Pax Ambiensis, (on the peace of Amiens, which he recited before the assembled academy at Harderwyk, and which was reprinted by Didot at Paris,) have a true poetical value, and are at the same time classically correct. He translated Blair's Rhetoric; Plutarch's Lives; Denon's work on Egypt; Schiller's Revolt of the Netherlands; and wrote a very useful classical hand-book of mythology, antiquities, and history. (Bibliotheca Classica, 1794.) He is also the author of a not very satisfactory history of the revolution in Holland, in 1813, of which there is a German translation.

BOSSCHAERT, (Thomas Willibrord,) an eminent painter, born at Bergen-op-Zoom, in 1613, and educated under Segers, at Antwerp, where then resided some of the greatest masters of the Flemish school. Having greatly profited there, his instructor advised him to visit Italy for farther improvement. After a residence of four years at Rome, he returned to the Low Countries, and acquired a reputation no less high than merited. His style nearly resembles that of Vandyck, both in history and portrait. His colouring is extremely tender and harmonious, his touch is free and spirited, his heads are graceful, and his finishing is often exquisite. Hence his works, though placed by those of Rubens and Vandyck, are still admired as noble specimens of the Flemish school. Bosschaert died at Antwerp in 1656. (Bryan. Pilkington.)

BOSSCHE, (William van der,) an eminent physician at Liège, in the seventeenth century. His only known work is, Historia Medica, in quâ Libris IV. Animalium Natura et eorum Medica Utilitas exactè et luculenter tractantur Brux. 1639, 4to.

BOSSE, (Abraham,) an able French engraver, and author upon artistical subjects, born at Tours, in 1611. He received a very good education there, and becoming eventually very intimate with the celebrated Desargues, he acquired a fund of geometrical knowledge which served him most essentially both as an artist and a writer. He engraved a great number of plates, chiefly from his own designs, in a bold masterly manner. Among his artistical works, the following have been reprinted:—Traité de diverses Manières de Graver en Taille douce. Manière de Dessiner les Ordres d'Architecture. Bosse died in his native town, in 1678. (Bryan. Biog. Univ.)

BOSSI, (Benign,) a designer and engraver, born in the Milanese, in 1727, and resident for some time at Dresden. Being under the necessity of leaving that place in the seven years' war, he went to Parma, and was patronized by the duke. (Bryan.)

BOSSIUS, (James,) a Flemish engraver, born about 1520, chiefly resident at Rome. His work is neat, but rather stiff; and although his drawing is not very correct, he has produced prints of considerable merit. (Bryan.)

BOSSO, (Donatus,) a Milanese advocate, born in 1436, author of two works, printed in a very rare folio volume, at Milan, in 1492. The former work, known as Chronica Bossiana, is a sort of compendious universal history from the world's beginning to the author's time; the latter is a history of the prelates of Milan, from the first to 1489. (Clement. Biog. Univ.)

BOSSO, (Jerome,) born at Pavia, in 1588, of a noble Milanese family, first professor of eloquence at Milan, afterwards of elegant literature at Pavia, known as author of a treatise on the Roman *toga*, and of some similar pieces to be found in Sallengre's Thesaurus of Roman Antiquities. (Biog. Univ.)

BOSSO, (Matthew,) an Italian writer of Latin, considerably noted in his day, born at Verona in 1427. He was sent early to Milan for education, and made a most satisfactory progress; but his friends became uneasy about his morals in a city so dissipated, and hastily recalled him to Verona. He soon discovered a very serious frame of mind, and, in 1451, became a canon regular in the congregation of St. John of Lateran. He subsequently filled several ecclesiastical employments with great credit; among them, a visitation of the Genoese nunneries, which had become extremely corrupt. As a reward for these services, Sixtus IV. thrice offered him a bishopric, but Bosso declined. So much did Laurence de' Medici value him, that he chose him for the solemn delivery of the ensigns of the cardinalate to his son John, afterwards Leo X., who had been enrolled in the sacred college when so young a boy, that his patron, Innocent VIII., made a bargain, to save appearances, that he should not assume the Roman purple until after the lapse of three years. Bosso died at Padua, in 1502, highly respected for scholarship, acuteness, eloquence, and moral worth. His epistles are the most interesting of his works, and have been several times reprinted. His dialogue, De Veris ac Salutaribus Animi Gaudiis, having become very scarce, was reprinted by Mabillon, in the Musæum Italicum, and it has been translated into Italian. His whole works were published at Bologna, in 1627, except the third book, or volume of epistles, which, on account of its extreme rarity, escaped the editor's notice. (Bayle. Chalmers. Biog. Univ.)

BOSSU, (René le,) an eminent French critic, born at Paris, March 16, 1631. He was a canon regular in the abbey of St. Geneviève, and, at one time, taught elegant literature in several religious houses, but at length retired from this monotonous drudgery to read and write according to the bent of his own inclinations. His leisure proved prolific, in 1674, of a parallel between the physical principles of Aristotle and those of Des Cartes. But he was not considered very successful in his intended reconciliation of the two philosophers, either from substantial differences between them, or his own imperfect acquaintance with their systems. In 1675 he published a dissertation on the epic poem, which long passed for a standard piece of criticism, and was translated into English in 1719. Its day is, however, gone, a fanciful train of thought, which has been carefully exposed, having diverted public attention from the sound observations which it really contains. Bossu died March 14, 1680. (Chalmers. Morhof.)

BOSSUET, (James Benign,) one of the most famous of Romish controversialists, born at Dijon, September 27, 1627, of an eminent legal family. His earlier education was conducted by the Jesuits in his native city, and a circumstance occurred to him when very young which strikingly marks the difference between protestant and Romish countries. A Latin Bible accidentally fell in his way, and he read it with such an interest as no lapse of years allowed him to forget. Among protestants, almost every reading child is first interested by the Bible. Had Bossuet lighted upon Scripture somewhat later than he did, he might, perhaps, have noticed how our Saviour treats the operation of men's traditions upon the ancient Jewish faith, and have thus been spoiled for advocating any religious system that makes large appeals to an unwritten word. But children chiefly read the Bible for the facts; and when Bossuet was becoming ripe for doctrinal inquiry, his mind was stored with prejudice and sophistry. His later studies were pursued at Paris, and with such brilliant success, that common fame pointed at him as a prodigy. His attention was principally bestowed upon Scripture and the fathers; and among the latter, Austin was his great authority. In 1652 he took his doctor's degree, and was ordained priest. Soon afterwards he removed to Metz, where he was canon, and subsequently grand archdeacon and dean. His abilities were soon put into requisition there by the bishop, who wished for a refutation of a catechism by Paul Ferry, a protestant minister of high character. Bossuet undertook this office, and performed it, not only to the satisfaction of his own party, but also in such a manner as to make a favourable impression upon his opponents. The conversion of the protestants was now a favourite scheme at court; and Anne of Austria, the queen mother, considered Bossuet, from his refutation of Ferry's catechism, as admirably fitted for a Romish mission in the diocese of Metz. He showed himself quite equal to the duty, having great success. There had long been, in fact, among the French, a growing disposition to profess the same religion that was generally professed by the great, and exclusively patronized in high quarters. Hence a man of Bossuet's abilities and address could find no great difficulty in thinning the ranks of French protestantism. His rural labours were varied occasionally by calls to Paris upon business for the chapter of Metz. In these visits to the capital he displayed pulpit eloquence of the highest order, and the queen mother followed him every where. By her means he was appointed to preach before the king in the Advent of 1661, and in the following Lent, an honour very unusual for a divine of 34. He acquitted himself, however, so as to secure a succession of similar distinctions, and in 1669 he was nominated bishop of Condom. He was consecrated to this see at Pontoise, in the general assembly of the clergy of France, Sept. 21, 1670, but he only held it about twelve months, finding the duties of a distant diocese quite incompatible with those of tutor to the dauphin, which he became immediately after his consecration. For his royal pupil Bossuet composed his discourse on universal history, and some other works, but he has not been considered so successful in tuition as he was in most of his undertakings. He might not, undoubtedly, have had materials to work upon of sufficient plasticity; but it is probable, besides, that his own disposition and habits wanted the pliancy required for giving instruction, especially to a prince. He acquitted himself, however, so much to the king's satisfaction, that he was appointed, in 1680, first almoner to the dauphiness, and in 1681, bishop of Meaux. Other honours flowed in upon him, and in 1697 he was made counsellor of state. He died at Paris, full of a controversy with the Socinians, April 12, 1704, and was buried in his cathedral at Meaux.

Of Bossuet's numerous works, the ablest has been thought his Discours sur l'Histoire Universelle, first published in 1681, and often reprinted. It has three divisions, of which the first is chronological, based on the labours of archbishop Ussher; the second is a series of reflections on the truth and condition of religion; the third is a comprehensive and noble view of the great political revolutions down to the time of Charlemagne. Every preceding view of a subject so immense had been superficial and uninteresting. It was reserved for the mighty genius of Bossuet to discern an unity and trace a coherence in the greater movements of human affairs, that group them into one instructive and delightful whole. Still it is this able man's controversial talents that have chiefly earned his fame. His refutation of Ferry's catechism, already mentioned, appeared in 1655. In 1671 appeared his Exposition de l'Eglise Catholique sur les Matières de Controverse; a work of small extent, but most carefully considered, which has been translated into various languages, and incessantly reprinted. It was written for the use of two brothers of the Dangeau family; and having been shown to Turenne, the most eminent protestant remaining in France, it induced him to become a Romanist. No work has been found in later years so serviceable to the papal church as this. It is confidently cited by Romish advocates as a complete answer to those who charge their system with indefensible absurdities. The author undoubtedly manages to keep baffling questions very much out of sight. He undertakes no defence of any doctrine unsanctioned by the council of Trent, and in this his ground is chosen fairly no less than judiciously. But then he maintains it unfairly, by declining any farther notice to all rites and usages, however general, or sanctioned by the regular discipline of his church, than the council obliges him to take. Hence he glides with a transient step over the invocation of departed spirits, and the religious veneration of images. Thus he pares down a system that may give tolerable satisfaction to inquiring minds, leaving unregarded the colossal mass of superstitions which meet a Romish population at every turn. It was impossible that acute advocates of the papal church should have contemplated without alarm this abandonment of their most vulnerable points to shift for themselves; and Bossuet himself appears to have had his own misgivings as to the safety of such a policy. Hence his exposition, short as it is, was not published until more than three years after it had been written. Some MS. copies of it were taken about the year 1667. In the early part of 1671, twelve or fourteen copies of it were printed, but as the author subsequently alleged, without his order or knowledge. They were, however, for the most part, returned to him after circulation among his friends, accompanied by various MS. notes. The hints thus communicated appear to have guided Bossuet in preparing for the press the first acknowledged edition of his important work, which appeared before the close of 1671. Three copies, however, of the suppressed edition were never returned; among them was one in the hands of Turenne. One of these copies came into the possession of archbishop Wake, and is now in the archiepiscopal library at Lambeth. Two others of them are at Paris, or were so lately. Much use was made of this suppressed edition by the protestant party, because it differs from the editions regularly published in some important particulars. It speaks of the invocation of saints as merely commended by the council of Trent for goodness and utility, without being put upon the footing of necessity, or positive commandment; and it says of the mass, that it may be *reasonably* called a sacrifice. Thus people were pretty much left to judge for themselves upon the wisdom of invoking the dead, and were at liberty to think the Romish communion service hardly more of a sacrifice than other services acceptably offered to God. This, it may be observed, is the doctrine approved by the distinguished Frenchmen whose conviction professedly rested upon Bossuet's MS. But it aimed blows at the heart of Romanism. Hence, probably, the notes of the author's friends protested against it, and his authorized edition contains no such dangerous matter. Still, it contains enough to surprise the mere herd of Romanists, really leaving their faith, as it is popularly professed, in a most unguarded state. At first, accordingly, the book seems to have found little or no favour at Rome. Clement X., under whose pontificate it was published, is said to have positively refused it his approbation. Towards the close of 1676, he died; and in 1678, the book was published at Rome, Innocent XI. being then pope. By that pontiff, it was formally, but cautiously, commended in a brief dated January 4, 1679. Great stress has been laid by protestant writers upon this tardy commendation, as well as upon the original suppressed edition, more, perhaps, than the cases will fairly warrant; but obviously both of the facts are important. Romish controversialists are now anxious to deny this, and to take their stand upon Bossuet's Exposition, finding it extremely useful in dealing with inquiring minds, while it has taken no effect at all upon the great mass of their people. There was an excellent answer to this famous tract published by La Bastide, one of the most eminent protestant ministers in France, which Bossuet was at length compelled to leave in possession of the field.

Another of Bossuet's more famous controversial works, is his Histoire des Variations des Eglises Protestantes, published in 1688, and often reprinted. Few things are more splendid in polemical writing than the exposure of Luther's weak points in this book. Nor does the illustrious bishop of Meaux ever fail to make the most of all the advantages afforded him by protestant religious history. But his theory may easily be used against himself. If variations in religious belief and practice are evidences that a church is not guided by the Divine Spirit, and if the vices or follies of teachers demonstrate unsoundness in the doctrines taught, then the church of Rome has abundantly forfeited claims to the confidence of mankind. Against the Variations, James Basnage wrote his famous Histoire des Eglises Reformées, Rotterd. 2 vols, 8vo. Bossuet replied to this in his Defence de l'Histoire des Variations; on which Basnage composed his great work, Histoire de l'Eglise de Jésus-Christ jusqu'à présent, Rotterd. 2 vols. fol. Bossuet's fame, however, was invulnerable in France, and he came to be regarded as the regular champion of the Roman church there. John Claude was equally regarded by the French protestants. The two had, accordingly, a regular conference in 1678, before madame Duras, a protestant lady, who, like most others of her condition in society, was veering towards the court religion. The dispute entirely turned on church authority, and Bossuet's arguments gave the lady a decent pretext for conforming to Romanism. Yet nothing can be more flimsy than his charge of presumption upon those who set up their individual judgments against the acquiescence of large masses. It is a sophism which, if good for any thing, would serve as a defence for paganism;

and it merely goes to stifle inquiry, because the bulk of men neglect it, or are incapable of it. Bossuet published an account of this conference, entitled, Conférence avec M. Claude sur la Matière de l'Eglise, Paris, 1683, 12mo. In answer to this, Claude wrote his Réponse au Livre de M. de Meaux, intitulé Conférence avec M. Claude, à la Haye, 1683, 8vo. The famed prelate of Meaux did not, however, stand forth upon every occasion as the champion of Rome. Lewis XIV. took upon himself the privilege of receiving the revenues of all vacant bishoprics in his kingdom, although immemorial usage had exempted many of them from the operation of this royal prerogative. Innocent XI. resisted this innovation, and Lewis convened, in consequence, the famous assembly of the Gallican clergy, in 1682. Bossuet preached at the opening of this assembly, and his sermon is one of the noblest efforts of his genius. He was afterwards commissioned to prepare the four articles, which the assembly, rather at the instigation, perhaps, of Colbert, than of its own accord, promulgated as the Gallican creed, on the limitations of papal authority. Of his conduct on this delicate occasion, he wrote an elaborate Latin defence in the years 1683 and 1684, but it was not published until 1730, when it appeared at Luxemburg, in 2 vols, 4to, with this title, Defensio Declarationis celeberrimæ quam de Potestate Ecclesiastica sanxit Clerus Gallicanus, 19 Martii, 1682, ab illus. ac rev. Jacobo Benigno Bossuet, Meldensi Episcopo, ex speciali jussu Ludovici Magni scripta. This work was put into the Roman index of prohibited books, a remarkable fate for even the posthumous progeny of a powerful intellect ever intent upon protecting the papal creed.

Bossuet was also engaged in controversy with the mystics. Madame Guyon's theory of a religious life within the breasts of individuals, having evidently, from its incessant reappearance under different forms, a strong affinity for certain minds, and being supported by the fair apostle's own unquestionable excellences, was making rapid way, even at court. Few watched its progress with more uneasiness than Bossuet. He had spent a laborious life in building up a system of observances, and he could not bear to hear that nothing was of much value but a heavenly cast of thought, which the world could neither see nor understand. He undertook, accordingly, to refute madame Guyon, whose influence had already exposed her to active persecution, and this embroiled him in a controversy with Fenelon, who admired her, and maintained that her principles were those of several eminent saints. By his work in her defence, entitled, Explication des Maximes des Saints sur la Vie intérieure, published in 1697, the bishop of Meaux was violently offended, and he never ceased from importunities to Lewis XIV. and Innocent XII., until, in 1699, the book was formally branded at Rome as erroneous. Fenelon's name was not mentioned, but either his humility or want of spirit led him to unreserved submission under the censures pronounced against his opinions. Bossuet published several works upon this question towards the close of the seventeenth century, but it was his misfortune to have a man for an opponent so amiable as Fenelon. His character suffers considerably by the contrast, and accordingly those who admire him, have reason to regret that madame Guyon was contemporary with himself. Perhaps, after all, his sermons, especially the funeral orations, are among the most striking evidences of this great man's genius; but it is his controversial pieces that keep Bossuet before the world. (Moreri. Hallam's Literature of Europe. Mosheim. Mendham's Literary Policy of the Ch. of Rome. Biog. Univ. Clement.)

BOSSUET, (James Benign,) nephew of the preceding, eventually bishop of Troyes. He was editor of his uncle's voluminous works, in which he inserted a large mass of correspondence, that might well be spared, relating to himself. He also published a judicious abridgement of the great Bossuet's work on the four articles of the clergy of 1682, and prepared a missal for his cathedral, containing innovations that excited a violent clamour. He died at Paris, July 12, 1743, aged 82. (Biog. Univ.)

BOSTON, (John,) a monk of St. Edmundsbury, referred to 1410, one of the first collectors of English lives. Having examined most of the libraries in the kingdom, he made a catalogue of authors, with short opinions of them. He also wrote a history of monachism. (Chalmers.)

BOSTON, (Thomas,) a Scottish divine, born at Dunse, March 17, 1676, and educated at Edinburgh. In 1699 he was ordained to the parish of Simprin, which in 1707 he exchanged for Etterick. He now devoted himself to the study of Hebrew, particularly to the Hebrew accents, concerning which he published a learned treatise in Latin. He is, however, better known by his Fourfold State, 1720; and in Scotland his Body of Divinity, 3 vols, 8vo, is still much esteemed. He left a memoir of his own life and times, printed in 1776. He died May 20, 1732. (Chalmers.)

BOSVILLE, (James,) from whom a tribe of gipsies is denominated "Bosville's Gang." He died January 30, 1708, and was buried in the churchyard of Rossington, near Doncaster, where a stone was erected to his memory, the two ends of which still remain. For a number of years the gipsies from the south made an annual pilgrimage to it, and among other ceremonies, poured a flagon of ale upon the grave. (Miller's Doncaster.)

BOSWELL, (James,) the friend and biographer of Johnson, born at Edinburgh, October 29, 1740. His father, named Alexander, was a judge, and called, according to Scottish usage, lord Auchinleck, from his estate. He wished the son to follow his own profession, and eventually induced him to do so, although long bent upon entering the army. After studying the law at Edinburgh, Glasgow, and Utrecht, and making the grand tour of Europe, young Boswell was called to the Scottish bar. He had previously been introduced to Dr. Johnson, whose acquaintance forms the main distinction of his life. He always entertained a great predilection for London, and removing thither in 1785, he was called to the English bar. He died in the metropolis, soon after a visit to Auchinleck, June 19, 1795. His own family was good, and he married a lady with a like recommendation, who died before him, leaving two sons and three daughters. Besides some pamphlets, Boswell published an Account of Corsica, with Memoirs of General Paoli; a Journal of Dr. Johnson's Tour to the Hebrides; and that eminent person's life. The last appeared in 1790, and is one of the most interesting biographies extant. It places before the reader, in a manner highly graphical, both Johnson and his biographer. The latter undoubtedly does not make any very dignified appearance, the exhibition of himself being generally that of an obsequious admirer and diligent chronicler; but he thereby forms an amusing contrast to the dogmatical dignity of the principal personage. Thus Boswell has furnished, partly at his own expense, one of the most entertaining books in the English language; and Mr. Croker has lately done good service, by editing, with additions, a work so worthy, upon several accounts, of public notice. (Chalmers.)

BOTALLI, (Leonard,) a celebrated physician, born at Asti, in Piedmont, who studied under Fallopius; and after serving as surgeon in the French army, settled in Paris in 1564. He was made physician in chief to Charles IX. and to the duke of Alençon, son of Henry II., whom he accompanied into England, and afterwards to the Low Countries, where this prince, as duke of Brabant and count of Flanders, held the reins of government. He subsequently became physician to Henry III. Botalli exercised considerable influence on the practice of physic; he freely urged the necessity of bleeding in many cases in which previously it had either been totally forbidden, or in which the greatest circumspection with regard to its employment had been exercised. His doctrines and his practice were condemned as heretical by the faculty of Paris, and were severely criticised by Bonaventura Granger. Botalli, however, sustained his opinions, and relied upon the authority of Hippocrates, Galen, and the Arabian physicians. He unquestionably carried his practice to excess; but he effected much good by dispelling vain fears generally entertained by the French practitioners of his day. His contributions to medical and surgical knowledge have been put together with notes, by J. Van Horne, under the title of Opera Omnia Medica et Chirurgica, Lugd. 1660, 8vo.

BOTERO, (John,) an Italian political writer, born at Bene, in Piedmont, in 1540, and at one time connected with the Jesuits; but he left their body in 1581, without having made his profession. He was afterwards, in succession, secretary to the sainted Charles Borromeo, envoy from his sovereign to the court of France, employed by the *Propaganda* to collect religious information in foreign countries, and tutor to the young Savoyard princes. He died at Turin, in 1617, chiefly celebrated for a political work, entitled Della Ragione di Stato, which has been translated into various languages, and was once extensively read. It justifies the massacre of St. Bartholomew, and all the atrocities of that age, but recommends the removal of obnoxious persons with as much silence and secrecy as possible. Botero had, however, thought, read, and observed, more than most men, and his views are sometimes luminous. Among his remarks deserving notice, is the inefficacy of encouraging matrimony for the purpose of increasing population, without a simultaneous provision for the people's maintenance, and the due nurture of children. Botero also published a geographical work, entitled, Relazioni Universali, describing, in a general manner, as much of the world as was then known. (Biog. Univ. Hallam's Literature of Europe, ii. 202, 493.)

BOTH, (John and Andrew,) two Dutch artists, brothers, of great celebrity, born at Utrecht early in the seventeenth century. Their father, a painter on glass, after teaching them the rudiments of design, placed them under Abraham Bloemart. They then went to Italy, and worked conjointly with the most complete success, John painting exquisite landscapes, which Andrew decorated with figures altogether worthy of them. The two brothers thus produced pictures of extraordinary merit, which appear like products of the same hand. Unfortunately their affectionate union was abruptly terminated by the death of Andrew, who fell into a canal at Venice, and was drowned. John immediately returned home, and painted landscapes in his native city, employing Polemburg to people them with figures. But he never got over his loss at Venice. In 1650, which was about five years afterwards, he died. (Bryan. Pilkington.)

BOTHWIDI, a Swedish prelate, the ecclesiastical adviser of Gustavus Adolphus, whom he accompanied in all his expeditions. He was born in 1575, and died in 1635, leaving several works, among them a Swedish funeral oration on Gustavus Adolphus, and a Latin piece, published during war with Russia, entitled, Utrum Moscovitæ sint Christiani. (Biog. Univ.)

BOTIN, (Andrew,) a Swedish historian, born in 1724, dead in 1790. He published, between 1754 and 1764, an excellent history of his country. The public was also indebted to him for a Swedish topographical work, observations on the national language, and a life of Birger. (Biog. Univ.)

BOTT, (John de,) an eminent architect, born in France, of protestant parents, in 1670. After the revocation of the edict of Nantes, he went into Holland, and was favourably received by the prince of Orange, eventually William III. of England. He died at Dresden, in 1745. (Chalmers.)

BOTT, (Thomas,) an English clergyman, born at Derby in 1688, of an ancient Staffordshire family, and brought up a dissenter. After being minister of a presbyterian congregation at Spalding, Lincolnshire, he removed to London, and for some time studied physic; but on the accession of George I. his devotion to whig principles induced him to take orders, and he obtained three benefices in Norfolk. In 1752 his faculties began to fail, and he removed to Norwich, where he died, September 23, 1754. His opinions very much coincided with Hoadly's, and might have passed for those of an ancient pagan philosopher converted to Christianity. He published several sermons and pamphlets; among them, remarks on bishop Butler's doctrine of necessity, and another, considered his best work, in answer to the first volume of Warburton's Divine Legation.

BOTTA, (Marc Antony,) a respectable Genoese painter of history and portrait, who died, aged seventy-six, in 1648. (Pilkington.)

BOTTALLA, (John Maria,) an Italian painter, who died at Milan, aged 31, in 1644, called *Il Raffaellino*, from his great veneration for Raphael's works, to which, however, his own bear no resemblance, being in the style of Peter of Cortona. (Pilkington. Bryan.)

BOTTANI, (Joseph,) an Italian landscape painter, of considerable reputation, in the style of Gaspar Poussin. He occasionally painted history. He died at Mantua, in 1784, aged 67. (Pilkington. Bryan.)

BOTTARI, (John Gaetan,) a learned Italian prelate, born at Florence, Jan. 15, 1689, and first known to the literary world as principal editor of the new edition of the *Vocabulario della Crusca*, which appeared in 1738 and following years, in six volumes folio. After presiding with credit over the grand-ducal press in his native city, he established himself at Rome in 1730, and was appointed keeper of the Vatican library. He was patronized by successive popes, and died at Rome, June 3, 1775. He was author and editor of numerous works; among them, of Vasari's Lives of Artists, which came from his hands much improved; and of the famous Vatican Virgil, with a learned preface of his own. This work was published in 1741, with the following title, Antiquissimi Virgiliani

Codicis Fragmenta et Picturæ, ex Vaticana Bibliotheca, ad priscas Imaginum Formas a Petro Sancte Bartoli incisæ. (Chalmers. Biog. Univ.)

BOTTONI, (Dominic,) an eminent physician, born at Leontini, in Sicily, October 6, 1641, who, after teaching philosophy at Naples, returned to his native island, where he died at the advanced age of ninety years. He is the first Sicilian philosopher associated with the Royal Society of London, of which he was admitted a corresponding member in 1697, having previously sent, Idea Historico-Physica de magno Trinacriæ Terræ-motu, published in its Transactions.

BOVADILLA, (Jerome,) an excellent Spanish painter of history and perspective, born at Antequera. He died in 1680, age 60. (Bryan.)

BOUCHARDON, (Esme,) a French sculptor, of distinguished ability, born at Chaumont, in Bassigni, in 1698. After greatly improving himself in Italy, he returned home, and adorned Paris with his works. He died July 17, 1762, much regretted, not only as a loss to the arts, but also as a man unusually disinterested and amiable. (Chalmers. Biog. Univ.)

BOUCHAUD, (Matthew Anthony,) a learned French jurisconsult, born at Paris, April 16, 1719, of an ancient Provençal family, allied to that of Gassendi. He was at college with d'Alembert, who obtained for him the office of supplying legal articles to the famous *Encyclopédie*, but his colleagues disagreed with him violently; rather a presumption that he did not share in their execrable opinions. Among these vexatious incidents he found relief in translating some of Apostolo Zeno's dramas from the Italian, and Brooke's novel of Julia Mandeville, from the English. In 1763 he appeared before the public in a graver attitude, and as an original author, publishing his Essai sur la Poésie Rythmique, which was reprinted, with other pieces, under the title of Antiquités Poétiques. He then produced a series of works connected with classical literature and his own profession. In 1766 appeared his Essai Historique sur l'Impôt du Vingtième sur les Successions, et de l'Impôt sur les Marchandises chez les Romains. He was now elected a member of the Academy of Inscriptions, and immediately showed his fitness for that compliment by producing a Mémoire sur les Sociétés que formèrent les Publicains pour la Levée des Impôts chez les Romains. About the same time he published some historical essays on laws, translated from the English; but France was not ripe for these deep speculations, which had attracted great notice in England, and Bouchaud's book was little regarded. In 1774, a professorship of natural and national law being founded in the Royal College of France, Bouchaud was chosen to fill it; but his only contribution to the fund of knowledge which he was thus employed to disseminate, appeared in the preceding year, entitled, Théorie des Traités de Commerce entre les Nations. In 1784, Bouchaud published a work, based on one by a German legal scholar, entitled, Recherches Historiques sur la Police des Romains, concernant les grands Chemins, les Rues, et les Marchés. Three years afterwards appeared his Commentaire sur la Loi des Douze Tables. This was reprinted, with considerable additions, at the expense of government, in 1803. Bouchaud closed his long and meritorious career, February 1, 1804, at the age of eighty-five. (Biog. Univ.)

BOUCHE, the surname of some Provençal authors.—*Honorius*, a clergyman, born at Aix, in 1598; left an historical topography of Provence, the best, perhaps, of any ancient French province; written originally in Latin, but translated by himself into French. He published it at Aix, in 1664.—His brother, *Balthazar*, a lawyer, wrote an excellent discussion on the jurisprudence of his province.—*Charles Francis*, probably of the same family, a lawyer, who figured in the States General of 1789, as an opponent of the clergy and an advocate of religious toleration; left some works upon the history of Provence, its famous men, and fiscal burthens. He died about 1794. (Biog. Univ.)

BOUCHEL, (Laurence,) one of the best French canonists, born in 1559, chiefly remarkable as compiler of, Decretorum Ecclesiæ Gallicanæ ex Conciliis, Paris, 1609, and 1621, fol.; and of Somme Bénéficiale, 1628, reprinted, in 1689, under the title of Bibliothèque Canonique, with great improvements by Blondeau, 2 vols, fol.—(Arnold,) a lawyer at Utrecht, where he died in 1641, having published a description of it. Its history, which he had founded upon a former work by Furnerius, was published two years after his death. Both works are in Latin. (Biog. Univ.)

BOUCHER, (Peter,) governor of Trois Rivières, in Canada, who, being sent to France, about the year 1664, to represent the wants of the colony, published, during his stay, an account of Canada, entitled, Histoire véritable et naturelle des Mœurs et Productions de la Nouvelle France; a superficial but accurate production. The author lived nearly 100 years. (Carter's Amer. Biog. Dict.)

BOUCHER, (Peter Joseph,) a medical practitioner at Lille, born May 10, 1715, distinguished by proficiency in anatomy. He was physician to the hospitals, which, after the battle of Fontenoy, in 1745, received a great number of the wounded, to whom Boucher paid great attention, and gave the results of his practice to the Royal Academy of Surgery. He died June 22, 1793, not having produced any extensive work, but many very important practical papers, some of which have been published by the Royal Academy of Sciences of Paris. He was elected a member of that body in 1751.

BOUCHER, (Francis,) a French painter and engraver, born in 1704, highly patronized in his day, but now little valued.—(Giles,) a Jesuit, who died at Tournay, in 1665, leaving some Latin works on the history of Belgium, and the early history of France. He is the first author who treated successfully the history of the French kings of the first race.—(John,) a fanatical divine on the Romish side, notorious for some violent publications, and an inflammatory sermon preached against Henry IV., May 12, 1593. He subsequently preached against that monarch's *simulated conversion, and the nullity of his pretended absolution.* These sermons were burnt by the hangman. Boucher soon afterwards was obliged to flee, and became archdeacon of the cathedral of Tournay. Having ventured upon a return to France, he would have been punished for his violence, had not Henry's clemency protected him. He showed himself quite unworthy of this forbearance, continuing at Tournay his old strain of writing. He died there very aged, about 1644.—Another John Boucher, a French observantine friar, published at Paris, in 1616, Le Bouquet Sacré, often reprinted, a fantastical account of his travels in Palestine, betraying gross ignorance, and describing things which he seems never to have seen.

BOUCHER, (Jonathan,) an English divine, born in Cumberland, March 12, 1738, who went to North America in his sixteenth year, and after returning to England for ordination, was in due time beneficed in Virginia. He subsequently exchanged his first preferment for other churches in succession, and he continued in America until the revolutionary war drove all such unbending loyalists as he was out of the country. His opinions upon the contest between Great Britain and her late colonies were eventually given to the world, in A View of the Causes and Consequences of the American Revolution, in thirteen discourses, preached in North America, between the years 1763 and 1775. In 1784, long after his return to England, he was presented to the vicarage of Epsom, in Surrey, by the learned, amiable, and conscientious John Parkhurst, author of the Greek and Hebrew Scripture Lexicons, who knew him only by character, but thought himself unable to discharge his trust as an ecclesiastical patron more satisfactorily, than in preferring a learned, worthy clergyman, who had abandoned home and living rather than violate his obligations as an Englishman. Subsequently Boucher published two assize sermons, and an anonymous pamphlet, subscribed A Cumberland Man, suggesting means of improving his native county. He also contributed importantly to Hutchinson's history of it. His chief attention was, however, given, during the last fourteen years of his life, to a glossary of ancient and provincial words, intended as a supplement to Johnson's Dictionary. This was left incomplete at his death, April 27, 1804, but a portion, containing words under the letter A, was published in 1807. The remainder was purchased of his family, in 1831, by the proprietors of the English edition of Dr. Webster's Dictionary, to form a supplement to that work. (Chalmers. Life of Parkhurst, prefixed to his Greek Lexicon. Allen's Americ. Biog. Dict.)

BOUCHET, (John,) the names of two French authors; the elder, born at Poitiers, in 1476, wrote poetry, now very rarely read, the Annals of Aquitaine, with the Antiquities of Poitou, printed in 1524, and again, with improvements, in 1644; and a folio volume of epistles, printed in 1545, esteemed the most curious of his works.—The other Bouchet, who died in 1684, was a genealogist, whose works are deemed valuable in France by those who take an interest in such inquiries. (Biog. Univ.)

BOUCHET, (Peter,) a distinguished surgeon of Lyons, where he was born January 6, 1752. He was the first to apply the hard knot in cases of internal polypi. He died January 6, 1794, exhausted by the labours consequent upon the siege of his native city.

BOUDET, (John Peter,) once an apothecary at Rheims, where he was born in 1748. There he became connected with a learned society, of which, in 1782, Pilâtre de Rozier was the professor of chemistry as applied to the arts. In 1783, upon the accident which caused that aëronaut's death, Boudet succeeded to his chair; but in 1785 he went to Paris, and when the revolution broke out, he espoused its principles. In 1793, the Committee of Public Health, upon the recommendation of Berthollet, named him inspector of the department of the east, for the collecting of saltpetre and the manufacture of gunpowder. His exertions in this capacity were so successful, that the Executive Directory, in 1798, made him apothecary-in-chief to the army destined for the expedition to Egypt, and he was attached to the commission of the sciences and the arts, known as the Egyptian Institute. General Kleber confided to him the direction of the pharmacy of the marine. Upon the return of the expedition to Paris in 1802, he was made apothecary-in-chief to the Hôpital de la Charité; he was afterwards appointed to the camp at Bruges, and received from the hands of Buonaparte the decoration of the legion of honour. In 1805 and 1807, he made the campaigns of Austria and Prussia. His age, and its attendant infirmities, prevented him from accompanying marshal Massena to Portugal, and he obtained leave to retire to his former appointment at La Charité, where he remained for some time. He is not much known as a writer, but he assisted in editing several works, and was particularly consulted upon the pharmacopœia for the use of the hospitals, &c. He wrote on the Prussian Blue, on Phosphorus, (published separately at Paris in 1815, 4to,) and an Historical Notice on the Art of Making Glass in Egypt, which was inserted in the Journal de Pharmacie, 1824. He died at the age of eighty, at Paris, in 1829.

BOUDEWYNS, (Michael,) a physician, born at Antwerp, who, after studying philosophy and theology, applied to medicine, and was received as M.D. at Paris in 1642. He settled in his native city, where he was chosen professor of anatomy and surgery. He died of an attack of apoplexy, October 29, 1681, having published, Est-ne decimestris Partus perfectissimus? Paris, 1642, 4to. Oratio de Sancto Lucâ Evangelistâ et Medico, Antuerp. 1660, 4to. Pharmacia Antuerpiensis Galeno-Chymica, &c. *ib.* Ventilabrum Medico-Theologicum, *ib.* 1666, 4to.

BOUDON, (Henry Maria,) godson to Henrietta Maria, daughter of Henry IV. and eventually queen of Great Britain. He was born in 1624, and became archdeacon of Evreux, where he died, in 1720, extensively venerated for piety, leaving several French works of a nature highly ascetic and mystic, but not written sufficiently well to maintain their ground even in France, and little likely to please foreign protestants. (Biog. Univ.)

BOUDOT, a name known in French bibliography.—*John*, a printer, who died at Paris in 1706, published a dictionary, Latin and French, often reprinted, extracted from a much longer dictionary, of which he bought the MS. from the author, Peter Nicholas Blondeau.—His elder son, also named *John*, who followed the same business, and died in 1754, amassed, with great skill, copious materials for a bibliographical work, which he thought of publishing, and for the compilation of which he was admirably qualified.—A younger brother of his, *Peter John*, known as the abbé Boudot, was in the Royal Library, and in conjunction with the abbé Sallier, compiled the catalogue of it. He also wrote an historical essay on Aquitaine, and defended the president Henault's Abregé Chronologique de l'Histoire de France, a work of which he appears to have been really in a great measure the author. He died at Paris, September 6, 1771. (Biog. Univ.)

BOUETTE DE BLEMUR, (Jacqueline,) a Benedictine nun, of good family, who took the veil in the celebrated abbey founded by the Conqueror's wife at Caen. She died March 24, 1696, having written the Benedictine Year, or lives of saints of her order for all the days of the year, with some other French religious books, which have gained her a place in biographical dictionaries, and which once had a certain degree of reputation. (Biog. Univ.)

BOUFLERS, the name of an estate in Picardy, between Hesdin and Abbeville, possessed by a family seated there from the twelfth century, which has produced several persons of note.—*Aléaume* de Bouflers was taken prisoner at the battle of Agincourt, in 1415, and after a detention of some length in England, ransomed by the payment of 5,000 livres.—*Lewis* de Bouflers, known as the *Strong*, brought up by his relation, John of Bourbon, duke of Enghien, uncle to Henry IV., was the Milo of his day, possessing a degree of strength and agility, very rarely conferred upon man. His unbounded confidence in these qualifications was, however, fatal to him at the siege of Pont-sur-Yonne, in 1533, where, hastily leaping the fosse and raising his visor to encourage others, he received a musket-ball near the eye, which killed him, after some hours of suffering, while still a mere youth. His brother *Adrian*, gentleman of the chamber to Henry III. was repeatedly in action during the civil wars of his day, and published, Considerations sur les Ouvrages du Créateur, ou Melanges Historiques, Paris, 1608. He died in 1622.—The great grandson of this gentleman, *Lewis Francis*, eventually duke of Bouflers, was the most illustrious member of this ancient house. He was born in 1644, brought up for the army, and rapidly became a distinguished officer. His early lessons in the art of war were learnt under Condé, Turenne, and other French generals of the first ability, so that few soldiers have risen to high commands with a better stock of military knowledge. The great glory of his life was the defence of Lisle, in 1708. In this he showed himself invariably brave, watchful, and modest, able to give orders in the midst of dangers with as much coolness as if he had been in his own private apartment. His care both of soldiers and citizens rendered him universally beloved; and although the siege lasted four months, he did not go to bed more than three times. He would have buried himself under the ruins of the place, had he not received orders from the king to surrender, that the garrison might be preserved. When he marched out, prince Eugene said to him, *I am proud of taking this place, but I should have been more so of defending it like you.* Lewis XIV. rewarded Bouflers for this admirable defence as if it had succeeded, making him a duke and peer of France, and granting the government of Flanders in reversion to his eldest son, then only ten years old. The veteran marshal might now have reasonably retired from service; but in the following year France was menaced by such dangers as made him think of being useful again, and he desired permission to go as an assistant to marshal Villars, an officer junior to himself. By him the chief command was immediately offered, but Bouflers modestly refused it, saying, *I merely came to help you with my advice and experience.* He rendered, however, most important service at the sanguinary battle of Malplaquet, in which Marlborough's usual success was purchased at such a price as rendered it unpalatable at home. Bouflers led the retreating French at the close of this desperately contested day, and in such order as greatly consoled them for the mortification of abandoning the field. He died at Fontainebleau, August 22, 1711. "In him," wrote madame de Maintenon, "the heart died last." (Moreri. Gifford's Hist. Fr. Biog. Univ.)

BOUGAINVILLE, (John Peter de,) a French miscellaneous writer, of considerable abilities, son of a notary at Paris, where he was born, December 1, 1722. His family came from Picardy. He received an excellent education, and early displayed such talents as gained him the notice of some eminent literary men. To this flattering distinction he substantiated his claim, by gaining, in 1745, the prize offered by the Academy of Inscriptions, and in the following year he was admitted a member of that body. He contributed seven dissertations to its memoirs, the most remarkable of which contains a French translation of Hanno's Periplus, and discusses, in a manner more complete than had hitherto been known, the discoveries and establishments of the Carthaginians on the coasts of Africa. Bougainville also translated cardinal Polignac's Anti-Lucretius; and although he is blamed for inexactitude, his work has been reprinted several times; nor has it been completely superseded by another translation of the same work, published in 1786, by de Bataut. In 1752, Bougainville published a parallel between Alexander's expedition to India and that of Kouli Khan; a book displaying erudition, thought, and imagination, but occasionally blemished by efforts to write finely. He died June 22, 1763, after a life of ill-health, caused by asthma. It has been said that he adverted to his infirmity when desirous of admission into the French Academy, observing, that, if elected, another opportunity must soon occur of supplying a vacancy made by his death, and that Duclos unfeelingly observed, *the academy has no concern with giving extreme unction.* But Duclos was not its secretary until 1755, and Bougainville became a member the year before. (Biog. Univ.)

BOUGAINVILLE, (Lewis Anthony, count of,) brother of the preceding, a circumnavigator of considerable renown, and as a seaman of science, well entitled to posthumous distinction. Nor should his fame be forgotten as an officer, displaying in battle considerable ability, conduct, and courage. He was born at Paris, November 11, 1729. Although he commenced his public career as an officer of cavalry, served in the capacity of aid-de-camp to the marquess of Montcalm in the memorable siege of Quebec, and ultimately became colonel of a brigade distinguished for its gallantry on all occasions, whether of attack or defence; still, singular to say, (and the remark has hitherto escaped historic note,) to him may be awarded the merit of being the *first* Frenchman who accomplished the circumnavigation of the globe. Bougainville's narrative of his voyage round the world was translated into English by P. R. Foster, and published in London in 1772, the same year in which the work in quarto made its appearance in Paris. According to concurring authorities, English as well as French, our subject volunteered the command of an expedition to the North Pole. But though his services were not accepted, still his ardent devotion to all matters connected with maritime discoveries induced him to submit to the consideration of the Royal Society of London (of which institution he had been admitted a member) a paper projecting two distinct routes, by which attempts might be made to reach the Pole, indicating that which to him seemed most desirable to adopt, and which he avowed as his determined intention to take, had he been entrusted with the sole control of the expedition. Captain Phipps, afterwards lord Mulgrave, undertook the voyage, but it would not appear that the polar navigator pursued the course which M. Bougainville considered as best calculated to ensure success. Nevertheless Phipps pushed northward as far as the 80th parallel of latitude.

On the opening of the war of 1778, Bougainville was appointed to the command of a ship of the line; and between the years 1779 and 1782, we find him participating in every encounter and general engagement which had been contested in the western world between the hostile fleets of England and of France. In the memorable conflict in which Rodney defeated the count de Grasse, April 12, 1782, *L'Auguste*, the ship commanded by Bougainville, suffered severely. This vessel, to employ the words of the most impartial, and, we might add, competent of French naval biographers, (M. Henequin, author of the *Biographie Maritime*,) "fut l'un de plus maltraités de la flotte Français." After displaying a cool and becoming bearing in battle, maintaining his station in the line to the last extremity, Bougainville, who was regarded by his companions in arms as an able and quick-sighted tactician, succeeded in rescuing, by a movement judicious as decisive, eight sail of his own immediate division from a position of imminent peril. These vessels he was fortunate enough to conduct in safety to the anchorage of St. Eustace. The count subsequently became a member of the Board of Longitude, as also one of the leading directors of La Section de Géographie et de Navigation.

The appellation of the "French Anson" has been given to Bougainville by more than one of his biographers; but, saving the attribute of personal courage common to both, there can be traced no other particulars in their respective characters, relative positions, or professional careers, which can in any way warrant the applicability of the style. In the first place, Bougainville never had to encounter the perils, privations, and disheartening disasters which attended the tedious and protracted voyages of Anson; and in the next, neither the services, nor in some instances the *disputed* discoveries of the French navigator, led to accumulation of wealth nor to consequential and responsible posts in the administration of the state affairs of his country; and lastly, in the particular of scientific attainment, the peer of England was not to be compared with the *savant* of France. Indeed, Anson was anything but a man of science. (See Anson.) After attaining the rank of contre-admiral, (vice-admiral,) Bougainville closed his earthly career at the advanced age of eighty-two, August 30, 1811.

BOUGEANT, (William Hyacinth,) a French Jesuit, of lively parts, and considerable application, born at Quimper, Nov. 4, 1690. After teaching eloquence and polite literature in some of the colleges of his order, he came to Paris, and published there, in 1739, a little sportive piece, entitled, Amusement Philosophique sur le Langage des Bêtes, founded upon an Indian fable. Of this both English and German translations appeared in due time; but popular opinion denounced it as unbecoming of a Jesuit, and the successful author was exiled to La Flèche, where he published a sort of retractation. He now turned his attention to graver pursuits, and writing history, excelled, perhaps, any Frenchman of his order in that branch of literature. His best work was not published until 1744, after his death. It was a history of the treaty of Westphalia, for which materials were found in the memoirs of the count of Avaux, one of the French plenipotentiaries. For this work he had paved the way, by publishing, in 1727, a history of the wars and negotiations preceding that famous treaty. The two works were reprinted uniformly in 1751, in 6 vols, 12mo, and form a valuable contribution to historical knowledge, although the author occasionally shows himself imperfectly master of his subject, and is rarely animated or clear unless in detailing the stirring events of war. Besides these works, Bougeant produced some of a religious, and several of a miscellaneous nature; mingling them with dramatic pieces in ridicule of Jansenism, and an ingenious attack upon Lenglet Dufresnoy's Usage des Romans, entitled, Voyage merveilleux du Prince Fanféredin dans la Romancie. This was reprinted in the Voyages Imaginaires. Probably these lighter works are those to which the genius of Bougeant was really best suited. He died at Paris, Jan. 7, 1743. (Biog. Univ.)

BOUGEREL, (Joseph,) a priest of the Oratory, born at Aix, in 1680, and honourably remembered for exposing himself during the plague at Marseilles. He died at Paris, in 1753, having published, in the preceding year, fourteen lives of illustrious natives of Provence, as a sample of a general biography of his more famous compatriots. He had published, in 1737, a life of Gassendi; and ten years before, a work for youth, on the topography and history of France. All his productions are distinguished by accuracy, but the writing is inferior. (Biog. Univ.)

BOUGUER, (Peter,) a celebrated French mathematician, born at Croissac, in Lower Brittany, February 16, 1698, and instructed in the exact sciences by his father, John Bouguer, who professed hydrography, and published a complete treatise on navigation, in the year after his son was born. This comprehensive and excellent work, reprinted in 1706, correctly delineates the state of navigation at that period. Young Bouguer proved such an apt pupil, that at fifteen, he detected an error in a professor of mathematics, who was so mortified that he immediately quitted the country. Within that year the elder Bouguer died, and the son, boy as he was, obtained his place, which he filled with distinguished reputation. In 1727 he gained a prize from the Royal Academy of Sciences for the best mode of masting ships; in 1729, for the best method of observing the heights of stars at sea; and in 1731, for the best means of observing the variation of the compass. In his piece on observing the stars at sea, he represents himself as the first who gave a legitimate solution of the curve traced by a ray of the sun descending through the atmosphere. Brook Taylor, however, had already, probably unknown to him, in his Methodus Incrementorum, obtained, by an elegant analysis, a fluxional equation, which gave all the points of the curve. Still, Bouguer's method was the first that was applied to use for astronomical purposes. In 1729 appeared his optical essay on the gradation of light, a subject on which his discoveries were eventually laid before English readers, by Dr. Priestley, in his History of Light and Colours. In 1730, Bouguer removed to Havre; in the following year he succeeded Maupertuis as associate-geometer; and in 1735, he was appointed pensioner-astronomer. In the May of this year he left France, with Godin and La Condamine, on a mission for measuring a degree of the meridian in South America. He was the soul of this expedition, from which he did not return until 1744, and which exposed him to a long series of personal inconveniences among the Cordilleras. His difficulties and discomforts were, however, abundantly made up to him by a great mass of important observations, which he communicated to the world in 1749, in his Théorie de la Figure de la Terre, a work deserving the utmost attention from students of astronomical and physical science. By this publication Bouguer's fame attained its height, but his popularity fell short of La Condamine's, who was more a man of letters than himself, and who, he fancied, took pains to appropriate praises that were really his own. This unworthy jealousy involved Bouguer in dissensions which displayed him disadvantageously, notwithstanding his unquestionable scientific eminence, and probably hastened his end. He died August 15, 1758. (Rees. Biog. Univ.)

BOUHIER, (John,) born at Dijon, March 16, 1673, began his studies under his father at the Jesuits' college of his native town, from whence at a fitting age he went to Orleans and Paris to go through a course of law. In 1692 he became a member of the parliament of

Dijon, and in 1704 its president, and three years afterwards he was elected a member of the academy on the condition of his leaving Dijon; but this his health did not permit him to do, as he was frequently attacked with fits of the gout, under which he at last sank, March 17, 1746. Within an hour of his death, when a friend who had come to see him was standing at his bedside, and was about to address him, he found the president in a state of apparently profound meditation, who made a sign to him not to disturb him, and with difficulty pronounced the words, "J'épie la mort,"—"I spy death." Besides his works on legal subjects, of which a complete edition was published by De Berry in 1787, fol., he wrote a great deal in the shape of dissertations on classical subjects, to be found in Le Journal de Trevoux, Le Mercure, and the Amœnitates Literariæ of Schelhorn, the whole amounting to fifty-six articles, of which a full account is given by Oudin, who published at Dijon, 1746, 4to, his Recherches et Dissertations sur Herodote; and amongst them is a dissertation on the origin of the Greek and Latin Alphabet, which Montfaucon printed in his Palæographia Græca, and another on the Therapeutæ mentioned by Philo Judæus, whom he endeavoured to show were not Christians, but a sect of philosophical Jews. Like the generality of law-writers, his style was rather wanting in elegance, and hence his wife told him that it was for him to think and for herself to put his thoughts on paper; and like the mass of French scholars since the time of Salmasius, he directed his attention to things rather than words, observing, to use his own expression, that "Critics have generally found it easier to alter a difficult passage, than to discover what its meaning might be without altering it;" and hence his own remarks turn rather upon historical questions than those relating to the language merely.

BOUHOURS, (Dominic,) a French critic and grammarian, born at Paris, in 1628, and made a Jesuit at sixteen. After teaching for a time in colleges of his order, he became tutor to the young princes of Longueville, and afterwards to Colbert's son. He died at Paris, after a life of incessant head-aches, May 27, 1702. His numerous works are very different in character, some being religious, others gay. Latterly he has been sometimes treated as a writer of little account, but his contemporaries quoted him with respect. One of his most popular productions, Entretiens d'Ariste et Eugène, first published in 1671, contains a dialogue between these two fictitious gentlemen upon the French language, which is really the most interesting of the whole series, and very naturally claims for the author's own tongue a superiority over every other. Another of his works, first published in 1687, and often reprinted, entitled, Manière de bien penser dans les Ouvrages d'Esprit, also in dialogue, shows acuteness and delicacy of discrimination, but a deficiency in warmth and sensibility, leading occasionally to judgments over strict and fastidious. Bouhours did, however, good service by exposing unmercifully all obscurity, exaggeration, and nonsense. As he was an acute and rigid critic, he necessarily gave a good deal of offence, and it was invidiously remarked, that although a fertile author, he had written very little that became a Jesuit. He endeavoured to silence such objections by publishing, in 1700, Pensées Ingénieuses des Pères de l'Eglise; but this gave a new triumph to his opponents, by proving clearly that he had read next to nothing of the fathers. (Biog. Univ. Hallam's Literature of Europe, iii. 475, iv. 509, 512.)

BOUILLE, (Francis Claud Amour, marquess of,) a distinguished French officer, chiefly memorable for an abortive attempt to save Lewis XVI. and his unfortunate family. The marquess was from Auvergne, and had an important command in the West Indies, during the American war, the duties of which he fulfilled very much to his honour. On the conclusion of peace, he travelled in England, and other countries of Europe. When the revolution broke out, Bouillé was in command at Metz, and he endeavoured earnestly to preserve order. Connected with upper life by birth, and attached to the throne by principle and affection, he was nevertheless far from an enemy to those political reforms which France really required, and was justified in demanding; but he saw them demanded in such a manner as made him tremble for the consequences. Hence he strove diligently and effectually to maintain the royal authority among the troops under his command. Nor would he take the new military oath, until importuned to do so by the king himself. Upon the loyal squadron led by him, Lewis calculated when attempting to escape, and if the royal movements had been sufficiently active, it might, apparently, have saved him. Bouillé was all night on horseback, with a body of men on whom he could rely, anxiously expecting the king's arrival; and it was with inexpressible anguish that, when arrived at Varennes, he found him to have left that place with an escort, that the tired horses of his own troop had no power to overtake. The marquess was now obliged to flee himself, and he wrote from Luxemburg an indiscreet letter, menacing the national assembly. This caused his proscription by the successful revolutionists, but he never came within their reach. After some wanderings upon the continent, he settled in England, where he died November 14, 1800. Three years before he published, Memoirs relating to the French Revolution, soon translated into German and French, and forming a most valuable contribution to the history of that great convulsion. (Chalmers. Biog. Univ. Alison, i. 230, 247.)

BOUILLET, (John,) a learned physician, born at Servian, near Beziers, March 6, 1690, to the academy of which place he was appointed professor of mathematics and secretary, upon the nomination of the king, in 1722, and he fulfilled his duties there for fifty-five years. He died August 13, 1777, having published many works, of which the following are the principal:—Avis et Remède contre la Peste, 1721, 8vo. Instruction sur la manière de traiter la Petite Vérole, 1733, 4to. Plan d'une Histoire Générale des Maladies, 1737, 4to. Elémens de Médecine Pratique, 1744, 2 vols, 4to. Suite des Elémens, 1746, 4to. Observations relatives à l'Anasarque, 1765, 4to.

BOUILLET, (John Henry Nicholas,) a physician, son of the preceding, born at Beziers, Dec. 6, 1729. He practised in his native place, and died about 1788, having published, besides other pieces—Mémoire sur les Avantages et les Inconvéniens de la Fièvre. Mémoire sur les Avantages de la Saignée à la Jugulaire; two excellent papers in the Mercure de France, 1750, 1755.

BOUILLON, (Henry de la Tour d'Auvergne, duke of,) an eminent French marshal during the civil dissensions under Henry IV. That monarch rewarded his services, when viscount of Turenne, by giving him the hand of Charlotte de la Marche, to whom her deceased brother had bequeathed the duchy of Bouillon, and the principality of Sedan, on condition that she married a protestant. Henry, as the lady's guardian, had been earnestly solicited by three dukes to set aside this testamentary disposition in favour of one of their sons. Turenne, however, henceforth known as duke of Bouillon, immediately gave a noble justification of his royal master's choice. On the very evening of his nuptials, he surprised Stenay, and took it from the Lorrainers by escalade. *Ventre St. Gris*, said Henry, when he heard of it, *I would make marriages of every day, if I could be sure of such wedding presents. I should soon get full possession of my kingdom*. Bouillon survived the heiress, and married again. By his second wife, a daughter of William, prince of Orange, he had his successor, and the great Turenne. After a life of great credit and activity, he died March 25, 1623. Some memoirs of his, reaching from 1560 to 1586, were published in 1666, but they only comprise a portion of the MS. A life of him by Marsollier, appeared at Paris in 1719, and it was reprinted in 1726. (Smedley's Hist. of the Ref. Rel. in France, ii. 310. Biog. Univ.)

BOULAINVILLIERS, (Henry, count of,) a French historian, of an ancient Picard family, but himself born in Normandy, October 11, 1658. He was a man of talent and research, but unsettled in his religious opinions, and possessed of such an extravagant affection for the feudal system as rendered him ridiculous. He died January 23, 1723, happily brought to a pious frame of mind, leaving numerous works, which he allowed to circulate freely in MS., and many of them have been printed, though none until after his death. Perhaps the most important is his bold and curious Histoire de l'Ancien Gouvernement de France, avec 14 Lettres Historiques sur les Parlemens, ou Etats Généraux, La Haye, 1727, 3 vols, 8vo; and published in English in 1739. The letters were printed separately in 1753. Another of his works, Etat de la France, extracted from official materials, prepared by order of Lewis XIV. for the duke of Burgundy's use, and accompanied by historical pieces on the ancient government of France down to Hugh Capet, was printed in London, in 1727, in 3 vols, fol.; at Rouen, (though London is named,) in 1737, in 6 vols, 12mo; and again in London, in 1752, in 8 vols, 12mo. The last is the best edition. Boulainvilliers besides wrote a life, or, as Mosheim says, "rather a fable of Mahomet," whom he describes as "one raised up by God to instruct mankind." This was published at London and Amsterdam in 1730; and again at

Amsterdam in 1731. It was also translated into English, Italian, and German. It is, however, an unfinished work, only going to the *hegira*, and a continuation has been added to it from Gagnier. The author's competence for such an undertaking may well be doubted, as he was no orientalist. His most exceptionable production, printed in 1731, is entitled, A Refutation of Spinoza's Doctrine, but is really an exposition and defence of it. (Biog.Univ. Mosheim, iv.41. Chalmers.)

BOULANGER, (John,) the names of two French artists, cousins, born at Troyes; one, a painter, in 1606: the other, an engraver, in 1613. The painter spent most of his life in Italy, and attained considerable eminence in history, his master being Guido Reni. The engraver made some considerable improvements in his art, and his prints are valuable. (Bryan.)

BOULANGER, (Nicholas Anthony,) the son of a tradesman at Paris, where he was born, November 11, 1722. His name and writings have been a good deal brought forward by the literary infidels of France. He was educated in the college of Beauvais, but left it with a very slender stock of knowledge. He had, however, a talent for the mathematics, and obtained employment as an engineer. He thus became concerned in various works, which brought under his notice a great number of geological facts, and these, filling him with reflections upon some great destruction of the globe by water, he proceeded to speculate upon the moral influence of such a frightful calamity on the fears of mankind. In prosecuting this train of thought, he applied himself to language, and acquired a superficial knowledge even of Hebrew and Syriac. But his information was quite insufficient for critical research. He thus had no difficulty in discerning allegory where sounder learning and humbler spirits can see nothing but fact. Scripture, subjected to a mind thus perverted, became a mass of riddles, which ingenuity was to explain so as to destroy religion. Perhaps, if he had lived to acquire more knowledge, and to digest it more thoroughly, he might have altered many of his opinions, but he died at thirty-seven, without having published anything. He left, however, various MSS. of which the infidels, then very busy in France, gladly took advantage. Still it was not until 1766, seven years after his death, that Boulanger's principal work, l'Antiquité devoilée, appeared. It was then brought forward by the baron of Holbach; and although free from direct attacks upon Christianity, aims really at its claims to implicit belief. The work is eloquent in places, and shows a powerful imagination, but at the same time deficiencies of judgment and critical acuteness. Other works under Boulanger's name subsequently appeared, but he probably merely left sketches of them, which men of his own cast of thought subsequently finished, producing at last mere startling paradoxes, of no real value whatever. Boulanger also wrote some articles in the *Encyclopédie*, one of which, on the *corvée*, is moderate and sensible. (Biog. Univ.)

BOULAY, the surname of some French authors.—*Cæsar Egasse du*, who died October 16, 1678, is eminent for a Latin history of the university of Paris, in six volumes, fol., which contains a mine of valuable information relating to that noble institution, and its famous men. He also wrote some other works relating to the same subject.—*N. du*, a learned canonist, published in 1740, a French history of his country's canon law, which gave great offence in some quarters.—*Charles Nicholas Maillet du*, who died in 1769, wrote upon the history of William the Conqueror, and some other pieces relating to the annals of his native country, Normandy. He wrote also some grammatical pieces and poems. (Biog. Univ.)

BOULLIAU, (Ishmael,) whose name is sometimes spelt, but improperly, with a final *d*, an eminent French astronomer and general scholar, born in Loudon, September 28, 1605, of protestant parents, but he abandoned their creed for the Romish at twenty-one, and took priest's orders four years afterwards. Besides his various learning, he was a man of business, and acted as agent for John Casimir, king of Poland, to the Dutch government, during the war between Sweden and Poland. He died Nov. 25, 1694, in the abbey of St. Victor, at Paris, to which he had retired. In 1638 he published a treatise De Natura Lucis. Subsequently appeared his Philolaus, seu de vero Systemate Mundi, 1639; Theonis Smyrnæi Mathematica, 1644, Gr. Lat. (the version and notes are his own.) Astronomia Philolaica, 1645. This laid him open to censure from Seth Ward, and Boulliau ingenuously confesses his mistake in the Astronomiæ Philolaicæ Fundamenta Explicata, 1657. In the same year appeared his De Lineis Spiralibus

Demonstrationes, and in 1667, his Ad Astronomos Monita duo, in which he reasonably explains the change of light observed in some stars, by a revolution on their axis discovering successively obscure or luminous portions. In the same year Boulliau published Ptolomæi Tractatus de Judicandi Facultate, et Animi Principatu, with a Latin version and notes of his own. Another work of ancient literature, the Astronomicon of Manilius, received the benefit of Boulliau's learning, in the edition published in 1655. In 1682, appeared his Opus Novum ad Arithmeticam Infinitorum. To general literature, Boulliau contributed in 1649 an edition of the Byzantine history by Ducas; to bibliography, an improved catalogue of Thuanus's library; and to his own profession, a tract establishing the uncertainty of St. Benign's history, together with an address on the Portuguese churches, which was proscribed by the inquisition. (Moreri. Biog. Univ.)

BOULLONGNE, the surname of some French artists. Two of them, named *Lewis*, were father and son, the former born in 1609, the latter in 1654. The former excelled most as a copyist of the best ancient pictures. The latter became a painter of great eminence, having profited by a residence at Rome more than most artists of his nation. His heads are fine, he draws correctly, and colours vigorously. His elder brother, *Bon*, born in 1640, excelled in what the Italians call *pasticci*, imitations, that is, of the style of other masters, without the servility of copies. He died in 1717, his brother Lewis in 1734. There were also two French female artists of this surname. *Magdalen*, born in 1644, painted history, but her strength lay in flowers and fruit. Her sister *Genevieve*, who died in 1708, aged sixty-eight, painted in the same style, and with equal merit. (Bryan. Pilkington.)

BOULTER, (Hugh,) an excellent prelate, born in or near London, January 4, 1671, and educated under Bonwicke, at Merchant Taylors' school, whence he removed to Christ Church, Oxford, a short time previous to the revolution. Immediately after that event he was elected demy of Magdalen college, together with Addison and Wilcox, afterwards bishop of Rochester. He subsequently became fellow, and continued resident till 1700, when he was made chaplain to sir Charles Hedges, secretary of state; he was shortly after appointed to a similar office in the household of archbishop Tenison, and was preferred to the rectory of St. Olave's, Southwark, and to the archdeaconry of Surrey. In 1719 he accompanied king George I. to Hanover, in the capacity of chaplain; he was also English tutor to prince Frederic, and drew up "a set of instructions" for his royal pupil, with which the king was so much pleased, that he made him dean of Christ Church and bishop of Bristol, to which see he was consecrated November 1719. He presided over it with great ability for about four years and a half, but whilst he was engaged in visiting his diocese, he received a letter informing him that the king had nominated him to the primacy of Ireland, vacant by the death of Dr. Lindsay. He was for some time very unwilling to accept this high but responsible dignity; the king, however, would hear of no denial, and the archbishop accordingly arrived in Ireland, November 3, 1724. In the discharge of his important duties he exhibited the utmost sagacity and energy. He engaged most earnestly in every scheme for the benefit of the people. In a time of scarcity he distributed vast quantities of corn—he increased, at his own expense, the number of clergy in populous places—provided for the education of their children, maintaining several of them at the university—he erected houses for the reception of clergymen's widows, and purchased an estate for the endowment of his institution—he also did a great deal for the augmentation of poor livings, on which he expended 30,000*l.*—he built a market-house at Armagh, and encouraged the formation of roads and canals to facilitate the intercourse and trade of the inhabitants—he was also a zealous advocate of the incorporated society for promoting English protestant working schools in Ireland; in addition to which his private charity was of the most extensive nature. He was likewise an able assistant at the council table, and was several times one of the lords justices of Ireland; in fact, the government of that country was, at one time, very much directed by him. Having business in London, in 1742, he was taken ill there, and after a struggle of two days, died at his house in St. James's-place, on Sept. 27, and was buried in Westminster abbey, where a handsome monument has been erected to his memory. He published a few Charges to his Clergy, and some occasional sermons, printed separately. In 1769, however, appeared two volumes of his letters to ministers of state, and others, giving accounts of Irish affairs from 1724 to 1738.

BOULTON, (Matthew,) an Englishman of the highest eminence in the mechanical arts, born at Birmingham, September 3, 1728. He became early famous for the manufacture of steel personal ornaments, of which great quantities were exported to France, whence many were brought back as trophies of French ingenuity. Having thus formed a larger business than could be conducted upon his original premises, he transferred his concerns, in 1762, to Soho, then a barren heath in the neighbourhood, but which he purchased in 1794, and it has become one of the most important manufactories ever known. Its extraordinary success resulted from the steam-engine, which Mr. James Watt, formerly of Glasgow, but eventually partner to Mr. Boulton at Soho, improved in a surprising manner, and from their manufactory, these wonderful machines were supplied to all parts of the kingdom. After a long life, which added materially to the wealth of his country by establishing her superiority in the mechanical arts, Mr. Boulton died, universally respected, at Soho, August 17, 1809. (Chalmers.)

BOULTON, (Richard,) a physician at Chester, in the beginning of the eighteenth century. He was of Brasennose college, Oxford, and published several works, but of his history nothing is known. Among his publications are:—A Treatise concerning the Heat of the Blood and the Use of the Lungs, Lond. 1698, 8vo. An Answer to Dr. Leigh's Remarks upon the same, Lond. 1698, 8vo. The Works of the Hon. Rob. Boyle Epitomized, Lond. 1699, 4 vols, 8vo. System of Rational and Practical Chirurgery, Lond. 1699, 1713, 8vo. The Theological Works of the Hon. Rob. Boyle Epitomized, with his Life prefixed, London, 1715, 3 vols, 8vo.

BOUQUET, (Martin,) an eminent French Benedictine, of the congregation of St. Maur, born at Amiens, June 6, 1685. He entered very early into his order, and was at one time librarian of the abbey of St. Germain-des-Pres; but finding the duties of this employment an interruption, he resigned it. In the earlier part of his life, he assisted the illustrious Mabillon during the printing of several works. Afterwards he made great preparations for an improved edition of Josephus, collating MSS. and correcting the text; but he found that Havercamp was employed upon the same work, and with a liberality worthy of Christianity, literature, and himself, he sent him all his collections. They proved very serviceable to that learned Hollander in the preparation of the Josephus which he produced, in 2 vols, fol. at Amsterdam, in 1726. Bouquet then turned his attention to a new edition of the ancient French historians. This had been projected by Colbert, in 1676, and at his death, Letellier, archbishop of Rheims, begged Mabillon to undertake it. He declined, and D'Auguesseau, then chancellor, confided it to Le Long, a priest of the oratory. On his death, in 1721, Bouquet was selected by the superior general of the congregation of St. Maur to proceed with the work. The first-fruits of his labours appeared in 1738, in 2 vols, fol., under the title of Rerum Gallicarum et Francicarum Scriptores. He subsequently produced six other volumes. His death occurred April 6, 1754; and since that event, seven or eight volumes more of this important collection have made their appearance. (Biog. Univ.)

BOURBON L'ARCHAMBAUD, *Borbonium Arcimbaldi*, the name of a town in France, within a short distance from Moulins, conspicuous for giving a family designation to the modern royal houses of France, Spain, and Naples. It first came to this illustrious race by the marriage of Robert, sixth son of Lewis IX., the sainted king of France, with Beatrice of Burgundy, only daughter and heiress of Agnes, lady of Bourbon in her own right. Beatrice died in 1310; her husband, Robert of France, born in 1256, died February 7, 1318. He held the great fief of Bourbon only as a barony; but it was made a duchy in 1327, in favour of his son Lewis. (Moreri. Biog. Univ.)

BOURBON, (Charles of,) generally known as the *Constable Bourbon*, born February 27, 1489, was the second son of Gilbert of Bourbon, count of Montpensier, descended from a third son of John, duke of Bourbon, taken prisoner at the battle of Agincourt, who never recovered his liberty, but died in England in 1434, after a detention of eighteen years. The constable's mother was Clara, daughter of Frederic Gonzaga, marquess of Mantua, by Margaret of Bavaria. His elder brother, Lewis, was killed at the siege of Naples, August 14, 1501, aged 18, without issue. Charles married, May 10, 1505, Susan, daughter and heiress of Peter, duke of Bourbon. He discovered early an intrepid spirit, and great military talents, which, being united with royal blood, rendered him a political character of considerable importance when a very young man. Hence Francis I. gave him the sword of constable when only in his twenty-sixth year. He proved himself every way worthy of such distinction, displaying, as governor of the Milanese, a frankness and affability which won every heart. Unhappily, however, for his peace and credit, he became embroiled with the duchess of Angoulême, mother of Francis I. She had been his friend, and to her influence he appears to have owed the dignity of constable; but she served him, it was reported, because she was enamoured of him. While his wife lived, he had every reason for neglecting her advances, but when that lady died, in 1521, the constable became fairly open for a new connexion, and the duchess of Angoulême is believed to have made a formal attack upon his heart, which he rejected. To this mortification is attributed a law-suit, commenced against him for the recovery of very large estates, part of which he held in right of his deceased wife, and part as a patrimonial inheritance. The judges, overawed by the duchess of Angoulême's authority, promised a provisional sentence, destitute of even the appearance of equity, by which the constable's possessions were sequestered. His rage now led him into the service of Charles V., with whose troops he got possession of the whole Milanese. The emperor was to grant him the investiture of this duchy. Bourbon's situation was, however, very difficult, from inability to pay his troops, Charles finding it impossible to send him the requisite remittances. To prevent them from mutinying, he led them to Rome, that all their disappointments might be more than compensated by the plunder of that wealthy city. On the 6th of May, 1527, the assault was made, and it fully answered the expectations of Bourbon's army. But he did not live to witness their satisfaction, being killed by a random shot, as he was planting a ladder to scale the walls. (Gifford's Hist. Fr. iii. 335, 350. Moreri.)

BOURBON, (Nicholas,) the names of two French Latin poets, an uncle and great-nephew, both born at Vandeuvre, near Bar-sur-Aube, the elder in 1503, the younger in 1574. Their name is written in Latin, *Borbonius*. The elder wrote epigrams, a poem called Ferraria, on the forge, (his father being a forge-master,) and a collection of moral distichs for youth, styled Pædalogia. The last were at one time thought so excellent, that they were printed with a commentary in 1571. In fact, Erasmus and other contemporary wits thought highly of Bourbon, who frequently visited England, and was much noticed there. Scaliger, however, speaks of him with contempt. His great-nephew and namesake is thought to have shone most in a poem on the assassination of Henry IV. entitled Diræ in Parricidam; but modern criticism is not favourable to it. Some, however, consider Bourbon to have been most successful in an ode on the Saviour. (Biog. Univ. Hallam's Literature of Europe, iii. 518.)

BOURCET, (Peter Joseph de,) a French military author, who died in 1780, aged 80, after seeing a great deal of service. In 1792 were published, Mémoires Historiques de la Guerre que les Français ont soutenue en Allemagne depuis 1757 jusqu'en 1762, 3 vols, 8vo. The first two volumes only of this work contain anything by Bourcet, but they are made up of fragments selected from his MSS. Another work of his was published in 1801, entitled, Mémoires Militaires sur les Frontières de la France, du Piémont, de la Savoye, depuis l'Embouchure du Var jusqu'au Lac de Genève. (Biog. Univ.)

BOURCHENU, (John Peter Moret de,) marquess of Valbonnais, who died in 1730, aged 79, is known for some French works on the history of Dauphiny, which are valuable, and have been reprinted with additions. The author had an adventurous curiosity in early youth, which led him to visit foreign countries, even against his father's wishes, but he was so shocked by witnessing a sea-fight on board an English ship of war, that he determined immediately upon studying the law, as his family desired. This determination led to some distinguished situations, but at fifty he became blind, and henceforth sought his gratifications in study with the help of an amanuensis. (Biog. Univ.)

BOURCHIER, (John,) grandson of Sir John Bourchier, fourth son of William, earl of Ewe. The knight married Margery, daughter and heiress of Richard Berners, commonly called lord Berners, of West Horseley, in Surrey, and in consequence of this marriage, was summoned to parliament under Henry VI.

His son, Humphrey, died before him, being killed at the battle of Barnet, in 1471, fighting for Edward IV. On his own death, in 1474, he was succeeded by Humphrey's son, named John, after himself. This John, who became, by his grandfather's death, baron Berners, and who is thought, with some probability, to have been born at Therfield, in Hertfordshire, was educated in the university of Oxford, as it seems, at Balliol college, where several young men of quality were then trained in academical learning. On quitting Oxford, he travelled abroad, and acquired a higher scale of accomplishments than was usual at that period. His first claim to public notice was established in an insurrection that broke out in Devonshire and Cornwall, under Michael Joseph, a blacksmith, about the year 1495. He thus gained a secure hold upon the affections of Henry VII. By Henry VIII. he was made chancellor of the exchequer for life, and he attended that monarch's sister into France, on her marriage with Lewis XII. He was appointed subsequently lieutenant of Calais and the marches adjoining. He died at Calais, aged about 65, in 1532, without male issue, but leaving two daughters, by Catharine, his wife, daughter to John, duke of Norfolk. He wrote On the Duties of the Inhabitants of Calais, and a comedy, called *Ite in Vineam meam,* acted in the great church at Calais after vespers. Bourchier is, however, more known as a translator. There are two editions, both undated, of a work by him, entitled, The hystory of the most noble and valyant knyght, Arthur of lytell brytayne, translated out of frensshe into englysshe by noble Johan Bourgheher, knyght, lorde Barners. Another of his translations, The Famous Exploits of Hugh of Burdeaux, reached a third edition in 1601. The Castle of Love, a romance from the Spanish, has been printed both in 12mo and 8vo. The Golden Boke of Marcus Aurelius, emperour and eloquent oratour, translated "at the instaunt desire of his nevewe, sir Frauncis Bryan, knighte," was reprinted frequently in the sixteenth century, the first impression, seemingly, being in 1534, the last in 1586. But Bourchier's most important work is a translation of Froissart, printed by Pynson, Lond. 1523, and subsequently, but without date, line for line with Pynson's edition by Myddleton. A new edition, very much improved, by Alderson, in two vols, 4to, appeared in 1812. (Wood's Athenæ, by Bliss. Banks.)

BOURCHIER, BOWSCHYRE, or BOWCER, (Thomas,) archbishop of Canterbury from the thirty-second year of Henry VI. to the second of Henry VII., was son of Sir William Bourchier, earl of Eux, (Eu,) in Normandy. He was educated at Neville's inn, Oxford, of which university he was chancellor from 1433 to 1437. His first dignity was dean of St. Martin's, London. From thence, in 1433, he was advanced to the see of Worcester. A year after the monks of Ely chose him for their bishop, which election was confirmed by the pope; but he was obliged to wait seven or eight years before the consent of the king could be obtained to his translation. He removed to Ely in 1443, and presided over that diocese for about ten years. In 1454 he was elected archbishop of Canterbury in the room of John Kemp, and in December of that year (Bentham says 1461) he was created cardinal priest of St. Cyriacus, in Thermis. In the year following he was made lord chancellor, an office which he held only for a few months. Richard duke of Gloucester contrived to make the archbishop an instrument of promoting his own ambitious designs. It was by his persuasion that the queen consented to deliver up the duke of York into the hands of the protector. He performed the marriage ceremony between Henry VII. and Elizabeth. He presided over the church as archbishop during thirty-two years, and those years some of the most troublous of any in our history. He died at Knowle, then an archiepiscopal residence, and was buried on the north side of the choir of his cathedral, near the high altar, in a marble tomb, bearing merely his name. Though Bourchier was undoubtedly a man of learning, no writings of his have descended to us, except a few synodical decrees; but he deserves mention as being the first introducer of printing into this country. The art had for some time been practised on the continent, but the greatest secrecy was observed respecting the manner in which the operation was conducted. The archbishop therefore persuaded Henry VI. to send Tournour and Caxton abroad in the guise of merchants, (which Caxton was,) to possess themselves, if possible, of this important secret, which with some difficulty they accomplished, having persuaded one of the compositors to carry off a set of types, and go over with them into England. On their return they set up a press at Oxford, which was in a few years followed by the erection of others at Westminster, St. Alban's, Worcester, and elsewhere.

BOURDALOUE, (Lewis,) one of the most illustrious of known preachers. He was born at Bourges, August 20, 1632, and became a Jesuit at sixteen. His talents were soon found admirably fitted for the pulpit, and being employed as a preacher in the country, he had so much success, that his superiors sent him to Paris in 1669, to take the usual course of preaching in their church of St. Lewis. It was then the most brilliant portion of Lewis the Fourteenth's reign. Every body was talking of Turenne's victories, magnificent court entertainments, and splendid flashes of genius from the pen either of Corneille or Racine. The young Jesuit, however, had abilities which defied every countervailing force. He shone forth immediately as the first of preachers, and other men of eminence could only divide with him the public admiration. This high distinction he retained, until advanced age rendered him unequal to extraordinary efforts in the pulpit. He then confined himself to the more private duties of a ministerial life, and in the discharge of these never was displayed a zeal more exemplary. Bourdaloue died at Paris, May 13, 1704, universally respected. Bretonneau, a brother Jesuit, published two editions of his works, one in 14 vols, 8vo, Paris, 1707, and following years, another in 15 vols, 12mo. The former has the preference. As a sermon writer, Bourdaloue is admirable. He is remarkably simple, earnest, and practical; he convinces rather than commands, and by convincing he persuades, for his discourses always tend to some duty, to something that is to be done or avoided. His sentences are short, interrogative, full of plain and solid reasoning, unambitious in expression, and wholly without that care in the choice of words and cadences which is to be detected in Bossuet and Fléchier. No one would call Bourdaloue a rhetorician; and though he continually introduces the fathers, he has not caught their vices of language. (Biog. Univ. Hallam's Literature of Europe, iv. 170.)

BOURDELIN, (Claud,) a celebrated physician, born at Senlis, June 21, 1667. He was carefully educated. At the age of seventeen he had translated Pindar and Lycophron, being profoundly versed in the Greek language; nor was he less fitted for the mathematics, understanding the whole of the conic sections of De la Hire without any help. Desirous of following the profession of his father, he commenced a course of medical study, and in 1692 was received as a doctor of the faculty of medicine of Paris. He visited England, made acquaintance with the most learned of his day, and was admitted a fellow of the Royal Society of London. He was also one of the associated anatomists of the Royal Academy of Sciences of Paris. Upon the death of Bourdelot he became chief physician to the duchess of Bourgundy. He resided at Versailles until his death, April 20, 1711, of a dropsy of the chest, leaving no works behind.

BOURDELOT, (John.) Of his life little is known, except that he was of a respectable family of Sens, and that when he became an advocate in the parliament of Paris, he attracted the attention of queen Mary of Medicis, by whom he was made her master of requests. At an early age he edited Lucian, at Paris, in 1615, to which he added some notes, where he alludes to his remarks on Petronius, that did not appear till 1618; and in the following year he published Heliodorus. He died suddenly at Paris, in 1638, and as he had no children, left his property to a nephew, whom he had adopted, together with a mass of papers, containing, amongst other things, a commentary upon Juvenal, some of which have never been published, says Moreri. His MS. notes on Æschylus are still extant on the margin of a copy of Stephens, amongst the books of Isaac Voss, at Leyden.

BOURDELOT, (Peter,) nephew of the preceding, son of Maximilian Michon, and Anne Bourdelot, whose name he obtained permission to adopt. He was born at Sens, February 2, 1610, studied surgery under his father, and afterwards philosophy and medicine at Paris. In 1641 he was appointed physician to the king, and in the following year admitted doctor of the faculty of medicine of Paris. He was an accomplished man, excelled in music, and a knowledge of the fine arts. By the death of his uncles he had become possessed of a very considerable library, and he assembled together the learned of all nations, and many individuals of high rank. By this means he acquired a celebrity that his talents did not merit. In 1651 he was called into Sweden to attend Christina in an illness which must have been hypochondriacal, as the interdiction of study and the engaging in amusing occupations seemed to remove the malady. He became a great favourite with the queen, and excited the jealousy of the court. Such representations were accordingly made not only to the court of France, but also to Christina herself, as occasioned him to be sent away from Sweden to France upon some secret negotiation. He returned to Paris with considerable wealth, and, according to Guy Patin, under the influence of Christina, obtained, through the cardinal Mazarin, the abbey of Massay. Henceforth he took the title of Abbé Bourdelot. He resumed his assemblies, and continued them until his death, February 9, 1685, from a gangrene, supervening upon a burn of the heel. He published:—Recherches et Observations sur les Vipères, Paris, 1670, 1671, 12mo; Du Mont Etna; Relation des Appartemens de Versailles. His Conférences were collected by the abbé Gallois, and published, Paris, 1765, 3 vols, 12mo.

BOURDIN, (Giles,) was born at Paris, in 1517, and after filling various situations of honour connected with the profession of a lawyer, under the reigns of Francis I. and his three successors, died of apoplexy, January 23, 1570. He was well versed in the dead and oriental languages; and when he was twenty-eight years old, amused himself with writing some Greek notes on a play of Aristophanes, to be found in the editions of Kuster and Dindorf. There is likewise a work of his under the title of Paraphrasis in Constitutiones Regias, 1539, of which Fontanon gave a French translation in 1606. Being very corpulent, and consequently lethargic, he seemed, during a conference, to be in a profound sleep; but like lord North, in after times, could give a reply in which he touched upon every point that had been urged. He left, in a MS. still preserved in the Royal Library at Paris, Mémoires sur les Libertés de l'Eglise Gallicane.

BOURDON, (Aimé,) a physician of Cambray, where he was born in 1638; he died December 21, 1706. He was an excellent anatomist, and published some papers in the Journal des Savans, and some anatomical works, particularly Nouvelles Tables Anatomiques, Paris, 1678, 1683, 1702, 1707, folio. Cambrai, 1707, folio. Nouvelle Description de toutes les Parties du Corps Humain et de leurs Usages, sur le Principe de la Circulation, et conformément aux Nouvelles Découvertes, Paris, 1684, 1687, 12mo.

BOURDON, (Sebastian,) an eminent French painter, born at Montpellier in 1616. His father, a painter on glass, first instructed him, but at eighteen he went into Italy, and formed an acquaintance at Rome with Andrew Sacchi, and Claud Lorraine, from whom he received many valuable lessons. After a residence of three years in the pontifical city, he went to Venice, and greatly improved himself by studying the works of Titian, especially his landscapes. On returning to France he soon made his way to distinguished patronage, but the civil war of the *fronde* diverted public attention from the fine arts, and in 1652 he went to Stockholm, where queen Christina most graciously received him, and gave him full employment. On her determination to abdicate, he returned into his own country, and he died at Paris, in 1671. He painted history, portrait, and landscape, but excelled most in the last, having formed a style both from Titian and Poussin. He had great fecundity of genius, and an uncommon facility, but his design wants correctness. He displayed also very considerable talents as an engraver. (Bryan.)

BOURGELAT, (Claud,) a celebrated veterinarian, born at Lyons, in 1712. He rendered much service to humanity and to science by the establishment of veterinary schools, of which he is to be regarded as the founder. He studied first with the Jesuits, afterwards embraced the profession of the law, pleaded for an unjust cause, and succeeded for his client, which excited in him so great a disgust of his profession that he abandoned it and became a musqueteer. He soon excelled in horsemanship, and was appointed to the Royal Academy of Lyons, which, under his direction, became a most celebrated school, and drew pupils from all parts of France, Denmark, Sweden, Prussia, Sardinia, and Switzerland. Intimate with the celebrated Ponteau and Charmeton, he turned his attention to the anatomy of the horse and domestic animals, dissected many with great care, and studied their diseases. With the assistance of Bertin, comptroller-general of the finances at Lyons, he, in 1672, established a veterinary school, and a short time after was named commissary-general of the royal stud. The success of the school at Lyons induced the government to establish others of the same description, and Bourgelat was called to Alfort, which became, and has continued to be, the principal seat of veterinary instruction. He was admitted a member of the Royal Academy of Sciences; also an associate of that of Berlin. He was highly esteemed, and held correspondence with Voltaire, Buffon, Frederic the Great, lord Pembroke, D'Alembert, Bonnet, Haller, and other celebrated men. He died January 3, 1779, having published—Le Nouveau Newkastle, ou Traité de Cavalerie, Lausanne et Genève, 1744, 12mo; Paris, 1747, 12mo; Lyon, 1771, 12mo. Elémens d'Hippiatrique, Lyon, 1750-53, 3 vols, 8vo. Translated into German by J. A. Gladbuch, Dantzic, 1772, 8vo. Précis Anatomique du Corps du Cheval, comparé à celui du Bœuf et du Mouton. This work was published in three parts at Paris, in 1766, 1768, and 1769, 8vo. It has gone through several editions, the best of which is that edited by Huzard, Paris, 1807, 2 vols, 8vo. Art Vétérinaire, ou Médecine des Animaux, Paris, 1767, 4to. Matière Médicale Raisonnée, Lyon, 1765, 1771, 8vo. Traité de la Conformation extérieure du Cheval, Paris, 1768-69, 8vo. The best edition is by Huzard, Paris, 1818, 8vo. Essai Théorique et Pratique sur la Ferrure, Paris, 1771, 1804, 1813, 8vo. Essai sur les Appareils et sur les Bandages propres aux Quadrupèdes, Paris, 1770, 1813, 8vo. Ecole Royale Vétérinaire, Paris, 1770, 4to. Mémoire sur les Maladies Contagieuses du Bétail, Paris, 1775, 4to. Règlement pour les Ecoles Vétérinaires de France, Paris, 1777, 8vo. He also wrote many articles in the Encyclopédie, in the works of Barberet, in the Recueil des Savans Etrangers de l'Acad. des Sciences, &c. &c.

BOURGEOIS, (Francis,) knight of the Polish order of merit, an English artist, chiefly known as the founder of the Dulwich picture gallery. His family was Swiss, but he was himself born in London, in 1756. He was originally meant for the army, his father having means of recommending him to the patronage of lord Heathfield; but a foreigner of no note as a horse painter, having given him, when a child, some instructions in the art, he became so attached to it that he resolved upon making painting his profession. He was now placed under Loutherbourg, whose style he adopted in his landscapes and sea pieces. In 1776 he went to Italy, and on his return, he exhibited some specimens of his abilities at the Royal Academy, which obtained him employment. In 1791 he was appointed painter to the king of Poland, who conferred upon him the honour of knighthood. For this appointment he was indebted to the king's brother, the prince primate, who had been much pleased, when in England, with his performances. In 1794 he was appointed his landscape painter by George III., who also confirmed his Polish honour. He died in London, January 8, 1811, in affluent circumstances, which he owed chiefly to a bequest of Noel Desenfans, an eminent picture-dealer, who, besides leaving him a considerable sum of money, left him a fine collection of pictures. The whole of these he conferred, by will, upon Dulwich college, adding to this noble legacy 10,000*l.* to keep them in due preservation, and 2,000*l.* for the repair of a gallery to receive them. Sir Francis Bourgeois also left to the master and chaplain of the college 1,000*l.* each, and all his other property to the foundation. The public wondered at such a bequest to an institution unconnected with the arts, at a distance of some miles from London; but it seems, that intentions had been at one time entertained of either forming a separate gallery for the pictures, in town, or of conferring them upon the British Museum. Real or fancied obstacles were in the way of either scheme. As an artist, Sir Francis was only second-rate, being defective in finishing, and a mannerist in colouring. (Chalmers. Pilkington.)

BOURGEOIS, (John,) a physician, born at Westerwitwert, near Groningen, June 13, 1618. He was received as a doctor of medicine at Angers, in 1645. and in the following year appointed to a chair of mathematics at the university of Groningen. A loss of sight, with which he was afflicted, did not prevent him from continuing his lectures until his death, which took place November 22, 1652. He published — Dissertatio de Catarrho, Angers, 1645, 4to. Oratio de Mercurio, Götting. 1646, 4to.

BOURGES, (Lewis de,) a celebrated physician, born at Blois, in 1482, and received as a doctor of medicine at Paris in 1504. He was physician in ordinary to Lewis XII., and afterwards to Francis I. and Henry II. He died in 1556, having published, Ergò Arthritis assumptis melius quam admotis curatur, Paris, 1553, 4to.

BOURGET, (John,) a learned French antiquary, born at Beaumains, near Falaise, in Lower Normandy, in 1724, and educated at Caen, both in grammar and academical learning. He became a Benedictine monk, and died at the close of 1775, in the abbey of his order, founded by William the Conqueror, St. Stephen's, at Caen. He was elected an honorary member of the Society of Antiquaries of London, January 10, 1765, and left copious MS. histories of some of the principal Norman abbeys. He resided for some time in the abbey of Bec, and compiled a very full account of that illustrious foundation, of which the history presented to Dr. Ducarel, in 1764, is only an abstract. (Chalmers.)

BOURGUET, (Lewis,) a naturalist, born at Nimes, April 23, 1678, but driven from France into Switzerland, by the revocation of the edict of Nantes. His father was a wealthy trader, and he wished the son to follow commerce, but a taste for natural history and antiquities found him through life his chief employment. He died December 31, 1742, having published some French works upon salts, crystals, and petrifactions. (Biog. Univ.)

BOURGUEVILLE, (Charles de,) born at Caen, in 1504, and long attached to the court of Francis I. He died in 1593, having lived, upon the whole, a studious life. The fruits of this appeared in a French translation of Dares Phrygius, made in his youth, and published at Caen, in 1573, together with some other works, no longer of any importance. One of his productions, however, the Antiquities of Neustria, and especially of Caen, printed there in 1588, and again at Rouen, in 1705, is valuable. (Biog. Univ.)

BOURIENNE, (Robert,) a military surgeon, born at Vinne-Merville, near Rouen, May 4, 1731. He completed his education at Paris, where he took his degree in 1749. In 1757 he was sent with the army into Germany, where he was placed at the head of the military hospitals, and remained until the peace in 1763. In the following year the king named him surgeon-major to the French troops in Corsica, and of the hospital of St. Omer; and in 1777 he was by brevet made consulting-surgeon of the army. In 1786 he settled in Paris, where he died March 16, 1804. He published the results of his practice in numerous excellent papers, in the Journal de Médecine, Chirurgie et Pharmacie, tom. 20, 36, 37, 39, 40, 41, 42, 43; and also in the Journal de Médecine Militaire, tom. 1, 3, 5, 6, 7.

BOURIGNON, (Antoinette,) a female enthusiast, born January 13, 1616, at Lisle, in Flanders, but so deformed that her friends deliberated, after her birth, whether she ought not to be made away with as a monster. As age advanced, her mother's repugnance to her increased; and being very much left to herself, she sought amusement in mystic theology, and accounts of the first Christians. This reading falling upon a mind of considerable acuteness, but undoubtedly tinged with insanity, she grew up a restorer of religion, in her own conceit, having imbibed a notion that real Christianity was extinct. Her father, however, who was a man of property, looked out a marriage for her, but she had conceived a most extravagant admiration of virginity, and when the time of her intended nuptials arrived, she escaped from home in man's attire. Eventually she inherited considerable wealth, which, no doubt, aided her materially in commanding public attention. She did not, however, gain any popularity by charitable gifts; on the contrary, she closed her purse against the poor, under pretence that any thing bestowed upon them would probably do no real service. She was, in fact, avaricious; but doctrines like hers have been at all times found so agreeable to a large portion of mankind, that her disciples became rather numerous. Religion, according to her, consists in an internal emotion or sensation of the soul, and not either in knowledge or practice. But such principles, however delightful to enthusiastic spirits, are so subversive of good order and rational piety, that the prophetess taught them in the face of unceasing opposition from the authorities. She was, accordingly, driven from one place to another, and was on her way to Holland, when she died at Franeker, in Friesland, October 30, 1680. One of her books, for she wrote several, The Light of the World, was published in English, in 1696, and her tenets were for a time highly popular in Scotland. (Bayle. Mosheim, iv. 380.)

BOURN, (Gilbert,) an English divine, conspicuous at the beginning of queen Mary's reign, son of Philip Bourn, of Worcestershire. He became a student in the university of Oxford, in 1524, and was elected fellow of All Souls college there in 1531. In the next year he proceeded in arts, being esteemed a good orator and disputant. In 1541 he was appointed one of the first prebendaries of Worcester, Henry VIII. having then substituted a capitular for a conventual foundation in that church. He proceeded B.D. June 30, 1543, and about the same time became chaplain to Bonner, bishop of London. By that prelate he was collated to the prebend of Wildland, in St. Paul's cathedral, September 12, 1545, which he resigned, in 1548, for that of Brownswood. In 1549 he had so far complied with the Reformation as to be appointed archdeacon of Bedford, in which dignity he was installed August 7 of that year. On the 6th of the following March, he was instituted to the valuable rectory of High Ongar, in Essex. All this professional success, however, under the protestant party, did not prevent Bourn from veering directly round on Mary's accession. He was appointed, accordingly, to preach at St. Paul's Cross, August 13, 1553, in the presence of the corporation of London, several of the nobility, and his old patron, bishop Bonner. He took for his text, the passage on which that prelate had discoursed from the same place four years before, warmly eulogized him, adverted to the hardships that he had recently undergone, and attacked severely king Edward's religious policy. As he proceeded, murmurs arose, women and boys became violently excited, and even some clergymen present encouraged the general disgust. At length, caps were thrown into the air, stones were levelled at the preacher, and some fiery zealot, probably an apprentice, completed the disgrace of his own party by hurling a dagger at the indiscreet author of so much confusion. Bourn, stooping down, avoided the deadly weapon, and his brother besought Bradford, eventually a martyr, to appease, if possible, the people's fury. The call being readily obeyed, a mild rebuke from one so well known, and so deservedly respected, soon quelled the spirit of outrage. The obnoxious preacher was then conducted between Bradford and Rogers, proto-martyr in the Marian persecution, into St. Paul's school, where he remained until the crowd dispersed. Bourn having thus established claims upon Mary's government, and having one to press them, in his uncle, Sir John Bourn, of Batenhall, in Worcestershire, then secretary of state, was elected bishop of Bath and Wells, March 28, 1554, and he continued in great favour all queen Mary's reign, being appointed president of Wales. Under Elizabeth, he was deprived for denying the royal supremacy. Being then committed to the free custody of the dean of Exeter, he gave himself entirely up to reading and devotion. He died at Silverton, in Devonshire, Sept. 10, 1569. (Wood. Newcourt.)

BOURN, (Immanuel,) a puritanical divine of the English church, born in Northamptonshire, December 27, 1590; and entered of Christchurch, Oxford, in 1607. He did not take the degree of M.A. until 1616. He first came into notice as curate of a London parish, of which a canon of Christchurch was incumbent. In 1622 he obtained the rectory of Ashover, in Derbyshire, which he held several years with great satisfaction to the puritanical party; when, however, the rebellion broke out in 1642, he sided with the presbyterians, and thus rendered himself obnoxious to the king's friends in his neighbourhood. By their means, his residence at Ashover could no longer be continued with comfort, and he removed to London, where he became preacher at St. Sepulchre's, and a great favourite with holders of his opinions. About the year 1656, he was preferred to the rectory of Waltham, in Leicestershire. But although his preferments and popularity were gained by puritanical views, he conformed on the Restoration; and in 1669, he was instituted to the rectory of Ailston, also in Leicestershire. He died December 27, 1672. He was well read in the fathers and schoolmen; and published, besides some occasional sermons, A Light from Christ, leading unto Christ by the Star of His Word; or, a Divine Directory for Self-Examination and Preparation for the Lord's Supper, 1645; Defence of Scriptures as the Chief Judge of Controversies, 1656; Vindication of the Honour due to Magistrates, Ministers, and Others, against the Quakers, 1659; Defence of Tythes, Infant Baptism, Human Learning, and the Sword of the Magistrate, against the Anabaptists; A Golden Chain of Directions to preserve Love between Husband and Wife, 1669. (Wood.)

BOURNE, (Robert,) born in 1769: M.D. Oxon, 1787. He read at one time Lectures on Chemistry, at Oxford, where he practised. He was afterwards appointed Aldrichian professor of medicine; and eventually, upon the death of Dr. Wall, in 1824, clinical professor of medicine. He died December 23, 1830, having published An Introductory Lecture to a Course on Chemistry, London, 1797, 8vo; Oratio in Theatro Coll. Reg. Med., Lond. ex. Harveii inst. habita, Lond. 1797, 4to. Cases of Pulmonary Consumption treated with Uva Ursi; to which are added some Practical Observations, London, 1805, 8vo.

BOURNE, (Vincent,) an elegant Latin poet, and a very amiable man; but so indolent as to mar his usefulness. He would not, however, increase his responsibilities by taking orders. He was admitted a scholar of Westminster school in 1710, and elected to Trinity college, Cambridge, in 1714. Of this noble institution he ultimately became fellow. He became M.A. in 1721. For many years he was an usher in Westminster school; and he died after a lingering illness, December 2, 1747. His writings, collected in 1772, under the title of Miscellaneous Poems, consist of originals and translations, most of which had been printed in his life-time. They are a lasting testimony to his talents. He was, probably, the best Latin poet of his day; and some of his pieces are scarcely inferior to Ovid or Tibullus. (Chalmers.)

BOURRU, (Esme Claud,) a physician, born at Paris, March 27, 1741. He took his doctor's degree in 1766, and in 1771 was elected librarian to the faculty, which office he held during four years. He was eminently qualified for this duty, and he made an exceedingly good catalogue of the books. In 1780 he was appointed to deliver a course of lectures on surgery, which he commenced on the 6th of February, by a discourse which was printed. In 1783 he delivered a course on pharmacy; and in 1787 he was elected dean of his faculty, the duties of which he discharged with such ability, that he was re-elected to the office until 1793, when the establishment was suppressed. In 1792 he appeared before the Legislative Assembly, of which Broussonnet was the president, to claim for medicine an exemption from the operation of the law of March 12, 1791. The Academy of Medicine being established in 1804, Bourru was nominated one of the members; he was chosen a vice-president in 1813. He was much beloved, and generally known as "Bourru bienfaisant." In 1819 he had an attack of apoplexy, from which, however, he recovered; but his health remained indifferent until his death, September 21, 1823. He published Num Chronicis Aquæ Minerales vulgo de Merlanges? Paris, 1765, 4to. L'Art de se traiter soi-même dans les Maladies Vénériennes, Paris, 1770, 8vo. Des Moyens les plus propres à éteindre les Maladies Vénériennes, Amst. (Paris,) 1771, 8vo. A quels points doit s'arrêter le Chirurgien dans les différentes Sciences dont l'Etude lui est nécessaire? Paris, 1780, 4to. Eloge du Médecin Le Camus. This was printed separately, and accompanying the works of Camus. Eloge funèbre de Guillotin, Paris, 1814, 4to. He made translations of Medical Observations and Inquiries, by a Society of Physicians of London, 1763-65, 2 vols, 8vo. Gilchrist on the Use of Sea-Voyages in Medicine, and particularly in Consumption, 1770, 2 vols, 12mo; and with Dr. Guilbert, Disquisitions on Medicines that dissolve the Stone, by Blackrie, 1775, 8vo. He was likewise one of the editors of the Journal Economique.

BOURSAULT, (Edmund,) a French dramatic writer and satirist, born at Muci-l'Evêque, in Burgundy, in 1638. His father was an officer and man of pleasure, contented with his own ignorance, and willing that his son's should be as great. Hence, when the boy came to Paris in 1651, he could not even speak any better language than the rustic dialect of his native province. He became, however, fond of reading, and thus removed pretty completely some of his most conspicuous intellectual disadvantages. He was, accordingly, ordered by Lewis XIV. to write a book for the education of the dauphin. This command produced his Véritable Etude des Souverains, Paris, 1671, a work of no great merit, but which so much pleased the king, that he would have made Boursault sub-preceptor to his son, had not ignorance of Latin obliged him to decline the appointment. He obtained, however, a pension for turning a gazette into verse, for the amusement of the court; but he lost this income by making a capuchin cut a ridiculous figure in his publication. The queen's confessor interfered, and the gazette was suppressed. He afterwards undertook another gazette, which was also suppressed in consequence of an attack upon king William, with whom France then desired peace. As a dramatic author, Boursault was more fortunate, although his tragedies are little esteemed. But his Esope à la Ville, and Esope à la Cour, had a great run; although the latter was not played until after his death, and some happy verses were retrenched which were capable of an injurious application to Lewis XIV., who was yet alive. Boursault's most successful production is, however, founded upon the Mercure Galant, a famous magazine of light periodical amusement, such as was then new in France, and which had a great sale. The editor objected to

Boursault's adoption of this title for his play; and the latter, accordingly, called it Comedie sans Titre. He makes his hero a temporary editor of this publication; and brings, in a series of detached scenes, a variety of applicants for his notice. Boursault, who had a kind heart, as well as a playful genius, was employed in the revenue department at Montluçon, where he died, September 15, 1701. His theatrical pieces have been printed collectively several times; the best edition is that of 1725, 3 vols, 12mo. (Biog. Univ. Hallam's Literature of Europe, iv. 478.)

BOURSIER, (Laurence Francis,) a French divine, born at Ecouen, in 1679, chiefly conspicuous in an abortive attempt to unite the Greek and Latin churches. His first hold upon public notice was gained by an anonymous work, printed in Holland, entitled L'Action de Dieu sur les Créatures. This was attacked by Malebranche, but it is an able piece of ratiocination, and proves the author to have been no contemptible metaphysician His principal claim to the notice of posterity rests, however, upon a memorial, drawn up in a single night, upon the means of uniting the Russian church to that of Rome. It was occasioned by the czar Peter's visit to the Sorbonne, in 1717, when the doctors of that institution addressed him on the advantages of such a union. He heard them courteously, and received Boursier's memorial; but the project failed, as might be expected. Boursier became subsequently involved in some of the religious controversies which agitated France in the earlier half of the eighteenth century, and he died under proscription, February 17, 1749. (Biog. Univ.)

BOUT, (Francis,) a Flemish painter of ability, who lived about the year 1700, and is best known in conjunction with N. Boudewyns, to whose landscapes he supplied figures, though he sometimes painted pictures entirely of his own composition, representing winter-pieces and views of the sea-strand. Bout also etched a few plates in a slight, painter-like manner. (Bryan.)

BOUTATS, the surname of a Flemish family of engravers.—*Frederic*, born at Antwerp, about 1620, engraved chiefly after his own designs; most of his works, which are not without merit, are portraits.—*Gaspar*, his younger brother, engraved almost entirely for the booksellers.—*Gerard*, another brother, still younger, settled at Vienna, and was appointed engraver to the university. His prints are mostly portraits.—*Philibert*, son of Frederic, born at Antwerp, about 1650, chiefly engraved portraits, and in rather a neat style. (Bryan.)

BOUTERWEK, (Frederic,) a meritorious academic teacher and writer, born 1766, at Ocker, near Goslar, educated first at Brunswick, and then for the law at Göttingen. He soon showed an exclusive attachment to polite literature, having already in his childhood been enchanted by the works of Horace among the ancients, and of Gellert and Klopstock among the moderns. He could not long resist the impulse to original production, and gave to the world, in 1791, a novel (Count Donamar,) in three parts; and a collection of poems, which he would fain have afterwards disavowed as youthful follies. Having been deceived in the hope of obtaining at Berlin or Hanover an appointment through the recommendation of Gleim, he became a "Privatdocent" at Göttingen, of the history of literature and philosophy; the latter he taught according to Kantean principles. He afterwards succeeded Feder as extraordinary professor of philosophy. Jacobi exercised considerable influence over him, and he published several works in the spirit of that energetic and singular writer, but they had no independent value, and are now deservedly forgotten. More important were his labours in the field of literary history; but even his *magnum opus*, The History of Poetry and Rhetoric since the End of the Thirteenth Century, though a meritorious production, is far from corresponding to our present requisitions, either in point of learning or criticism. The most valuable portion of it, perhaps, is that comprising the literature of Spain and Portugal. It is not to be denied, however, that Bouterwek was a man of considerable taste and talent in description. His death took place August 9, 1828, at Göttingen. For a tolerably complete list of his works, see Wolf's Encyclopedia of German Literature.

BOUVARD, (Charles,) a physician, born at Montoire, near Vendôme, in 1572, educated at the university of Angers, and distinguished by his knowledge of anatomy and botany. In 1604 he was admitted a doctor of medicine; and in 1625 named professor at the Royal College. Upon the death of John Héroard, in 1628, he was made first physician to the king, and superintendent of the botanic garden. The king ennobled him in 1629, which elated him so much beyond propriety, that he became involved in disputes with the faculty of Paris. He died October 25, 1658, at the age of 86. He is reported to have been a strong advocate for bleeding, and to have performed that operation on Lewis XIII. forty-seven times in one year. In the administration of purgatives he was no less liberal. He published—Historicæ hodiernæ Medicinæ Rationalis Veritatis, &c. 4to. Description de la Maladie, de la Mort, et de la Vie de Madame la Duchesse de Mercœur, décédée le 6 Septembre, 1625, Paris, 4to. This is written in verse.

BOUVART, (Michael Philip,) a celebrated French medical writer, born at Chartres, Jan. 11, 1711. His father, a well-educated physician, intimately acquainted with the ancient languages, gave him such instruction as enabled him to terminate his general education at the early age of fourteen. He then attended the lectures of Hunault, and of other professors at Paris during three years, at the expiration of which time he went to Rheims, and there took a doctor's degree in 1730. He returned to his native place, commenced practice, and was appointed to the Hôpital de la Charité in that city; but the sphere was too limited for the ambition of Bouvart, who quitted it for Paris, where he fixed himself in 1736. Here he submitted to various examinations, and displayed his acquaintance with anatomy, physiology, and medical science in general. In 1743 the Royal Academy of Sciences admitted him into their body; and in 1745 he was made professor of physiology by the faculty of medicine. He opened his course by a Latin oration, which was greatly admired. In the same year he was removed to a chair of medicine in the Royal College of France, the functions of which he performed with great success until 1756, when his health obliged him to retire. Upon the death of Senac, he was offered the appointment of first physician to the king; but desirous of devoting his time to the education of his children, and to the maintenance of his own independence, he declined the honour intended for him. He was, however, occasionally consulted by the king and the court. In 1768 or 1769, letters of nobility and the order of St. Michael were given to him. From 1784 his health gradually declined, and he died January 19, 1787. The writings of Bouvart are insufficient to give an idea of the reputation that he enjoyed. According to his contemporaries, his great faculty evinced itself in the quickness of his diagnosis, and the accuracy of his prognosis. In the delivery of the latter he is described as being rude, and oftentimes brutal; which, however, has been generally ascribed to the inflexibility of his character, and his scrupulous adherence to truth. He, notwithstanding, by his manners appears to us at this day somewhat in the light of an empiric. An anecdote is related of him which places his benevolence in a good point of view. He was called to attend upon a banker, whose illness was occasioned by pecuniary embarrassment, which being ascertained by Bouvart, he left as his prescription a note for 20,000 francs. Much of his celebrity seems to have been acquired by ability in polemical writing. His causticity and learning eminently qualified him to excite attention, and he was engaged in numerous disputes with his contemporaries, Tronchin, Bertin, Petit, &c. His works are, An Ossa Innominata, in Gravidis et Parturientibus diducantur? Paris, 1739, 4to. De Experientiæ et Studii Necessitate in Medicina, *ib.* 1747, 4to. De Dignitate Medicinæ, *ib.* 1747, 4to. Examen d'un Livre de Tronchin de Colica Pictonum, &c. *ib.* 1758, 4to. Lettre d'un Médecin de Province à une Médecin de Paris, Chalons, 1758, 4to. Directed against Savirotte. Mémoire à Consulter, Paris, 1764, 4to. Consultation contre les Naissances prétendues tardives, *ib.* 1764, 8vo. Consultation sur une Naissance, *ib.* 1765, 8vo; written in reply to Le Bas, Bertin, and A. Petit. Lettre pour servir de Réponse à une Lettre à M. Bouvart, par M. Petit, *ib.* 1769, 8vo. The lectures of Bouvart were printed at Amsterdam, under the title of De Reconditâ Febrium Intermittentium, tum remittentium Naturâ, lib. ii. 1759, 8vo. There is also a paper in the Memoirs of the Academy of Sciences, by Bouvart, entitled, Mémoire sur le Sénéka, ou Polygala de Virginie.

BOUVET, (Francis Joseph,) baron, a vice-admiral of France. He was born at L'Orient, April 23, 1753, and entered the sea service of his sovereign in 1779. His professional career will be found succinctly, though not over accurately, recorded, in the Biographie Maritime of M. Henequin, published in Paris; but it may be here stated that when filling the office of rear-admiral commanding a division of the Gallic revolutionary fleet, he took a prominent part in the *grand combat*, as the French proudly designate the memorable and well-sustained conflict which terminated in the defeat of their formidable force, June 1, 1794. On that occasion the *Terrible*, of 110 guns, bore the flag of Bouvet; and though that vessel became a considerable sufferer in the action, having lost her main and mizen-masts, and was much shattered in her hull, still the rear-admiral contrived to secure a timely retreat, and carry back his ship to the port of Brest. In 1796 he was selected, with two other active and zealous flag-officers (Nielly and Richery,) to accompany admiral Morard de Galles in the conduct and escort of the ill-fated force which the authority of France sought to co-operate with the rebels of Ireland. The failure and disasters which attended the invading force in the neighbourhood of Bantry Bay and other portions of the Irish coast, will be found fully detailed in vol. ii. of James's Naval History. Fortunately for Bouvet, following the example of the admiral-in-chief, he disobeyed the directions of the minister of marine, and embarked on board the *Immortalité* frigate, instead of on board the *Droits-de-l'Homme*, the battle ship appointed to receive his flag. The melancholy fate that befel that noble vessel and her numerous crew, presents one of the most deplorable cases of disaster recorded in the naval annals of Europe. The subsequent services of Bouvet are unworthy of note. He died at Brest, July 21, 1832.

BOUVIER, (Andrew Maria Joseph,) a physician, born at Dole in 1746. He studied at Besançon, at the university of which place he received the degree of M.D. in 1776, taking for the subject of his thesis An Musica per se Medicas habeat Vires? in which he admits the advantages to be derived from the employment of music in some mental disorders, but repudiates its use as a regular method of treatment. He established himself at Versailles, and availed himself of the advantages which arose from his connexion with the Count de Buffon, the friend of his uncle Gentil, a celebrated agriculturist. He obtained the confidence of the minister, and was appointed physician to the service directed for investigating the nature of epidemics. In this occupation, and in the acquirement of a knowledge of mathematics and history, he passed his time. He made many notes in the course of his extensive reading, which are preserved in the library of Dole. He was greatly attached to music, performed on several instruments, and composed some masses, symphonies, and other small pieces. He was also passionately fond of declamation, piqued himself upon his ability in reciting verses, and was a good critic upon the talents of the different actors at the theatres and the court. From the continued enjoyment of these elegant amusements, however, the state of the political world at length obliged him to withdraw. He quitted Versailles in 1790, and retired to one of the least populous divisions of Paris, where he had the good fortune to remain unnoticed. He was afterwards named physician to the queen-mother, and received the decoration of the Legion of Honour. At the return of the Bourbons he was made consulting physician to the house of St. Denis, and honorary physician to the Garde Meuble. As age advanced, he abandoned his former tastes, and devoted himself to the cultivation of agriculture and domestic economy. He made many experiments at his garden at Vaugirard, and he printed accounts of them in the journals. In October, 1827, whilst standing with his back to the fire, his clothes ignited, and he was much burnt. This accident proved fatal to him, December 27, at which time he had reached the age of 81 years. He left by will his library, his MSS., his paintings, and his busts of four great physicians who had honoured him with their friendship, MM. Corvisart, Lepreux, Desserserts and Percy, to the library of Dole. He contributed many papers to the Journal de Médecine, by Sedillot, and besides published:—Expériences et Observations sur la Culture et l'Usage de la Spergule, Paris, 1798, 12mo. De l'Education des Dindons, *ib.* 12mo. Quelques Notions sur la Race des Bœufs sans Cornes, *ib.* 1799, 12mo. Observations sur les Participes et sur la Cacographie de M. Boinvilliers, *ib.* 1805, 12mo. Mémoire sur cette Question: Est-il vrai que le Médecine puisse rester étranger à toutes les Sciences, et à tous les Arts qui n'ont pas pour But d'éclairer la Pratique? *ib.* 1807, 8vo. Extrait d'un Mémoire sur l'Hydropisie Aiguë des Ventricules du Cerveau, *ib.* 1807, 8vo.

BOUZI, (surnamed Taj-al-Molouk, the *Crown of Kings*,) succeeded his father, Togtekin, the redoubted enemy of the crusaders, in the principality of Damascus, A.D. 1128, (A.H. 522.) His name is frequently written *Bouri*, but the orthography here followed seems most probably correct, as William of Tyre calls him *Bezeuge;* in Arabic characters the difference consists merely in the presence or absence of a single punctuation. The year after his accession his capital narrowly escaped capture by treachery. The Ismailis, or Assassins, who were harboured and protected by his vizir Tahir Mazdegani, had entered into a compact to betray Damascus to the Franks of Jerusalem; but the plot was discovered; 6,000 of the infamous sectaries, with their patron, the treacherous vizir, were delivered over to slaughter; and the Franks, who had advanced towards the city, were repulsed with severe loss. This achievement is the principal event of the short reign of Bouzi, of whom we find little else recorded, excepting some petty hostilities with Amad-ed-Deen Zenki, father of the famous Noor-ed-Deen. But the massacre of the Assassins, noticed above, had marked the prince of Damascus for the revenge of their brethren. He was waylaid, and stabbed in two places, and died of his wounds, after lingering nearly a year, A.D. 1131, (A.H. 526.) He is said by Abul-Feda to have been a prudent and valiant prince, and a worthy successor of his father. His son, Ismaïl Shams-al-Molouk, succeeded him. (Abul-Feda. De Guignes. William of Tyre. Van Hammer's History of the Assassins.)

BOWDEN, (John,) professor of moral philosophy in Columbia college, New York, was elected bishop of Connecticut, but declined the office. He published The Apostolic Origin of Episcopacy, 2 vols, 8vo, 1808, and died in 1817. (Carter's Amer. Biog. Dict.)

BOWER, (Archibald,) a literary man, who once made considerable noise, born at or near Dundee, January 17, 1686, descended, as he said, from an ancient family in the county of Angus. At the age of sixteen he was sent to the college at Douay, whence, in 1706, he removed to Rome, and was admitted a Jesuit in 1712. He was then sent to lecture at Fano; and having studied divinity at Rome, he was appointed reader of philosophy in the college of Arezzo. He afterwards became professor of rhetoric, and member of the inquisition at Macerata. Here, according to his own account, he became so disgusted with the scenes of torture which he was compelled to witness, that he determined upon making his escape. For this purpose he obtained leave to pay a visit to the shrine of the Virgin at Loretto, when finding a suitable opportunity, he diverged from the high road, and succeeded, but with considerable difficulty, in reaching England safely. After several conferences with Dr. Clarke and Dr. Berkeley, bishop of Cloyne, he renounced his connexion with the church of Rome, but declined joining any protestant communion. He was made librarian to queen Caroline; and edited the Historia Literaria, the parent of our modern reviews. He wrote also the Roman history in the Universal History; and lastly, he published the History of the Popes, a work which drew down upon him the most scurrilous abuse from the Romish party. He is said to have become reconciled to the Jesuits, and to have separated from them a second time; and he fell into great disrepute by the publication of his correspondence with that society. A most desperate attack was made upon him from all quarters, which he sustained and rebutted with great spirit. His character was described as a sensualist and a hypocrite, the truth of his narrative of his escape from Macerata was impugned, and every thing which the most envenomed hostility could invent seems to have been tried to ruin his literary and private reputation. Nevertheless no tangible accusation was brought against him. He seems to have spent a long life in working industriously for his subsistence; and if his writings display no brilliancy of genius, they are at least useful, and some of them interesting. He died September 3, 1766, at the advanced age of 80 years, and was buried in the churchyard of St. Mary-le-bone. His wife some time after attested to his dying in the protestant faith, a point much disputed at the time. Judging from his life, it would appear that, although he disliked the cruelties of the inquisition, he was not prepared to acquiesce in the principles of the reformation, except in a very qualified degree. His writings, besides those above mentioned, consist chiefly of pamphlets, published in his own defence against the calumnies with which he was assailed.

BOWLE, (John,) a learned English clergyman, born in 1725, and so devoted to Spanish literature, that his friends commonly called him Don Bowles. He was educated academically at Oriel college, Oxford, and proceeded M.A. July 6, 1750. He became vicar of Idmeston, Wilts, where he died October 26, 1788. His great work is an edition of Don

Quixote, in six small quarto volumes, Lond. 1781, a bold undertaking for one who had never been in Spain; but it did not meet with such a favourable reception as he had expected. He was a member of the Antiquarian Society, and wrote several papers in the Archæologia. He also afforded valuable assistance to Granger's history, and to the edition of Shakspeare by Johnson and Steevens.

BOWYER, (George,) a British admiral, the descendant of an ancient family in Berkshire, who, according to Charnock, have long held extensive possessions. The year in which our subject was born would seem to be unknown to his biographer. It would appear, however, that after serving the usual probationary period, he received his lieutenant's commission in the year 1758, and that he attained his post-rank at the close of the year 1762. He subsequently served under Byron, when that enterprising officer commanded on the North American and West Indian station, during which period he participated in several sharp encounters with the enemy. In the action with the French fleet off Granada, July 6th, 1779, the *Albion*, Bowyer's ship, occupied a prominent position in the line of battle, being the *next* in succession astern to the commander-in-chief. In the month of December following, he eminently distinguished himself in an attack made by admiral Sir Hyde Parker on a French squadron in Port Royal bay. Sir Hyde, in his official account of this encounter, speaks of Bowyer in terms of the highest praise.

In the engagement which took place off Martinique, with De Guichen, April 1780, Bowyer took a prominent part; and in the two skirmishes on the 15th and 19th of the May succeeding, closing the naval campaign in that quarter for the current year, our subject acquired additional honours. "The van," says Sir George Rodney, in his public despatch, "led by that good and gallant officer, captain Bowyer, about seven in the evening, reached their (the enemy's) centre, and was followed by rear-admiral Rowley's squadron. The *Albion* and *Conqueror*," adds Rodney, "suffered much in this last action." Early in 1783 Bowyer commissioned the *Irresistible*, one of the ships stationed at Chatham to guard the Medway. At the general election, 1784, he was chosen representative for Queenborough, for which place he continued to sit during the whole of that parliament; and in 1785 became one of the board of officers appointed to investigate the proper system of defence to be adopted for the better security of the dockyards of Portsmouth and Plymouth. In 1787, according to a custom but recently abolished, Bowyer, as one of the most distinguished of the senior captains on the list of the navy, attained for his past services the nominal appointment of colonel of marines for the Portsmouth division, and in 1799, immediately after the commencement of the French revolutionary war, he was raised to the rank of rear-admiral of the white, and appointed to command a division of the channel fleet under earl Howe. Nothing material took place till the memorable encounter followed by the glorious victory obtained over the French fleet, June 1, 1794. On this occasion, the *Barfleur*, 98, bore the flag of Bowyer, the rear-admiral having then for his captain the since far-famed and incomparable Collingwood. In this severe and well-contested struggle, a struggle which to this day the French designate by the distinctive appellation of "*Le Grand Combat*," the gallant subject of this sketch had the misfortune to lose a leg. On his recovery, he was presented with a gold chain and medal, and on the 16th of August following, he was created a baronet of Great Britain, with a pension of 1000*l*. per annum, by way of "remuneration" for his loss of limb. Sir George, it would seem, never again served afloat. When and where he died the writer has not been able to ascertain.

BOWYER, (William,) a learned English printer, born in London, Dec. 19, 1699, educated under Ambrose Bonwicke, the eminent non-juring schoolmaster, at Headley, near Leatherhead, in Surrey, and subsequently at St. John's college, Cambridge, of which house he was admitted a sizar in June, 1716, but it does not appear that he took a degree. In 1722 he entered into business with his father, who was an eminent printer, and who had married a daughter of Thomas Danks, employed in printing the London Polyglott. Bowyer soon rose to the head of his profession, having not only the habits and abilities fitted for commanding success in any condition, but also a degree of scholarship long very unusual in a printing-office, though evidently of great utility there. He was thus enabled to bring out, with every recommendation to public confidence, various important works, acting in some cases as editor, and in others making additions. One of his most important contributions to literature was an excellent edition of the Greek Testament, published in 1763, in 2 vols, 12mo, under the following title, Novum Testamentum Græcum, ad fidem Græcorum solum Codicum MSS. nunc primum expressum, adstipulante Joanne Jacobo Wetstenio, juxta Sectiones Jo. Alberti Bengelii divisum; et nova inter-punctione sæpius illustratum. This sold rapidly, although it pretended to no superiority of type or paper, but rested solely upon intrinsic merit. The conjectural emendations are a very valuable addition to the New Testament, and were extremely well received by scholars. A second edition of the Conjectures on the New Testament, with very considerable additions, was published in 1772, a third in 1782, and a fourth in 1812. In 1774, Bowyer published a new edition of Hederic's Greek Lexicon, with numerous additions of his own, distinguished by an asterisk. In the same year appeared an anonymous work on the origin of printing, for which the world appears to have been principally indebted to Bowyer. That learned printer and estimable man died November 18, 1777. (Chalmers.)

BOXHORN, (Marc Zeur,) the son of James Zeur, a minister of Bergen-op-Zoom, by Anne Boxhorn, born Sept. 12, 1612. Having lost his father when he was only six years old, he was brought up by and took the name of his grandfather Boxhorn, whose real name was however Bockerinck, according to the *Bibliotheca Belgica* (p. 841), and who had been a Romish priest. He changed his religion after he became a father by a female whom Foppens calls Sibylla Stylvia, a Calvinist, whose zeal against the Romanists made her prophesy that Breda would never be recovered from the Spaniards, unless the figure of the Virgin Mary, which stood in some public place, was removed. On the fall of Breda, where he had been appointed the minister to a protestant church, the grandfather retired to Leyden, and superintended the education of his grandson; and such was the rapid progress made by the youth in his studies, that at the age of seventeen he wrote some greatly admired verses on the taking of Bois-le-duc by the Dutch, and upon some other victories gained by his countrymen. In 1631 he gave an edition of the Historiæ Augustæ Scriptores, in 4 vols, 12mo; and in 1632, Plinii Panegyricus and Suetonius; and in the following year, Poetæ Satyrici Minores, all with notes, and with a rapidity of which history affords scarcely any parallel, and which led Salmasius to anticipate no little fame for him as a future scholar. Nor was he altogether deceived, for though Boxhorn lived to repent of these precocious publications, yet they led to his appointment to the chair of eloquence, when he was barely of age, and subsequently to those of jurisprudence and history, when the two last were vacated by the veteran, Daniel Heinsius. During the zenith of his reputation, queen Christina made him great offers to go to Sweden; but he preferred remaining at Leyden, where he closed his brief but brilliant career on October 3, 1653, after a tedious illness, occasioned, it is said, by the immoderate use of tobacco, which he used to smoke when reading and writing, and for that purpose had a hole made in the brim of his hat to hold his pipe. Despite, however, the praises bestowed upon him by Salmasius, a rupture took place between them, which was carried to such length by Boxhorn, that he refused during his last illness to receive the parties to whom Salmasius had given letters of recommendation; while in the case of a similar quarrel with Reinesius, who had found fault with some of his notes in private, and spoken contemptuously of his learning, he was called "Trago-ceros," in allusion to his name, which means, like the Greek compounds, "Goat's horn." Foppens, and Chalmers after him, has given a list of his works, extending to fifty-six articles, amongst which the most generally interesting for philologists of after times, is perhaps the Gallicarum Originum Liber, published by his successor, Hornius, Amst. 1654, 4to. His sympathy for fallen majesty was shown by an oration printed at Leyden, in 1642, in honour of a visit paid to that place by Henriette Maria. This exposed him to the censures of the republicans of England. Nor did he make himself less obnoxious to believers in Christianity, by asserting that he had arrows in his quiver which he could direct even against our Saviour. He married the daughter of Peter Davelaar, by whom he left two children.

BOYCE, (William,) an eminent English musician, chapel-master and organist to George II. and III., born in London, February 7, 1710. His father was a joiner and cabinet-maker, and his musical education, begun as a singing-boy at St. Paul's, was completed under Dr. Greene, to whom he was apprenticed, and who bequeathed his MSS. to him. After a considerable course of professional success, he was made doctor of music in 1749. In 1757 he was appointed master of the king's band, and in the following year organist of the Chapel Royal. He published, with assistance from Hayes and Howard, at great expense to himself, three volumes of cathedral music, being a collection in score of the best compositions for that service by English musicians during the preceding two centuries, a publication intended by Dr. Greene. Dr. Boyce died, worn out by gout, Feb. 7, 1779, and was buried under St. Paul's. He has the merit of neither pillaging Handel, nor imitating him servilely. His works have an original and sterling worth, founded on a study of the best masters, foreign and domestic; but his style is unblended, and has a character of its own, clear and easy, without extraneous or heterogeneous ornament. (Chalmers.)

BOYD, (Hugh, or Hugh Macauley,) a political writer, whose claims to notice rest on attempts once made to prove him the author of Junius. He was the second son of a gentleman in the county of Antrim, and educated at Trinity college, Dublin, with a view to the bar. His habits were, however, unsteady and extravagant, so that, although he married a rich wife, and obtained a situation in the east under lord Macartney, he never followed any regular profession, or occupied a station thoroughly respectable. He died in 1791, and his various political writings were published collectively, both in 1798 and 1800, with a view to his identification with Junius. The attempt, however, proved a total failure. Boyd, indeed, like other contemporary writers of ephemeral politics, was evidently an imitator of Junius; but his imitations are among the most feeble that came forward. (Chalmers.)

BOYD, (Mark Alexander,) a Scottish writer of Latin verse, which once gained considerable applause. He was son of Robert Boyd, of Pinkill, in Ayrshire, who early left him an orphan, and his education was conducted by his uncle, James Boyd, then an object of popular prejudice, because he was archbishop of Glasgow. The nephew proved an unapt, headstrong scholar, and his friends advised him, after a sufficient experience of his youthful follies, to go abroad, and become a soldier. He consented, and went to France, where, however, he applied himself once more to study, but notwithstanding, he took part in the military movements that supported Henry III. and received a shot in the ankle. At length he returned to Scotland, and died at Pinkill, his paternal seat, in April 1601, in the thirty-eighth or thirty-ninth year of his age. He seems to have made himself a highly accomplished man, who could appear with credit either as a scholar or a soldier, and he left various MSS. behind him. Of these, the *Hymni* and *Epistolæ Heroidum*, have been published in the Delitiæ Poetarum Scotorum, Amst. 1637, and were at one time placed upon a level with the best models, whether ancient or modern, but later critics have come to no such favourable conclusion. (Chalmers.)

BOYD, the name of a Scottish noble family, of considerable note in the history of that country. The first of that house who became conspicuous was named Robert, rendered by great qualities for business acceptable to James II., by whom he was called to parliament as baron Boyd of Kilmarnock. His first appearance in history is under the year 1459, when he went with other persons of distinction to Newcastle, to prolong the truce with England, just then expired; which was done for nine years. Upon the death of James II., in 1460, lord Boyd was made justiciary, and became the most influential statesman during the ensuing minority, acquiring, in a short course of time, the offices of regent and lord great chamberlain. He was thus enabled to obtain in marriage for his son the king's sister, Mary Stuart, and to have him created earl of Arran. Such splendid fortune, however, only raised a conspiracy against the Boyds, which ended in their ruin, Sir Alexander, lord Boyd's brother, being beheaded; and he would himself undoubtedly have undergone the same fate, had he not fled into England, where he died in 1470. His son, the earl of Arran, took refuge on the continent, and died at Antwerp, the lady Mary Stuart having been previously divorced from him, and married to James, lord Hamilton. A descendant of this family, William Boyd, fourth earl of Kilmarnock, was beheaded on Tower-hill, August 18, 1746, aged 42, for his share in the rebellion of the preceding year. He seems to have been allured into this unhappy enterprise, chiefly by the desperate condition of his pecuniary affairs, and he met death with firmness and propriety. (Biog. Brit.)

BOYD, (Robert, 1578—1627,) a Scotch divine, descended from Robert Boyd, earl of Arran. He graduated at Edinburgh, and then spent some time in study in France, where he was ordained a minister of the reformed church. The university of Montauban appointed him professor of philosophy; but this office he resigned in 1608, upon his appointment to a professorship at Saumur. He had now acquired such reputation, that king James invited him to accept the divinity chair at Glasgow, which he filled with great advantage to the university. He could not, however, countenance king James's attempts to restore episcopacy in Scotland; he therefore resigned his preferment, and retired to an estate of which he was possessed at Carrick, where he died, January 5, 1627. He wrote a Latin commentary on the Ephesians, much esteemed for the elegance of its style. (Chalmers.)

BOYDE, (Zachary,) a clergyman of the kirk of Scotland in the sixteenth century. His statue stands in a niche in front of the university of Glasgow, to which he was a liberal benefactor. His character was very learned and pious, but withal very eccentric. In proof, he turned the whole Bible into rhyme, in the vulgar dialect of the country, to be published for the benefit, as he said, of the lower orders; and he left a large sum of money to the college, which was then, by reason of the reformation, on the verge of ruin, for its re-establishment, ("nova erectio," as called in the charter of James VI. in 1577,) on the express condition, according to the current tradition, of having his metrical version printed. But his executors took so very different a view of the work and its utility, that out of pure respect to the Scriptures, it has been ever since kept carefully locked up, and shown only as a curiosity; and in this, it is said, they have certainly acted wisely.

BOYDELL, (John,) an English engraver, chiefly memorable as a most important patron of his art, and the liberal undertaker of a Shakspeare, magnificently embellished. He was born at Stanton, in Shropshire, January 19, 1719. His grandfather was a doctor in divinity, who held two livings in Derbyshire; his father was a land-surveyor, who meant him for his own business; in Dr. Boydell's time he had been intended for the church. His taste for engraving arose from seeing a print by Toms, a very indifferent artist, of Hawarden castle, the seat of the Glynnes, in Flintshire. He was extremely struck by the accuracy with which a building, well known to him, was thus represented on paper, and although then twenty-one, he resolved upon walking to London, and becoming an engraver. His father was much displeased, but young Boydell persevered, and coming up to the metropolis, bound himself apprentice to Mr. Toms for seven years. Before his time expired he had surpassed his master, and the last year he purchased from him. About 1745 he published six small landscapes, designed and engraven by himself, in most of which a bridge was introduced, and the set was hence known as the *Bridge Book*. Eventually he became a print-seller, and effected a complete revolution in that branch of business. He found engraving at an ebb miserably low, English professors of it doing little else than figure hunting lords and squires in jockey-caps, with other such subjects, taken from the sporting habits then almost engrossing the aristocracy. The few men of fortune who had any taste for such refinements, procured prints of a higher character from abroad, and considerable sums were annually sent out of England for this purpose. Boydell succeeded in reversing this. He brought forward Woollet, and other artists, who gradually so raised the fame of England for engraving, that continental nations made every year large remittances to himself for the works that he exported. In 1786 he conceived his noble design of publishing a series of prints for the illustration of Shakspeare. It was suggested at a dinner-party, in which an observation arose upon an opinion among foreigners that England had no talent for historical painting. Boydell maintained that it was otherwise, nothing more being wanted than a suitable subject, and adequate encouragement. A subject was then proposed in Shakspeare's immortal dramatic scenes, and the great printseller himself undertook to give the requisite encouragement. The result was the painting of that series of beautiful pictures, long exhibited in London, as the Shakspeare Gallery, and the engravings from them, which accompany a magnificent edition of the mighty dramatist's theatrical works. This gallery Boydell intended to leave as a legacy to the country; but the interruptions of continental trade, produced by the wars that sprang out of the French revolution, so crippled his resources, that he was compelled to dispose of it by lottery, under parliamentary authority. He lived to see every ticket sold, but not until the prizes were drawn, dying in December 1804, universally respected. He was alderman of the ward, that of Cheap, in which he lived, and served the office of lord mayor in 1790. (Chalmers.)

BOYER, (Abel,) a lexicographer and miscellaneous writer, born of a protestant family of respectability, at Castres, in Languedoc, June 13, 1667. On the revocation of the edict of Nantes, he followed his uncle into Holland, and under the pressure of want, entered the army. His relations, however, soon induced him to abandon it, and he went through a regular course of study at the university of Franeker. In 1689 he came to England, in the hope of a speedy permission to settle finally in his native country; an expectation then general among the exiled French. Being disappointed, he transcribed Camden's letters from the Cottonian library for Dr. Smith, who afterwards published them. In 1692 he became tutor to Allen, eldest son of Sir Benjamin Bathurst; and for his use prepared a French grammar, which was printed, and long continued a standard work. He had hoped for some situation through the Bathurst family, but his politics, like those of the French refugees generally, were Whig, while his patrons took the opposite side. Boyer, who had acquired sufficiently the English tongue, now became author by profession, and produced several historical works, which have considerable value, since they contain various documents rarely to be seen elsewhere—as the Political State of Great Britain, published in volumes, from 1710 to 1729; a History of William III., 3 vols, 8vo; Annals of the Reign of Queen Anne, 11 vols, 8vo; and a Life of Queen Anne, fol. His name is, however, chiefly remembered as compiler of the French Dictionary, 1699, 4to, of which, as well as his French Grammar, he lived to see several editions, and which long kept possession of the public eye. He died November 16, 1729, at a house that he had built in Five-fields, Chelsea, and was buried in Chelsea church-yard. (Chalmers.)

BOYER, (Alexis,) a celebrated French surgeon, born at Uzerche, in Limousin, March 30, 1757. His parents were in humble circumstances, and only able to teach him to read and write. He engaged himself as an assistant to a surgeon in the country, where he compounded medicines, and occasionally bled the patients. He obtained, however, the means of going to Paris, and there studied anatomy sufficiently to enable him to commence teaching it. He successfully competed for several prizes in the practical school, and afterwards assisted his master, Desault, in the demonstrative part of his lectures on anatomy, at the Hôtel Dieu. In 1787 he contended at the Hôpital de la Charité for the situation of *chirurgien gagnant-maîtrise*, an office afterwards suppressed; and in 1794 arranged for that of second surgeon. He now commenced lectures on anatomy, physiology, and surgery. In 1795 he became professor of operative surgery, and then filled a clinical chair at the Ecole de Santé, an institution formed of the chief physicians and surgeons of Paris. His reputation increased and his practice became extensive. Bonaparte made him his first surgeon, and he accompanied him into Poland, made the campaign of 1807, received the decoration of the Legion of Honour, and was created a baron. He was afterwards appointed professor of practical surgery to the faculty of medicine of Paris, and surgeon-in-chief of the Hôpital de la Charité. Upon the restoration of the Bourbons, Lewis XVIII. named Boyer one of his consulting surgeons, and the Royal Academy of Sciences admitted him a member in 1824. Being deeply affected by the loss of his wife, in 1832, his health sensibly declined under this grief, and he died November 25, 1833. Baron Boyer rendered great services to surgery; his writings are lucid and methodical, distinguished by great penetration and acute observation. He published—Traité complet d'Anatomie, Paris, 1796, 4 vols, 8vo; of which the fourth edition appeared in 1815. Leçons sur les Maladies des Os, Paris, 1803, 8vo; of which an English translation, by Farrell, was published at London, 1807, 2 vols, 8vo. Traité des Maladies Chirurgicales, et des Opérations qui leur conviennent, Paris, 1814, 6 vols, 8vo; second edition, 1818; third, 1822-28, 11 vols, 8vo. The latter with an analytical table. Boyer also printed some papers in the Memoirs of the Medical Society of Emulation of Paris, and assisted Corvisart and Leroux in editing the Journal de Médecine, &c.

BOYER, (John Baptist Nicholas,) a French physician, born at Marseilles, August 5, 1693. He studied with the Fathers of the Oratory at Marseilles, and afterwards went to Constantinople with his uncles, who were desirous of engaging him in commercial pursuits; but his inclination leading him to the study of medicine, he was, after a second voyage to the east, permitted to go to Montpellier, where he was received as a doctor of medicine in 1717, maintaining a thesis on small-pox inoculation, as he had seen it practised at Constantinople, and the introduction of which he contended would be of importance to France. He then visited Paris, contracted friendship with Chirac, Dodart, and Helvetius, and in 1720, when the plague was desolating his native place, he was one of the three physicians selected to treat that epidemic. He conducted his mission with such zeal and success, that in 1723 he received the brevet of a pension, and was named physician to the regiment of guards. In 1728 he was received as an M.D. by the faculty of Paris, and in 1730 sent to Madrid to attend upon the French ambassador. Four years afterwards the cardinal de Fleury entrusted to him the care of the French troops engaged at the siege of Philipsburg, and in the same year he was made physician to the parliament. In 1742 he was again engaged to arrest the progress of an epidemic which had broken out in the environs of Paris. The acquaintance that he possessed on pestilential diseases occasioned him again to be employed, in 1745, and also in 1747, at Châblis, at Beaumont, and in the environs of Beauvais. He received an additional pension for his services; and upon the return of the disease in 1750, he again hastened to Beauvais, and is said to have been the means of saving the lives of more than three thousand of the inhabitants. The gratitude of the citizens was displayed by an annual present of a sheep! His pension was, however, again augmented, and he was made professor of pharmacy, had letters of nobility, and received the order of St. Michael. In 1755 he went to Montargis, to subdue another epidemy. In 1756 he was elected dean of his faculty, and continued in office during three years, and engaged himself in making a new edition of the Codex Medicamentarius, or Parisian Pharmacopœia, published in 1758, 4to. He was made inspector-general of military hospitals, physician in ordinary to the king, of the city of Paris, of Vincennes, and also of the Bastille. He was likewise named one of the royal censors, a singular appointment for a man who had devoted his time entirely to medical pursuits. In the exercise of his various duties, he, however, gained the good will of all, for he was a man of ability in his profession, and highly esteemed for his philanthropy and virtue. He was a member of the Royal Society of London. He died April 2, 1768, and was interred at St. Sulpice. He published, Relation Historique de la Peste de Marseille, Cologne, 1721, 12mo. An deprimendæ Cataractæ expectanda Maturatio, Paris, 1728, 4to; also printed by Haller, in his Disput. Chirurg. tom. ii. Utrum in Gravidis totus Uterus æqualiter extenditur? *ib.* 1729, 4to. Méthode Indiquée contre la Maladie qui vient de règner à Beauvais, Paris, 1730, 4to. Méthode à suivre dans le Traitement des différentes Maladies Epidémiques qui règnent le plus ordinairement dans la Généralité de Paris, Paris, 1761, 1762, 12mo. There are also various academical pieces by Boyer, which it is unnecessary to specify.

BOYLE, the surname of an ancient family, long seated in Herefordshire. The immediate ancestor of the family that has attained conspicuous notice, was *Roger*, a younger brother, sometimes said, but erroneously, to have descended from Sir Philip Boyle, a knight of Aragon, who signalized himself at a tournament in the reign of Henry VI. He was born in Herefordshire, married Joan, daughter of Robert Naylor, Esq., of Canterbury, October 16, 1565; and died at Preston, near Feversham, in Kent, March 24, 1576; his wife dying March 20, 1586. Both are buried at Preston. Their second and youngest son, *Richard*, usually known as the Great Earl of Cork, the first of the family who acquired rank and fortune in Ireland, was born at Canterbury, Oct. 3, 1566, and educated at Benet, or Corpus Christi college, Cambridge, where he rose early, studied hard, and lived temperately. He then became a law student in the Middle Temple, and afterwards clerk to Sir Richard Manwood, chief baron of the exchequer; but finding his fortune in England unequal to his wants and spirit, he determined to visit Ireland in quest of a better, and accordingly reached Dublin, June 23, 1588. His entire property then was 27*l.* 3*s.* in money, a diamond ring, a bracelet of gold, his clothes, rapier, and dagger; but being in the prime of life (22), graceful and accomplished, he soon won his way; and first to the heart of one of the two daughters and co-heiresses of William

Apsley, of Limerick, Esq., whom he married in 1595, and who died in childbirth in 1599, leaving him a widower and childless, with 500*l.* per annum in land, besides money. Beginning now to make purchases in Munster, he excited considerable envy. Sir Henry Wallop, then treasurer in Ireland; Sir Robert Gardiner, chief justice of the King's Bench; Sir Robert Dillam, chief justice of the Common Pleas; and Sir Richard Bingham, chief commissioner of Connaught; conspired against him, and each wrote to queen Elizabeth, charging him with being in league with the king of Spain, and with other unfounded crimes. Having intimation of this, he was preparing to return to England, and anticipate his enemies by an audience with the queen, when the general rebellion broke out in Munster, the rebels seizing his estates and laying them waste, so that he could not now calculate upon one penny of certain revenue from them. Thinking himself ruined, he returned to his chambers in the Temple to resume the law; but was soon recommended to, and received by the earl of Essex, who was going out as governor, to Ireland. This roused anew the jealousy of Sir H. Wallop, who renewed his complaints against him to the queen; in consequence of which he was committed close prisoner to the Gate House. Thus thrown upon his integrity, he boldly, but humbly, petitioned the queen to be examined before *herself* in council. She, though strongly prejudiced, consented; when he first answered the allegations brought against him, then delivered a plain straight-forward statement of his own proceedings in Ireland during his entire residence there; and lastly, laid open the conduct of Sir H. Wallop, and his mode of passing his accounts. The queen was more than satisfied, and in strong language expressed her indignation at his accusers, and her will to employ him, and that Wallop "should be treasurer no longer." She instantly chose a new treasurer, (Sir G. Carey,) commanded Boyle to be released and indemnified for all his costs, gave him her hand to kiss, and told him to attend the court; appointed him a few days afterwards clerk of the council of Munster, and bade him repair to Sir G. Carey. He was, of course, well received by Sir George, and was with him at the memorable siege of Kinsale, whence he was despatched to the queen with the news of the victory there obtained. He lost no time: "I left my lord president (says he) at Shannon castle, near Cork, on the Monday morning, about 2 o'clock, and the next day (Tuesday) I delivered my packet, and supped with Sir Robert Cecil, then chief secretary, at his house in the Strand, who, after supper, held me in discourse until 2 o'clock in the morning; and by seven that morning called upon me to attend him to court, where he presented me to her majesty in her bed-chamber." The queen was well-pleased and very gracious, and dismissed him with despatches for Ireland, where he rejoined Sir George at the siege of Beer-haven castle. After that place was carried, and the western parts of the province reduced, Sir George sent him again to England, to gain permission for himself to lay before her majesty a full account of her affairs in Ireland. While in England at this time, Mr. Boyle, at the instance of his friend, Sir George, purchased the whole of Sir Walter Raleigh's estates in Munster, including the castle of Lismore; they had yielded Sir Walter little, but when peace was restored were made very valuable by Mr. Boyle. Returning again to Ireland, in 1603, he married Catharine, only daughter of Sir Jeffery Fenton, chief secretary of state in Ireland. The anecdote told of this being the result of a singular and long-standing engagement, made when the bride was but two years old, seems very doubtful; dates, at least, seem to discredit it. He was, however, knighted on the wedding-day, by his friend Sir George Carey, then holding the appointment of lord president of Munster. On March 12, 1606, he was sworn a privy counsellor to James I., for the province of Munster; and from this time his honours and estates multiplied. On February 15, 1612, he was sworn a privy counsellor of state of the kingdom of Ireland; in 1616 he was created lord Boyle, baron of Youghall; in 1620 he was created lord viscount Dungarvan, and earl of Cork; in 1629, (October 26,) he was sworn one of the lords justices for the government of Ireland, in conjunction with his son-in-law, lord viscount Loftus. So fast and thick did honours wait upon him! On February 16, 1629-30, he felt a severe bereavement in the death of his lady, at Dublin, who was interred in St. Patrick's cathedral. He speaks of her as "the crown of all his happiness; for she was a most religious, virtuous, loving, and obedient wife unto me all the days of her life, and the happy mother of all my hopeful children." In 1631 he was made lord high treasurer of Ireland, and the honour was further made *hereditary* in his family. In 1641, when the great rebellion broke out in Ireland, he distinguished himself by his great efforts, bravery, and military skill; he turned his castle of Lismore into a fortress, (which was besieged by 5,000 Irish, and defended by Lord Broghill, who obliged them to raise the siege;) he raised a small army, chiefly of his servants and protestant tenantry, put them under the command of his four sons—defended therewith the province of Munster—took several strong castles—killed, at least, 3,000 of the enemy—maintained all this at his own expense, and in the true spirit of the patriot, when all his ready money was gone, converted his plate into coin. "Cari sunt parentes, cari liberi, propinqui, familiares; sed omnes omnium caritates patria una complexa est." Well might the Irish for years, almost generations, afterwards echo his praises with their own native warmth, and tell of his valour and loyalty, and the splendour in which he lived, and the excellent order of his family, and his generous patronage of merit, and the good that he did in a thousand ways beside. He died Sept. 15, 1644, aged 78 years, as he had lived, literally in the service of his country, leaving the character of having been a dutiful son, an excellent husband, a tender father, and a firm friend in private life; and in public life, one of the greatest of statesmen and patriots. Though no peer of England, he was, for his transcendant abilities and public services, admitted to sit in the House of Lords, "ut consiliarius."

Two things contributed not a little to increase his fame—1. his prosperous family; 2. his prosperous estate.—1. His prosperous family. His children were fifteen—seven sons and eight daughters; of whom his youngest, Margaret, was born at Westminster when he was in his sixty-fourth year. His eldest son, Roger, died at the age of nine years, and was buried at Deptford, in Kent; his second son, Richard, succeeded to the earldom; his son Lewis was created baron of Bandon, and viscount Kinelmeaky; Roger was baron of Broghill, and earl of Orrery; and Francis was lord Shannon; and Robert, though without a title, was the distinguished christian philosopher. Of his daughters, Alice was married to the earl of Barrimore; Sarah, to lord Digby; Lettice, to lord Goring; Mary, to the earl of Warwick; Joan, to the earl of Kildare; Dorothy, to lord Loftus; and Catharine, to lord Ranelagh. Rarely, if ever, has it been the lot of any father to be the founder of such a family, so numerous and so distinguished. He had taken great care of their education, and his recorded prayer for them was, "The great God of heaven, I do humbly beseech to bless all these my children with long and religious lives, and that they may be fruitful in virtuous children and good works, and continue till their lives' end loyal and dutiful subjects, and approve themselves good patriots and members to the commonwealth; which is the prayer and charge of me their father."—2. His prosperous estate. He became rich, not as some, by hoarding, but more wisely by *spending*, and that even on estates which had ruined the prior owners. He judiciously, benevolently, and nobly *laid out* his money in effecting improvements, which soon returned it with increase, and he thus acquired little short of a principality. When some time afterwards Cromwell saw the prodigious improvements that he had made, so much beyond any thing that he expected to see in Ireland, he declared, that if there had been an earl of Cork in every province, it would have been impossible for the Irish to have raised a rebellion. Nor do any but fair means seem to have been used to acquire it; no oppression, rapine, or injustice. He himself thus ascribes it to the Fountain of all mercies—"The blessing of God, whose heavenly providence guided me hither, hath enriched my weak estate in the beginning with such a fortune as I need not envy any of my neighbours, and addeth no care nor burthen of my conscience thereunto." With this the motto placed under his arms well corresponds, "God's providence is my inheritance." He left memoirs of his life, entitled, True Remembrances, published in Dr. Birch's Life of the Hon. Mr. Boyle.

Richard, second but oldest surviving son of the great earl, succeeded to the title. He was born at Youghall, Oct. 20, 1612; married Elizabeth, sole daughter and heiress of the earl of Cumberland, by whom he had two sons, Charles, (commonly called lord Clifford,) and Richard, killed at sea in the Dutch war. He was renowned for his loyalty to Charles I., whom, in his troubles, he supplied with both troops and money, and continued faithful to him to the last, when he had to compound for his estate. He was created lord Clifford of Lanesborough; and after the Restoration, which he promoted to his utmost, Charles II., in further consideration of his faithful services, created him earl of Burlington, in 1663. He died January 15, 1697-8, aged 86 years.

Roger, fifth son of the great earl, born April 26, 1621. At the age of fifteen he entered Dublin college, where he gained a good report; thence he travelled with his tutor on the continent, visiting first the court of France, where he saw Lewis XIV. in his nurse's arms; and then Italy. On his return he was much admired at the English court, and in great favour with both the earl of Northumberland, and also the earl of Strafford; of whom the former appointed him to the command of his own troop in his expedition to the North, and by the interest of the latter he was created lord Broghill. He soon after married lady Margaret Howard, sister to the earl of Suffolk. Repairing with his bride to Ireland, he arrived there the very day on which the great rebellion broke out. His father gave him the command of a troop of horse, raised by him against the rebels. He was ordered, with his brothers, to join the lord president St. Leger; and he successfully defended his father's castle of Lismore, when besieged by 5,000 rebels, under Sir R. Beling, compelling them to raise the siege. He also, for some time, acted against the rebels under the parliamentary commissioners; but on the murder of the king, retired in disgust to his seat at Marston, in Somersetshire, where he lived in seclusion until 1649. This, however, ill suited his public spirit; he could not brook to see his country ruined and his own estate lost, and do nothing; to sit still any longer was impossible. He therefore determined to go and apply to Charles II., on the continent, for a commission to raise forces to restore his majesty and recover his estate, under pretence of visiting Spa for his health; and having provided himself with money, he reached London on his way. Unfortunately he had trusted some false friends with his design; the committee of state became acquainted with it, and resolved to make an example of him. Cromwell, then a member of the committee, and general of the parliamentary forces, with his wonted discernment, asked, and with some difficulty obtained, leave of the committee to try to gain over lord Broghill. In consequence his lordship received a very unlooked for and very unwelcome visit from Cromwell, with whom he had never before exchanged even a word. Cromwell told him that he was discovered; and when the design was disowned, produced copies of his confidential letters, which reduced him to the necessity of asking Cromwell's pardon and direction. The future protector immediately offered him, in very complimentary terms, the command of a general officer, exempt from all oaths and engagements, and that he should not be obliged to draw his sword against any but the Irish rebels. Lord Broghill was not displeased with this turn of so awkward an affair, and not unwilling, of course, to serve against the rebels, but begged time to consider of Cromwell's proposal. That could not be. Cromwell at once told him he must determine that very instant, for "he was himself returning to the committee, who were still sitting, and if his lordship rejected their offer, had determined to send him immediately to the Tower." Lord Broghill finding that he had no alternative, and won by Cromwell's frankness, gave him his word and honour that he would faithfully serve him against the Irish rebels. Accordingly, by Cromwell's instructions, he passed over into Ireland, where he was heartily welcomed, and soon at the head of a well-appointed regiment; and on Cromwell landing, he joined him at Wexford. He was cautioned to beware of Cromwell, but he judged it better to act with him in generous confidence, which Cromwell appears to have appreciated, nor to have ever given him cause to repent of it. He consequently became a very valuable and efficient ally, and frequently distinguished himself by noble exploits, especially at the siege of Clonmel, in 1650. On that occasion he first routed, with only 2,000 horse and no infantry, a body of 5,000 men coming to relieve Clonmel, making their general a prisoner; he next manœuvred the castle of Carrigdroghid into a surrender, by fabricating the *appearance of artillery* at a distance, and sending a threat of no quarter unless they surrendered before the arrival of his cannon! though he had, in reality, but a single gun!! the rest being large trunks of trees drawn by his baggage horses, the appearance of which, at a distance, sufficiently deceived the enemy. He then hastened, by forced marches, to Cromwell himself before Clonmel, who was in great distress from sickness among his troops and the repulses of the garison; and relieved him, when to all appearance nothing else could have rescued him and his army from destruction. This seasonable and efficient succour raised lord Broghill greatly in Cromwell's esteem; he ran to him, embraced him, applauded him, congratulated him; and then, thus reinforced, took Clonmel in the depth of winter.

Cromwell, embarking for England, left Ireton commander-in-chief, and lord Broghill at the head of a flying camp in Munster. His lordship was very active, very gallant, and very successful, taking several places, and routing the enemy many times. This, of course, made him very popular, and Ireton is reported to have become jealous and suspicious, and to have said to one or two of his friends, "We must take off Broghill, or he will ruin us all." His lordship also received a letter from Ireton's chaplain, apprising him that Ireton intended to destroy him. In consequence his lordship prudently kept his distance, until obliged to join Ireton at the siege of Limerick, where he distinguished himself by a very gallant action. With 600 foot and 400 horse, he was ordered by Ireton to attempt the forlorn hope of preventing lord Muskerry from joining the pope's nunçio, who was advancing to relieve Limerick. By forced marches he came up with Muskerry before he had joined, and, against three times his own number, fell resolutely upon him. The conflict was desperate, and for some time so much in favour of the rebels, that they even offered lord Broghill quarter. This he nobly refused, bravely exposing himself in the very hottest of the fight. His refusal of quarter provoked the enemy to *single* him out for a mark, and he was hardly brought off by a very brave act of one of his lieutenants. The English, thus roused, now resolved either to conquer or die with their noble commander, redoubled their fury and their action, and at length completely routed the enemy, killing 600 on the field, and taking many prisoners. His lordship is said, on this occasion, also to have added a dexterous artifice to his unparalleled bravery. In the heat of the action he desired those about him to repeat what he said, and then cried out as loud as he could, "They run, they run." The first line of the Irish looked round to see if their rear was broken; and the rear seeing the faces of their comrades, and hearing the shouts of the English, imagined that the first line was routed, and fled. The result was, that Ireton took Limerick, and died a few days after; by which last event his lordship was freed from all danger thence.

Cromwell being proclaimed protector, sent for lord Broghill to England, made him one of his privy council, and admitted him to great intimacy and confidence; insomuch that he is said to have conferred with Cromwell on a project that he had formed (sufficiently hazardous even to hint to such a jealous character) of restoring the old constitution by a match between Charles II. and the protector's daughter; to which Cromwell at first gave ear, but, recollecting himself, quashed it as impracticable, "for (said he) Charles can never forgive me the death of his father."

Lord Broghill was next sent by Cromwell to preside in Scotland; a commission from which he would fain have been excused, and to which he consented only on the condition of being recalled at the end of one year, and being allowed an opportunity of vindicating himself before Cromwell acted upon any complaints that might be brought against him. This condition Cromwell honourably fulfilled, and was fully satisfied with lord Broghill's administration there.

Lord Broghill very kindly employed his influence with the protector for the aid or protection of his old friends who still remained opposed to Cromwell; he was allowed, even at Cromwell's suggestion, to save the marquess of Ormond when he had come secretly to London on the king's business; and he saved lady Ormond from Cromwell's resentment by undeceiving him as to forged letters palmed upon him for hers; he also considerably mitigated the severity with which the house of commons had intended to treat lord Clanricard.

During all this time he is said by some to have kept up a constant correspondence with Charles II.; to have been, in fact, carrying on two games, and to have obtained Charles's concurrence in his scheme of marriage above-mentioned, though he never dared to let Cromwell know of it. All this seems, however, very doubtful; his lordship was not the man to act this double part—too open, noble, frank, and generous in his disposition; and he would scarcely have ventured on the risk, after the proof he had had in his own case of Cromwell's penetration and complete system of espionage. The truth, perhaps, is this. Lord Broghill was in principle a cavalier; but driven by circumstances, *nolens volens*, to join Cromwell, and seeing no probability whatever of Charles's restoration, he transferred his mind and services to Cromwell, generously and honestly; his employment under Cromwell being chiefly against a common enemy, the Irish rebels, whom both parties equally detested. Cromwell gained upon him by favours and confidence, and he felt the constraint of both gratitude and honour. His reported scheme of restoration was one which secured the protector's interests no less than those of Charles, and at that juncture was probably the only one at all feasible. While in Cromwell's service he was faithful; but also ready to return to his majesty's service, if honourable circumstances should arise and call for it, of which he had little or no hope.

On Oliver's death, lord Broghill was chosen, by Richard Cromwell, one of the three constituting his cabinet council, and a member of the parliament called by him. Without consulting his council, the new protector had unwisely consented to a meeting of a general council of officers. Lord Broghill blamed him for it, but conceded to his request to be present at the meeting, to prevent mischief as far as he could. Above five hundred officers met, and his lordship fought Richard's battle single-handed. Desbrough, in a long canting speech, proposed to purge the army by a test oath, and was loudly cheered; on silence being restored, Broghill rose and protested against the imposition of any test whatever, as being a restraint often condemned by their own declarations; arguing, that if they once came to put tests on themselves, they would soon come to have them put upon them by others, and so would lose their liberty of conscience. He then added, that if they persisted in having some test, he would propose another in defence of the established government, and that if that test were rejected by them, he would move it next day in the House of Commons. After some further management, the result was that both tests were withdrawn; exactly what his lordship wished. He advised Richard to dissolve the council immediately, and drew up a speech for him to deliver upon the occasion; which was actually spoken the next day when he did dissolve them. Being provoked, they attacked his lordship in the House of Commons, and moved an address to the protector, to know who had advised him to dissolve the council of war without the consent of his parliament. His friends made signals to lord Broghill to withdraw from the threatening storm; but no, he was not to be daunted; and when his enemies had vented their ire, he boldly proposed another address, to be presented to the protector at the same time, to know who advised the calling of a council of officers without the consent of parliament. This was carried by acclamation; and Fleetwood had the mortification of seeing himself again baffled by the tactics of his lordship. Still, however, considering Richard's power and person both in danger from these refractory officers, lords Broghill, Howard, and some others told him that he must at once strike a bold stroke, and that if he would give them sufficient authority, they would either reduce his enemies to obedience, or cut them off. Richard, startled by the proposal, with more of the benevolence of a good man than the policy of an autocrat, replied, that "he thanked them, but that he neither had done nor would do any person any harm; and that rather than a drop of blood should be spilt on his account, he would lay down that greatness which was but a burthen to him." This was the upshot of the whole; lord Broghill would withstand the cabal no longer, and Richard resigned.

Released now from all obligations to the Cromwells, and being under none to those assuming the government, whose schemes he had discernment to see would soon prove abortive, he set himself to plan and prosecute the return of Charles. He therefore resumed his command in Munster. The committee of safety sent seven commissioners into Ireland, with strict injunctions to watch lord Broghill, and if possible confine him. With that view they summoned him to Dublin, and required him to engage, on the forfeiture of his life and estate, that there should be no commotion in his province. He at once saw the dilemma in which they had put him: if he refused, he was in their power; if he engaged, his enemies themselves had only to raise a disturbance in the province. He asked for time to consider: none could be given. However, he outwitted them; promising compliance if they would put the whole power of Munster into his hands, otherwise "he must appeal to all the world how cruel and unreasonable it was to expect him to answer for the behaviour of those over whom he had no command." The commissioners were embarrassed; and not daring to take the harsh step of imprisoning him on account of his just popularity, they agreed to send him back to his province quietly. He then engaged in behalf of the king, 1. his own officers; 2. the governor of Limerick; 3. Sir Charles Coote, then commanding in the north of Ireland. He sent his brother, lord Shannon, to the king in Flanders with the information, and a messenger to general Monk, in Scotland. Coote began operations earlier than intended, and precipitated the affair; but lord Broghill would not fail him: they acted together, and Ireland was secured.

On the restoration, lord Broghill went to England to congratulate the king, but to his surprise was coolly received. Having discovered the cause in the machinations of Coote, he set the king right, who then became very gracious towards him, and he was soon created by letters patent, dated September 5, 1660, earl of Orrery, made also a privy counsellor, and lord president of Munster. His vigour was now on the decline, abated by fever, gout and age; but in 1665 he went over to England at the king's request, and healed a breach between him and his brother, the duke of York. Returning to Ireland, he and two others were made lords justices for the government of Ireland, with power to call a parliament for the settlement of that kingdom; and he drew up with his own hand that famous act of settlement which passed in that parliament. He also, by his wise and active measures, rendered abortive the plan of a descent upon Ireland by the Dutch and French, formed by the duke of Beaufort. So high likewise was the opinion of his judicial talents, that it is said the seals were offered to him on the fall of Clarendon, but that the gout prevented his acceptance of them. A quarrel with his old friend, the duke of Ormond, arising from mutual jealousies, assumed a public and serious aspect. The earl was impeached, but defended himself, and the prosecution came to nothing; however, it caused him to retire to his presidency of Munster. On the "Bill of Exclusion," he would not consent to alter the succession, but would have laid restrictions on the duke of York sufficient to protect his protestant subjects. To the last the king often sought his counsel, and he as often passed and repassed to and from England. His last voyage to England, however, was for medical advice; but he died from gout, October 16, 1679, aged fifty-nine years, leaving two sons and five daughters.

During the peace which followed the restoration, he employed himself in composition, chiefly dramatic, at the request and for the amusement of the king and his gay companions. His plays met, of course, with applause at court, and might therefore answer so far their temporary purpose; but he had consulted his reputation better by declining this intercourse with the muses, for as a poet he cuts but a poor figure. His attempt also of tragedy in *rhyme* is in bad taste, and a great mistake. His plots, too, overstep probability, his narratives are at variance with history, and the whole is deficient in a moral. The dramas are in two vols. He wrote besides several poems,—1. on the restoration; 2. a political poem, entitled A Dream, in which he represents the genius of France persuading Charles to govern on French principles; and then introduces the ghost of his father dissuading him from it, *because* a king's chief treasure and only real strength are in *the affections of his people*; 3. on the death of Cowley; 4. poems on most of the festivals of the church, well meant, but poorly executed. He also wrote Parthenissa, a romance, in 1 vol. fol., dedicated to Henrietta Maria, sister to Charles II., by whose command the last of the six parts into which it is divided was written. Also The Art of War, a thin folio, dedicated to the king, useful at the time, but now obsolete. His best composition is, An Answer to a scandalous Letter, by Peter Walsh, &c., written when he was one of the lords justices. He also drew up an account of the various scenes in court or camp in which he himself had taken part; but it was lost or suppressed, to the great disappointment of the public. He was a decided protestant; and a noble instance is on record of his fidelity to his principles. Soon after the restoration the Irish papists petitioned Charles to restore them to their estates. The protestants selected the earl of Orrery with seven others to oppose the petition before the king in council. The Irish advocates offered the earl a bribe of 8,000*l*. in money, and to settle estates of 7,000*l*. per annum upon him and his heirs, if he would not appear against them at the council-board. He rejected the proposal with disdain, saying, "That since he had the honour to be employed by the protestants, he would never be so base as betray them." When the cause was solemnly heard, he boldly maintained before the king, that "his protestant subjects were the first who formed an effectual party for restoring him; that the Irish had broken all the treaties made with them, and *offered the kingdom of Ireland to the pope*, the king of Spain, and the king of France." He then proved his assertions by producing several original papers signed by the Irish supreme council. His majesty in consequence dismissed the Irish advocates in displeasure. The earl strictly adhered to the established church, and was a great favourite with many of her prelates, though he hesitated not to tell them that "he thought them a little too stiff in some points; he wished to see an union between the church and dissenters, and he conceived it highly barbarous to persecute men for any opinions which were not utterly inconsistent with the good of the state." He was a generous patron of merit, and liberal to the poor, for whom he built and endowed several almshouses and schools; of a compassionate mind, for on one occasion, when Ireton had determined to destroy the men, women, and children, in an Irish barony, because, after being pardoned, they had rebelled a second time, lord Broghill never left him till he had persuaded him to lay aside so cruel a design; of a generous and faithful temper, and of great integrity of principle. A very prominent characteristic also was his great presence of mind, united with amazing tact and deep manœuvre; the more hardly he was pressed, the more ready he appeared ever able to extricate himself dexterously, yet uprightly. His credit, indeed, ever stood high for bravery and military skill as a soldier, for consummate talent as a statesman, and for generous fidelity as a friend.

BOYLE, (Robert,) styled emphatically *the great Christian philosopher*, brother of the preceding, seventh son and fourteenth child of the *great earl of Cork*, born at his father's seat, Lismore castle, in the province of Munster, Ireland, January 25, 1627. The first rudiments of learning he acquired in his father's house, Latin being taught him by one of the chaplains, and French by a native of the country, who formed part of the establishment; but in 1635 he was sent to Eton, where the earl's friend, Sir Henry Wotton, was then provost. He remained in that noble seminary between three and four years, but his progress at length became rather unsatisfactory, and he was removed as a private pupil into the house of Mr. Douch, rector of Stalbridge, in Dorsetshire, an estate recently purchased by lord Cork. He subsequently received instructions from M. Marcombes, a Frenchman, who was more of a man of the world than a scholar, and with whom he afterwards travelled on the continent. His return home was impeded by the troubled politics of the British isles, which intercepted his resources; but after some pecuniary difficulties, he reached England in 1644. His father was then dead, but he had left him the Stalbridge estate, with property in Ireland; but such were the public confusions of the times, that he could not even reach Dorsetshire until after an interval of nearly four months; he procured, however, protections for both his estates from the powers in being. At Stalbridge Boyle chiefly resided from March 1646 to May 1650, diligently employed in study; natural philosophy, especially chemistry, being the main object of his attention. During this time he was an active member of a society of learned men, termed by him the *Invisible College*, which privately met at various places, first in London, afterwards in Oxford, for the discussion and investigation of experimental philosophy, not excluding other subjects of liberal inquiry, with the exception of religion and politics. This small assemblage of superior minds, which was driven to a degree of secrecy for fear of alarming the unsettled authorities, produced the Royal Society after the restoration. In 1652 he went into Ireland upon his private affairs, but availed himself of the opportunity to make various researches in natural history, especially into the island's mineral wealth, of which he formed a very high opinion. A silver mine, indeed, was then farmed of the state, and Boyle seems readily to have believed an assertion made by some experienced men, that *no country in Europe was so rich in mines as Ireland, if the inhabitants had industry enough to seek them, and skill to use them.* After his return to England, which was probably, according to his intentions, in the latter end of June, 1654, he went to reside at Oxford, in order to prosecute his studies with the greater advantage, and continued there for the most part until April 1668, when he settled in London, at his sister, lady Ranelagh's, in Pall Mall. At Oxford he chose to live in a private house rather than a college, considering it more healthy, and being undoubtedly more convenient for his experiments. He lodged with an apothecary, named Crosse, evidently a person of superior mind, as he was intimately acquainted with Fell, eventually bishop of Oxford, and founded with his own wealth an hospital near Ampthill, as a retreat for thirteen decayed citizens of Oxford. It was only within the precincts of that noble university that Boyle could then have lived with any satisfaction to himself. There he found a spirit of rational piety and sound learning, supported by the influence and example of Wilkins, warden of Wadham, who was a man of excellent temper and superior abilities. There were also resident Dr. John Wallis and Dr. Seth Ward, the Savilian professors of geometry and astronomy, Dr. Thomas Willis, the physician, then student of Christchurch, Christopher Wren, the great architect, then fellow of All Souls, Dr. Goddard, warden of Merton, Dr. Ralph Bathurst, then fellow of Trinity, but afterwards president and dean of Wells. With these eminent men Boyle held constant intercourse, and regular meetings were established for the discussion of philosophical subjects. The whole party became thoroughly convinced that a satisfactory knowledge of nature could only be gained by experiment, and accordingly they severally addicted themselves to that mode of study, and communicated their discoveries to each other. Boyle came to the task with no common stock of mathematical and chemical learning. Of the Aristotelian philosophy, when applied to natural objects, he had no opinion, considering it fitter for words than things, and hence unlikely to aid any man in physical research. He would not even study the Cartesian philosophy for many years, although it was become a general object of attention, lest he should be so biassed by any theory, as to lose sight of his great principle, that nature will never be understood without a long series of careful experiments. One object with Boyle in giving up himself to such inquiries, was the benevolent hope of rendering them popular, that men might be thus diverted from frivolous amusements and hateful contentions, to pursuits that would interest individuals and benefit society. A principal fruit of his Oxford researches was a great improvement in the air-pump, of which he has therefore been considered as the inventor, and which was perfected for him in 1658, or 1659, by Robert Hooke, afterwards Gresham professor of geometry, but then living with Boyle as his chemical assistant. Of this instrument he made important use in demonstrating the elasticity of the air, and in laying the foundations of a satisfactory theory of its nature and properties.

Boyle's attention at Oxford was not, however, wholly given to experimental knowledge. His religious frame of mind also inclined him to branches of learning connected with Scripture, and hence he spent a good deal of time with Hyde, the orientalist, of Queen's, and other scholars whose strength lay in philology, divinity, and general literature, especially with Dr. Thomas Barlow, the Bodleian librarian, and subsequently bishop of Lincoln, a scholar more than usually conspicuous for reading and memory. He kept up also an active correspondence with a great number of individuals eminent for knowledge both at home and abroad; among them with the learned and amiable Evelyn. In 1659, Boyle came to know that Robert Sanderson, afterwards bishop of Lincoln, was in very distressed circumstances, having lost his preferments as an adherent to the royal cause. He therefore lost no time in conferring upon him a pension of 50*l*. a year, then an income of some account, with a view that he should apply himself to the writing of cases of conscience, for which he had already shown qualifications of a very superior kind. In November, 1659, the fruits of this liberality appeared in the publication of Dr. Sanderson's treatise, De Obligatione Conscientiæ, with a dedication highly but justly complimentary to his generous and discerning patron.

On the restoration, Boyle was most favourably received at court, and Clarendon wished him to enter the church. But he rather shrank from the responsibility of such a step, and he thought himself, besides, more likely to serve religion as a layman than as one whose profession gave him a direct interest in its support. He published accordingly, in 1660, a piece finished so early as 1648, entitled, Some Motives and Incentives to the Love of God, pathetically discoursed of in a Letter to a Friend; a work reprinted several times, and translated into Latin. In 1662 a lease for thirty-one years of certain forfeited impropriations in the counties of Mayo, Galway, and Tipperary, was granted to Boyle, without his knowledge; but he immediately determined upon relinquishing any private benefit from this act of royal favour, appropriating two-thirds of its net proceeds to the religious and temporal wants of the parishes whence the revenue was to arise. He did accordingly print at his own expense the Church Catechism and the New Testament in Irish. The remaining third of his grant he set aside as a contribution to the Society for Propagating the Gospel in New England and the parts adjacent, incorporated after the restoration on the basis of a former society established by parliamentary authority in 1649. Of the new society, Boyle was appointed governor. In 1663 the Royal Society was incorporated by letters patent, and Boyle was named in the charter as one of the council. He had been principally concerned in giving rise to that learned and useful body, and he continued through life one of its most active and distinguished members. The statesmen of his time would fain have connected him with learning in such a way as to make a pecuniary acknowledgment of his services to it, and accordingly he was nominated, in 1665, provost of Eton; but his disinterested spirit shone forth again, and he declined the honourable appointment. As if to make himself useful in every possible way, Boyle became a director of the East India Company, and was instrumental in procuring its charter. Nor did he fail to sit in committee on its affairs while his health allowed. When that failed, he still continued anxious to awaken in his brother commissioners an anxiety to spread Christianity in India; and in 1677 he printed, at his own expense, 500 copies of the Four Gospels and the Acts of the Apostles in the Malay language, for dispersion among those who understood it. In a similar spirit, he sent, some years before, into the Levant, an impression of Pocock's Arabic translation of Grotius *De Veritate*, made and printed at his own expense. Boyle's fame upon the continent caused, in 1677, a selection of his works to be published at Geneva, in Latin, under the title of Roberti Boyle, nobilissimi Angli, et Societatis Regiæ dignissimi Socii, Opera varia, 4to. It was a publication without the author's consent or knowledge; and although flattering to him, yet exhibiting a disorder in the arrangement of his productions, that he would gladly have seen avoided. His prominence in all matters connected with science, joined to noble birth and admirable principles, naturally pointed him out as fit for president of the Royal Society, and to that honour he was elected November 30, 1680, but he found himself unable to accept it without taking some oaths which his extreme conscientiousness made him wish to decline. Hence he denied himself the satisfaction of presiding over a body which had so long filled him with the liveliest interest; but his letter of excuse shows him to have deeply felt the compliment. About the same time he rendered pecuniary assistance to Burnet, while compiling his valuable History of the Reformation, a work which, though imperfect, and insufficiently polished in style for extensive modern reading, was an important addition to the literature of England, as it was more complete than Heylin's history, more protestant in spirit, and fortified by an immense documentary apparatus. It is only those who know the expense of historical research, and the narrow circumstances general among such as are able and willing to undertake it, that can justly appreciate the liberality of Boyle towards Burnet. The revolution found the health of this great and good man very much impaired; it also entirely cut off his resources from Ireland. He determined accordingly upon relinquishing his presidency of the Society for Propagating the Gospel, as no longer able to satisfy himself in attention to its affairs, or to render it that pecuniary assistance which its efficiency required. His letter of resignation is dated August 22, 1689. He was, in fact, now admonished, by general decays of his health, and a difficulty of seeing by candle-light, to look upon that future state, for which nearly all his life had been a preparation, as nearly approaching. The immediate prelude to his passage from the world was the death of his dear sister, Catharine, viscountess Ranelagh, in whose pious, affectionate, and intellectual society he had lived more than the last twenty-three years of his life. He did not survive her above a week, but died Dec. 30, 1691, in the sixty-fifth year of his age. The brother and sister were buried by each other in the church of St. Martin-in-the-Fields. Robert Boyle was tall, but slender, and pale. His health was delicate, which made him very cautious in facing the external air; and he was guided by the thermometer in fixing upon one among his various cloaks to wear abroad. He never married, although he had one opportunity, if not two, of making an advantageous connexion. His diet was remarkably simple, and to this self-denial some attributed the age that he attained, which, although far from long, seemed greater than his constitution promised. Witness is borne to his piety by every thing recorded of him; but it may be noted, in addition to what has been already said, that he never mentioned God without making a decided pause in the conversation. So confirmed was this reverential habit, that Sir Peter Pett, who knew him for almost forty years, declared himself able to recollect no one instance of his failure in it. A desire to render his own happy frame of mind more general among men, made him in the last year of his life, by a codicil to his will, found a lecture, afterwards called from him *Boyle's Lecture*, for providing a succession of clergymen, each appointed for three years, who should be ready with answers to objectors against Christianity, and preach eight sermons in its defence.

No Englishman of the seventeenth century raised himself to a reputation so high in experimental philosophy as Robert Boyle. It has even been remarked, that he was born in the very year of Bacon's death, as if meant by nature to succeed him. This would imply an extravagance of eulogy, if it aimed at placing the geniuses of these two great men upon a level; but it really keeps within the bounds of reason, if Boyle be viewed in his true light, as the most faithful, the most patient, and the most successful disciple that carried forward Bacon's experimental philosophy. His works fill five folio, or six large 4to vols. They have been abridged by Dr. Shaw, and may be divided into theological or metaphysical, and physical or experimental. Among the former may be mentioned his Disquisition into the Final Causes of Natural Things, his Free Inquiry into the received Notion of Nature, his Discourse of Things above Reason, his Considerations about the Reconcileableness of Reason and Religion, his Excellency of Theology, and his Considerations on the Style of Scripture. His chemical and experimental writings, however, form more than two-thirds of his works. His metaphysical treatises, to use that epithet in a large sense, or rather his treatises concerning natural theology, are very perspicuous, very free from system, and such as display an independent love of truth. His Disquisition on Final Causes was a well-timed vindication of that palmary argument against the paradox of the Cartesians, who had denied the validity of an inference, from the manifest adaptation of means to ends in the universe, to a general providence. Boyle takes a more philosophical view of the principle of final causes than had been adopted by many divines, who weakened the argument itself by narrowly speaking of man as the sole object of Providence in the creation. His greater knowledge of physiology led him to perceive that there are both animal, and what he calls cosmical ends, in which man has no concern. Besides being almost an inventor of the air-pump, he improved the thermometer, already made, however, an accurate instrument of investigation by Newton, who entertained the highest regard for him and his abilities. Boyle's mathematical knowledge was not very considerable; but we are indebted to him for some of the principles of hydrostatics. In chemistry he particularly shone, being the first investigator, neither connected with pharmacy nor mining, that had paid it any striking degree of attention. His Sceptical Chemist, published in 1661, did much to overturn the theories of Van Helmont's school, that of the iatro-chemists, then in its highest reputation; raising doubts as to the existence, not only of the four elements of the Peripatetics, but also of those which later chemistry had substituted. He thus was as usual in advance of his age, and held a lamp by which posterity might safely guide its steps to farther discoveries. He showed himself, in fact, upon all occasions equally sagacious and good. He was not, indeed, entirely free from that credulity which prevailed universally in his age; but no man was more laborious and intelligent, no one less trammelled by previous system, no one more anxious for the discovery of truth, or more disinterested in all that he undertook. (Birch's Life of Boyle. Hallam's Literature of Europe, iv. 566. Bishop Mant's Hist. of the Church of Ireland, i. 670.)

BOYLE, (Charles,) earl of Orrery, second son of Roger, second earl of Orrery, by lady Mary Sackville, daughter to Richard, earl of Dorset and Middlesex, born at Chelsea, in 1676, and entered at fifteen at Christ church, Oxford. Aldrich, then dean, completed, at his request, the compendium of logic, long used at Oxford, and originally drawn up for another pupil, but left imperfect. In the preface to the finished work, young Boyle is called *Magnum Ædis nostræ ornamentum.* On leaving college he became member for Huntingdon, but his return was disputed, and the warmth with which he supported it in the house of commons involved him in a duel, that left him with such wounds as made him seriously ill, from loss of blood, for several months. On the death of his elder brother, Lionel, August 23, 1703, he became the fourth earl of Orrery, and in 1706 he married lady Elizabeth Cecil, daughter to the earl of Exeter, by whom he had his only son, John, who succeeded him. He chose the army as a profession, and rose to the rank of major-general. He was employed also as a diplomatist, and was envoy in Flanders while the treaty of Utrecht was pending, in which situation he displayed considerable address. To reward him he was created an English peer, as baron of Marston, in Somersetshire. On the accession of George I. he retained his influence, and was made a lord of the bed-chamber, but refusing to vote invariably for the ministry, his regiment was taken from him while the king was at Hanover, and he then resigned his post at court. He subsequently made no great figure as a politician, being but an indifferent speaker, although he regularly attended parliament, when in town. He was, however, arrested in 1722, as implicated in Layer's plot, and detained six months in custody. Nor would he have been released at the end of that time, had not Dr. Mead deposed that longer imprisonment was likely to ruin his constitution. He was released on bail, and on a subsequent inquiry into his case, it was found impossible to criminate him. He died rather unexpectedly, August 28, 1731, much beloved as a very agreeable man, and with a high character for talents and acquirements. His chief claim upon the notice of posterity rests upon the name of Phalaris. He is the Boyle who waged unequal war, seemingly, rather than in reality, with Bentley, upon the genuineness of the epistles that have passed as that author's. (See the article Bentley, where, however, Boyle's name is erroneously given as *Robert*.) This literary peer also wrote a comedy, called, As you find it; and from him was named the astronomical instrument styled an orrery, not that he invented it, but because one of the first was made for him, and Sir Richard Steele, ignorant that it was really the invention of Graham, gave it his name, as an honour due to one by whom he thought such a curious machine had been contrived. (Biog. Brit. Chalmers.)

BOYLE, (John,) son of the preceding, earl of Orrery, and by death of a relative, in 1753, earl of Cork, chiefly known as a biographer of Swift. He was born January 2, 1707, educated first under Fenton, the poet, afterwards at Westminster and Christ church, Oxford. In 1728 he married lady Harriet Hamilton, third and youngest daughter of George, earl of Orkney, a connexion originally agreeable to his father, but eventually the cause of so much dissension, that the old earl left his library and fine collection of scientific instruments away from him to Christ church, Oxford. He also left an embarrassed estate, encumbered by several considerable legacies. The father and son, at length, were reconciled, and the former determined upon altering his will, but the suddenness of his death prevented him. On the younger earl's entrance into public life, he made a trial of parliamentary oratory, declaiming, in the house of lords, against standing armies, and other objects of popular dislike; but although he received many compliments, he never became much of a politician. His health, perhaps, was too delicate, and certainly his private affairs gave him a great deal of occupation. They took him too very much into Ireland, where, in fact, he resided, with little intermission, some years together; a circumstance that interests posterity, because it made him acquainted with dean Swift. The results of this connexion have been given to the public in a series of letters, containing Remarks on the Life and Writings of Dr. Swift, dean of St. Patrick's, Dublin. Lord Orrery was much censured for this publication, because it details a great mass of matter derogatory to Swift, which became known to him while he was acting as his friend. But it is desirable to know the real character of a man so conspicuous as Swift, and there is no reason to suppose it unfairly drawn by the noble letter-writer. Lord Orrery also edited some works of his ancestors, and produced various literary effusions himself. His last work, Letters from Italy, was not published until 1774. It was then edited, with his life prefixed, by the Rev. John Duncombe. He died November 16, 1762. (Chalmers.)

BOYLE, (Richard,) third earl of Burlington, and fourth earl of Cork, of the same family as the preceding, holding the earldom of Cork immediately before him. He was born April 25, 1695, and married, March 21, 1721, lady Dorothy Savile, elder of the two daughters and coheirs of William, marquis of Halifax. By this marriage he left an only daughter, who married the duke of Devonshire. Lord Burlington was an excellent architect, the liberal patron of Kent, whom he really surpassed in taste, but whose fame he was far more desirous to extend than his own. After designing various buildings, both public and private, and aiding some of the former liberally with his purse, he died Dec. 3, 1753. (Chalmers.)

BOYLE, (Hamilton,) earl of Cork and Orrery, second, but eldest surviving son of the subject of the last article but one. He was born in 1730, and educated at Westminster and Christ church. He died January 17, 1764, having secured himself a place among noble authors by contributing Nos. 60 and 170 to the World. He has thus left reason for believing that, had his life been prolonged, he would have come up to the intellectual standard of his very able family. (Chalmers.)

BOYLE, (Henry,) great-grandson of the first earl of Cork, and third son of Charles, lord Clifford of Lanesborough, (who did not live to be earl,) by Jane, youngest daughter of William Seymour, duke of Somerset. He became a distinguished politician towards the close of king William's reign, and was appointed chancellor of the exchequer in March 1701. He continued in that office until February 11, 1708, when he exchanged it for that of secretary of state, in the room of Harley, eventually earl of Oxford. It was under the ministry of which he thus formed a part, that Marlborough dazzled all Europe by his victories. After the battle of Blenheim, regret was expressed in the cabinet that so great successes should want a pen adequate to their celebration, and lord Halifax mentioned Addison to the lord treasurer, Godolphin, as possessed of the requisite powers. Godolphin sent Boyle to him, and as the poet was then but indifferently provided for, he readily undertook to celebrate Marlborough's triumphs in verse. The result was his poem, entitled The Campaign. (See the article ADDISON.) In 1710, Boyle was one of the managers at Dr. Sacheverell's trial, but upon the change of his ministry, he lost his post of secretary, which was conferred upon St. John, afterwards viscount Bolingbroke. In 1714, after the accession of George I., he was created baron Carleton, of Carleton, Yorkshire, and was appointed, soon afterwards, president of the council. He died unmarried, March 14, 1725, when his title became extinct. His house in Pall Mall he left to Frederic, prince of Wales, and his successors. It was, accordingly, known many years as the habitation of George IV. before he came to the throne, and its site, still preserving lord Carleton's name, is now covered by some of the handsomest residences in London. (Chalmers. Bank's Baronage.)

BOYLSTON, (Zabdiel, 1680—1766,) an eminent American physician, who first introduced inoculation for the small pox amongst his countrymen; he wrote several works, principally relating to this subject. (Carter's Amer. Biog. Dict.)

BOYS, (Edward,) a learned English clergyman, of a good Kentish family, educated at Eton and Corpus Christi college, Cambridge, of which college he was elected fellow in 1631, and was presented to the rectory of Mautboy, in Norfolk, in 1640. He was much admired as a preacher, and was a great favourite of bishop Hall, through whose influence he became chaplain to Charles I. A posthumous volume of sermons forms the whole of his printed works. He died either in 1665, or 1667.

BOYS, or rather BOIS, (John,) as appears from Peek's Desiderata Curiosa, born at Nettlestead, in Suffolk, Jan. 3, 1560, the son of William Bois, rector of West Stowe, near Bury St. Edmund's, by whom he was taught the first rudiments of learning. So precocious were the talents of the child, that he could read Hebrew when he was five years old. From his father's roof he was sent to Hadley school; and at the age of fourteen went to St. John's college, Cambridge, where there was only another freshman who could even read Greek. He found there, however, an able and assiduous instructor in Andrew Dounes, under whom he made so rapid a progress, that when he offered himself a candidate for a scholarship, he sent in, not as usual a Latin, but a Greek letter, addressed to the senior fellows; and as the library of his college was too small to satisfy his thirst for reading, he had recourse to the public library, where, during the summer months, he used to stay from four in the morning till eight in the evening. It was his intention originally to study medicine, but as he fancied himself affected with every disease in turn of which he read the symptoms, he gave up the idea and went into the church, being ordained deacon on June 21, 1583, and next day priest by a dispensation. Appointed the Greek lecturer in his college, he held the office for ten years; and during that period, gave a lecture daily at four A.M., which even the fellows of the college were wont to attend. At the age of 36, he married the daughter of Mr. Holt, whom he succeeded as the rector of Boxworth, in Cambridgeshire. But as his wife was a bad economist in house-keeping, he became so involved as to be compelled to sell, at a great sacrifice, his library, which contained, he said, every Greek book, great or small; and so much was he afflicted with the loss, that he had some idea of leaving his country; but being soon reconciled to his lot, he continued to reside on his living, which he held forty-seven years, and was a widower during only the last two years of that lengthened period. When James I. directed a new translation to be made of the Bible, he was one of the parties fixed upon to take a share in it; and not only performed his own portion, the Apocrypha, but likewise that assigned to another party, whose name has however never transpired. As a reward for his labours he was to have been one of the fellows of Chelsea college, which it was then in contemplation to found; but as the project died away, he obtained even less remuneration than he did for the assistance he rendered Sir Henry Savile in getting up the edition of St. Chrysostom, for which he received merely a copy of the work; although had Sir Henry lived longer, he would have been repaid by a fellowship at Eton. It was owing, however, in all probability, to his double disappointment, that bishop Andrews bestowed, unsolicited, on him a prebendal stall in Ely cathedral, in 1615, and thus enabled him to pass the last twenty-eight years of his life in easy retirement; which was first interrupted by the death of his wife in 1641, and two years afterwards by his own, on Jan. 14, 1643, at the advanced age of eighty-four. Although he left behind him a great mass of MSS., the only work he published was Johannis Boisii Veteris Interpretis cum Beza aliisque recentioribus Collatio, in iv. Evangeliis et Actis Apostolorum, Lond. 1655, 4to; the object of which was to defend the vulgate version of the New Testament. When he was a young man he received from Dr. Whitaker three rules for avoiding the diseases to which literary men are subject—1. to read standing; 2. not to read near a window; and 3. not to go to bed with the feet cold: and by following these and some other sanatory precepts, his life was not only prolonged to a great age, but it is said that when he died his brow was without wrinkles, his sight quick, his hearing sharp, his countenance fresh, his head not bald, and his body sound.

BOYS, (John,) an English divine, born in 1571, of a family that came into Kent at the Conquest, educated at Corpus Christi college, Cambridge, from whence he was elected fellow of Clare hall. Sir John Boys, his uncle, presented him to the livings of Bettishanger and the adjoining parish of Tilmanstone, near Deal; and archbishop Whitgift collated him to the mastership of Eastbridge hospital, in Canterbury. He now became distinguished as a theologian and as a "painful" preacher, proceeded to the degree of D.D., and was appointed by James I., dean of Canterbury, May 1619. This dignity, however, he did not enjoy long, dying suddenly in his study, Sept. 26, 1625, at the age of fifty-four. His chief work is his Postils, or a series of Discourses on the Epistles, Gospels, &c. of the Christian Year. He was a violent opponent of popery, and was the author of a profane parody on the Lord's Prayer, beginning Papa noster qui es Romæ.

BOYS, (William,) a Kentish antiquary, descended from the family so long known among the gentry of that county, born at Deal, September 7, 1735, and many years an eminent surgeon at Sandwich. His father, a commodore in the navy, was lieutenant-governor of Greenwich hospital. His own circumstances were easy, and he was thus able to indulge that taste for antiquarian research and collections which distinguished him through life. He wrote various papers upon his favourite subjects, but no work of any considerable length, except Collections for a History of Sandwich, with notices of the other Cinque Ports, and of Richborough, the first part of which appeared in 1788, and the second in 1792. It is of the quarto size, and is an elaborate and valuable work, filling, in the whole, 877 pages. Mr. Boys made himself very useful in the magisterial and other public business of his town and neighbourhood. He was twice married, and had a large family. He died of apoplexy, March 15, 1803. (Chalmers.)

BOYSE, (Joseph,) a protestant dissenting minister, born at Leeds, in 1660, and educated for his profession partly in the north, and partly near London. In 1683 he became coadjutor with Dr. D. Williams, in Dublin, who was shortly after succeeded by Mr. Thomas Emlyn, but the heterodoxy of Mr. Emlyn's opinions on the doctrine of the Trinity induced Mr. Boyse to renounce the connexion with him. The latter years of Mr. B.'s life were embittered by much physical suffering; he died in 1728, but the precise time is not known. His works were published in 1728, in 2 vols, fol.; they consist of 71 sermons, 6 dissertations on the doctrine of justification, and a paraphrase on some portions of the New Testament. One of his sermons, published separately, on the office of a christian bishop, was ordered to be burnt by the Irish parliament, in Nov. 1711. He wrote also several controversial pieces in opposition to Mr. Emlyn. (Chalmers. Biog. Brit.)

BOYSE, (Samuel,) only son of the preceding, born in 1708, and chiefly known as author of The Deity, a poem that once had some reputation. His father intended him for a dissenting minister, and sent him with that view to Glasgow for education. He there contracted an imprudent marriage, the prelude to a life of extreme imprudence, and consequent misery. The first steps in this unhappy course were the less acutely felt while his father lived, because, partiality for an only son, induced the old minister even to embarrass his own circumstances for the purpose of maintaining him. But when death deprived young Boyse of his parent, he soon began to feel the ruinous effects of reckless improvidence. As, however, he possessed a fair share of genius and information, he might have emerged from distress by the intervention of powerful friends, whom he contrived to interest in his behalf, had not an inveterate sensuality rendered him incapable of receiving a substantial kindness from any one. His first struggles were undergone in Edinburgh, whither he removed in 1730. Seven years afterwards he went to London, where he earned a precarious subsistence by mendicancy and composition. His principal employer was Cave, original proprietor of the Gentleman's Magazine. But it was impossible to place any dependence upon him, although his principles at bottom never seem to have been radically corrupt; but he was enslaved by such a greediness of animal pleasures, that charitable contributions, raised under his most urgent necessities, only tempted him into some extravagant carousal. He died in London, in the depths of distress, in May, 1749. His poem, called The Deity, published in 1740, was written while his condition was wretched in the extreme, and had the good fortune to be noticed by two writers, both very popular, but with very different classes of readers. Hervey calls it, in his Meditations, "a beautiful and instructive poem;" Fielding extracts a few lines from it in Tom Jones, and says that they are taken from "a very noble poem, called The Deity." Such commendations kept up its credit, and a third edition of it appeared in 1752. It is described as "irregular and monotonous, but containing striking proofs of poetical genius." (Chalmers.)

BOYSEN, (Frederic Everard,) born at Halberstadt, April 7, 1620, the son of a learned theologian, studied the oriental languages under Michaelis, at Halle, and applied himself with great assiduity to the works of the rabbis and the Talmud. He is the author of an Ancient History, in 10 vols, Halle, 1767-72, full of polemical, philological, and useless critical digressions, in defence of which he was led into a long and noisy controversy with the noted Nicolai, the Berlin bookseller, and editor of the Allg. Deuts. Bibliot. He also published several works on the history and antiquities of Magdeburg. His General Historical Magazine, (6 parts, Halle, 1767-70,) contains some valuable materials for the history of Germany. His contributions to Hebrew philology, and comments on the Bible in the original, were received with approbation; but his most valuable performance was a German translation of the Koran, with excellent and learned notes. He wrote his own life, which abounds in petty details, digressions, and proofs of his vanity and self-complacency, but is not without some good practical remarks.

BOZE, (Claud Gros de,) a French antiquary, born at Lyons, January 28, 1680, and elected, in spite of his youth, secretary to the Academy of Inscriptions, June 24, 1706. He edited the first fifteen vols of its memoirs, and wrote most of the *Eloges* to be found in them; satisfactory proofs of his ability to compose with elegance. These historical panegyrics have been printed separately, in 12mo. Boze also published a second edition, with a continuation, of the medallic history of Lewis XIV.; a treatise, now rare, on the Jewish jubilee, and some other works of less importance. He died Sept. 10, 1753. (Biog. Univ.)

BOZIO, (Thomas,) a priest of the Oratory, of the congregation of St. Philip Neri, died at Rome, in 1610, leaving the following works against Machiavelli—De Imperio Virtutis. De Robore bellico, Rom. 1593; Cologne, 1594, 1601. De Ruinis Gentium et Regnorum. De Antiquo et novo Italiæ Statu, Rom. 1594; Cologne, 1595. Bozio also wrote, De Signis Ecclesiæ Dei, libri xxiv. Rom. 1591, 2 vols, fol.; reprinted both there and at Cologne. Annales Antiquitatum, intended to fill ten vols, but the author lived only to finish two. De Jure Divino, Rom. 1600.—His brother, named *Francis*, of the same congregation, wrote a work, refuted by William Barclay, maintaining extravagant ultramontane pretensions, entitled, De Temporali Ecclesiæ Monarchia, Cologne, 1602, 4to. (Biog. Univ.)

BRABECK, (Frederic Maurice, Baron, and afterwards Count, von,) born 1728, at the seat of his family, Brabeck, in Westphalia, educated for the church, received preferment as canon at Hildesheim and Paderborn. A lover of art and literature, he spent his income in travelling for information and improvement. In 1785, on the election of a coadjutor to the episcopal prince of Hildesheim, a great portion of the chapter declared for Brabeck, but from despising the intrigues necessary for success, he was not chosen. On the death of the head of his family without children, he being its next and sole surviving representative, obtained a dispensation, quitted holy orders, and married. The retirement which he now sought was disturbed by political duties. Various abuses in the principality of Hildesheim demanded the convocation of a diet, as a member of which Brabeck declared himself warmly for their correction, and expressed himself also energetically to the same effect in a note addressed to his fellow-members. This well-intentioned zeal was misinterpreted. He was accused of revolutionary tendencies, and even brought to trial on that account, but acquitted. From this time his quiet remained unruffled, and he devoted himself again to his favourite pursuits. He formed a collection of paintings, celebrated throughout Germany, and set on foot, without any view to profit, but merely for the improvement of the public taste, an establishment for publishing plates of paintings in his and other galleries; this was afterwards removed to Degsau, munificently supported by the duke and others, and, under the name of the Chalcographic Society, was productive of excellent effect. Brabeck died childless, 1814, and with him his family was extinguished. Besides some pamphlets, in answer to the charges above alluded to, he was the author of a few works on art and other subjects, which have now lost their importance.

BRACCIOLI, (John Francis,) an Italian painter, who died at Ferrara, in 1762, aged 64. He was first pupil to Parolini, afterwards to Crespi. (Bryan.)

BRACCIOLINI, (Francis,) an Italian poet of some eminence, born at Pistoia, of a noble family, November 26, 1566. In 1605, he had the offer of a canonry, and this decided him to the ecclesiastical profession. He now went to Rome, and found employment with Maffeo Barberini, soon afterwards a cardinal, and eventually pope, as Urban VIII. This personage took Bracciolini with him, when he went as nuncio into France, and on attaining the pontificate, recommended him as secretary to his brother, cardinal Anthony Barberini. During Urban's reign, the poet lived at Rome in considerable reputation, though accused of sordid avarice, but on his death, he retired into his own country, where he died August 31, 1645. Bracciolini left many poems, but only two of any particular account. Of these, La Croce Racquistata, an epic, originally published at Paris, in 1605, has been ranked immediately after the works of Tasso and Ariosto; but no such estimate is placed upon it in modern times. Its action turns upon the recapture of the true cross from the Persians, by the emperor Heraclius; no very promising theme for a genius of any real elevation. The poem has, however, been often reprinted. Bracciolini's other more considerable production is Lo Scherno degli Dei, a mock heroic, ridiculing the heathen mythology. It was first printed in 1618, four years before Tassoni's Secchia rapita; but it does not therefore follow, as Bracciolini wished people to believe, that Lo Scherno was really the model of mock heroics. The truth is that Tassoni finished his piece in 1615, and afterwards allowed it freely to circulate in MS. (Biog. Univ.)

BRACELLI, (James,) an Italian historian, born towards the end of the fourteenth century, at Sarzano, in Tuscany, then belonging to the Genoese. His countryman, pope Nicholas V. would have employed him as secretary, but he declined, and the people of Genoa recompensed his devotion to their service by appointing him their chancellor. He died in 1460, leaving in Latin, which has been compared with Cæsar's, a history of the war between the Spaniards and Genoese, from 1412 to 1444. This was first published at Paris, in 1520, and has been several times reprinted. He also wrote some other works relating to the Genoese states. Some of them are to be seen in the Thesaurus of Græevius; and a small treatise of his on the principal families of Genoa has been inserted by Mabillon, in his Iter Italicum. (Biog. Univ.)

BRACELLI, (John Baptist,) an Italian painter and engraver, born at Genoa, who died young in 1609. He was a pupil of Paggi, and painted history in that master's style. There are some architectural plates of his, which are neat, but stiff. (Bryan.)

BRACKEL, a commodore in the Dutch navy, a brave and meritorious seaman, slain in battle in the year 1665, (some authorities say 1664,) while defending with a resolute spirit a valuable convoy from the vigorous and successful assault of a British force under admiral Thomas Allen. (*Vide* ALLEN, Sir Thomas, where by a misprint Brackel's name appears as *Bracknel.*)

BRACTON, (Henry of,) an ancient English legal writer, called *John* by bishop Nicholson, who seems to have confounded him with John Breton, bishop of Hereford about his time, author of a large work upon the laws of England. Of Henry Bracton's history scarcely anything certain is known. Sir William Pole, in a MS. description of Devonshire, pronounces him to have been a native of that county; and Prince, in his Worthies of Devon, adopting the statement, places his birth at Bracton, or Bratton, near Oakhampton. His surname is variously written in ancient records, which call him Bratton, Breton, Bretton, Briton, Britton, and Brycton. He appears to have studied at Oxford, and to have taken the degree of doctor of laws there. Sir William Dugdale tells us, that in the 29th of Hen. III., that is, about 1244, Henry of Bracton and others were constituted justices itinerant for the counties of Nottingham and Derby, and in the 30th of the same reign, for the counties of Northumberland, Westmoreland, Cumberland, and Lancaster. In another place, Dugdale recites a writ, bearing date in the 38th of Hen. III., granting Bracton the custody of the house of William de Ferrers, earl of Derby, to serve him for a town residence until that peer should come of age. He was, therefore, living in 1253, and probably much later, as he has been said to have filled the office of chief justice during twenty years. Leland found him described as chief justice in a MS. of his work. If this description be correct, and lord Derby's house was assigned to him at the time of his appointment, which may reasonably be supposed, and also the length of his official tenure be correct, he must have died about the year 1273, which is, on several accounts, highly probable. His work, entitled De Legibus et Consuetudinibus Angliæ, as it is one of the most ancient, so also it is one of the most accurate and methodical treatises upon English law. It was not printed until 1569, but the MS. copies of it in circulation were so numerous, that no degree of care usual in that age could make out a genuine text from any or all of them. In 1640, however, it was printed again, and great pains were then taken to collate the various MSS. The work is in five books, evidently after the model of the emperor Justinian, whose matter, indeed, is very frequently brought forward, and his laws quoted, sometimes to the letter, just as if they were part of the known common law of England. In many places, too, whole sentences are transcribed from Glanvil. One of the best MSS. of this venerable law-book was burnt in the fire which unfortunately so much damaged the Cotton library at Ashburnham house, Oct. 23, 1731. (Biog. Brit. Nicholson's Historical Library, 224.)

BRADBURY, (Thomas,) a dissenting minister, whose fame rests chiefly upon his wit, or, perhaps, rather buffoonery. He was born in 1677, at Wakefield, in Yorkshire, and seems to have carried the dry oddity not uncommonly affected by natives of that county, to a reprehensible extreme. He began to preach at the age of eighteen, and after some probation in the north, was chosen, in 1707, pastor of a congregation in Fetter-lane, London, where he preached with great popularity for twenty years; but a quarrel arising, he was invited to succeed his brother wit, Daniel Burgess, of New-court, Carey-street. His biographer's remark upon this circumstance is, "This pulpit a second time presented a phenomenon as rare *as it is beneficial*, wit consecrated to the services of serious and eternal truth."—(Bogue, vol. ii. p. 403.) Among the standing objects of his mirth was the religious poetry of Dr. Watts. He thus used, accordingly, to give out a hymn from that writer, it may be hoped only when in a sillier mood than common, "Let us sing one of Dr. Watts's Whims." At another time, preaching before an association of ministers at Salter's-hall, on the

Arian controversy, he exclaimed, "You who are not ashamed to own the deity of our Lord follow me to the gallery," to which he immediately bent his way; but some of the opposite party beginning to hiss, he turned round, and said, "I have been pleading for him who bruised the serpent's head; no wonder the seed of the serpent should hiss." His favourite meal was supper, after which he entertained his company with "The Roast-Beef of Old England," in singing which he was considered to excel. His works consist of fifty-four sermons, in three volumes, 8vo. They are many of them entirely occupied with politics, so that it has been said, "One would imagine from these discourses the Bible written only to confirm by divine authority the benefits accruing to this nation from the accession of king William III." Bradbury died Sept. 9, 1759.

BRADFORD, (John,) an eminent English martyr, born at Manchester, soon after the accession of Henry VIII. Being of a respectable family, he received a good education, and particularly excelled as an accountant, a qualification which procured him the place of clerk or secretary to Sir John Harrington, treasurer and paymaster of the English forces in France. After holding this situation for some years, his conscience smote him concerning a large defalcation in his accounts. Whether he had wilfully appropriated the money to himself, or whether he had committed an error of inadvertence, or whether he had participated in or connived at certain fraudulent practices, then common, by others, cannot now be ascertained; the consequence was that he made restitution of the money, and relinquished his employment. Some attribute his conduct in this matter to a sermon of bishop Latimer, but others think that the sermon alluded to was not preached till after the restitution had been made. Having now to seek a new way of life, Bradford, about 1547, began to study law in the Temple, where he continued for some time, but finding divinity more congenial to his taste, he removed in 1548 to Catharine hall, Cambridge, where his proficiency in learning was found so great, that in little more than twelve months he was admitted to the degree of M.A., and soon afterwards elected fellow of Pembroke. He was ordained deacon in 1550, and almost immediately became celebrated as a preacher. Bishop Ridley, his patron, gave him a stall in St. Paul's, and he was also appointed one of the royal chaplains, an office which he did not hold long, as the death of Edward took place the next year. Bradford was among the earliest victims of Mary's intolerance. He was accused of exciting a tumult at St. Paul's Cross, whereas really the disorder arose from a violent discourse preached by Gilbert Bourn. (See Bourn.) Bradford, in fact, was the means of protecting Bourn from the populace, exasperated by his indiscreet attack upon the reformation. He was, however, committed to prison in the Tower, where he remained for a year and a half; but not being put under very close restraint, he continued, by his writings and discourses to all comers, to promote the spread of protestant opinions. In 1554 he was removed to Southwark, and examined by Gardiner, bishop of Winchester, then chancellor, Bonner, of London, and some others. The result was, that he was sentenced to death. But the Romish party, being earnestly desirous of acquiring the services of so eminent a person, used every effort in their power to effect his conversion, and delayed the execution of the sentence for several months; but all their endeavours proving ineffectual, he was on the 1st of July, 1555, brought to the stake in Smithfield, in company with a youth named John Lyefe, and there burned as a heretic. He seems to have been a man of mild and amiable manners, of keen feelings, and of great boldness and zeal. His writings consist chiefly of sermons, tracts, letters, meditations, and prayers. They have recently been printed in 12mo by the Religious Tract Society.

BRADFORD, (Samuel,) an able English prelate, born in London, December 20, 1652, educated at St. Paul's school and Benet College, Cambridge. He did not take his degree in due course, having at the proper time some scruples about subscription. These he eventually surmounted, and entered into orders. Being employed in educating the grandson of archbishop Tillotson, this introduction, joined to real merits of his own, led him to a series of distinguished preferments. In 1718, he was promoted to the see of Carlisle, from which, in 1723, he was translated to that of Rochester, holding with it, *in commendam*, the deanery of Westminster. He died May 17, 1731, having published in 1699 a course of sermons preached at Boyle's lecture, on the Credibility of the Christian Religion from its intrinsic evidence. He also printed separately twenty-three occasional sermons, and assisted in the publication of Tillotson's works. (Chalmers.)

BRADLEY, (James,) an eminent English astronomer, born at Shireborn, in Gloucestershire, in 1692, educated at Northleach grammar school, and Balliol college, Oxford. M.A. June 21, 1717, D.D. by diploma, February 22, 1741. He was ordained in 1719, and instituted in the same year to the vicarage of Bridstow, in Herefordshire, he being then chaplain to the bishop, who has the patronage of that preferment. About the same time was obtained for him from the crown, by the Hon. Mr. Molyneaux, the small sinecure rectory of Llandewy Welfry, in Pembrokeshire. He thus had every prospect of rising in his profession, but a devotion to astronomy, united with a conscientious desire to decline emoluments where he was unwilling to undertake duties, turned him away from the thought of clerical advancement. He served, however, for a time, the curacy of Wanstead, in Essex, a parish of which his maternal uncle and mathematical instructor, Dr. James Pound, was the rector. In such society his peculiar talents rapidly attained maturity, and on the death of Dr. Keil, in 1721, he succeeded to the Savilian professorship of astronomy at Oxford. Bradley having now secured a provision entirely agreeable to his inclinations, bent every energy to discharge its duties effectively, and hence found himself no longer able to hold with satisfaction ecclesiastical preferment. He resigned accordingly both his vicarage and his Welsh sinecure, although the latter would have been retained by most men, even of tender conscience, without hesitation. The earliest conspicuous result of his entire devotion to astronomical pursuits was his famous theory of the aberration of fixed stars, completed by him about the year 1727, and published in No. 406 of the Philosophical Transactions. This theory, being based upon the most accurate observations, was admitted by all the great mathematicians, and gave Bradley an influence with Newton, and others of high consideration in the scientific world. In 1730 he was appointed lecturer in astronomy and experimental philosophy, in the university of Oxford, and he continued to hold that situation until within a few years of his death, when ill health rendered him no longer capable of its duties. In February, 1742, he had the honour of succeeding Dr. Halley as astronomer royal, a distinguished appointment, which that great man had intended to resign in his favour, if life had been a little longer spared him. Bradley's opportunities for observation were now of the best kind; and in 1747, his ability to profit by such advantages was conspicuously shown in his important discovery of the nutation of the earth's axis. In 1748, he availed himself of the annual visit paid by the Royal Society to the Observatory at Greenwich, to represent the want of better instruments. In consequence, a grant of 1000*l.* was made by George II., and the Observatory was furnished with a scientific apparatus, worthy of such a noble institution, and of an enlightened nation. In 1751, Bradley received an offer of the vicarage of Greenwich; but although it is a valuable preferment, and his residence in the park appeared excellently fitted for enabling him to fulfil its duties, his conscientious objections interposed, and he declined it. The king would not, however, allow him to suffer materially by a refusal so honourable, but generously conferred upon him a pension of 250*l.* a year, which was continued after his death to the astronomer royal. Bradley's exertions never abated until within two years of his decease, when his bodily strength declined, and a depression of spirits made him fear the loss of reason, a calamity which, however, he escaped. In June, 1762, he was attacked with a suppression of urine, arising from inflammation of the kidneys, under which he sank at Chalford, in Gloucestershire, on the 13th of the following month. He was not only one of the greatest astronomers of his age, but also a very amiable man; and although generally silent, capable of delivering himself with great precision and perspicuity. He published several papers in the Philosophical Transactions, but the world knew little of him as an author. He left, however, thirteen folio and two quarto volumes of observations, made during twenty years at the Royal Observatory, which were, after his death, taken away by the guardians of his only daughter, a minor, as property from the publication of which she was entitled to any benefit that might accrue. But the government thought otherwise, and commenced a suit for the recovery of the MSS., which was abandoned on the young lady's marriage, her husband giving them to the university of Oxford. That learned body published a portion of them in a splendid volume in 1798. (Rees.)

BRADLEY, (Richard,) an English writer upon gardening and agriculture, who gained considerable popularity in the eighteenth century, and has the merit of being one of the first who treated the subjects of his pen in a philosophical manner. His introduction to the public was through two papers in the Philosophical Transactions; one upon the motion of the sap in vegetables, the other upon the tendency of melons to become mouldy. Having been elected member of the Royal Society, he next aspired to the professorship of botany at Cambridge, which he succeeded in obtaining, Nov. 10, 1724, but by discreditable artifices. When elected, he was found all but wholly ignorant of the learned languages, and indisposed for the reading of lectures. This duty, therefore, was, under permission of the university, fulfilled by Dr. Martyn. Besides his neglect, Bradley's general conduct gave so much just offence that thoughts were entertained of dismissing him from the professorship; but his death, Nov. 5, 1732, prevented this severity. His publications fill two vols. in folio, four in quarto, and nearly twenty in octavo. Among them, his New Improvement of Planting and Gardening, both philosophical and practical, 1717, 8vo, was reprinted several times, as was his Gentleman's and Gardener's Kalendar. His Philosophical Account of the Works of Nature was an instructive and entertaining work, that long kept its ground, which may be said also of his General Treatise of Husbandry and Gardening, and of his Practical Discourses concerning the Four Elements, as they relate to the Growth of Plants. His Dictionarium Botanicum, 1728, 8vo, has been considered as the first work of the kind produced in England; and his Historia Plantarum Succulentarum, published from 1716 to 1727, was a contribution to exotic botany, which good judges were sorry to see discontinued from want of sufficient encouragement. (Chalmers.)

BRADSHAW, (Henry,) an early English poet, born in Chester, where he died in 1513. Having a taste for learning and religion in early youth, he entered, while a boy, the Benedictine monastery of St. Werburg, in his native city. As his age advanced, he was sent to Gloucester, now Worcester, college, Oxford, whence he returned to his cell at St. Werburg's, after studying theology among the novices of his order. Besides some historical works, he translated from the Latin a metrical life of St. Werburg, printed by Pynson, in 1521, and now a volume of the utmost rarity. He is thought also to be the author of The Lyfe of Saynt Radegunde, printed by Pynson, but not bearing the writer's name. This is inferred from a comparison of that work with the St. Werburg. Bradshaw speaks of his performance with extreme modesty, declining all appearance of competition with Chaucer, Lydgate, (he calls him Ludgate,) Barkley, or Skelton, and his versification is considered inferior to Lydgate's worst manner, but his matter is rendered attractive by a happiness of description, a vein of moral purity, and a tinge of legendary lore. (Wood's Athenæ, by Bliss. Chalmers.)

BRADSHAW, (John,) known as the *President Bradshaw*, because he presided in the court which condemned Charles I. He was of an ancient Lancashire family, but his branch of it was seated either in Cheshire or Derbyshire. Of his life before he became a student at Gray's-inn nothing is known; but, being called to the bar, he obtained a considerable degree of chamber practice among the parliamentarian party, to the politics of which he was warmly addicted. Clarendon describes him as a man of some ability, but insolent and ambitious. His competence being seconded by his politics, he was entrusted with a parliamentary prosecution in 1644; in 1646, he had with others the custody of the great seal, by a vote of the commons; in 1647, he was made chief justice of Chester by a vote of both houses; in the same year he was named by parliament one of the counsel to prosecute judge Jenkins; and in October, 1648, he was raised to the rank of sergeant. When the king's death, by judicial forms, was decided upon at the end of that year, the new sergeant does not seem to have been immediately marked out for any very prominent part, as his name was not in the first list of commissioners for that purpose; but when the lords rejected the proposal, the names of six peers, originally placed in the commission, were erased, and Bradshaw's, with those of five others, substituted. On Jan. 10, 1649, the commissioners for trying the king met in the painted chamber, and chose Bradshaw for their president. It has been said that he was very much surprised by this choice, and at first resolved upon declining a distinction so very responsible and invidious. But he certainly seemed, when fairly entered upon the duties of his office, altogether fit for them. No opportunities, indeed, were given him of displaying any qualifications strictly professional, as the king denied any authority to his court, and was besides unprovided with means of making a good legal defence. In self-possession, however, Bradshaw showed no deficiency, which is a point of great importance under circumstances so difficult as his at that time. The general opinion is that he behaved with brutality and insolence; and undoubtedly he betrayed none of that feeling which the miserable spectacle before him would have raised in every generous breast. The rewards conferred upon him prove that he was thought to have served his party most importantly. He had a gratuity of 5,000*l.*, the deanery in Westminster for a town house, for a country seat, Summer-hill, in Kent, belonging to Ulic De Burgh, marquess of Clanricard and earl of St. Alban's, lord Cottington's estate in Wiltshire, with other landed property, making up altogether a rental of 4,000*l.* a year, and the chancellorship of the duchy of Lancaster. He was, however, a thorough republican, and hence an enemy to the supreme authority of Cromwell, who removed him accordingly from the chief-justiceship of Chester. On the protector's death, Bradshaw regained some of his former importance, and was elected president of the council. He would have been made commissioner of the great seal, had not his failing health obliged him to decline. He died November 22, 1659, fully impressed with a belief that Charles was justly executed, and declaring that, if such a thing were necessary again, he would be one of the first to undertake it. He was buried with great pomp in Westminster Abbey, but his body did not rest long in its grave, being very foolishly and indecently exposed on a gibbet, with those of Cromwell and Ireton. In spite of this, an idle tale found its way into circulation, that he went abroad, and died in Jamaica. (Chalmers. Kennet. Hume. Lingard. Neal.)

END OF VOL. IV.

RICHARD CLAY, PRINTER, BREAD STREET HILL.

CPSIA information can be obtained
at www.ICGtesting.com
Printed in the USA
BVHW081606220819
556561BV00017B/3775/P